EMPATH

PRESERVING CULTURES

WHY STUDY HISTORY?

HISTORY THROUGH OBJECTS

IDENTITY

THE HUMAN EPIC GLOBAL CITIZENSHIP

STORYTELLING

WHY STUDY HISTORY? EMPATHY

IDENTITY CIVILIZATION

STORIES MAKING HISTORY

EMPOWERMENT

SAVING OUR PAST

EMPATHY

HISTORY THROUGH OBJECTS

CIVILIZATION

PRESERVING CULTURES

GLOBAL CITIZENSHIP

PRESERVING CULTURES

EMPATHY

OUR HUMAN STORY

CIVILIZATION THE HUMAN EPIC

WHO OWNS THE PAST

STORIES MAKING HISTORY

EMPOWERMENT

GLOBAL CITIZENSHIP

SAVING OUR PAST

EMPOWERMENT

PRESERVING CULTURES

SAVING OUR PAST

WHY STUDY HISTORY?

GLOBAL CITIZENSHIP

IDENTITY

THE HUMAN EPIC

STORYTELLING

OUR HUMAN STORY

EMPOWERMENT

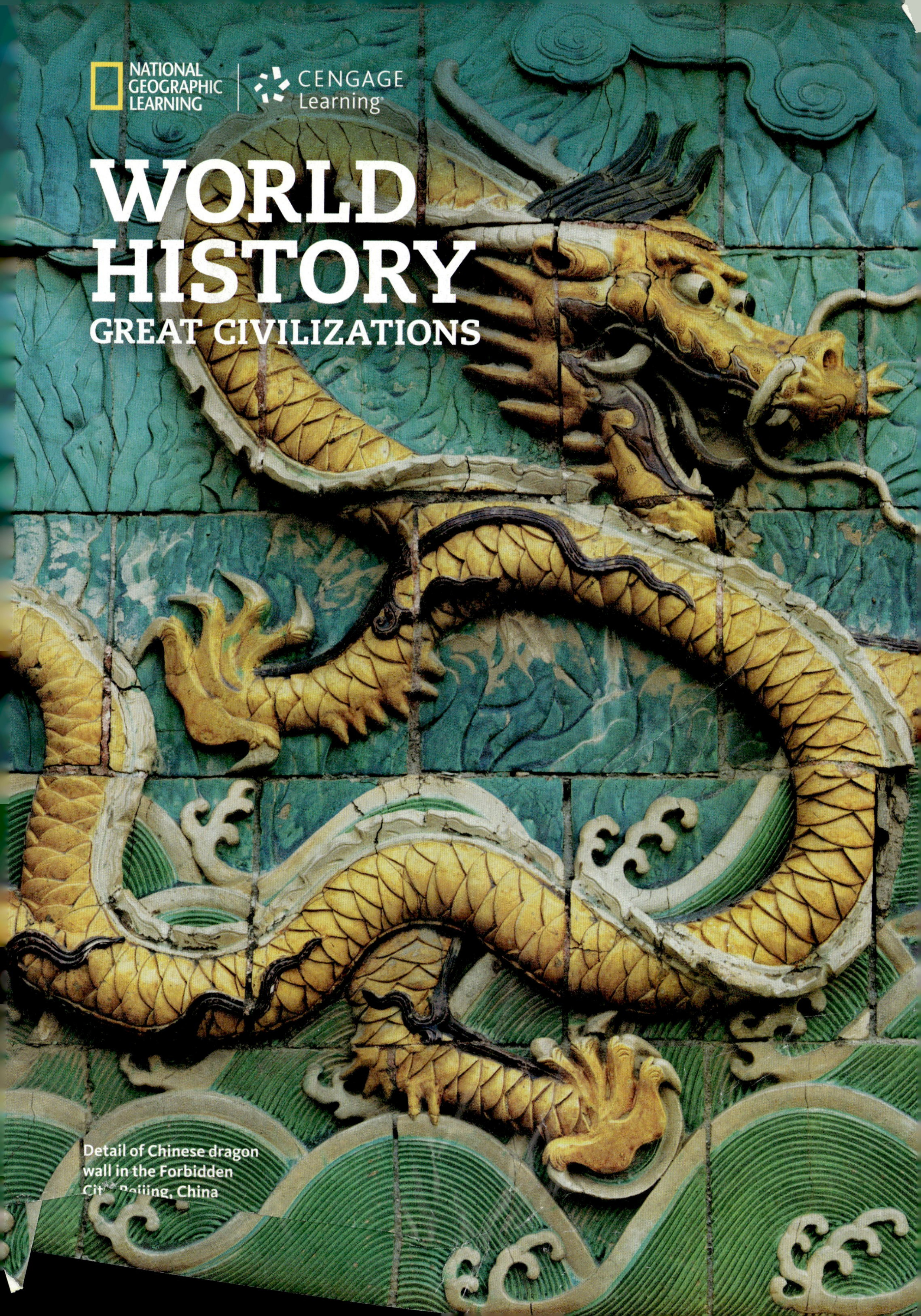
NATIONAL GEOGRAPHIC LEARNING
CENGAGE Learning
WORLD HISTORY
GREAT CIVILIZATIONS

Detail of Chinese dragon wall in the Forbidden Cit[illegible] Beijing, China

Acknowledgments

Grateful acknowledgment is given to the authors, artists, photographers, museums, publishers, and agents for permission to reprint copyrighted material. Every effort has been made to secure the appropriate permission. If any omissions have been made or if corrections are required, please contact the Publisher.

Photographic Credits

Front Cover: ©Neale Clark/Robert Harding World Imagery/Alamy

Acknowledgments and credits continue on page R46.

Visit National Geographic Learning online at NGL.Cengage.com

Visit our corporate website at www.cengage.com

Printed in the USA.

Quad/Graphics , Versailles , KY

ISBN: 978-12853-52305

18 19 20 21 22 23 24

10 9 8 7 6 5 4 3

NATIONAL GEOGRAPHIC

Program Consultants

Fredrik Hiebert

Dr. Fred Hiebert is a National Geographic Explorer and Archaeology Fellow. He has led archaeological expeditions at ancient Silk Roads sites across Asia and underwater in the Black Sea. Hiebert rediscovered the lost Bactrian gold in Afghanistan in 2004 and was curator of National Geographic's exhibition *Afghanistan: Hidden Treasures from the National Museum, Kabul*, which toured museums throughout the world. Hiebert curated National Geographic's exhibition *Peruvian Gold: Ancient Treasures Unearthed* and, most recently, the exhibition *The Greeks: Agamemnon to Alexander the Great.*

Christopher P. Thornton

Dr. Chris Thornton is the Lead Program Officer of Research, Conservation, and Exploration at the National Geographic Society, and Director of the UNESCO World Heritage Site of Bat in the Sultanate of Oman. Thornton works closely with NGS media to promote grantees and other scientists, overseeing research grants in anthropology, archaeology, astronomy, geography, geology, and paleontology. He also manages the Society's relationship with academic conferences around the world.

Jeremy McInerney

Dr. Jeremy McInerney is chairman of the Department of Classical Studies at the University of Pennsylvania. McInerney recently spent a year as Whitehead Professor in the American School of Classical Studies in Athens, Greece. He has excavated at Corinth, on Crete, and in Israel. Author of *The Cattle of the Sun: Cows and Culture in the World of the Ancient Greeks* (2010), McInerney has received top teaching awards, including the Lindback Award for Distinguished Teaching.

Program Consultants

Michael W. Smith

Dr. Michael Smith is the Associate Dean for Faculty Development and Academic Affairs in the College of Education at Temple University. He became a college teacher after 11 years of teaching high school English. His research focuses on how experienced readers read and talk about texts, as well as what motivates adolescents' reading and writing. Smith has written many books and monographs, including the award-winning *"Reading Don't Fix No Chevys": Literacy in the Lives of Young Men*.

Peggy Altoff

Peggy Altoff's long career includes teaching middle school and high school students, supervising teachers, and serving as adjunct university faculty. Peggy served as a state social studies specialist in Maryland and as a K–12 coordinator in Colorado Springs. She was president of the National Council for the Social Studies (NCSS) in 2006–2007 and was on the task force for the 2012 NCSS National Curriculum Standards.

David W. Moore

Dr. David Moore is a Professor Emeritus of Education at Arizona State University. He taught high school social studies and reading before entering college teaching. His noteworthy co-authored publications include the *Handbook of Reading Research* chapter on secondary school reading, the first International Reading Association position statement on adolescent literacy, and *Developing Readers and Writers in the Content Areas (6e)*.

NATIONAL GEOGRAPHIC

Program Writer

Special thanks to Jon Heggie for his extensive contributions to *National Geographic World History: Great Civilizations*. Heggie became fascinated with history as a small child, a passion nurtured by his parents and educators. He studied history at Oxford University and received his Post Graduate Certificate in Education from Bristol University. Heggie has taught English and History at a number of schools in the UK and has written for *National Geographic* magazine for the past ten years. He is currently working on a number of history projects and serving as the editor of the recently launched National Geographic *History* magazine.

Reviewers of Religious Content

The following individuals reviewed the treatment of religious content in selected pages of the text.

Murali Balaji
Hindu American Foundation
Washington, D.C.

Dr. Charles C. Haynes
Director, Religious Freedom
Center of the Newseum Institute
Washington, D.C.

Munir Shaikh
Institute on Religion and
Civic Values
Fountain Valley, California

National Geographic Society

The National Geographic Society contributed significantly to *National Geographic World History: Great Civilizations*. Our collaboration with each of the following has been a pleasure and a privilege: National Geographic Maps, National Geographic Education and Children's Media, National Geographic Missions programs, and National Geographic Studios. We thank the Society for its guidance and support.

We BELIEVE in the power of science, exploration, and storytelling to change the world.

NATIONAL GEOGRAPHIC

Unit Explorers

Each unit in this book opens and closes with a National Geographic Explorer discussing the content presented in the unit and explaining his or her own related work in the field. Within the Student eEdition, you can watch video footage of each Unit Explorer "on location" to expand and enhance your world history learning experience.

Nina Burleigh
Journalist/Author

Christopher DeCorse
Archaeologist
National Geographic
Grantee

Steven Ellis
Archaeologist
National Geographic
Grantee

Francisco Estrada-Belli
Archaeologist
National Geographic
Grantee

Fredrik Hiebert
Archaeologist
National Geographic
Fellow

Louise Leakey
Paleontologist
National Geographic
Explorer-in-Residence

Albert Lin
Research Scientist/Engineer
National Geographic
Emerging Explorer

Jodi Magness
Archaeologist
National Geographic
Grantee

William Parkinson
Archaeologist
National Geographic
Grantee

Aziz Abu Sarah
Cultural Educator
National Geographic
Emerging Explorer

Maurizio Seracini
Cultural Heritage
Engineer
National Geographic
Fellow

Christopher Thornton
Archaeologist
National Geographic
Lead Program Officer of Research,
Conservation, and Exploration

NATIONAL GEOGRAPHIC

Chapter Explorers

In the chapters of this book, National Geographic Explorers tell the story of their work as it relates to the time in history you're learning about. Archaeologists, photographers, and writers explain their historical and cultural findings and the process involved in making the important discoveries that help us understand more about the past—and the future.

Caroline Alexander
National Geographic
Writer/Journalist

Beverly Goodman
Geo-Archaeologist
National Geographic
Emerging Explorer

Fredrik Hiebert
Archaeologist
National Geographic
Fellow

Patrick Hunt
Archaeologist
National Geographic
Grantee

Christine Lee
Bio-Archaeologist
National Geographic
Emerging Explorer

Sarah Parcak
Archaeologist
National Geographic
Fellow

Jeffrey Rose
Archaeologist
National Geographic
Emerging Explorer

William Saturno
Archaeologist
National Geographic
Grantee

Hayat Sindi
Science Entrepreneur
National Geographic
Emerging Explorer

Dave Yoder
Photojournalist
National Geographic
Grantee

NATIONAL GEOGRAPHIC

Featured Explorers

Throughout the Student eEdition, National Geographic Featured Explorers take part in informal "video chat" style interviews to explain and discuss their fieldwork and explore high-interest topics covered in the book. Other Featured Explorers tell the story of important and ongoing world events in the Stories Making History section.

Salam Al Kuntar
Archaeologist
National Geographic Emerging Explorer

Nicole Boivin
Archaeologist
National Geographic Grantee

Steve Boyes
Conservation Biologist
National Geographic Emerging Explorer

Michael Cosmopoulos
Archaeologist, National Geographic Grantee

Jeff Gusky
National Geographic Photographer

Sarah Parcak
Archaeologist
National Geographic Fellow

Thomas Parker
Archaeologist
National Geographic Grantee

Matt Piscitelli
Archaeologist
National Geographic Grantee

Max Salomon
National Geographic Producer

Anna Secor
Political Geographer
National Geographic Grantee

Shah Selbe
Conservation Technologist
National Geographic Emerging Explorer

Soultana Maria Valamoti
Archaeologist, National Geographic Grantee

Simon Worrall
National Geographic Writer

Xiaobai Angela Yao
Geographer
National Geographic Grantee

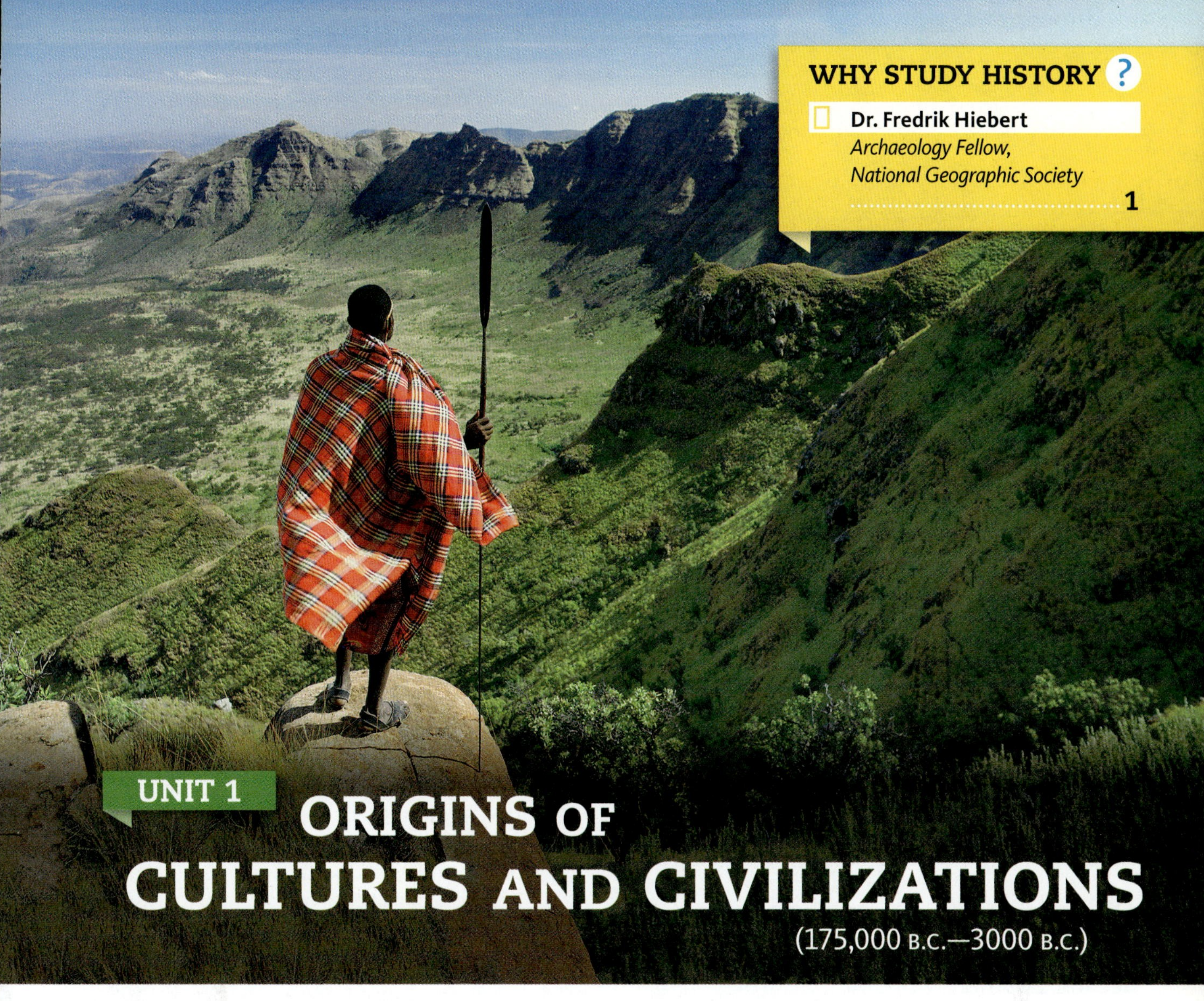

WHY STUDY HISTORY ?

UNIT 1

ORIGINS OF CULTURES AND CIVILIZATIONS

(175,000 B.C.–3000 B.C.)

UNIT 2

EARLY CIVILIZATIONS

(3000 B.C.—A.D. 535)

WHY STUDY HISTORY ?
Dr. Fredrik Hiebert
Archaeology Fellow, National Geographic Society
198

UNIT 3
GREEK
CIVILIZATION
(2000 B.C.—323 B.C.)

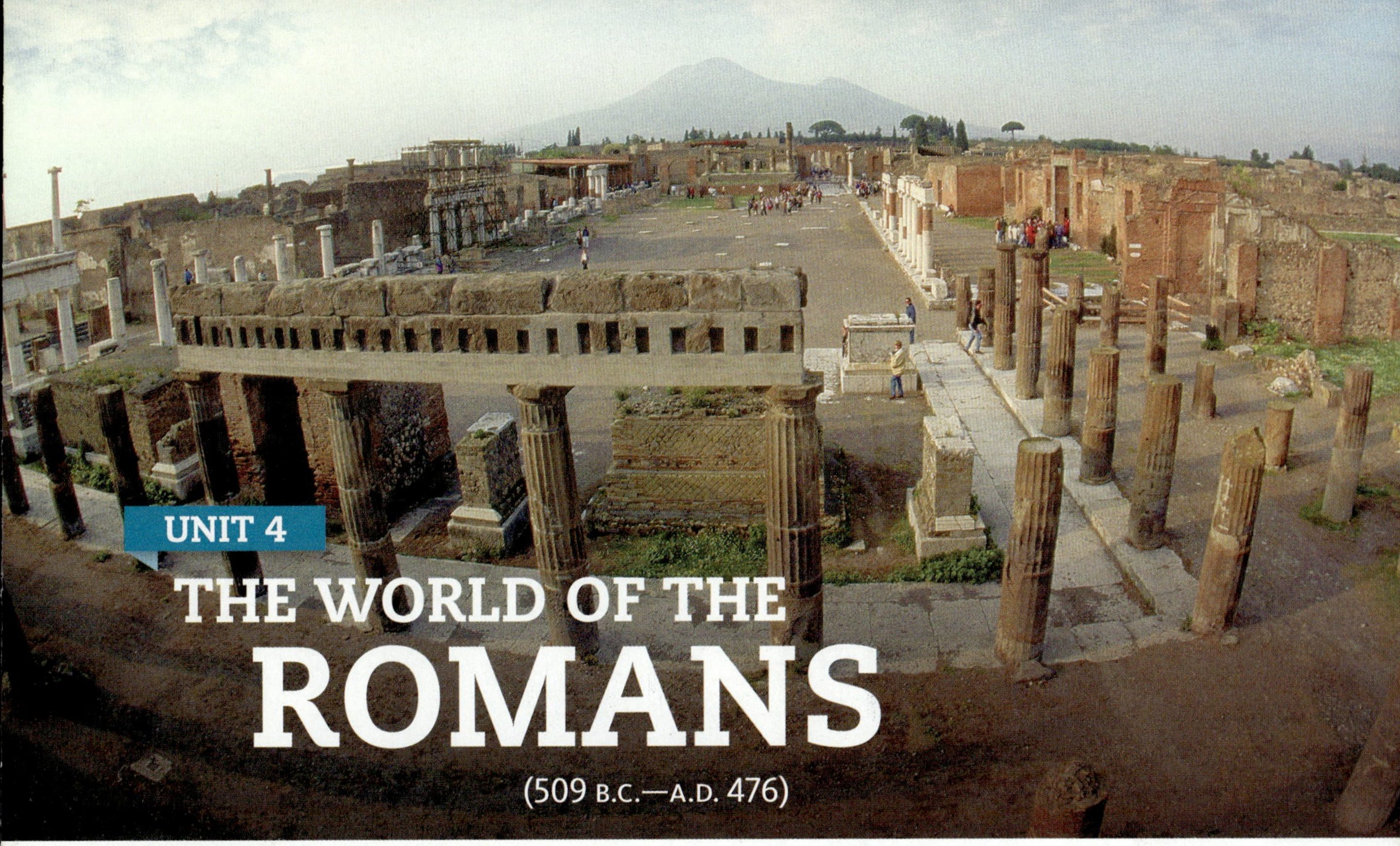

UNIT 4

THE WORLD OF THE ROMANS

(509 B.C.—A.D. 476)

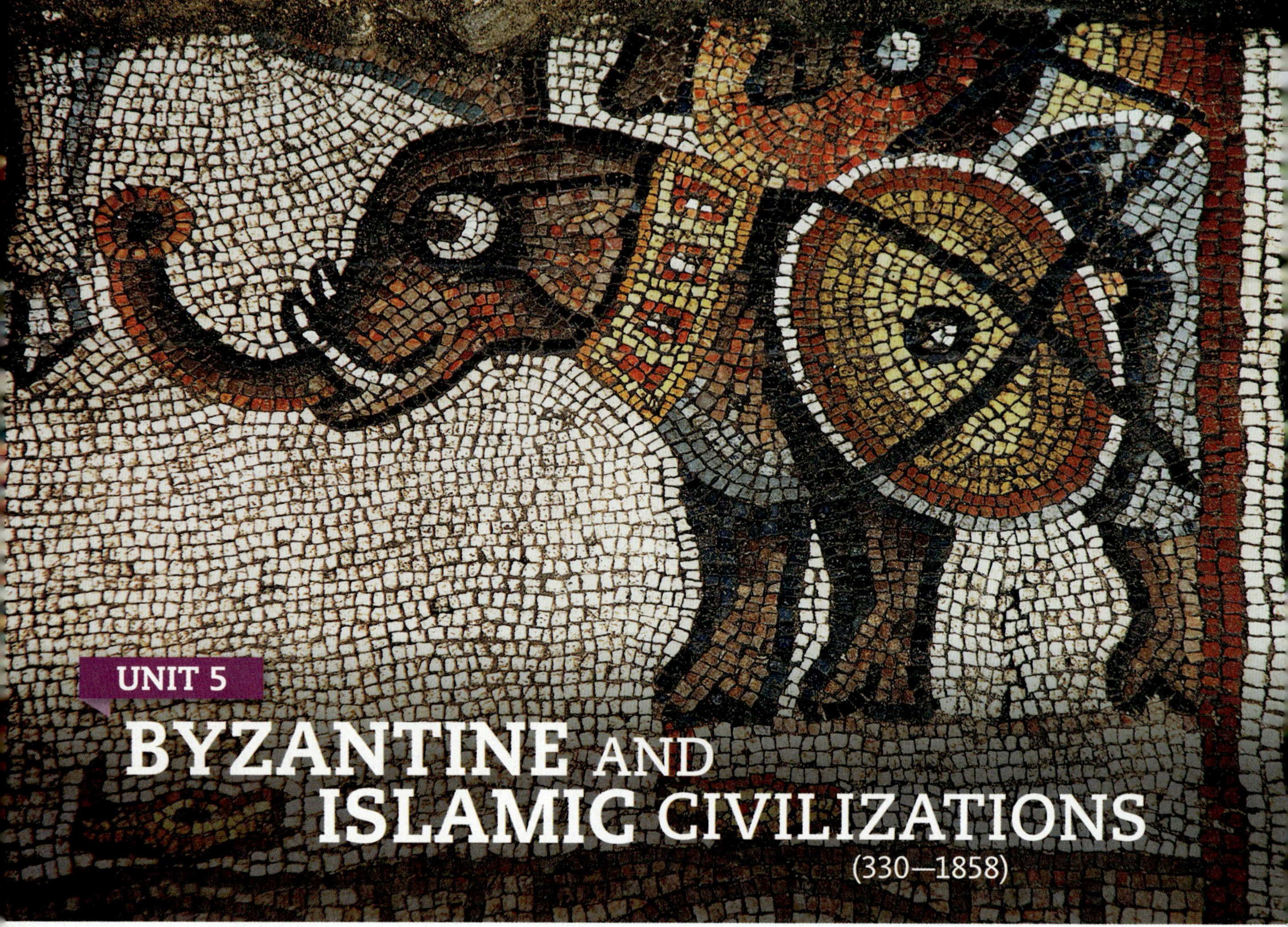

UNIT 5

BYZANTINE AND ISLAMIC CIVILIZATIONS

(330–1858)

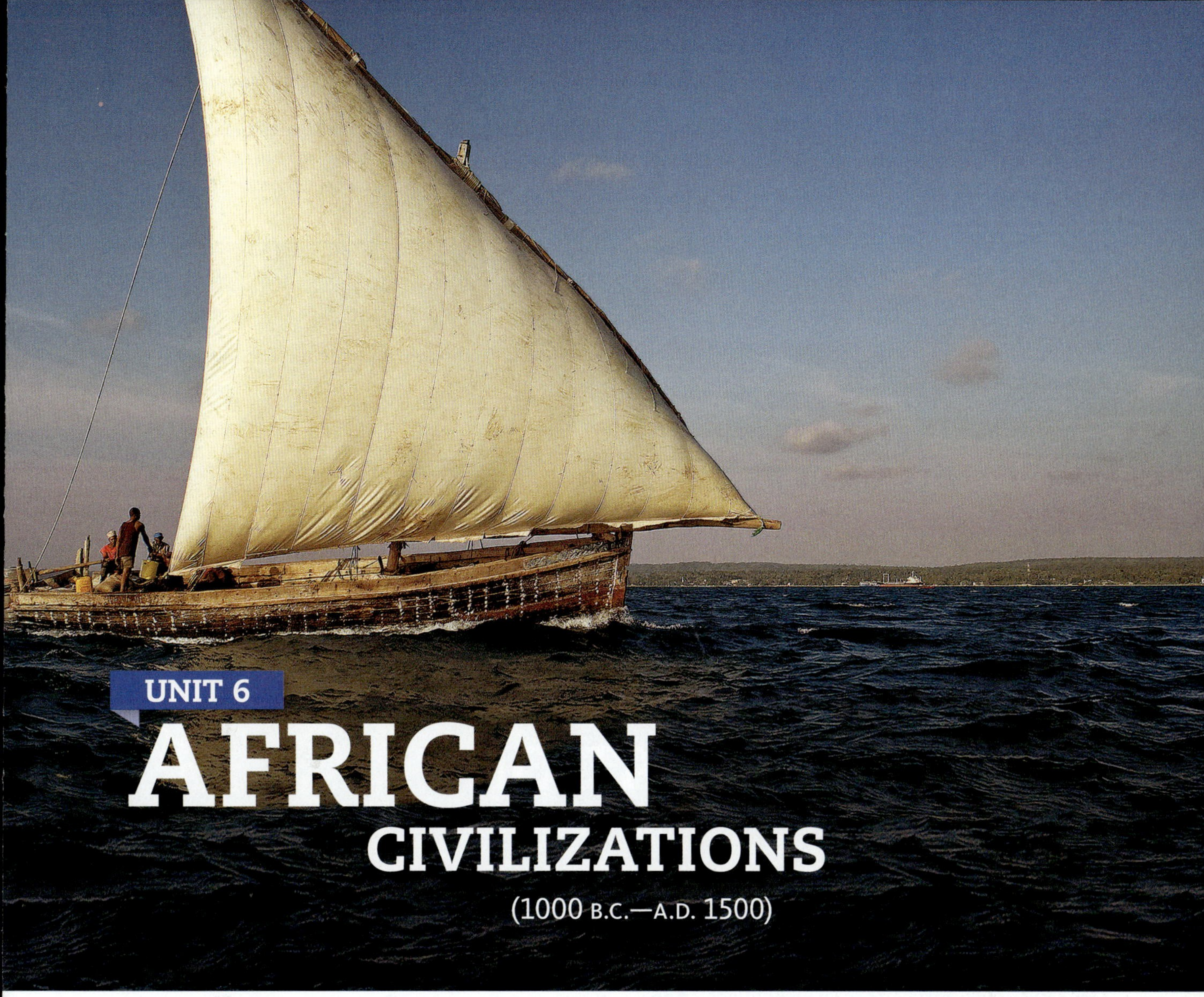

UNIT 6
AFRICAN CIVILIZATIONS
(1000 B.C.—A.D. 1500)

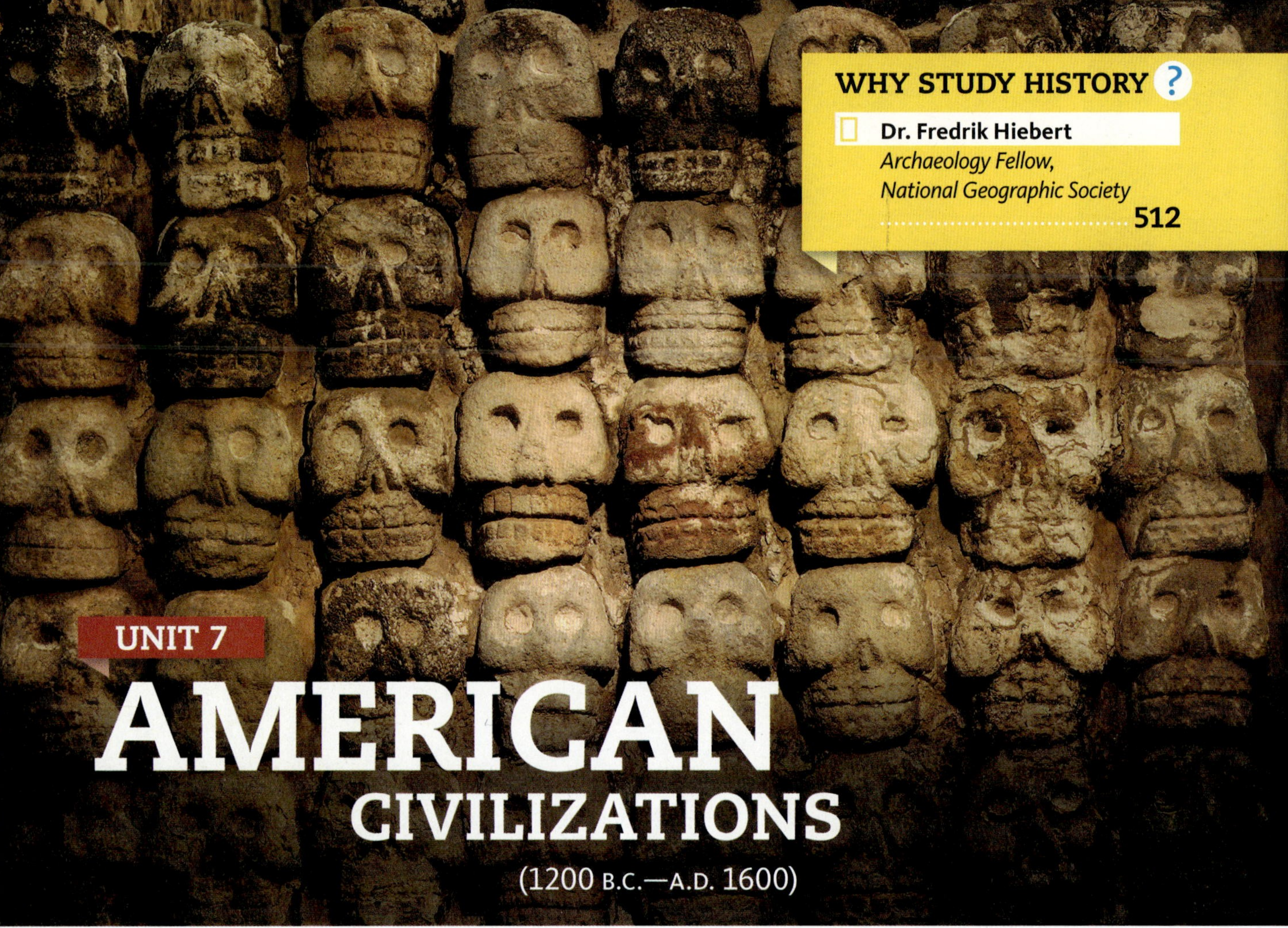

WHY STUDY HISTORY ?

UNIT 7

AMERICAN CIVILIZATIONS

(1200 B.C.—A.D. 1600)

UNIT 8
EMPIRES OF ASIA
(400–1912)

WHY STUDY HISTORY ?
Dr. Fredrik Hiebert
Archaeology Fellow,
National Geographic Society
690
UNIT 9
MEDIEVAL AND
RENAISSANCE EUROPE
(500—1700)

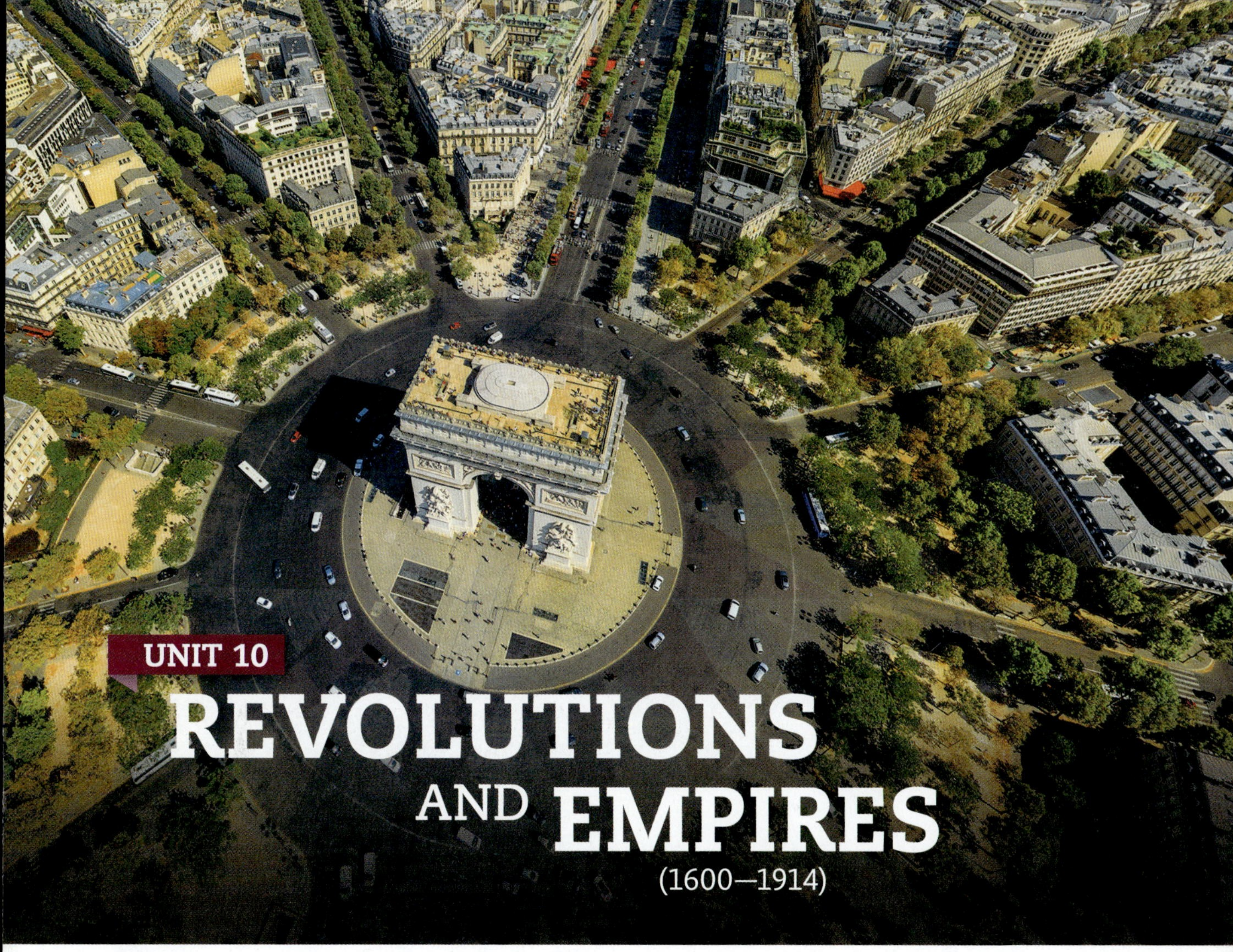

UNIT 10

REVOLUTIONS AND EMPIRES

(1600–1914)

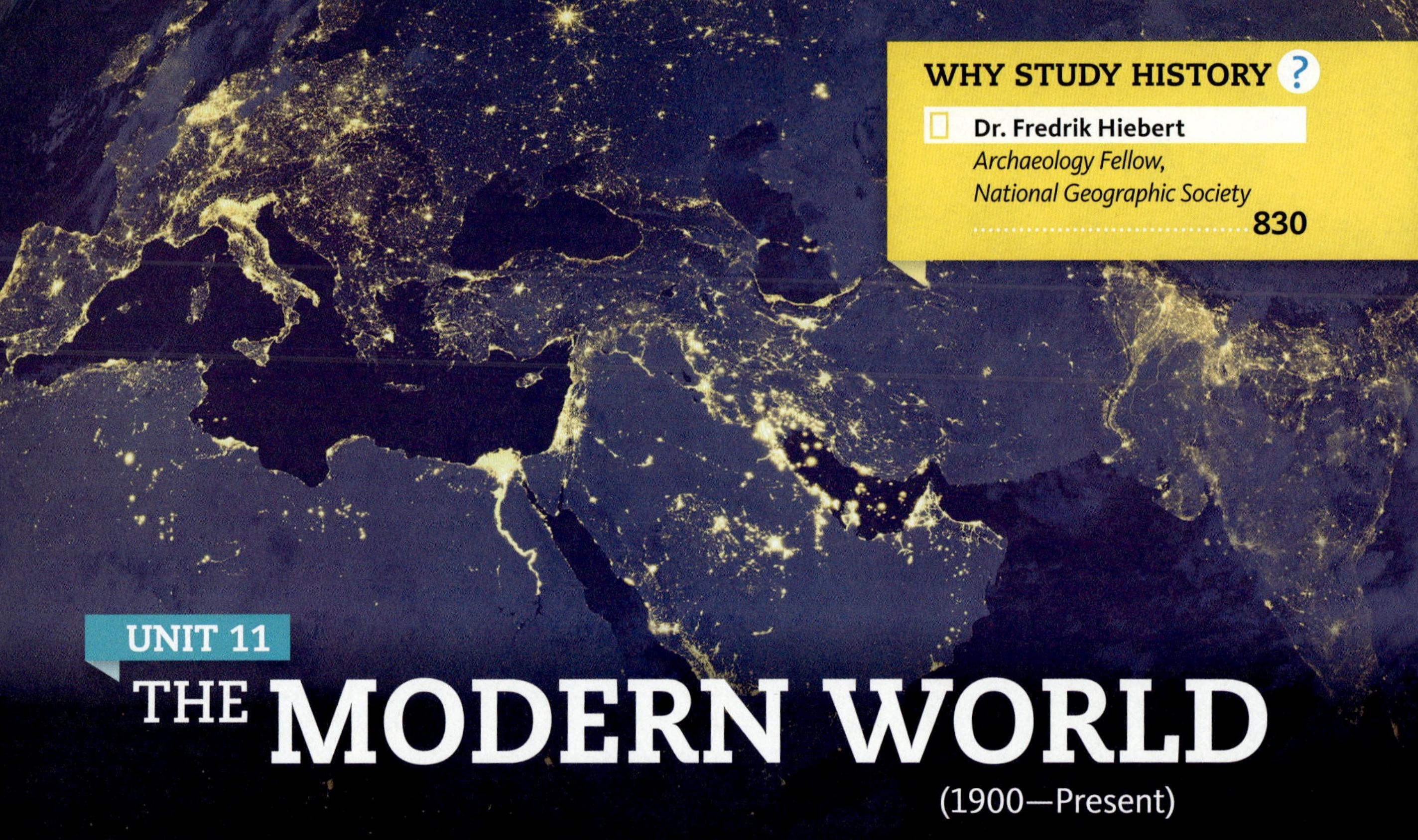
WHY STUDY HISTORY ?
Dr. Fredrik Hiebert
Archaeology Fellow, National Geographic Society
830

UNIT 11 THE MODERN WORLD

(1900—Present)

STORIES MAKING HISTORY

The world changes on a daily basis, and National Geographic is there. Join five National Geographic voices as they tell the stories of five current global events. Learn about these newsworthy topics, discuss what might come next, and think about how these events impact you, the place you live, and the people you know—your global citizenship.

Special Features

NATIONAL GEOGRAPHIC EXPLORER LESSONS

Hayat Sindi

PRIMARY AND SECONDARY SOURCES: OBJECTS AND EXCERPTS

Passport Medallion

PROFILES

Statue of Julius Caesar

HISTORY THROUGH OBJECTS

MAPS

DOCUMENT-BASED QUESTIONS

TIME LINES, CHARTS, MODELS, GRAPHS, INFOGRAPHICS

MOMENTS IN HISTORY

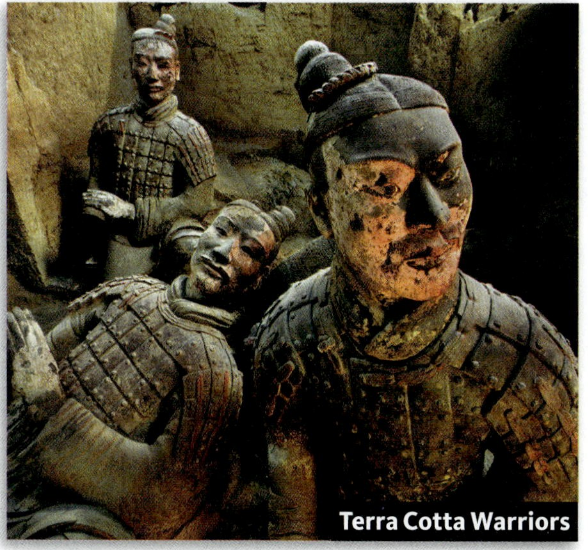
Terra Cotta Warriors

WHY STUDY HISTORY?

Hi! I'm Fred Hiebert, National Geographic's Archaeology Fellow. We're about to embark on a journey all over the world and back through time—the history of the world as we know it today.

So why do we study past civilizations? The basis of civilization is identity—who we are and what we stand for. We express identity by creating unique ways to be housed and fed and to thrive. The basic building blocks of civilization are the same around the world: what kinds of plants and animals to tend and consume, how to find enough water, and how to survive the changes of the seasons. All core civilizations— from China, India, and Mesopotamia, to Europe and Mesoamerica—struggled with these issues.

Look at the sculptures shown below. These prehistoric "selfies" reveal a universal need to think about ourselves—in relation to the environment, the future, our religious beliefs—that dates from the earliest civilizations.

THE HUMAN EPIC

Historians, archaeologists, and anthropologists constantly update the story of human civilizations as new data surfaces from the latest dig site or the most recent scholarship. The Framework of World History at right is only one way to think about how human identity developed—there are many pathways from the past to the present.

I've lived and worked all over the world in lots of different cultures, and I know first-hand that you and others your age are more alike than you are different. You share the same need to understand yourself, your family, and your community and the same urge to hope and plan for your future. Your generation may be one of the first to truly be considered global citizens.

ARTEMIS
This Greek marble sculpture dating back to the 4th century B.C. is known as *Artemis Hunting*.

NEFERTITI
The bust of this famous Egyptian queen and wife of Pharaoh Akhenaten was sculpted more than 3,300 years ago.

Fred Hiebert

Watch the Why Study History video

The ancient cave painting in the background is located in Snake Cave in Australia. An Aboriginal artist created it by blowing pigment over his or her hand, leaving a blank hand shape.

TERRA COTTA BUDDHA
This 5-foot tall statue was discovered at the site of Hadda in Afghanistan.

FRAMEWORK OF WORLD HISTORY

The model below is one way to view the development of civilizations. For all cultures, it's not just the famous leaders who make history—it's all of us, through small actions that grow into world-changing events and ideas.

1 CORE CIVILIZATIONS

Humans begin to think about where they live, what they eat, and what they believe in—and plan for the future. Across the centuries and in all world cultures, humans use these building blocks to think about who they are and where they come from—the beginning of identity.

2 PRIMARY CIVILIZATIONS

Humans develop more effective responses to their environment, creating irrigation and other farming methods that make agriculture more predictable and more productive. People are able to form groups and move together, and eventually cities develop.

3 SECONDARY CIVILIZATIONS

Human understanding of identity comes into focus, and writing develops partly as an expression of identity. Codes of law and better rulers come to the forefront as cultures take on characteristics that embody those identities.

4 WORLD SYSTEMS

Civilizations reach out to each other, and trade develops along what would eventually be called the Silk Roads. The urge to move results in new road systems, new country borders with border guards, and new systems of taxation.

WHY STUDY HISTORY ?

TO BECOME A GLOBAL CITIZEN

As you study world history, you're going to meet some National Geographic Explorers along the way—men and women who are making incredible contributions to our lives through their work. Studying world history is part of what they do because they believe they can add to our understanding of the human story. Here are just a few.

MICHAEL COSMOPOULOS ▶
Cosmopoulos directs two major excavations exploring the origins of states and social complexity in Greece.

◀ WILLIAM SATURNO
Saturno supervises excavations in the jungles of Guatemala and determines the architectural history of a site by studying the little pieces that remain.

LOUISE LEAKEY ▲
Paleontologist Louise Leakey is responsible for some of the most important hominid fossils discovered in East Africa in the past two decades.

BECOME PART OF THE GLOBAL CONVERSATION!

Think About It

1. In what ways are you a global citizen?
2. Describe a situation or problem in which you think people should strive for global citizenship. What actions do you think should be taken to solve the problem?
3. Pick one action you named above and explain how you would go about accomplishing it. Develop a detailed action plan that could be put in place to make this happen.

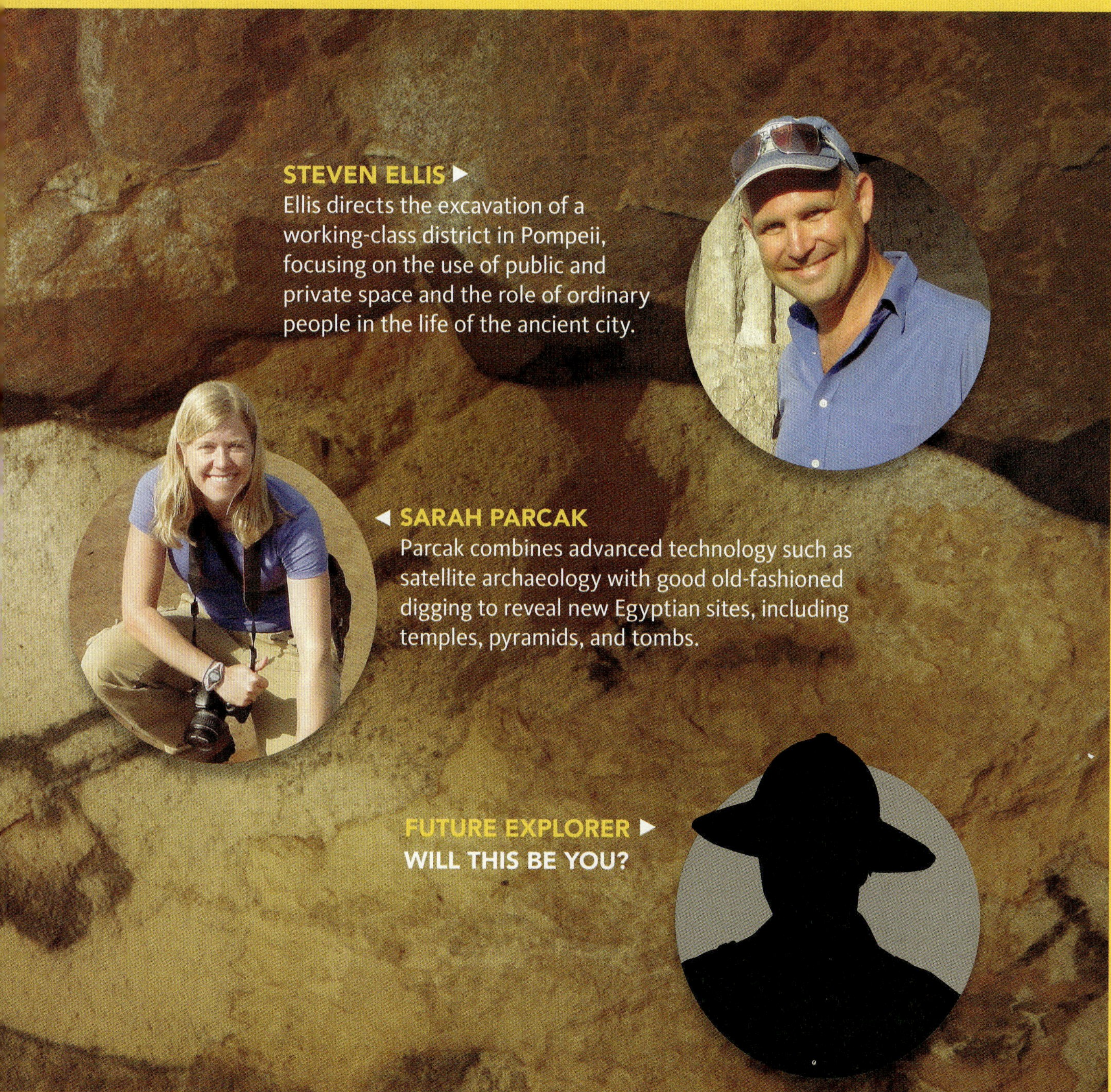
STEVEN ELLIS ▶
Ellis directs the excavation of a working-class district in Pompeii, focusing on the use of public and private space and the role of ordinary people in the life of the ancient city.
◀ SARAH PARCAK
Parcak combines advanced technology such as satellite archaeology with good old-fashioned digging to reveal new Egyptian sites, including temples, pyramids, and tombs.
FUTURE EXPLORER ▶
WILL THIS BE YOU?

Write About It

SYNTHESIZE What does **identity** mean to you? Answer this question in two or three paragraphs in your notebook. Be sure to include your definition of identity, explain the various parts that make up your identity, and describe how you express your identity. Then designate a spot in your notebook where you can record how your understanding of identity changes as you read each chapter.

MAKE CONNECTIONS What different types of identities do you notice in your school and community? Create a chart that represents these identities and write your description of each.

ASK AND ANSWER QUESTIONS Imagine that you are at a panel discussion that includes the Explorers shown above. Write three questions you would like to ask the panel, including specific questions for individual Explorers.

UNIT 1

ORIGINS OF CULTURES AND CIVILIZATIONS

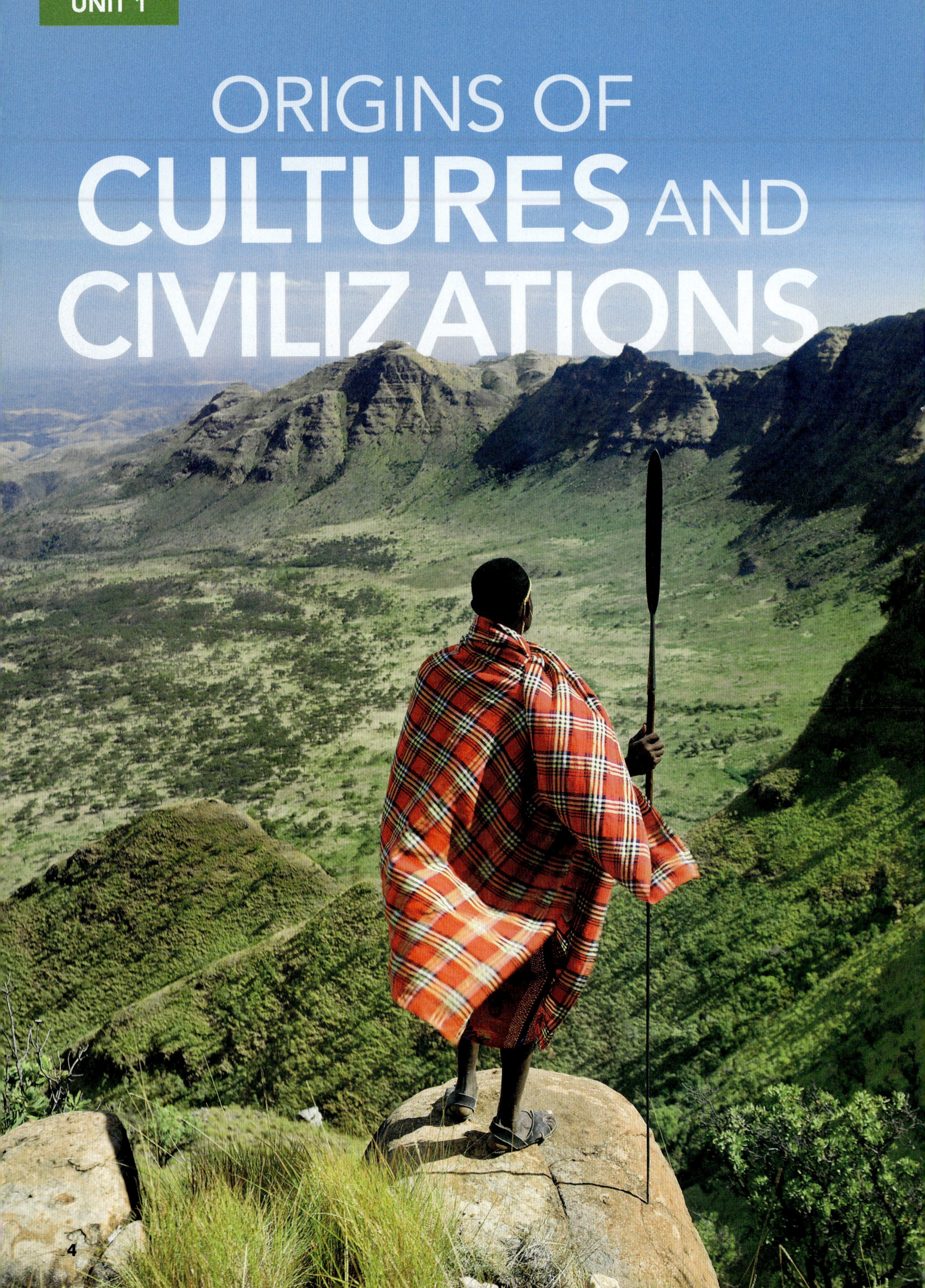

NATIONAL GEOGRAPHIC

ON **LOCATION** WITH

Louise Leakey

Paleontologist

One of the first jobs of a paleontologist is finding a good place to dig. We look for places where fossilized bones, buried long ago by rivers and lakes, have been brought to the surface by tectonic activity and erosion. Lake Turkana in Kenya's Great Rift Valley is the world's best field laboratory for fossil discoveries going back several million years. My family has been working in this profession for three generations, uncovering the bones of human ancestors and other animals that lived in this region in the past. I'm Louise Leakey, and I help investigate and share the human story.

‹ **CRITICAL VIEWING** A shepherd gazes out over East Africa's Great Rift Valley. How might the geography of the valley help archaeologists carry out their work?

UNIT 1
TIME LINE OF WORLD EVENTS

The World

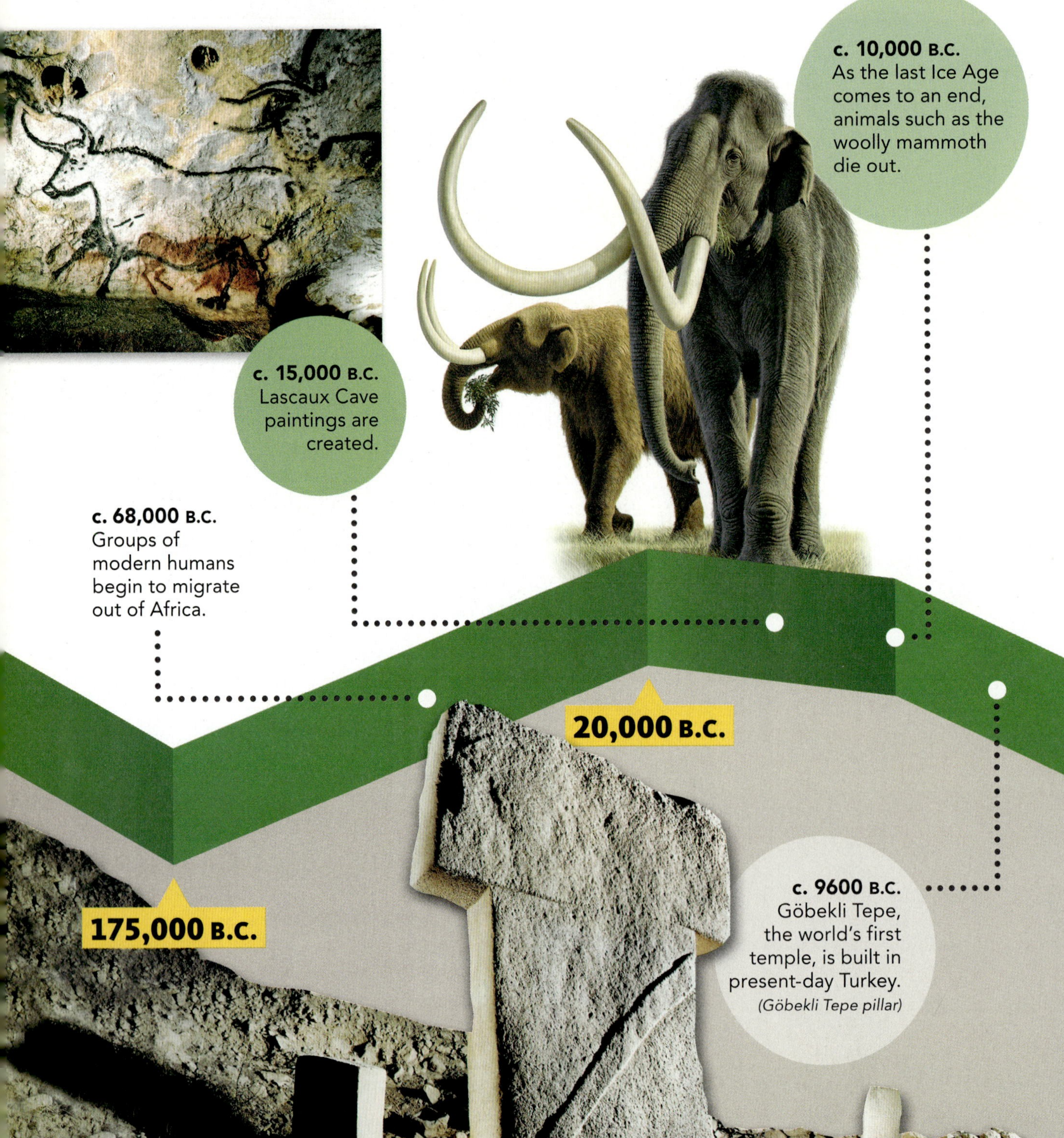

c. 10,000 B.C.
As the last Ice Age comes to an end, animals such as the woolly mammoth die out.

c. 15,000 B.C.
Lascaux Cave paintings are created.

c. 68,000 B.C.
Groups of modern humans begin to migrate out of Africa.

20,000 B.C.

175,000 B.C.

c. 9600 B.C.
Göbekli Tepe, the world's first temple, is built in present-day Turkey.
(Göbekli Tepe pillar)

COMPARE TIME LINES

What similar events took place within 1,000 years in Egypt and Mesoamerica?

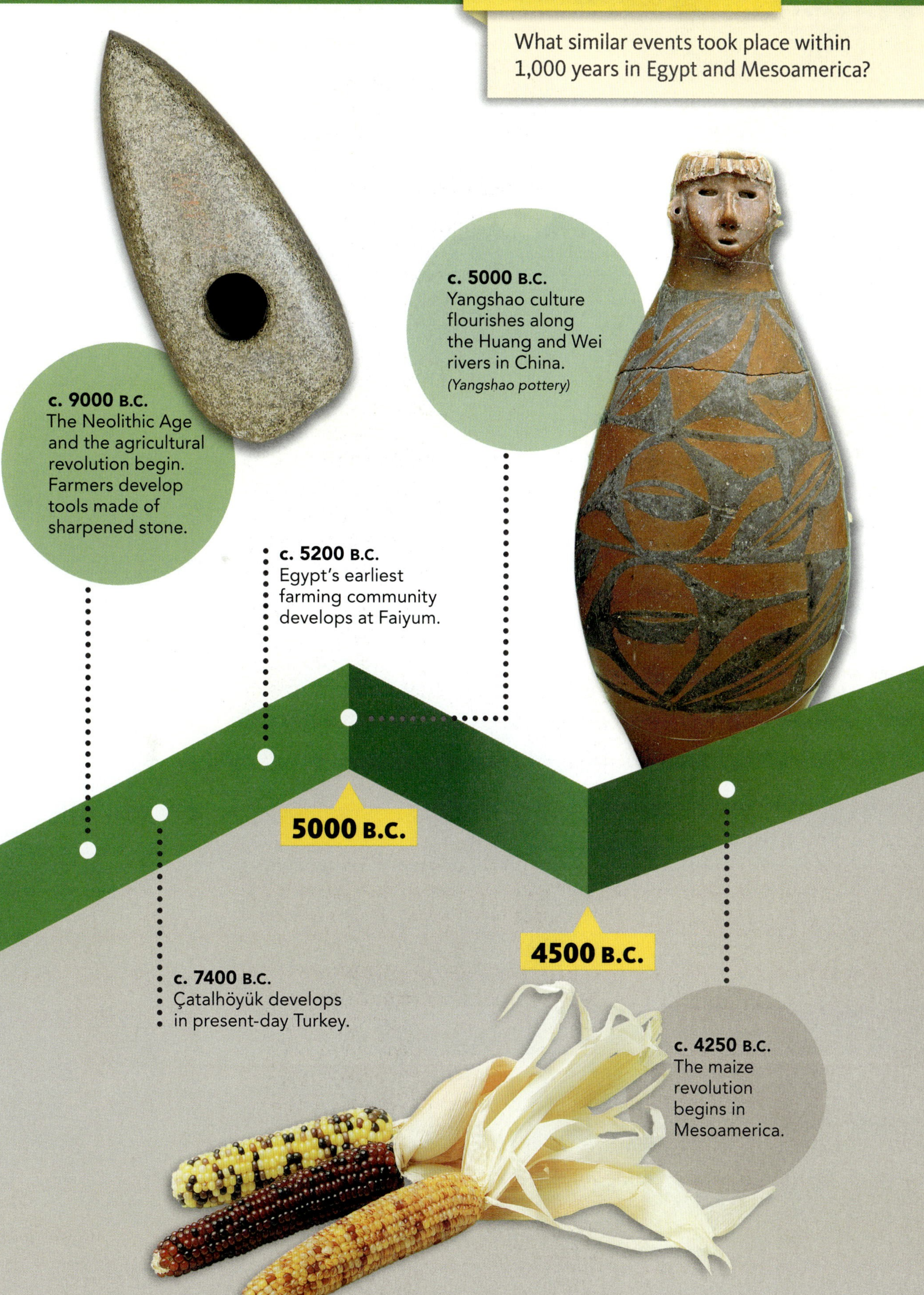

c. 9000 B.C.
The Neolithic Age and the agricultural revolution begin. Farmers develop tools made of sharpened stone.
c. 7400 B.C.
Çatalhöyük develops in present-day Turkey.
c. 5200 B.C.
Egypt's earliest farming community develops at Faiyum.
c. 5000 B.C.
Yangshao culture flourishes along the Huang and Wei rivers in China.
(Yangshao pottery)
5000 B.C.
4500 B.C.
c. 4250 B.C.
The maize revolution begins in Mesoamerica.

UNIT 1
GEOGRAPHY IN HISTORY

THE LAST ICE AGE

18,000 B.C.–10,000 B.C.

For much of history, Earth has been a cold place. It has endured long periods, called Ice Ages, during which temperatures dropped and slow-moving masses of ice called glaciers formed. The last Ice Age, which began more than two million years ago, reached its height in 18,000 B.C. Around this time, glaciers covered large areas of the world. By 12,000 B.C., the overall temperature of Earth had warmed, and much of the ice had melted. By 10,000 B.C., our world looked much the way it does now and had a climate similar to today's. As you can see in the photos, glacial movement also formed bodies of water and landforms that still make up Earth's landscape.

What continents were not affected by the last Ice Age? How can you tell?

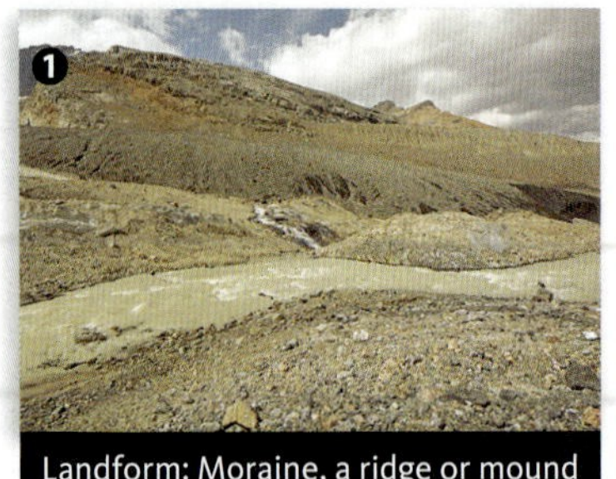

1

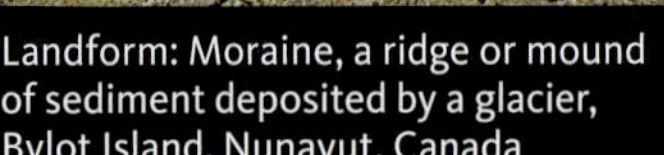

Landform: Moraine, a ridge or mound of sediment deposited by a glacier, Bylot Island, Nunavut, Canada

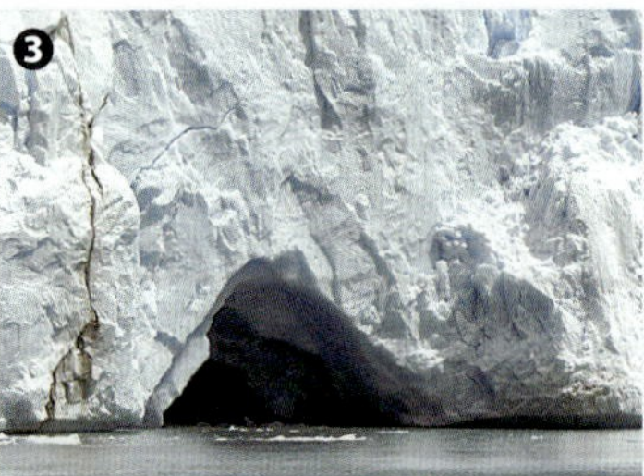

3

Landform: Glacier cave, Patagonia, Argentina

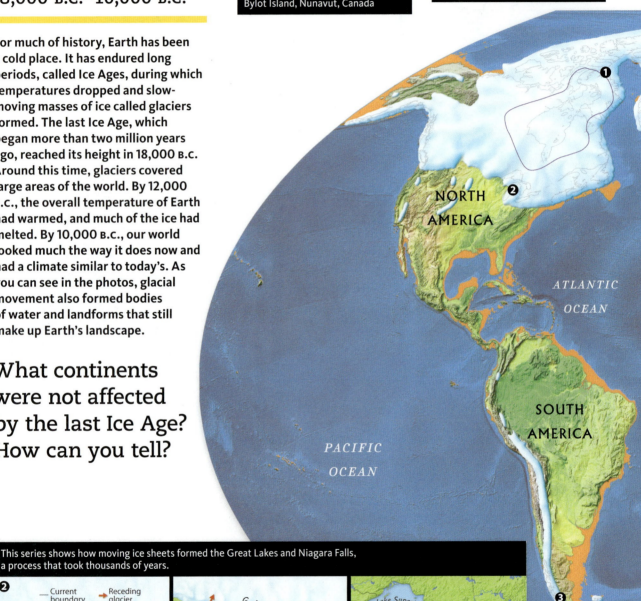

1
2
NORTH AMERICA
ATLANTIC OCEAN
SOUTH AMERICA
PACIFIC OCEAN
3

This series shows how moving ice sheets formed the Great Lakes and Niagara Falls, a process that took thousands of years.

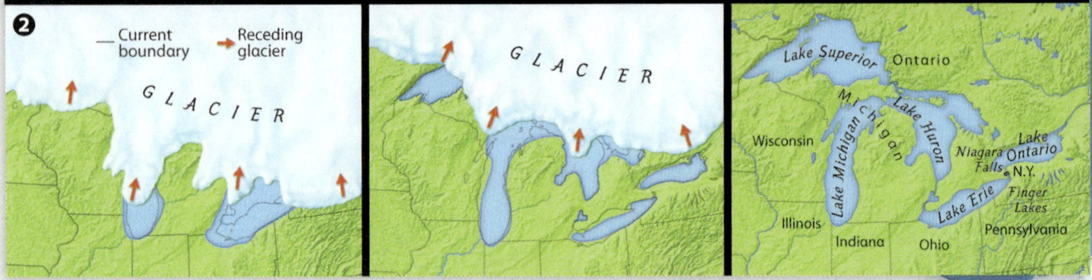

2
Current boundary
Receding glacier
GLACIER
GLACIER
Lake Superior
Ontario
Michigan
Lake Huron
Wisconsin
Lake Michigan
Niagara Falls
Lake Ontario
N.Y.
Lake Erie
Finger Lakes
Illinois
Indiana
Ohio
Pennsylvania

4
Landform: Fjord, a deep glacial trough that filled with seawater, Norway

5
Landform: Glacial valley, Fagaras Mountains, Romania

6
Landform: Sediment-filled glacier, Karakoram, Himalaya

ARCTIC OCEAN

ASIA

PACIFIC OCEAN

AFRICA

INDIAN OCEAN

AUSTRALIA

Extent of ice coverage, c. 18,000 B.C.

Extent of ice coverage, c. 10,000 B.C.

Land area, c. 18,000 B.C.

Modern land area

0 1,000 2,000 kilometers

0 1,000 2,000 miles

Winkel Tripel projection

CHAPTER

1 THE DEVELOPMENT OF HUMAN SOCIETIES

175,000 B.C. – 3000 B.C.

SECTION 1

THE PALEOLITHIC AGE

KEY VOCABULARY
- anthropologist
- archaeologist
- artifact
- culture
- drought
- fossil
- land bridge
- megafauna
- migration
- oasis
- technology

NAMES & PLACES
- Beringia
- *Homo sapiens*
- Ice Age
- Lascaux Cave
- Paleolithic Age
- Sahara

SECTION 2

THE NEOLITHIC AGE

KEY VOCABULARY
- agriculture
- domestication
- fertile
- hunter-gatherer
- nomad
- oral history
- primary source
- secondary source

NAMES & PLACES
- Fertile Crescent
- Neolithic Age

READING STRATEGY

ORGANIZE IDEAS: COMPARE AND CONTRAST

When you compare and contrast two or more things, you note their similarities and differences. Use a Venn diagram like this one to help you compare and contrast Paleolithic and Neolithic people as you read the chapter.

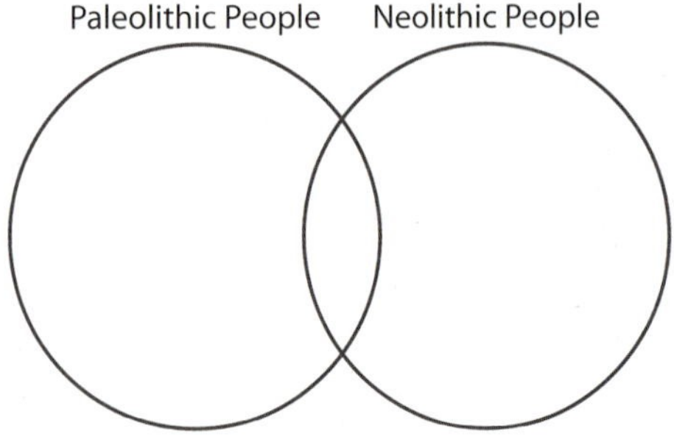

Paleolithic People
Neolithic People

This rock art found in the North African country of Algeria dates back at least 8,000 years.

1.1 Discovering Prehistory

You probably think your parents are pretty old. Well, think again. They actually belong to the newest human species on the planet—*Homo sapiens*, or "wise man"—and so do you. We'll begin our story with this species.

MAIN IDEA

The evidence uncovered by scientists helps us learn about our early human history.

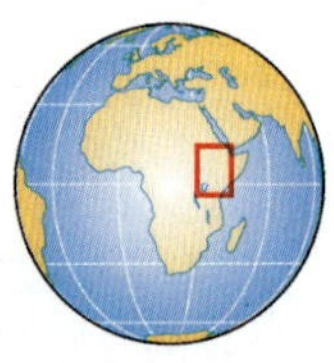

Great Rift Valley

A rift valley is created in places where Earth's outer layer, or crust, has split apart. In East Africa's Great Rift Valley, this action has produced valleys that average 30 to 40 miles wide. The area has provided archaeologists with a wealth of human fossils because the soil in the valley helped preserve the remains.

GEOLOGIC AND ARCHAEOLOGICAL TIME

Earth is incredibly old: somewhere around 4.5 billion years old. Yet ***Homo sapiens*** (HOH-moh SAY-pee-uhnz) has existed for only about the last 200,000 years. Scientists know this because they have found fossils and artifacts that belonged to this species. **Fossils** are the remains, such as bones and teeth, of organisms that lived long ago. **Artifacts** are human-made objects, such as stone tools. These items provide some of the best clues to prehistory, or the time before written records existed.

Scientists called **archaeologists** search for, discover, and then interpret artifacts left behind by *Homo sapiens*. Archaeologists are like the crime scene investigators of history. They piece together evidence that tells the story of what happened at a site hundreds, thousands, or even hundreds of thousands of years ago.

Archaeologists sometimes use geologic techniques to find out how old fossils and artifacts are. For example, they can figure out how old an artifact is based on how deeply it is buried in layers of dirt. In a site that hasn't been disturbed over time, dirt builds up in layers, with younger layers covering the older ones. Archaeologists know that fossils and artifacts lying in the deepest layers are the oldest.

ORIGINS IN AFRICA

Early *Homo sapiens* looked very much like humans do today. It is now widely accepted that the species first appeared in Africa. Earlier hominins, or human-like species, are believed to have lived in Africa for millions of years before *Homo sapiens*.

In 1967, a team of archaeologists led by Richard Leakey found the earliest fossils of modern humans. The team discovered two *Homo sapiens* skulls near the Omo River in the Great Rift Valley of East Africa. The skulls were originally thought to be 130,000 years old, but a more recent dating has determined them to be about 195,000 years old.

Homo sapiens lived during the **Paleolithic** (pay-lee-uh-LIHTH-ihk) **Age**, a period that began around 2.5 million B.C. and ended around 8000 B.C. The period is also called the Old Stone Age because the people living then made simple tools and weapons out of stone. It was a time of dramatic changes in geography and climate. It was also a time when modern human development—and human history—began.

Homo sapiens fossils have been found in East Africa's Great Rift Valley, shown here.

REVIEW & ASSESS

1. **READING CHECK** What kinds of evidence do archaeologists uncover to learn about early modern humans?
2. **DETERMINE WORD MEANINGS** *Paleo* means "old." What do you suppose *lithic* means?
3. **MAKE INFERENCES** What does the fact that early *Homo sapiens* made tools suggest about this group?

Critical Viewing Friends and neighbors in a community in China sit down to a lavish banquet. What do details in the photo tell you about the community's cultural behaviors?

1.2 The Elements of Culture

Maybe you've heard the saying "You are what you eat," but did you know that you are also what you speak, what you wear, and what you believe? All of these behaviors—and many others—help identify you with your particular blend of cultures.

MAIN IDEA

Studying the culture of *Homo sapiens* in the Paleolithic Age helps reveal how people lived.

WHAT IS CULTURE?

Culture is a big part of human development. All the elements that contribute to the way of life of a particular group of people make up culture. These elements include language, clothing, music, art, law, religion, government, and family structure. Culture is passed down from parents to children and greatly affects our behaviors and beliefs. It influences people to do things in a particular way, such as eating or avoiding certain foods. It unifies a group and distinguishes that group from others.

Language, art, toolmaking, and religion are the elements that were most important in defining early cultures. Even early *Homo sapiens* communicated through speech, created cave paintings, made and used tools, and buried the dead. However, groups of people often did things slightly differently. These differences reflect each group's technical knowledge, artistic styles, and available natural resources.

WHY STUDY CULTURE?

As you've learned, cultural behaviors are passed down from generation to generation, but they can also change over time or—like the ability to make stone tools—be nearly lost altogether. In part, scientists study prehistoric cultures to learn how these cultures differ from modern cultures and discover what they all have in common. Information about modern cultures is often provided by archaeologists called **anthropologists**.

The artifacts archaeologists uncover help them piece together a picture of early humans' cultural behavior and daily life. For example, by studying tools uncovered at a prehistoric site, archaeologists learn how advanced the people who made them were and what jobs they needed to do. In addition, comparing artifacts from different sites can explain why one group was more successful than another.

Comparing artifacts from different time periods helps explain how people changed and developed. This knowledge helps us see thousands of years into the past so we can better understand the present and predict the future.

REVIEW & ASSESS

1. **READING CHECK** What do artifacts, such as stone tools, reveal about the culture of early *Homo sapiens*?
2. **SUMMARIZE** How do archaeologists and anthropologists work together?
3. **DRAW CONCLUSIONS** What might the discovery of tools used primarily as weapons suggest about a group of early humans?

1.3 Changing Environments

Today, climate change is forcing us all to make some adjustments—from switching off lights to turning off faucets. Still, we're not the first humans to be affected by shifting climate patterns. A big change in their environment drove Paleolithic people to take steps that would transform the world forever.

MAIN IDEA

A changing climate forced Paleolithic people to move to new places and develop new tools to survive.

COMPARING TOOLS

The stone tool on the left was made about 100,000 years ago. The fishhook made from bone on the right dates back about 42,000 years. You can see that early humans' technical skill had come a long way in about 60,000 years.

FINDING NEW HOMES

About 100,000 years ago, much of Africa had a very unstable climate. Some places became warmer and wetter, while others became hot and dry. These climate changes greatly altered the landscape in which Paleolithic people lived.

Archaeologists have discovered that East Africa suffered a terrible **drought** between 100,000 and 75,000 years ago. This long period of dry, hot weather had a huge impact on the landscape. Rivers and vast lakes shrank and left people struggling for survival. The plants they ate became scarce, and the animals they hunted disappeared. At the same time, previously uninhabitable areas became livable and attractive. For example, the **Sahara**, which is one of the harshest deserts on Earth today, turned into an **oasis**, or a green area where plants can grow. These environmental changes may have encouraged some of the 10,000 Paleolithic people living in East Africa at the time to leave their homeland. They began their long **migration**, or movement, first to the Sahara in North Africa and then into the wider world.

ADAPTING TO NEW CONDITIONS

As people migrated, they responded to some of the challenges of their new environments by using technology. **Technology** is the application of knowledge, tools, and inventions to meet people's needs.

Critical Viewing Paleolithic people first lived on savannas like this one. Savannas are areas of flat grassland where animals roam. What might have made the savanna a welcoming environment?

The ability to capture and control fire was a particularly valuable technology. In addition to providing much-needed warmth and light, fire helped Paleolithic people scare away enemies and drive animals into traps. Cooking meat made it easier to digest and killed bacteria.

Paleolithic people also used technology to develop tools that helped them adapt to new environments and climates. Simple tools had been used for millions of years, but *Homo sapiens* refined them to create a really effective tool kit. A hard stone called flint was especially useful, as it could be split into hard, razor-sharp flakes. Early humans learned to design a tool to perform a particular task, such as chopping wood, carving meat, or skinning animals.

Over time, tools grew increasingly advanced. Humans crafted fishhooks out of bone and sewing needles out of ivory. These specialized tools helped our ancestors survive in an amazing range of new habitats and climates—from arctic areas to deserts.

REVIEW & ASSESS

1. **READING CHECK** What led some Paleolithic people to leave their home in East Africa thousands of years ago and migrate to new places?
2. **DETERMINE WORD MEANINGS** What context clues tell you that *uninhabitable* means "unlivable"?
3. **MAKE INFERENCES** Think about the adaptations Paleolithic people made to survive in new conditions. What can you infer about their intelligence?

1.4 Moving into New Environments

More than 60,000 years ago, the world witnessed movement on a scale never seen before as our restless ancestors began leaving Africa in waves. They set out on a worldwide migration that would permanently populate the entire planet.

MAIN IDEA

Between 70,000 and 10,000 B.C., Paleolithic people migrated from Africa and settled throughout the world.

SPREAD OF EARLY HUMANS

As you have learned, the changing climate made Paleolithic people search for homes outside of Africa. They first migrated into Southwest Asia around 70,000 years ago. The region was warm and tropical and provided lush vegetation and abundant wildlife.

In time, people spread across the rest of the world. From Asia they reached Australia around 50,000 years ago. By about 40,000 years ago, early humans had arrived in Europe. Around 30,000 years ago, *Homo sapiens* reached Siberia on the edge of eastern Asia.

The last continents to be populated were the Americas. This final migration may have been made possible by the **Ice Age**. At its height around 20,000 years ago, the Ice Age trapped so much water as ice that the sea level was nearly 400 feet lower than it is today. This trapped ice created **land bridges** that allowed humans to walk across continents. Many scientists have proposed the theory that hunters crossed the **Beringia** (beh-RIN-gee-uh) land bridge, which connected Siberia with North America, in a series of migrations between 20,000 and 15,000 years ago.

Scientists believe that during a period of glacial melting around 12,000 years ago, more travelers pushed southward through Central America and South America. However, new evidence has emerged that challenges this timing. The genes of some South American people suggest that their ancestors arrived from Australia 35,000 years ago, and *Homo sapiens* footprints in Central America have been dated to 40,000 years ago. These findings might support the theory that the earliest Americans arrived in boats, rather than by land bridge.

IN SEARCH OF FOOD

People migrated to many of these places, possibly in hot pursuit of the animals they liked to eat. Some of these creatures were **megafauna**, which means "large animals." Megafauna included the woolly mammoth, giant ground sloth, and saber-toothed cat, which are shown below.

Megafauna

Humans hunted herds of woolly mammoths in northern Asia and parts of Europe and North America. The giant ground sloth and saber-toothed cat lived primarily in North and South America.

Woolly Mammoth

Giant Ground Sloth

Saber-Toothed Cat

EARLY HUMAN MIGRATION: 100,000–14,000 YEARS AGO

This map shows what Earth might have looked like many thousands of years ago. The purple shading indicates areas that were covered in ice from the Ice Age. The green shading shows land that once existed but has since eroded, or worn away.

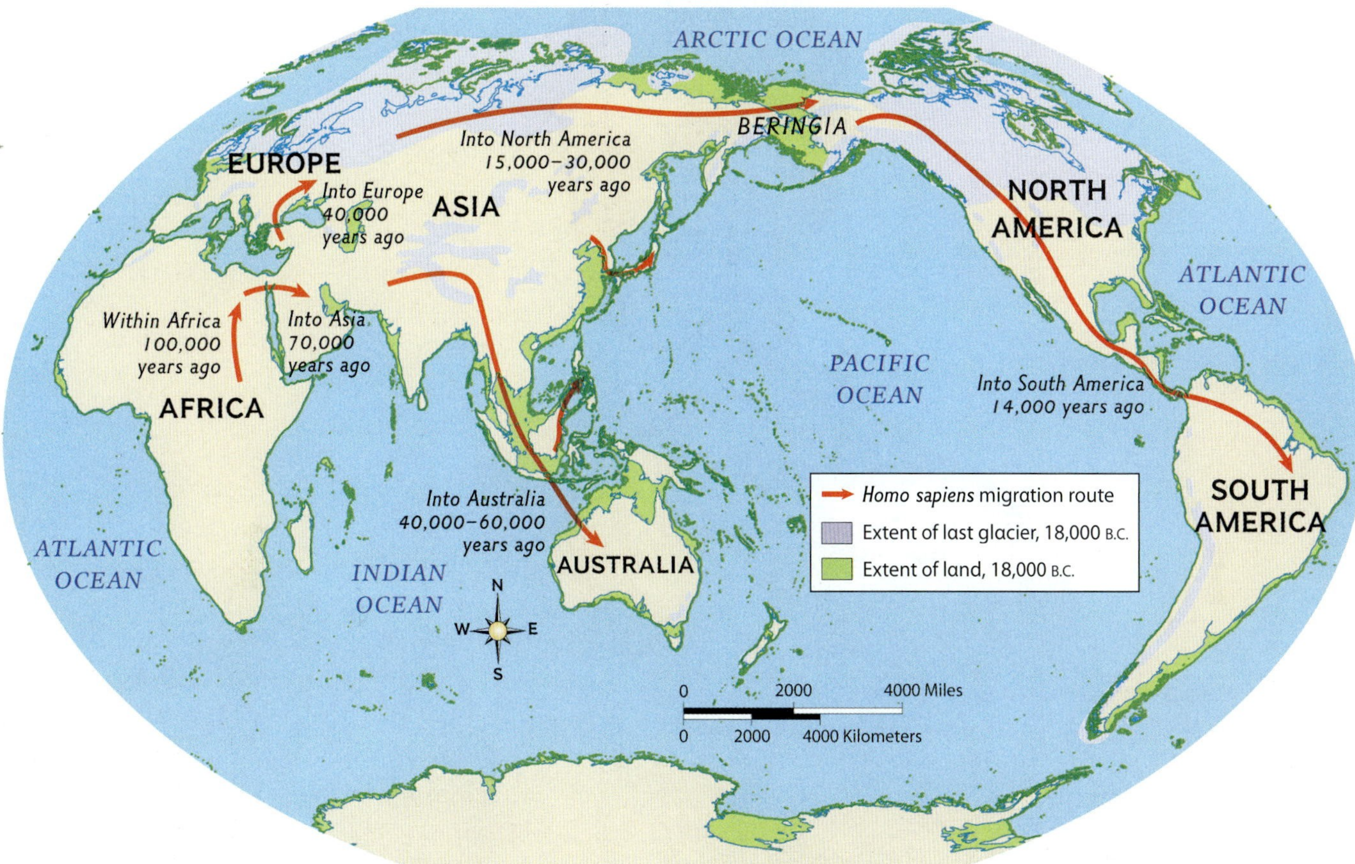
ARCTIC OCEAN
EUROPE
Into Europe 40,000 years ago
ASIA
Into North America 15,000–30,000 years ago
BERINGIA
NORTH AMERICA
ATLANTIC OCEAN
Within Africa 100,000 years ago
Into Asia 70,000 years ago
AFRICA
PACIFIC OCEAN
Into South America 14,000 years ago
Into Australia 40,000–60,000 years ago
AUSTRALIA
Homo sapiens migration route
Extent of last glacier, 18,000 B.C.
Extent of land, 18,000 B.C.
SOUTH AMERICA
ATLANTIC OCEAN
INDIAN OCEAN
N
W
E
S
0
2000
4000 Miles
0
2000
4000 Kilometers

The woolly mammoth, a relative of the modern elephant, was one of the largest megafauna. It stood between 9 and 11 feet tall and weighed as much as six tons. Its curved tusks grew up to 13 feet long.

At five tons, the giant ground sloth wasn't much smaller than the woolly mammoth. However, the sloth was fairly harmless. It mostly used its long claws to tear leaves and bark, not other animals.

There was more reason to fear the saber-toothed cat with its two huge, swordlike teeth. This creature was smaller than a modern lion but much heavier, weighing more than 400 pounds.

These megafauna became extinct, or died out, about 11,000 years ago. Many scientists believe they were overhunted or wiped out by climate change as the Ice Age began to come to a close.

REVIEW & ASSESS

1. **READING CHECK** What food did Paleolithic people eat when they migrated to Asia and other parts of the world?
2. **INTERPRET MAPS** What challenges do you think people encountered as they moved into the new environments shown on the map?
3. **FORM OPINIONS** Do you think the Americas became populated by land bridge, by boat, or by a combination of the two? Explain your position.

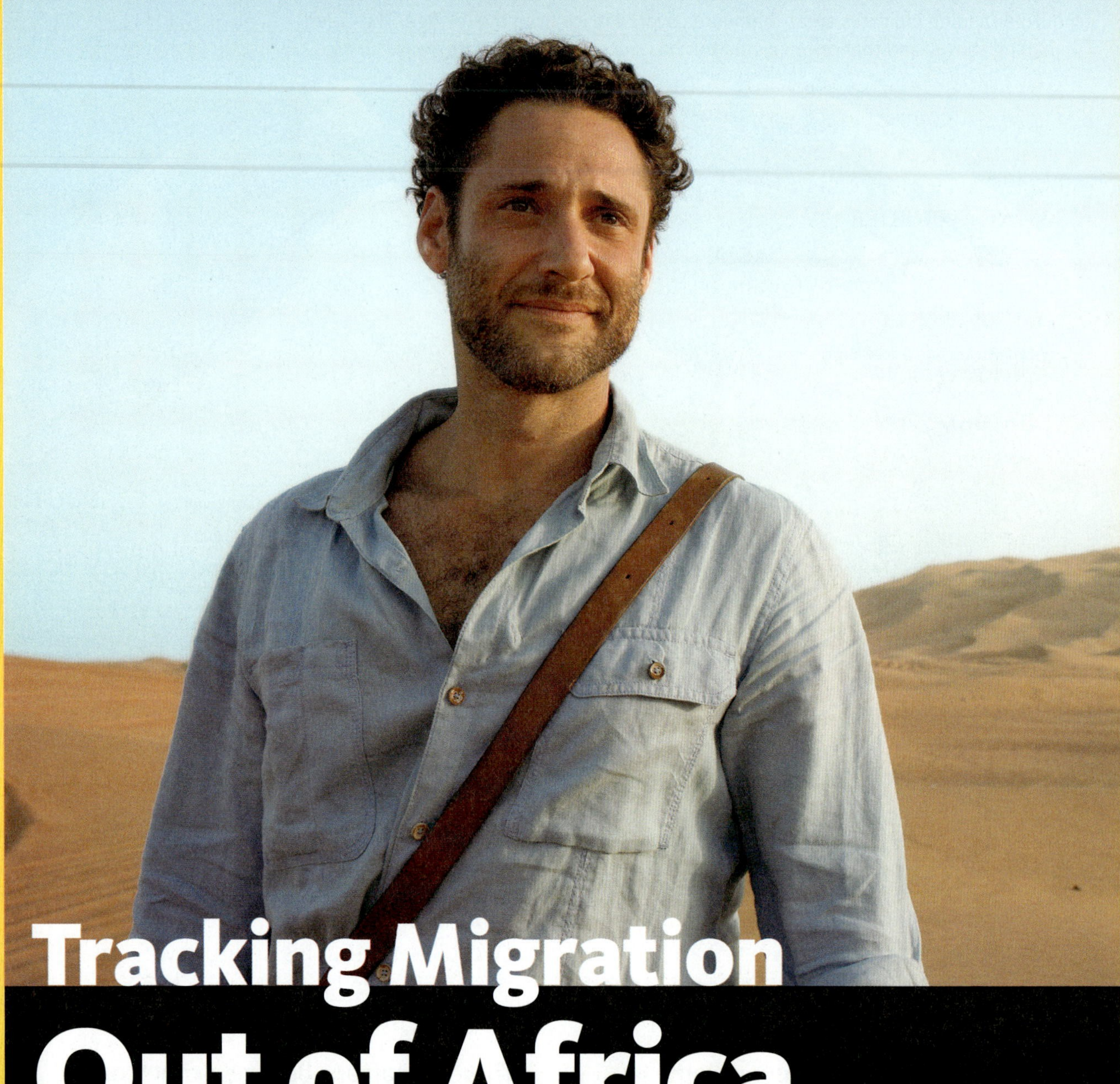

Tracking Migration Out of Africa

Archaeologist **Jeffrey Rose** lives in a desert truck stop in the Southwest Asian country of Oman. He spends his days with his team of experts, sifting through rocks in 100-degree heat. Occasionally, he finds what he's looking for: small, sharp, egg-shaped stones. That may not sound like much, but his finds may dramatically rewrite our earliest history. Rose is looking for evidence to support his theory about who first migrated out of Africa and what route was taken. After years of exploration, he thinks he might have found the answer.

^ Jeffrey Rose has conducted work in many parts of Southwest Asia, including this desert outside of Dubai, United Arab Emirates.

MAIN IDEA

Jeffrey Rose has found evidence to support a new theory about which Paleolithic people first left Africa and what route they took.

LOOKING FOR EVIDENCE

National Geographic Explorer Jeffrey Rose conducted his search in Oman. Geneticists—scientists who study DNA and heredity—have suggested that the first humans to leave Africa traveled through Ethiopia to Yemen and Oman, following the coast of the Arabian Peninsula. Rose went to Oman hoping to find archaeological evidence of this migration.

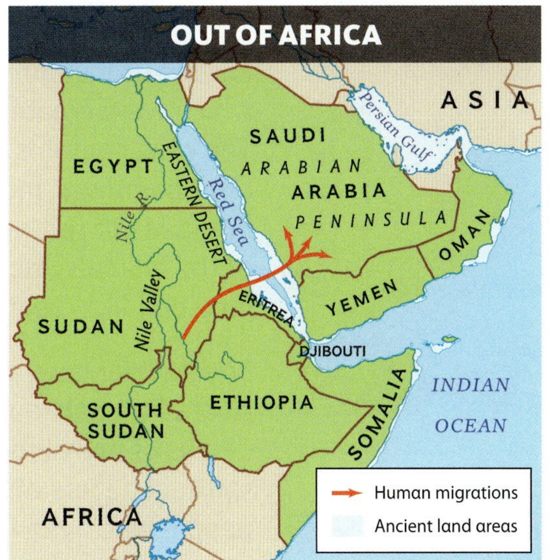
OUT OF AFRICA
ASIA
Persian Gulf
SAUDI
ARABIAN
ARABIA
PENINSULA
EGYPT
EASTERN DESERT
Red Sea
Nile R.
OMAN
YEMEN
ERITREA
SUDAN
Nile Valley
DJIBOUTI
INDIAN
OCEAN
SOUTH
SUDAN
ETHIOPIA
SOMALIA
AFRICA
Human migrations
Ancient land areas

He recorded the earliest traces of humans: discarded flint tools. "Our geologist constantly reads the landscape to tell us where Paleolithic humans would have found water and flint. Find those and you find early people," Rose says. However, after years of surveying, he'd found no African-style artifacts and no evidence of Paleolithic humans on the Arabian Peninsula coast.

HITTING THE JACKPOT

Then in 2010, on the final day at the last site on his list, Rose hit the jackpot. He found a stone spear point with a design unique to people of the Nubian Complex, who had lived in the Nile Valley in North Africa. "We had never considered that the link to Africa would come from the Nile Valley and that their route would be through the middle of the Arabian Peninsula rather than along the coast," says Rose. Yet it made sense that people would migrate to Arabia from the Nile Valley. As Rose points out, "It's logical that people moved from an environment they knew to another that mirrored it." By the end of 2013, he had found more than 250 Nubian Complex sites in Oman.

When Rose dated the artifacts, he discovered they were roughly 106,000 years old, a point in time when people of the Nubian Complex flourished in Africa. The puzzle pieces fit. "Geneticists have shown that the modern human family tree began to branch out more than 60,000 years ago," says Rose. "I'm not questioning *when* it happened, but *where*. I suggest the great modern human expansion to the rest of the world was launched from Arabia rather than Africa." Rose's evidence suggests that perhaps it was a two-stage process. Paleolithic people might have left North Africa for Arabia more than 100,000 years ago. Then about 40,000 years later, they left Arabia and began to settle the rest of the world.

Now Rose wants to know why it was people of the Nubian Complex who spread from Africa. "What was it about their technology and culture that enabled them to expand so successfully," he wonders, "and what happened next?" As Rose says, "We've always looked to the beginning and wanted to understand how we got here. That's what it means to be human."

REVIEW & ASSESS

1. **READING CHECK** What theory has Jeffrey Rose proposed about the migration of Paleolithic people?
2. **INTERPRET MAPS** What body of water did the Nubians cross to get to the Arabian Peninsula?
3. **MAKE INFERENCES** Why would resources of water and flint have been important to early humans?

1.6 Cave Art

It wasn't all about tools in the Paleolithic Age. Early humans had an artistic side as well. Prehistoric graffiti appears on cave walls all over the world. It turns out that the urge for artistic expression is almost as old as humankind itself.

MAIN IDEA

Cave paintings reveal much about Paleolithic people and their world.

ANCIENT ARTISTS

Art is an important part of culture. It shows a capacity for creativity, which separates humans from animals. Very early humans may have collected pretty rocks, carved wood, or painted pictures of themselves and their surroundings.

However, around 35,000 years ago, an artistic explosion occurred when humans began painting detailed images on cave walls. Examples have been found across the world, but it took archaeologists a long time to accept that the cave paintings had been created during the Paleolithic Age. They found it hard to believe that prehistoric people had the ability, time, or desire to produce such beautiful works of art.

The subjects of these cave paintings vary quite a bit, which is not surprising since they were created over a span of 25,000 years. The paintings often depict side-view images of animals, including woolly mammoths and horses. Some images feature everyday scenes, such as deer being hunted by men with spears. Other images consist of lines, circles, and geometric patterns.

One type of image that appears all over the world is considered by many to be one of the most moving: handprints. An artist often created this image by blowing paint through a reed over the hands—leaving behind the imprint of people who lived thousands of years ago.

GLIMPSE INTO AN EARLY WORLD

The **Lascaux Cave** in France has some of Europe's most amazing cave paintings, which were created about 17,000 years ago. The cave contains about 600 beautifully clear paintings, mostly of animals, many in shades of red, yellow, and brown. Some of the animals, including a nearly 17-foot-long bull-like creature, are now extinct.

Spectacular cave and rock paintings in Australia's Kakadu National Park show details of daily life and also reflect the spiritual beliefs of Aborigines, the earliest people who lived in Australia. These beliefs include a strong connection to the land and nature, which is still shared by the people who live in the region today.

The Sahara is also rich in rock art. The Tassili-n-Ajjer (tuh-sill-ee-nah-JAIR) mountain range in North Africa has spectacular paintings showing the once abundant wildlife and grasslands of this now barren desert. The Cave of the Hands in Argentina contains an incredible wall of handprints, as shown on the next page.

Despite many theories, it is unclear why Paleolithic people created such beautiful images in dark and hard-to-reach caves. Some researchers believe that most early art was actually created outdoors but has long since faded away. While we are unlikely to ever fully understand the meaning of Paleolithic art, it does provide insight into the lives and culture of our ancestors.

Researchers believe that this painting from the Cave of the Hands in Argentina shows the handprints of 13-year-old boys.

REVIEW & ASSESS

1. **READING CHECK** What do cave paintings reveal about Paleolithic people?
2. **INTEGRATE VISUALS** What different purposes might cave art have served in the Paleolithic world?
3. **COMPARE AND CONTRAST** What does the rock art in North Africa reveal about how that region has changed from the Paleolithic Age to today?

2.1 Nomadic Hunter-Gatherers

When you're hungry, you probably raid the fridge or head for the store. When Paleolithic people were hungry, they tracked down an animal, killed it with their handmade weapons, and then cooked it over a fire they had to carefully start and keep going. That's what it took to survive every day.

MAIN IDEA

Paleolithic people were constantly on the move to find food.

MOVING WITH THE SEASONS

The Paleolithic world had no farms or stores, but it did have a rich variety of foods. People just had to search them out. During the Paleolithic Age, humans lived as hunter-gatherers. A **hunter-gatherer** hunts animals and gathers wild plants to eat. These tasks were made easier and safer by the fact that early humans worked together and shared the jobs.

Most hunter-gatherer groups were small—around 30 people. The men hunted, often herding large animals into traps or over cliffs. Meanwhile, the women and young children gathered fruits and nuts. Scientists have learned a great deal about hunter-gatherers by studying the body and belongings of a later hunter known as the Iceman, seen at right.

Because the animal herds moved with the seasons, so did the groups hunting them. People who move from place to place like this are called **nomads**. Nomadic hunter-gatherers traveled light. They carried all their possessions with them, including stone tools and clothing.

As hunter-gatherers traveled in areas outside of Africa, they learned to adapt to their new environments—especially the cold. They made needles that enabled them to sew warm clothes out of animal skins. Caves offered the best protection from the worst winter weather. However, people also made shelters of wood, bone, and animal skins, which provided temporary camps.

FOLLOWING THE HERDS

Nomadic hunter-gatherers followed herds of megafauna as the animals moved from place to place. The herds migrated with the seasons and entered new environments created by the changeable Ice Age climate. For example, the Beringia land bridge allowed herds of woolly mammoths to cross into North America, with hunter-gatherers following close behind.

It wasn't easy to kill an animal as big as a woolly mammoth. It took intelligence, teamwork, and special tools. Paleolithic people developed deadly new weapons, including barbed harpoons, spear-throwers, and bows and arrows. These weapons allowed them to kill from a distance, which made the task safer and more efficient. The rewards were also great. A woolly mammoth could feed the group for months.

As humans spread around the world, various human groups competed for resources. Conflict would have been most common during cold periods when food and shelter were scarce. It's likely that in warmer periods of plentiful food, human groups interacted more happily, sharing their technology and culture. This interaction helped spread new ideas and paved the way for a remarkable new stage in human development.

THE ICEMAN

The Iceman lived around 3300 B.C. More than 5,000 years later, hikers found his frozen body in the Alps in Europe. His clothing, his tools, and even the contents of his stomach have helped scientists understand how prehistoric people lived. The graphic here offers some clues as to how he might have died.

1 The Iceman perches on a cliff. He tests the copper blade of his ax and the flint points of his dagger with satisfaction. They're razor sharp. He searches below for his prey. With any luck, he'll bring goat meat back to his community tonight.

2 Suddenly an arrow pierces the Iceman's shoulder. Another hunter has shot him from behind. The Iceman falls off the cliff into the snowbank below.

3 Desperately the Iceman rises and struggles to fight off his attacker, but he's too weak. He falls back down but manages to crawl into a cave in the ice. As the Iceman dies, snow begins to fall. Snow and ice will hide him from view for the next 5,000 years.

REVIEW & ASSESS

1. **READING CHECK** Why were Paleolithic people constantly moving from place to place?
2. **INTEGRATE VISUALS** What words would you use to describe hunter-gatherers such as the Iceman?
3. **ANALYZE CAUSE AND EFFECT** What impact did the changing climate have on hunter-gatherers?

2.2 The Beginnings of Domestication

A pet poodle might lick your hand and follow you everywhere, but dogs weren't always man's best friend. All dogs are descended from wolves. Humans transformed some of these wild animals into loyal helpers, which marked a major breakthrough in learning to control their environment.

MAIN IDEA

Early humans took control of their environment by raising useful plants and taming animals.

CHANGING CLIMATE

Around 14,000 years ago, Earth grew warmer, and the ice sheets melted. These changes raised sea levels, created freshwater lakes, and increased global rainfall. Large areas of land became covered with water. As a result, land bridges disappeared, and coastal waters formed that were full of fish. Animals moved, adapted, or died as their habitats, or environments, changed.

These environmental changes also began to transform the ways that hunter-gatherers lived in some areas. The warmer, wetter climate encouraged the development of forests and grasslands and resulted in longer growing seasons. These conditions proved to be perfect for the growth of grasses. In time, people learned to raise other plants and animals, making them useful to humans. This development, called **domestication**, led to the beginning of farming.

TAMING PLANTS AND ANIMALS

Hunter-gatherers had grown plants to increase their productivity long before the ice began to melt. Now the improved climate made growing plants even easier. After scattering seeds in wet ground, hunter-gatherers knew they could return and harvest the plants the following year. Some foods, especially grains from cereals such as wheat and barley, could be stored to feed people and animals year-round.

At about the same time, humans began to tame animals. The earliest domesticated animals were dogs. All around the world, wild wolf pups were caught and

Critical Viewing Young nomadic girls corral sheep for milking in northeastern Afghanistan. What details in the photo tell you that the animals have been domesticated?

bred for hunting and protection. Other animals were domesticated for food: first sheep and goats, then pigs and cattle. As well as providing meat, milk, and wool, some domesticated animals could carry heavy loads and pull carts.

Although most humans remained nomadic, the warmer climate provided certain areas with such abundant resources that some hunter-gatherer groups decided to settle down. For example, areas around estuaries made perfect places to live. An estuary is formed where a river feeds into the ocean. The combination of fresh water, salt water, and land provided people with a year-round supply of food. Settling down to live permanently in such places would bring about a great change that allowed humans to make their next big leap forward.

REVIEW & ASSESS

1. **READING CHECK** How did humans use the plants and animals they domesticated?
2. **ANALYZE CAUSE AND EFFECT** How did the warmer climate and increased rainfall in some places affect people's ability to grow plants for food?
3. **FORM OPINIONS** What do you think were some of the advantages of the settled life over the nomadic one?

2.3 The Agricultural Revolution

If you wanted to grow some crops, you'd probably look for a warm place with a reliable supply of water and soil full of nutrients. Thousands of years ago, a number of river valleys satisfied all of these conditions. They were at the heart of an important change in the way people lived.

MAIN IDEA

Humans settled down and farmed along river valleys and developed new farm tools and methods.

NORTH AMERICA
ATLANTIC OCEAN
TEHUACÁN
PACIFIC OCEAN
SOUTH AMERICA
N
W
E
S
0
1000
2000 Miles
0
1000
2000 Kilometers

THE SICKLE

The sickle, which developed during the Neolithic Age, was crucial to harvesting certain grains. The tool was so important that in some places, people made sickles all the same size so that the tools could be repaired easily and quickly.

FERTILE RIVER VALLEYS

Imagine that a great change took place all over the world and transformed forever the way people lived. That is exactly what happened when farming largely replaced hunting and gathering. The slow shift to growing food began around 10,000 B.C. and ended around 8000 B.C. By then, many people had discovered that they could live year-round on what they farmed, rather than on what they found.

This shift in the way people lived is called the agricultural revolution. **Agriculture** is the practice of growing plants and rearing animals for food. The shift to agriculture also ushered in a new period known as the **Neolithic Age**, which began somewhere between 10,000 B.C. and 8000 B.C. In the early stages of this period, people began to build farming villages.

Many of the earliest farming villages were in an area called the **Fertile Crescent**. This region stretches from the Persian Gulf to the Mediterranean Sea. It includes the fertile, flat floodplains along the Tigris and Euphrates rivers in Southwest Asia. **Fertile** soil encourages the growth of crops and plants. The region provided a steady food supply. People were able to settle down and enjoy a much more comfortable lifestyle.

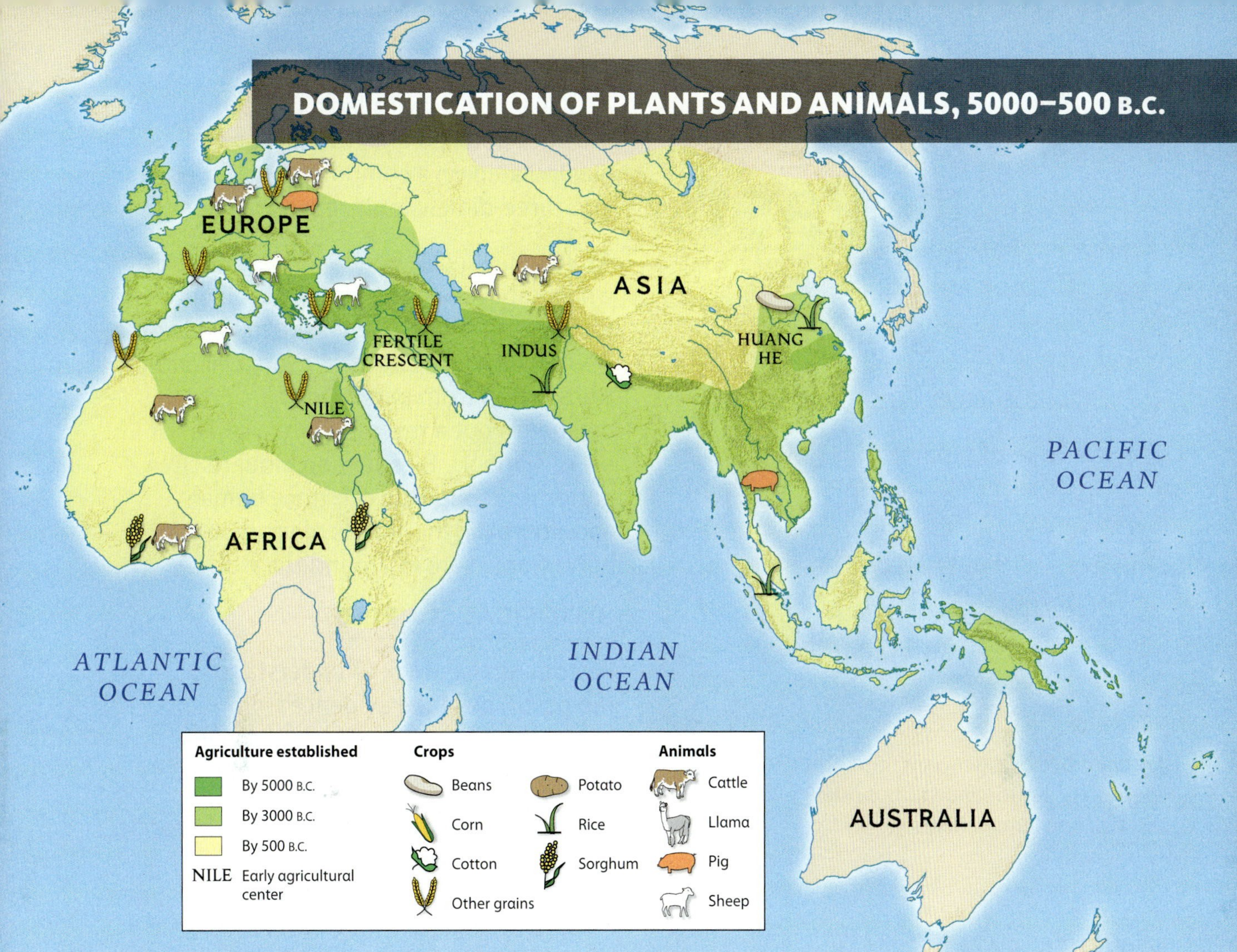
DOMESTICATION OF PLANTS AND ANIMALS, 5000–500 B.C.
EUROPE
ASIA
AFRICA
AUSTRALIA
FERTILE CRESCENT
INDUS
HUANG HE
NILE
PACIFIC OCEAN
ATLANTIC OCEAN
INDIAN OCEAN
Agriculture established
By 5000 B.C.
By 3000 B.C.
By 500 B.C.
NILE Early agricultural center
Crops
Beans
Corn
Cotton
Other grains
Potato
Rice
Sorghum
Animals
Cattle
Llama
Pig
Sheep

NEW FARM TOOLS AND METHODS

Even so, farming was very hard work. To make it easier, Neolithic people developed specialized tools. They fashioned hoes for digging the soil and plows for preparing the land to plant seeds. They also made curved sickles that cut through the stalks of grain and millstones that ground the grain into flour.

Farmers used domesticated animals to make their new tools more efficient. For example, they tied cattle to the plows and led the animals up and down the rows. In addition to helping turn over the soil, the cattle left behind manure that fertilized the land.

Neolithic people also developed new technology for the home. They made clay pots and hardened them in kilns, or ovens. The kilns could also be used to heat and melt the metal from rocks—a process called smelting. The liquid metal was then cast in molds to create metal tools, which eventually began to replace stone tools. The Stone Age had come to a close.

REVIEW & ASSESS

1. **READING CHECK** What new farm tools did humans develop during the agricultural revolution?

2. **INTERPRET MAPS** Along what geographic feature had most agriculture developed by 5000 B.C.?

3. **DRAW CONCLUSIONS** In what ways was the agricultural revolution an important breakthrough in human history?

2.4 Studying the Past

Look around. Everything you can see tells a story. At a glance, the shape, size, age, and use of a particular object provide some clues to its history. However, with a team of scientists, you could learn a whole lot more.

MAIN IDEA

Archaeologists, historians, and other specialists gather and study evidence to tell the story of human history.

SCIENTIFIC DATA

As you have learned by reading this chapter, archaeologists piece together clues to tell the story of what happened in a particular place at a particular time. It is detective work, and like detectives, they rely on other specialists to help them find and analyze the evidence.

Some of these specialists include geologists, who can tell the story of a landscape by analyzing rocks and fossils. When geologists investigate rock layers, they sometimes uncover prehistoric plant and animal remains. These remains can reveal what the environment was like. The bones they find provide information about human health and diet. Geologists can also help archaeologists locate deeply buried artifacts.

Other specialists called radiologists study x-ray images to look beneath the surface of objects to show what the eye cannot see, especially in bones and rusty metal. An advanced x-ray called a CT scan provides detailed images that can be manipulated on a computer and turned into three-dimensional representations.

As you may recall, geneticists are scientists who study genes, the biological blueprints for all living things. Genes are made up of DNA, which is encoded in every cell and transmitted from parent to child. *Encode* means "to put a message into a code," or set of symbols. By studying modern DNA patterns, geneticists can trace human ancestry back thousands of years to see how people spread around the world.

HISTORICAL SOURCES

Historians also work to understand the past. They take evidence from many different sources to explain what happened and when and why it did.

Some of the sources historians use include primary sources. A **primary source** is a document or other object that was created by someone who witnessed or lived through a historical event. These sources include letters, maps, paintings, and tools. Primary sources are very important, but they are not always completely reliable. The opinions of the author may distort, or misrepresent, the facts.

Historians also use **secondary sources**, documents or other objects created after an event by someone who did not see it or live during the time when it occurred. These are interpretations of events, often based on primary sources. History books and biographies are secondary sources. **Oral history** is an unwritten account of events that is often passed down through the generations as stories or songs.

Different historians can interpret the same evidence in very different ways. In addition, new evidence is continually being discovered. That means that history—especially the details—is always changing.

PRIMARY SOURCE: THE ROSETTA STONE

The Rosetta Stone, which stands nearly four feet high and weighs about 1,700 pounds, is a primary source from ancient Egypt. It is not from the Paleolithic Age. Instead, the three different types of writing carved onto it date back to 196 B.C. The stone was discovered in 1799, but no one could read the first two scripts until a scholar cracked the code in 1822.

HIEROGLYPHIC

Hieroglyphs are pictures that can represent people, objects, animals, plants, sounds, and ideas.

DEMOTIC

Demotic writing is an ancient Egyptian script that, like hieroglyphs, scholars could not read or write before 1822.

GREEK

The three scripts mostly contain the same text, so scholars used the Greek writing to read the other two.

REVIEW & ASSESS

1. **READING CHECK** How do archaeologists, historians, and other specialists work together to study historical evidence?
2. **ANALYZE LANGUAGE USE** How does the phrase "it is detective work" help explain the nature of an archaeologist's job?
3. **COMPARE AND CONTRAST** What is the difference between a primary source and a secondary source?

CHAPTER 1 Review

VOCABULARY

For each pair of vocabulary words, write one sentence that explains the connection between the two words.

1. **fossil; artifact**
   Both fossils, the remains of living organisms, and artifacts, human-made objects, provide helpful clues to understanding our history.
2. **archaeologist; anthropologist**
3. **culture; oral history**
4. **anthropologist; culture**
5. **hunter-gatherer; nomad**
6. **migration; land bridge**
7. **agriculture; fertile**
8. **primary source; secondary source**

READING STRATEGY

9. **ORGANIZE IDEAS: COMPARE AND CONTRAST** If you haven't already, complete your Venn diagram to compare and contrast the lives of Paleolithic and Neolithic people. Then answer the question.

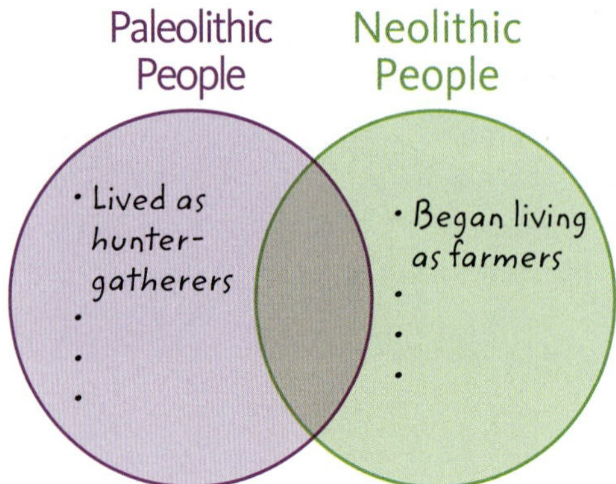
Paleolithic People
Neolithic People
• Lived as hunter-gatherers
•
•
•
• Began living as farmers
•
•
•

In what ways did the lives of Paleolithic and Neolithic people differ? In what ways were they the same?

MAIN IDEAS

Answer the following questions. Support your answers with evidence from the chapter.

10. What do archaeologists learn about early modern humans by studying their fossils and artifacts? **LESSON 1.1**
11. What effect did a catastrophic drought in East Africa have on *Homo sapiens* thousands of years ago? **LESSON 1.3**
12. Why were the Paleolithic people who left Africa probably attracted to the region of Southwest Asia? **LESSON 1.4**
13. How did groups of hunter-gatherers work together? **LESSON 2.1**
14. What were some of the first plants and animals domesticated by humans? **LESSON 2.2**
15. Why is the development of farming called the agricultural revolution? **LESSON 2.3**
16. What sources do historians use to study the past? **LESSON 2.4**

CRITICAL THINKING

Answer the following questions. Support your answers with evidence from the chapter.

17. **MAKE INFERENCES** What factors do you think were essential to the survival of humankind?
18. **COMPARE AND CONTRAST** How was the culture of prehistoric *Homo sapiens* similar to our own?
19. **DRAW CONCLUSIONS** What does the domestication of plants and animals suggest about the development of humans?
20. **YOU DECIDE** Some historians think that the agricultural revolution was the most important event in human history. Others claim that the ability to control fire was the most important. Which development do you think was more important? Support your opinion.

INTERPRET MAPS

Study the map of the Fertile Crescent. Then use the map to answer the questions that follow.

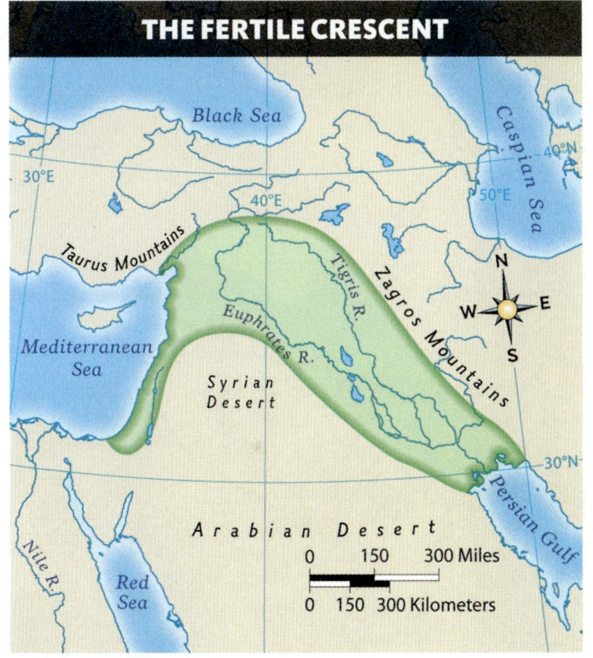
THE FERTILE CRESCENT
Black Sea
Caspian Sea
30°E
40°E
50°E
40°N
30°N
Taurus Mountains
Tigris R.
Zagros Mountains
Euphrates R.
Mediterranean Sea
Syrian Desert
Persian Gulf
Arabian Desert
Nile R.
Red Sea
N
S
E
W
0 150 300 Miles
0 150 300 Kilometers

21. The Fertile Crescent is the area shown in green on the map. Why do you think the Fertile Crescent was so narrow?

22. What rivers were vital to the development of early farming in the Fertile Crescent?

23. What bodies of water bordering the region probably contributed to its fertility?

24. MAP ACTIVITY Sketch your own physical map of the Fertile Crescent. Be sure to label all bodies of water, deserts, and mountains. Use a different color for each type of physical feature. How does your map help you visualize the Fertile Crescent and its surrounding area?

ANALYZE SOURCES

Study this cave painting of two bison, or buffalo-like animals, from the Lascaux Cave in France. Then answer the question.

25. What details in the cave painting suggest that the Paleolithic artist who created it was highly skilled?

WRITE ABOUT HISTORY

26. EXPLANATORY Many new developments occurred during the Neolithic Age. Write a paragraph in which you describe one important development and explain how it changed the way people lived during that period.

TIPS

- Take notes from the chapter on the development you chose.
- State your main idea clearly at the beginning of the paragraph.
- Support your main idea with relevant facts, definitions, specific details, and examples.
- Use vocabulary you learned from the chapter.
- Provide a concluding statement about the significance of the development you chose.

CHAPTER 2

ORIGINS OF CIVILIZATION

10,000 B.C. – 3000 B.C.

SECTION 1

EARLY VILLAGES

KEY VOCABULARY

clan
cultural diffusion
cultural hearth
maize
matrilineal
metallurgy
staple
surplus

NAMES & PLACES

Banpo
Çatalhöyük
Faiyum
Mesoamerica
Nile River Valley
Oaxaca
Yangshao

SECTION 2

THE SEEDS OF CIVILIZATION

KEY VOCABULARY

city
civilization
government
record keeping
religion
scribe
specialized worker
temple
trade

NAMES & PLACES

Göbekli Tepe

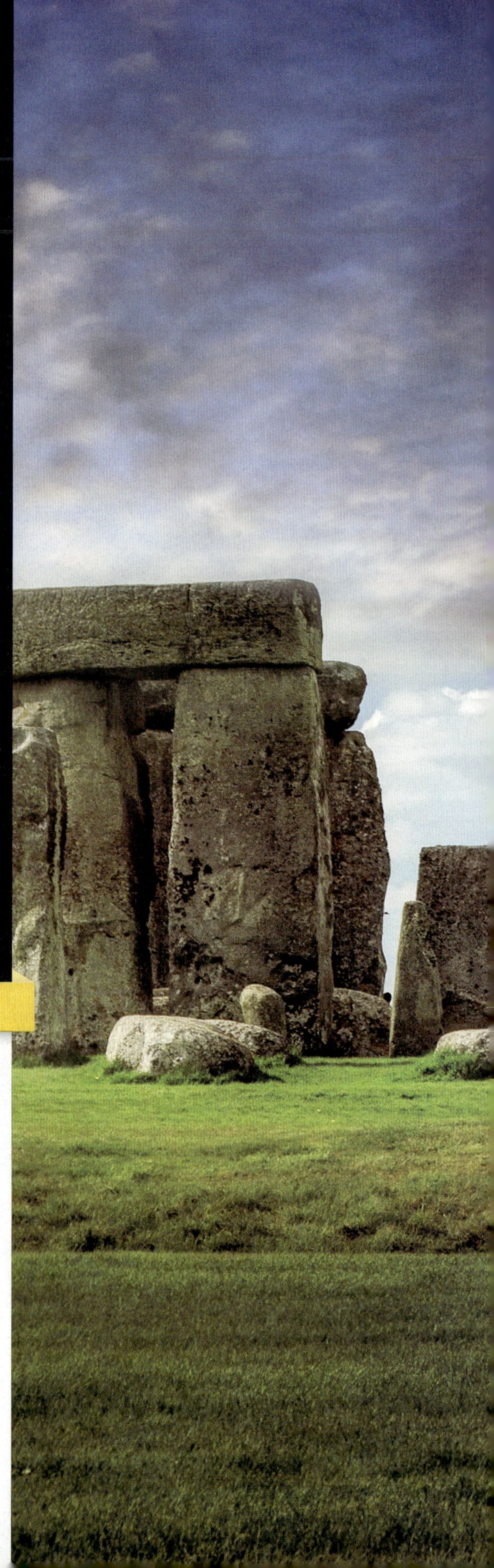

READING STRATEGY

IDENTIFY MAIN IDEAS AND DETAILS When you identify a text's main idea and supporting details, you state the most important idea about a topic and determine which facts support that idea. As you read the chapter, use a diagram like this one to find a main idea and supporting details about cultural hearths.

Cultural Hearths

Main Idea:
Detail:
Detail:
Detail:

Stonehenge is an ancient stone circle that still stands on the Salisbury Plain in England. Archaeologists believe that work on this mysterious site began around 3000 B.C.

1.1 Centers of New Ideas

Where do new ideas come from, and how do they spread? Today's trends start with ideas that catch on all over the world. About 12,000 years ago, ideas began to spread in the same way. Groups of people living in different places invented new ways of doing things. These groups created the world's early cultural hearths.

MAIN IDEA

Cultural hearths promoted the spread of new ideas, practices, and technology in different parts of the world.

WHAT IS A CULTURAL HEARTH?

New ideas, practices, and technology began in places called **cultural hearths**. Remember that culture is a group's way of life, including the group's behaviors, beliefs, language, and customs. Ancient cultural hearths spread ideas and practices that influenced the way people did everyday things, from planting crops to burying their dead.

New practices emerged in several cultural hearths around the same time. Between 8000 and 5000 B.C., people living in different parts of the world began to develop new ways of community living. They began to practice new methods of domesticating animals and plants and living in settled communities. As settled societies thrived, they began to form organized governments. People living in settled communities also built places of worship and expressed themselves artistically.

Despite being separated by thousands of miles, ancient cultural hearths shared similar geographic features. These features included mild climates, fertile land, and access to rivers. Such favorable conditions allowed agriculture to flourish and attracted new people to the area. As populations grew and migrated to other places, they took the new cultural practices with them.

FOUR CULTURAL HEARTHS

Several cultural hearths developed during the Neolithic period. In this chapter, you will learn about four of them, specifically the cultural hearths that emerged in Southwest Asia, China, Mesoamerica, and North Africa.

As you can see on the map, these cultural hearths were located in widely scattered parts of the world. For example, Mesoamerica, in present-day Mexico and Central America, was thousands of miles away from Banpo, in China. Keep in mind that people living in these cultural hearths did not have the benefit of modern communication or transportation. Thousands of years ago, new ideas and practices emerged in and spread from very different places around the same time—without the benefit of the Internet or air travel.

Each of these cultural hearths made an important contribution to surrounding cultures and regions. Simultaneously, the people living in these cultural hearths accepted new ideas themselves. They learned new ways of doing things from people who traveled from other places, and they absorbed the new ideas into their own cultures. Later cultures would build upon the foundations established by these ancient cultural hearths.

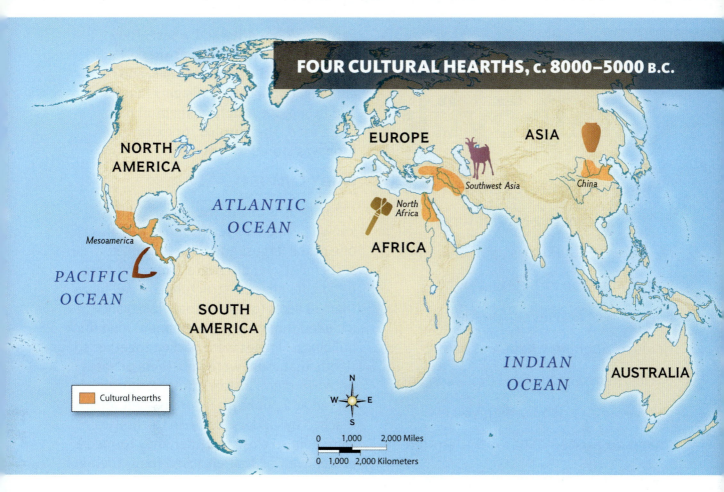

FOUR CULTURAL HEARTHS, c. 8000–5000 B.C.

NORTH AMERICA
EUROPE
ASIA
AFRICA
SOUTH AMERICA
AUSTRALIA
ATLANTIC OCEAN
PACIFIC OCEAN
INDIAN OCEAN
Mesoamerica
North Africa
Southwest Asia
China
Cultural hearths
N
S
E
W
0 1,000 2,000 Miles
0 1,000 2,000 Kilometers

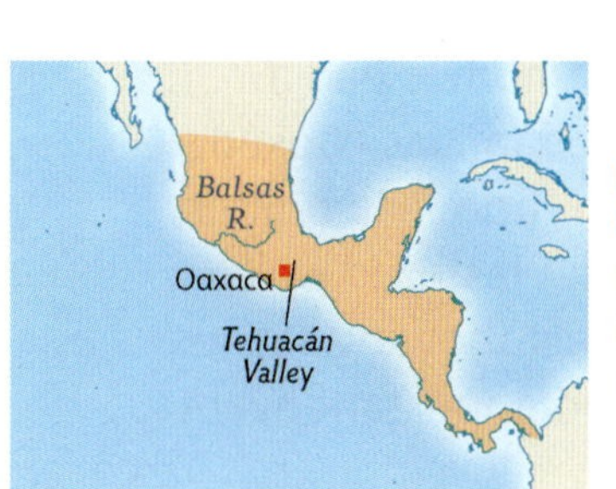
Balsas R.
Oaxaca
Tehuacán Valley

Mesoamerica: Oaxaca
Farmers in Oaxaca introduced an important new crop: maize.

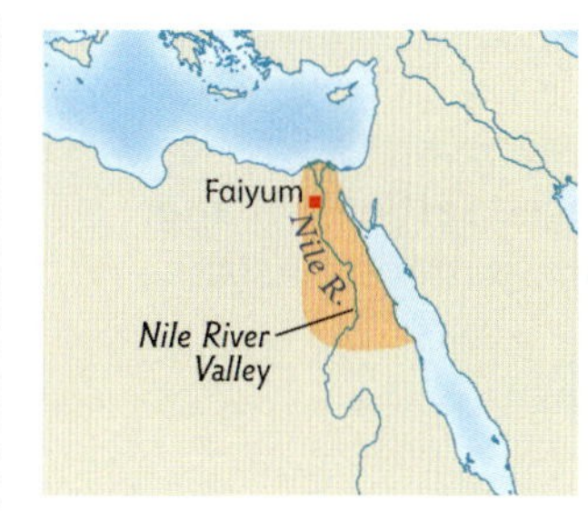
Faiyum
Nile R.
Nile River Valley

North Africa: Faiyum
Faiyum farmers adopted techniques from cultures across the Mediterranean.

Çatalhöyük
Göbekli Tepe
Tigris R.
Fertile Crescent
Euphrates R.

Southwest Asia: Çatalhöyük
Builders at Çatalhöyük demonstrated advanced construction techniques.

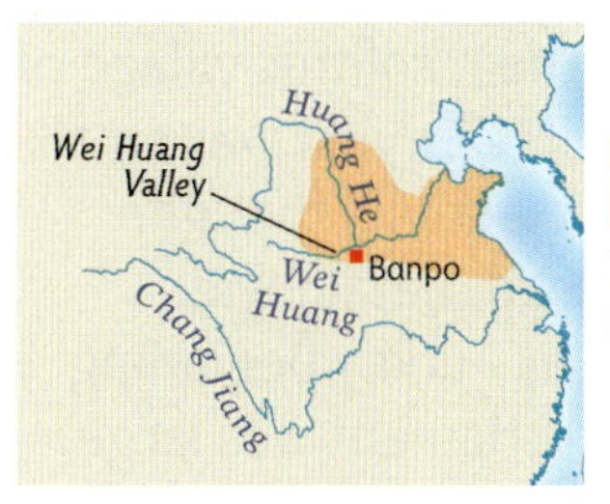
Huang He
Wei Huang Valley
Banpo
Wei Huang
Chang Jiang

China: Banpo
Yangshao potters at Banpo created functional, beautiful pottery.

REVIEW & ASSESS

1. **READING CHECK** What is a cultural hearth?
2. **DESCRIBE** What geographic features did ancient cultural hearths share?
3. **INTERPRET MAPS** Near what rivers did these four ancient cultural hearths emerge?

1.2 Southwest Asia: Çatalhöyük

Imagine you are a traveler crossing central Turkey 9,000 years ago. Suddenly, you stumble on an amazing sight: hundreds of houses surrounded by fields of ripening wheat and barley, enclosures of cattle, and thousands of people—more people than you ever imagined existed. What is this strange place? It's Çatalhöyük.

MAIN IDEA

Çatalhöyük was an advanced settlement and an early cultural hearth in Southwest Asia.

AN AGRICULTURAL VILLAGE

By modern standards, the Neolithic village of **Çatalhöyük** (chah-tuhl-HOO-yuk) was small and simple. To Neolithic people, though, it was incredibly advanced. Çatalhöyük developed in present-day Turkey beginning around 7400 B.C. This settlement was large, both in size and population. Çatalhöyük still fascinates people thousands of years later because of the rich cultural material left behind by those who lived there.

The people who built Çatalhöyük relied on farming for food. A stable food supply contributed to population growth and Çatalhöyük's agriculture eventually supported as many as 10,000 people. Farmers grew barley and wheat. They also raised livestock such as sheep, goats, and cattle for meat, milk, and clothing. Çatalhöyük's villagers hunted and fished, too, but farming produced more food. The **surplus**, or extra, food was stored for later use.

EARLY CULTURE

Çatalhöyük is one of the world's oldest known permanent settlements. It is also one of the largest and most advanced settlements yet discovered from this time period. Its physical structure covered more than 30 acres (or 27 football fields) and included thousands of permanent mud brick buildings. Houses were packed together so tightly that there were no streets or yards between them. Instead, the flat rooftops served as a public plaza, or an open square, reached by ladders. Because the houses were built so close together, they formed a protective wall that enclosed the settlement.

People entered their homes through doors in the roofs. Most homes had a single main room where families cooked, ate, and slept. The main room had built-in benches and a fireplace. Plastered walls were covered with murals showing scenes of hunting, daily life, and important events.

At Çatalhöyük, archaeologists found evidence of religious practices and artistic expression. Horned bulls' heads mounted on walls and symbolic clay figures suggest that the villagers worshipped gods. Villagers also buried their dead, a fact revealed by human remains discovered beneath the floors of homes. The presence of pottery, cloth, cups, and bone utensils as well as tools and jewelry shows artistic expression. Archaeologists even found lead and copper, a sign of very early **metallurgy**, or metalworking. This was an important technological advance.

Discoveries at Çatalhöyük continue even today. Each new find sheds more light on the people who lived in this ancient settlement.

IMAGINING ÇATALHÖYÜK

Çatalhöyük was unknown to modern people until its discovery in the 1950s. Since then, archaeologists have carefully excavated the site. Their discoveries have revealed details of a unique settlement and culture. This illustration shows what archaeologists think Çatalhöyük might have been like. The cutaways let you peek inside the homes.

REVIEW & ASSESS

1. **READING CHECK** What archaeological evidence demonstrates that Çatalhöyük was an advanced culture?

2. **IDENTIFY MAIN IDEAS AND DETAILS** Why did the people of Çatalhöyük build their dwellings so close together?

3. **ANALYZE VISUALS** Based on the illustration, what might have been some advantages to living at Çatalhöyük?

1.3 China: Banpo

About 1,000 years after the development at Çatalhöyük, a lightbulb went off on the other side of the world. Thousands of miles from Southwest Asia, another center of new ideas developed in China's rich river valleys.

MAIN IDEA

The Yangshao culture developed as a cultural hearth in northern China.

RIVER VALLEY AGRICULTURE

Around 5000 B.C., warmer, wetter weather prompted the development of cultural hearths in the fertile river valleys of China. As in Çatalhöyük, people here domesticated pigs, chickens, and dogs. They hunted and fished, too.

In southern China, which has a relatively warm climate, people began to settle in villages. Farmers grew rice, which they had domesticated from the wild rice that grew in the Chang Jiang (chahng jyahng) Basin.

Farming villages also developed farther north in the Huang He (hwahng huh) Basin. However, the colder, drier climate in the north was less favorable for growing rice. Farmers there domesticated wild millet instead. Millet is a tiny, yellow grain. It grows fast and is a low-maintenance, or easy-to-grow, crop. It was an important part of the diet of ancient people in northern China.

YANGSHAO CULTURE

The **Yangshao** (yahng-shou) culture was one of China's Neolithic cultural hearths. The Yangshao lived along the Huang and Wei (way) rivers from about 5000 to 3000 B.C. Archaeologists have discovered more than 1,000 Yangshao sites in northern China.

One of the best-known Yangshao sites is **Banpo**, a large farming village. This village contained many small houses that faced a community building in a central square. Archaeologists determined that Banpo houses were rebuilt many times. People may have abandoned the village when the fields were exhausted of nutrients and then later returned when the land recovered. Banpo villagers grew millet as their **staple**, or main crop. They also grew a fibrous plant called hemp and cultivated silk, which they crafted into textiles.

The Yangshao at Banpo left behind a unique style of pottery that demonstrates their artistry. Yangshao potters created bowls and vessels, or containers, that they formed by hand and baked in kilns, or ovens, just outside Banpo village. The Yangshao's painted pottery commonly features geometric designs. Other examples include shaped vessels used for food storage.

Archaeologists found many of these vessels and other useful items buried with the dead in neatly arranged graves. These "grave goods," as they are called, suggest that the Yangshao people believed in a link between the living and the dead, though their specific religious beliefs remain unknown. Because most graves contained similar grave goods, archaeologists believe that most people probably had equal status in society.

Early Yangshao graves also suggest that people were arranged into **clans**, or family groupings, when buried. These clans were **matrilineal**, which means they traced descendants through the mother rather than the father.

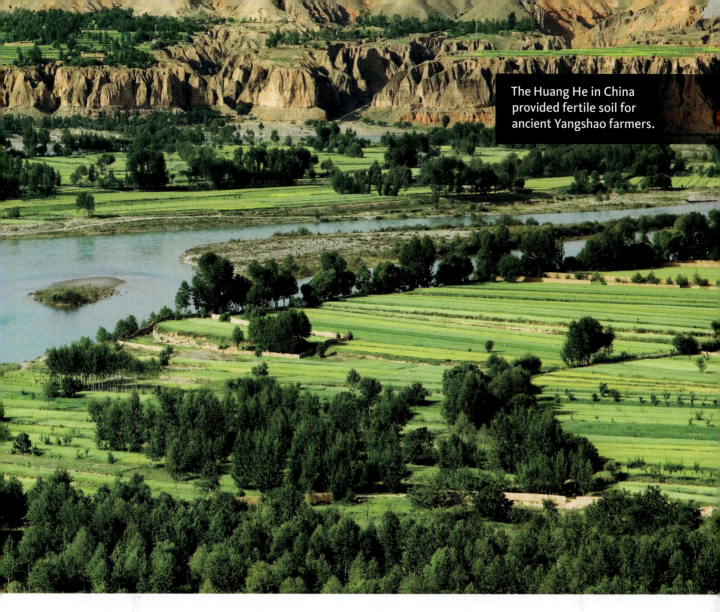

The Huang He in China provided fertile soil for ancient Yangshao farmers.

By about 3200 B.C. Yangshao culture had evolved into Longshan (lung-shan) culture. The Longshan crafted useful tools and beautiful objects from jade—a hard green or white stone. Longshan artists produced a distinctive black pottery using pottery wheels, and craftspeople made tools out of copper. The Longshan also established trade networks on which later Chinese cultures would build.

Yangshao Pottery

Formed in the shape of an owl, this tripod pottery vessel was used to serve food.

REVIEW & ASSESS

1. **READING CHECK** What is unique about the Yangshao culture?
2. **COMPARE AND CONTRAST** Why did farmers grow different types of crops in the southern and northern river basins of China?
3. **DETERMINE WORD MEANINGS** Based on its definition, what does the word part *matri-* mean?

1.4 Mesoamerica: Oaxaca

Around the time the Yangshao were farming in China, another cultural hearth was forming across the Pacific in Mesoamerica. The people there were developing an important crop that you might recognize—corn.

MAIN IDEA

Maize domestication helped make Mesoamerica an important cultural hearth.

MESOAMERICAN NOMADS

Mesoamerica, which means "middle America," refers to the ancient geographic and cultural region that reached from central Mexico south through Central America. This region was another important Neolithic cultural hearth, similar in some ways to Çatalhöyük in Southwest Asia and Banpo in China.

For thousands of years, Mesoamericans traveled in small nomadic groups, moving from place to place with the seasons. They gathered wild plants but did little farming. For brief periods, these Mesoamericans may have tended small patches of land. However, they didn't settle in permanent sites, build permanent homes, or form villages. Eventually, though, Mesoamericans began to domesticate wild plants. In this way, they resembled people living in cultural hearths in other parts of the world.

CRADLE OF THE MAIZE REVOLUTION

One of the main plants Mesoamericans domesticated was **maize**, or what we know as corn. A cave is an unlikely place to find clues about an important development in farming, but that is where archaeologists found traces of an ancient plant. In fact, caves and rock shelters scattered across southern Mexico revealed the earliest signs of domestication in North America.

Archaeologists found prehistoric corncob fragments in the highland caves of **Oaxaca** (wah-HAH-kah) and the Tehuacán (tay-wah-KAHN) Valley. The pieces had been preserved for thousands of years by the region's hot, dry conditions. These fragments, which date to around 4250 B.C., came from an early variety of domesticated maize. Archaeologists also found stone tools for grinding the hard maize kernels into flour for baking. The first varieties of maize were probably neither juicy nor yellow, but they were easily harvested and stored, which made them a useful food source.

So where did maize come from? After decades of debate, scientists believe that maize was domesticated from a wild Mexican grass called teosinte (tay-uh-SIN-tay) that is native to the area around the Balsas River. Teosinte kernels are easily knocked off the plant, making it a difficult crop to harvest. However, hundreds of years of domestication solved this problem. Domestication also increased the number and size of kernels on the teosinte plant. Over time, it came to resemble modern corn.

As maize became a more productive crop, Mesoamericans relied on it for their annual food supply. By 2000 B.C., the maize revolution had taken place, and maize farming was widespread in Mesoamerica. Little did these farmers know they had invented a food that people would still enjoy thousands of years later.

DOMESTICATING CORN

Teosinte, the wild relative of modern corn, produced much smaller kernels. Note the size of the cobs of the teosinte plant as compared to a quarter. Now compare a quarter to the size of modern corn. In domesticating this plant, ancient farmers slowly began to encourage fewer branches on the plant. Less branching meant the plant could divert more energy into fewer cobs, which then grew larger. In addition, the hard kernel of the teosinte plant eventually gave way to the softer kernel we recognize as modern corn.

TEOSINTE
MODERN CORN

REVIEW & ASSESS

1. **READING CHECK** How did the domestication of maize help Mesoamerica become a cultural hearth?
2. **SUMMARIZE** How do archaeologists know that Mesoamericans domesticated maize?
3. **INTEGRATE VISUALS** Based on the illustration and text, what changes did domestication bring about to teosinte?

This photo of Faiyum today shows how access to a water source determines where crops can grow and people can live.

1.5 North Africa: Faiyum

Long before building their extraordinary pyramids, the ancient Egyptians laid the building blocks of an advanced culture on the floodplains of the Nile River in North Africa. As in other cultural hearths, agriculture was at the root of cultural development in ancient Egypt, whose farmers adapted ideas from places far and wide.

MAIN IDEA

Early farmers established the Nile River Valley as an important cultural hearth.

MIGRANTS FROM THE SAHARA

As you may recall from the previous chapter, the Sahara was a tropical grassland 10,000 years ago. Then the climate changed drastically. Seasonal rains shifted south, and the grasslands dried into desert. This dramatic change forced people to migrate to more fertile lands with steadier water supplies.

The same climate shift that transformed the Sahara transformed the narrow **Nile River Valley**. Its swamps dried up, making the land usable and this fertile valley a perfect place for farming. The Nile floodplain was ideal for the agriculture that would later support a large population.

EGYPT'S EARLIEST FARMING VILLAGE

Faiyum (fy-YOOM) is an oasis about 50 miles south of present-day Cairo. Dating from around 5200 B.C., it is considered Egypt's earliest farming community. At Faiyum, archaeologists discovered storage pits for grain, postholes for building foundations, and the ruins of clay floors and fireplaces. They also stumbled upon a 7,000-year-old, Neolithic-era wood and flint sickle used for farming and left in a storage bin.

The agricultural practices used at Faiyum were not native to the Nile River Valley, though. According to archaeologists, people from neighboring cultures introduced new practices to Faiyum farmers. Grains of wheat and barley and bones of sheep and pigs found at Faiyum came from across the Mediterranean Sea or the Sinai Desert where domestication was already well established. People from these areas likely brought the domesticated grains and animals to the Nile River Valley.

The process by which cultures interact and spread from one area to another is called **cultural diffusion**. This process allowed Faiyum farmers to benefit from the skills of other cultures. It also helped establish the Nile River Valley as an important cultural hearth.

REVIEW & ASSESS

1. **READING CHECK** Why were early farmers attracted to the Nile River Valley?
2. **SUMMARIZE** How did a climate shift that took place 10,000 years ago change the Sahara and Nile River Valley?
3. **DRAW CONCLUSIONS** What impact did neighboring cultures have on the farmers at Faiyum?

2.1 Paths to Civilization:

Göbekli Tepe

An old riddle asks: Which came first, the chicken or the egg? Archaeologists have posed their own riddle: Which came first, organized agriculture or organized religion? Like most riddles, this one can't be easily answered.

MAIN IDEA

Throughout history, different cultures have traveled different paths to civilization.

THE WORLD'S FIRST TEMPLE

Over time, cultural hearths around the world transformed into civilizations. A **civilization** is an advanced and complex society. Two important markers of civilization are agriculture and organized **religion**, or the belief in and worship of gods and goddesses.

About 11,600 years ago in southeast Turkey on the edge of the Fertile Crescent, at least 500 people came together to create **Göbekli Tepe** (guh-bek-LEE TEH-peh), the world's first **temple**, or place of worship. Ancient builders formed massive limestone pillars into T shapes and arranged them into sets of circles.

The tallest pillars stood as high as 18 feet and weighed 16 tons. Keep in mind that Göbekli Tepe's builders did all this before the invention of the wheel. Stone workers carved ferocious animals onto the pillars after they were in place. Once completed, the immense pillars and the frightening images of deadly animals flickering in the firelight must have been an awesome sight.

Göbekli Tepe represents an important event in the development of organized religion. As one of the first known examples of monumental architecture, or large structures built for an identified purpose, it was specifically dedicated for religious use. Its commanding views over fertile plains, evidence of ceremonies, and high levels of artistic expression all suggest a religious purpose.

Göbekli Tepe is also remarkable because archaeologists believe that hunter-gatherers, not settled farmers, built it. The structures at Göbekli Tepe were constructed miles from any Neolithic settlement, water source, or agricultural land. The absence of harvest symbols found in later farming cultures reinforces the theory that hunter-gatherers—not a settled people—built Göbekli Tepe.

THE MEANING OF GÖBEKLI TEPE

Archaeologists argue over the meaning of Göbekli Tepe. Evidence found there has changed the way some think about the human transition from hunter-gatherer to farmer. For a long time, archaeologists thought that the need to ensure good harvests led to the belief in and worship of gods and goddesses. In other words, agriculture developed before religion. However, Göbekli Tepe turns that argument around, suggesting that here, at least, humans developed organized religion before farming. In this case, perhaps the need to feed religious gatherings led to the development of agriculture.

The fact is that in some places, agriculture came before religion; in others, religion came first. Göbekli Tepe teaches us that different cultures forged different paths to civilization. Either way, by 6000 B.C., both organized religion and agriculture—two of the fundamental building blocks of civilization—had been established in the Fertile Crescent.

Göbekli Tepe's builders constructed the site without the benefit of the wheel. They relied on human muscle—and lots of it—to move the 16-ton limestone pillars from as far as a quarter mile away.

PATHS TO CIVILIZATION

HUNTER-GATHERER → **FARMER**

A warmer climate leads to more vegetation and wildlife, allowing for . . . › Agriculture; Domestication of plants and animals; Permanent settlement *which led to* › Religion

Curiosity about the natural world encourages the beginnings of . . . › Religion *which led to* › Agriculture; Domestication of plants and animals; Permanent settlement

REVIEW & ASSESS

1. **READING CHECK** How does Göbekli Tepe show that organized religion sometimes developed before agriculture?

2. **IDENTIFY MAIN IDEAS AND DETAILS** What features made Göbekli Tepe such an important achievement?

3. **INTEGRATE VISUALS** Based on the diagram and description of the pillars in the text, what might the hunter-gatherers who visited Göbekli Tepe have worshipped?

2.2 Traits of Civilization

You might hear the word *civilization* a lot, but do you understand what it means? All civilizations, whether past or present, have certain things in common. So, what is a civilization?

MAIN IDEA

A civilization is a complex society that is defined by five key traits.

Cultural hearths prepared the way for the next development in human history: civilization. Ancient cultures around the world transformed into complex civilizations at about the same time, and they had five traits, or characteristics, in common: cities, complex institutions, specialized workers, record keeping, and improved technology.

CITIES

The first civilizations were born in **cities**. More than just large population centers, early cities were political, economic, and cultural centers for the surrounding areas. Cities often contained monumental architecture usually dedicated to religion or government. The city's heart was its trading center, where farmers and merchants met to conduct business. **Trade**, or the exchange of goods, allowed some civilizations to grow very rich. Some merchants traveled long distances to trade goods with other groups. Over time, they established trade routes, which helped spread ideas and practices.

COMPLEX INSTITUTIONS

As cities developed, complex institutions such as government and organized religion emerged as ways to manage resources and populations. **Government**, or an organization set up to make and enforce rules in a society, provided leadership and laws. Organized religion bound communities together through shared beliefs.

SPECIALIZED WORKERS

Food surpluses made possible by the agricultural revolution led to settled communities and to another key characteristic of civilizations: **specialized workers**. Specialized workers performed jobs other than farming. Some people specialized in pottery, metalworking, weaving, or toolmaking. Others became government officials, priests, teachers, soldiers, or merchants.

RECORD KEEPING

As societies developed, they had to manage information. **Record keeping**, or organizing and storing information, became an important job. Specialized workers called **scribes** recorded business transactions, important events, customs, traditions, and laws. The first writing systems used pictographs that looked like the things they represented, such as wavy lines for water. Eventually, complex writing systems helped people record important information and abstract ideas. As writing developed, so did calendar keeping.

IMPROVED TECHNOLOGY

The fifth key characteristic civilizations have in common is improved technology. As cultures became more complex, people developed new tools and techniques to solve problems and survive. Advances in technology included metalworking methods, inventions such as the wheel and the plow, and tools to create everyday items, such as the potter's wheel.

FIVE TRAITS OF CIVILIZATION
COMPLEX INSTITUTIONS
SPECIALIZED WORKERS
RECORD KEEPING
CITIES
IMPROVED TECHNOLOGY

Giant's Tower, a temple in Malta, demonstrates evidence of complex institutions.

Specialized workers crafted this blue gemstone and gold necklace in ancient Iraq.

Pictographs carved on this clay tablet predated writing systems we recognize today.

Potters used the wheel long before it would be attached to vehicles around 3000 B.C.

The great city of Ur was one of the busiest and most powerful trading centers of the ancient world.

REVIEW & ASSESS

1. **READING CHECK** What key traits, or characteristics, define civilizations around the world?
2. **DRAW CONCLUSIONS** In what ways were cities essential to the development of civilizations?
3. **ANALYZE CAUSE AND EFFECT** What is the connection between food surpluses and specialized workers?

HISTORY THROUGH OBJECTS

2.3 NEW TECHNOLOGY

Ancient tools and technology reveal much about the cultures that used them. As early cultures advanced toward civilization, the design and manufacture of tools improved. Materials used to make tools also changed. For example, with the development of metallurgy, strong metals such as bronze allowed for the transition from stone to metal tools. Better and more complex tools developed by ancient people demonstrated the emergence of civilization around the world. Based on what you see here, what purpose did many early tools serve?

Spearhead
Metals such as bronze improved a weapon's strength.

Arrowhead
Arrowheads of flint or other stone were tied to arrows and used for hunting.

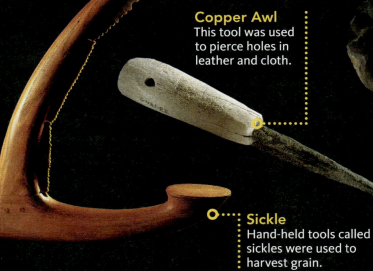

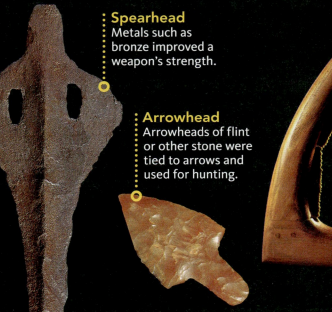

Copper Awl
This tool was used to pierce holes in leather and cloth.

Sickle
Hand-held tools called sickles were used to harvest grain.

Flint Tool
Flint is a hard stone that can be shaped into a sharp point.

Harpoon
Reindeer antlers provided the bone for this hunting tool.

Flint Knife
The intricate handle on this knife was carved from a hippopotamus tooth.

Kitchen Utensil
This fork-shaped utensil made of bone was found at Çatalhöyük.

Flint Stone
When hit, flint stones helped spark fire.

Pottery
Pottery vessels of all shapes held liquids and food.

Bronze Ax Head
Axes were used for chopping and hunting.

Stone Hoe
This stone hoe, dated around 7000 B.C., is an example of an early agricultural tool.

Bone Needle
Needles made of bone were used for sewing and weaving.

Wheel
Early wheels were constructed simply: wooden disks with holes for axles.

CHAPTER 2

Review

VOCABULARY

Use each of the following vocabulary words in a sentence that shows an understanding of the term's meaning.

1. **cultural hearth**
   A cultural hearth is a place from which new ideas and technology spread to surrounding areas.
2. **surplus**
3. **metallurgy**
4. **matrilineal**
5. **maize**
6. **temple**
7. **cultural diffusion**
8. **government**
9. **specialized worker**
10. **civilization**

READING STRATEGY

11. **IDENTIFY MAIN IDEAS AND DETAILS** If you haven't already, complete your diagram to determine a main idea and supporting details about cultural hearths. Then answer the question.

Cultural Hearths

Main Idea: Cultural hearths promoted the spread of new ideas, practices, and technology around the world.
Detail:
Detail:
Detail:

What is a cultural hearth? What impact did the four main cultural hearths have on the ancient world?

MAIN IDEAS

Answer the following questions. Support your answers with evidence from the chapter.

12. Why are cultural hearths referred to as centers of new ideas? LESSON 1.1
13. In what way was agriculture central to the people who built Çatalhöyük? LESSON 1.2
14. How did natural resources and climate influence the formation of cultural hearths in China? LESSON 1.3
15. In what ways did the Faiyum farmers demonstrate cultural diffusion? LESSON 1.5
16. What key characteristics do civilizations around the world share? LESSON 2.2

CRITICAL THINKING

Answer the following questions. Support your answers with evidence from the chapter.

17. **EVALUATE** What are some of the factors that contribute to the development of civilization?
18. **DRAW CONCLUSIONS** How did cultural hearths help lead to the emergence of civilization?
19. **MAKE INFERENCES** Why do you think government became necessary as cities developed?
20. **COMPARE AND CONTRAST** How did the lifestyles of hunter-gatherers compare with those of settlers of early agricultural communities?
21. **MAKE INFERENCES** Why is it significant that hunter-gatherers built Göbekli Tepe as a place of worship?
22. **FORM OPINIONS** Do you think agriculture or religion developed first? Support your opinion with evidence from the chapter.
23. **YOU DECIDE** Which of the five traits of civilization do you consider the most important? Support your opinion with evidence from the chapter.

INTERPRET MAPS

Study the map of the locations of the Yangshao and Longshan cultures that developed in China's cultural hearth. Then answer the questions that follow.

24. Which river was vital to the development of the Yangshao culture?

25. Why might the Longshan culture have expanded east from the Yangshao culture?

26. **MAP ACTIVITY** Create your own sketch maps of the other cultural hearths discussed in this chapter. Label the areas and bodies of water. Then study the maps and note the cultural hearths' physical similarities and differences.

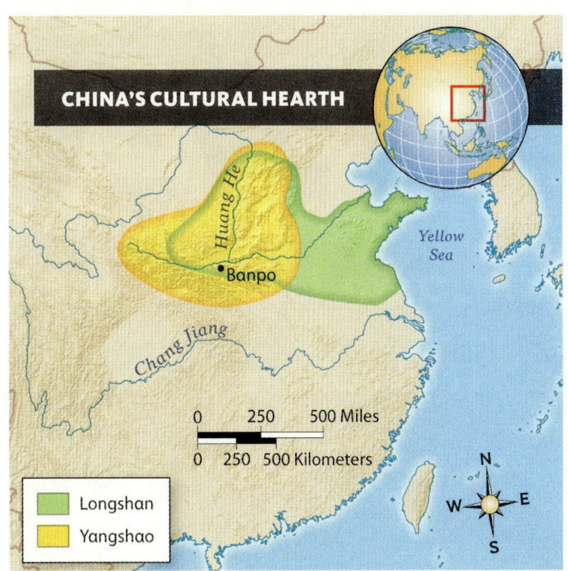

CHINA'S CULTURAL HEARTH
Huang He
Banpo
Yellow Sea
Chang Jiang
0 250 500 Miles
0 250 500 Kilometers
Longshan
Yangshao
N
S
E
W

ANALYZE SOURCES

The dagger below is made of carved and chipped stone. Archaeologists who discovered it at Çatalhöyük believe it was made around 6000 B.C. Study the artifact. Then answer the question that follows.

27. What information might archaeologists learn about the skills of the Neolithic people who created the dagger? Use evidence from the chapter to support your answer.

WRITE ABOUT HISTORY

28. **EXPLANATORY** Choose two cultures discussed in this chapter. Write a 3-paragraph explanatory essay that compares and contrasts the cultures in terms of their agricultural and technological developments.

TIPS

- Take notes from the lessons about the two cultures you chose.
- State your main idea and supporting details in a clear, well-organized way.
- Use appropriate transitions to clarify the relationships among ideas.
- Use at least two vocabulary words from the chapter.
- Provide a concluding statement that wraps up the information about the two cultures.

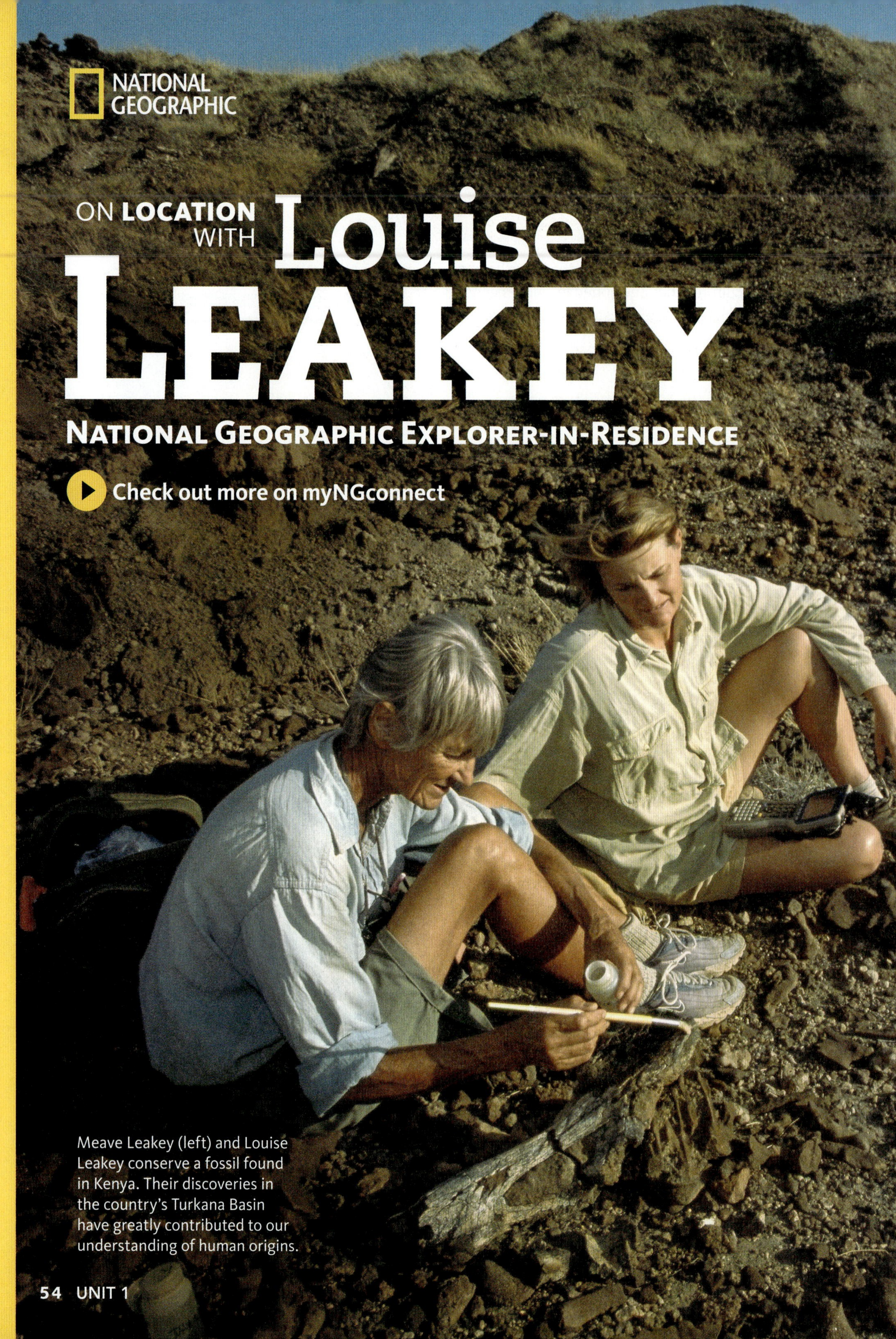
NATIONAL GEOGRAPHIC

ON **LOCATION** WITH Louise

LEAKEY

NATIONAL GEOGRAPHIC EXPLORER-IN-RESIDENCE

Check out more on myNGconnect

Meave Leakey (left) and Louise Leakey conserve a fossil found in Kenya. Their discoveries in the country's Turkana Basin have greatly contributed to our understanding of human origins.

ALL IN THE FAMILY

I've spent quite a bit of time on my hands and knees, carefully excavating the remains of our ancestors and other animals. I have been fortunate to have done this work alongside my mother, Meave Leakey. She is also a highly acclaimed paleontologist, so there's a lot to live up to! This is what happens when you're born into a family famous for finding prehuman fossils. My grandfather, Louis Leakey, made important discoveries in Tanzania, at Olduvai Gorge, that helped explain the human fossil record. I remember when my father, Richard Leakey, discovered a well-preserved 1.6-million-year-old skeleton of *Homo erectus*, one of our ancestors that left Africa for the first time 1.8 million years ago. I was twelve years old at the time, and they compared my teeth with the teeth of this skeleton, the Nariokotome Boy, to determine that it was about the same age as I was.

Louise Leakey uses GPS to locate fossils in Kenya. You can explore many of her family's fossil discoveries at www.africanfossils.org.

EARLY HUMAN FOSSILS

My mother and I continue with our field work, on the east side of Lake Turkana in Kenya's Rift Valley. We organize and coordinate the search for fossil remains in extensive fossil deposits in northern Kenya. During every expedition, we discover and collect exciting new fossils that help us answer important questions about the past. These fossils are kept at the Turkana Basin Institute or in the National Museums of Kenya. In 1999, we organized a National Geographic-sponsored expedition to the Turkana Basin. It was there that my mother and I uncovered a 3.3-million-year-old human skull and part of a jaw. The skull is very flat, and that makes it different from anything else ever found. In fact, it is so different that we believe it belongs to an entirely new branch of early human that we named *Kenyanthropus platyops*. To prove this beyond doubt, we still need to find more remains, ideally another intact skull! From this same site, the earliest stone tools known to the world have recently been announced, which strongly suggests that this species was also the earliest tool maker.

WHY STUDY HISTORY?

"When you look at the state of the world today, with its many conflicts and ethnic divisions, it's hard to believe that we are a single species with a common ancestor. We have to understand our past to contemplate our future. The fossils in east Africa are our *global heritage.*" —Louise Leakey

NATIONAL GEOGRAPHIC

Scotland's Stone Age Ruins

BY ROFF SMITH

Adapted from "Scotland's Stone Age Ruins," by Roff Smith, in *National Geographic*, August 2014

Orkney is a fertile, green archipelago off the northern tip of Scotland. Five thousand years ago, people there built something unlike anything they had ever attempted before. They had Stone Age technology, but their vision was millennia ahead of their time.

The ancient people of Orkney quarried thousands of tons of sandstone and transported it several miles to a grassy hill. There they constructed a complex of buildings and surrounded them with imposing walls. The complex featured paved walkways, carved stonework, colored facades, and slate roofs. Many people gathered here for seasonal rituals, feasts, and trade.

Archaeologist Nick Card says the recent discovery of these stunning ruins is turning British prehistory on its head. "This is almost on the scale of some of the great classical sites in the Mediterranean, like the Acropolis in Greece, except these structures are 2,500 years older." Only a small part of the site has been excavated, but this sample has opened a window into the past. It has also yielded thousands of artifacts, including ceremonial mace heads, polished stone axes, flint knives, stone spatulas, and colored pottery. Archaeologists have also discovered more than 650 pieces of Neolithic art at the site.

"Nowhere else in all Britain or Ireland have such well-preserved stone houses from the Neolithic survived," says archaeologist Antonia Thomas. "To be able to link these structures with art, to see in such a direct and personal way how people embellished their surroundings, is really something."

Sometime around the year 2300 B.C., it all came to an end. Climate change may have played a role. Or perhaps it was the disruptive influence of a new toolmaking material: bronze.

Whatever the reason, the ancient temple was deliberately destroyed and buried under stone and trash. Card surmises, "It seems that they were attempting to erase the site and its importance from memory, perhaps to mark the introduction of new belief systems."

For more from National Geographic
Check out "First Americans" on myNGconnect

UNIT INQUIRY: CREATE A CULTURAL SYMBOL

In this unit, you learned about the origins of early human cultures and civilizations. Based on your understanding of the text, what elements of culture developed in early human societies? How did those elements help make each society unique?

ASSIGNMENT Create a symbol that represents the culture of an early human society you studied in this unit. The symbol should reflect one or more cultural characteristics that made that early society unique. Be prepared to present your cultural symbol and explain its significance to the class.

Plan As you create your symbol, think about specific characteristics that were unique to the society you have selected. For example, what elements of culture defined and unified early Stone Age humans? What customs, social structure, arts, tools, and major achievements distinguished them from other groups of early humans? You might want to use a graphic organizer to help organize your thoughts. Identify the early society and at least one specific detail about different characteristics of its culture. ▶

Produce Use your notes to produce detailed descriptions of the elements of culture that defined the early human society you selected. You might want to draw or write descriptions of visual icons for each element.

Present Choose a creative way to present your cultural symbol to the class. Consider one of the following options:

- Write an introduction to the cultural symbol that describes the early human society it represents.
- Create a multimedia presentation showing different elements of the society's culture and what made it unique.
- Paint a flag of your symbol using colors that also express significance or meaning to the culture.

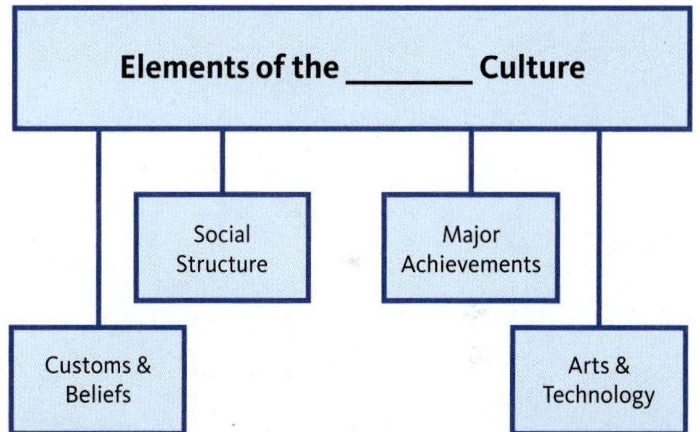

Elements of the _______ Culture
Social Structure
Major Achievements
Customs & Beliefs
Arts & Technology

RAPID REVIEW
UNIT 1

ORIGINS OF CULTURES AND CIVILIZATIONS

TOP TEN

1. Humans originated from a common ancestor who lived in Africa 60,000 years ago.
2. For thousands of years, humans lived in small, nomadic groups, hunted wild animals, and gathered edible plants.
3. Farming produced food surpluses that allowed rapid population growth and job specialization.
4. Agriculture encouraged people to group together in villages that grew into more complex cities.
5. Cultural hearths emerged around the world during the Neolithic period.

6-10. **NOW IT'S YOUR TURN** Complete the list with five more things to remember about the origins of cultures and civilizations.

EARLY CIVILIZATIONS

NATIONAL GEOGRAPHIC

ON **LOCATION** WITH

Christopher Thornton

Archaeologist

Lead Program Officer, Research, Conservation, and Exploration, National Geographic

The past is a window to the future. Early civilizations differ in many ways from those today, but there are also many similarities between then and now. Studying early civilizations is exciting because of what we can learn from the ancients, and also because what we know—or think we know—is always changing. I'm Christopher Thornton, and I time travel between the past and present. Join me on my journey!

‹ **CRITICAL VIEWING** This painted bas-relief shows ancient Egyptian king Thutmose III wearing the Atef crown, which was worn during religious rituals. What details in the artwork convey the king's strength and power?

UNIT 2
TIME LINE OF WORLD EVENTS

Early Civilizations

Mesopotamia, Egypt, Israel, India, and China

c. 3500 B.C.
The world's first civilization arises in Sumer. *(stringed instrument from Ur)*

c. 3100 B.C.
Upper and Lower Egypt are united under a single ruler. *(Horus, Egyptian sky god)*

c. 2500 B.C.
Harappan civilization develops in the Indus Valley.

2334 B.C.
Sargon the Great conquers Sumer and creates the world's first empire.

c. 1790 B.C.
Hammurabi issues his Code of Laws at Babylon.

c. 1600 B.C.
The Shang dynasty emerges along the Huang He in China.

1500 B.C.

c. 1470 B.C.
Hatshepsut becomes Egypt's first female pharaoh.

c. 1250 B.C.
Moses leads the Hebrews out of Egypt.
(Hebrew text scroll)

c. 1000 B.C.
Aryan civilization spreads through the northern Indian subcontinent.

3500 B.C.

COMPARE TIME LINES

What can you infer about the Qin dynasty in China based on this time line?

600 B.C.

563 B.C.
Siddhartha Gautama, the Buddha, is born.

587 B.C.
Jerusalem falls to the Babylonians, beginning the Babylonian Exile.

c. 269 B.C.
Asoka becomes ruler of the Maurya Empire and eventually rules by Buddhist principles.

c. 221 B.C.
The Qin dynasty begins with the reign of Shi Huangdi.

200 B.C.

202 B.C.
The Han dynasty comes to power.
(Han bronze dragon)

A.D. 100

A.D. 105
The Chinese invent paper.

A.D. 320
Chandra Gupta I establishes the Gupta Empire, which oversees India's golden age.
(Gupta gold coin)

UNIT 2
GEOGRAPHY IN HISTORY

FIRST CIVILIZATIONS
3500 B.C.–1800 B.C.

Most of the world's earliest civilizations, including Mesopotamia, Egypt, India, and China, developed in fertile river valleys. The good soil made the river valleys ideal for growing crops. By contrast, the Hebrews established their civilization along the Mediterranean. However, what really set them apart was their belief in one God. This belief would influence the rest of the world for centuries.

What landforms separated the civilizations?

ANCIENT MESOPOTAMIA

Water sources:	Tigris and Euphrates rivers, Mediterranean Sea
Civilizations and empires:	Sumer, Akkadia, Babylon, Assyria, Chaldea, Phoenicia, Persia
Significant leaders:	Sargon, Hammurabi, Nebuchadnezzar II, Cyrus
Legacy:	farming, writing, government, law, shipbuilding, math

EUROPE
Black Sea
Caucasus Mts.
Caspian Sea
Mediterranean Sea
Tigris
Mesopotamia
Euphrates
Persian Gulf
Egypt
Nile
Red Sea
AFRICA

ANCIENT EGYPT

Water sources:	Nile River
Civilizations and empires:	Egypt, Kush
Significant leaders:	Khufu, Ahmose, Hatshepsut, Ramses II, Piankhi
Legacy:	writing, math, science, medicine, art, architecture

JUDAISM & ISRAELITE KINGDOMS

Water sources:	Mediterranean Sea
Civilizations and empires:	Israel, Judah
Significant leaders:	Abraham, Moses, Saul, David, Solomon
Legacy:	education, religion, philosophy

0 250 500 750 1000 kilometers
0 250 500 750 1000 miles
ASIA
China
Huang (Yellow)
Chiang Jiang (Yangtze)
Himalaya
India
Indus
Ganges
Arabian Sea
Bay of Bengal
South China Sea
INDIAN OCEAN

ANCIENT CHINA	
Water sources:	Huang He, Chang Jiang
Civilizations and empires:	Shang, Zhou, Qin, Han
Significant leaders:	Shi Huangdi, Liu Bang, Empress Lü, Emperor Wudi
Legacy:	philosophy, government, navigation, farming, writing, textiles, art

ANCIENT INDIA	
Water sources:	Indus River, Ganges River, Indian Ocean
Civilizations and empires:	Harappa, Aryan, Maurya, Gupta
Significant leaders:	Chandragupta Maurya, Asoka, Chandra Gupta I
Legacy:	religion, art, medicine, math

CHAPTER

3 ANCIENT MESOPOTAMIA

3000 B.C. – 500 B.C.

SECTION 1

SUMER

KEY VOCABULARY	NAMES & PLACES
artisan	Euphrates River
city-state	Mesopotamia
cuneiform	Sargon the Great
empire	Sumer
famine	Tigris River
irrigation	
polytheism	
ritual	
silt	
social class	
tribute	
ziggurat	

SECTION 2

BABYLONIA AND LATER CIVILIZATIONS

KEY VOCABULARY	NAMES & PLACES
alliance	Cyrus the Great
colony	Darius I
legacy	Hammurabi
province	Nebuchadnezzar II
raw material	
satrap	
tolerance	

READING STRATEGY

MAKE INFERENCES When you make inferences, you use what you already know to figure out the meaning of the text. As you read the chapter, use a chart like this one to make inferences about why civilization developed in Mesopotamia.

I notice...	I know...	And so...

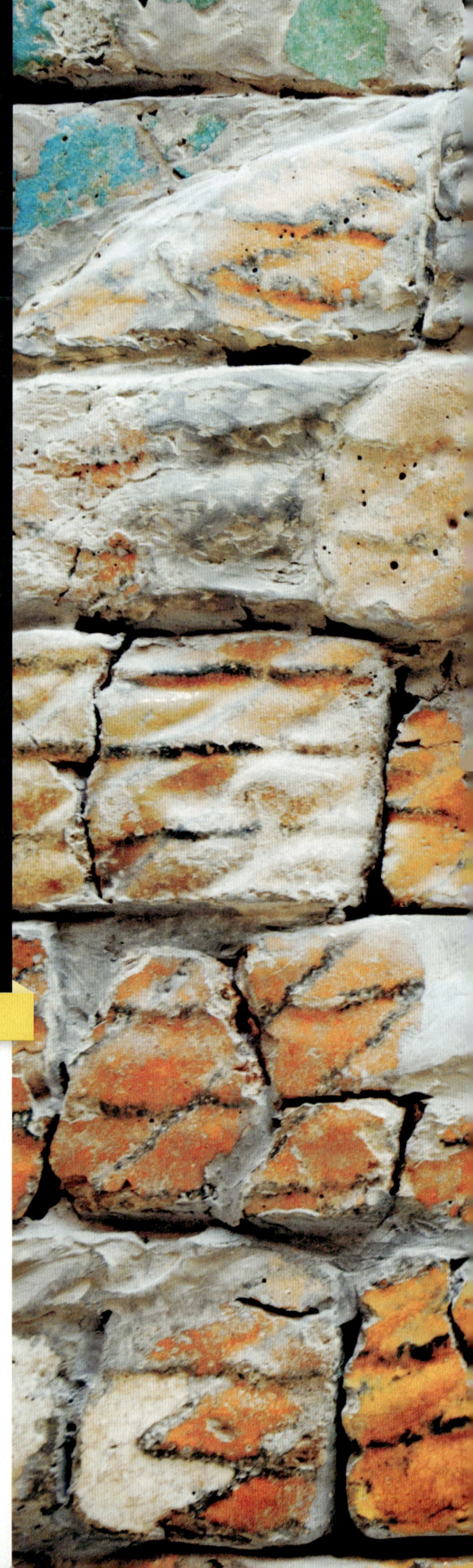

Fierce lions decorated the walls of the street that passed through the Ishtar Gate. Standing 38 feet high and featuring hundreds of dragons and bulls, the Ishtar Gate was the entryway to the city of Babylon in Mesopotamia.

1.1 The Geography of Ancient Mesopotamia

Long after Çatalhöyük was settled, Southwest Asia was home to another group of people. They lived between two flowing rivers in a fertile land. Because of the advances in government, culture, and technology that took place there, the region is often called a "cradle of civilization."

MAIN IDEA

The geography of Mesopotamia helped create the conditions for civilization.

THE LAND BETWEEN THE RIVERS

As you have learned, the Fertile Crescent sweeps its way across Southwest Asia. In the west it bends down the coast of the Mediterranean. In the east it follows the course of the **Tigris** (TY-gruhs) **River** and the **Euphrates** (yu-FRAY-teez) **River** until they merge and empty into the warm waters of the Persian Gulf. Today this river valley lies mostly in the country of Iraq. Historians call this flat, fertile area **Mesopotamia** (meh-suh-puh-TAY-mee-uh), which means "land between the rivers." The people who once lived there are known as Mesopotamians.

The people of Mesopotamia called the Tigris "swift river" because it flowed fast. The Euphrates flowed more slowly. It frequently changed course, leaving riverside settlements without water. Both rivers flooded unpredictably. Mesopotamians never knew when or how much water would come. Too much, too little, or too late spelled disaster for crops.

On the plus side, the often-destructive floodwaters deposited **silt**, an especially fine and fertile soil, that was excellent for agriculture. In this way, the rivers brought life to the otherwise dry land of Mesopotamia and supported the early civilization that was developing there. As farming thrived in this river valley, populations grew and cities developed.

FARMING IN THE FERTILE CRESCENT

Farming began as early as 9800 B.C. in the Fertile Crescent. It eventually spread throughout Mesopotamia. However, Mesopotamia was far from perfect for agriculture. In addition to flooding, farmers had to deal with hot summers and unreliable rainfall. However, the region's fertile soils promised plentiful crops, such as wheat, barley, and figs—if the people could come up with a way to control the water supply.

Irrigation, or watering fields using human-made systems, was the answer. Farmers in Mesopotamian villages cooperated to dig and maintain irrigation canals that carried water from the rivers to the fields. Farmers also stored rainwater for later use and built walls from mounds of earth to hold back floodwaters. The people developed important new technology, such as the ox-driven plow, a tool that broke up the hard-baked summer soil and prepared large areas for planting. These creative methods enabled farmers to use the rich soil to their advantage.

The result was a reliable and abundant agricultural surplus. The ample food fed the area's growing population. Because food was plentiful, the people of Mesopotamia could afford to develop art, architecture, and technology. The agricultural surpluses allowed a great civilization to develop.

ANCIENT MESOPOTAMIA, 2500 B.C.
30°E
35°E
40°E
45°E
50°E
45°N
40°N
35°N
Black Sea
Caspian Sea
Caucasus Mountains
Rivers' Source
The Tigris and Euphrates rivers have their source in the mountains of Asia Minor (present-day Turkey).
Mountain Snow and Rain
Melting snow (from the mountains north of the Fertile Crescent) and rain flooded the Tigris and Euphrates rivers. This flooding deposited rich soil on riverbanks.
ASIA MINOR
Taurus Mountains
ASIA
MESOPOTAMIA
Nineveh
Ashur
Tigris R.
Euphrates R.
Zagros Mountains
PERSIA
Mediterranean Sea
Byblos
Sidon
Tyre
Mt. Lebanon Ra.
Syrian Desert
Jerusalem
Dead Sea
Babylon
Susa
Umma
Lagash
Uruk
SUMER
Ur
0 100 200 Miles
0 100 200 Kilometers
Giza
Nile R.
EGYPT
Deserts
The Syrian and Arabian deserts created an open area, which made it easy for enemies to attack cities in the Fertile Crescent. As a result, people built walls around their cities for protection.
Persian Gulf
Fertile Crescent
Mesopotamia
Ancient coastline (about 5000 B.C.)
ARABIAN DESERT
Red Sea
Tropic of Cancer

REVIEW & ASSESS

1. **READING CHECK** How did the Tigris and Euphrates rivers make the growth of civilization in Mesopotamia possible?

2. **INTERPRET MAPS** What forms the borders of Mesopotamia?

3. **IDENTIFY MAIN IDEAS** What new methods and technology did farmers in Mesopotamia use to take advantage of the fertile soil?

1.2 City-States Develop

The present-day location that was once Mesopotamia is made up of windswept deserts. It's hard to imagine that 5,500 years ago this dusty land was filled with people living their busy city lives. The city streets were not just filled with people—there were also buildings and temples so tall they seemed to rise up to the heavens.

MAIN IDEA

The city-states of Sumer formed Southwest Asia's first civilization.

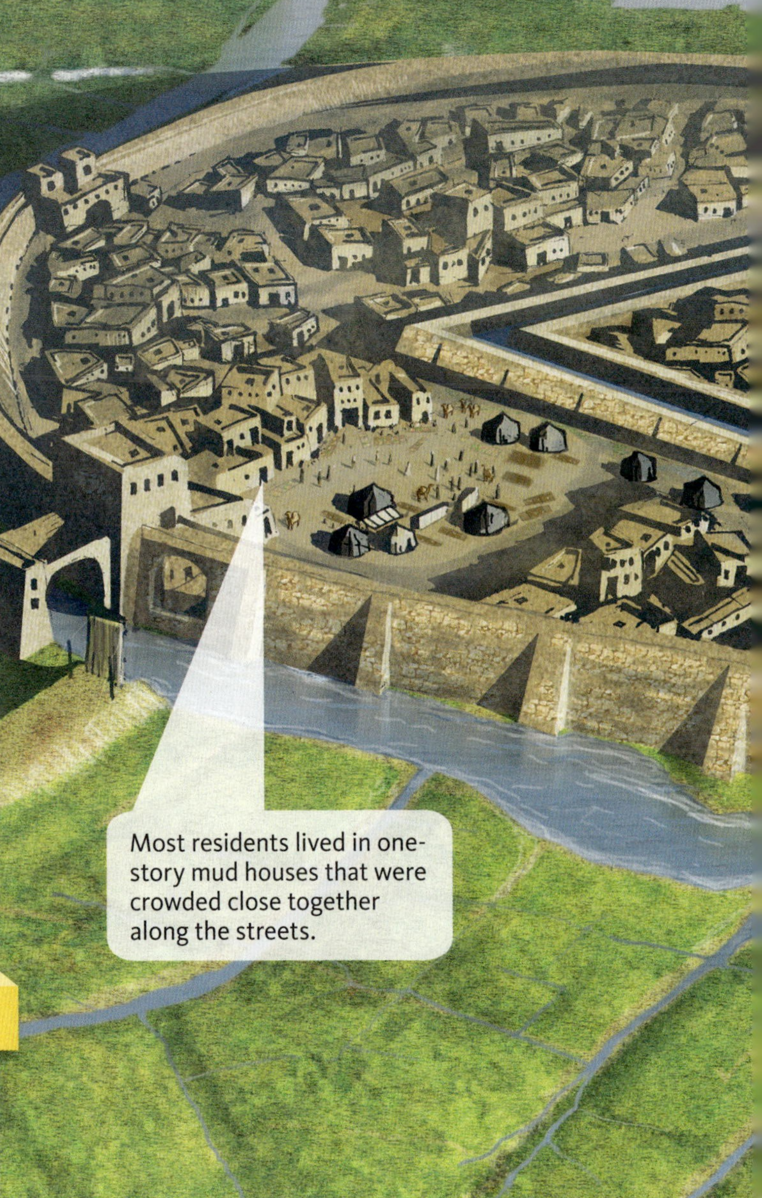

Most residents lived in one-story mud houses that were crowded close together along the streets.

SUMER

Around 3500 B.C., Mesopotamia's first civilization arose in **Sumer** (SOO-mur), an area in the southern part of the region. (See the map in Lesson 1.1.) Sumer was not controlled by a single, unified government. Instead, the area was made up of a dozen advanced, self-governing city-states. A **city-state** included the city and its surrounding lands and settlements. These units developed when villages united to build major irrigation projects.

Most of Sumer's 12 city-states, including Ur, were built on the Tigris or Euphrates rivers. City-states also clustered close to the coast of the Persian Gulf, where the people developed fishing and trade. Frequent wars were fought between city-states to protect fertile land, limited natural resources, and profitable trade routes.

CENTERS OF CIVILIZATION

Surplus food gave Sumerians time to learn new skills and encouraged trade. Though Sumer had productive farmland, the area lacked important natural resources, such as tin and copper. These resources had to be acquired through trade. When combined, tin and copper produce bronze, a strong metal used by Sumerians to create tools and weapons. Because of the importance of bronze, the period around 3000 B.C. is called the Bronze Age.

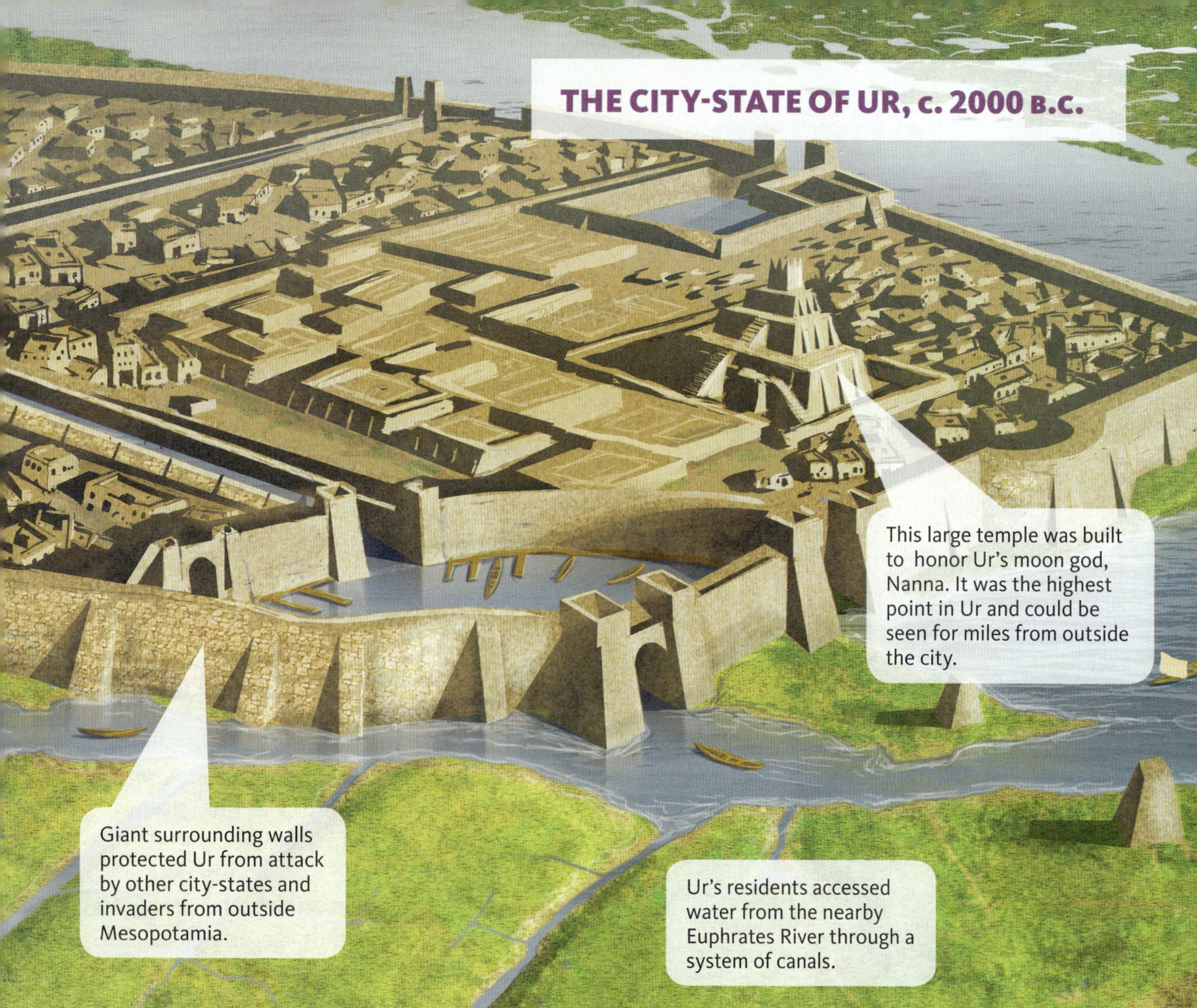
THE CITY-STATE OF UR, c. 2000 B.C.
This large temple was built to honor Ur's moon god, Nanna. It was the highest point in Ur and could be seen for miles from outside the city.
Giant surrounding walls protected Ur from attack by other city-states and invaders from outside Mesopotamia.
Ur's residents accessed water from the nearby Euphrates River through a system of canals.

Surplus food also led to a growth in population. New government systems had to be established to meet the challenge of managing so many people. Kings arose to provide strong leadership, and administrators supervised taxes and kept order. Because of the wealth created by agricultural surpluses, Sumerians could afford to support these government administrators.

Sumerian society was organized by **social class**, an order based on power and wealth. Kings ruled at the top, with priests just beneath them. Next came administrators, scribes, merchants, and **artisans**, or people who are skilled at making things by hand. These groups in turn looked down on farmers and less-skilled workers. However, even people at the bottom of this system ranked higher than Sumerian slaves.

REVIEW & ASSESS

1. **READING CHECK** How did the organization of Sumerian society affect the way different roles were viewed by others?
2. **INTEGRATE VISUALS** In what ways did the rivers support agriculture and the city-states?
3. **ANALYZE CAUSE AND EFFECT** How did food surpluses encourage local and long-distance trade?

1.3 Religion in Sumer

In the blazing sun, Sumerian priests carry food offerings step by step to the top of the great temple. The purpose of this feast is to secure the gods' favor for another day. In the dangerous and unpredictable world of Sumer, it's important to keep the gods on your side.

MAIN IDEA

Sumerians took religion seriously and built monumental structures to please their gods.

VOTIVE STATUES

To demonstrate their devotion to the gods, Sumerians placed small statues called votives in temples. Sumerians believed that while they worked on earthly activities like farming or fishing, the statues would pray on their behalf.

LAND OF MANY GODS

Sumerian lives depended on natural forces they could not control, including rivers that flooded and changed course. The people worshipped hundreds of gods, who they believed could control these forces. A belief in many gods is called **polytheism**.

Sumerians believed that their gods ruled the earth and had created humans to serve them. They also believed that the gods possessed superhuman powers. Unfortunately, the gods could use these powers to cause droughts, floods, and disease. For example, Ishkur was a storm god who was believed to have the power to cause destructive rains and floods whenever he liked.

To keep the gods happy, Sumerian priests tried to please them. Everyone paid a temple tax, which was offered to the gods in elaborate public **rituals**, or formal series of acts always performed in the same way. By observing natural events, including the movement of the sun, moon, and stars, priests tried to predict what the gods were planning. These observations helped the Sumerians develop a calendar, astronomy, and mathematics.

OFFERINGS AT THE TEMPLES

City-states were important religious centers. The most important building within a city-state was a huge pyramid-shaped temple called a **ziggurat** (ZIH-guh-rat). *Ziggurat* means "mountaintop." Every city was dedicated to a major deity, a god or goddess, who was its guardian. Sumerians believed that the deity lived in a shrine, or sacred place, on top of the ziggurat. People reached the shrine by climbing long, external flights of stairs.

Priests were responsible for conducting religious practices at the ziggurat. These practices included various rituals, such as offering food to the city god or goddess. A statue representing the deity was placed in a space called the adytum (A-duh-tuhm), or holy place. A meal was set on a table before the statue. Sumerians believed that the god or goddess would eat the meal.

Priests also performed purification, or cleansing, rituals using holy water. This purification process was often used on kings before they entered shrines where the deities were believed to dwell.

Critical Viewing Priests climbed 100 or more steep steps to the shrine at the top of a ziggurat to worship the city god. Why would the shrine have been positioned so high?

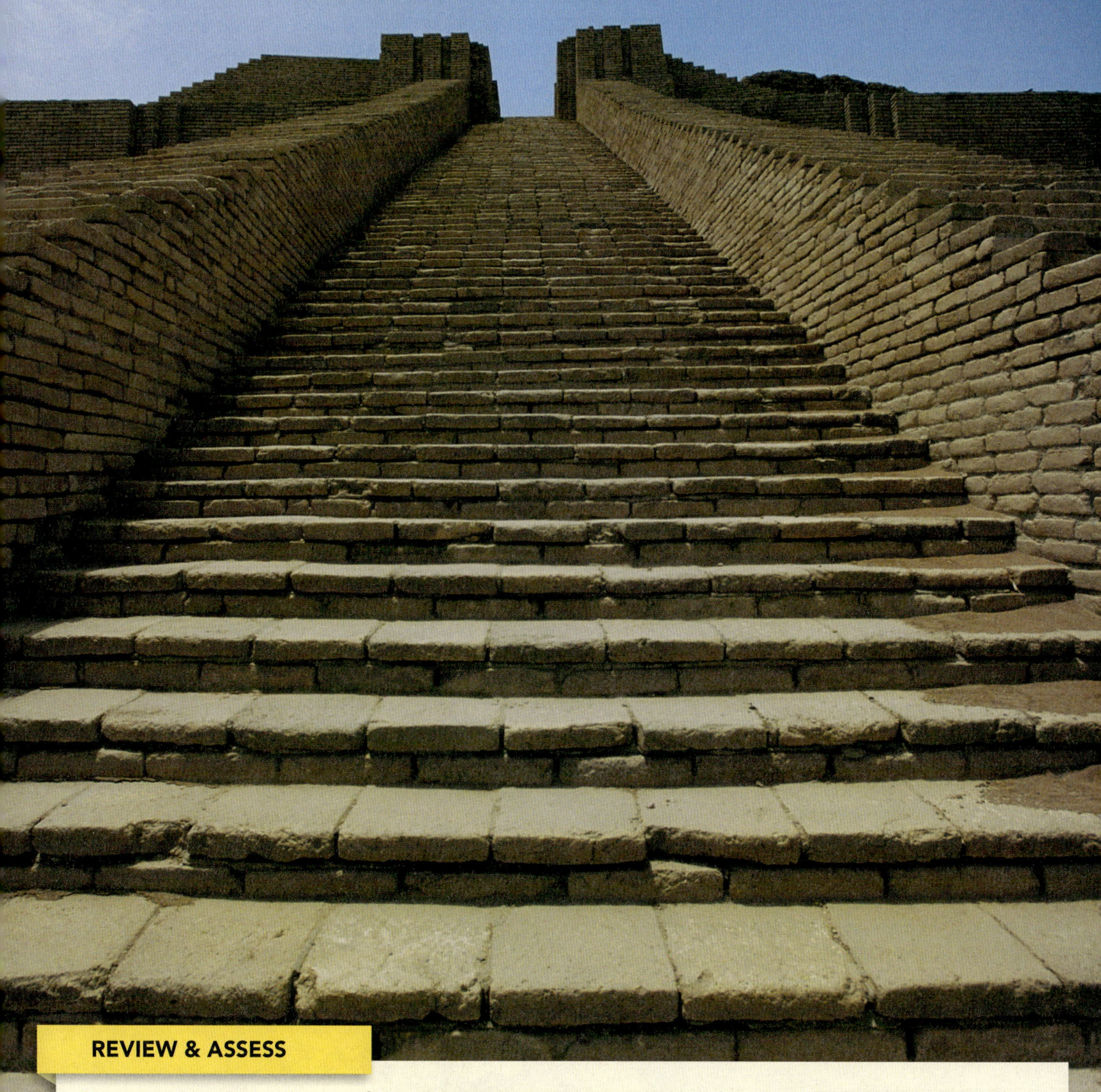

REVIEW & ASSESS

1. **READING CHECK** What religious practices did Sumerians observe to serve and please their gods?

2. **DETERMINE WORD MEANINGS** What context clues in the text tell you what *superhuman* means?

3. **MAKE INFERENCES** Why do you think Sumerians thought that cleansing was necessary before entering shrines?

1.4 DOCUMENT-BASED QUESTION

Sumerian Writing

Sumerians invented the earliest form of writing, known as pictographs, or images of objects. Detailed pictographs evolved into symbols called **cuneiform** (kyoo-NEE-uh-fawrm), which, over time, represented sounds rather than objects. Scribes began forming words and combining them into sentences in religious and scientific works and in stories. This change marked the beginning of written history and a major step forward in the development of civilization.

This 20th-century illustration depicts Gilgamesh arriving at the palace of the goddess Siduri-Sabitu in his search for immortality.

DOCUMENT ONE

Primary Source: Artifact

Cuneiform Tablet, Northern Iraq, c. 600s B.C.

Scribes used reeds, or sharpened blades of grass, to carve the wedge-shaped cuneiform symbols—600 in all—into wet clay tablets that were then dried. This tablet describes a flood scene from *The Epic of Gilgamesh*, explained in more detail below.

CONSTRUCTED RESPONSE Why did the Sumerians dry the clay cuneiform tablets?

DOCUMENT TWO

Primary Source: Epic

from *Gilgamesh*, translated by Stephen Mitchell

The Epic of Gilgamesh is the world's oldest recorded story. The author is unknown. Gilgamesh was probably a real king of Uruk. In the story, he sets off on a fantastic adventure with his loyal friend Enkidu. This passage describes their encounter with a monster.

CONSTRUCTED RESPONSE Why would the Sumerians record a story about their king encountering a monster?

They came within sight of the monster's den.

He was waiting inside it. Their blood ran cold.

He saw the two friends, he grimaced, he bared his teeth, he let out a deafening roar.

He glared at Gilgamesh. "Young man," he said, "you will never go home. Prepare to die."

DOCUMENT THREE

Primary Source: Creation Story

from *The Epic of Creation*, translated by Stephanie Dalley

This Babylonian creation story by an unknown author explains how the world was formed. In this passage, the chief god, Marduk, creates the stars and a 12-month calendar.

CONSTRUCTED RESPONSE Why might Babylonians want to tell and record their story of the creation of the world?

He [Marduk] fashioned stands for the great gods.

As for the stars, he set up constellations corresponding to them.

He designated the year and marked out its divisions,

Apportioned three stars each to the twelve months.

SYNTHESIZE & WRITE

1. **REVIEW** Review what you have learned about Sumerian writing and the world's oldest stories.
2. **RECALL** On your own paper, write down the main idea expressed in each document.
3. **CONSTRUCT** Construct a topic sentence that answers this question: What did the Sumerians' cuneiform writing system make possible?
4. **WRITE** Using evidence from the documents, write a paragraph that supports your topic sentence from Step 3.

1.5 Sargon Conquers Mesopotamia

Have you heard the expression, "Uneasy lies the head that wears a crown"? It applied well to Sargon the Great. He conquered many peoples, lands and cities, including Sumer. As ruler, Sargon was expected to keep his people safe, peaceful, happy, and fed. His role involved much responsibility. It was not easy being in charge of what was, at that time, the world's largest civilization.

MAIN IDEA

Sargon conquered Sumer and other lands in Mesopotamia to create the world's first empire.

AN OUTSIDER TAKES OVER

Sargon the Great was an ancient Mesopotamian ruler who has inspired stories for nearly 4,500 years. It is difficult to separate fact from fiction about his life. According to one story about his childhood, Sargon's mother was a royal priestess who abandoned him as a baby. A humble gardener from Kish raised him after finding him in a basket floating in a river.

Kish was a city-state in Akkad (AH-kahd), an area in central Mesopotamia. Akkadians and Sumerians shared a similar culture but had different ethnic origins and spoke different languages. Before becoming a ruler, Sargon was a servant to the king of Kish. After serving in the royal court, Sargon became a powerful official in Kish and eventually overthrew the king.

While Sargon gained power, Sumer was weakened by internal wars and invasions. In 2334 B.C., Sargon's armies swept through Sumer, conquering it completely. They also took control of northern Mesopotamia. These conquests created the world's first **empire**, a group of different lands and people governed by one ruler. Sargon's empire stretched from the Mediterranean Sea to the Persian Gulf. He ruled the Akkadian Empire from Akkad, his now long-lost capital city.

EMPIRE AND EXPANSION

The Akkadian Empire lasted 150 years, and Sargon ruled for 56 of them. He personally led the fight to expand the empire and claimed to have won 34 battles and taken 50 rulers prisoner. Sargon was an effective warrior and skilled at managing people and projects.

In the lands he conquered, Sargon allowed the people to keep their local rulers and customs. However, they had to obey him and pay a protection tax called a **tribute**. Sargon's policy helped keep peace and win the loyalty of people throughout his empire. He also introduced standard weights and measures and made Akkadian the official language of the government.

Sargon's powerful empire brought prosperity to his people and encouraged trade. Akkad's farmers managed agriculture so well that 100 years went by without **famine**, or widespread hunger. Sargon's wars were spread over large areas. As a result, Akkad traded with distant suppliers for timber, metal, and other raw materials Mesopotamia lacked. His wars concentrated

AKKADIAN EMPIRE, 2334–2200 B.C.

Reign of Sargon
(2334–2279 B.C.)

- Sargon's Empire
- Ancient coastline (about 5000 B.C.)

0 100 200 Miles
0 100 200 Kilometers

on controlling trade centers and protecting natural resources, such as cedar forests.

Despite Sargon's abilities, the empire became too big to control. After he died, his sons took over but were unable to maintain order. City-states rebelled, and a great deal of time and effort went into trying to keep the peace. Enemies from the northeast raided the empire's unprotected borders. Famine returned, spreading suffering and unrest among the people. By 2200 B.C., the Akkadian Empire had come to an end.

SARGON THE GREAT

To guarantee loyalty from the governors who ruled parts of his empire, Sargon gave trusted relatives powerful positions. To keep control of his army, he created a group of professional soldiers whose sole purpose was to fight for him.

‹ This sculptured head is believed to depict Sargon with his crown and long beard.

REVIEW & ASSESS

1. **READING CHECK** What measures did Sargon take to unite his empire?
2. **INTERPRET MAPS** Where were most of the cities of the empire located? Why do you think that was so?
3. **DRAW CONCLUSIONS** What conclusions can you draw about Sargon's abilities as a ruler?

2.1 Hammurabi's Code of Laws

Would you know how to play a game if you didn't know its rules? Probably not. This is how people from Mesopotamia must have felt when it came to following laws enforced by rulers. Though they did exist, laws were not laid out in a clear fashion. This changed when a king decided it was time to literally spell out the laws for his people.

MAIN IDEA

Hammurabi changed civilization by organizing laws and displaying them.

NEW EMPIRE IN MESOPOTAMIA

After the fall of Sargon's Akkadian Empire, a tribe called the Amorites invaded western Mesopotamia around 2000 B.C. They established their capital at Babylon (BA-buh-lahn), a city-state overshadowed by powerful neighbors. (See the map in Lesson 1.5.) Then in 1792 B.C., **Hammurabi** (ha-muh-RAH-bee) became the sixth king of Babylon. Hammurabi was Babylon's most influential and powerful ruler. He expanded the kingdom and established his Babylonian Empire across Mesopotamia and other parts of the Fertile Crescent.

Hammurabi spent the first 29 years of his rule working on domestic improvements. These included directing large projects, such as creating straight streets, strong city walls, magnificent temples, and efficient irrigation canals. Hammurabi also skillfully built up a network of **alliances**, or partnerships. This helped him conquer all of Mesopotamia in just eight years and claim the title "King of Sumer and Akkad."

HAMMURABI'S CODE

Hammurabi was a skillful ruler, but he is best remembered for his Code of Laws. His vast empire contained many different peoples who all followed different laws. To help unite his empire, Hammurabi took the best existing laws, added new rules, and then organized them into a clear, written system. The Code of Laws marked a major step forward for civilization. The code helped bring justice to everyday life. It also serves as an important primary source for historians because it offers insight into Babylonian society, including its structures, priorities, problems, and attitudes.

The Code of Laws was often applied based on a person's social class. For example, landowners could be fined more heavily than slaves. Hammurabi also laid down detailed laws about agriculture and the buying and selling of goods, highlighting the importance of these activities.

Three experienced judges heard cases. They listened to statements, examined evidence, and heard from witnesses. The judges even assumed the defendant's innocence. Guilt had to be proven. (Courts in the United States today also assume that people are innocent until proven guilty.) Hammurabi's Code of Laws influenced later legal systems, including those of ancient Greece and Rome.

After Hammurabi's death in 1750 B.C., the first Babylonian Empire declined rapidly and disappeared about 150 years later. However, Hammurabi's achievements ensured that Babylon remained a center of political, cultural, and religious importance for centuries to come.

CODE OF HAMMURABI

Hammurabi's Code of Laws was carved into an eight-foot-high stone slab, called a stela (STEE-luh), for everyone to see and read. An introduction announced its purpose: "To prevent the strong from oppressing the weak and to see that justice is done to widows and orphans."

The code's 282 laws covered all aspects of life and dictated specific penalties for specific crimes. Punishments were often as brutal as the crime. For example, a son's hand would be cut off for striking his father, and those who robbed burning houses were burned alive. Additional examples of the numbered laws include the following:

196 If a man put out the eye of another man, his eye shall be put out.

197 If he [a man] break another man's bone, his bone shall be broken.

This top portion of the stela shows King Hammurabi receiving the Babylonian laws from Shamash, the god of justice.

REVIEW & ASSESS

1. **READING CHECK** How was Hammurabi's court system similar to the one we have today?
2. **IDENTIFY MAIN IDEAS AND DETAILS** What details illustrate the improvements Hammurabi made as Babylon's king?
3. **MAKE INFERENCES** Why was Hammurabi's Code of Laws displayed in public for everyone to see?

2.2 The Assyrians and the Chaldeans

For 1,000 years after Hammurabi, Mesopotamia came under the rule of empire after empire. Then around 1000 B.C., the region shook with the sounds of an approaching army: marching feet, pounding hooves, frightening war cries. The Assyrian army had arrived.

MAIN IDEA

The Assyrians and then the Chaldeans conquered Mesopotamia.

THE ASSYRIAN EMPIRE

The Assyrians (uh-SIHR-ee-uhnz) were a people of northern Mesopotamia who developed a different culture. They were united by their worship of the god Ashur, for whom the Assyrian capital was named. (See the map in Lesson 1.5.) A strong agricultural economy and a large professional army helped the Assyrians conquer all of Mesopotamia, parts of Asia Minor, and even the rich state of Egypt by 650 B.C.

Destructive iron weapons gave Assyrian armies an advantage over their enemies, whose weapons were made of a weaker bronze. The armies also had horse-drawn chariots and soldiers who used bows and arrows while riding horses. Assyrian soldiers were experts at capturing cities. It was not uncommon for soldiers to kill or enslave captured people and then burn their cities to the ground.

Villages, towns, and cities answered to the unforgiving Assyrian king, who held absolute power. Even the highest officials were closely watched. The government sometimes forced rebellious people to move to faraway lands. In time, however, the Assyrian Empire grew too big, and its subjects became tired of being treated so unfairly and violently. By about 626 B.C., the Assyrians were weakened by internal power struggles. This made it possible for a people known as the Chaldeans (kal-DEE-unz) to eventually defeat them.

CHALDEANS OVERTAKE THE ASSYRIANS

The Chaldeans were a seminomadic people who originally came from southern Babylonia. After overthrowing the Assyrians in 612 B.C., the Chaldeans became the ruling power of Babylon and extended their rule over all of Mesopotamia. **Nebuchadnezzar II** (ne-byuh-kuhd-NE-zuhr) was the most famous Chaldean king. Under his rule, which lasted for 43 years, the New Babylonian Empire included Mesopotamia and all of the Fertile Crescent.

Though he was often cruel, Nebuchadnezzar also made improvements to Babylon by rebuilding the city and adding incredible beauty to it. From miles away, the Tower of Babel, a soaring seven-story multicolored ziggurat, inspired awe. Visitors entered the inner city through the colorful Ishtar Gate with its gleaming blue-glazed bricks and images of dragons and bulls.

The king's most famous accomplishment was the Hanging Gardens of Babylon. Pumps operated by slaves irrigated a large, leveled terrace of trees and plants. The terrace formed a green mountain that seemed to float in the city. Although his empire outlasted him by fewer than 25 years, Nebuchadnezzar had built a monumental city fitting its name: Babylon, Gate of God.

Critical Viewing This painting shows what the Hanging Gardens of Babylon might have looked like. What reaction might the gardens have inspired in visitors?

from *Wonders of the Past*, J. A. Hammerton, ed., 1923

REVIEW & ASSESS

1. **READING CHECK** In what ways were the rule of the Assyrians and the Chaldeans similar and different?

2. **MAKE INFERENCES** Why do you think the two empires did not last very long?

3. **ANALYZE LANGUAGE USE** What does "the terrace formed a green mountain that seemed to float in the city" mean?

PHOENICIAN SHIP

The Phoenicians sailed their ships in the Mediterranean and beyond. Through trade, the Phoenicians also had contact with Mesopotamia. They established **colonies**, or outposts of people from one land who live in another land, in places as far away as Spain. Phoenicia's most famous colony was Carthage in North Africa.

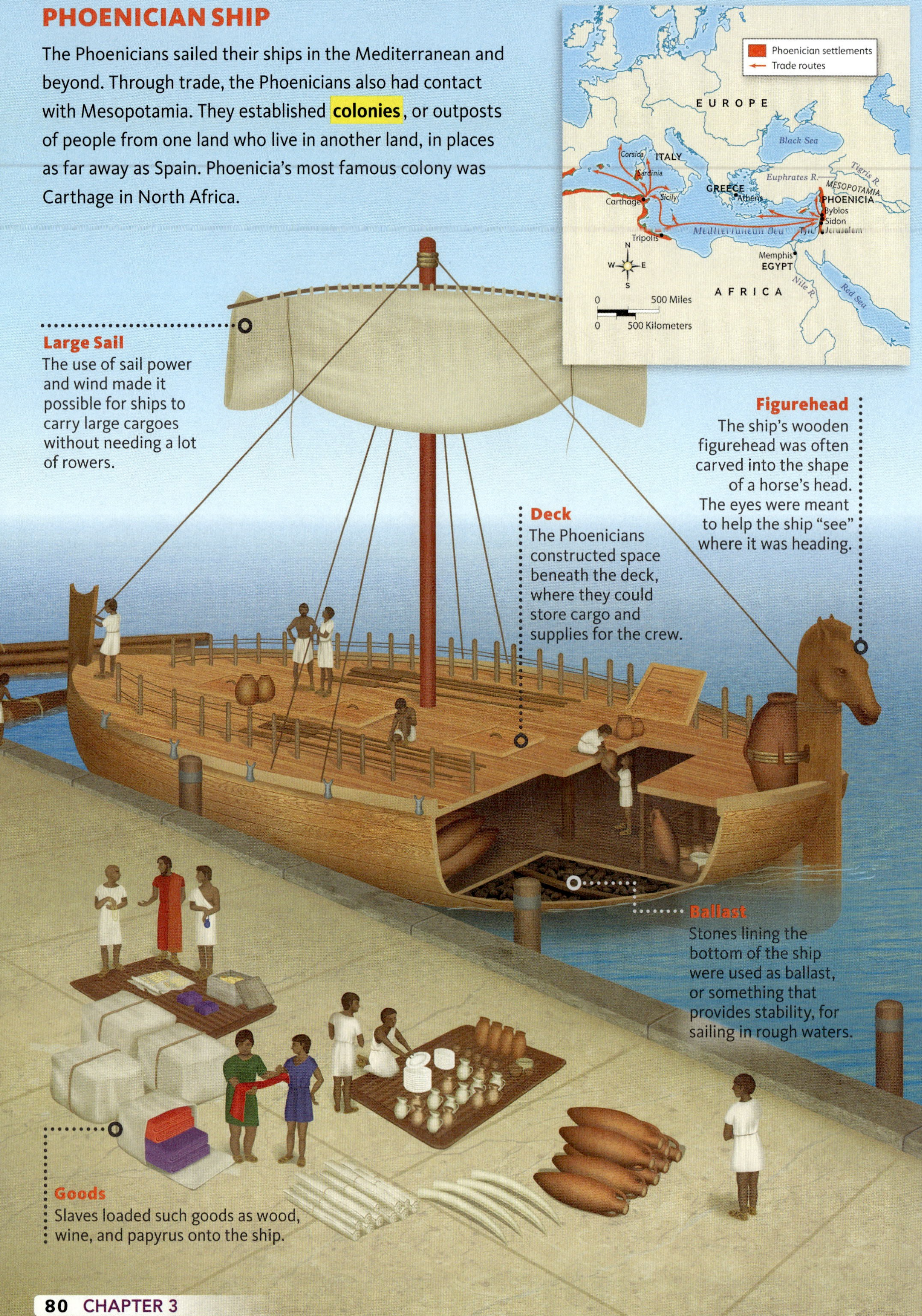
Phoenician settlements
Trade routes
EUROPE
Black Sea
Corsica
ITALY
Sardinia
Euphrates R.
Tigris R.
MESOPOTAMIA
GREECE
Athens
PHOENICIA
Carthage
Sicily
Byblos
Sidon
Tyre
Jerusalem
Mediterranean Sea
Tripolis
Memphis
EGYPT
N
W
E
S
AFRICA
Nile R.
Red Sea
0 500 Miles
0 500 Kilometers
Large Sail
The use of sail power and wind made it possible for ships to carry large cargoes without needing a lot of rowers.
Figurehead
The ship's wooden figurehead was often carved into the shape of a horse's head. The eyes were meant to help the ship "see" where it was heading.
Deck
The Phoenicians constructed space beneath the deck, where they could store cargo and supplies for the crew.
Ballast
Stones lining the bottom of the ship were used as ballast, or something that provides stability, for sailing in rough waters.
Goods
Slaves loaded such goods as wood, wine, and papyrus onto the ship.

2.3 The Phoenicians

Do you have a well-traveled friend who always has interesting information about places you've never been? You can think of the Phoenicians as this worldly friend. While conducting trade throughout the Mediterranean and Mesopotamia, the Phoenicians spread cultural practices from one stop on their trade route to the next.

MAIN IDEA

Through their extensive trade network, the Phoenicians spread different cultures throughout the Mediterranean and beyond.

A TRADING PEOPLE

The narrow strip of coast along the eastern Mediterranean (present-day Lebanon) contained many natural resources and had good harbors. This combination was perfect for the development of industry and trade. About 1000 B.C., independent city-states emerged in the area. They shared cultural similarities, including language and a trading economy. The Greeks called the people from these city-states Phoenicians (fih-NEE-shuhnz), which means "purple dye people." The Phoenicians processed local shellfish into a purple dye used to color fabric. This dye was their most famous trade good. They exported wood from their highly desired cedar trees to Egypt and Mesopotamia. From other lands, they imported **raw materials**, or substances from which other things are made. Phoenician artisans crafted these materials into luxury goods for trade.

Phoenicia's most important export was its culture. To record trade transactions, the Phoenicians used their own 22-letter alphabet, which was adapted from Sumerian cuneiform. Each symbol from the Phoenician alphabet stood for a sound. First the ancient Greeks adopted the Phoenician alphabet, then the ancient Romans modified it to form the basis of our modern Western alphabet.

SHIPBUILDERS AND SEAFARERS

The Phoenicians were also skilled shipbuilders and sailors. They built strong, wide ships. Powered mainly by wind and a large, square sail, these ships carried huge cargoes thousands of miles. The Phoenicians became one of the first Mediterranean peoples to sail on the Atlantic Ocean. They sailed north to Britain, west to the Azores (nine volcanic islands located in the mid-Atlantic), and possibly even around Africa.

Despite their talents and enormous wealth, the Phoenicians were militarily weak and were eventually absorbed into the New Babylonian Empire. However, they performed a valuable service by spreading different cultures from one area to another. Their accomplishments show the importance of trade in building civilizations.

REVIEW & ASSESS

1. **READING CHECK** What goods and ideas did the Phoenicians spread through their sea trade network?
2. **ANALYZE VISUALS** Why might ballast have been important to the condition of goods transported by ship?
3. **MAKE INFERENCES** Why would the Phoenicians have established trading colonies in faraway places?

2.4 Persian Leaders

Palaces in the Persian Empire were built with diverse materials: bricks from Mesopotamia, timber from Phoenicia, ebony and silver from Egypt. This mix of materials was a deliberate celebration of the Persian Empire's rich ethnic diversity—a diversity that was encouraged by the wise leadership of two men.

MAIN IDEA

Under the rule of Cyrus and Darius I, the Persian Empire united different peoples and cultures.

CYRUS THE GREAT

The region of Persia was located in what is present-day southwestern Iran, just east of Mesopotamia. Around 700 B.C., the Persians were ruled by a people called the Medes (meedz). Then in 550 B.C., a Persian king known as **Cyrus the Great** led a successful uprising against the Medes. In 539 B.C., he captured the Babylonian Empire. Cyrus continued to add to his empire until it stretched from Afghanistan to the Aegean Sea, including Mesopotamia. Under Persian rule, these lands enjoyed 200 years of peace and economic well-being.

The secret of Cyrus's success was **tolerance**, or sympathy for the beliefs and practices of others. After winning a war, he showed mercy to conquered kings by allowing them to keep their thrones. Cyrus demanded only tribute that defeated people could afford, sparing them great hardships. He also honored local customs, religions, and institutions. His tolerance won him widespread respect and acceptance from conquered subjects.

DARIUS EXPANDS THE EMPIRE

After Cyrus's death around 529 B.C., his son Cambyses (kam-BY-seez) became king and added Egypt and Libya to the empire. The next king, **Darius I** (duh-RY-uhs), ruled Persia at its height. Darius expanded the empire until it grew to about 2,800 miles, stretching from India in the east to southeastern Europe in the west, with the Fertile Crescent in the middle.

Like Cyrus, Darius was a wise ruler. He avoided problems that had weakened other empires. For example, he divided his empire into 20 smaller **provinces**, or administrative districts, that were ruled by governors called **satraps** (SAY-traps). They helped him maintain control of his huge empire. Darius introduced regular taxation and fixed each province's tribute at only half of what the people could afford to pay. He also introduced a form of currency, which made it easier to pay taxes and buy goods.

Understanding that communications were essential to good government, Darius built the 1,500-mile-long Royal Road, running from Susa in Persia to Sardis in Anatolia (present-day Turkey). Other roads connected all 20 provinces so that messengers could carry his orders anywhere in under 15 days. The roads helped unify the blend of people and cultures that made up the Persian Empire.

Darius also built a new capital, called Persepolis, for his empire. Decorated with palaces and jeweled statues, Persepolis was meant to symbolize the magnificence of the Persian Empire—the largest, most stable, and most powerful empire of ancient Mesopotamia.

CYRUS THE GREAT

Job: Rebel and king of the Persian Empire

Education: Unknown; legend says a herdsman or a wild dog raised him

Home: Pasargadae, a city in ancient Persia

In this relief from ancient Persepolis, representatives from different regions of the Persian Empire carry gifts for the Persian king. The gifts are meant to symbolize their loyalty.

FRIENDS

Cyrus's friends included almost everyone he ruled.

TRIVIA

Cyrus remains a highly respected figure for modern Iranians, and his simple tomb is still visited by millions of people every year.

REVIEW & ASSESS

1. **READING CHECK** How did Cyrus and Darius each rule diverse groups of people peacefully?
2. **CONTRAST** In what ways did the governing policies of Cyrus and Darius differ from those of Assyrian rulers?
3. **SEQUENCE EVENTS** Identify four significant events, in order, that occurred while Cyrus and Darius ruled.

2.5 The Legacy of Mesopotamia

As you check your calendar, text a friend, or ride your bike, you probably aren't thinking about the people who walked the earth more than 3,000 years ago. But if it weren't for the people of ancient Mesopotamian civilizations, you might not be able to do any of these things.

MAIN IDEA

Mesopotamian civilizations were responsible for major cultural and technological developments.

CULTURAL DEVELOPMENTS

The advances developed in ancient Mesopotamia form the region's **legacy**—or the things, both cultural and technological, left to us from the past. Mesopotamia's cultural legacy touches our lives every day. For example, the written word took important leaps forward with Sumer's development of pictograph and cuneiform writing and then with the spread of the Phoenician alphabet.

Mesopotamia also left us a legacy in forms of government. The city-state unit that developed in Sumer, Babylon, and Phoenicia became an important governmental form in the ancient world. Equally important were the styles of government that emerged. Hammurabi highlighted the importance of law. His Code of Laws influenced later legal systems. Cyrus the Great demonstrated the power of tolerance to future leaders. Finally, the use of provinces, governors, and good communications are still essential to modern governments.

TECHNOLOGICAL ADVANCES

It is easy to take Mesopotamia's technological advances for granted because they seem so commonplace to us today. Yet at the time, Mesopotamian technology clearly furthered the development of human civilization. During the Bronze Age, tools and weapons became more effective than ever before. Strong axes, swords, and daggers were crafted from bronze.

Mesopotamian technology also had an impact on agriculture and on land and sea travel. The ox-drawn plow made it easier to cultivate large areas of land. Irrigation techniques pioneered by the Sumerians are still used around the world. The wheel revolutionized transportation and trade on land. Phoenician shipbuilding and navigation did the same at sea by spreading Phoenicia's Mesopotamian-influenced culture.

With advances like the abacus, people from Mesopotamia laid the foundations of mathematics and science. The abacus is a device that uses sliding beads for counting. The Mesopotamians were also among the first to perform complex calculations and develop a calendar. Additionally, they devised number systems based on 60, which is what we use today to keep track of time.

The application of mathematics made it possible for Mesopotamians to build larger and more complex buildings, including Mesopotamia's cultural and technological masterpiece, the ziggurat. So the next time you ride in a car, use a tool, or see a skyscraper, thank ancient Mesopotamia.

MATCH-UP: THEN AND NOW

These images show Mesopotamian inventions and their current forms—the ones we are familiar with today. Can you pair each Mesopotamian invention with its modern-day match?

a

b
Sarah
Yeah but gonna leave now. What you up to ?
I'm going into town later
Send

c

d

e

f

g

h

MATCH-UP KEY

a. Phoenician merchant ship
e. Cargo ship
c. Abacus
g. Calculator
d. Message written in cuneiform on clay tablet
b. Text message on cell phone
h. Model of Sumerian plow
f. Tractor

REVIEW & ASSESS

1. **READING CHECK** What are examples of Mesopotamia's cultural and technological legacy?
2. **INTEGRATE VISUALS** What other modern items would you add to the images above to illustrate Mesopotamia's legacy?
3. **FORM OPINIONS** Which cultural or technological advance from ancient Mesopotamia do you think is most important? Explain and support your choice.

CHAPTER 3

Review

VOCABULARY

Match each word in the first column with its definition in the second column.

WORD	DEFINITION
1. city-state	**a. a pyramid-shaped temple with a shrine at the top**
2. artisan	**b. the governor of a district**
3. polytheism	**c. an order based on power and wealth**
4. ziggurat	**d. a person skilled at making things by hand**
5. social class	**e. an administrative district**
6. province	**f. a self-governing city that controlled the surrounding land**
7. satrap	**g. things left to us from the past**
8. legacy	**h. the belief in many gods**

READING STRATEGY

9. **MAKE INFERENCES** If you haven't already, complete your chart to make inferences about why civilization developed in Mesopotamia. Then answer the question.

I notice . . .	I know . . .	And so . . .
Two rivers flowed through Mesopotamia	Rivers provide water to sustain agriculture.	

Consider the traits of civilization that you learned about in Chapter 2. How did they develop in the region?

MAIN IDEAS

Answer the following questions. Support your answers with evidence from the chapter.

10. How did the geography of Mesopotamia contribute to the development of civilization? **LESSON 1.1**
11. What caused city-states to develop in Sumer and form the world's first civilization? **LESSON 1.2**
12. What purpose did the ziggurat serve in each Sumerian city-state? **LESSON 1.3**
13. What is important about the empire Sargon created in Mesopotamia? **LESSON 1.5**
14. What did Hammurabi establish to help unite his vast empire? **LESSON 2.1**
15. What factors helped the Assyrians of northern Mesopotamia conquer all of Mesopotamia? **LESSON 2.2**
16. How did Phoenician sea traders affect Mesopotamian culture? **LESSON 2.3**
17. In what ways were Cyrus and Darius wise rulers? **LESSON 2.4**

CRITICAL THINKING

Answer the following questions. Support your answers with evidence from the chapter.

18. **DRAW CONCLUSIONS** How might unpredictable natural forces, such as floods, have influenced the development of polytheism in Sumer?
19. **IDENTIFY MAIN IDEAS AND DETAILS** What are three details that support the idea that Sargon was a highly skilled administrator?
20. **ANALYZE CAUSE AND EFFECT** What led to Hammurabi's Code of Laws?
21. **SUMMARIZE** What were the important achievements of Mesopotamian civilizations?
22. **YOU DECIDE** Were the punishments in Hammurabi's Code of Laws appropriate? Support your opinion with evidence from the text.

INTERPRET CHARTS

Study the chart comparing letters in the Phoenician, early Greek, early Latin, and modern English alphabets. Then answer the questions that follow.

Phoenician	Early Greek	Early Latin	Modern English
			A
			B
			C
			D
			E
			F
		H	H

23. Which letter is most similar in all four alphabets?

24. What conclusions can you draw about language in the ancient world?

ANALYZE SOURCES

Read the following translation of an Assyrian king's description of one of his raids. Then answer the question.

> I carried off his silver, gold, possessions, property, bronze, iron, tin, . . . captives of the guilty soldiers together with their property, his gods together with their property, precious stone of the mountain, his harnessed chariot, his teams of horses, the equipment of the horses, the equipment of the troops, garments with multi-colored trim, linen garments, fine oil, cedar, fine aromatic plants, cedar shavings, purple wool, red-purple wool, his wagons, his oxen, his sheep—his valuable tribute which, like the stars of heaven, had no number.

25. Based on this passage, what can you conclude about the nature of Assyrian attacks on city-states in Mesopotamia?

WRITE ABOUT HISTORY

26. ARGUMENT Of all the achievements of Mesopotamian civilizations, which one do you think has had the most significant and lasting impact on the modern world? Write a persuasive essay outlining your argument.

TIPS

- Take notes about the many important achievements of Mesopotamian civilizations discussed in the chapter.
- State your argument in a clear, persuasive way.
- Present strong evidence to support your argument.
- Use vocabulary words from the chapter as appropriate.
- Provide a concluding statement that wraps up the argument presented.

CHAPTER

4 ANCIENT EGYPT

3000 B.C. – 500 B.C.

SECTION 1

A SOCIETY ON THE NILE

KEY VOCABULARY
cataract
delta
dynasty
pharaoh
vizier

NAMES & PLACES
Lower Egypt
Menes
Nile River
Upper Egypt

SECTION 2

THE OLD AND MIDDLE KINGDOMS

KEY VOCABULARY
hierarchy
mummy
pyramid

NAMES & PLACES
Ahmose
Hyksos
Khufu
Middle Kingdom
Old Kingdom
Re

SECTION 3

THE NEW KINGDOM

KEY VOCABULARY
barter

NAMES & PLACES
Hatshepsut
Kush
New Kingdom
Nubia
Ramses II

SECTION 4

THE EGYPTIAN LEGACY

KEY VOCABULARY
hieroglyph
papyrus
scribe

READING STRATEGY

DRAW CONCLUSIONS
When you draw conclusions, you use the facts in a text to make educated guesses. As you read the chapter, use an organizer like this one to draw conclusions about the importance of ancient Egypt's geographic features.

Conclusion
Evidence | Evidence

Egyptian ruler Ramses II built this massive temple at Abu Simbel to honor Egypt's gods—and himself. Each of the four 66-foot statues is an image of Ramses.

1.1 The Geography of Ancient Egypt

"Hail to thee, O Nile! Who manifests thyself over this land and comes to give life to Egypt!" These words written 4,000 years ago emphasize the importance of the Nile River to Egyptians: No Nile, no life, no Egypt. It was that simple.

MAIN IDEA

The Nile was the source of life in Egypt's dry, barren deserts.

THE GIFT OF THE NILE

The **Nile River** was central to the civilization that developed in Egypt. At around 4,132 miles in length, it is the world's longest river. It flows northward from sources deep in Africa to the Mediterranean Sea. Six **cataracts**, rock formations that create churning rapids, break the river's smooth course. The 550 miles from the most northerly cataract to the Mediterranean Sea formed ancient Egypt's heartland, which was divided into two distinct regions: the Upper (southern) Nile and the Lower (northern) Nile. The Lower Nile region included the Nile Delta, next to the Mediterranean. A **delta** is an area where a river fans out into various branches as it flows into a body of water.

The Nile was generally a peaceful river. Its current carried ships gently downstream, while the winds above it usually blew upstream, making it easy for ships to row downstream or sail upstream.

Water was the Nile's greatest gift. Without it there could be no agriculture in Egypt's desert. Every year faraway rains sent a surge of water downstream to Egypt, swelling the river with the annual flood.

Unlike the rivers of Mesopotamia, the Nile's flood was predictable, occurring every summer. The waters spilled over the riverbanks, depositing another great gift: silt, or very fine particles carried from upriver. The silt-enriched soil was fertile, or full of nutrients to support abundant crops. This soil made agriculture extremely productive—a key to the development of Egyptian civilization. With good management and a little luck, the soil delivered huge harvests.

THE BLACK LAND AND THE RED LAND

Egypt's climate was consistently dry, and sunshine was plentiful. Seven months of hot, sunny weather were followed by a

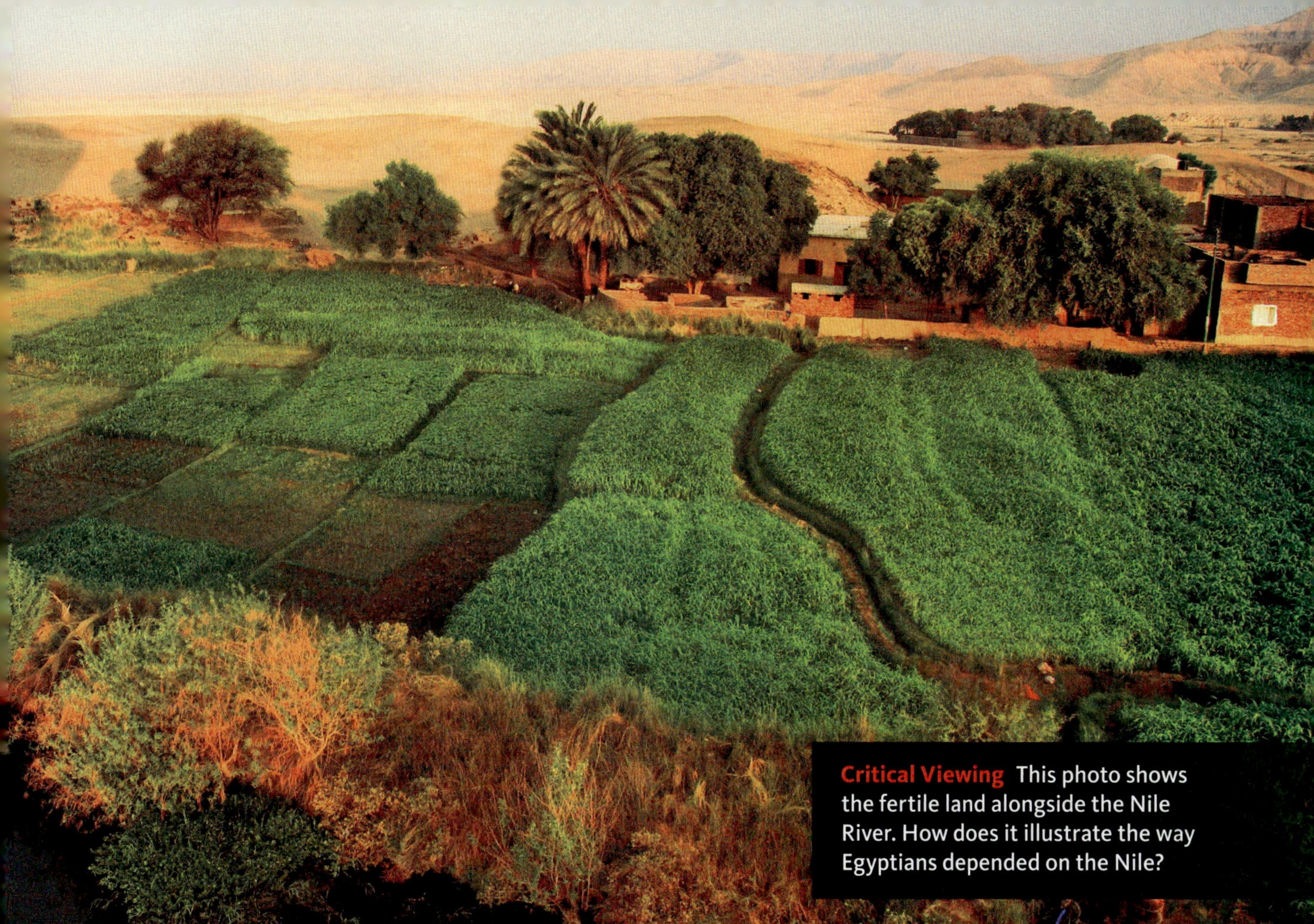

Critical Viewing This photo shows the fertile land alongside the Nile River. How does it illustrate the way Egyptians depended on the Nile?

winter of mild, sunny weather. The lack of rainfall created a landscape of striking contrast, made up of regions called the "black land" and the "red land."

The black land was the narrow stretch that ran along both sides of the Nile. There, the river's waters and nourishing dark silt allowed plants to grow and people to live.

The red land was a vast, scorching desert that surrounded the Nile. This desert formed a powerful barrier against invasion and helped separate Egypt from the world beyond. The seemingly empty desert also held a treasure trove of raw materials, including stone for building and gold. The only major resource Egypt lacked was timber.

Egypt's geography, its climate, and—above all—the Nile River all played parts in the kind of civilization that Egypt would become. The land was rich in resources, produced a huge food surplus, and had well-protected borders. In addition, Egypt was a crossroads for trade, lying along important trade routes connecting Africa, the Mediterranean, the Red Sea, and the Middle East. The scene was set for Africa's most famous civilization of ancient times.

REVIEW & ASSESS

1. **READING CHECK** Why was the Nile River essential to life in ancient Egypt?
2. **ANALYZE CAUSE AND EFFECT** What effect did the annual flooding of the Nile River have on the development of agriculture in Egypt?
3. **COMPARE AND CONTRAST** What did the black and red lands have in common? How were they different?

1.2 Agriculture Develops

It's August, and all that can be seen of the flooded fields is water lapping at the stones marking each farmer's boundary. In the dark of night, a farmer paddles nervously out and shifts the stones to steal a few feet from his neighbor. It's a profitable but serious crime—the penalty is death. Farmland in Egypt is so valuable that some are willing to risk it.

MAIN IDEA

Agriculture encouraged the development of communities and kingdoms in Egypt.

THE FERTILE NILE DELTA

Five thousand years ago, the lives of most Egyptians revolved around farming. Along with raising livestock, Egyptians grew a wide variety of crops such as wheat, barley, beans, lentils, peas, onions, and leeks. Fruits included grapes, dates, figs, and watermelons. Farmers grew flax to make cloth. Fish and birds were plentiful, and even poor Egyptians could eat well.

The cycles of the river dictated the farming year. From July to October, the fields were flooded, so farmers did other work. When the floods receded, farmers plowed the soft ground, scattered seeds, and used animals to trample the seeds into the soil. The growing crops were carefully watered through irrigation. Farmers captured floodwater in artificial lakes and channeled it to the fields. Later, the shaduf (shuh-DOOF) made irrigation easier. This tool was a long pole with a bucket on one end and a weight on the other. Farmers could use a shaduf to effortlessly lift water to their fields. The grain harvest started in mid-March. During the hot summer that followed, farmers prepared their fields before the next flood.

Irrigation and the Nile's fertile soil allowed for extremely productive farming. As in Mesopotamia, successful farming generated surpluses, which led to population growth, trade, and specialized jobs. Building and maintaining irrigation networks took a lot of labor, so farmers grouped together to create larger communities. Leadership was needed to coordinate and manage these increasingly complex societies. As villages grew into towns, village chiefs became kings.

TWO KINGDOMS ARISE

Some historians believe that by around 3200 B.C., two kings ruled over two separate kingdoms—**Upper Egypt** and **Lower Egypt**. Lower Egypt was the Nile Delta region with its wide expanse of fertile land and access to the Mediterranean Sea. Upper Egypt was the long, narrow stretch of the Nile south of modern Cairo and hemmed in by desert.

The Nile served as a superhighway, encouraging contact between Upper and Lower Egypt. Movement along the Nile was easy, and all the villages and towns were located near the great river. Goods and ideas were traded freely between the kingdoms, unifying Egyptians economically and culturally. Unlike Mesopotamia, Egypt would come to be a strong, unified state rather than a group of city-states.

However, Upper Egypt and Lower Egypt remained proudly distinct. Even after Egypt was united, it was represented by a double crown. Every time Egypt descended into disorder, the two kingdoms were usually on opposite sides of the power struggle.

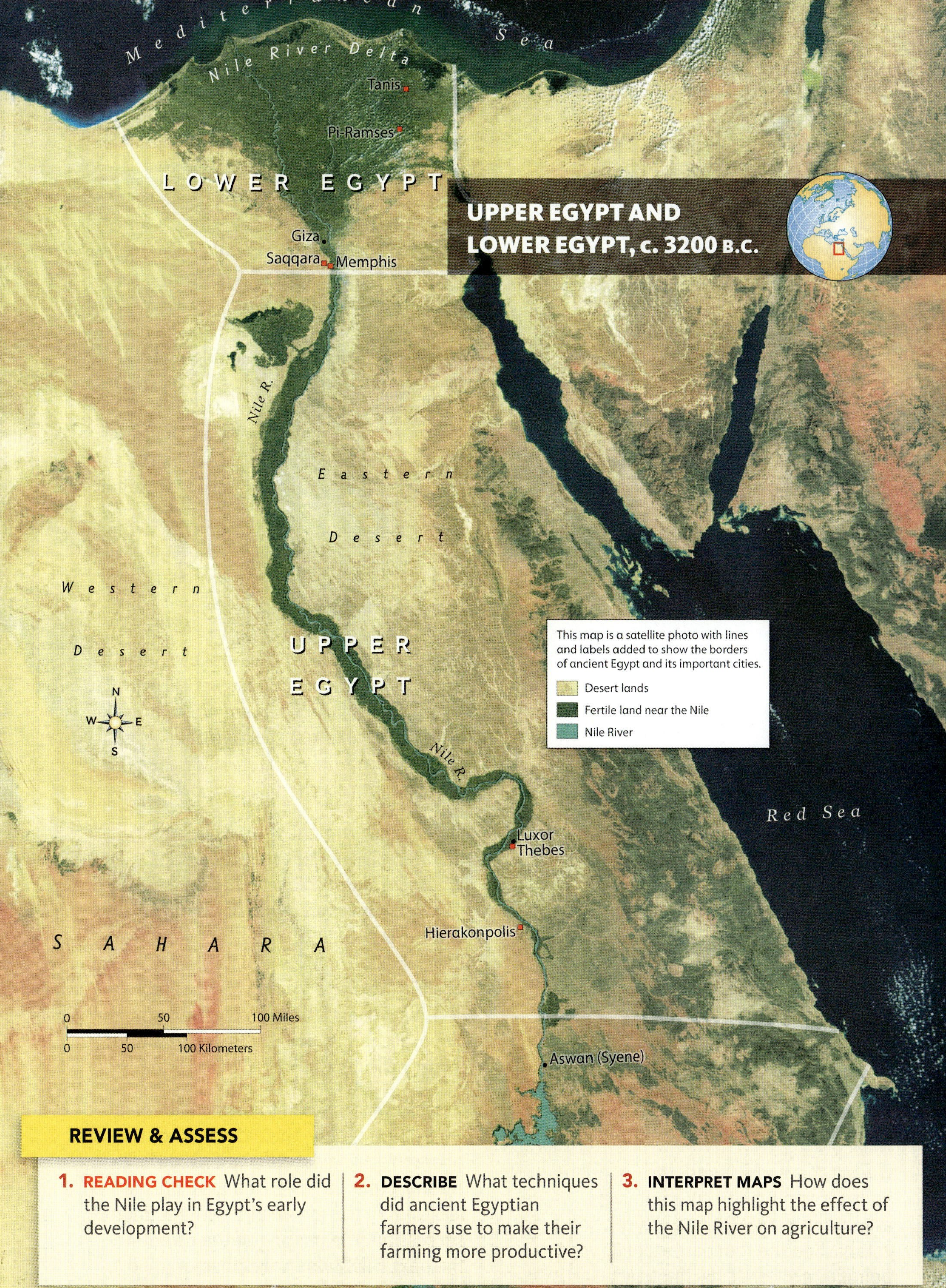
UPPER EGYPT AND LOWER EGYPT, c. 3200 B.C.
Mediterranean Sea
Nile River Delta
Tanis
Pi-Ramses
LOWER EGYPT
Giza
Saqqara
Memphis
Nile R.
Eastern Desert
Western Desert
UPPER EGYPT
Nile R.
Luxor
Thebes
Hierakonpolis
Aswan (Syene)
Red Sea
SAHARA
N
S
E
W
0 50 100 Miles
0 50 100 Kilometers
This map is a satellite photo with lines and labels added to show the borders of ancient Egypt and its important cities.
Desert lands
Fertile land near the Nile
Nile River

REVIEW & ASSESS

1. **READING CHECK** What role did the Nile play in Egypt's early development?

2. **DESCRIBE** What techniques did ancient Egyptian farmers use to make their farming more productive?

3. **INTERPRET MAPS** How does this map highlight the effect of the Nile River on agriculture?

1.3 Egypt Unites

Egypt's ancient civilization was unified for close to 3,000 years—twelve times as long as the United States has been a country. Of course, ancient Egypt witnessed its share of good rulers and good times and bad rulers and bad times. Still, ancient Egypt will be long remembered for its wealth and power.

MAIN IDEA

Strong kings united Egypt and ruled with the authority of gods.

DYNASTIES BEGIN

Egypt was governed by a long series of strong rulers. Exactly how Egypt united under a single ruler is uncertain. Tradition says that around 3100 B.C., the king of Upper Egypt conquered Lower Egypt and became ruler of all Egypt. Historians believe this king was called **Menes** (MEH-nehz). The complete unification of Egypt was probably a process that took place over the reigns of the kings who followed Menes. A double crown that combined the white crown of Upper Egypt with the red crown of Lower Egypt symbolized the newly unified country.

During this early period, the Egyptians built a magnificent new capital city at Memphis (MEHM-fihs). They also established the foundations of Egypt's political, economic, technological, artistic, and religious practices. The first kings founded a ruling **dynasty** (DY-nuh-stee)—a series of rulers from the same family. Egypt had 31 dynasties and was ruled by a total of more than 330 kings.

PHARAOHS RULE

Even though Egyptians did not call their kings **pharaoh** (FEHR-oh) until after 1000 B.C., the title is generally used for all Egyptian kings. The people used the term because they were afraid to speak the king's name. Why did the pharaoh inspire such fear in his subjects? He had complete authority over all religious, civil, and military matters. He exercised absolute power of life and death over everyone. A pharaoh was more than a man; he was worshipped as the son of Egypt's gods and a living god himself.

In Egypt, religion and government strongly overlapped. The pharaoh's main religious role was to keep harmony by maintaining communication between Egypt's people and their gods. He was high priest of every temple and led the most important ceremonies, especially the New Year rituals to ensure bountiful harvests. With this godly role came risk. Success reinforced the pharaoh's power. Defeat, disease, or famine threatened his authority.

On the government side, the pharaoh dictated all the important decisions. He also led his armies into battle as commander-in-chief. However, much of his day-to-day work was actually done by his **viziers** (vuh-ZEERZ), or chief officials. At first each pharaoh had one vizier. Later pharaohs had two viziers—one ran Upper Egypt and the other ran Lower Egypt. Thousands of lesser officials supported the viziers.

Most pharaohs were men and had many wives. Commonly, the eldest son of the pharaoh's principal wife inherited the throne. He often ruled alongside his father, learning on the job and ensuring a smooth succession (the passing of the throne to the next ruler) when the pharaoh died.

Critical Viewing This carving shows a pharaoh wearing the double crown of Egypt. Why was it important for the pharaohs to wear the double crown?

REVIEW & ASSESS

1. **READING CHECK** What made the pharaohs of ancient Egypt so strong and powerful?
2. **DRAW CONCLUSIONS** Why would disease or famine threaten the pharaoh's authority over the people?
3. **ANALYZE LANGUAGE USE** Why does the text refer to Egypt's rulers as *strong*?

1.4 NATIONAL GEOGRAPHIC EXPLORER SARAH PARCAK

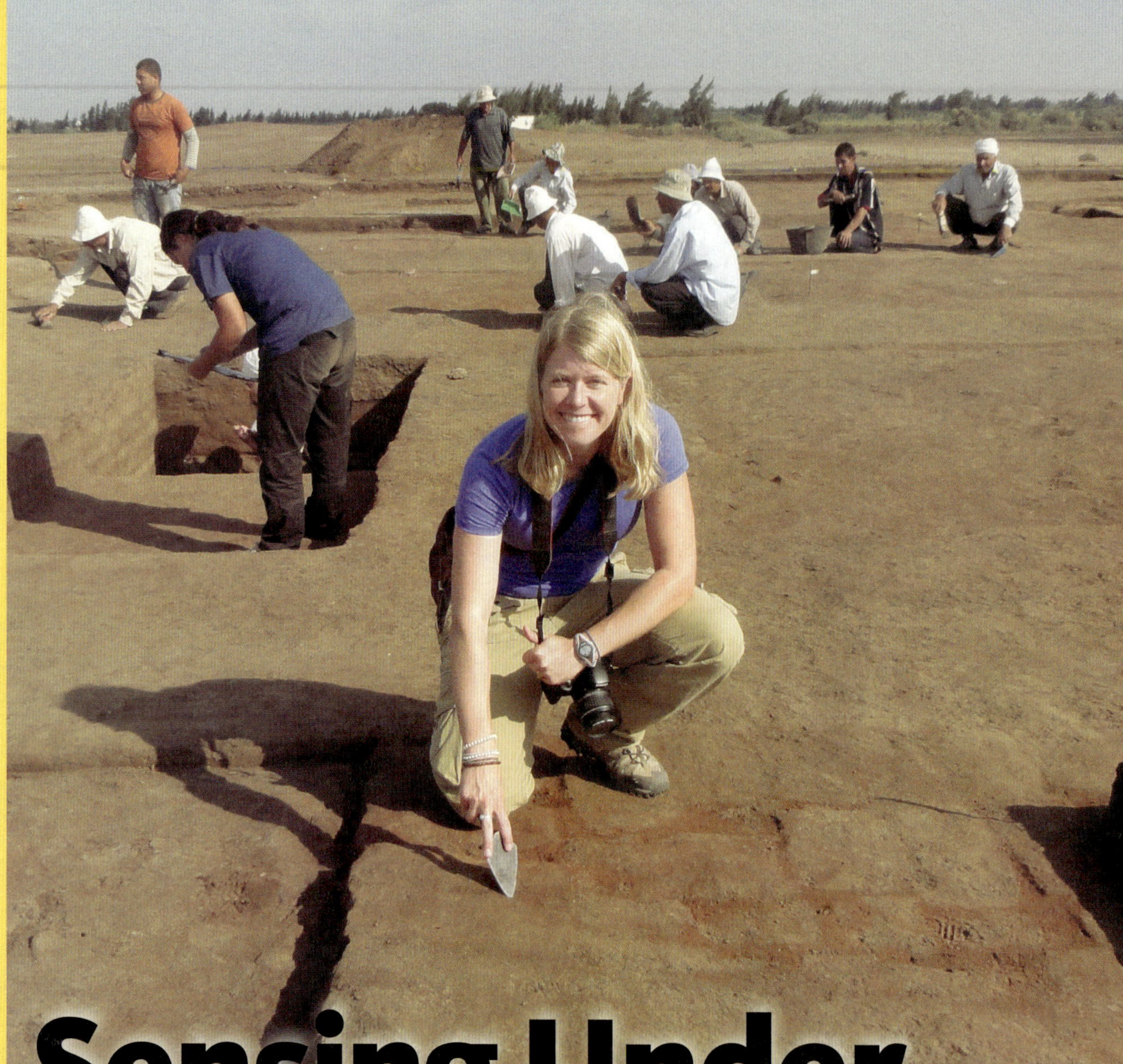

Sensing Under the Surface

"Indiana Jones is so old school," laughs National Geographic Explorer **Sarah Parcak**. "I'm sorry, Indy, but things have moved on!" Parcak should know—she's a leading specialist in satellite archaeology. She is pioneering technology that archaeologists never would have dreamed of decades ago.

^ After identifying the likely location of an ancient city, Sarah Parcak and her team head for the site to begin the hands-on excavation. Together, technology and muscle power are revealing ancient Egypt.

MAIN IDEA

Sarah Parcak uses satellite imagery to guide her archaeological excavations in Egypt.

SATELLITE TECHNOLOGY

Sarah Parcak prepares for another tough day of searching beneath Egypt's desert for evidence of ancient Egyptian civilization and its people's daily lives. However, instead of digging, she boots up her laptop.

Parcak relies on remote sensing, using powerful infrared cameras mounted on satellites. These cameras use invisible rays of light to pinpoint even small objects buried beneath sand, soil, vegetation, or new buildings. "The Egyptians built with mud-bricks, which are denser than the surrounding soil," explains Parcak. "The infrared picks out this denser material. Computer programs refine the detail until we start to see recognizable shapes—houses, streets, temples, tombs, and pyramids. It's a real 'wow' moment."

A satellite image of the Great Pyramid of Giza

Yet these revelations only happen after painstaking processing and analysis. "We don't just grab an image, flip it into the computer, and press a button. I've spent more than 10,000 hours of my life staring at satellite imagery to understand what I'm seeing," says Parcak. This effort pays off, saving enormous amounts of time and money. Before leading an expedition to Egypt, Parcak analyzed satellite imagery to figure out exactly where to dig. Within three weeks, she found about 70 sites. With traditional methods, this research would have taken around three and a half years.

MAPPING TANIS

Parcak's hard work has uncovered the main settlement area of Tanis, an important city in the eastern part of the Nile Delta. Over the centuries, Tanis was flooded and buried beneath Nile silt. Until recently only a tiny area had been excavated, but archaeologists, with the help of remote sensing, are changing that. Parcak turned the cameras onto Tanis with startling results. "We've created a map of this ancient city that's so clear it looks like something you'd use to navigate a town today," she says.

Excavations on the ground are proving the value of remote sensing. Scientists found an 80 percent match between the satellite image and the houses they unearthed. "This isn't just another 'gee whiz' toy," Parcak claims. "Less than one percent of ancient Egypt has been discovered and excavated, and, with the pressures of urbanization [the growth of cities], we're in a race against time. We need to use the most advanced tools to explore, map, and protect our past." Right now, satellites are just the tools for the job.

REVIEW & ASSESS

1. **READING CHECK** How does satellite imagery help guide Sarah Parcak's archaeological excavations in Egypt?
2. **COMPARE AND CONTRAST** What advantages does satellite archaeology have compared to more traditional methods of archaeology?
3. **MAKE INFERENCES** Why do you think urbanization creates a problem for the discovery and exploration of ancient Egyptian sites?

2.1 The Old Kingdom

It is taller than the Statue of Liberty, twice the area of the U.S. Capitol building, double the volume of the Rose Bowl Stadium, and 4,500 years older than all of them. For thousands of years, the Great Pyramid of Khufu was the largest structure on the planet.

MAIN IDEA

Old Kingdom pharaohs demonstrated their power by building monumental pyramids.

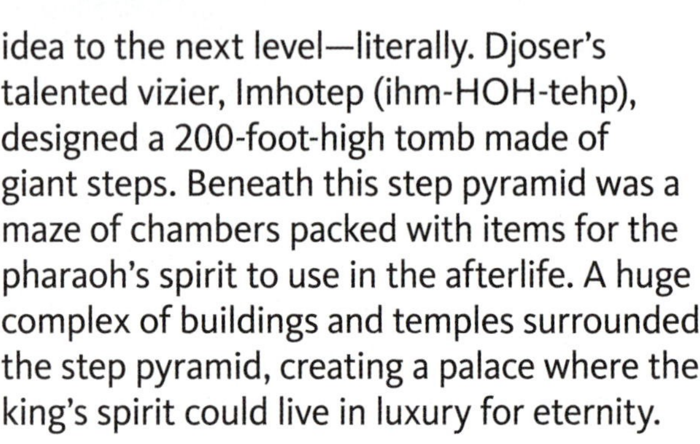

PYRAMIDS ALONG THE NILE

The **Old Kingdom** was Egypt's first great period of unity and prosperity, lasting from around 2700 B.C. to 2200 B.C. During these centuries, Egypt prospered under effective pharaohs, a strong central government, and an efficient administration. As Egyptian power grew, trade, technology, building, writing, and art also flourished. The pharaohs used their enormous wealth and power to build the **pyramids** (PEER-uh-mihdz), massive monumental tombs to house their dead bodies. The pyramids represented the Egyptian belief that life is a passageway to the afterlife, an existence believed to follow death. As a result, people made careful preparations for death.

Egyptian kings were originally buried beneath low mud-brick buildings. Around 2650 B.C., King Djoser (JOH-sur) took this idea to the next level—literally. Djoser's talented vizier, Imhotep (ihm-HOH-tehp), designed a 200-foot-high tomb made of giant steps. Beneath this step pyramid was a maze of chambers packed with items for the pharaoh's spirit to use in the afterlife. A huge complex of buildings and temples surrounded the step pyramid, creating a palace where the king's spirit could live in luxury for eternity.

THE GREAT PYRAMID

In Giza (GEE-zuh), near Cairo, the Great Pyramid of **Khufu** (KOO-foo) dominates the skyline. It is so extraordinarily huge that historians once assumed Khufu had been a cruel tyrant who used brutal methods to build it. In fact, he probably employed farmers unable to farm during the annual floods. Even so, Khufu must have commanded exceptional power and wealth to build his Great Pyramid.

The great pyramids of Giza dwarf the human figures nearby. These imposing structures would have awed the average Egyptian in ancient times, just as they amaze visitors today.

The pyramids were an impressive achievement for a civilization with limited technology. Using copper tools, ropes, sleds, and ramps, some 18,000 workers quarried, cut, and precisely placed 2.3 million two-and-a-half-ton limestone and granite blocks. It took 20 years. The pyramid they built was symmetrical—all sides were the same. It covered 571,158 square feet and stood 481 feet high. Deep inside were Khufu's tomb and treasure. Two other large pyramids were built in Giza by Khufu's successors, Menkaure (mehn-KO-ray) and Khafre (KAH-fray). Khafre also built the Great Sphinx (sfihnks), a symbol of divine power with a lion's body and Khafre's head. The sphinx was carved out of a huge piece of limestone.

The Great Pyramid was a powerful symbol of the pharaoh's status as a living god and the unity of religion and government in Egypt. A proper burial within the great tomb would ensure the pharaoh's smooth passage to life after death. Until then, a vast city of pyramid builders surrounded Giza. Here, too, were palaces and government buildings that allowed the pharaoh to run the country while building his home for the afterlife.

REVIEW & ASSESS

1. **READING CHECK** Why did Old Kingdom pharaohs build pyramids?
2. **DESCRIBE** What was new and different about the design of King Djoser's burial building?
3. **DRAW CONCLUSIONS** What do the pyramids reveal about Egyptian society?

2.2 Daily Life and Religion

There's a saying that "you can't take it with you" when you die. But Egyptians did! In fact, they were buried with everything they might need in the afterlife. The graves of wealthy Egyptians contained food, furniture, and jewelry. The Egyptians were ready for anything.

MAIN IDEA

The Egyptians had strong beliefs about religion and burial that affected all social classes.

Eight Gods of Ancient Egypt

Horus Sky god

Hathor Goddess of love, birth, and death

Re God of the sun (sometimes called Ra)

Nut Sky goddess

Anubis God of the dead

Osiris God of agriculture and judge of the dead

Isis Wife of Osiris and mother of Horus

Thoth God of writing, counting, and wisdom

EGYPTIAN SOCIETY

Ancient Egypt's society was a **hierarchy** (HY-rar-kee), meaning that people belonged to different social classes and each class had a rank in society. The social structure resembled Egypt's pyramids. At the top was the pharaoh, the all-powerful ruler and living god.

Beneath the pharaoh came the priests and nobles who ran the country and army. At the next step in the pyramid were all the officials and scribes who kept the government running smoothly by collecting taxes, organizing building projects, and keeping records. Beneath the officials and scribes were craftsmen and merchants. Farmers formed the next layer, and at the bottom came unskilled laborers and slaves who did all the hardest work.

Unlike in Mesopotamia, Egyptian women shared some rights with men. They could own property, conduct business, and take part in court cases. Poorer women often worked alongside their husbands, but they could do almost any job. Still, a woman's main role was to be a wife and raise children.

EGYPTIAN GODS

Like the people of Mesopotamia, the Egyptians believed in multiple gods. Modern scholars know 1,500 of them by name. The Egyptians believed that the gods controlled every aspect of life and death. The most important god was **Re** (RAY), the sun god, who created the world. The Egyptians also worshipped Osiris (oh-SY-rihs), the god of the underworld. The god Anubis (uh-NOO-bihs) weighed each dead person's heart against the weight of an ostrich feather. If the person was good, his or her heart would weigh the same as the feather, and the person would be admitted to the afterlife.

These beliefs encouraged Egyptians to lead good lives and take burial seriously. They believed a dead person's spirit needed food and a body to live in. The spirit would need to recognize the body after death. That is why the bodies of pharaohs and other powerful people were preserved as **mummies**. Specialized workers removed and preserved the internal organs (except for the heart, which Anubis had to weigh). Then the workers dried out the body and wrapped it in linen. Last, the body was placed in a coffin, and priests performed special rituals that were intended to give life to the mummy.

Critical Viewing The jackal-headed god Anubis often appears on tomb walls. Why did Egyptians paint this god on their tombs?

REVIEW & ASSESS

1. **READING CHECK** How was Egyptian society organized?

2. **COMPARE** How were the ancient Egyptians' religious beliefs similar to those of the people of Mesopotamia?

3. **DRAW CONCLUSIONS** How did religion affect daily life in ancient Egypt?

2.3 DOCUMENT-BASED QUESTION

Life, Death, and Religion

The majority of ancient Egyptians could not read or write. Still, a vast amount of writing has survived in the form of official records, business transactions, religious texts, technical manuals, and stories. These documents tell us a lot about life in ancient Egypt.

The ancient Egyptian *Book of the Dead* helped archaeologists learn much about the civilization's religious beliefs. Here, a section of the book illustrates a vision of the afterlife that closely resembles the living world.

DOCUMENT ONE

Primary Source: Poem

from *Hymn to the Nile*, c. 2100 B.C., translated by Paul Guieysse

Hymn to the Nile is a religious poem. It may have been read aloud at festivals celebrating the annual Nile flood. It has about 200 lines divided into 14 verses, although historians are not sure how the verses should be read. The hymn praises the Nile as the source of all life in Egypt. It expresses the people's joy when the flood brings water and silt and their misery when the flood fails. The author is unknown.

Hail to thee, O Nile!
Who manifests [reveals] thyself over this land, and comes to give life to Egypt!
Mysterious is thy issuing forth from the darkness, on this day whereon it is celebrated!
Watering the orchards created by Re, to cause all the cattle to live, you give the earth to drink, inexhaustible one!

CONSTRUCTED RESPONSE Why might ancient Egyptians have wanted to praise the Nile River each year by reciting this religious poem?

DOCUMENT TWO

Primary Source: Sacred Text

from the *Book of the Dead*, 1240 B.C., translated by E.A. Wallis Budge

The *Book of the Dead* was a series of texts that contained around 200 spells for helping the dead reach the afterlife. The texts were usually placed in the coffin or in the mummy's wrappings. This passage describes the sun god's journey as he rises and sets each day.

The gods are glad [when] they see Re in his rising; his beams flood the world with light. The majesty of the god, who is to be feared, sets forth and comes unto the land of Manu [a sacred place]; he makes bright the earth at his birth each day; he comes unto the place where he was yesterday.

CONSTRUCTED RESPONSE What does this passage suggest about Re's role in ancient Egyptian beliefs?

DOCUMENT THREE

Primary Source: Artifact

Sun God Re in Falcon Form, Ancient Egypt

This statue depicts Re, god of the sun and creator of Earth.

CONSTRUCTED RESPONSE What can you infer about Re's connection to nature from his representation in this statue?

SYNTHESIZE & WRITE

1. **REVIEW** Review what you have learned about ancient Egyptian religious beliefs from the text and these documents.
2. **RECALL** On your own paper, write down the main idea expressed in the artifact and in each document.
3. **CONSTRUCT** Construct a topic sentence that answers this question: What did the Egyptians believe about their gods' control of their world?
4. **WRITE** Using the evidence from the artifact and documents, write an informative paragraph that supports your topic sentence in Step 3.

2.4 The Middle Kingdom

First comes the thunder of hooves, then the whistling of arrows. Through the dust of battle bursts a line of horse-drawn chariots. From these wheeled wooden platforms, enemy archers rain arrows into your ranks before crashing through them, scattering your Egyptian army. These foreign war machines are effective; it's time to adopt, adapt, and fight back.

MAIN IDEA

The Middle Kingdom was strong and peaceful between periods of weakness and foreign rule.

CONFLICT AND STABILITY

The peace and prosperity of the Old Kingdom gave way to chaos and war between rival Egyptian groups around 2200 B.C. Building monumental tombs had drained the royal treasury. Water shortages and famines made the people doubt the pharaoh's power as a living god. The kingdom descended into a long period of conflict within its borders.

Then, around 2040 B.C., a king named Mentuhotep II (mehn-too-HOH-tehp) reunited the kingdom and launched a new era of peace and prosperity known as the **Middle Kingdom**. This period lasted until about 1650 B.C. During the Middle Kingdom, the pharaohs restored the power of the centralized government. Farmers expanded agriculture into new regions, and the building of great monuments, including pyramids, resumed.

The pharaohs also pursued an active foreign policy to increase Egypt's wealth. Trade expanded greatly. Egypt's trade network reached to several nearby lands and possibly as far as East Africa. To support and expand the prosperity of the Middle Kingdom, the pharaohs increased Egypt's military power. In the northeast, they conquered lands along the eastern Mediterranean. They also extended Egypt's southern border further up the Nile by leading successful military campaigns against the kingdoms of Nubia (NOO-bee-uh).

INVADERS

Egypt's wealth made a tempting target. One group of foreigners, the **Hyksos** (HIHK-sohs), came to live in Egypt and rose to power in Lower Egypt. The Hyksos brought an end to the Middle Kingdom.

Hyksos means "rulers of foreign lands," and, from their capital Avaris (AH-var-ihs) in the Nile Delta, they controlled much of Egypt for more than 100 years. The Hyksos probably ruled pretty much as the pharaohs had, adopting native ways and practices. Even so, native Egyptians resented being under foreign rule. Finally, in Upper Egypt, King **Ahmose** (AH-mohz) rebelled. The Hyksos brought to the battlefield deadly new tools including horse-drawn chariots, powerful new bows, curved swords, and body armor. Ahmose adopted these deadly weapons and threw the invaders out of Egypt.

Although Ahmose reunited Egypt under native Egyptian rule, he faced new challenges. Egypt had been largely on its own for centuries, but now the pharaohs had to deal with the wider world. Armed with their new military might, the pharaohs set out to forge an empire.

Critical Viewing This pendant depicts the pharaoh Ahmose being purified by the gods Re and Amun. Why is the pharaoh shown with the gods?

REVIEW & ASSESS

1. **READING CHECK** Who were the Hyksos?
2. **ANALYZE CAUSE AND EFFECT** Why did the pharaohs lose control of the Old Kingdom?
3. **SEQUENCE EVENTS** What events marked Egypt's movements back and forth between disorder and order?

This statue shows Hatshepsut wearing the false beard traditionally worn by the male pharaohs.

3.1 Hatshepsut Expands Trade

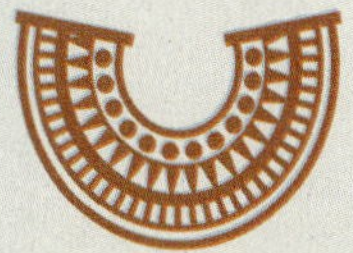

At any grocery store, you can find exotic fruits from distant lands right alongside the crunchy apples from a nearby orchard. Like you, the ancient Egyptians had access to food and other goods from near and far.

MAIN IDEA

Under a great female pharaoh, Egypt grew wealthy through conquest and trade.

EGYPT'S GREAT FEMALE RULER

On the heels of the defeat of the Hyksos came the **New Kingdom**, which spanned nearly 500 years from 1550 B.C. to 1070 B.C. This period of prosperity saw Egypt grow more powerful than ever as it built a mighty empire. Its large professional army expanded the empire northeast into Palestine and south into Nubia. Plunder from war and taxes from conquered lands made Egypt rich, but so did trade. Under the rule of **Hatshepsut** (haht-SHEHP-soot), history's earliest well-known female ruler, trade flourished.

Hatshepsut came to power sometime around 1470 B.C. After her husband the pharaoh died, she ruled with her stepson, Thutmose III (thoot-MOH-suh), who was very young. Hatshepsut played a smart political game and won enough support to be crowned sole king. She performed all the religious, military, and political functions of the pharaoh, and she even dressed as a king.

TRADE AND EXPANSION

Like other pharaohs, Hatshepsut fought wars to expand the empire, but she also promoted trade. Egypt had abundant resources to **barter**, or exchange, for things the land couldn't produce—especially timber and exotic luxuries. These goods traveled along trade routes and pathways established by traders over land and sea. Hatshepsut sent expeditions as far as East Africa. Egyptian merchants and traders bartered Egyptian beer, wine, food, and manufactured goods for myrrh trees, incense, ebony, ivory, leopard skins, and monkeys. The wealth generated through these expeditions stimulated Egypt's economy and funded great building projects.

Back in Egypt, Hatshepsut moved the capital city to Thebes and ordered many great monuments constructed to celebrate her rule. After 15 years in power, she disappeared suspiciously, possibly murdered by her stepson. Thutmose III became a mighty pharaoh in his own right and tried to erase Hatshepsut's name from all monuments and records. Luckily for future generations, he did not entirely succeed. Instead, a solid trail of clues has allowed historians to reconstruct Hatshepsut's remarkable reign.

REVIEW & ASSESS

1. **READING CHECK** In what ways did Egypt prosper during the reign of Hatshepsut?
2. **DRAW CONCLUSIONS** Why did the pharaohs engage in trade with other countries?
3. **FORM AND SUPPORT OPINIONS** What details support the opinion that Hatshepsut was an ambitious leader?

3.2 BIOGRAPHY

RAMSES II

RULED
1279 B.C. – 1213 B.C.

The women and children wail, and the men look up to the sun god in desperation. After ruling for 66 years, the pharaoh is dead. Most Egyptians have known no other king, and the dead pharaoh wasn't just any ruler. He was **Ramses II**—also known as Ramses the Great, a man who earned his title. Egypt was never more powerful than during Ramses' long reign.

- **Job:** Pharaoh of Egypt
- **Education:** Ruled alongside his father, Seti I
- **Home:** Pi-Ramses

FINEST HOUR

He led Egypt's army against the Hittites at the Battle of Kadesh around 1274 B.C.

WORST MOMENT

He saw 12 of his sons die before he did.

FRIENDS

The people loved him, affectionately calling him Sese (SEH-say), a nickname for "Ramses." He had about 200 wives and more than 100 children.

TRIVIA

His mummified nose was stuffed with peppercorns to keep its distinctive shape. When his mummy was exhibited in Paris, it received the Presidential Guard of Honor reserved for visiting royalty.

A LONG AND POWERFUL REIGN

Lasting 66 years, Ramses' (RAM-zeez) reign was one of the longest in Egyptian history. Ramses expanded Egypt's empire south into Nubia, west into Libya, and into the eastern Mediterranean. There he clashed with another ancient people, the Hittites (HIH-tyts).

The Hittites had a powerful empire centered around present-day Turkey, and they also sought to control the eastern Mediterranean. In his fifth year as pharaoh, Ramses fought a huge battle against the Hittites at Kadesh (kay-DEHSH). The battle stopped the Hittites' advance, but war with the Hittites dragged on for more than 15 years. At last, Ramses wrote letters to the Hittite king and negotiated a peace treaty. Peace with the Hittites and Egypt's territorial expansion helped Ramses create a strong economy.

Ramses went on to carve his legacy in stone and make himself unforgettable. First he built a new capital city, which he

Critical Viewing Visitors at a museum in Memphis, Egypt, marvel at a statue of Ramses II. What does the size of this statue say about how Ramses was viewed in his day?

called Pi-Ramses (puh-RAM-zeez). Then he commissioned an awesome number of temples, monuments, and statues. At Abu Simbel (ah-boo SIHM-buhl) in Egyptian-controlled Nubia, Ramses had two cavernous temples carved out of the rock cliff face. His massive tomb at Thebes had a long wait for him—Ramses outlived 12 sons, dying in 1213 B.C. at more than 90 years of age.

THE NEW KINGDOM ENDS

Egypt's power was at its peak under Ramses the Great. After his death, several challenges emerged. Members of the ruling dynasty clashed with each other. In addition, Egypt was repeatedly invaded by a group known as the Sea Peoples. Although they never conquered Egypt, the Sea Peoples waged a lengthy war that left Egypt's civilization weak and unstable.

In the years following the New Kingdom, Egypt was conquered and controlled by various foreign powers. First the Libyans and then the Nubians seized large areas of land. Later, another people from Southwest Asia, the Persians, conquered Egypt. After 332 B.C., Egypt came under the control of the Macedonians, a people from the Greek peninsula. The final pharaohs were all Macedonians, right down to the last one, the famous Cleopatra VII. When Rome conquered Egypt in 30 B.C., Cleopatra committed suicide. It was a suitably dramatic end to 3,000 years of pharaohs.

REVIEW & ASSESS

1. **READING CHECK** What weakened Egypt's power after the death of Ramses II?
2. **MAKE INFERENCES** Why did peace with the Hittites help strengthen Egypt's economy?
3. **COMPARE AND CONTRAST** Think about Ramses II and Hatshepsut. What did these two strong pharaohs have in common?

HISTORY THROUGH OBJECTS

3.3 TUT'S TREASURES

In 1922, archaeologist Howard Carter broke through into tomb KV62 in the Valley of the Kings. There he discovered the first-ever intact royal tomb and treasures beyond the wildest imagination. The discovery turned an otherwise unremarkable pharaoh, Tutankhamen (too-tang-KAH-muhn), into a worldwide superstar. Sometime after 1330 B.C., Tutankhamen became pharaoh at the age of eight—he died just nine years later. The unique and priceless treasures of Tutankhamen's tomb have taught us a lot about the boy king, the pharaohs, and ancient Egypt. What do these treasures reveal about the ancient Egyptians' views of the afterlife?

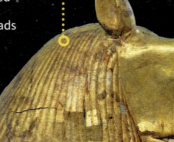

Funerary Mask
The magnificent gold mask was placed over the mummy's head inside the coffin.

Bed for a Pharaoh
The tomb contained a bed with gold hippopotamus heads for bedposts.

Bracelet
The lavish gold bracelet is adorned with a scarab beetle made of lapis lazuli, a precious stone.

Ointment Jar
The alabaster jar held precious oil for the pharaoh's spirit to use in the afterlife.

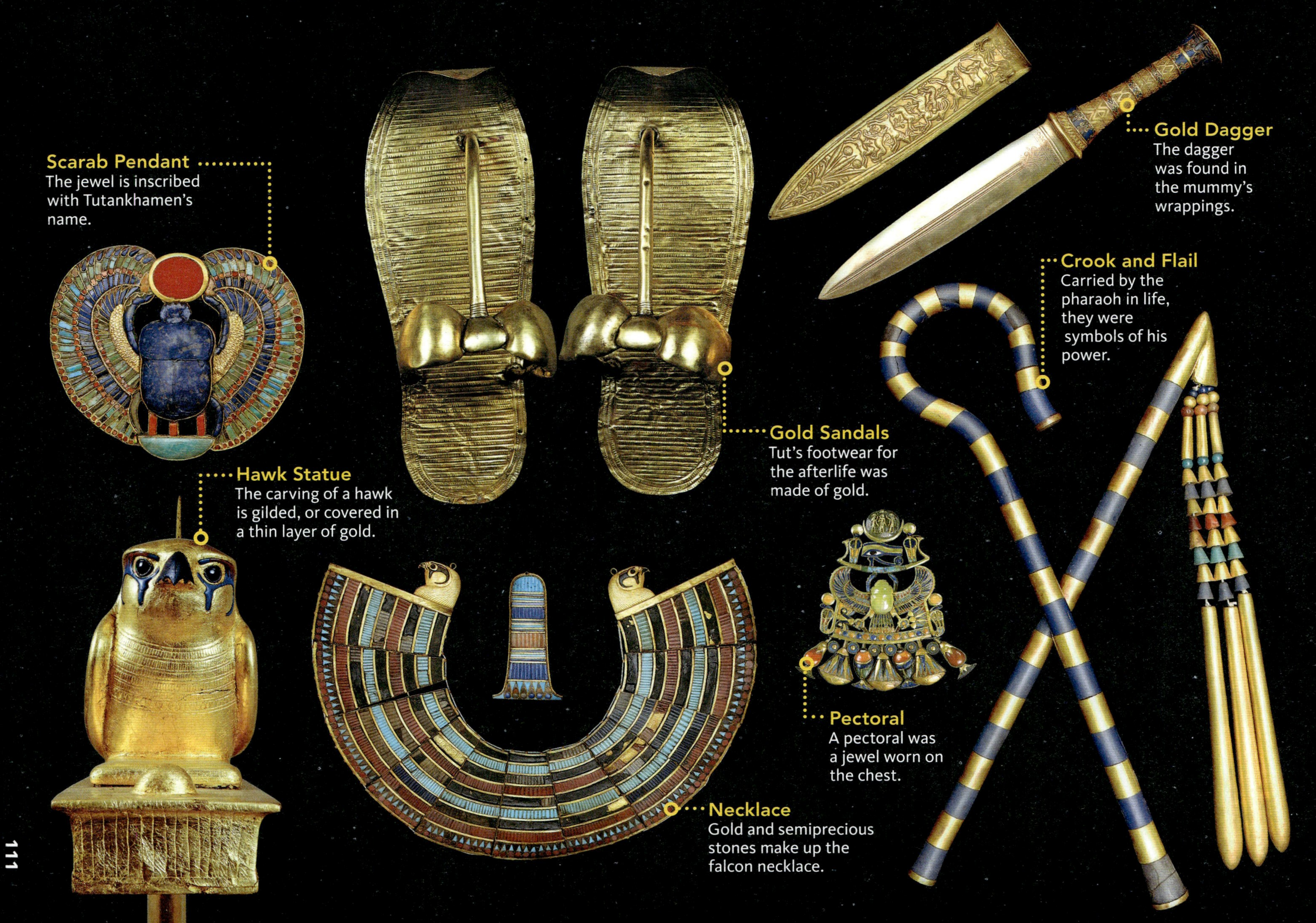
Scarab Pendant
The jewel is inscribed with Tutankhamen's name.
Hawk Statue
The carving of a hawk is gilded, or covered in a thin layer of gold.
Gold Sandals
Tut's footwear for the afterlife was made of gold.
Necklace
Gold and semiprecious stones make up the falcon necklace.
Pectoral
A pectoral was a jewel worn on the chest.
Gold Dagger
The dagger was found in the mummy's wrappings.
Crook and Flail
Carried by the pharaoh in life, they were symbols of his power.

3.4 The Rise of Kush

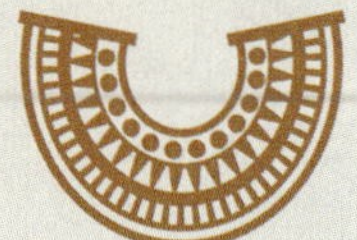

How well do you know your neighbors? How do their lives affect yours? From annoyingly loud parties to borrowing tools or exchanging gifts, neighbors interact. Egypt couldn't ignore its closest neighbor, Nubia.

MAIN IDEA

The Nubian kingdom of Kush followed Egypt as a center of power, culture, and trade.

KUSH CONTROLS EGYPT

Just south of Egypt, across the first cataract of the Nile, lay the land of **Nubia**. Rich in gold, copper, and other important resources needed by Egypt, Nubia also provided a critical trade route for exotic goods from central Africa. This helps explain why the histories of Egypt and Nubia are so deeply connected. Early Nubia was a collection of chiefdoms dominated by Egypt. Later, when stronger Nubian kingdoms emerged, Egypt took more active control of its southern neighbor. It conquered and colonized large areas of Nubia, and Nubia's people adopted many Egyptian practices and customs during a thousand years of direct rule. Eventually, however, the tables were turned.

In the generations following the reign of Ramses II, the Nubian kingdom of **Kush** asserted its independence. It grew strong and ambitious. The Kushite king, Piankhi, invaded Egypt, sweeping north to take control of Thebes, Memphis, and Upper and Lower Egypt. In 728 B.C., Piankhi united the kingdoms of Egypt and Kush under a new line of Kushite kings.

Piankhi did not think of himself as a foreign conqueror but as a traditional pharaoh reviving Egyptian traditions. The Kushite kings styled themselves as pharaohs and continued classic Egyptian religious, social, and political practices. They built pyramids, mummified their dead, and worshipped Egyptian gods.

Eventually, the Kushite kings came into conflict with the iron-weapon wielding superpower of Assyria to the northeast of Egypt. In the course of the war, Kush lost control of Egypt to the Assyrians. Some of the fighting was fierce; the city of Thebes was destroyed before the Kushite kings abandoned Egypt.

TRADE IN IRON AND GOLD

After being pushed out of Egypt, Kush continued to flourish as an independent power. Its capital, Napata (nah-PAH-tuh), had a palace and a temple to the Egyptian god Amun (AH-muhn), one of the creator gods. The city's strategic location across two major trade routes ensured that Kush remained an important center of international trade. The Kushites had stores of gold, and they began to mine and produce iron as well.

Around 590 B.C., the Kushite capital moved south to another important trading city called Meroë (MAIR-oh-ee). Here the Egyptian influence continued with royal pyramids and temples to Amun and the goddess Isis. The Nubians expanded their kingdom and opened up many new trading routes, especially for iron.

Iron was increasingly important in the ancient world because it was used to make strong tools, and Meroë had abundant supplies of iron ore. Because of its resources, the city remained an important economic and political center for several centuries.

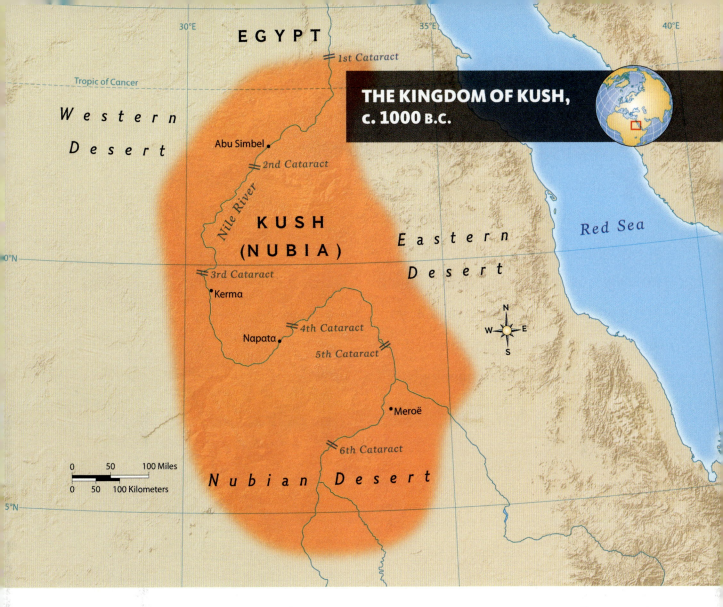

THE KINGDOM OF KUSH, c. 1000 B.C.

EGYPT
1st Cataract
Tropic of Cancer
Western Desert
Abu Simbel
2nd Cataract
Nile River
KUSH (NUBIA)
Eastern Desert
Red Sea
3rd Cataract
Kerma
4th Cataract
Napata
5th Cataract
Meroë
6th Cataract
Nubian Desert
30°E
35°E
40°E
20°N
15°N
N
S
E
W
0 50 100 Miles
0 50 100 Kilometers

GOLD

The importance of gold to Nubia is clear from its name. *Nub* was the Egyptian word for gold, and Nubia was rich with it. Skilled goldsmiths turned gold ore into intricate jewelry, such as this pendant of the goddess Isis.

REVIEW & ASSESS

1. **READING CHECK** In what ways did Kush follow Egypt as a center of power, culture, and trade in Africa?
2. **MAKE INFERENCES** Would life have changed a great deal for Egyptians living under the rule of the Kushite kings? Why or why not?
3. **INTERPRET MAPS** Why do you think Kushite kings established the kingdom's two capital cities—Napata and later Meroë—along the Nile River?

4.1 Hieroglyphs and Papyrus

You might be able to guess the meaning of some foreign words. But try reading a store bar code. The seemingly random arrangement of lines is actually a unique writing system telling you the product and price. To read it, you need to crack the code. Egyptian writing was just as baffling until archaeologists discovered the key—a slab of rock called the Rosetta Stone.

MAIN IDEA

The Egyptians valued writing and wrote for many purposes.

COMMON HIEROGLYPHS

Sun
(or day)

R
(a mouth symbol)

S
(a folded cloth symbol)

N
(water ripple)

WRITING AND WRITERS

Egyptian writing developed sometime before 3000 B.C., and it used **hieroglyphs** (HY-ruh-glihfs) instead of letters. A hieroglyph could be a picture representing an object, or it could represent a sound or an idea. By combining hieroglyphs, the Egyptians formed words and sentences.

The hieroglyphic writing system was very complex. There were nearly 800 hieroglyphs, no vowels, and very complicated rules. Few people mastered the skill of writing in hieroglyphs.

These special people were known as **scribes**, or professional writers, and they were among the most highly respected people in Egypt. It took five years of intense training to become a scribe, but the benefits made up for the hard work. Scribes were powerful, well paid, and had many privileges.

Reading and writing were just part of a scribe's job. Scribes were also skilled in art, mathematics, bookkeeping, law, engineering, and architecture. All scribes were important, but a really talented scribe could move up in Egypt's social hierarchy. One royal scribe eventually became the pharaoh Horemheb.

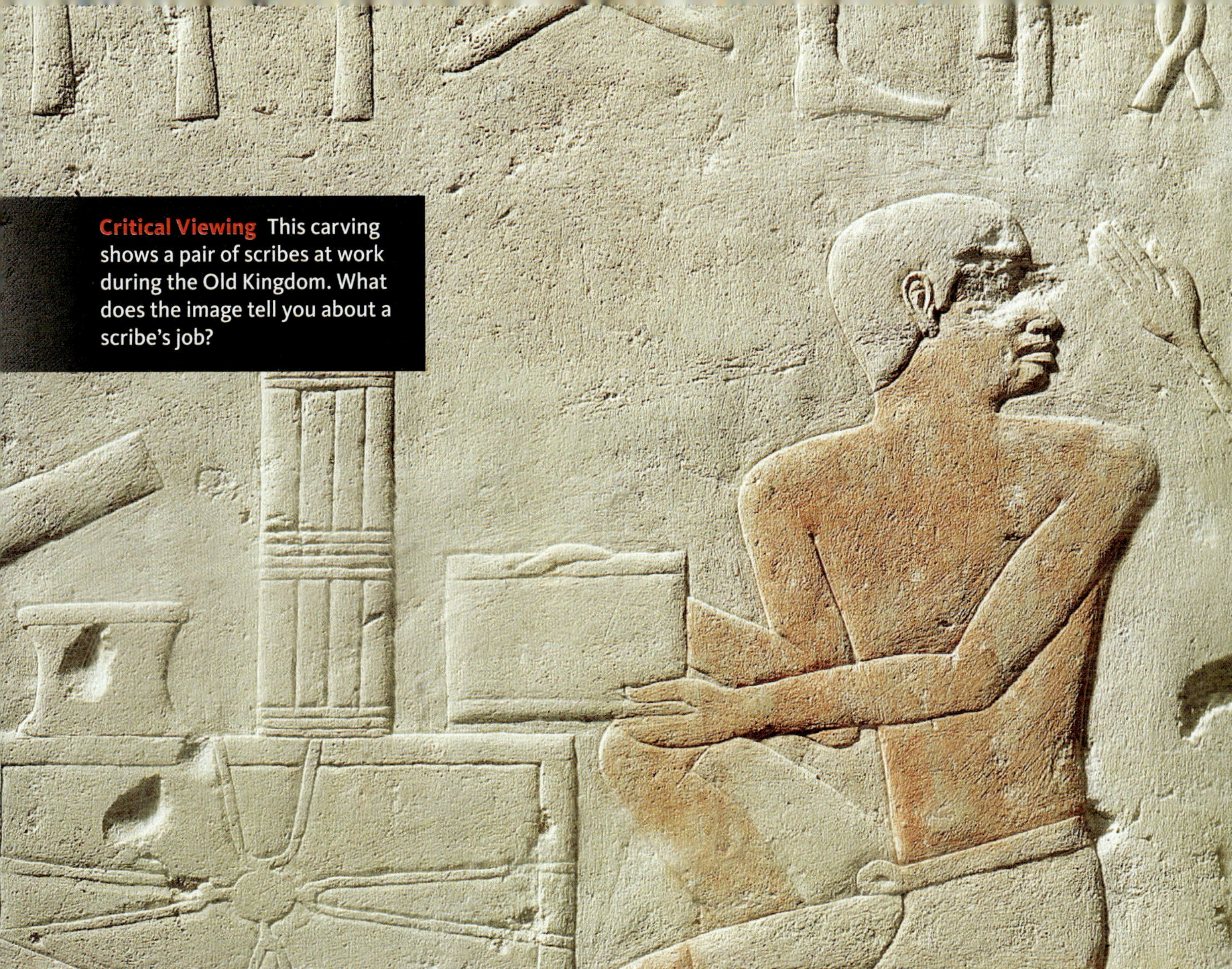

Critical Viewing This carving shows a pair of scribes at work during the Old Kingdom. What does the image tell you about a scribe's job?

PAPER AND THE ROSETTA STONE

Hieroglyphs were painted and carved on tombs, temples, and monuments. For important documents, the Egyptians used sheets of a paperlike material called **papyrus** (puh-PY-ruhs), made from reeds that grew along the banks of the Nile. Sheets of papyrus could be glued together to make scrolls—some scrolls were several yards long. Papyrus was light and easy for a scribe to carry.

Eventually, the Egyptians abandoned the old forms of writing. For many years, scholars tried to crack the code of the hieroglyphs. Then, in A.D. 1799, a slab of rock was discovered near Rosetta, Egypt. On it was carved the same text in hieroglyphs, another form of writing, and Greek. Because scholars understood Greek, they were able to figure out what the hieroglyphs meant. Thanks to the Rosetta Stone, historians can read hieroglyphs and learn about the lives of the people who produced them.

REVIEW & ASSESS

1. **READING CHECK** How much time did it take to become a scribe in ancient Egypt?
2. **IDENTIFY MAIN IDEAS AND DETAILS** What details support the idea that scribes were among the most highly respected people in Egypt?
3. **MAKE INFERENCES** What does the complexity of the hieroglyphic writing system tell us about the role of scribes?

4.2 Medicine, Science, and Mathematics

The priest chants magic spells while the doctor applies a fragrant lotion to your wound. He carefully bandages it and gives you a foul-smelling medicine sweetened with honey. You gag on it, but the chances are you'll live. The ancient Egyptians were advanced medical practitioners for their time.

MAIN IDEA

Egyptians put their advanced knowledge of medicine, science, and mathematics to practical use.

CANOPIC JARS

Canopic (kuh-NOH-pihk) jars contained the internal organs of a mummified body. The head-shaped lids on the jars represent the sons of the god Horus.

MEDICINE

Egypt had the most advanced medical practices in the ancient world. Some ancient Egyptian science was so accurate that it formed the foundation of later medical practices in Europe. The Egyptians had developed a detailed understanding of anatomy through mummifying bodies. They identified the heart as the most important organ and the pulse as its "voice."

Doctors provided medicines made from plants and minerals, set broken bones, and even performed surgery. Researchers have found medical texts written on papyrus that give doctors instructions and advice for treating a variety of illnesses. Texts and carvings also show some of the surgical tools that doctors used to treat their patients. Magical spells to heal different illnesses were also considered part of medical treatment.

SCIENCE AND MATHEMATICS

Ancient Egyptians were gifted astronomers as well as talented doctors. Astronomy is the branch of science that studies the sun, moon, stars, planets, and space. By making observations of the moon, ancient Egyptian astronomers developed a 365-day calendar. It had 24-hour days, 10-day weeks, 3-week months, and 12-month years. The extra five days were added as birthdays for five gods and were considered unlucky.

The Egyptians were also excellent mathematicians. Like us, they used a decimal counting system that included fractions. However, they did not use zero. Egyptian mathematicians established several key principles of geometry, accurately calculating angles and areas. They could calculate the area of a circle and the volume of a pyramid or cylinder. These skills made it possible to design big buildings like the pyramids.

Less visible but equally impressive was their mastery of the mathematics needed to run an empire. Scribes accurately calculated how many workers would be needed for building projects and how much food they would eat. Similar assessments estimated trade profits, crop yields, and taxes. Along with trade and military might, math and science were foundations of ancient Egypt's civilization.

Critical Viewing
The mummy of Ramses II lies in the Cairo Museum. How did making mummies like this one advance medical knowledge?

REVIEW & ASSESS

1. **READING CHECK** How did ancient Egyptians put their advanced knowledge to practical use?
2. **MAKE CONNECTIONS** How was the calendar invented by the Egyptians similar to our modern calendar?
3. **SYNTHESIZE** How did science and mathematics help advance ancient Egyptian civilization?

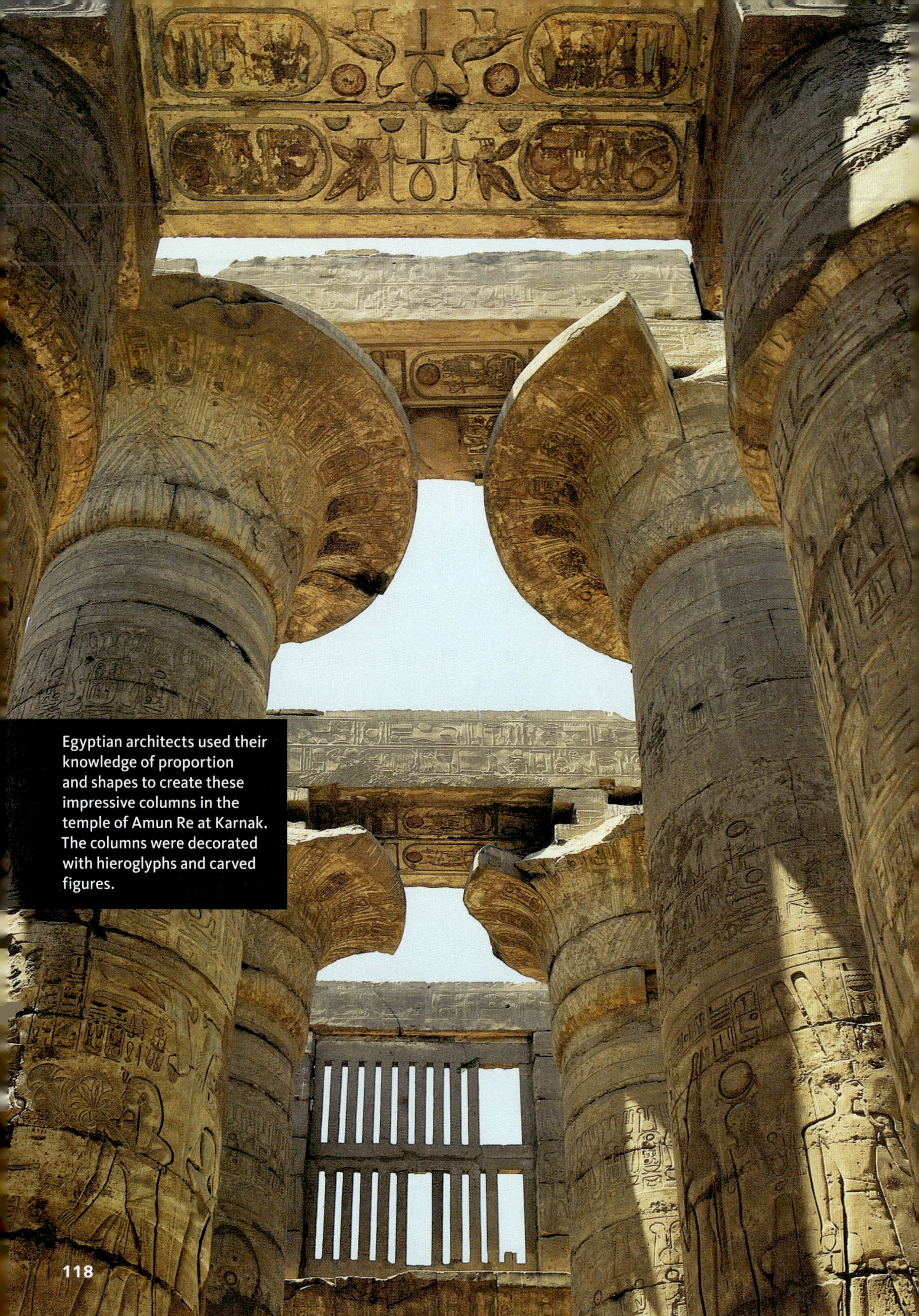
Egyptian architects used their knowledge of proportion and shapes to create these impressive columns in the temple of Amun Re at Karnak. The columns were decorated with hieroglyphs and carved figures.

4.3 Art and Architecture

The figures in ancient Egyptian paintings look awkward with their bodies facing the viewer, heads and feet facing right. Surely the artist didn't believe people really look like this!

MAIN IDEA

The ancient Egyptians created distinctive art and architecture.

A DISTINCTIVE ART STYLE

Ancient Egyptian art is easily recognizable. That is because artists used a distinctive style called frontalism. According to this style, the head and legs were drawn in profile, but the shoulders, chest, and arms were drawn as if they were facing front. The result looked pretty unnatural, but realism wasn't the goal. Most portraits were painted for religious purposes, which made it important to show as much of the body as possible. Frontalism achieved this goal.

Artists arranged each figure in a painting precisely to achieve balance and order. To get the sizes and proportions right, they followed a strict formula. Typically the human body was divided into three equal parts: from foot to knee, from knee to elbow, and from elbow to hairline. A figure's waist appeared exactly halfway up the body.

Most paintings showed scenes from everyday life. These included pharaohs performing religious rituals, fighting battles, or feasting, and ordinary people at work or play. Artists painted and carved figures and scenes like these in great temples, monuments, and tombs. This ancient art has revealed much about Egyptian life and beliefs.

ARCHITECTURE AND SACRED SHAPES

Egyptian architects also used clever techniques to make their soaring temples and other buildings look impressive. The architects used grid lines to create precise designs. They also applied mathematics to their designs using the "golden ratio." This mathematical formula helped architects achieve the most pleasing proportions—what looks good, in other words. The Greeks borrowed and developed the formula, and the golden ratio is still used today.

Certain geometric shapes, such as squares and triangles, were considered sacred, so architects included these in their designs. The most important shape, though, was the pyramid, which dominated Egyptian architecture throughout the civilization's 3,000-year history. In addition to the Great Pyramid of Khufu, architects built many other pyramids all over Egypt. Small pyramids even topped the tombs of the skilled craftspeople who built Egypt's great monuments.

REVIEW & ASSESS

1. **READING CHECK** What makes ancient Egyptian art and architecture stand out?
2. **DRAW CONCLUSIONS** What do Egyptian art and architecture reveal about the place of religion in ancient Egyptian society?
3. **DETERMINE WORD MEANINGS** How does the base word *front* clarify the meaning of the *frontalism* style of art?

CHAPTER 4 Review

VOCABULARY

Use each of the following vocabulary words in a sentence that shows an understanding of the word's meaning.

1. **cataract**
   Cataracts make river travel difficult because boats must navigate around these rapids.
2. **dynasty**
3. **pharaoh**
4. **hierarchy**
5. **mummy**
6. **hieroglyph**
7. **scribe**
8. **papyrus**

READING SKILL

9. **DRAW CONCLUSIONS** If you haven't already, complete your organizer to draw conclusions about the importance of ancient Egypt's geographic features. Then answer the question.

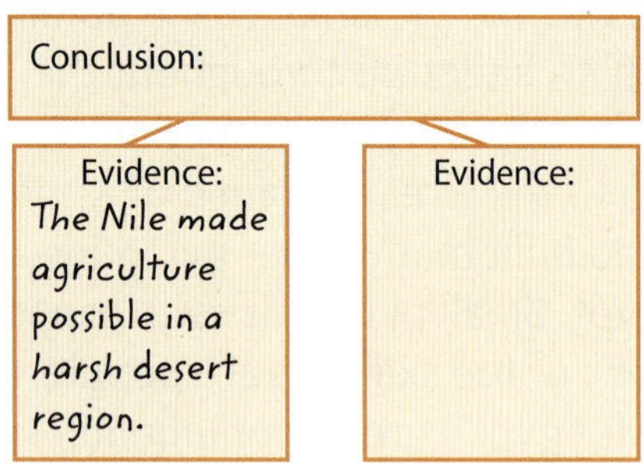

Conclusion:
Evidence:
The Nile made agriculture possible in a harsh desert region.
Evidence:

How did the Nile River affect civilization in ancient Egypt? Explain.

MAIN IDEAS

Answer the following questions. Support your answers with evidence from the chapter.

10. Why was Egyptian agriculture dependent on the Nile? **LESSON 1.1**
11. What was the relationship between Upper Egypt and Lower Egypt? **LESSON 1.2**
12. What was the role of the pharaoh in Egyptian life? **LESSON 1.3**
13. How did the Great Pyramid of Khufu demonstrate the pharaoh's power? **LESSON 2.1**
14. How were the classes of Egyptian society organized? **LESSON 2.2**
15. What contributions did Hatshepsut make to Egypt during her reign? **LESSON 3.1**
16. In what ways were Kush and Egypt connected? **LESSON 3.4**
17. Why was it desirable to be a scribe in ancient Egypt? **LESSON 4.1**

CRITICAL THINKING

Answer the following questions. Support your answers with evidence from the chapter.

18. **SYNTHESIZE** How did the pharaohs use Egypt's resources to increase the country's wealth and power?
19. **DRAW CONCLUSIONS** What impact did the Nile have on Egypt's trade industry?
20. **ANALYZE CAUSE AND EFFECT** How did the absolute power of the pharaohs contribute to Egypt's cycles of order and disorder?
21. **MAKE GENERALIZATIONS** What position did women have in Egyptian society?
22. **YOU DECIDE** The Egyptians had many important achievements in math, science, art, and architecture. Which achievement do you think left the greatest legacy, and why?

INTERPRET DIAGRAMS

Study the cross-section diagram of the interior of King Khufu's Great Pyramid at Giza. Then answer the questions that follow.

GREAT PYRAMID AT GIZA

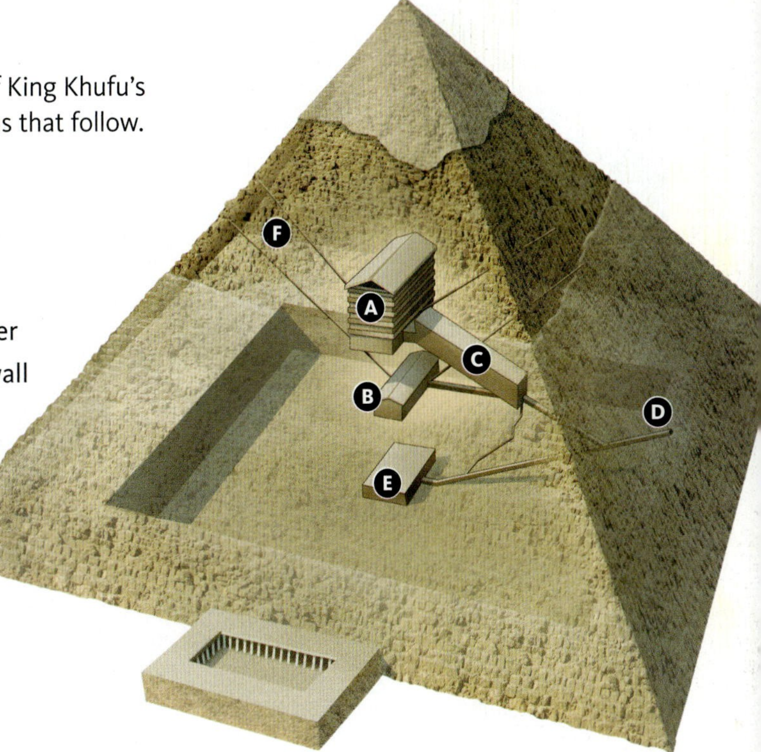
F
A
C
B
D
E

- **A King's Chamber,** where Khufu was buried
- **B Queen's Chamber,** which was found empty
- **C Grand Gallery,** leading to the King's Chamber
- **D Entrance,** which was sealed off by a heavy wall
- **E Unfinished Chamber,** built underground, beneath the pyramid
- **F Air Vents**

23. What features of the pyramid might help discourage tomb robbers?

24. What features of the pyramid were created to help the workers who built it?

ANALYZE SOURCES

Read the following translation of advice from an ancient Egyptian father to his son, who is training to be a scribe. Then answer the question.

> I have compared the people who are artisans and handicraftsmen [with the scribe], and indeed I am convinced that there is nothing superior to letters. Plunge into the study of Egyptian Learning, as you would plunge into the river, and you will find that this is so. . . . I wish I were able to make you see how beautiful Learning is. It is more important than any trade in the world.

25. What conclusions can you draw about the role of scribes in ancient Egyptian society?

WRITE ABOUT HISTORY

26. NARRATIVE Ramses II was one of the key figures from ancient Egypt. Suppose you were a scribe who was alive then. Write an eyewitness account that tells about the greatest achievements of Ramses II.

TIPS

- Take notes from the chapter about the reign of Ramses II and his achievements.
- Make an outline of the achievements and events you will include.
- Be sure to include details and examples.
- Use at least two vocabulary words from the chapter.
- Provide a concluding statement that summarizes why Ramses II was an effective pharaoh.

CHAPTER

5 JUDAISM AND THE ISRAELITE KINGDOMS

2000 B.C. – A.D. 70

SECTION 1
THE FOUNDING OF JUDAISM

KEY VOCABULARY
- confederation
- covenant
- kosher
- monotheism
- rabbi
- synagogue
- tribe

NAMES & PLACES
- Abraham
- Deborah
- Exodus
- Hebrew Bible
- Judaism
- Moses
- Talmud
- Ten Commandments
- Torah

SECTION 2
KINGDOMS AND EXILE

KEY VOCABULARY
- exile

NAMES & PLACES
- Cyrus the Great
- David
- Diaspora
- Hanukkah
- Israel
- Judah
- Solomon
- Zealots

READING STRATEGY

IDENTIFY MAIN IDEAS AND DETAILS When you identify a text's main idea and details, you state the most important idea about a topic and list facts that support that idea. As you read the chapter, use a web like this one to identify beliefs and practices of Judaism.

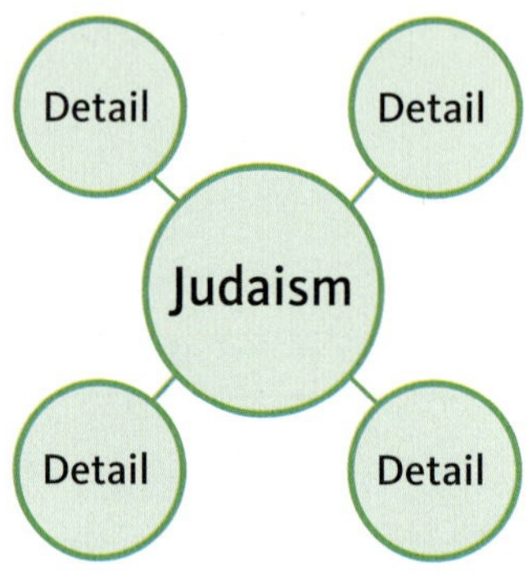

Detail
Detail
Judaism
Detail
Detail

Jerusalem is the religious center of Judaism. The Old City of Jerusalem is shown here.

1.1 Abraham and Moses

While mighty empires rose and fell, a group of shepherds grew into a small nation. These people never ruled a powerful empire. But they were bound together by a strong religious faith, and their influence has been greater than that of many empires. These people are known by various names, including Hebrews, Israelites, and Jews.

MAIN IDEA

Abraham and Moses were important leaders of **Judaism**, the first religion based on the worship of a single God.

THE PROMISED LAND

The Hebrews were a people who settled in Canaan (KAY-nuhn) around 1800 B.C. Canaan was on the eastern coast of the Mediterranean Sea. This region was later called Israel and also Palestine. The Hebrews differed from all other ancient people in an important way: they practiced **monotheism**, the worship of a single God. All other ancient people practiced polytheism, which you may recall is the worship of many gods. Monotheism was a significant development in religion and has had a great impact on cultures around the world.

Most of what we know about the Hebrews comes from the **Hebrew Bible**, a collection of ancient religious writings. According to these writings, God told **Abraham**, a Mesopotamian shepherd, to take his family and settle in Canaan. The region would be their Promised Land—a land that would belong to Abraham and his family forever. Abraham's descendants would have a special **covenant** (KUHV-uh-nuhnt), or religious agreement, with God. According to the covenant, God would protect the Hebrews if they accepted no other god and did what God asked.

The early Hebrews led a quiet, seminomadic life in Canaan. Seminomadic people move frequently with their flocks, but they often return to one place where they grow crops.

THE EXODUS

The land of Canaan sometimes became too dry for growing crops. According to the Hebrew Bible, a devastating drought, or dry period, caused such a severe shortage of food that the Hebrews left Canaan and settled in northern Egypt, perhaps around 1650 B.C. Here, the pharaoh enslaved them to work on his building projects. Around this time, the Hebrews became known as the Israelites.

The Hebrew Bible relates that the Israelites endured centuries of suffering before God chose a man named **Moses** to help them escape from Egypt. The Israelites returned to Canaan in a journey from slavery to freedom called the **Exodus**, possibly in the 1200s B.C. According to the Bible, the Israelites traveled through the desert for 40 years before finally returning to Canaan. Along the way Moses climbed Mount Sinai (SY-ny), where God gave him the **Ten Commandments** and other laws. This religious, moral, and civil code reaffirmed and expanded the Israelites' covenant with God. Today, the Ten Commandments form the basis of many modern laws, such as the law against stealing another person's property.

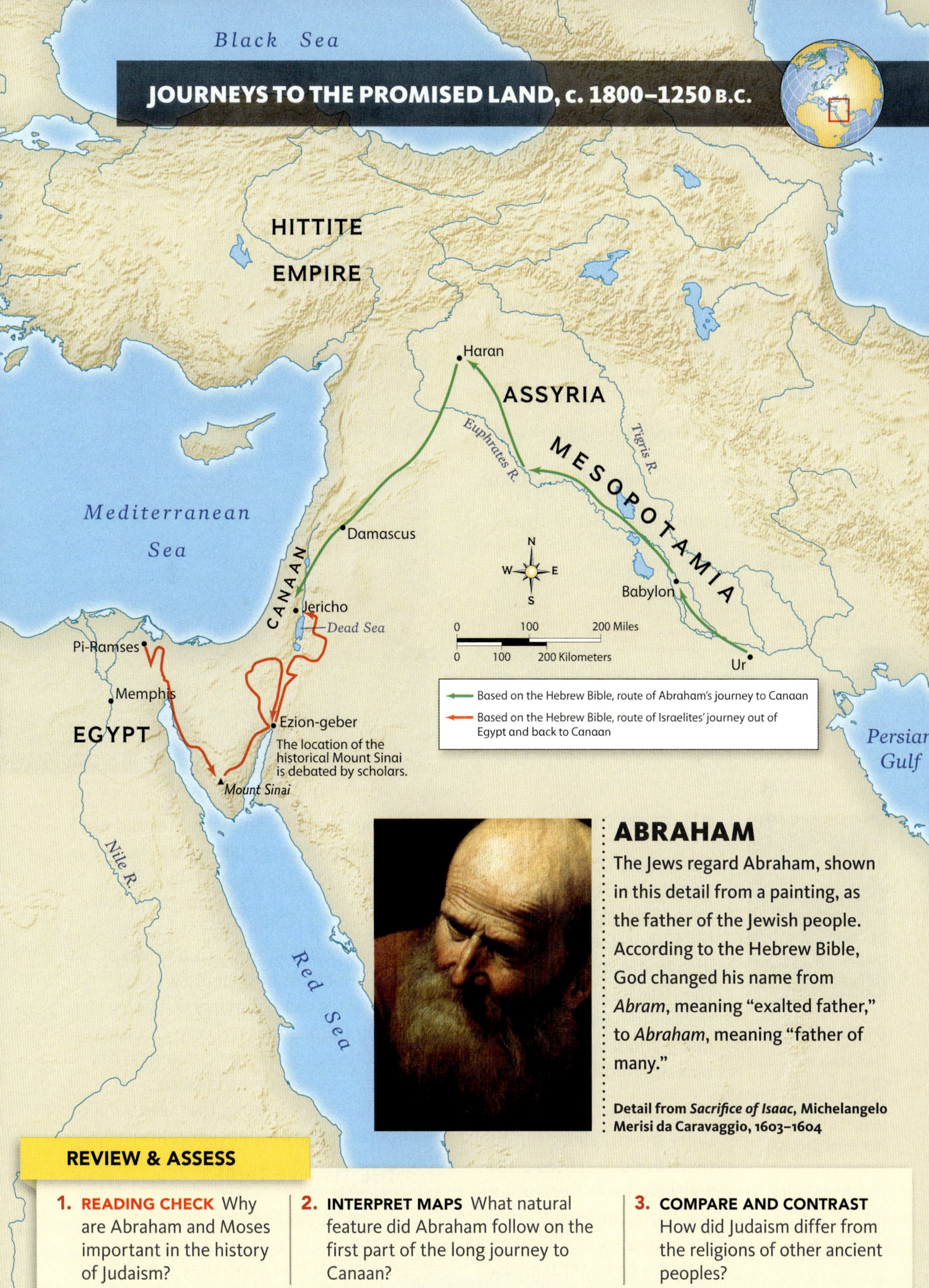

JOURNEYS TO THE PROMISED LAND, c. 1800–1250 B.C.
Black Sea
HITTITE EMPIRE
Haran
ASSYRIA
Euphrates R.
Tigris R.
MESOPOTAMIA
Mediterranean Sea
Damascus
CANAAN
Jericho
Dead Sea
Babylon
Ur
N
W
E
S
0 100 200 Miles
0 100 200 Kilometers
Based on the Hebrew Bible, route of Abraham's journey to Canaan
Based on the Hebrew Bible, route of Israelites' journey out of Egypt and back to Canaan
Pi-Ramses
Memphis
EGYPT
Ezion-geber
The location of the historical Mount Sinai is debated by scholars.
Mount Sinai
Persian Gulf
Nile R.
Red Sea

ABRAHAM

The Jews regard Abraham, shown in this detail from a painting, as the father of the Jewish people. According to the Hebrew Bible, God changed his name from *Abram*, meaning "exalted father," to *Abraham*, meaning "father of many."

Detail from *Sacrifice of Isaac*, Michelangelo Merisi da Caravaggio, 1603–1604

REVIEW & ASSESS

1. **READING CHECK** Why are Abraham and Moses important in the history of Judaism?

2. **INTERPRET MAPS** What natural feature did Abraham follow on the first part of the long journey to Canaan?

3. **COMPARE AND CONTRAST** How did Judaism differ from the religions of other ancient peoples?

1.2 A Distinct Culture

I You need a lot of nerve to go against a common belief. Abraham had this courage. But his strong belief ended up leading his people down a path filled with intolerance and harsh treatment, which continue in some places today. As you will see, acting out of strong belief became an important part of the distinct culture of the Israelites.

MAIN IDEA

As the Israelites fought to win control of their Promised Land, their religious beliefs and practices set them apart from the Canaanites.

DEBORAH

Deborah was the Israelites' only female judge. At the Battle of Mount Tabor around 1125 B.C., she led the Israelites to victory against a Canaanite king.

BELIEF IN ONE GOD

The belief in one God is central to Judaism. This idea may seem normal to many people today, but it was a radical idea in the ancient world. The Israelites were the first people to reject polytheism, making Judaism the world's oldest monotheistic religion.

Belief in one God helped unify the Israelites, but their beliefs and practices also set them apart from other ancient cultures. According to the Hebrew Bible, God gave Moses a code of religious practices that governed most aspects of life. The Israelites did not worship idols, or false gods. They ate only certain foods. They did not work on the Sabbath, a weekly day of rest. While they traded with other peoples, they tried to keep a distinct cultural identity. Most Israelites did not marry outside their faith, and they were careful not to adopt foreign customs. They generally avoided the cultural diffusion, or mixing, that was a major part of many other civilizations.

THE TWELVE TRIBES

According to the Hebrew Bible, when the Israelites returned to Canaan from Egypt, they consisted of 12 **tribes**, or extended family

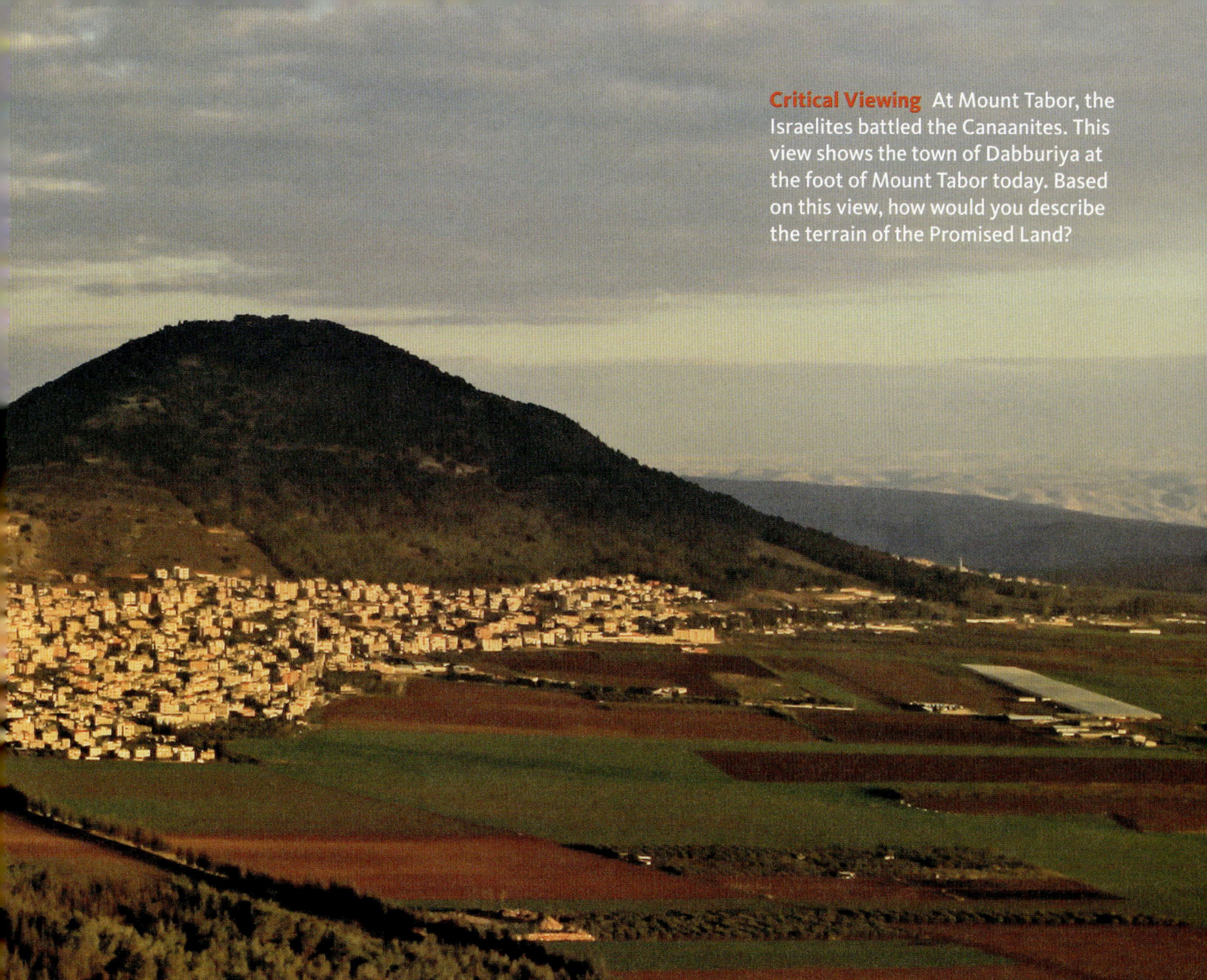

Critical Viewing At Mount Tabor, the Israelites battled the Canaanites. This view shows the town of Dabburiya at the foot of Mount Tabor today. Based on this view, how would you describe the terrain of the Promised Land?

units. Each tribe was descended from a son of Jacob, Abraham's grandson. Since Jacob was also called Israel, the tribes were called the Twelve Tribes of Israel, and Jacob's descendants were called Israelites. They referred to Canaan as the Promised Land.

Moses had died before the Israelites returned to Canaan. The Bible describes how a new leader named Joshua brought the Israelites into the Promised Land around 1250 B.C. Joshua went to war against local people known as the Canaanites, who practiced polytheism. After battling for about 200 years, the Israelites conquered most of Canaan. The tribes then divided up the conquered lands among themselves. They lived separately but acted together as a loose **confederation**, or group of allies. Powerful leaders called judges came to head the confederation of tribes. The judges directed battles, made decisions on policy, and helped keep the tribes united.

REVIEW & ASSESS

1. **READING CHECK** What was a major difference between the Israelites and the Canaanites?
2. **IDENTIFY MAIN IDEAS AND DETAILS** According to the text, how was Israelite society organized?
3. **MAKE INFERENCES** How did the Israelites maintain a distinct cultural identity?

1.3 Beliefs and Texts of Judaism

Your teachers probably have high expectations of you. At the very least, they'd like you to act responsibly and follow the class rules. Likewise, the Israelites believed that God had high expectations of them and wanted them to follow his rules. These rules were written down and covered almost every aspect of their lives.

MAIN IDEA

The Israelites followed religious teachings written down in their holy books.

JEWISH BELIEFS AND PRACTICES

The Hebrew Bible describes how Moses transmitted a religious code that governed the lives of the Israelites. It addressed all aspects of life, including how to worship God, how to treat all members of society well, and what to eat. For example, they could eat only **kosher** foods, foods that were specially prepared according to Jewish dietary laws. According to these laws, animals had to be killed humanely, dairy and meat could not be eaten together, and pork and shellfish were not allowed.

Judaism stressed the importance of treating others well. It promoted social justice, equality, and the holiness of human life. The Israelites also highly valued education, charity, and hospitality, or the kind treatment of guests. In addition, Israelite women were treated well for the time. Religious teachings told husbands to love and respect their wives, who were considered to be the heart of the family.

In time, Jews began gathering to worship in buildings called **synagogues** (SIHN-uh-gahgs), meaning "places of assembly." A spiritual leader called a **rabbi**, or "teacher," usually conducted services. Rabbis upheld Jewish customs and provided guidance for living a Jewish life.

An important practice of Judaism is the observance of a weekly day of rest known as the Sabbath. It begins at sunset on Friday and ends on Saturday night. On the Sabbath, the Jewish community gathers for prayer and to read from sacred texts. Families enjoy festive meals, and people leave behind weekday work and concerns.

SACRED TEXTS

The Hebrew Bible consists of 24 books in three sections: the **Torah**, Prophets, and Writings. The Torah consists of the five books of Moses. The name *Torah* means "the teachings." Jews believe that the Torah contains the word of God as revealed to Moses on Mount Sinai. The Torah includes religious and moral guidance covering most areas of life. In fact, it forms the basis of all Jewish law. Every synagogue has a Torah scroll, handwritten on parchment, which is treated with enormous respect and read from beginning to end over the course of a year. The Torah and other Jewish laws are discussed and explained in the **Talmud**, a collection of writings by early rabbis.

The books in the Hebrew Bible also make up the Old Testament of the Christian Bible, though the books are ordered, divided, and sometimes named differently. Many stories related in the Hebrew Bible and in the Christian Bible also appear in the Qur'an, the holy book of Islam. For example, stories about Abraham appear in all three texts.

This page from a Hebrew Bible dated A.D. 1299 is written in Hebrew script.

REVIEW & ASSESS

1. **READING CHECK** What are some important beliefs and texts of Judaism?

2. **MAKE GENERALIZATIONS** What were important values in Judaism, and why might they have stood out in the ancient world?

3. **DRAW CONCLUSIONS** Why do you think the Torah is treated with great respect by Jews?

1.4 DOCUMENT-BASED QUESTION

Writings from the Hebrew Bible

Judaism was originally based on an oral tradition, in which stories are passed down by word of mouth. After the Israelites developed writing, they wrote down their religious texts. In 1947, a shepherd discovered a set of texts near the Dead Sea. Later known as the Dead Sea Scrolls, these texts included portions of the Hebrew Bible dating from around 150 B.C.

In this part of a painting by Italian artist Guido Reni, Moses is shown with one of the two tablets containing the Ten Commandments.

Moses with the Tablets of the Law, Guido Reni, 17th century

DOCUMENT ONE

Primary Source: Sacred Text

from the Book of Genesis

Genesis is the first book of the Hebrew Bible. In this excerpt, God speaks to Abraham and tells him to bring his family to the land of Canaan.

CONSTRUCTED RESPONSE What does God promise Abraham?

Go forth from your native land and from your father's house to the land that I will show you. I will make of you a great nation, and I will bless you.

Genesis 12:1–2

DOCUMENT TWO

Primary Source: Sacred Text

from the Book of Exodus

Exodus is the second book of the Hebrew Bible. It describes the oppression of the Israelites in Egypt and their escape from slavery to freedom during the Exodus. It also depicts Moses' experience on Mount Sinai, where God gave Moses the Ten Commandments. According to the Bible, these laws were written on two stone tablets. This excerpt details the Ten Commandments.

CONSTRUCTED RESPONSE What do the first four commandments have in common? What do the last six have in common?

The Great Isaiah Scroll, one of the Dead Sea Scrolls

Ten Commandments

1. I the Lord am your God. . . . You shall have no other gods besides Me.
2. You shall not make for yourself a sculptured image [idol].
3. You shall not swear falsely by the name of the Lord your God.
4. Remember the Sabbath day and keep it holy.
5. Honor your father and your mother.
6. You shall not murder.
7. You shall not commit adultery.
8. You shall not steal.
9. You shall not bear false witness against your neighbor.
10. You shall not covet [desire] . . . anything that is your neighbor's.

Exodus 20:2–14

SYNTHESIZE & WRITE

1. **REVIEW** Review what you have learned about the covenant made between God and the Israelites.
2. **RECALL** On your own paper, write down the main idea expressed in each document above.
3. **CONSTRUCT** Construct a topic sentence that answers this question: What did God promise the Israelites?
4. **WRITE** Using evidence from the documents, write an explanatory paragraph that supports your topic sentence from Step 3.

2.1 Israel and Judah

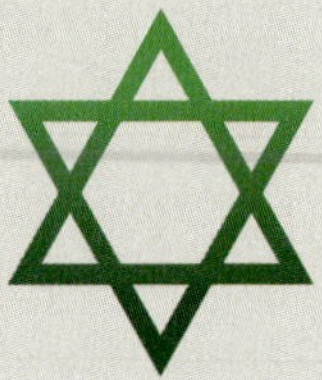

Twelve friends decide to go to a movie, but everyone has different ideas about what to see. Finally, they agree to put one person in charge—a natural-born leader. His decision is quick and readily accepted. For a similar reason, the Israelites swapped decision-making by judges for rule by a single strong king.

MAIN IDEA

The Israelites united under a line of kings, but they later became divided and were defeated by external powers.

DAVID

David, a simple shepherd, attracted attention when he killed a gigantic warrior called Goliath using only his shepherd's sling and stones. David became one of the Israelites' greatest kings. His emblem, the six-pointed star called the Star of David or Shield of David, became a symbol of Judaism and modern Israel.

A LINE OF KINGS

The Israelites realized they needed greater unity and stronger leadership when they were attacked by another people called the Philistines (FIH-luh-steens), who lived in the area. The Israelites appointed a king named Saul to rule. In 1020 B.C., Saul defended Israel against the Philistines and other enemies.

When Saul died, **David** was crowned king. David united the tribes and continued the fight against the Philistines and other enemies. He captured Jerusalem and made it his capital, starting its transformation into one of history's most important cities.

David's son **Solomon** inherited a peaceful kingdom. He built a great stone temple in Jerusalem. Solomon's Temple became the focus of religious life. Solomon used trade and taxes to fund other huge building projects. However, most of the tax burden fell on the northern tribes, who came to resent Solomon's rule. Once again, trouble began.

Soon war broke out between the northern and southern tribes. Around 922 B.C., Israel was divided into two kingdoms: **Israel** in the north and **Judah** in the south. The northern kingdom consisted of ten of the original tribes, while the southern kingdom consisted of the remaining two. The kingdoms sometimes fought each other and sometimes formed alliances against common enemies. Eventually, Judaism and the Jewish people would be named after Judah.

INVADED AND CONQUERED

In 722 B.C., the Assyrian Empire conquered Israel. The ten tribes of Israel were scattered to other lands and disappeared from history. Judah, though, survived and was able to fight off Assyria.

However, Judah soon found itself the battleground between two warring groups: the Egyptians and the New Babylonians. Egypt conquered Judah first. Then the New Babylonian army, led by King Nebuchadnezzar, overran Judah.

Judah rebelled. In 597 B.C., the king responded by invading Jerusalem. He moved the elite members of society to Babylon, leaving the poor behind. In 586 B.C., Nebuchadnezzar's army destroyed Jerusalem, including Solomon's Temple. For the Jews, the age of kings was over.

SOLOMON'S TEMPLE

According to the Hebrew Bible, King Solomon built a magnificent temple in Jerusalem with walls and a floor of cedarwood overlaid in gold. The Bible indicates that Solomon's Temple housed the Ark of the Covenant, a container holding the stone tablets with the Ten Commandments. This reconstruction is based on descriptions of the Temple in the Hebrew Bible.

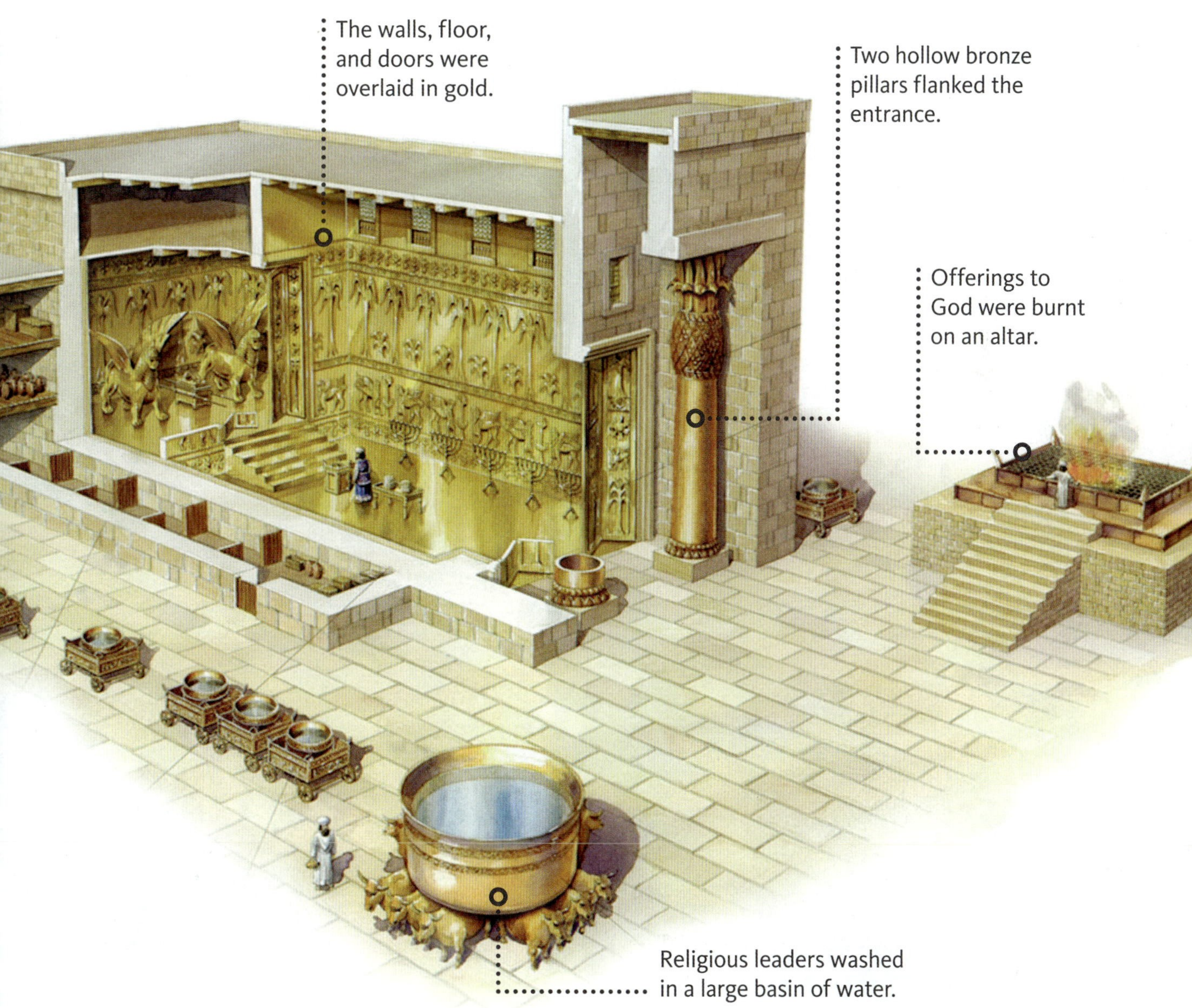

The walls, floor, and doors were overlaid in gold.
Two hollow bronze pillars flanked the entrance.
Offerings to God were burnt on an altar.
Religious leaders washed in a large basin of water.

REVIEW & ASSESS

1. **READING CHECK** What events mark the rise and fall of the Jews' age of kings?

2. **IDENTIFY PROBLEMS** What was one source of conflict between the northern and southern tribes of the Israelites?

3. **MAKE INFERENCES** What do you think the destruction of Solomon's Temple meant to the Israelites?

Jews come to pray at Jerusalem's Western Wall, a remnant of the Second Temple. Many visitors leave written prayers in cracks in the wall.

2.2 Exile and Return

In Psalm 137, from a book in the Hebrew Bible, captures the terrible upheaval the Jews suffered when they were forced to leave Judah and live in Babylon: "By the rivers of Babylon, there we sat, sat and wept, as we thought of Zion [Israel]. How can we sing of the Lord on alien [foreign] soil?" But the Jews found a way, and they grew stronger as a result of the experience.

MAIN IDEA

While in Babylon, the Jews maintained, developed, and strengthened their identity and religion.

BABYLONIAN CAPTIVITY

The removal of some of the Jewish people from their homeland to faraway Babylonia was a deeply distressing experience. Their captivity, called the Babylonian Exile, lasted about 50 years. **Exile** is the forced removal from one's native country. During the exile, Jews built their first synagogues. Any remaining tribal divisions disappeared, to be replaced by a sense of religious and social unity among the Jewish people. Scribes started writing down the holy texts in a new script that is still used today. Most importantly, the Jews found that it actually was possible to "sing of the Lord on alien soil." Although they had lost control of the Promised Land, the Jews held on to their cultural identity and their religious faith.

CYRUS THE GREAT OF PERSIA

The Jews' efforts to maintain their faith were aided when **Cyrus the Great**, king of the Persian Empire, conquered Babylon in 539 B.C. As you may remember, Cyrus became known as "the Great" because of his impressive military conquests and wise rule. He adopted a policy of tolerance, allowing conquered people to keep their own customs and beliefs.

While Judah remained under Persian control, Cyrus freed the Jewish people in Babylon and encouraged them to return to their homeland and rebuild the Jewish state. Because of his policy of tolerance, Cyrus became a hero to the Jews.

Many of the Jewish people decided to stay in Babylonia. They formed a large Jewish community that thrived for centuries and remains in small numbers in present-day Iran and Iraq. However, in 538 B.C., about 42,000 Jews returned to Judah. There, they began rebuilding the temple in Jerusalem, called the Second Temple. Religious leaders began to refine Judaism into something like its modern form. In particular, they finalized the Hebrew Bible, which became the central document of the Jewish faith, and began public readings of the Torah.

REVIEW & ASSESS

1. **READING CHECK** Why did Cyrus the Great become a hero to the Jews?
2. **IDENTIFY DETAILS** While in exile, how did the Jews maintain their identity?
3. **MAKE INFERENCES** Why did a large number of Jews return to Judah in 538 B.C.?

2.3 The Diaspora

If you moved to another country to live, you might adopt its language and customs to get along. But when Jews settled abroad, most tried hard to keep practicing their own religion and customs. The ability of the Jewish people to preserve their religion and heritage has been one of the most remarkable achievements in world history.

MAIN IDEA

The Syrians and then the Romans tried to destroy Judaism but ultimately failed.

YOHANNAN BEN ZAKAI

When the Romans destroyed the Second Temple, a Jewish teacher named Yohannan Ben Zakai asked permission to establish a school to teach Jewish scholars. The school was important in preserving Jewish traditions. Today, Jews regard Zakai as a great hero.

SYRIAN CONTROL

After the Persians, competing foreign powers controlled Judah. By about 300 B.C., Egypt took over the Jewish homeland. The Egyptian rulers tolerated Judaism and largely left Judah alone.

In 198 B.C., a Syrian empire, the Seleucids, conquered Judah. The Seleucids treated the Jews well until 168 B.C., when the Seleucid king tried to force the Jews to worship Greek gods. He dedicated the Second Temple to the Greek god Zeus. Outraged Jews rebelled, led by a family called the Maccabees. Their small army fought hard, defeated the Seleucids, and rededicated the Second Temple to Judaism.

ROMAN RULE

Judah's freedom from foreign rule did not last long. In 63 B.C., Rome seized control of the region. At first the Romans allowed the Jews to rule themselves. In time, however, Rome took direct control of Judah and insisted that Jews worship the Roman gods. Many Jews, including revolutionaries called **Zealots**, favored armed rebellion.

War finally broke out in A.D. 66. Unfortunately, Jewish resistance was no match for the powerful Roman army. Rome's soldiers destroyed much of Jerusalem, including the Second Temple. By A.D. 70, the war was almost over. The Zealots fought on from the mountaintop fortress of Masada, but the Roman army eventually crushed the revolt.

After the rebellion, many Jews were forced to leave Jerusalem and settle in new places. The migration of Jews to places around the world, which began with the Babylonian Exile, is called the **Diaspora** (dy-AS-puh-ruh). Yet even after leaving their homeland, Jews kept their religion alive and maintained a strong connection to the land of Israel. The rabbis transformed Judaism into a home- and synagogue-based religion that could be practiced anywhere. By holding on to their religion and customs, the dispersed Jews ensured Judaism would become a worldwide religion.

The legacy of the Jewish people is important in world history. Judaism was the first monotheistic religion. Its emphasis on justice and morality influenced later religions, including Christianity. Judaism also had a great influence on other aspects of Western civilization, such as law.

JEWISH DIASPORA, A.D. 70–500

- Major Jewish settlements, A.D. 500
- Routes of Jewish Diaspora

North Sea
Colonia Agrippina (Cologne)
EUROPE
Mediolanum (Milan)
Genoa
Ravenna
Black Sea
Oescus
Tarraco
Rome
Thessalonika
Pergamum
Edessa
ASIA
Ephesus
Athens
Antioch
Mediterranean Sea
Carthage
Babylon
Jerusalem
Cyrene
Alexandria
AFRICA
EGYPT
0 200 400 Miles
0 200 400 Kilometers

HANUKKAH

One of the holiday traditions Jews continued to celebrate after the Diaspora is **Hanukkah.** The holiday commemorates religious freedom and the rededication of the Second Temple to Judaism.

According to tradition, the Temple had only enough holy oil to burn for one day, but the oil lasted eight days. This event is symbolized by a special menorah used for Hanukkah. The Hanukkah menorah has eight main holders for candles, plus a ninth holder for the candle that is used to light the others.

REVIEW & ASSESS

1. **READING CHECK** How were Syrian rule and Roman rule of Judah similar?
2. **INTERPRET MAPS** In what direction did most Jews travel during the Diaspora?
3. **DRAW CONCLUSIONS** Why did Judaism become a worldwide religion?

2.4 NATIONAL GEOGRAPHIC EXPLORER **BEVERLY GOODMAN**

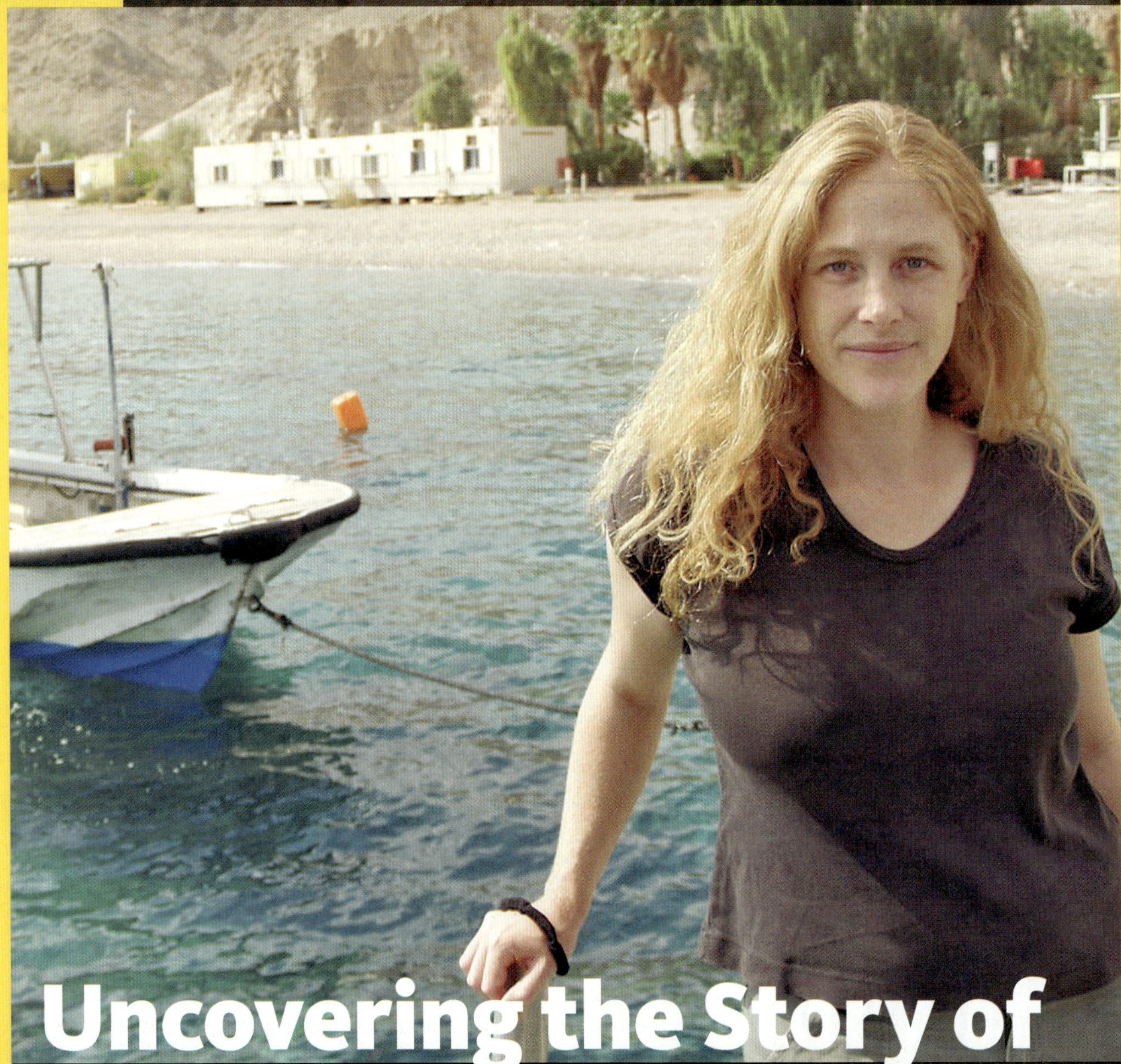

Uncovering the Story of Caesarea's Port

In the first century B.C., Judea was a province of Rome and was ruled by a Roman-appointed king named Herod. He founded the city of Caesarea on the coast of what is now Israel. Sometime in the A.D. 100s, the city's port was mysteriously destroyed. That's where National Geographic Explorer Beverly Goodman comes in. Goodman is a geo-archaeologist, a scientist who investigates ancient cultures by applying the tools of earth science. By studying broken seashells, she concluded that a natural disaster destroyed Caesarea's port.

^ Beverly Goodman, shown above, studies archaeological sites along the Mediterranean coast.

MAIN IDEA

Geo-archaeologist Beverly Goodman has shown that a natural disaster likely destroyed the ancient port of Caesarea.

ISRAEL'S ANCIENT COASTLINE

Goodman's research focuses on the complex interaction between nature and humans along coastlines. "No place is more vulnerable than our coasts," she explains. Her findings from the port of Caesarea prove this thesis while ringing alarm bells that echo across 2,000 years.

An aerial view of the ruins of Caesarea

At the end of the first century B.C., King Herod built a huge harbor at Caesarea to tap into the valuable trade between the East and ancient Rome. Caesarea had no geographic features useful for a harbor, so Herod relied on "modern" technology.

Herod's builders used waterproof concrete to build huge breakwaters, or walls extending out from the coast. These breakwaters created a deepwater harbor where sailing ships could shelter from great storms. Nevertheless, the harbor could not escape the sea's deadliest force. That force came in the form of a tsunami (su-NAH-mee), a giant ocean wave caused by an underwater earthquake, a volcanic eruption, or a landslide. Tsunamis have threatened humans for as long as people have lived on the world's coastlines.

A 2,000-YEAR-OLD DISASTER

Before Goodman began her investigation, no researchers had ever found physical evidence of a major disaster. Scholars had always thought that the harbor had disappeared because of the builders' poor workmanship and inferior materials. However, when Goodman began exploring the coastline, she uncovered an unusual concentration of shell fragments. "Instead of the normal half-inch layer, this band of shells was more than three feet deep!" she said.

To gather more evidence, she developed a new way of taking deep-sea core samples, sinking hollow tubes into the seabed and then pulling them out to show the layers of deposits. The layers can be read like tree rings. Analysis and dating suggested that a single, sudden, and violent event caused the shell concentrations. Goodman concluded that a major tsunami had destroyed Herod's great harbor.

Goodman is now putting her findings to the test. She's examining other archaeological sites around the Mediterranean region, looking for signs of tsunami damage. Goodman's research could help save lives in the future. "Analyzing the causes and effects of ancient environmental events like tsunamis can help tell us which types of coast are at greatest risk, and what kind of damage to expect in the future," Goodman explains. "I hope I'm collecting clues that will help us avoid catastrophic consequences down the line."

REVIEW & ASSESS

1. **READING CHECK** What natural disaster likely destroyed the ancient port of Caesarea?
2. **IDENTIFY MAIN IDEAS AND DETAILS** What findings support Goodman's conclusion about the cause of the port's destruction?
3. **MAKE CONNECTIONS** Why does Goodman's discovery have important implications for other sites on the Mediterranean?

CHAPTER 5 Review

VOCABULARY

Match each word in the first column with its definition in the second column.

WORD	DEFINITION
1. exile	a. a Jewish spiritual leader and teacher
2. tribe	b. the belief in only one God
3. monotheism	c. a place where Jews assemble to worship
4. covenant	d. an extended family unit
5. rabbi	e. a period of forced absence from one's homeland or native country
6. synagogue	f. a religious agreement with God

READING STRATEGY

7. IDENTIFY MAIN IDEAS AND DETAILS If you haven't already, complete your web to identify beliefs and practices of Judaism. Then answer the question.

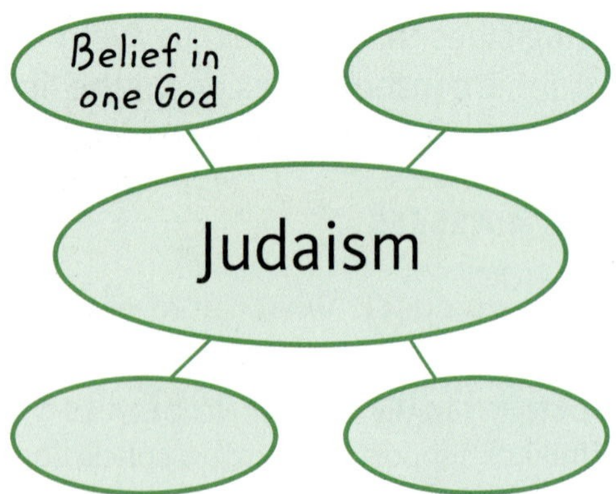
Belief in one God
Judaism

What are some of the beliefs and practices of Judaism? What is one way in which Judaism differs from other ancient religions?

MAIN IDEAS

Answer the following questions. Support your answers with evidence from the chapter.

8. What did the Israelites believe God wanted them to do in order to fulfill their special covenant? **LESSON 1.1**

9. What important religious belief set the Israelites apart from other ancient cultures? **LESSON 1.2**

10. Why is the Torah the most important holy book in Judaism? **LESSON 1.3**

11. What did Saul achieve as the first king of the Israelites? **LESSON 2.1**

12. Who was David, and what were his major accomplishments? **LESSON 2.1**

13. How did Cyrus the Great's policy of tolerance affect Jews during their exile in Babylon? **LESSON 2.2**

14. What was the Diaspora? **LESSON 2.3**

15. What natural disaster likely destroyed King Herod's harbor at Caesarea 2,000 years ago? **LESSON 2.4**

CRITICAL THINKING

Answer the following questions. Support your answers with evidence from the chapter.

16. MAKE CONNECTIONS How did the Jews develop and maintain their cultural identity?

17. DRAW CONCLUSIONS Why did the Israelites believe that the Ten Commandments reaffirmed their covenant with God?

18. EVALUATE Why was the Exodus such an important event in Jewish history?

19. ANALYZE CAUSE AND EFFECT What effect did the Diaspora have on the religion of Judaism?

20. YOU DECIDE Who do you think was the most important person in the history of the Jewish people? Why?

INTERPRET TIME LINES

Study the time line of selected events in Jewish history. Then answer the questions that follow.

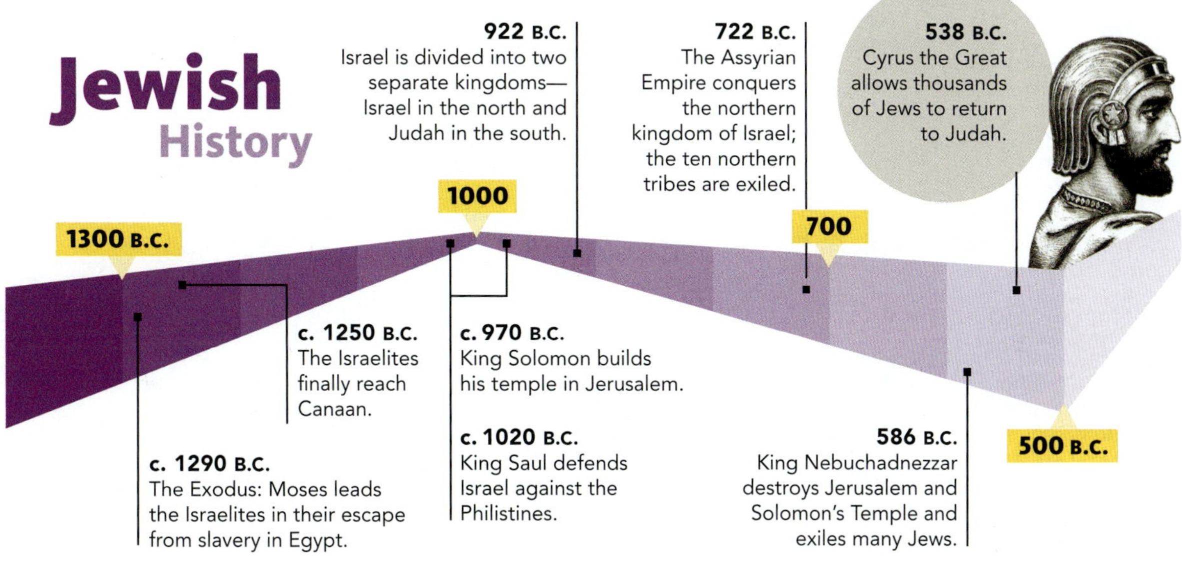

Jewish History
1300 B.C.
c. 1290 B.C.
The Exodus: Moses leads the Israelites in their escape from slavery in Egypt.
c. 1250 B.C.
The Israelites finally reach Canaan.
c. 1020 B.C.
King Saul defends Israel against the Philistines.
1000
c. 970 B.C.
King Solomon builds his temple in Jerusalem.
922 B.C.
Israel is divided into two separate kingdoms—Israel in the north and Judah in the south.
722 B.C.
The Assyrian Empire conquers the northern kingdom of Israel; the ten northern tribes are exiled.
700
586 B.C.
King Nebuchadnezzar destroys Jerusalem and Solomon's Temple and exiles many Jews.
538 B.C.
Cyrus the Great allows thousands of Jews to return to Judah.
500 B.C.

21. Who destroyed the First Temple and exiled the two tribes of Judah to Babylon?

22. Which empire destroyed the northern kingdom of Israel?

ANALYZE SOURCES

Read the following psalm, or sacred song, from the Hebrew Bible. Then answer the question.

> The Lord is my shepherd; I lack nothing. He makes me lie down in green pastures; he leads me to water in places of repose [calm]; he renews my life; he guides me in right paths as befits his name. Though I walk through a valley of deepest darkness, I will fear no harm, for you are with me; your rod and your staff—they comfort me. You spread a table for me in full view of my enemies; you anoint [rub] my head with oil; my drink is abundant. Only goodness and steadfast love shall pursue me all the days of my life, and I shall dwell in the house of the Lord for many long years.
>
> Psalms 23:1–6

23. What qualities does the author attribute to God in this psalm?

WRITE ABOUT HISTORY

24. ARGUMENT Which one of the Ten Commandments do you think has had the greatest impact on society? Make a list of some of its important effects on society.

TIPS

- Reread the Ten Commandments in Lesson 1.4. Choose the one that you think has had the greatest impact on society.
- Write down the commandment. Under it, list at least three effects of this commandment on society.
- If you can think of more than three effects, add them to the list.
- Use vocabulary from the chapter as appropriate.
- If you have difficulty identifying three effects, you might draw evidence from informational texts. For example, you might look up the Ten Commandments in an encyclopedia or another reference book.

CHAPTER

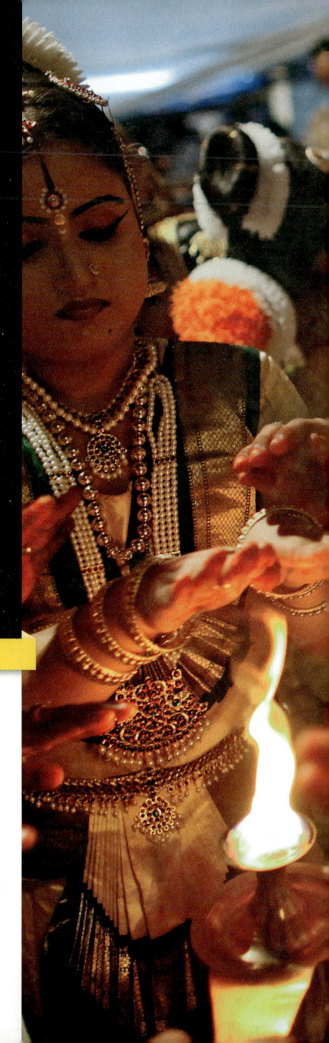

6 ANCIENT INDIA

2500 B.C. – A.D. 535

SECTION 1

INDUS RIVER CIVILIZATIONS

KEY VOCABULARY
caste system
dharma
epic poem
karma
monsoon
nirvana
planned city
reincarnation
subcontinent
yoga

NAMES & PLACES
Aryans
Brahmanism
Buddhism
Ganges River
Harappa
Hinduism
Indus River
Mohenjo-Daro
Sanskrit
Siddhartha Gautama
Vedas

SECTION 2

INDIAN EMPIRES

KEY VOCABULARY
golden age
inoculation

NAMES & PLACES
Asoka
Ayurveda
Chandragupta Maurya
Chandra Gupta I
Kalidasa
Mohandas Gandhi

READING STRATEGY

ORGANIZE IDEAS: ANALYZE CAUSE AND EFFECT
When you analyze cause and effect, you note the consequences of an event, an action, or a condition. As you read the chapter, use a graphic organizer like this one to identify the effects of the Aryan migrations on Indian civilization.

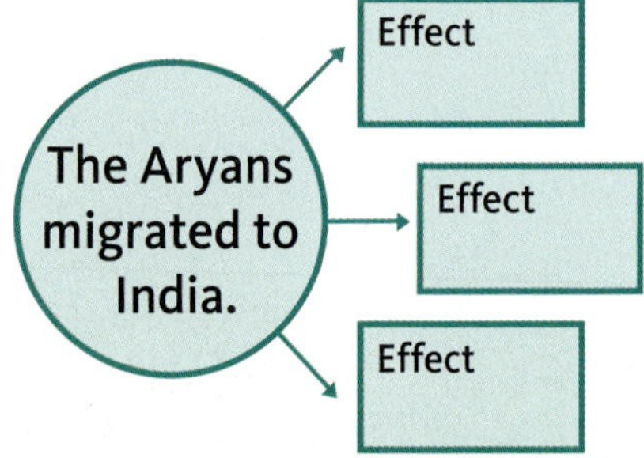
The Aryans migrated to India.
Effect
Effect
Effect

Schoolgirls offer a prayer before a performance of Indian classical dance in honor of Lord Shiva, one of the three major Hindu male deities.

THE INDIAN SUBCONTINENT
60°E
70°E
80°E
90°E
100°E
40°N
30°N
20°N
10°N
Tropic of Cancer
Syr Darya
Naryn R.
Toxkan R.
Yarkant R.
Zarafshon R.
Tejen R.
Panj R.
HINDU KUSH
Harirud R.
Helmand R.
Indus R.
H I M A L A Y A
Tongtian (Yangtze) R.
Lancang (Mekong) R.
Nu (Salween) R.
Brahmaputra R.
Jhelum R.
Chenab R.
Ravi R.
Harappa
Sutlej R.
Sarasvati R.
Mohenjo-Daro
THAR DESERT
The Sarasvati River has dried up and disappeared
Mt. Everest 29,035 ft (8,850 m)
Ghaghara R.
Ganges R.
Yamuna R.
Chambal R.
Chindwin R.
INDIA
Mahi R.
Narmada R.
Tapi R.
Mahanadi R.
Mouths of the Ganges
Wainganga R.
Godavari R.
Bhima R.
Krishna R.
DECCAN PLATEAU
WESTERN GHATS
EASTERN GHATS
Tungabhadra R.
Cauvery R.
Irrawaddy R.
Arabian Sea
Bay of Bengal
SRI LANKA
INDIAN OCEAN
Elevation
feet meters
10,000+ 3,050+
5,000 1,524
2,000 610
1,000 305
500 152
0 0
Below sea level
Dry monsoon winds
Wet monsoon winds
N S E W
0 200 400 Miles
0 200 400 Kilometers

1.1 The Geography of Ancient India

Geographically, India has it all. If you were to travel around India, you could climb snowcapped mountains, cross wide grassy plains, hack through dense tropical forests, sail down mighty rivers, and skirt around sun-scorched deserts. You might travel under a bright blue sky or get soaked by seasonal rains.

MAIN IDEA

South Asia's physical geography affected the development of Indus Valley civilizations.

MOUNTAINS, RIVERS, AND MONSOONS

Present-day India, Bangladesh, Bhutan, Nepal, and Pakistan make up the large landmass, or **subcontinent**, of South Asia. This diamond-shaped landmass was originally an island. However, 40 million years ago, the large moving plates on which the continents lie drove the subcontinent into Asia. As the lands collided, they pushed Earth's crust upward to form the Himalaya, a 1,500-mile mountain range.

The Himalaya are the world's highest mountains. Many Himalayan peaks rise about 24,000 feet. Thirty peaks, including Mount Everest—Earth's highest point—are over 25,000 feet high.

On either side of the Himalaya lie lower mountain ranges, including the Hindu Kush, which separates what was once northwest India from present-day Afghanistan. These northern mountains form a natural barrier against invaders. The Arabian Sea, Indian Ocean, and Bay of Bengal have provided further protection. The Deccan Plateau, which contains smaller mountain systems, makes up much of southern India.

The two major rivers of northern India, the **Indus** and the **Ganges**, both start in the Himalaya. Like the Tigris and the Euphrates in Mesopotamia, these rivers provide water for irrigation and deposit fertile soil for farming.

Strong seasonal winds called **monsoons** have long been an important element of the subcontinent's climate. These winds bring a dry season in winter. In summer, they bring a wet season with heavy rainfall.

INDUS RIVER VALLEY

Physical characteristics of the Indus River Valley offered nearly ideal conditions for agriculture. The valley's fertile soil and plentiful water supply most likely encouraged nomadic herdsmen to settle there and farm. Villages emerged. Then, around 2500 B.C., some villages grew into cities—and a civilization developed.

REVIEW & ASSESS

1. **READING CHECK** How did physical geography affect the development of Indus Valley civilizations?
2. **INTERPRET MAPS** What physical feature separates India from the continent of Asia?
3. **MAKE INFERENCES** What positive and negative effects might the summer monsoons have had on farmers?

1.2 Harappan Civilization

Historians have studied ancient Egyptian civilization for many centuries. But evidence of ancient India's great civilization was not discovered until the early 20th century. Then, in 1921, archaeologists unearthed an Indian culture every bit as vast and sophisticated as that of ancient Egypt: the Harappan civilization.

MAIN IDEA

One of the world's earliest and most advanced civilizations emerged in ancient India's Indus River Valley.

WELL-PLANNED CITIES

Around 2500 B.C., civilization developed in the Indus Valley. Fertile soil and irrigation delivered food surpluses that generated wealth. As populations boomed, villages grew into large cities. **Mohenjo-Daro** (moh-HEHN-joh DAHR-oh), one of the civilization's major cities, covered over 250 acres. Another important city, **Harappa** (huh-RA-puh), gave the Harappan civilization its name. These cities were the largest of their time. Their influence spread across a 500,000-square-mile area, which was greater than that of either ancient Egypt or Mesopotamia.

Indus Valley cities were among the world's first **planned cities**. Many were built with the same layout and the same features. Such cities had an eastern housing and business area guarded by defensive walls. To the west were public buildings, as well as structures that may have been used to store grain. Main roads as straight as rulers intersected at right angles with streets exactly half their width. Wells were another common feature. People used bricks that were all the same size to build houses. Homes had indoor plumbing with a bathroom and a toilet that emptied into excellent underground sewers.

Archaeologists have found similarly styled pottery, jewelry, toys, and tools at more than 1,000 Harappan sites. These similar goods demonstrate strong cultural ties among people living hundreds of miles apart. The similarities also suggest that the Harappan civilization was a single state with a strong central government. However, historians have no idea how it was ruled.

AN ADVANCED CULTURE

In fact, there is a lot historians do not know about Harappan civilization because archaeologists have not figured out its writing system. It seems to be based, at least in part, on pictograms, like Sumerian cuneiform. The only writing found is on small items such as pottery, tools, and tiny square stone seals. Traders probably pressed these seals into soft clay to leave their mark on trading goods. Traders also used stone cubes as standard weights and measures.

The Harappans were long-distance traders, using boats and possibly the world's first wheeled vehicles. Their enormous trade network stretched over the mountains into what are now Afghanistan, Iran, and Iraq. There, archaeologists have found records of Harappan copper, gold, and ivory.

Historians know little about Harappan religion. In fact, much about the Harappans remains a mystery.

Critical Viewing This photo shows the ruins of Mohenjo-Daro. What detail indicates that the high mound had a specific purpose?

REVIEW & ASSESS

1. **READING CHECK** What is one characteristic of the advanced culture of Harappan civilization?

2. **INTEGRATE VISUALS** What details in the photo support the conclusion that Harappa was an advanced civilization?

3. **MAKE INFERENCES** Why do you think it is important to use standard weights and measures in trade?

1.3

Aryan Migrations

Historians believe the Indus Valley suffered a series of earthquakes from which the Harappan civilization never recovered. Other forces were also in play. Eventually, migrations of Aryan people from the north led to the establishment of another great Indian civilization.

MAIN IDEA

After the Harappan civilization declined, Aryan immigrants forged a new Indian civilization.

HARAPPAN SEAL

Found at Mohenjo-Daro, this soft stone seal was probably used to mark trade goods. The marks at the top are an example of the Harappan language, which archaeologists have not yet learned to read.

END OF HARAPPA

A combination of natural forces probably contributed to the Harappan civilization's downfall. First agriculture declined when rainfall diminished. Then earthquakes caused flooding and drastically changed the course of rivers. One river, the Sarasvati, no longer flowed near Harappan cities. With reduced access to river water for irrigation, agriculture became more difficult.

As food supplies declined, people abandoned the cities. By 1900 B.C., a simple village way of life had largely replaced the Harappans' advanced urban civilization.

According to many historians, around 1500 B.C., waves of new people began crossing the Hindu Kush into India. The migrants were a collection of tribes called **Aryans**, meaning "noble ones." They belonged to the Indo-European people who had populated central Asia. (Some scholars have begun to dispute this theory, however. They believe that the Aryans were descendants of earlier Indus civilizations and were not foreign invaders at all.)

The Aryans were seminomadic herders of horses and cattle and were also fierce warriors. They built only basic houses but rode horses and used wheeled chariots.

Around 1000 B.C., what became known as Vedic civilization expanded south and east. There the people adopted agriculture, cleared the forests to cultivate crops, and settled down in villages. The villages grouped together into chiefdoms and then into kingdoms. As they conquered and mixed with native people, the Aryans had a huge cultural impact on religion, class, and language.

IMPACT ON INDIAN SOCIETY

The Aryans worshipped many gods from nature. They also had gods for friendship and for moral authority. To keep their gods happy, Aryan priests, or Brahmans, performed complicated rituals in **Sanskrit**, the Aryan language. Their religion came to be called **Brahmanism** (BRAH-muh-nih-zuhm).

In time Brahmanism's rituals and hymns were recorded in sacred texts called the **Vedas**. The oldest text is the Rig Veda, which contains 1,028 melodic hymns.

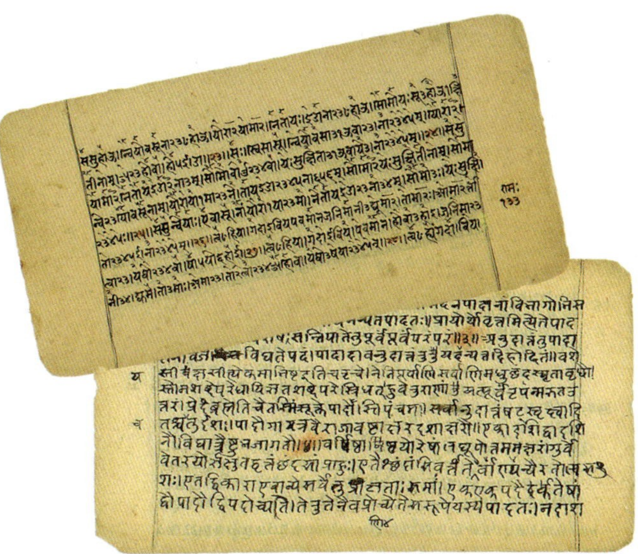

VEDAS

The Vedas are four sacred texts that were probably composed between 1500 and 1200 B.C. For a thousand years, people passed the Vedas down orally.

After a written form of Sanskrit emerged, people were finally able to write down the Vedas. These texts tell historians what life might have been like in the Vedic period.

ARYAN MIGRATIONS, c. 1500 B.C.

Aryan migration

Brahmanism grew powerful because the priests established beneficial relationships with kings. The Brahmans preached that the gods granted the right to rule to the kings. In return the kings upheld the authority of the Brahmans.

Over time, a social class system developed that determined how people lived. Priests were at the top, followed by warriors and nobles. Freemen, farmers, and traders were third in importance. At the bottom were slaves, laborers, and artisans. Non-Aryans made up most of the lowest class. Many centuries later, another group developed that was considered even lower.

The Aryan hierarchy developed into a rigid **caste system** that was hereditary and could never be changed. People's castes dictated the kind of work they did and whom they could marry. The caste system even dictated what people could eat. Such definitions applied to people's children as well.

REVIEW & ASSESS

1. **READING CHECK** Who were the Aryans?
2. **INTERPRET MAPS** What physical features did the Aryan migrations pass through?
3. **DETERMINE WORD MEANINGS** What does *waves* mean in the sentence, "Around 1500 B.C. waves of new people began crossing the Hindu Kush into India"?

1.4 Hindu Beliefs and Practices

If you are into computer games, you might have an online avatar, a character that represents you. The concept of avatars is nothing new. The Hindu god Vishnu had many avatars, including a godlike hero called Krishna. Unlike your avatar, Vishnu's avatars were versions of himself in various forms.

MAIN IDEA

Over 5,000 years, Hinduism absorbed and integrated many beliefs found throughout South Asia.

GODS AND SACRED TEXTS

The religion that grew out of Aryan beliefs and practices is **Hinduism**, the world's third largest religion. Hinduism developed over many centuries. Its many gods and goddesses, or deities, combine to form Brahman, a universal spirit. The three most important Hindu deities are Brahma, Vishnu, and Shiva.

Female deities include Saraswati, goddess of knowledge, science, and the arts, and Parvati, who is both a goddess and the beautiful wife of Shiva. She meditated for years in the Himalaya to attract his attention. Lakshmi, wife of Vishnu, is the goddess of wealth and prosperity. People who seek success worship Lakshmi.

The Vedas are Hinduism's holiest books, but two **epic poems**, or long narrative poems, are also important. One, called *Mahabharata* (mu-HAH-bahr-AH-tuh), teaches the importance of living and acting righteously. The other poem, the *Ramayana* (rah-mah-YAH-nuh), tells the story of Rama, the perfect king, who fought evil forces in the world.

Within the *Mahabharata* is a spiritual poem called Bhagavad Gita (BAH-gah-vuhd GEET-ah), or "Song of the Lord." In this poem Krishna praises duty. He also encourages action over inaction, knowledge over ignorance, belief over disbelief, and good over evil. This poem remains popular as a source of spiritual guidance and inspiration.

BELIEFS AND PRACTICES

Hindus occasionally worship in temples, but the home is the center of religious activity. Many homes have a temple room or corner where family members worship. Many Hindus still observe certain cultural practices related to the caste system, such as marrying within one's caste. They also believe the soul is eternal and is reborn in different bodies over different life cycles. This is known as **reincarnation**.

According to Hindu beliefs, people's actions and conduct create **karma**, which determines the kind of life into which they will be reborn. The karma of someone who leads a good and moral life leads to rebirth into a better life. A life filled with misdeeds creates bad karma, which leads to rebirth into a life of greater hardship and suffering. The ultimate goal of a Hindu is to end this cycle of rebirth by living selflessly and eliminating material desires.

There are many paths to the perfect life. One path involves the practice of **yoga**—a series of exercises intended to help a person achieve spiritual insight. An important idea underlying such practices is to seek and know the truth.

These women in northern India are throwing flowers in the air to celebrate the Hindu festival of Holi, which marks the coming of spring.

HINDU DEITIES

Brahma, *the Creator:* Brahma created the universe, the world, and the human race. His four heads represent the four Vedas.

Vishnu, *the Preserver:* Vishnu contains and balances good and evil. It is his job to maintain the divine order of the universe. If evil is winning, Vishnu comes to Earth in human form to restore the balance.

Shiva, *the Destroyer:* Shiva is responsible for all forms of change, from giving up bad habits to death. He is closely associated with yoga.

REVIEW & ASSESS

1. **READING CHECK** Who are the three most important gods in Hinduism, and what is the role of each?
2. **MAKE INFERENCES** How might the concept of karma guide a Hindu during his or her lifetime?
3. **ANALYZE LANGUAGE USE** How does knowing that *carne* refers to "flesh" help you understand the word *reincarnation*?

1.5 DOCUMENT-BASED QUESTION
Hindu Sacred Texts

The Bhagavad Gita and the *Ramayana* are two of Hinduism's most famous and popular sacred texts. They tell exciting stories about great warriors having heroic adventures, while also teaching important religious and moral lessons. People in ancient India originally memorized these epic poems and passed them down orally, as they did the Vedas.

This painting shows the Lord Krishna, an avatar of Vishnu, and Prince Arjuna as they head into battle.

DOCUMENT ONE

Primary Source: Sacred Text

from the Bhagavad Gita, translated by Stephen Mitchell

The Bhagavad Gita is a 700-verse poem describing a conversation between Vishnu's avatar Krishna and the hero Arjuna. In this excerpt, Krishna speaks to Arjuna before a great battle. Krishna tells the warrior about the soul—the "it" in the poem.

CONSTRUCTED RESPONSE According to Krishna, what is special about a soul?

The sharpest sword will not pierce it;
the hottest flame will not singe [burn] it;
water will not make it moist;
wind will not cause it to wither [die].

It cannot be pierced or singed,
moistened or withered; it is vast,
perfect and all-pervading [everywhere],
calm, immovable, timeless.

DOCUMENT TWO

Primary Source: Epic Poem

from the *Ramayana*, a retelling by William Buck

The *Ramayana* is a love story in which the good king Rama, an avatar of Vishnu, rescues his kidnapped wife Sita from Ravana, the evil ruler of an island off India's southeastern coast. In this passage, Rama speaks to his brother after they learn that their father has died.

CONSTRUCTED RESPONSE What comfort might his brother take from Rama's words?

Life is passing as a river ever flowing away, never still, never returning. Life is changeable as the flashing lightning, a pattern of as little meaning, and impermanent. . . . Life is bright and colored for a passing moment like the sunset. Then it is gone and who can prevent it going?

DOCUMENT THREE

Primary Source: Sacred Text

from the Rig Veda, translated by Wendy Doniger

The Rig Veda is a series of 1,028 hymns grouped into 10 books. It is also the oldest of the Hindu sacred texts. This excerpt from a poem in Book 10 addresses a person who has just died.

CONSTRUCTED RESPONSE According to the passage, what happens to a person after death?

May your eye go to the sun, your life's breath to the wind. Go to the sky or to earth, as is your nature; or go to the waters, if that is your fate. Take root in the plants with your limbs.

SYNTHESIZE & WRITE

1. **REVIEW** Review what you have learned about Hinduism, the Bhagavad Gita, the *Ramayana*, and the Rig Veda.
2. **RECALL** On your own paper, write down the main idea expressed in each document.
3. **CONSTRUCT** Construct a topic sentence that answers this question: What do the passages from the Bhagavad Gita, the *Ramayana*, and the Rig Veda suggest about Hinduism's attitude toward life and death?
4. **WRITE** Using evidence from the documents, write an explanatory paragraph that answers the question in Step 3.

1.6 Siddhartha and Buddhism

Like many people, you might very much want to own the latest cell phone or tablet. But what if someone told you that your desire for such material possessions would only bring you suffering? That's exactly what a man who lived about 2,500 years ago said.

MAIN IDEA

Buddhism emerged in India around 500 B.C.

EIGHTFOLD PATH

Right View: See and understand things as they really are

Right Intention: Commit to ethical self-improvement

Right Speech: Tell the truth and speak gently

Right Action: Act kindly, honestly, and respectfully

Right Livelihood: Earn a living in a moral, legal, and peaceful way

Right Effort: Focus your will onto achieving good things

Right Mindfulness: Value a good mind

Right Concentration: Single-mindedness

THE LIFE OF BUDDHA

Earlier in this chapter, you learned about the development of Hinduism in India. Another major religion, called **Buddhism**, also began there. Buddhism is based on the teachings of **Siddhartha Gautama** (sih-DAR-tuh GOW-tuh-muh). According to tradition, Siddhartha was born in 563 B.C. He was a prince who lived a life of luxury in what is now Nepal.

Siddhartha enjoyed his life until, at the age of 29, he came across an old man, a sick man, a dead man, and a holy man who was poor but very happy. These men made Siddhartha think about suffering brought on by old age, disease, and death and wonder what had made the holy man so happy. Siddhartha gave up his wealth, his wife, and his child to search for the answer to this question. Then, after six years of wandering, he meditated beneath a tree and finally understood how to be free from suffering. Because of this revelation, or understanding of truth, Siddhartha came to be known as the Buddha, or "Enlightened One."

BUDDHIST BELIEFS

The Buddha spent the rest of his life teaching what he had learned. Much of what he taught is contained in a set of guidelines called the Four Noble Truths. The first truth teaches that all life is suffering. The second truth is that the cause of suffering is desire. The third truth teaches that the end of desire means the end of suffering; the fourth, that following the Eightfold Path can end suffering. The Eightfold Path is also called the Middle Way because it promotes a

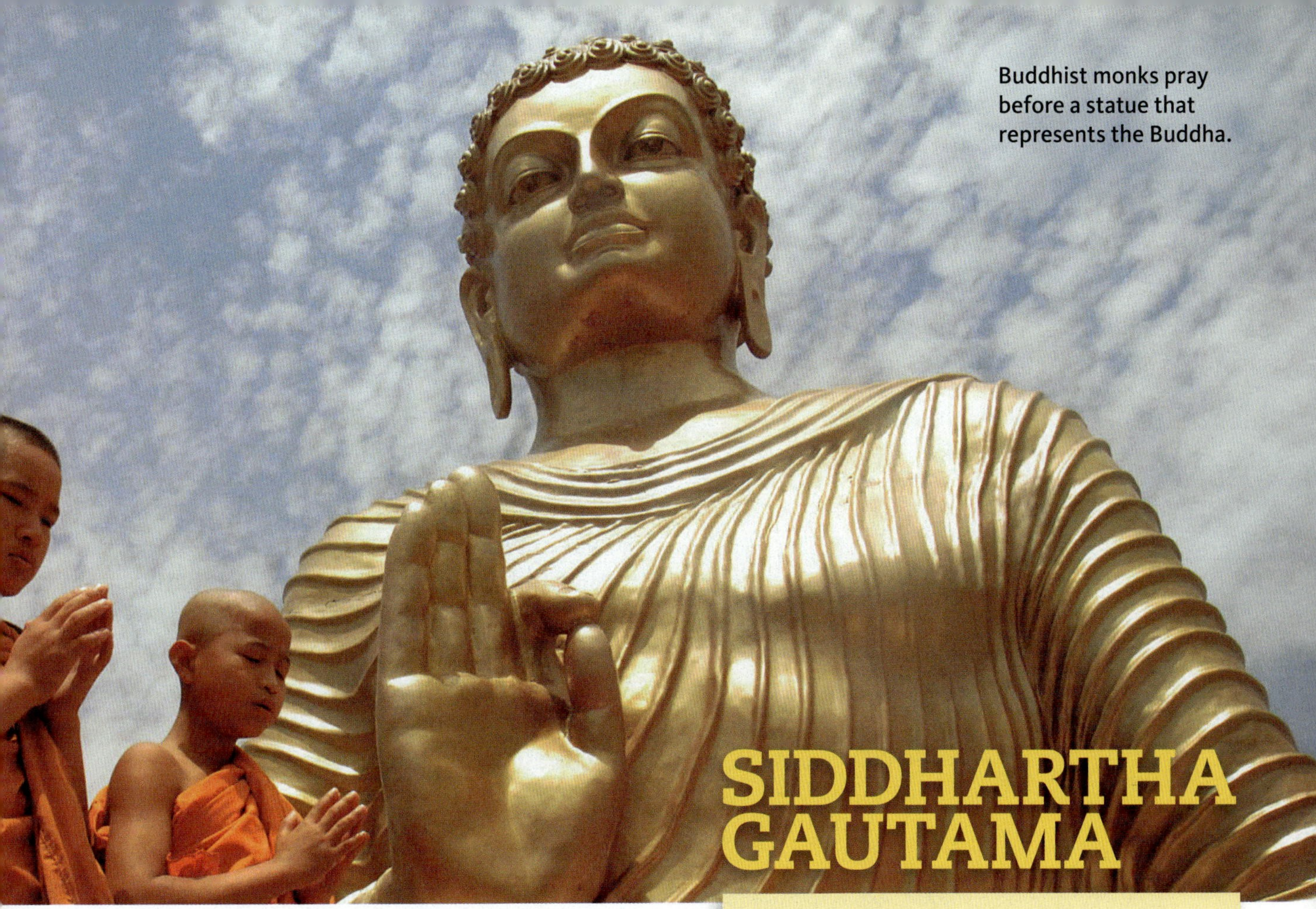

Buddhist monks pray before a statue that represents the Buddha.

SIDDHARTHA GAUTAMA

life balanced between happiness and self-denial. Like Hindus, the Buddha believed in reincarnation. He taught that following the Eightfold Path would lead to **nirvana** (nihr-VAH-nuh), a state of bliss or the end of suffering caused by the cycle of rebirth.

The totality of the Buddha's teachings are known as the **dharma** (DUHR-muh), or divine law. The Buddha taught that a person of any caste could attain nirvana, and he also promoted nonviolence. Buddhism spread throughout Asia and beyond. After the Buddha died, his remains were buried under eight mound-like structures called stupas.

Job: Prince, poor man, Enlightened One, and founder of Buddhism
Education: Princely pursuits followed by soul searching
Home: Northeast India

FINEST HOUR

He finally achieved enlightenment after 49 days of intense meditation.

WORST MOMENT

He struggled to find the answers he sought, despite putting himself through much suffering and hardship.

MILESTONE

The Buddha is said to have received enlightenment at the age of 35.

REVIEW & ASSESS

1. **READING CHECK** Who is Siddhartha Gautama and what did he seek to learn?
2. **DRAW CONCLUSIONS** What is the purpose of the Four Noble Truths and the Eightfold Path?
3. **MAKE INFERENCES** Why do you think Buddhism became popular in ancient India?

2.1 The Maurya Empire

Bite into oven-hot food and you'll burn your tongue. But nibble away at the cooler edges and you can eventually eat the whole meal. That's the principle one king applied to defeat some weaker kingdoms until he was strong enough to conquer them all.

MAIN IDEA

The Maurya Empire united much of India under a single ruler.

A UNITED INDIA

Earlier in this chapter, you read about the Aryans who migrated to India. The Aryans established many kingdoms in the subcontinent. For hundreds of years, no major power arose. Then, around 550 B.C., a kingdom called Magadha in northeast India grew powerful.

Chandragupta Maurya (chuhn-druh-GUP-tuh MOWR-yuh) became king of Magadha around 325 B.C. Believed to have been a soldier, Chandragupta gained power with the help of Kautilya, a Brahmin who plotted Chandragupta's rise. Once Chandragupta became king, he conquered many of the other kingdoms and established an empire. His Maurya Empire united most of northern India and was the first great Indian empire.

Chandragupta established a strong central government. He used taxes to pay for a network of spies and a large army to crush troublemakers. Then, somewhat surprisingly, Chandragupta gave up the throne in 297 B.C. Instead of continuing to rule his empire, he chose to become a monk committed to nonviolence.

THE BUDDHIST KING

Around 269 B.C., **Asoka** (uh-SHOH-kuh), Chandragupta's grandson, became king. At first he earned a reputation for cruelty. His unprovoked attack on another Indian kingdom caused the deaths of hundreds of thousands of people. In the aftermath of so much violence, Asoka underwent a dramatic change. He converted to Buddhism and began to rule using Buddhist principles about peace.

Asoka made a pilgrimage to all the Buddhist holy places in northern India, preaching to his subjects as he traveled. He actively encouraged the spread of Buddhism by sending missionaries to preach abroad. This practice helped Buddhism reach other countries such as Sri Lanka and China, where it is still very popular today.

Asoka had his Buddhist policies inscribed on rocks and tall pillars across his empire. The inscriptions were written in the appropriate regional languages. These policies encouraged everyone to live good lives. State officials monitored moral conduct.

Asoka built more than 1,000 stupas in honor of the Buddha. He donated to charity and built hospitals for animals as well as for humans. To govern his vast empire effectively, Asoka built good roads with plenty of shade and water. These roads were useful for trade and allowed his instructions, inspectors, and armies to travel quickly.

Although Asoka may have been India's greatest king, his well-run empire did not last long. After his death, the Maurya Empire collapsed into many warring kingdoms.

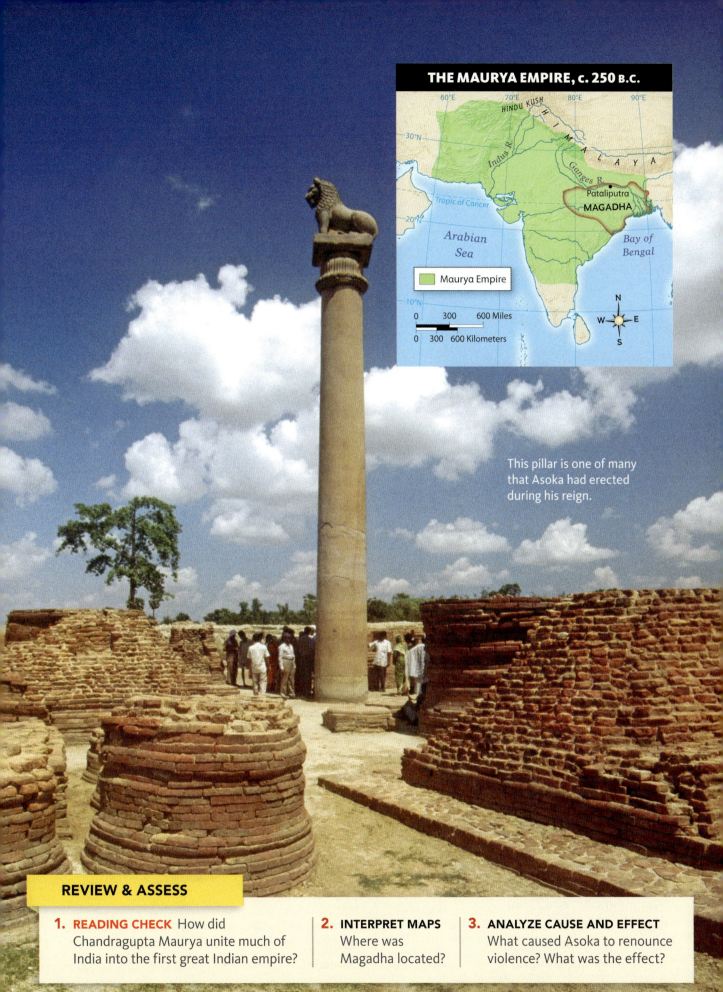

THE MAURYA EMPIRE, c. 250 B.C.
60°E
70°E
80°E
90°E
HINDU KUSH
HIMALAYA
30°N
Indus R.
Ganges R.
Pataliputra
MAGADHA
Tropic of Cancer
20°N
Arabian Sea
Bay of Bengal
Maurya Empire
10°N
0 300 600 Miles
0 300 600 Kilometers
N
W
E
S

This pillar is one of many that Asoka had erected during his reign.

REVIEW & ASSESS

1. **READING CHECK** How did Chandragupta Maurya unite much of India into the first great Indian empire?

2. **INTERPRET MAPS** Where was Magadha located?

3. **ANALYZE CAUSE AND EFFECT** What caused Asoka to renounce violence? What was the effect?

THE GUPTA EMPIRE, c. A.D. 400
60°E
70°E
80°E
90°E
30°N
20°N
10°N
HINDU KUSH
HIMALAYA
Indus R.
Ganges R.
Ayodhya
Pataliputra
MAGADHA
Tropic of Cancer
Arabian Sea
Bay of Bengal
Gupta Empire
0 300 600 Miles
0 300 600 Kilometers
N
S
E
W

Dedicated to the god Vishnu, the Dashavatar Temple in northern India is an example of Gupta architecture.

2.2 The Gupta Empire

History has some weird coincidences. Two of India's greatest empires began in Magadha with a king called Chandragupta. But the kings weren't related. And both empires began around 320, although the Maurya Empire began in 320 B.C. and the Gupta in A.D. 320.

MAIN IDEA

The Gupta Empire brought 200 years of peace and prosperity to India.

A WISE RULER

The collapse of the Maurya Empire led to 500 years of fighting in India. Despite this disorder, the period brought continued economic, social, and cultural progress. Then around A.D. 320 a new unifying power arose. A leader in Magadha called **Chandra Gupta I** began gaining new land and established the Gupta Empire. A dynasty of strong Gupta kings continued to expand the empire until it covered most of northern India. Instead of establishing a strong central government like the Mauryas did, the Guptas allowed the defeated kings to continue to rule. In exchange the Guptas required obedience and tribute, or payment, from the defeated kings.

A series of strong, wise, and long-lived Gupta rulers brought India 200 years of political stability, peace, and prosperity. The expanding empire and its extensive trade routes spread Indian cultural influences around Asia and beyond. Hinduism was reestablished and eventually became India's main religion.

A GOLDEN AGE

Chandra Gupta II, grandson of Chandra Gupta I, ruled during India's **golden age**, a period of great cultural achievement. **Kalidasa** (kah-lih-DAH-suh), the greatest poet in Chandra Gupta II's court and one of India's greatest writers, composed poems and plays in Sanskrit. Scribes, or writers, finally wrote down the spoken stories, including the *Mahabharata* and the *Ramayana*.

Indian artists painted and sculpted statues of Hindu deities. Architects designed and built elegant new temples. Metalworking, improved dramatically. A 24-foot iron pillar weighing more than 6 tons still stands in Delhi some 1,500 years after being installed.

Medical understanding also increased. **Ayurveda** (y-uhr-VAY-duh), a traditional guide to medicine, diet, exercise, and disease, developed and remains an alternative form of healing. In medicine, as in many other areas, ancient Indian knowledge and culture reached far around the world.

REVIEW & ASSESS

1. **READING CHECK** How did the Gupta kings bring peace to their empire?
2. **INTERPRET MAPS** In which directions did the Gupta Empire spread out from Magadha?
3. **FORM AND SUPPORT OPINIONS** Which achievement during India's golden age do you think was most significant? Explain your answer.

2.3 The Legacy of Ancient India

Martin Luther King, Jr., championed nonviolent protest to win rights for African Americans. His methods were inspired by the nonviolent protests of Mohandas Gandhi, who helped India gain its independence in 1947. And Gandhi took his nonviolent principles from Hinduism and Buddhism. In that way alone, Indian thinking has had an immense impact on the modern world.

MAIN IDEA

The achievements of ancient India have influenced much of the world.

RELIGION

Two major religions had their origins in India: Hinduism and Buddhism. These religions remain important and influential in much of the modern world. Today four out of five Indians are Hindu, which greatly affects the country's culture. Although the caste system is now officially illegal, some people still observe certain cultural practices according to caste. The idea of reincarnation is especially widespread. Ancient Sanskrit texts continue to teach ethics through stories. Millions of people in many countries practice Hinduism, including more than two million people in the United States alone.

A number of great leaders, including **Mohandas Gandhi** (moh-HUHN-dahs GAHN-dih), have encouraged the Hindu and Buddhist principle of nonviolence. People throughout the world engage in nonviolence to protest injustice. Many vegetarians, people who do not eat meat, follow the Hindu and Buddhist principle of nonviolence toward animals. Today around one percent of India's population is Buddhist. However, Buddhism thrives in countries such as Sri Lanka, Thailand, Vietnam, Japan, Korea, and China. Buddhism also has a following in Europe and in the United States.

ARTS AND SCIENCE

You've learned that religion influenced Indian writing. The *Mahabharata* and the Bhagavad Gita are popular around the world. Religion also influenced Indian architecture, an influence that spread to other parts of the world. The temple of Angkor Wat in Cambodia, a country in Asia, is considered one of the world's greatest architectural achievements. The building's elaborate style evolved from ancient Indian architecture. Similar examples can be found in Myanmar (Burma), Vietnam, and Thailand.

Ancient India also contributed much to the fields of science and mathematics. Indians were among the first to practice **inoculation**, which stimulates mild forms of disease in people so that they do not develop more serious forms. Inoculation has greatly reduced the threat of smallpox.

Indian mathematicians created the decimal system and numerals (the number symbols we use today). They also developed the concept of zero, which is crucial to mathematics and computing. Indian astronomers, scientists who study the sun, moon, stars, and planets, accurately calculated the length of the solar year. They also asserted that Earth traveled around the sun and proved that the world was round 1,000 years before Columbus's voyage to America.

LEGACIES OF ANCIENT INDIA

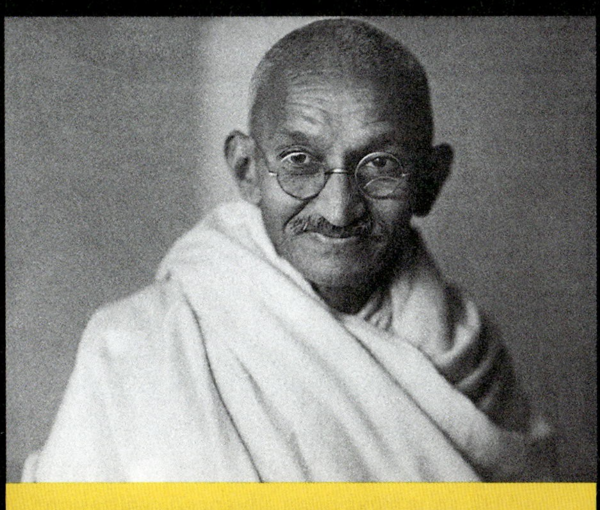

KAZAKHSTAN
UKRAINE
BLACK SEA
TURKEY

Moral Conduct

Mohandas Gandhi's understanding of the Bhagavad Gita inspired his nonviolent protests in the mid-twentieth century against the British rule of India.

Science

Ancient astronomers determined that Earth is round. They also correctly calculated the length of the solar year.

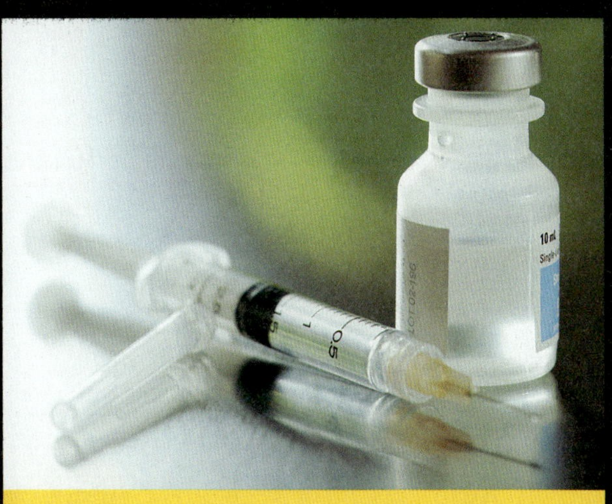
10 mL

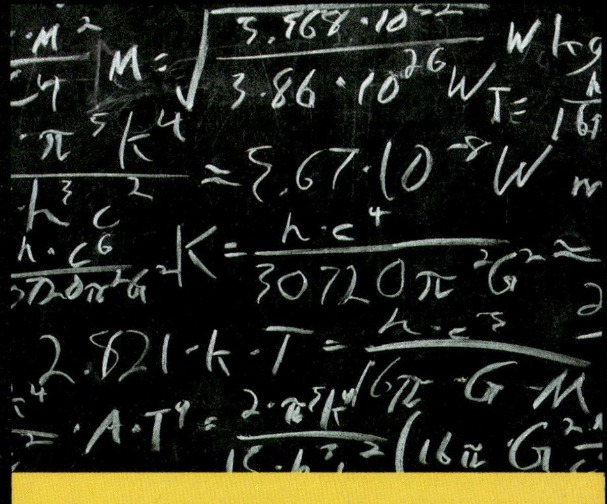

Medicine

Inoculation protects people's health by increasing one's resistance to disease. It has virtually eliminated smallpox.

Mathematics

Mathematicians of ancient India devised both the decimal system and numerals. They were the first to use zero.

REVIEW & ASSESS

1. **READING CHECK** How did ancient India influence religion in other parts of the world?
2. **SEQUENCE EVENTS** How did mathematicians in ancient India contribute to the age of computers?
3. **MAKE CONNECTIONS** What is the legacy of India's ancient Sanskrit texts?

CHAPTER

6 Review

VOCABULARY

On your paper, write the vocabulary word that completes each of the following sentences.

1. Today, five countries make up the Indian ______, which is separated from the rest of Asia by the Himalaya.
2. Strong seasonal winds called ______ shape India's climate.
3. The *Ramayana* is an example of an ______.
4. Ancient Indians had a social hierarchy that developed into a rigid ______.
5. Hindus believe in ______, which means that when a person dies, his or her soul is reborn in another body.
6. According to Hindu teachings, ______ is the practice of breathing exercises as a path to spiritual insight.
7. The totality of the Buddha's teachings are known as the ______, or divine law.
8. Buddhists believe that the Eightfold Path leads to the end of suffering, or ______.

READING STRATEGY

9. **ORGANIZE IDEAS: ANALYZE CAUSE AND EFFECT** If you haven't already, complete your organizer to identify the effects of the Aryan migrations on Indian civilization. Then answer the question.

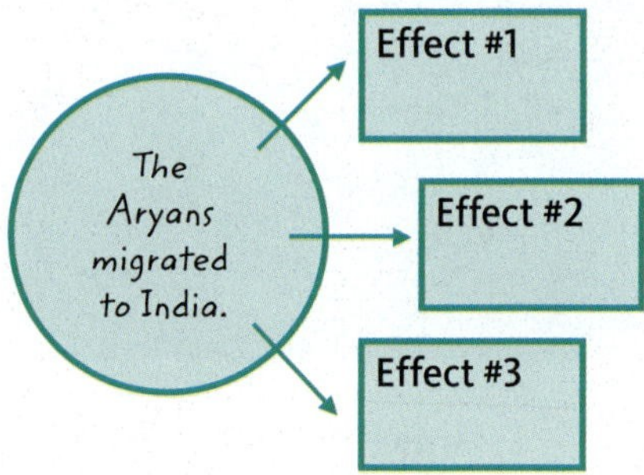
The Aryans migrated to India.
Effect #1
Effect #2
Effect #3

How did the Aryans change civilization in ancient India?

MAIN IDEAS

Answer the following questions. Support your answers with evidence from the chapter.

10. How did geographic features contribute to the development of the Harappan civilization? **LESSON 1.1**
11. In what way were the cities of Mohenjo-Daro and Harappa signs of an advanced civilization? **LESSON 1.2**
12. Who were the Aryans? **LESSON 1.3**
13. How did Hinduism develop in India? **LESSON 1.4**
14. What did Siddhartha Gautama achieve? **LESSON 1.6**
15. How did Asoka spread Buddhism? **LESSON 2.1**
16. In what ways was the reign of Chandra Gupta II a golden age? **LESSON 2.2**
17. What Hindu beliefs and values still deeply influence people's behavior in India today? **LESSON 2.3**

CRITICAL THINKING

Answer the following questions. Support your answers with evidence from the chapter.

18. **ANALYZE CAUSE AND EFFECT** How did the Guptas establish and maintain their empire?
19. **MAKE CONNECTIONS** What did early Indus Valley civilizations have in common with other ancient river valley civilizations?
20. **EVALUATE** How important were the contributions of ancient India to the fields of science and mathematics? Support your evaluation with evidence from the chapter.
21. **COMPARE AND CONTRAST** How are Hindu and Buddhist beliefs similar? How are they different?
22. **YOU DECIDE** What do you think were Asoka's two greatest leadership qualities? Support your opinion with evidence from the chapter.

INTERPRET CHARTS

Study the chart of the caste system that developed in ancient Indian society. Then answer the questions that follow.

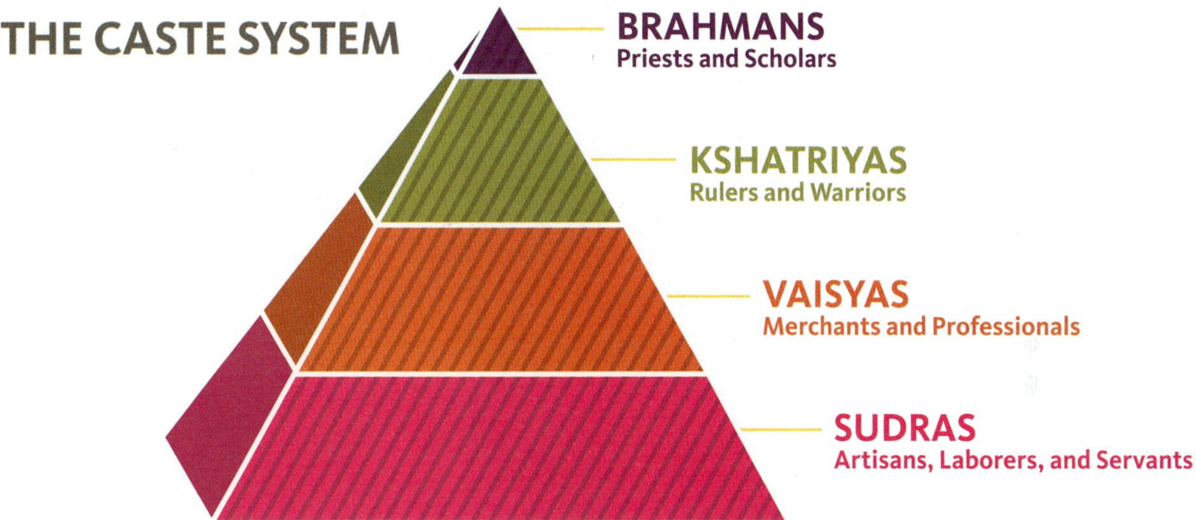
THE CASTE SYSTEM
BRAHMANS
Priests and Scholars
KSHATRIYAS
Rulers and Warriors
VAISYAS
Merchants and Professionals
SUDRAS
Artisans, Laborers, and Servants

23. To which caste did most Indians belong?

24. Which caste was the smallest? Why do you think this was so?

ANALYZE SOURCES

Read the following words spoken by the Buddha. Then answer the question.

> Hold fast to the truth as a lamp. Hold fast as a refuge [place of safety] to the truth. Look not for refuge to anyone besides yourselves. . . .
>
> And whosoever, . . . either now or after I am dead, shall be a lamp unto themselves, . . . shall look not for refuge to anyone besides themselves—it is they . . . who shall reach the very topmost Height!—but they must be anxious to learn.
>
> from *The Last Days of Buddha*, trans. T.W. Rhys David

25. In the passage, the Buddha is telling his followers how to act. What is his message?

WRITE ABOUT HISTORY

26. INFORMATIVE Suppose you are writing a pamphlet for a museum exhibit about India. Write a short essay that explains the lasting influence of ancient India on religion.

TIPS

- Develop an outline that shows how ancient India's influence on religion continues to this day.
- Write the introductory paragraph of your essay using your outline as a guide.
- Develop the topic with relevant, well-chosen facts, concrete details, and examples.
- Use vocabulary from the chapter to explain your ideas.
- Provide a concluding statement that summarizes the information presented.

CHAPTER

7 ANCIENT CHINA

2000 B.C. – A.D. 220

SECTION 1
RIVER DYNASTIES

KEY VOCABULARY
dynastic cycle
dynasty
filial piety
isolate
oracle bone

NAMES & PLACES
Chang Jiang
Confucianism
Daoism
Huang He
Legalism
Mandate of Heaven
Shang
Warring States
Zhou

SECTION 2
CHINA'S EMPIRES

KEY VOCABULARY
bureaucracy
emperor
peasant
silk
terra cotta

NAMES & PLACES
Great Wall
Han
Qin
Shi Huangdi

SECTION 3
EAST MEETS WEST

KEY VOCABULARY
barter
caravan
cultural diffusion
maritime

NAMES & PLACES
Silk Roads

READING STRATEGY

ANALYZE LANGUAGE USE
When you analyze language use, you note how specific word choices indicate the author's point of view and purpose. As you read the chapter, use concept clusters like this one to analyze the language used to describe the philosophies of Confucianism, Daoism, and Legalism.

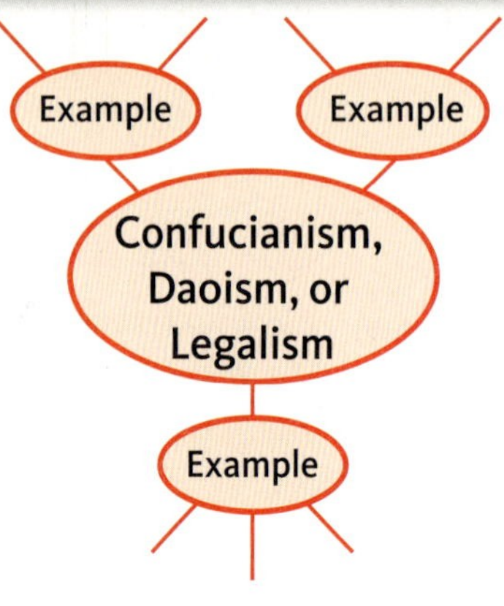
Example
Example
Confucianism, Daoism, or Legalism
Example

福

The lion's dance, a Chinese tradition for more than 1,000 years, is performed during a New Year's celebration in Beijing, China's capital.

1.1 The Geography of Ancient China

At about 240 years of age, the United States may seem like an old civilization, but it's young compared to China. The Chinese civilization has continued for more than 5,000 years. China's geography helped set the stage for the early development of its civilization.

MAIN IDEA

China's deserts, mountains, and rivers helped shape its civilization.

NATURAL BARRIERS

In the beginning of its growth, natural barriers somewhat **isolated**, or cut off, China's civilization from much of the rest of the world. As a result, ancient China developed differently from other early civilizations, with relatively little outside cultural influence. This early isolation helped unify Chinese culture and allowed China to establish a firm foundation for its civilization.

Some of China's natural barriers included vast deserts. The Gobi to the north and the Taklimakan (tah-kluh-muh-KAHN) to the west discouraged invaders and peaceful immigrants alike. The Himalaya, Tian Shan, and Pamir mountain ranges formed a significant obstacle in the west. The waters of the Pacific Ocean, Yellow Sea, and East China Sea on China's east coast separated the region from its nearest neighbors, Japan and Korea.

MAJOR RIVERS

Like the ancient civilizations of Mesopotamia, Egypt, and India, China's civilization arose along fertile river valleys. It developed on the land between China's two great rivers: the **Huang He** (hwahng huh) and the **Chang Jiang** (chahng jyahng).

The 3,395-mile-long Huang He lies in northern China. It is also called the Yellow River because of its high concentration of yellow silt, or fine, fertile soil. The river deposits this silt along its floodplains, creating good farmland. However, the Huang He is unpredictable. Its course, or the direction in which a river flows, has changed many times. Throughout China's history, heavy rains have also caused the river to flood—with deadly results.

At about 4,000 miles long, the Chang Jiang, or Yangtze, in central China is the third longest river in the world. Like the Huang He, the Chang Jiang carries fertile yellow silt. Unlike the Huang He, the Chang Jiang maintains a relatively predictable course. For thousands of years, the river helped unify China by serving as a useful transportation and trade network within its borders.

The area between the two rivers, called the North China Plain, is the birthplace of Chinese civilization. In Chapter 2, you read about the Yangshao culture, which developed along the Huang He. Another important culture in the area was the Longshan, which developed around 3200 B.C. Other advanced Chinese cultures arose in other river valleys. These cultures include the Liangzhu (lyahng-jew) and the Hongshan. Archaeologists have uncovered beautifully carved jade objects from these cultures in other parts of China. All of these ancient cultures contributed to the development of China's unique civilization and to the rise of its earliest rulers: the Shang and the Zhou.

ANCIENT CHINA, 1300–600 B.C.
Shang dynasty, 1300 B.C.
Zhou dynasty, 600 B.C.
Present-day China
70°E
80°E
90°E
100°E
110°E
120°E
130°E
50°N
40°N
30°N
20°N
10°N
Tropic of Cancer
N
S
E
W
TIAN SHAN
Taklimakan Desert
PAMIR
HIMALAYA
GOBI
HONGSHAN CULTURE
Huang He (Yellow R.)
Wei He
NORTH CHINA PLAIN
LIANGZHU CULTURE
Chang Jiang (Yangtze R.)
Xi Jiang
KOREA
JAPAN
Yellow Sea
East China Sea
South China Sea
PACIFIC OCEAN
0 200 400 Miles
0 200 400 Kilometers

REVIEW & ASSESS

1. **READING CHECK** How did China's natural barriers affect the early development of its civilization?

2. **INTERPRET MAPS** Into what large body of water do the Huang He and Chang Jiang flow?

3. **MAKE INFERENCES** What might have been the advantages and disadvantages of China's early isolation from other civilizations?

1.2 Shang and Zhou Dynasties

According to Chinese tradition, a ruler named Yu learned to control the floodwaters of the Huang He and established China's first dynasty, the Xia (shee-AH). But no archaeological evidence of this dynasty has ever been found. The first dynasty for which evidence does exist is the Shang.

MAIN IDEA

The Shang and Zhou dynasties developed many cultural behaviors and beliefs that have become part of Chinese civilization.

CHINA'S FIRST DYNASTY

The **Shang** dynasty emerged along the banks of the Huang He around 1600 B.C. A **dynasty** is a line of rulers from the same family. The Shang developed many cultural behaviors and beliefs that rulers would continue throughout much of Chinese civilization. They established an ordered society with the king at the top, warlords coming next, and farmers at the bottom. The farmers helped advance agriculture in China and grew crops such as millet, wheat, and rice.

The Shang also developed a system of writing using about 3,000 characters. These characters became the basis for modern Chinese writing. They first appeared on **oracle bones**, which are animal bones used to consult the many gods the Shang people worshipped. Priests carved a question on a bone and then heated it. They believed that the pattern of cracks that resulted revealed the gods' answer.

In addition to their gods, the Shang people worshipped the spirits of their dead ancestors. The Shang believed these spirits influenced everything from the king's health to farmers' harvests. To keep the spirits happy, priests conducted special ceremonies, often using beautifully decorated bronze vessels. Shang craftspeople were among the most skilled metalworkers at that time. They also built elaborate tombs for the dead.

THE DYNASTIC CYCLE

In time, the Shang dynasty began to weaken. Around 1045 B.C., the **Zhou** (joh) overthrew the Shang and became China's longest ruling dynasty, lasting about 800 years. The rise of the Zhou also marked the beginning of China's classical period, a time of great social and cultural advances that lasted for about 2,000 years. The Zhou adopted many of the Shang's cultural practices, including ancestor worship and the use of oracle bones. However, the Zhou also developed a concept, known as the **Mandate of Heaven**, to be a guiding force for rulers. They believed that a king could rule only as long as the gods believed he was worthy. The mandate led to a pattern in the rise and fall of dynasties in China called the **dynastic cycle**.

During the first 200 years or so of their rule, the Zhou established a strong central government. However, during the last 500 years of the dynasty, the Zhou divided their lands among local lords. Eventually the ruling lords grew too powerful and independent. They fought among themselves and disobeyed the Zhou kings. By 475 B.C., China had descended into a time of constant war called the **Warring States** period. In 256 B.C., the last Zhou king was finally overthrown.

THE DYNASTIC CYCLE
1 The people believe that the gods approve of the new dynasty.
2 The dynasty weakens.
3 Disasters occur.
4 The people believe that the gods no longer approve of the dynasty.
5 The dynasty is overthrown.
6 A new dynasty re-establishes order.

REVIEW & ASSESS

1. **READING CHECK** What were some of the religious beliefs and practices of the Shang people?

2. **INTEGRATE VISUALS** Based on the diagram and what you've read in the lesson, what do you think happened after the Zhou dynasty fell?

3. **DRAW CONCLUSIONS** How might the Mandate of Heaven have helped the Chinese people accept dynastic changes?

1.3 Chinese Philosophies

"What you do not wish for yourself, do not do to others." Sound familiar? You may have heard this saying before—or another version of it. It's a simple but powerful guide for moral behavior, and it was written 2,500 years ago by a man called Confucius.

MAIN IDEA

Chinese philosophers developed important ideas on how society should be organized.

CONFUCIANISM

As you've read, China began to fall into disorder during the Zhou dynasty. By the time Confucius was born in 551 B.C., China was already experiencing unrest. A teacher and government official, Confucius believed that Chinese society was breaking down as a result of the constant conflict. In an effort to restore order, he taught that people should respect authority and one another.

Confucius' teachings formed the basis of a belief system known as **Confucianism**. His teachings focused on the duties and responsibilities in the following five relationships: father and son, older brother and younger brother, husband and wife, friend and friend, and ruler and subject. Confucius also promoted education, family unity, and **filial piety**, or the respect children owe their parents and ancestors.

Confucius died believing he had failed to restore order to society. Yet after his death, his students collected his teachings in a book called the *Analects*, and Confucian ideas spread. In time Confucius' teachings became required reading for all government officials. Today Confucianism influences millions of people. The philosophy has been a unifying force in Chinese culture and civilization.

DAOISM AND LEGALISM

Another man called Laozi (low-dzuh) is believed to have lived around the same time as Confucius. He founded a belief system called **Daoism**, which emphasizes living in harmony with nature and the Dao. *Dao* means "the Way" and is believed to be the driving force behind everything that exists. Daoists seek order and balance in their lives by merging, or blending, with nature "like drops of water in a stream."

Critical Viewing Followers write comments and questions to Confucius on notes that bear his image. What do the notes suggest about the lasting influence of Confucius?

In contrast with both Confucianism and Daoism, **Legalism** emphasizes order through strong government and strictly enforced laws. Legalism developed after 400 B.C. This philosophy does not have a founder, but Han Feizi (fay-zee) set down its ideas around 260 B.C. He maintained that people were naturally bad and needed to be controlled through the threat of harsh punishment. As you will see, a Chinese dynasty would arise that would govern according to this philosophy.

YIN
dark
cold
soft
water
YANG
light
hot
hard
fire

DAOIST YIN-AND-YANG SYMBOL

This symbol is often used in Daoism to show how seemingly opposite forces form a whole. Daoists believe that everything contains aspects of both yin and yang. The symbol shows some of the aspects of each force.

REVIEW & ASSESS

1. **READING CHECK** What are the basic beliefs of Confucianism?
2. **ANALYZE LANGUAGE USE** What Daoist idea does the phrase "blending with nature like drops of water in a stream" help convey?
3. **COMPARE AND CONTRAST** How does Legalism's attitude toward people's nature differ from that of both Confucianism and Daoism?

1.4 DOCUMENT-BASED QUESTION

Contrasting Belief Systems

You've seen that the suffering caused by weak government and conflict in China led many to think about the best ways to ensure an orderly and peaceful society. As a result, China produced some of the world's greatest philosophical thinkers and writers. Their ideas were so powerful that they not only shaped the future of China for 2,000 years but also continue to influence world thinking today.

Children dressed in traditional clothing perform in China during a celebration of Confucius' birthday.

DOCUMENT ONE

from *Analects of Confucius*, translated by Simon Leys

The *Analects*, a collection of Confucius' ideas, sayings, and stories, was probably recorded by many people over many years. In this passage from the *Analects*, a lord asks Confucius (often referred to as "the Master") how to govern his people.

CONSTRUCTED RESPONSE What details in the passage support the idea that Confucius believed rulers had to set a good example for their people?

Primary Source: Philosophical Teaching

Lord Ji Kang asked: "What should I do in order to make the people respectful, loyal, and zealous [enthusiastic]?" The Master said: "Approach them with dignity and they will be respectful. Be yourself a good son and a kind father, and they will be loyal. Raise the good and train the incompetent [those unable to do a good job], and they will be zealous."

DOCUMENT TWO

from *Dao de Jing*, translated by Stephen Mitchell

The *Dao de Jing* is a key text of Daoism. In general, it stresses inaction over action and silence over words. This passage explains the power of the Dao.

CONSTRUCTED RESPONSE According to the passage, how can powerful people live peaceful, happy lives?

Primary Source: Philosophical Teaching

The Dao never does anything,
yet through it all things are done.
If powerful men and women
could center themselves in it,
the whole world would be transformed
by itself, in its natural rhythms.
People would be content
with their simple, everyday lives,
in harmony, and free of desire.

DOCUMENT THREE

from *Han Feizi: Basic Writings*, translated by Burton Watson

Han Feizi lived from 280 to 233 B.C. He did not believe Confucianism was the answer to the chaos brought about in China during the Warring States period. In this passage from a collection of his writings, Han Feizi describes the role of rulers.

CONSTRUCTED RESPONSE What does the passage suggest about the kind of ruler and government Legalism supported?

Primary Source: Philosophical Teaching

Discard wisdom, forswear [reject] ability, so that your subordinates [those beneath you] cannot guess what you are about. Stick to your objectives and examine the results to see how they match; take hold of the handles of government carefully and grip them tightly. Destroy all hope, smash all intention of wresting [taking] them [the handles of government] from you; allow no man to covet [desire] them.

SYNTHESIZE & WRITE

1. **REVIEW** Review what you have learned about Confucianism, Daoism, and Legalism.
2. **RECALL** On your own paper, write down the main idea expressed in each document.
3. **CONSTRUCT** Write a topic sentence that answers this question: What ideas about leadership do each of the ancient Chinese philosophies convey?
4. **WRITE** Using evidence from the documents, write a paragraph to support your answer from Step 3.

2.1 BIOGRAPHY

SHI HUANGDI

259 B.C. – 210 B.C.

The flames rise higher as officials toss more books onto the fire. Their emperor, Shi Huangdi, has ordered them to burn any writing that contains ideas he doesn't like. High on the list is anything to do with Confucianism. Shi Huangdi is a cruel but skilled ruler—and he intends his dynasty to last for 10,000 generations.

Job: First emperor of China

Home: Kingdom of Qin

FINEST HOUR

After unifying and expanding China, he became its first emperor.

WORST MOMENT

He supposedly died after taking pills he thought would keep him alive forever.

HOBBIES

He built a huge tomb for himself filled with life-size statues of warriors and horses.

GREATEST FEAR

Convinced that his enemies wanted to kill him, he slept in a different apartment in his palace every night.

A RUTHLESS RULER

China's Warring States period finally ended when the leader of the **Qin** (chin) kingdom defeated all other kingdoms around 221 B.C. The leader's name was Ying Zheng, and he united the kingdoms to form an empire. He would come to call himself **Shi Huangdi** (shee hwahng-dee), meaning "first emperor." An **emperor** is the ruler of an empire.

Shi Huangdi established his government based on Legalist ideas. He set up his capital in Xianyang (shee-ahn-yang) and built magnificent palaces in the city to demonstrate his power. The emperor then forced thousands of China's most powerful families to relocate to the capital so he could keep an eye on them.

In addition, Shi Huangdi divided his empire into 36 areas governed by officials he himself had selected. He also followed Legalist ideas by punishing anyone who disagreed with or criticized him. Shi Huangdi is said to have put to death hundreds of Confucian scholars.

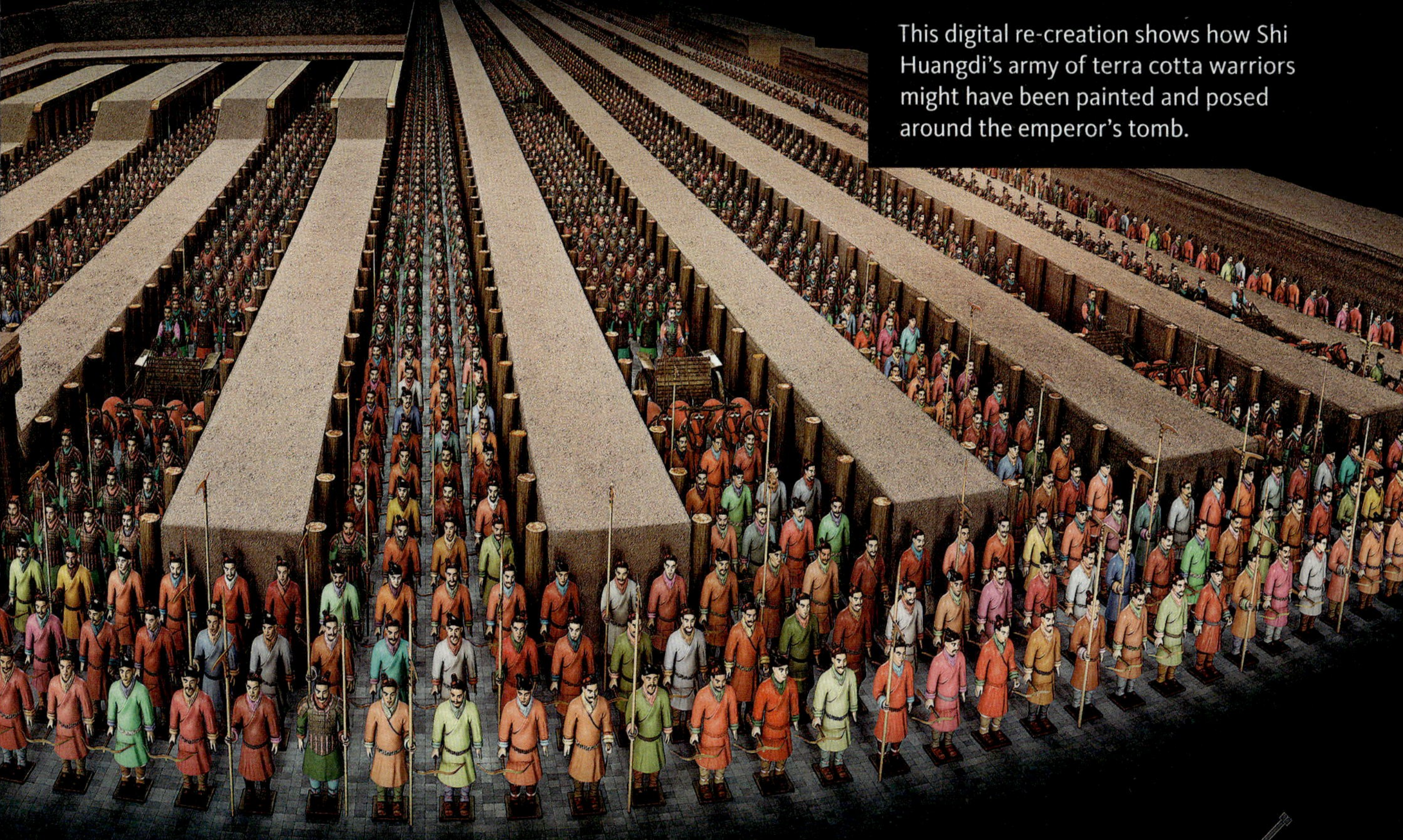

This digital re-creation shows how Shi Huangdi's army of terra cotta warriors might have been painted and posed around the emperor's tomb.

A UNIFIED EMPIRE

Although his methods were cruel, Shi Huangdi brought order to China. He made sure units used to weigh and measure items throughout the empire were standardized, or the same, to ensure that buyers were not being cheated. He also brought a single writing system and currency, or form of money, to China.

As Shi Huangdi conquered new lands and expanded his empire, he made further improvements that united his territory. He had thousands of miles of roads built to link different parts of the empire. These roads were all constructed at the same width. He also built canals and irrigation systems. Shi Huangdi's most famous construction project was the **Great Wall** of China, which you will learn more about in the next lesson. Many historians believe these structures were built by forced labor and funded by high taxes.

Shi Huangdi's rule came to an end when he died in 210 B.C. Throughout his reign, the emperor had feared being murdered by assassins. It seems he believed evil spirits could also attack him in the afterlife. As a result, Shi Huangdi had an army of **terra cotta**, or baked clay, warriors buried beside his tomb to protect him. The burial site probably forms his greatest legacy—an odd twist of fate for a man who spent much of his life trying to cheat death.

REVIEW & ASSESS

1. **READING CHECK** How did Shi Huangdi link the new lands of his empire?
2. **DRAW CONCLUSIONS** What are the benefits of using a single currency within a country?
3. **FORM OPINIONS** What do you think was Shi Huangdi's greatest achievement? Why?

2.2 The Great Wall

Groaning under the weight of another brick, you set it in place on the wall. You didn't volunteer for this work, and you won't be paid very much for it either. It's possible you'll even die working on the wall. But under Shi Huangdi's rule, you do as you're told.

MAIN IDEA

Shi Huangdi began building the Great Wall to keep invaders out of China.

KEEPING OUT INVADERS

While mountains, deserts, and seas protected most of China, part of its northern border was vulnerable, or open to attack. Riding on horseback, nomadic tribes from Central Asia often swept over the border, destroying farms, villages, and towns. Small walls had been built along the border during the Warring States period, but Shi Huangdi decided to join them into one long wall that would stretch over 2,500 miles.

The emperor forced hundreds of thousands of **peasants**, or poor farmers, to build his wall. He also conscripted soldiers and prisoners to perform the backbreaking labor, often in extreme conditions. Many of the laborers died from exhaustion, hunger, and disease. After Shi Huangdi's death, the wall fell into disrepair. However, later rulers built and extended it. In fact, work on the wall continued into the 1600s.

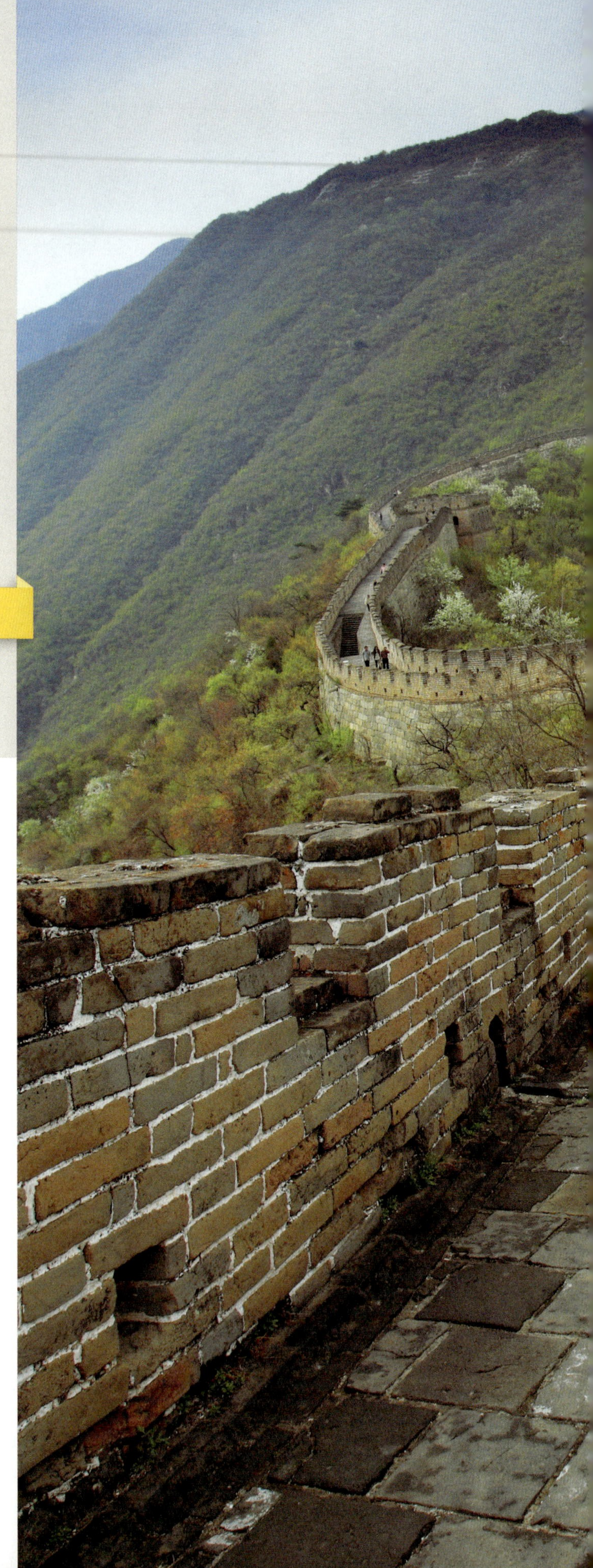

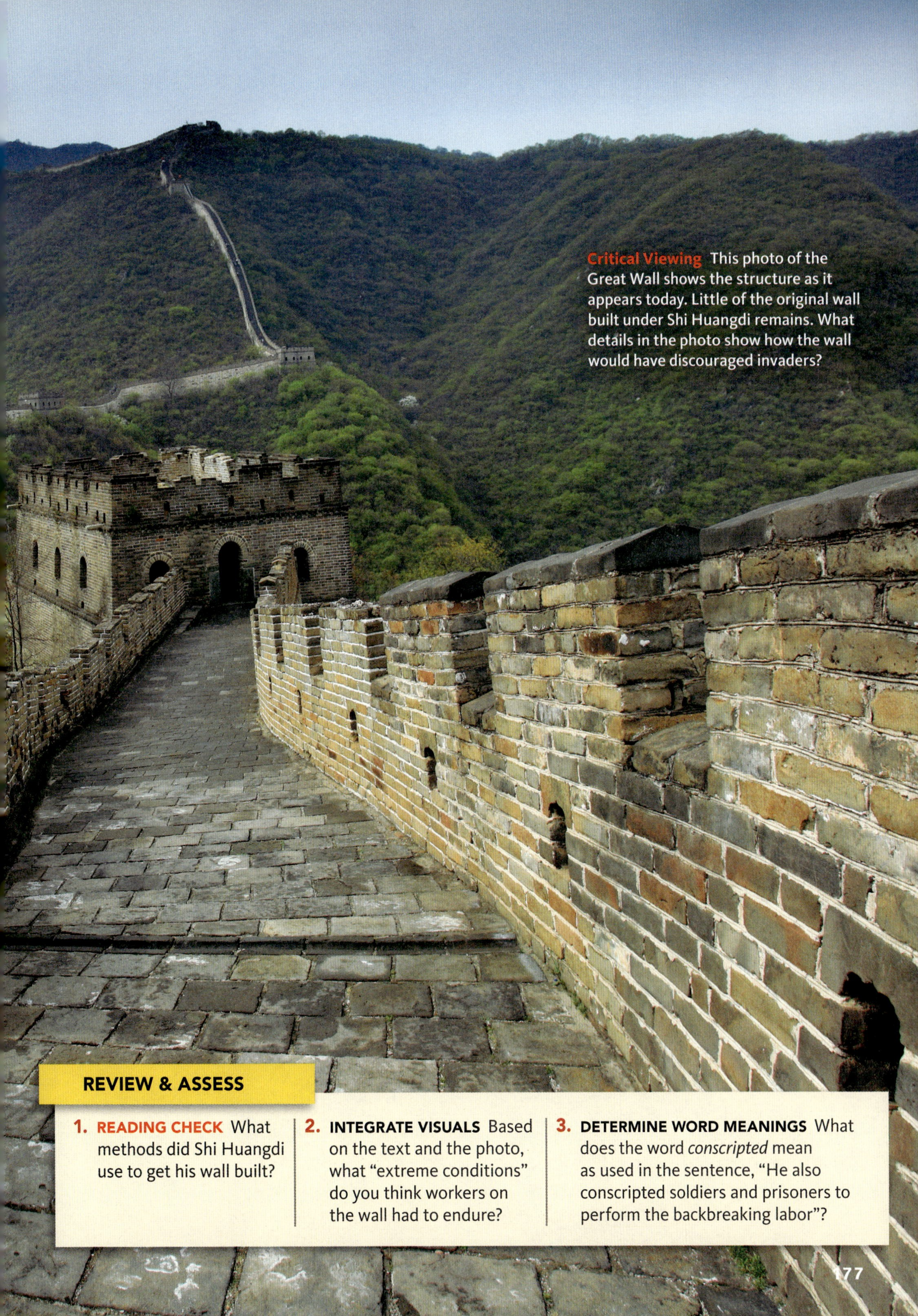

Critical Viewing This photo of the Great Wall shows the structure as it appears today. Little of the original wall built under Shi Huangdi remains. What details in the photo show how the wall would have discouraged invaders?

REVIEW & ASSESS

1. **READING CHECK** What methods did Shi Huangdi use to get his wall built?
2. **INTEGRATE VISUALS** Based on the text and the photo, what "extreme conditions" do you think workers on the wall had to endure?
3. **DETERMINE WORD MEANINGS** What does the word *conscripted* mean as used in the sentence, "He also conscripted soldiers and prisoners to perform the backbreaking labor"?

2.3 MOMENTS IN HISTORY
Terra Cotta Warriors

209 B.C.

On the morning of March 29, 1974, farmers digging a well in a village near Xi'an (shee-ahn), China, made an incredible discovery. They found a body—but one made of baked clay. It was one of an estimated 8,000 life-size terra cotta warriors that had been created to protect Shi Huangdi more than 2,000 years ago. The army of warriors—and their chariots and horses—stood in battle formation, ready to fight Shi Huangdi's battles in the afterlife. Historians estimate that more than 700,000 laborers worked for 38 years to complete the project around 209 B.C. As wonderful as the warriors are, archaeologists believe even greater treasures lie in the emperor's tomb itself, which remains unexplored. What details in the statues help make the warriors look lifelike?

2.4 The Han Dynasty

Maybe you've gotten in trouble for coming to class late, but that predicament would be nothing next to this: In 209 B.C., some farmers arrived late to sign up for their required military service, and they were sentenced to death. The farmers got away and spurred thousands of others to rebel against the Qin dynasty.

MAIN IDEA

Han dynasty rulers reformed the government, expanded the empire, and brought prosperity to China.

GOVERNMENT

After Shi Huangdi died, his son became emperor but proved to be a weak ruler. The farmers who escaped their death sentence fueled a bloody rebellion that brought about the collapse of the Qin dynasty. Rebels struggled for power until Liu Bang (lee-oo bahng), a peasant from the Han kingdom, seized control and began the **Han** dynasty in 202 B.C.

Han emperors introduced practices that were less cruel than those of Shi Huangdi. They lowered taxes and put an end to laws that were especially harsh. They also required lighter punishments for crimes.

You may recall that Shi Huangdi had forced workers to labor for years on his building projects. The Han, on the other hand, had peasants work for only one month per year to build roads, canals, and irrigation systems.

The Han rulers also replaced Legalism with Confucianism and used Confucius' teachings as a guide. Furthermore, they valued the well-educated and obedient officials Confucianism produced. As a result, the officials they appointed had to pass an examination that tested their knowledge of Confucianism. The rulers established their government based on a **bureaucracy**, in which these appointed officials ran the bureaus, or offices.

Later Han rulers included Liu Bang's wife, who came to be known as Empress Lü. Women were not allowed to rule as emperor in ancient China, but Lü found a way around that restriction. After her husband died in 195 B.C., Lü placed their young son on the throne and ruled in his name. When she outlived her son, she held on to power by crowning a couple of infants emperor and ruling in their place. After Lü died in 180 B.C., all of her relatives were executed by a group of rival court officials. They made sure that no other member of her family could rule again.

Emperor Wudi (woo-dee), who ruled from 141 to 87 B.C., was another notable emperor. He used military conquests to expand the empire's boundaries—nearly to the size of present-day China. His reign lasted 54 years, which set a record that would not be broken for more than 1,800 years.

DAILY LIFE

China prospered under the Han dynasty. Many merchants, government workers, and craftspeople lived in large houses in the cities. Like modern cities, these were crowded places filled with restaurants, businesses, and places of entertainment. Some cities had populations of up to 500,000 people.

HAN DYNASTY, 206 B.C.–A.D. 220
70°E
80°E
90°E
100°E
110°E
120°E
130°E
30°N
20°N
10°N
Tropic of Cancer
TIAN SHAN
Taklimakan Desert
PAMIR
HIMALAYA
INDIA
Huang He (Yellow R.)
Wei He
Chang Jiang (Yangtze R.)
Anyang
Luoyang
Ch'ang-an (Xi'an)
Hao
Yellow Sea
East China Sea
South China Sea
PACIFIC OCEAN
N
S
E
W
0 200 400 Miles
0 200 400 Kilometers
Han dynasty
Qin dynasty
Great Wall
Important Han city

Most of the Chinese people, however, were peasants. They lived in small mud houses in villages close to their farms. Some peasants could not afford farm animals and so pulled their plows themselves. They had few possessions and barely produced enough to feed their own families. For the most part, peasants lived on the rice, wheat, and vegetables they grew on their farms.

Perhaps because the Han leaders ruled more wisely than Shi Huangdi had, their dynasty lasted about 400 years—until A.D. 220. Most Chinese people today are proud of their ancient civilization and of the contributions made during the Han dynasty in particular. As a result, many Chinese call themselves "people of the Han" in recognition of the dynasty's great achievements.

REVIEW & ASSESS

1. **READING CHECK** What government reforms did the Han rulers put in place?
2. **INTERPRET MAPS** How does the size of the Qin dynasty compare to that of the Han?
3. **COMPARE AND CONTRAST** How did the lives of poor peasants and rich merchants differ?

THE LEGACY OF CHINA'S EARLY COMPASS

Over the centuries, people have used the technology behind ancient Chinese inventions to develop their own inventions. For example, this Chinese compass from the Han dynasty paved the way for the development of the items shown below. The compass wasn't used for navigation, but it did show direction. The spoon is a special type of magnet that aligns with Earth's poles and can point in the eight main directions marked on the plate.

Sextant from the 1700s
Developed in the 1730s, the sextant measured the angle between a star and the horizon, enabling navigators to determine latitude.

World War II Radio Receiver
This navigational device was used on ships and planes during World War II. The device determines the direction of incoming radio signals.

Present-Day GPS Receiver
A global positioning system, or GPS, device uses satellite information to determine the location of almost any place on or near Earth.

2.5 The Legacy of Ancient China

Ancient China's contributions to world civilization are so many and so varied that it's difficult to know where to begin. But consider that whenever you read a book, you're looking at one of China's most important inventions: paper.

MAIN IDEA

Early Chinese achievements, including inventions, cultural contributions, and ideas, left the world a lasting legacy.

INVENTIONS

Although historians believe the use of paper in China goes back even further, China is officially said to have invented paper in A.D. 105. The invention transformed writing. The ancient Chinese made paper from tree bark, plant fibers, and old rags. It was cheap to produce and easy to write on. The availability of paper allowed ideas to spread farther and faster than ever.

During the Han dynasty, the ancient Chinese also invented the first compass (shown opposite). The Chinese sometimes used the instrument to determine the best location for burials. However, this early compass would eventually lead to the development of the navigational compass, which made exploration of distant lands possible.

As you have learned, most Chinese worked as farmers. Many benefited from early agricultural inventions, such as an improved plow, a wheelbarrow, and a harness that fitted around a horse's neck.

CULTURE AND IDEAS

Not all of ancient China's contributions were strictly practical. One of its most valued inventions is the beautiful textile, or cloth, called **silk**. The Chinese developed the technique for making silk and kept it secret for thousands of years. (Hint: It had something to do with worms.) Demand for silk grew until it became China's most traded good. It is still a prized textile today.

Chinese craftspeople worked in metals as well. Remember reading about the advanced bronze sculptures developed during the Shang dynasty? Hundreds of years later, the Chinese would also teach the world to cast iron. This process involves heating iron until it becomes liquid and then pouring it into a mold to solidify into different shapes.

Finally, Chinese philosophies remain one of ancient China's greatest legacies. One of these philosophies—Confucianism—got a boost from the invention of paper. Confucian ideas were among the first spread by China's new writing material. Today, Confucianism continues to influence thinking, just as Chinese inventions make our lives easier.

REVIEW & ASSESS

1. **READING CHECK** What were a few of the inventions that ancient China contributed to world civilization?
2. **ANALYZE CAUSE AND EFFECT** What impact did agricultural advancements probably have on ancient China's food production and economy?
3. **FORM OPINIONS** Which ancient Chinese invention, cultural development, or idea do you think is the most significant? Explain your reasons.

3.1 The Silk Roads

The desert sun beats down on your back as you trudge wearily across the sand. Peering ahead, all you see is a long line of camels, each loaded with bundles of silk. Still, you know that the profit you'll make from trading these goods will make your journey worthwhile.

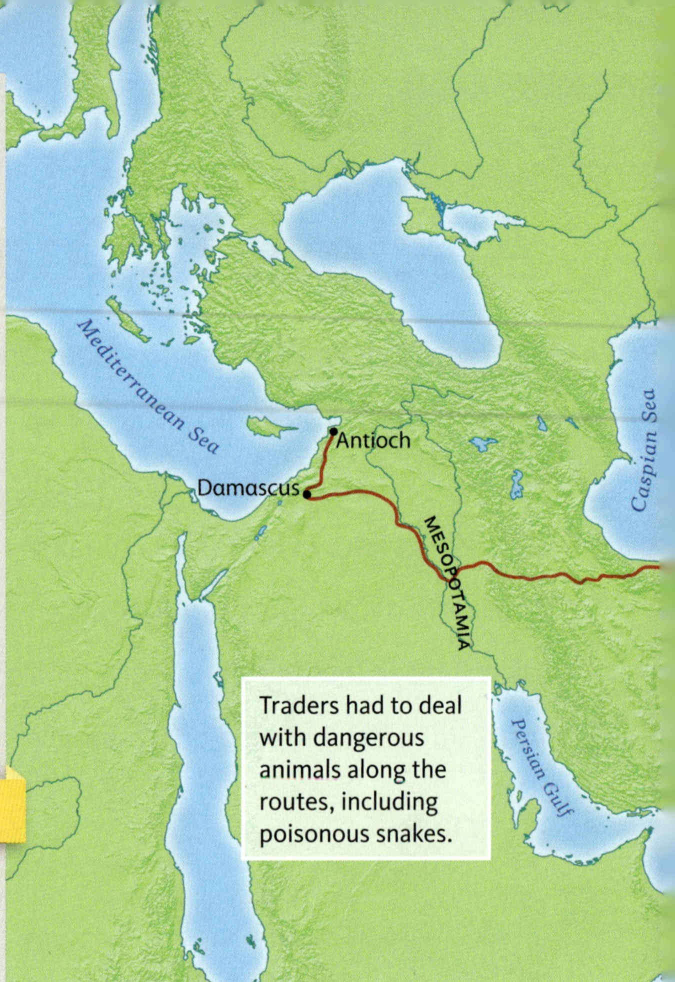

Mediterranean Sea
Antioch
Damascus
MESOPOTAMIA
Caspian Sea
Persian Gulf

Traders had to deal with dangerous animals along the routes, including poisonous snakes.

MAIN IDEA

The Silk Roads were some of the world's most important international trade routes.

CAMELS

Camels sometimes bite and spit, but they're terrific on a long journey—like one along the Silk Roads. They can store fat in their humps and survive without eating or drinking for days. When they get a chance to drink, however, they can take in as much as 25 gallons of water at one time.

ROUTES ACROSS ASIA

You have learned about ancient China's legacy of inventions, culture, and ideas. However, a series of international trade routes called the **Silk Roads** is also one of China's great legacies. The Silk Roads had been well established by 100 B.C., but the name for the routes was coined many centuries later. A German geographer came up with the name because silk was the main good China traded on the routes. The Silk Roads brought great wealth to China and its trading partners.

The Silk Roads began as a network of local overland routes. These eventually joined to form a huge network that connected China with the rest of Asia, Europe, and Africa. The main route stretched more than 4,000 miles and ran from China through Central Asia and Mesopotamia. Other land routes branched off the main road. Some of these routes brought traders to northern India.

The Silk Roads also included **maritime**, or sea, routes. Traders could sail along these routes to the Mediterranean Sea and to Europe. Other maritime routes led across the Indian Ocean to East Africa and across the Pacific Ocean to Korea, Japan, and Southeast Asia.

A DEMANDING JOURNEY

Chinese goods might have traveled thousands of miles, but Chinese traders did not. They traded their goods somewhere around Kashgar, near China's western border. They may have passed

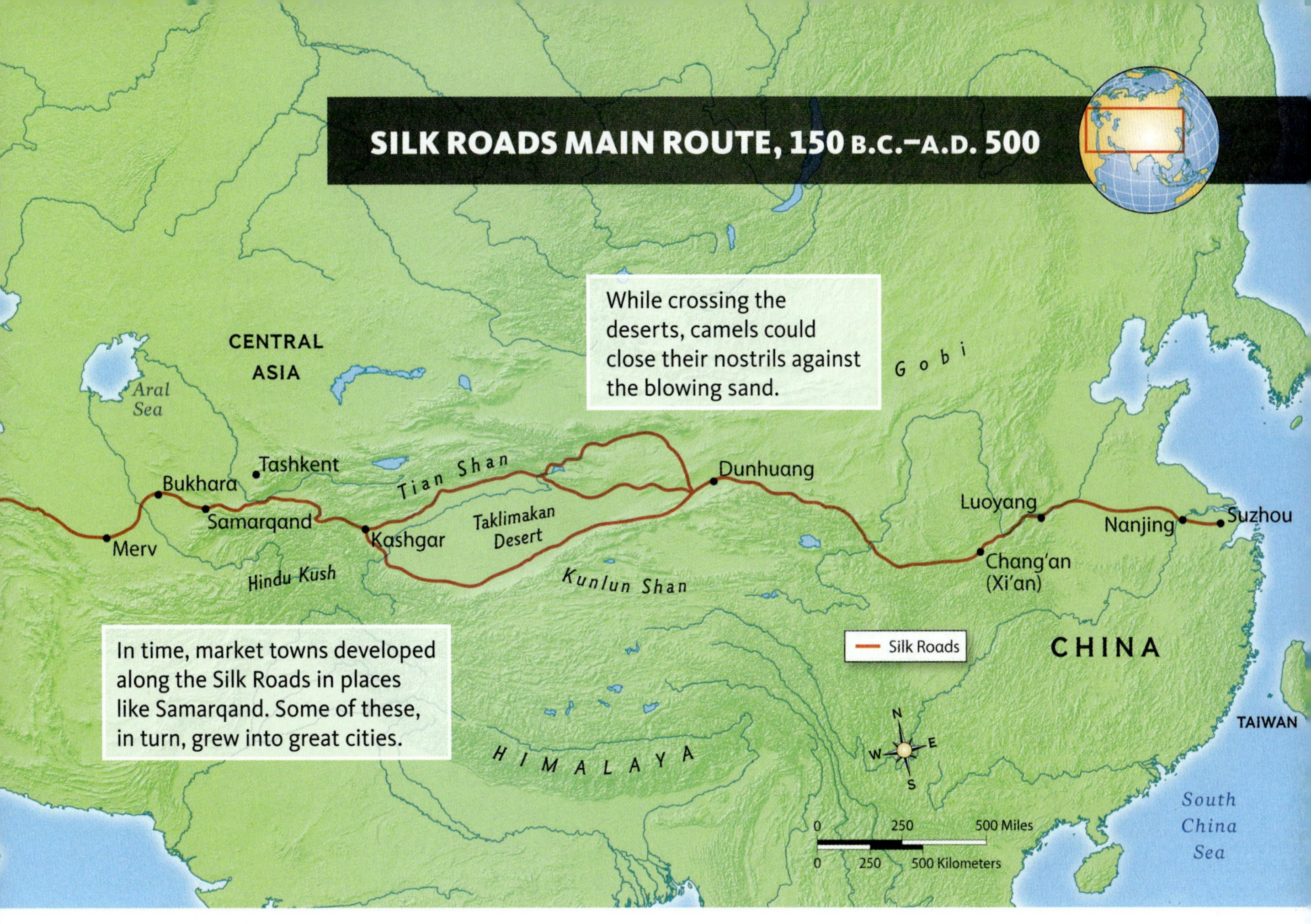
SILK ROADS MAIN ROUTE, 150 B.C.–A.D. 500
While crossing the deserts, camels could close their nostrils against the blowing sand.
In time, market towns developed along the Silk Roads in places like Samarqand. Some of these, in turn, grew into great cities.
CENTRAL ASIA
Aral Sea
Gobi
Tashkent
Bukhara
Samarqand
Merv
Kashgar
Hindu Kush
Tian Shan
Taklimakan Desert
Kunlun Shan
Dunhuang
Luoyang
Nanjing
Suzhou
Chang'an (Xi'an)
Silk Roads
CHINA
TAIWAN
HIMALAYA
South China Sea
N
E
S
W
0 250 500 Miles
0 250 500 Kilometers

their goods along to Central Asian nomads. The nomads, in turn, may have gone on to trade the goods with other merchants from Asia, Africa, and Europe. The goods probably changed hands so many times that no one knew where they originated.

Actually, few traders made the entire journey from one end of the main Silk Roads route to the other. The trip over the rugged terrain would have taken at least six months. At best, traders followed rough paths or tracks. At worst, they scaled ice-covered mountain passes or encountered sandstorms as they crossed scorching-hot deserts.

These difficult conditions made camels the ideal pack animals because they were strong, sure-footed, and tough. They could carry huge loads—about 400 to 500 pounds of goods—for long distances in the driest, hottest weather.

The traders on the Silk Roads usually walked alongside the camels and traveled in groups called **caravans**. They found safety in numbers. The valuable caravans created a tempting target for the bandits and thieves who often lay in wait along the routes. After all, a single camel carried more wealth than most people could possibly imagine.

REVIEW & ASSESS

1. **READING CHECK** What continents were connected by the Silk Roads?

2. **INTERPRET MAPS** Why do you think the main route of the Silk Roads divided in two between the cities of Dunhuang and Kashgar?

3. **MAKE INFERENCES** What impact do you think the Silk Roads had on China's economy?

3.2 Trade on the Silk Roads

In the late 1930s, archaeologists discovered two sealed rooms in Begram, Afghanistan, an ancient city on the Silk Roads. Inside they found decorative bowls from China, ivory statues from India, and glassware from Europe. Stored away about 2,000 years ago, the objects illustrate the worldwide trade that flowed along the Silk Roads.

MAIN IDEA

Many different goods and ideas from three continents were traded on the Silk Roads.

GOODS

As you have learned, silk was China's chief trade good. Production of the fabric was not easy, though. Silk is made from the cocoons, or protective coverings, of silkworms, which live only on mulberry trees. Chinese workers had to remove strands of silk from the cocoons by hand and spin them into thread. Even so, the process was worth the trouble. Demand for the rare fabric allowed Chinese merchants to charge high prices for it. In fact, silk was so valuable that the Chinese government sometimes used it to pay its soldiers.

In addition to silk, China traded paper, highly polished decorative items called lacquerware, and objects made of iron or bronze. In return for these goods, Chinese merchants often sought gold, silver, and olive oil. One of the items the Chinese especially valued was Central Asian horses.

Market towns sprang up all along the Silk Roads. Major market towns in China included Chang'an, where the main route began, and Kashgar. A dazzling variety of items, including Central Asian rugs, Indian spices, and European wool, landed in the stalls in these towns. Traders from these and many other places used different currencies. Many had no money at all. As a result, the traders often **bartered**, or exchanged, items for other goods.

INVENTIONS AND IDEAS

Goods were not all that passed along the Silk Roads. With so many traders from so many parts of the world, the routes served as a network for the exchange of inventions and ideas as well. You have already learned that the process by which ideas spread from one culture to another is called **cultural diffusion**. By this process, Chinese ideas about papermaking, metalwork, and farming techniques began to spread beyond China's borders. In time, these ideas and inventions reached as far as Western Europe.

China also absorbed new ideas. Chief among these was Buddhism. You might remember that Buddhism began in India around 500 B.C. Indian merchants introduced Buddhist ideas to Chinese traders and even established Buddhist shrines along the Silk Roads.

Buddhism's ideas about ending suffering appealed to the Chinese, and eventually the religion became an important part of Chinese life. Many Chinese blended its practices with Confucianism. From China, Buddhism would spread throughout East Asia. Other ideas also reached China, including Greek and Indian styles in sculpture, painting, and temple building. All of these ideas enriched Chinese culture and civilization.

Critical Viewing It took artists more than 90 years to carve this Giant Buddha in southwest China, the largest carved stone Buddha in the world. What qualities does the Buddha's face convey?

REVIEW & ASSESS

1. **READING CHECK** What were some of the goods and ideas exchanged on the Silk Roads?
2. **DRAW CONCLUSIONS** Why do you think Buddhism's ideas about ending suffering might have appealed to the ancient Chinese?
3. **MAKE INFERENCES** Why were Chinese traders able to demand high prices for their silk?

3.3 GOODS FROM THE SILK ROADS

Imagine a market filled with delicate silk and gold and jewels that catch the sunlight. Rows of foods, including grapes, olive oil, spices, and honey, tempt you as you stroll along the stalls. Horses and camels stare back at you with bored expressions as they wait under a tent for potential buyers. Because of the long distances, difficulties, and dangers along the Silk Roads, only the finest and most expensive goods were traded. Very few of the actual goods traded have survived, but as you can see, the types of wares exchanged can still dazzle the eye. Who probably bought these goods in the markets?

Rugs and Blankets Nomads from Central Asia used wool from their sheep and camels to weave the rugs and blankets they traded.

Ivory Asian traders bartered ivory plaques, like this one, carved from elephant tusks.

Grapes European merchants traded grapes, which were used to make wine.

Spices
Spices were used to flavor food but were also believed to cure many diseases.
The design on a rug traded on the Silk Roads often represented the nomadic tribe to which the weaver belonged.
The spices shown here include cinnamon, coriander, and pepper. In ancient times before refrigeration, these and other spices were used to mask the flavor of food that had spoiled.
Silk
A pound of silk was as valuable as a pound of gold on the Silk Roads.
Pottery
Korean celadon, like this pottery jug, probably traveled to China over the maritime routes.
Honey
Northern European merchants sold honey on the Silk Roads. This image shows honey in a honeycomb.

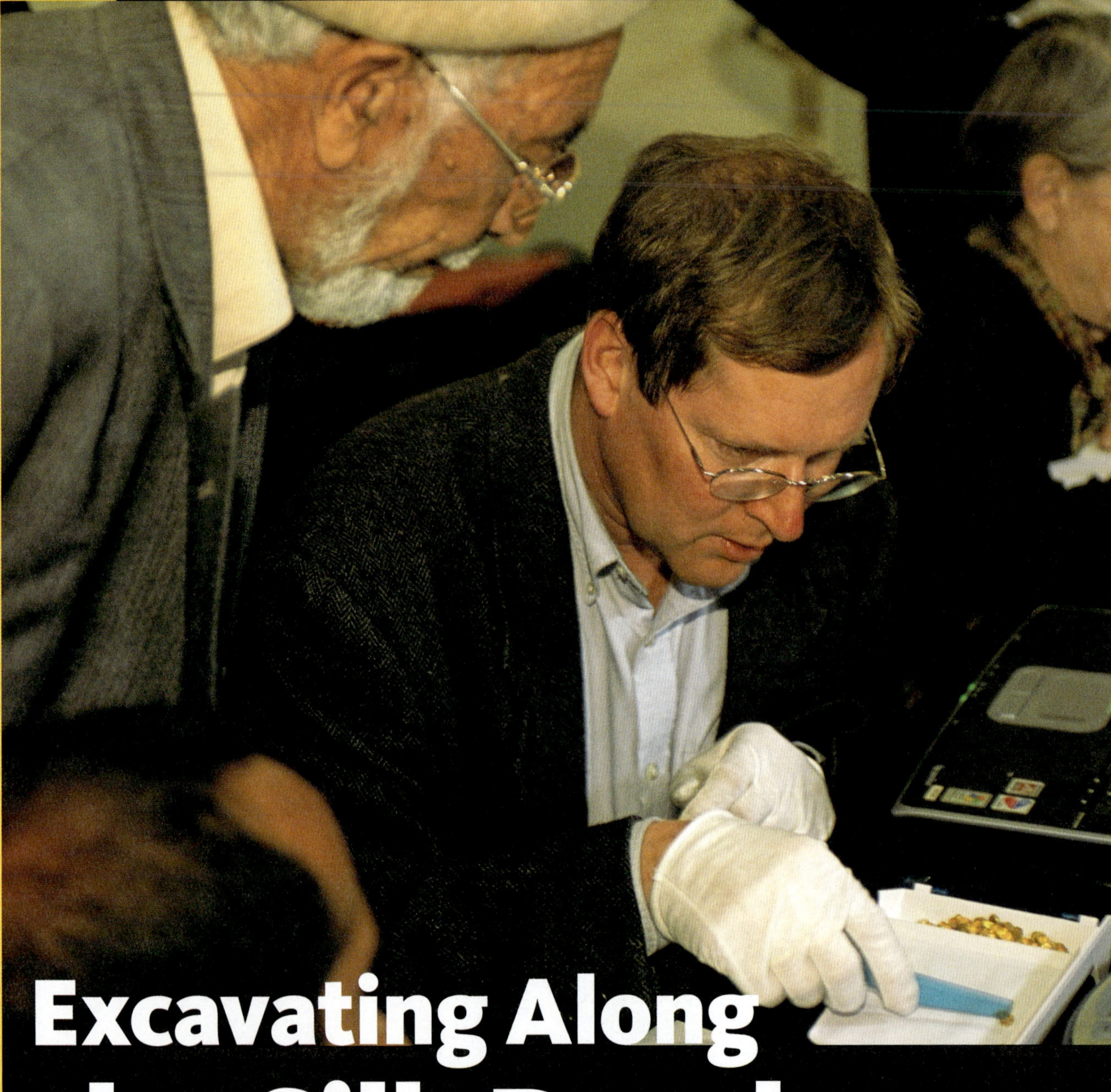

Excavating Along the Silk Roads

Fredrik Hiebert likes to challenge accepted ideas. "As an archaeologist," he says, "my main job is to try to make the textbooks go out of date. History is a living thing, and we're always rewriting it." Some of Hiebert's major excavations, or archaeological digs, have been in Turkmenistan, a country in Central Asia. Based on his discoveries there, Hiebert has concluded that traders began traveling along the Silk Roads about 4,000 or 5,000 years ago—much earlier than historians had once thought.

^ Fredrik Hiebert's study of the ancient trade routes led him to Afghanistan, where he uncovered a golden treasure. Here he examines some of the artifacts.

MAIN IDEA

Archaeologist Fredrik Hiebert's explorations have uncovered lost gold and challenged ideas about when trading began on the Silk Roads.

CONNECTED CULTURES

National Geographic Explorer Fredrik Hiebert has been conducting excavations at Silk Roads sites—like cities in Turkmenistan—for more than 20 years. "Historians thought the Silk Roads had emerged about 100 B.C.," says Hiebert. "But when we dug deeper into Silk Roads cities, we found they'd been built on much older Bronze Age settlements, which contained artifacts from as far away as India and Mesopotamia. This means that long-distance trade along the Silk Roads took place 2,000 years before we'd thought it had started."

Necklace from the Bactrian Hoard

The realization didn't surprise Hiebert. He believes that ancient cultures were always connected. "It's easy to argue that ancient cultures were isolated by geography and the lack of transport," he claims, "but that really didn't stop people from traveling and trading. They just did it more slowly."

LOST GOLD

Hiebert's explorations of the Silk Roads have also taken him to Afghanistan, which borders Turkmenistan in the south. In 1988, a Russian archaeologist told him about 21,000 pieces of ancient gold that he'd excavated ten years earlier near the Afghan region of Bactria. He later showed Hiebert photos of the collection, which came to be known as the Bactrian Hoard. The gold had belonged to nomads who herded and traded along the Silk Roads around the first century B.C. The collection was placed in a museum in Afghanistan. However, after war erupted in the country in 1978, the gold disappeared. The Russian archaeologist believed it was lost forever.

"Fast-forward to 2003 when I heard rumors of ancient gold hidden in the Afghan presidential palace," Hiebert continues the story. "I thought: Could it be the Bactrian Hoard?" Working with the National Geographic Society, Hiebert persuaded the Afghan authorities to let him open the safes where he thought the treasure might be found. Inside were all 21,000 pieces of gold, including a necklace, shown here, that Hiebert recognized from the photos he had seen of the hoard.

"Against all odds it had survived intact, thanks to a few dedicated museum workers who had kept it secret for so many years," Hiebert says. His study of the gold revealed more evidence of cultural connections. The items were imitations of Chinese, Greek, and Indian artifacts traded on the Silk Roads. The gold is beautiful and valuable beyond measure, but that's not what most interests Hiebert. As he says, "We don't actually search for treasure. We search for knowledge—that's our real gold."

REVIEW & ASSESS

1. **READING CHECK** When does Hiebert believe trade along the Silk Roads first took place?
2. **IDENTIFY MAIN IDEAS AND DETAILS** What evidence did Hiebert find to support his ideas about cultural connections on the Silk Roads?
3. **ANALYZE LANGUAGE USE** What does Hiebert suggest about knowledge when he compares it to gold?

CHAPTER 7

Review

VOCABULARY

Complete each of the following sentences using one of the vocabulary words from the chapter.

1. During China's early development, physical features such as mountains and deserts helped *isolate* China.
2. The Han dynasty's government was based on a ______ run by appointed officials.
3. Rather than sell silk for money, Chinese merchants would ______ it for gold.
4. According to the ______, a dynasty is overthrown once it has lost the approval of the gods.
5. Many historians believe that hundreds of thousands of ______ were forced to build the Great Wall.
6. Confucius taught that children should show their parents ______.
7. Traders on the Silk Roads often traveled in groups called ______.

READING STRATEGY

8. **ANALYZE LANGUAGE USE** If you haven't already, complete your concept clusters to analyze language used to describe Confucianism, Daoism, and Legalism. Then answer the question.

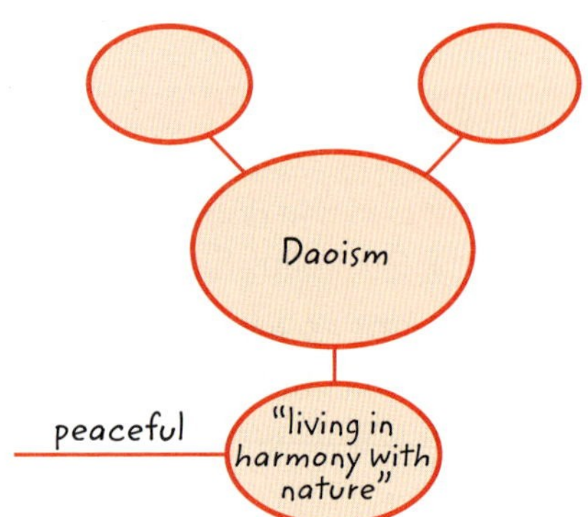
Daoism
peaceful
"living in harmony with nature"

Based on the author's choice of words, how would you describe the overall theme of each philosophy?

MAIN IDEAS

Answer the following questions. Support your answers with evidence from the chapter.

9. Why did civilization in ancient China first develop with relatively little cultural influence from the outside world? **LESSON 1.1**
10. What was the Mandate of Heaven? **LESSON 1.2**
11. How did Shi Huangdi organize his empire? **LESSON 2.1**
12. Why did Shi Huangdi begin building the Great Wall? **LESSON 2.2**
13. How did Han rulers bring Confucianism into their government? **LESSON 2.4**
14. What were the benefits of traveling on the Silk Roads in camel caravans? **LESSON 3.1**
15. How did trade on the Silk Roads encourage the process of cultural diffusion? **LESSON 3.2**

CRITICAL THINKING

Answer the following questions. Support your answers with evidence from the chapter.

16. **SUMMARIZE** How did China establish one of the world's oldest continuous civilizations?
17. **DRAW CONCLUSIONS** How did the dynastic cycle help ensure the rise of new dynasties throughout China's early history?
18. **MAKE INFERENCES** Why do you think Shi Huangdi was drawn to Legalist ideas rather than Confucian ideas?
19. **COMPARE AND CONTRAST** What did the governments under the Qin and Han dynasties have in common? How did they differ?
20. **MAKE INFERENCES** What role do you think the Silk Roads played in the Han dynasty's prosperity?
21. **YOU DECIDE** Do you think Shi Huangdi was an effective emperor? Why or why not? Support your opinion with evidence from the chapter.

INTERPRET MAPS

Study the map showing the spread of Buddhism. Then answer the questions that follow.

THE SPREAD OF BUDDHISM
JAPAN
KOREA
East China Sea
CHINA
Huang He (Yellow R.)
Chang Jiang (Yangtze R.)
Indus R.
Brahmaputra R.
Ganges R.
Tropic of Cancer
PACIFIC OCEAN
30°N
150°E
30°E
Arabian Sea
INDIA
SOUTHEAST ASIA
Khmer
Mekong R.
Bay of Bengal
South China Sea
0 400 800 Miles
0 400 800 Kilometers
Origin of Buddhism
Present-day boundaries shown
60°E
90°E
120°E
Equator 0°
N
E
S
W

22. Why do you think Buddhism spread to China before Korea and Japan?

23. What other region shown on the map was influenced by Buddhism?

ANALYZE SOURCES

Study this bronze statue of a flying horse, one of the finest examples of art from the Han dynasty. Then answer the question.

24. What details in the statue make it appear as if the horse is actually flying?

WRITE ABOUT HISTORY

25. ARGUMENT Which Chinese philosophy might be most effective as the basis for a governing policy? Choose one of the philosophies—Confucianism, Daoism, or Legalism—and create a bulleted list of arguments you might use in a debate on the subject.

TIPS

- Take notes from the lessons about each philosophy and its application in ancient Chinese government.
- Study the excerpt from each philosophy's teachings in Lesson 1.4.
- Consider what each philosophy offers governments and the people they rule.
- Use vocabulary terms from the chapter.
- Organize your ideas into a bulleted list of arguments. Include points that might counter, or answer, arguments proposed by the opposing side.

NATIONAL GEOGRAPHIC

ON **LOCATION** WITH

Christopher THORNTON

NATIONAL GEOGRAPHIC LEAD PROGRAM OFFICER, RESEARCH, CONSERVATION, AND EXPLORATION

Check out more on myNGconnect

Christopher Thornton directs excavations at the archaeological site of Bat in Oman. He has uncovered information that is providing new insights into the social history of the region.

EARLY PASSION

I'd always planned to major in chemistry in college, but in my freshman year, I took a seminar on archaeological chemistry and got hooked! From that moment on, archaeology became my passion and my career.

Today I specialize in late prehistory in Southwest Asia, from the beginning of agriculture to the rise of empires. I love working in this region because, while people's lives have been modernized, their cultures remain fairly traditional. You get a sense of "the old ways" while still enjoying hot showers!

Chris Thornton works near a 4,500-year-old Bronze Age monument in northwestern Oman at the site of Bat.

DIGGING FOR CLUES

Because this region had very limited literacy during the late prehistoric and early historic periods, it needs an archaeologist's eye to investigate and figure out what was going on then. One of the key questions I'm trying to answer is how and why people living in harsh regions like present-day Oman managed to create relatively large settlements 4,000 years ago but, 1,000 or so years later, were content to live in much smaller areas. A clue lies in copper.

Mesopotamian texts from the Bronze Age refer to modern Oman as "Magan," noting that it was then a major producer of copper for the entire region. Most archaeologists believed that the people of Magan were being exploited by traders from Mesopotamia and the Indus Valley. However, for nine years, my team and I have been excavating a site called Bat in northwestern Oman. In the course of our digs, we've discovered not only evidence of copper production, but also indications of the local use of copper in tools, weapons, and jewelry. This suggests that despite the harsh geography of the region, the people of Magan were a very important part of the Bronze Age economic trade networks that led to the rise of cities. This puts a whole new slant on the history of the region.

Now we hope to find clues that will help us understand how the adoption of farming led to early settled villages in Magan, and how these eventually grew into the large centers we find by 2200 B.C. These are the kind of answers we keep digging for.

WHY STUDY HISTORY ?

“History helps us *to understand the similarities* between apparently different nations, peoples, and cultures. Studying history lets us look back on all that we have accomplished and to consider where we are going now!” —Christopher Thornton

NATIONAL GEOGRAPHIC

China's Ancient Lifeline

BY IAN JOHNSON

Adapted from "China's Ancient Lifeline," by Ian Johnson, in *National Geographic*, May 2013

Barges sailing the Grand Canal have knit China together for 14 centuries. They carried grain, soldiers, and ideas between the economic heartland in the south and the political capitals in the north.

Old Zhu, as everyone calls him, is a modern barge captain. Barge captains live by tough calculations that determine whether they get rich or are ruined. One captain said, "The product owners set the price, the moneylenders set the interest, and the government officials set the fees. All we can do is nod and continue working."

On paper, the Grand Canal runs 1,100 miles between Beijing and the southern city of Hangzhou. But for nearly forty years, part of its course has been too dry for shipping. Today, the waterway's main commercial section is the 325 miles from Jining to the Yangtze.

Emperor Yang of the Sui dynasty built the original canal system. Ancient China's main rivers ran west to east, and he needed a way to move rice from south to north to feed his armies. The emperor forced one million workers to build the canal. It took six years to complete and many workers died, but goods began to flow. The Grand Canal also moved culture. Emperors inspecting the canal took some local customs back to the capital.

Along one section, Old Zhu pointed and said, "That's the old Grand Canal, or what's left of it," pointing to a channel about 15 feet wide curving between a small island and the bank. Today, local governments aim to boost tourism and development by beautifying the canal. But beautification can also destroy. In Yangzhou, the makeover required leveling nearly every canal-side building.

In 2005, a small group of citizens campaigned for the Grand Canal to become a UNESCO World Heritage site. "Every generation wants the next generation to look at its monuments," said Zhu Bingren, who co-wrote the proposal. "But if we wipe out the previous generations' work, what will following generations think of us?"

For more from National Geographic
Check out "Faces of the Divine" on myNGconnect

UNIT INQUIRY: WRITE A CREATION MYTH

In this unit, you learned about the development of early civilizations in Mesopotamia, Egypt, India, and China. Based on your understanding of the text, what crucial roles did geography and natural resources play in the development of early civilizations? What other factors were important to their growth and longevity?

ASSIGNMENT Write a creation myth for one of the civilizations you learned about in this unit. The narrator of your creation myth should be a geographic feature or a natural resource—such as a river—that was vital to the civilization's development. Be prepared to present your creation myth to the class and explain your choice of narrator.

Plan As you write your creation myth, think about the essential roles geography and natural resources played in that civilization's development. To describe the civilization, answer from the narrator's point of view the questions *Who? What? Where? When? Why?* and *How?* Try to incorporate these descriptions in your myth. You might want to use a graphic organizer to help organize your thoughts. ▶

Produce Use your notes to produce detailed descriptions of the factors that were important in the development of the civilization you selected. Begin your creation myth with an engaging introduction to capture your audience's attention.

Present Choose a creative way to present your myth to the class. Consider one of these options:

- Create a multimedia presentation using illustrations or photographs of the civilization's geography to produce a sense of place.
- Dress in costume and play the role of an ancient storyteller for an oral presentation of the myth.
- Illustrate cover art featuring the narrator of the creation myth.

Who?	______________________
What?	______________________
Where?	______________________
When?	______________________
Why?	______________________
How?	______________________

RAPID REVIEW
UNIT 2
EARLY CIVILIZATIONS
TOP TEN

1. Farming in the fertile lands of Mesopotamia led to the emergence of city-states such as Sumer and Ur.
2. The fertile farmland along the Nile River enabled the development of ancient Egyptian civilization.
3. Judaism was the first monotheistic religion.
4. Several important religions developed in India, including Hinduism and Buddhism.
5. Ancient China spread innovative forms of government, philosophy, technology, writing, and art via trade routes.

6-10. **NOW IT'S YOUR TURN** Complete the list with five more things to remember about early civilizations.

WHY STUDY HISTORY ?

TO LEARN ABOUT THE BUILDING BLOCKS OF CIVILIZATION

In Units 1 and 2, you've learned about the origins of culture and how the building blocks of civilization allowed humans to move from individuals struggling to survive to groups creating a life together. All early civilizations faced the same challenges—and the urge to establish an identity was key to their survival.

The record of human occupation involves the study of stones, bones, and artifacts that go back hundreds of thousands of years. Archaeologists rely on that record to learn about the way we've lived on this earth. Artifacts represent people's identity. When an artifact is looted, or excavated illegally, we lose the context for that artifact—where it was found and who created it. It becomes lost to history. The human record is a non-renewable resource that can never be replaced.

Fred Hiebert

Watch the Why Study History video

WHAT COMES NEXT? PREVIEW UNITS 3–7

3

ACROPOLIS

GREEK CIVILIZATION

Learn how the Greeks left a legacy in government, art, and architecture that would have an impact on all civilizations.

4

POMPEII

THE WORLD OF THE ROMANS

See how the Roman developments in government, engineering, and religion continue to affect your life today.

5

MOSAIC, HUQOQ, ISRAEL

BYZANTINE AND ISLAMIC CIVILIZATIONS

Explore the judicial and artistic contributions of the Byzantine civilizations and the rise of Islamic traditions and empires.

KEY TAKEAWAYS UNITS 1 AND 2

PATTERNS IN HISTORY: SIMILAR DEVELOPMENTS ACROSS LOCATIONS

All centers of civilization develop the same basic structures:

- the beginnings of social organization that lead to governments
- origins of religion as a way to make sense of the world
- the development of crafts that lead to technology
- basic economies that lead to today's economy

GOVERNMENT

Advancements include the rise of dynasties, such as those in Egypt and China; the creation of laws, including Hammurabi's Code; and the building of cities.

MOVEMENT OF PEOPLE AND IDEAS

People adapt to new places, environments, and climates, from the earliest exodus from Africa to migrations in India.

TRADE

Peoples and cultures gradually intermingle, a first step toward global citizenship.

ARTISTIC EXPRESSION

Cave art, including the handprints shown here, become early expressions of identity.

TECHNOLOGY & INNOVATION

Tools, settlements, and the development of agriculture increase chances of survival.

6
DHOW

AFRICAN CIVILIZATIONS

Learn how African peoples successfully adapted to the extreme environments in which they lived to found great trading civilizations.

7
AZTEC SKULLS

AMERICAN CIVILIZATIONS

Study the sophisticated cultures that developed in the Americas and their similarities and differences to earlier cultures.

AS YOU READ ON

History is more than just one fact after another. Keep in mind the key takeaways from Units 1 and 2. Be sure to ask "how" and "why," and not just "what." Watch as the human story continues with the civilizations that may be most familiar to you: the Greek, Roman, Byzantine, and Islamic civilizations.

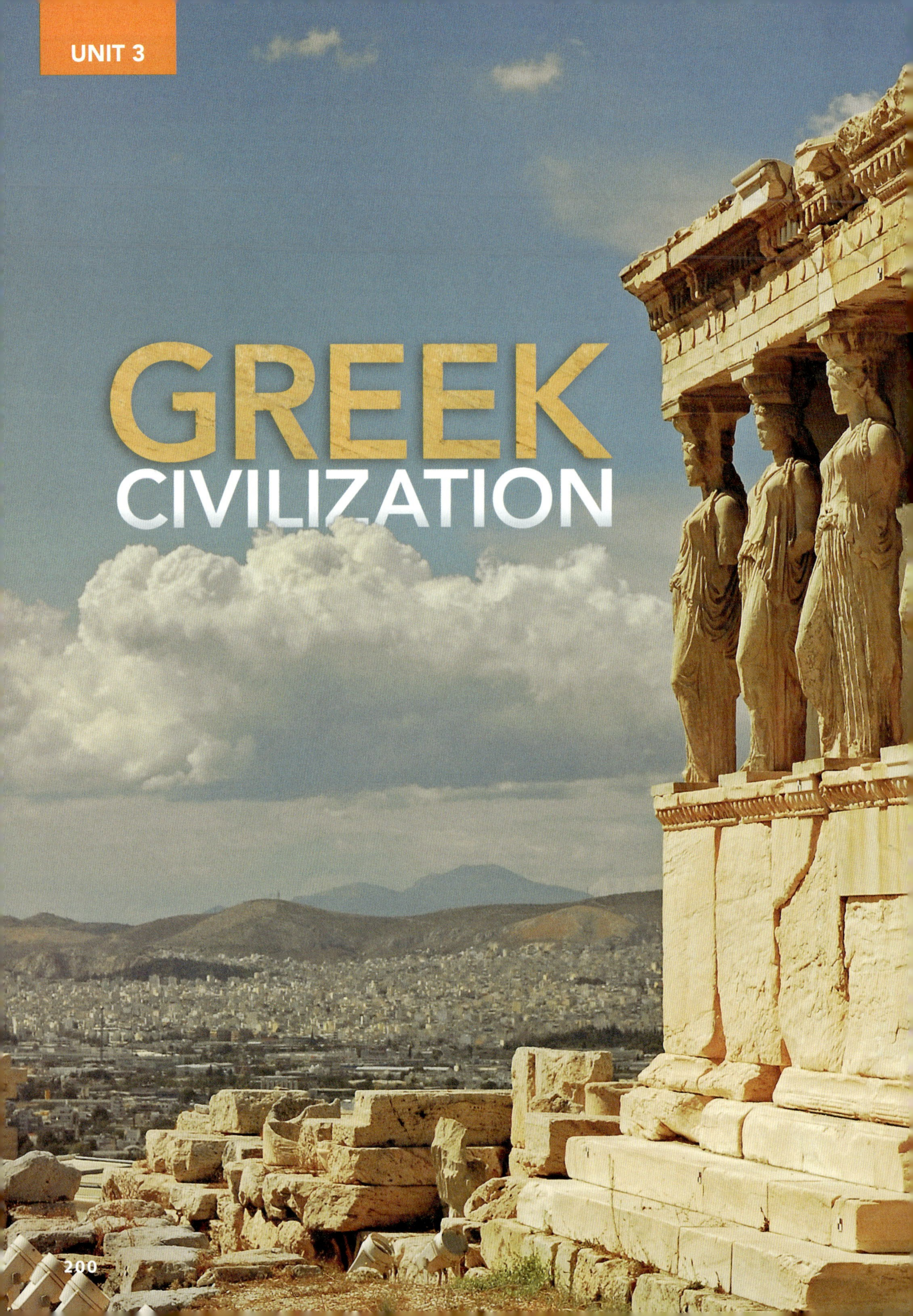
UNIT 3
GREEK
CIVILIZATION

ON **LOCATION** WITH

William Parkinson

Archaeologist

All around the world, before there were governments and formal countries, most people lived in small farming villages. As individual societies grew, they also became more complex. The city-states that emerged in Greece between the ninth and sixth centuries B.C. developed as distinct cultures. However, they were united by certain characteristics, too. I'm William Parkinson, and I work with the Field Museum in Chicago and National Geographic. Welcome to the world of Greek civilization!

< **CRITICAL VIEWING** Built during the Peloponnesian Wars, the Caryatid Porch of the Erechtheion is lined with statues of maidens. It is one of the most beautiful features of the Acropolis. What function do these statues serve in the porch?

UNIT 3
TIME LINE OF WORLD EVENTS

Greek Civilization

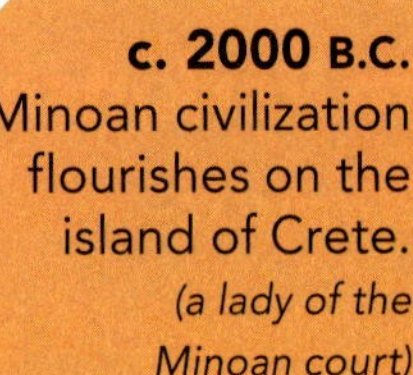

c. 2000 B.C.
Minoan civilization flourishes on the island of Crete.
(a lady of the Minoan court)

c. 1450 B.C.
Mycenaean civilization thrives on the Greek mainland and takes control of Crete, ending Minoan civilization.
(Lion Gate of Mycenae)

2000 B.C.

1500 B.C.

The World

c. 2000 B.C.
EUROPE
Stonehenge is built in England.

1790 B.C.
ASIA
Hammurabi's Code is issued in the Babylonian Empire.

1300 B.C.
ASIA
The kingdom of Israel is established by the Hebrews.

1279 B.C.
AFRICA
Ramses II begins 66-year reign in Egypt.

1200 B.C.
AMERICAS
Olmec culture rises in the Americas.
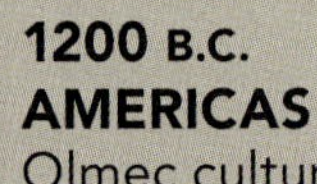
(Olmec stone head)

COMPARE TIME LINES

What happened in the world just before democracy was established in Athens?

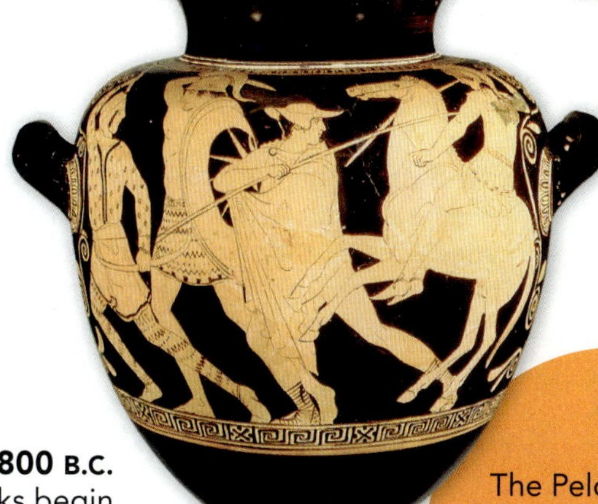

334 B.C.
Alexander the Great enters Asia Minor in order to conquer Persia. He dies in 323 B.C., marking the end of the Classic Age. *(gold coin with Alexander's profile)*

431 B.C.
The Peloponnesian War between Athens and Sparta begins. *(Greek pot with scene from Peloponnesian War)*

800 B.C.
Greeks begin using an alphabet. Literature is written down, including the *Iliad* and *Odyssey*.

1000 B.C.

c. 750 B.C.
Phoenicia develops into wealthy city-states, including the colony of Carthage.

c. 500 B.C.
The first democracy is established in Athens.

1100s B.C.
ASIA
The Zhou dynasty rules China.
(Zhou vessel)

500 B.C.

509 B.C.
EUROPE
The Roman Republic is established.

551 B.C.
Confucius is born in China.

ANCIENT GREECE c. 500 B.C.

The area colored orange on the map may look like a small and fragmented collection of peninsulas and islands, but these areas of land formed one of the most sophisticated cultures and civilizations the world has ever known: the civilization of ancient Greece. Not even its geography stood in Greece's way. Greek traders used the waters of the Mediterranean to secure and control trade routes. Mountains made travel and communication difficult, but independent city-states formed around them. The city-states are labeled with dots on the map. In the city-state called Athens, a form of government developed that would change the world: democracy.

What empire might have challenged Greek power in the region?

Bosporus
Sea of Marmara
Dardanelles
Mount Olympus
GREECE
PERSIAN EMPIRE
Aegean Sea
Ionian Sea
Delphi
Thebes
Megara
Corinth
Athens
Mycenae
Argos
Olympia
Sparta
Delos
Ephesus
Miletus
Sea of Crete
Knossos
Crete
Mediterranean Sea
0 25 50 75 100 kilometers
0 25 50 75 100 miles

THE OLYMPICS

The first Olympic Games took place in 775 B.C. and lasted one day. Today's games include 28 different sports in summer and 7 in winter and last a couple of weeks. The early games had just a few events, not all of which are played today. You can read about the original events in the early Greek Olympics below. Emperor Theodosius banned the games in A.D. 393, calling them a "pagan cult." The first modern Olympics took place in 1896.

Running Contestants ran the 200-meter dash, 400-meter dash, and long distance events.

Jumping Athletes carried stone weights that they threw at the end of their jump to increase their distance.

Discus Athletes tossed a heavy disk made of stone, or later, of heavy metal.

Boxing Athletes fought one another using wrapped straps around their hands to strengthen their punches.

Equestrian Horse races and chariot-driven races took place in the Hippodrome, an ancient Greek stadium.

Pentathlon The pentathlon included five events: long jump, javelin throw, discus throw, foot race, and wrestling.

Pankration This event was a blend of wrestling and boxing and had few rules.

CHAPTER 8

ANCIENT GREECE

2000 B.C. – 480 B.C.

SECTION 1
EARLY GREECE

KEY VOCABULARY
- acropolis
- agora
- aristocracy
- epic poem
- hero
- labyrinth
- monarchy
- myth
- oligarchy
- polis
- raw material
- tyrant

NAMES & PLACES
- Homer
- Minoan
- Mycenaean
- Odysseus
- Trojan War

SECTION 2
SPARTA AND ATHENS

KEY VOCABULARY
- alliance
- democracy
- helot
- trireme

NAMES & PLACES
- Athens
- Darius I
- Solon
- Sparta
- Thermopylae
- Xerxes

READING STRATEGY

ORGANIZE IDEAS: COMPARE AND CONTRAST
When you compare and contrast information in a text, look for words such as *also*, *and*, or *too* to signal comparisons and *but*, *however*, or *unlike* to signal contrasts. As you read the chapter, use a graphic organizer like this one to compare and contrast life in Sparta and Athens.

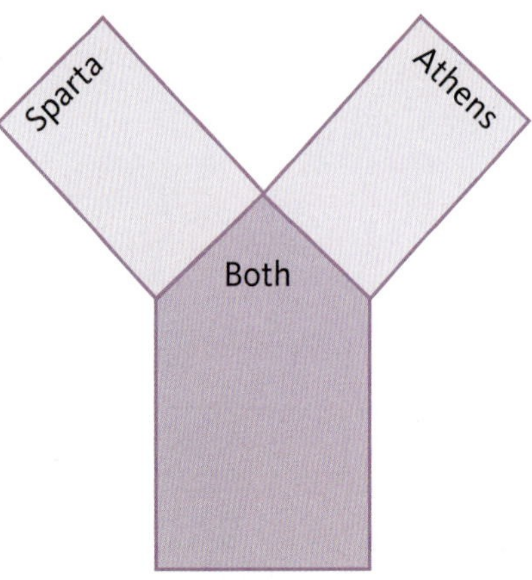

Sparta
Athens
Both

The Temple of Aphaia, goddess of sailors and hunters, was built on the island of Aegina around 500 B.C.

1.1 Mysterious Minoans

You step forward and grasp the horns of the huge panting bull. Its head twitches; your muscles tighten in anticipation. Blocking out the cheers of the crowd, you spring over the bull's back and land behind the enormous animal. In ancient Crete such deadly games as bull-leaping are your way of worship.

MAIN IDEA

The Minoans established the earliest civilization in ancient Greece.

ANCIENT DISASTER

Around 1600 B.C., a volcano called Thira (THIH-ruh) erupted on an island 70 miles north of Crete. The eruption destroyed most of the island and caused death and destruction across the Mediterranean. Scholars disagree about whether this eruption caused the decline of Minoan civilization, but this is one possibility.

MINOAN CIVILIZATION

Historians trace the origins of Greek civilization to Crete, a mountainous island about 150 miles off the coast of mainland Greece. Neolithic farmers settled there around 7000 B.C. and agriculture flourished. By 2000 B.C., a sophisticated **Minoan** (mih-NOH-uhn) civilization had emerged, centered on cities governed from magnificent royal palaces.

Though the Minoans left behind written records, historians cannot read their language. Their knowledge of Minoan civilization is pieced together through archaeology and the writings of ancient Greek historians. There are also many myths about this civilization. **Myths** are very old stories told to explain events or to justify beliefs and actions. The word *Minoan* comes from a mythical Cretan king named Minos (MY-nuhs). According to the myth, Minos built a **labyrinth** (LAB-uh-rinth), or maze, beneath his palace. A monstrous Minotaur (MIHN-uh-tawr)—half man, half bull—lived in this labyrinth and was offered regular sacrifices of unlucky humans. Unlikely? Perhaps, but archaeological evidence confirms that a powerful Minoan king built a labyrinth-like palace, and Minoans did in fact worship bulls and perform sacrifices.

CITIES AND CULTURE

The Minoans grew wealthy through trade across the Mediterranean. One of the Minoans' strengths was that they were expert sailors. Their well-built ships carried olive oil, wine, cloth, pottery, and metalwork to Greece, Egypt, Cyprus, and Spain. The Minoans returned from trading voyages with important **raw materials**, or substances from which other products are made, such as tin, gold, pearls, and ivory. Minoans spread their culture throughout Greece and along the coasts of the Aegean (ee-JEE-uhn) Sea. Their strong navy controlled the seas, making the Minoans feel so safe they did not build city walls.

The great palace at Knossos (NAW-suhss) dominated Crete. The size and complexity of the palace may have encouraged some people to believe it was Minos's labyrinth. Home to almost 20,000 people, Knossos was more like a city than a palace. It was the center of Minoan culture, religion, and economy. The palace included a central courtyard for ceremonies, hundreds of rooms,

This painting from the palace of Knossos shows bull-leaping.

and even advanced plumbing. It also provided workshops for Minoan artisans and storerooms for surplus crops, such as grains. Minoans worked to support the palace and enjoyed a relatively prosperous life.

Minoan religion was polytheistic, which means that people believed in many gods and goddesses. Lifelike Minoan wall paintings suggest forms of worship involving bull-leaping, boxing, wrestling, and dancing as well as sacrifices to pacify the gods.

Mysteries surround the end of the Minoans. Around 1500 B.C., Minoan civilization declined sharply and its palaces fell into ruins. Possible causes for their collapse include natural disasters such as earthquakes, tidal waves, or volcanic eruptions. Some historians think all three factors—as well as an invasion by people from mainland Greece—contributed to the Minoans' decline. By 1450 B.C., a new civilization would overtake the Minoans.

REVIEW & ASSESS

1. **READING CHECK** What were some of the traits of the earliest civilization in ancient Greece?
2. **DRAW CONCLUSIONS** What does the great palace at Knossos reveal about the Minoan civilization?
3. **ANALYZE CAUSE AND EFFECT** How did trade help the Minoans develop wealth?

1.2 Mycenaean Civilization

The fascinating thing about history is often what we *don't* know. Though we know the Mycenaeans overtook the Minoans, we don't know for sure what caused their own violent end. Along with the Minoans, the Mycenaeans helped lay the foundation of Greek civilization.

MAIN IDEA

After copying Minoan culture, the Mycenaeans conquered the Minoan people.

CONQUERORS

Around 2000 B.C., a new group of people from farther east settled in mainland Greece. They became known as **Mycenaeans** (my-SEE-nee-uhnz) based on the name of their main city, Mycenae (my-SEE-nee). The early Mycenaeans established villages throughout Greece, picked up influences from Minoan culture which had spread there, and spoke an early version of the Greek language.

After invading Crete in 1500 B.C, the Mycenaeans adopted Minoan culture. The Mycenaeans copied Minoan art, architecture, religion, writing, trade, metalworking, and shipbuilding. Elements of Minoan and Mycenaean culture became part of the foundation of Greek civilization.

The Mycenaeans had an aggressive streak, though, and they eventually turned against the Minoans. The Mycenaeans seized and conquered lands across the eastern Mediterranean and Greece. Around 1450 B.C., they conquered the Minoans, taking their treasure, land, people, and palaces.

RICH KINGS

The city of Mycenae was the center of Mycenaean civilization. Built high on a hill, the city was surrounded by thick walls that protected houses, storerooms, and a grand palace. The Mycenaeans protected Mycenae and other cities with great stone walls—so huge that later Greeks believed they were built by mythical giants called Cyclopes (SY-klohps). A network of good roads connected Mycenae to other important cities.

While most Mycenaean farmers lived in simple mud-brick houses in the countryside, important officials, artisans, and traders lived in three-story stone houses in cities. Warriors had it even better. Mycenaean kings gave elite warriors fine houses and lands to rule. Everyone else worked to support the warriors.

Extensive trade and wars made Mycenaean kings rich. The fierce Mycenaean military, wearing metal armor and driving fast-moving chariots, raided and conquered surrounding people. Yet at the height of its power, around 1200 B.C., the Mycenaean civilization came to a violent end. Suddenly most Mycenaean cities and towns were mysteriously destroyed.

Historians have several theories about why Mycenaean civilization declined. One theory suggests that natural disasters caused shortages that turned cities against one another or led to peasant uprisings. Another theory suggests that Mycenaean cities were invaded by the mysterious Sea Peoples. The Sea Peoples were seaborne and land raiders who had also attacked the ancient Egyptians and fought the Hittites of Mesopotamia.

MYCENAEAN TRADE ROUTES, c. 1250 B.C.

Mycenaean Greece
Mycenaean city
Other city
Trade route

GREECE
Ionian Sea
Orchomenos
Euboea
Gla
Thebes
Athens
Mycenae
Tiryns
Peloponnesus
Pylos
Lesbos
Troy
Aegean Sea
Chios
Samos
ANATOLIA
Rhodes
Crete
Knossos
Cyprus
Mediterranean Sea
EGYPT
0 100 200 Miles
0 100 200 Kilometers
N W E S
40°N 35°N 20°E 25°E 30°E 35°E

Whatever the cause of the collapse, the end of Mycenaean civilization meant that ancient Greece entered a period of decline that lasted until about 950 B.C. The people abandoned cities, trade halted, and the economy floundered. During this time, the ancient Greeks also stopped keeping written records.

Without written records, historians know little about this 400-year period of Greek history. Luckily, though, the Greeks would learn to write again and record some of the greatest stories ever told.

MASK OF AGAMEMNON

This gold funeral mask discovered at Mycenae in 1876 is called the Mask of Agamemnon, named after the mythical Greek king. The mask most likely covered the face of a Mycenaean leader, though archaeologists are unsure which leader it was.

REVIEW & ASSESS

1. **READING CHECK** How did the Mycenaeans become so powerful?
2. **COMPARE AND CONTRAST** In what ways were the Mycenaeans similar to and different from the Minoans?
3. **INTERPRET MAPS** Describe the route Mycenaean traders used to reach Egypt from Tiryns.

1.3 The Age of Heroes

A good story needs an exciting plot, a little suspense, fascinating characters, and an exotic location. The ancient Greeks knew this and invented stories filled with adventure, romance, revenge, and intense action. This was the age of heroes.

MAIN IDEA

The ancient Greeks created a strong storytelling tradition.

HOMER'S EPIC POEMS

The ancient Greeks believed in many gods, goddesses, monsters, and heroes. Stories about these characters were told and retold. About 750 B.C., a man named **Homer** emerged. Historians do not know much about Homer, but tradition says he was a blind bard who lived in ancient Greece. A bard is a poet who tells stories as a rhythmic chant accompanied by music.

Homer composed two of the world's greatest stories, the *Iliad* and the *Odyssey*. Both are **epic poems**, or long poetic stories. Every epic poem has a **hero**, or a character who faces a challenge that demands courage, strength, and intelligence. Homer's epic poems dramatized how gods and goddesses influenced the lives of humans. They also helped establish the characteristics of Greek gods and goddesses.

The *Iliad* and the *Odyssey* followed a strong Greek storytelling tradition that mixed history, religion, and fantasy. These epic poems also united the Greeks through pride in their shared past and set the stage for future Western literature.

HEROIC DEEDS

The setting for Homer's epic poems was the **Trojan War**, which historians believe was fought between the Greeks and the Anatolian city of Troy around 1200 B.C. The *Iliad* tells of events in the final weeks of the war. According to the story, the Trojan War started because Paris, the prince of Troy, ran away with Helen, the wife of Menelaus (mehn-uh-LAY-uhs), the king of Sparta.

The *Odyssey* tells the story of the Greek hero **Odysseus** (oh-DIH-see-uhs). After ten years of fighting the Trojan War, Odysseus suggests that the Greeks play a trick on the Trojans. The Greeks leave a huge wooden horse as a gift and pretend to sail away from Troy. The Trojans drag the horse into the city, not knowing that Odysseus and his men are hiding inside. That night, Odysseus and his men sneak out of the horse. They open the city gates to Greek soldiers waiting outside. The Greeks take the city and recover Helen.

The *Odyssey* also tells the story of Odysseus's journey home after the war. He has many adventures involving creatures such as a one-eyed Cyclops and the Sirens—women whose singing lures sailors to crash their ships onto rocks.

FACT OR FICTION?

For thousands of years Troy and the Trojan War were considered nothing more than myths. However, Homer's stories inspired archaeologists to explore Greece. In the 1820s, they discovered the remains of a great city in Turkey. It matched Homer's description of Troy and had been violently destroyed about the same time, so Homer's war may have actually happened.

Critical Viewing The *Odyssey* captured artists' imaginations long after Homer lived. What part of the action does this painting depict?

The Trojan Horse, Henri Paul Motte, 1874

REVIEW & ASSESS

1. **READING CHECK** What is the setting for Homer's epic poems, the *Iliad* and the *Odyssey*?

2. **IDENTIFY MAIN IDEAS AND DETAILS** In Greek epic poems, why do heroes take action and what traits do they have?

3. **FORM AND SUPPORT OPINIONS** What details about the Trojan War do you think are fact and which are fiction?

1.4 City-States

Though ancient Greek cities seemed to lie quiet for 400 years, around 800 B.C. they began to thrive again. Eventually they would extend their influence across the Mediterranean.

MAIN IDEA

Ancient Greek city-states established different ways of governing as they gained power.

CITIES AND CITY-STATES

As population, trade, and wealth grew, the ancient Greeks began to build cities near coastlines for trade and on hilltops for defense. Greek cities were distinct from one another, each with its own personality. However, these ancient cities shared certain similarities, too.

The highest point in an ancient Greek city was the **acropolis** (uh-KRAHP-uh-lihs), or upper city. This stone-walled fortress was the city's last line of defense against invasion. From the acropolis one could see houses and narrow streets and easily spot the open space of the **agora**, the city's marketplace and social center for sports, festivals, and meetings.

A powerful city grew into an even more powerful city-state, also called a **polis** (POH-luhs). As you may recall, a city-state is an independent political unit in which a dominant city rules the surrounding area. A number of Greek city-states emerged after 750 B.C. Some city-states grew larger than others. Smaller towns and villages supplied food, trade goods, labor, and soldiers for the city-states.

Geographic isolation influenced how city-states developed in ancient Greece. High mountains surrounded plains and valleys, separating cities from one another. The mountains made it more challenging for some city-states to communicate and engage in trade with other city-states.

City-states developed at the same time all over ancient Greece, but they did so in different ways. Although they shared a common language, religion, heritage, and culture, city-states remained independent from one another. Each city-state had its own sets of customs and laws. Even more, citizens identified themselves as Athenians or Spartans—not as Greeks.

Critical Viewing The ruins of a temple called the Parthenon still stand atop the Acropolis in Athens. What details in this photo convey the advantages of the Acropolis's location?

EARLY GOVERNMENT

Greek city-states were as different as they were independent. Each city-state established its own way of governing its citizens. One form of governing was a **monarchy**, a government ruled by a single person, such as a king. Another form was an **aristocracy**, a government ruled by a small group of elite, landowning families.

Aristocratic rule was soon challenged by a growing merchant class. As trade expanded, the merchants became more powerful. The 600s saw increasing tensions involving aristocratic landowners and an uneven distribution of wealth. These tensions led to fighting and civil strife. Sometimes powerful men took advantage of the situation and seized power as **tyrants**. Some tyrants were ruthless, but others made positive changes, including giving farms to the landless and work to the unemployed. Not everyone favored their rule, though. In order to take power from tyrants, merchants formed an **oligarchy**, or a government ruled by a few powerful citizens.

Eventually, some city-states, such as Athens, wanted to give citizens a greater voice and began to experiment with a new type of government. You will read more about this government later in the chapter.

REVIEW & ASSESS

1. **READING CHECK** How were ancient Greek city-states alike and different?
2. **DETERMINE WORD MEANING** Based on what you have read, from what ancient Greek word do you think the word *politics* originates?
3. **ANALYZE CAUSE AND EFFECT** How did the geography of Greece influence the development of city-states?

1.5 Colonization and Trade

The ancient Greeks were always on the look out for fertile land and materials such as timber, metals, and luxury goods. Together these prompted the Greeks to trade and settle around parts of the Mediterranean where they could control the land.

MAIN IDEA

Ancient Greeks spread their culture around the Mediterranean and Black seas.

NEW SETTLEMENTS

Growing city-states meant growing populations and new problems. The hot, dry, and mountainous Greek countryside did not have enough usable farmland to feed everyone. As hunger fueled unrest, the leaders of city-states had two choices. They could fight other city-states for space or they could reduce their own populations.

Most did both. Between 750 and 550 B.C., the city-states waged wars with one another for control over limited natural resources. They also sent people overseas to establish new colonies in places with better farmland and valuable raw materials. Remember, a colony is an area controlled by a distant ruler. City-states selected their colonists by lottery and often prevented them from returning to Greece. The rulers wanted to make sure the new colonies would stay populated.

Greek city-states established hundreds of colonies in the Mediterranean region. Most colonies were situated on or near the coastlines of the Black and Mediterranean seas. They were located in present-day Spain, France, and Italy, in North Africa, and on the islands of Sardinia, Corsica, and Cyprus.

The new colonies were self-governing, but they maintained close political and economic links with their parent city-states. Although colonists adopted some local ways, they remained proudly Greek in their culture and outlook. They shared a common language, worshipped the same gods, and took part in Greek festivals such as the Olympic Games.

WATER HIGHWAYS

Colonies served many purposes for the ancient Greeks. Overall, they allowed access to land and resources not available in Greece. Some colonies were specifically set up to secure and control trade routes.

The Mediterranean and Black seas were relatively easy to navigate. Because most colonies were positioned near good harbors, sea trade flourished throughout the region. Expert sailors on well-built merchant ships carried raw materials such as silver and tin from present-day Spain and France back to Greece.

The flow of new resources to and from these colonies stimulated the production of goods. These goods were then traded at home and abroad. Trade boosted Greece's growing economy, as did the introduction of coins after 600 B.C.

Wide-ranging sea trade also encouraged cultural diffusion, or the spread of ideas from one culture to another. This dual exchange of goods and ideas was important in shaping civilizations in the ancient world. For example, the ancient Egyptians welcomed learning about Greek military skills. Ancient Greece had a strong cultural influence on early Rome and carried Mediterranean culture as far away as

GREEK TRADE, c. 500 B.C.

Region of Greek influence
Major trade route
Greek trade goods found
0 200 400 Miles
0 200 400 Kilometers
N
S
E
W
ATLANTIC OCEAN
EUROPE
AFRICA
ASIA
ANATOLIA
ITALY
GREECE
EGYPT
Black Sea
Mediterranean Sea
Ionian Sea
Aegean Sea
Danube
Olbia
Panticapaeum
Phasis
Trapezus
Byzantium
Abydos
Phocaea
Miletus
Al Mina
Athens
Corinth
Sparta
Crete
Cyprus
Cyrene
Sicily
Gela
Syracuse
Spina
Massilia
Hemeroscopium
20°W
10°W
0°
10°E
20°E
30°E
40°E
30°N
40°N

present-day France. The ancient Greeks also incorporated ideas from other cultures. Elements of Egyptian culture influenced Greek art and architecture. Some historians think that ancient Greeks may have gotten their ideas of city-states, colonization, and sea trade from the Phoenicians.

One of the major effects of cultural diffusion in the ancient Mediterranean was the Greek adoption of the Phoenician alphabet. The Greeks made changes to the Phoenician alphabet, which then became the foundation of the modern alphabet we use today.

GREEK POTTERY IN ITALY

Tuna fish decorate this pottery cup found in the Apulia region, in the heel of Italy's boot. The cup may have been produced there by Greek colonists, or it may have been a trade good. Archaeologists believe the cup dates to about 500 B.C. In what ways does this cup represent Greek colonization and trade?

REVIEW & ASSESS

1. **READING CHECK** Why did the ancient Greeks establish colonies in the Mediterranean region?
2. **ANALYZE CAUSE AND EFFECT** In what ways did trade and cultural diffusion shape the ancient Greek world?
3. **INTERPRET MAPS** How far north did Greek influence reach as a result of trade?

2.1 Sparta's Military Society

One of the greatest rivalries in the ancient world was between the city-states of Athens and Sparta. The Athenians, whom you'll learn about in the next lesson, emphasized culture and learning. The Spartans, though, were the fierce warriors of ancient Greece. They fought hard and could handle more pain than anyone. They were almost unbeatable, thanks to tough military training.

MAIN IDEA

Sparta was a powerful ancient Greek city-state devoted to war.

STRONG WOMEN

This bronze sculpture from Sparta reflects the expectation that Spartan girls and women be tough. Girls' education focused on physical strength and athletic skills, and Spartan girls learned how to defend themselves.

SPARTAN SOCIETY

The Spartans lived in one of the most fertile areas of southern Greece. The city-state of **Sparta** was located in the Eurotas river valley, protected by mountains that made attacking this city-state difficult. This physical separation may have led to an outlook and values in sharp contrast with those of other ancient Greek city-states.

Spartan government was an unusual blend of rule by kings, elected officials, and the ruling class. Two kings who shared power ruled Sparta. Together, they led Sparta's armies into battle. Real power rested with the five officials who were elected each year by an assembly of Spartan citizens. In addition, the two kings and a council of elders, made up of 28 men over 60 years of age, proposed laws. The Spartans' unique government helped maintain a balance of power and prevent revolts.

Spartan society was a rigid hierarchy. Groups of citizens were ranked by importance based on wealth and power. Elite, landowning families of Sparta formed the upper class. A second class included free noncitizens from the villages around Sparta. They were farmers and traders and sometimes served in the army.

The lowest social class was made up of the **helots**, or state-owned slaves captured from conquered lands. Helots farmed the Spartans' land and were only allowed to keep a tiny portion of their harvest. The helots outnumbered the Spartans, and fear of helot uprisings was a main reason for Sparta's military society. The army was at the center of everything in Sparta—and everything in Sparta was centered on the army.

DAILY LIFE

Spartan soldiers considered it an honor to die in battle for Sparta, but they did not die easily. At seven years of age, all boys were taken from their families and raised by the state to be soldiers. Their training was brutal. They wore thin tunics and no shoes, even in winter. Their meals were purposely small and nasty so that they had to steal food to survive but were punished if caught.

Such intense physical training and endless military drills created strong and obedient

Critical Viewing King Leonidas of Sparta was a heroic Spartan soldier. How does this statue of him celebrate Spartan values?

soldiers. At age 20, they joined a military mess, or regiment, a commitment that dominated the rest of their lives.

Family life supported Sparta's military values. Women's primary role was to produce future soldiers for the state, and husbands and wives spent much time apart. One result of this separation was that Spartan women lived their daily lives independent of men. Spartan women could also own property.

Sparta's extraordinary commitment to war transformed this city-state into an ancient power, but this success came at a price. Although Sparta boasted the best soldiers, it claimed few artists, philosophers, or scientists, unlike its rival Athens.

REVIEW & ASSESS

1. **READING CHECK** What was one reason Sparta developed a military society?
2. **SUMMARIZE** In what ways was Sparta's government unique?
3. **ANALYZE CAUSE AND EFFECT** What effect did Sparta's commitment to the military have on other aspects of its society and culture?

DAILY LIFE IN ATHENIAN ART

The art on ancient Greek pots allows a glimpse into daily life in ancient Greece. Study each pot. Then decide what you think the art portrays. Compare your ideas with the descriptions of the art below.

1. Athletes throw a ball to a trainer.
2. A servant attends to a woman tying a shoe.
3. A merchant watches over his goods.
4. A priest and an acolyte [assistant] light a fire.
5. A young woman combs her hair.
6. An athlete learns how to throw a discus.

2.2 Athens's Democratic Society

The city-state of Athens was named for its devotion to Athena, the Greek goddess of wisdom. Ancient Athenians developed one of the world's great forms of government.

MAIN IDEA

The culturally rich city-state of Athens developed democracy.

DAILY LIFE

The daily lives of people in ancient **Athens** helped shape their approach to governing. Citizenship was open to adult men who had been born in Athens. Foreign-born residents could live in Athens. However, they did not generally become citizens, vote, or own property—even though they paid taxes and fought in the army. Slaves were at the bottom of society.

Athenian women were firmly controlled by their husbands. Wealthy women ran the household and raised children, but they could not go out alone. Poorer women had more freedom but had to work for wages.

Children were raised much differently in Athens than in Sparta. Athenians valued education, and boys attended school if their families could afford it. After a well-rounded education, Athenian boys went through two years of military training in preparation for citizenship. Athenian girls did not attend school, but they learned household skills at home. Poor children worked from an early age.

BEGINNINGS OF DEMOCRACY

Even as the city-state of Athens thrived, many Athenians felt they had little voice in their government. Unlike Sparta, Athens replaced its monarchy with an aristocracy. Trouble arose when aristocratic families began to fight with each other and farmers started to protest decreasing wealth and land. A time of increasing strife and, on occasion, violence in Athens followed. A harsh code of laws made things worse.

In 594 B.C., the aristocrats responded to the crisis by granting special powers to a trusted man named **Solon**. He improved conditions for the poor by limiting the power of the aristocracy and allowing an assembly of free citizens to pass laws. In 508 B.C., Athens established **democracy**, a form of government in which citizens have a direct role in governing.

Athenians were less devoted to war than were Spartans. Although their citizen-soldiers were capable, they did not form a professional army. To defend itself, Athens joined forces with other city-states, including Sparta. In 490 B.C., the Persians attacked Greece from the east. The resulting war would test Spartans and Athenians alike.

REVIEW & ASSESS

1. **READING CHECK** What role do citizens play in a democracy?
2. **ANALYZE CAUSE AND EFFECT** What steps did Solon take to reform Athens's government?
3. **INTEGRATE VISUALS** How do the depictions of ancient Greek women on the pots fit with the text's description of them?

2.3 Uniting Against the Persians

When the Persians attacked Greece, they triggered the Persian Wars. We know much about these wars from the ancient Greek historian Herodotus. Modern historians consider him to be reliable even though it's likely that he exaggerated the size of the Persian threat. Whatever the numbers, these wars changed the course of Greek history.

MAIN IDEA

City-states in ancient Greece united to drive back invasions by the Persian Empire.

26.2

The modern marathon has its roots in the Persian Wars. According to one legend, upon defeating the Persians at Marathon, Miltiades sent his best runner to Athens to announce the victory. After he reported the news, the runner collapsed and died.

The distance from Marathon to Athens was just over 24 miles. Today's race measures 26.2 miles.

IONIAN REVOLT

In 546 B.C., the Persian Empire conquered Ionia, an area of Greek colonies on the west coast of present-day Turkey. Life under Persian rule was not especially harsh, but the Ionians wanted to regain their independence. They rebelled in 499 B.C. with the support of Athens. Despite Athenian help, Persia crushed the Ionian revolt in 494 B.C. The Persian emperor **Darius I** vowed to punish Athens as revenge for helping Ionia.

In 490 B.C., the Persian army landed at Marathon, just over 24 miles east of Athens. Knowing they were outnumbered by at least two to one, the Athenians knew their strategy would have to be clever—and bold. As the Persian foot soldiers stood in formation, the Greek general Miltiades (mihl-TY-uh-deez) ordered his troops to lock shields and advance at a full run. The Greeks charged into the surprised Persians, forced them back to their ships, and claimed victory over them.

DEFEAT OF THE PERSIAN EMPIRE

Ten years after the Battle at Marathon, **Xerxes** (ZURK-seez), Darius's successor, invaded Athens. In 480 B.C., hundreds of Persian ships and more than 150,000 soldiers went on the attack. Athens was ready this time—and it did not have to face the Persians alone. Athens had forged strong **alliances**, or partnerships, with other Greek city-states, including Sparta. Because the Athenians needed more time to prepare for battle, King Leonidas of Sparta occupied the important mountain pass of **Thermopylae** (thur-MAHP-uh-lee). Leonidas's small army fought off the Persians, giving the Greeks time to assemble further south.

The Athenians fought on. At the Battle of Salamis (SAL-uh-mihs) a small fleet of Greek warships called **triremes** (try-REEMZ) faced the Persian navy. The Greeks lured the Persians into a trap in the strait at Salamis and destroyed nearly a third of the Persian fleet. In 479 B.C., a large and united Greek army finally defeated the Persians at the Battle of Plataea. After this, the Persians left Greece and never invaded again. Although the war flared on and off for a few more decades, Greece was safe. Athens and Sparta emerged triumphant as the most powerful city-states in Greece.

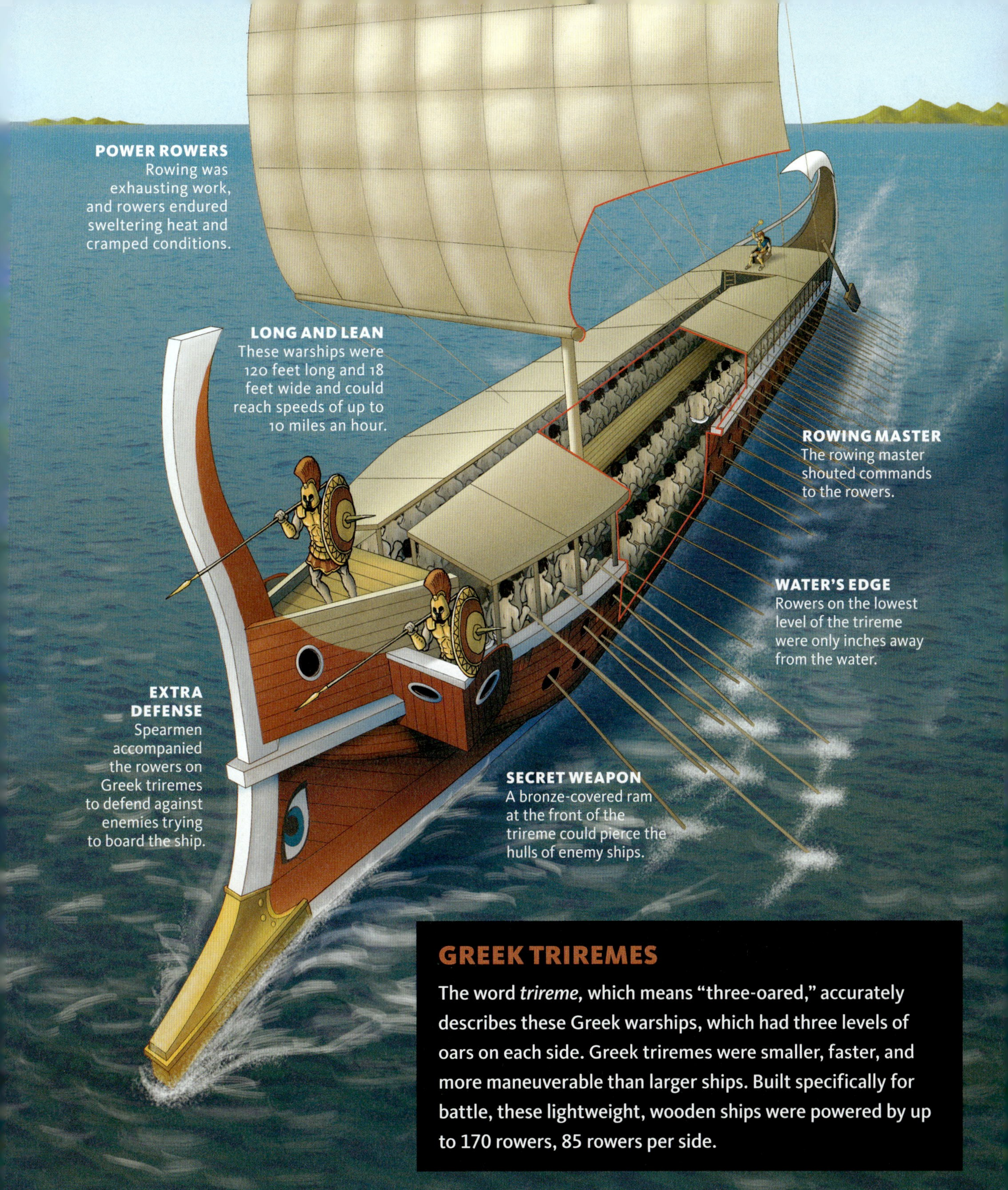

POWER ROWERS Rowing was exhausting work, and rowers endured sweltering heat and cramped conditions.

LONG AND LEAN These warships were 120 feet long and 18 feet wide and could reach speeds of up to 10 miles an hour.

ROWING MASTER The rowing master shouted commands to the rowers.

WATER'S EDGE Rowers on the lowest level of the trireme were only inches away from the water.

EXTRA DEFENSE Spearmen accompanied the rowers on Greek triremes to defend against enemies trying to board the ship.

SECRET WEAPON A bronze-covered ram at the front of the trireme could pierce the hulls of enemy ships.

GREEK TRIREMES

The word *trireme,* which means "three-oared," accurately describes these Greek warships, which had three levels of oars on each side. Greek triremes were smaller, faster, and more maneuverable than larger ships. Built specifically for battle, these lightweight, wooden ships were powered by up to 170 rowers, 85 rowers per side.

REVIEW & ASSESS

1. **READING CHECK** How were the Greeks able to defeat the Persians at the Battle of Salamis?
2. **COMPARE AND CONTRAST** How did the size and strategy of the Greek army contrast with that of the Persians?
3. **ANALYZE VISUALS** Why do you think triremes were effective warships?

2.4 MOMENTS IN HISTORY
The Battle of Thermopylae

480 B.C.

Heroic events inspire exciting movies. Here, outnumbered Spartan soldiers force Persians over a cliff in a scene from the 2007 film *300.* At the Battle of Thermopylae in 480 B.C., 6,000 Greek soldiers led by Spartans fought off more than 100,000 Persian soldiers. Exhausted, the soldiers battled bravely, but their strength was running out. King Leonidas of Sparta realized the battle was lost and ordered most of the soldiers to withdraw. He and his 300 elite Spartans stayed behind to protect the retreating army and delay the Persians. It meant certain death. The ensuing battle was fierce. When swords broke, the Spartans fought with bare hands. None escaped alive. Thanks to the sacrifice of the 300, the Greeks were able to regroup and eventually defeat the Persians. How do the actions of Leonidas and the 300 reflect the culture of Sparta?

CHAPTER 8 Review

VOCABULARY

Complete each of the following sentences using one of the vocabulary words from the chapter.

1. According to an ancient myth, King Minos of Crete built a large maze, or ______, beneath his palace.
2. The *Odyssey* is a(n) ______ that was written by Homer and tells the many adventures of Odysseus.
3. ______ is the Greek word for city-state.
4. In ancient Greek city-states, the ______ was the city's marketplace and social center.
5. Typically built on a hilltop, the ______ was a city's last line of defense.
6. During the Persian Wars, Athens formed ______ with other Greek city-states.
7. In Spartan society, ______ were slaves from conquered regions.
8. Gold and tin are examples of ______.

READING STRATEGY

9. **ORGANIZE IDEAS: COMPARE AND CONTRAST** If you haven't already, complete your graphic organizer to compare and contrast life in Sparta and Athens. Then answer the question.

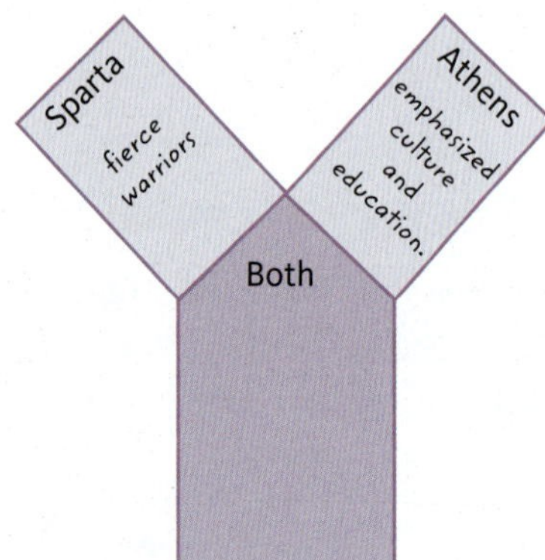

Sparta
fierce warriors
Athens
emphasized culture and education.
Both

How was life in Sparta and Athens similar? How was it different?

MAIN IDEAS

Answer the following questions. Support your answers with evidence from the chapter.

10. Where did the Minoan civilization settle and flourish? LESSON 1.1
11. How did the Mycenaeans gain wealth and power in the Mediterranean? LESSON 1.2
12. What are epic poems and what kinds of stories do they tell? LESSON 1.3
13. What was the function of the polis as it developed in Greek civilization? LESSON 1.4
14. How did sea trade affect ancient Greek civilization? LESSON 1.5
15. What were the advantages and disadvantages of Sparta's military society? LESSON 2.1
16. How did the roles of Athenian men and women differ? LESSON 2.2
17. What caused the Persian Wars? LESSON 2.3

CRITICAL THINKING

Answer the following questions. Support your answers with evidence from the chapter.

18. **SYNTHESIZE** What were some of the developments that led to the establishment of a cultured and influential civilization in ancient Greece?
19. **COMPARE AND CONTRAST** How were the Minoan and Mycenaean civilizations alike? How were they different?
20. **DRAW CONCLUSIONS** Why were epic poems and their heroes important to the ancient Greeks?
21. **EVALUATE** Why was the Greek adoption of the Phoenician alphabet an important development?
22. **YOU DECIDE** Which city-state—Athens or Sparta—had the most effective system of government? Support your opinion with evidence from the chapter.

INTERPRET MAPS

Study the map of the Persian Wars. Then answer the questions that follow.

PERSIAN WARS, 499–497 B.C.
Sea of Marmara
40°N
1. Athenian army defeats Persian army.
2. Greek force, led by Spartans, falls to Persian army.
Aegean Sea
Thermopylae 480 B.C.
Marathon 490 B.C.
4. Greeks defeat Persians, ending the war.
Plataea 479 B.C.
Salamis 480 B.C.
Athens
Sardis
Miletus
Sparta
3. Greek fleet defeats Persian navy.
Persian Wars, 499–479 B.C.
Greek states
Persian Empire
1st Persian invasion, 490 B.C.
2nd Persian invasion, 480 B.C.
Major battle
N
W
E
S
0 100 200 Miles
0 100 200 Kilometers
20°E
25°E
30°E
35°N
Crete

23. How did the routes of the first and second Persian invasions differ?

24. Which of the major battles shown was a naval battle?

ANALYZE SOURCES

Read the following description of Darius I, the emperor of Persia, written by Herodotus after the Ionian revolt.

> Darius did, however, ask who the Athenians were, and after receiving the answer, he called for his bow. This he took and, placing an arrow on it, shot it into the sky, praying as he sent it aloft, "O Zeus, grant me vengeance on the Athenians."
>
> Then he ordered one of his servants to say to him three times whenever dinner was set before him, "Master, remember the Athenians."

25. What does this description of Darius I reveal about him?

WRITE ABOUT HISTORY

26. INFORMATIVE Suppose you have been asked to participate in a radio program that examines important topics from history. Write a paragraph to inform your audience about the beginnings of democracy in ancient Greece between 600 and 500 B.C.

TIPS

- Take notes from the lesson about Athens's democratic society.
- Introduce the topic clearly.
- Develop the topic with relevant, well-chosen facts, concrete details, and examples.
- Use vocabulary from the chapter to explain democratic ideas.
- Provide a concluding statement that summarizes the information presented.

CHAPTER

9 CLASSICAL GREECE

480 B.C. – 323 B.C.

SECTION 1

THE GOLDEN AGE OF GREECE

KEY VOCABULARY	NAMES & PLACES
direct democracy	Cleisthenes
golden age	Delian League
immortal	Parthenon
mythology	Pericles

SECTION 2

THE PELOPONNESIAN WAR

KEY VOCABULARY	NAMES & PLACES
plague	Peloponnesian War
siege	Thucydides
truce	

SECTION 3

ALEXANDER THE GREAT

KEY VOCABULARY	NAMES & PLACES
catapult	Alexander the Great
cosmopolitan	Philip II
Hellenistic	
phalanx	

SECTION 4

THE LEGACY OF ANCIENT GREECE

KEY VOCABULARY	NAMES & PLACES
comedy	Aesop
jury	Aristotle
philosophy	Homer
representative democracy	Plato
tragedy	Socrates

READING STRATEGY

DETERMINE WORD MEANINGS Many English words are based on Greek words. This chart shows some common Greek roots and their meanings. As you read the chapter, write down examples of words you find that include these roots.

Root	Meaning
cosm-	universe
-cracy	government
dem-	people
-logy	speech
myth-	story
phil-	love
poli-	city
soph-	wise

Cape Tainaron, located at the southernmost point of Greece, was known in ancient times as the "Gate to Hades," or what the Greeks thought of as hell.

1.1 Pericles and Democracy

When you go out with your friends after school, how does your group decide what to do? Does one friend make this decision? Do two or three take charge? Or do you all have a say? If you all weigh in, that's democracy, a concept that began in Athens more than 2,500 years ago.

MAIN IDEA

Athens established the world's first democracy.

ELECTED BY LOTTERY

Athenians used this machine, known as a *kleroterion*, to elect officials. Each eligible male placed a token with his name on it in one of the slots. A series of balls were then released from a tube to determine whose tokens would be chosen.

SEEDS OF DEMOCRACY

As you may recall from the previous chapter, the leader Solon made life better for the poor. He canceled their debts, freed enslaved farmers, and abolished unfair payments to greedy landowners.

Solon also reduced the power of the aristocracy. He organized citizens into four classes based on wealth. Rich men still had more power, but all male citizens, rich and poor, were allowed to join the assembly and help elect leaders. Solon also created a council chosen by lottery, or chance, from the assembly. Solon made Athenian government fairer, but it was not yet a true democracy.

Around 500 B.C., a leader named **Cleisthenes** (KLYS-thuh-neez) took things further. Under his rule, the assembly members debated openly and heard court cases. Citizens were organized into groups based on where they lived. Each group sent 50 representatives a year to the Council of 500. The council proposed laws and debated policies, and the assembly voted on them. The citizens were now fully engaged in government. This was democracy—but a limited one. Only male property owners born in Athens could participate. Women, foreigners, and slaves had no political rights.

ATHENS'S GREATEST LEADER

Pericles (PEHR-uh-kleez), one of Athens's greatest leaders, expanded this limited democracy into one that would allow all male citizens to participate in government. He transferred the remaining powers of the aristocrats to the assembly. He paid jurors, which allowed poor citizens to take time off to serve the state. This idea was later extended to all public officials, who previously were unpaid. Pericles also opened up powerful political positions to the middle classes. Neither social class nor poverty was a barrier to political power anymore. Athens now had a **direct democracy**, in which citizens gathered together to vote on laws and policies.

Pericles was also determined to glorify Athens by transforming it from a city ravaged by the Persian Wars to a center of learning, creativity, and beauty. By encouraging the work of great thinkers and artists, Pericles guided Athens through a **golden age**—a period of great cultural achievement.

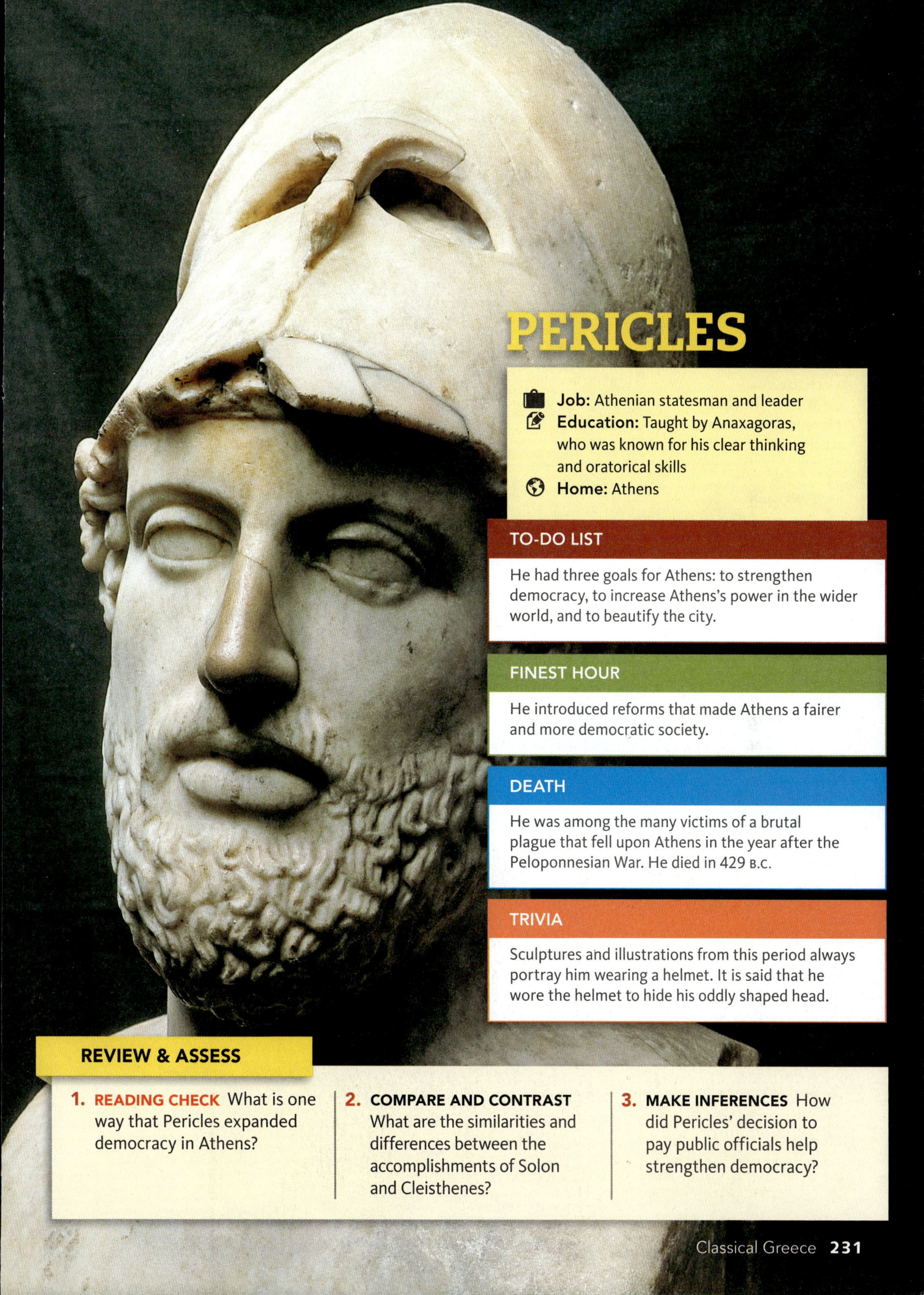

PERICLES

Job: Athenian statesman and leader
Education: Taught by Anaxagoras, who was known for his clear thinking and oratorical skills
Home: Athens

TO-DO LIST

He had three goals for Athens: to strengthen democracy, to increase Athens's power in the wider world, and to beautify the city.

FINEST HOUR

He introduced reforms that made Athens a fairer and more democratic society.

DEATH

He was among the many victims of a brutal plague that fell upon Athens in the year after the Peloponnesian War. He died in 429 B.C.

TRIVIA

Sculptures and illustrations from this period always portray him wearing a helmet. It is said that he wore the helmet to hide his oddly shaped head.

REVIEW & ASSESS

1. **READING CHECK** What is one way that Pericles expanded democracy in Athens?
2. **COMPARE AND CONTRAST** What are the similarities and differences between the accomplishments of Solon and Cleisthenes?
3. **MAKE INFERENCES** How did Pericles' decision to pay public officials help strengthen democracy?

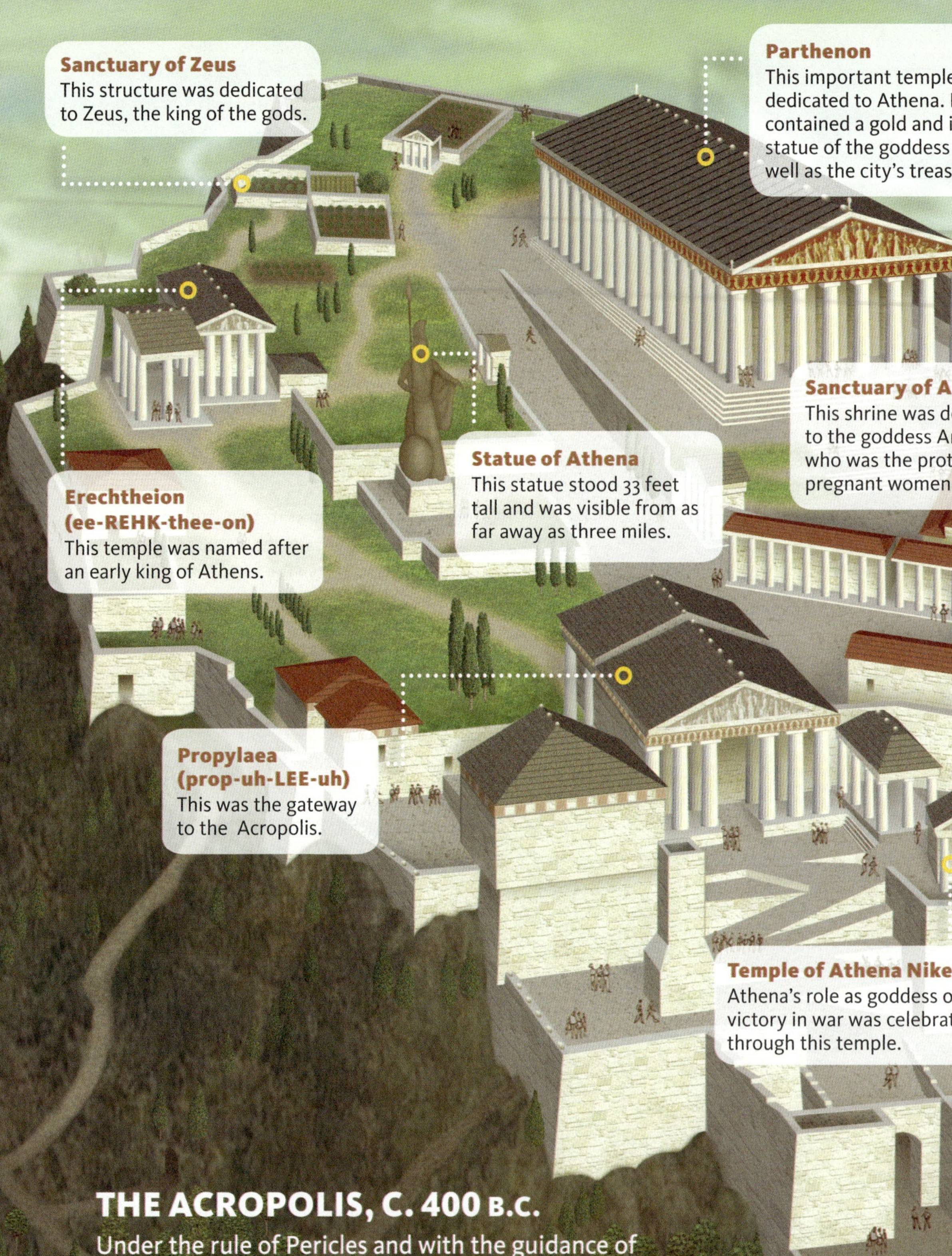
Sanctuary of Zeus
This structure was dedicated to Zeus, the king of the gods.
Parthenon
This important temple was dedicated to Athena. It contained a gold and ivory statue of the goddess as well as the city's treasury.
Sanctuary of Artemis
This shrine was dedicated to the goddess Artemis, who was the protector of pregnant women.
Statue of Athena
This statue stood 33 feet tall and was visible from as far away as three miles.
Erechtheion (ee-REHK-thee-on)
This temple was named after an early king of Athens.
Propylaea (prop-uh-LEE-uh)
This was the gateway to the Acropolis.
Temple of Athena Nike
Athena's role as goddess of victory in war was celebrated through this temple.

THE ACROPOLIS, C. 400 B.C.

Under the rule of Pericles and with the guidance of sculptors and artists, the Acropolis of Athens was constructed on a rocky hill in the center of the city. The fortress loomed high over the rest of Athens, and the most important buildings and temples were situated there. The Acropolis was easier to defend from invading armies than was the rest of the city.

1.2 The Athenian Empire

The war with Persia made the Greeks realize that there really is strength in numbers. So Athens and numerous other city-states joined forces to protect themselves against enemies. But Athens was always the strongest of the city-states, and it soon became apparent that Athenians had their own interests in mind.

MAIN IDEA

Athens grew into a powerful empire and was rebuilt to reflect its important status.

THE DELIAN LEAGUE

To defend themselves from Persia, which still posed a possible threat, Athens and the other city-states formed an anti-Persian alliance. The **Delian** (DEE-lee-uhn) **League**, formed in 478 B.C., was based on the island of Delos, where funds were kept to fight future wars with Persia. Each city-state contributed cash, ships, or soldiers and had equal votes in the league's council. However, Athens was always the league's leader and took control over the other city-states in the alliance.

Pericles used the league's money to build Athens's powerful navy. This naval force allowed Athens to rule the Mediterranean region and the Delian League. In 454 B.C., the league's treasury was moved from the island of Delos to Athens. The other city-states in the alliance were now powerless against Athens.

The Spartans were not happy that the Athenians were gaining so much power. Although distracted by regular slave revolts, Sparta remained a major power. It established its own network of alliances called the Peloponnesian League. Resentment built between the two leagues, causing tension to run dangerously high.

REBUILDING THE CITY

Meanwhile, Athens was still in ruins from the Persian Wars. The Delian League began funding the rebuilding of Athens, which would be grander than ever.

The city walls were rebuilt. Then Pericles rebuilt the Acropolis with richly decorated temples and monuments. One structure on the Acropolis was the **Parthenon** (PAHR-thuh-nahn), the awe-inspiring temple that was dedicated to Athens's goddess, Athena. The city's leaders poured money into beautifying the city with the finest architecture, art, and sculpture. Pericles transformed Athens into one of the most magnificent cities in the ancient world. It was a fitting capital for a powerful empire.

REVIEW & ASSESS

1. **READING CHECK** How did the Delian League make Athens more powerful?
2. **ANALYZE CAUSE AND EFFECT** How did the Spartans respond to the creation of the Delian League?
3. **INTEGRATE VISUALS** Why do you think the Parthenon was located on the Acropolis?

1.3 Religion and the Gods

Greek gods and goddesses may seem more like cartoon superheroes than divine deities. According to Greek belief, the gods looked and acted like humans: They married, had children, got jealous, and started wars. But they did it all with fantastic superpowers! Ordinary people had to either keep them happy or face their wrath.

MAIN IDEA

The Greeks believed that the many gods they worshipped could strongly influence daily life.

BELIEFS

Greek gods played an important role in ancient Greece. The gods were considered **immortal**, or able to live forever. Like the Mesopotamians and Egyptians, the Greeks believed that unhappy gods showed their displeasure by causing problems in people's lives. Greeks obtained the gods' help by leaving offerings outside temples—the gods' earthly homes. Temples were usually impressive stone buildings housing a statue of the god. A city's biggest temple was dedicated to its patron god, who protected it.

There were hundreds of Greek gods. According to Greek belief, the top 12 gods were the Olympians, or the ones who lived in luxury on Mount Olympus, the highest mountain in Greece. A holy day, celebrated with colorful and noisy public festivals, was dedicated to each god and goddess. These special days involved great processions, offerings, poetry recitals, and competitive sports, including the original Olympic Games. For private worship, most Greek homes had small altars where people would pray to the gods.

MYTHS

The Greeks had a close relationship with their gods, who often got involved in human affairs. This is how Greek religion blended with **mythology**—a collection of stories that explained events, beliefs, or actions. In Greek myths, the gods, kings, heroes, and ordinary people had amazing adventures together. The gods often rewarded or punished humans for their deeds. These stories were written down to form a group of exciting tales that are still popular today. One of these myths appears on the next page.

The 12 Olympians

Zeus King of the gods

Hera Queen of the gods

Aphrodite Goddess of love and beauty

Apollo God of the sun and music

Ares God of war

Artemis Goddess of the moon and hunting

Athena Goddess of wisdom and war

Demeter Goddess of the harvest

Dionysus God of wine

Hephaestus God of fire and metalworking

Hermes Messenger of the gods

Poseidon God of the sea

THE MYTH OF DAEDALUS AND ICARUS

On the island of Crete, there lived a skilled craftsman named Daedalus. Daedalus wanted to leave the island with his son, Icarus, but the king would not let him go. So he came up with a plan to escape. He took feathers and wax and constructed two pairs of wings that would allow him and Icarus to fly like the birds.

As Daedalus attached the wings to his son's arms, he told Icarus to follow him closely. "If you fly too low, the sea will soak the wings. If you fly too high, the sun will burn them," he warned.

The father and son were soon flying through the air. Icarus grew excited and began to fly higher and higher in spite of his father's warning. Apollo, the god of the sun, decided to teach the boy a lesson, and soon the wax holding Icarus's wings together was melting away. Icarus tumbled down to the water below. Daedalus could only watch helplessly as his beloved son was claimed by the sea.

When he safely reached land, Daedalus built a shrine to Apollo and hung his wings on it. He never tried to fly again.

REVIEW & ASSESS

1. **READING CHECK** What role did gods and goddesses play in the lives of the ancient Greeks?

2. **MAKE INFERENCES** What lesson do you think Apollo was trying to teach Icarus?

3. **DRAW CONCLUSIONS** Why were myths important to ancient Greek culture?

2.1 War Breaks Out

As Athens became wealthier and more powerful, other city-states, especially Sparta, became suspicious and fearful of Athens's future plans. Athens and Sparta had created very different societies. Athens championed a democratic government, while Sparta focused on military strength. These differences contributed to a growing distrust that exploded into war.

MAIN IDEA

Rivalry between Sparta and Athens plunged Greece into war.

TENSIONS RISE

In addition to societal differences, Sparta resented Athens's use of money from the Delian League. Remember, Athens had used this money, intended to protect all of the city-states, for its own benefit. When the city-states protested this inequality and attempted to free themselves from Athenian rule, Pericles punished them. By 431 B.C., Sparta had had enough of Athenian aggression and declared war on Athens. The **Peloponnesian War** had begun.

Sparta had a strong army and Athens had a strong navy. This contrast in military strength forced the two sides to develop very different plans for winning the war. Athens, under Pericles, avoided fighting Sparta and its allies on land and planned to attack from the sea. Athens withdrew behind its strong city walls. Its ships kept the city stocked with supplies and were also used to raid its enemies' land.

Meanwhile, Sparta marched its army into Athenian lands expecting a big battle, but the Athenian army stayed protected behind the city walls. The frustrated Spartans attempted to weaken the Athenian economy by burning its crops. Though the walls protected Athenians from the Spartans, they could not prevent a devastating attack from an unexpected enemy.

A PLAGUE STRIKES ATHENS

In 430 B.C., Athenians began suffering from rashes, headaches, vomiting, and fever. This was probably an outbreak of typhoid fever, a highly infectious disease. In the narrow streets of Athens, overcrowded with refugees from the countryside, the fever quickly became a deadly **plague**, or a disease that causes many deaths. In four years the plague killed one in three Athenians—about 60,000 people—including Pericles. Disease was doing more damage than Sparta's soldiers.

Elsewhere the war raged on with brutal acts committed by both sides. It was typical for a captured city to have all its male citizens executed and its women and children enslaved. Despite all the deaths, the war seemed unwinnable. Athens was dominant at sea and Sparta ruled on land, but neither was able to overpower the other. In 421 B.C., Athens signed a **truce**, or an agreement to stop fighting. Sparta and Athens entered a period of peace, but it would not last for long.

THE PELOPONNESIAN WAR, 431–404 B.C.

Black Sea
THRACE
Sea of Marmara
MACEDONIA
422 B.C.
429 B.C.
405 B.C.
410 B.C.
411 B.C.
406 B.C.
Aegean Sea
PERSIAN EMPIRE
Sardis
Ionian Sea
424 B.C.
Thebes
Corinth
Athens
407 B.C.
418 B.C.
Miletus
Delos
425 B.C.
Sparta
Crete
Mediterranean Sea
20°E
25°E
30°E
40°N
35°N
N
S
E
W
0 50 100 Miles
0 50 100 Kilometers

Legend
Sparta and allies
Athens and allies
Neutral states
Spartan victory
Athenian victory

MYRTIS, A VICTIM OF PLAGUE

Myrtis is the name given to the remains of an 11-year-old Athenian girl who died of the plague around 430 B.C. Her body was found in a mass grave in a subway tunnel in the 1990s. Myrtis's skull was in good enough condition to be reconstructed. Scientists built up layers of artificial skin and muscle tissue and gave her brown eyes and hair and an appropriate hairstyle for the age. Myrtis's reconstruction is probably very close to what she actually looked like. It is rare and exciting to be able to look into the eyes of someone who lived some 2,500 years ago.

REVIEW & ASSESS

1. **READING CHECK** What caused tensions between Athens and Sparta? What did these tensions lead to?
2. **COMPARE AND CONTRAST** How did Sparta's and Athens's war strategies differ?
3. **INTERPRET MAPS** How did geography give Sparta an advantage during the war?

2.2 The Defeat of Athens

Both Sparta and Athens wanted to control all of Greece. Sparta thought its soldiers, with their strict military training, would crush any opponent. Athens attempted to dominate the region by building a powerful navy. But Sparta and Athens failed to notice that their constant warring was causing Greece to slowly fall apart.

MAIN IDEA

After many years of fighting, Greece found itself in a weakened and vulnerable state.

THE WAR DRAGS ON

The truce was supposed to last 50 years. Instead it ended in only two. Sparta and Athens were drawn back into war over the rich lands of Sicily, a fertile island near Italy that the Greeks had colonized. A dispute between a pro-Athenian colony and a pro-Spartan colony prompted Athens to invade.

In 414 B.C., Athens laid **siege** to Syracuse, Sicily's strongest and richest city. In a siege, soldiers surround a city in an attempt to take control of it. The invasion of Syracuse was disorganized, and Athens made many mistakes. Spartan reinforcements arrived and attacked the Athenians on land and sea. The Spartans sank all 200 of Athens's ships, and killed or enslaved 40,000 soldiers.

Meanwhile, Sparta seized control of the land around Athens, cutting off the Athenians' agricultural and economic resources. With Athens weakened, its allies revolted. Athens's situation just kept getting worse. The city-state had no good leaders left, and its naval fleet had been completely destroyed by Sparta.

In 412 B.C., Sparta strengthened its forces by allying with its old enemy Persia. The Spartan army steadily advanced on Athens, deliberately causing refugees to flee to the already overcrowded city. Blocked by Spartans on land and sea, a desperate Athens had only two choices: surrender or starve. In 404 B.C., Athens surrendered and the Peloponnesian War was finally over.

SPARTA IS VICTORIOUS

Sparta's fellow members in the Peloponnesian League wanted Athens to be completely destroyed and its people enslaved, but Sparta rejected these calls for revenge. Still, surrendering to Sparta was humiliating to the proud Athenians. The long walls linking Athens to the sea were torn down, and the Athenian navy was reduced to just 12 ships. As a final insult, Sparta replaced Athenian democracy with an oligarchy, a government made up of a small group of people. It was run by tyrants who ruled in a ruthless and controlling way. This form of leadership caused further conflicts within democracy-loving Athens.

The once powerful city of Athens was reduced to a second-rate state. However, Athens was not alone in its suffering. The long war had been costly in men, money, and resources to all the city-states involved. Greece as a whole was left weakened and vulnerable. To repair the damage, the city-states needed to cooperate with one another. Unfortunately, the end of the war did not stop conflicts from erupting. The city-states were soon warring among themselves again. In its weakened condition, Greece was a prime target for attack.

Critical Viewing Spartan soldiers raise their weapons for battle. What does the illustration suggest about how Spartan soldiers fought?

Spartan Warriors, Howard David Johnson, 2013

REVIEW & ASSESS

1. **READING CHECK** What finally caused Athens to surrender to Sparta, ending the Peloponnesian War?

2. **DETERMINE WORD MEANINGS** How does knowing that *olig-* means "few" and *arch-* means "ruler" clarify the meaning of *oligarchy*?

3. **ANALYZE CAUSE AND EFFECT** What were the effects of the Peloponnesian War on the Greek city-states?

2.3 DOCUMENT-BASED QUESTION

Athenian Democracy

In 431 B.C., Pericles delivered an oration, a kind of formal speech, at a large public funeral held in honor of Athenian soldiers who had died fighting in the Peloponnesian War. Pericles used the opportunity to inspire the living to keep fighting for Athens. He talked about the many reasons that Athenians could be proud of their great city, including all of the advantages that came with living in a democratic society.

The Age of Pericles, Philipp von Foltz, 185

Critical Viewing An artist imagines what the scene might have looked like as Pericles delivered his oration. How do the Athenians appear to react to Pericles' words?

DOCUMENT ONE

Primary Source: Speech

from *History of the Peloponnesian War* by Thucydides (translated by Rex Warner)

Thucydides (thoo-SIH-duh-deez) was a Greek historian and general best known for his historical account of the events of the Peloponnesian War. As an Athenian military commander, he failed to prevent the capture of an important city from Sparta and was exiled for 20 years. During this time, he was able to witness events firsthand and interview participants much as a modern journalist would. His account provides a detailed record of Pericles' funeral oration. In this excerpt, Pericles reminds Athenians of the power they have as members of a democratic society.

CONSTRUCTED RESPONSE According to Pericles, what was special about the Athenian system of government?

> Our constitution is called a democracy because power is in the hands not of a minority but of the whole people. When it is a question of settling private disputes, everyone is equal before the law; when it is a question of putting one person before another in positions of public responsibility, what counts is not membership of a particular class, but the actual ability that the man possesses. No one, so long as he has it in him to be of service to the state, is kept in political obscurity because of poverty.

DOCUMENT TWO

Primary Source: Artifact

Ostracon, Greece, c. 400s B.C.

Ostracism was an enforced banishment. Athenians used it to prevent an individual from gaining too much power. Each citizen carved the name of someone he believed to be dangerous on a piece of pottery called an ostracon, seen at right. If the same name appeared often enough, the named person had to leave Athens. He did not lose citizenship, property, or wealth, but he was forbidden to return for ten years.

CONSTRUCTED RESPONSE What does the practice of ostracism tell you about Athenian values?

SYNTHESIZE & WRITE

1. **REVIEW** Review what you have learned about democracy in Athens from the text and the sources above.
2. **RECALL** On your own paper, write down the main idea expressed in the speech and artifact.
3. **CONSTRUCT** Write a topic sentence that answers this question: What was most important in Athenian democracy—the individual or the community?
4. **WRITE** Using evidence from the speech and artifact, write an argument to support your answer to the question in Step 3.

3.1 Philip of Macedonia

Your king wants to conquer Greece, located just south of your homeland. Weakened from internal fighting, Greece has become a prime target for attack. You and your fellow soldiers grip your 18-foot-long spears tighter as Greek soldiers approach. You are terrified, but you trust King Philip II. His military skills are extensive. In his capable hands, the act of war is turned into an art.

MAIN IDEA

Greece became unified under the military influence of Philip II.

CONQUEROR OF GREECE

The Greeks didn't think much of the kingdom of Macedonia (ma-suh-DOH-nee-uh), located just north of Greece. They dismissed its residents as uncultured foreigners. However, in 359 B.C., **Philip II** seized the Macedonian throne. He was an intelligent general and a clever politician—skills he combined with ambition, determination, and ruthlessness. An inspiring king, Philip completely controlled all political, military, legal, and religious matters.

Philip admired many things about Greece, including its ideas and art. He set his sights on uniting the Greek city-states with his own kingdom to create a combined kingdom strong enough to conquer the Persian Empire—his ultimate goal.

Philip built a powerful professional army and used new warfare methods. For example, he placed large groups of soldiers close together, forming an almost unstoppable battle formation called a **phalanx** (FAY-langks). Each soldier carried a spear that was much longer than the enemy's. The soldiers stood close to one another so that their shields overlapped, making it difficult for the enemy to attack them. Another new method of waging war was the use of war machines like the **catapult**, which hurled huge stones to shatter city walls.

Philip conquered the lands around Macedonia and seized Greek colonies that were rich in natural resources like gold mines, increasing his wealth. Greek city-states were still weak from the Peloponnesian War and were constantly quarrelling among themselves.

They were no match for Philip's strong army, great wealth, and political skill. By 348 B.C., Philip had won control of much of Greece. Any remaining Greek resistance crumbled when Athens and the strong city-state of Thebes fell to Philip at the Battle of Chaeronea (kair-uh-NEE-uh) in 338 B.C. Philip had united Greece for the first time ever. However, his son, **Alexander the Great**, would soon surpass his achievements.

YOUNG ALEXANDER

Born in 356 B.C., Alexander demonstrated his courage at a young age. One story tells how 12-year-old Alexander bravely stepped up to a nervous wild horse named Bucephalus (byoo-SEHF-uh-luhs), spoke gently to calm him down, and then rode him. Philip proudly announced that Macedonia would never be big enough for such a brave boy—and he was right.

Alexander trained for war with "the companions," a group of aristocratic sons

The Battle of Issus, House of the Faun, Pompeii, c. 80 B.C.

Critical Viewing This mosaic fragment shows Alexander the Great in battle. What do the details in this picture help you infer about Alexander's character?

who became his loyal lifelong friends. His most important training came from his father, who took Alexander into battle with him. This gave his son firsthand experience in planning and carrying out a war.

The Greek scientist and great thinker Aristotle (A-ruh-stah-tuhl) was Alexander's tutor. He taught him geography, science, and literature. Alexander was greatly influenced by Homer's *Iliad* and kept a copy of it under his pillow. He wanted to be like the *Iliad*'s courageous hero, Achilles (uh-KIH-leez). According to myth, Achilles was one of the greatest warriors Greece had ever known.

Alexander soon became a warrior himself. At the age of 16, he was fighting off invasions and founding cities. In 336 B.C., Philip was assassinated, and 20-year-old Alexander became king.

The people of Thebes rebelled after Philip's death. They thought Macedonia would become weak without him. They could not have been more mistaken. Alexander marched into Greece to assert his leadership. He destroyed Thebes, terrifying all of Greece into submission. Alexander was well on his way to becoming "the Great."

REVIEW & ASSESS

1. **READING CHECK** What was Philip II's key achievement in Greece?
2. **ANALYZE CAUSE AND EFFECT** Why were the Greek city-states unprepared for an attack by Philip II?
3. **IDENTIFY MAIN IDEAS AND DETAILS** What evidence from the text demonstrates that Philip II was an intelligent general?

3.2 BIOGRAPHY

ALEXANDER THE GREAT

356 B.C. – 323 B.C.

According to legend, the city of Gordium in Asia Minor contained a knot so complex that it was impossible to untie. Whoever could unravel the Gordian knot would conquer Asia. When Alexander saw the knot, he drew his sword and asked, "What does it matter how I untie it?" He then sliced the knot in two.

- **Job:** King of Macedonia and general of the army
- **Education:** Taught by Aristotle, the great Greek thinker and scientist
- **Home:** Born in Pella, Macedonia

FINEST HOUR

He led his unbeaten army to conquer lands as far east as India.

WORST MOMENT

In a drunken rage, he murdered his friend Cleitus.

FRIENDS

- Ptolemy (boyhood friend and general in the army)
- Hephaestion (lifelong friend and second-in-command)
- His soldiers

ENEMIES

- Thebans (Greek warriors)
- Darius (Persian king)
- Porus (Indian king)

TRIVIA

To honor his beloved horse, Alexander named a city in present-day India after him: Bucephala.

ALEXANDER'S TRIUMPHS

In 334 B.C., Alexander set out to fulfill his father's plans to conquer Persia. Philip was a skilled politician and general, but Alexander was even more gifted. He was a military genius who never once lost a battle. Alexander invaded and freed Persian-controlled Anatolia (present-day Turkey). Then he marched his army south toward Egypt, taking control of Persia's Mediterranean naval bases along the way. Persia responded with an attack from its huge army. However, Alexander cleverly forced the battle to occur on a narrow coastline, which destroyed Persia's advantage of having more soldiers.

When Alexander arrived in Egypt, the people, who had been living under Persian rule, greeted him as a liberator and crowned him pharaoh. Here, as elsewhere, Alexander won the support of conquered people by honoring local traditions. While in Egypt, he founded Alexandria, the first of many cities to bear his name. As a center of education,

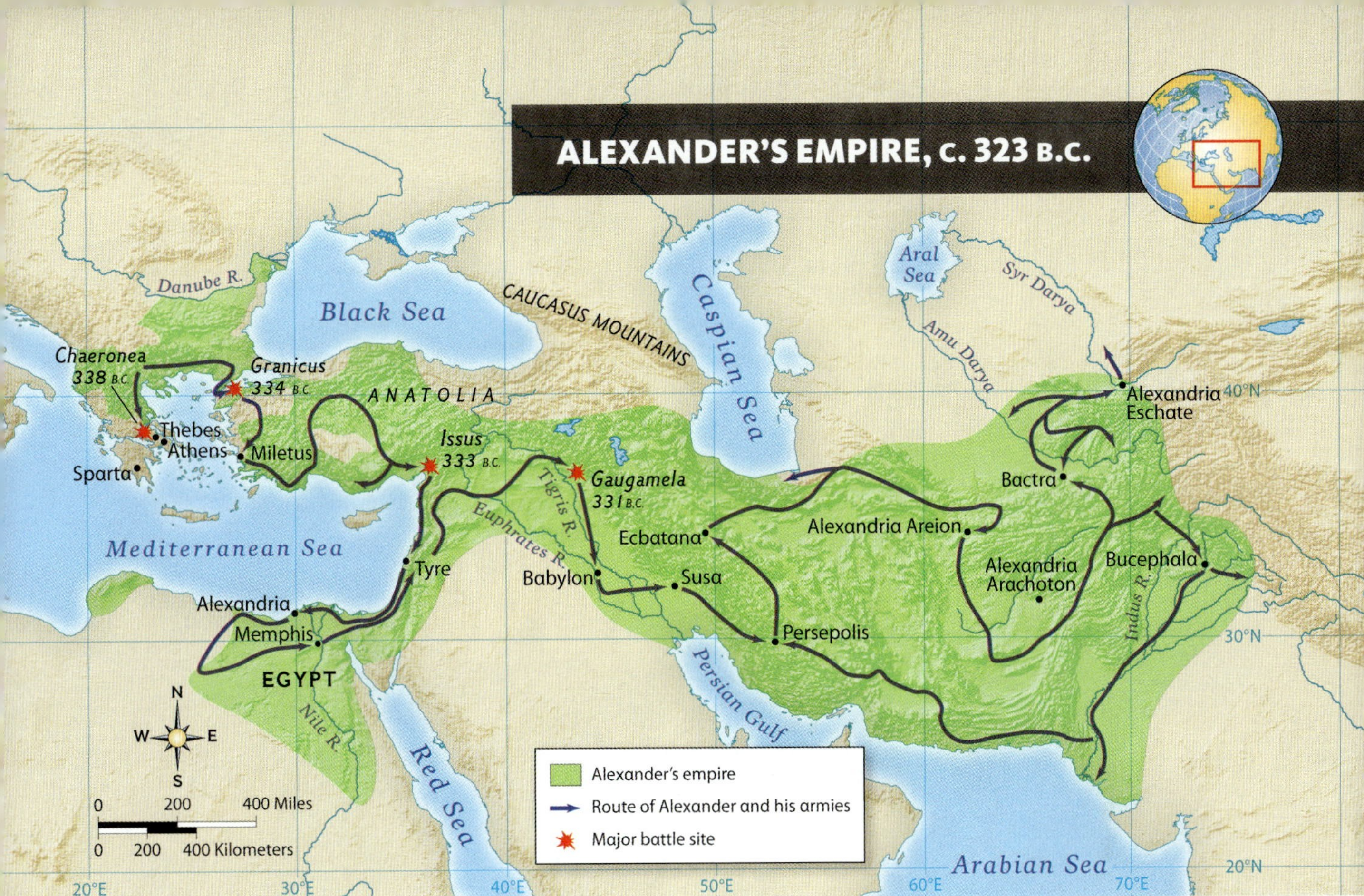
ALEXANDER'S EMPIRE, c. 323 B.C.
Danube R.
Black Sea
CAUCASUS MOUNTAINS
Caspian Sea
Aral Sea
Syr Darya
Amu Darya
Chaeronea 338 B.C.
Granicus 334 B.C.
ANATOLIA
Thebes
Athens
Miletus
Sparta
Issus 333 B.C.
Gaugamela 331 B.C.
Tigris R.
Euphrates R.
Mediterranean Sea
Tyre
Babylon
Susa
Ecbatana
Alexandria Areion
Alexandria Eschate
Bactra
Alexandria Arachoton
Bucephala
Indus R.
Persepolis
Alexandria
Memphis
EGYPT
Nile R.
Red Sea
Persian Gulf
Arabian Sea
Alexander's empire
Route of Alexander and his armies
Major battle site
0 200 400 Miles
0 200 400 Kilometers
40°N
30°N
20°N
20°E
30°E
40°E
50°E
60°E
70°E

culture, and trade, Alexandria was one of the most important cities in the ancient world.

In 331 B.C., Alexander defeated the Persians near Babylon and soon controlled the rest of the Persian Empire. Instead of returning home to celebrate, Alexander and his soldiers continued east. They conquered present-day Afghanistan and Uzbekistan before turning toward what is now India, which was then thought to be the edge of the world. In 326 B.C., Alexander crossed the Indus River and won a number of bloody battles, but his soldiers had had enough. Deeply homesick after 11 years away, they wanted to return home. Alexander reluctantly agreed. Over the course of 13 years, Alexander had carved out an empire stretching 3,000 miles from Europe to India. Legend says that he wept because he had no more worlds to conquer.

ALEXANDER'S DEATH

Thousands of soldiers died during the long trip home. Alexander himself did not survive the return journey. In 323 B.C., he became sick with a fever while in Babylon and died a few days later at the age of 32. His generals fought each other for control of the empire, which eventually fell apart. Alexander's empire was replaced with four kingdoms: the Egyptian, Macedonian, Pergamum (PUR-guh-muhm), and Seleucid (suh-LOO-suhd) kingdoms.

REVIEW & ASSESS

1. **READING CHECK** How did Alexander the Great win the support of the people he conquered?
2. **COMPARE AND CONTRAST** How were Philip II and Alexander similar and different as leaders?
3. **INTERPRET MAPS** What physical feature marks the eastern extent of Alexander's empire?

This statue, known as *Winged Victory of Samothrace*, is an example of Hellenistic sculpture from the second century B.C. It depicts Nike, the Greek goddess of victory. The head and arms of the statue have been lost.

3.3 The Spread of Hellenistic Culture

People enjoy going to museums to check out new exhibits. The library is the perfect quiet spot for research and reading. Sports fans gather in stadiums to be entertained by sporting events. Theaters showcase the latest dramatic play for an eager audience. Thousands of years ago, ancient Greeks enjoyed these very same activities.

MAIN IDEA

Alexander's conquests spread Greek culture across Asia.

CULTURAL BLEND

Hellas is Greek for "Greece," and the three centuries after Alexander's death are called the **Hellenistic** era because the known world was dominated by Greek culture. Alexander founded Greek colonies wherever he went, and Greek culture spread from these centers through cultural diffusion. Thousands of Greek colonists carried Greek practices and ideas to the plains of Persia, deserts of Egypt, mountains of Afghanistan, and river valleys of northern India. Each area adopted and adapted Greek culture differently, blending it with its own culture.

Alexander founded more than 70 cities, each with Greek designs and features such as temples, gymnasiums, and theaters. These cities flourished, cementing Greek influence in faraway places for centuries. The ultimate Hellenistic city was Alexandria, Egypt's new capital.

WORLDLY ALEXANDRIA

Alexandria became one of the largest, wealthiest, and most cultured cities in the ancient world. Many parks and open spaces created a pleasant environment, and the main streets were lined with colonnades, a series of columns that support a roof to provide shade. Alexandria's multiethnic mix of Greeks, Egyptians, Jews, and others created a **cosmopolitan**, or worldly, atmosphere.

In addition to housing Alexander's tomb and countless temples, Alexandria also had many magnificent buildings, including a museum used as a research center and a library known as the Great Library. It boasted a copy of every book written in Greek—some 500,000 scrolls. The library drew scholars and scientists from around the world. Meanwhile, Alexandria's wealth attracted the best artists, sculptors, writers, and musicians. The city was the cultural and trade center of the Hellenistic world.

REVIEW & ASSESS

1. **READING CHECK** How did Alexander spread Greek culture across Asia?
2. **DRAW CONCLUSIONS** What made Hellenistic culture unique?
3. **IDENTIFY MAIN IDEAS AND DETAILS** In what ways was Alexandria the cultural center of the Hellenistic world?

4.1 Philosophy and Literature

What is right? What is wrong? What is good? What is bad? We all think we know the answers, but do we really? These are some of the questions posed by Greek thinkers over 2,000 years ago. Today we are still searching for the answers.

MAIN IDEA

Greek ideas and writings remain influential today. They are the foundation of Western thought.

SOCRATES, PLATO, AND ARISTOTLE

Philosophy comes from a Greek word meaning "love of wisdom." Philosophers try to understand the universe and our place in it. Instead of explaining the world through gods and myths, they use logic and reason. Greek city-states provided an open environment where philosophers excelled. They also studied and taught other subjects, such as science, math, and biology.

Socrates (SAH-kruh-teez) was an Athenian philosopher interested in ethics, or the study of right and wrong. He challenged people to think more deeply, asking probing questions like, "What is justice?" His question-and-answer teaching style became known as the Socratic method. Socrates' methods made him unpopular among the leaders of Athens. He was accused of not believing in the official gods and of encouraging young Athenians to rebel. He was put on trial, found guilty, and sentenced to death.

Socrates taught **Plato** (PLAY-toh), one of the most influential philosophers in history. Plato believed that this world was a shadow of a superior world. He disliked democracy, believing instead that philosopher-kings should rule. Plato founded an elite academy, where he taught **Aristotle**, the tutor of Alexander the Great.

Aristotle searched for understanding by examining the world closely. He categorized everything, laying the foundations for the study of biology, law, physics, and politics. Aristotle opened an academy, the Lyceum, where anyone could study a wide range of subjects. Together these three Greek philosophers formed the basis of modern Western philosophy, mathematics, and science and continue to influence our thinking.

EPICS AND HISTORIES

Homer was the most famous writer of epic poetry, a form of poetry that combines elements of drama and narrative. With their mythical beasts, interfering gods, and adventurous heroes, Homer's epics about the Trojan War—the *Iliad* and the *Odyssey*—continue to entertain modern readers. Another Greek writer still popular today was a slave called **Aesop** (EE-sahp). He wrote a series of fables, or short stories with animals as the central characters. Each fable taught a moral lesson.

The Greeks were among the first people to research their past and write it down accurately. When the Greek historian Herodotus (hih-RAH-duh-tuhs) wrote a history of the Persian Wars, he made sure to check his sources and to understand the significance of the events he described. He is considered the father of history. Similarly, Thucydides wrote an accurate account of the Peloponnesian War, while Xenophon (ZEH-nuh-fuhn) described life in Greece. They provided useful insights into ancient Greece and created a model for the future study of history.

Aristotle
Aristotle believed in studying the world as it is, including politics and biology.
Socrates
Socrates taught his pupils to question everything and to think for themselves.
Plato
Plato believed that all things on Earth were lesser versions of their ideals in heaven.

THE SCHOOL OF ATHENS (Detail)

The Renaissance artist Raphael worked on this fresco over a three-year period. It was painted on a wall in the pope's palace in Rome. The painting shows the greatest thinkers of classical Greek society. There are mathematicians, natural philosophers, artists, and scientists. They all lived at different times, but Raphael painted them under one roof. The two central figures are Plato and Aristotle, who have had a lasting effect on Western thought.

Detail from *The School of Athens*, Raphael, A.D. 1511

REVIEW & ASSESS

1. **READING CHECK** What are some of the subjects that ancient Greek thinkers studied and taught?
2. **DRAW CONCLUSIONS** What was unique about Aristotle's philosophy?
3. **ANALYZE CAUSE AND EFFECT** How did Herodotus and Thucydides influence the writing of history?

4.2 Arts and Architecture

A well-known ancient Greek tyrant cruelly enjoyed burying his enemies alive. Surprisingly, actors performing a Greek play were able to make him cry during sad scenes. The tyrant would weep for the suffering the actors mimicked onstage. Greek drama was powerful.

MAIN IDEA

The Greeks developed forms of art and architecture that are still appreciated today.

GREEK MASKS
Greek actors hid their faces with masks that represented the faces of a play's characters. Since three actors played multiple roles, the masks helped the audience recognize character changes.

DRAMA AND SCULPTURE

The Greeks loved the theater. Plays sometimes lasting entire days were performed in huge semicircular theaters, or amphitheaters. Greek drama evolved from plays honoring the god Dionysus (dy-uh-NY-suhs) into two main forms. **Comedy** was humorous and often mocked famous people. **Tragedy** was serious, with characters suffering before an unhappy ending.

Only three male actors performed each play, which required each actor to play many parts. The chorus, a group of actors who spoke, sang, and danced together, narrated the story. Costumes, props, and music brought the action to life.

The greatest Greek playwrights were Sophocles (SAH-fuh-kleez), Aeschylus (EHS-kuh-luhs), and Euripides (yu-RIH-puh-deez), who all wrote tragedies, and Aristophanes (a-ruh-STAH-fuh-neez), who wrote comedy.

Greek sculptors were dedicated to capturing the human form in their art. They carved sculptures from marble, wood, and bronze. The sculptures were painted to look amazingly alive. The Colossus of Rhodes was a 100-foot-tall bronze statue of the sun god Helios, similar in style to the Statue of Liberty. It was once considered one of the Seven Wonders of the Ancient World, but the original no longer stands. In fact, many of the best examples of Greek sculpture are actually newer Roman copies of Greek originals.

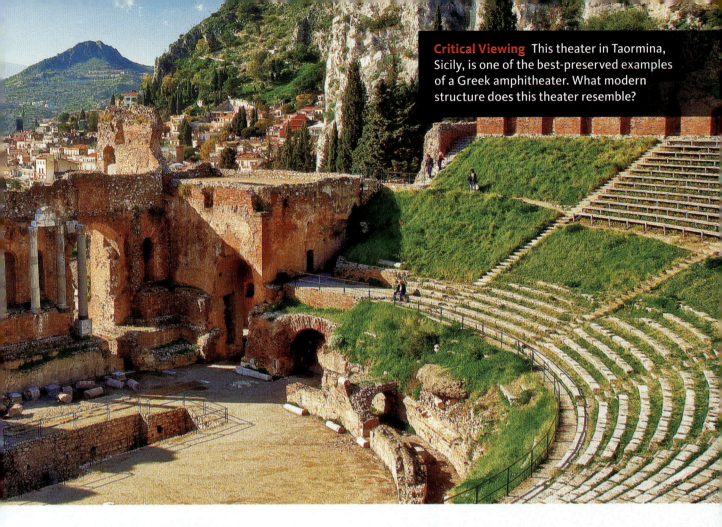

Critical Viewing This theater in Taormina, Sicily, is one of the best-preserved examples of a Greek amphitheater. What modern structure does this theater resemble?

COLUMNS AND TEMPLES

Ancient Greek architecture was a democratic art. It expressed beauty and harmony for everyone to enjoy. Temples were designed to be admired from outside, and all followed a similar plan. The temple usually faced east, toward the sunrise. The main room was rectangular and contained a statue of the temple god. Columns supported the roof. The features of Greek architecture continue to influence the style of buildings today. The Supreme Court Building in Washington, D.C., is a good example of this influence.

THREE COLUMN TYPES

Doric
Mainland, western colonies

Corinthian
More rarely found

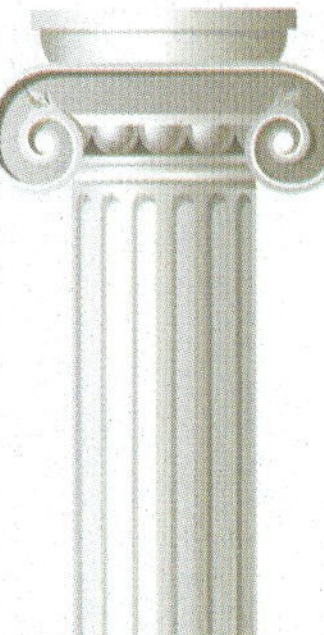

Ionic
Eastern Greece and the islands

REVIEW & ASSESS

1. **READING CHECK** What art forms did the Greeks develop that we still appreciate today?

2. **COMPARE AND CONTRAST** What is the difference between the two main forms of Greek drama—comedy and tragedy?

3. **IDENTIFY MAIN IDEAS AND DETAILS** The text states that Greek architecture was a democratic art form. What evidence supports this claim?

4.3 MOMENTS IN HISTORY
The Parthenon

432 B.C.

The Parthenon, one of the world's most recognizable buildings, was completed in 432 B.C. It took workers almost 15 years to build this magnificent marble temple, which honored Athena, goddess and protector of Athens. Like much Greek architecture, the Parthenon was made to be looked at from the outside. Its elegant proportions communicated a sense of harmony and balance. Inside, towering from floor to ceiling, was a 33-foot gold and ivory statue of Athena. The Parthenon was both an expression of Athens's wealth and a symbol of its cultural, political, and military superiority. What details in the Parthenon's design help convey these ideas?

4.4 Democracy and Law

Sometimes we might take our system of government for granted. However, our democracy is a legacy that has been passed down to us from thousands of years ago. Our modern ideas of democracy, justice, and citizenship all have their roots in ancient Greece.

MAIN IDEA

The Constitution of the United States was influenced by ancient Greek ideas.

GOVERNMENT OF THE PEOPLE

Ancient Greece was the birthplace of democracy and citizenship. Thousands of Greek citizens met regularly to vote on policies and laws. Greek colonies in Italy spread democracy to the ancient Romans, who carried it around the ancient world. They firmly established Greek political ideas in Europe. From these ideas evolved our modern ideas about government and civic life.

Ancient Greece also laid the foundations of American constitutional democracy. The cornerstone of Greek democratic ideas was that political power should rest with the people. The Greeks established the concept of citizenship with its rights and responsibilities toward the state and a duty to participate in politics and civic life.

The Greeks also embraced the principle of political equality, in which one citizen has one vote and where officials are paid, allowing the poor to serve as well as the rich. The Greeks put checks and balances into place. They limited terms of office and separated the three key branches of government—lawmaking, executive, and judicial—to prevent any one branch from becoming too powerful.

The **representative democracy** of the United States is based on the Greek system. Because the U.S. population is so large, its millions of citizens cannot vote directly on policies. Instead, citizens exercise their political power by electing representatives to vote on their behalf.

RULE OF LAW

Greek democracy was built on the rule of law. Greek citizens proposed and voted on laws that were enforced in courts. These courts established innocence or guilt through trials by **jury**. A jury is a group of people chosen to decide guilt or innocence in a trial. Greek jurors were selected randomly so that the results would be impartial. They also were paid so that even poor citizens could take part.

In Greek trials, the accuser and the accused represented themselves. There were no lawyers. Both parties had the same amount of time to speak, and both relied on witnesses. Under oath, witnesses sometimes testified to events but usually provided character statements.

Both sides presented their case, but they did not sum up the evidence, as lawyers do in court cases today. Nor was the jury allowed to discuss the case. Instead, jurors voted immediately by placing metal discs called ballots into a pot. The jury also passed sentence. Some penalties were automatic, such as death for murder, but more involved fines. Few people were actually imprisoned. There were no appeals, and the entire process was completed in a day.

Critical Viewing
Supporters of immigration rights march through downtown Los Angeles. How are these people demonstrating citizenship?

REVIEW & ASSESS

1. **READING CHECK** Why were jury members chosen randomly and why were they paid?

2. **ANALYZE CAUSE AND EFFECT** What ancient Greek ideas laid the foundation for the U.S. system of government?

3. **COMPARE AND CONTRAST** What are the differences between ancient Greek trials and modern trials in the United States?

CHAPTER 9

Review

VOCABULARY

Use each of the following vocabulary words in a sentence that shows an understanding of the meaning of the word.

1. **direct democracy**
   Athens's government was a direct democracy, in which citizens voted for or against laws.
2. **immortal**
3. **plague**
4. **siege**
5. **philosophy**
6. **comedy**
7. **tragedy**
8. **jury**

READING STRATEGY

9. **DETERMINE WORD MEANINGS** Copy the chart below and add your examples of words that include each Greek root. Then write a paragraph about Greek culture that includes each word.

Root	Meaning	Example(s)
cosm-	universe	
-cracy	government	*democracy*
dem-	people	*democracy*
-logy	speech	
myth-	story	
phil-	love	
poli-	city	
soph-	wise	

MAIN IDEAS

Answer the following questions. Support your answers with evidence from the chapter.

10. How did Athens become a powerful empire after the Persian Wars? **LESSON 1.2**
11. Why did the Greeks make offerings to the gods and goddesses they worshipped? **LESSON 1.3**
12. What caused the outbreak of the Peloponnesian War between Athens and Sparta? **LESSON 2.1**
13. How did Sparta defeat Athens and end the Peloponnesian War? **LESSON 2.2**
14. What was Phillip II's most important achievement in Greece? **LESSON 3.1**
15. Why did Alexander's conquests end? **LESSON 3.2**
16. How is Hellenistic culture an example of cultural diffusion? **LESSON 3.3**
17. What evidence is there that the ideas of the Greek philosophers and writers are still important today? **LESSON 4.1**

CRITICAL THINKING

Answer the following questions. Support your answers with evidence from the chapter.

18. **DRAW CONCLUSIONS** What are three ways in which Greek influences are felt today?
19. **ANALYZE CAUSE AND EFFECT** How did the plague contribute to the failure of Pericles' war strategy against the Spartans?
20. **EVALUATE** What factors contributed to Philip II's success in conquering and unifying Greece?
21. **YOU DECIDE** Where would you rather have lived—Athens or Sparta? Why? Support your opinion with details from the chapter.

INTERPRET MAPS

Study the map of the Hellenistic world after Alexander's death, when his empire broke apart. Then answer the questions that follow.

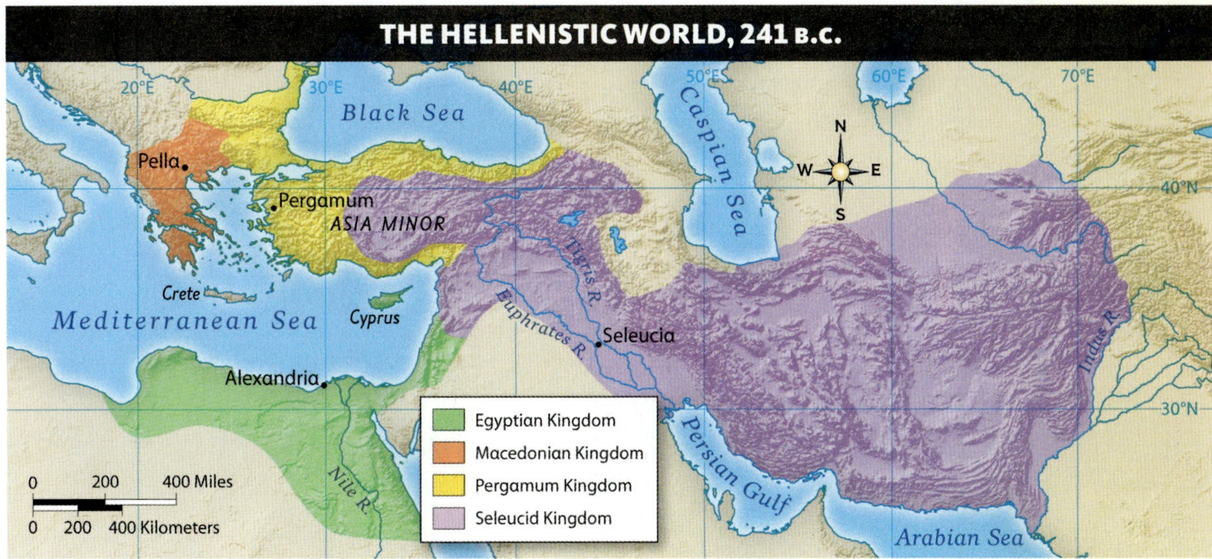

THE HELLENISTIC WORLD, 241 B.C.
20°E
30°E
40°E
50°E
60°E
70°E
40°N
30°N
Black Sea
Caspian Sea
N
W
E
S
Pella
Pergamum
ASIA MINOR
Tigris R.
Euphrates R.
Crete
Mediterranean Sea
Cyprus
Seleucia
Alexandria
Indus R.
Nile R.
Persian Gulf
Arabian Sea
Egyptian Kingdom
Macedonian Kingdom
Pergamum Kingdom
Seleucid Kingdom
0 200 400 Miles
0 200 400 Kilometers

22. Into what four kingdoms did Alexander's empire separate?

23. Which kingdom appears to have the least territory?

ANALYZE SOURCES

Read the following excerpt from the American Declaration of Independence. Then answer the question.

> We hold these truths to be self-evident, that all men are created equal, that they are endowed by their Creator with certain unalienable Rights, that among these are Life, Liberty, and the pursuit of Happiness.

24. How are the thoughts on democracy expressed by the authors of the Declaration of Independence similar to those of the Athenians?

WRITE ABOUT HISTORY

25. INFORMATIVE Write a three-paragraph speech for new American citizens explaining how democratic concepts developed in Greece laid the foundation for democracy in the United States.

TIPS

- Take notes from the lessons about Pericles and democracy and the legacy of ancient Greece.
- Introduce the topic clearly.
- Develop the topic with relevant, well-chosen facts, concrete details, and examples.
- Use vocabulary from the chapter as appropriate.
- Use appropriate transitions to clarify the relationships among concepts.
- Provide a concluding statement that summarizes the information presented.

ON **LOCATION** WITH
William PARKINSON

NATIONAL GEOGRAPHIC GRANTEE

Check out more on myNGconnect

In the field, Parkinson uses hi-tech equipment like this Real-Time-Kinetic GPS. It makes accurate maps by communicating with multiple satellites at one time.

FROM VILLAGE TO CITY

Like many kids who grew up in the Midwest, I loved searching for arrowheads in the fields and woods. Finding them made me want to learn more about people who lived long ago. Lucky for me, I had excellent college professors who encouraged me to study archaeology, and now I'm living my dream!

Today, I study how small farming villages turned into big cities. From an archaeological perspective, cities are weird. Until about 8,000 years ago humans lived in small groups and moved around as hunter-gatherers. Today, more than half of all humans live in cities. This has dramatic implications for our future. Archaeologists have done a good job explaining human development from hunter-gatherers to settled farmers. However, we still don't really understand how those early villages turned into massive cities.

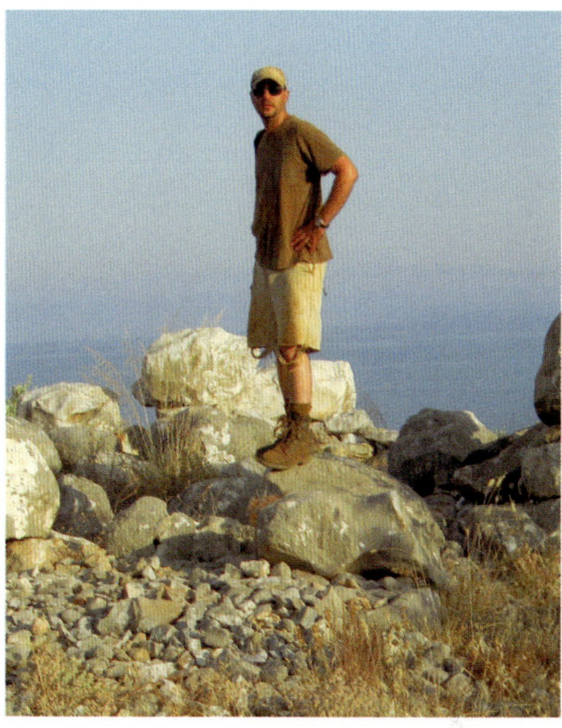

Bill Parkinson explores a coastline while conducting an archaeological survey in Diros Bay, Greece.

A TEAM SPORT

In Europe and the Near East, the turning point came during the Neolithic and the Bronze Ages. My team has been excavating an ancient farming village in Greece, just outside a big cave called Fox Hole Cave. This cave was used for rituals and habitation during the Neolithic period, when the first farmers emerged in southeastern Europe. Greek archaeologists have explored this cave for 40 years, and we wanted to build on their great work. Archaeology is a team sport that relies on the collaboration of many different specialists, so we brought together an international crew to study the cave.

Our excavations show that people built an agricultural settlement at the site about 6,000 years ago. This settlement gives us greater insight into how early agricultural villages developed. I'm studying a similar site from the same time period in Hungary, so we're able to compare and contrast how societies changed over time in different parts of the world. Now we are publishing the results of our research, another crucial part of archaeology. Soon we'll be back in the field, hunting for the next clues about how ancient villages transformed into cities.

WHY STUDY HISTORY ?

“Nothing can describe how exciting it is to put your trowel in the ground and uncover something nobody has seen for several thousand years. ***It never gets old.***” —William Parkinson

NATIONAL GEOGRAPHIC

Greek Statues Sparkle Once Again

BY A. R. WILLIAMS

Adapted from "2,500-Year-Old Greek Statues Sparkle After Facelift," by A. R. Williams, news.nationalgeographic.com, June 19, 2014

Four marble maidens from ancient Greece have gotten a makeover. Using a specially designed laser, conservators have stripped away the black grime that covered the statues. Sculpted in the late fifth century B.C., the figures served as columns for the Erechtheion, one of the temples that stood on the Acropolis. The maidens, known as the Caryatids, stand more than seven and a half feet tall and hold the roof of the Erechtheion's south porch on their heads.

As Athens rapidly industrialized over the past century, the Caryatids suffered from the effects of air pollution. Their golden hue turned dark, and their features began to dissolve under the constant assault of acid rain. In 1979 the figures were moved to protect them from further damage. Cement replicas were installed in their place on the Erechtheion's porch.

The Caryatids got their makeover in the public gallery of the Acropolis Museum. Conservators focused on one figure at a time in a makeshift room whose walls were sheets of heavy fabric hung from a frame. A video monitor outside allowed visitors to see the statues slowly changing color. The curtain walls protected museumgoers' eyes from the laser system that conservators, wearing protective goggles, used to clean the statues. This system uses two pulsed beams of radiation—one infrared and the other ultraviolet—to zap away dust, soot, minerals, and metals.

Conservators and technicians considered several different kinds of cleaning, including chemicals and micro-sandblasting. The dual-wavelength laser system was the best option. It allows for safe, controlled cleaning that leaves the marble's ancient patina intact.

A future project may reveal even more of the maidens' original beauty. Their clothing was once brightly painted. However, centuries of winter rain have washed away all visible traces of pigment. Modern imaging techniques can peer into the invisible parts of the light spectrum and find long-faded hues. The result may be even more dazzling than the maidens' current makeover.

For more from National Geographic
Check out "Behind the Tomb" on myNGconnect

UNIT INQUIRY: DEFINE GOOD CITIZENSHIP

In this unit, you learned about ancient Greek civilization and its influence on our modern world. Based on your understanding of the text, what new form of government was central to Greek civilization? What role did citizenship play in Greek civilization and government?

ASSIGNMENT Create your own definition for good citizenship. Your definition should include a clear statement of what constitutes good citizenship and why it is important today. Be prepared to present your definition to the class and explain your reasoning.

Plan As you write your definition, think about the active role citizens played in ancient Greek civilization and government. Also think about the rights and responsibilities ancient Greek citizens had and how those ideas have influenced our ideas about citizenship today. You might want to use a graphic organizer to help organize your thoughts. ▶

Produce Use your notes to produce descriptions of the elements that make up your definition of good citizenship.

Present Choose a creative way to present your definition to the class. Consider one of these options:

- Create a video presentation using examples from everyday life showing good citizens "in action" in their community.
- Design a good citizenship medal to present to someone who exemplifies what it means to be a good citizen.
- Design a good citizenship brochure that outlines citizens' rights and responsibilities.

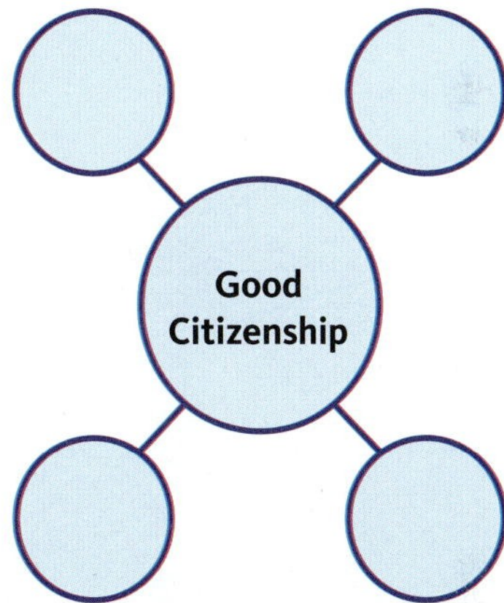
Good Citizenship

RAPID REVIEW
UNIT 3
GREEK CIVILIZATION TOP TEN

1. The Minoans and the Mycenaeans were the first advanced Greek civilizations.
2. Ancient Greek city-states established colonies and trade networks throughout the Mediterranean.
3. The city-state of Athens developed the world's first democracy.
4. Alexander the Great conquered Persia, Egypt, Afghanistan, and India, building a vast empire that spread Greek culture.
5. The ancient Greeks influenced Western art, architecture, literature, philosophy, science, medicine, government, and law.

6-10. **NOW IT'S YOUR TURN** Complete the list with five more things to remember about Greek civilization.

THE WORLD OF THE ROMANS

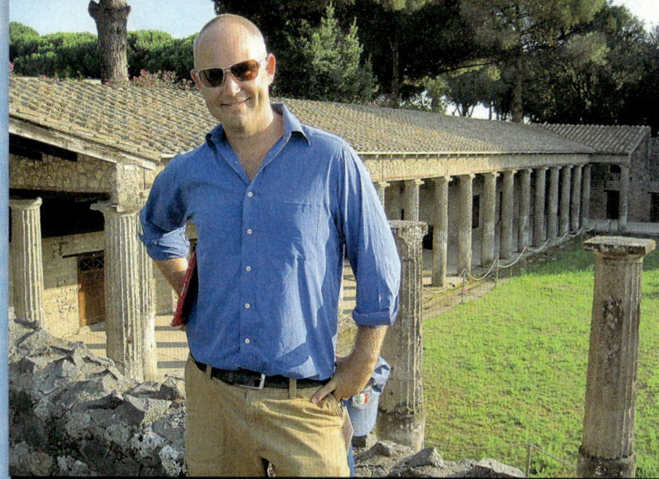

NATIONAL GEOGRAPHIC

ON **LOCATION** WITH

Steven Ellis

Archaeologist

Have you ever heard the expression "All roads lead to Rome?" Well, 2,000 years ago, all roads actually did lead to Rome. Though it began as a small town on the Tiber River in Italy, in only a few centuries Rome came to dominate the Mediterranean and build a civilization that stretched from northern Europe to Syria. I'm Steven Ellis, and I work with National Geographic. Welcome to the world of the Romans!

< **CRITICAL VIEWING** The ruins of Pompeii, seen here in the shadow of Mount Vesuvius, continue to reveal much about the lives of the ancient Romans. What details do you notice in the photo that resemble features you might see in a town or city today?

UNIT 4

TIME LINE OF WORLD EVENTS

Ancient Rome

800 B.C.

753 B.C.
According to legend, Romulus founds the city of Rome. *(illustration of Romulus on a coin)*

509 B.C.
Rome becomes a republic.

100 B.C.

44 B.C.
Julius Caesar is assassinated by a group of Roman senators.

The World

750 B.C.
EUROPE
Greek city-states flourish with shared Greek identity but individual loyalties, customs, and governments.

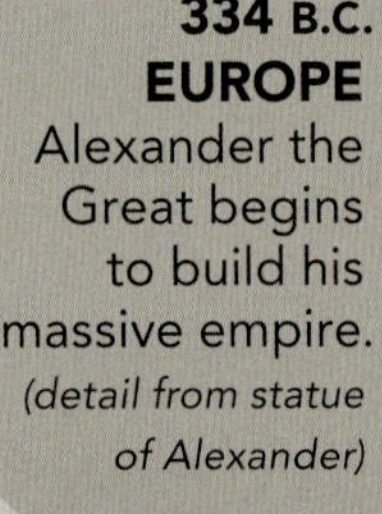

334 B.C.
EUROPE
Alexander the Great begins to build his massive empire.
(detail from statue of Alexander)

COMPARE TIME LINES

What other world event happened around the time Rome became an empire?

A.D. 26–29
Jesus preaches religious ideas that will form the basis of Christianity.

A.D. 476
Invasions bring about the fall of the Western Roman Empire.
(painting of the sack of Rome)

27 B.C.
Rome becomes an empire, and Augustus becomes its first emperor.

A.D. 177
The Roman Empire reaches its greatest extent, stretching over parts of Europe, Asia, and Africa.

A.D. 395
The Roman Empire is divided into the Eastern and Western empires.

A.D. 100

A.D. 300

A.D. 500

10 B.C.
ASIA
The Silk Roads connect China to the Mediterranean.

A.D. 250
AMERICAS
The Maya build great cities and make significant advances in learning.
(Maya pyramid)

A.D. 300s
AFRICA
The kingdom of Aksum in East Africa reaches its height under Ezana.

UNIT 4
GEOGRAPHY IN HISTORY

FROM REPUBLIC TO EMPIRE

146 B.C.–A.D. 117

Find Rome on the map. That's how it began: as a small dot in a land once known as Italia. Actually, Rome was even smaller, since it began as a village of farmers. But the Romans developed a civilization that grew to become one of the greatest empires the world has ever seen.

At its full extent, the Roman Empire stretched over three continents. It was held together by taxes, the powerful Roman army, and an amazing network of roads. Through periods of peace and war, Rome remained the center of the Western world for hundreds of years.

What body of water probably helped link the Roman Empire?

Hadrian's Wall

Time Line of Good and Bad Emperors

"Bad" emperor
Historians traditionally call the first three emperors below "bad" because they abused their power.

"Good" emperor
The other five emperors are considered "good" because, like Augustus, they presided over a period of peace and ruled wisely.

Caligula
A.D. 37–41
- Reigned as a cruel tyrant
- Insisted on being treated as a god

Nero
A.D. 54–68
- Committed many murders
- Did nothing while much of Rome burned

Domitian
A.D. 81–96
- Ruled as a dictator
- Murdered many of his enemies

Nerva
A.D. 96–98
- First emperor chosen for the job
- Tried to end tryannical rule

0 50 100 150 200 250 kilometers
0 50 100 150 200 250 miles
Places on the map are labeled with their early Latin names.
The Arch of Constantine, Rome
Detail of Trajan's column, A.D. 113, Trajan's Forum, Rome
As a vassal of Rome, this kingdom managed much of its internal affairs, but Rome controlled its foreign affairs.
Volga
E
Sarmatia
Dniester
Dnieper
BOSPORAN KINGDOM
Caucasus Mts.
Caspian Sea
Lake Sevan
ARMENIA A.D. 114–117
Lake Van
Black Sea
DACIA
Danube
MOESIA INFERIOR
MOESIA SUPERIOR
THRACIA
Byzantium (Constantinople)
BYTHINIA ET PONTUS
CAPPADOCIA
Parthia
ASSYRIA A.D. 116–117
ASIA
Asia Minor
MESOPOTAMIA A.D. 115–117
Tigris
Euphrates
Persian Gulf
MACEDONIA
Aegean Sea
ASIA
GALATIA
EPIRUS
LYCIA
CILICIA
SYRIA
Athens
ACHAEA
Sparta
Tripolis
Ionian Sea
CYPRUS
CRETA
JUDAEA
Jerusalem
Dead Sea
Sea
ARABIA
Alexandria
Ptolemais
Nile
CA
CYRENE
AEGYPTUS
Red
The curled fingers were part of a statue that stood in Arabia around A.D. 160.
Roman Territory, 201 B.C.
Gains by 100 B.C.
Area ruled by the time of Julius Caesar's death, 44 B.C.
Area ruled by the time of Caesar Augustus' death, A.D.14
Gains by Emperor Trajan, A.D. 117 (Roman Empire at its greatest extent)
Region temporarily held by Rome, with dates
Vassal of Rome
Fortified frontier

Trajan
A.D. 98–117

- Brought Empire to greatest extent
- Created aid program for the poor

Hadrian
A.D. 117–138

- Fortified the Empire's borders
- Enforced peace

Antoninus Plus
A.D. 138–161

- Reigned over period of peace and prosperity
- Specified that Marcus Aurelius succeed him

Marcus Aurelius
A.D. 161–180

- Fought off invaders
- Reigned as a just and lawful man

CHAPTER

10 THE ROMAN REPUBLIC

509 B.C. – 44 B.C.

SECTION 1
EARLY ROME

KEY VOCABULARY	NAMES & PLACES
consul	Aeneas
dictator	Cicero
legend	Cincinnatus
patrician	Etruscans
peninsula	Forum
plebeian	Romulus and Remus
republic	Senate
tribune	Tiber River
veto	Twelve Tables

SECTION 2
SOCIETY AND CULTURE

KEY VOCABULARY	NAMES & PLACES
aristocracy	Council of Plebs
pantheon	
patriarchy	

SECTION 3
THE ARMY AND EXPANSION

KEY VOCABULARY	NAMES & PLACES
legionary	Carthage
province	Hannibal
	Punic Wars

SECTION 4
THE END OF THE REPUBLIC

KEY VOCABULARY	NAMES & PLACES
civil war	First Triumvirate
reform	Julius Caesar

Temple of Venus and Rome

READING STRATEGY

ORGANIZE IDEAS: COMPARE AND CONTRAST When you read, you often compare and contrast one thing with another to help you understand new information. As you read the chapter, use a Venn diagram like this one to compare and contrast the lives of rich people and poor people in the Roman Republic.

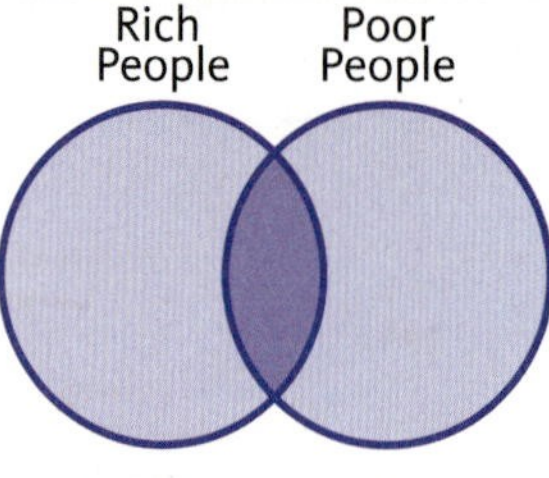
Rich People
Poor People

Painting of gladiators in the Colosseum

Claudian Aqueduct

This model of Rome shows the city as it might have looked in A.D. 312.

1.1 The Geography of Ancient Rome

If you wanted to build a Mediterranean empire, you'd probably start from Rome. The city lies near the heart of the sea. Geographically, it's the best place to begin a conquest of the Mediterranean.

MAIN IDEA

Rome's location had many geographic advantages that helped it grow and become powerful.

THE ITALIAN PENINSULA

Italy lies on a **peninsula**, or land surrounded by water on three sides, in the Mediterranean Sea. It is shaped like a boot and looks as though it is kicking a football—the island of Sicily—toward North Africa. Italy is attached to the rest of Europe by a massive range of snow-covered mountains called the Alps.

Another mountain range, the Apennines (A-puh-nynz), runs down the center of Italy. These mountains slope through wooded hills to sunny coastal plains and the blue waters of the Mediterranean. In time, the Romans would come to call the Mediterranean *Mare Nostrum* (MAHR-ay NOHS-truhm), or "Our Sea."

Rome was founded on seven hills on the volcanic west coast of Italy. The Romans embraced the advanced cultures of their neighbors to the north and south. Ideas adopted from these cultures helped Rome flourish and grow strong.

THE CITY OF ROME

Rome's geography helped it survive and thrive. What first made Rome important was its strategic position. It was located at a key crossing point of the **Tiber** (TY-bur) **River**.

The location was also a natural stopping point on the valuable trade routes running north to south and inland from the sea. The city was far enough from the coast to escape deadly attacks by pirates and enemies but close enough to benefit from the Mediterranean's busy sea trade. Olive oil and wine were among Rome's most commonly traded items.

The circle of seven hills on which Rome was built rose above the river and also provided protection against attack. These seven hills became Rome's center. Romans built important government buildings there. The hills were also home to religious temples and entertainment facilities. Roads branched off from this area to the outside world.

The land around the city had fertile soil, a good water supply, and a mild climate. These qualities helped Rome's agriculture flourish and support the large population needed to wage and win wars in the ancient world. As the Roman historian Livy boasted, "With good reason did gods and men choose this site for founding a city."

Rome's central location helped it take over much of Italy. Then Italy's central location helped Rome become a powerful force in the Mediterranean. Around the sea, the riches of Europe, Southwest Asia, and North Africa were temptingly close. Control of the Mediterranean seemed within the grasp of a strong, ambitious, and determined civilization like Rome.

THE HILLS OF ROME
Alta Semita
Quirinal Hill
Viminal Hill
Clivus Patricus
Esquiline Hill
Temple of Jupiter
Capitoline Hill
Senate House
Forum
Regia
Palatine Hill
Caelian Hill
Via Appia
Circus Maximus
Tiber River
Aventine Hill
N
E
W
S
ALPS
0
100 Miles
0
100 Kilometers
Apennines
Corsica
Rome
ITALY
Sardinia
40°N
Sicily
Mediterranean Sea
10°E

REVIEW & ASSESS

1. **READING CHECK** How did Rome's geographic advantages help the city grow and gain power?

2. **FIND MAIN IDEAS AND DETAILS** What physical features helped protect Rome from invasion?

3. **INTERPRET MAPS** Where did the Romans build most of their buildings? What might be a good reason for this location?

1.2 The Founding of Rome

Three thousand years ago, a few small huts stood scattered across the hills that overlooked the Tiber River's swampy floodplain. Within just 250 years, this humble landscape was transformed into the heart of a mighty empire.

MAIN IDEA

Rome grew from a tiny village to a city between 753 and 509 B.C.

MYTHICAL BEGINNINGS

The Romans loved stories, especially bloody ones with great heroes. One of the most popular **legends**, or stories about famous people and events in the past, was about the founding of Rome. Not only did the story contain a hero and plenty of blood, but it also linked Rome to the great civilization of ancient Greece.

According to the legend, a Trojan hero named **Aeneas** (ih-NEE-uhs) was the ancestor of Rome's founders—the twin brothers **Romulus** (RAHM-yuh-luhs) and **Remus** (REE-muhs). As babies, the brothers were abandoned. They were rescued by a wolf and raised by a shepherd. When they grew up, the brothers founded their own city. In 753 B.C., Romulus became the first king of the city, which he named Rome, after himself.

Research actually supports a part of the story of Romulus and Remus. Archaeologists have uncovered ruins suggesting that the hills around Rome contained many small villages in 1000 B.C. Some of these villages merged with villages in the valleys to create a larger settlement around 750 B.C. This was early Rome.

EARLY ROMANS

At this time, Italy was a patchwork of different peoples with their own rulers, customs, and languages. Most of Rome's original residents were Latins, who came from an area around the Tiber River called Latium. The Latins were not united, and their many cities were often at war with one another as well as with neighboring peoples. In its early days, Rome was a small village in a violently competitive world.

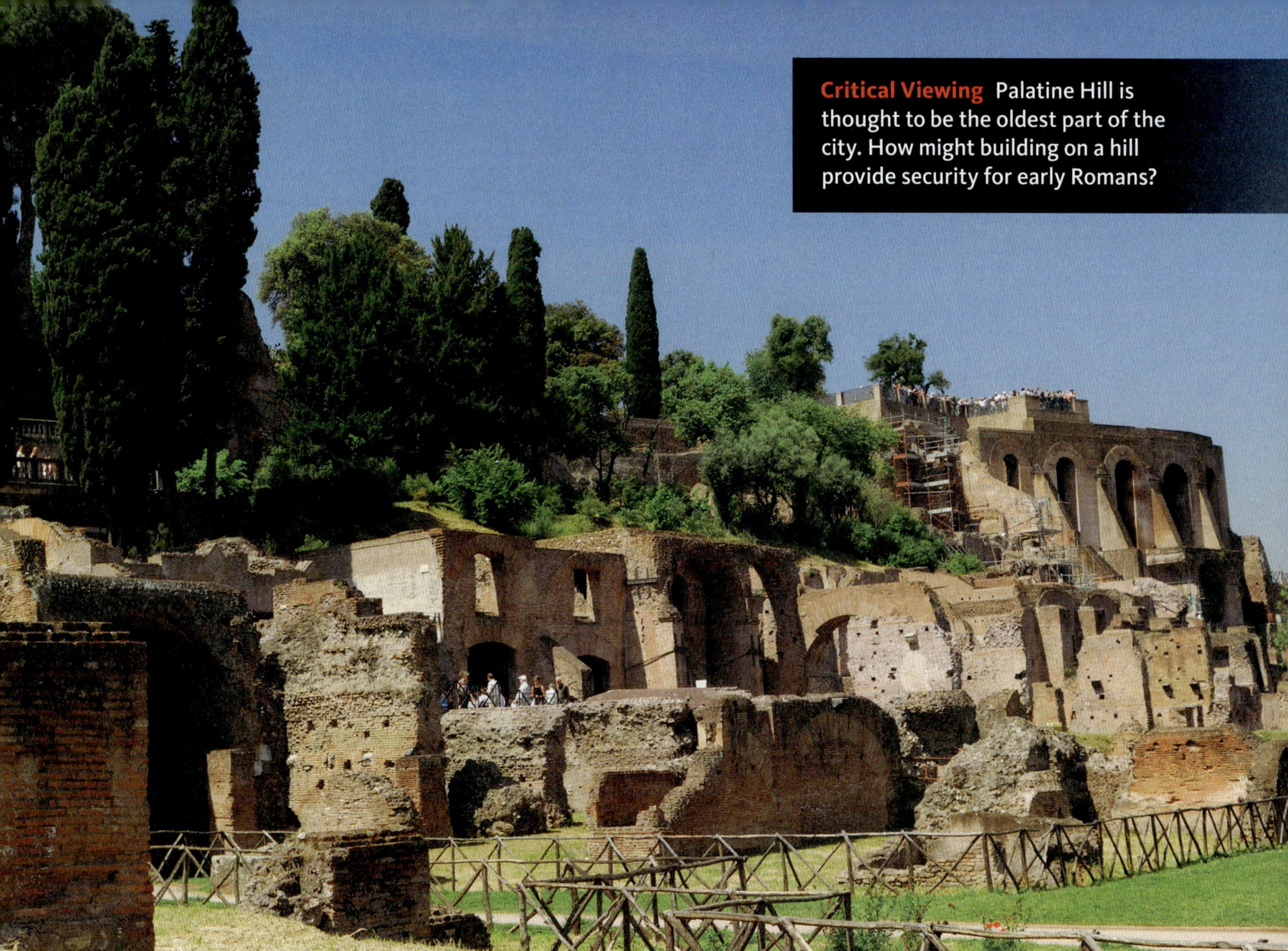

Critical Viewing Palatine Hill is thought to be the oldest part of the city. How might building on a hill provide security for early Romans?

What helped make Rome strong was that it welcomed people from many different lands. Foreigners of different classes and professions settled in the city and helped it grow in size and strength. The people who most influenced early Rome were the Greeks to the south and the **Etruscans** (ih-TRUHS-kuhnz) to the north.

The Greeks dominated the Mediterranean and had many colonies in southern Italy. Through travel and trade, they introduced the Romans to important advances in agriculture, architecture, and learning. The Romans learned to grow olives and modified the Greek alphabet for writing. Roman poets copied the Greek style of the long epic poem.

The Etruscans were expert traders, metalworkers, and engineers. Three Etruscan kings who came to rule Rome brought these professional skills with them. They laid out the city's streets in a grid plan around a central square. The Etruscans replaced mud huts with stone houses and built Rome's first temples and public buildings. By 509 B.C., Rome was becoming the city we still see traces of today.

REVIEW & ASSESS

1. **READING CHECK** How did people from different cultures help Rome develop into a city?
2. **IDENTIFY MAIN IDEAS AND DETAILS** According to legend, how was Rome founded?
3. **MAKE INFERENCES** What does the willingness to adopt other peoples' ideas suggest about Roman values?

1.3 Republican Government

You wouldn't have wanted to meet the Etruscan king Tarquin the Proud in a dark alley. He ruled as a tyrant—a cruel ruler—and had many of his opponents killed. In 509 B.C., the people of Rome overthrew Tarquin and established a new form of government.

MAIN IDEA

Rome developed a republican form of government that protected the rights of ordinary citizens.

THE YOUNG REPUBLIC

In a **republic**, citizens vote for their leaders. Only free adult men were citizens in Rome, but not all citizens were equal. Roman society was divided into two groups: the patricians and the plebeians. The **patricians** (puh-TRIH-shuhnz) were wealthy landowners. The **plebeians** (plih-BEE-uhnz), who included poorer farmers and craftsmen, made up the majority of Rome's citizens but were under-represented in the government.

The plebeians wanted a say in how Rome was run. As a result, in 494 B.C., they went on strike. The plebeians left the city, shutting down Roman shops and businesses, and set up their own government. Economic activity came to a halt. Once the patricians started losing money, they became frightened and agreed to share their power. In time, the plebeians were allowed to elect their own representatives, called **tribunes**, who fought to protect the rights of ordinary citizens.

The plebeians had one more demand. Because Rome's laws were not written down, the patricians often interpreted them to favor their rich friends. The plebeians fought back. They insisted that the laws be not only written down but carved into bronze tablets and displayed for all to see. These laws became known as the **Twelve Tables**. They protected all Roman citizens from injustice. Some of these laws are the basis of our own laws today.

ROMAN GOVERNMENT

Rome's new, more representative government contained three branches. An executive branch led the government and the army, a legislative branch made the laws, and a judicial branch applied the laws.

The Romans put checks and balances in place to prevent any one branch from becoming too powerful. They also replaced the position of king with two leaders called **consuls**. The consuls had the authority of a king but for only one year. They shared power so equally that the consuls had the right to **veto**, or reject, each other's decisions.

The legislative branch was made up of the **Senate**, elected judicial officers, and two assemblies. The Senate advised the consuls. The assemblies represented the plebeians. In the beginning, most of the 300 members of the Senate were patricians. Over time, however, plebeians were also allowed to participate.

Senators often spoke out about issues in the Senate House and in public squares. Delivering such speeches was a highly valued skill in Rome. One of Rome's most brilliant speakers was **Cicero** (SIH-suh-roh), who often used his speeches to attack those who he believed were a threat to the republic.

Critical Viewing In this painting, Cicero delivers a speech before the Senate. What qualities does the artist try to convey in his portrayal of Cicero?

Cicero Denounces Catiline, Cesare Maccari, 1888

In times of crisis, the Romans appointed **dictators** who had complete control but were expected to give up power after danger had passed. One such Roman dictator was **Cincinnatus** (sihn-suh-NA-tuhs). In 458 B.C., Rome's army was facing defeat by a fierce enemy, and the Senate wanted Cincinnatus to take charge. He accepted the dictatorship, defeated the enemy, and then surrendered his power and returned to his farm. The example set by Cincinnatus was celebrated by the Romans, who valued the idea of civic duty—putting service to the community ahead of personal interest.

REVIEW & ASSESS

1. **READING CHECK** How did the Roman government come to protect the rights of the citizens?
2. **COMPARE AND CONTRAST** In what ways are the governments of the Roman Republic and the United States similar?
3. **DRAW CONCLUSIONS** Why was it important to the plebeians to have Roman laws written down?

The ruins of the Roman Forum represent different periods of Rome's ancient history. Here older ruins of buildings surround the Arch of Titus. The Colosseum stands in the background.

1.4 The Roman Forum

The Roman Forum was the place to be. It was the place to meet, shop, do business, worship, celebrate, and be entertained. This public square was one of the liveliest and most important places in all of Rome.

MAIN IDEA

The Roman Forum was the political, religious, economic, and social center of the Roman Republic.

BURIAL GROUND TO PUBLIC SQUARE

The **Forum** developed over several centuries in a valley between the Palatine and Capitoline hills. In heavy rain, the banks of the Tiber River would burst, flooding the marshy valley. Long before Rome was founded, this scrap of swamp had been used as a burial ground. However, once Rome began to grow and its population spilled down the hills, the swamp became a piece of desirable real estate. Around 600 B.C., an Etruscan king built a sewer to drain the area and created an open public square paved with pebbles. The Roman Forum was born.

Everyone came to the Forum. It was the city's open-air market, where Romans could buy everything from local fruit and vegetables to imported Greek pottery. Rome's oldest road, the Via Sacra, looped through the Forum. Along the road, the early kings of Rome built a royal residence, shops, houses, and temples dedicated to their many gods and goddesses. At first these buildings were little more than mud huts or raised-earth platforms. Over time, these were replaced with permanent structures, and the Forum became the center of Rome's religious, economic, and social activity.

THE CENTER OF ROME

After the republic was founded, the Forum also became the center of Roman politics. Although the Forum's open space remained small, huge public and government buildings sprang up around it. The Temple of Saturn, dedicated to one of Rome's most important gods, became the treasury, holding the growing riches of the republic. The Curia was the meeting place of the Roman Senate. Political activity, ranging from public speeches to rioting mobs, took place at the Forum. Because it was where ordinary Romans gathered, the Forum was the perfect place to display the Twelve Tables.

The Forum also provided a setting for public spectacles. Crowds came to watch theatrical performances and athletic games. Even the funerals of important men were held at the Forum.

In later centuries, the Forum's buildings were transformed from brick to marble, and great bronze statues were added. Later rulers built other public places, but none ever rivaled the importance of the great Roman Forum.

REVIEW & ASSESS

1. **READING CHECK** Why did the ancient Romans gather in the Forum?
2. **IDENTIFY MAIN IDEAS AND DETAILS** How did the Forum change over time?
3. **MAKE INFERENCES** How did the Roman Forum reflect the democratic values of the Roman Republic?

2.1 Men and Women

Growing up in Rome wasn't easy. There were no laws to protect children. Boys were expected to head their own families one day, but most girls never had any real control over their futures.

MAIN IDEA

Men and women had different roles in Roman society.

MEN IN ANCIENT ROME

If you were born a boy in Rome, you already had a head start in life. Rome was a **patriarchy** (PAY-tree-ahr-kee), or a society in which men have all the power. Only men could vote or hold public office, fight in wars, and perform important ceremonies. In Rome's patriarchy, men were in charge of everything—especially the family.

The family was at the core of Roman society. At the head of every family was the senior male, the *paterfamilias* (pa-tur-fuh-MIH-lee-uhs). He made all decisions. He could put family members on trial and punish them—even execute them. The Twelve Tables eventually limited the power of the paterfamilias, but he still had a lot of control over his family.

Boys from poorer families received little education and often could not read or write. Instead they went out to work beginning at an early age. Wealthier families sent their sons to school. Classes started at dawn, and teachers, who were often Greek slaves, taught reading, writing, and arithmetic. Public speaking was another important lesson. Long poems had to be memorized, and mistakes were often punished with a beating.

After the age of 14, boys destined for government jobs continued their education with private tutors at home. At the age of 17, boys were considered to be men and registered as Roman citizens in the Forum.

WOMEN IN ANCIENT ROME

Roman women had more rights than women in ancient Greece, but those still didn't amount to much by modern standards. Roman women were subject to the authority of men—their husbands, fathers, or brothers. They could not vote or hold public office, though they could eventually own property and manage their own businesses and finances. A wife could also manage her husband's business, and women with powerful husbands had some political influence.

In Rome, a woman's main role was to be a good wife and mother. For many, this meant doing the daily domestic chores of spinning yarn, making clothes, cooking, cleaning, and looking after the children. Sometimes women would have paying jobs as well. In wealthier families, the wife managed the household and its finances, but slaves did all the physical labor.

If they were lucky, some girls from wealthy families learned basic reading, writing, and arithmetic at home. However, they mostly learned household skills to prepare them for married life, which could begin when girls were as young as 12. Most marriages had little to do with love but were arranged to benefit the family. However, divorce was easy and acceptable, and ambitious politicians might remarry many times to gain support from increasingly important families.

Critical Viewing This fresco, a style of painting on fresh plaster, shows a Roman woman and man holding writing tools. Based on the details you can see in the fresco, what conclusions can you draw about these people?

Portrait of Terentius Neo and His Wife, artist unknown, A.D. 1st century

REVIEW & ASSESS

1. **READING CHECK** What was a woman's role in Roman society?

2. **DETERMINE WORD MEANINGS** How does knowing that *pater* is Latin for "father" help clarify what *patriarchy* and *paterfamilias* mean?

3. **COMPARE AND CONTRAST** How did roles differ for boys and girls in Rome?

2.2 Rich and Poor

If you were rich in Rome, life was good, but if you were poor, life was miserable. The huge gap between rich and poor was reinforced by a rigid class structure that kept all Romans firmly in their places.

MAIN IDEA

Roman society was divided among different classes of people.

CLASS DIVISIONS

At the top of society was the **aristocracy**, the small group of wealthy patricians who owned most of the land and dominated the government. The majority of citizens were plebeians. Some were well-off and owned farms or businesses, but many were very poor. At the bottom was Rome's huge population of slaves.

The wealthiest families lived in luxurious country estates. These were built around elegant courtyards and decorated with works of fine art. Slaves did the hard work, leaving the homeowners free to conduct business, take part in politics, or spend time on their hobbies.

Most poor Romans lived and worked on small farms. Often, the wealthy used their money to buy up land and create huge farms worked entirely by slaves. This practice forced many farmers off their farms and into the city to look for work. There they lived in overcrowded buildings and worked at manual labor for very low wages.

Romans' diets also differed greatly. The poor used cheap pottery bowls to eat porridge or bread with vegetables. Meat was a luxury. Only the largest houses had kitchens, so even wealthier plebeians relied on restaurants for hot food. There they could eat fish, cooked meat, and vegetables and perhaps a dessert of sweet pastries. The very rich enjoyed lavish banquets with dozens of courses, including exotic foods.

Around 287 B.C., the plebeians finally achieved political equality when their representative assembly, the **Council of Plebs**, was allowed to make laws for all citizens. However, the patricians continued to dominate society.

SLAVES IN THE REPUBLIC

Slaves were the largest class in Rome, but they had the fewest rights. They were considered property to be bought and sold. Some slaves were prisoners from Rome's conquests. However, most were bought from foreign traders.

Slaves were very useful in Rome's economy. Most worked at manual labor, from household chores to construction work or agriculture. Skilled slaves might be craftspeople, while educated slaves might be teachers, doctors, or managers of their master's business. The worst slave jobs were in the mines or factories, where the work was tough, the conditions were harsh, and the life expectancy was short.

Some slaves were treated well, but others suffered very badly. Excessive punishments could spark rebellion. A slave named Spartacus led the most famous rebellion in 73 B.C. For about two years, his slave army fought the Roman soldiers and controlled large areas of the countryside. When Spartacus was finally defeated, 6,000 of his followers were executed as a warning to other slaves.

A WEALTHY ROMAN FAMILY'S HOME

The diagram below shows four key areas in a house belonging to a wealthy family. While the house contained rooms for the family's private use, much of the space was designed for business and social gatherings.

1 ENTRANCE HALL
The front door opened up on a large entrance hall. Most mornings clients seeking favors waited here for the chance to pay their respects to their patron, or financial supporter.

3 OFFICE
This room was located behind the reception area and functioned as the patron's office. The room could also be used for family gatherings.

1
2
3
4

2 RECEPTION ROOM
In this large, airy space, the patron showed off his wealth and received visitors. The rectangular space beneath the opening in the roof served to collect rainwater.

4 COURTYARD
A roofed porch enclosed the courtyard garden. The space often included fountains, benches, and sculptures. In the richest homes, the porch's inner walls were often decorated with frescoes.

REVIEW & ASSESS

1. **READING CHECK** How did the lives of the Roman classes differ?
2. **INTEGRATE VISUALS** In what ways might plebeian or slave homes have differed from the home illustrated above?
3. **MAKE INFERENCES** How do you think the patricians reacted at first to the plebeians' political equality?

2.3 Gods and Beliefs

To Romans, the wrath of their gods was always present. They felt that honoring the gods—or at least not upsetting them—was a matter of life and death.

MAIN IDEA

Religious worship was an important part of Roman life.

Ten Gods of Ancient Rome

Jupiter King of the gods

Saturn God of agriculture

Mercury Messenger of the gods

Apollo God of poetry and music

Mars God of war

Neptune God of the sea and earthquakes

Ceres Goddess of the harvest

Juno Goddess of women; wife of Jupiter

Diana Goddess of the moon and the hunt

Venus Goddess of love and beauty

ROMAN WORSHIP

Roman religion was based on a **pantheon** (PAN-thee-ahn), or group of many gods, most adopted from the ancient Greeks. These gods had Roman names and were believed to have human traits and to control areas of Roman life. For example, Jupiter was the king of the gods. Juno was the goddess of women, marriage, childbirth, and children. Mars was the god of war, and Venus was the beautiful goddess of love.

The pantheon constantly grew to include the gods of people Rome conquered. Later, the Romans worshipped their rulers as gods after their death. Some rulers claimed to be living gods, but this claim made them very unpopular.

Romans worshipped their gods almost anywhere. Nearly every home had a shrine where the paterfamilias would make daily offerings to the gods that protected his family and his house. Priests managed temples for the most important gods. The priests conducted the rituals that Romans believed would secure the gods' favor.

The Roman calendar had many religious festivals that attracted huge audiences. The government funded many of them to ensure that the gods granted Rome good harvests or victories in war. These festivals included colorful processions, feasts, music, dance, theater, and sports.

THE ROMAN WAY

Roman gods had human traits that often highlighted the qualities most prized by the Romans. The Romans were a very practical and ambitious people, so they valued qualities that would help them achieve success. They considered the Greek virtues of beauty, grace, and elegance as nice but not essential. Instead, they preferred qualities like discipline, strength, and loyalty. Discipline and strength helped Romans endure hardship and overcome problems. Loyalty bound strong individuals together into even more powerful groups.

These valued qualities emphasize an important aspect of the Roman personality—*gravitas* (GRA-vuh-tahs). Having gravitas means being solemn and serious. Romans respected people who acted with great consideration, determination, and energy. These characteristics helped the people of the Roman Republic accomplish remarkable achievements in war, politics, law, commerce, and engineering. These qualities came to be known as "the Roman Way."

Trevi Fountain, Nicola Salvi and Giuseppe Pannini, 1762

Critical Viewing A statue of Neptune, god of the sea, stands above the flowing water of Rome's Trevi Fountain. What details in the statue convey the qualities that the ancient Romans admired?

REVIEW & ASSESS

1. **READING CHECK** Why was the worship of gods an important part of Roman life?
2. **SUMMARIZE** In what ways did the Romans expect the gods to affect daily life?
3. **DRAW CONCLUSIONS** What qualities did the Romans value? Why did they value these qualities more than others?

3.1 The Roman Army

War in the ancient world was extremely physical, and the Romans were good at it. The republic developed a formidable fighting force of well-trained professional soldiers called the legion. It was the ultimate weapon of ancient warfare.

XV

MAIN IDEA

Organization and training brought Rome's army military success.

THE ROMAN LEGION

It was a privilege to serve in Rome's legions. At first only property-owning citizens could join, and they had to supply their own weapons. A legion contained around 4,200 men, and each consul led an army of two legions. When the battle season finished in October, everybody went home.

Yet as the republic fought longer wars farther from Rome, citizens who owned property became reluctant to serve. In 107 B.C., the consul Marius (MAIR-ee-uhs) found himself short of recruits, so he allowed poor, landless citizens to volunteer. The government supplied their equipment, which included a bronze helmet, mail armor, a short sword, a javelin, and an oval shield. These men became professional soldiers known as **legionaries**.

Marius also reorganized the legions for maximum strength and flexibility. He often grouped squads of men into 100-man centuries, or units. These units, in turn, were grouped into 600-man cohorts, or divisions. Ten cohorts made up a legion, now 6,000 strong. This command structure gave Roman generals control over large numbers of men, and it continues to be a model for modern military organization.

The legions became an efficient military machine that Rome used to conquer its enemies and expand its territory. Rome recruited additional soldiers from the regions it defeated, which led to more military might and manpower. If a Roman army was defeated, Rome would send an even bigger army the next time. This stubborn determination made Rome unstoppable.

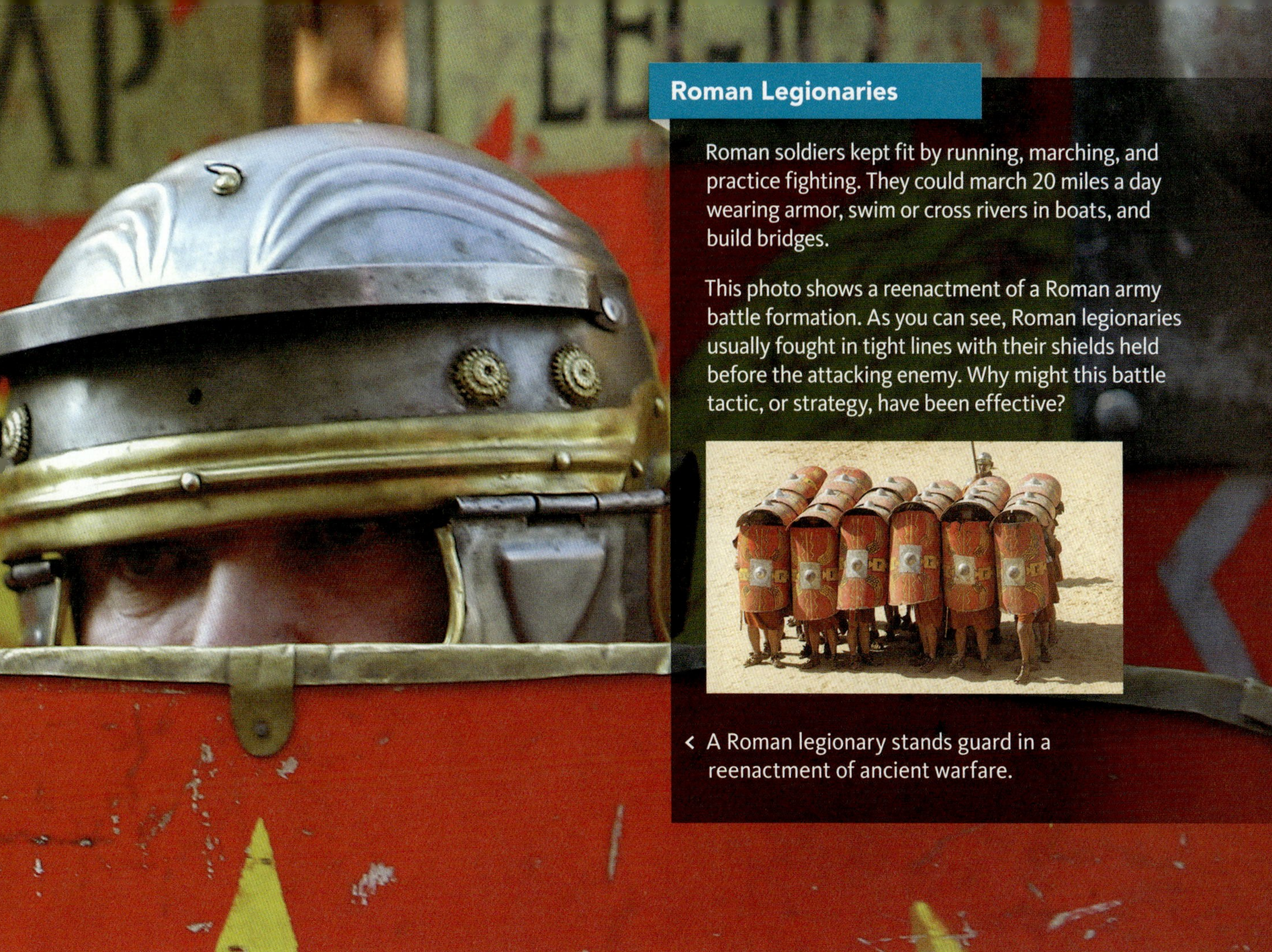

Roman Legionaries

Roman soldiers kept fit by running, marching, and practice fighting. They could march 20 miles a day wearing armor, swim or cross rivers in boats, and build bridges.

This photo shows a reenactment of a Roman army battle formation. As you can see, Roman legionaries usually fought in tight lines with their shields held before the attacking enemy. Why might this battle tactic, or strategy, have been effective?

‹ A Roman legionary stands guard in a reenactment of ancient warfare.

LIFE OF A LEGIONARY

Legionaries joined young and served for a maximum of 16 years. A recruit had to pass a physical inspection. Then in front of the legion's revered flag, the eagle, he swore an oath to serve the republic. This oath inspired a powerful sense of duty to comrades, to commanders, and to Rome itself.

Daily life revolved around a squad that trained, marched, and fought together. Soldiers built strong bonds of friendship and loyalty through sharing a tent, duties, and meals. When off duty, a legionary might play games or visit the public baths. However, duty always came first. While bravery led to rewards, failure led to severe punishment.

Training was key to the legions' success. Legionaries learned to carry out complicated instructions in the chaos of battle. At the end of each day, they built a fortified camp with deep ditches and high walls called palisades. Over time, they also built the straight roads and strong bridges that connected the republic and carried its men into battle.

REVIEW & ASSESS

1. **READING CHECK** How did the Roman army's organization and training lead to success?
2. **IDENTIFY MAIN IDEAS AND DETAILS** What were the duties of a legionary?
3. **SUMMARIZE** What changes did Marius make to the Roman army?

3.2 HISTORY THROUGH OBJECTS

ROMAN ARMOR

"The infantry soldier carries so much equipment that he differs little from a mule," said an observer from the first century A.D. Along with his armor, shield, and weapons, which combined weighed some 50 pounds, a soldier had to carry food, tools, and personal belongings that could double the weight. Based on what you see here, what might have been some challenges that Roman soldiers encountered on and off the battlefield?

Hooded Cloak
Wool kept soldiers warm.

Stake
Each soldier carried two to build a palisade.

Iron Pick
Picks were used in camp construction.

Canteen
Canteens held *posca*, a mixture of vinegar and water.

Javelin
The heavy javelin was thrown at close range and was designed to bend on impact.

Sword
Legionaries wore it on the right; officers wore it on the left.

Galea, or Helmet
The iron helmet followed a design used by warriors from Gaul.

The ridge protected against vertical sword strikes.

Wide cheek flaps protected the face but left ears exposed to hear orders.

A wide projection shielded the neck and deflected blows from behind.

Breastplate
Made of steel plates bound by leather straps, it weighed about 20 pounds and was lined with padding for comfort.

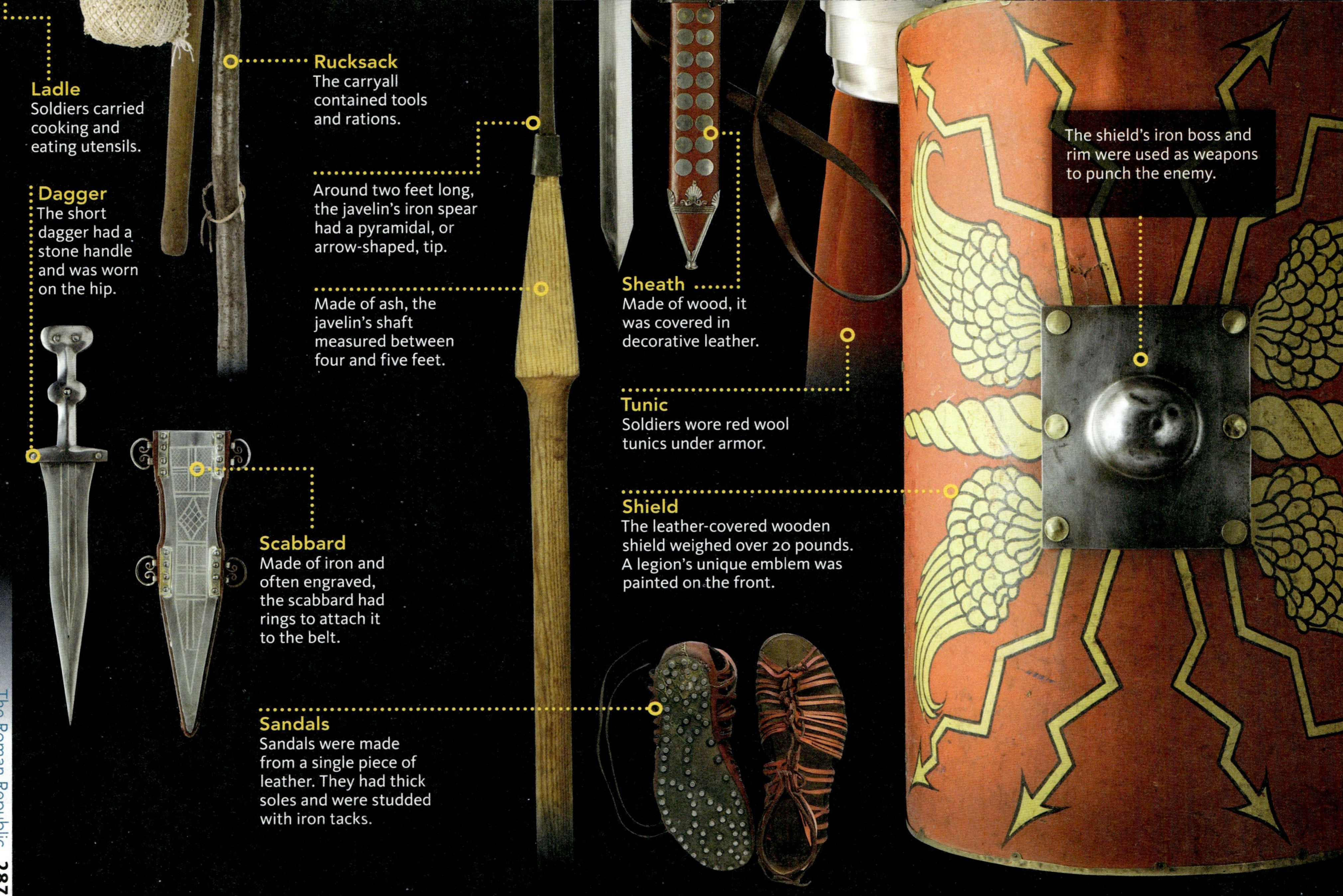
Ladle
Soldiers carried cooking and eating utensils.
Dagger
The short dagger had a stone handle and was worn on the hip.
Rucksack
The carryall contained tools and rations.
Around two feet long, the javelin's iron spear had a pyramidal, or arrow-shaped, tip.
Made of ash, the javelin's shaft measured between four and five feet.
Scabbard
Made of iron and often engraved, the scabbard had rings to attach it to the belt.
Sandals
Sandals were made from a single piece of leather. They had thick soles and were studded with iron tacks.
Sheath
Made of wood, it was covered in decorative leather.
Tunic
Soldiers wore red wool tunics under armor.
Shield
The leather-covered wooden shield weighed over 20 pounds. A legion's unique emblem was painted on the front.
The shield's iron boss and rim were used as weapons to punch the enemy.

3.3 Hannibal and the Punic Wars

To win in the big leagues, you've got to take on the champion. In 264 B.C., Rome turned its might against the Mediterranean superpower of Carthage. The two enemies fought a series of wars, called the **Punic** (PYOO-nihk) **Wars**, that lasted, off and on, for about 100 years.

MAIN IDEA

Rome and Carthage fought the Punic Wars for control of the Mediterranean Sea.

War Elephants

Hannibal's war elephants were the "battle tanks" of the ancient world. Their size and power made them a terrifying and innovative battle weapon. Normally gentle creatures, however, the elephants had to be provoked and prodded to attack.

THE FIRST PUNIC WAR

The North African city of **Carthage** was immensely rich. It had grown from a Phoenician colony (*Punic* is Latin for "Phoenician") into a trading empire. Carthage had established colonies and trading ports around the western Mediterranean, and the city controlled valuable mineral resources in North Africa and present-day Spain. In time, Rome began to compete with Carthage for control of the sea.

The First Punic War broke out in 264 B.C. over the strategic island of Sicily (see the map in Section 3.5). The war was fought mainly at sea, but Carthage's navy was vastly superior to Rome's. After suffering a key defeat, Rome quickly built a fleet of 120 powerful warships that beat the Carthaginian navy in almost every battle. These victories allowed Rome to occupy the important islands of Sicily, Sardinia, and Corsica. In 241 B.C., Carthage surrendered to Rome. Its defeated general was Hamilcar Barca, the father of a young boy named **Hannibal**.

THE SECOND PUNIC WAR

When Hannibal was a child, he promised his father that he would always hate Rome. When he became a Carthaginian general, he made good on that promise. After Hannibal attacked one of Rome's allies in southern Spain, the Second Punic War began in 218 B.C. While the Romans planned a counterattack,

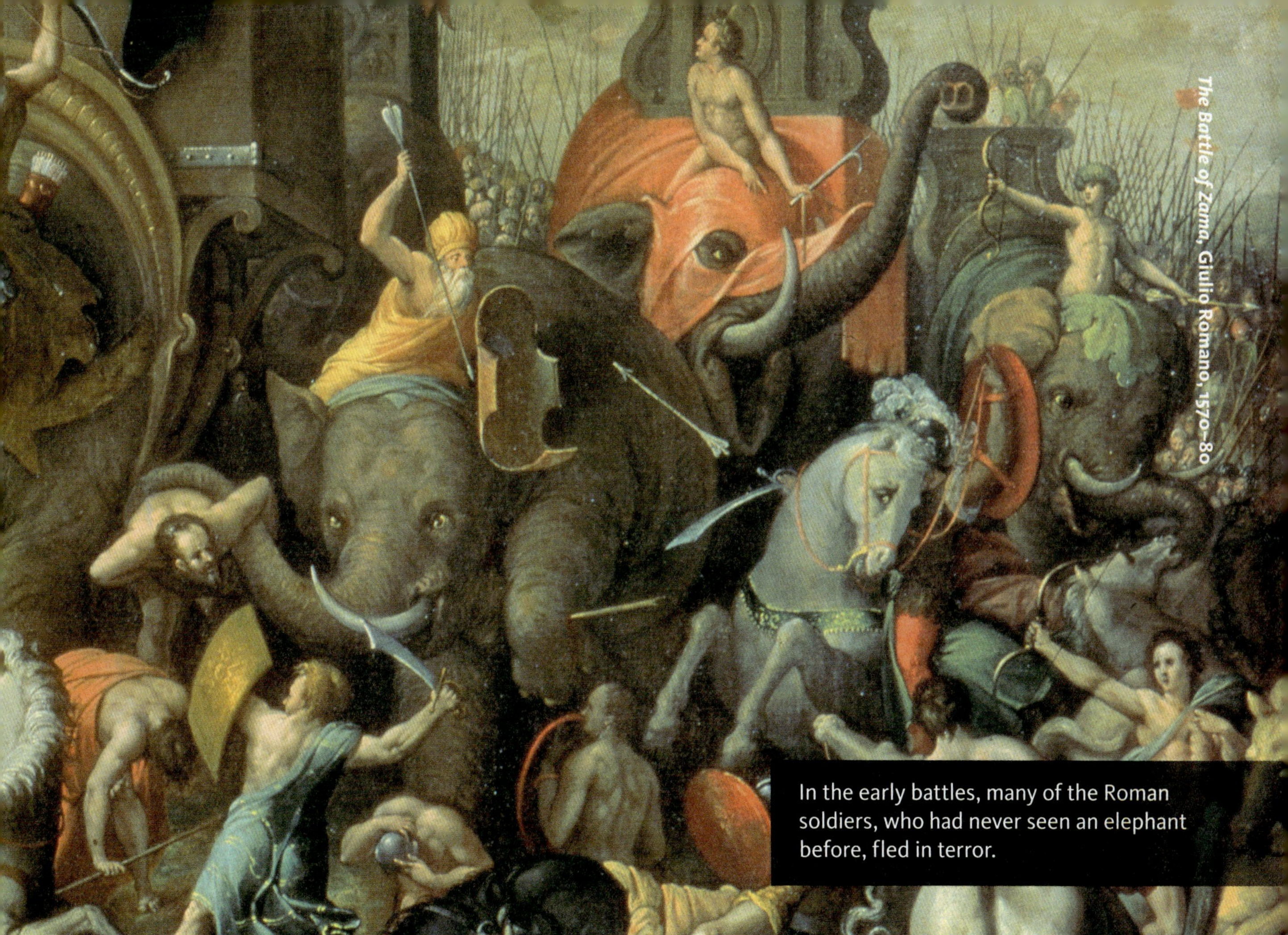
The Battle of Zama, Giulio Romano, 1570–80

In the early battles, many of the Roman soldiers, who had never seen an elephant before, fled in terror.

Hannibal outsmarted them. He led about 60,000 soldiers and a herd of war elephants out of Spain and across the Alps to invade the Italian Peninsula by land. This astonishing action caught the Romans by surprise. Hannibal swiftly defeated the Roman army in battle after battle as he swept south toward Rome itself.

By 216 B.C., Hannibal was in southeast Italy, facing a huge Roman army at Cannae (KA-nee). Although outnumbered, Hannibal defeated the legions. His brilliant tactics are still studied at military academies today.

Rome fought on, however, and steadily wore down Hannibal's army. In 205 B.C., the Roman general Scipio (SIHP-ee-oh) was elected consul. He invaded North Africa in a plan devised to draw Hannibal out of Italy. It worked. Hannibal left Italy to defend his homeland. At the Battle of Zama (ZAY-muh) in 202 B.C., Hannibal and Scipio faced each other in a desperate fight. They were both brilliant generals, but after a long, bloody battle, Hannibal was defeated and later fled abroad to Asia Minor in present-day Turkey. In 201 B.C., the Second Punic War ended, and Rome once again ruled the western Mediterranean.

REVIEW & ASSESS

1. **READING CHECK** What events led Rome to fight two wars with Carthage?
2. **COMPARE AND CONTRAST** How were the two Punic Wars alike and how were they different?
3. **DRAW CONCLUSIONS** Why was Hannibal's trek through the Alps such an astonishing accomplishment?

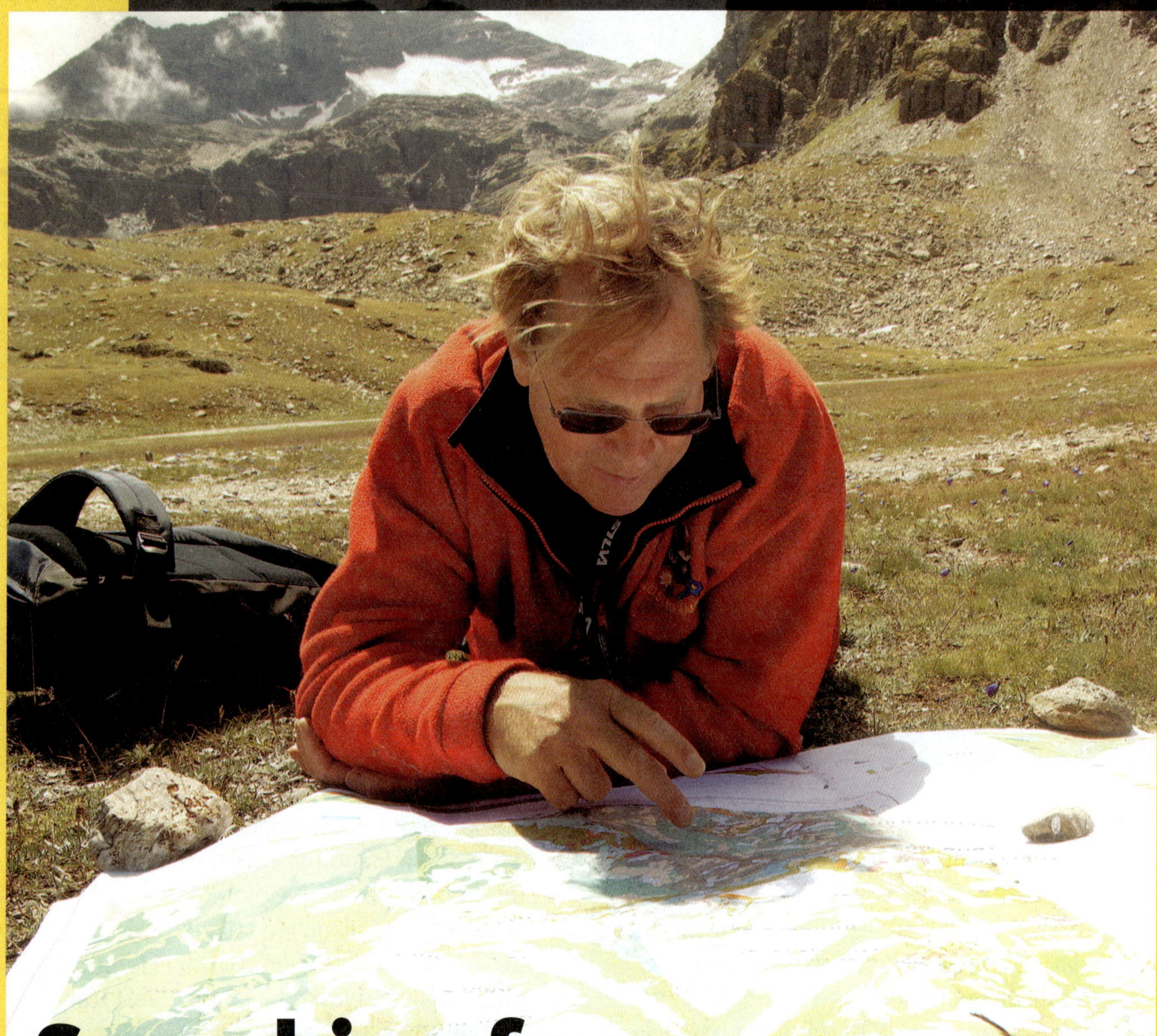

Searching for Hannibal's Route

Patrick Hunt is a man on a mission to solve one of history's mysteries: Where did Hannibal cross the Alps? One of the most daring military maneuvers of all time, Hannibal's invasion of Italy in 218 B.C. required marching about 40,000 men and 37 elephants across these rugged mountains in winter. Hannibal didn't leave a map behind though. "For the last decade plus, we've been trying to pinpoint Hannibal's route," says Hunt. Because of his research, now he's close to an answer.

^ Patrick Hunt theorizes that Hannibal used the Col du Clapier-Savine Coche mountain pass, shown above, to cross the Alps into Italy.

MAIN IDEA

Geo-archaeologist Patrick Hunt is rediscovering the route of Hannibal's army.

HANNIBAL'S FOOTSTEPS

Patrick Hunt is a National Geographic grantee and the director of the Hannibal Expedition. Since 1994, he has used everything from ancient literature to satellite imaging to find the mountain pass Hannibal traveled. "It's like looking for a needle in a haystack," Hunt says, "but it's not just for the sake of mystery." The Alps were considered impassable in winter. Historians know Hannibal crossed them, but they don't know how because they don't know where. If someone were to find the route, historians might begin to understand how Hannibal achieved this amazing military feat.

HANNIBAL'S ROUTE
GAUL
ALPS
EUROPE
Col du Clapier-Savine Coche
Rhône R.
PYRENEES
IBERIAN PENINSULA
ITALY
Adriatic Sea
Corsica
Rome
Sardinia
Balearic Is.
Mediterranean Sea
Carthage
AFRICA
0° 10°E 40°N
N S E W
0 200 Miles
0 200 Kilometers

The Roman historians Polybius (puh-LIH-bee-uhs) and Livy (LIH-vee) wrote accounts of Hannibal's campaign. Although they use few place-names, they describe the geographic features Hannibal saw and the distances he traveled each day. Hunt uses these clues to work out probable routes. "It's a bit like sleuthing," he admits. "We've been over close to 30 Alpine passes, mostly on foot, constantly comparing how they fit the descriptions."

A SCIENTIFIC APPROACH

Geo-archaeology applies earth sciences such as geography and geology to archaeology. These sciences are vital to Hunt's search because he has to factor in 2,000 years of change. Mountains may look different because of erosion; climate changes may have moved the snow line. "The first thing we do on-site is to examine the basic rock types to check how stable the geology is," he says. "The more stable it is, the less likely it is to have changed much." It's a scientific approach and a physically challenging one, too. Several team members have suffered broken bones because of the treacherous working conditions.

Through a process of elimination, Hunt is now confident he knows most of Hannibal's route. The view from the summit of the Col du Clapier-Savine Coche fits perfectly with the descriptions in the ancient texts. "Now we're looking for physical evidence, and we are focused on the campsites," he explains. "Ash has a chemical signature that lasts over 2,000 years. We think we've found the ash of Hannibal's camps and have pinpointed a major summit campground. Now we're looking at stone deposits that may mark graves. An elephant burial would be fantastic!"

"Hannibal is very close to my heart," asserts Hunt. "He lost close to 40 percent of his men crossing the Alps. That would be unacceptable today, but Hannibal went on to defeat the Romans multiple times. This is a man who wins battle after battle but ultimately doesn't win the war."

REVIEW & ASSESS

1. **READING CHECK** What tools is Patrick Hunt using to determine Hannibal's route through the Alps?
2. **INTERPRET MAPS** In what ways did the Alps both protect Rome and help Hannibal attempt a sneak attack?
3. **MAKE INFERENCES** What knowledge of geography and maps might Hannibal have had in order to believe his campaign over the Alps could be successful?

3.5 Rome Expands

The geographic location of Rome made it the perfect place to begin building a Mediterranean empire. By 146 B.C., Rome had proved this point at the expense of its conquered neighbors. Its navy ruled the seas, its army dominated the land, and many once-great countries were now run by a Roman governor.

ATLANTIC OCEAN
GAUL
PYRENEES
IBERIAN PENINSULA
Balearic Is.
40°N
30°N
0°
W
Controlled by Carthage, 264 B.C.
Controlled by Rome, 264 B.C.
Added to Rome, 146 B.C.
Carthaginian land added to Rome, 146 B.C.

MAIN IDEA

Between 264 and 146 B.C., Rome's armies conquered a vast amount of land stretching from the Iberian Peninsula to Greece.

The Catapult

The catapult was one of the Roman army's most effective weapons. It was capable of launching 60-pound rocks, long wooden beams, and even vats of fire. This powerful war machine relied on a system of tension and release to hurl missiles 500 to 1,000 feet across battlefields.

THE THIRD PUNIC WAR

After the Second Punic War, Carthage focused on trade and began to grow very rich. This worried the Romans, who were still suspicious of their old enemy. The famous Roman statesman Cato the Elder visited Carthage and was alarmed by its wealth, which he believed would be used to fight Rome. Cato shared his fears with the Senate in a unique way. Whenever he spoke, whatever the subject, he always ended with the dramatic exclamation *"Carthago delenda est"* ("Carthage must be destroyed").

Roman leaders eventually ordered the city of Carthage to be abandoned. Bullied into a corner, Carthage declared war. After decades of conflict, Rome decided that only the total destruction of its old enemy would do.

In 149 B.C., Rome laid siege to Carthage, surrounding it and stopping its food supply. Roman soldiers battered the city with huge rocks hurled from catapults and then stormed its shattered walls. The starving defenders fought bravely, but the Romans' victory was inevitable—and their revenge was merciless. The Romans sold Carthaginian survivors as slaves and destroyed every building. Carthage ceased to exist. Carthage and its adjoining lands were renamed the Roman **province** of Africa. The Iberian Peninsula, which Carthage had controlled, eventually became the Roman province of Hispania.

ROMAN EXPANSION, 264–146 B.C.
EUROPE
ALPS
ITALY
Adriatic Sea
Corsica
Rome
Sardinia
MACEDONIA
GREECE
Corinth
ASIA
Sicily
Carthage
Mediterranean Sea
AFRICA
0
200
400 Miles
0
200
400 Kilometers
10°E
20°E
30°E
40°N
30°N

THE MACEDONIAN WARS

While Hannibal was rampaging through Italy in the Second Punic War, Philip V of Macedonia launched the First Macedonian War against Rome. Because Rome's army was focused on Hannibal, Rome could not fight against Macedonia and was forced to make peace. However, after Hannibal's defeat, two legions of battle-hardened Roman warriors invaded Macedonia, starting the Second Macedonian War.

The legions were pitched against the Macedonian phalanx, a solid body of troops bristling with long spears. The phalanx was strong, but it lacked the flexibility of the legion—and this flaw proved decisive. Once past the spears, fresh Roman reserves would fight ferociously until they destroyed the enemy army. These tactics defeated Philip's army in 197 B.C., ending the war. Macedonia later became a Roman province. Rome also destroyed the city of Corinth and conquered Greece, turning it into a Roman province in 146 B.C.

Roman power now extended from the Iberian Peninsula to the islands of Greece. Control of this vast area made Rome the new superpower of the ancient world.

REVIEW & ASSESS

1. **READING CHECK** In what order did the events of the Punic and Macedonian wars occur?
2. **INTERPRET MAPS** How did the defeat of Philip of Macedonia help Rome dominate the Mediterranean?
3. **ANALYZE LANGUAGE USE** How does Cato's exclamation about Carthage convey the Romans' fear of their enemy?

4.1 The Republic in Crisis

Politics in Rome had often been crooked, selfish, and occasionally even violent. But after 133 B.C., the corruption and greed spiraled out of control and threatened the survival of the republic.

MAIN IDEA

The Roman Republic collapsed into civil war following a series of major events.

ATTEMPTS AT REFORM

Expansion following the Punic Wars brought great wealth to the Roman Republic, but this wealth was not evenly distributed among the people. Roman generals returned with great riches from the conquered territories. They used their new wealth to buy large areas of farmland, which drove many small farmers out of business. Unemployment and poverty became common in the republic, but the rich ignored the problems of the poor.

In 133 B.C., the tribune Tiberius Gracchus (ty-BIHR-ee-uhs GRA-kuhs) proposed a bill to take land from the rich and give it to the poor for farming. He knew the senators would reject his bill, so he had it approved by the plebeian assembly instead.

The Senate was furious at being bypassed. In response, members of the Senate arranged to assassinate, or murder, Tiberius. Ten years later his brother, Gaius (GAY-uhs) Gracchus, tried to introduce **reforms**, or changes to make things better, in the Senate. He, too, was assassinated.

In 107 B.C., the people elected the army general Marius as consul. As you have learned, he allowed landless citizens to join the army. When these soldiers retired, they relied on the generosity of their generals to support them, which made them more loyal to their commanders than to the state.

BATTLES FOR CONTROL

Marius's reforms did not help him when a general named Sulla rose up against him. Sulla was a brilliant general with political ambitions of his own. He marched his army into Rome, starting a **civil war**, or war between groups in the same country, and took control of the Senate. Marius fled, and Sulla set himself up as dictator of Rome. He created a list of his enemies and had many of them killed.

When Sulla left Rome to fight in the east, Marius led his army into Rome and attacked Sulla's supporters. Sulla invaded Rome a second time and regained control. By 81 B.C., he was declared dictator once again.

In the following decades, crises arose that forced the Senate to give extraordinary powers to two generals named Pompey (PAHM-pee) and Crassus. You have read about the slave rebellion that spread throughout the republic in 73 B.C. Pompey and Crassus combined their two large armies to put down the rebellion.

By 63 B.C., the republic was in chaos, and the consul Cicero argued strongly for reducing the powers of the army and restoring the government's system of checks and balances. However, his words failed to persuade Rome's leaders.

FACTORS THAT WEAKENED THE REPUBLIC

- Greed of the rich
- Inequality between rich and poor
- Failed reforms
- Ambitious generals and powerful armies
- Soldiers' shifting loyalty to their generals
- Civil war

Critical Viewing Sulla, shown he[illegible] horseback, never lost a battle. W[illegible] qualities of a successful general a[illegible] conveyed in this painting?

Sulla at Orchomenos, R. Weibezahl, 1832

REVIEW & ASSESS

1. **READING CHECK** What happened when Marius and Sulla fought over Rome?

2. **IDENTIFY MAIN IDEAS AND DETAILS** What problems led to civil war in Rome?

3. **FORM OPINIONS** Could Roman leaders have helped the republic survive? Why or why not?

4.2 BIOGRAPHY

GAIUS JULIUS CAESAR 100 B.C. – 44 B.C.

Julius Caesar is by far the most famous Roman. He overcame obstacles to success with his military brilliance, political cunning, and amazing speeches. When his power-sharing triumvirate collapsed, he led his army into Rome and was voted dictator for life by the frightened Senate. Caesar's rule marked the end of the republic.

- **Job:** Dictator for life
- **Education:** Taught by Greek tutors
- **Home:** Rome

FINEST HOUR

His conquest of Gaul was his most impressive military achievement.

WORST MOMENT

His enemies finally won when dozens of them joined in stabbing him to death.

FRIENDS

- Cleopatra VII, Queen of Egypt
- Commoners of Rome
- Veteran soldiers

TRIVIA

His most noted connection was with Egypt's last queen, Cleopatra VII. Both a love affair and a political alliance, their relationship was short lived. It began in 48 B.C. and ended with Caesar's assassination in 44 B.C.

THE FIRST TRIUMVIRATE

Generals Crassus and Pompey were elected consuls in 70 B.C. However, they soon made themselves unpopular with the Senate by seizing much of its power for themselves. As a result, the Senate turned to a rising political star, **Julius Caesar**.

Caesar had already proved himself as a politician and general. Pompey and Crassus used their influence to have him elected consul. In return, Caesar persuaded the Senate to pass Pompey and Crassus' legislation. This political alliance became known as the **First Triumvirate** (try-UHM-vuh-ruht)—a sharing of power between three people. The triumvirate lasted for about seven years but was always an uneasy alliance full of suspicions and jealousies.

The triumvirate granted Caesar a huge army, which he used to conquer Gaul (present-day France). This conquest extended Roman territory north and made Caesar very popular with the people. He also

Many movies and television series have focused on the life of Julius Caesar. Here, actor Ciarán Hinds portrays Caesar in the 2005 television series *Rome*.

won immense wealth and the fierce loyalty of his soldiers.

END OF THE REPUBLIC

In 53 B.C., Crassus died, and the triumvirate collapsed. Law and order in Rome broke down. To end the chaos, the Senate appointed Pompey sole consul. This, however, resulted in a power struggle between Caesar in Gaul and Pompey in Rome. To regain control, Caesar led his army into Rome, sparking a bloody civil war. In August 48 B.C., Caesar defeated Pompey and declared victory.

Many Romans expected Caesar to restore the republic, but he had other ideas. Backed by his army, he ruled alone. Caesar declared himself dictator for life and introduced reforms that were popular with the people, such as creating jobs for the poor. But the Senate hated his reforms. On March 15, 44 B.C., a group of senators assassinated Caesar.

Another civil war followed Caesar's death. Fourteen years later, the Roman Republic transformed into a monarchy and, ultimately, an empire.

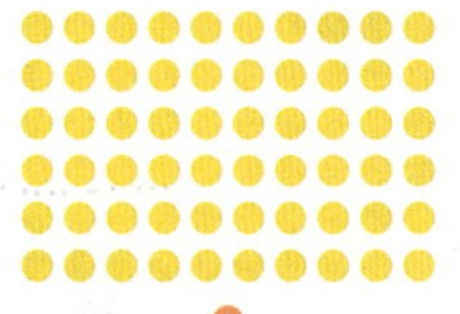

Et tu, and tu, and tu, and tu, and tu?

Julius Caesar was assassinated by about 60 senators under a statue of his old enemy Pompey. According to legend, as Caesar died, he cried out to a man who he had thought was his friend, *"Et tu, Brute?"* ("And you, Brutus?")

REVIEW & ASSESS

1. **READING CHECK** What were Caesar's major successes and failures?
2. **SUMMARIZE** Why was Caesar assassinated, and what happened after he was killed?
3. **COMPARE AND CONTRAST** How does Caesar's career as a general compare with his role as a leader?

4.3

DOCUMENT-BASED QUESTION

The Assassination of Julius Caesar

Caesar's assassination commanded much attention right after his death—and for many centuries after that. The ancient Romans commemorated, or remembered, the date with special coins. Historians who lived in later years tried to describe Caesar's death, and playwrights dramatized the event. We may never know all the details of his death, but the story and fate of a leader who became too hungry for power still fascinates us.

Critical Viewing The woman fainting in the painting is a soothsayer, or a fortune-teller, warning Caesar not to go to the Senate. What elements of this painting forewarn of a terrible event?

Julius Caesar on His Way to the Senate on the Ides of March, Abel de Pujol, c. 1850

DOCUMENT ONE

Primary Source: Artifact

Silver Denarius of Marcus Junius Brutus, Macedonia, 43–42 B.C.

This commemorative coin, called a denarius, shows the profile of Marcus Brutus, Caesar's former friend and assassin. The reverse features two daggers and a "cap of liberty." Underneath are the words EID MAR, or Ides of March. In the Roman calendar, the ides referred to the day that fell in the middle of the month.

BRVT
IMP
L.PLAET.CEST
EID·MAR

CONSTRUCTED RESPONSE What did Roman leaders want people to remember about Caesar when they saw the commemorative coin?

DOCUMENT TWO

Secondary Source: Biography

from *The Lives of the Twelve Caesars*, by Gaius Suetonius Tranquillus, translated by J.C. Rolfe

In Volume 1 of his biography, written in the second century A.D., Suetonius describes Caesar's assassination by a group of senators who called themselves "the liberators."

CONSTRUCTED RESPONSE What does the violence of Caesar's death tell about the liberators' view of Caesar?

When he saw that he was beset [surrounded] on every side by drawn daggers, he muffled his head in his robe . . . with the lower part of his body also covered . . . [H]e was stabbed with three and twenty wounds, uttering not a word . . . All the conspirators made off, and he lay there lifeless.

DOCUMENT THREE

Secondary Source: Drama

from William Shakespeare's *Julius Caesar*

In this excerpt from Act 3, Scene 2 of Shakespeare's play *Julius Caesar,* written in 1599, Mark Antony, a Roman politician and general, speaks at Caesar's funeral.

CONSTRUCTED RESPONSE According to Mark Antony, why was Caesar assassinated?

Friends, Romans, countrymen, lend me your ears;
I come to bury Caesar, not to praise him.
The evil that men do lives after them;
The good is oft interred [buried] with their bones;
So let it be with Caesar. The noble Brutus
Hath told you Caesar was ambitious:
If it were so, it was a grievous [serious] fault,
And grievously hath Caesar answer'd it.

SYNTHESIZE & WRITE

1. **REVIEW** Review what you have learned about the Roman Republic, Julius Caesar, and Caesar's assassination.
2. **RECALL** On your own paper, write down the main idea expressed in each document and in the photograph of the coin.
3. **CONSTRUCT** Construct a topic sentence that answers this question: What do the Roman leaders' actions and words tell about their view of Caesar?
4. **WRITE** Using evidence from the documents, write a paragraph that supports your answer to the question in Step 3.

4.4 MOMENTS IN HISTORY
The Ides Of March

The Assassination of Julius Caesar, Vincenzo Camuccini, 1798

MARCH 15, 44 B.C.

Julius Caesar met a violent end on this date, known as the Ides of March. After Caesar's assassination, the Ides of March came to represent an unlucky or ill-fated day, which is why today we hear, "Beware the Ides of March!" every March 15. In this dramatic painting, Caesar reaches out for help. He appears unable to believe that his own countrymen, most of whom he had handpicked to be senators, would assassinate him. What other details in the painting does the artist include to illustrate the intensity of the moment?

CHAPTER 10 Review

VOCABULARY

For each pair of vocabulary words, write one sentence that explains the connection between the two words.

1. **patrician; plebeian**
   At first wealthy patricians held much of the power, but over time the plebeians, who made up most of Rome's citizens, could also hold office.
2. **consul; veto**
3. **republic; tribune**
4. **aristocracy; patrician**
5. **plebeian; tribune**
6. **consul; dictator**
7. **legionary; province**
8. **civil war; reform**

READING STRATEGY

9. **ORGANIZE IDEAS: COMPARE AND CONTRAST** If you haven't already, complete your Venn diagram to compare and contrast the lives of rich people and poor people in the Roman Republic. Then answer the question.

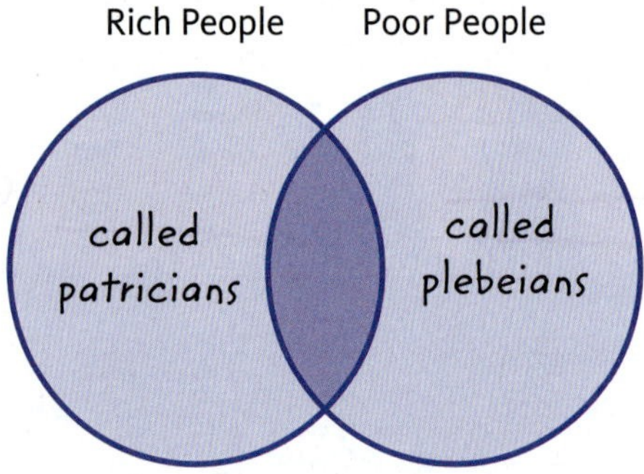
Rich People
Poor People
called patricians
called plebeians

How did the lives of the rich and poor differ in the Roman Republic? Did they share any similarities?

MAIN IDEAS

Answer the following questions. Support your answers with evidence from the chapter.

10. What geographic advantages helped Rome grow into a city? **LESSON 1.1**
11. How did different cultures help transform Rome from a small village into a city? **LESSON 1.2**
12. What was the purpose of the Twelve Tables? **LESSON 1.3**
13. What was the role of men in Rome's patriarchal society? **LESSON 2.1**
14. Why were slaves important to the Roman economy? **LESSON 2.2**
15. What factors made the Roman army successful? **LESSON 3.1**
16. What did Rome gain from its battles with Carthage during the Punic Wars? **LESSON 3.3**
17. What was the First Triumvirate? **LESSON 4.2**

CRITICAL THINKING

Answer the following questions. Support your answers with evidence from the chapter.

18. **MAKE INFERENCES** Based on what you've learned about ancient Rome, what factors helped the republic develop into a mighty power?
19. **DRAW CONCLUSIONS** Why did the Romans replace the position of king with two consuls and give each the right to veto?
20. **COMPARE AND CONTRAST** How did the lives of the rich and poor differ in the Roman Republic?
21. **IDENTIFY MAIN IDEAS AND DETAILS** What details in the chapter support the idea that the Roman Senate had a great deal of power?
22. **YOU DECIDE** Was Julius Caesar a great leader? Was he a dictator who abused his power? Did he fall somewhere in between? Support your opinion with evidence from the chapter.

INTERPRET CHARTS

Study the chart comparing the governments of the Roman Republic and the United States. Then answer the questions that follow.

GOVERNMENT	ROMAN REPUBLIC	UNITED STATES
Executive Branch	Led by two consuls elected for a one-year term; led government and army	Led by a president elected for a four-year term; heads government and military
Legislative Branch	• Senate of 300 members • Senate advised consuls and set policies • Two assemblies made laws and selected officials	• Senate of 100 members • House of Representatives of 435 members • Laws approved by both groups
Judicial Branch	• Eight judges oversaw courts and governed provinces	• Supreme Court of nine justices • Supreme Court interprets the Constitution and federal law
Legal Code	• Twelve Tables basis of Roman law • Twelve Tables established laws protecting citizens' rights	• U.S. Constitution basis of U.S. law • Constitution established individual rights of citizens and powers of government

23. In what ways are the branches of each government similar?

24. What do the legal codes of each government protect?

ANALYZE SOURCES

Read the following translation from one of the Twelve Tables. Then answer the question.

> TABLE VII: Rights Concerning Land
>
> The width of a road extends to 8 feet where it runs straight ahead, 16 round a bend . . .
>
> Persons shall mend roadways. If they do not keep them laid with stone, a person may drive his beasts where he wishes . . .
>
> Should a tree on a neighbor's farm be bent crooked by a wind and lean over your farm, action may be taken for removal of that tree.
>
> It is permitted to gather up fruit falling down on another man's farm.

25. Why do you think the Romans included so much detail in the laws of the Twelve Tables?

WRITE ABOUT HISTORY

26. ARGUMENT What arguments might a senator favoring Julius Caesar's assassination make? What arguments might a senator opposing his assassination make? Create an outline that lists points supporting each side.

TIPS

- Take notes from the chapter about Caesar's actions as a ruler and the manner of his death.
- Consider who benefited from Caesar's reforms and who benefited from his death.
- Consider how the Romans might have felt when Caesar declared himself dictator for life.
- Use vocabulary from the chapter in your outline.
- List the points that support assassination in the first part of your outline. List the points that support opposition to the assassination in the second part.

CHAPTER

11 THE ROMAN EMPIRE AND CHRISTIANITY

44 B.C. – A.D. 476

SECTION 1
LIFE DURING THE EMPIRE

KEY VOCABULARY	NAMES & PLACES
aqueduct	Augustus
arch	Colosseum
emperor	Pax Romana
fresco	Pompeii
gladiator	
mosaic	

SECTION 2
CHRISTIANITY

KEY VOCABULARY	NAMES & PLACES
catacomb	Christianity
epistle	Constantine
missionary	Gospels
parable	Jesus
pope	New Testament
	Paul
	Roman Catholic Church
	Twelve Apostles

SECTION 3
DECLINE AND FALL OF THE EMPIRE

KEY VOCABULARY	NAMES & PLACES
barbarian	Attila
tetrarchy	Diocletian

SECTION 4
THE LEGACY OF ROME

KEY VOCABULARY	NAMES & PLACES
bas-relief	Latin
oratory	Virgil

The Colosseum is made of stone and concrete. Early Roman theaters were built into hillsides for extra support, but the Colosseum is a freestanding structure.

READING STRATEGY

ORGANIZE IDEAS: SEQUENCE EVENTS

When you sequence events, you place them in the order in which they occurred. As you read the chapter, use a time line like this one to keep track of key people and events in the Roman Empire.

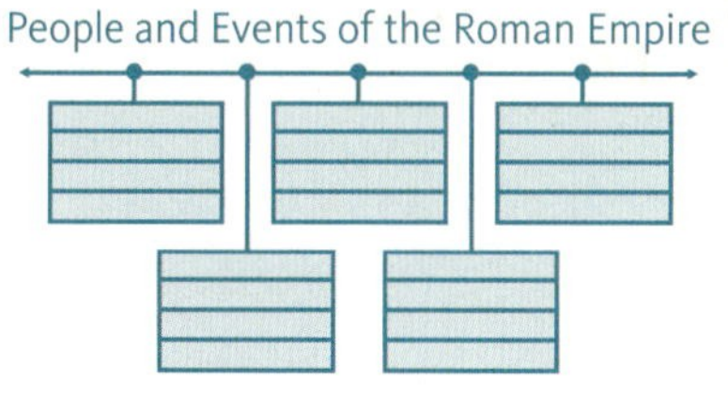
People and Events of the Roman Empire

Spectators entered and exited through 76 gates that sat just inside the 80 arches surrounding the ground floor.

The Roman Colosseum was opened in A.D. 80 and is still standing today.

1.1 Augustus and the Pax Romana

When Julius Caesar was assassinated, Romans rolled their eyes and thought, "Here we go again." After decades of dictatorships and civil wars, they hoped for stability in the empire. They got it, but the republic was dead. A new type of leader was about to rule Rome for the next 500 years.

MAIN IDEA

Augustus transformed Rome from a violent republic into a peaceful empire.

A NEW EMPIRE

After Caesar's death, his heir, Octavian, found himself at the center of a deadly power struggle. At 18 years old, he had to kill or be killed. He survived and thrived. Octavian defeated his rivals, killed Caesar's assassins, and crushed revolts. He emerged victorious, immensely rich, and all-powerful. In 31 B.C., he became Rome's sole ruler. Four years later, the Senate gave him the name **Augustus**, or "exalted one."

Augustus was smarter than Caesar had been. He used his wealth and political skill to take control of the army and secure the people's support. He also won over the Senate, which awarded him dictator-like powers. He did all this while working within the law and appearing to uphold republican ideals. The Senate, among other institutions, continued, but Augustus controlled its decisions. He was the supreme ruler in Rome, or its **emperor**. His powers were granted for life and could be passed to a successor, which was something that made the Romans uneasy. They didn't want to return to the harsh rule of kings. However, the people accepted Augustus because he moved slowly, carefully, and legally. Above all, he finally brought peace to Rome.

PEACE UNDER AUGUSTUS

Augustus' reign began the **Pax Romana**, or "Roman Peace"—200 years of peace and prosperity enjoyed across the empire. The Pax Romana was possible because Augustus tackled some long-standing problems. The poor thanked Augustus for guaranteeing free handouts of grain. Most of the people might not have noticed that Augustus' newly paid officials were improving government. However, everyone took immense pride in his transformation of Rome into an impressive capital with magnificent marble monuments. Meanwhile, Augustus' new laws were restoring order, and he actively encouraged art, literature, and education.

Augustus also cleverly prevented any threat that might have been posed by the army. He cut its size in half but kept out-of-work veterans happy with grants of land. Soldiers still serving were kept constantly busy defending and expanding the empire's frontiers. The army also now had standardized pay and conditions and a new oath of loyalty to the emperor himself.

The elite Praetorian (pree-TAWR-ee-uhn) Guard were the only soldiers stationed in Rome, and they were committed to upholding the emperor's authority. In addition, to protect the empire's coasts and shipping trade, Augustus created Rome's first permanent navy. All of these changes helped ensure long-term stability for the empire and for many Roman emperors to come.

GAIUS OCTAVIAN

AUGUSTUS

Job: First emperor of Rome

FINEST HOUR

Augustus was able to peacefully pass on all his imperial powers. He left a secure, stable, and prosperous empire to his adopted son Tiberius.

WORST MOMENT

A major military embarrassment occurred in A.D. 9 when Germanic barbarians destroyed three Roman legions.

TRIVIA

Although often ill, Augustus lived to be 77. Shortly before he died, the month of August was named after him.

Augustus of Pirmaporta, c. 20–17 B.C.

REVIEW & ASSESS

1. **READING CHECK** What is the Pax Romana?
2. **IDENTIFY MAIN IDEAS AND DETAILS** What are three things Augustus did to secure people's support?
3. **MAKE INFERENCES** Why do you think Augustus was careful to reward soldiers and reduce the size of the army?

1.2 Growth and Trade

During the Pax Romana, you could travel easily and safely across the entire Roman Empire. By A.D. 117, that meant you could cross most of the known western world. It was a merchant's dream, and the economy boomed as Romans enjoyed goods imported from almost everywhere.

MAIN IDEA

As the Roman Empire expanded, trade became easier and the economy boomed.

IMPERIAL EXPANSION

Under Augustus, the Roman army became the mightiest in the world. Its relentless march expanded the empire's frontiers and cultural influence farther than ever before. Soldiers in forts on three continents—Europe, Asia, and Africa—protected the empire's frontiers from attacks by numerous enemies. The soldiers could be soaking in the rains of northern Britain, sweltering in the deserts of southern Egypt, battered by Atlantic winds in western Spain, or swimming in the waters of the Red Sea.

Some of the frontier military camps became permanent settlements. Soldiers stationed at these settlements often stayed in the community when they retired. This practice helped expand Roman culture and influence in the region.

The Roman Empire did not always rely on military conquest to expand its borders. If an area looked like it would be difficult or costly to conquer outright, Augustus would support a local ruler. In return, the territory would be required to provide the empire with military aid if needed. In this way, Augustus was able to expand the empire while saving the expense of an all-out war. This arrangement also made it easier for Augustus to invade the territory in the future if he felt that it was necessary.

A network of roads, bridges, and tunnels built by soldiers connected these far-flung frontiers. It allowed the army to march swiftly across great distances and quickly crush trouble wherever it arose. The roads helped the army keep order, but they also benefited everyone in the empire. The official mail service used the roads to keep information flowing across the empire. Rest areas and inns for overnight stays were built at regular intervals. Everyone in the empire could travel farther, faster, more easily, and more safely than ever before.

A BOOMING ECONOMY

These excellent roads also stimulated the economy by making it easy to transport and sell goods throughout the empire—basic goods as well as luxuries. Even citizens with limited incomes could afford African olive oil and Spanish salted fish. This flow of goods around the empire created a thriving economy as well as a sense of community. Roman merchants gained great benefits from all of this trade.

Rome's craftspeople produced beautiful objects that archaeologists have found as far away as Vietnam, but what flowed out of the empire most was money. The city of Rome itself was the main consumer of imports, or goods brought from other places. Rome especially needed food to feed its huge population. Agriculture, though still Rome's largest industry, was focused on luxuries such as fruit.

ROMAN TRADE, c. A.D. 117
EUROPE
BRITAIN
GAUL
SPAIN
ATLANTIC OCEAN
AFRICA
EGYPT
Rome
Black Sea
Mediterranean Sea
Red Sea
To China
To India
Tropic of Cancer
60°N
40°N
20°N
0°
20°E
40°E
N
S
E
W
Roman Empire at its height, c. A.D. 117
Trade routes
Slave trade
Goods traded
Gems
Grain
Marble
Metals
Olive oil
Spices
Textiles
Timber
Wild animals
Wine
0 300 600 Miles
0 300 600 Kilometers

The most important Roman goods in terms of the quantity traded were wine, olive oil, and grain. Traders moved these bulky goods by ship before transferring them to slower ox-drawn carts. Adventurous traders looked far beyond the empire's borders. These merchants would sail east to India or travel the Silk Roads to China. There they sought to trade wool, gold, and silver for luxuries such as silks, spices, and gems.

The introduction of a standard currency, or money, throughout the empire made it easier to conduct trade as well as collect taxes and pay soldiers. The empire made coins called *denarii* (dih-NAIR-ee) out of silver and *sesterces* (SEHS-tuhrs) out of brass. Roman coins were accepted not only in the empire but also beyond. The expanded empire and the Pax Romana were certainly good for business.

REVIEW & ASSESS

1. **READING CHECK** What factors encouraged trade in the Roman Empire?

2. **INTERPRET MAPS** From which locations in the empire did Rome import grain to feed its citizens?

3. **ANALYZE CAUSE AND EFFECT** What were two positive effects of the flow of goods throughout the empire?

1.3 Roman Engineering

Step outside your door and you'll see a road. Follow the road and you'll reach a city. In the city, you'll find large concrete buildings. Two thousand years ago, Roman engineers were perfecting the techniques that enabled the building of these "modern" constructions.

MAIN IDEA

The Romans were skilled engineers who helped transform how things were built.

ROMAN INVENTIONS

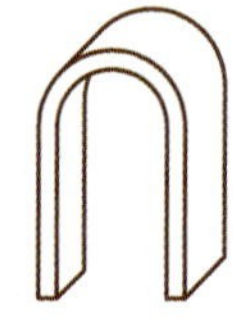

Arch
A curved structure over an opening

Vault
An extended series of arches

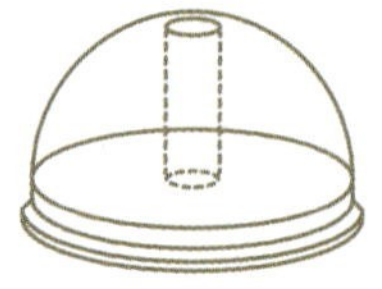

Dome
A rotated series of arches

ROADS

Before the Romans began building their network of roads, travel generally meant following dirt tracks. Rome's first great road was the Appian Way built in 312 B.C. It connected Rome with southern Italy. As the empire expanded, its armies built new roads back to the capital—which is where the saying "All roads lead to Rome" comes from.

The army used specialized tools and lots of human power to build roads. Soldiers marked the route, dug foundations, and built up the road with several layers of material. The center of the road was slightly higher than the edges, which helped rain run into drainage ditches. Where possible, the soldiers built the road wide and straight, making marches shorter and easier. Engineers developed special techniques to overcome obstacles. Roads sometimes included bridges over rivers or tunnels through hills. Every mile a milestone marked the distance to major cities. By A.D. 300, the Romans had built about 53,000 miles of roads.

ARCHES AND AQUEDUCTS

Concrete is not usually very interesting, but at the time of Augustus it transformed construction. The Romans developed a new, stronger type of concrete and used it to build huge freestanding structures, like the Pantheon in Rome. This building, shown on the next page, was built in 27 B.C. as a temple to all the gods of ancient Rome.

Roman architecture was modeled on Greek architecture, but the use of arches, vaults, and domes created a distinctive Roman style. An **arch**, or curved structure over an opening, is strong and inexpensive to build. Lengthening an arch creates a vault, and joining a circle of arches at their highest point creates a dome.

Long stone channels called **aqueducts** (AK-wih-duhkts) carried clean water from hilltops into cities and towns. The engineers' precise calculations over long distances ensured a steady flow of water. Rome received 35 million cubic feet of water every day. While most of an aqueduct ran underground, sometimes huge arched bridges were built to carry the water across valleys. Many of these magnificent structures still stand as reminders of Roman engineering ability: building big and building to last.

Critical Viewing This interior photo of the Pantheon shows the oculus—the opening in the center of the dome. What mood did Roman architects create using a tall dome with an opening at the top?

REVIEW & ASSESS

1. **READING CHECK** What techniques and constructions did Roman engineers develop?
2. **SUMMARIZE** What was the process Roman soldiers used to build roads?
3. **MAKE INFERENCES** How did aqueducts help unify the empire?

1.4 The Colosseum

Just as you might go to a stadium to watch a ball game, the Romans went to an amphitheater for entertainment—but the "games" they watched were far more dangerous than the toughest sports we see today.

MAIN IDEA

The Colosseum was the stage for brutal games to entertain the Roman people.

1 DAY AND NIGHT
During the day, a huge canvas awning provided welcome shade, and a hanging light lit the action at night.

A COLOSSAL STADIUM

The **Colosseum** in Rome was the world's largest amphitheater. The emperor Titus (TY-tuhs) opened it in A.D. 80. The building was designed to seat 50,000 spectators. An expertly engineered network of arches carried the structure's huge weight of stone.

Violent death was what Romans came to see at the Colosseum. In the morning, exotic animals hunted down defenseless criminals. After a break to clear the bodies, the main event began—the gladiators.

The **gladiators**, usually slaves or criminals, fought each other to the death. A successful gladiator might win fame, fortune, and his freedom.

The games, which could last 100 days, were usually paid for by the emperor. He hoped they would distract the poor from their problems.

Modern sports stadiums copied the Colosseum's design of tiered seating encircling a central stage.

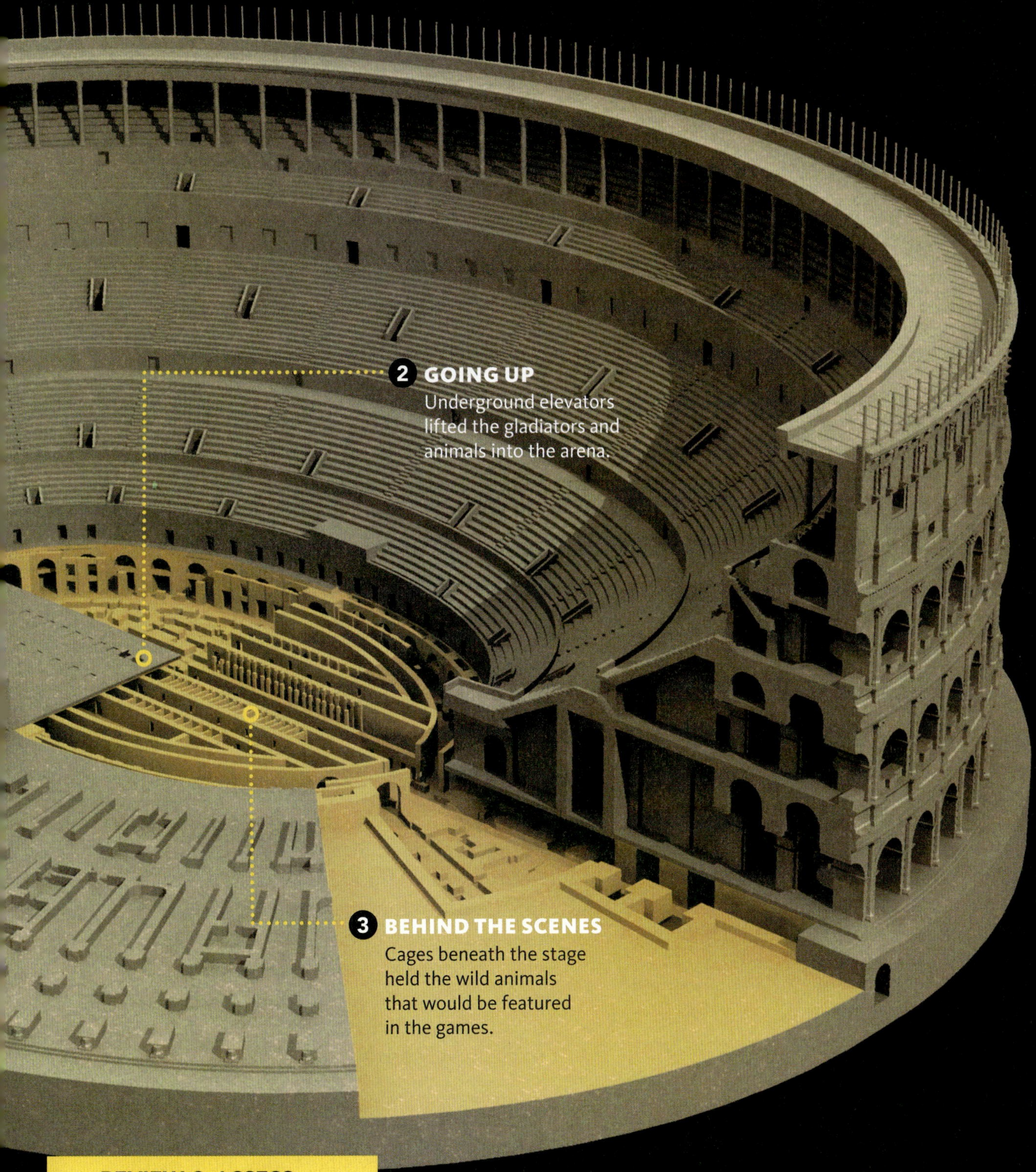

2 GOING UP
Underground elevators lifted the gladiators and animals into the arena.

3 BEHIND THE SCENES
Cages beneath the stage held the wild animals that would be featured in the games.

REVIEW & ASSESS

1. **READING CHECK** What were some of the games that took place at the Colosseum?
2. **MAKE CONNECTIONS** How did the Colosseum influence the design of modern sports stadiums?
3. **MAKE INFERENCES** Why do you think the emperor might have wanted to distract the poor from their problems?

1.5 Villas and Frescoes

Whether you rented rooms in a block of apartments or were rich enough to own a house, summer in the city of Rome was seriously hot for everyone. Summer also brought the risk of deadly diseases. There was no air conditioning to keep you cool and no antibiotics if you got sick. If you were really rich, you'd head for the fresh, clean air of your country home.

MAIN IDEA

Wealthy Romans lived in luxurious country houses called villas.

LIFE IN A ROMAN VILLA

Villas were large country houses designed to impress. Visitors entered through huge doors into a bright central courtyard. This was the main living room, where Romans would relax and entertain. They knew their guests would admire expensive features such as fountains, magnificent marble statues, and portraits of important ancestors. Many other rooms for working, eating, and sleeping stood beyond the courtyard.

Roman interior designers favored large rooms with high ceilings. Usually there were only a few pieces of very fine furniture, which were often beautifully carved or decorated. A very expensive design feature in Roman villas was mosaic (moh-ZAY-ihk) floors. A **mosaic** contains tiny colored stone cubes set in mortar to create a picture or design. A mosaic floor was a work of art, and keeping it clean was essential. Villas had many slaves who did all the work, from tending the fields to cleaning, cooking, and serving meals.

The Villa Adriana at Tivoli (TIH-vuh-lee) near Rome is a luxurious example of a country house that is still visible today. Built by the emperor Hadrian, it formed a vast group of 30 buildings, many copied and named after places Hadrian had admired on his travels. Covering an area equal to about 270 football fields, the villa included a theater, a stadium, baths, a library, and a palace.

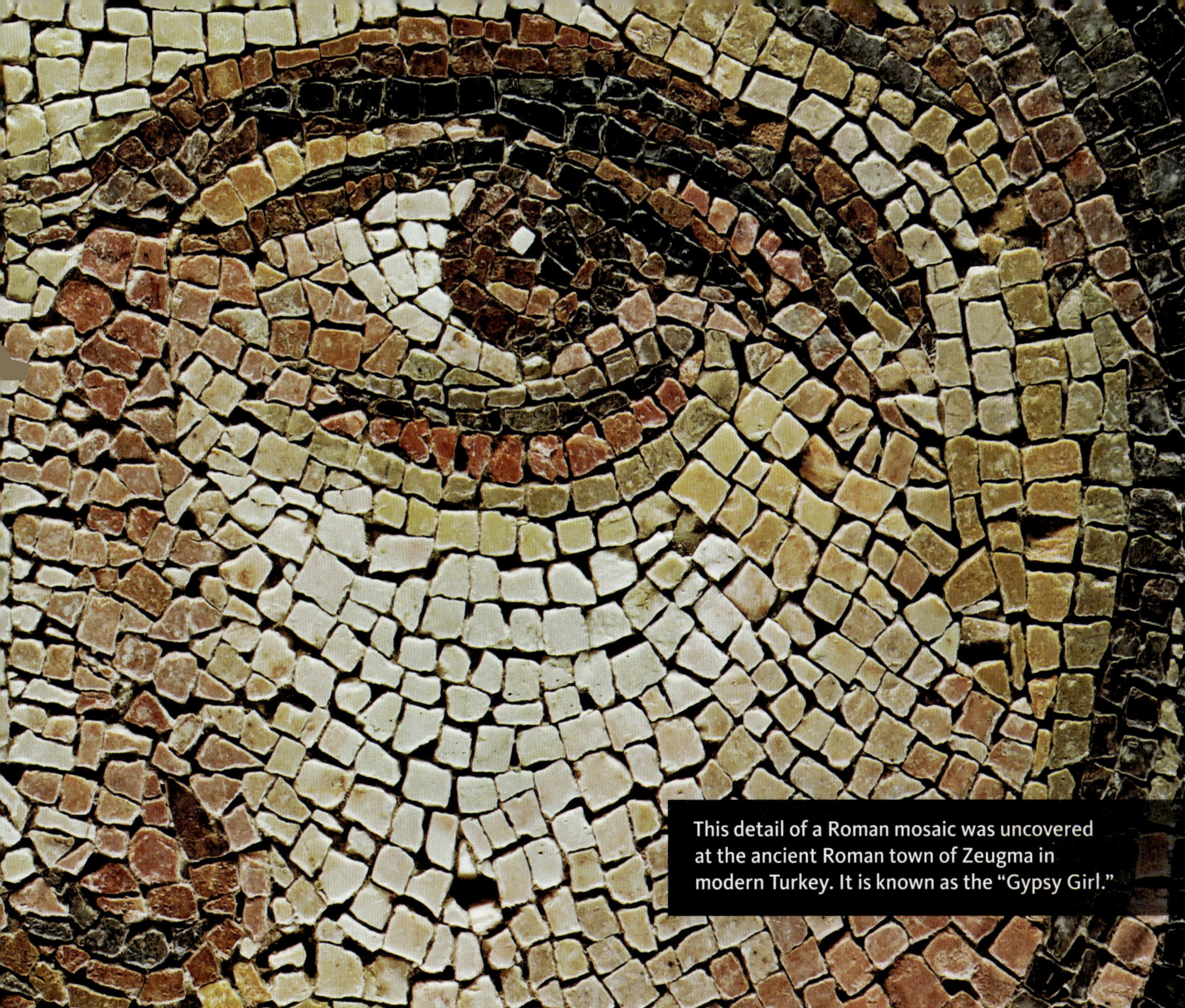

This detail of a Roman mosaic was uncovered at the ancient Roman town of Zeugma in modern Turkey. It is known as the "Gypsy Girl."

FRESCOES

The Romans learned the art of painting frescoes from the ancient Greeks. A **fresco** is a picture painted directly onto the wall while the plaster is still wet. Rich Romans covered their walls with these paintings. Talented Greek artists were often employed to paint these frescoes.

Roman frescoes could show a variety of scenes such as landscapes, famous battles, and views of everyday life. Some pictures even included family members, posed to show off wealth and status. The Romans were great lovers of art, which they used to emphasize their position in society. To rich Romans, appearance was everything.

REVIEW & ASSESS

1. **READING CHECK** What kinds of luxurious features did the villas of wealthy Romans often have?
2. **MONITOR COMPREHENSION** For what purpose did wealthy Romans employ talented Greek artists?
3. **SYNTHESIZE** What was the relationship between art and status in Roman culture?

1.6 Pompeii

As dawn broke on August 24, A.D. 79, the citizens of **Pompeii** (pahm-PAY) rolled out of bed and dressed for another day. Around noon, a dog was chained to a post, a crate of new pottery waited to be unpacked, and a kettle was filled with water. Then disaster struck. Within days, the whole city became a "living" history—entombed in ash for 1,900 years.

MAIN IDEA

The ruins and remains of Pompeii provide insight into everyday Roman life.

MODERN VESUVIUS

Mount Vesuvius is still an active volcano, and about 2.4 million people live in nearby Naples and its suburbs.

Vesuvius has erupted several times since the destruction of Pompeii. The last eruption was in 1944. Experts believe it is not a question of *if* the volcano will erupt again, but *when*.

DISASTER STRIKES

Pompeii was an average city resting in the shadow of Mount Vesuvius (vuh-SOO-vee-uhs), a volcano on Italy's western coast. The paved streets of the city followed an orderly pattern, and citizens there had all the civic comforts expected. Some 20,000 people worked, played, ate, slept, and lived within Pompeii's city walls until the afternoon of August 24, A.D. 79.

The Roman writer Pliny the Younger was near Pompeii that day. He had once described the city as "one of the loveliest places on Earth." After the events that occurred in Pompeii, he described a nightmare.

A violent explosion brought the city to a standstill. Pliny watched in horror as Mount Vesuvius erupted, shooting gas mixed with rock and ash high into the sky and creating an immense black cloud that blocked out the sun. Panic-stricken citizens fled as ash rained down.

As lava crept toward the city, fires raged and buildings collapsed. A vast volcanic ash cloud swept in to suffocate the city, burying its people and their possessions nearly 25 feet deep. A cloud of poisonous gas overtook and killed anyone who had not yet escaped. Over the next few days, lightning, earthquakes, and tidal waves followed. Finally after three days, Vesuvius went quiet—as silent as the deserted city of Pompeii.

This man died fleeing the eruption of Mount Vesuvius, which rises in the background. Pompeians' final moments were preserved by the ash from the volcano and then revealed using plaster casts.

A CITY PRESERVED

The volcanic ash that buried Pompeii also helped preserve its contents. The city's ruins were first discovered in the late 1500s. By 1861, archaeologists began carefully uncovering and working to protect their extraordinary find. Removing the ash, the scientists found houses, shops, and public buildings that contained mosaics, frescoes, and even graffiti. Many of the items had obviously been abandoned suddenly, in the first moments of the eruption. These artifacts offer a revealing glimpse into everyday Roman life. The ash preserved items such as leather shoes, wooden furniture, food, and a library of scrolls.

The ash also preserved some of its victims. It hardened around the bodies. Over time the bodies decayed and left behind an empty space. By pouring plaster into these spaces, archaeologists created exact casts of people, animals, and plants at their moment of death. All the discoveries are moving reminders of how suddenly death came to the city of Pompeii and froze it in time under a blanket of ash.

REVIEW & ASSESS

1. **READING CHECK** What items in Pompeii were preserved after the eruption?
2. **SEQUENCE EVENTS** What was the order of events that occurred in Pompeii on August 24, A.D. 79?
3. **ANALYZE CAUSE AND EFFECT** How were the ruins of Pompeii preserved?

2.1 The Origins of Christianity

A man named Jesus who lived in Nazareth was a Jew whose beliefs became a threat to Jewish and Roman leaders. His teachings formed the foundation of a religion that has powerfully shaped the world for over 2,000 years.

MAIN IDEA

Christianity developed in Jewish communities and was based on the teachings of Jesus.

JEWISH ROOTS

As the empire expanded, the Romans were usually tolerant of the many different religions practiced throughout the empire. As long as people worshipped their emperor as a god, they could follow whatever faith they liked. This was not a problem for most religions. The exception was Judaism, the religion of the Jewish people.

As you've already learned, the Romans captured the Jewish city of Jerusalem in 63 B.C. This brought the Jewish people under Roman control. At first the Romans allowed the Jews to worship one God. Over time, tensions grew. Rome began to enforce emperor worship, and the tensions exploded into conflict. In A.D. 70, Rome defeated the Jews, who then scattered throughout the empire. This helped spread a new religion that was developing in the Jewish community: Christianity.

JESUS OF NAZARETH

Christianity is based on the teachings of **Jesus**, a man born into a poor family in Judea around 6 B.C. Most of what we know about Jesus' teachings comes from the four **Gospels**. These books were written after Jesus' death by four of his followers—Matthew, Mark, Luke, and John. The Gospels are part of the **New Testament**, which presents the history, teachings, and beliefs of Christianity. According to historical record, Jesus was a practicing Jew and worked as a carpenter. When he was about 30 years old, he began to teach ideas that differed from Jewish practices. Biblical accounts claim that Jesus could perform miracles, such as healing the sick.

In time, Jesus traveled around Judea preaching and gathering disciples, or followers. He chose his closest followers, known as the **Twelve Apostles**, to help spread his teachings. He often used **parables** (short stories about everyday life) to make his religious or moral points. In his Sermon on the Mount, Jesus declared that love for God and charity toward all people were more important than following Jewish law. He also promised that those who sought God's forgiveness for their sins would go to heaven after death. To his followers, Jesus became Christ, "the anointed one." They believed he was the promised Messiah—the one who would free them.

According to Christian writings, Jesus criticized Jewish practices while visiting Jerusalem during the Jewish observance of Passover. Jesus was arrested and turned over to Roman authorities. Pontius Pilate, the Roman governor of Judea, sentenced Jesus to death by crucifixion—being nailed to a cross and left to die. Jesus' body was buried, and then, according to the Gospel accounts, he was resurrected, or rose from the dead, and ascended into heaven. For Christians, the resurrection signals victory over sin and death. The man called Jesus was gone, but Christianity was just beginning.

The Last Supper, Leonardo da Vinci, 1498

1 2 3 4 5 6 7 8 9 10 11 12 13

THE LAST SUPPER

Leonardo da Vinci completed this painting in 1498. It was painted directly on the wall of a church in Milan, Italy.

Jesus and his Twelve Apostles have gathered for a final Passover supper. The painting depicts the moment when Jesus tells his Apostles that one of them will betray him. Da Vinci captures a range of emotions among the Apostles and a sense of calm in Jesus. According to Christian belief, the Apostle Judas would betray Jesus after the meal. The next day Jesus was put to death.

LEGEND

1. *Bartholomew*
2. *James Minor*
3. *Andrew*
4. *Judas*
5. *Peter*
6. *John*
7. *Jesus*
8. *Thomas*
9. *James Major*
10. *Philip*
11. *Matthew*
12. *Thaddeus*
13. *Simon*

REVIEW & ASSESS

1. **READING CHECK** What were some of Jesus' teachings?
2. **SEQUENCE EVENTS** What were the key events in the life of Jesus?
3. **MAKE INFERENCES** What do you think makes parables an effective way to teach Christian ideas?

2.2 Christianity Spreads

Faith is very personal. We follow a particular religion (or no religion) for different reasons. Early Christians were the same way. Christianity had broad appeal and attracted a wide mix of people. They all believed that Jesus was the Messiah.

MAIN IDEA

Christianity attracted many followers and spread throughout the Roman Empire.

North Sea
BRITAIN
Rhine R.
ATLANTIC OCEAN
GAUL
SPAIN
20°W
10°W
0°
50°N
40°N
30°N
0
200
400 Miles
0
200
400 Kilometers
N
S
E
W

APPEAL OF CHRISTIANITY

At first all Christians were practicing Jews who still met in synagogues, places for Jewish worship. However, soon Christianity placed less emphasis on the laws of Judaism and welcomed Gentiles (GEHN-tylz), or non-Jews. As a result of the split from Judaism, Christianity grew and developed its own identity.

Christianity appealed to a lot of people. The religion's main appeal was the promise of salvation made possible by the sacrifice of Jesus. Many followers were also attracted by Christianity's rejection of the Roman focus on wealth and image. They preferred Jesus' focus on living simply and peacefully, sharing property, and providing charity to help the less fortunate. The poor liked the way Christian communities shared their wealth and established hospitals, schools, and other public services to improve their lives. Women and slaves liked Christianity because it treated them more like equals than other religions and Roman society did. Finally, many people embraced the idea of a personal relationship with God.

SPREADING THE WORD

In spite of Christianity's broad appeal, the religion's survival was far from certain, and it could easily have faded away. Instead it thrived because Jesus' followers spread his teachings fast and far. Through the Roman road network, Christianity spread rapidly in Jewish communities across the empire. Another big break was that the Romans confused Christianity with Judaism, and so they ignored the new religion, which allowed it to grow.

Even so, life as a Christian wasn't easy. The Romans often persecuted, or

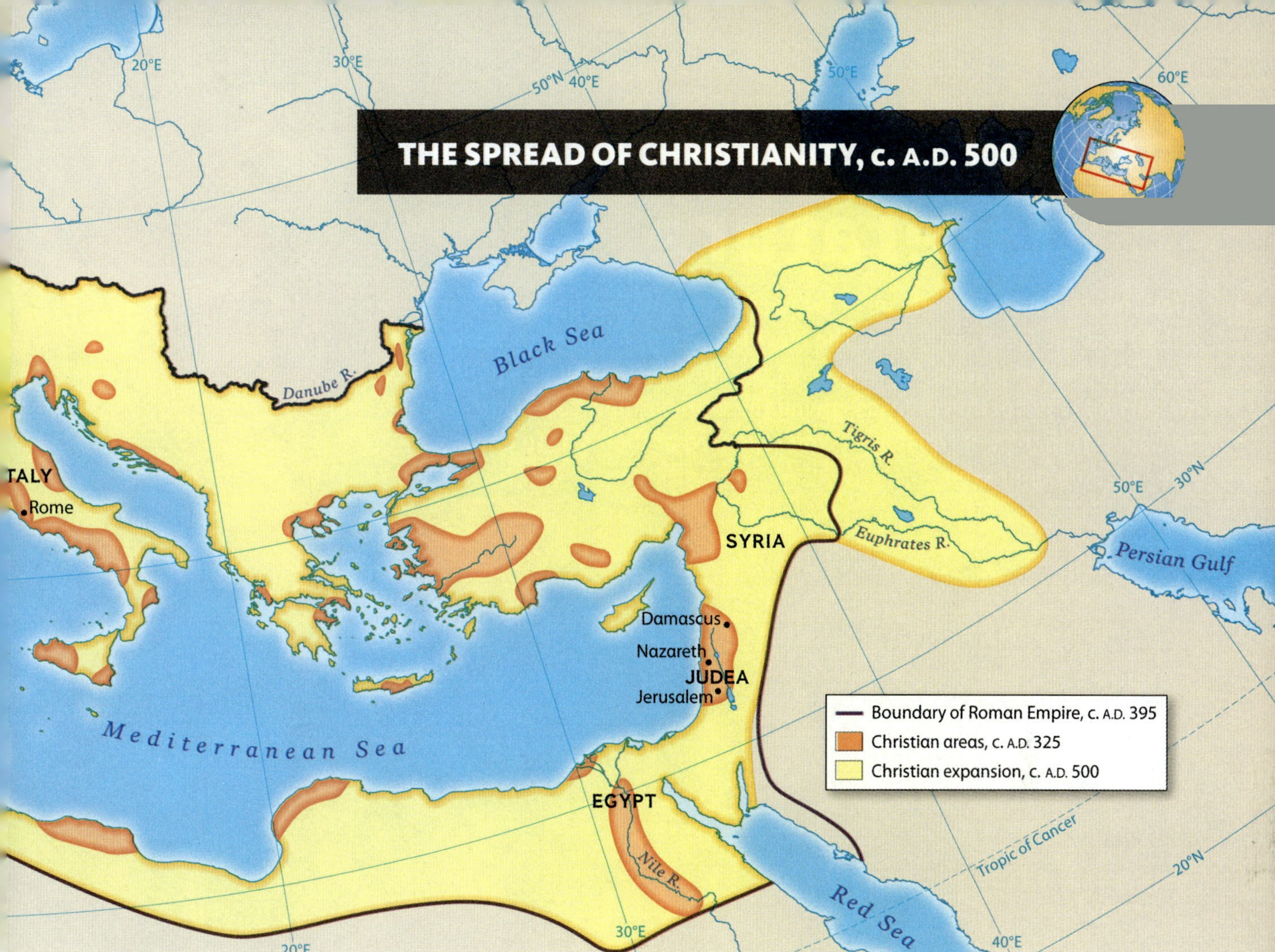
THE SPREAD OF CHRISTIANITY, c. A.D. 500
20°E
30°E
40°E
50°N
50°E
60°E
Black Sea
Danube R.
ITALY
Rome
Tigris R.
Euphrates R.
SYRIA
50°E
30°N
Persian Gulf
Damascus
Nazareth
JUDEA
Jerusalem
Mediterranean Sea
EGYPT
Nile R.
Red Sea
Tropic of Cancer
20°N
30°E
40°E
20°E
Boundary of Roman Empire, c. A.D. 395
Christian areas, c. A.D. 325
Christian expansion, c. A.D. 500

punished, Christians for their beliefs. However, one of Christianity's fiercest persecutors, a man named **Paul**, eventually became its biggest champion.

Paul was most responsible for spreading early Christianity. He was a well-educated Jew and a Roman citizen. He converted to Christianity while traveling on the road to Damascus. According to Paul's own account, he had a vision in which Jesus was revealed to him as the Son of God. As a result, Paul became a **missionary**, a person who travels to another country to do religious work.

He began spreading Jesus' teachings. Paul was often arrested, but he always escaped to preach again. He wrote many letters, or **epistles** (ih-PIH-suhls), explaining Jesus' teachings by answering specific questions. According to tradition, Paul was killed in a Roman massacre of Christians in A.D. 64. By then, Roman leaders realized that Christianity was a separate religion from Judaism and a popular religion—too popular. Fearful that Christianity might threaten the stability of the empire, Roman rulers made the religion's practice illegal.

REVIEW & ASSESS

1. **READING CHECK** How did Christianity spread throughout the Roman Empire?
2. **INTERPRET MAPS** What natural features served as the northern border for Christian expansion by A.D. 500?
3. **MAKE INFERENCES** Why was Paul an effective spokesperson for spreading the teachings of Christianity?

2.3 DOCUMENT-BASED QUESTION

New Testament Literature

The Christian Bible is made up of two parts: the Old Testament (or Hebrew Bible) and the New Testament. The New Testament includes the Gospel of Luke and Paul's Epistles. At the core of the New Testament teaching is the death and resurrection of Jesus, giving the world a "new covenant" (new testament) that would enable all who repented of their sins to enter the kingdom of heaven.

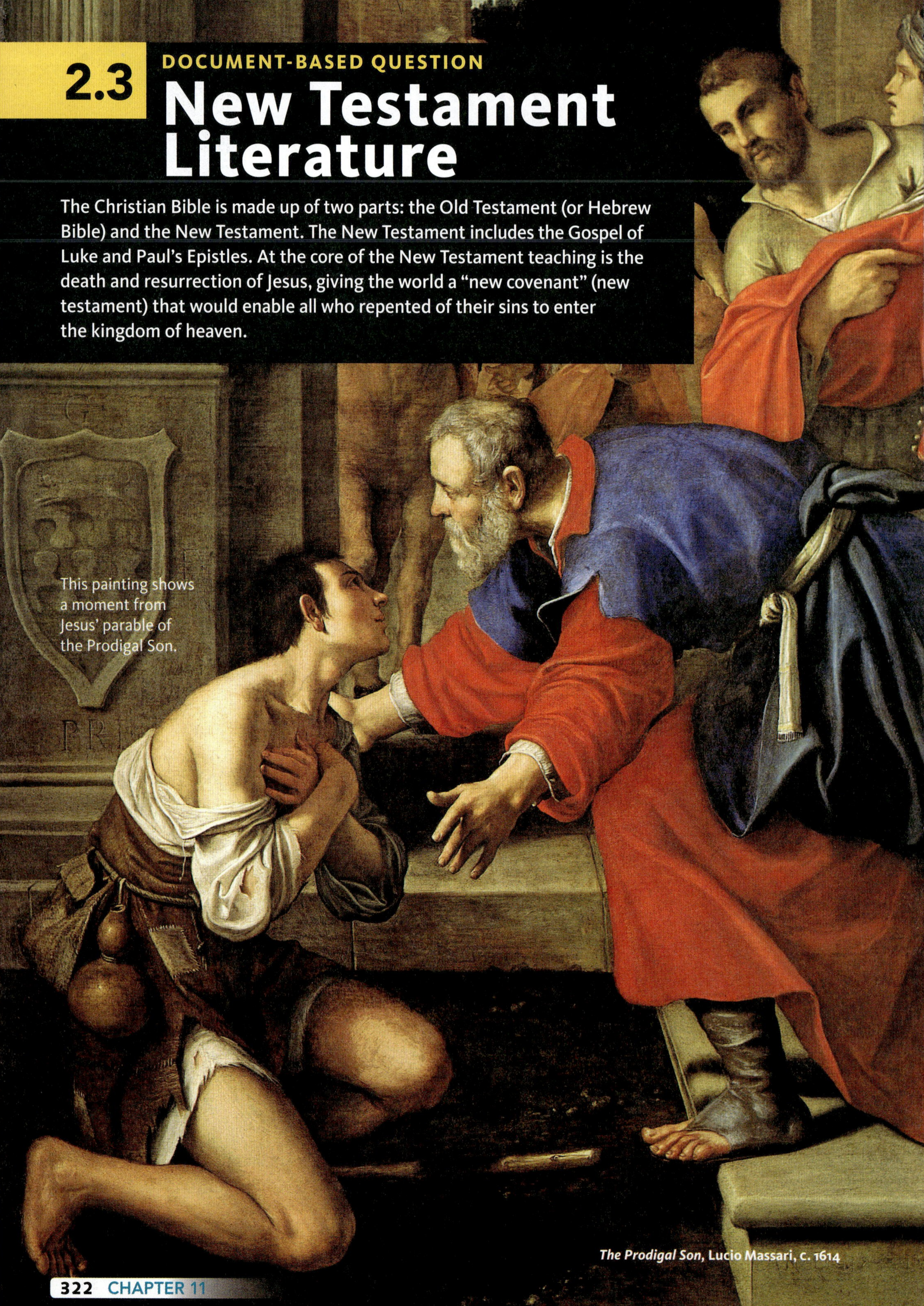

This painting shows a moment from Jesus' parable of the Prodigal Son.

The Prodigal Son, Lucio Massari, c. 1614

DOCUMENT ONE

Primary Source: Sacred Text

The Parable of the Good Samaritan

This parable was recorded in the Gospel of Luke in the first century A.D. The Samaritans (suh-MEHR-uh-tuhns) were a community of people who were generally distrusted by the Jews, the audience of the parable. According to the Gospel of Luke, Jesus tells this parable to answer the question "Who is my neighbor?"

CONSTRUCTED RESPONSE How does the Samaritan's response to the beaten man differ from the responses of the priest and Levite?

***Good Samaritan*, Julius Schnorr von Carolsfeld, 1860**

A man was going down from Jerusalem to Jericho, when he fell into the hands of robbers. They stripped him of his clothes, beat him, and went away, leaving him half dead. A priest happened to be going down the same road, and when he saw the man, he passed by on the other side. So too, a Levite [a Jew], when he came to the place and saw him, passed by on the other side. But a Samaritan, as he traveled, came where the man was; and when he saw him, he took pity on him. He went to him and bandaged his wounds, pouring on oil and wine. Then he put the man on his own donkey, took him to an inn, and took care of him. The next day he took out two silver coins and gave them to the innkeeper. "Look after him," he said, "and when I return, I will reimburse you for any extra expense you may have."

Luke 10:30–35

DOCUMENT TWO

Primary Source: Sacred Text

from Paul's Epistle to the Galatians

Paul wrote his letter to the Galatians (guh-LAY-shuhnz) in the first century A.D. The Roman province of Galatia contained a number of early Christian communities. In his letter, Paul stresses some important ideas of the Christian faith.

CONSTRUCTED RESPONSE What important Christian ideas is Paul stating in this epistle?

You all are sons of God through faith in Christ Jesus, for all of you who were baptized . . . have clothed yourselves with Christ. There is neither Jew nor Greek, slave nor free, male nor female, for you are all one in Christ Jesus.

Galatians 3:26–28

SYNTHESIZE & WRITE

1. **REVIEW** Review the ideas expressed in the parable of the Good Samaritan and Paul's Epistle to the Galatians.
2. **RECALL** On your own paper, write down the main idea expressed in each document.
3. **CONSTRUCT** Write a topic sentence that answers this question: What are some fundamental Christian ideas about how people should treat one another?
4. **WRITE** Using evidence from the documents and from the chapter, write a paragraph that supports your answer to the question in Step 3.

2.4 The Early Christian Church

Being different can make you a target for attacks. Early Christians were violently attacked, but their courage and determination ensured Christianity's survival.

MAIN IDEA

In time, Christianity became the official religion of the Roman Empire.

CONSTANTINE

Constantine was very generous to his supporters. Historians have suggested that he could afford to be so generous only because he robbed temples and used tax money for his own purposes. It is also clear that some of his supporters gained favor by faking conversions to Christianity.

THE CONVERSION OF CONSTANTINE

As you have learned, Christians were often persecuted by their Roman rulers. In A.D. 35, a Christian named Stephen became the first of thousands of Christian victims. He was killed for his religious beliefs. Roman leaders punished Christians for refusing to worship the emperors.

This persecution only got worse. In A.D. 64, the emperor Nero blamed Christians for a great fire that swept through Rome. He had thousands of Christians put to death. Just being a Christian became punishable by death. As a result, worshippers were forced to meet in secret. They buried their dead in hidden underground chambers called **catacombs** (KA-tuh-kohms).

In A.D. 312, Christian persecution had reached its highest point when an amazing change began. On the eve of a battle for control of the empire, a young Roman leader named **Constantine** prayed for help. He believed his prayers were answered with a vision of the Christian cross. The vision led him to paint a symbol on his soldiers' shields. Constantine went on to win the battle. As a result, he immediately put an end to Christian persecution.

Constantine made many other changes after he became emperor. He built churches in Roman lands and declared Sunday the Christian day of rest. He even had Christian symbols placed on coins. Constantine ruled for a long time. However, it was only after Constantine's rule that the emperor Theodosius officially closed all the temples to the Roman gods and made Christianity the official religion of Rome.

Catacombs

Catacombs are underground burial chambers. They often have tunnels with spaces cut into the walls for the bodies. Some catacombs also have large chambers where funeral feasts were held. There are about 40 early Christian catacombs around Rome, and they are the most extensive of any known catacomb system in the world. Shown below is the Catacomb of Priscilla in Rome, Italy.

‹ Saint Peter's Basilica, in present-day Vatican City

FORMATION OF THE EARLY CHURCH

With the legalization of Christianity, Christian communities could openly share their beliefs. Church leaders from across the empire held councils, or meetings, to discuss Christianity and the writings of religious scholars. Their discussions helped them define Christian beliefs and practices.

Christian practices were then communicated to Christian churches throughout the empire and beyond. Each church was led by a priest, and groups of churches were overseen by a bishop. The first bishop of Rome, according to Christian tradition, was the apostle Peter, who died for his beliefs in A.D. 64. Constantine had a church, St. Peter's Basilica, built over the apostle's tomb. The photo above shows the basilica, which was rebuilt in the 1600s. In time the bishop of Rome became the most important bishop, or **pope**. He was seen as the leader of the unified church, known as the **Roman Catholic Church**.

Church leaders standardized Christian beliefs into a common creed, or statement of beliefs. One such statement was the definition of God as a Holy Trinity: the union of Father, Son (Jesus), and Holy Spirit. Worship in the Christian church focused on some common sacraments, or religious ceremonies, such as baptism, an individual's acceptance by the church. As Christianity grew more structured and became more organized, it became a powerful religion.

REVIEW & ASSESS

1. **READING CHECK** How did Christianity become the official religion of the Roman Empire?
2. **DESCRIBE** How was the leadership of the early church organized?
3. **DRAW CONCLUSIONS** In what way did their persecution help unite the Christians?

3.1 The Third Century Crisis

Despite the occasional unbalanced emperor, the Roman Empire ran smoothly for 200 years. Then things began to fall apart. Disputes over who should be emperor caused the return of political violence and civil war. In some years, four or even six emperors were on the throne. By A.D. 235, the Roman world had plunged into a crisis.

MAIN IDEA

Military problems led to a crisis in the Roman Empire.

MILITARY PROBLEMS

So what went wrong? Arguably the empire had physically outgrown the emperor's ability to govern it. At its height, the Roman Empire stretched from Scotland to the Sahara, an area about half the size of the United States. This vast expanse, with huge geographic and cultural differences, was very difficult to govern effectively.

Defending such a large area also proved difficult. Rome faced attacks on two fronts at the same time, which drained money and resources all across the empire. In the east, Rome fought the powerful Parthian Empire from Persia, while Germanic tribes raided Rome's northern borders.

Meanwhile, warring groups within the empire once again fought to decide who would be emperor. Civil wars bled the empire of desperately needed food, money, and soldiers. As emperors fought expensive wars they could not win, enemies from outside the empire attacked. With so many Roman soldiers engaged in warfare, the invaders plundered, or stole riches from, the unguarded interior. It was a sure sign of trouble when cities, including Rome, rebuilt their long-neglected defensive walls. These military problems provoked further political and social problems.

POLITICAL, ECONOMIC, AND SOCIAL PROBLEMS

War was not only dangerous for soldiers; it was disruptive for everyone. Emperors were blamed for not protecting the empire, and they were regularly replaced or murdered. Fifty different emperors ruled between A.D. 235 and 285. People living in what would become Spain, France, and Britain preferred to trust local rulers. They broke from Rome to form a separate Gallic Empire. These events weakened imperial authority and prevented the strong, decisive, and long-term action needed to restore order.

This constant warfare also ruined the economy. Trade was interrupted, and the empire had to rely on its inadequate agricultural resources. The people suffered food shortages and higher taxes. Wars are expensive, and the emperors expected the people to pay for them. Even heavier taxes were enforced when the imperial currency lost value. This affected rich and poor but mostly the poor.

Ordinary people grew angry, criminal organizations grew, and outbursts of mob anger increased. It even became difficult to recruit local officials. Nobody wanted these jobs because people risked a beating for doing them. In these unstable times, good citizenship took second place to looking after oneself.

DECLINE OF THE ROMAN EMPIRE

Illustration of a parade honoring victories of Emperor Augustus

Military Reasons

- Fighting the Parthian Empire in the east
- Fighting Germanic tribes in the west
- Fighting civil wars at home

Stone relief showing a government bureaucrat at work

Political Reasons

- Difficult to govern huge empire
- Frequently changing emperors
- Power gained by local leaders

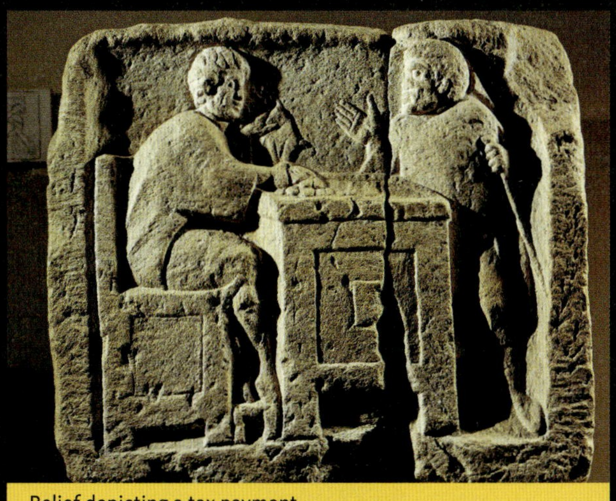
Relief depicting a tax payment

Economic Reasons

- Trade interrupted
- People heavily taxed
- Lower value of currency

Illustration of a Roman party with the poor waiting on the rich

Social Reasons

- Unrest from gap between rich and poor
- More criminal organizations
- Civic responsibility no longer important

REVIEW & ASSESS

1. **READING CHECK** Why did the size of the Roman Empire cause military problems?
2. **ANALYZE CAUSE AND EFFECT** What was the result of the emperors' expensive wars?
3. **DRAW CONCLUSIONS** How did Rome's military problems lead to political, social, and economic problems?

3.2 Eastern and Western Roman Empires

The Roman Empire was too big for one person to manage. Unfortunately that didn't stop ambitious men from trying and failing. Then Rome's luck changed. In A.D. 284, the throne was seized by an emperor who had the sense and strength to make the big changes that could keep the empire alive.

MAIN IDEA

In A.D. 285, the Roman Empire was divided into the Western Roman Empire and the Eastern Roman Empire.

DIOCLETIAN DIVIDES THE EMPIRE

The new emperor was named **Diocletian** (dy-uh-KLEE-shuhn), and he had a lot on his plate. He faced endangered frontiers, overstretched armies, economic collapse, weak imperial authority, and widespread unrest. However, Diocletian had a radical plan: In A.D. 285, he divided the empire in two. Diocletian ruled the Eastern Roman Empire, and his trusted friend Maximian ruled the Western Roman Empire. Each man appointed a junior emperor to rule with him. This rule by four emperors, called a **tetrarchy** (TEH-trahr-kee), worked really well at first.

Each emperor focused on his specific region while cooperating to introduce reforms. Together they increased the army to 400,000 men and reorganized and strengthened the frontier forces. They also created a mobile field army ready to tackle trouble wherever it broke out. On the political front, Diocletian and Maximian reformed government administration and divided the provinces into more manageable units. To promote unity, they enforced emperor worship and the Latin language everywhere. They encouraged economic recovery by reforming tax laws, controlling inflation, and stabilizing the currency. The empire was on the road to recovery, and after 20 years, Diocletian and Maximian retired, letting the junior emperors take over. However, this was as good as the tetrarchy got.

CONSTANTINE MOVES THE CAPITAL

You've learned that the emperor Constantine made the practice of Christianity legal in the empire. Before he did that, he had to fight to become emperor. Constantine's father was emperor of the Western Roman Empire. When Constantine's father died in A.D. 306, however, the tetrarchy refused his claim to be western emperor, sparking a civil war. Constantine won the war and became emperor of east and west. However, Constantine was more interested in the eastern half of his empire.

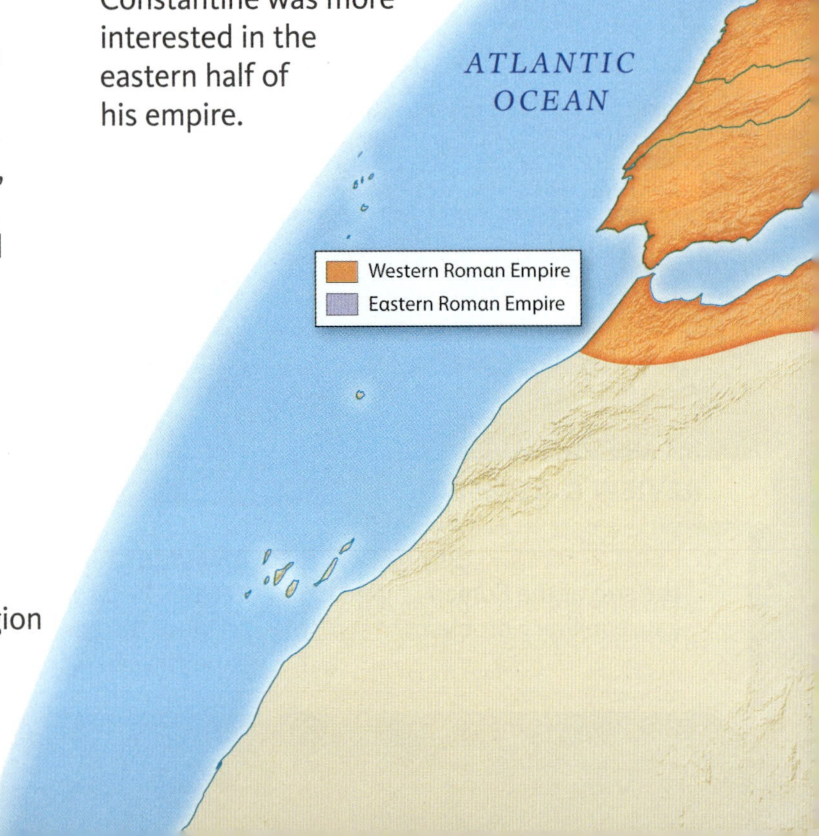

ATLANTIC OCEAN

Western Roman Empire
Eastern Roman Empire

Rome's importance had long been decreasing. Emperors no longer lived in Rome, and Italy had lost its privileged status.

The differences between east and west were increasing. The east produced more people, more food, more taxes, and more soldiers, while the west just grew weaker. So Constantine moved the capital from Rome to the ancient Greek city of Byzantium, which he renamed Constantinople. (Today the city is called Istanbul.) He built his new capital on the strategically important Bosporus, a narrow stretch of water separating Europe and Asia.

Constantine also continued the reforms begun by earlier emperors, earning the title "the Great." However, his sons plunged the empire into another civil war. The emperor Theodosius later reunited the empire, but the division of east and west became permanent after his death in A.D. 395. From then on, the fortunes and futures of the two empires were very different.

ROMAN EMPIRE: EAST AND WEST, c. A.D. 395
NATURAL BORDERS The Rhine and Danube rivers on the northern border of the Roman Empire were difficult to cross, which made it easier for the Roman army to defend the empire.
CONSTANTINOPLE Constantine's new capital on the Bosporus provided easy access to many resources and allowed the empire to control trade.
ROME Diocletian's decision to rule the Eastern Roman Empire made it clear that Rome was no longer the center of political power.
EUROPE
Rhine R.
Danube R.
Black Sea
Bosporus
Constantinople
Rome
ASIA
AFRICA
Mediterranean Sea
N
S
E
W

REVIEW & ASSESS

1. **READING CHECK** Why did Diocletian divide the Roman Empire in two?
2. **INTERPRET MAPS** In what ways was Rome's location similar to that of Constantinople?
3. **IDENTIFY PROBLEMS AND SOLUTIONS** What was Diocletian's plan for ruling the vast empire more efficiently?

Attila the Hun Raising Aquila, Tancredi Scarpelli, 1930

Critical Viewing This painting shows Attila the Hun attacking a Roman city. In what ways has the artist made Attila seem very fierce?

3.3 End of the Western Roman Empire

If you lived in the Western Roman Empire in A.D. 375, you'd be unhappy with the way things were going. While the west struggled to rule itself, feed itself, pay its bills, and defend its borders, you would enviously watch the Eastern Roman Empire grow richer, stronger, and more stable. However bad things got, you could never imagine a world without the Roman Empire—but that reality was just 101 years away.

MAIN IDEA

Invaders attacked the Western Roman Empire and caused its downfall.

FOREIGN INVADERS

Diocletian and Constantine only delayed the end of the Western Roman Empire. The end came in the form of **barbarians**, a Greek word Romans used to describe all people outside of the empire. Three main tribes of barbarians would finally tear the Western Roman Empire apart. The Visigoths (VIH-zuh-gahths) and Vandals were Germanic tribes from northern Europe. Looking for better farmland, both groups migrated south toward the Roman frontier.

The Huns formed the third tribe of barbarians. Migrating from Asia, they were nomads, or wandering cattle herders. Their skill with horses and bows made them a ferocious fighting force. Beginning in A.D. 445, a man named **Attila** was their sole ruler.

THE WESTERN ROMAN EMPIRE FALLS

Attila and his army swept into Europe. Forced into the Western Roman Empire by the Huns, the Visigoths soon invaded Italy. Around the same time, the Vandals invaded Gaul and then Spain. By now the emperor, who had few Roman soldiers to call on, had to enlist barbarian fighters to defend the empire.

On August 24, 410, the Visigoths shocked the world by sacking, or destroying, Rome. They then conquered Gaul and Spain, driving the Vandals into North Africa. Then came Attila. The Huns attacked Gaul in A.D. 451, and the emperor relied on barbarian armies to fight them. Rome had lost control. In A.D. 476, the last emperor quietly left the throne.

The Western Roman Empire was broken up into many Germanic kingdoms, and the Eastern Roman Empire became known as the Byzantine Empire. The Roman Empire was over. Historians argue about why the Western Roman Empire fell. Did it end naturally because of internal failings? Was it brought down by external forces? Or was it simply transformed into something new?

REVIEW & ASSESS

1. **READING CHECK** What three barbarian tribes invaded Roman territory, leading to Rome's downfall?
2. **SEQUENCE EVENTS** What events led to the fall of the Western Roman Empire?
3. **DRAW CONCLUSIONS** Why were so many tribes able to invade the Western Roman Empire?

4.1 Latin and Literature

Students learning Latin have a rhyme: "Latin is a language as dead as dead can be. First it killed the Romans, and now it's killing me." But Latin is not dead. Latin is still used—especially by scientists and doctors. In fact, you use Latin words every day. It's part of Rome's legacy, or heritage.

MAIN IDEA

The Latin language spread across the empire and influences the way we speak and write today.

AN INFLUENTIAL LANGUAGE

As you've learned, the Roman Empire had dozens of languages, but the language spoken in Rome was **Latin**. Although Greek was also commonly used, Latin was established as the official language for international communication, government, law, and trade. It was used for official business from Britain to Egypt.

The Romans brought writing to northern Europe, and we still use the Latin alphabet today. However, back then the alphabet had only 22 letters. The letters *i* and *j* were interchangeable, as were *u* and *v*. The letters *w* and *y* did not exist at all.

After the Roman Empire fell, the Latin language lived on. Over time, new languages, called Romance languages, developed from Latin. These languages include French, Italian, Spanish, and Portuguese. Each language is distinctive but shares a common root in Latin, the "Roman" in *Romance*. The English language was greatly influenced by the Romance languages and uses many Latin words, including *campus, census, curriculum, index, item, sponsor,* and *stadium.*

ORATORY, POETRY, AND PHILOSOPHY

In addition to language, Rome left behind a legacy in literature, featuring speeches, poetry, and philosophical works. **Oratory**, or public speaking, was especially prized, and promising young men were trained in the art of argument and persuasion. As you learned previously, Cicero was one of Rome's greatest orators, and his speeches are still studied by serious students of public speaking.

The Romans also loved poetry, which was based on Greek traditions. The ultimate poem was the epic, a long story describing a hero's adventures. The most celebrated Roman epic was **Virgil's** *Aeneid* (uh-NEE-uhd), which fills 12 volumes. Written between 30 and 19 B.C., it tells the story of Aeneas, the legendary founder of Rome.

Roman philosophy was another extension of Greek ideas. Philosophy is the study of reality, knowledge, and beliefs. Ethical and religious arguments interested Romans more than theory and speculation. The Greek Stoic (STOH-ihk) philosophy was especially influential in Roman life. It stressed a practical approach to life in which people performed their civic duty and accepted their circumstances—good or bad.

The Roman Catholic Church became the keeper of Roman literature for centuries after the empire fell. It preserved works that could be used to educate young men in morality, government, and law. A 15th-century fascination with the ancient world revived the popularity of Roman literature and has ensured its widespread circulation ever since.

LATIN AND ENGLISH

Many English words have Latin roots, or origins. Examine the prefixes and suffixes listed. What words can you add?

-ty, -ity

FORMS NOUNS FROM ADJECTIVES

Similarity
Technicality

Sub-

UNDER

Submarine ›
Subway

Re-

AGAIN

Rebuild
Remake

-ation

FORMS NOUNS FROM VERBS

Celebration
Formation

Pre-

BEFORE

Preview
Prepay

Dis-

NOT ANY

Disbelief
Disrespect

-ment

FORMS NOUNS FROM VERBS

Entertainment
Statement

-ible, -able

FORMS ADJECTIVES FROM VERBS

˄ *Flexible*
Likable

Post-

AFTER

Postgame
Postwar

-fy, -ify

FORMS VERBS AND MEANS "TO MAKE"

‹ *Purify*
Humidify

LEGEND

 Prefix  Prefix Definition  Suffix  Suffix Explanation Example Words

REVIEW & ASSESS

1. **READING CHECK** How has the English language been influenced by Latin?
2. **SEQUENCE EVENTS** What sequence of events helped keep Latin alive?
3. **MAKE INFERENCES** How did Roman ideas about philosophy support the ancient Roman approach to life?

4.2 Art, Architecture, and Law

The Romans shaped the ancient world for a thousand years. But what have they ever done for us? Well, quite a lot actually. If you know what to look for, you can spot Rome's legacy in modern-day art, architecture, and law.

MAIN IDEA

The Romans developed many ideas that continue to influence our lives today.

ART AND ARCHITECTURE

As with their philosophy, Romans preferred a realistic approach to art. The paintings and statues that decorated their homes showed people and things as they really looked. Like the Romans, people today often display realistic family portraits, although photos have generally replaced statues.

The Romans also made mosaics and frescoes popular on floors and walls around the world. Roman frescoes can be compared to modern murals and even some street art. The Roman **bas-relief** (bah-ruh-LEEF) is a realistic sculpture with figures raised against a flat background. These sculptures appear on monuments such as the National World War II Memorial in Washington, D.C. The photo on these pages is an example of a Roman bas-relief carved into the side of a sarcophagus, or stone coffin.

Rome's architectural influence is everywhere. Starting from the ground up, the Romans showed the world the benefit of an extensive, well-built, and well-maintained all-weather road network. European roads still follow Roman routes and sometimes cross original Roman bridges.

When a new Roman town was created, city planners took into account the city's climate and geography. The Romans always tried to establish a grid pattern for the streets. That means that the streets formed a network of intersecting horizontal and vertical lines. Many towns and cities use this pattern today.

Like the Romans, modern builders rely on concrete to build strong, tall, and unusual buildings. Roman architectural styles such as columns, arches, and domes can be seen in the U.S. Capitol and other buildings. Many modern stadiums follow the design perfected in the Colosseum.

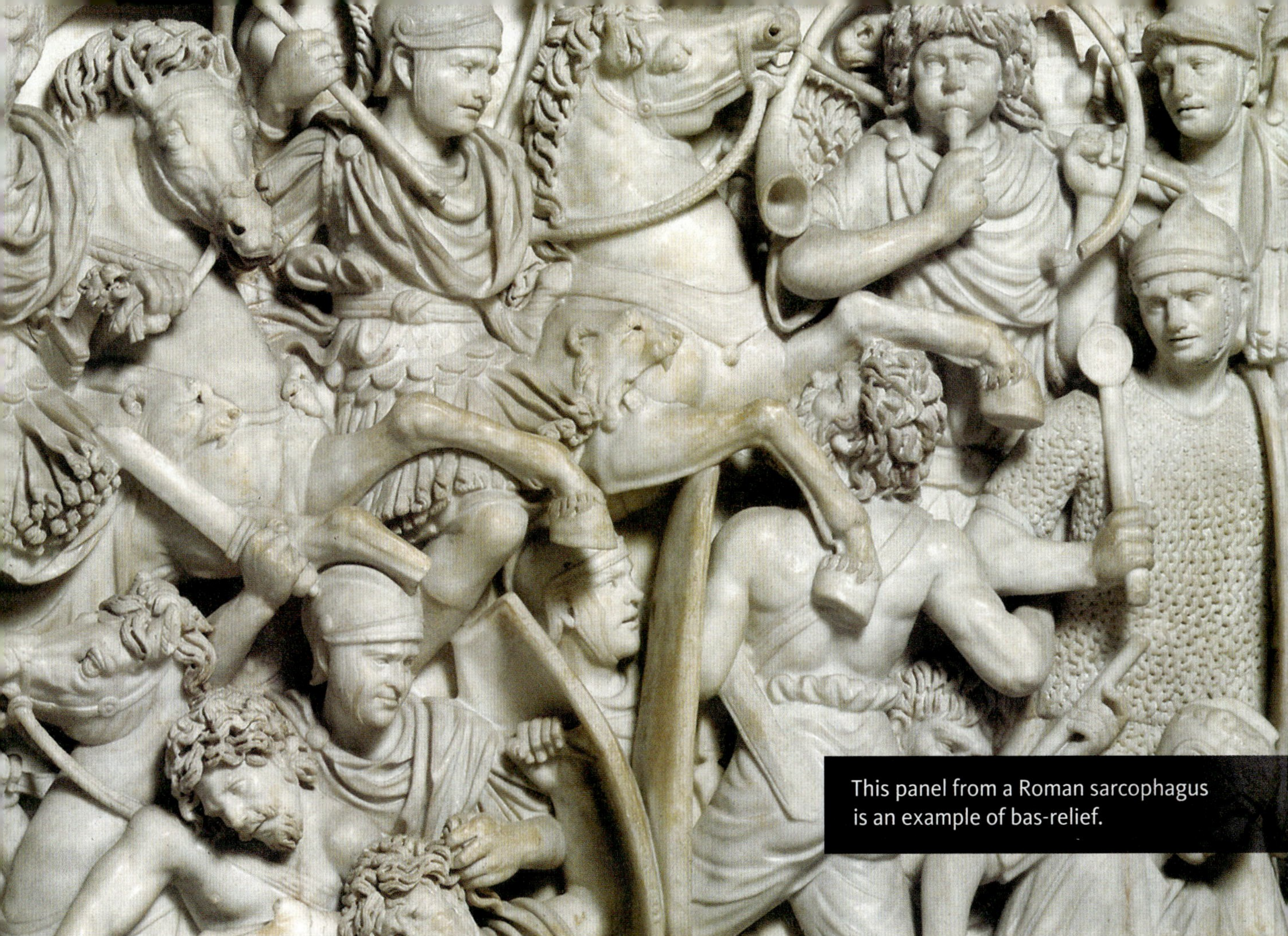

This panel from a Roman sarcophagus is an example of bas-relief.

LAW AND GOVERNMENT

Rome even influences the way people today live. Roman ideas of civic duty are encouraged in the United States and elsewhere. The structure of the U.S. government reflects elements of the Roman Republic, including representative assemblies and the system of checks and balances. Roman laws are the basis of law codes around the world, including that of the United States. The ideas of a fair judge, presumption of innocence, and equality under the law also come from the Romans.

The Latin language is still very much a part of modern law and other fields and professions. Legal documents, science papers, and memorial inscriptions are rich with Latin text. As you learned earlier, many everyday English words have their roots in Latin. Studying Latin can also make it easier to learn other modern languages that have Latin roots.

So don't just think about the legacy of Rome, search it out. It's in our language, laws, government, art, and architecture. The Romans are everywhere.

REVIEW & ASSESS

1. **READING CHECK** What Roman achievements in art and architecture influence our lives today?
2. **MAKE CONNECTIONS** How has the government of the Roman Republic influenced the structure of the U.S. government?
3. **COMPARE AND CONTRAST** How are the layouts of many towns and cities today similar to those in ancient Rome?

4.3 MOMENTS IN HISTORY

The Roman Aqueduct

A.D. 52

The system of aqueducts that supplied water to Rome and its empire was a major feat of engineering. In the capital city itself, 11 aqueducts carried fresh water from the area's surrounding rivers and lakes, some as far as 57 miles away. Not all of these structures were architectural masterpieces like the Claudian Aqueduct (shown here), which was completed in A.D. 52. Many consisted of simple underground pipes through which water flowed to various tanks throughout the city. The Roman aqueduct system fell apart after the breakdown of the empire, but the basic engineering principles behind its construction are still in use today.

CHAPTER 11 Review

VOCABULARY

Match each word in the first column with its definition in the second column.

WORD	DEFINITION
1. aqueduct	a. the practice and skill of public speaking
2. fresco	b. thousands of tiny colored stone cubes set in plaster to create a picture or design
3. parable	c. a painting done on plaster walls
4. barbarian	d. a system of government in which there are four rulers
5. oratory	e. a member of a tribe outside the empire
6. bas-relief	f. a simple story told to make a moral point
7. tetrarchy	g. a stone channel that carries water
8. mosaic	h. a sculpture with figures raised against a flat background

READING SKILL

9. **ORGANIZE IDEAS: SEQUENCE EVENTS** If you haven't already, complete your time line of key people and events in the Roman Empire. Then answer the question.

People and Events in the Roman Empire

31 B.C. Augustus became emperor

Which person or event do you think had the greatest impact on the Roman Empire? Why?

MAIN IDEAS

Answer the following questions. Support your answers with evidence from the chapter.

10. What was accomplished during the Pax Romana? LESSON 1.1

11. What effect did safe seas and a network of excellent roads have on the Roman Empire's economy? LESSON 1.2

12. What role did Constantine play in the growth of Christianity? LESSON 2.4

13. Why did Diocletian divide the Roman Empire into the Eastern and Western Roman Empires? LESSON 3.2

14. How did Roman ideas about government and law influence the government of the United States? LESSON 4.2

CRITICAL THINKING

Answer the following questions. Support your answers with evidence from the chapter.

15. **FORM AND SUPPORT OPINIONS** What was the main reason the Roman Empire became so powerful and long lasting?

16. **SYNTHESIZE** What steps did Augustus take to secure the support of the Roman people and bring peace to the Roman Empire?

17. **EVALUATE** What role did technology play in Roman architecture?

18. **ANALYZE CAUSE AND EFFECT** How did the Roman Empire's vast geographic expanse become a serious disadvantage in the third century? What was the effect of this disadvantage?

19. **MAKE CONNECTIONS** How did the Latin language influence the Romance languages and English?

20. **YOU DECIDE** Do you think Augustus was a great emperor or a clever politician? Support your opinion with evidence from the chapter.

INTERPRET MAPS

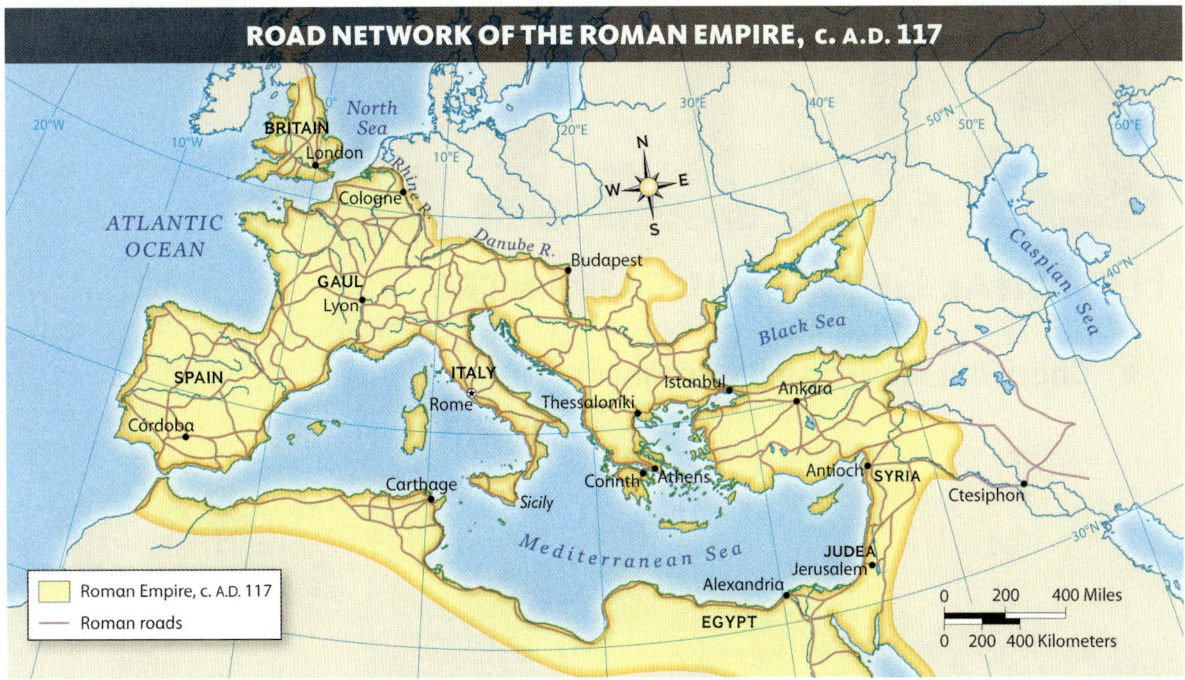

ROAD NETWORK OF THE ROMAN EMPIRE, c. A.D. 117
North Sea
BRITAIN
London
Rhine R.
Cologne
ATLANTIC OCEAN
Danube R.
Budapest
GAUL
Lyon
Black Sea
Caspian Sea
SPAIN
Córdoba
ITALY
Rome
Istanbul
Ankara
Thessaloniki
Carthage
Sicily
Corinth
Athens
Antioch
SYRIA
Ctesiphon
Mediterranean Sea
JUDEA
Jerusalem
Alexandria
EGYPT
Roman Empire, c. A.D. 117
Roman roads
0 200 400 Miles
0 200 400 Kilometers
N
S
E
W

21. Where is Rome located in relation to the rest of the Roman Empire?

22. In A.D. 117 how far north and how far south did the Roman Empire extend?

ANALYZE SOURCES

Read the following selection from Jesus' Sermon on the Mount. Then answer the question.

> Blessed are the poor in spirit, for theirs is the kingdom of heaven.
>
> Blessed are the meek, for they will inherit the Earth.
>
> Blessed are the merciful, for they will be shown mercy.
>
> Blessed are the pure in heart, for they will see God.
>
> —Matthew 5:3–8

23. SYNTHESIZE How might these teachings from Jesus have helped guide people to lead their lives during the Roman Empire?

WRITE ABOUT HISTORY

24. EXPLANATORY Many social, political, and economic problems contributed to the decline and fall of the Roman Empire. Put yourself in the position of a senator at that time. Write a speech explaining three of these problems.

TIPS

- Take notes as you review the portion of the chapter about the decline and fall of the Roman Empire.
- State your main idea and supporting details in a clear, well-organized way.
- Present evidence to support your explanation.
- Use vocabulary from the chapter to explain the problems.
- Make a concluding statement based on your explanation of and evidence about the decline and fall of the Roman Empire.

ON LOCATION WITH Steven ELLIS

NATIONAL GEOGRAPHIC GRANTEE

Check out more on myNGconnect

Archaeologist Steven Ellis surveys the ruins of Pompeii. His project focuses on the city's common people, which is a new approach to archaeological excavation.

NOT JUST DIGGERS

That's the misconception that annoys us the most! I dig up cities, yes, but it's what I learn from those cities that is important. Discovering artifacts is pretty cool, but piecing them together to tell a 2,000-year-old human story—that's what I find really exciting.

Pompeii is better preserved than any other Roman site, and because it's a city, you can relate to it more easily than, say, the pyramids. It's also got the drama of its sudden death, but we want to uncover its life. Pompeians lived in houses and went to shops and schools. I love that familiar urban element. They also had very different rules and did things differently. I think it's fascinating to try and recognize those similarities and differences.

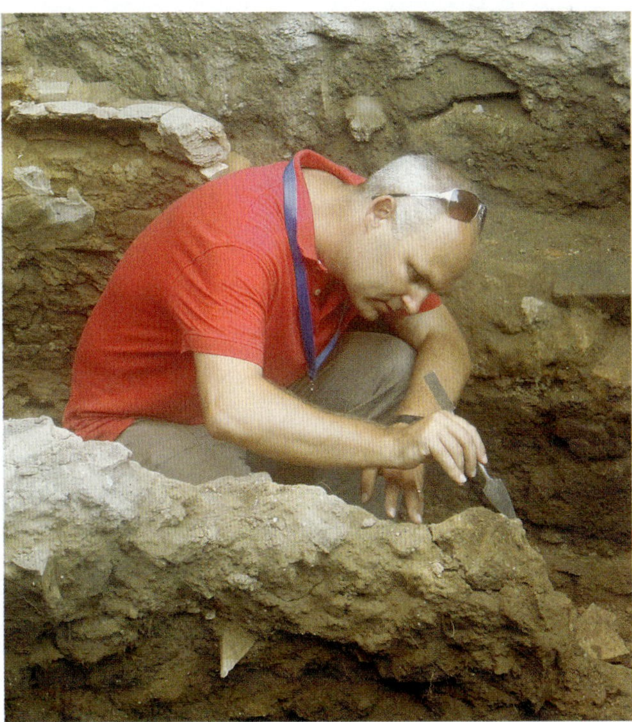

Archaeologists like Steven Ellis spend long hours in the field, carefully uncovering signs of past civilizations.

TELLING THE HUMAN STORY

For 200 years we've mostly looked at what the rich were doing by unearthing the grandest buildings. I'm using archaeology to tell the story of ordinary people, the other 98 percent of the population. It's a fairly new approach. I was the youngest archaeological director at Pompeii, and I was also the new guy with new questions. I said, "I want to work in areas that you've ignored." So I'm looking at shops, bars, restaurants, and houses. They don't have fine art, but they do have bones, seeds, and pieces of pottery that tell us a story. Some of our discoveries are pretty obvious, like the fact that poor people lived in smaller houses and ate cheaper foods off cheaper plates. But they're expanding our understanding of Roman society beyond just the rich and revealing the complex layers of life in the middle and working classes.

Excavating in poorer communities is incredibly gratifying because you've got to work harder at it. The rich lived in the best houses, with the best decorations and the most stuff. This all survived better, so it's easier to uncover and study. I'm proud that we are excavating the stories of families whose histories would otherwise never be told.

WHY STUDY HISTORY ?

"I study history because it's fascinating and ***because I can***. In some countries, people are forbidden to study their own history, and that's a tragedy. I love finding out how similar or different people were from us." —Steven Ellis

NATIONAL GEOGRAPHIC

Rethinking Nero

BY ROBERT DRAPER

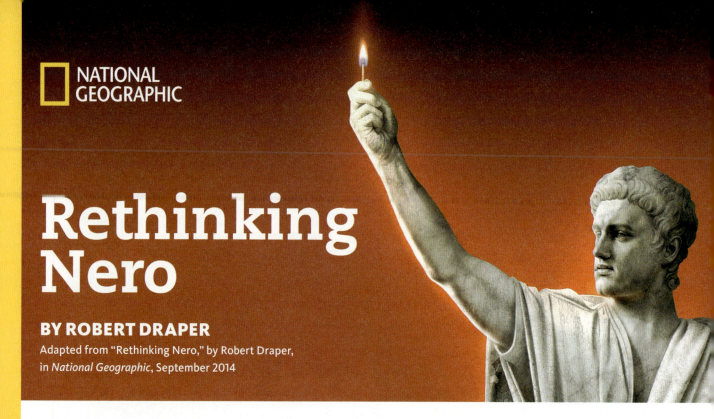

Adapted from "Rethinking Nero," by Robert Draper, in *National Geographic*, September 2014

As the city of Rome burned in A.D. 64, the infamous emperor Nero allegedly sat around playing his violin. He also may have killed two of his wives, his mother, and his stepbrother. In the accounts of many historians, he is described as a murderer and a lunatic. But now some scholars are rethinking Nero's reputation.

In 2007, archaeologist Fedora Filippi discovered the base of a column while digging under a busy street in Rome. Burrowing further, she encountered a portico and the edge of a pool. After a year of analysis, she concluded that she had discovered the enormous public gymnasium built by Nero a few years before the Great Fire. At first her discovery garnered little attention. But it was an important find. "The gymnasium was part of a big change Nero brought about in Rome," Filippi says. "Before, such baths were only for the aristocrats. This changed social relations because it put everyone on the same level, from senators to the horsemen."

Nero's gymnasium and events early in his reign suggest that he was a reformer who desired the admiration of his people. He ended the secret trials of the previous emperor, issued pardons, and was reluctant to sign death warrants. He praised Greek culture, encouraging Greek-style contests of athletics and poetry. Instead of looting other countries to gain wealth, Nero taxed wealthy Romans to raise funds, a practice that made him unpopular with the most powerful members of society. These early accomplishments likely alienated him from the Roman senators. But his own outrageous behavior later in his reign is the reason why he went down in history as a madman.

"Nero was a fool obsessed with his own power, but a fool can also be charming and interesting," says Roman archaeologist Andrea Carandini. He became powerful by appealing to the popular desires and prejudices of his people. In turn, he cherished the masses who adored him.

Romans themselves were conflicted about their ruler. "He was a monster," says Roberto Gervaso, author of the biographical novel *Nerone*. "But that's not all he was."

For more from National Geographic
Check out "Roman Frontiers" on myNGconnect

UNIT INQUIRY: BUILD AN EMPIRE

In this unit, you learned about ancient Rome and its legacy. Based on your reading, what factors can help make an empire great? What factors can lead to its decline?

ASSIGNMENT Design an empire that you think would be successful today. The empire should have a geographic location, a government, an economy, a social structure, and its own culture. Be prepared to present your empire and explain it to the class.

Plan As you build your empire, think about ancient Rome—what made it successful and what made it grow weak. Make a list of these factors and try to incorporate or avoid them in your own empire. Use a graphic organizer like this one to help organize your thoughts. ▶

Produce Use your notes to produce detailed descriptions of the elements of your empire. Write them in outline or paragraph form.

Present Choose a creative way to present your empire to the class. Consider one of these options:

- Create a multimedia presentation using photos to represent different elements of your empire.
- Write an introduction to a travel guide that describes your empire.
- Draw a map of your empire to accompany the description of its overall structure.

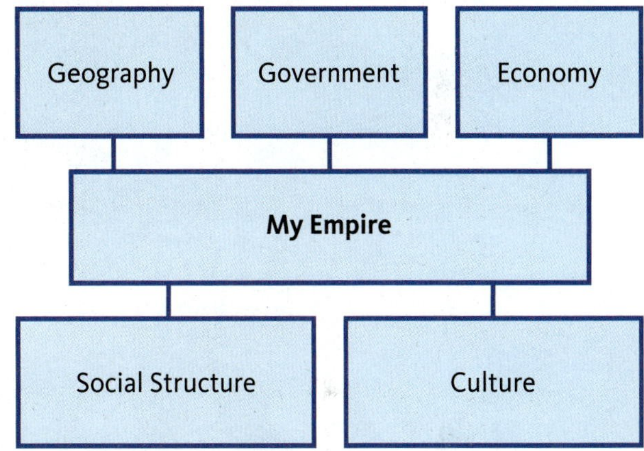
Geography
Government
Economy
My Empire
Social Structure
Culture

RAPID REVIEW
UNIT 4

THE WORLD OF THE ROMANS TOP TEN

1. In the Roman Republic, power was shared between elected consuls and assemblies to prevent individuals from becoming too powerful.
2. After many civil wars, Rome became an empire ruled with absolute authority by a single emperor.
3. The wise rule of the emperor Augustus ushered in the Pax Romana, 200 years of peace and prosperity.
4. The Colosseum hosted spectacular and bloody games where gladiators fought to the death.
5. Romans spoke Latin, and we still use many Latin words today.

6-10. **NOW IT'S YOUR TURN** Complete the list with five more things to remember about the world of the Romans.

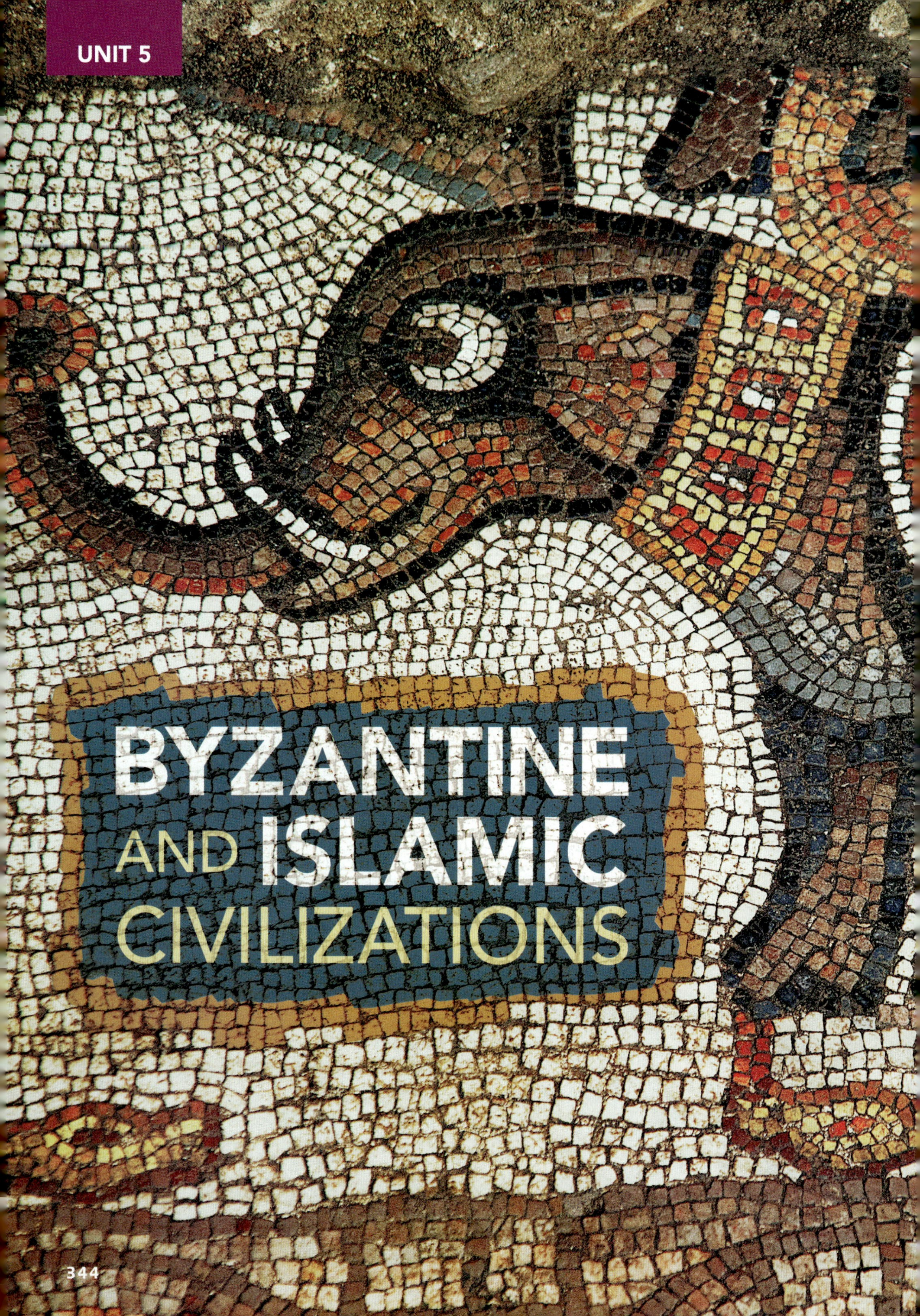

BYZANTINE AND ISLAMIC CIVILIZATIONS

NATIONAL GEOGRAPHIC

ON **LOCATION** WITH

Jodi Magness

Archaeologist

People say that the Roman Empire fell in 476, and a part of it did. But the empire lived on in the East. This part became known as the Byzantine Empire, but its citizens called themselves Romans. In the 600s, Muslim Arabs invaded Southwest Asia and conquered some of the territory held by the Byzantines, including Palestine. I'm Jodi Magness, and I excavate archaeological sites in Israel. Join me as we dig through the history of the Byzantine and Islamic civilizations!

< **CRITICAL VIEWING** Jodi Magness discovered a 5th-century synagogue and this Byzantine-inspired mosaic of an elephant at a site in Israel. What does the mosaic suggest about the skill of its artist?

UNIT 5
TIME LINE OF WORLD EVENTS

Byzantine and Islamic Civilizations

527
Justinian begins his rule of the Byzantine Empire.
(mosaic of Justinian)

630
Muhammad unites much of Arabia under Islam.

750
Muslim rule spreads Islam over parts of Asia, Africa, and Europe.
(page from the Qur'an)

1054
Christianity splits, and the Eastern Orthodox Church forms in Byzantium.

500

800

The World

618
ASIA
Tang dynasty begins in China.

800
EUROPE
Charlemagne unites and rules much of Western Europe.

c. 1000
AMERICAS
Inca civilization arises in South America.
(gold Inca figurine)

COMPARE TIME LINES

What world event occurred soon after the Byzantine Empire came to an end?

1200

1215
EUROPE
England's Magna Carta lays the groundwork for later democratic developments.

1312
AFRICA
Mansa Musa begins rule of Mali.

1400

1453
Ottoman Turks capture Constantinople, and the Byzantine Empire comes to an end.
(Suleyman I, Ottoman ruler)

1492
AMERICAS
Christopher Columbus sails to the Americas.

1501
The Safavid Empire arises in Persia.

1556
Akbar the Great leads Muslim India to a golden age.

1600

mid-1600s
Mughal emperor Shah Jahan builds the Taj Mahal in India.

UNIT 5

GEOGRAPHY IN HISTORY

BYZANTINE AND EARLY MUSLIM EMPIRES, 565–750

EUROPE
France
Alps
Spain
ABBASSID EMPIRE
Córdoba
Granada
Rome
BYZANTINE EMPIRE
Mediterranean Sea
Black Sea
Constantinople (Istanbul)
Caucasus Mts.
Caspian Sea
Aral Sea
ASIA
Persia
Baghdad
Damascus
Jerusalem
Alexandria
Cairo
Egypt
UMAYYAD EMPIRE
ABBASSID EMPIRE
Persian Gulf
Arabian Peninsula
Medina
Mecca
Red Sea
AFRICA
Himalaya
Agra
India
Arabian Sea
Bay of Bengal
INDIAN OCEAN

Byzantine Empire, 565
Umayyad Empire, 661
Abbassid Empire, 750

BYZANTINE & MUSLIM EMPIRES 565–1683

After the Western Roman Empire fell in 476, invaders overran its lands. But the eastern part of the empire, which came to be known as the Byzantine Empire, survived. The empire reached its height in 565.

The Byzantine Empire's power was soon overshadowed by a Muslim state that arose in Arabia. Over many centuries, Muslim armies conquered lands in Europe, Asia, and Africa. Muslim leaders established empires there and spread their Islamic faith.

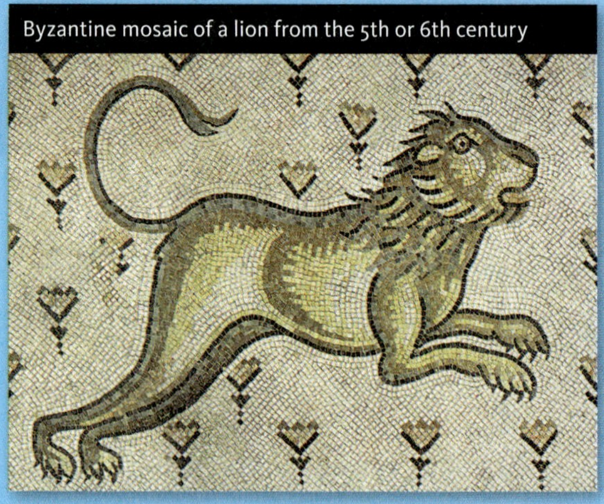
Byzantine mosaic of a lion from the 5th or 6th century

On which continent were the later Muslim empires mostly located?

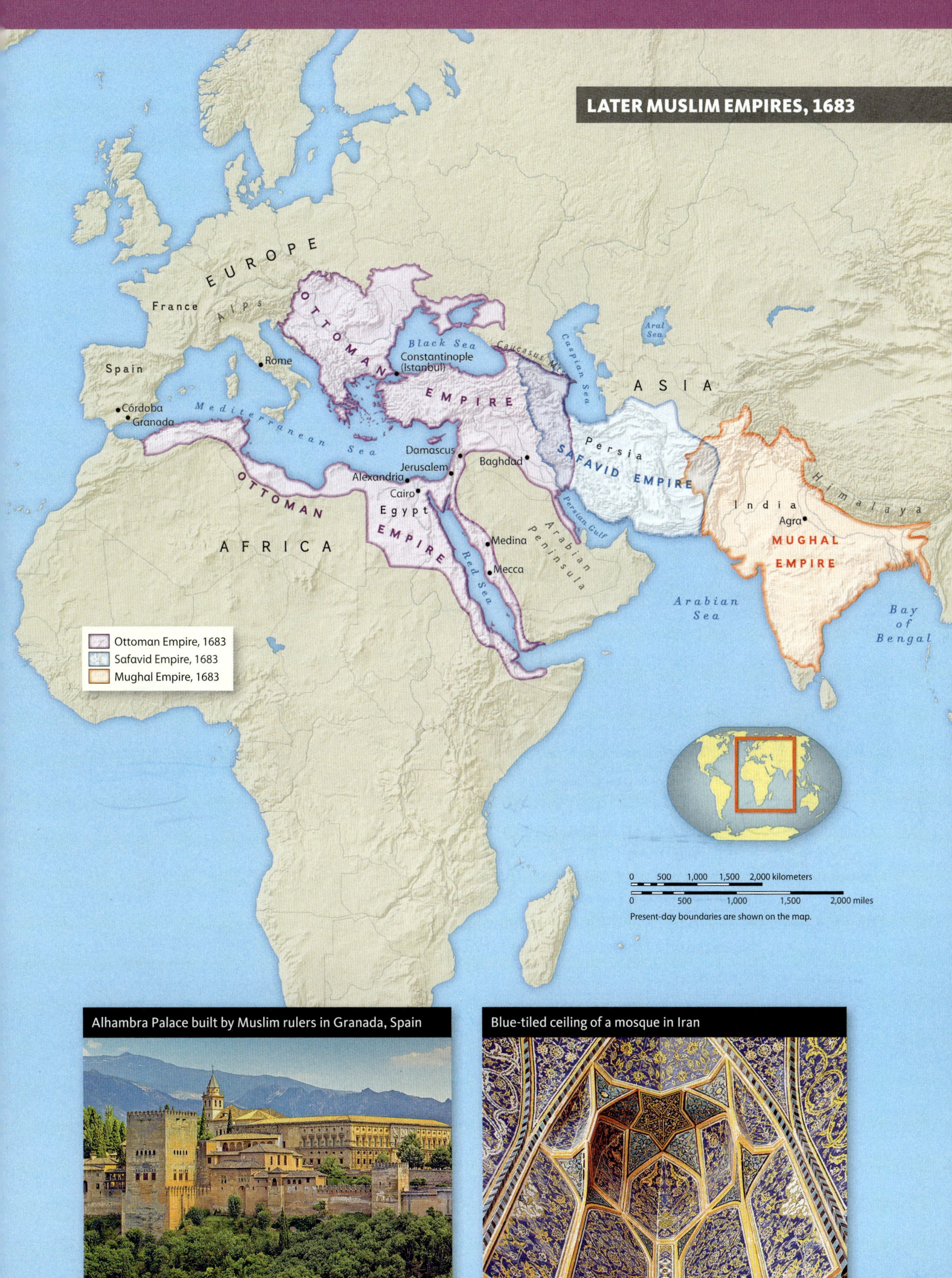

LATER MUSLIM EMPIRES, 1683
EUROPE
France
Alps
Spain
Córdoba
Granada
Rome
Mediterranean Sea
OTTOMAN EMPIRE
Black Sea
Constantinople (Istanbul)
Caucasus Mts.
Caspian Sea
Aral Sea
ASIA
Persia
SAFAVID EMPIRE
Damascus
Jerusalem
Alexandria
Baghdad
Cairo
Egypt
OTTOMAN EMPIRE
AFRICA
Medina
Mecca
Red Sea
Arabian Peninsula
Persian Gulf
Arabian Sea
India
Agra
MUGHAL EMPIRE
Himalaya
Bay of Bengal
Ottoman Empire, 1683
Safavid Empire, 1683
Mughal Empire, 1683
0 500 1,000 1,500 2,000 kilometers
0 500 1,000 1,500 2,000 miles
Present-day boundaries are shown on the map.

Alhambra Palace built by Muslim rulers in Granada, Spain

Blue-tiled ceiling of a mosque in Iran

CHAPTER

12 THE BYZANTINE EMPIRE

330 – 1435

SECTION 1

THE EARLY EMPIRE

KEY VOCABULARY
- crossroads
- diversity
- divine
- heresy

NAMES & PLACES
- Bosporus
- Constantinople
- Hagia Sophia
- Justinian
- Justinian Code
- Theodora

SECTION 2

THE LATER EMPIRE

KEY VOCABULARY
- creed
- excommunicate
- icon
- patriarch
- schism

NAMES & PLACES
- Eastern Orthodox Church

READING STRATEGY

ORGANIZE IDEAS: ANALYZE CAUSE AND EFFECT
Analyzing cause and effect means figuring out why things happen. Often, an effect will have several contributing causes. As you read the chapter, use a diagram like this one to take notes and to think about what people and events caused the Byzantine Empire to grow and thrive.

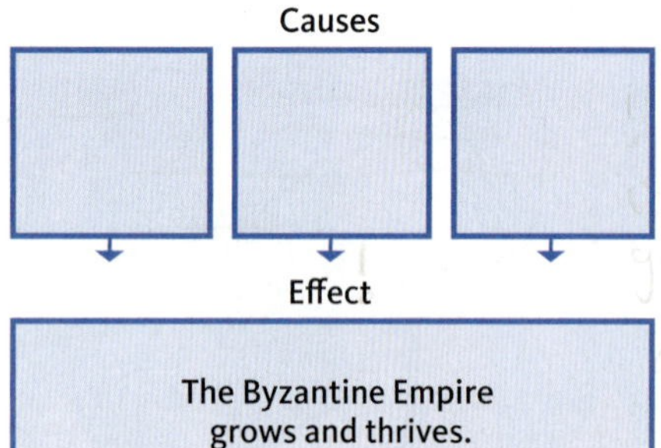

Causes
Effect
The Byzantine Empire grows and thrives.

The Hagia Sophia dominates the skyline of Istanbul in present-day Turkey. Originally built as a church by a Byzantine emperor, it later became a mosque and is now a museum.

1.1 The Geography of the Byzantine Empire

The Western Roman Empire fell in A.D. 476, but that's not the end of its story. For a thousand years after that date, the glory of Rome lived on in the Byzantine Empire.

MAIN IDEA

The Byzantine Empire was well located for trade but open to attack.

CONNECTING EAST AND WEST

From law to architecture, the Byzantine (BIHZ-unh-teen) Empire's achievements were extraordinary. One reason for those achievements was the empire's location at the **crossroads** of Europe and Asia, the place where the trade routes from each continent met. As a result of the empire's geography, many influences came together to create the Byzantine civilization.

As you may recall from the previous chapter, the emperor Diocletian divided the Roman Empire in A.D. 293. The Eastern Roman Empire became known as the Byzantine Empire because its capital was built on the old Greek town of Byzantium (buh-ZAN-tee-uhm). In fact, the Byzantine Empire is often referred to as Byzantium. By A.D. 330, the emperor Constantine had transformed Byzantium into a grand "New Rome." He named the city **Constantinople**, or city of Constantine. Today it is called Istanbul.

While the Western Roman Empire was ripped apart by invading barbarians, the Byzantine Empire managed to survive similar attacks. A series of strong emperors fought off Byzantium's enemies and strengthened the empire. Thus, the Byzantine Empire continued the traditions of Roman civilization for another thousand years after the collapse of the Western Roman Empire. The people we now call Byzantines proudly called themselves Romans.

Constantinople occupied one of the ancient world's most important geographic locations. At the heart of the empire was the small but important land link between Asia and Europe that permitted trade between east and west. The empire itself reached into both continents. Its heartland was in what are now Greece and Turkey.

Constantinople was also located on the **Bosporus**, a strait that links the Black Sea with the Mediterranean. The city was a major trade center for goods traveling by land and sea from all over the world. Constantinople and the Byzantine Empire grew rich on this trade. The city also attracted people from many parts of the world. They came to trade goods from their homelands and wound up living in the bustling city. These immigrants gave Constantinople the cultural **diversity**, or variety, for which it was famous.

EXPANDING THE EMPIRE

The Byzantine Empire's location brought problems as well as advantages. Although Constantinople itself was well protected, the rest of the empire was surrounded by enemies. To the north and west were many barbarian kingdoms forcefully pressing on Byzantium's borders. To the east was an age-old enemy, the powerful and hostile Persian Empire.

The rich resources and great wealth of Byzantium made it a tempting target for raids and invasions. With no strong geographic barriers to prevent invasion by enemies, the empire was dangerously

THE BYZANTINE EMPIRE, A.D. 527–565
10°W
0°
10°E
20°E
30°E
40°E
50°N
40°N
30°N
SLAVS
FRANKS
EUROPE
GOTHS
GOTHS
HUNS
Black Sea
Ravenna
DALMATIA
ITALY
Corsica
Rome
Sardinia
MACEDONIA
Bosporus
Constantinople
Nicaea
ANATOLIA
PERSIAN EMPIRE
Cartagena
Sicily
Carthage
Athens
NUMIDIA
Mediterranean Sea
Cyprus
SYRIA
Crete
Damascus
Jerusalem
AFRICA
N
W
E
S
TRIPOLITANIA
CYRENAICA
Alexandria
EGYPT
Red Sea
The Byzantine Empire before Justinian
Expansion under Justinian
0
250
500 Miles
0
250
500 Kilometers

exposed. Its long borders were constantly under attack by invading neighbors.

The Byzantine Empire needed strong leadership to hold it together in the face of so many threats. Over a thousand years, its borders grew and shrank, depending on the ability of its rulers and the eagerness of its enemies to wage war. At its greatest extent, the empire completely encircled the Mediterranean Sea.

Probably the greatest Byzantine ruler was one of its earliest—**Justinian**, the emperor from A.D. 527 until his death in 565. He not only recaptured lost Byzantine lands but also reconquered large areas of the old Western Roman Empire. His armies defeated the Persians and reconquered North Africa, Italy, and parts of Spain. For a brief time, Justinian reunited the Eastern and Western Roman Empires. He built up the strength of the Byzantine Empire, even while Rome was being overrun by invaders. Justinian's legacy of leadership remained influential throughout the time of the Byzantine Empire and beyond.

REVIEW & ASSESS

1. READING CHECK Why was Constantinople's geographic location an advantage for trade?

2. ANALYZE CAUSE AND EFFECT What caused the Persian Empire and other enemies to attack and invade Byzantium?

3. INTERPRET MAPS How far west did the borders of the Byzantine Empire expand after Justinian's conquests?

1.2 Justinian and Theodora

There's a popular saying that two heads are better than one. This was certainly true of Justinian's reign. Justinian became Byzantium's greatest emperor thanks in part to the support and intelligence of his wife, Theodora.

MAIN IDEA

Justinian and Theodora ruled over a golden age for Byzantium.

A POWERFUL RULER

Justinian was born in A.D. 482 or 483 to a peasant farmer. It was a humble beginning, but Justinian's uncle rose to become a great general and then emperor. The uncle educated Justinian, gave him important jobs, and appointed him as his successor. It was a smart choice. Justinian was intelligent, talented, and ambitious. He modeled himself on the old Roman Caesars. After he became emperor in 527, Justinian worked to bring a golden age to Byzantium.

In many ways, Justinian proved to be a powerful and effective leader. As you have read, he greatly expanded the empire's borders. Within those borders, he made major improvements in the areas of government, construction, and law. He reformed Byzantine government to improve efficiency and get rid of corruption. Justinian also started an ambitious construction program. He ordered the building of the **Hagia Sophia** (HY-uh soh-FEE-uh), a church in Constantinople that today is considered a masterpiece of Byzantine architecture. He also sponsored many other civic projects in the city, including a magnificent new building for the Senate.

Justinian was a dedicated Christian actively involved in issues of faith. He punished those he found guilty of **heresy** (HAIR-uh-see)—beliefs contrary to church teachings—including Jews. For example, he prohibited Jews from building synagogues and reading the Bible in Hebrew.

Justinian also worked hard to settle the differences of opinion that divided the early church. For example, groups within the church had different beliefs about whether Jesus Christ was fully **divine** (having the nature of a god) and should be worshipped as an equal to God. This disagreement continued long after Justinian's death.

Justinian's reform of the law was far more successful. He reorganized and standardized confusing Roman laws and had the surviving laws written down clearly and logically in a single work called the **Justinian Code**. This remarkable work has formed the basis of European law until modern times.

A COURAGEOUS EMPRESS

Of all Justinian's advisors, the most influential was his wife, **Theodora**. An actress when she was young, Theodora was part of a lower social class, so Justinian had to have the law changed to marry her. Together, they formed an unstoppable team who shared power as nearly equal co-rulers.

Theodora was extremely bright and energetic. Justinian admired her intelligence and deeply respected her opinions. As a result, she had a huge influence on imperial policy. Theodora was probably behind the laws passed to protect women, children, and some Christian minority groups.

This sixth-century mosaic shows Justinian in the center with religious leaders on his right and government officials on his left.

Theodora even saved Justinian's crown. In 532, some of Justinian's opponents turned a riot between rival sports fans into a widespread rebellion against his policies. As Justinian prepared to flee the city, Theodora refused to leave. Her courageous determination to stay and fight the rebels inspired Justinian. He ordered the army to crush the rebellion, which led to the deaths of 30,000 protesters. Order was restored, along with the emperor's authority. Following these events, Justinian decided to rule more carefully in the future.

SPORTS, POLITICS, AND PASSIONS

The people of Byzantium passionately followed the sport of chariot racing. More than just entertainment, the races were a focus of life and politics in the city. The people were bitterly divided in their support of the two main chariot teams—the Blues and the Greens. Races were an emotional standoff between supporters who often became violent. Justinian and Theodora both supported the Blues.

REVIEW & ASSESS

1. **READING CHECK** In what areas did Justinian make major improvements during his reign?

2. **IDENTIFY MAIN IDEAS AND DETAILS** What evidence from the text shows that Justinian's law reforms were successful?

3. **ANALYZE VISUALS** What can you infer about Justinian's reign from the people portrayed in the mosaic?

1.3 MOMENTS IN HISTORY
The Hagia Sophia

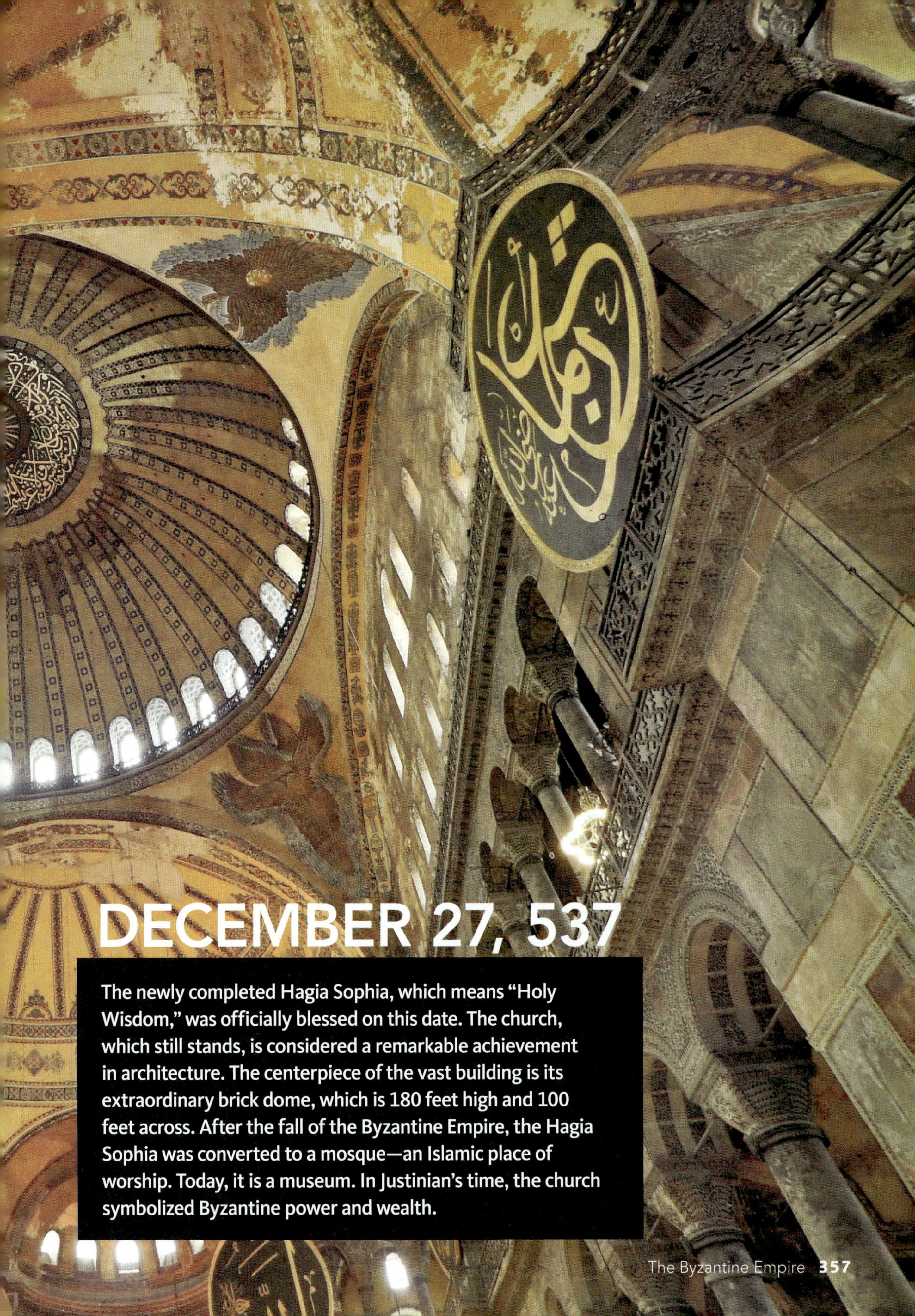

DECEMBER 27, 537

The newly completed Hagia Sophia, which means "Holy Wisdom," was officially blessed on this date. The church, which still stands, is considered a remarkable achievement in architecture. The centerpiece of the vast building is its extraordinary brick dome, which is 180 feet high and 100 feet across. After the fall of the Byzantine Empire, the Hagia Sophia was converted to a mosque—an Islamic place of worship. Today, it is a museum. In Justinian's time, the church symbolized Byzantine power and wealth.

CONSTANTINOPLE: THE HEART OF THE EMPIRE

Constantinople was the vibrant center of the Byzantine Empire. Beginning with Constantine, the emperors adorned the city with numerous churches, monuments, and civic buildings. Every day, thousands of people from all around the ancient world thronged the streets, buying, selling, and socializing.

Emperor Constantine built the first strong wall around Constantinople. As the city expanded, later emperors built walls farther out.

The Mese was the main street of Constantinople. Lined with shops, it led from the Hagia Sophia through the city's forums.

Like Rome, Constantinople had forums where people met to do business. The oval Forum of Constantine was one of these.

The Hagia Sophia overlooked the Bosporus and commanded a view of the entire city as well.

Emperor Constantine built the Hippodrome, the largest stadium of its time. It could seat some 60,000 people.

1.4 Life in Constantinople

You had to like people to enjoy living in Constantinople. It was the world's largest city, with its 500,000 inhabitants packed tightly together. The people of the city considered it the new Rome.

MAIN IDEA

Constantinople was a lively capital city modeled on ancient Rome.

THE CAPITAL CITY

Like Rome, Constantinople relied on resources from outside the city for its survival. The people consumed grain imported from Egypt and water piped in from more than 70 miles away.

Surrounded by the sea on three sides, Constantinople expanded to the west as it constantly attracted new people. Its strategic location on the Bosporus made it the richest and most influential city of its time. Merchants and traders from many parts of Europe and Asia brought in a constant flow of business and goods.

Like the residents of Rome, many of Constantinople's residents lived in poor conditions. They relied on government handouts of bread. Just a short walk away, though, spectacular public buildings and magnificent monuments inspired civic pride. As in Rome, a Senate house, public baths, triumphal arches, columns, and statues reflected the wealth and glory of the empire.

The city's people would frequently cram into the huge Hippodrome, a massive arena almost 1,500 feet long, to watch chariot races. The track was decorated with treasures from ancient Greece and Egypt. The emperor supervised the games from the imperial box, just as in Rome.

ROMAN CULTURAL INFLUENCE

Constantinople reflected everything that was glorious about ancient Rome. Its design, architecture, and monuments all reinforced the fact that the Byzantines considered themselves Roman. They saw themselves as the true inheritors of Roman cultural traditions—far more than Rome itself. Indeed, the Byzantine emperors brought many great monuments from Roman Italy, Africa, and Greece to adorn the capital.

Constantinople was also a center of cultural diversity because it was a center of trade. People who came from abroad to trade sometimes settled in the city. Greece was a strong influence as well. Greek, not Latin, was the people's language and the official language of the state. However, the Justinian Code, based on Roman law, continued as the basis for the Byzantine legal system. In this way, Byzantium helped preserve Greek and Roman learning for later generations.

REVIEW & ASSESS

1. **READING CHECK** What was one way in which Constantinople modeled itself on ancient Rome?
2. **MAKE INFERENCES** Why was trade with other regions necessary for Constantinople?
3. **INTERPRET VISUALS** What details in the drawing illustrate the idea that Constantinople was a busy, wealthy city?

2.1 The Church Divides

It's Saturday afternoon in the Hagia Sophia. Just before the service, three men burst in, march up to the altar, slam down a piece of paper, shout in a foreign language, and storm out. You've just witnessed the Christian church being split in two—forever.

MAIN IDEA

Christianity in the East and the West developed differently, causing arguments and finally a split.

EAST VERSUS WEST

When the old Roman Empire divided, the cultures of its eastern and western empires developed very differently. Arguments arose over Christian religious practices. In the East, the emperor was seen as God's representative on Earth. The emperor had a great deal of influence over the church and its leader, the **patriarch**. The first patriarchs of Constantinople were bishops under the governance of the pope. Over time, however, they became more independent of Rome.

The West did not have an emperor after 476, when the Roman Empire fell. As you may recall, the pope in Rome grew extremely powerful and claimed absolute authority over all western Christians, even kings. He then claimed authority over the eastern Christians, which led to a long power struggle with the Byzantine emperors. With different leaders and with very little contact, eastern and western Christians drifted apart in their beliefs and practices.

One key conflict was a disagreement about the Holy Trinity—the Father, the Son, and the Holy Spirit. The western church adopted a **creed**, or statement of belief, that claimed the Holy Spirit comes from the Father and the Son—God and Jesus. The eastern church maintained the belief that the Holy Spirit comes only from the Father.

Another major clash was over **icons**, images of Jesus and the saints. Many Christians had icons, and some began to pray to them. In the East, the emperor banned icons and ordered that they be destroyed. In the West, the pope rebuked the emperor and condemned the destruction of the icons. Religion was an extremely important topic to the Byzantine people. They believed their eternal salvation depended on proper understanding of God and the Bible. As a result, these religious disagreements brought about strong feelings.

THE EAST-WEST SCHISM

Growing disagreements created suspicion and hostility between eastern and western Christians. Finally, the pope's representatives in Constantinople announced that the Byzantine patriarch was **excommunicated**—no longer part of the church. They made this announcement by placing the letter of excommunication on the altar of the Hagia Sophia. The furious patriarch then excommunicated the pope. In 1054, the church split in what is called the East-West Schism (SKIH-zuhm) or the Schism of 1054. A **schism** is a separation. The Roman Catholic Church remained in the West, and the **Eastern Orthodox Church** developed in Byzantium.

Followers of each religion shared some important common ground. They both based their beliefs on Jesus and the Bible, and they both worshipped in churches with services led by priests and bishops. However, in

THE SCHISM OF 1054

Eastern Orthodox Church
Roman Catholic Church

20°W 10°W 0° 10°E 20°E 30°E 40°E 50°E 60°E
60°N 50°N 40°N 30°N

NORWAY
SWEDEN
SCOTLAND
DENMARK
ENGLAND
EASTERN SLAVIC PRINCIPALITIES
POLAND
HOLY ROMAN EMPIRE
FRANCE
HUNGARY
KINGDOM OF NAVARRE
BURGUNDY
KINGDOM OF LEÓN
KINGDOM OF ARAGON
CROATIA
KINGDOM OF CASTILLE
CATALONIA
Black Sea
Corsica
PAPAL STATES
Rome
Constantinople
Nicaea
Sardinia
BYZANTINE EMPIRE
Sicily
Crete
Cyprus
Mediterranean Sea
Jerusalem
0 250 500 Miles
0 250 500 Kilometers

the Roman Catholic Church, the pope had authority over all the clergy and even kings. Priests could not marry, and services were conducted in Latin. In the Eastern Orthodox Church, the emperor had spiritual authority over the clergy, priests could marry, and services were conducted in Greek.

ΟΒ
IC
XC
ΤΔ

ICONS

The word *icon* comes from the Greek word for "image." Many icons were painted on wood, but some were made from mosaic tiles, ivory, and other materials. Although Byzantine emperors banned icons more than once, people kept them in their homes and businesses and placed them in churches.

REVIEW & ASSESS

1. **READING CHECK** What was one principal difference between the eastern and western churches?

2. **DETERMINE WORD MEANINGS** How does knowing that *ortho* refers to "correct" and *dox* refers to "opinion" clarify the meaning of the word *orthodox*?

3. **INTERPRET MAPS** What does the map add to the text's description of the Schism of 1054?

HISTORY THROUGH OBJECTS

2.2 BYZANTINE MOSAICS

The Byzantine Empire developed an influential artistic culture. Its distinctive style is well represented by the remarkable mosaics found in churches such as the Hagia Sophia. Covering entire walls and ceilings, Byzantine mosaics stood out for their exceptional quality and craftsmanship. Large expanses of gold-backed glass created a rich glow. Natural stone cubes helped create vibrant, detailed scenes. The breathtaking results still awe viewers today.

SALVS MVNDI

Sant'Apollinare
The Basilica of Sant'Apollinare in Classe in Ravenna, Italy, is an excellent example of Byzantine mosaic art. The church was built in the sixth century. The area around its altar is covered with an elaborate mosaic scene showing Saint Apollinaris outdoors, surrounded by lambs.

Mosaic Technique
To make a mosaic, the artist spreads a layer of plaster onto a surface and sets the cubes into the plaster before it dries.

Natural Coloring
Byzantine mosaic artists were able to create highly detailed and realistic pictures of people and animals. In this image of Saint Apollinaris, stone tesserae create natural tones and shadows on the face.

Realistic Animals
The artists used naturally white stone cubes to depict the snowy white sheep in the scene.

Cubes Up Close
These present-day mosaic cubes, or tesserae, give an idea of the shapes the Byzantines used in their mosaics. Like the Byzantine tesserae, modern cubes also come in many colors.

Dazzling Gold
The pieces in this mosaic from another church in Ravenna are made of gold leaf sandwiched in clear glass. They are precisely angled to reflect light in different directions and create a sparkling effect.

2.3 The End of an Empire

On May 29, 1453, the last Byzantine emperor died fighting as his enemies swarmed through his capital's shattered walls. That day, the Byzantine Empire ended. It was a heroic finale for an empire that had survived against the odds for a thousand years.

MAIN IDEA

After Justinian, the empire experienced invasions and another golden age before it finally collapsed.

GREEK FIRE

The Byzantine army had a secret weapon: Greek fire. It was liquid fire soldiers could propel at enemy troops. It burned with an incredible intensity, and not even water could extinguish it.

The formula for making Greek fire was a closely guarded secret that died with the empire.

DEBTS AND INVASIONS

After Justinian died in 565, the debts the emperor had taken out to pay for his many wars nearly bankrupted the empire. In addition, the plague, which had already attacked during Justinian's time, made a return. Rats arriving aboard grain ships from Egypt carried the deadly disease, and it spread quickly through the overcrowded city. At the height of the plague, perhaps 10,000 people died every day.

As if that weren't enough, Byzantium's old enemies, including the Persians, renewed their attacks on the empire's borders. And then, in 634, the Byzantine Empire confronted a new rival. The religion of Islam had united Arab tribes, who formed a mighty Muslim army. This army conquered Egypt—a disaster for Constantinople's grain supply. By 711, the Arabs had conquered Syria, Egypt, parts of Southwest Asia, North Africa, and the Persian Empire.

NEW GOLDEN AGE AND FALL

Still, the Byzantine Empire was not yet down or out. By the early 1000s, the empire had entered a new golden age. Under the leadership of Basil II, Byzantium regained more control over trade, restored many of Constantinople's buildings and institutions, and spread Christianity among Slavic peoples to the north.

The empire's prosperity was short-lived, however. In 1096, an army of Christian Europeans launched a series of wars called the Crusades to fight the spread of Islam. The Crusaders soon came into conflict with Byzantine leaders. In 1204, they sacked Constantinople and occupied the city until 1261.

In time, the Byzantine Empire became a shadow of its former power—and then came the Turks, a people who had migrated into the region. By 1450, the Turks, who were Muslims, controlled all the lands around Constantinople. The city stood alone and surrounded.

In 1453, Mehmed II, the Turkish ruler, launched an army of 100,000 men against Constantinople's walls. The city's defenders, in contrast, numbered 7,000. On May 29, 1453, the Turks launched a final assault. They broke through the city's walls and killed the last Byzantine emperor, Constantine XI, as he charged into the invading army. By nightfall, Constantinople was under Turkish control.

The Capture of Constantinople in 1204, Jacopo Robusti Tintoretto, 16th century

Critical Viewing This painting shows the invasion of Constantinople by the Crusaders. Based on this painting, how would you describe the battle?

REVIEW & ASSESS

1. **READING CHECK** What was one factor that led to the decline and collapse of the Byzantine Empire?
2. **ANALYZE CAUSE AND EFFECT** Why was the plague able to spread so quickly throughout Constantinople?
3. **SEQUENCE EVENTS** What events took place in Byzantium during the 1000s?

CHAPTER 12 Review

VOCABULARY

Match each word in the first column with its meaning in the second column.

WORD	DEFINITION
1. divine	a. an image of Jesus or another holy figure
2. patriarch	b. a belief that goes against church teachings
3. heresy	c. having the nature of a god
4. icon	d. variety
5. diversity	e. a leader of the Eastern Orthodox Church

READING SKILL

6. ORGANIZE IDEAS: ANALYZE CAUSE AND EFFECT If you haven't already, complete your diagram to identify the factors that caused the Byzantine Empire to grow and thrive. Then answer the question.

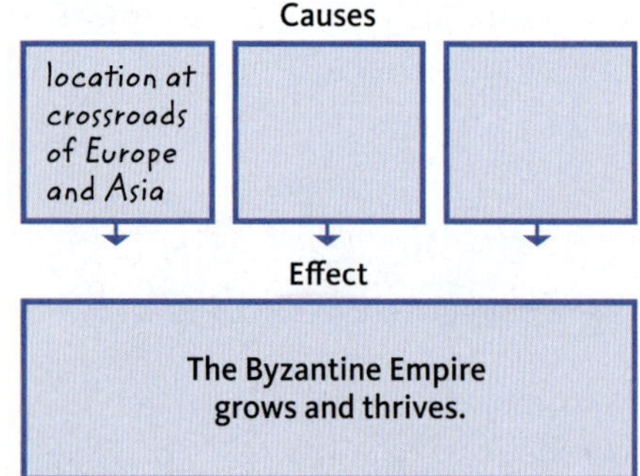

Causes
location at crossroads of Europe and Asia
Effect
The Byzantine Empire grows and thrives.

What conditions made it possible for the Byzantine Empire to grow, thrive, and enter a golden age?

MAIN IDEAS

Answer the following questions. Support your answers with evidence from the chapter.

7. In what ways was the location of Constantinople important to the growth of the Byzantine Empire? **LESSON 1.1**
8. In what ways did the Justinian Code improve on the Roman laws that it replaced? **LESSON 1.2**
9. What actions did Justinian take to bring a golden age to Byzantium? **LESSON 1.2**
10. Why did the Byzantines use ancient Rome as the model for their capital city, Constantinople? **LESSON 1.4**
11. How did the Byzantine emperor affect the religious life of the empire? **LESSON 2.1**
12. What effect did the plague have on the Byzantine Empire? **LESSON 2.3**

CRITICAL THINKING

Answer the following questions. Support your answers with evidence from the chapter.

13. **DRAW CONCLUSIONS** How do events that took place during the Byzantine Empire still affect the present-day world?
14. **SYNTHESIZE** How did the Byzantine Empire carry on the culture and traditions of the old Roman Empire?
15. **ANALYZE CAUSE AND EFFECT** Why was the Byzantine Empire a target for invaders throughout its long history?
16. **MAKE GENERALIZATIONS** How does geographic location help determine whether a city will become wealthy and powerful?
17. **YOU DECIDE** What was Justinian's greatest accomplishment? Support your opinion with evidence from the chapter.

INTERPRET DIAGRAMS

Study the diagram below to compare and contrast the two branches of Christianity that developed after the East-West Schism. Then answer the questions that follow.

The East-West Schism

Roman Catholic Church
- Led by the pope
- Pope had authority over all Christians, including kings and emperors
- Priests could not marry
- Services conducted in Latin
- Worship and use of icons promoted by the pope

Similarities
- Faith based on belief in Jesus and the Bible
- Services held in churches led by priests and bishops

Eastern Orthodox Church
- Led by the patriarch
- Emperor had authority over all church officials
- Priests could marry
- Services conducted in Greek
- Some believed the worship of icons should be forbidden

18. In what way did the pope have greater influence in the West than patriarchs did in the East?

19. How were the faiths of both branches of Christianity similar?

ANALYZE SOURCES

The historian Procopius was present at and recorded the events of a rebellion in 532. Read his account of Theodora's speech to Justinian as the emperor prepared to flee Constantinople. Then answer the question that follows.

> I believe that flight, now more than ever, is not in our interest even if it should bring us to safety. . . . For one who has reigned it is intolerable to become a fugitive. May I *never* be parted from the purple [the imperial color]! May I *never* live to see the day when I will not be addressed as Mistress by all in my presence! Emperor, if you wish to save yourself, that is easily arranged. . . . But consider whether, after you have saved yourself, you would then gladly exchange safety for death.

20. What does this this speech suggest about Theodora's character and influence?

WRITE ABOUT HISTORY

21. INFORMATIVE Suppose you are in the court of the emperor Justinian. Write an explanation for your fellow citizens of how Theodora influences Justinian's rule of the Byzantine Empire.

TIPS
- Take notes from the lessons about Justinian and Theodora.
- Write a topic sentence that clearly introduces your main idea about Theodora and Justinian.
- Choose relevant facts, concrete details, and examples for your explanation.
- Use vocabulary from the chapter where appropriate.
- Organize your details, facts, and examples clearly and logically.
- Provide a concluding statement that summarizes the information presented.

CHAPTER

13 THE ISLAMIC WORLD

600 – 1858

SECTION 1
THE ROOTS OF ISLAM

KEY VOCABULARY	NAMES & PLACES
caliph	Bedouin
clan	Islam
imam	Mecca
mosque	Muhammad
oasis	Muslim
pilgrimage	Qur'an
prophet	Sunna
shari'a	

SECTION 2
MUSLIM DYNASTIES AND EMPIRES

KEY VOCABULARY	NAMES & PLACES
bureaucracy	Abbasids
janissary	Mughals
mercenary	Ottomans
shah	Safavids
sultan	Shi'ite
tolerance	Suleyman I
	Sunni
	Umayyads

SECTION 3
THE LEGACY OF ISLAMIC CULTURE

KEY VOCABULARY	NAMES & PLACES
arabesque	al-Zahrawi
calligraphy	Ibn Rushd
medieval	Omar Khayyám
minaret	

READING STRATEGY

IDENTIFY MAIN IDEAS AND DETAILS

When you identify a text's main idea, you must support it with evidence from the text. As you read the chapter, use a web like this one to note evidence that supports the following idea: Islamic culture has had a lasting influence on the world.

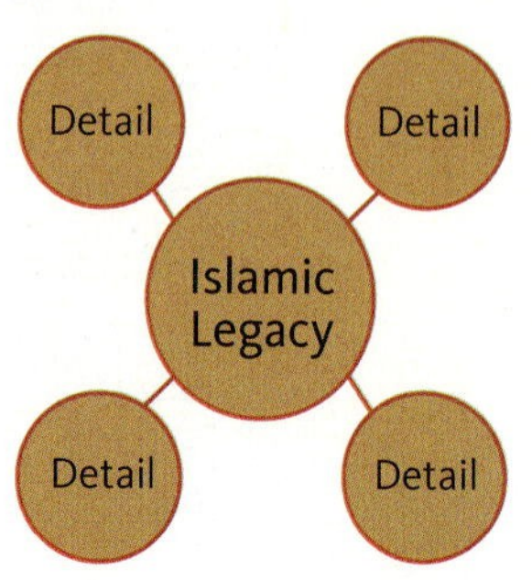
Detail
Detail
Islamic Legacy
Detail
Detail

The Great Mosque of Córdoba in Spain is a magnificent example of Muslim architecture. Its prayer hall is noted for its many double arches and columns.

1.1 Trading Crossroads

People living on the Arabian Peninsula in the 600s had to be tough. Their homeland was mostly a sea of sun-scorched sand that offered little shelter, shade, or water. But its location—at a spot where three continents meet—proved to be an advantage.

MAIN IDEA

The Arabian Peninsula became an important crossroads for trade among the continents of Asia, Africa, and Europe by the early 600s.

DESERT LIFE

The huge rectangle of the Arabian Peninsula, also known as Arabia, is one of the hottest and driest places on Earth. Almost the entire 1.2 million square miles is scorching desert and dry, flat land. Rain falls in few places, making water scarce and precious. Much of the peninsula gets only three to five inches of rain a year.

The region's harsh climate has long placed limits on farming. Many of Arabia's early inhabitants made their living as nomadic herders called **Bedouin** (BEH-duh-wuhn). They constantly moved their sheep, goats, and cattle among sources of water and grazing land. *Bedouin* is an Arabic word meaning "desert dweller."

In the 600s, the Bedouin were organized into tribes based on **clans**, or groups of related families who believed they shared a common ancestor. Each tribe formed an extended family to which members were fiercely loyal. Tribe members owned land and most property together, and each tribe had an elected leader called a sheikh (SHAYK). The tribes often fought one another to maintain or gain control of areas of the desert. As a result, the tribesmen became strong and skilled warriors.

GROWTH OF CITIES

The only place life could flourish in Arabia was at an **oasis**. An oasis is an isolated, reliable source of water in a desert where plants can grow. The oases were like stepping stones across the vast desert. They naturally attracted people, who then built permanent settlements. Anyone crossing the desert had to visit the oases, which became useful places to trade.

Because of its central location, Arabia became an important crossroads connecting routes from Asia, Africa, and Europe. Merchants led camels carrying silks, spices, metals, and other products along these trade routes. As a result, some oases grew into rich market towns and then into cities.

Arabia's most important city was **Mecca**, which became a center for both trade and religion. The various Arab tribes worshipped different nature gods. These beliefs were polytheistic, or based on the existence of multiple gods. Most Arabs also recognized the existence of a supreme God, called Allah (AL-luh) in Arabic. According to ancient Islamic tradition, the religious leader known in the Hebrew Bible as Abraham had stopped at Mecca and built a shrine called the Ka'aba (KAH-buh). Although Abraham dedicated the Ka'aba to the one supreme God, the shrine came to include representations of many Arabian tribal gods. Mecca became an important site for polytheistic Arabs. People from all over the peninsula made a **pilgrimage**, or journey, to worship there.

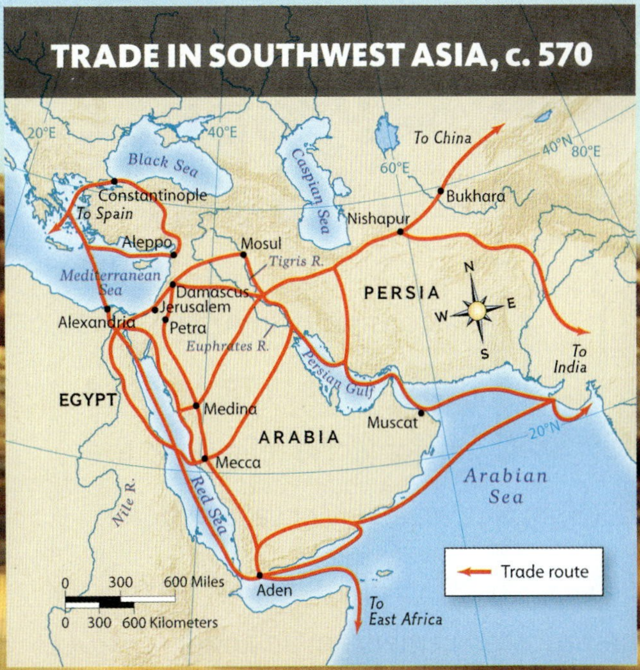

TRADE IN SOUTHWEST ASIA, c. 570

←	Trade route

Critical Viewing Sand dunes like these cover much of the Arabian Peninsula. What dangers might traders have faced as they crossed the vast desert?

REVIEW & ASSESS

1. **READING CHECK** How did Arabia's location contribute to its development as an important trading crossroads?

2. **ANALYZE CAUSE AND EFFECT** How did Arabia's physical geography influence the Bedouin's way of life?

3. **INTERPRET MAPS** Find Mecca on the map. Why is Mecca's location good for trade?

1.2

The Prophet of Islam

An oasis city in Arabia became the birthplace of a major world religion in the 600s. In a cave near Mecca, a middle-aged merchant heard messages that he reported came from an angel named Gabriel. The merchant began preaching those messages and united Arabia under a new religion.

MAIN IDEA

Muhammad was a great religious, political, and military leader who preached the religion of Islam and unified much of Arabia.

THE LIFE OF MUHAMMAD

Today the religion of **Islam** has about 1.5 billion followers worldwide. Its prophet, **Muhammad**, was born into a family of Mecca's ruling tribe about 570. A **prophet** is a teacher believed to be inspired by God. As a young man, Muhammad gained a reputation for intelligence, honesty, and kindness. He worked as a trader for a wealthy widow and merchant named Khadijah (kah-DEE-juh). She was so impressed by Muhammad's virtues that she married him.

Muhammad had a deep interest in religion. He periodically retreated to a cave outside of Mecca to pray. When he was about 40 years old, he had the first of many religious experiences. As he prayed in his cave, he heard a voice that he identified as the angel Gabriel. The main message was that people could achieve salvation, or go to heaven, in the afterlife only by worshipping and obeying the one true God. Muhammad thereafter rejected the polytheism that was common in Mecca. Instead, he followed the teaching attributed to Abraham, who said that there is only one God.

In 613, Muhammad began to preach that only the God of Abraham should be worshipped and obeyed, not the traditional tribal gods. In Arabic, *Islam* means "submission to the will of God." The name for a follower of Islam, **Muslim**, means "one who has submitted to God."

THE LEADERSHIP OF MUHAMMAD

Muhammad's teachings about the one true God threatened Mecca's political leaders. They supported traditional religion and benefitted from the city's position as a pilgrimage center for polytheistic Arabs. The leaders made life difficult for Muhammad and his followers, who then fled to the Arabian city of Yathrib. This event became known as the Hijrah (HEEJ-rah). The year of Muhammad's flight, 622, marks the beginning of the Muslim calendar. Yathrib was later renamed Medina (muh-DEE-nuh).

Muhammad and his followers were given leadership of Medina, where they established an Islamic community called the umma (OO-muh). Muhammad made loyalty to the umma more important than that to a tribe. He began uniting Arabia's many quarrelling tribes under Islam.

The ruling tribes of Mecca tried to crush this movement. However, in 630, Muhammad conquered Mecca, removed all idols at the Ka'aba, and dedicated the shrine to the God of Abraham. This victory and others helped spread Islam. By 632, when Muhammad died, most Arab tribes had joined the umma. Muhammad had proved himself a great religious, political, and military leader.

Muslims from all over the world journey to pray at the Ka'aba. This shrine takes the form of a stone cube and contains a holy rock called the Black Stone.

REVIEW & ASSESS

1. **READING CHECK** On what main belief did Muhammad base the religion of Islam?

2. **ANALYZE CAUSE AND EFFECT** Why did Muhammad and his followers move from Mecca to Medina?

3. **IDENTIFY DETAILS** The text states that Muhammad was a great religious, political, and military leader. What details in the text support this claim?

1.3 Beliefs and Laws

Could you point toward the direction of your home no matter where you were, even if you were in a faraway city? Muslims must be able to point toward the holy city of Mecca wherever they happen to be. It's an important aspect of a Muslim's daily life, which revolves around faithfully following Islamic religious practices.

MAIN IDEA

Islamic religious practices are based on Islam's holy book and the life of Muhammad.

THE QUR'AN AND THE SUNNA

The holy book of Islam is called the **Qur'an** (kuh-RAN). Muslims believe that the Qur'an contains the flawless words of Allah as revealed to Muhammad by the angel Gabriel. The Qur'an teaches that there is only one God, whom all Muslims should worship. According to the Qur'an, God is the creator and is merciful and compassionate. Islam teaches that God will judge individuals for their good and bad actions and send them to heaven or hell on a final judgment day. The Qur'an states how Muslims should behave. For example, the Qur'an promotes charity and forbids gambling and drinking alcohol.

Muslims believe that Muhammad demonstrated perfectly how to apply the Qur'an in daily life. The words and actions attributed to Muhammad, called the **Sunna** (SOON-uh), were written down by his followers. Muslims rely on both the Qur'an and the Sunna as guides. For example, the Qur'an instructs Muslims to wash before prayer but does not explain how. However, accounts of the Sunna claim to describe how Muhammad washed for prayer, so Muslims carefully follow this description.

Together, the Qur'an and the Sunna form the basis of Islamic law, which is called **shari'a** (shah-REE-ah). This system of law is comprehensive. It covers all aspects of human behavior, including family life, community life, moral conduct, worship, and business.

Early Muslims recognized Islam's link to the other monotheistic religions of Judaism and Christianity. They regarded Jews and Christians as "people of the book" because they consider Abraham a prophet and had a holy book with teachings similar to those of the Qur'an. Muslims believed the Qur'an was the final book of revelations from the same God that Jews and Christians worshipped. They regarded Muhammad as the final prophet of God.

EVERYDAY PRACTICES

Muslims apply their religious beliefs to their daily lives by following a set of duties called the Five Pillars of Islam. Additional Islamic customs guide their daily lives. For example, Muslims avoid eating certain meats and eat meat only from animals that are killed in a humane way.

Each Islamic community centers on a **mosque**, a Muslim place of worship. The main weekly service is on Friday afternoon. Worshippers wash themselves before entering a mosque and kneel on special prayer mats facing Mecca. A religious teacher called an **imam** leads the weekly service, which includes prayer and a sermon. Mosques also serve as centers of education and social work.

Critical Viewing A group of Bedouin in Saudi Arabia stop for evening prayer. According to the Five Pillars of Islam, in what direction should these Muslims be facing as they pray?

THE FIVE PILLARS OF ISLAM

All believers of Islam are called upon to carry out the following duties.

1 **Faith** Testify to this statement of faith: "There is no god but God, and Muhammad is His Prophet."

2 **Prayer** Pray five times a day, facing toward Mecca.

3 **Alms** Donate a portion of one's wealth to help people in need.

4 **Fasting** Eat and drink nothing between dawn and sunset during the Islamic holy month of Ramadan.

5 **Pilgrimage** Perform the hajj (haj), or pilgrimage to Mecca, at least once in a lifetime if able.

REVIEW & ASSESS

1. **READING CHECK** What is one practice that Muslims follow based on the Qur'an?
2. **SYNTHESIZE** How are the Qur'an and the Sunna related?
3. **MAKE GENERALIZATIONS** What are some links among Judaism, Christianity, and Islam?

1.4 DOCUMENT-BASED QUESTION

The Qur'an and Hadith

The Qur'an, Islam's holy book, provides religious guidance to Muslims on all aspects of life, from saying prayers to conducting business. Muslims also look to the Sunna, or Muhammad's example, to guide their behavior. Accounts of what Muhammad reportedly said, did, or approved were recorded by his followers after his death and are called hadith (huh-DEETH). The word *hadith* can refer either to a specific account of Muhammad's words and actions or to all the accounts in general.

This Persian painting shows the angel Gabriel. Muslims believe that Gabriel revealed the words of the Qur'an to Muhammad.

DOCUMENT ONE

Primary Source: Sacred Text

from the Qur'an

Muslims consider the Qur'an to be the words of God revealed in human language. In this excerpt, God speaks using the pronoun *We*, even though God is a single being. This use of *We* serves to emphasize the majesty and authority of God. This excerpt and the following one focus on why God created diversity among people.

CONSTRUCTED RESPONSE According to the Qur'an, who are the noblest human beings?

> O mankind, We have created you male and female, and appointed you groups and tribes, that you may know one another. Surely the noblest among you in the sight of God is the most godfearing of you. God is All-knowing, All-aware.
>
> Qur'an 49:13

DOCUMENT TWO

Primary Source: Sacred Text

from the Qur'an

As this excerpt suggests, tolerance of diversity is an important value in the Qur'an. In this excerpt, the pronoun *He* is used to refer to God. Muslims believe that God has no gender. The use of *He* is simply a custom.

CONSTRUCTED RESPONSE According to the Qur'an, why did Allah create a world of diversity?

> If God had willed, He could have made you one nation; but [He willed otherwise] that He may try [test] you in what has come to you. So be you forward [active] in good works; unto God shall you return, all together.
>
> Qur'an 5:54

DOCUMENT THREE

Primary Source: Sacred Text

Hadith

The Qur'an strongly warns Muslims to prepare for a day of judgment, when the worthy will go to paradise and the unworthy will suffer in hell. This hadith offers guidance on how to behave on Earth in order to attain paradise.

CONSTRUCTED RESPONSE According to this hadith, what should Muslims do to be worthy of entering paradise on the Last Day?

> Anyone who believes in God and the Last Day [of Judgment] should not harm his neighbor. Anyone who believes in God and the Last Day should entertain his guest generously. And anyone who believes in God and the Last Day should say what is good or keep quiet.
>
> Sahih Al-Bukhari, 6018

SYNTHESIZE & WRITE

1. **REVIEW** Review what you have learned about the Qur'an and hadith.
2. **RECALL** On your own paper, write down the main idea expressed in each of the three documents.
3. **CONSTRUCT** Write a topic sentence that answers this question: According to sacred Islamic writings, how should people behave?
4. **WRITE** Using evidence from the documents, write an informative paragraph that supports your topic sentence.

The Prophet's Mosque in Medina, Saudi Arabia, contains the tomb of Muhammad and is a holy site for Muslims.

1.5 After Muhammad

If your classroom teacher were suddenly called away, is there a student in your class who could take control and keep everyone focused on the lesson? After Muhammad died, Muslims needed a leader to keep the community focused. After a period of uncertainty, the Muslim state met the challenge.

MAIN IDEA

The Muslim state recovered from a period of disorder after Muhammad's death and soon expanded to form a powerful empire.

NEW LEADERS

In 632, the Muslim state in Arabia almost collapsed when Muhammad died without naming a successor. His followers disagreed over how to choose a leader. Then a few leading Muslims acted decisively. They appointed Muhammad's father-in-law, Abu Bakr (uh-boo BA-kuhr), as **caliph** (KAY-lihf), which means "successor." He promised to follow Muhammad's example.

As the first of many caliphs, Abu Bakr served as the supreme religious, political, and military leader of a growing Muslim empire. Though he ruled for just two years, he was critical to the survival of Islam. He crushed rebellions that could have destroyed the young state. His strong leadership kept all of Arabia united under Islam.

ISLAM SPREADS

The early caliphs succeeded in establishing a large Muslim empire that stretched thousands of miles from the Mediterranean region into Central Asia. The Muslims faced two great superpowers in the region. The Byzantine Empire ruled Syria and Egypt, while the Persian Empire ruled Iran and Iraq. However, these two rival empires had become exhausted by fighting long and bitter wars. Meanwhile, the Muslim empire had developed a skilled, disciplined, and enthusiastic army. By 652, just 20 years after Muhammad's death, the Muslims had conquered Syria, Palestine, Iraq, Iran, Egypt, and various parts of North Africa. (A map of Muslim conquests appears in the Chapter Review.)

The Qur'an forbade the conquering caliphs from forcing their new non-Muslim subjects to convert to Islam. Instead of being persecuted, or mistreated, as they had been under Byzantine and Persian rule, Jews, Christians, and those of other faiths were allowed to follow their own religious customs with some restrictions. Even so, many people chose to convert to Islam. Some people were genuinely attracted by Islamic ideas and customs. Other people converted for practical reasons of social, political, and economic gain.

REVIEW & ASSESS

1. **READING CHECK** How did Muhammad's death in 632 affect the Muslim state he had established?
2. **ANALYZE CAUSE AND EFFECT** Why were the Muslims able to conquer the powerful Byzantine and Persian Empires in just 20 years?
3. **MAKE GENERALIZATIONS** Why did many Jews, Christians, and other non-Muslims convert to Islam in the growing Muslim empire?

2.1 The Umayyads and the Abbasids

Running an empire is hard work. There are complicated issues to understand, mountains of paperwork to complete, and tough decisions to make. The caliphs lost interest and let others govern while they enjoyed luxurious lifestyles. Their actions lost them both respect and control of their empire.

MAIN IDEA

Opposing groups competed for power in the Muslim empire, and a major split developed in Islam in the late 600s.

UMAYYAD EXPANSION

Despite its military successes, the Muslim community could not maintain unity as various groups struggled for power. The last three of the first four caliphs were assassinated. After the last one, Ali, was murdered in 661, a family known as the **Umayyads** (oo-MY-yadz) gained power.

The Umayyads established a hereditary system of succession, with the title of caliph automatically passing within the clan, usually from father to son. They also moved the capital of the Muslim empire to Damascus in Syria, which made it easier to control conquered lands. However, many Muslims felt the new capital was too far from Islam's heartland near Medina.

These unpopular actions helped split Islam into two branches. The majority group, the **Sunni** (SU-nee), accepted Umayyad rule. They believed that any Muslim could be caliph. The other group, the **Shi'ite** (SHEE-yt), believed that only members of Muhammad's family, especially Ali and his descendants, could rule as caliph. This major division in Islam remains today.

Despite this split, the Umayyads expanded the Muslim empire, which spread Islam into new areas. To govern their growing territory, the Umayyads set up an efficient **bureaucracy**, a system of government with specialized departments. They also divided the empire into provinces governed by Muslim rulers. A postal service connected the provinces, and a strong army kept order. These actions helped unite the diverse empire. However, many Muslims believed that the Umayyads put too much emphasis on gaining wealth and power.

ABBASID RULE

Opposition to the Umayyads grew until rebel groups overthrew them in 750. A rival clan called the **Abbasids** (AB-uh-sihdz), who were descendants of Muhammad's uncle, took control of the empire. Non-Arab converts and Shi'ites lent support to the Abbasids, who moved the capital to Baghdad in central Iraq.

The Abbasids ruled during a prosperous golden age in Muslim history, but the caliphs were isolated from the people. Government was left to trusted advisers who held the empire together through force. They built a huge army that relied on mainly Turkish **mercenaries**, or hired soldiers.

Eventually, a group called the Seljuk (SEHL-jook) Turks converted to Islam and came to control the government of the Muslim empire. Then, in 1258, an invading group from Central Asia called the Mongols stormed Baghdad and killed the last Abbasid caliph.

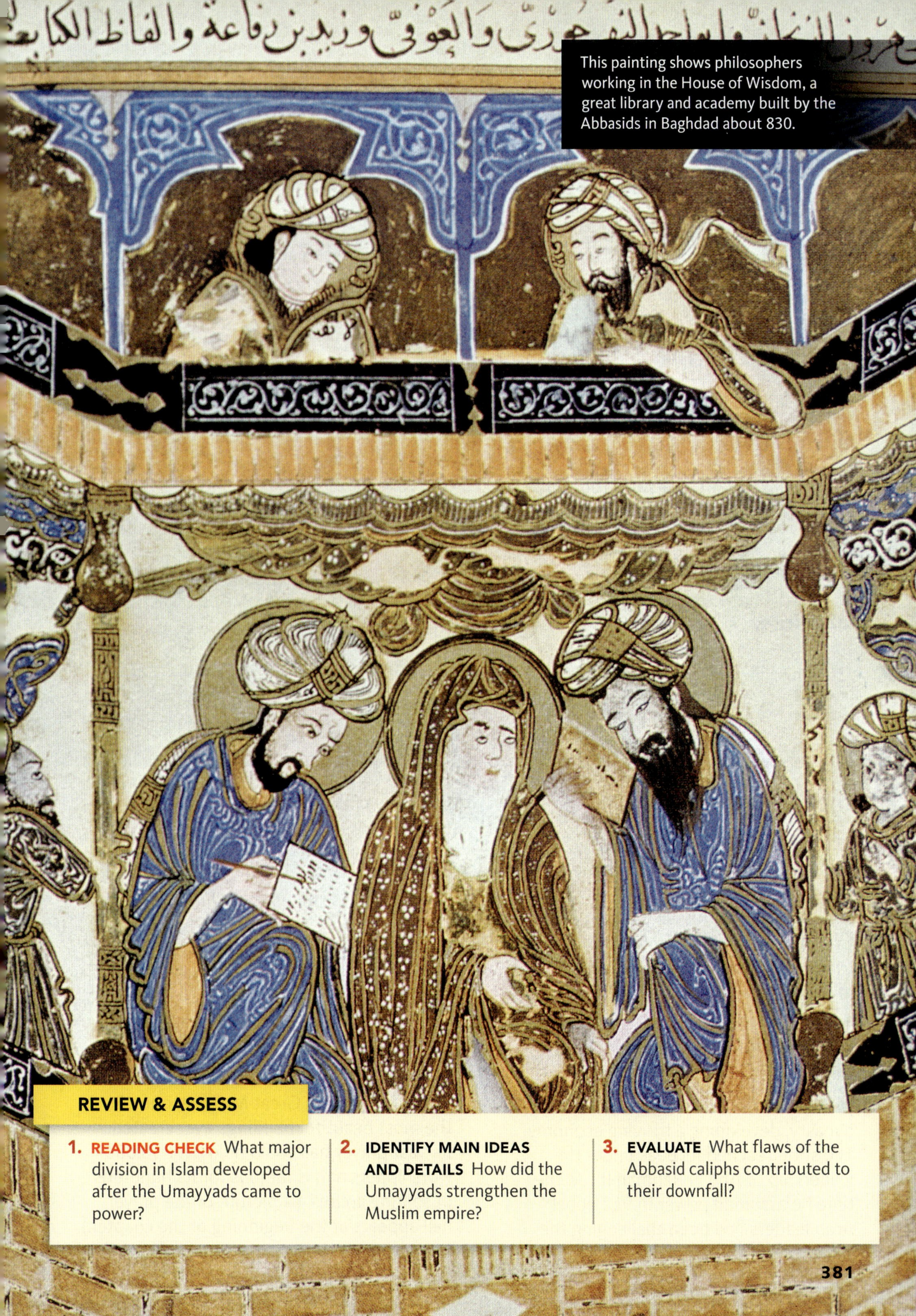

This painting shows philosophers working in the House of Wisdom, a great library and academy built by the Abbasids in Baghdad about 830.

REVIEW & ASSESS

1. **READING CHECK** What major division in Islam developed after the Umayyads came to power?
2. **IDENTIFY MAIN IDEAS AND DETAILS** How did the Umayyads strengthen the Muslim empire?
3. **EVALUATE** What flaws of the Abbasid caliphs contributed to their downfall?

2.2

Muslim Spain

When they overthrew the Umayyads in 750, the Abbasids ruthlessly hunted down and killed members of the Umayyad family. But they missed one important person. An Umayyad prince escaped to Spain and soon founded a rival Muslim dynasty that was destined for fame.

MAIN IDEA

The Umayyads transformed Muslim Spain into a center of power, learning, and culture between 756 and 1031.

THE UMAYYADS RETURN

Muslims had first conquered Spain in 711, and much of the region came under Umayyad control by 750. The last surviving Umayyad prince, Abd al-Rahman, fled to this region in 755 and founded an Umayyad dynasty in 756. From the city of Córdoba, he established a powerful, independent state called al-Andalus (al-an-duh-LUS) and refused to acknowledge Abbasid authority in Baghdad.

Al-Andalus flourished under the Umayyad dynasty, developing a thriving economy. The state reached its peak under the leadership of Abd al-Rahman III. At the time he assumed power in 912, rebel Arab leaders had been challenging the authority of the Umayyad dynasty. However, Abd al-Rahman III vigorously fought the rebels and proclaimed himself caliph in 929, directly competing with the Abbasids. His strong leadership preserved Umayyad power, and all of Muslim Spain was united under his rule by 933.

A GREAT CAPITAL

Abd al-Rahman III transformed Córdoba into one of the largest and greatest cities in the world. He built a series of lavish palaces and extended the Great Mosque, one of the most beautiful buildings ever created. Its vast prayer hall could hold over 50,000 worshippers and is famous for its hundreds of soaring arches. (A picture of the prayer hall appears at the beginning of the chapter.)

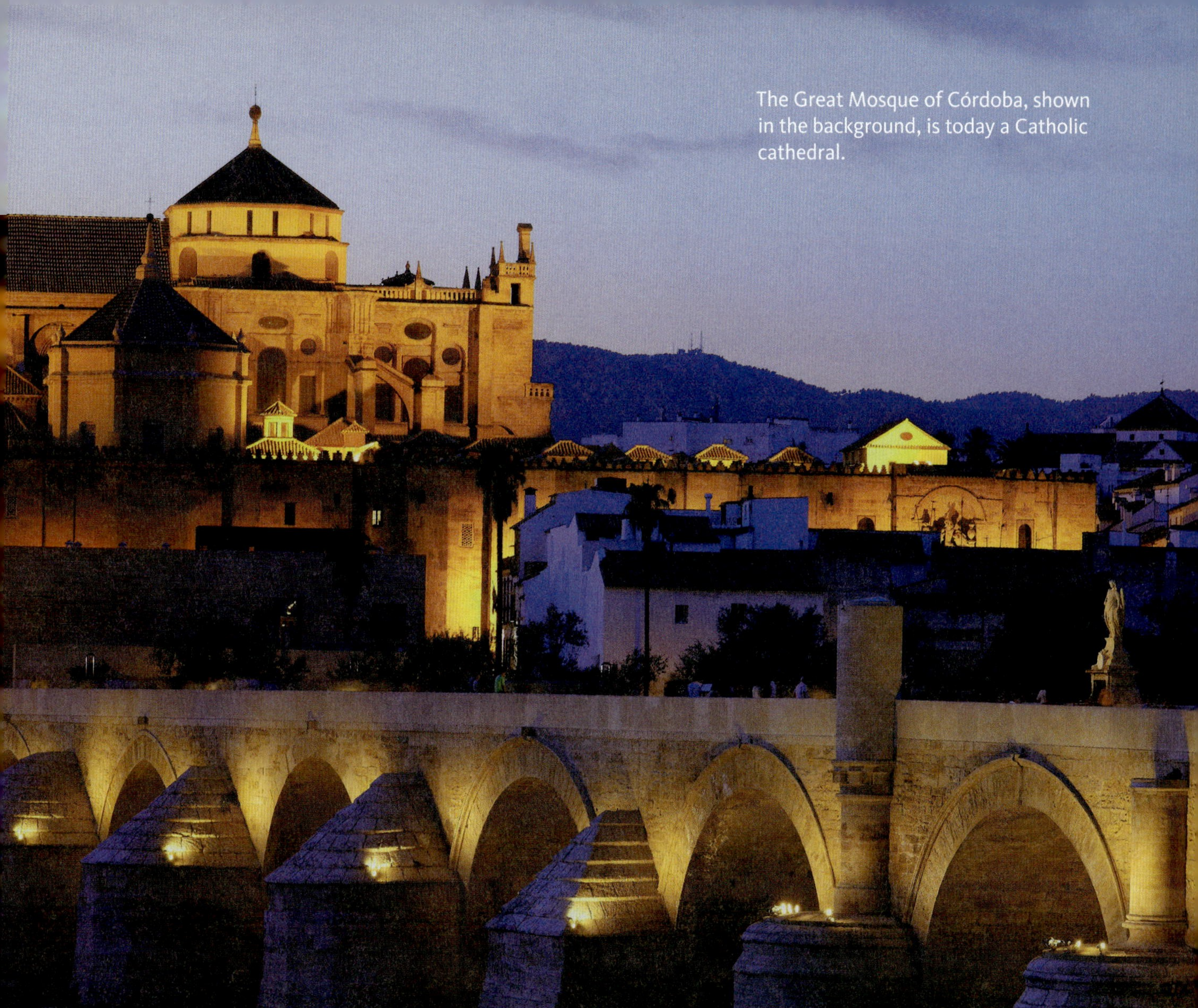

The Great Mosque of Córdoba, shown in the background, is today a Catholic cathedral.

Córdoba became most celebrated as a center of learning. Its huge library was said to contain about 400,000 books. In Córdoba, Christians, Jews, and Muslims lived together under a government that practiced religious **tolerance**, or sympathy for the beliefs and practices of others. In this rich intellectual environment, many advances in science, philosophy, medicine, and the arts were made.

Muslim rulers of al-Andalus faced many challenges, however. After the death of Abd al-Rahman III in 961, civil war erupted. Al-Andalus split into many small Muslim kingdoms after 1031. The increasingly powerful Christian kings of northern Spain steadily took over more of al-Andalus. In 1492, the Christians captured Granada, Spain's last Muslim city, ending almost 800 years of Muslim rule in western Europe.

REVIEW & ASSESS

1. **READING CHECK** How did the Umayyad dynasty transform Muslim Spain?
2. **DRAW CONCLUSIONS** Why did Córdoba become an international center of learning in the 900s?
3. **SEQUENCE EVENTS** What series of events ended almost 800 years of Muslim rule in Europe?

2.3 MOMENTS IN HISTORY
The Alhambra

JANUARY 2, 1492

Paradise on Earth—that's what Muslim rulers intended the Alhambra to represent. This fortified palace dominates the Spanish city of Granada. Begun around 860, the palace was expanded and perfected by Muslim rulers over the course of many years. The Alhambra is considered one of the greatest surviving examples of Islamic architecture. On January 2, 1492, Muslim rulers surrendered Granada to forces of the Spanish rulers Ferdinand and Isabella. Thereafter, Christian kings used the Alhambra as a royal palace for centuries. Based on this photograph, how would you describe Islamic architecture?

2.4 The Ottoman Empire

In the 1500s, one Muslim leader became the most powerful monarch in the world. A devout Muslim, Suleyman I oversaw one of the largest empires in history—and one of the longest lasting. This empire included the lands of Persia, Byzantium, and Egypt as well as parts of eastern Europe.

MAIN IDEA

A Muslim state known as the Ottoman Empire became the largest empire in the world in the 1500s.

SULEYMAN THE LAWGIVER

Suleyman I reformed the legal system in the Ottoman Empire. He cracked down on corruption and passed laws to protect non-Muslims. His commitment to justice earned him the title Suleyman the Lawgiver.

A VAST EMPIRE

While al-Andalus was in decline, a new Muslim power was arising to the east. A dynasty of Turkish Muslims, known as the **Ottomans**, emerged as frontier warriors against the Byzantines in Anatolia, or what is now Turkey, around the 1290s. These warriors and their leader, Osman, captured many Byzantine cities, fueling the Ottomans' expansion into the Balkans in southeastern Europe. In 1453, the Ottomans ended the Byzantine Empire by capturing Constantinople. This city, renamed Istanbul, became the Ottomans' capital and the center of their highly efficient government. The Ottomans continued to build an empire as they challenged the Safavid Empire, a rival Muslim power, and then captured Syria, Palestine, and Egypt from other Muslim rulers.

The Ottoman rulers were called **sultans**. The greatest of them was **Suleyman I**, known as Suleyman the Magnificent. He ruled the Ottoman Empire at the height of its power and grandeur, from 1520 to 1566. He led a powerful navy and a large army well-equipped with guns and cannons, which helped him conquer vast portions of northern Africa and eastern Europe. Only bad weather made him turn back from besieging the Austrian capital of Vienna.

However, military conquest wasn't Suleyman's only interest. He was also a celebrated poet, a talented goldsmith, and a generous patron of the arts. His rule inspired a cultural era that made Istanbul the artistic center of the Muslim lands. Suleyman commissioned work on restoration of the Grand Mosque in Mecca. He built magnificent mosques and palaces, transforming Istanbul's skyline with many buildings still seen there today.

DAILY LIFE

The Ottoman Empire steadily declined after the reign of Suleyman I, but it lasted into the early 1900s. One reason for its long life was its religious tolerance, which helped reduce internal conflict. Jews and Christians enjoyed religious and cultural freedom in return for paying a tax and being loyal to the state. They were organized into large self-governing communities, whose leaders worked with the Ottoman government to ensure positive relations. These communities prospered.

OTTOMAN EMPIRE, c. 1683
ATLANTIC OCEAN
FRANCE
SPAIN
PORTUGAL
AUSTRIA
Vienna
POLAND
HUNGARY
CRIMEA
Belgrade
Danube R.
Adriatic Sea
Black Sea
Caspian Sea
Rome
Naples
ITALY
BALKANS
Constantinople (Istanbul)
GREECE
Athens
ANATOLIA
Algiers
ALGIERS
Tunis
TUNIS
Crete
Cyprus
SYRIA
MESOPOTAMIA
Tigris R.
Euphrates R.
Baghdad
SAFAVID EMPIRE
Tripoli
Mediterranean Sea
Damascus
PALESTINE
Jerusalem
AFRICA
TRIPOLI
Cairo
EGYPT
Persian Gulf
Medina
Tropic of Cancer
Mecca
ARABIA
Red Sea
Nile R.
50°N
40°N
30°N
0°
10°E
20°E
30°E
40°E
50°E
N
S
E
W
0 300 600 Miles
0 300 600 Kilometers

Many "people of the book," or Jews and Christians, played important roles in the Ottoman Empire. Like other civilizations, the empire had different social classes. The Ottomans relied heavily on special slaves to staff the government and army. These slaves attained elite status and became rich and powerful. Many senior government officials were technically slaves. Slaves also made up the **janissaries**, a group of highly trained and disciplined soldiers in the Ottoman army who received the best equipment and benefits. To form the janissary corps, the government took young boys from non-Muslim villages, educated them, and trained them to fight for the sultan.

As elsewhere in the world, women in the Ottoman Empire led more restricted lives than men did. Lower-class women had more access to public areas than did upper-class women, who were often kept isolated from the outside world. Upper-class women influenced elite culture and royal policies, and they used their wealth to promote the arts, architecture, and charitable causes.

REVIEW & ASSESS

1. **READING CHECK** What were some of the major achievements of Suleyman I?
2. **MAKE INFERENCES** How did the Ottoman Empire benefit from practicing religious tolerance?
3. **INTERPRET MAPS** Along what major seas did the Ottoman Empire extend?

2.5 The Safavid and Mughal Empires

As Islam spread over parts of three continents—Asia, Africa, and Europe—rival dynasties arose that challenged one another. The Ottoman Empire was the largest empire of its time, but it faced strong rivals in Persia and India.

MAIN IDEA

Rival Muslim empires arose in Persia and India during the time of the Ottoman Empire.

THE SAFAVID EMPIRE

The Ottomans formed the largest Muslim empire of the time. However, it was not the only one. The **Safavids** (suh-FAH-vihdz), a Shi'ite dynasty, became rivals of the Sunni Ottomans.

The Safavid Empire arose when a youthful leader named Ismail united the Persian kingdoms into an independent state in 1501. He took the Persian title for king, **shah**. Ismail rapidly expanded Persia's borders north and west by boldly invading Ottoman lands. The Safavids and Ottomans went on to fight a long war that lasted more than 100 years. They battled mainly over control of Mesopotamia's fertile plains. Over and over again, the Safavids gained and lost possession of this land.

Located at the center of international trade routes, the Safavid Empire developed a strong economy. The Safavids used their wealth to build fabulous palaces and mosques and schools, hospitals, roads, and bridges. They made their new capital of Esfahan into one of the most magnificent cities in the world. It had more than 160 mosques and more than 270 public baths.

The Safavids also made Persia into a cultural center by encouraging the immigration of Shi'ite scholars and attracting craftspeople, artists, and traders of many nationalities. The government actively supported both art and industry, resulting in a rich mix of beautiful textiles, carpets, and other products. Europeans eagerly imported these products from Safavid merchants.

The Safavids actively spread Shi'ite Islam. They established it as the dominant Islamic faith in the Caucasus (a region between the Black and Caspian Seas) and in western Asia.

The Safavid Empire reached its peak between 1588 and 1629, during the reign of Shah Abbas I. It then declined steadily under the leadership of weak shahs. In 1722, a group of Afghan warriors invaded the Safavid Empire, which resulted in its downfall.

THE MUGHAL EMPIRE

The Safavid Empire was wedged between two other Muslim empires—the Ottoman Empire to the west and the Mughal Empire to the east. The **Mughals** (MOO-guhlz) were nomads from Central Asia who invaded India. In 1526, troops headed by a Mughal leader named Babur swept out of Central Asia and conquered north and central India. Babur laid the foundation of the Mughal Empire, which eventually stretched across almost the entire subcontinent.

In 1556, the Mughal leader Akbar the Great came to the throne at the age of 13 and led Muslim India to a brilliant golden age. Akbar doubled Babur's conquests and stabilized the empire by establishing a loyal governing class and an effective modern

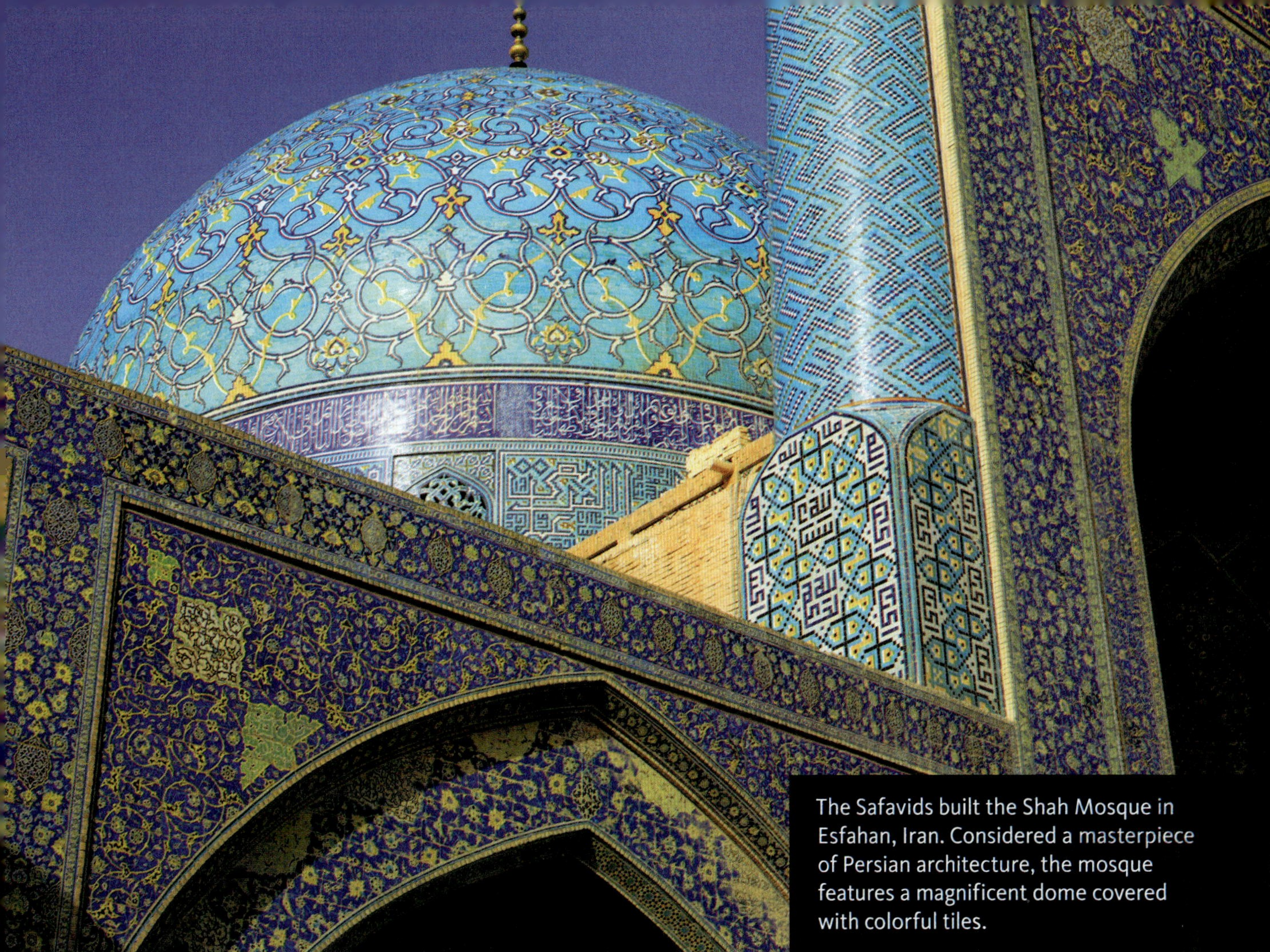

The Safavids built the Shah Mosque in Esfahan, Iran. Considered a masterpiece of Persian architecture, the mosque features a magnificent dome covered with colorful tiles.

government. He also allowed different religions to flourish in the empire. He even tried to end traditional conflicts between Muslims and Hindus by creating a new religion that mixed elements of both. His library was vast and included books in English, Greek, Persian, Hindi, and Arabic, and his court was cultured and learned.

The Mughal Empire reached its peak under Akbar's grandson, Shah Jahan, who reigned from 1628 to 1658. The empire became most famous for its dazzling splendor and wealth. Shah Jahan collected thousands of precious jewels and exported magnificent Indian art to Europe. He commissioned India's most famous building, the Taj Mahal, in memory of his beloved wife, who had died at a young age. Built of white marble, the monument served as a testament to the power and glory of Mughal rule. (This majestic tomb is pictured in Lesson 3.3.)

Mughal power eventually began to decline, however, as rebellious Hindus and European countries sought to gain control of India. In 1857, the British, who by then had gained control, sent the last Mughal ruler into exile.

REVIEW & ASSESS

1. **READING CHECK** What Muslim empires were rivals of the Ottoman Empire, and where were they located?
2. **COMPARE AND CONTRAST** How were the Safavid and Mughal Empires similar? How were they different?
3. **IDENTIFY PROBLEMS AND SOLUTIONS** How did Akbar the Great deal with the problem of religious conflicts?

3.1 Science and Philosophy

The knowledge in a book is useless if nobody reads it. But when people read a book and share its knowledge with others, the knowledge can become incredibly valuable. The leaders of various Muslim empires opened up whole libraries and shared their books with the world to stimulate learning. By doing so, Muslim empires advanced both science and philosophy.

MAIN IDEA

Under the leadership of Muslim dynasties, science and philosophy made important advances that spread across the world.

MATHEMATICS AND ASTRONOMY

Medieval times, which spanned from the 500s to the 1500s, saw the rise and fall of many Muslim empires. The vast extent of these empires and their religious tolerance allowed for a unique blending of cultures. Medieval Muslim leaders and scholars played a key role in preserving and building on the intellectual works of ancient Greece, Persia, and India. In this way, they helped build a foundation for modern civilization.

The field of mathematics provides an important example. Muslim scholars revived interest in the works of such Greek mathematicians as Euclid and Archimedes and further developed their ideas in geometry, trigonometry, and algebra. To simplify mathematics, they used the decimal number system and encouraged its adoption as the world's standard number system.

Muslim scholars also built upon ancient learning to extend their understanding of the universe. They constructed observatories to plot the movement of the stars, which enabled them to calculate dates for religious ceremonies and contributed to advances in navigation.

MEDICINE AND IDEAS

The Muslim quest for knowledge helped make the form of medicine practiced in Muslim lands the most advanced in the world. Following the Qur'an's instruction to care for the sick, Muslims built many hospitals. Muslim, Jewish, and Christian doctors collected the best available medical knowledge and organized it into reference books. These works helped spread the most advanced medical practices of the time throughout much of the world. They provided the basis for many Western medical treatments for centuries.

One of the most influential works was a 30-volume medical encyclopedia produced around 1000 by an Arab Muslim physician in al-Andalus known as **al-Zahrawi** (al-zuh-RAH-wee). This encyclopedia recommended treatments for a wide range of illnesses and included in-depth descriptions of surgeries. Al-Zahrawi pioneered surgical procedures and invented instruments, some of which are still used today.

Another Muslim physician from al-Andalus known as **Ibn Rushd** (ih-buhn RUSHT) wrote influential books on medicine. He was also a famous philosopher. His detailed studies of the Greek philosophers Aristotle and Plato were crucial in keeping alive the works of these two great thinkers. In his writings, Ibn Rushd tried to harmonize the ideas of Aristotle and Plato with Islam.

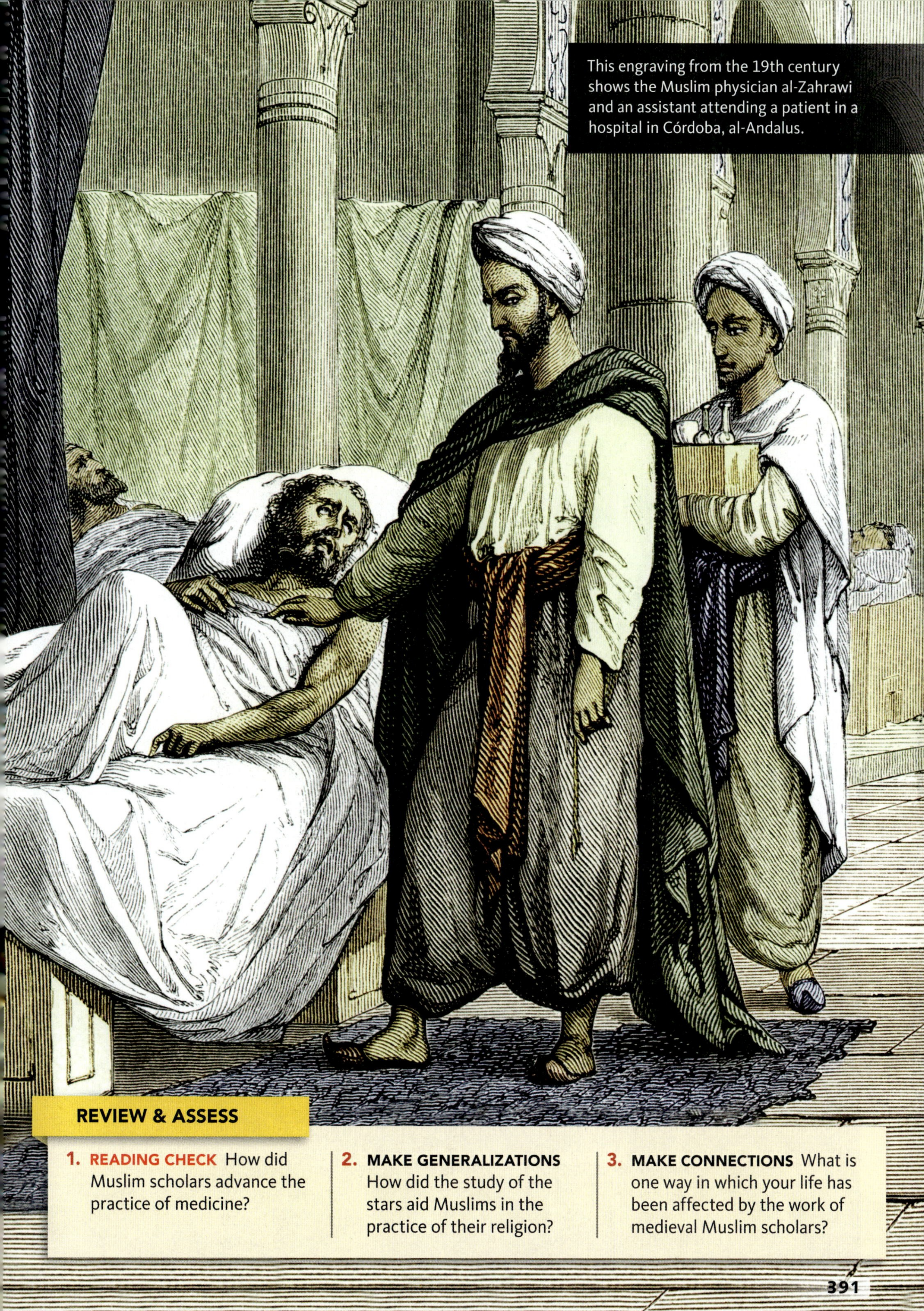

This engraving from the 19th century shows the Muslim physician al-Zahrawi and an assistant attending a patient in a hospital in Córdoba, al-Andalus.

REVIEW & ASSESS

1. **READING CHECK** How did Muslim scholars advance the practice of medicine?

2. **MAKE GENERALIZATIONS** How did the study of the stars aid Muslims in the practice of their religion?

3. **MAKE CONNECTIONS** What is one way in which your life has been affected by the work of medieval Muslim scholars?

Aiding People Through Science

Hayat Sindi is acclaimed as one of the most influential Muslim women in the world. She is proud of her culture and its legacy of learning. "I've always admired people who do something for society," she says. One of her contributions fits on the tip of her finger. It's a tiny piece of paper that is helping save millions of lives around the world.

^ As a co-founder of Diagnostics for All, Hayat Sindi has traveled around the world. This photograph shows her in Brooklyn, New York.

MAIN IDEA

Scientist Hayat Sindi is following Muslim tradition by promoting a medical device that benefits the world's poor people.

MEETING CHALLENGES

A fundamental belief of Islam is that the healthy should care for the sick, just as the wealthy should look after the poor. This belief motivated medieval Muslims to build hospitals and provide medical care to all groups of people at a time when medical care was extremely limited. The work of National Geographic Explorer Hayat Sindi carries on this tradition in the modern world. "Science can be such a powerful way to help humanity," says Sindi, a practicing Muslim from Mecca. "I'm using it to bring easy, affordable health diagnoses to the world's poorest people."

Postage-stamp-sized diagnostic tests developed by a scientific team at Harvard

Sindi was raised in a traditional Muslim family. Her passion for science drove her to leave Saudi Arabia, where women are not allowed to drive or vote. Even taking a job requires a male relative's permission. She traveled to England, where she taught herself English and won a place studying science at King's College in London. She went on to study at the University of Cambridge, the University of Oxford, the Massachusetts Institute of Technology, and Harvard University. "It was quite a journey," she says, "but when people tell me things are impossible, it just gives me energy."

A MISSION TO SAVE LIVES

Sindi's journey was certainly worth it. Today a medical invention she co-invented is helping millions of people from various ethnic groups and religions. "Essentially we've created a medical laboratory that can be taken anywhere because it's made of paper and is the size of a postage stamp," explains Sindi. The paper is etched with tiny channels that carry a single drop of saliva or other body fluid to tiny wells filled with chemicals. The chemicals change color, providing information on medical conditions, such as how well a person's liver is functioning.

The test costs less than a dime and requires no medical training to interpret. It is saving lives by identifying medical conditions early enough to be treated. "It's a tool that allows the poorest people in the most medically challenged places to get the tests they need," explains Sindi.

Just as Muslim physicians compiled books of medical knowledge and pushed the boundaries of medical understanding, Sindi is using the latest technology to ensure that more people receive better care. Sindi believes passionately in bringing science to everyone. "For me science is a universal language that transcends [rises above] nationality, religion, and gender. It can help solve any problem our world faces." Perhaps Muslim scholars before her felt the same way.

REVIEW & ASSESS

1. **READING CHECK** How does the medical device Sindi promotes benefit poor people?
2. **COMPARE AND CONTRAST** How is Sindi's work similar to the work of medieval Muslim physicians?
3. **DISTINGUISH FACT AND OPINION** Is the following statement a fact or an opinion: "[Science] can help solve any problem our world faces"? Explain your answer.

3.3 Architecture, the Arts, and Literature

Have you ever drawn your name or other words in an artistic way? If so, you have something in common with medieval Muslim artists. These artists considered beautiful writing to be one of the highest forms of art and an expression of their religion, Islam. The Qur'an provided the passages for this beautiful writing.

MAIN IDEA

Medieval Muslim dynasties produced distinctive forms of architecture, art, and writing that are highly admired today.

BUILDING AND DESIGN

In medieval Islamic civilization, beautiful writing appeared not only in books but also in buildings. Those buildings, especially mosques, displayed many architectural features that were developed from Roman, Egyptian, Byzantine, and Persian models. However, the style of architecture soon became recognized as distinctly Islamic.

A typical mosque was topped by a large dome and had one or more **minarets**. These extremely tall, slender towers were designed to dominate the skyline and call attention to the importance of the mosque. From a minaret, a Muslim official known as a muezzin (moo-EH-zuhn) would call out a summons to prayer.

The inside of a mosque also had distinctive features. Under the dome was the prayer hall, a large open area designed to appear spacious and full of light. Set into one wall was the mihrab (MEE-ruhb), an often richly decorated archway that indicated the direction of Mecca. While sharing these common features, mosques also incorporated local influences, so they varied in design in different locations.

The decoration inside a mosque was often elaborate, featuring elegant writing called **calligraphy** and abstract design known as **arabesque**. Arabesque consists of patterns of flowers, leaves, vines, and geometric shapes. The patterns often repeat in a seemingly endless way, representing the Muslim belief in the infinity of God's creation. Muslim artists did not portray human figures or animals. According to an interpretation of the Qur'an, the depiction of people and animals imitates God's act of creation. Muslims feared the display of such works might encourage the worship of images.

LITERATURE

Besides distinctive architecture and art, medieval Islamic civilization also produced significant works of literature. Muslims consider the Qur'an to be the greatest literary work in the Arabic language. The best-known popular work of literature is *The Thousand and One Nights*, a collection of entertaining stories from India, Persia, and Arabia. It features such well-known characters as Aladdin and Sinbad the Sailor.

Muslims admired poetry more than any other form of literature. A four-line rhyming poem known as a quatrain was made popular by the Persian poet **Omar Khayyám** (ky-YAM), who lived from 1048 to 1131. *The Rubáiyát of Omar Khayyám*, a selection of his quatrains, is considered a masterpiece of world literature.

Critical Viewing The Taj Mahal in India was built in the mid-1600s by the Mughal emperor Shah Jahan. What features of Muslim architecture are apparent in the building's exterior?

REVIEW & ASSESS

1. **READING CHECK** What is a distinctive feature of the exterior architecture of a typical mosque?
2. **DRAW CONCLUSIONS** Would you expect to find statues in a mosque? Why or why not?
3. **EVALUATE** What qualities of Muslim architecture and art do you find most appealing?

3.4 HISTORY THROUGH OBJECTS

ISLAMIC ART

Islamic art features cultural influences from across vast empires. More importantly, it reflects the values and teachings of Islam. Muslim artists initially created calligraphy to beautify the Qur'an. The intricate floral and geometric patterns of arabesque emerged partly in response to an interpretation of the Qur'an. That interpretation discouraged the depiction of people and animals in art.

Mihrab
This archway comes from a mosque in Iran built in the 1300s. It features a mosaic of colorful tiles decorated with arabesque and calligraphy.

Caftan
This caftan, a long garment, belonged to Bayezid II, an Ottoman sultan who ruled from 1481 to 1512.

Stained Glass
This stained glass window appears in the Blue Mosque, which was built in the 1600s in Istanbul, Turkey.

Ceramic Plate
This decorated plate was made in the 1700s in Morocco.

Tile
This Turkish tile from about 1530 features floral patterns.

Calligraphy
This page of calligraphy comes from a Qur'an produced in Cairo, Egypt, around 1310.

CHAPTER **13** Review

VOCABULARY

Use each of the following vocabulary words in a sentence that shows an understanding of the word's meaning.

1. **oasis**
   An oasis was the only source of water for traders crossing the vast desert.
2. **medieval**
3. **mosque**
4. **pilgrimage**
5. **caliph**
6. **sultan**
7. **janissary**
8. **minaret**

READING STRATEGY

9. **IDENTIFY MAIN IDEAS AND DETAILS** If you haven't already, complete your web with details that illustrate the legacy of Islamic culture. Then answer the question.

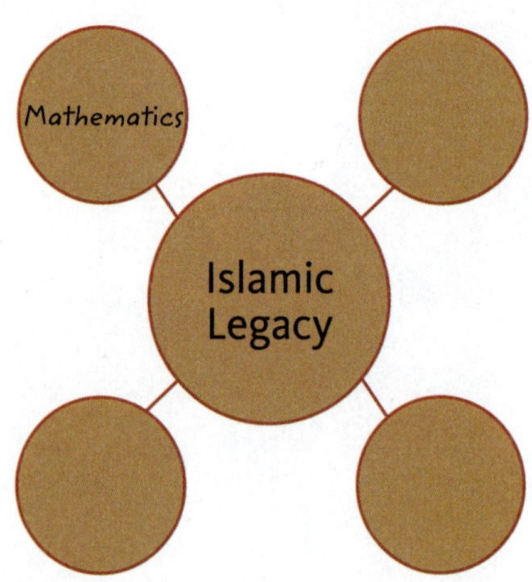
Mathematics
Islamic Legacy

How is the influence of Islamic culture apparent in the present day?

MAIN IDEAS

Answer the following questions. Support your answers with evidence from the chapter.

10. How were the Bedouin in Arabia organized in the 600s? **LESSON 1.1**
11. Who was Muhammad? **LESSON 1.2**
12. What happened to the Muslim state after Muhammad's death in 632? **LESSON 1.5**
13. Why did Muslims split into two main sects in the late 600s? **LESSON 2.1**
14. What dynasty transformed Muslim Spain into a center of Islamic culture between 756 and 1031? **LESSON 2.2**
15. Who ruled the Ottoman Empire at its peak, and what were his major achievements? **LESSON 2.4**
16. What major contributions did medieval Muslim scholars make to the field of mathematics? **LESSON 3.1**
17. What are the advantages of the medical invention Hayat Sindi promotes? **LESSON 3.2**

CRITICAL THINKING

Answer the following questions. Support your answers with evidence from the chapter.

18. **DRAW CONCLUSIONS** What is one major way in which medieval Muslim scholars helped build a foundation for modern civilization?
19. **ANALYZE CAUSE AND EFFECT** How did the Qur'an affect the development of Islamic art?
20. **MAKE INFERENCES** How did its geographic location contribute to the growth of the Safavid Empire?
21. **YOU DECIDE** Which of the Muslim empires was the greatest? Be sure to explain what you mean by "great."

INTERPRET MAPS

Study the map that shows the spread of Islam. Then answer the questions that follow.

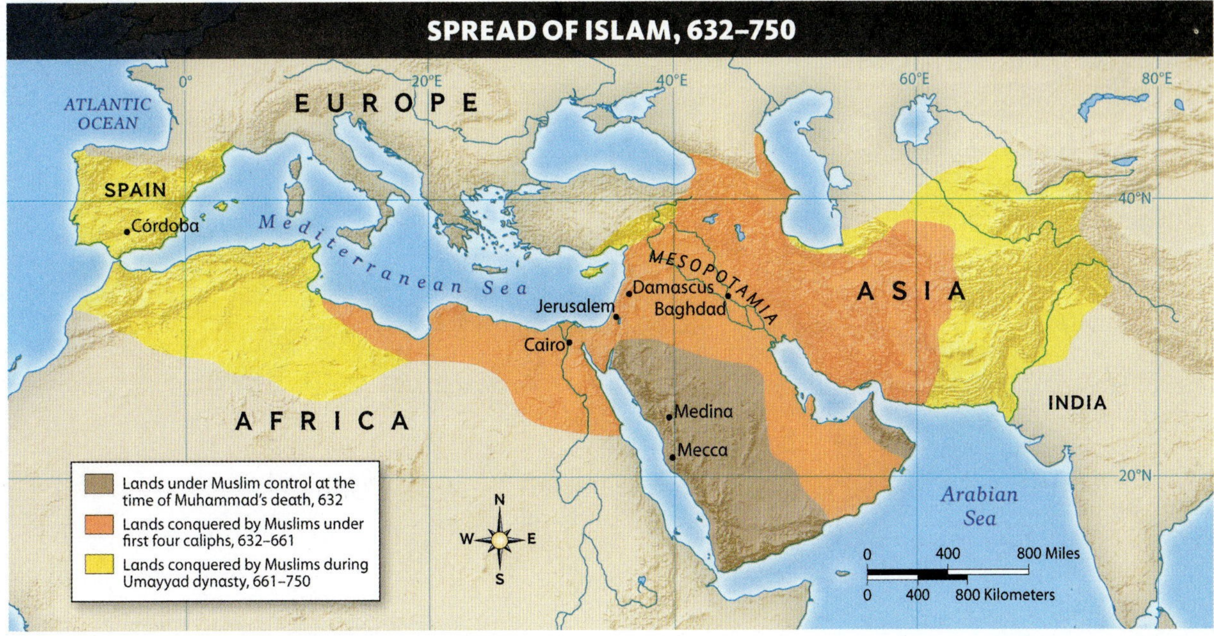

SPREAD OF ISLAM, 632–750
ATLANTIC OCEAN
EUROPE
SPAIN
Córdoba
Mediterranean Sea
Jerusalem
Damascus
Baghdad
MESOPOTAMIA
ASIA
Cairo
AFRICA
Medina
Mecca
INDIA
Arabian Sea
0°
20°E
40°E
60°E
80°E
40°N
20°N
Lands under Muslim control at the time of Muhammad's death, 632
Lands conquered by Muslims under first four caliphs, 632–661
Lands conquered by Muslims during Umayyad dynasty, 661–750
N
S
E
W
0 400 800 Miles
0 400 800 Kilometers

22. Across what region had Islam spread by the time of Muhammad's death in 632?

23. To what continents had Islam spread by 661?

ANALYZE SOURCES

Read this part of an oath that was written by Moses Maimonides, a physician in Muslim Spain. Then answer the question that follows.

> May I never see in the patient anything but a fellow creature in pain. Grant me the strength, time and opportunity always to correct what [learning] I have acquired, always to extend its domain [sphere]; for knowledge is immense and the spirit of man can extend indefinitely to enrich itself daily with new requirements. . . . Oh, God, Thou has appointed me to watch over the life and death of Thy creatures; here am I ready for my vocation and now I turn unto my calling.

24. How do Maimonides' ideas about knowledge reflect achievements in Muslim Spain during its golden age?

WRITE ABOUT HISTORY

25. INFORMATIVE Write a brief encyclopedia article that compares the main beliefs of Islam with those of Judaism and Christianity.

TIPS

- Take notes on the beliefs of Islam described in Lesson 1.3.
- State the main idea about the similarities among the beliefs of Islam, Judaism, and Christianity in your beginning sentence.
- Develop the main idea by using relevant, well-chosen facts about the beliefs of each religion.
- Use appropriate transition words, such as *likewise, similarly,* and *also,* to clarify the similarities among the three religions' beliefs.
- Provide a concluding statement that follows from and supports the facts you have presented on the three religions' beliefs.

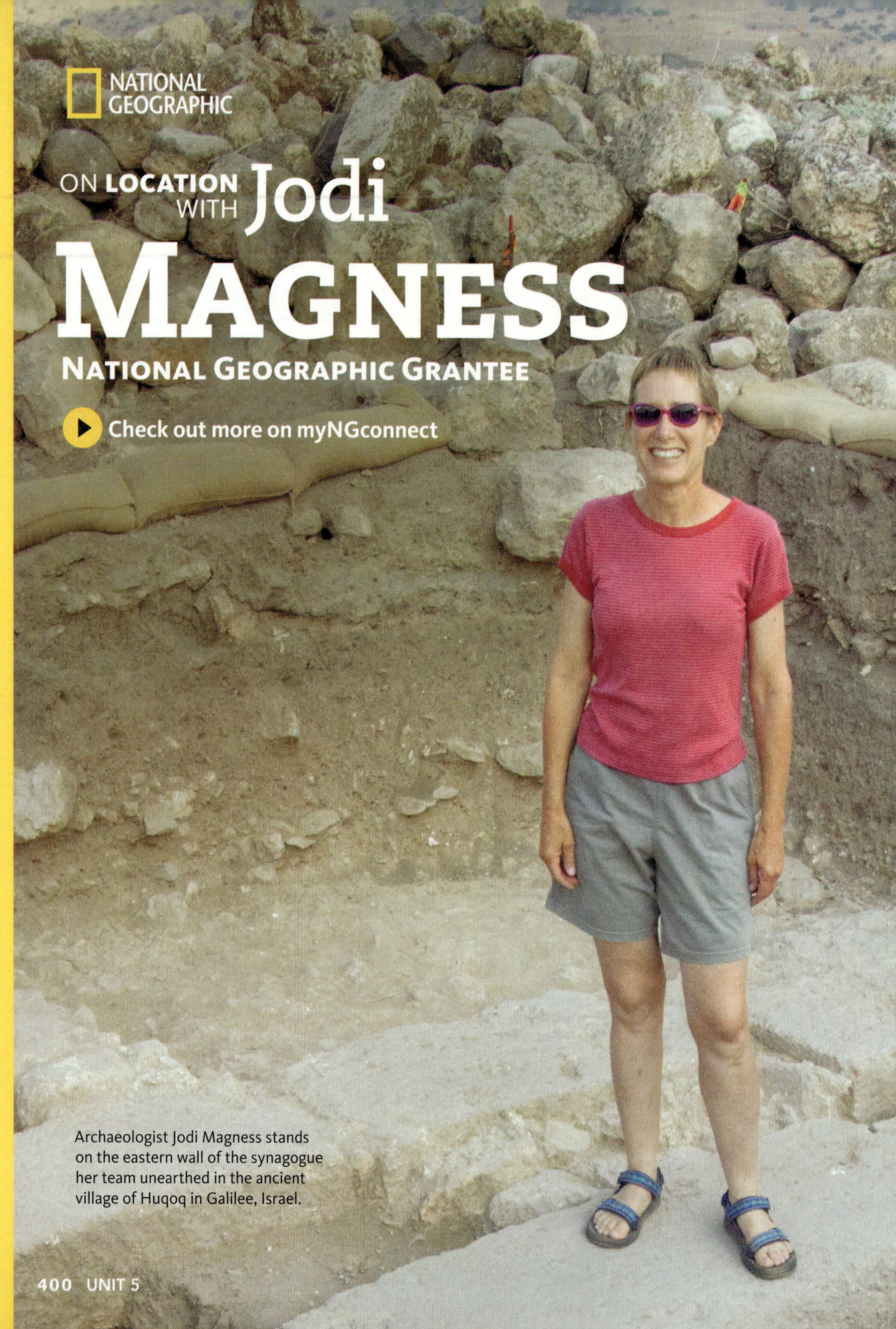

NATIONAL GEOGRAPHIC

ON LOCATION WITH Jodi MAGNESS

NATIONAL GEOGRAPHIC GRANTEE

Check out more on myNGconnect

Archaeologist Jodi Magness stands on the eastern wall of the synagogue her team unearthed in the ancient village of Huqoq in Galilee, Israel.

EXPLORING IN ISRAEL

I was just 12 when I decided I wanted to become an archaeologist. It is a passion I'm lucky enough to pursue as my career. I've taken part in over 20 excavations around the Mediterranean Sea. I now specialize in the history of ancient Palestine, the area that includes modern Israel, Jordan, and the Palestine territories. It's a land rich in history, and it's allowed me to study the city of Jerusalem, the fortress of Masada, and the Roman Army. But things really took off in 2011 when I came to study the ancient village of Huqoq (hoo-KOKE) in Galilee, Israel.

We were hunting for the remains of a fifth century synagogue. It was a big, overgrown site but our very first sounding came down right on the synagogue's eastern wall. We weren't able to use technologies like ground-penetrating radar to find the synagogue because it is covered by the bulldozed ruins of a modern village. We remove one rock at a time and record everything we do because you can never put the stones back the way they were.

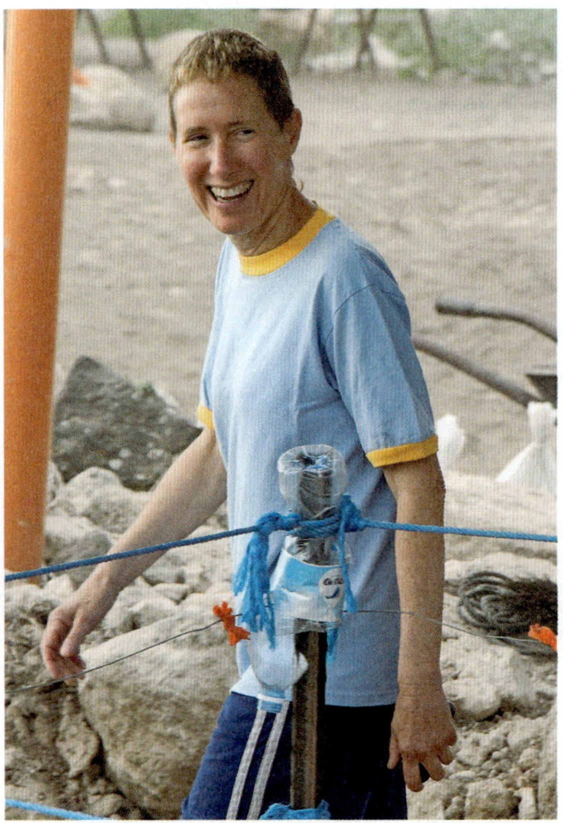

Jodi Magness and her team are challenged by the summer heat, scorpions, and snakes in Huqoq.

HIDDEN MOSAICS

This is especially important because of what we are finding—mosaic floors made up of thousands of tiny cubes of stone. The very first mosaic that peered out of the dirt was the face of a woman. We've also uncovered spectacular mosaics depicting stories from the Hebrew Bible. We found a beautiful depiction of Samson taking revenge on the Philistines using foxes to carry torches and set fire to their fields. There's another mosaic showing Samson carrying the gate of Gaza in an incredible act of strength. We've even found one mosaic with elephants (see pages 344–345), which indicates that this is not a story from the Hebrew Bible. It might tell the story of Alexander the Great. So far, we have only uncovered a small part of the synagogue, and we hope our continued excavation will reveal more mosaics.

WHY STUDY HISTORY ?

"The mosaics we are uncovering in Huqoq are not only beautiful, they are helping other archaeologists, scholars, and the general public to *better understand ancient Judaism*. Every year we come back and discover more, so it's really an extraordinary experience." —Jodi Magness

NATIONAL GEOGRAPHIC

The Stolen Past

BY KAREN LANGE

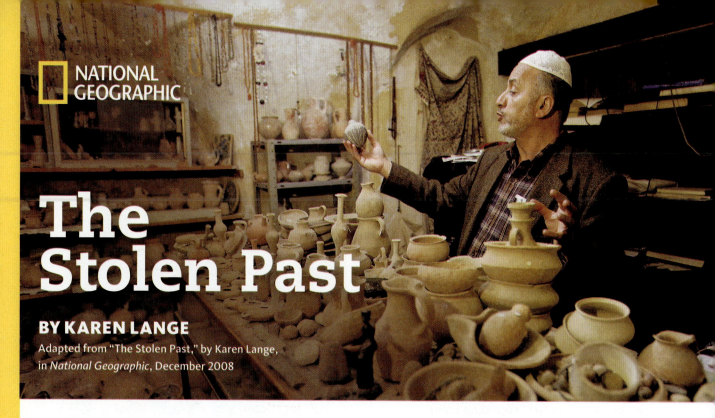

Adapted from "The Stolen Past," by Karen Lange, in *National Geographic*, December 2008

For a thousand years, the ruins of Khirbet Tawas, a Byzantine jewel, stood southwest of Hebron. Then, in 2000, the second intifada began. As Palestinians fought Israeli troops, the West Bank became all but ungovernable. Soon the Israelis set up a web of security checkpoints, sealed off the region, and barred most Palestinians from working inside Israel. Jobless men looked for cash wherever they could find it. Armed with shovels, a small band descended on Khirbet Tawas. The looters searched for anything they could sell: Byzantine coins, clay lamps, glass bracelets.

Looters have overrun not just Khirbet Tawas but countless other archaeological sites located in the West Bank. They attack ancient sites with backhoes and small bulldozers, scraping away the top layer of earth across areas the size of several football fields. Guided by metal detectors—coins often give away the location of other goods—they take anything of value.

The West Bank is a cradle of civilization and a crossroads of empires. For Jews, Christians, and Muslims, it is sacred ground. Yet this priceless legacy is swiftly being lost. Archaeologist Salah Al-Houdalieh says, "They are destroying a cultural heritage that belongs to every Palestinian, to every human being."

Few jobs, inadequate law enforcement by both Palestinian and Israeli authorities, and demand for artifacts just across the border in Israel have created the perfect storm for looting.

Some looted artifacts are bought by middlemen who supply shops in Israel. Tourists eager to take home a piece of the Holy Land unknowingly support the trade. Other artifacts are smuggled into Jordan, then on to dealers elsewhere, who in turn sell the artifacts to outlets in Israel.

Alarmed by the spike in looting, Palestinian lawmakers have proposed increasing the maximum prison sentence for damaging archaeological sites from three years to five. Yet political circumstances and deep mutual distrust continue to hamper police on both sides of the border.

For more from National Geographic
Check out "The Wells of Memory" on myNGconnect

UNIT INQUIRY: MAKE AN IDEA MAP

In this unit, you learned about many cultural contributions of the Byzantine Empire and medieval Islamic civilizations. Based on your understanding of the text, what impact did these cultural contributions have on civilization as they spread throughout the world? How do medieval cultural contributions continue to make a major impact on our civilization today?

ASSIGNMENT Create an idea map that illustrates the cultural impact one of the major contributions of the Byzantine Empire or medieval Islamic civilizations has had (and continues to have) on our civilization today. Be prepared to present your idea map to the class and explain how the contribution or achievement is an example of cultural diffusion from medieval civilization to today.

Plan As you create your idea map, think about the many cultural achievements and contributions made by the Byzantine Empire and medieval Islamic civilizations. Select one major contribution or achievement that you think has had an impact on today's civilization. You might want to use a graphic organizer to help organize your thoughts. ▶

Produce Use your notes to produce descriptions of different ways the contribution or achievement you selected has impacted the world today. You might want to write them in outline or paragraph form.

Present Choose a creative way to present your idea map to the class. Consider one of these options:

- Create a multimedia presentation using photos to illustrate different ways the medieval contribution/achievement impacts our civilization today.
- Write an introduction to your idea map that explains the significance of cultural diffusion in medieval civilization and the modern world.
- Draw a physical map to show the location where the contribution/achievement originated.

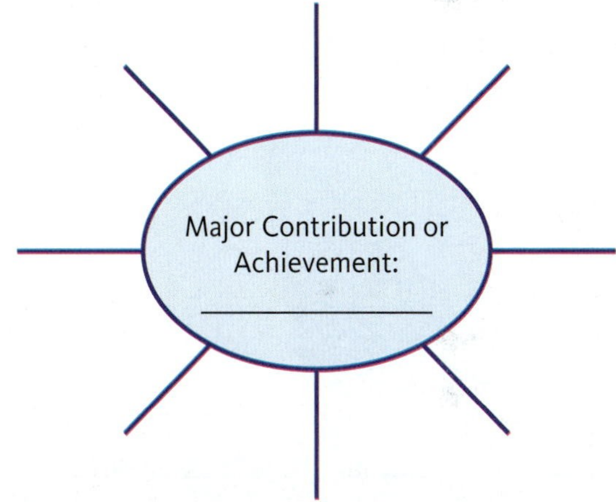
Major Contribution or
Achievement:

RAPID REVIEW
UNIT 5

BYZANTINE AND ISLAMIC CIVILIZATIONS

TOP TEN

1. Byzantium was a center of trade and learning and the largest city in the medieval world.
2. The Roman Catholic Church split with the Eastern Orthodox Church in 1064.
3. Muhammad was a political and religious leader who founded Islam.
4. Islam spread across Southwest Asia, North Africa, India, and Europe through conquest and trade.
5. Islamic scholars made important advances in mathematics, astronomy, medicine, science, art, architecture, and literature.

6-10. **NOW IT'S YOUR TURN** Complete the list with five more things to remember about Byzantine and Islamic civilizations.

UNIT 6

AFRICAN CIVILIZATIONS

NATIONAL
GEOGRAPHIC

ON **LOCATION** WITH

Christopher DeCorse

Archaeologist

The story of Africa is an ancient one. The natural resources and movement of people across this huge continent have made the exchange of goods and ideas a major theme throughout its long history. Crossing the vast Sahara and sailing the waters of the Indian Ocean, Africans created some of the most successful trading networks in history. I'm Christopher DeCorse, and I'm an archaeologist and National Geographic Grantee. Join me on a journey to explore the civilizations of Africa!

< **CRITICAL VIEWING** Ships like this African dhow carried goods in and out of coastal trading cities. Why would a ship like this be good for sailing the open sea?

UNIT 6
TIME LINE OF WORLD EVENTS

African Civilizations

c. 1000 B.C.
The Bantu begin their slow migration across sub-Saharan Africa.

c. 500 B.C.
The Nok people develop iron tools and terra cotta sculpture. *(terra cotta Nok head sculpture)*

c. A.D. 100
Aksum emerges as a prosperous trading kingdom in present-day Ethiopia.

c. 300
The introduction of camels in North Africa allows for trans-Saharan trade.

1000 B.C.

A.D. 100

The World

552 B.C.
ASIA
Confucius is born in northeast China.

c. 500 B.C.
AMERICAS
The Zapotec build the city of Monte Albán overlooking the Oaxaca Valley. *(statuette of a Zapotec god)*

COMPARE TIME LINES

What two cultures had become highly developed by about 500 B.C.?

c. 500
The trading kingdom of Ghana emerges west of the Sahara.

c. 1230
The empire of Mali is founded by Sundiata Keita.

c. 1300
East African city-states, including Kilwa, arise along the East African coast.
(ruins at Kilwa)

1324
Mansa Musa makes his pilgrimage to Egypt. *(illustration of Mansa Musa from an illuminated map)*

1400
The kingdom of Kongo emerges in the rain forests south of the Congo River.

1250

1500

1095
EUROPE
Pope Urban II initiates the first crusade to the Holy Land.

IMP CONSTANTINVS P F AVG

330
EUROPE
Emperor Constantine makes Constantinople the capital of the Eastern Roman Empire.
(profile of Constantine on a gold coin)

1453
ASIA
Ottoman Turks capture Constantinople, ending the Byzantine Empire.

UNIT 6
GEOGRAPHY IN HISTORY

AFRICA

Land Use & Resources
2014

Africa is a huge land area that encompasses a wide variety of physical features and cultures. Trade has long been a part of many of these cultures, fueling the rise of kingdoms across the continent. West African civilizations were built on the trade of gold, salt, and slaves. The Indian Ocean trade made the ancient kingdom of Aksum a mighty power and later helped found the great city-states of East Africa.

With its plentiful natural resources, Africa plays a major role in international trade today. The highly detailed National Geographic map on the next page shows the continent's resources and land use systems. Many African nations are important trading partners of the United States. The graph below shows how much the United States spends on goods received from Africa (imports) and how much it earns on goods sent to Africa (exports).

What natural resources are found in West Africa?

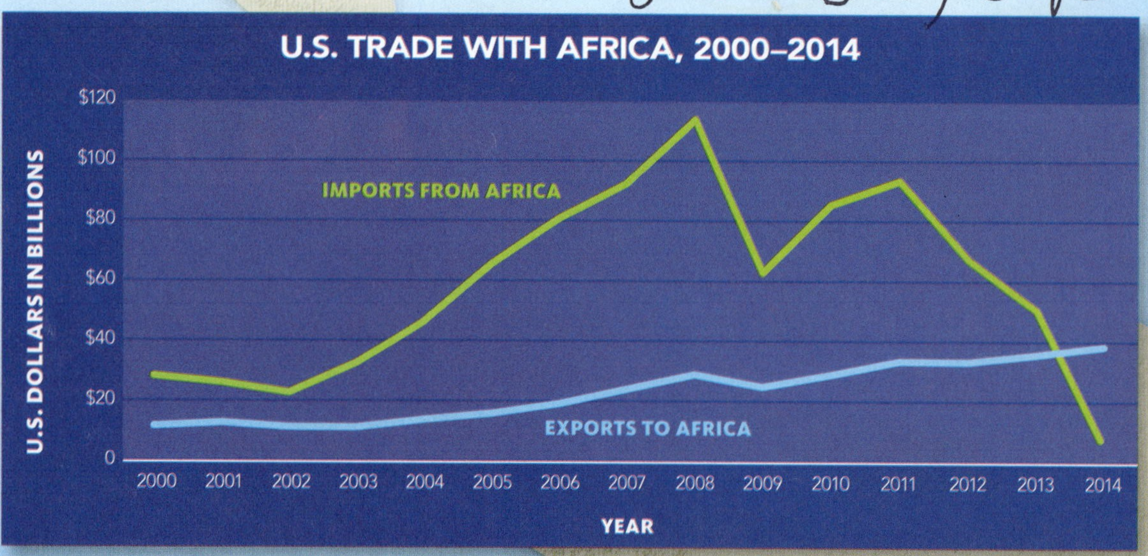
U.S. TRADE WITH AFRICA, 2000–2014
U.S. DOLLARS IN BILLIONS
$120
$100
$80
$60
$40
$20
0
IMPORTS FROM AFRICA
EXPORTS TO AFRICA
2000 2001 2002 2003 2004 2005 2006 2007 2008 2009 2010 2011 2012 2013 2014
YEAR

Imports Oil is among the top items imported to the United States from Africa, including that drilled from this oil rig in South Africa.

Exports The top items exported to Africa from the United States are machinery and equipment, including agricultural machines.

Mediterranean Sea
Red Sea
Nile R.
Niger R.
Lake Chad
Congo R.
Lake Turkana
Lake Victoria
Lake Tanganyika
Lake Malawi
Zambezi R.
ATLANTIC OCEAN
Land Use
Agriculture
Barren land
Forest
Grassland
Shrub & sparse vegetation
Wetland
Major Resources
Bauxite (Aluminum ore)
Coal
Copper
Diamonds
Fish
Forest products
Gold
Iron ore
Natural gas
Oil
Uranium
Other minerals
0 250 500 750 1000 kilometers
0 250 500 750 1000 miles
Source: Food and Agriculture Organization (FAO)

CHAPTER

14 NORTH AND WEST AFRICA

1000 B.C. – A.D. 1500

SECTION 1
NORTH AFRICA

KEY VOCABULARY
caravan
commodity
desertification
savanna
scarcity
trans-Saharan

NAMES & PLACES
Berbers
Djenné
Sahara
Timbuktu

SECTION 2
WEST AFRICA

KEY VOCABULARY
griot
iron
mansa
oral tradition
terra cotta

NAMES & PLACES
Ghana
Iron Age
Mali
Mansa Musa
Nok
Sub-Saharan Africa
Sundiata Keita

READING STRATEGY

ANALYZE LANGUAGE USE
When you analyze language use, you determine the impact of the language a writer uses. Use a chart like this one to analyze the impact of language in the introductory paragraphs of the lessons in the chapter.

Language Example	What It Suggests

A woman wearing a traditional Songhai headdress poses in front of a decorative curtain in the town of Gao in northern Mali. The Songhai Empire was one of the great trading civilizations that flourished in West Africa between the 10th and 16th centuries A.D.

1.1 A Vast and Varied Land

The way that some modern maps are drawn magnifies the size of countries in the Northern Hemisphere. This projection disguises the huge scale of Africa, which is larger than the United States, Europe, Japan, and China combined. North Africa alone is a huge area that includes the Sahara, the world's largest desert.

MAIN IDEA

North Africa has a variety of landforms, including the vast Sahara.

THE LARGEST DESERT IN THE WORLD

The northern part of Africa borders the Mediterranean Sea. (See the map in Lesson 1.2.) At the entrance to the Mediterranean, North Africa lies only ten miles south of Europe. Lining the coast of North Africa are the rugged Atlas Mountains. For centuries, people have lived in villages scattered throughout these mountains.

South of the Atlas Mountains lies the **Sahara**, an important geographic feature of North Africa. Sahara, which means "desert," is the largest desert in the world. It stretches more than 3,000 miles across North Africa, spanning the continent from the Red Sea in the east to the Atlantic Ocean in the west. Covering 3.5 million square miles, the Sahara is about the size of the continental United States, Alaska, and Hawaii combined. With its hot summers and warm winters, the Sahara is one of the hottest and driest places on Earth.

The Sahara's soaring mountains and vast seas of shifting sand provide a dramatic contrast to the desert's mostly flat and rocky terrain. In addition to the Atlas Mountains, two other mountain ranges, the Ahaggar and Tibesti, rise in the Sahara's interior.

For thousands of years, people found the Sahara almost impossible to cross. As a result, the peoples of North Africa, with their Mediterranean and Southwest Asian influences, developed independently from those living on the rest of the continent.

THE GREEN SAHARA

The hot, dry Sahara seems an unlikely place to find fossils of fish and rock paintings of lakes, forests, and herds of cattle. However, the Sahara has both, which offer clues to its past. The Sahara was not always a desert. Thirty million years ago, the Sahara was an ocean full of fish and whales. Over time, climate change drained the seas to leave lush tropical grasslands called the **savanna**. Many thousands of years ago, the Sahara was green. People farmed there and herded cattle.

Beginning around 5300 B.C., seasonal rains shifted southward. The Sahara's lakes, rivers, and grasslands dried up. As rain became scarce and temperatures soared up to 130°F, the Sahara's fertile soil dried, baked, and became unproductive. This process, called **desertification**, created the desert that exists today.

People and animals began migrating to better land with steady water supplies. Some people moved north, others south. Still others headed east toward the Nile River Valley, where they built one of Africa's greatest civilizations—Egypt, which you learned about in Chapter 4.

Critical Viewing The Gao region of Mali is located in the southern Sahara along the Niger River, shown here. What traits of this area might enable people to live here?

REVIEW & ASSESS

1. **READING CHECK** What major landforms are found in North Africa?

2. **IDENTIFY MAIN IDEAS AND DETAILS** Why did North Africa develop independently from the rest of the African continent?

3. **ANALYZE CAUSE AND EFFECT** What effect did climate change have on the geography and climate of the Sahara?

1.2 Trans-Saharan Trade

The camel caravan snakes back and forth for miles across the desert. Thousands of camels trudge surefooted across the Saharan sand despite being loaded down with Mediterranean goods for trade. The caravan is a merchant's ticket to profit, but first the merchant must survive the journey.

MAIN IDEA

As North Africa developed a strong economy, trade between native and foreign communities brought the riches of the Sahara to Europe.

BERBER TRADERS

Trade in North Africa began with the **Berbers**. They were native to the region, and they lived in communities spread throughout areas in present-day Egypt, Libya, Tunisia, Algeria, and Morocco. Most Berbers farmed or herded cattle. Others lived as desert nomads or dwelled in the mountains. Despite these differences, they shared a broad Berber culture.

Around 800 B.C., the Phoenicians and Greeks arrived in North Africa and founded cities on the coast. The Phoenicians used these cities as staging areas for trade with Spain. One such city, Carthage, increasingly controlled Berber lands and peoples. Numidia, an early Berber kingdom, reacted to this invasion by helping the Romans overthrow Carthage.

Although clashes between Berbers and foreign rulers continued, trade relationships developed between the people of the desert and the people of the North African coast. The Berbers took an active role in this trade. Traveling along routes in the Sahara, they transported slaves, salt, semiprecious stones, and other goods for the Mediterranean market. In exchange, they received food, cloth, horses, weapons, and other manufactured goods.

A DIFFICULT PASSAGE

Carrying goods on trade routes in the desert was difficult and dangerous. Historians believe that around A.D. 300, the introduction of camels began to transform trade in North Africa, and the animals started to make large-scale **trans-Saharan** trade possible. That is, trade now crossed the Sahara. Camels were able to carry heavy loads over long distances and difficult terrain. They also needed little food and water.

Many independent merchants sought safety in numbers by traveling in a group called a camel **caravan**. Caravans had hundreds or even thousands of camels. Led by highly paid Berber guides, caravans would set off from North African cities and head into the Sahara. To avoid the worst of the desert heat, caravans only traveled in winter and most often at night.

Few merchants crossed the entire Sahara. Instead they exchanged their goods at an oasis, where they could find water. From there, other merchants would take the goods to the next oasis, and so on across the desert. In this way, trade routes connecting North and West Africa developed across the Sahara. The oases grew into towns and cities that became wealthy as centers of trade. However, the dangers of caravan travel remained. The possibility of dying from getting lost or from being caught in a sandstorm was just as real as the threat of attack by desert nomads. Trans-Saharan trade was a risky business.

NORTH AND WEST AFRICAN TRADE ROUTES, A.D. 800–1500

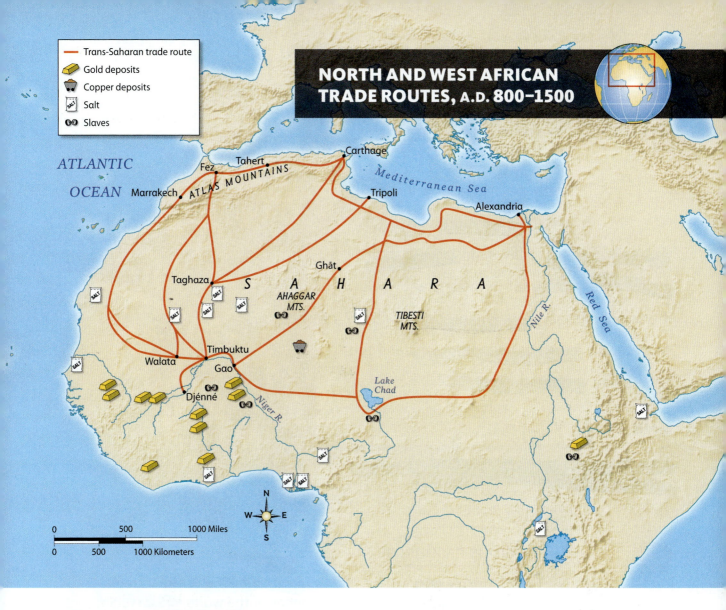

Trans-Saharan trade route
Gold deposits
Copper deposits
Salt
Slaves

ATLANTIC OCEAN
Mediterranean Sea
Red Sea
ATLAS MOUNTAINS
SAHARA
AHAGGAR MTS.
TIBESTI MTS.
Nile R.
Niger R.
Lake Chad
Fez
Tahert
Carthage
Marrakech
Tripoli
Alexandria
Ghāt
Taghaza
Timbuktu
Walata
Gao
Djénné
SALT
N S E W
0 500 1000 Miles
0 500 1000 Kilometers

TODAY'S MOUNTAIN BERBERS

Berbers now living in urban areas often lose touch with their traditions. However, the way of life of Berbers living in the Atlas Mountains of North Africa has remained basically unchanged for centuries.

Mountain Berber homes are simple structures of stone and wood. The ground floor is most often a stable, perhaps housing a cow or a few chickens. Their owners occupy the floor above. Instead of power tools, farmers use scythes and other hand tools. They plow using mules and harvest by hand.

Although mountain Berbers see few strangers, they are friendly and hospitable. They often greet Westerners with the ancient term *Arrumi*, meaning "Roman."

REVIEW & ASSESS

1. **READING CHECK** What was trans-Saharan trade?
   trade over the Sahara
2. **FORM AND SUPPORT OPINIONS** Was travel by caravan worth the risk? Support your opinion.
   because there was rich resources on the other side
3. **INTERPRET MAPS** What valuable goods were exchanged on the trans-Saharan trade routes?
   gold salt

1.3 Gold, Salt, and Slaves

"Pass the salt, please" is an everyday expression we use without thinking. Today, salt is so common we hardly notice it, but in the ancient world it was unbelievably rare and precious. Salt was literally worth its weight in gold, and the Sahara had vast quantities of it.

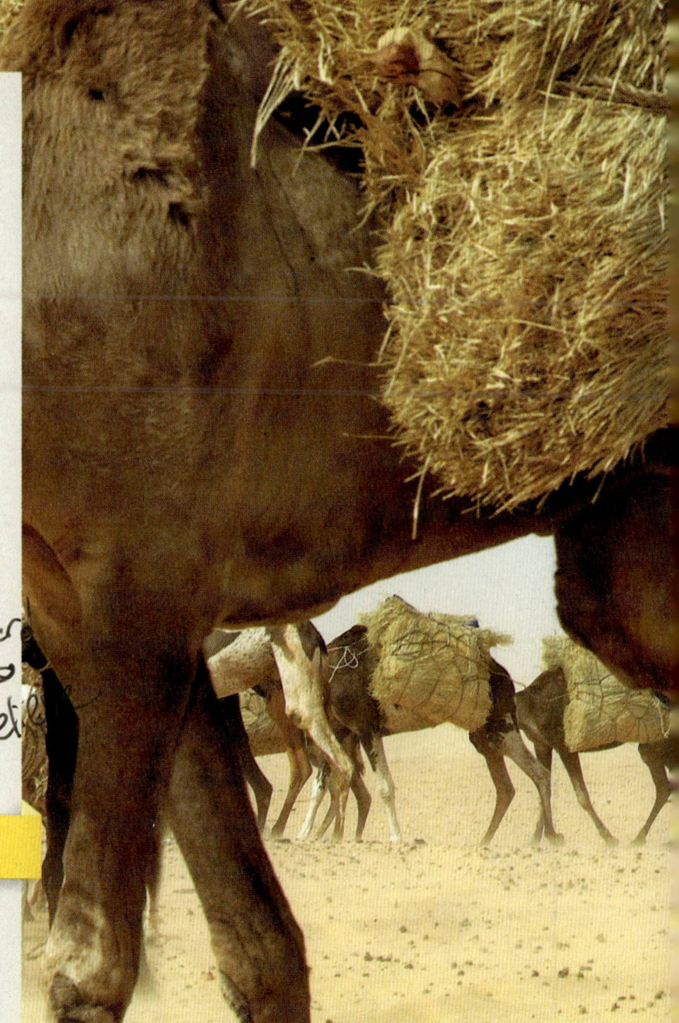

MAIN IDEA

Africa had many valuable resources that fostered trade with the Mediterranean world and beyond.

SALT

Too much salt is unhealthy, but a limited amount is crucial to a healthy body.

Salt assists in hydration, circulation, muscle contraction, and digestion. It's important to replace salt lost through perspiration.

PRECIOUS RESOURCES

Two of Africa's most valuable **commodities**, or trade goods, were gold and salt. Beginning in the 400s, these goods were traded for hundreds of years. The Western Sudan, the name for all of northern Africa west of Lake Chad, was especially rich in gold deposits.

Each year, perhaps a ton of gold crossed the Sahara, finding its way to Europe and Asia. African gold stimulated the flow of silk from China and spices from India. European kings used African gold to make coins.

Salt was worth almost as much as gold. Before there were refrigerators to keep food cold, people used salt to preserve meat and other foods. In some areas of the world, preservation with salt is still practiced. In much of the ancient world, salt was rare. Its **scarcity**, or small supply, made salt valuable. Africa, though, had large salt deposits, thanks to the Sahara. The desert had once been a shallow sea. As its waters dried up, salt deposits were left, especially in western Africa. Laborers extracted, or dug out, 200-pound slabs of salt, which they carved into blocks. Camels carried salt blocks hundreds of miles to be traded at a huge profit.

AFRICAN SLAVE TRADE

The labor needed for mining gold and salt came largely from slaves, who were traded across the desert beginning in the 600s. Like the

Critical Viewing A camel caravan moves through the desert. What does the image show about how camels are useful to traders?

Atlantic slave trade that would emerge in the 1500s, the trans-Saharan slave trade was a harsh and horrible business. Most slaves came from the Niger Delta region. (See the map in Lesson 1.2.) Once captured, they were chained together and forcibly marched through the desert.

The slave trade increased dramatically when Muslim traders arrived in North Africa in the 600s. However, the desert's vast expanse always limited the slave trade. Many slaves died during the terrible journey. The survivors were exchanged for trade goods, especially horses. A good horse was extremely valuable in the desert and cost a large number of slaves.

While some slaves were sold for labor, others satisfied a growing demand for slaves in the Mediterranean world. There, slaves were likely to become domestic servants, soldiers, artisans, or even important government officials. Nonetheless, these people had been taken from their families and cruelly treated, with little hope of ever returning home. It was a particularly brutal aspect of Africa's history.

REVIEW & ASSESS

1. **READING CHECK** Why were salt and gold such valuable resources?
2. **SEQUENCE EVENTS** What happened to greatly increase the slave trade?
3. **IDENTIFY MAIN IDEAS AND DETAILS** According to the text, what happened to slaves who reached North Africa?

1.4 Islam Spreads to Africa

The mighty Muslim general Uqba fought his way across North Africa during the A.D. 600s. After his great triumphs, he rode his horse into the Atlantic Ocean, saying, "Oh God, if the sea had not prevented me, I would have galloped on forever . . . upholding your faith and fighting the unbelievers." Such determination helped assure the place of Islam in Africa.

MAIN IDEA

Islam spread through North and West Africa, affecting African culture.

MALI'S ANCIENT MANUSCRIPTS

Timbuktu and Djenné are home to hundreds of thousands of manuscripts dating back to the 1100s. These handwritten works contain invaluable insight into the history of Africa and Islam.

CONQUEST AND TRADE

After the prophet Muhammad's death in A.D. 632, Islam spread from its origins on the Arabian Peninsula to many other parts of the world. By 642, Arab armies had conquered Egypt. Over the next several centuries, Muslims would spread Islam throughout North and West Africa. At first, few Berbers converted to Islam, but eventually many did so. In time, most North Africans were Muslim. During the 1000s and the 1100s, first the Almoravids (al-muh-RAH-vuhdz) and then the Almohads (al-muh-HAHDZ) founded Berber dynasties that united northwestern Africa.

When the Arabs invaded North Africa, trans-Saharan trade with West Africa expanded greatly. Using camel caravans, Berber merchants carried their goods and religion across the Sahara. Many West African merchants saw a trading advantage and converted to Islam.

By the 1000s, West African rulers also began to convert to Islam, as did some of their subjects. Others continued their traditional beliefs, sometimes mixing them with Islamic practices. Muslim merchants established Islam as far away as the East African coast. By 1500, Islam had spread across North Africa, West Africa, and along the coast of East Africa.

THE IMPACT OF ISLAM

As Islam spread, so did Islamic culture. By the 1300s, Muslim leaders ruled several empires, and mosques were common in North and West Africa. Traditional mosque architecture was cleverly adapted to Africa's climate and materials. Builders used mud and even salt blocks. They created impressive buildings like the mud-built mosque in **Djenné** (jeh-NAY), shown opposite. Builders also designed rectangular mud-brick houses with flat roofs.

The Arabic language also spread. Literacy increased through the teaching of the Qur'an, and mosques became important centers of learning. Scholarship thrived. Cities like **Timbuktu** and Djenné became famous centers for Muslim art, literature, and science. Scholars in Timbuktu collected and wrote down Islamic teachings in many fields of knowledge, including astronomy, medicine, law, and mathematics.

Critical Viewing The Great Mosque of Djenné, Mali, is an architectural wonder. What distinctive features does the image show?

REVIEW & ASSESS

1. **READING CHECK** How did Islam spread throughout North and West Africa?

2. **MAKE INFERENCES** Why might West African merchants have viewed conversion to Islam as a trading advantage?

3. **ANALYZE LANGUAGE USE** How does the phrase "cleverly adapted" help explain the use of traditional mosque architecture in Africa?

NOK TERRA COTTA SCULPTURES

These heads were sculpted out of terra cotta by the Nok. The first such head was discovered in the small Nigerian town of Nok in 1943. Some archaeologists think the heads were once attached to bodies sculpted in standing, sitting, or kneeling positions.

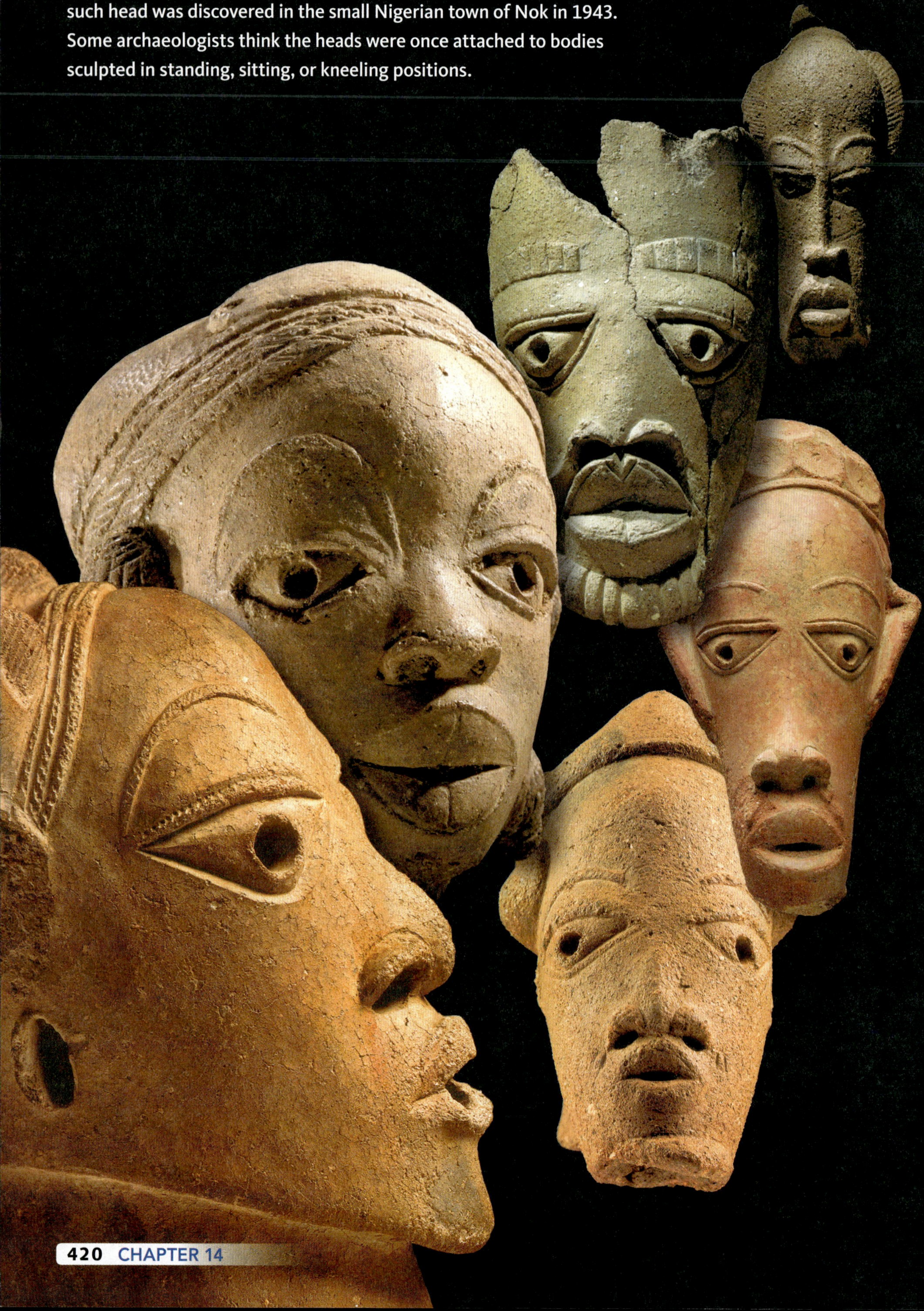

2.1 Nok Culture and Iron Technology

You put more wood into the blazing furnace and blow into it through long clay tubes. The injection of air makes the fire burn even hotter, and your body is almost scalded by the heat. But the results will be worth it when you succeed in extracting precious iron from rock.

MAIN IDEA

The Nok developed art forms and iron tools that brought great changes to West Africa.

THE NOK

West Africa juts out like the hump of a camel into the Atlantic Ocean. The region is part of **Sub-Saharan Africa**, which stretches south of the Sahara to the southern tip of the continent.

The **Nok** people settled in what is now the country of Nigeria. (See the map in Lesson 2.2.) Around 500 B.C., the Nok were among the first in West Africa to make tools from **iron**, a metal that is found in rock.

Nok artists also used **terra cotta**, which is fire-baked clay, to create unusual sculptures of humans. The sculpted heads of Nok figures, which are about 12 inches high and cone-shaped, are all that remain. These sculptures are the oldest known figurative sculptures south of the Sahara. They have elaborate hairstyles, triangular eyes, oversized features, and exaggerated expressions. This style heavily influenced West African art for centuries.

AFRICA'S IRON AGE

What archaeologists call the **Iron Age** was an important period during which the use of superior iron tools and weapons began and spread. The Nok were probably the first sub-Saharan people to smelt iron. They may have developed smelting independently or learned it through contact with other cultures.

Smelting is the process used to extract iron from a type of rock called iron ore. Using extraordinarily high temperatures, the iron is literally melted out of the rock. The Nok built clay furnaces with two chambers, one for the fire and the other for the ore. Smelters used clay pipes to blow air into the fire and increase its heat. Then they drained the liquid iron into stone molds to make strong iron tools and weapons.

The Nok used iron axes, picks, and hoes to clear huge areas of land for farming. With an increased food supply, the population grew.

At its peak, Nok culture covered about 350,000 square miles. However, deforestation, or cutting down forests, damaged the local ecosystem. At the same time, overuse made the soil infertile. Due to these geographic changes, Nok culture declined after about A.D. 200.

REVIEW & ASSESS

1. **READING CHECK** What Nok developments brought change to West Africa?
2. **ANALYZE CAUSE AND EFFECT** How did the use of iron tools affect Nok culture?
3. **DRAW CONCLUSIONS** How did the Nok use raw materials to advance their culture?

2.2 The Kingdom of Ghana

During the 700s, Arab traders from North Africa began to cross the Sahara more frequently. When they reached West Africa, they talked glowingly of a "land of gold," where the king wore a hat made of gold and the horses were draped in stunning gold cloth. This was the land of Ghana, and for centuries, it was the wealthiest kingdom in West Africa.

MAIN IDEA

Trade, especially in gold, spurred the development of the powerful kingdom of Ghana in West Africa.

A KINGDOM OF GOLD

South of the Sahara was a region of grasslands that was ideally suited for agriculture. Iron tools helped the farmers grow more food, which fed more people and allowed the population to increase. The people lived in villages, each of which had its own chief. Over time, the villages banded together to form the kingdom of **Ghana**.

By A.D. 500, Ghana had become the first great trading state in West Africa. Traders arrived there bringing salt and other commodities. The capital of Ghana, Koumbi-Saleh (KUHM-bee SAHL-uh), stood midway between Africa's main sources of salt, most of which were in the Sahara, and West Africa's gold mines, which Ghana controlled. This control and a favorable location made Ghana's traders the ideal middlemen for trans-Saharan trade. (Middlemen are people who buy goods from one person and sell them to another.) The trade brought Ghana's traders wealth and power.

Ghana's kings made their money by taxing salt and other trade goods as they entered and departed Ghana. Ghana's rulers also strictly controlled the flow of gold. All gold nuggets automatically belonged to the king, and only gold dust could be traded. These rules ensured that gold remained scarce, which kept gold prices high. Trade goods also included textiles, weapons, horses, and even bananas. As trans-Saharan trade expanded, caravans carrying goods grew longer, sometimes numbering several hundred camels.

THE COMING OF ISLAM

Like all societies, Ghana was affected by outside influences. During the 700s, Arab traders brought Islam and Islamic laws to West Africa. Traders and others learned to speak and write in Arabic. Up to that point, people living in West Africa had not had a written language.

Around 1050, the Almoravids, whom you learned about earlier in this chapter, attacked Ghana and tried to force the leaders to become Muslims. The leaders fought back, but they had been greatly weakened by constant war. In 1076, the Almoravids captured Koumbi-Saleh.

In addition, Ghana's soil was worn out and could no longer support the population. By the early 1200s, Ghana's traders and farmers were migrating to richer lands to the south and west. The kingdom of Ghana had come to an end. However, Ghana's "land of gold" had played a major role in the development of trade and civilization in West Africa.

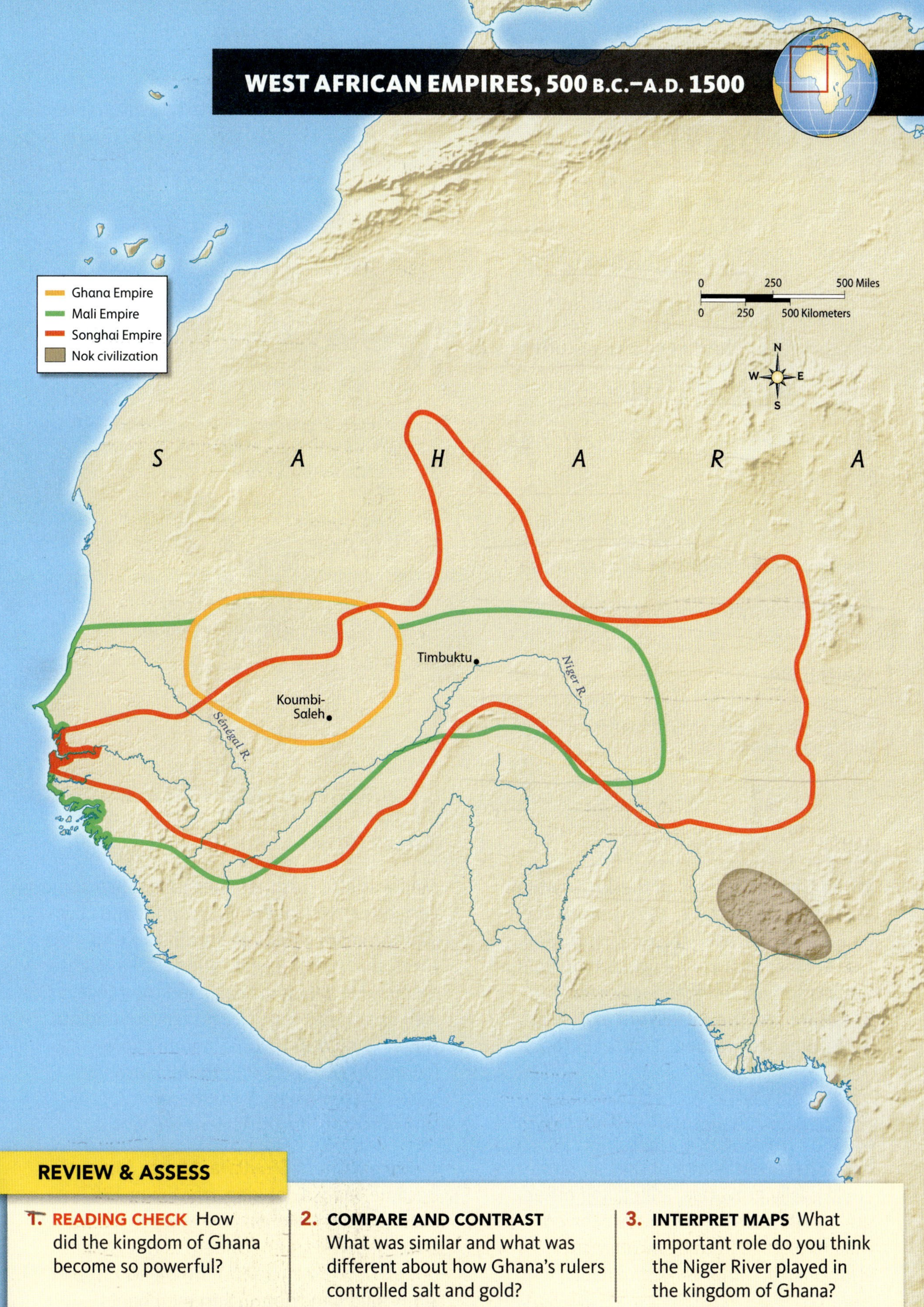
WEST AFRICAN EMPIRES, 500 B.C.–A.D. 1500
Ghana Empire
Mali Empire
Songhai Empire
Nok civilization
0
250
500 Miles
0
250
500 Kilometers
N
S
E
W
S A H A R A
Timbuktu
Koumbi-Saleh
Senegal R.
Niger R.

REVIEW & ASSESS

1. **READING CHECK** How did the kingdom of Ghana become so powerful?

2. **COMPARE AND CONTRAST** What was similar and what was different about how Ghana's rulers controlled salt and gold?

3. **INTERPRET MAPS** What important role do you think the Niger River played in the kingdom of Ghana?

2.3 The Empire of Mali

"This man flooded Cairo with his [gifts]. He left no . . . holder of a royal office without the gift of a load of gold." This man, Mansa Musa, gave away so much gold that it led to a decline in the precious metal's value and ruined the Egyptian economy! African kings could grow unbelievably rich.

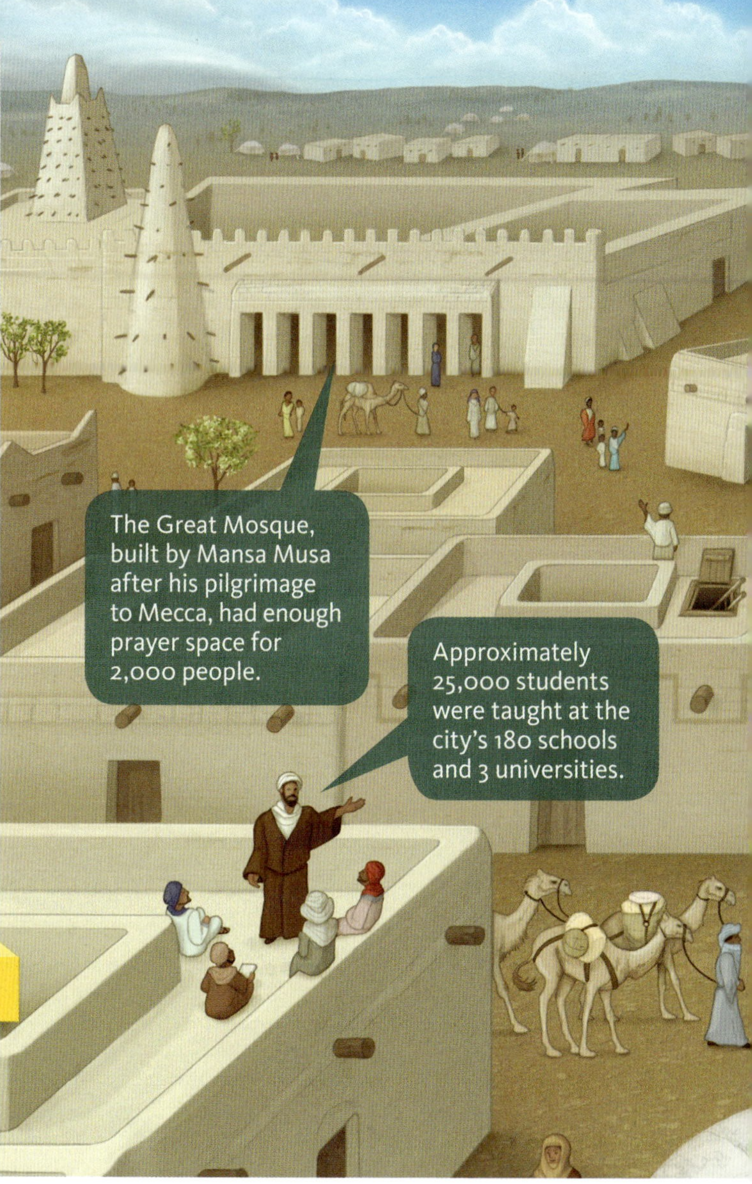

The Great Mosque, built by Mansa Musa after his pilgrimage to Mecca, had enough prayer space for 2,000 people.

Approximately 25,000 students were taught at the city's 180 schools and 3 universities.

MAIN IDEA

Like Ghana, the powerful empire of Mali was built on trade and gold.

THE EMERGENCE OF MALI

When Ghana declined in the 1200s, it left West Africa without a major power. Then a new power arose—the empire of **Mali**. Like Ghana, Mali built its wealth on gold, but it also boasted great achievements in culture and the arts. Word of Mali's achievements reached as far as Europe.

Located along the west coast of Africa, Mali had several geographic advantages. Much of the land was a savanna. The region received plenty of rain, so farmers could easily grow rice, millet, and other grains. Agricultural surpluses allowed Mali to engage in trade, acquire art, and construct impressive buildings.

MALI'S GREAT LEADERS

Mali was also fortunate because it had some very effective leaders. Popular legend claims extraordinary things of **Sundiata Keita** (sun-JAHT-ah KAY-tah), who founded the mighty empire. He brought peace and tolerance, as well as law and order, to his lands. Sundiata ruled from 1230 to 1255 and became incredibly rich by taxing trade. However, it was **Mansa Musa** (MAHN-sah MOO-sah) who introduced Mali to the world.

A descendant of Sundiata, Mansa Musa became **mansa**, or king, of Mali in 1307. Musa enlarged the empire and controlled trans-Saharan trade. Under his rule, Mali's population grew to about 40 million. Subject kings paid him tribute, and merchants

TIMBUKTU, c. 1500
Most people lived in houses made of brick. Living quarters were dark and stuffy.
A traveler's inn, or funduq, provided food and water for merchants and their animals.
Camel caravans brought goods such as salt, cloth, copper, and books to trade for gold.

paid him taxes. Musa owned all of Mali's abundant gold and was fabulously wealthy.

A devout Muslim, Musa provided strong support for the arts, learning, and Islam. He encouraged the trading city of Timbuktu to develop as a center of Islamic learning. He oversaw the construction of the city's Great Mosque, one the oldest mosques in Sub-Saharan Africa. Musa laid the groundwork for Timbuktu's emergence in the 1500s as the scholarly and religious center of West Africa. Although Musa ably ruled his vast empire, his successors were weak. As a result, Mali shrank to almost nothing as smaller kingdoms broke away and Berber nomads captured Timbuktu. One of the newly independent kingdoms, Songhai, eventually surpassed Mali in size and splendor.

REVIEW & ASSESS

1. **READING CHECK** In what ways were Mali and Ghana similar and different?
2. **DRAW CONCLUSIONS** What enabled Mansa Musa to support the arts and learning?
3. **SEQUENCE EVENTS** What events led to the decline of Mali?

2.4 The Oral Tradition

You are exploring the past by reading this book. Written history is often considered the most accurate. But until very recently, people in much of the world, including Africa, didn't write down their history. Instead, special performers spoke or sang stories of the past, passing them from generation to generation.

MAIN IDEA

Africa has a rich tradition of oral history.

AN EPIC OF OLD MALI

One of the most famous griot stories is *Sundiata: An Epic of Old Mali.* This epic describes how Sundiata, the Lion King, defeated his enemies to found the empire of Mali. There is good evidence to suggest that at least some of the story is true.

ORAL HISTORY

Most early African civilizations, such as Ghana and Mali, did not develop a writing system until Muslim traders brought the Arabic language and writing system. Before the arrival of these traders, Africans passed on histories and stories orally, a method that historians call the **oral tradition**. In this manner, history, culture, and social values were transmitted from one generation to the next.

A class of special storytellers emerged to relate the stories of villages, families, and kings. Known in West Africa as **griots** (GREE-ohz), they spent years painstakingly memorizing family trees and learning stories.

Griots dramatically told their tales at public ceremonies, where excited crowds gathered to listen and learn. Stories about their ancestors and the exploits of kings were especially popular. Much of what historians know about early African history has been passed down through this oral tradition. It was not until the early 1900s that scholars wrote down these stories, fables, songs, and poems.

GRIOT TRADITION

Griots were highly respected members of African society who carried out many different roles. Most were men, but some were women. Griots served as historians, educators, and advisors. They also served as genealogists, or people who know how family members are related to one another and to their ancestors.

Griots were accomplished performers who could captivate their audiences. They often played drums or stringed instruments, such as the 21-string kora. Other musicians sometimes accompanied them as they told their stories.

Some griots wore costumes and masks. As the stories unfolded, actors and dancers sometimes interpreted the action. These dramatic aspects of griot performances added to the tales' excitement and helped make them more memorable.

In West Africa, the griot tradition is still very much alive. Famous griots are treated like rock stars, and the tradition has had a huge influence on modern West African music. In Western countries, young musicians with African roots are making the tradition their own.

Critical Viewing The griot is seated before a percussion instrument called a balafon. What instruments popular in the West are similar to the balafon?

Balafon
The balafon is a traditional African instrument made of wood and gourds.

Kora
The kora is a stringed instrument with a rounded back similar to that of a mandolin.

Koni
The koni has two strings and is made of wood and leather.

REVIEW & ASSESS

1. **READING CHECK** Why was oral tradition important in West Africa?

2. **ANALYZE LANGUAGE USE** How does the word *captivate* describe the ability of griots to perform?

3. **DRAW CONCLUSIONS** What might be the advantages and disadvantages of passing down history through oral tradition?

2.5 DOCUMENT-BASED QUESTION

Trans-Saharan Travelers

Written accounts of early Africa have largely come from Muslim sources. Many manuscripts were kept in cities like Timbuktu and are still waiting to be studied. These accounts, written by people who were actually there, offer insights into early Africa and its place in the world.

This painting from a 13th-century manuscript shows a caravan of pilgrims.

DOCUMENT ONE

Primary Source: Historical Account

from Al-Umari's account of Mansa Musa's visit to Cairo in 1324

Al-Umari, an Arabic historian, visited Egypt not long after Mansa Musa's famous visit. He was able to interview many firsthand witnesses to the event. His descriptions of Mansa Musa and his enormous wealth have greatly contributed to our knowledge of Mali. In this passage, Al-Umari recounts the experience of a government official who met the legendary ruler.

CONSTRUCTED RESPONSE What evidence from the text demonstrates that Mansa Musa was an immensely wealthy and religious man?

> *From the beginning of my coming to stay in Egypt I heard talk of the arrival of this sultan Musa on his Pilgrimage. . . . I asked the emir Abu . . . and he told me of the opulence [wealth], manly virtues, and piety of his sultan. "When I went out to meet him [he said] on behalf of the mighty sultan al-Malik al-Nasir, he did me extreme honour and treated me with the greatest courtesy. . . . Then he forwarded to the royal treasury many loads of unworked native gold and other valuables. I tried to persuade him to . . . meet the sultan, but he refused persistently saying: 'I came for the Pilgrimage and nothing else. I do not wish to mix anything else with my Pilgrimage.'"*

DOCUMENT TWO

Primary Source: Atlas

from the *Catalan Atlas*, c. 1375

Mansa Musa's pilgrimage to Mecca literally put West Africa on the map. Stories of his extraordinary wealth stimulated international interest in West Africa, the land of gold. This made it a feature of medieval maps such as the *Catalan Atlas*, which gives West Africa considerable prominence. Abraham Cresques, a mapmaker, created the atlas in Majorca, an island that is part of Spain.

CONSTRUCTED RESPONSE Based on the map, what can you conclude about Mansa Musa's importance to West Africa?

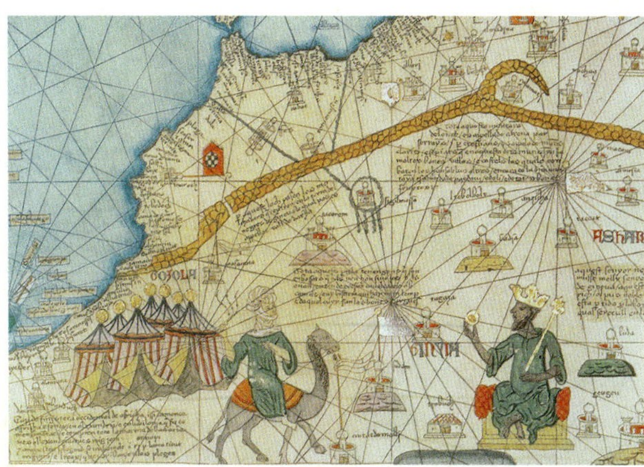
Detail showing West Africa and Mansa Musa (right)

SYNTHESIZE & WRITE

1. **REVIEW** Review what you have learned about West Africa and Mansa Musa in this chapter.
2. **RECALL** On your own paper, write down the main idea expressed in each primary source.
3. **CONSTRUCT** Write a topic sentence that answers this question: How did Mansa Musa affect Mali and the rest of the world?
4. **WRITE** Using evidence from the sources, write an argument to support the answer to the question in Step 3.

CHAPTER

14 Review

VOCABULARY

Match each word in the first column with its definition in the second column.

WORD	DEFINITION
1. desertification	**a.** a tradable good
2. trans-Saharan	**b.** an area of lush tropical grasslands
3. caravan	**c.** the practice of passing stories by spoken voice
4. commodity	**d.** across the Sahara
5. scarcity	**e.** a West African storyteller
6. savanna	**f.** the process by which fertile land becomes a desert
7. griot	**g.** people traveling together
8. oral tradition	**h.** a shortage of something

READING STRATEGY

9. ANALYZE LANGUAGE USE If you haven't already, complete your chart to analyze language in at least three introductory paragraphs. Then answer the question.

Language Example	What It Suggests
The caravan is a merchant's ticket to profit, but first the merchant must survive the journey.	*The trip across the Sahara was very dangerous.*

How does the writer's use of language in these examples help you understand what life was like in North and West Africa between 1000 B.C. and A.D. 1500?

MAIN IDEAS

Answer the following questions. Support your answers with evidence from the chapter.

10. How did the geography and climate of the Sahara change over a long period of time? **LESSON 1.1**

11. What impact did the development of trade between early colonists and Berbers have on North Africa? **LESSON 1.2**

12. What valuable resources in Africa fostered trade? **LESSON 1.3**

13. How did Islam spread throughout North and West Africa? **LESSON 1.4**

14. What new technology was developed by the Nok people of West Africa? **LESSON 2.1**

15. What factors led to the emergence of the powerful kingdom of Ghana? **LESSON 2.2**

16. Why does Africa have a rich tradition of oral history? **LESSON 2.4**

CRITICAL THINKING

Answer the following questions. Support your answers with evidence from the chapter.

17. SYNTHESIZE How did technology contribute to both the rise and the decline of Nok culture?

18. ANALYZE CAUSE AND EFFECT What effect did desertification have on the people and animals who inhabited the Sahara?

19. SEQUENCE EVENTS How did vast salt deposits develop in the Sahara?

20. DRAW CONCLUSIONS What was the cultural legacy of the spread of Islam in North and West Africa?

21. YOU DECIDE If you were a trader in West Africa, would you rather have a pound of salt or a pound of gold? Support your opinion with evidence from the chapter.

INTERPRET MAPS

Study the map that shows the spread of ironworking in Africa. Then answer the questions that follow.

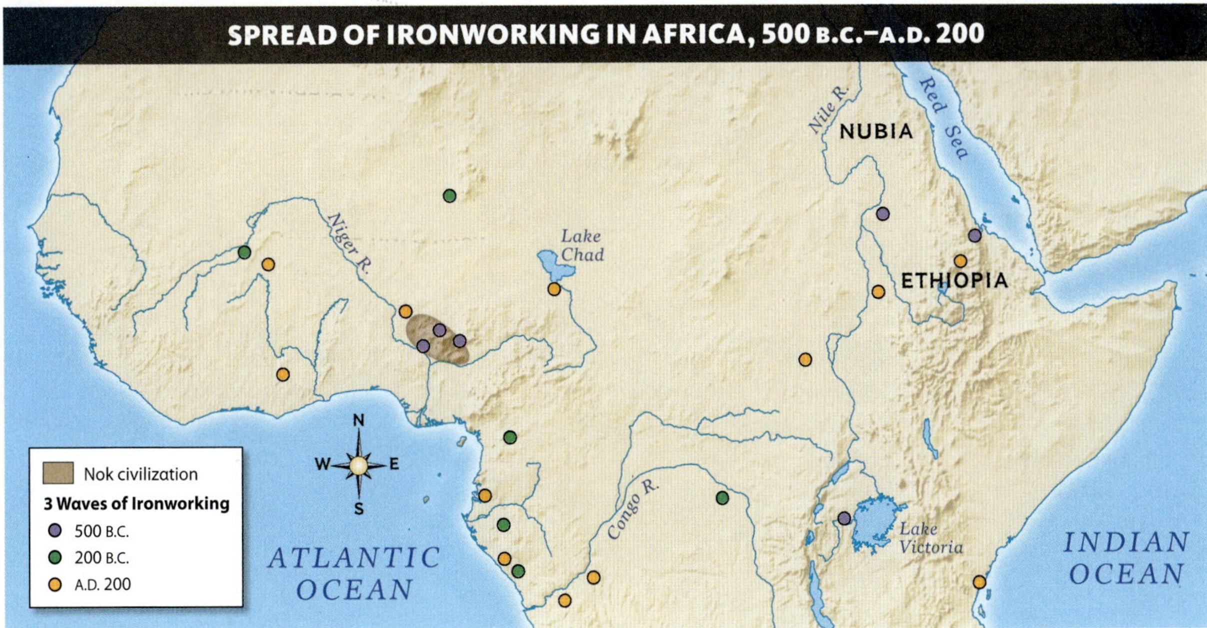
SPREAD OF IRONWORKING IN AFRICA, 500 B.C.–A.D. 200
Nile R.
NUBIA
Red Sea
Niger R.
Lake Chad
ETHIOPIA
Nok civilization
3 Waves of Ironworking
500 B.C.
200 B.C.
A.D. 200
ATLANTIC OCEAN
Congo R.
Lake Victoria
INDIAN OCEAN

22. In what areas of Africa did people develop ironworking at the same time as the Nok?

23. Where did ironworking spread between 500 B.C. and 200 B.C?

ANALYZE SOURCES

Alvise Cadamosto was an Italian explorer who wrote one of the earliest known accounts of West Africa. Read his description of the salt-gold trade in the 1450s.

> Having reached these waters [the upper Niger] with the salt, they proceed in this fashion: all those who have the salt pile it in rows, each marking his own. Having made these piles, the whole caravan retires half a day's journey. Then there come another [group] who do not wish to be seen or to speak . . . they place a quantity of gold opposite each pile and then turn back, leaving salt and gold. When they have gone [those] who own the salt return: if they are satisfied with the quantity of gold, they leave the salt and retire with the gold. . . . In this way, by long and ancient custom, they carry on their trade without seeing or speaking to each other.

24. What is distinctive about how transactions in the salt-gold trade were carried out?

WRITE ABOUT HISTORY

25. NARRATIVE Suppose you were able to travel to the trading city of Timbuktu at the time of its greatest influence and importance. Write a brief account of your time there and describe what you see.

TIPS

- Take notes from the lesson about the empire of Mali.
- Select relevant, well-chosen facts, concrete details, and examples that will be the basis of your narrative.
- Use transitions to make your account of your trip clear to readers.
- Use vocabulary from the chapter as appropriate.

CHAPTER

15 EAST, CENTRAL, AND SOUTHERN AFRICA

1000 B.C. – A.D. 1500

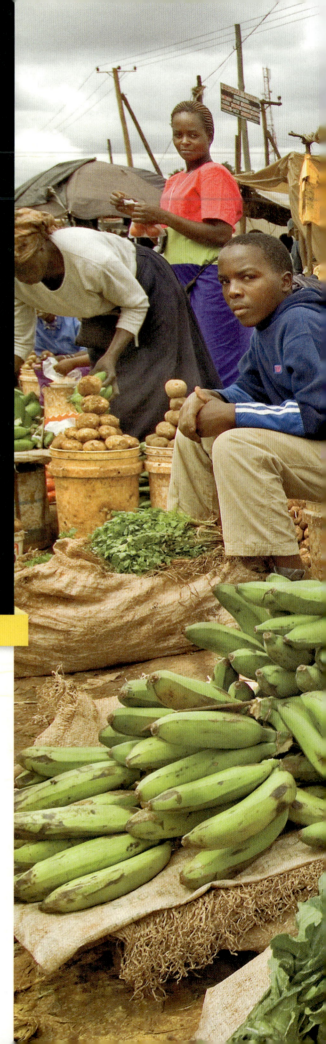

SECTION 1

EAST AFRICA

KEY VOCABULARY
city-state
dhow
hub
mariner
monsoon
sultan

NAMES & PLACES
Aksum
Ezana
Kilwa
Swahili

SECTION 2

CENTRAL AND SOUTHERN AFRICA

KEY VOCABULARY
deplete
lingua franca
migration
tribute

NAMES & PLACES
Afonso I
Bantu
Great Zimbabwe
Kongo
Shona

READING STRATEGY

ORGANIZE IDEAS: ANALYZE CAUSE AND EFFECT
When you analyze cause and effect, you note the consequences of an action. Often, a cause will have multiple effects. As you read the chapter, use a diagram like this one to identify effects of the Bantu migrations across sub-Saharan Africa.

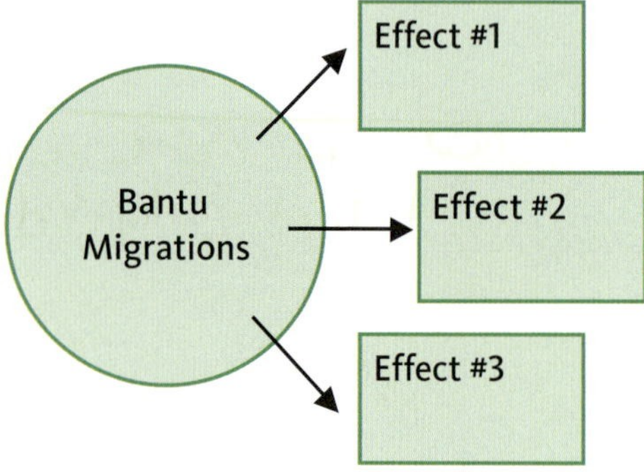
Bantu Migrations
Effect #1
Effect #2
Effect #3

Farmers sell their produce next to one of the main roads on the outskirts of Nairobi, Kenya.

1.1 The Kingdom of Aksum

Around A.D. 250, a Persian prophet listed the four great empires in the world: Rome, Persia, China, and Aksum. Two thousand years ago, Aksum was the jewel of East Africa. It was an organized and prosperous kingdom built on trade.

MAIN IDEA

The prosperous kingdom of Aksum rose to power in East Africa.

IVORY TRADE

Ivory comes from the tusks of animals, especially elephants. Ivory exports, such as this mask, brought the African elephant close to extinction. Today these exports are regulated, but illegal trade still threatens elephants.

THE RISE OF AKSUM

The geography of East Africa made it ideally suited for trade. The region is shaped like a rhinoceros horn, earning it the nickname the Horn of Africa. The Red Sea connects East Africa with the Persian Gulf, the Mediterranean Sea, and the Indian Ocean. These bodies of water can carry Africa's vast resources around the world. From very early times, trade was central to East Africa's development.

Aksum (AHK-soom) began around 500 B.C. in what is now Ethiopia. By A.D. 100, Aksum had emerged as a prosperous trading kingdom. Its territory stretched from the Sahara to the Red Sea, where ports enabled it to dominate trade with Arabia, Persia, India, China, and Europe.

Around A.D. 350, King **Ezana** (AY-zah-nah) of Aksum conquered its great trading rival, Kush (which you read about in Chapter 4), and seized control of the valuable ivory trade. He also converted to Christianity and made it the official religion of Aksum. Ezana declared his faith on a solid stone pillar called a stela (STEE-luh). Aksum's kings built these monuments as symbols of their power.

TRADE AND ISOLATION

Aksum's location made it a major international trading **hub**, or center. The kingdom's economy grew through the trade of ivory, spices, and slaves. Aksum spent its wealth on textiles, metal, and olive oil from its trading partners. Its wealth also fueled cultural achievements. Artisans produced luxury goods, and the kingdom minted its own coins. Aksum developed a written language, which was used to create a rich body of literature. However, this time of prosperity did not last.

Beginning in the A.D. 500s, regional wars and Arab expansion closed off some of Aksum's key trade routes. The kingdom also suffered the effects of deforestation, droughts, and overfarming, which reduced the availability of food. Aksum declined, and Muslim invaders shrank its borders. Christian Aksum became surrounded by Muslim territories.

By A.D. 800, Christians in the region had retreated into the mountains of Ethiopia. Isolated, the Christians were mostly left alone, and their legacy still thrives there today.

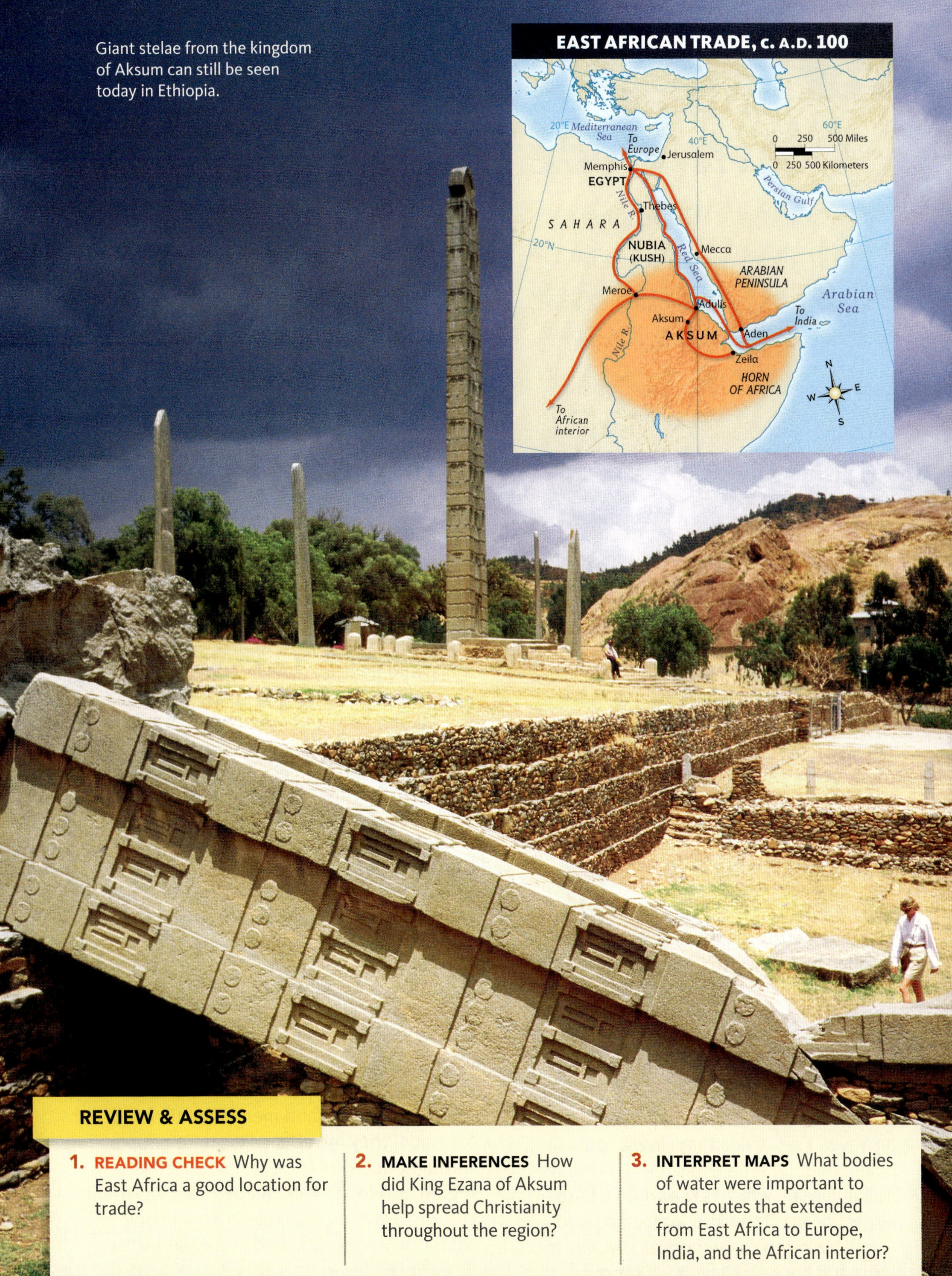

EAST AFRICAN TRADE, c. A.D. 100
20°E
Mediterranean Sea
To Europe
Jerusalem
40°E
60°E
0 250 500 Miles
0 250 500 Kilometers
Memphis
EGYPT
Persian Gulf
Nile R.
Thebes
SAHARA
20°N
NUBIA (KUSH)
Mecca
Red Sea
ARABIAN PENINSULA
Arabian Sea
Meroe
Adulis
Aksum
AKSUM
To India
Aden
Nile R.
Zeila
HORN OF AFRICA
To African interior
N
E
S
W

Giant stelae from the kingdom of Aksum can still be seen today in Ethiopia.

REVIEW & ASSESS

1. **READING CHECK** Why was East Africa a good location for trade?

2. **MAKE INFERENCES** How did King Ezana of Aksum help spread Christianity throughout the region?

3. **INTERPRET MAPS** What bodies of water were important to trade routes that extended from East Africa to Europe, India, and the African interior?

1.2

Indian Ocean Trade

In 1980, an adventurer recreating the legendary voyage of Sinbad the Sailor came to a halt near the island of Sri Lanka. The winds propelling his ship suddenly stopped, and for 35 days he went nowhere. Ancient East African sailors could have predicted this occurrence because they understood exactly when the Indian Ocean's winds blew—and when they did not.

MAIN IDEA

The Indian Ocean was a key part of East Africa's far-reaching trade network.

MONSOON WINDS

The East African coast became important for trade because the area could easily be reached by land or sea. Traders could bring goods from inland areas and load them onto ships in the Red Sea. However, even experienced sailors clung to coastlines because their ships and navigational skills were not good enough to sail safely out to sea. Beginning around A.D. 800, however, East African **mariners**, or sailors, developed the skills and ships to cross the Indian Ocean, which is the world's third largest ocean. They also learned how to use the wind to carry them all the way to India and back—if they timed it right.

From April to October, strong winds called **monsoons** blow northeast from Africa toward India. Between November and March, the winds reverse direction and blow southwest from India to Africa. They are extremely reliable and make it possible for a sailing ship to make the long journey from Africa to India and back. Even with the winds, however, the round trip could take as long as a full year.

Sailors learned to predict these winds and plan their journeys around them. Merchants who needed to move their goods between Africa and India hired experienced sailors who knew the winds. This trade across the Indian Ocean helped the economic development of both regions.

INDIAN OCEAN TRADE NETWORK

Over time, mariners and merchants continued working together to create an extensive trade network around the Indian Ocean. This network directly linked East Africa with Arabia, Persia, India, and Southeast Asia. Traders could transport goods to Europe, the Middle East, and even China.

New sailing technology made the trade network possible. Trading goods across the ocean required a sturdy ship that could carry a large amount of goods. In the Indian Ocean trade, that ship was called a **dhow** (dow). Dhows not only carried goods, but they also transported important elements of culture, such as language and religion.

With the expansion of trade, more Muslim merchants settled on the East African coast and married into local ruling families. Coastal villages grew into important trading towns controlled by Muslim rulers called **sultans**. As Muslim sailors and merchants traveled for trade, they introduced Islam to people throughout East Africa. As a result, the region developed a distinctive African-Arabic culture. It was an example of how people from other regions would influence Africa.

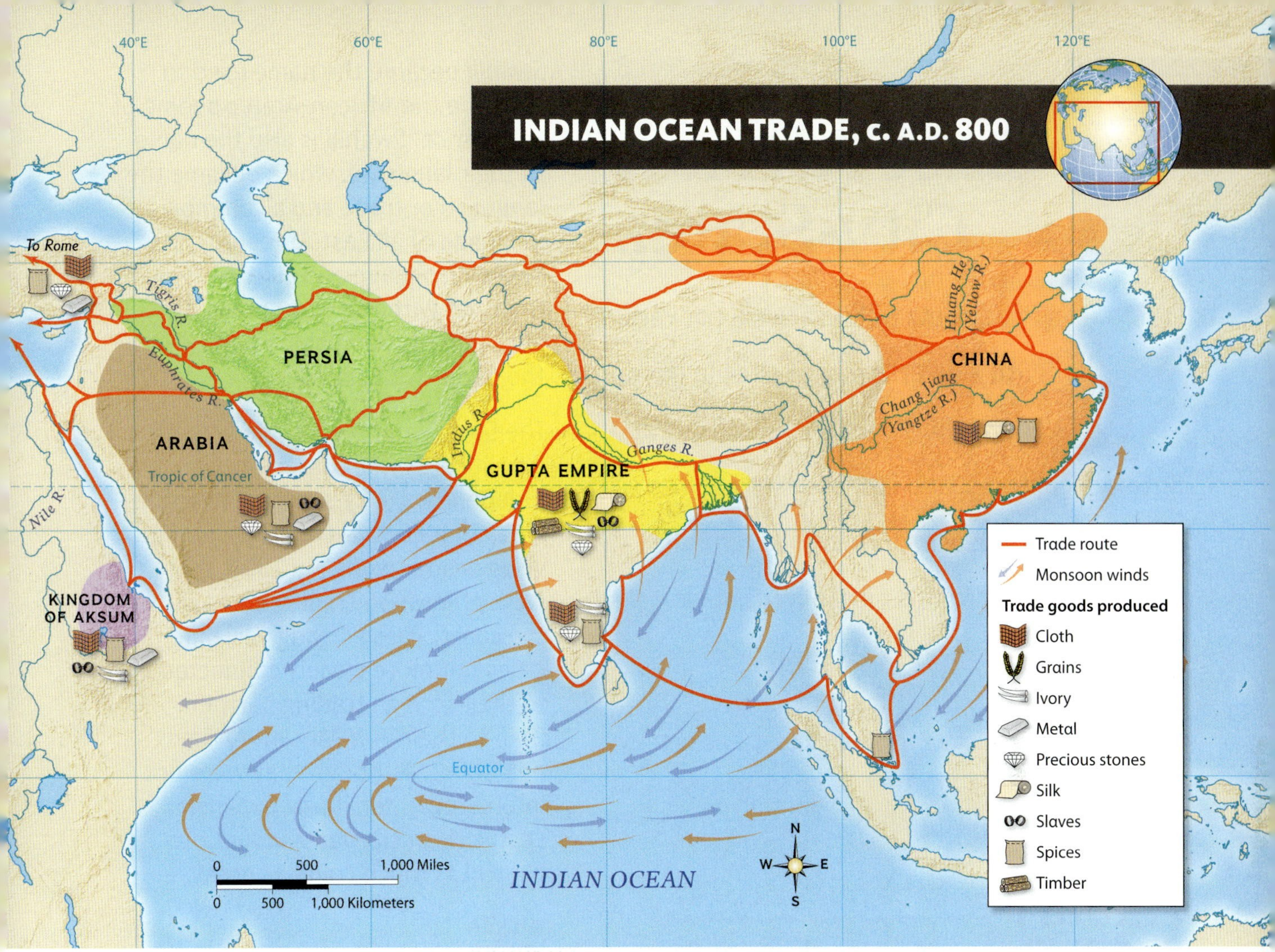

INDIAN OCEAN TRADE, c. A.D. 800

40°E 60°E 80°E 100°E 120°E 40°N

To Rome
Tigris R.
Euphrates R.
PERSIA
ARABIA
Tropic of Cancer
Nile R.
KINGDOM OF AKSUM
Indus R.
GUPTA EMPIRE
Ganges R.
CHINA
Huang He (Yellow R.)
Chang Jiang (Yangtze R.)
Equator
INDIAN OCEAN

0 500 1,000 Miles
0 500 1,000 Kilometers

N W E S

Trade route
Monsoon winds

Trade goods produced

- Cloth
- Grains
- Ivory
- Metal
- Precious stones
- Silk
- Slaves
- Spices
- Timber

DHOW SHIPS

Dhows typically had long, thin hulls and triangular sails that were good at catching the monsoon winds. The winds were critical for successful voyages.

The early dhows were able to carry relatively large shipments of trade goods. They would travel across the Indian Ocean, trade their cargo, and return to Africa with silks and other valuables.

Today many types of dhows are still used along the East African coast.

REVIEW & ASSESS

1. **READING CHECK** How did monsoon winds affect trade between Africa and India?

2. **IDENTIFY MAIN IDEAS AND DETAILS** How did trade networks across the Indian Ocean develop?

3. **INTERPRET MAPS** What products did East Africans produce to trade with other countries?

1.3 East African City-States

The streets of Kilwa were packed with a diverse mix of people from all over the world. Their different clothing, customs, and languages made for an exciting atmosphere. Trade brought all these influences to this vibrant city-state.

MAIN IDEA

City-states with a distinctive culture developed in East Africa.

Habari "Hello"

SWAHILI TODAY

Today, Swahili is an official language of Tanzania and a common language among many East African peoples. There are about 15 major Swahili dialects, or variations of the language. More than 30 million people speak Swahili. The word above is Swahili for "hello."

TRADE ON THE COAST

As Arab merchants settled in East African towns, they brought Islam. As you have read, these Arabic immigrants married local ruling families, and Muslims came to control trade.

The Arabs encountered Africans who spoke Bantu languages. The Bantu, whom you will learn more about in the next lesson, were people who migrated from West Africa into sub-Saharan Africa. These migrations began more than two thousand years ago. The Bantu established trade networks. In time, their trade networks grew.

As a result, East Africa had a rich mix of cultures. The East African and Arabic Muslim cultures combined to form the unique **Swahili** (swah-HEE-lee) culture. *Swahili* became the name used to describe the African-Arabic people of East Africa. Swahili is also the name of their language, which became the language of trade and a common language of all East Africans. The Swahili language and culture, together with the widespread adoption of Islam, helped unify the people of East Africa.

The Swahili people also developed a political system based on independent **city-states**. These are cities that control the surrounding villages and towns. By 1300, there were at least 35 trading cities along the coast. These strongly Islamic cities felt more closely connected to their foreign trading partners than to their non-Muslim African neighbors. Although they were not interested in territorial expansion, East African city-states fought to control as much trade as possible.

KILWA

One of the richest and most powerful city-states in Africa was **Kilwa**. (See the map in the Chapter Review.) It was located on an island that was as far south along the East African coast as trading ships could reach in one season. Any merchants from southern Africa had to come to Kilwa if they wanted foreign goods. Africa's main sources of gold were also south of Kilwa, which meant that the city-state controlled the overseas trade in gold.

To reinforce its control of the gold trade, Kilwa took over the port of Sofala. Sofala was farther south than Kilwa, but Sofala was closer to the gold mines. By controlling Sofala, Kilwa could more easily move gold to its ports for the arrival of seasonal trading ships.

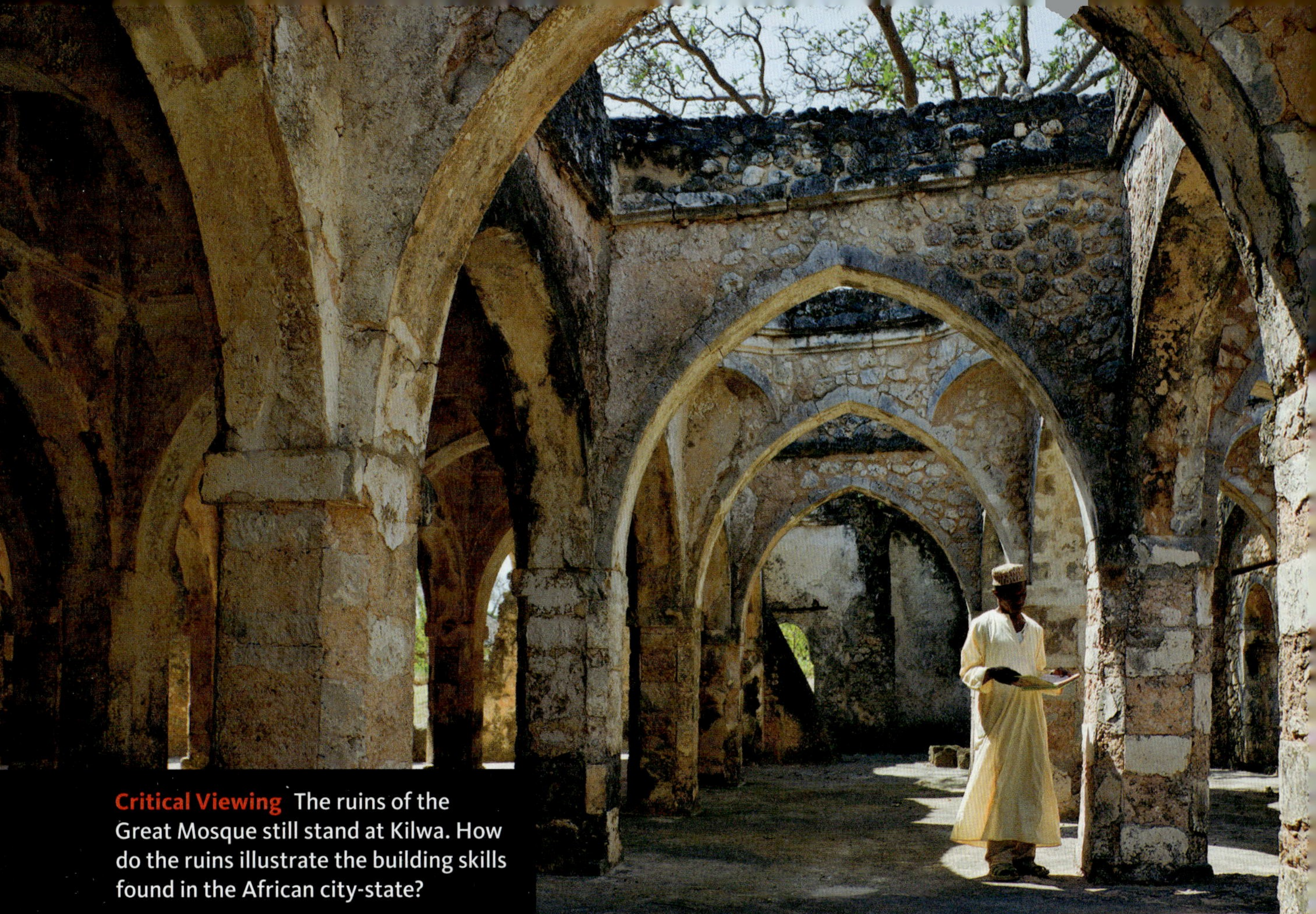

Critical Viewing The ruins of the Great Mosque still stand at Kilwa. How do the ruins illustrate the building skills found in the African city-state?

Kilwa's social classes were rigid, and it was difficult to move from one class to another. This was true for most East African city-states. Kilwa's sultan stood at the top of the society. Below the sultan were Muslim merchants, who were taxed heavily by the sultan but still grew rich. Merchants built ornate palaces, mosques, and homes of coral stone. Below the merchants were the majority of the townspeople, who were artisans, officials, and sailors. At the bottom of society were non-Muslim farmers, fishers, and, below them, slaves.

Kilwa and other East African city-states thrived for centuries until the arrival of the Portuguese in the late 1400s. These European explorers and traders stumbled upon the previously unknown East African trade network. They quickly recognized that the network moved a great deal of wealth. Just as quickly, they decided they wanted a piece of that wealth. Through political pressure and sometimes direct force, the Portuguese gained increasing control over East Africa's city-states, coastline, and commerce.

REVIEW & ASSESS

1. **READING CHECK** What effect did trade have on the culture of East African city-states?
2. **ANALYZE CAUSE AND EFFECT** What factors helped Kilwa become one of the richest and most powerful city-states in Africa?
3. **ANALYZE LANGUAGE USE** The text uses the word *stumbled* to describe how the Portuguese discovered Kilwa's trade network. What does this word suggest about this discovery?

2.1 Bantu Migrations

More than two thousand years ago, people in western Africa started migrating east and south, spreading their language and culture. These were the Bantu-speaking people, and their migration is one of the great stories in African history. They have played a major role in the development of sub-Saharan Africa—and they show the role that migration has played in world history.

MAIN IDEA

The Bantu populated much of Africa.

MOVEMENTS EAST

Bantu means "people" and is a general name for many different peoples of Africa who speak more than 500 different languages yet share a common ancestry. By studying the different Bantu languages, linguists, people who study human speech, know that the Bantu originated in western Africa around present-day Nigeria and Cameroon.

The **migration**, or movement, of the Bantu people was slow through the dense forest at the equator but accelerated across the open savanna. By the end of the A.D. 300s, Bantu speakers dominated all of sub-Saharan Africa except in the southwest, where the dry and hot climate was much more harsh.

The earliest Bantu speakers were probably fishers and farmers. Along the way, they learned how to work metals to create tools and weapons. The Bantu carried their metalworking skills with them. They traveled in small family groups and chose the best land for farming.

The Bantu's numbers grew, thanks to their mastery of iron, which allowed them to prepare land for planting crops. They relied on a method in which they used iron tools and fire to clear land for cultivation. They adapted the environment to better suit their needs. When the soil was exhausted, they simply moved to the next fertile area.

One crop that became widespread actually originated from Indonesia—bananas. Bananas became a staple crop in East Africa, where more varieties have developed than anywhere else in the world. Communities had rapid population growth if they had good growing conditions, plentiful rainfall, and an absence of the disease-carrying tsetse flies.

The Bantu spread across Africa in phases. Their migration was not constant and the speed of their migration could be altered by many factors including vegetation, disease, and climate.

IMPACT OF THE MIGRATIONS

At the time the Bantu began migrating, hunter-gatherers populated most of Africa, but both populations remained relatively low. As a result, there was plenty of room for the Bantu and hunter-gathers to coexist peacefully—or to avoid each other if they wanted.

At times, the Bantu and the people they encountered even helped each other by exchanging information. One skill the Bantu learned along the way was how to raise animals. When arguments over territory did occur, however, the Bantu's iron weapons gave them a clear and deadly advantage.

BANTU MIGRATIONS, 2000 B.C.–A.D. 500
Benue R.
Niger R.
Uele R.
from 2000 B.C.
from 2000 B.C.
CONGO BASIN
Congo R.
Equator
Lake Victoria
1000 B.C.–A.D. 500
Lake Tanganyika
A.D. 1–500
A.D. 1–500
Lake Malawi (Lake Nyasa)
ATLANTIC OCEAN
INDIAN OCEAN
Comoros
Madagascar
Zambezi R.
Namib Desert
KALAHARI DESERT
Limpopo R.
Tropic of Capricorn
Orange R.
Vaal R.
Paths of migrations
Bantu homeland, c. 2000 B.C.
Northwestern Bantu region, by A.D. 500
Eastern Bantu region, by A.D. 500
Western Bantu region, by A.D. 500
0 400 800 Miles
0 400 800 Kilometers
0°
20°S
20°E
40°E
60°E

As they migrated, the Bantu had a great impact on the people of eastern and western Africa. They married into local families and spread the technology of making weapons and tools from iron, bronze, and copper. They also affected how people organized and governed themselves. Some of these influences are felt in Africa even today.

At the same time, the Bantu who migrated down the east coast of Africa also absorbed the influences of Arabic settlers. As you have read, this led to the region's distinctive African-Arabic culture and the Swahili language. Swahili became the widespread language of trade and a **lingua franca** (LING-gwuh FRANG-kuh), or a language commonly used by many different groups of people.

REVIEW & ASSESS

1. **READING CHECK** What is one impact the Bantu-speaking people had on Africa?
2. **COMPARE AND CONTRAST** In what ways were the Bantu different from other groups of people who lived in Africa at this time?
3. **INTERPRET MAPS** What physical features may have limited Bantu migration into the far south and southwest?

2.2 Great Zimbabwe

Meeting Great Zimbabwe's king means walking a narrow path between towering stone walls. Reaching out, you can easily touch each wall, but the sky is just a sliver high above you. You feel closed in, fearful, and very, very small. And that's the idea. These imposing stone structures express the enormous power of the king.

MAIN IDEA

Great Zimbabwe was a wealthy trading empire that expressed its power through enormous stone structures.

A SOUTHERN TRADING CITY

One group of the Bantu-speaking migrants that you learned about in the previous lesson settled on a plateau between two rivers in southern Africa. They were the **Shona** (SHOH-nuh), who established **Great Zimbabwe**. The site of their capital was probably chosen for its climate and agricultural potential. But it was also on the route traders used to carry gold to the coast, where Kilwa was located. (See the map in the Chapter Review.) Great Zimbabwe and Kilwa thrived and grew together. Great Zimbabwe's rulers grew rich and powerful by taxing trade goods. They controlled a vast empire with more than 300 towns.

GREAT STONE HOUSES

Great Zimbabwe's rulers expressed their power and wealth through extraordinary stone structures. *Zimbabwe* means "place of stone houses" in Bantu, and over 300 zimbabwes are scattered throughout southern Africa.

The ruins of Great Zimbabwe are still impressive today. The Great Enclosure is an imposing circular wall over 30 feet tall and 15 feet thick. The stones are cut so carefully and wedged in so tightly that they hold together without mortar. Behind the wall lived Great Zimbabwe's elite, separated from the ordinary people.

The massive circular wall in Great Zimbabwe surrounds an area known as the Great Enclosure.

After A.D. 1450, however, Great Zimbabwe declined and was abandoned. The arrival of Portuguese traders on the coast shifted the gold trade away from Great Zimbabwe, which led to a decrease in wealth. Historians also theorize that the city's citizens may have **depleted**, or used up, the local resources, such as soil, water, and wood.

SHONA SCULPTURE

The only surviving sculptures from Great Zimbabwe are stylized birds carved out of soapstone. The bird was adopted as the symbol of present-day Zimbabwe. Modern Shona have revived traditional sculpture by carving pieces influenced by their Great Zimbabwe traditions.

REVIEW & ASSESS

1. **READING CHECK** What was the source of Great Zimbabwe's wealth?
2. **DESCRIBE GEOGRAPHIC INFORMATION** How did the location of Great Zimbabwe affect its role as a trading civilization?
3. **IDENTIFY MAIN IDEAS AND DETAILS** According to the text, what key factors probably led to the decline and abandonment of Great Zimbabwe?

NOROEGA
PONTVS EVXINVS
MARE
MARE
MEDITERRANEVM
IERVSALEM
AFRICA
NILVS
ARABIA
OPRES
TE IOÃ
ÆTIOPIA
PALVDES
TROPI CVS

This Portuguese map from the mid-1500s shows how European countries viewed Africa—as territory to be used. The flags across Africa represent areas claimed by European countries.

2.3 The Kingdom of Kongo

"Great and powerful, full of people, having many vassals [loyal landowners]." This is how Portuguese explorers described the African kingdom of Kongo. They were soon responsible for changing every bit of that description.

MAIN IDEA

Kongo grew rich on the gold trade but would lose everything to the Europeans.

KINGDOM OF THE RAIN FOREST

The kingdom of **Kongo** emerged in the rain forests south of the Congo River around 1400. Like other regions of Africa, Kongo was influenced by migrating Bantu speakers who took advantage of the area's fertile soil. The people also knew how to make weapons and tools from iron and copper. They eventually formed a loose partnership of farming villages. Wise kings known as *manikongo* (MA-nuh-kahng-go) led the people and united the kingdom, which expanded through conquest, marriages, and treaties.

By the 1480s, the *manikongo* ruled more than half a million people in a large and well-ordered state. The *manikongo* grew wealthy through an organized tribute system. In this system, local rulers took **tribute**, or goods and services, from their subjects and passed them on to the king and his royal court. The tribute system actually increased trade and strengthened the economy.

The people of Kongo were not only good farmers, but they were also skilled metalworkers, potters, and weavers. Kongo's kings also sought to improve their understanding of science and the arts. When the Europeans arrived, the *manikongo* saw it as an opportunity to make great leaps in understanding. They were wrong.

THE ARRIVAL OF THE PORTUGUESE

In 1483, the Portuguese arrived in Kongo. An alliance was arranged, and, eight years later, the king converted to Christianity. The king's son, **Afonso I** (uh-FOHN-soo), became *manikongo* in 1509. He was a devout Christian and strongly pro-Portuguese. With Portuguese soldiers and weapons, Afonso extended his kingdom and took many prisoners, who were sold to the Portuguese as slaves.

However, the Portuguese wanted more than Kongo's many natural resources. They wanted cheap labor and began enslaving the people of Kongo. Afonso tried to resist slavery, but despite his best efforts, the slave trade grew. The drain of people, especially the agricultural workforce, greatly weakened the kingdom. For the next four centuries, European and American slavery would have a devastating impact on all of Africa.

REVIEW & ASSESS

1. **READING CHECK** What caused the kingdom of Kongo to weaken and lose its wealth and power to Portugal?
2. **DESCRIBE GEOGRAPHIC INFORMATION** What role did the location of Kongo play in the kingdom's settlement and prosperity?
3. **SEQUENCE EVENTS** Describe the turning points in the interaction between Kongo and Portugal.

CHAPTER 15 Review

VOCABULARY

Use each of the following vocabulary words in a sentence that shows an understanding of the term's meaning.

1. **hub**
   Aksum's prime location made it a hub of international trade.
2. **monsoon**
3. **dhow**
4. **city-state**
5. **migration**
6. **deplete**
7. **lingua franca**

READING STRATEGY

8. **ORGANIZE IDEAS: ANALYZE CAUSE AND EFFECT** If you haven't already, complete your diagram to identify effects of the Bantu migrations across sub-Saharan Africa. Then answer the question.

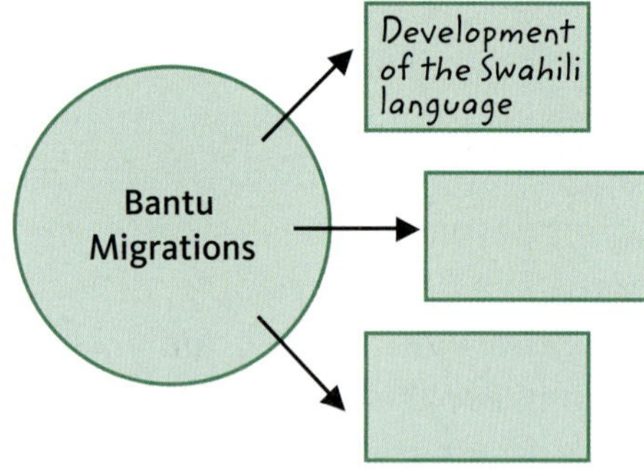
Development of the Swahili language
Bantu Migrations

How did the Bantu migrations affect culture in sub-Saharan Africa?

MAIN IDEAS

Answer the following questions. Support your answers with evidence from the chapter.

9. Why was East Africa a good location for trade? **LESSON 1.1**
10. What helped sailors navigate across the Indian Ocean? **LESSON 1.2**
11. How did Kilwa become an important trading city? **LESSON 1.3**
12. How did the Bantu come to populate much of sub-Saharan Africa? **LESSON 2.1**
13. What was the purpose of Great Zimbabwe's imposing stone structures? **LESSON 2.2**
14. What effect did the arrival of the Portuguese have on the kingdom of Kongo? **LESSON 2.3**

CRITICAL THINKING

Answer the following questions. Support your answers with evidence from the chapter.

15. **IDENTIFY MAIN IDEAS AND DETAILS** What evidence demonstrates that Aksum made many cultural achievements while it was an international trading hub?
16. **ANALYZE CAUSE AND EFFECT** How did advances in sailing make long-distance trade across the Indian Ocean possible?
17. **DRAW CONCLUSIONS** In what way was Swahili the result of the blending of cultures?
18. **MAKE INFERENCES** How did their method of farming influence the Bantu's movement across Africa?
19. **ANALYZE CAUSE AND EFFECT** What impact did Portugal have on the development of the kingdom of Kongo?
20. **YOU DECIDE** What was the greatest cultural achievement of eastern, central, and southern Africa? Support your opinion with evidence from the chapter.

INTERPRET MAPS

Study the map that shows the location of kingdoms and city-states in sub-Saharan Africa. Then answer the questions that follow.

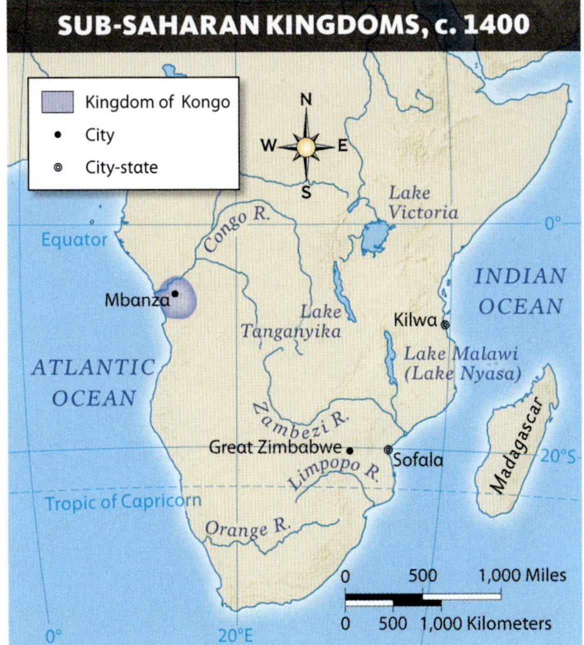
SUB-SAHARAN KINGDOMS, c. 1400
Kingdom of Kongo
City
City-state
N
W
E
S
Lake Victoria
Congo R.
Equator
0°
INDIAN OCEAN
Mbanza
Lake Tanganyika
Kilwa
ATLANTIC OCEAN
Lake Malawi (Lake Nyasa)
Zambezi R.
Madagascar
Great Zimbabwe
Sofala
20°S
Limpopo R.
Tropic of Capricorn
Orange R.
0 500 1,000 Miles
0 500 1,000 Kilometers
0°
20°E

21. What do trading city-states—such as Sofala and Kilwa—have in common?

22. What rivers could traders from Great Zimbabwe have used to trade with Mbanza?

ANALYZE SOURCES

Look at the photograph below of one of the 11 medieval Christian churches of Lalibela, Ethiopia, all of which were carved and chiseled out of rock. Known as House of St. George, this church is isolated from the other 10 churches.

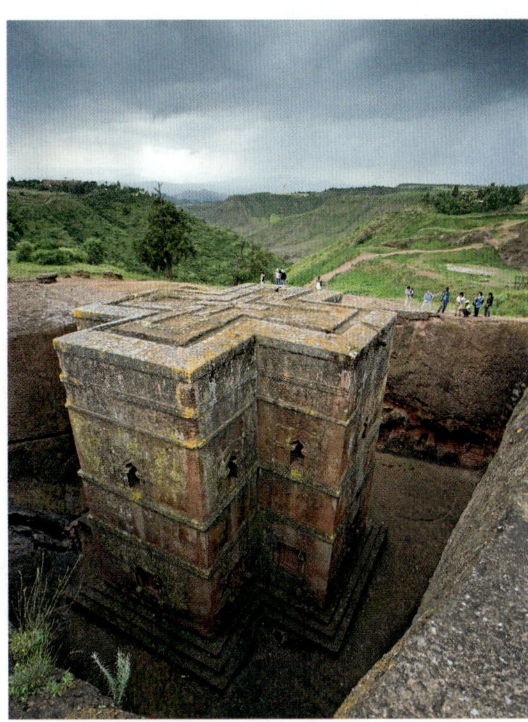

23. What is unique about the construction of this church?

WRITE ABOUT HISTORY

24. INFORMATIVE Write an outline of the causes and effects of the slave trade between the kingdom of Kongo and Portugal.

TIPS

- Take notes from the lesson about the kingdom of Kongo.
- List your topic at the beginning of the outline.
- Create two sections under the topic: one to focus on causes and another to focus on effects.
- List relevant facts, concrete details, and examples under each section of the outline.
- Use at least two vocabulary words from the chapter in your outline.

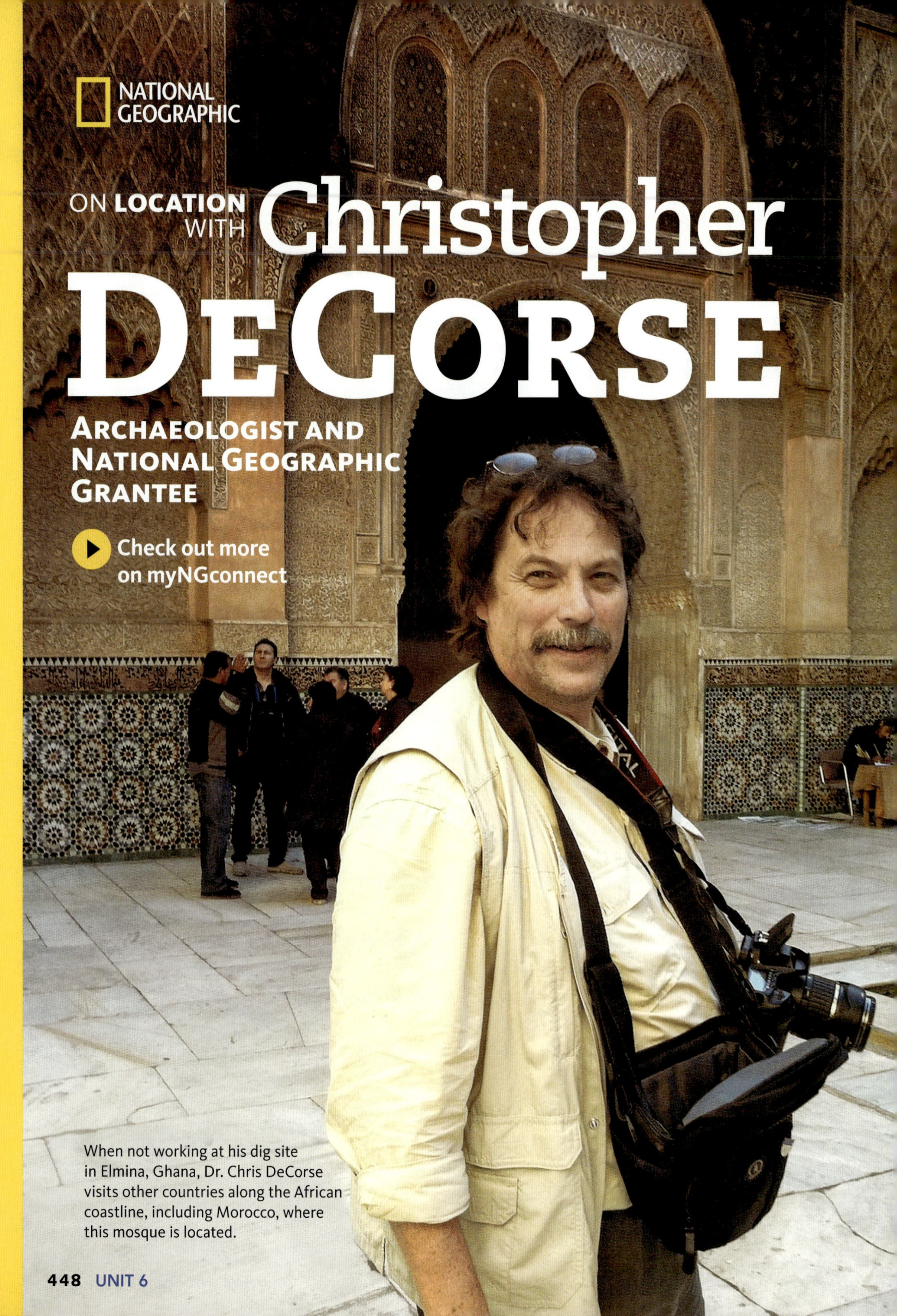
NATIONAL GEOGRAPHIC

ON LOCATION WITH Christopher DeCorse

Archaeologist and National Geographic Grantee

Check out more on myNGconnect

When not working at his dig site in Elmina, Ghana, Dr. Chris DeCorse visits other countries along the African coastline, including Morocco, where this mosque is located.

EARLY INTEREST

Who isn't fascinated by archaeology? Lost civilizations, undisturbed tombs, and golden idols captivate us all! When I was five years old, my grandfather took me to museums and I was entranced by the models and displays. My parents indulged my interest with family trips to archaeological sites, taking the bus in our muddy field clothes with our digging equipment—people thought we were nuts. By sixth grade I had decided to be an archaeologist in Africa.

Chris DeCorse and his team visit Freetown, Sierra Leon, the capital city and a major African port in the Atlantic Ocean.

EXCAVATING ELMINA

Africa is believed to be the place where humankind likely emerged, but many parts of the vast continent remain largely unexplored by archaeologists. Given the lack of early written information about most of sub-Saharan Africa, archaeology is the key to revealing a relatively unknown past. I really want to know what the civilizations and societies of the region were like before the Europeans arrived in the 15th century. I'd also like to know how this area was changed by the Atlantic trade, and especially the slave trade that brought millions of Africans to the Americas. Archaeology holds the answers to these questions.

My research into the African settlement of Elmina in coastal Ghana allows me to examine the interactions and exchanges of Africans and Europeans over the past 500 years. In 1482, the Portuguese built a castle next to an existing African settlement. It was the first and largest European outpost in sub-Saharan Africa, and a center of European trade for the next four centuries. By studying the growth of the African settlement of Elmina from a small village to a town of perhaps 20,000, we can chart the changes in the lives of its inhabitants.

Previous studies had suggested there would be few traces of the early Elmina settlement, but I discovered a remarkably preserved site filled with intact artifacts from the town's occupants. While the vast majority of archaeological artifacts are rarely exciting to the average person, every bit of broken pottery or fragment of iron has a story to tell and forms part of the bigger story of how this West African trading city developed. Elmina was part of a changing landscape that marks the emergence of the modern world.

WHY STUDY HISTORY ?

“*History is part of modern life;* it shaped the world we live in and it continues to influence the present in a myriad of ways. Sites like Elmina are a testament to the exchanges that have shaped the modern world.” —Christopher DeCorse

NATIONAL GEOGRAPHIC

The Telltale Scribes of Timbuktu

BY PETER GWIN

Adapted from "The Telltale Scribes of Timbuktu," by Peter Gwin, in *National Geographic*, January 2011

Abdel Kader Haidara is one of Timbuktu's leading historians. He is also a man obsessed with the written word. Books, he said, are part of his soul, and books, he is convinced, will save Timbuktu. Words form the muscle that hold societies upright, Haidara argues. Consider the Qur'an, the Bible, the American Constitution, but also letters from fathers to sons, last wills, or blessings. Thousands of words infused with emotions fill in the nooks and corners of human life. "Some of those words," he says triumphantly, "can only be found here in Timbuktu."

Haidara's family controls Timbuktu's largest private library. The collection of around 22,000 manuscripts dates back to the 11th century. Most are written in Arabic, but some are in Haidara's native Songhai. Others are written in Tamashek, the Tuareg language.

The mosaic of Timbuktu that emerges from its manuscripts describes a city made wealthy by its position at the intersection of the trans-Saharan caravan routes and the Niger River. As its wealth grew, the city built grand mosques, attracting scholars who formed academies and imported books from throughout the Islamic world. New books arrived, and scribes copied facsimiles for the private libraries of local teachers and their wealthy patrons.

Timbuktu's downfall came when one of its conquerors valued knowledge, too. When the Moroccan army arrived in 1591, its soldiers looted the libraries and sent the books back to the Moroccan ruler. The remaining collections were scattered. Scholars estimate many thousands of manuscripts lie buried in the desert or forgotten in hiding places, slowly yielding to heat, rot, and bugs.

Three new state-of-the-art libraries have been constructed to collect, restore, and digitize Timbuktu's manuscripts. Haidara heads one of these new facilities. When asked about tensions in the region, he points to pages riddled with tiny holes and remarks, "Criminals are the least of my worries. Termites are my biggest enemies."

For more from National Geographic
Check out "Rift in Paradise" on myNGconnect

UNIT INQUIRY: CREATE A LOCAL TRADE EXCHANGE

In this unit, you learned how trade influenced the growth and cultures of African civilizations. Based on your understanding of the text, what natural resources were Africa's most valuable commodities? For what other goods were these commodities traded? How did Africa's valuable resources stimulate trade in the region and throughout the world?

ASSIGNMENT Create a local trade exchange that focuses on selling a commodity that is plentiful in your local area in exchange for goods and/or services that are needed in your local area. Be prepared to present your trade exchange plan to the class and explain how it will benefit the growth of your community.

Plan As you create your local trade exchange, think about some of the trade items that were highly valuable to African trading kingdoms—salt, for example. To begin creating your local trade exchange, identify trade items (goods and services) that are plentiful in your community, as well as goods and services that are needed. You might want to use a graphic organizer to help organize your thoughts. ▶

Produce Use your notes to produce descriptions of the goods and services you will sell and buy through your local trade exchange. Think about the value of these goods and services and why they are important to your community.

Present Choose a creative way to present your local trade exchange to the class. Consider one of these options:

- Create a multimedia presentation to promote the local goods and services for sale on your trade exchange.
- Write an advertisement for a media site that describes your local trade exchange and its importance to the community.
- Draw a map of your community and provide icons in the map key to identify commodities that are traded on the exchange.

Trade Commodities

Goods and Services to Sell	
Goods and Services to Buy	

RAPID REVIEW
UNIT 6

AFRICAN CIVILIZATIONS

TOP TEN

1. Berbers from North Africa established profitable trans-Saharan trade routes with West Africa for gold, salt, and slaves.
2. The Nok people were the first to raise cattle and use iron, and they dominated West Africa.
3. The empires of Ghana and Mali grew powerful by controlling trans-Saharan trade routes.
4. Wealthy civilizations emerged on the East African coast as the monsoon winds helped a sea trade develop in the Indian Ocean.
5. Groups of people in Central Africa migrated east and south, carrying with them their Bantu language and iron making skills.

6-10. **NOW IT'S YOUR TURN** Complete the list with five more things to remember about African civilizations.

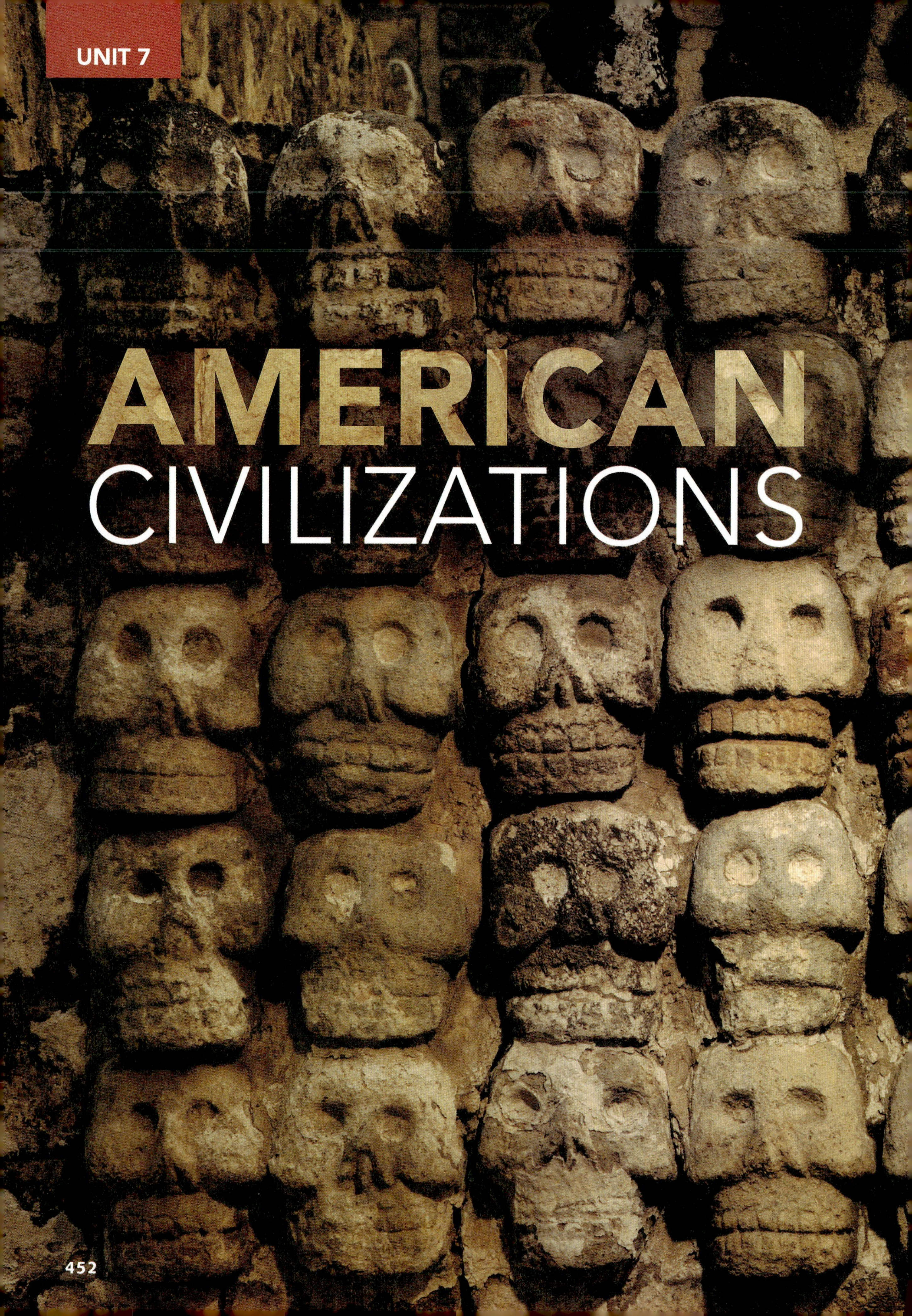

AMERICAN CIVILIZATIONS

NATIONAL GEOGRAPHIC

ON **LOCATION** WITH

Francisco Estrada-Belli

Archaeologist

When I was seven years old, my parents introduced me to one of the most amazing American civilizations in history: the Maya. As an archaeologist, I've rediscovered lost cities in the jungles of Guatemala and have learned much about Maya culture and history. Part of my job is teaching Guatemalan children about the Maya and instilling a sense of pride in their homeland. My name is Francisco Estrada-Belli, and I'm a National Geographic Explorer. Join me in exploring the many civilizations of the Americas.

< **CRITICAL VIEWING** The Tzompantli, or "Wall of Skulls," is located at the Maya site of Chichén Itzá on the Yucatán Peninsula. What does this carving tell you about the Maya culture?

UNIT 7
TIME LINE OF WORLD EVENTS

American Civilizations

1200 B.C.
The Olmec civilization begins in Mesoamerica.

500 B.C.
The Zapotec build Monte Albán.

A.D. 250
The Maya Classic Period begins.
(carving on a Maya stele)

900
The ancient Pueblo build Pueblo Bonito.

1200 B.C.

A.D. 500

1045 B.C.
ASIA
Zhou dynasty begins 800-year rule in China.

500 B.C.
ASIA
Buddhism emerges in India. *(Indian Buddha sculpture)*

476
EUROPE
The Western Roman Empire falls.

The World

COMPARE TIME LINES

How long after the Olmec arose did the Zhou dynasty begin in China?

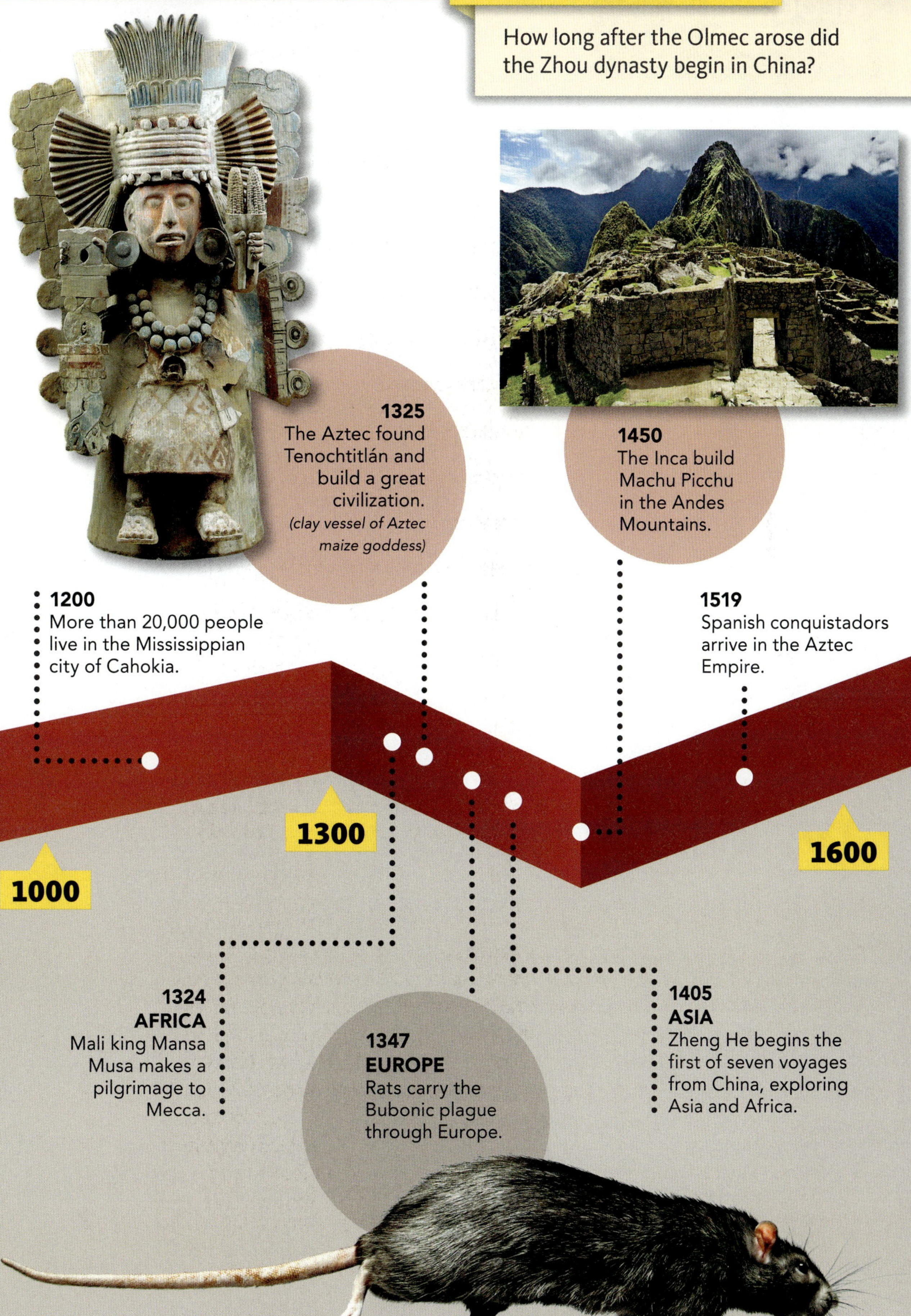

1000
1300
1600

1200
More than 20,000 people live in the Mississippian city of Cahokia.

1325
The Aztec found Tenochtitlán and build a great civilization.
(clay vessel of Aztec maize goddess)

1450
The Inca build Machu Picchu in the Andes Mountains.

1519
Spanish conquistadors arrive in the Aztec Empire.

1324
AFRICA
Mali king Mansa Musa makes a pilgrimage to Mecca.

1347
EUROPE
Rats carry the Bubonic plague through Europe.

1405
ASIA
Zheng He begins the first of seven voyages from China, exploring Asia and Africa.

Early North American Civilizations, c. 1400
Arctic & Subarctic
California
Eastern Woodlands
Great Basin
Great Plains
Northwest Coast
Plateau area
Southwest
Southeast
NORTH AMERICA
Gulf of Alaska
Hudson Bay
ROCKY MOUNTAINS
Great Lakes
Appalachian Mountains
Colorado R.
Mississippi R.
Rio Grande
see inset
Gulf of Mexico
PACIFIC OCEAN
ATLANTIC OCEAN
MESOAMERICA
Caribbean Sea
see inset
Amazon R.
SOUTH AMERICA
ANDES
PACIFIC OCEAN
Paraná R.
ATLANTIC OCEAN

AMERICAN CIVILIZATIONS

900 B.C.–A.D. 1532

The first civilizations in the Americas arose in Mesoamerica. From the Olmec to the Aztec, these civilizations spanned thousands of years and left their imprint on the region and the world. Early South American civilizations developed in the Andes Mountains around the time of the Maya. They adapted to the challenges of their rugged, dry environment and built great centers of power. Hundreds of different civilizations populated North America. Their civilizations did not develop in the same way as those in other parts of the Americas, but they were just as sophisticated.

What South American civilization thrived during the time of the Aztec?

EARLY MESOAMERICAN CIVILIZATIONS
Gulf of Mexico
YUCATÁN PENINSULA
Caribbean Sea
PACIFIC OCEAN
Early Mesoamerican Civilizations
Olmec, c. 900 B.C.
Zapotec, c. 500 B.C.
Maya, c. A.D. 900
Aztec, c. A.D. 1519

EARLY SOUTH AMERICAN CIVILIZATIONS
AMAZON
BASIN
Amazon R.
Marañón R.
Ucayali R.
Madre de Dios R.
Cuzco
Lake Titicaca
ANDES
PACIFIC OCEAN
Early South American Civilizations
Moche, c. A.D. 700
Nazca, c. A.D. 600
Wari, c. A.D. 1000
Sican, c. A.D. 1400
Inca, c. A.D. 1532

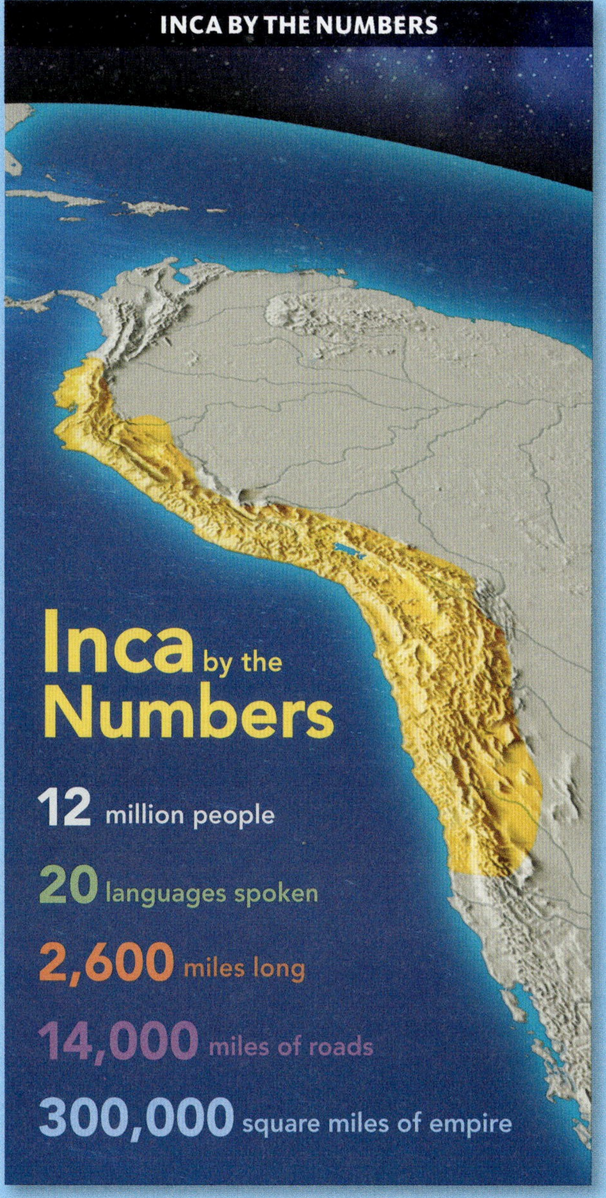
INCA BY THE NUMBERS
Inca by the Numbers
12 million people
20 languages spoken
2,600 miles long
14,000 miles of roads
300,000 square miles of empire

CHAPTER

16 MESOAMERICA

1200 B.C. – A.D. 1521

SECTION 1
THE OLMEC AND THE ZAPOTEC

KEY VOCABULARY
cacao
highland
lowland
maize
mother culture
slash-and-burn agriculture
terrace

NAMES & PLACES
Mesoamerica
Monte Albán
Olmec
Yucatán Peninsula
Zapotec

SECTION 2
THE MAYA

KEY VOCABULARY
codex
creation story
glyph

NAMES & PLACES
El Mirador
Maya
Popol Vuh

SECTION 3
THE AZTEC

KEY VOCABULARY
chinampa
communal
conquistador
noble
serf

NAMES & PLACES
Hernán Cortés
Moctezuma II
Templo Mayor
Tenochtitlán
Teotihuacán

READING STRATEGY

IDENTIFY MAIN IDEAS AND DETAILS

When you identify key topics in a text, you need to support them with details from the text. As you read the chapter, use diagrams like this one to identify details about each Mesoamerican civilization.

Main-Idea Diagram

Main Idea: Olmec Civilization
Detail:
Detail:
Detail:
Detail:
Detail:

The Temple of the Great Jaguar at Tikal, Guatemala, served as a tomb for a Maya ruler. Its steep staircase is divided into nine levels and may represent the nine levels of the underworld in Maya religious belief.

1.1 The Geography of Mesoamerica

You walk among the ruins, gazing at the remains of temple complexes, carved stone sculptures, and towering pyramids. Are you visiting a city that thrived during the time of ancient Egypt? No. You're in the middle of a jungle in a region of North America known as Mesoamerica.

MAIN IDEA

Geographic factors greatly influenced the development of civilizations in Mesoamerica.

HIGHLANDS AND LOWLANDS

Thousands of years ago, advanced civilizations arose in **Mesoamerica**, which stretches from southern Mexico into part of Central America. The region's climate and fertile land helped the civilizations thrive.

Mesoamerica's landscape is divided into two main geographic areas: **highlands**, or land high above the sea, and **lowlands**, or land that is low and level. The highlands lie between the mountains of the Sierra Madre, a mountain system in Mexico, and consist of fairly flat and fertile land. This land was good for agriculture, but it also posed some challenges for its early residents. They were rocked from time to time by volcanic eruptions and powerful earthquakes. The lowlands are less active. They lie along the coast of the Gulf of Mexico. They are also found in the jungles of the **Yucatán** (you-kuh-TAN) **Peninsula**, which is located between the Gulf of Mexico and the Caribbean Sea.

If you hiked from the lowlands to the highlands, you would experience a wide variety of climates, from tropical rain forests to very cold, dry zones in the higher mountains. In general, the climate in the highlands is cooler and drier than that in the lowlands, where it can rain more than 100 inches a year. The lowlands are also crisscrossed by many rivers. Some of these rivers flood during heavy seasonal rains and wash fertile silt onto their floodplains.

AGRICULTURE

Early Mesoamerican farmers learned what crops would grow well in the different climates of the highlands and lowlands. In the drier highland areas, the main crops included **maize** (also known as corn), squash, and beans. These three crops are often called the Three Sisters because they benefit from being planted close together. The beans grow up the maize stalks, while the squash spreads over the ground, preventing the growth of weeds. Farmers in the lowlands grew these three crops as well as palm, avocado, and **cacao** (kuh-COW) trees. Cacao beans were used to make chocolate. Sometimes the beans were even used as money.

Mesoamerica's farmers developed different agricultural practices in the region's varied landscapes. In drier areas, farmers redirected the course of streams to irrigate their fields. In the dense lowland jungles, farmers cleared fields through a technique known as **slash-and-burn agriculture**, shown on the opposite page. These agricultural techniques helped ancient cultures produce food surpluses and allowed people to do jobs other than farming. As a result, civilizations began to arise in Mesoamerica more than 3,000 years ago—first the Olmec and later the Zapotec.

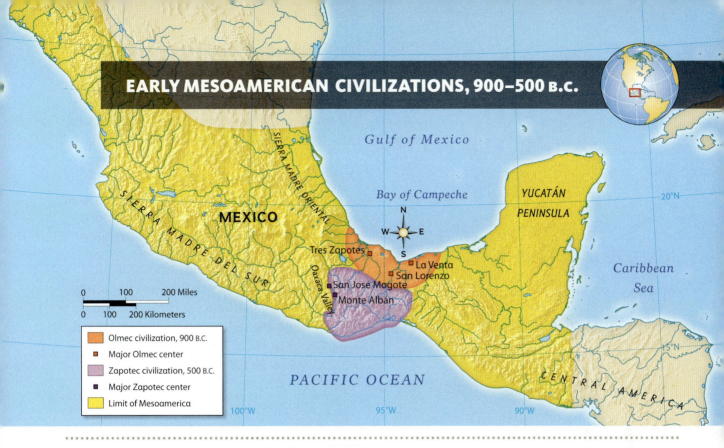

EARLY MESOAMERICAN CIVILIZATIONS, 900–500 B.C.

Gulf of Mexico
Bay of Campeche
YUCATÁN PENINSULA
MEXICO
SIERRA MADRE ORIENTAL
SIERRA MADRE DEL SUR
Tres Zapotes
La Venta
San Lorenzo
San José Mogote
Monte Albán
Oaxaca Valley
Caribbean Sea
PACIFIC OCEAN
CENTRAL AMERICA
20°N
15°N
100°W
95°W
90°W
N S E W
0 100 200 Miles
0 100 200 Kilometers

- Olmec civilization, 900 B.C.
- Major Olmec center
- Zapotec civilization, 500 B.C.
- Major Zapotec center
- Limit of Mesoamerica

SLASH-AND-BURN AGRICULTURE

1 Slash
Wooded areas and jungles are too thick to plant crops. Farmers slash, or cut down, trees.

2 Burn
Fallen trees and leaves are burned to clear the land. Ash produced by the fires is used as fertilizer.

3 Fertilize and Plant
Cleared land is fertilized with ash. Farmers plant crops such as maize and squash.

4 Migrate
Farmers move on to new locations after soil on cleared land becomes less productive.

REVIEW & ASSESS

1. **READING CHECK** What geographic factors influenced the development of civilizations in Mesoamerica?
2. **INTERPRET MAPS** Why do you think the Olmec and Zapotec civilizations developed along coastal areas?
3. **COMPARE AND CONTRAST** How did agricultural techniques differ in Mesoamerica's highlands and lowlands?

1.2

Olmec Culture

After a long search, the foreman has finally found the right rock. It's huge and heavy. He directs his men to begin their work. Their task: to haul the rock 50 miles through the jungle to the city where an artist will carve it into a sculpture. Their challenge: to move the rock without using a wheeled cart or animals. Welcome to the world of the Olmec.

MAIN IDEA

The Olmec civilization that arose in Mesoamerica was one of the region's earliest civilizations and influenced later cultures.

JAGUAR GOD

The Olmec worshipped many gods, but one of the most important was the jaguar god. When Olmec priests visited the spirit world, the priests believed they transformed into powerful jaguars.

OLMEC CITIES

The **Olmec** (AHL-mehk) culture began along Mexico's Gulf Coast around 1200 B.C. The development of this culture led to the birth of Mesoamerica's first civilization.

Like the ancient civilizations of Mesopotamia, Egypt, India, and China, the Olmec emerged on the floodplains of rivers. Heavy rains caused these rivers to flood and deposit fertile silt on their plains. The rich soil allowed farmers to grow abundant crops. In time, the culture's economy expanded and cities, including San Lorenzo, La Venta, and Tres Zapotes, began to develop. (See the map in Lesson 1.1.)

Olmec cities contained pyramids and temples built on earthen mounds. The Olmec also built courts where athletes played a game that was a sort of combination of modern soccer and basketball. You will learn more about this game later in the chapter.

Archaeologists have also found extraordinary works of art in Olmec cities. Chief among these are the huge stone heads the Olmec carved out of rock. The heads stand as tall as 10 feet and can weigh up to 20 tons. They are believed to represent different Olmec rulers.

DAILY LIFE AND LEGACY

Workers, including those who hauled the rocks for the stone sculptures, and farmers made up most of Olmec society. They were at the bottom of the civilization's class structure. Rulers were at the top, followed by priests, merchants, and artists. The farmers and workers lived in simple houses made of wood or mud. The upper classes lived in more elaborate stone structures and wore fine clothes and precious jewelry.

Archaeologists are not sure why, but around 400 B.C., the Olmec civilization disappeared. However, elements of the civilization's legacy can be seen in later civilizations. The Olmec had established an extensive trade network. In addition to the exchange of goods, the trade routes carried Olmec culture throughout Mesoamerica. As new civilizations arose, their people were influenced by Olmec art and religious practices. As a result, many archaeologists consider the Olmec to be the **mother culture** of Mesoamerica.

Critical Viewing The rock this head was carved out of may have been rolled onto a log raft and floated downriver. Why might Olmec laborers have chosen to use this method to move the head?

REVIEW & ASSESS

1. **READING CHECK** What geographic features played a key role in the development of Olmec civilization?
2. **INTERPRET VISUALS** What does the stone head suggest about the power and authority of Olmec rulers?
3. **DRAW CONCLUSIONS** What conclusions can you draw about daily life for most of the Olmec people?

The Zapotec and Mixtec Civilization, Diego Rivera, 1945

Critical Viewing This mural by Mexican artist Diego Rivera shows Zapotec artists at work. What details in the mural convey class differences in the society?

1.3 The Zapotec and Monte Albán

As the Olmec declined, the Zapotec people were developing an advanced society to the southwest. Although their culture reflected Olmec influence, the Zapotec developed their own distinct and powerful civilization. They became a leading player in Mesoamerica.

MAIN IDEA

The Zapotec established a civilization and controlled the Oaxaca Valley for more than 1,000 years.

PEOPLE OF THE VALLEY

The **Zapotec** people would build one of the first major cities in Mesoamerica, but their beginnings were humble. They developed their society in the Oaxaca (wuh-HAH-kah) Valley, a large, open area where three smaller valleys meet. (See the map in Lesson 1.1.) This fertile area, with its river, mild climate, and abundant rainfall, proved excellent for growing crops, especially maize.

For centuries, the Zapotec lived in farming villages located throughout the Oaxaca Valley. Then, around 1300 B.C., a settlement called San José Mogote (san ho-ZAY moh-GOH-tay) emerged as the Zapotec center of power. Leaders built temples there and had artists decorate them with huge sculptures. In time, nearly half of the Zapotec people lived in San José Mogote.

URBAN CENTER

Around 500 B.C., the center of power shifted when the Zapotec built a city known now as **Monte Albán** (MAHN-tay ahl-BAHN) high atop a mountain. The site overlooked the Oaxaca Valley. Its location helped the Zapotec defend themselves against their enemies. Monte Albán must have been a spectacular sight. The city's rulers flattened the top of the mountain and built great plazas on it filled with pyramids, palaces, and even an astronomical observatory.

Monte Albán became the center of the Zapotec civilization. There, the Zapotec built magnificent tombs in which they buried the bodies of wealthy people wearing their gold jewelry. The Zapotec believed the deceased would carry the jewelry into the afterlife. Artificial **terraces**, or stepped platforms built into the mountainside, provided additional area for building and agriculture.

Around A.D. 750, Monte Albán's power began to weaken. By 900, the city had disappeared. Economic difficulties may have caused the decline, but no one knows for sure. Like the fall of the Olmec, the decline of the Zapotec civilization remains a mystery.

REVIEW & ASSESS

1. **READING CHECK** What geographic features of the Oaxaca Valley encouraged the development of the Zapotec civilization?
2. **MAKE INFERENCES** How do you think the location of Monte Albán helped the Zapotec defend themselves from their enemies?
3. **DETERMINE WORD MEANINGS** What does *deceased* mean in the phrase, "the deceased would carry the jewelry into the afterlife"?

2.1 Maya Social Structure

Can people be made of corn? According to Maya tradition, they can. But it took the Maya gods a while to figure out how to do it. At first, they made people out of things like mud and wood, but these creatures couldn't speak. Finally, the gods mixed their blood with maize flour. The result? Walking, talking human beings. No wonder the early Maya called themselves "the people of the maize."

MAIN IDEA

Maya society was structured according to a class system, and religion shaped daily life.

CLASS SYSTEM

The **Maya** emerged around the same time as the Zapotec. Their culture began to develop to the east of the Zapotec in areas of present-day southern Mexico and Central America around 1500 B.C. These areas included lowlands in the north, highlands in the south, the forests of the Yucatán Peninsula, and the tropical jungles of Mexico and Guatemala.

Like Olmec farmers, Maya farmers developed successful agricultural practices. They produced surpluses of crops, including beans, chili peppers, cacao beans, and, of course, maize, which the Maya considered sacred. These surpluses allowed some people to become priests, merchants, and craftspeople and some villages to gain great wealth. Wealthier villages with religious ceremonial centers arose around 500 B.C. In time, these villages grew into cities.

The development of Maya cities produced a class system with four main classes. At the top was the king, who performed religious ceremonies and was believed to have descended from the gods. Next came priests and warriors. The priests decided when farmers could plant and when people could marry. They also conducted important religious rituals and ceremonies. Warriors were well respected and well trained.

Merchants and craftspeople followed these upper classes. Craftspeople made articles out of pottery and designed buildings and temples. The merchants sold and traded goods—often with buyers in other Maya cities. Finally, farmers—who made up the majority of the population—and slaves were at the bottom of the heap. Most of the slaves were prisoners of war. They were given the worst jobs and were often killed when their masters died.

DAILY LIFE

Class determined where people lived and how they dressed. People who belonged to the upper classes lived in stone buildings and wore colorfully decorated clothes and jewelry. Farmers wore plain clothes and lived in mud huts.

While the wealthy enjoyed a comfortable lifestyle, farmers worked hard in the heat to grow their crops. On hillsides they carved out terraces on which to grow their maize, cacao beans, and chili peppers. In drier areas they dug channels that carried river water to their fields. In addition to doing their own work, sometimes farmers had to tend the king's fields and build monuments and temples in his cities.

MAYA MAIZE GOD

The maize god was one of the most important Maya gods. The god often appeared as a handsome young man with hair made of maize silk. The god represented the cycle of life (birth, death, rebirth) as well as the cycle of maize (planting, harvesting, replanting).

MAYA CIVILIZATION, A.D. 250–900

Eventually the Maya learned how to track seasonal changes. This knowledge helped them predict the best time to plant and harvest their crops. You will learn more about how the Maya measured time later in the chapter.

Above all, however, the farmers looked to their gods to control the weather and increase their harvests. Religion was central to everyone's lives, and the Maya worshipped many gods, including the gods of fire, sun, war, rain, and maize. (You can learn more about the importance of the maize god in the feature above.) All of these gods were thought to influence every aspect of the people's lives—in both good and bad ways.

To please the gods, the Maya made frequent offerings of food, animals, plants, and precious objects. As you have already learned, the Maya believed that the gods had given their blood to create people. In return, the Maya sometimes offered their own blood or made human sacrifices to honor the gods. Just as maize nourished people, the Maya believed that blood nourished the gods. Rather than sacrifice one of their own, however, the Maya often sacrificed a member of the lowest class in their society: a slave.

REVIEW & ASSESS

1. **READING CHECK** What were the four main classes of early Maya society?
2. **INTERPRET MAPS** On what geographic landform were many of the major Maya cities located?
3. **COMPARE AND CONTRAST** How did the daily life of farmers differ from that of people belonging to the wealthier classes?

2.2

Maya Cities

In the 1800s, explorers battled mosquitoes, illness, and thick jungle growth in their search for the ruined remains of the Maya civilization. Their efforts paid off. When they came upon the half-buried monuments in the ancient Maya city of Copán, one of the explorers—John Lloyd Stephens—was so fascinated by what he saw that he purchased the site on the spot.

MAIN IDEA

The Maya built sophisticated cities that contained impressive structures and artwork.

CLASSIC PERIOD

Many of the great Maya cities lay hidden beneath the jungle growth for centuries. One of the earliest of these cities was **El Mirador**, which has been called the "cradle of the Maya civilization." (See the map in Lesson 2.1.) The city flourished from about 300 B.C. to A.D. 150 and was home to as many as 200,000 people. Most Maya cities, however, developed during the Classic Period, which lasted between A.D. 250 and 900. These cities included Copán (koh-PAHN), Tikal (tee-KAHL), Chichén Itzá (chee-CHEHN ee-TSAH), and Palenque (pah-LEHNG-keh). Although each was an independent city-state ruled by a king, trade linked the city-states. Merchants from the cities exchanged goods such as salt and jade jewelry and often paid for them with cacao beans.

Most Maya cities followed a similar layout. A large plaza in the center of the city served as both a public gathering place and market. Each city also contained a palace for the king, administrative buildings, temples, and stepped pyramids. The pyramids rose hundreds of feet in the air and were lined with steep staircases. Many of the pyramids featured platforms at the top. Priests conducted ceremonies on the platforms so that the entire population could witness them.

The Maya built temples on the top of some of the pyramids. A huge ball court was constructed at the foot of at least one of these pyramids in each city to allow athletes to play the sacred Mesoamerican ball game. The Maya played this game, which began with the Olmec, to honor their gods. The illustration on the opposite page shows Maya athletes in action on the court.

CULTURE AND ART

Like the ball game, many other aspects of Maya culture and art were linked to religion. Artists made sculptures that honored and brought to life the various Maya gods. They also carved stone slabs called stelae to honor their kings. Artists carved a king's likeness on the slab and recorded his actions on it as well—actually setting his story in stone.

All of these stories were probably passed down orally from generation to generation. This oral tradition continued long after the great Maya civilization had come to an end. It may have been weakened by war, food shortages, or overcrowding. For whatever reason, by A.D. 900, the Maya had abandoned many of their cities. When Spanish conquerors arrived in the 1500s, only weakened city-states had been left behind—a shadow of their former glory.

MESOAMERICAN BALL GAME

The game the Maya and other Mesoamerican peoples played on a court like this one was much more than a game. It was often a matter of life and death. The captain of the losing Maya team probably climbed the temple steps to be sacrificed to the gods.

Players weren't allowed to touch the ball with their hands. They could only bounce the ball off their knees, hips, and elbows.

The solid ball was hard enough to break bones, so the players wore some heavy padding.

The goal of the game was to launch the ball through a stone ring. Since this wasn't easy, a game could go on for days.

REVIEW & ASSESS

1. **READING CHECK** What was the layout of most of the great Maya cities?

2. **INTEGRATE VISUALS** Based on the illustration and what you have learned about the Mesoamerican ball game, what qualities were probably necessary to play the game?

3. **MAKE INFERENCES** How do you think the Maya reacted as they witnessed a religious ceremony performed at the top of a towering pyramid?

2.3 NATIONAL GEOGRAPHIC EXPLORER WILLIAM SATURNO

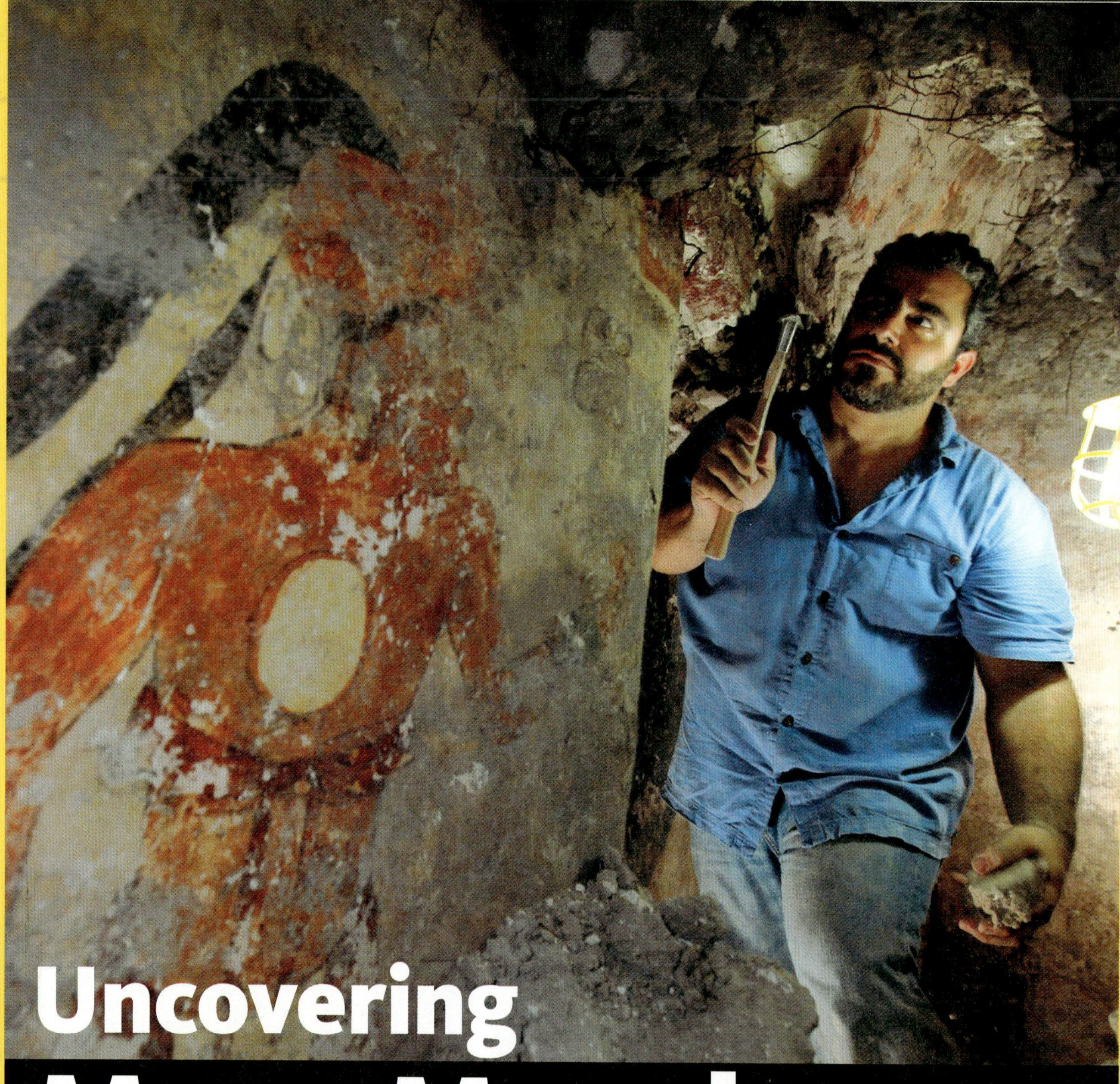

Uncovering Maya Murals

Sometimes you're just lucky. Ask **William Saturno**. He had spent three days—instead of the three hours he thought the trip would take—trudging through the jungles of Guatemala looking for carved Maya monuments. During the search, he and his team had been lost and near death. When a pyramid appeared in the midst of the dense undergrowth, Saturno ducked inside it to escape the terrible heat. He turned around to find a stunning Maya mural of the maize god looking right back at him. Now Saturno's lucky find is rewriting Maya history.

^ William Saturno is dedicated to preserving and interpreting the remains of the early Maya. In this photo, he removes debris from a mural he uncovered at the Maya site of Xultún.

MAIN IDEA

Archaeologist William Saturno's discoveries have challenged ideas about the early Maya and provided insight into their way of thinking.

A LUCKY FIND

National Geographic Explorer William Saturno has spent his life studying the Maya and searching out the civilization's secrets. His greatest discovery occurred in 2001, when he found the mural at a site he later named San Bartolo.

Saturno spent several years excavating the wall painting, which represented the Maya creation story in graceful and sophisticated detail. However, when Saturno dated the work of art, he found that it had been created around 100 B.C.—more than 300 years before the Maya Classic Period had even begun. As Saturno says, "Clearly Maya painting had achieved glory centuries before the great works of the Classic Maya."

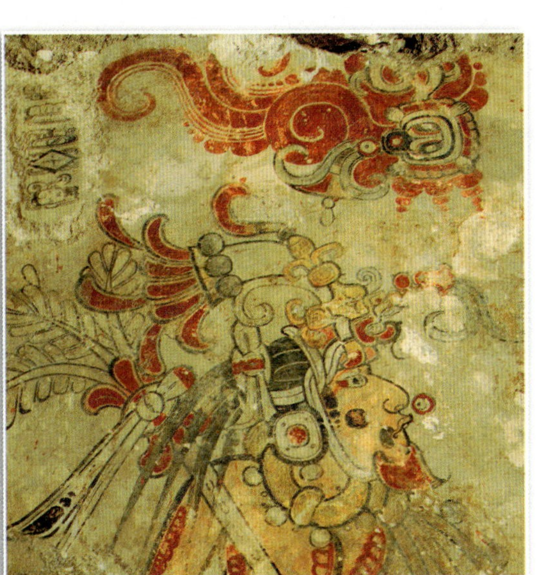

Portrait of a scholar in the San Bartolo mural

The far end of the mural revealed another surprise—the portrait of a king. "Some scholars thought that at this early stage in Maya history, the Preclassic, city-states had not yet evolved into full-fledged monarchies, with all the trappings seen later," explains Saturno. "But here was a king, named and titled, receiving his crown. In short, this one chamber upended much of what we thought we knew about the early Maya."

ROOM OF WONDER

About ten years later and just five miles from San Bartolo, Saturno got lucky again. He was digging under a mound in the Maya site of Xultún (shool-tuhn) when a student assistant claimed he'd found traces of paint on a wall. "I was curious," Saturno says. "So I excavated to the back wall, and I saw a beautiful portrait of a king. There he was in Technicolor, with blue feathers."

After more painstaking work, Saturno uncovered an entire room with paintings of other figures and a wall covered with columns of numbers. He thinks that mathematicians had been using the walls like a whiteboard to see whether the movements of the moon and planets matched the dates they had calculated. The mural and numbers dated back to about A.D. 750, around the time Xultún was beginning to decline.

According to Saturno, the Maya knew the collapse of their city had begun. Still, as he says, "They wanted to tie events in their king's life to larger cosmic cycles. They wanted to show that the king would be okay and that nothing would change. We keep looking for endings. It's an entirely different mind-set. I would never have identified this nondescript [uninteresting] mound as special. But this discovery implies that special things are everywhere."

REVIEW & ASSESS

1. **READING CHECK** Why are William Saturno's discoveries so remarkable?
2. **DRAW CONCLUSIONS** Saturno emphasizes the luck he's had in his explorations, but what other qualities must he possess to carry out his work?
3. **ANALYZE LANGUAGE USE** Saturno says that the Maya had "an entirely different mind-set." What do you think he is suggesting about how the Maya viewed the world?

2.4 Legacy of the Maya

In 2012, the prediction went viral: On December 21, the world was going to end. The prediction was based on the Maya calendar, which some people claimed would end on that day. But the date simply marked the completion of a 5,125-year cycle. The Maya had calculated that a new cycle would begin on the 22nd.

MAIN IDEA

Important advances in mathematics, astronomy, and writing allowed the Maya to create their calendar.

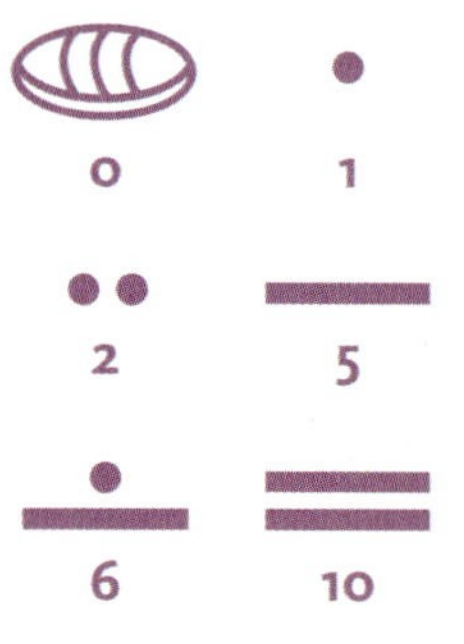

0
1
2
5
6
10

MAYA NUMBERS The Maya represented numbers using only three symbols: a shell for zero, a dot for one, and a bar for five. A few of the numbers are shown above. Try using the symbols to create some simple subtraction problems.

MATH AND ASTRONOMY

The Maya were superb mathematicians. Like the people of ancient India, they developed the concept of zero. They also developed a sophisticated number system using positions to show place value and to calculate sums up to the hundreds of millions.

Such calculations were used to record astronomical observations as well. Maya astronomers observed the sun, moon, planets, and stars and were able to predict their movements with great accuracy—all without the aid of any instruments. Instead, they studied the sky from temples and observatories. Astronomers used their observations to calculate the best times for planting and harvesting crops and for religious celebrations.

These astronomical observations and calculations were used to develop an elaborate 365-day calendar that was nearly as accurate as our own. Remember the room that William Saturno uncovered in Xultún? The mathematical calculations on its walls were probably used to work out dates in the calendar.

WRITING SYSTEM AND BOOKS

Archaeologists gained a better understanding of the Maya people's scientific achievements and culture

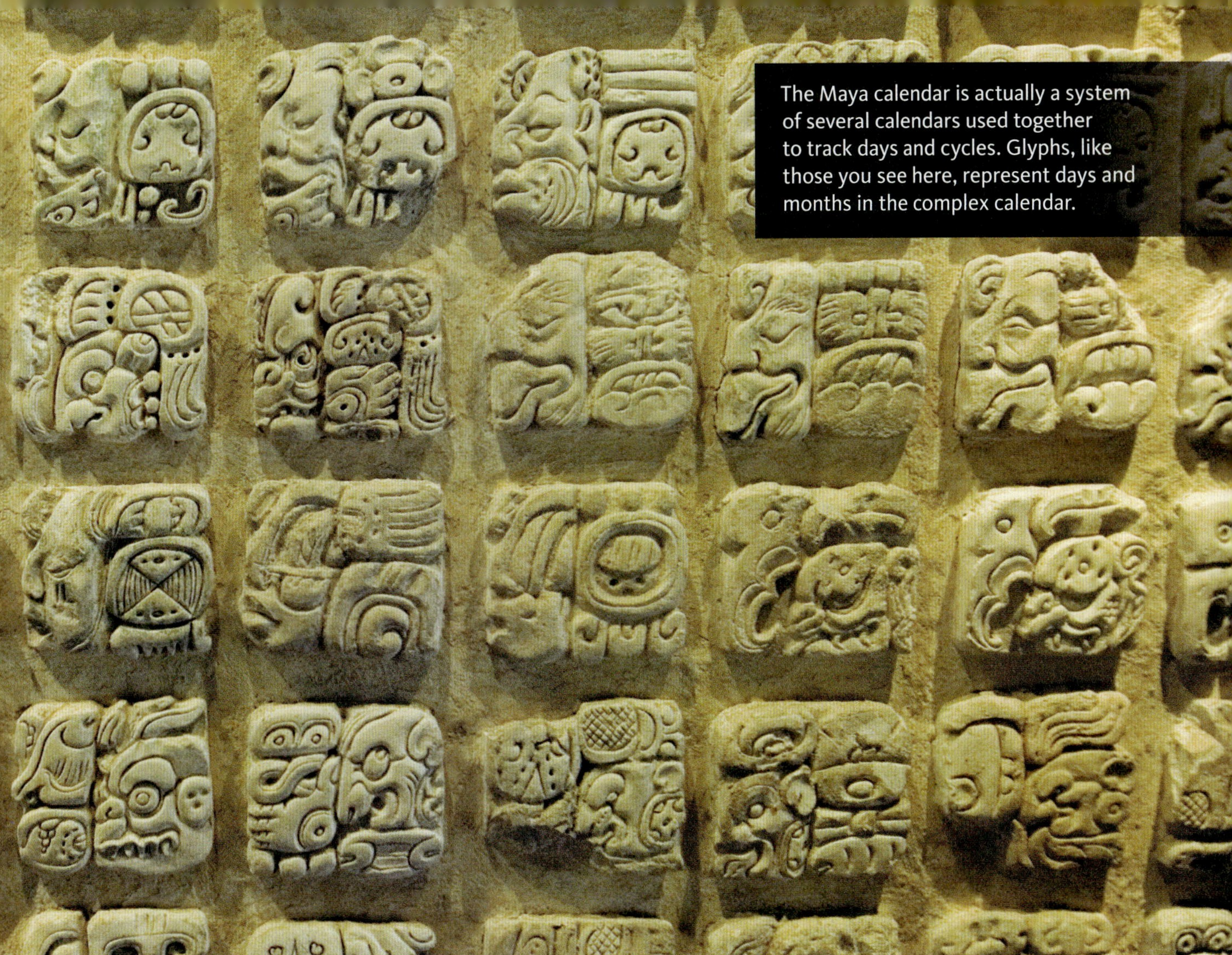

The Maya calendar is actually a system of several calendars used together to track days and cycles. Glyphs, like those you see here, represent days and months in the complex calendar.

once they began to crack the code of their writing system. The Maya used symbolic pictures called **glyphs** (glihfs) to represent words, syllables, and sounds that could be combined into complex sentences.

The Maya carved glyphs into their monuments, stelae, and tombs. Maya writers, called scribes, also used them to record their people's history in a folded book made of tree-bark paper called a **codex**. The Spanish conquerors destroyed most of the codices in the 1500s. However, after the Spanish arrived, the Maya wrote other books in which they recorded Maya history and culture. The most famous of these books is called the ***Popol Vuh***, which recounts the Maya creation story.

As you've already learned, the Maya civilization had greatly declined by A.D. 900. However, Maya people today still keep their culture alive. Many of them speak the Maya languages and tell their ancestors' stories. They are a living legacy of the Maya civilization.

REVIEW & ASSESS

1. **READING CHECK** What important mathematical ideas did the Maya develop?
2. **IDENTIFY MAIN IDEAS AND DETAILS** According to the text, why did Maya astronomers study the sun, moon, planets, and stars?
3. **ANALYZE CAUSE AND EFFECT** What breakthrough helped archaeologists gain a better understanding of Maya history and culture?

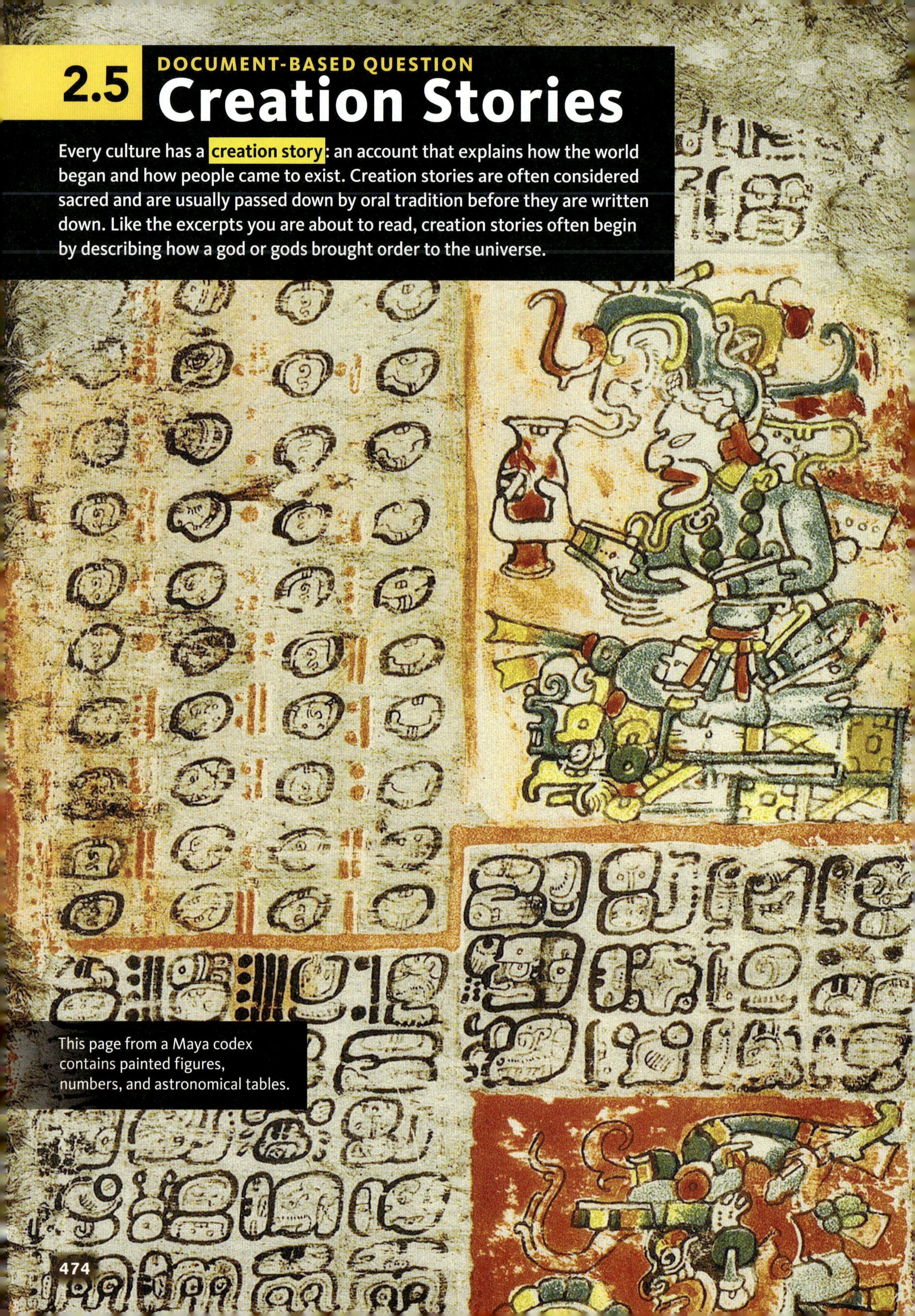

2.5 DOCUMENT-BASED QUESTION

Creation Stories

Every culture has a **creation story**: an account that explains how the world began and how people came to exist. Creation stories are often considered sacred and are usually passed down by oral tradition before they are written down. Like the excerpts you are about to read, creation stories often begin by describing how a god or gods brought order to the universe.

This page from a Maya codex contains painted figures, numbers, and astronomical tables.

DOCUMENT ONE

Primary Source: Sacred Text

from the *Popol Vuh*, translated by Dennis Tedlock

Spanish conquerors destroyed much of Maya culture in the 1500s. To preserve their sacred stories for future generations, Maya scribes wrote them down in the *Popol Vuh*. In this passage, two Maya gods form Earth from a world that contains only the sea.

CONSTRUCTED RESPONSE According to this passage, how did the Maya gods form Earth?

"Let it be this way, think about it: this water should be removed, emptied out for the formation of the earth's own plate and platform . . ." they said. And then the earth arose because of them, it was simply their word that brought it forth. For the forming of the earth they said, "Earth." It arose suddenly, just like a cloud, like a mist, now forming, unfolding.

DOCUMENT TWO

Primary Source: Sacred Text

from the Book of Genesis

Genesis is the first book of the Hebrew Bible, a collection of sacred Jewish texts. It is also the first book of the Old Testament in the Christian Bible. Followers of both religions believe in a single God. In this passage from Genesis, which means "the origin, or beginning," God creates night and day.

CONSTRUCTED RESPONSE In this excerpt, what was the world like before God brought light to the earth?

When God began to create heaven and earth—the earth being unformed and void [empty]. . .—God said, "Let there be light"; and there was light. God saw that the light was good, and God separated the light from the darkness. God called the light Day, and the darkness He called Night. And there was evening and there was morning, a first day.

DOCUMENT THREE

Primary Source: Myth

from *Pan Gu Creates Heaven and Earth*, translated by Jan and Yvonne Walls

Pan Gu is a god in an ancient Chinese creation story that has been told and passed down for more than 2,000 years. According to the story, Pan Gu created heaven and earth. In this passage, Pan Gu bursts from a disordered universe that is shaped like an egg.

CONSTRUCTED RESPONSE In this myth, what elements formed heaven and what elements formed the earth?

Pan Gu, an enormous giant, was being nurtured [cared for] in the dark chaos of that egg. . . . Then one day he woke and stretched himself, shattering the egg-shaped chaos into pieces. The pure lighter elements gradually rose up to become heaven and the impure heavier parts slowly sank down to form the earth.

SYNTHESIZE & WRITE

1. **REVIEW** Review what you have learned about the creation stories and religious beliefs of early civilizations.
2. **RECALL** On your own paper, write down the main idea expressed in each document.
3. **CONSTRUCT** Write a topic sentence that answers this question: What are some common characteristics of creation stories?
4. **WRITE** Using evidence from the documents, write a paragraph to support your answer in Step 3.

3.1 Tenochtitlán: An Aztec City

Thriving cities, massive temples, fierce warriors, strong armies. These are only a few characteristics of the Mesoamerican civilization called the Aztec. The Aztec were nomads from a mysterious land known as Aztlán—the origin of the name *Aztec*. Starting from only an island city in a swamp, the Aztec founded a powerful empire.

MAIN IDEA

The Aztec developed a mighty empire in central Mexico.

SETTLING IN CENTRAL MEXICO

Around A.D. 1300, Aztec nomads migrated into the Valley of Mexico, a thriving and populous region in the central part of Mexico. When the Aztec arrived, the valley was dominated by rival city-states. The Aztec settled there, adopted local ways, and served powerful kings as farmers and warriors. Then, in 1325, the Aztec founded their own city, **Tenochtitlán** (tay-nohch-teet-LAHN). Today Tenochtitlán is known as Mexico City.

The Aztec built Tenochtitlán on two islands in a swamp in the western part of Lake Texcoco. To feed their growing population, they constructed artificial fields called **chinampas** (chee-NAHM-pahz). Chinampa farmers piled layers of mud and vegetation to raise the soil level above the water. Then they planted trees alongside to mark off planting areas. Finally, they covered the areas with more soil, dug up from the bottom of the lake. Farmers planted maize, beans, and different kinds of squash on the chinampas. These remarkable fields produced many crops, and the Aztec population thrived.

One advantage of living in a lake was that canoes made transport easy, so trade flourished. In time, the Aztec established a twin city called Tlatelolco (tlaht-el-OHL-koh) in the northern part of Lake Texcoco. Tlatelolco had a huge marketplace. Every day, thousands of people crossed the lake in canoes and visited Tlatelolco's bustling market.

BUILDING AN EMPIRE

The Aztec developed into skilled warriors. At first they fought for other kings, but then they overthrew their masters and began fighting for themselves. They allied with two other cities, Texcoco and Tlacopan (tlaht-oh-PAHN), to form a powerful Triple Alliance that the Aztec would control by 1428. Well-trained Aztec armies marched steadily through Mesoamerica, forcing hundreds of small city-states to surrender to Aztec rule.

Aztec bureaucrats, or government officials, kept order and enforced the supply of tribute to Tenochtitlán. Tribute, or a payment for protection, was made in food, raw materials, goods, or labor. Over time, the Aztec grew rich and commanded a vast empire stretching from the Pacific Ocean to the Gulf of Mexico. Around six million people lived in the Aztec Empire at its height.

By 1519, about 200,000 people lived in Tenochtitlán, which had become the largest city in Mesoamerica. It was one of the most magnificent cities of its time. The pyramid of **Templo Mayor**, or the Great Temple, towered above the city. Dozens more temples and many beautiful palaces surrounded Templo Mayor. Four roads

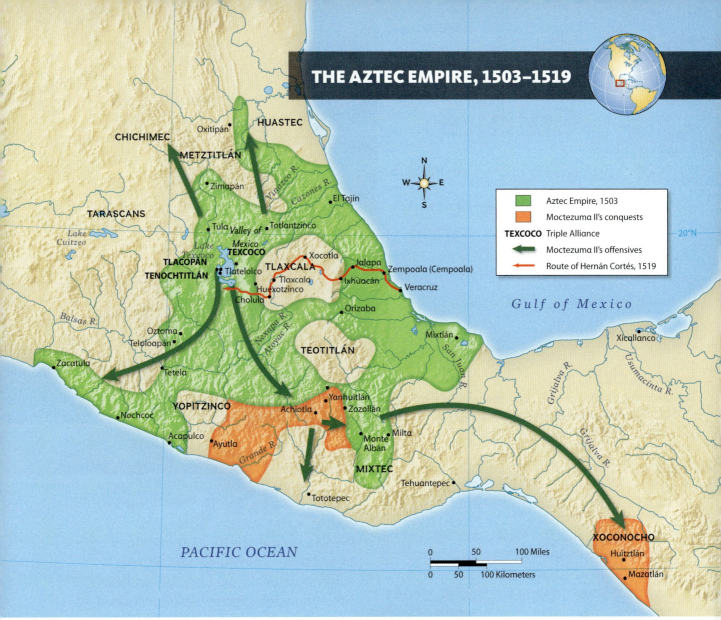

THE AZTEC EMPIRE, 1503–1519

Aztec Empire, 1503
Moctezuma II's conquests
TEXCOCO Triple Alliance
Moctezuma II's offensives
Route of Hernán Cortés, 1519

divided the city into quarters, each with distinct neighborhoods, leaders, farmland, markets, and temples. The island city was crisscrossed by canals and connected to the mainland by long causeways, or roads across the water. When Spanish explorers arrived in 1519, they marveled at Tenochtitlán's size and splendor.

PRECIOUS MASKS

This turquoise mask depicts the Aztec god Quetzalcoatl (kweht-sahl-koh-AHT-uhl), believed to be part bird, part snake. Aztec sculptors carved masks from volcanic rock and precious stones such as turquoise and jade.

REVIEW & ASSESS

1. **READING CHECK** What features made Tenochtitlán an awe-inspiring city?

2. **ANALYZE CAUSE AND EFFECT** How were the Aztec able to develop productive farm fields in the swampy lands around Tenochtitlán?

3. **INTERPRET MAPS** Use the map scale to determine how far the Aztec Empire extended from north to south in 1503.

3.2 Aztec Culture

In any big city, you will find people from all walks of life. The same was true for the great Aztec city of Tenochtitlán, where you might have met nobles, priests, soldiers, artisans, and slaves.

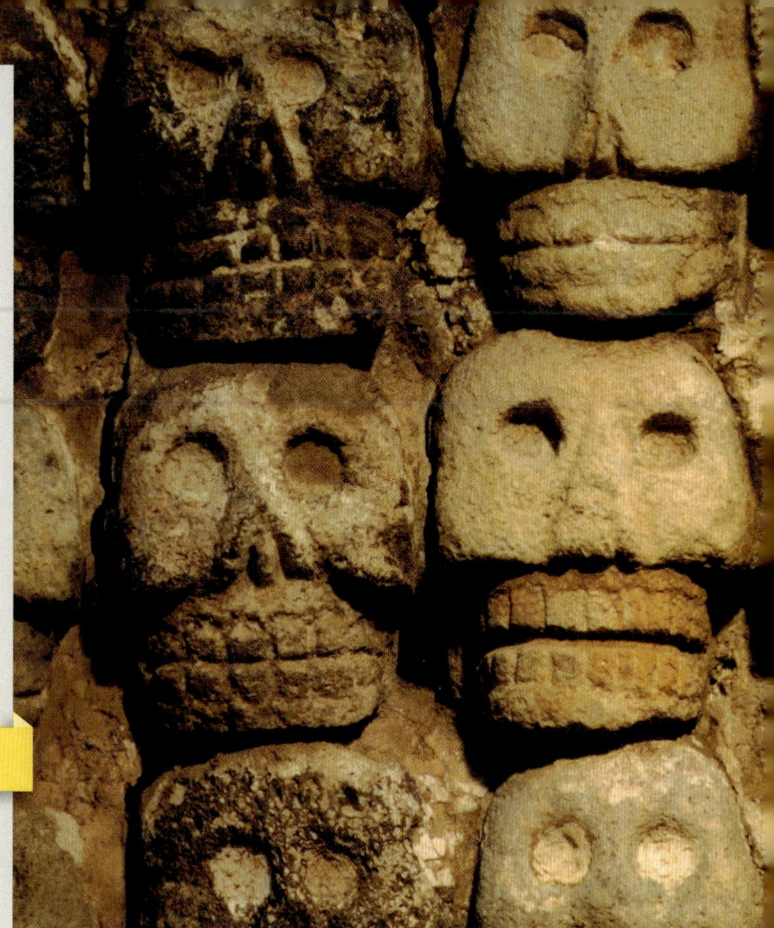

MAIN IDEA

Class structure and religious practices defined Aztec society.

CLASS STRUCTURE

The emperor was the most powerful person in Aztec society. He controlled all political and spiritual matters and served for life. Below him were the **nobles**. Nobles were the smallest but most powerful class. They inherited their status and held the top jobs as generals, priests, tax collectors, and judges. Some nobles even governed cities for the Aztec emperor.

Most Aztec belonged to the commoner class, which included merchants and artisans, farmers, and soldiers. Merchants and artisans were highly respected, and they lived in their own communities. Merchants traveled throughout the empire, trading goods. Artisans made and sold jewelry, ornaments, and clothes. Many Aztec were farmers who worked **communal**, or shared, land and had to give part of their harvest as a tax to the empire. Others were professional soldiers, some of whom gained wealth and privilege by distinguishing themselves on the battlefield.

Serfs and slaves occupied the lowest level of Aztec society. **Serfs** lived and worked on the private land of nobles. In addition to providing agricultural labor, serfs performed household tasks for landowners. Slaves were considered property and were usually prisoners of war. Slave status was not based on race, and children of slaves were born free.

AZTEC GODS

Religion was central to all classes of Aztec society. The Aztec were polytheistic. They worshipped as many as 1,000 gods and built hundreds of magnificent temples and religious structures in Tenochtitlán to honor those gods. Though people's individual homes were simply constructed, they almost always featured a shrine to the gods.

The Aztec followed many traditions that they shared with other Mesoamerican cultures. They believed they could please the gods with offerings and sacrifices. Some of these sacrifices were human.

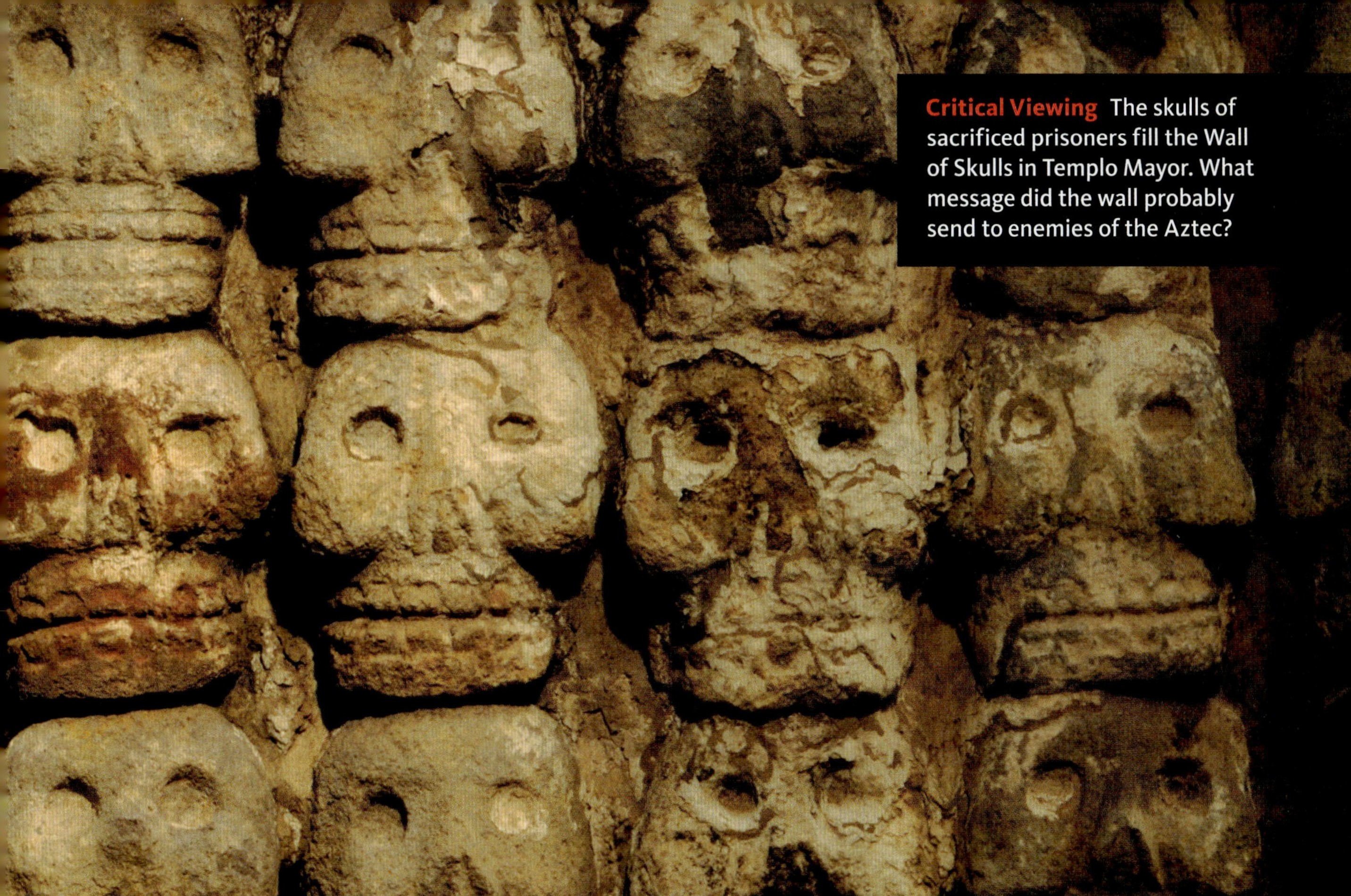

Critical Viewing The skulls of sacrificed prisoners fill the Wall of Skulls in Templo Mayor. What message did the wall probably send to enemies of the Aztec?

Most of the human sacrifices were prisoners of war. The Aztec considered themselves "the People of the Sun" and believed they nourished the sun with these sacrifices.

An important site for the Aztec was **Teotihuacán** (tay-oh-TEE-wah-khan), or "the place where the gods were born." Teotihuacán was located north of Tenochtitlán and built by an earlier people. This once-great city became sacred to the Aztec, who came later. The Aztec built onto the ruins they found there and revived worship at its many temples, including two vast pyramids dedicated to the sun and moon.

WARRIOR SCHOOLS

This Aztec sculpture depicts an Eagle Warrior. Much of the success of the Aztec Empire was due to its fierce warriors. All boys attended military training schools from a young age. At these schools, boys learned to fight in formation and use weapons.

REVIEW & ASSESS

1. **READING CHECK** Which social class in Aztec society had the most members?
2. **DRAW CONCLUSIONS** Why do you think merchants and artisans were highly respected members of the commoner class?
3. **COMPARE AND CONTRAST** In what ways were some Aztec religious practices similar to practices of other Mesoamerican cultures?

3.3 Aztec Defeat and Legacy

The Aztec founded thriving cities, developed rich cultures, and built a strong military. However, their empire lasted barely 200 years. It came to a sudden end when the Spanish arrived in the early 1500s.

MAIN IDEA

European invaders defeated the Aztec, who left behind a rich cultural legacy.

END OF THE EMPIRE

Aztec power depended on the empire's huge military, which conquered many people and then demanded tribute from defeated populations. Constant wars and regular rebellions, though, kept the Aztec Empire unstable. The unrest in the empire was made worse by the rule of **Moctezuma II** (mok-tih-ZOO-muh), who became emperor in 1502. He considered himself an equal to the gods. He also kept pressuring defeated peoples for more and more tribute to pay for his luxurious, wasteful lifestyle. Until 1519, he crushed one rebellion after another. Then the unthinkable happened.

That year **conquistadors** arrived from Europe. Conquistadors were Spanish conquerors who were greedy for gold and other riches from South and Central America. Although few in number, they were able to overpower the Aztec with superior weapons, such as guns and cannons, as well as horses. Aztec warriors armed with spear throwers and swords were no match for Spanish conquistadors. Spanish invaders also brought diseases such as smallpox that would eventually kill millions of native people throughout the Americas.

Believing the Spanish would liberate them from the tyranny of their rulers, some Aztec joined the conquistadors' leader, **Hernán Cortés**, in his battles. (See Cortés' route on the map in Lesson 3.1.) The conquest ended with a great siege of Tenochtitlán in 1521. The Spanish surrounded and systematically destroyed the great city. They rebuilt over the ruins, and that city became present-day Mexico City, Mexico.

AZTEC LEGACY

Because of their ruthless approach to conquest, the Spanish destroyed Aztec buildings, art, and literature. However, some Aztec ruins, artifacts, and writings survived the conquest. Archaeologists and historians study them to learn more about the Aztec.

The Aztec built huge monuments, especially temples for their gods. Aztec temples were positioned to line up with the sun and stars. The Aztec were skilled astronomers who could predict the movements of the sun, moon, planets, and stars. Like the Maya, the Aztec believed these movements directly affected their lives. They also used complex calendars to chart and record events, such as important religious rituals and the planting and harvesting of crops.

Aztec writing also gives archaeologists and historians a picture of their society. The Aztec recorded historical events, and they wrote inspiring speeches, poetry, legends, and prayers to their gods. Glyphs represented words that were painted into codices. Although few of the original codices survived, many were copied and translated by Spanish scholars. These colorful books offer a detailed and artistic picture of Aztec society.

Portrait of Montezuma II, European School, 16th century

This painting of Moctezuma II reflects how Europeans viewed him. Moctezuma expanded the Aztec Empire and made Tenochtitlán its capital city.

REVIEW & ASSESS

1. **READING CHECK** What factors caused instability and unrest in the Aztec Empire?

2. **DRAW CONCLUSIONS** How were the Spanish conquistadors able to defeat the powerful Aztec?

3. **MAKE INFERENCES** Why are Aztec codices important to archaeologists and historians?

CHAPTER 16 Review

VOCABULARY

On your paper, match the vocabulary word in the first column with its definition in the second column.

WORD	DEFINITION
1. terrace	**a.** a civilization that greatly influences other civilizations
2. mother culture	**b.** a stepped platform built into a mountainside
3. codex	**c.** a symbolic picture used to represent a word, syllable, or sound
4. glyph	**d.** a Spanish conqueror who overpowered the Aztec
5. chinampa	**e.** a folded book made from tree-bark paper
6. conquistador	**f.** an artificial field

READING STRATEGY

7. IDENTIFY MAIN IDEAS AND DETAILS If you haven't already, complete your diagram for each Mesoamerican civilization. Then answer the question.

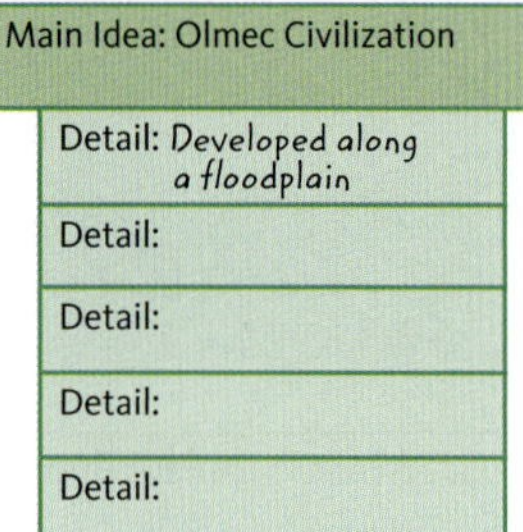
Main-Idea Diagram
Main Idea: Olmec Civilization
Detail: Developed along a floodplain
Detail:
Detail:
Detail:
Detail:

What feature do you think was the greatest legacy of each civilization? Explain.

MAIN IDEAS

Answer the following questions. Support your answers with evidence from the chapter.

8. Why is the Olmec civilization considered to be Mesoamerica's mother culture? **LESSON 1.2**

9. Why is Monte Albán considered one of the first major cities in Mesoamerica? **LESSON 1.3**

10. Which groups of people made up the largest social class in the Maya civilization? **LESSON 2.1**

11. During what time period did most of the great Maya cities develop? **LESSON 2.2**

12. What did the Maya use to develop their elaborate 365-day calendar? **LESSON 2.4**

13. Describe the class structure of society in the Aztec Empire. **LESSON 3.2**

14. How did instability contribute to the end of the Aztec Empire? **LESSON 3.3**

CRITICAL THINKING

Answer the following questions. Support your answers with evidence from the chapter.

15. ANALYZE CAUSE AND EFFECT What happened as a result of the Olmec's trade network?

16. DRAW CONCLUSIONS What conclusions can you draw about cacao beans based on the fact that the Maya often used them to pay for goods?

17. COMPARE AND CONTRAST What are some of the similarities surrounding the decline of the Zapotec and Maya civilizations?

18. COMPARE AND CONTRAST What distinguishes the Aztec from the early river valley civilizations of Mesopotamia, Egypt, India, and China?

19. FORM AND SUPPORT OPINIONS In your opinion, was Moctezuma II an effective leader of the Aztec Empire? Why or why not?

20. YOU DECIDE What do you think is the Maya civilization's greatest legacy? Support your opinion with evidence from the chapter.

INTERPRET VISUALS

Study the images of a Maya pyramid and an ancient Egyptian pyramid. Then answer the questions that follow.

Maya pyramid

Egyptian pyramid

21. How are the pyramids alike, and how do they differ?

22. What challenges did both pyramid styles present to the people who built them?

ANALYZE SOURCES

This jade mask was placed over the face of King Pacal, a great ruler of Palenque, when he died. The mask shows the king's own features.

23. The Maya highly valued jade and often used it to represent the maize god. Study the mask. Why do you think the Maya associated jade with the maize god?

WRITE ABOUT HISTORY

24. EXPLANATORY How were the Olmec, Zapotec, Maya, and Aztec civilizations similar? How did they differ? Write a paragraph comparing and contrasting the civilizations for tourists who are planning to visit some of the civilizations' archaeological and historic sites. Consider such aspects of the civilizations as religion, art, architecture, daily life, social structure, and the sciences.

TIPS

- Take notes from the lessons about the Olmec, Zapotec, Maya, and Aztec civilizations. You might jot down your comparisons in a chart using the aspects listed above as headings in the chart.
- State your main idea clearly at the beginning of the paragraph. Support your main idea with relevant facts, details, and examples.
- Use vocabulary from the chapter in your paragraph.
- Provide a concluding statement about the similarities and differences among the Olmec, Zapotec, Maya, and Aztec civilizations.

CHAPTER

17 SOUTH AND NORTH AMERICA

100 B.C. – A.D. 1600

SECTION 1

PERUVIAN CULTURES

KEY VOCABULARY	NAMES & PLACES
geoglyph	Atahualpa
quarry	Francisco Pizarro
quinoa	Machu Picchu
terrace farming	Moche
	Nasca
	Pachacuti
	Sicán
	Wari

SECTION 2

NORTH AMERICAN CULTURES

KEY VOCABULARY	NAMES & PLACES
adobe	Algonquin
confederation	Cahokia
kiva	Cherokee
mound builder	Creek
potlatch	Great Plains
shaman	Iroquois
totem pole	Mesa Verde
wigwam	Pueblo Bonito

READING STRATEGY

ORGANIZE IDEAS: SEQUENCE EVENTS In this chapter, the sequence of historical events is divided by geographic location. First you'll learn about events in South America, and then you'll learn about events in North America. Use a time line like this one to place all the events in the chapter in order so you can see what was happening in both locations at a specific time.

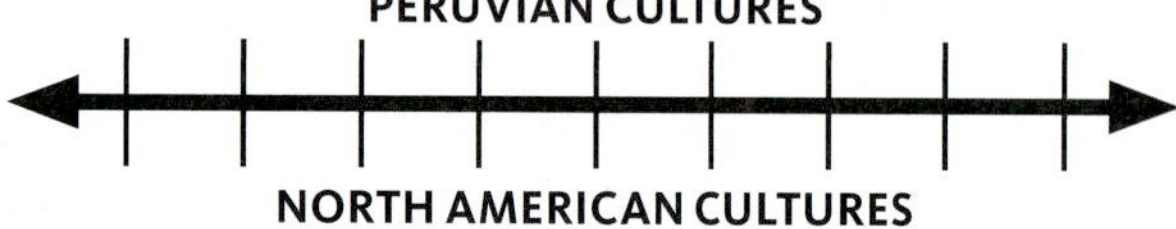
PERUVIAN CULTURES
NORTH AMERICAN CULTURES

The fine-line art that wraps around this Moche stirrup pot shows warriors running to the top of a mountain and back down again.

(Banco Central de Reserva Del Perú, Lima, Perú)

1.1 Pre-Inca Cultures

Humans have treasured gold for centuries. When people mold gold into necklaces and bracelets, the beautiful finish outshines all other metals. In the northern and western parts of South America, four cultures developed extraordinary skill in working with gold and other precious metals. These cultures lived in present-day Peru, which the Inca would dominate by A.D. 1400.

MAIN IDEA

Beginning around A.D. 100, four complex cultures thrived in Peru.

THE MOCHE AND THE NASCA

On the northwest coast of South America, the **Moche** (MOH-chay) culture flourished between A.D. 100 and 700. Their land was harsh—a desert that was squeezed between the Andes Mountains to the east and the Pacific Ocean to the west. Like other pre-Inca cultures and the Inca who came later, the Moche showed great creativity in adapting to this challenging environment. To irrigate the farm fields in their arid region, they built complex irrigation systems. They also developed a strong military and ruled nearly 400 miles of the Peruvian coast.

The Moche were also artists, as shown by the artifacts archaeologists have discovered. Moche artisans created beautiful ceramics, or bowls, statues, and other objects made from clay and then hardened under intense heat. The artisans decorated the vessels with detailed line drawings of animals and people, such as rulers and warriors. Just as impressive was Moche artists' work with gold, which they shaped into exquisite jewelry. One pair of solid gold peanuts looked just like the real things—except they were three times larger.

In south Peru, the **Nasca** culture thrived from about A.D. 200 to 600. It was one of the earliest complex cultures in South America. Nasca artisans were as highly skilled as those of the Moche culture, creating magnificent jewelry from gold, silver, and copper. They also formed ceramic pottery and decorated it with intricate designs from nature, such as birds and fish.

The Nasca left behind a mystery, though. They created enormous **geoglyphs**, or large geometric designs and shapes drawn on the ground. The shapes often took the form of animals or birds. The dry climate where the Nasca lived helped preserve the geoglyphs. However, archaeologists are still not absolutely certain what the purpose of the designs was.

THE WARI AND THE SICÁN

The greatest military power among pre-Inca cultures was the **Wari** culture, which dominated the high desert of central Peru from about A.D. 500 to 1000. With their strong military, the Wari overran the Nasca and other people and established the first empire in the region of the Andes Mountains. The Wari were also skilled farmers. To cultivate crops on the rugged terrain of the Andes, they created terraced fields, or flat fields dug out of the sides of hills.

In a recent find at El Castillo, a Wari city along the Peruvian coast, archaeologists

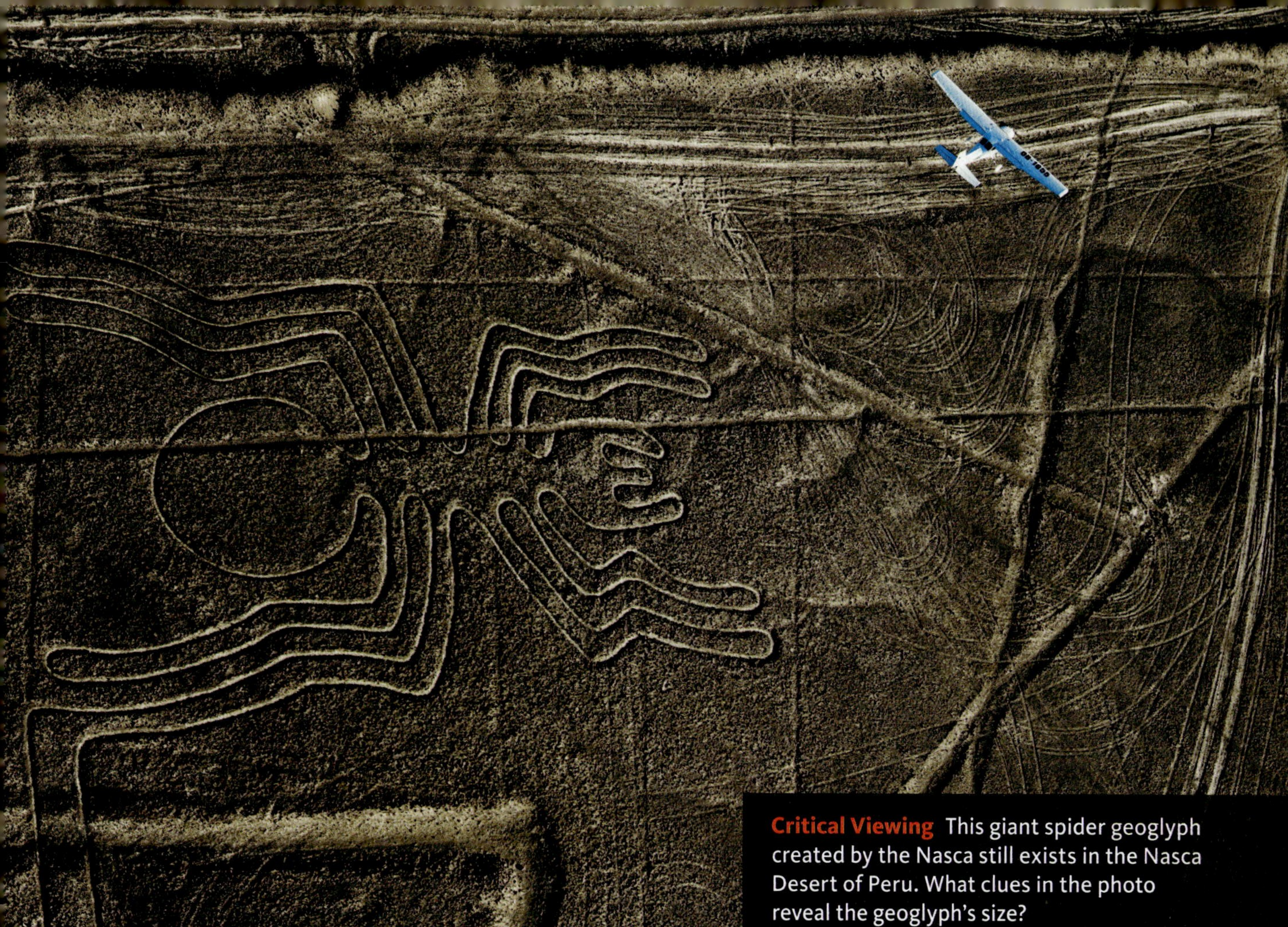

Critical Viewing This giant spider geoglyph created by the Nasca still exists in the Nasca Desert of Peru. What clues in the photo reveal the geoglyph's size?

unearthed a royal tomb that revealed a great deal about Wari culture. The tomb contained the remains of four queens or princesses and other members of the nobility. Buried with the remains were golden earrings, copper axes, and silver bowls. The discovery indicates that not only did the Wari worship their ancestors but they were, like other pre-Inca cultures, gifted artisans with precious metals.

While the Wari ruled central Peru, the **Sicán** culture flourished in the mountains of northern Peru from about A.D. 800 to 1400. The Sicán created delicate jewelry from gold, silver, and copper. They perfected a technique of pounding gold into extremely thin sheets. Archaeologists found two strips of metal that were only 0.006 inches thick—almost as thin as a piece of paper.

The Sicán showed great respect for the creatures of the natural world. Artists created a mural that was decorated with waves, fish, the sun, and the moon. When the Sicán buried the dead, they prepared them for the next world by burying them with gold, copper, and shells to carry water. This practice revealed their belief in an afterlife.

REVIEW & ASSESS

1. **READING CHECK** Where did the pre-Inca cultures live?
2. **SUMMARIZE** What have discoveries of tombs revealed about pre-Inca cultures?
3. **COMPARE AND CONTRAST** In what ways were these four pre-Inca cultures similar?

1.2 HISTORY THROUGH OBJECTS

PERUVIAN GOLD

Pre-Inca Peruvians were master artisans who created fine jewelry and adornments with precious metals such as gold, silver, and copper. They also made pottery that was both beautiful and functional. The artifacts shown here were part of a special exhibition by the National Geographic Museum in partnership with the government of Peru. What common themes do you notice in the artifacts featured below?

Nasca Bee
Pre-Inca artisans decorated clothing with gold appliqués like this bee, which mimics a Nasca geoglyph of the same shape.
(Banco Central de Reserva Del Perú, Lima, Perú)

Diadem
This Moche headpiece, called a diadem, symbolizes power and authority. It is 12 inches wide, made from a single sheet of copper, and coated with gold.
(Museo Larco Lima-Perú)

El Tocado
The Sicán crafted this headdress with movable parts and radiating feathers. Note the enormous gold ear spools on each side.
(Y. Yoshii/PAS)

Nose Ornament
Gold and silver are fused together in this bi-metal piece. Cats, which represented strength and fierceness, made frequent appearances in pre-Inca art.
(Banco Central de Reserva Del Perú, Lima, Perú)

Moche Mask
When copper is exposed to the elements, it changes in color from a shiny red-brown to a pale green, as it did on this funeral mask.
(Museo Larco Lima-Perú)

1.3 Inca Society and Government

The civilization known as the Inca began as a small mountain culture that lived high in the Andes Mountains. In only a few hundred years, the Inca had conquered large parts of South America and governed a huge empire.

MAIN IDEA

The Inca created and controlled a large empire in South America.

ORGANIZED EMPIRE

About the same time as the Aztec emerged in Mesoamerica, the Inca began their conquest of western South America. In A.D. 1200, the Inca were one of many small states occupying the Urubamba Valley, high in the Andes Mountains of present-day Peru. By 1440, the Inca ruled the region.

Under the leadership of the emperor **Pachacuti** (pah-chah-KOO-tee), the empire expanded rapidly. The name *Pachacuti* means "he who changed the world"—and this ambitious man certainly did that. Pachacuti conquered and ruled widespread areas through a powerful military and a strong central government. He also transformed the Inca capital, Cusco (KOO-skoh), into an impressive stone city of 100,000 people.

The Inca Empire stretched 2,600 miles from present-day Colombia to Argentina and included about 12 million people who spoke more than 20 languages. Despite its size, the Inca Empire was well organized. The hierarchy of Inca society helped rulers maintain tight control of the large empire.

At the top, the emperor had absolute power. Below him, four regional officials called prefects oversaw provincial governors, district officers, and local chiefs. Foremen supervised ten families each and helped carry out the policies of the emperor. The Inca government viewed the empire's subjects as a resource, like gold or timber. It demanded that whole populations relocate if the state needed their labor elsewhere. Commoners farmed communal land and worked on state-owned farms while also serving in the army or on building projects.

In order to manage the many details involved in running an empire, the Inca also had a large bureaucracy, or system of state officials. In fact, for every 10,000 Inca, there were 1,331 administrators. These administrators kept detailed records about all parts of the empire, from population to farm animals to trade.

MOUNTAIN LIFE

Like other early civilizations, the Inca Empire was built on agriculture. However, farming was difficult in the steep Andes. The Inca made up for the lack of flat farmland with a type of farming called **terrace farming**. They cut flat steps, or terraces, on the sides of mountains and then built stone walls to keep the terraces in place. Terrace farming produced potatoes, maize, and **quinoa** (KEEN-wah), a high-protein grain native to the Andes. In addition to farming, the Inca raised llamas and alpacas for meat and wool and for transporting goods and people across the mountains.

Inca religious rituals centered on the need to guarantee a good harvest. The Inca worshipped their emperor as the son of Inti, the sun god, and believed the emperor helped humans communicate with the gods.

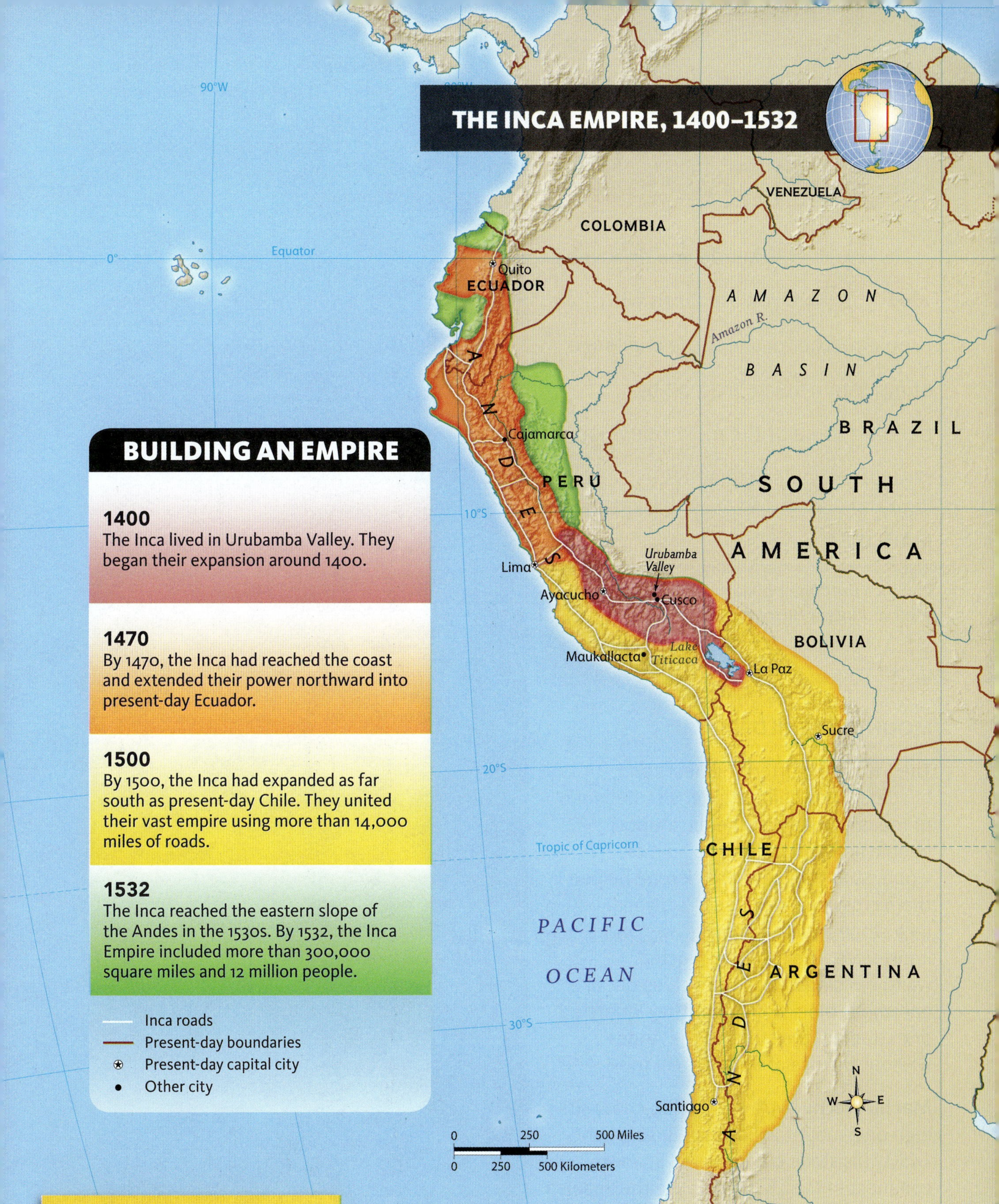

THE INCA EMPIRE, 1400–1532

VENEZUELA
COLOMBIA
Quito
ECUADOR
AMAZON BASIN
Amazon R.
BRAZIL
Equator
ANDES
Cajamarca
PERU
SOUTH AMERICA
Urubamba Valley
Lima
Ayacucho
Cusco
BOLIVIA
Lake Titicaca
Maukallacta
La Paz
Sucre
Tropic of Capricorn
CHILE
PACIFIC OCEAN
ARGENTINA
Santiago
90°W
0°
10°S
20°S
30°S
0 250 500 Miles
0 250 500 Kilometers
N S E W

BUILDING AN EMPIRE

1400
The Inca lived in Urubamba Valley. They began their expansion around 1400.

1470
By 1470, the Inca had reached the coast and extended their power northward into present-day Ecuador.

1500
By 1500, the Inca had expanded as far south as present-day Chile. They united their vast empire using more than 14,000 miles of roads.

1532
The Inca reached the eastern slope of the Andes in the 1530s. By 1532, the Inca Empire included more than 300,000 square miles and 12 million people.

- Inca roads
- Present-day boundaries
- Present-day capital city
- Other city

REVIEW & ASSESS

1. **READING CHECK** How did Pachacuti unify and control the Inca Empire?
2. **ANALYZE CAUSE AND EFFECT** What method did the Inca use to farm in the Andes Mountains?
3. **INTERPRET MAPS** What physical features limited eastward and westward expansion of the Inca Empire?

1.4 Inca Architecture

What do you do when you are faced with a problem? The Inca met the challenge of mountain living head-on by building some of the most remarkable structures you can imagine.

MAIN IDEA

The Inca used their building skills to adapt to their mountain surroundings.

MOUNTAIN BUILDERS

The Inca were gifted engineers and builders. They built an extensive network of roads that helped them transport people and goods. Bridges built of wood, stone, and even thick rope helped them cross rivers and deep canyons. Inca stone architecture was even more impressive. The Inca constructed walls, buildings, and entire cities out of enormous blocks of stone. They **quarried**, or extracted, the stone in the Andes without the use of iron or steel tools.

Machu Picchu (MAH-choo PEE-choo) sits high on a mountain in Peru. Built around 1450, this stone city survived Spanish conquest in the 1530s because the Spanish never found it. Machu Picchu included religious temples, royal residences, and homes for workers as well as waterworks and terraces for farming. Aqueducts made of stone carried water to the city—just as aqueducts carried water in ancient Rome.

Critical Viewing Machu Picchu sits 8,000 feet above sea level. Why might the Inca have built this city in such a remote place?

REVIEW & ASSESS

1. **READING CHECK** Why are the Inca known as highly skilled engineers and builders?
2. **MAKE INFERENCES** How did bridges and roads help the Inca manage their empire?
3. **DRAW CONCLUSIONS** Why did Machu Picchu survive the Spanish conquest?

1.5 MOMENTS IN HISTORY
The Inca and Spanish Meet

1532

This 20th-century mural in Cajamarca, Peru, depicts the 1532 meeting of the Spanish conquistador **Francisco Pizarro** and **Atahualpa** (ah-tah-WAHL-pah), the Inca emperor. Pizarro had just 180 men with him, but they had the advantage of horses and superior metal weapons. Shortly after the meeting, Pizarro's men captured Atahualpa and killed his unarmed attendants. The Spanish ruled the Inca through Atahualpa for almost a year—and then executed him. By 1539, the Spanish had conquered the territory of the fallen empire. What details in the mural convey Atahualpa's power as emperor?

2.1 Northwest Coast Cultures

North America is made up of vastly different landscapes, including rain forests, mountains, deserts, prairies, and woodlands. The hundreds of Native American cultures varied as much as North America's geography. In the Pacific Northwest, the forests and seacoast provided a hospitable environment for several cultures.

MAIN IDEA

Native American cultures of the Pacific Northwest thrived in a land of plentiful rainfall and dense forests.

NORTHWEST COAST TRIBES

Thirty distinct cultures lived in the Pacific Northwest region. This narrow strip of mountains and woodland followed the coast from present-day northern California to Alaska. It was one of the most densely populated parts of North America. The lakes, rivers, and ocean provided fish, shellfish, and whales. The forests offered plentiful plants and game. With such abundance, populations grew, and complex societies developed without any need to farm.

Along the southern coast of what is now the state of Alaska, the Tlingit (KLING-kit) people developed a thriving culture that was closely tied to the Pacific Ocean and the many rivers. In fact, the word *Tlingit* means "the People of the Tides." The Tlingit were superb sailors and fishers, and their most important food was salmon.

Because the Pacific Northwest receives ample rainfall, forests carpet the region. As a result, wood was central to Tlingit culture. Around A.D. 500, the Tlingit developed tools for splitting and carving wood. With those tools, they built permanent homes and crafted everyday necessities such as plates and utensils. They also used tools and fire to carve dugout canoes from logs. The canoes, some as long as 60 feet, were seaworthy and could sail for miles into the Pacific Ocean, allowing the Tlingit to hunt for whales.

Two other important Northwest Coast tribes—the Kwakiutl (kwahk-ee-YOU-tuhl) and the Haida (HIGH-dah)—lived south of the Tlingit. Both lived by hunting and gathering but settled in permanent villages. They used the forests' cedar trees to build large family houses. Like the Tlingit, they also built excellent seagoing canoes.

These tribes also traded extensively with neighboring cultures. Over time, trade allowed some families to become wealthy, and social classes developed. Social rank became hereditary and certain families had great influence based on their wealth and ancestry. These families demonstrated and shared wealth through gift-giving ceremonies called **potlatches**, in which they gave away gifts and food to their communities.

TOTEM POLES AND MASKS

The skillful wood carvings of Northwest Coast cultures reveal their relationship to the natural world and their belief in a spirit world. One example of their artistry is found in the intricate masks they carved and painted and then wore at ceremonies. A **shaman**, or a person who is believed to be able to help others communicate with the spirit world, guided the mask carving and led the ceremonies.

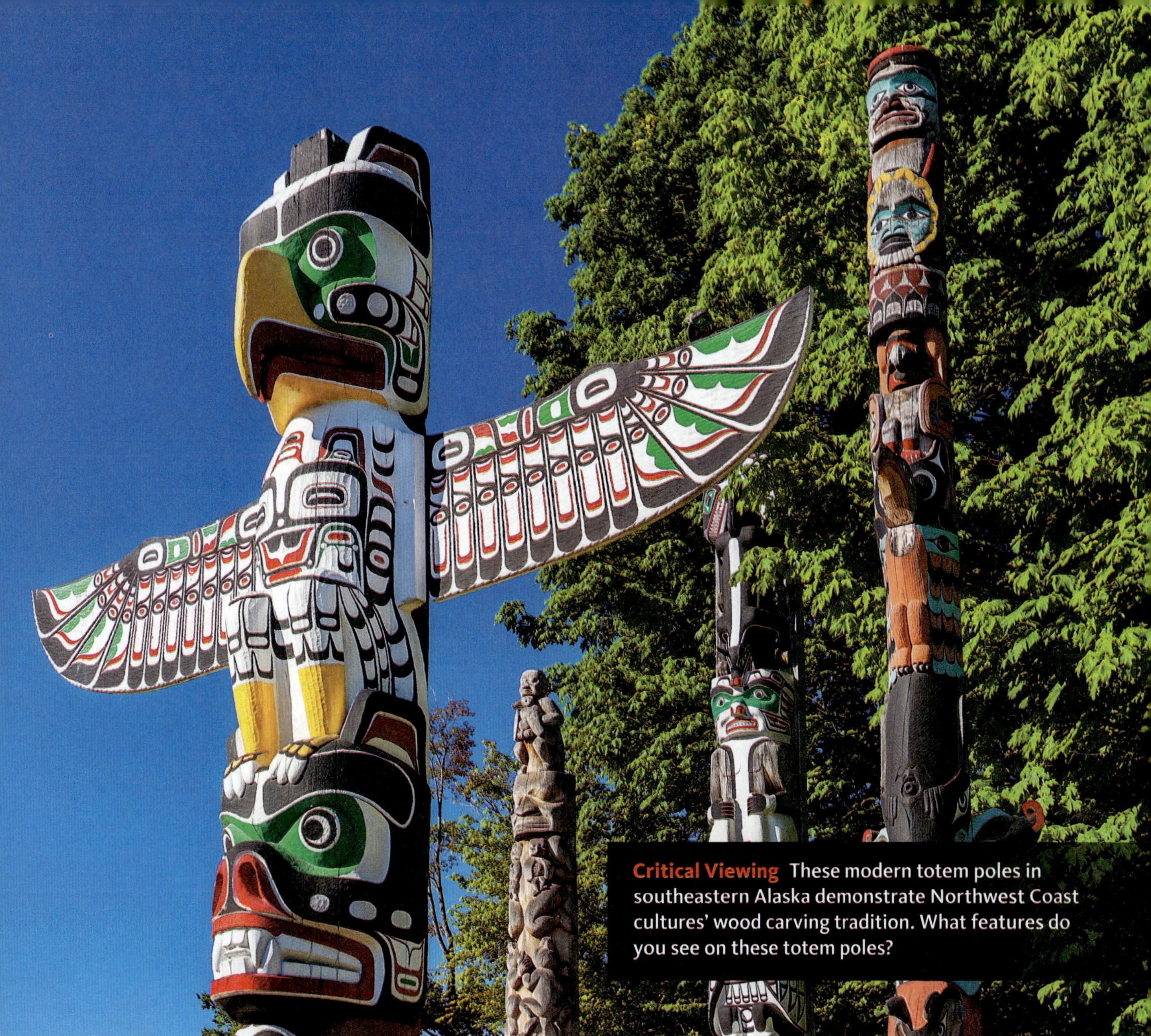

Critical Viewing These modern totem poles in southeastern Alaska demonstrate Northwest Coast cultures' wood carving tradition. What features do you see on these totem poles?

Totem poles are another example of Northwest Coast wood carving artistry. Totem poles are tall, elaborately carved and painted tree trunks that honor a revered being or guardian associated with a family. Totem pole carvings included colorful representations of animals of the region, such as bears, whales, and eagles. Other carvings included human figures, such as chiefs or ancestors and supernatural spirits. Totem poles told stories and legends as well as family and tribal histories. Wood rots easily in the region's damp climate, so few totem poles have survived more than 100 years. However, totem pole carving remains a Northwest Coast tradition today.

REVIEW & ASSESS

1. **READING CHECK** In what ways did the geography of the Pacific Northwest influence the culture of the Tlingit people?
2. **DRAW CONCLUSIONS** What was the function of the potlatch in the Kwakiutl and Haida societies?
3. **EVALUATE** What role did totem poles and masks play in the cultures of Pacific Northwest tribes?

2.2 The Ancient Pueblo

The American Southwest could not be more different from the Pacific Northwest. The Southwest is a harsh land of mountains and deserts, where temperatures can reach a scorching 120 degrees Fahrenheit. In this forbidding land, the ancient Pueblo developed a vibrant culture that was closely tied to the land.

MAIN IDEA

The ancient Pueblo adapted to their environment by farming the arid land and building complex structures.

DESERT DWELLERS

As early as 1000 B.C., the ancient Pueblo began to farm in various parts of the arid Southwest desert. They inhabited the Four Corners region, where present-day Arizona, Colorado, Utah, and New Mexico come together. Little by little, they began to build villages with permanent structures on high plateaus or in canyons. Some structures were dwellings made of stone and **adobe**, a clay used for building. Farm fields surrounded the villages. Using a technique called dry farming, the ancient Pueblo grew crops on the dry land, using very little water. The three staples of their diet were corn, beans, and squash.

The ancient Pueblo were skilled artisans who created baskets and pottery that were beautiful yet practical. They wove lightweight baskets and threaded together different materials to create brightly colored patterns. They used the baskets to carry objects and even to cook by placing hot stones in the baskets to heat the food. As they settled in permanent villages, the ancient Pueblo began to create extraordinary pottery, which was heavier but more permanent than baskets. They molded clay into jars, bowls, and pitchers.

PUEBLO BONITO AND MESA VERDE

One of the most impressive ancient Pueblo settlements was **Pueblo Bonito**, located in Chaco Canyon in northern New Mexico. It housed as many as 1,200 people and had more than 600 rooms and 30 kivas. **Kivas** were circular-shaped chambers in the ground used for ceremonies and social gatherings. Construction on Pueblo Bonito began around A.D. 850 and continued for another 200 years. The ancient Pueblo abandoned Pueblo Bonito sometime during the 1200s. Archaeologists are not sure why, but they believe that a severe drought may have forced people to migrate to other parts of the Southwest.

By 1200, the ancient Pueblo who lived in present-day southwestern Colorado built a series of dwellings into the sides of cliffs at **Mesa Verde**. They did this to defend themselves from invaders and provide protection from rain and the intense sun. Using advanced architectural skills, they built structures with several stories underneath cliff overhangs. The largest dwelling, Cliff Palace, featured more than 200 rooms and housed about 250 people. In all, the dwellings at Mesa Verde sheltered as many as 5,000 people.

The ancient Pueblo abandoned Mesa Verde by about 1300. In the late 1800s, two local ranchers discovered the ruins there, and in 1906, it became a U.S. National Park.

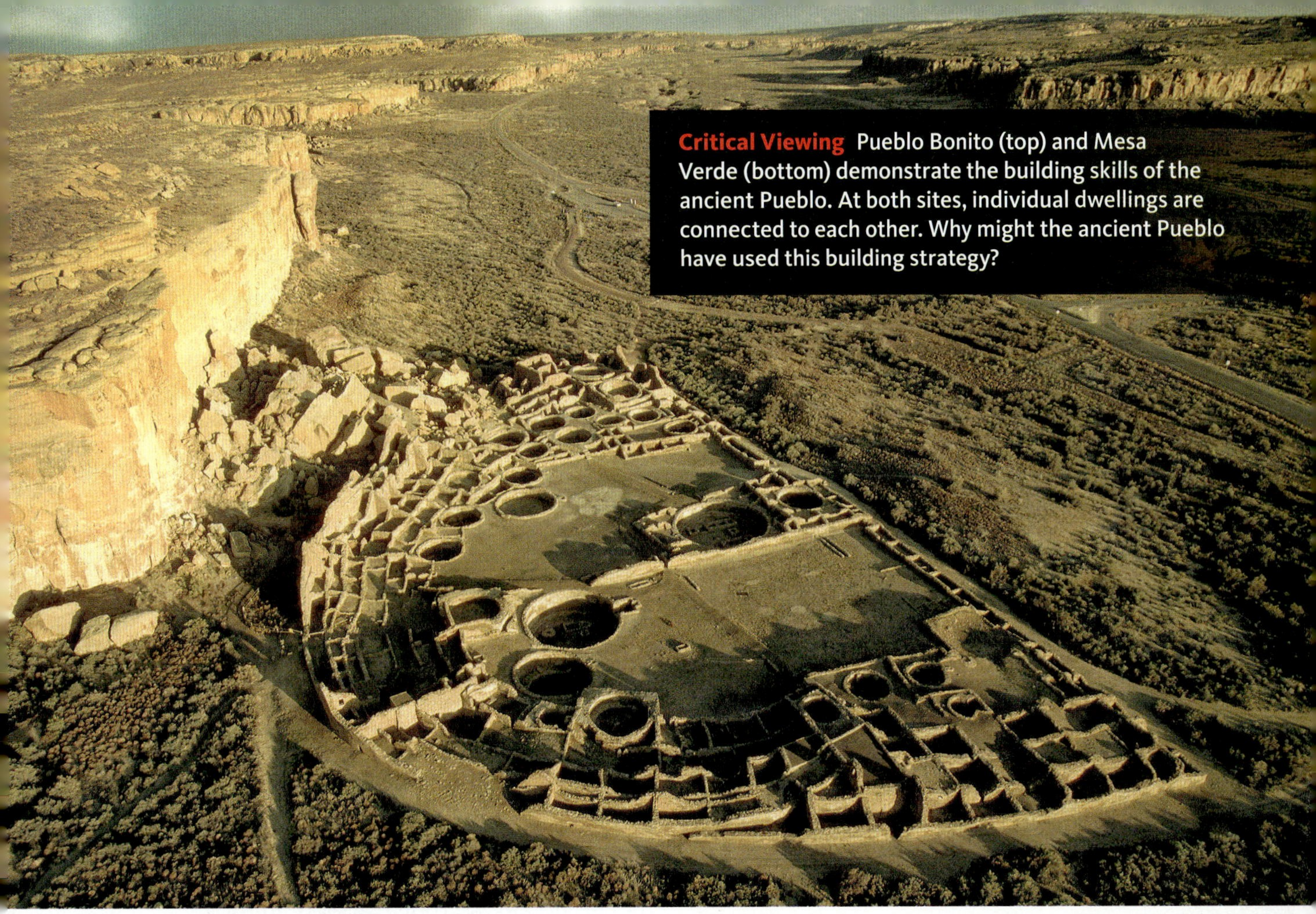

Critical Viewing Pueblo Bonito (top) and Mesa Verde (bottom) demonstrate the building skills of the ancient Pueblo. At both sites, individual dwellings are connected to each other. Why might the ancient Pueblo have used this building strategy?

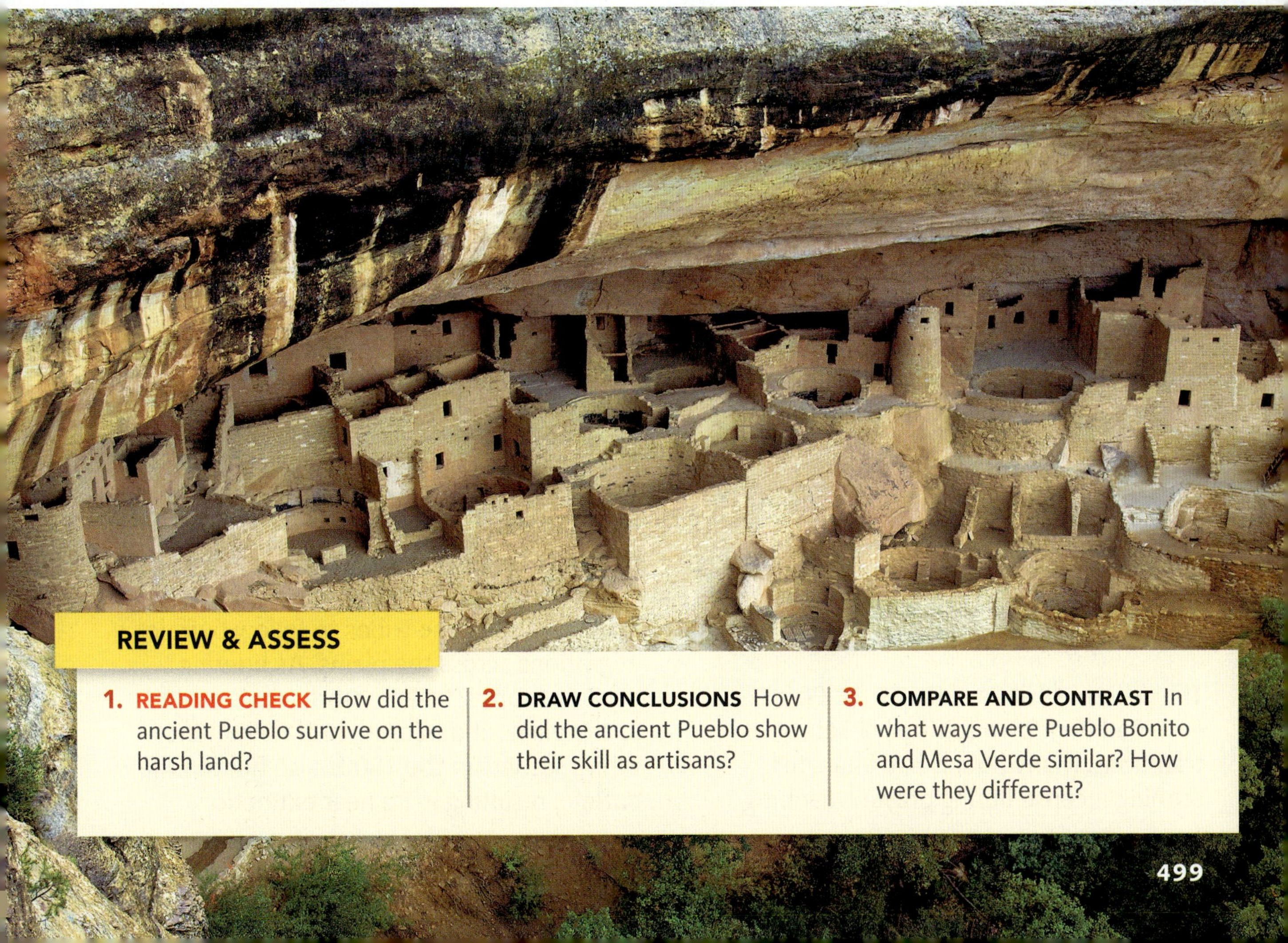

REVIEW & ASSESS

1. **READING CHECK** How did the ancient Pueblo survive on the harsh land?
2. **DRAW CONCLUSIONS** How did the ancient Pueblo show their skill as artisans?
3. **COMPARE AND CONTRAST** In what ways were Pueblo Bonito and Mesa Verde similar? How were they different?

2.3 Peoples of the Great Plains

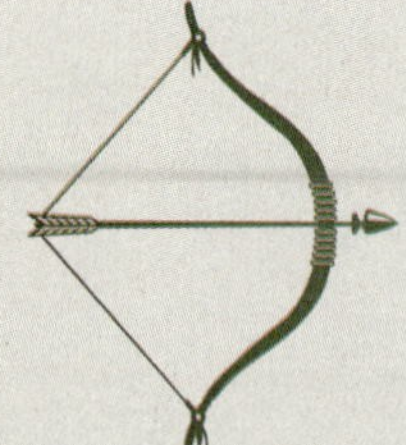

Hunting might be a sport for some people in the 21st century, but for early Great Plains cultures, hunting was key to survival. Farming on dry grasslands did not always produce good harvests. So Great Plains tribes relied on other natural resources, such as the buffalo.

MAIN IDEA

Native Americans on the Great Plains depended on the land and especially on the buffalo for survival.

PLAINS DWELLERS

The **Great Plains** is a wide area of flat, windswept grasslands that stretches north from present-day Texas into Canada. Early tribes settled along the region's major rivers and established permanent villages.

To survive the bitter winters, some tribes built earth lodges out of soil and grasses to house whole families. They relied mostly on hunting, gathering, and fishing because farming was not easy on the dry grasslands of the plains.

The different tribes of the Great Plains each had their own spiritual beliefs and traditions. Many homes had altars for burning incense during prayers. Farming communities practiced religious ceremonies centered on a good harvest. Hunting tribes had ceremonies focused on visions and spirit beings that might enhance their hunting abilities. For example, young men participated in vision quests where they put their bodies through strenuous ordeals. The goal was to achieve a trancelike state and have a vision—often of an animal. Shamans would interpret their visions.

Another important spiritual practice for Great Plains people was the Sun Dance. The Sun Dance was an annual ceremony of drumming, dancing, singing, and praying for harmony among people and giving thanks for prosperity.

BUFFALO HUNTERS

One animal was central to the livelihood and the culture of the Great Plains people—the buffalo. Large herds grazed on the wide-open grasslands, and nomadic tribes followed their migrations. These tribes had no horses, so they traveled on foot.

Because buffalo are more aggressive than cattle, they will attack if provoked. Hunting buffalo was a risky business. Hunters agitated the herd into a thunderous stampede. Then they drove the buffalo over cliffs or into corrals where they killed the animals with arrows or spears.

Buffalo were a useful resource. Great Plains people ate buffalo meat raw, roasted, or as smoked jerky. They used buffalo skins for clothes and tents, bones for tools, sinew, or tendons, for bowstrings, boiled hooves for glue, and even buffalo dung for fuel.

In the 1500s, the Spanish introduced horses to North America, and some Great Plains people began to use them to hunt. Horses allowed the tribes to follow buffalo migrations across the plains. As hunting became more efficient, more tribes moved to the plains and became buffalo hunters. White settlers in the 1800s also hunted the buffalo, resulting in its near extinction.

Critical Viewing Before 1500, about 50 million buffalo roamed freely on the plains. By 1889, commercial hunting with horses and guns had reduced buffalo numbers to just 1,000. How might this overhunting have affected tribes on the Great Plains?

REVIEW & ASSESS

1. **READING CHECK** Why were buffalo important to the people of the Great Plains?
2. **ANALYZE CAUSE AND EFFECT** How did the introduction of the horse to North America affect life for tribes on the Great Plains?
3. **COMPARE AND CONTRAST** How were the religious practices of Great Plains tribes similar? How did they differ?

2.4 The Mound Builders and Cahokia

The Mississippi River Valley and prairies and woodlands further east supported many different Native American cultures. Some built mounds, others built cities—including one of the largest cities in North America.

MAIN IDEA

Native Americans from the Great Lakes to the Gulf of Mexico developed complex societies, large cities, and organized governments.

MOUND BUILDERS

East of the Mississippi River, woodlands and prairies covered the lands that stretch between the Great Lakes and the Gulf of Mexico. Between 1000 B.C. and A.D. 500, the Adena and then the Hopewell lived in this region. They are known as **mound builders** because they built huge mounds of earth. The mounds served religious and ceremonial purposes. Some mounds, such as the Great Serpent Mound built by the Adena in southern Ohio, formed the shape of animals.

The mound builders relied mostly on hunting and gathering, but they also tamed wild plants and farmed crops such as barley. Maize—called corn today—appeared around A.D. 100, probably brought there by traders. The Adena and Hopewell cultures developed highly organized and complex societies. Living in villages that dotted the region, they hunted, farmed, and traded. The Hopewell culture collapsed by A.D. 500 for reasons that remain unknown.

From 800 to 1700, a different mound building culture—the Mississippians—emerged in the Mississippi River Valley. The Mississippians eventually populated the region from present-day Ohio, Indiana, and Illinois, south to the Gulf of Mexico. Like the Adena and Hopewell, Mississippians built mounds that had sloping sides, steps, and flat tops. However, the Mississippians built their mounds around a central plaza, where they held feasts and ceremonies.

The fertile floodplains of the Mississippi River Valley supported farming. Because of the fertility of their lands, the Mississippians grew ample quantities of maize, beans, and squash. They also hunted, skillfully using bows and arrows. Because of their plentiful food, Mississippian settlements supported large populations. In fact, they were the most populous Native American settlements north of Mexico.

CAHOKIA

The largest and most complex city that the mound builders created was at **Cahokia**, in southwest Illinois. Cahokia contained more than 120 mounds covering 6 square miles and supported more than 30,000 people. A series of stockades surrounded much of the city and a grand plaza provided space for ceremonies and celebrations.

The centerpiece of Cahokia was Monks Mound, which rose 100 feet above the flat prairie and covered 16 acres. This mound contained 814,000 cubic yards of soil—enough to fill 45,000 dump trucks. The Cahokians moved all this earth without the use of dump trucks, though. They used baskets instead.

Building the mounds required a highly organized society. A powerful chief who lived in a palace on top of one of the mounds ruled the city. Archaeologists believe that

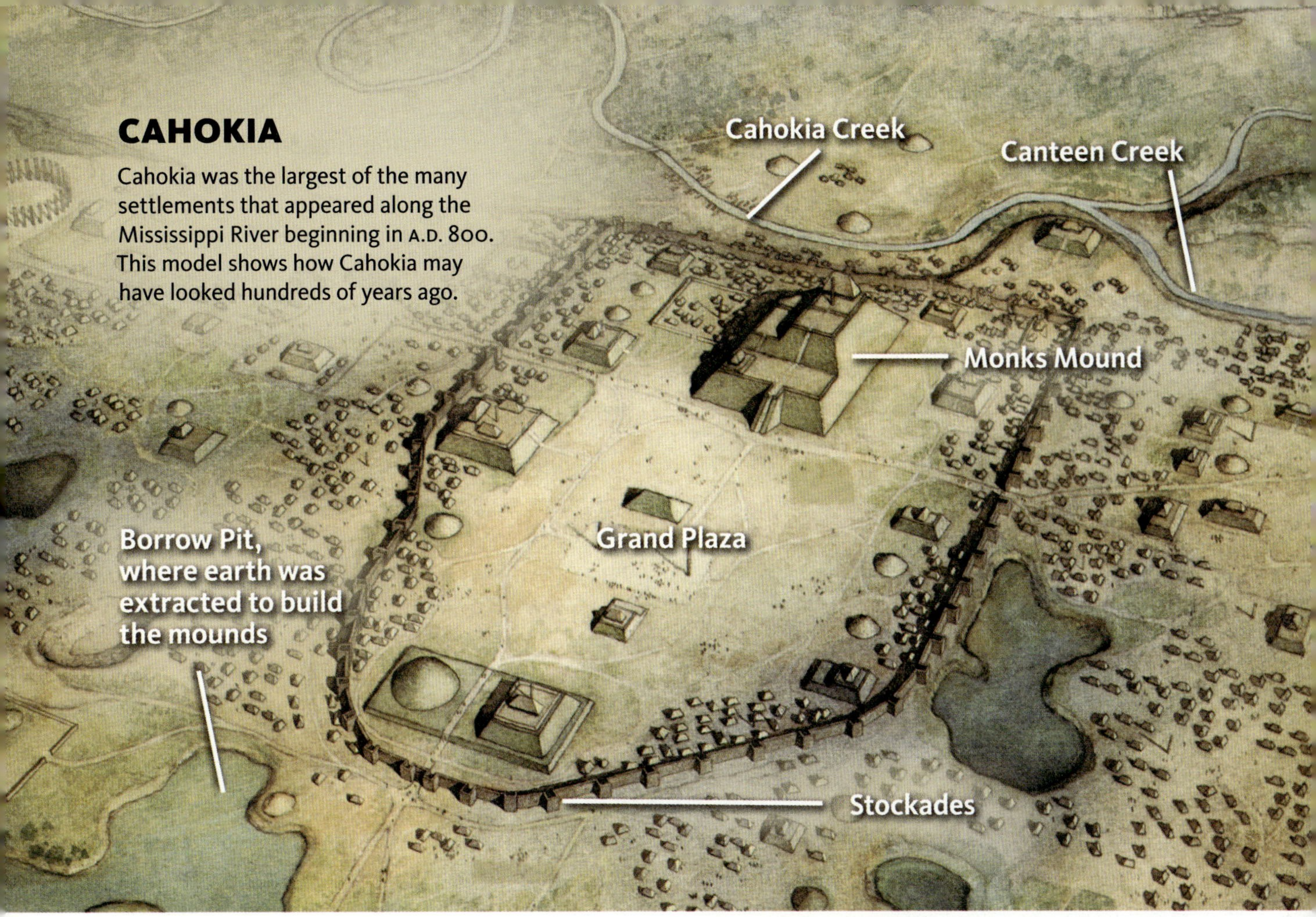

CAHOKIA

Cahokia was the largest of the many settlements that appeared along the Mississippi River beginning in A.D. 800. This model shows how Cahokia may have looked hundreds of years ago.

Cahokia Creek

Canteen Creek

Monks Mound

Grand Plaza

Borrow Pit, where earth was extracted to build the mounds

Stockades

when the chief died, the people destroyed the palace, added more earth to the mound, and built a new palace for the next ruler.

Cahokians engaged in widespread trade with other Mississippian cities and towns. Using the Mississippi River and other waterways, they exchanged freshwater pearls, silver, copper, beads, and pottery.

By 1400, Cahokia had been abandoned. Archaeologists are not sure why, but many think this once-mighty city may have been weakened by less abundant crop production, disease, overpopulation, or warfare.

Archaeologists found this artifact, called the Rattler Frog Pipe, in a burial mound near Cahokia. They think it may represent a shaman in an amphibian disguise.

REVIEW & ASSESS

1. **READING CHECK** What purposes did mounds serve in the Adena, Hopewell, and Mississippian cultures?
2. **DRAW CONCLUSIONS** How was agriculture important to the way of life of Mississippian cultures?
3. **ANALYZE VISUALS** Based on the text and illustration of Cahokia, what purpose might the stockades have served?

2.5 Cultures in the East and Southeast

Like cultures in the Pacific Northwest, Native Americans who lived on the opposite side of North America relied on the plentiful wood and game from the forests and woodlands that surrounded them. Over time, they developed sophisticated ways of governing themselves.

MAIN IDEA

Native American cultures in the East and Southeast developed complex political organizations.

THE CHEROKEE AND THE CREEK

The **Cherokee** lived in the forests of the present-day states of Georgia, Tennessee, North Carolina, and South Carolina. They built permanent log cabins using the wood from the forests that surrounded them. The Cherokee hunted deer, elk, and bear, and they also farmed, growing crops such as corn, beans, and squash.

Individual Cherokee villages formed complex alliances with each other and with other cultures. During wartime, some villages were known as "red towns," where the people held war councils and ceremonies. Other villages were considered "white towns," or towns devoted to peace. Spanish explorers arrived in the mid-1500s, and British colonists moved into the region in the 1700s. The Cherokee traded extensively with both groups, exchanging furs and animal hides for horses, fabrics, and firearms.

The **Creek** lived south and west of the Cherokee, in what are now the states of Alabama, Mississippi, Florida, Georgia, South Carolina, and Tennessee. Like the Cherokee, the Creek formed alliances with different tribes that spoke related languages.

The Creek had great respect for fire. Each settlement had a permanent fire, which the people believed was a symbol of the life-giving powers of the sun. The female head of each household lit a fire from the village's flame and then carried it to her family. With this custom, the Creek developed a strong sense of unity within the community.

An important custom that the Cherokee and the Creek shared was the Green Corn Ceremony. Corn was an important crop for both groups. The Cherokee and Creek held this ceremony when their corn first ripened, in early to mid-summer. Over a period lasting from four to eight days, they feasted, held dances, and repaired buildings. At the height of the ceremony, they relit the sacred fire at the center of the village's plaza.

THE ALGONQUIN AND THE IROQUOIS

The **Algonquin** and **Iroquois** dominated the woodlands of the Northeast, in present-day southern Canada, upper New York, and Pennsylvania. Each culture included different tribes with their own languages and customs. The woodlands provided wood, plants, and animals, but they could not support enough farming to sustain large cities.

Instead, farmers in temporary villages relied on slash-and-burn techniques. Algonquin and Iroquois farmers burnt fields out of the forests and grew crops such as corn, beans, and squash until the soil was exhausted, or depleted of nutrients. Entire villages would then move on and create new fields elsewhere.

This reproduction shows what an Iroquois longhouse may have looked like. Like wigwams, longhouses had domed roofs and were covered with tree bark for protection.

The Algonquin lived in **wigwams**, or domed huts built on a framework of poles and covered with skins or bark. Wigwams could be quickly moved and easily adapted to the changing weather. The Algonquin farmed for much of the year, but in winter moved around because they were hunting game. Chiefs led villages made up of related families. Villages traded and formed loose **confederations**, or groups of allies, to help each other through war or hardship.

In contrast to the Algonquin, the Iroquois developed a more formal political structure. They called themselves the "people of the longhouse." They lived in villages of longhouses, in which as many as 10 families lived. Iroquois tribes fought each other until the 1500s, when they formed the Iroquois League. This agreement formally bound together five tribes—Onondaga, Seneca, Mohawk, Oneida, and Cayuga—in a representative and democratic alliance.

REVIEW & ASSESS

1. **READING CHECK** What was the function of the Green Corn Ceremony in Cherokee and Creek culture?
2. **COMPARE AND CONTRAST** How did the political structures of the Algonquin and Iroquois differ?
3. **MAKE INFERENCES** How might the Iroquois League have helped end fighting among the Iroquois tribes?

CHAPTER 17 Review

VOCABULARY

Use each of the following vocabulary words in a sentence that shows an understanding of the term's meaning.

1. **quinoa**
   The Inca grew quinoa, a high-protein grain native to the Andes Mountains.
2. **wigwam**
3. **totem pole**
4. **terrace farming**
5. **adobe**
6. **confederation**
7. **potlatch**
8. **quarry**
9. **geoglyph**

READING STRATEGY

10. **ORGANIZE IDEAS: SEQUENCE EVENTS**
    If you haven't already, complete your time line to sequence events that occurred in civilizations in South and North America. Then answer the question.

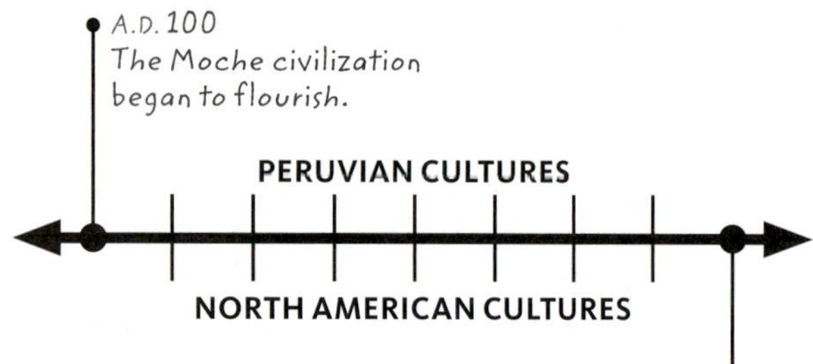

A.D. 100
The Moche civilization began to flourish.
PERUVIAN CULTURES
NORTH AMERICAN CULTURES
A.D. 500
The Tlingit developed tools for splitting and carving wood.

What event affected civilizations in both South and North America in the 1500s?

MAIN IDEAS

Answer the following questions. Support your answers with evidence from the chapter.

11. What have archaeologists learned about pre-Inca cultures from various discoveries in Peru? **LESSON 1.1**
12. Why did the Inca Empire develop rapidly under the leadership of Pachacuti? **LESSON 1.3**
13. What factors helped Machu Picchu survive the Spanish conquest? **LESSON 1.4**
14. On what natural resources did Northwest Coast cultures rely? **LESSON 2.1**
15. How did the beginning of pottery making signal a shift in ancient Pueblo culture? **LESSON 2.2**
16. Why were buffalo important to the people of the Great Plains? **LESSON 2.3**
17. What made it possible for the Mississippi River Valley to support large cities? **LESSON 2.4**

CRITICAL THINKING

Answer the following questions. Support your answers with evidence from the chapter.

18. **EVALUATE** Were the cultures in South and North America successful in adapting to their environments? Explain your answer.
19. **COMPARE AND CONTRAST** Consider what you have learned in previous chapters of this book. What distinguishes the Inca from the early river valley civilizations of Mesopotamia, Egypt, India, and China?
20. **MAKE INFERENCES** Why was a network of roads important to the success of the Inca Empire?
21. **ANALYZE CAUSE AND EFFECT** How were complex societies in the Pacific Northwest able to develop and grow without farming?
22. **YOU DECIDE** Did the size of the Inca Empire contribute to its fall? Support your opinion with evidence from the chapter.

(Banco Central de Reserva Del Perú, Lima, Perú)

INTERPRET VISUALS

Study the photograph showing farming terraces built by the Inca. Then answer the questions that follow.

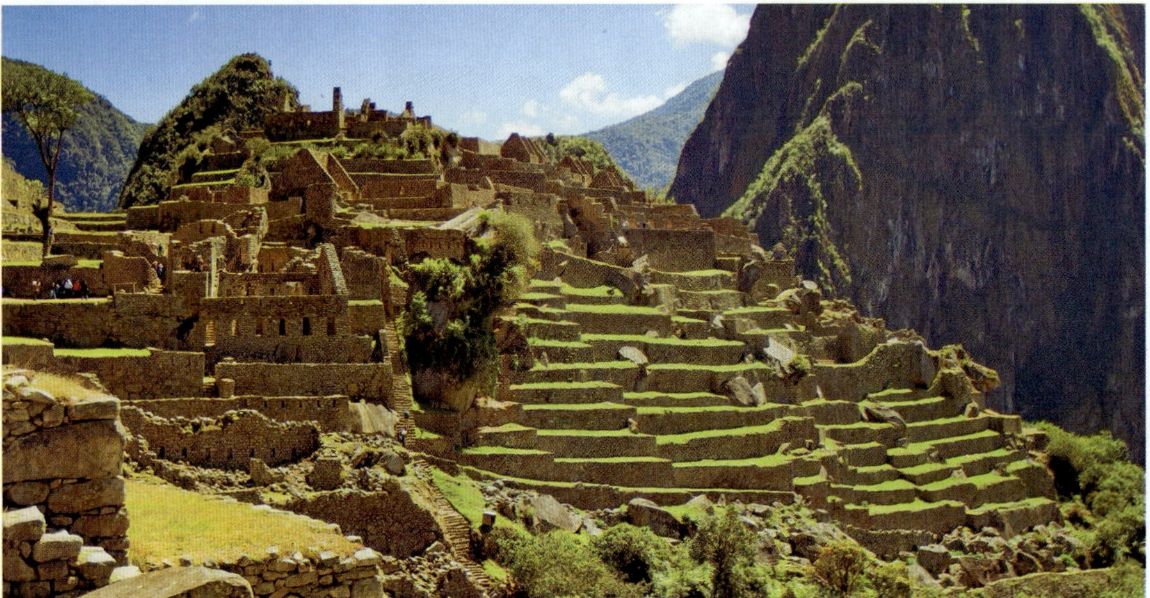

23. Use details in the photo to describe the method of terrace farming the Inca used.

24. Why might Inca farmers have preferred flat surfaces on which to grow crops?

ANALYZE SOURCES

While on an expedition in the Andes in 1911, American explorer Hiram Bingham and his guide discovered a city that had been hidden for nearly 400 years: Machu Picchu. Read the passage and then answer the question.

> We were confronted with an unexpected sight, a great flight of beautifully constructed stone-faced terraces, perhaps a hundred of them, each hundreds of feet long and ten feet high. . . . The flowing lines, the symmetrical arrangement of the [large stones], and the gradual gradation of the [layers], combined to produce a wonderful effect, softer and more pleasing than that of the marble temples of the Old World.
>
> from *Lost City of the Incas*, by Hiram Bingham, 1952

25. What were Bingham's impressions of the architecture at Machu Picchu?

WRITE ABOUT HISTORY

26. INFORMATIVE Suppose you are contributing to a booklet about Native American cultures. Write a paragraph that explores the impact of the Spanish use of guns and horses on either the Inca or the people of the Great Plains.

TIPS

- Take notes from the lessons about the Inca or the Great Plains peoples.
- Begin the paragraph with a clear topic sentence.
- Develop the paragraph with supporting details and examples of the impact of Spanish guns and horses on your chosen group.
- Use vocabulary from the chapter as appropriate.
- Conclude with a sentence about how changes resulting from the introduction of guns and horses affected the Inca or people of the Great Plains.

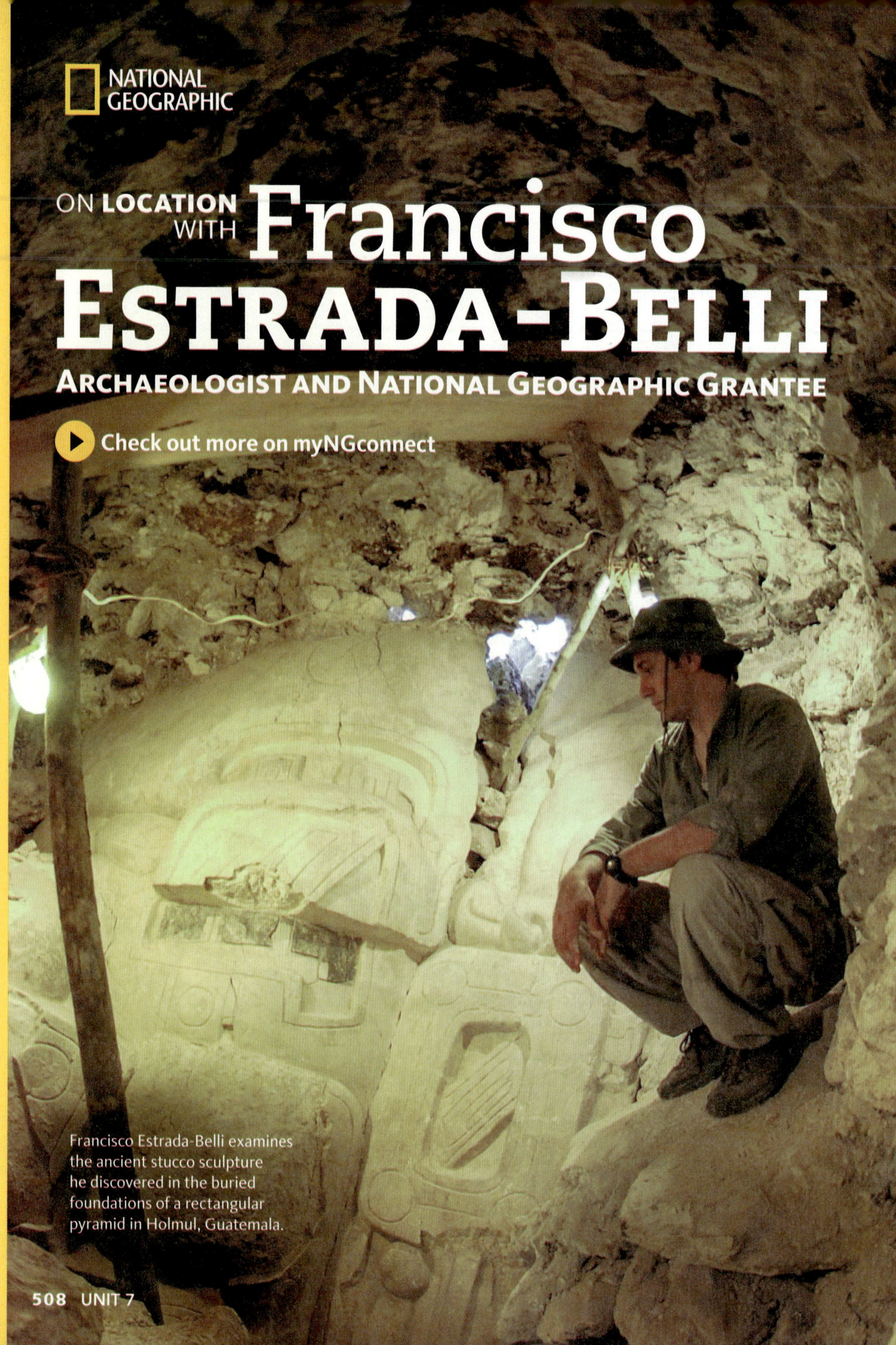

NATIONAL GEOGRAPHIC

ON LOCATION WITH Francisco ESTRADA-BELLI

ARCHAEOLOGIST AND NATIONAL GEOGRAPHIC GRANTEE

Check out more on myNGconnect

Francisco Estrada-Belli examines the ancient stucco sculpture he discovered in the buried foundations of a rectangular pyramid in Holmul, Guatemala.

HIDDEN CITIES

Exploring lost Mayan cities hidden deep in the jungles of Guatemala—that's my job! Every year we discover additional sites to explore to learn more about the Maya civilization, which thrived in Central America for nearly 1,500 years. It seems incredible, but in Guatemala you can still hack your way through the vegetation and come face-to-face with a long lost city.

As a child I visited the magnificent Mayan ruins of Tikal. I had so many questions! How did the Maya build such a great civilization in a jungle? Why did they leave their city? That's why I became an archaeologist: to try and answer some of those questions. I wanted to shed light on the beginnings of Maya civilization, so I chose to study the buried Maya city of Holmul, which had been partially excavated a hundred years ago and then forgotten. It was a good place to start. Exploring nearby, I found another lost Maya city called Cival. This turned out to be one of the earliest cities the Maya built, around 800 B.C. This was over 1,000 years before classic Maya civilization blossomed in cities like Tikal. By showing the complexity and innovation of early Maya settlements, including their architecture, our findings challenge the common belief that the early Maya were simple village farmers.

BURIED SCULPTURES

We've made many important discoveries, including a massive sculpture buried beneath a temple's rubble at Holmul. The site already had been ransacked by looters,

Archaeology can be messy. Here, Estrada-Belli uses a tractor to tow a car through the muddy Guatemalan jungle.

and if they had dug for another ten minutes, they might have found the sculpture. It's amazingly well-preserved—it even has a little color left on it—and it had almost been lost forever. That makes me feel as if we really rescued the past. I feel like I have made a really important contribution.

I love sharing all this new knowledge with others, not just academics but ordinary people and students. I want to help the modern Maya who live in the area, especially the children, reconnect with their glorious Maya past. Right now, they have little or no knowledge of their heritage, and I believe that people who know their past can live a better life.

WHY STUDY HISTORY?

"The past is irreplaceable, but the past is disappearing because of development, looting, and erosion. I study history because *the past is not a luxury, but instead a necessity* for cultures and for humanity as a whole to be able to live in peace." — Francisco Estrada-Belli

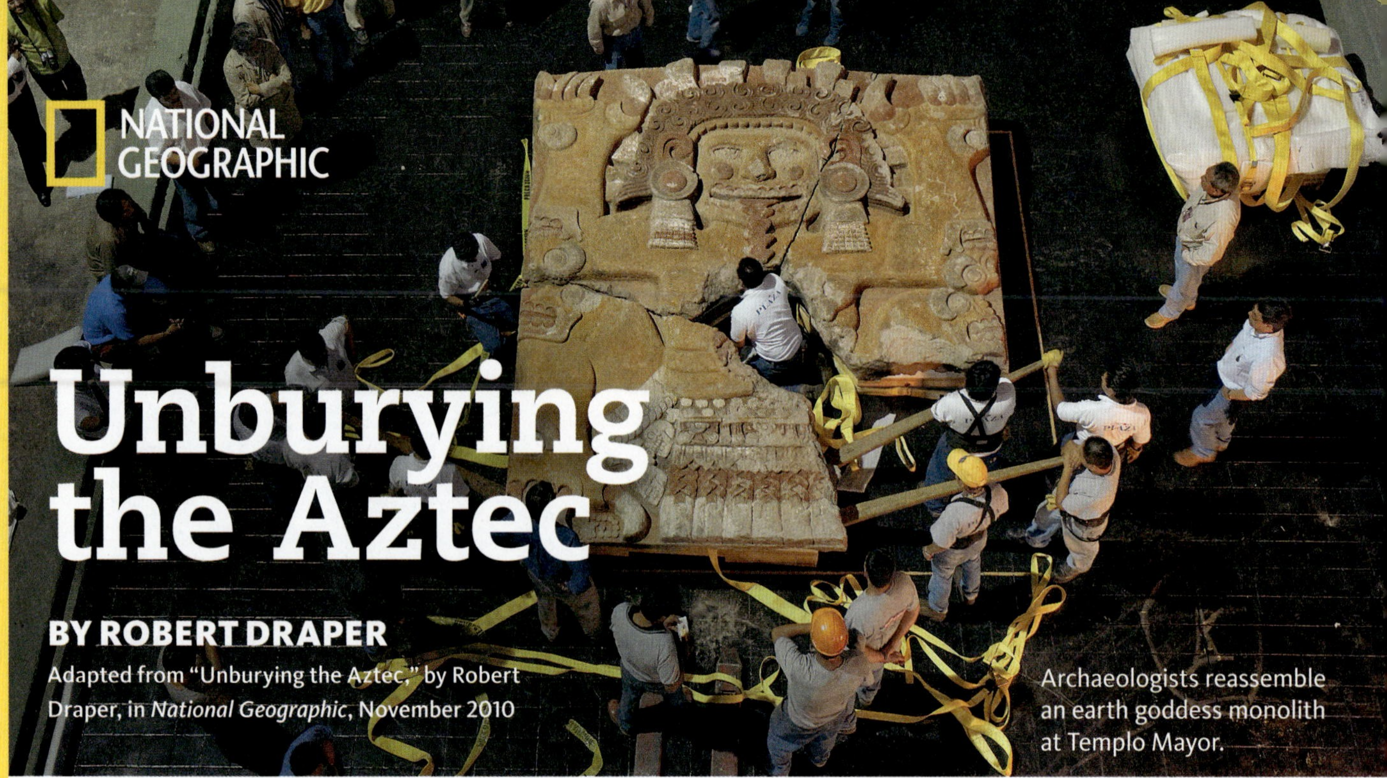
NATIONAL
GEOGRAPHIC

Unburying the Aztec

BY ROBERT DRAPER

Adapted from "Unburying the Aztec," by Robert Draper, in *National Geographic*, November 2010

Archaeologists reassemble an earth goddess monolith at Templo Mayor.

Archaeologist Leonardo López Luján might be on the verge of a major discovery. Since the Spanish conquest of Mexico in 1521, no Aztec emperor's remains have been discovered. Yet historical records say that three Aztec rulers were cremated and their ashes buried at the foot of Templo Mayor, in present-day Mexico City.

In 2008, López Luján unearthed a 12-ton monolith representing an earth goddess near Templo Mayor. Immediately, López Luján noticed that the monolith depicted a figure holding a rabbit, with ten dots above it. In the Aztec writing system, 10-Rabbit is 1502—the year that the empire's most feared ruler, Ahuitzotl (ah-WEE-tzoh-tuhl), died. López Luján is convinced that Ahuitzotl's tomb is somewhere near where the monolith was found.

Aztec power was fleeting. They ruled their empire for less than a century before the Spanish demolished it. The Aztec maintained what some scholars call "a cheap empire." The conquered were allowed to continue governing themselves as long as they paid tribute.

Ahuitzotl assumed the throne in 1486. As the eighth emperor, he stretched the empire to its breaking point. His armies made 45 conquests over 16 years, conquering areas along the Pacific coast, down into present-day Guatemala. He also sealed off trade from rivals to the west and increased control over subjugated territories. "He was more forceful, more brutal," says archaeologist Raúl Arana. "When people didn't want to pay tribute, he sent in the military. With Ahuitzotl, the Aztec went to the maximum expression of everything. And perhaps it was too much. All empires have a limit."

López Luján's work at the Templo Mayor site is slow, partly because of the challenges excavating in a modern city. Urban archaeologists have to dig around sewer and subway lines, avoid underground telephone, fiber optic, and electric cables, and maintain security for a dig in the middle of a city. "Sooner or later, we'll find Ahuitzotl's tomb," López Luján hopes. Whether or not he does, the Aztec mystique will continue to occupy modern Mexico's imagination.

For more from National Geographic
Check out "People of the Horse" on myNGconnect

UNIT INQUIRY: DESIGN AN ADAPTATION STRATEGY

In this unit, you learned how civilizations in North and South America adapted to the environments in which they lived. Based on your understanding of the text, what were the environments like in which these different civilizations lived? In what ways did people adapt to survive or become better suited to their environment?

ASSIGNMENT Design an adaptation strategy that you think would be helpful to people moving to a new environment. The strategy should identify the specific environment, such as a new school, neighborhood, or city. The strategy should also include a series of actions/steps people could take to adapt to their new environment. Be prepared to present your strategy to the class and explain how it will help people adapt successfully to the new environment.

Plan As you design your strategy, think about the role adaptation has played in the survival and success of past civilizations. Adaptation—no matter when and where it occurs—does not happen overnight. Think about the steps that would ensure successful adaptation in a new environment today. You might want to use a graphic organizer to help organize your thoughts. ▶

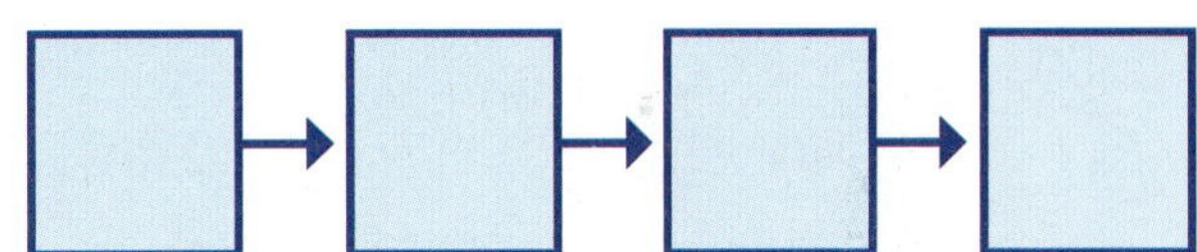

Produce Use your notes to produce descriptions of the elements of your adaptation strategy. You might want to write them in outline or paragraph form.

Present Choose a creative way to present your strategy for adaptation to the class. Consider one of these options:

- Create a multimedia presentation using photos to illustrate the series of actions/steps in your strategy.
- Write a slogan for your strategy that communicates the importance of successful adaptation in a new environment.
- Describe how a potential problem or difficulty in the new environment might be turned into an opportunity.

RAPID REVIEW UNIT 7

AMERICAN CIVILIZATIONS TOP TEN

1. The Maya developed an advanced writing system, and they studied mathematics and astronomy.
2. The Aztec Empire grew powerful through conquest by its formidable army.
3. Spanish conquistadors used steel weapons and horses to overthrow the Aztec and the Inca.
4. The Inca established a massive empire that included more than 12 million people.
5. The Mississippians built many cities in the Mississippi River Valley, including Cahokia.

6-10. **NOW IT'S YOUR TURN** Complete the list with five more things to remember about American civilizations.

WHY STUDY HISTORY ?

TO UNDERSTAND THE SIMILARITIES AND DIFFERENCES AMONG CIVILIZATIONS

You just plowed through five units introducing civilizations with similar but different languages, cultures, and religions. As global citizens, our call to action is to understand that each civilization has its own unique identity. Recognizing the inherent worth and equality of all civilizations and cultures—and, in fact, of all people—is at the heart of global citizenship.

On the Framework of World History chart at the beginning of this text, the civilizations in Units 3, 4, and 5 fall under "World Systems." The Greek, Roman, Byzantine, and Islamic civilizations continued to build on the foundations that early civilizations had established. Some of the civilizations in Africa and the Americas fall under the second and third levels of that chart. Yet all these civilizations established sophisticated cultures. Understanding the similarities and differences among them is one reason we study history.

Fred Hiebert
Watch the Why Study History video

WHAT COMES NEXT? PREVIEW UNITS 8–9

8
HORSE RACE, MONGOLIA

EMPIRES OF ASIA

Follow the inventions and advancements in technology that would open the globe to exploration and trade, cause an explosion in communication, and make human conflict more deadly.

9
SAN GIOVANNI

MEDIEVAL & RENAISSANCE EUROPE

Learn how the cultures and empires of medieval and Renaissance Europe further developed technology and artistic expression to set the stage for today's modern, global world.

KEY TAKEAWAYS UNITS 3–7

PATTERNS IN HISTORY: SIMILAR DEVELOPMENTS ACROSS LOCATIONS

- Continued environmental adaptations in Africa and the Americas improve agricultural production.
- Trade takes off on a global scale, including trans-Saharan movement of gold and salt and Indian Ocean trade between East Africa and Asia.

GOVERNMENT

- In Europe, emphasis shifts to protecting ordinary people, with the development of democracy in ancient Greece and Rome.
- Mighty empires form in Mali and Aksum in Africa.
- In the Americas, the Maya and Inca rise to power.

MOVEMENT OF PEOPLE AND IDEAS

- Hellenistic culture spreads through the empire-building of Alexander the Great.
- Roman culture spreads through colonization and trade.
- Islamic culture spreads through trade and conquest.

ARTISTIC EXPRESSION

- In Europe, new art forms include more realistic "selfies" in statues from ancient Greece; mosaics and frescoes of ancient Rome; and calligraphy and arabesques of Islam.
- The Nok in Africa produce terra cotta sculptures.

TECHNOLOGY & INNOVATION

Engineering and architectural developments include

- columns and temples from ancient Greece
- improved concrete and arches from ancient Rome
- the iron technology of the Nok
- the monumental structures of the Maya, Aztec, and Inca

These massive Roman aqueducts in Segovia, Spain, are evidence of ancient Roman technological advances in arch-building.

AS YOU READ ON

You've got a whole backdrop of complex civilizations to draw on as you read about key civilizations in Asia in Unit 8. Think about how these civilizations helped set the stage for the deep changes that would occur by the 1600s (Unit 9).

Remember that as global citizens, you know that throughout history all civilizations made enduring contributions to the human community. The diversity of those cultures and their contributions is what makes our world a rich and exciting place to live.

EMPIRES OF ASIA

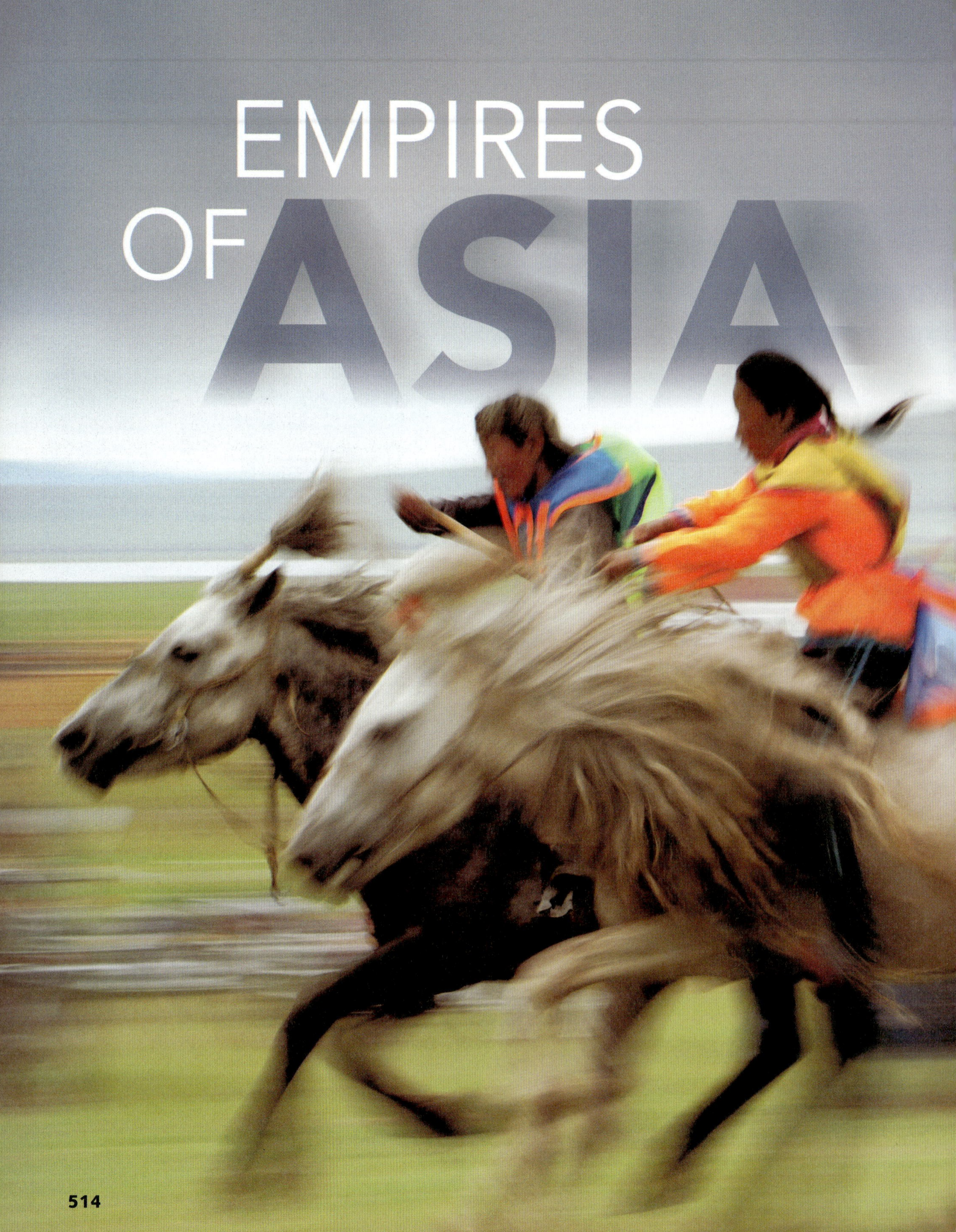

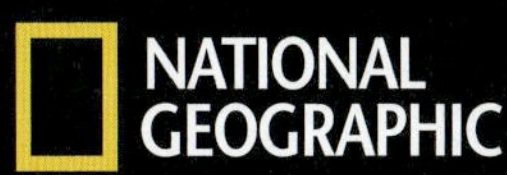

ON **LOCATION** WITH

Albert Lin

Research Scientist/Engineer

Looking for the unknown burial ground of the Mongol emperor Genghis Khan is a big challenge. The vast and unending steppe landscape of Mongolia makes it hard to know where to search. Add to that the fact that the Mongolians consider the tomb of their great leader to be sacred and off-limits to the traditional methods of archaeology—digging in the earth. I'm Albert Lin, and I'm using innovative technology such as satellite imagery and remote sensors to search for Genghis Khan's tomb without ever touching a shovel.

‹ **CRITICAL VIEWING** Children race horses across Central Mongolia during a summer festival. What can you infer about the geography of this region?

UNIT 8
TIME LINE OF WORLD EVENTS

Asian Civilizations

China, Japan, Korea, and Southeast Asia

676
Korea is united for the first time under the Silla kingdom.
(Silla crown)

581
Wendi reunifies China under the Sui dynasty.

938
The Dai Viet state (Vietnam) gains independence from China.

1000

900

500

800
EUROPE
Charlemagne becomes the first Holy Roman Emperor.

1096
EUROPE
Christians begin the First Crusade to recapture the Holy Land.
(illustration of Crusader)

c. 570
ASIA
The prophet Muhammad is born in Mecca.

The World

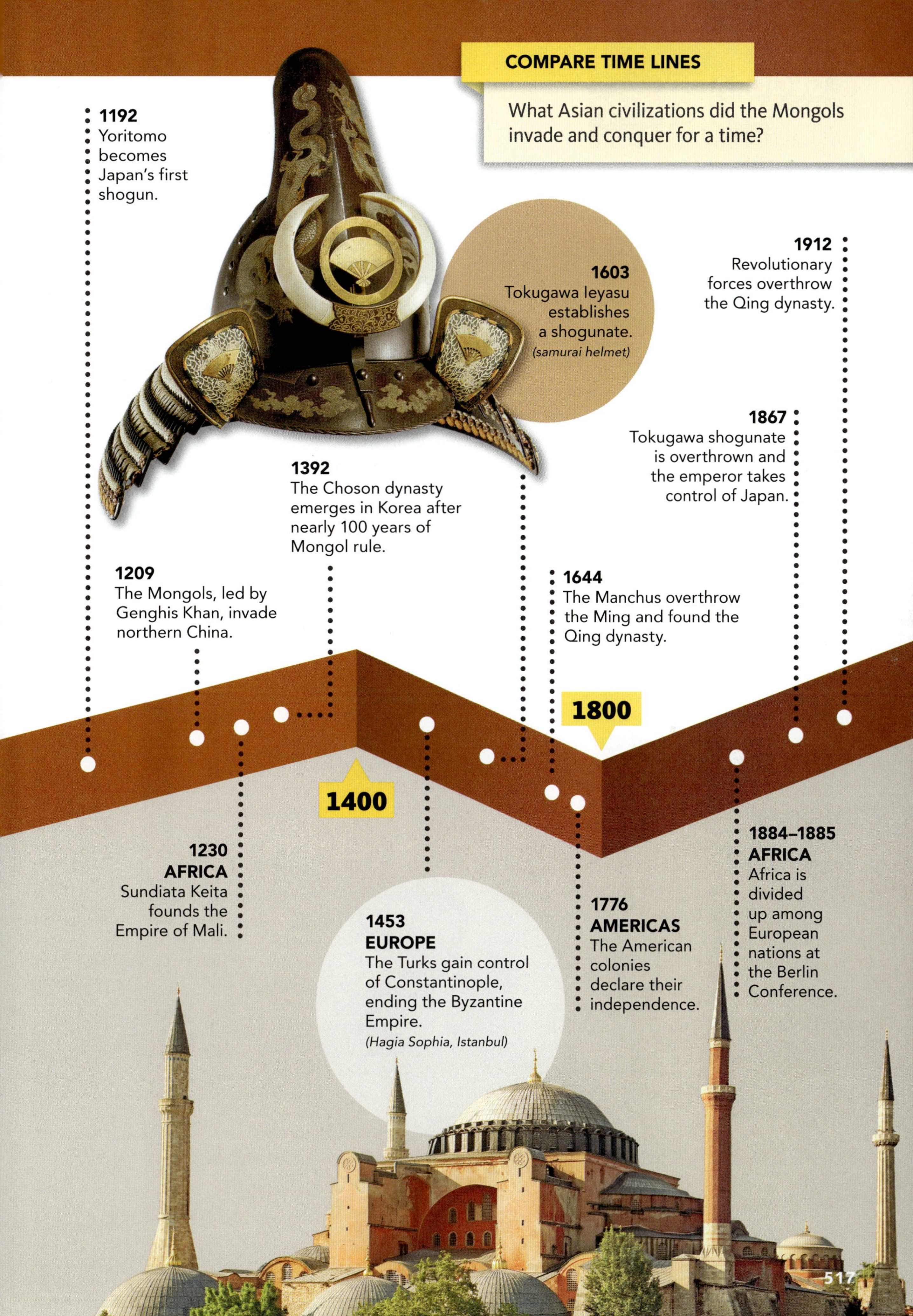
COMPARE TIME LINES
What Asian civilizations did the Mongols invade and conquer for a time?
1192
Yoritomo becomes Japan's first shogun.
1209
The Mongols, led by Genghis Khan, invade northern China.
1230
AFRICA
Sundiata Keita founds the Empire of Mali.
1392
The Choson dynasty emerges in Korea after nearly 100 years of Mongol rule.
1400
1453
EUROPE
The Turks gain control of Constantinople, ending the Byzantine Empire.
(Hagia Sophia, Istanbul)
1603
Tokugawa Ieyasu establishes a shogunate.
(samurai helmet)
1644
The Manchus overthrow the Ming and found the Qing dynasty.
1776
AMERICAS
The American colonies declare their independence.
1800
1867
Tokugawa shogunate is overthrown and the emperor takes control of Japan.
1884–1885
AFRICA
Africa is divided up among European nations at the Berlin Conference.
1912
Revolutionary forces overthrow the Qing dynasty.

UNIT 8
GEOGRAPHY IN HISTORY

Empires of Asia 1100–1200

Between 1100 and 1200, many great empires existed almost side by side in Asia. The Song dynasty, with its many inventions and booming economy, made China the world's most advanced society of the time. Chinese ideas had influenced kingdoms on the Korean Peninsula for centuries. However, the Koryu dynasty adapted Chinese practices, including the idea of a centralized government, to meet their own needs. In the 1200s, both China and the Koryu were conquered by the Mongols, who would establish the largest land empire in history.

East of the Korean Peninsula lay Japan, which was under military rule in the 1100s. In the strictly structured society of Japan at that time, armies of samurai fought to protect their ruler. Far to the south, the Khmer Empire dominated much of Southeast Asia. Intensive rice production was the foundation of Khmer prosperity and power. Only the Dai Viet also ruled in the region. This state began a thousand years of independence for Vietnam.

Where were most of the Asian empires located?

Bay of Bengal

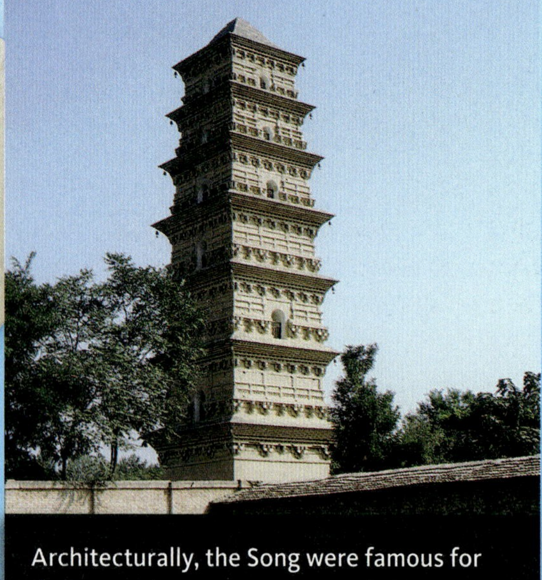

Architecturally, the Song were famous for their pagodas.

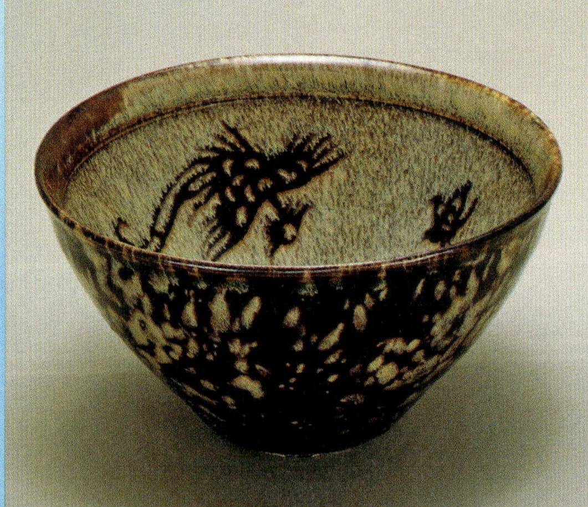

Tea, sipped from bowls like this one, became popular under the Song, and rice became an important crop.

Karakorum
MONGOL HOMELAND
GOBI
Huang He (Yellow R.)
Yangtze R.
Mekong R.
Kaifeng
Yangzhou
Hangzhou
SONG DYNASTY (CHINA)
Chang Jiang (Yangtze R.)
Guangzhou
KORYU DYNASTY (KOREA)
JAPAN
Heian (Kyoto)
Sea of Japan
Yellow Sea
East China Sea
PACIFIC OCEAN
DAI VIET (VIETNAM)
Hanoi
Hainan
KHMER
Angkor
Mekong R.
South China Sea
Philippines
Borneo
Sumatra
Celebe
Empires of Asia
Japan, 1100
Khmer, 1100
Koryu Dynasty (Korea), 1100
Mongol homeland, 1200
Song Dynasty (China), 1100
Da Viet (Vietnam), 1200
Grand Canal
Great Wall
0 200 400 600 800 kilometers
0 200 400 600 800 miles

CHAPTER

18 DYNASTIES OF CHINA

581 – 1912

SECTION 1

A GOLDEN AGE OF PROSPERITY

KEY VOCABULARY	NAMES & PLACES
commerce	Song
movable type	Sui
nirvana	Taizong
porcelain	Tang
reincarnation	Wendi
reunify	Yangdi
staple	

SECTION 2

THE MONGOL EMPIRE

KEY VOCABULARY	NAMES & PLACES
khanate	Genghis Khan
steppe	Kublai Khan
	Marco Polo
	Yuan

SECTION 3

THE MING DYNASTY

KEY VOCABULARY	NAMES & PLACES
isolationism	Hongwu
	Manchus
	Ming
	Qing
	Yongle
	Zheng He

READING STRATEGY

DRAW CONCLUSIONS When you draw conclusions, you support them with evidence from the text. Use a graphic organizer like this one to draw conclusions about the impact of the Tang, Song, and Ming dynasties on Chinese civilization.

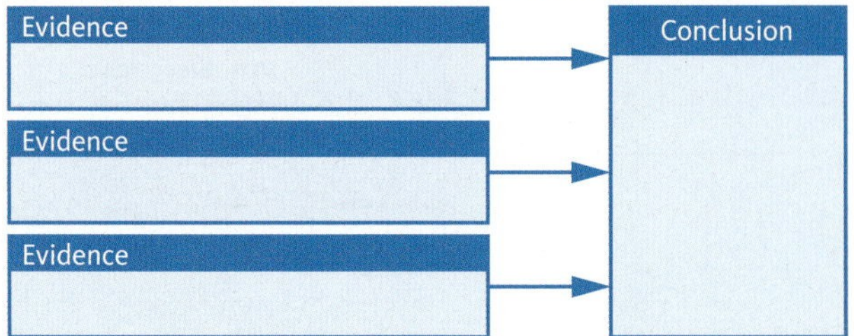
Tang, Song, or Ming Dynasty
Evidence
Evidence
Evidence
Conclusion

故宫博物院

The north gate of Beijing's Forbidden City, known as the Gate of Divine Prowess, served as an entrance and exit for China's empresses.

1.1 Reunification Under the Sui Dynasty

A famous Chinese proverb says, "After a long split, a union will occur; after a long union, a split will occur." This saying reflects the belief that Chinese history has been a series of cycles alternating between strength and weakness. After a period of unrest, a strong leader establishes a powerful dynasty. It flourishes and then eventually declines until the people rebel and a new dynasty gains power. This dynastic cycle is a repeating theme in Chinese history.

MAIN IDEA

The short-lived Sui dynasty reunified China after centuries of civil war.

WENDI'S RULE

The Han dynasty, which began its rule of China in 206 B.C., ruled China for centuries, until weak rulers, rebellions, and powerful warlords caused its collapse in A.D. 220. China was plunged into nearly 400 years of civil war among many small kingdoms. The state belief system of Confucianism declined, though its ethical ideals and Chinese culture survived.

Then, in 581, the dynastic cycle turned again. A general named **Wendi** seized power and established a new dynasty called the **Sui** (sway). Wendi's conquests allowed him to **reunify**, or join together again, northern and southern China. He then faced the enormous challenge of restoring order across a vast and culturally diverse land.

To reunify China, Wendi strengthened the central government, limiting the power of local nobles and the bureaucracy. The government selected new officials by written examination and made sure they better reflected China's diverse ethnic groups. The military was organized and brought under Wendi's control.

Wendi also issued a new law code that combined northern and southern traditions. He gave farming land to former soldiers, established agriculture in the border regions of the empire, and extended the canal system. Wendi encouraged religious tolerance but also promoted the popular religion of Buddhism. When he died unexpectedly in 604, he left a strong empire for his son and successor, **Yangdi**.

THE GRAND CANAL

Yangdi loved luxury and built extravagant palaces in his new eastern capital at Luoyang (lu-WOH-YAHNG). Yangdi extended some of his father's useful public projects, such as restoring and expanding the Great Wall to help protect China's long and vulnerable northern border, and building state granaries to protect the food supply.

He also built the Grand Canal, connecting the southern Chang Jiang with the northern Huang He. This incredible 1,200-mile waterway had a road alongside it and became a vital communication link. It united China's economy, allowing southern China's plentiful resources to flow north where the government and armies were located. However, it came at a cost. Millions of peasants were forced to work on it, and many of them died.

SUI AND TANG DYNASTIES, 581–907
Beijing
Luoyang
Xi'an
Huang He (Yellow R.)
Grand Canal
Yangzhou
Hangzhou
CHINA
Chian Jiang (Yangtze R.)
Yellow Sea
East China Sea
PACIFIC OCEAN
South China Sea
INDIAN OCEAN
Sui dynasty, 581–618
Tang dynasty, 618–907
Grand Canal
Great Wall
Boundary of modern China
0 200 400 Miles
0 200 400 Kilometers
N
S
E
W

The people of China hated this forced labor and the high taxes imposed by both Wendi and Yangdi to pay for such projects. Yangdi also launched expensive and unsuccessful wars against Korea. The military campaign required more money and service from his unhappy subjects.

Yangdi grew increasingly unpopular until, in 611, a famine finally pushed the people to rebel. It was the dynastic cycle at work. Rich and poor rose up against Yangdi's harsh rule, and he was assassinated. The Sui dynasty proved to be short-lived. In 618, a new dynasty—the Tang—rose to power. These leaders would continue to unify China.

REVIEW & ASSESS

1. **READING CHECK** What is the Sui dynasty known for?
2. **MAKE INFERENCES** How did the Sui dynasty reflect the pattern of the dynastic cycle?
3. **INTERPRET MAPS** How might the Grand Canal have improved China's trade network?

1.2 The Spread of Buddhism

When bad things happen, it's common to question our beliefs and re-examine our understanding of the world. In trying to make sense of the suffering, we might find comfort in the spirituality of religion—the belief that a higher power can end the misery. The Chinese people found comfort in religion when they most needed it.

MAIN IDEA

In troubled times, many Chinese turned to Buddhism.

BUDDHISM IN CHINA

The collapse of the Han dynasty in A.D. 220 plunged China into chaos for a period that would last hundreds of years. In such troubled times, many Chinese turned from the practical belief system known as Confucianism to a new, more spiritual religion—Buddhism.

As you learned in Chapter 6, Buddhism was based on an understanding of life founded by Siddhartha Gautama in India around 500 B.C. He taught that the keys to a good life were revealed in the Four Noble Truths: Life is full of suffering; the cause of suffering is desire and ignorance; to end the cycle of desire is to end suffering; and one can be free of desires by following the Eightfold Path. The path promoted a balanced life in which the sum of a person's deeds, or karma, results in **reincarnation**, or rebirth, into another life. Through good karma over successive lifetimes, a person could reach the state of **nirvana**—an end of reincarnation and the suffering of life.

Foreign traders and missionaries brought Buddhism to China during the first century A.D. During the collapse of the Han dynasty and the civil war that followed, Buddhism's teachings provided comfort and offered a clear path beyond suffering. Buddhist texts were translated, and Buddhist practices were adapted into a distinctive Chinese form, which became very popular among all classes of people.

Over the following centuries, Buddhism's popularity rose and declined, but emperors often promoted it to gain the people's support, as Wendi had done. This promotion included building magnificent monuments and not taxing Buddhist religious lands. Meanwhile, Buddhism continued to spread rapidly across the east and southeast areas of Asia, especially Korea and Japan.

IMPACT ON CONFUCIANISM

After the chaotic period of civil war ended, Confucianism made a comeback during the 600s. The government reintroduced traditional Confucian-style tests for the civil service. Confucian principles of respect, responsibility, loyalty, and duty to family and the state became popular once again.

In contrast, Buddhism encouraged moral behavior but played down the importance of obedience to outside authority in favor of inner guidance. Daoism, which emphasized our essential unity with nature, also had a strong following. These three competing belief systems became interwoven. Confucianism's concern with earthly duty influenced the religious spirituality of Buddhism and Daoism. As a result, Confucianism once more emerged as an important part of Chinese society.

Critical Viewing This Buddhist cave painting from China shows a seated figure meditating. What do the details in this painting suggest about Buddhism?

REVIEW & ASSESS

1. **READING CHECK** After the collapse of the Han dynasty, why did many Chinese turned to Buddhism?

2. **SEQUENCE EVENTS** How was Buddhism first introduced in China?

3. **COMPARE AND CONTRAST** How do the main principles of Confucianism and Buddhism differ?

1.3 Tang and Song Dynasties

A picture is worth a thousand words—but it often does not last as long. Only words remain to capture the brilliance of Chinese painting from this era. For example, legend tells how the acclaimed Tang artist Wu Daozi (woo dow-dzuh) painted a mural that was so lifelike, he walked into it and disappeared forever.

MAIN IDEA

Under the Tang and Song dynasties, China grew and prospered.

THE TANG DYNASTY

Although unpopular, the Sui dynasty established solid foundations of government for future dynasties to build on. After the rulers of the **Tang** dynasty seized power in 618, they continued the Sui policy of tolerance toward China's many religions and cultures. They encouraged economic growth through agricultural reform and trade. The dynasty also strengthened the government by using civil service examinations to select government officials. These well-educated scholar-officials carried out government policy. They helped keep the government stable from one emperor to the next.

These reforms helped the Tang expand the empire into central and southern Asia. (See the map in Lesson 1.1.) Meanwhile, literature and art flourished in a golden age. Few paintings survive, but beautiful sculptures reveal the talent of the artists of this period. Also, around 48,000 poems exist from this time. Tang officials were encouraged to write poetry.

Taizong (ty-johng) was the second Tang emperor and an admired figure in Chinese history. From 626 to 649, he used Confucian ideas to organize his government. Later, Wu Zhao (woo jow), the wife of Taizong's son and successor Gaozong, became China's only official female emperor by ruthlessly eliminating her rivals, including her own children. Despite the stormy succession, Wu Zhao had inherited a peaceful and well-run country. Her policies were sensible, improved the life of the people, and helped strengthen the empire. Later Tang emperors were less successful. Political instability sparked a long civil war in which millions died. Poor rulers, corruption, and rebellion weakened Tang authority until the dynasty lost power in 907. Once again, China plunged into chaos.

THE SONG DYNASTY

In 960, over 50 years later, the **Song** dynasty restored order. Though the Song rulers did not expand the territory of the empire, they introduced domestic improvements that made Song China the world's most advanced society of the time. Confucianism again became the state philosophy. Art and literature thrived while technology led to new inventions. Agriculture expanded with new techniques in drainage, irrigation, and terrace farming. Strains of rice from Southeast Asia doubled the harvest, and rice became China's **staple**, or main crop. In a short period, from 750 to 1100, China's population doubled to 100 million.

Meanwhile, this growth led to more rapid trade, and China's economy boomed. Farmers grew sugar cane, tea, bamboo, and hemp for trade, and the traditional crafts of

Critical Viewing These glazed ceramic camels were made during the Tang dynasty. Why do you think camels were important to the dynasty?

silk, paper, and ceramics grew in popularity. Improved roads and canals carried goods within China, while bigger ships carried exports overseas. For the first time, the state made more money from trade than from agriculture. Because of the strong economy, China started banks and printed the world's first paper money. Economic prosperity led to the growth of cities, which became busy centers of culture and **commerce**, or the buying and selling of goods.

REVIEW & ASSESS

1. **READING CHECK** How did China change during the Song dynasty?
2. **MAKE INFERENCES** How did reforms introduced under the Tang dynasty contribute to China's golden age?
3. **ANALYZE CAUSE AND EFFECT** How did the growth of trade during the Song dynasty affect China?

1.4 The Legacy of Chinese Inventions

Imagine using dimes to buy a car. Maybe you'd start counting but soon give up. Dollar bills are far more convenient. Printed money was a Chinese invention, as were printed books, porcelain, navigational compasses, and gunpowder. All these new inventions were created during the Tang and Song dynasties. It's difficult to imagine our world without these items.

MAIN IDEA

Chinese inventions have helped shape the world we live in today.

PRINTING AND PAPER MONEY

The Chinese had invented paper around A.D. 100. About five hundred years later, they contributed another bookmaking breakthrough—block printing. This technique involved carving the text in reverse to stand out on a block of wood. The block was painted with ink and pressed onto paper to create a printed page. Carving the blocks for each page of each book was a long process.

Around 1041, the innovation of **movable type**, which used individually carved characters, made it easier and cheaper to print books. The new widespread distribution of books helped spread government regulations, literature, and the ideas of Confucianism and Buddhism.

Meanwhile, China's booming population and economy created a large demand for coins—by 1085 six billion coins were minted per year. The coins were too bulky for large transactions, so merchants began exchanging paper notes as IOUs. The money stayed in a bank but was owned by whoever held the note. Around 1100, the first government-backed currency was issued. Over time, the use of bank seals and increasingly complex designs helped discourage counterfeiting.

GUNPOWDER, THE MAGNETIC COMPASS, AND PORCELAIN

Gunpowder was an accidental discovery by Chinese alchemists attempting to turn worthless metals into gold. These early chemists found that sulfur, saltpeter, and charcoal made a powerful explosive when mixed together. The military found that gunpowder confined in an iron tube could shoot objects great distances. This discovery led to the development of cannons, guns, and fireworks. Later, Chinese armies used gunpowder in Central Asia, and the secret spread.

The Chinese had long used magnetic compasses for ceremonies, but in the 1100s they began using them for navigation. A sliver of magnetized iron hanging from a silk thread or floating in water would point north and south. This property allowed sailors to tell their direction without the sun or stars. Longer sea journeys also became possible, which increased China's maritime trade.

One especially prized trade item was **porcelain**—a strong, light, and nearly see-through ceramic. Porcelain's closely guarded secret was the blending of unique minerals and a glaze at very high temperatures. Because of these secret techniques, porcelain—or china, as it came to be called—was incredibly rare and precious.

CHINESE INVENTIONS

Antique block characters for printing

Movable Type

The Chinese created block characters for use in movable type, a development that made printing easier. Artisans carved characters as individual clay tablets that could be arranged on a board to form text. After printing, the characters could be reused.

Song porcelain vase with celadon glaze

Porcelain

Techniques for creating porcelain were perfected during the Tang dynasty and reached the height of artistry under the Song. The formula used to create porcelain was a closely guarded secret.

Ancient Chinese nautical compass

Compass

The ancient Chinese had developed a compass that was used in rituals. During the Song dynasty, they discovered the secret to making a magnetic compass used for navigation.

Fireworks display

Gunpowder

After the invention of gunpowder, the military experimented with explosive arrows, grenades, rockets, and land mines, and finally developed firearms and fireworks.

REVIEW & ASSESS

1. **READING CHECK** What inventions occurred during the Tang and Song dynasties?
2. **DRAW CONCLUSIONS** Why did the invention of movable type help increase the spread of ideas?
3. **ANALYZE CAUSE AND EFFECT** How did the use of magnetic compasses for navigation affect China's trade?

2.1

BIOGRAPHY

GENGHIS KHAN

A.D. 1162 – 1227

Forget Rome or Britain. It was the Mongols who ruled the largest land empire in history. It stretched from present-day Korea to Hungary and included more than 100 million people of widely differing cultures. And the Mongols conquered all this territory in less than 100 years, thanks to the determination of one man—Genghis Khan.

Job: Universal ruler
Education: His harsh childhood
Home: Near the Onon River
Real Name: Temujin

FINEST HOUR

When he died, Genghis Khan had united the nomadic tribes, conquered China, and extended his rule over all of central Asia.

WORST MOMENT

The death of his father, a defeated Mongol chieftain, left young Temujin and his mother to eke out a living on the harsh steppe.

FRIENDS

Jamuka was a friend and rival whom Temujin later defeated to become universal ruler.

TRIVIA

It is said that Temujin was born grasping a clot of blood in his hand, which has been viewed throughout history as a mixed sign—an omen of his future fame (and notoriety).

THE MONGOL CONQUEST

The Mongols were a loose collection of independent nomadic tribes from the **steppes**—or vast, grassy plains—of northwest China. They spent their lives roaming, raiding, herding, and fighting across this landscape.

A child named Temujin (TEH-moo-juhn) was born on this landscape. He was the son of a defeated Mongol chieftain, and his childhood was harsh. However, Temujin was ambitious, clever, charismatic, and a great warrior. He became a tribal leader and, in 1206, the Mongol people gave him the title **Genghis Khan** (JEHNG-gihs KAHN), meaning "universal ruler."

Despite conflicts among the tribes, there was one thing they all needed—more grazing lands. Genghis Khan organized the diverse bands into a powerful military machine that would sweep mercilessly across Asia in one of history's most impressive conquests.

THE YUAN EMPIRE, 1294
EUROPE
Venice
Kiev
Moscow
RUSSIAN PRINCIPALITIES
Danube R.
Mediterranean Sea
Constantinople
Black Sea
Volga R.
GOLDEN HORDE (KIPCHAK KHANATE)
ASIA
Lake Baikal
Aral Sea
Caspian Sea
Alexandria
Antioch
Tyre
Tigris R.
Euphrates R.
Baghdad
Lake Balkhash
CHAGATAI KHANATE
KHANATE OF THE GREAT KHAN
Karakorum
GOBI
Huang He (Yellow R.)
Beijing
KOREA
Sea of Japan (East Sea)
Bukhara
Samarkand
Kashgar
Dunhuang
Yellow Sea
ILKHANATE
Kabul
Luoyang
Nanjing
Hangzhou
East China Sea
Red Sea
ARABIA
Indus R.
HIMALAYA
TIBET
Chang Jiang (Yangtze R.)
INDIA
Ganges R.
Arabian Sea
AFRICA
N
W
E
S
South China Sea
Silk Roads
Route of Marco Polo
Great Wall
Border of Mongol Empire
0
500
1000 Miles
0
500
1000 Kilometers

In 1212, Genghis Khan and the Mongols invaded northern China, destroying more than 90 cities and killing their inhabitants. Turning west, he destroyed an empire in what is now Iran. He then invaded southern Russia and, in 1215, destroyed China's capital.

When Genghis Khan died around 1226, he had conquered much of central Asia. Four of his sons shared his vast empire, dividing it into four **khanates**, or regions, and expanded their rule into Europe and southern China.

KUBLAI KHAN

China's next great leader was Genghis Khan's grandson, **Kublai Khan** (KOO-bluh KAHN). He rose to become leader of the Mongol Empire in 1264. Kublai Khan was determined to add to his empire by conquering all of southern China. By 1271, he had succeeded, giving the Mongols control over most of China. That year he declared himself emperor, adopting the dynastic name **Yuan** (yoo-ahn) and preparing to help his army meet new challenges.

REVIEW & ASSESS

1. **READING CHECK** How did the Mongols gain power?
2. **COMPARE AND CONTRAST** How were Genghis and Kublai Khan alike?
3. **INTERPRET MAPS** Which cities in the northwest were part of the Mongol Empire?

2.2 Life in Yuan China

You love your country but hate your rulers. The Mongols are in charge, and they discriminate against you. You pay higher taxes than foreigners, receive less justice, and are excluded from the best jobs—all because you're Chinese.

MAIN IDEA

The Mongols set up strict rules to control China.

YUAN GOVERNMENT

Kublai Khan adopted a less destructive approach to governing than that of his predecessors, trying to win over the Chinese people and preserve conquered towns instead of destroying them. Even so, any resistance was brutally punished. During the 1270s, Song loyalists continued to fight the Mongols in southern China. The Mongols defeated the Song uprising of 200,000 troops—and then killed the entire population of Hangzhou (hahng-joh) city. To avoid further suffering, remaining officials of the Song dynasty surrendered in 1279.

Kublai Khan was now ruler of all China—the first to unite all China since the end of the Tang dynasty, which ended in 907—and its first foreign ruler ever. He would rule for 15 years, until his death in 1294. His Yuan dynasty led China for a century, but it was not an easy time for the Chinese.

The Mongols were more used to fighting than governing, and controlling a country as large and sophisticated as China demanded a highly organized government. Under the Yuan dynasty, Chinese government continued much as before, with a strong central state built around a bureaucracy with Confucian rituals and ceremonies.

The big difference was that the Mongols excluded Chinese people from higher positions to stop them from having too much power. Instead, Mongols and foreigners, especially Muslims, received the top jobs. Foreigners migrated to China, including the famous Italian merchant **Marco Polo**, who served as a tax collector and special envoy to the emperor. However, Chinese scholars still had a strong unofficial influence, and Kublai Khan relied on Chinese advisors.

SOCIAL CLASSES

Most Chinese hated living under the Mongols, who treated them as second-class citizens in their own country. Society was divided into four classes. At the top were the Mongols, followed by non-Chinese foreigners. Then came the northern Chinese, who had lived longest under Yuan rule. At the very bottom of society were the southern Chinese, who made up 80 percent of the population.

Many peasant farmers in the bottom bracket of society were forced off their land when they could not pay their taxes. Unable to feed their families, many sold themselves into slavery far from home. The government forced peasants to work on extravagant imperial projects. The Yuan dynasty rebuilt Beijing as a wealthy city filled with magnificent palaces and pleasure gardens enjoyed by rich foreigners.

All this luxury came at a cost for the Chinese. The Mongols feared rebellion because of the pressures they placed on the Chinese. Looking for signs of revolt, agents working for the government kept a close eye on neighborhoods. They forced

People in China still use the Grand Canal, shown in this photograph, to move goods up and down the river.

every ten Chinese families to share a single knife. The government banned meetings and fairs and prevented the Chinese from going out at night or playing sports, thinking it was too much like military exercise.

The Yuan dynasty did make significant contributions, though. During its reign, trade and agriculture expanded. The Yuan built roads and extended the Grand Canal. The Mongol postal service provided efficient communication, and the government introduced an accurate calendar of 365.2 days. Also, with many Chinese scholars out of work, they had more time to write, and Chinese literature flourished.

Still, the Chinese remained hostile to Mongol rule and formed secret societies to plot rebellions. After Kublai Khan's death in 1294, the Yuan dynasty gradually declined. There were seven emperors in 40 years, none of them as gifted as Kublai Khan. Rebellions started to break out, and, by 1368, China was poised for yet another change in dynasties.

REVIEW & ASSESS

1. **READING CHECK** How did the Mongols treat the Chinese under their rule?
2. **MAKE INFERENCES** Why did Kublai Khan exclude the Chinese from important jobs in government?
3. **ANALYZE CAUSE AND EFFECT** Under the Yuan dynasty, how did the Mongols open China to foreigners?

2.3

DOCUMENT-BASED QUESTION

Travels on the Silk Roads

Under the Mongols, China continued to produce goods that were popular all around the world, especially silk and porcelain. The Mongols wanted to encourage commerce, and their control of China and all the lands that connected it to Europe helped trade flourish. The ancient trade routes, the Silk Roads, were revitalized, and new routes reached north to the Mongol capital of Karakorum. From here, great caravans could now travel in safety and ease across the lush plains that had previously been too dangerous because of tribal wars and banditry.

In this illustration from Marco Polo's book of his travels, traders bring spices from the western part of the Mongol Empire to the east.

from *Book of the Wonders of the World* by Marco Polo and Rustichello, 15th century

DOCUMENT ONE

Secondary Source: History Text

from *Genghis Khan and the Making of the Modern World* by Jack Weatherford

Anthropologist Jack Weatherford presents a fairly positive view of the rule of the Mongols. Silk was one of China's most valued exports, and here Weatherford notes how Genghis Khan shaped its distribution.

CONSTRUCTED RESPONSE Why might the people living on the steppes benefit from Genghis Khan's rerouting of exports through their territory?

> A river of brightly colored silk flowed out of China. It was as though Genghis Khan had rerouted all the different twisting channels of the Silk Route, combined them into one large stream, and redirected it northward to spill out across the Mongol steppes.

DOCUMENT TWO

Primary Source: Travel Account

from *Travels* by Marco Polo

Marco Polo was a merchant from Venice whose adventures in Asia have become the most celebrated of the medieval world. His colorful descriptions of life in Mongol China paint a vivid picture of the court of Kublai Khan.

CONSTRUCTED RESPONSE Why would using experts to determine prices make trade fairer and easier?

> Several times a year, parties of traders arrive with pearls and precious stones and gold and silver and other valuables, such as cloth of gold and silk, and surrender them all to the Great [Kublai] Khan. The Khan then summons twelve experts . . . and bids them examine the wares that the traders have bought and pay for them what they judge to be their true value.

DOCUMENT THREE

Primary Source: Artifact

Passport Medallion, c. 1300

Kublai Khan issued a medallion like the one at right to Marco Polo before he set off on his travels. It acted as a passport, helping Marco Polo access difficult areas and secure help and supplies from subjects of the Khan.

CONSTRUCTED RESPONSE How might Marco Polo have helped expand China's foreign contact and trade during the Mongol Empire?

SYNTHESIZE & WRITE

1. **REVIEW** Review what you have learned about the Mongol Empire.
2. **RECALL** On your own paper, write down the main idea expressed through each document and artifact.
3. **CONSTRUCT** Write a topic sentence that answers this question: During the Mongol Empire, how did Genghis Khan and Kublai Khan promote and increase trade?
4. **WRITE** Using evidence from the documents and artifact, write an informative paragraph to support the answer to the question in Step 3.

3.1 Return to Chinese Rule

After a challenging period of Mongol rule, the Chinese people found an unlikely rescuer in a peasant who led China's rebellion. China's next two emperors set out to restore the country to greatness. The Ming dynasty's capital was a spectacular new seat of power that would be used continuously for 500 years.

MAIN IDEA

The Ming dynasty restored China to greatness.

A NEW LEADERSHIP

By the 1360s, Mongol rule had weakened and rebellions broke out. The son of a peasant, Zhu Yuanzhang (joo yoo-ahn-jahng), emerged as a leader. In 1368, the rebels began driving the Mongols north of the Great Wall, eventually bringing an end to Mongol rule. Zhu declared himself **Hongwu** (hung-woo), or the first emperor of the **Ming** dynasty.

The Chinese again ruled China, and Hongwu set out to restore the country to greatness. He could be paranoid, controlling, and cruel, but he worked hard to improve the lives of peasants. Hongwu rebuilt China's agriculture system and supported the growth of manufacturing. He cut government spending and established efficient taxation. He based his rule on the principles of the Tang and Song dynasties, restoring Confucian values. Notices in villages outlined government policy and expectations of moral behavior.

Hongwu's son **Yongle** (yung-loh) was, like his father, a suspicious, ruthless, and tyrannical ruler. However, he also effectively continued his father's work rebuilding China. Yongle sponsored sea expeditions and encouraged local governments to build schools for commoners. He also sponsored great literary works and led armies to suppress China's neighbors.

IMPERIAL PALACE

Like many Chinese emperors, Yongle moved the imperial capital—this time north, to Beijing. This location placed Yongle near his supporters and closer to his armies guarding China's borders. Beijing was well organized. It was laid out in a grid aligned with the points of the compass and surrounded by 14 miles of 40-foot walls. To feed the vast numbers of people who flocked to the capital, Yongle extended the Grand Canal even farther, using advanced engineering to carry boats uphill.

At Beijing's heart was the Imperial Palace, or Forbidden City—so named because few were admitted and only with the emperor's permission. The Forbidden City would be the center of imperial power and government for the next 500 years. It took an estimated one million workers nearly 15 years to complete the palace, which was an architectural marvel. The huge complex boasted hundreds of buildings that towered over Beijing. It included luxurious private residences for the imperial family and more than 100,000 servants. The city's rectangular, symmetrical, and compass-aligned design was said to be in perfect harmony with the world. It remains the world's largest palace—the perfect place for the emperor to fulfill his role as a connection between the will of heaven and the practical rule of Earth.

FORBIDDEN CITY

Governments are often housed in imposing buildings that reflect the power of politics. But few are as impressive as the Imperial Palace in Beijing.

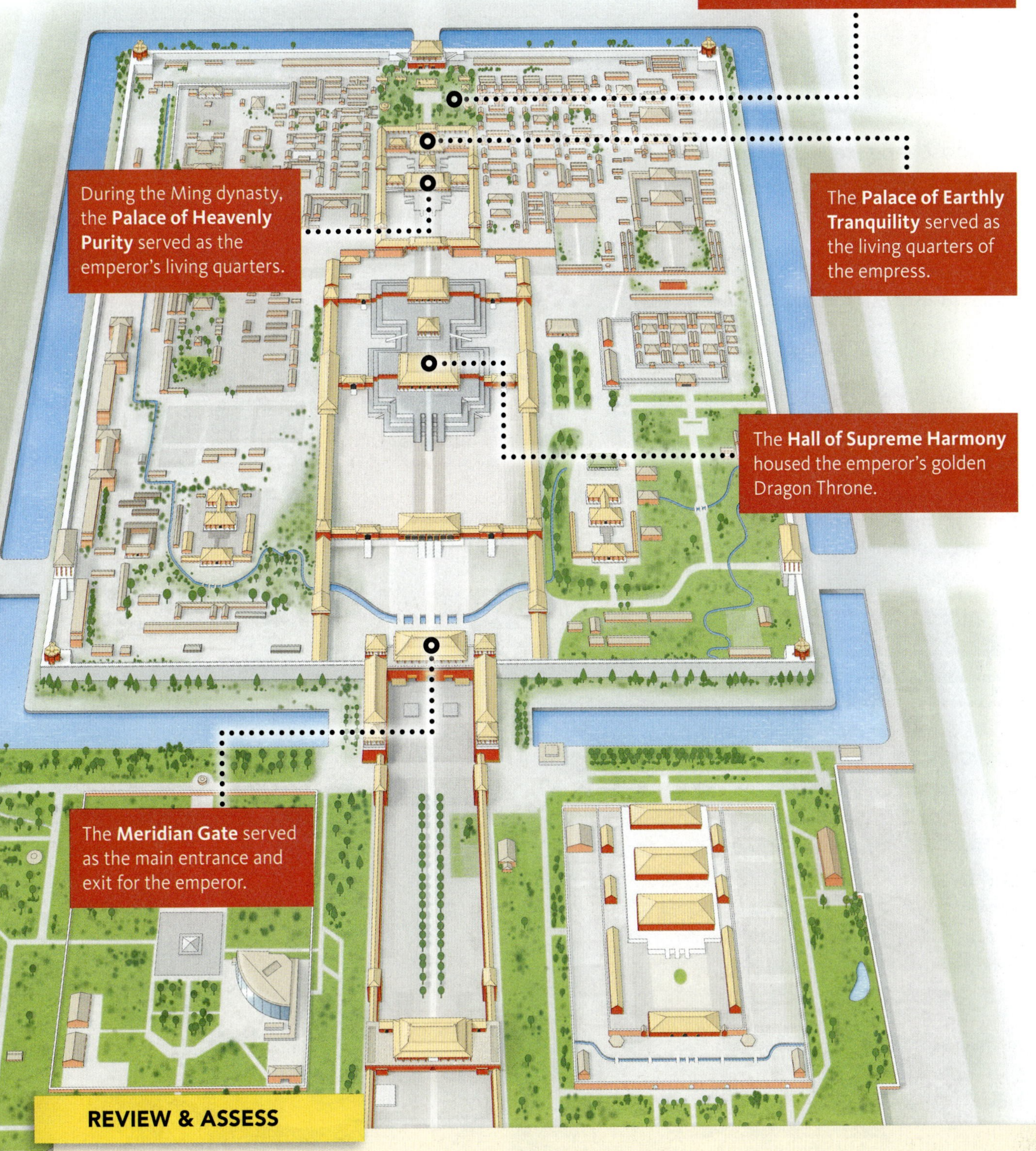

The **Imperial Garden** was filled with fragrant flowers, plants, and trees as well as sculptures and pavilions.
During the Ming dynasty, the **Palace of Heavenly Purity** served as the emperor's living quarters.
The **Palace of Earthly Tranquility** served as the living quarters of the empress.
The **Hall of Supreme Harmony** housed the emperor's golden Dragon Throne.
The **Meridian Gate** served as the main entrance and exit for the emperor.

REVIEW & ASSESS

1. **READING CHECK** How was the Ming dynasty established?

2. **ANALYZE CAUSE AND EFFECT** Why did Yongle move the imperial capital to Beijing?

3. **INTERPRET VISUALS** What did the impressive architecture of the Forbidden City symbolize?

3.2 Zheng He's Explorations

The sea beckoned to a young Chinese Muslim named **Zheng He** (jung huh), who rose through the ranks of the navy and, in 1405, began a series of seven voyages to Asia and Africa. His success was built on the accuracy of Chinese navigation—the best in the world.

MAIN IDEA

Chinese ships and navigational tools allowed China to spread its power and influence by sea.

THE VOYAGES OF ZHENG HE

Zheng He's expeditions included more than 300 ships and nearly 30,000 sailors. This show of force was about more than exploration and trade. It also communicated political power. Zheng He's main mission was to glorify Yongle by asserting Chinese control over trade routes and weaker countries. For three decades, Zheng He sailed 40,000 miles around Southeast Asia, East Africa, and the Middle East.

His ships returned to China laden with treasure and exotic luxuries such as gold, gems, rare spices, giraffes, and zebras. These expeditions established China's international reputation as goods and ideas were exchanged with more countries than ever before. However, not everyone was happy that China was reaching out to other lands.

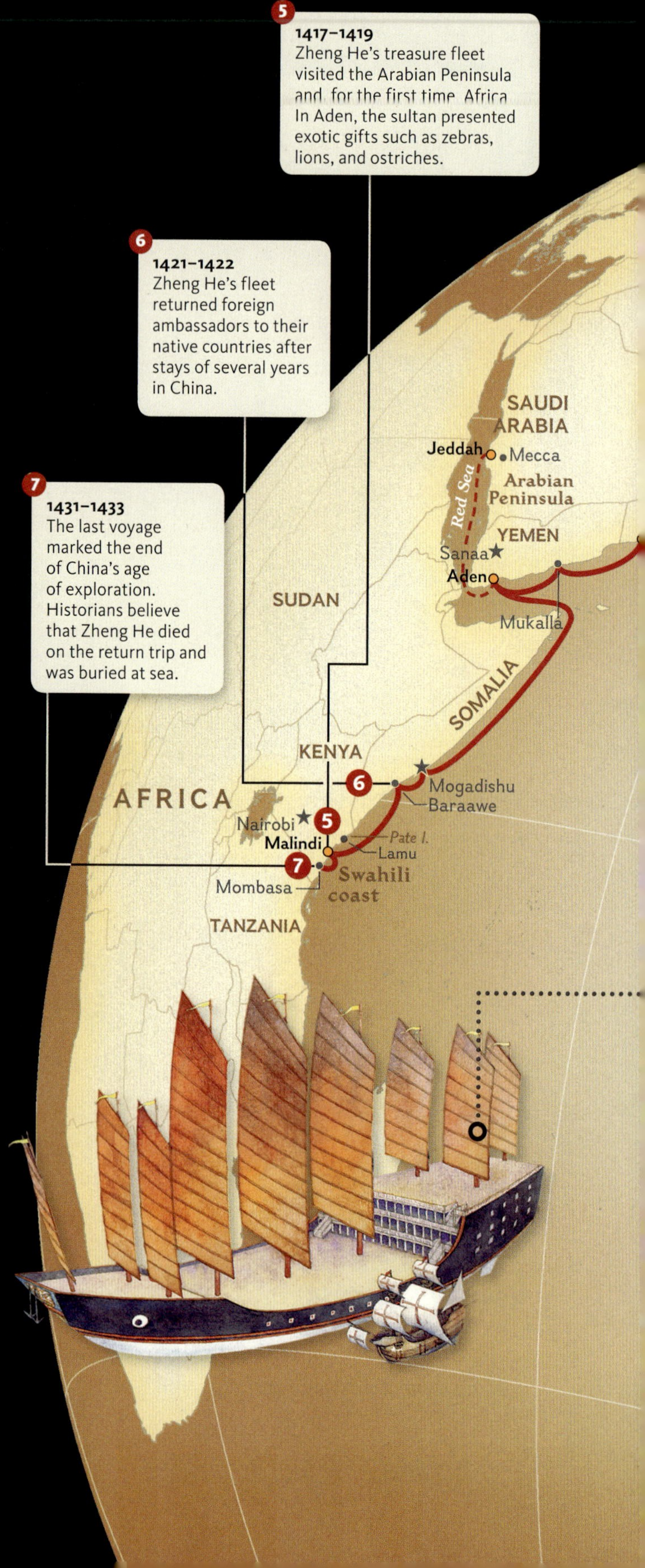

5 **1417–1419**
Zheng He's treasure fleet visited the Arabian Peninsula and, for the first time, Africa. In Aden, the sultan presented exotic gifts such as zebras, lions, and ostriches.

6 **1421–1422**
Zheng He's fleet returned foreign ambassadors to their native countries after stays of several years in China.

7 **1431–1433**
The last voyage marked the end of China's age of exploration. Historians believe that Zheng He died on the return trip and was buried at sea.

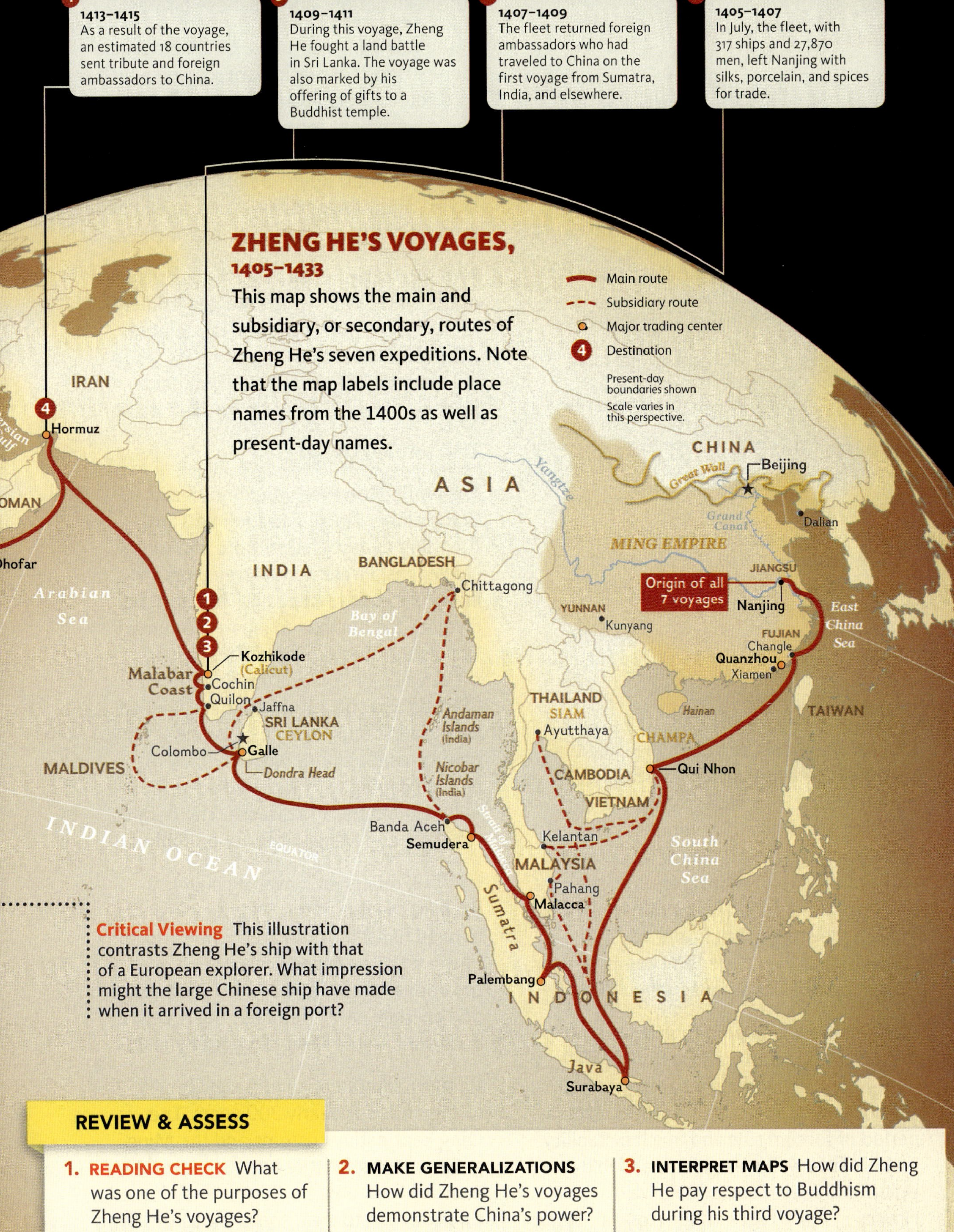
1413–1415
As a result of the voyage, an estimated 18 countries sent tribute and foreign ambassadors to China.
1409–1411
During this voyage, Zheng He fought a land battle in Sri Lanka. The voyage was also marked by his offering of gifts to a Buddhist temple.
1407–1409
The fleet returned foreign ambassadors who had traveled to China on the first voyage from Sumatra, India, and elsewhere.
1405–1407
In July, the fleet, with 317 ships and 27,870 men, left Nanjing with silks, porcelain, and spices for trade.
ZHENG HE'S VOYAGES, 1405–1433
This map shows the main and subsidiary, or secondary, routes of Zheng He's seven expeditions. Note that the map labels include place names from the 1400s as well as present-day names.
Main route
Subsidiary route
Major trading center
Destination
Present-day boundaries shown
Scale varies in this perspective.
IRAN
Hormuz
Persian Gulf
OMAN
Dhofar
Arabian Sea
INDIA
BANGLADESH
Chittagong
Bay of Bengal
ASIA
Yangtze
CHINA
Great Wall
Beijing
Grand Canal
Dalian
MING EMPIRE
JIANGSU
Origin of all 7 voyages
Nanjing
YUNNAN
Kunyang
FUJIAN
Changle
Quanzhou
Xiamen
East China Sea
TAIWAN
Hainan
Kozhikode (Calicut)
Malabar Coast
Cochin
Quilon
Jaffna
SRI LANKA CEYLON
Colombo
Galle
Dondra Head
MALDIVES
Andaman Islands (India)
Nicobar Islands (India)
THAILAND SIAM
Ayutthaya
CHAMPA
Qui Nhon
CAMBODIA
VIETNAM
INDIAN OCEAN
EQUATOR
Banda Aceh
Semudera
Strait of Malacca
Kelantan
MALAYSIA
Pahang
Malacca
South China Sea
Sumatra
Palembang
INDONESIA
Java
Surabaya

Critical Viewing This illustration contrasts Zheng He's ship with that of a European explorer. What impression might the large Chinese ship have made when it arrived in a foreign port?

REVIEW & ASSESS

1. **READING CHECK** What was one of the purposes of Zheng He's voyages?

2. **MAKE GENERALIZATIONS** How did Zheng He's voyages demonstrate China's power?

3. **INTERPRET MAPS** How did Zheng He pay respect to Buddhism during his third voyage?

3.3 China Turns Inward

An ostrich is believed to bury its head in the sand to avoid seeing its enemies. But that doesn't stop its enemies from seeing it—or attacking it. China could have learned a valuable lesson on what not to do from this bird.

MAIN IDEA

China isolated itself from the world, but foreign influences still brought the downfall of the dynastic system.

ISOLATION POLICY

China's great explorer, Zheng He, died during his seventh voyage and was buried at sea. His death marked the end of China's maritime expeditions. There were competing government factions for and against exploration, and when the emperor Zhengtong (jung-tung) took power in 1435, he stopped all future voyages, claiming that they were too expensive and they imported dangerous foreign ideas.

The Chinese considered themselves the most civilized people on Earth. They felt they were surrounded by barbarians and did not need the rest of the world. After a period of foreign rule and much instability in their history, it was understandable that the Chinese reacted this way. However, the effect of Zhengtong's decision was to surrender control of the region's seas and trade to ambitious European nations and Japanese pirates.

In the following centuries, China entered a long period of **isolationism**, during which it rejected foreign contact and influences. The government took up a defensive attitude and geared the economy toward self-sufficiency. Rulers banned foreign trade, kicked out foreigners, and tried to eliminate foreign influences from Chinese society.

Symbolic of this effort was the extension of the Great Wall, which the government rebuilt entirely in stone and completed with 25,000 watchtowers along its 5,500-mile length. The wall was a formidable physical sign of China's defensive isolation.

THE LAST DYNASTY

The world, however, would not leave China alone. Starting in the mid-1500s, the Ming dynasty faced more and more challenges. Pirate raids were common along the southeast coast. The Mongols invaded the north, and Japan conquered Chinese-protected Korea. The cost of these wars, on top of a lavish imperial lifestyle and corruption at court, spelled financial difficulties. The peasants paid taxes for all this while they were already coping with widespread crop failures, famine, and disease. The people rebelled, and Ming authority crumbled.

In 1644, rebels took over Beijing. In despair, the last of the Ming emperors hanged himself from a tree. Tribes north of the wall, the **Manchus**, united and took advantage of the confusion to seize power. They easily defeated the rebels and founded the **Qing** (chihng) dynasty.

China would remain under the Qing's foreign rule for nearly 300 years. The Qing kept native customs and the Ming government structure but also introduced some of their own traditions. They forced Chinese men to wear their hair as the Qing did, in a long braid. The Qing continued

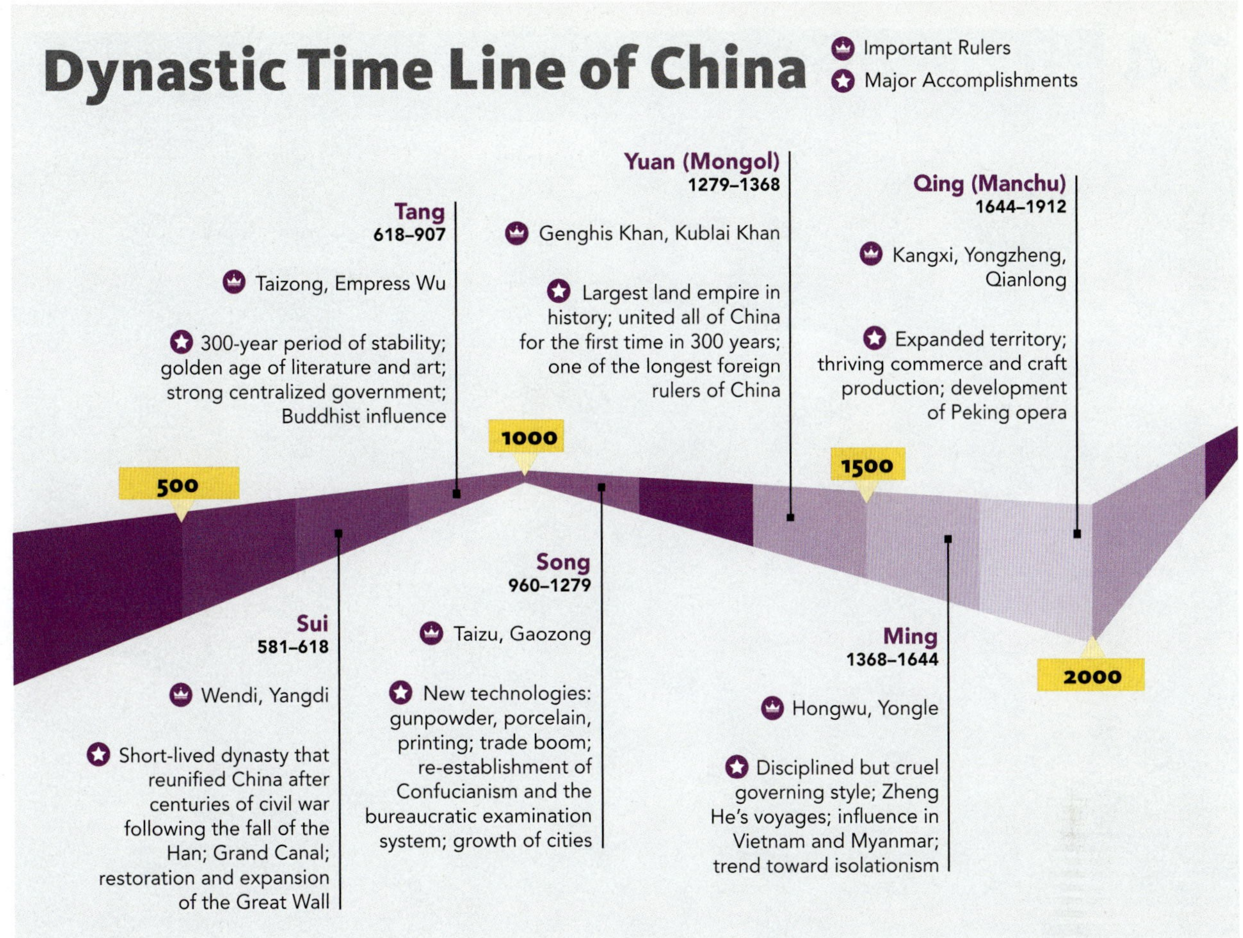
Dynastic Time Line of China
Important Rulers
Major Accomplishments
Sui
581–618
Wendi, Yangdi
Short-lived dynasty that reunified China after centuries of civil war following the fall of the Han; Grand Canal; restoration and expansion of the Great Wall
Tang
618–907
Taizong, Empress Wu
300-year period of stability; golden age of literature and art; strong centralized government; Buddhist influence
Song
960–1279
Taizu, Gaozong
New technologies: gunpowder, porcelain, printing; trade boom; re-establishment of Confucianism and the bureaucratic examination system; growth of cities
Yuan (Mongol)
1279–1368
Genghis Khan, Kublai Khan
Largest land empire in history; united all of China for the first time in 300 years; one of the longest foreign rulers of China
Ming
1368–1644
Hongwu, Yongle
Disciplined but cruel governing style; Zheng He's voyages; influence in Vietnam and Myanmar; trend toward isolationism
Qing (Manchu)
1644–1912
Kangxi, Yongzheng, Qianlong
Expanded territory; thriving commerce and craft production; development of Peking opera
500
1000
1500
2000

China's isolationism, although they did embark on some successful wars that expanded the empire by the end of the 18th century. With peace and prosperity, the population started to increase again, reaching 300 million by 1800. At that time, many Chinese began to migrate to new lands that the Ming had conquered earlier.

Since 1514, European traders had been traveling to China. The Europeans were building strong trading colonies across Asia. The Qing tried to restrict European trade and refused to buy European goods. During the late 1700s, frustrated British merchants began smuggling the drug opium into China. They soon had a successful trade, but addiction ruined countless Chinese lives. The resulting Opium Wars weakened China internally and internationally. European powers seized Chinese territories and took control of the economy. After 1850, a string of rebellions weakened China, and, in February 1912, revolutionary forces overthrew the Qing dynasty. Two thousand years of imperial rule had come to a decisive end.

REVIEW & ASSESS

1. **READING CHECK** How did China try to isolate itself from foreign influences?
2. **COMPARE AND CONTRAST** How did China's policy toward the outside world at the beginning of the Ming dynasty differ from that at the end of the Ming Dynasty?
3. **INTEGRATE VISUALS** How does the time line illustrate the recurring theme of the "dynastic cycle" in Chinese history?

Exploring China's Diverse Cultures

"When I was little I would identify the pieces of our Thanksgiving turkey and then reassemble the bones after the meal," laughs Christine Lee, a bioarchaeologist and a National Geographic Explorer. "My parents thought I was going to be a doctor!" Instead, she entered a relatively new science, bioarchaeology, which combines biology and archaeology, using the tools of both sciences to find out about the way ancient people lived.

^ This pit of human skulls was found during the excavation of Zhengzhou, a city from the Shang period about 3,750 years ago. Burial customs varied among several distinct cultures in early China.

MAIN IDEA

Bioarchaeology is providing insights into ancient China and Mongolia.

SKELETAL SECRETS

Christine Lee uses biological techniques to examine human skeletons found in archaeological sites. These new techniques allow researchers to piece together clues that tell the stories of long-dead individuals and groups. It is amazing what Dr. Lee can learn from even a single tooth.

A skeleton reveals even more. "Bones can tell me a person's sex, age, and whether they worked hard or had an easy life," she says. "Were they right- or left-handed, did they walk long distances, ride horses, or spend lots of time kneeling? Did they have arthritis, leprosy, tuberculosis? Did they get kicked by a cow, fall off a horse, break their nose in a fight? Bones show me all this and more," says Dr. Lee. By comparing particular skeletal characteristics across populations, she can see how ancient peoples were connected. She can also find details that provide clues to ancient people's ancestral origins, movements, and marriages.

Dr. Christine Lee in the field

PUZZLES FROM THE PAST

Dr. Lee has worked all over the world but has a particular interest in Asia. In Mongolia, she was the lead bioarchaeologist on a team excavating a cemetery of the Xiongnu (shung-noo) people. These were the nomads whose raids drove China to build the 2,000-mile-long Great Wall to keep them out. The dig site was in the middle of the desert, a thousand miles from the Mongolian capital. "We stopped in a village and asked for directions and were told the site was cursed," she says. "When we got there it was eerily quiet . . . I always said if I ever felt the skeletons didn't want me there I would leave. I decided we could study the skeletons when they were brought to the museum—then we left."

Back at the museum, Dr. Lee's studies highlighted cultural differences between the ancient Xiongnu and their Chinese neighbors to the south. "The ancestors of today's Mongolians rode horses, ate meat, and had a certain cowboy wildness compared to the rigid society and structure on the other side of the Great Wall," she notes. This cultural contrast was reinforced by her excavations of another independent kingdom, the Dian (dee-ahn), a city society of farmers and fishers in southern China. Dr. Lee's findings suggest that the Xiongnu and the Chinese had very little interaction and almost never intermarried.

Dr. Lee feels a responsibility to uncover the stories of these cultures in China's history: "When I look at a 2,000-year-old skull it's like I'm saying, 'Don't worry. I will tell the world about you—I'll describe what your life was like and prove it had meaning.'"

REVIEW & ASSESS

1. **READING CHECK** How is bioarchaeology helping scientists gain insights into ancient China and Mongolia?
2. **IDENTIFY MAIN IDEAS AND DETAILS** What can Dr. Lee tell about ancient people's lives from their bones?
3. **COMPARE AND CONTRAST** According to Dr. Lee's studies, what important cultural differences existed between the Xiongnu people and their Chinese neighbors?

CHAPTER **18** Review

VOCABULARY

On your paper, write the vocabulary word that completes each of the following sentences.

1. General Wendi's conquests managed to ______ north and south China and establish a strong new dynasty called the Sui.
2. During the Song dynasty, agricultural techniques improved and rice became China's ______.
3. A strong, nearly see-through ceramic called ______ was an especially valuable trade item.
4. The Mongols were a loose collection of nomadic tribes who roamed, raided, herded, and fought across the vast ______ of northwest China.
5. During Emperor Zhengtong's rule, China pursued a policy of ______, rejecting foreign contact and influences.
6. The goal of Buddhism is to achieve ______, an end of reincarnation and the suffering of life.

READING STRATEGY

7. **DRAW CONCLUSIONS** If you haven't already, complete your graphic organizer to draw conclusions about the impact of the Tang, Song, and Ming dynasties on Chinese civilization. Then answer the question.

Tang Dynasty

Evidence		Conclusion
Encouraged economic growth through agriculture and trade	→	
Evidence	→	
Evidence	→	

Which dynasty do you think had the greatest impact on Chinese civilization? Explain your reasoning.

MAIN IDEAS

Answer the following questions. Support your answers with evidence from the chapter.

8. What happened after the collapse of the Han dynasty in A.D. 220? **LESSON 1.1**
9. Why did many Chinese turn away from traditional Confucianism and embrace Buddhism? **LESSON 1.2**
10. What factors contributed to China's growth during the Tang and Song dynasties? **LESSON 1.3**
11. How did the Mongols gain power in China? **LESSON 2.1**
12. During the Yuan dynasty, how did the Mongols treat the Chinese under their rule? **LESSON 2.2**
13. How did the Ming dynasty restore Chinese rule to China? **LESSON 3.1**
14. What were the goals of Zheng He's voyages through Asia and Africa? **LESSON 3.2**
15. Why did China adopt a policy of isolationism during the Ming dynasty? **LESSON 3.3**

CRITICAL THINKING

Answer the following questions. Support your answers with evidence from the chapter.

16. **ANALYZE CAUSE AND EFFECT** Why was Wendi able to win the support of China's population?
17. **ANALYZE CAUSE AND EFFECT** How did Buddhism and Daoism influence Confucianism?
18. **EVALUATE** Which ancient Chinese invention benefitted people most: moveable type, porcelain, gunpowder, or the compass?
19. **SEQUENCE EVENTS** Describe the order of events in the Mongol creation of the world's largest empire.
20. **MAKE INFERENCES** How did Zheng He's maritime expeditions expand Chinese influence and demonstrate China's power and wealth?
21. **YOU DECIDE** Was Mongol rule good or bad for China? Support your opinion with evidence from the chapter.

INTERPRET VISUALS

Study the photograph of the seated Buddha statues in the Yungang Grottoes, a UNESCO World Heritage site in the Shanxi province of China. Then answer the questions that follow.

22. What spiritual qualities are conveyed through these statues of Buddha?

23. Why do you think these statues were carved in such a large scale?

ANALYZE SOURCES

Read the following poem, written by Li Po, one of the most popular Chinese poets of the Tang dynasty.

Zazen on Ching-t'ing Mountain

The birds have vanished down the sky.
Now the last cloud drains away.

We sit together, the mountain and me,
Until only the mountain remains.

24. What is one Daoist or Buddhist ideal that is reflected in this poem?

WRITE ABOUT HISTORY

25. EXPOSITORY Suppose you are a historian being interviewed about China. The interviewer asks you, "How did the Great Wall become a symbol of China's policy of isolationism at the end of the Ming dynasty?" Write your answer in a brief paragraph.

TIPS

- Take notes from Lesson 3.3, "China Turns Inward."
- Begin the paragraph with a clear topic sentence.
- Develop the paragraph with supporting details and examples of the steps China took to pursue its policy of isolationism, particularly the expansion and fortification of the Great Wall.
- Use at least two vocabulary terms from the chapter.
- Conclude with an explanation of why the Great Wall became a symbol of China's policy of isolationism.

CHAPTER

JAPANESE CIVILIZATION

400 – 1868

SECTION 1

EARLY JAPAN

KEY VOCABULARY
archipelago
aristocracy
calligraphy
clan
embassy
regent
ritual

NAMES & PLACES
Prince Shotoku
Ring of Fire
Shinto

SECTION 2

JAPANESE ART AND CULTURE

KEY VOCABULARY
haiku
kabuki
meditation
noh

NAMES & PLACES
Matsuo Basho
Murasaki Shikibu
Sei Shonagon
Zen Buddhism

SECTION 3

JAPANESE FEUDALISM

KEY VOCABULARY
bushido
daimyo
feudalism
samurai
shogun
shogunate
vassal

NAMES & PLACES
Tokugawa Ieyasu

READING STRATEGY

MAKE INFERENCES To make an inference, you combine what the text says with what you already know. As you read this chapter, think back to what you read about Chinese culture in the previous chapter. Use a graphic organizer like the one below to make inferences about how the Japanese felt about Chinese culture.

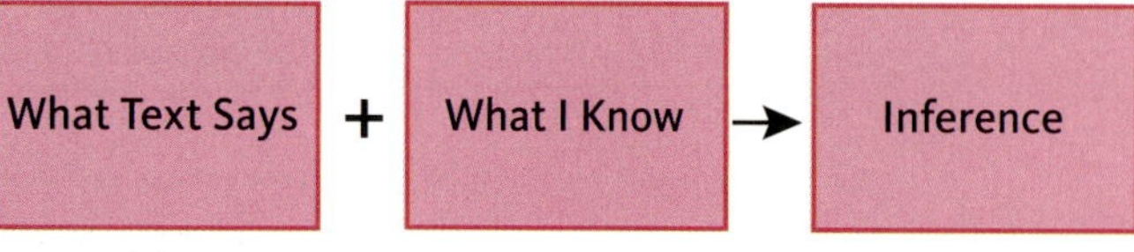
What Text Says
+
What I Know
Inference

Mount Fuji, on the island of Honshu, is the highest mountain in Japan. Many Japanese regard the mountain as sacred.

1.1 The Geography of Japan

From studying its geography, no one would expect Japan to have become the industrial superpower it is today. This small country consists of thousands of isolated, mostly mountainous islands. Japan has little land for agriculture and few natural resources or navigable rivers. In addition, catastrophic natural disasters are common.

MAIN IDEA

Japan's geography has greatly affected its historical and cultural development.

AN ISLAND NATION

Japan is an **archipelago** (AHR-kuh-peh-luh-goh), or group of islands, located in the vast Pacific Ocean. The country's thousands of islands stretch out in a long arc along the east coast of Asia.

Most of Japan's population lives on four main islands: Hokkaido (hoh-KY-doh), Honshu (HAHN-shoo), Shikoku (shih-KOH-koo), and Kyushu (keh-shoo). These four islands have a total area of about 145,000 square miles—roughly the size of the state of Montana—and thousands of miles of coastline. Honshu is by far Japan's largest island. Along with Kyushu, it has been the historic heartland of political, economic, and social development in Japan.

Japan's neighbor, South Korea, is more than 120 miles away. China is about 500 miles away. Japan's isolation has had a huge impact on its culture. For much of its history, Japan was far enough away from mainland Asia to escape invasions and major migrations. As a result, the Japanese nation developed largely from one ethnic group. This common ethnicity gave the Japanese a strong sense of unity.

However, Japan's nearest neighbors still influenced the country's culture. Japan imported many ideas and institutions from China and Korea and adapted them to form a unique Japanese culture. You will learn more about China's influence on Japan later in this chapter.

A MOUNTAINOUS LAND

The islands of Japan are actually the peaks of mostly submerged mountains and volcanoes. Japan lies along the **Ring of Fire**, an area of intense earthquakes and volcanic activity that arcs around the basin of the Pacific Ocean. About 1,500 earthquakes and thousands of volcanic eruptions rock Japan every year.

Because of underwater earthquakes, Japan also is at risk from huge ocean waves called tsunamis (su-NAH-mees). In addition, destructive storms called typhoons (ty-FOONS) are common. In the Atlantic Ocean, these storms are called hurricanes.

Japan's mountainous terrain limits the amount of space available for farming and for building homes. Only about 12 percent of the country's land can be farmed, and Japan's population is crowded onto a few coastal plains.

Apart from seafood and vast forests, Japan lacks any important natural resources, such as metals or coal. However, its geographic difficulties have helped make the Japanese a hardy people.

GEOGRAPHY OF JAPAN

120°E
130°E
140°E
30°N
Hokkaido
N
W
E
S
Sea of Japan
(East Sea)
CHOSON
DYNASTY
(KOREA)
Yellow
Sea
Honshu
JAPAN
Edo (Tokyo)
Fuji
PACIFIC
OCEAN
Heian (Kyoto)
Nara
Shikoku
Kyushu
CHINA
Elevation
feet meters
10,000+ 3,050+
5,000 1,524
2,000 610
1,000 305
500 152
0 0
0 100 200 Miles
0 100 200 Kilometers
RING OF FIRE
ASIA
NORTH
AMERICA
JAPAN
PACIFIC OCEAN
SOUTH
AMERICA
AUSTRALIA
0 2,000 Miles
0 2,000 Kilometers
Ring of Fire
Volcano active within
the past 12,000 years

REVIEW & ASSESS

1. **READING CHECK** What is the relationship between Japan's geography and its culture?

2. **ANALYZE CAUSE AND EFFECT** How did Japan's geography affect where people settled?

3. **INTERPRET MAPS** What are some advantages and disadvantages of Japan's location and terrain?

1.2 Early Beliefs and Cultures

Many people feel a great sense of awe when they witness a vibrant sunset, a stunning mountain view, or another wonder of nature. In early Japan, the beauty of the natural world became the basis of a religion.

MAIN IDEA

Religion was at the center of a society organized into family groups in early Japan.

TRADITIONAL RELIGION

With its rugged mountains and lush forests, Japan has an especially beautiful landscape. Its breathtaking views inspired Japan's most ancient religion, **Shinto** (SHIHN-toh), which means "way of the gods."

Shinto is based on the belief that spiritual powers reside in nature. Followers of Shinto worship divine spirits or gods called *kami*. The religion recognizes millions of kami, ranging from the sun, moon, and storms to individual animals, trees, streams, and rocks. Anything in nature that inspires a sense of religious wonder is considered a kami or the home of a kami. Followers of Shinto regard mountains as especially important homes for Shinto gods. Perhaps because of its size, Mount Fuji, near Tokyo, has long been considered particularly sacred.

Shinto has no founder, no holy scriptures, no moral code, and no clear date of origin. It also does not have elaborate temples. Instead, worshippers focus on simple shrines, or places that are considered sacred. Gates called torii (TAWR-ee-ee) often mark a shrine's entrance.

Shinto worship is relatively simple. Worshippers typically visit a shrine, purify themselves by washing, clap their hands to attract the god's attention, and then whisper a short prayer. Shinto priests perform more elaborate **rituals**, or religious ceremonies, that often involve bells, music, and dancing.

SOCIAL STRUCTURE

People from Siberia and Korea first settled Japan about 30,000 years ago. The first culture, the Jomon (JOH-mahn), emerged about 10,000 years ago. The Jomon people were hunters, gatherers, and fishers who lived in caves and shallow pit dwellings. They made simple pottery, baskets, and clothes from natural materials. Around 3000 B.C., they began basic farming.

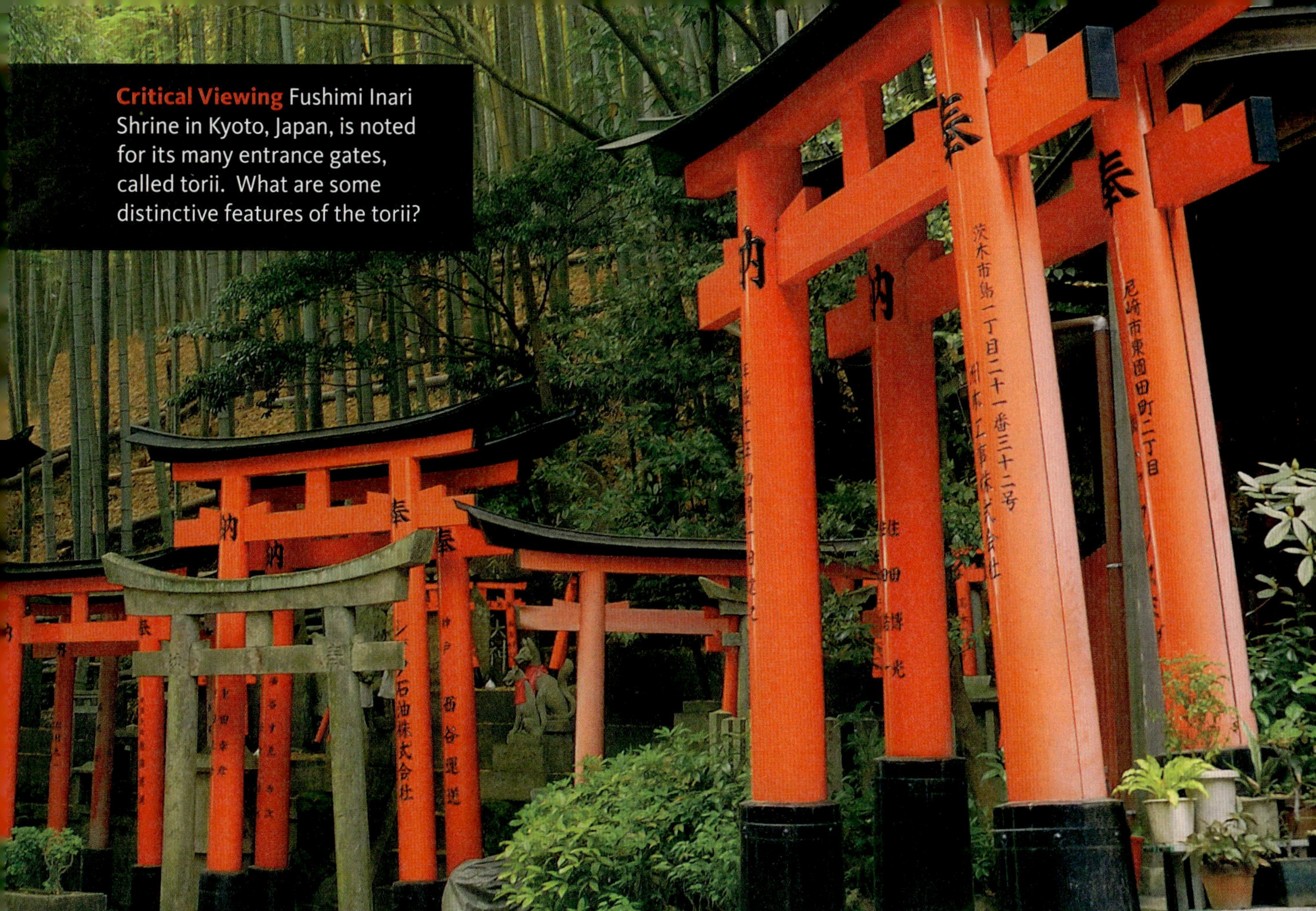
奉
奉
茨木市島一丁目二十一番三十二号
尼崎市東園田町二丁目

Critical Viewing Fushimi Inari Shrine in Kyoto, Japan, is noted for its many entrance gates, called torii. What are some distinctive features of the torii?

About 300 B.C., a new wave of immigrants with a significantly more advanced culture—the Yayoi (YAH-yoy)—arrived from mainland Asia. They knew how to grow rice, work metal, and weave. Their skills changed Japan dramatically. As farming flourished, people built villages that grew into larger communities.

A powerful **clan** ruled each community. A clan is a group of families who share a common ancestor. Each clan had a chief who was a religious leader or a mighty warrior. The chief, who could be male or female, headed a social class system in which a small **aristocracy**, or group of wealthy people, was supported by many farmers, artisans, and slaves.

After A.D. 300, the power of the aristocracy increased. This growth in power was reflected in the large tombs built for people of high social status. Vast earthen mounds covered the tombs. The largest of these tombs rivals Egypt's great pyramids in scale.

The Shinto religion served as a strong unifying factor in early Japanese society. The worship of particular gods bound together families, clans, and regions. Later, Shinto would help unite Japan's many independent kingdoms under a single leader.

REVIEW & ASSESS

1. **READING CHECK** What inspired the development of the ancient Japanese religion called Shinto?
2. **DESCRIBE** What are some distinctive features of the Shinto religion?
3. **ANALYZE CAUSE AND EFFECT** How did the Yayoi culture affect Japan?

This bronze statue stands before the entry gate of Horyu-ji, a Buddhist religious center founded by Prince Shotoku in the 600s.

1.3 Prince Shotoku

"In a country, there are not two lords; the people have not two masters. The sovereign is the master of the people of the whole country." In this strong statement, **Prince Shotoku** (shoh-toh-ku) of Japan sent a clear message to the people. He wanted them to know that Japan was now a united nation under a single ruler, or sovereign.

MAIN IDEA

Between 593 and 622, Prince Shotoku unified Japan under a Chinese model of centralized government and promoted other Chinese ideas.

A POWERFUL CLAN

Before the 400s, hundreds of Japan's independent clans ruled their own territories and often battled one another. Amid the many clans, one grew increasingly powerful: the Yamato (YAH-mah-toh). The Yamato rode into battle on horses, recently introduced from Korea. With their military superiority, they won control over many of the clans. By the 400s, these clans had united under the leadership of a Yamato emperor and his successors. To support the idea that they were the rightful rulers of Japan, the Yamato claimed their line of emperors was directly descended from the chief Shinto deity, the sun goddess Amaterasu (ah-mah-teh-RAH-soo). The Yamato effectively established a hereditary monarchy, in which rule passes from one member of a royal family to another.

In 593, Japan took another political leap. Empress Suiko (soo-EE-koh) won the throne and named her 21-year-old nephew, Prince Shotoku, as her **regent**. A regent is a person who rules when a monarch or emperor is unable to do so. However, Shotoku held most of the real power in Japan. He established the Japanese practice of having both a ruler in name only and an actual ruler. Between 593 and 622, Shotoku and Suiko laid the foundations of Japanese government.

CENTRALIZED GOVERNMENT

Greatly impressed by China's culture, Prince Shotoku introduced Chinese ideas and practices to help unite the Japanese people and strengthen imperial control over them. The religion of Buddhism and a centralized government were among these ideas and practices.

In 604, Shotoku issued Japan's first constitution, which skillfully mixed Confucian and Buddhist ideas. The constitution emphasized obedience to the emperor and the emperor's duty to care for his subjects. Shotoku introduced ideas for Japanese government that lasted for centuries.

REVIEW & ASSESS

1. **READING CHECK** How did Prince Shotoku unify the Japanese people?
2. **MAKE INFERENCES** Why do you think Prince Shotoku stressed the fact that Japan had only one ruler?
3. **FORM AND SUPPORT OPINIONS** What do you consider to be Prince Shotoku's greatest accomplishment? Why?

1.4 Influences from China

When you see a hairstyle you like, you might decide to copy it. But you might change it slightly to fit your own taste, type of hair, or facial shape. In a similar way, the Japanese copied aspects of Chinese culture but adapted them to suit Japan's culture.

MAIN IDEA

From the early 600s to the 800s, Japan adopted ideas from China's civilization and adapted them to fit Japanese culture.

SPREADING NEW IDEAS

To learn about Chinese culture, Japan sent many embassies to China. An **embassy** is a group of official representatives from one country who have been sent on a mission to another country. Between 607 and 839, Japan sent hundreds of people on more than 12 official missions to China. They brought back knowledge that influenced many aspects of Japanese life, including agriculture, art, government, religion, and technology.

As a result, China's influence extended to such everyday practices as drinking tea, cooking, and gardening. Even the name the Japanese use to refer to their country, *Nippon*, comes from the Chinese language. *Nippon* means "Land of the Rising Sun" and refers to Japan's location east of China—toward the rising sun.

China had a major impact on Japanese writing, even though the Japanese and Chinese languages are completely unrelated. For example, most Chinese words are just one syllable, while Japanese words combine many syllables. The differences made it extremely difficult to write Japanese using the Chinese alphabet, so at first the Japanese wrote in the Chinese language. Later, the Japanese added new characters to the Chinese alphabet, which made writing Japanese much easier.

The Chinese also influenced how the Japanese viewed writing. Initially, the Japanese considered writing to be a purely functional activity, useful for such purposes as keeping records. Japanese aristocrats did not bother to learn to write. However, interaction with China encouraged writing for cultural reasons, such as telling stories. The Japanese began to use writing to create religious, philosophical, and literary works. They also adopted the practice of **calligraphy**, or beautiful writing, from China.

ADAPTING INFLUENCES

The Japanese did not simply imitate everything Chinese. They carefully selected what suited them and then adapted it to their own needs, which led to a distinctive Japanese culture. For example, the Japanese copied the Chinese civil service system, which established a hierarchy, or ranking, of government officials. In China, government officials earned their positions based on examinations and good work. However, members of Japan's aristocracy wanted to keep power to themselves. In Japan, the emperor appointed government officials based on heredity, not on ability.

Japan continued adopting and adapting Chinese practices into the early 800s. By then, however, Japan's own culture was flourishing. After 839, Japan no longer sent any major missions to China. Nevertheless, China's influence on Japanese culture can still be seen today.

These students are participating in an annual calligraphy contest in Tokyo.

REVIEW & ASSESS

1. **READING CHECK** How does Japan's name reflect the influence of the Chinese?
2. **MAKE INFERENCES** How does the Japanese system of writing demonstrate Japan's tendency to adopt—and adapt—ideas from China?
3. **COMPARE AND CONTRAST** What was a major difference between the civil service systems in China and Japan?

2.1 Literature and the Arts

If you look at a time line of early English literature, you'll notice that all the best known authors—like William Shakespeare—are male. That's *not* the case with early Japanese literature. Two of the most famous authors are female, and one introduced a new form of literature to the world.

MAIN IDEA

Japan's rich cultural heritage includes unique forms of literature and art.

BONSAI

The Japanese imported the tradition of bonsai (bohn-SY) from China. To create a bonsai, a gardener painstakingly prunes and trains an ordinary plant to grow into a miniature tree that perfectly reflects its full-size relative.

LITERATURE AND DRAMA

A Japanese woman named **Murasaki Shikibu** (MOO-rah-SAH-kee SHEE-kee-boo) wrote the world's first novel in the 1000s. Her novel, *The Tale of Genji*, paints a vivid picture of life at the emperor's court. Her much admired masterpiece is still read today.

Another female writer of the same time, **Sei Shonagon** (SAY SHOW-nah-gohn), wrote a collection of reportedly true stories about court life called *The Pillow Book*. The book's title probably comes from the practice of keeping paper by the bedside for writing down thoughts.

Other Japanese writers developed a form of poetry called **haiku** (HY-koo), which has 17 syllables in three unrhymed lines of 5, 7, and 5 syllables. Traditional haiku evokes aspects of nature and often employs striking comparisons. One of the great masters of haiku was **Matsuo Basho** (MAHT-soo-oh bah-SHAW). In 1666, he abandoned his warrior life to write verses inspired by Buddhism. His poetry provided deep insights into human nature, turning haiku into a popular and beloved art form.

In the field of drama, Japan developed two forms that are still popular today. **Noh** (noh) emerged in the 1300s and **kabuki** (kuh-BOO-kee) in the 1600s. Noh grew out of Shinto rituals and often retold well-known folktales. Performing on a simple wooden stage, the actors wore elaborate masks and many layers of clothing to appear larger than life. Their movements were deliberately slow and choreographed to music to create a powerful effect.

Kabuki developed as a contrast to noh and was more lively and understandable. The actors performed on a large stage with trapdoors, revolving sections, and a raised walkway for dramatic effects. They wore luxurious costumes that reflected their characters' status. Their elaborate makeup highlighted important facial expressions, such as smiling or frowning.

PAINTING AND GARDENING

As you have learned, the Japanese adopted the Chinese art of calligraphy, which is traditionally produced with a brush and ink. China also influenced painting in Japan. Japanese artists adapted a form of Chinese ink painting to create paintings called *suiboku*

Critical Viewing In kabuki, actors wear elaborate makeup and costumes. What emotion is emphasized by the makeup on the actor in the foreground?

(soo-ee-BOH-koo), using bold strokes of black and white ink. Artists later created vibrant watercolors and prints. Early Japanese painting focused on religious subjects, but landscapes, scenes of daily life, legends, and battles also became popular.

Following the Shinto tradition of seeking harmony with nature, the Japanese became dedicated gardeners. They developed various types of gardens with the aim of creating symbolic miniature landscapes. Paradise gardens re-created the Buddhist idea of paradise. Dry-landscape gardens consisted of carefully chosen stones arranged in raked gravel as a focus for meditation. Stroll gardens featured carefully designed landscapes along a walking path. Tea gardens had neatly trimmed plants along a short path leading to a special house for drinking tea.

REVIEW & ASSESS

1. **READING CHECK** What new forms of literature and drama did the Japanese develop?
2. **COMPARE AND CONTRAST** How are the literary works of Murasaki Shikibu and Sei Shonagon similar?
3. **MAKE GENERALIZATIONS** How did Japanese gardens reflect both Shinto and Buddhist ideas?

2.2 DOCUMENT-BASED QUESTION

Poetry and Prose

During the Heian (HAY-ahn) period, from 794 to 1185, Japan enjoyed a golden age in literature. The ruling class in the capital city of Heian, modern Kyoto (kee-OH-toh), filled their time with cultural pursuits. Both male and female aristocrats, including warriors, engaged in writing as a cultural activity. The common literary subjects of nature and beauty had wide appeal to Japanese audiences. Literature also flourished during the later Edo (eh-doh) period, from 1603 to 1867.

This woodblock print by Japanese artist Utagawa Kunisada (1786–1864) depicts a scene from *The Tale of Genji.*

DOCUMENT ONE

Primary Source: Diary

from *The Pillow Book* by Sei Shonagon

In keeping with the traditional Japanese love of nature, artists and writers found a source of inspiration in the changing seasons. Here, Sei Shonagon paints a timeless portrait of the seasons to set the scene at the start of *The Pillow Book*.

CONSTRUCTED RESPONSE Which parts of the day does Sei Shonagon find most beautiful in the spring and summer seasons? Why?

In spring, the dawn [is most beautiful]—when the slowly paling mountain rim is tinged with red, and wisps of faintly crimson-purple cloud float in the sky.

In summer, the night—moonlit nights, of course, but also at the dark of the moon, it's beautiful when fireflies are dancing everywhere in a mazy [confused] flight.

DOCUMENT TWO

Primary Source: Novel

from *The Tale of Genji* by Murasaki Shikibu

Prince Genji is the central character in Murasaki's novel. Although most of the story is told in prose, Murasaki includes many poems that are spoken by the characters. Here, the writer sets the scene as Genji says farewell to a former love.

CONSTRUCTED RESPONSE How does the writer use images of nature to express Genji's feelings?

No one could ever convey all that passed between those two [Genji and the lady], who together had known such uncounted sorrows. The quality of a sky at last touched by dawn seemed meant for them alone.

"Many dews attend any reluctant parting at the break of day but no one has ever seen the like of this autumn sky," Genji said.

DOCUMENT THREE

Primary Source: Poetry

Haiku by Matsuo Basho

A traditional haiku has 17 syllables, arranged in three lines of 5, 7, and 5 syllables, though the syllable count is sometimes lost in translation, as in the one shown here. In the 1600s, Matsuo Basho developed haiku into a distinct art form.

CONSTRUCTED RESPONSE What feelings about nature does this haiku express?

The quiet pond
A frog leaps in,
The sound of water

SYNTHESIZE & WRITE

1. **REVIEW** Review what you have learned from this chapter about Japanese literature.
2. **RECALL** On your own paper, write down the main idea expressed in each document above.
3. **CONSTRUCT** Write a topic sentence that answers this question: What can you infer about early Japanese authors' relationship to nature?
4. **WRITE** Using evidence from the documents, write a paragraph that supports your topic sentence in Step 3.

2.3

Zen Buddhism

The world's religions prescribe a variety of ways for people to seek salvation, enlightenment, or meaning in life. Many encourage followers to study holy books, perform rituals, say prayers, and do good deeds. A religion called **Zen Buddhism**, which took root in Japan in the 1100s, takes a different approach. Its followers focus on clearing their minds and simplifying their lives.

MAIN IDEA

In the 1100s, Zen Buddhism developed a small but elite following that allowed it to greatly influence Japanese culture.

A NEW FORM OF BUDDHISM

Buddhism originally spread to Japan in the 500s. Over time, many sects, or forms, of Buddhism emerged, the best-known being Zen Buddhism. This sect arrived from China in the 1100s.

While traditional Buddhists sought salvation by studying scriptures, performing rituals, and doing good deeds, Zen Buddhists focused on **meditation**. In fact, *Zen* is the Japanese pronunciation of the Chinese word *Ch'an*, which roughly translates as "meditation." In meditation, a person remains still and enters a trancelike state of thought. True meditation requires self-discipline and concentration. For Zen Buddhists, the goal is to achieve inner peace and to realize that there is something divine in each person. To help focus and escape worldly distractions, Zen Buddhists embrace simplicity in all things, including home furnishings, food, clothing, and art.

INFLUENCE ON CULTURE

Zen Buddhism influenced Japanese culture far more than any other form of Buddhism. Many Japanese poets and artists, for example, embraced the religion's guiding principles of simplicity, understatement, and grace. The content and form of haiku reflect not only these principles but also the religion's focus on the present moment. Artists inspired by Zen Buddhism challenged themselves to convey complex natural scenes with as few brushstrokes as possible, using only black ink on white paper. A typical painting might capture the essence of a mountain-filled landscape.

You read about the different types of Japanese gardens in a previous lesson. These gardens were all influenced by Zen Buddhism. For example, the religion inspired gardeners to create dry-landscape gardens, also called viewing gardens, that represented the world in miniature. In these gardens, simple objects typically stood for something much bigger. An arrangement of rocks might convey a waterfall, or a collection of pebbles might depict a stream. Ryoanji (roh-AHN-gee) Temple in Kyoto has a celebrated Zen viewing garden. It consists of a rectangle of raked sand and 15 pebbles surrounded by clay walls and tall trees.

The main purpose of Zen viewing gardens was to promote a calm state of mind for meditation. As a result, the gardens made a perfect setting for the highly ritualized Zen tea ceremony. This ceremony involved drinking bitter tea in precisely

Critical Viewing A Buddhist monk meditates by a Zen viewing garden. What mood or state of mind might such a garden inspire?

three and a half sips while sitting on the floor of a bare hut. The simplicity of the tea ceremony focused attention on the beauty of an everyday activity.

Many people considered Zen Buddhism a difficult religion to practice. However, Zen Buddhism won a strong following among the warrior class that was developing in Japan. The religion's focus on simplicity, self-discipline, and the contemplation of life and death appealed to warriors, who regularly faced deadly challenges on the battlefield. Their support ensured Zen Buddhism an important place in Japanese society.

REVIEW & ASSESS

1. **READING CHECK** Which guiding principles of Zen Buddhism had an impact on Japanese society and culture?
2. **COMPARE AND CONTRAST** How do traditional Buddhism and Zen Buddhism differ?
3. **MAKE INFERENCES** How do Zen viewing gardens reflect the values of Zen Buddhism?

3.1 Samurai and Shoguns

The year is 1195. A Japanese warrior strides confidently past a group of peasant farmers. He looks magnificent in his colorful and decorative armor. But with his swords and spears, he is also deadly. The warrior hardly notices the peasants, but they bow their heads anyway. They know their place in Japanese society.

MAIN IDEA

Between 1192 and 1867, powerful military families ruled Japan with the support of armies of hired warriors.

FEMALE WARRIORS

Some Japanese women were well-trained, skillful fighters. Women of the samurai class were expected to defend their homes from attack by enemy warriors. A few female warriors also rode into battle.

A STRUCTURED SOCIETY

By the mid-1000s, the power of the central government in Japan was fading. The emperor's responsibilities were limited to religious functions. The real rulers of Japan were the **daimyo** (DY-mee-oh), the leaders of large landowning families.

As the power of the central government decreased, the daimyo grew stronger and more independent. They transformed their local estates into self-governing states, wielding the power of life and death over those under them.

Each daimyo had an army of hired warriors called **samurai** (SAM-uh-ry). Individual samurai swore allegiance to a daimyo and were duty-bound to fight for their lord. In return, the samurai received money and land. The samurai were **vassals** of the daimyo. A vassal is a person who receives land from a feudal lord in exchange for obedience and service.

This order of allegiance, called **feudalism**, was the main system of government in medieval Europe as well as Japan. The greatest daimyo came to command the allegiance of many lesser lords and their armies, creating powerful rival groups that battled for control of Japan.

Critical Viewing Samurai line up for battle in this scene from the 2003 movie *The Last Samurai*. How might an enemy facing these samurai feel?

MILITARY RULE

Japan's daimyo fought one another until the Minamoto (MEE-nah-moh-toh) family defeated them all. In 1192, the family's leader, Yoritomo (yoh-REE-toh-moh), became **shogun**, which means "general." As shogun, Yoritomo effectively governed Japan, and the emperor became a figurehead. The Minamoto family began a long line of hereditary rulers. The dynasty held power until the 1300s.

The warrior culture of this period was based on a strict code of behavior called **bushido** (buh-SHEE-doh), or "the way of the warrior." Bushido fused aspects of three religions: Shinto's devotion to family and ruler, Zen Buddhism's focus on inner peace and fearlessness, and Confucianism's service to state and country. The code promoted loyalty, bravery, and honor, much like the code of chivalry followed by knights, a warrior class that arose in Europe around the 800s.

REVIEW & ASSESS

1. **READING CHECK** What were the roles of the emperor, the daimyo, and the samurai in feudal Japan?
2. **IDENTIFY PROBLEMS AND SOLUTIONS** What problem in Japan's central government did feudalism help solve?
3. **MAKE INFERENCES** What were some benefits and drawbacks of being a samurai?

3.2 HISTORY THROUGH OBJECTS

TOOLS OF THE SAMURAI

A samurai riding into battle on horseback must have been quite a sight. The colorful, complicated armor was made to be both beautiful and useful. The armor included metal or leather scales laced together to protect the warrior's body while allowing quick, easy movement. A samurai was armed with two swords, a long curved one and a short one, as well as a spear or gun.

Armor A great deal of care and effort went into making the elaborate armor for a samurai.

Coat This surcoat from the 1700s was made to be worn over armor.

Spear This spear from the 1800s is made of iron, wood, and crushed mother of pearl.

Sword Samurai highly valued their razor-sharp swords.

Gun
The Portuguese introduced the first guns into Japan in the 1500s.
Face and Neck Guard
Samurai wore terrifying masks like this one.
Helmet Crest
The creature depicted in this helmet crest has the head of a tiger and the body of a fish.
Helmet
This helmet from about 1550 is made of iron, wood, leather, gilt copper, and lacing.

3.3 Unification and Isolation

In some developing countries today, people protest against Western influence on their cultures. They fear losing their own unique cultures as their countries become more and more westernized. In the 1600s, Japan's rulers not only complained, they did something. They closed the country's doors to foreigners.

MAIN IDEA

After centuries of intense power struggles, Japan was reunified in the 1600s under a strong central government that rejected contact with foreigners.

THE WARRING STATES PERIOD

Japan faced a major threat in 1274: invasion by the Mongols, the great Asian superpower you learned about in the previous chapter. The Mongols had already conquered China and Korea. Now the Mongol leader Kublai Khan wanted to control Japan, too. In their initial attack, the Mongols captured many outlying islands. Then they retreated after a typhoon wrecked many of their ships.

Kublai Khan did not launch another invasion of Japan until 1281. However, this time he assembled the largest seaborne invasion force the world had yet seen—4,400 ships carrying about 150,000 men. The daimyo put aside their differences and focused all their resources on defeating the Mongols. The Japanese warriors fought the invaders for about two months. Then a typhoon smashed into the Mongol fleet, killing tens of thousands. Japan claimed that heaven had saved the country by sending a *kamikaze*, or "divine wind," to stop the Mongols.

Instead of unifying Japan, however, this victory against the Mongols tore the country apart. A vast amount of money had been spent on the defense, but the Japanese gained no valuable rewards to repay the nobles and warriors. This inability to pay undermined the shogun's authority. Steadily, the daimyo seized control of their regions and then ruled them independently. Japan became divided among some 300 daimyo, all plotting and fighting for power.

This period of the "Warring States" lasted from 1467 until 1568. Then a powerful leader named Oda Nobunaga (oh-dah noh-boo-nah-gah) brought most of Japan under his control. In 1603, a leader named **Tokugawa Ieyasu** (toh-koo-gah-wah ee-yeh-yah-soo) finally broke the power of the daimyo and reunified all of Japan under a **shogunate**, or rule by a shogun.

THE TOKUGAWA SHOGUNATE

Ieyasu's rule ushered in a period of stability and peace that lasted nearly 300 years. Ieyasu and his successors feared that foreign contact was corrupting the people and upsetting the traditional balance of power. As a result, by 1639, the shoguns had begun a national policy of isolation and cut Japan off from outside influence. They stopped almost all foreign trade and travel and expelled certain groups of foreigners, including Europeans and Christians. Japan's isolation continued for more than 200 years. Then, in 1854, the United States pressured Japan to reopen for foreign trade. In 1867, the Tokugawa shogunate was overthrown and the emperor took control of Japan.

TOKUGAWA IEYASU

Job: Shogun of all of Japan
Education: Learned the art of war and government while being held hostage by a neighboring clan
Home: Ruled from Edo (present-day Tokyo)

FINEST HOUR

He defeated the rebellious daimyo at the Battle of Sekigahara in 1600 to become shogun of Japan.

TRIVIA

Ieyasu built a castle at Edo that was gradually expanded until it became the world's largest at the time. The families of the daimyo were forced to live in mansions around the castle. Ieyasu effectively made the families hostages to guarantee good behavior by the daimyo.

This print shows a busy street in Edo during the period of Japan's isolation from the West.

Fuji from Suruga Street, Yedo, Ando Hiroshige

REVIEW & ASSESS

1. **READING CHECK** What were the key events in Japan's unification and isolation?
2. **ANALYZE CAUSE AND EFFECT** Why did the Tokugawa shogunate decide to isolate Japan from foreign influence?
3. **FORM AND SUPPORT OPINIONS** Do you think a policy of isolation was wise for Japan? Why or why not?

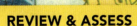

CHAPTER 19 Review

VOCABULARY

Use each of the following vocabulary words in a sentence that shows an understanding of the word's meaning.

1. **archipelago**
   Japan is an archipelago, or chain of islands, located in the Pacific Ocean.
2. **daimyo**
3. **clan**
4. **regent**
5. **haiku**
6. **samurai**
7. **shogun**
8. **bushido**

READING STRATEGY

9. **MAKE INFERENCES** If you haven't already, complete the graphic organizer to make inferences about how the Japanese viewed Chinese culture. Then answer the question.

What Text Says
The Japanese added new characters to the Chinese alphabet.

+

What I Know
The Chinese had developed an alphabet for the Chinese language.

↓

Inference

Based on what you've read, how did the Japanese view Chinese culture? Support your response with evidence from the chapter.

MAIN IDEAS

Answer the following questions. Support your answers with evidence from the chapter.

10. In what ways did Japan's geography affect its sense of unity? **LESSON 1.1**
11. What belief forms the basis of Japan's ancient religion of Shinto? **LESSON 1.2**
12. What ideas did Japan borrow from China's civilization? **LESSON 1.4**
13. What new forms of literature and drama did the Japanese develop? **LESSON 2.1**
14. What is the goal of meditation in Zen Buddhism? **LESSON 2.3**
15. How did Japan come to be ruled by powerful military families between 1192 and 1867? **LESSON 3.1**
16. How was Japan reunified after the Warring States period? **LESSON 3.3**

CRITICAL THINKING

Answer the following questions. Support your answers with evidence from the chapter.

17. **MAKE INFERENCES** How does the Zen tea ceremony reflect the religion's value of simplicity?
18. **ANALYZE CAUSE AND EFFECT** Why was the Shinto religion a strong unifying factor in early Japanese society?
19. **DRAW CONCLUSIONS** Which government probably had more qualified officials—the Chinese or the Japanese? Why?
20. **COMPARE AND CONTRAST** How did Japan open itself to other cultures? How did it close itself off?
21. **MAKE GENERALIZATIONS** How did feudalism benefit both the daimyo and vassals?
22. **YOU DECIDE** Was China's influence on Japan beneficial or harmful? Support your opinion with evidence from the chapter.

INTERPRET CHARTS

Study this chart, which illustrates Japan's society in the feudal period. Then answer the questions that follow.

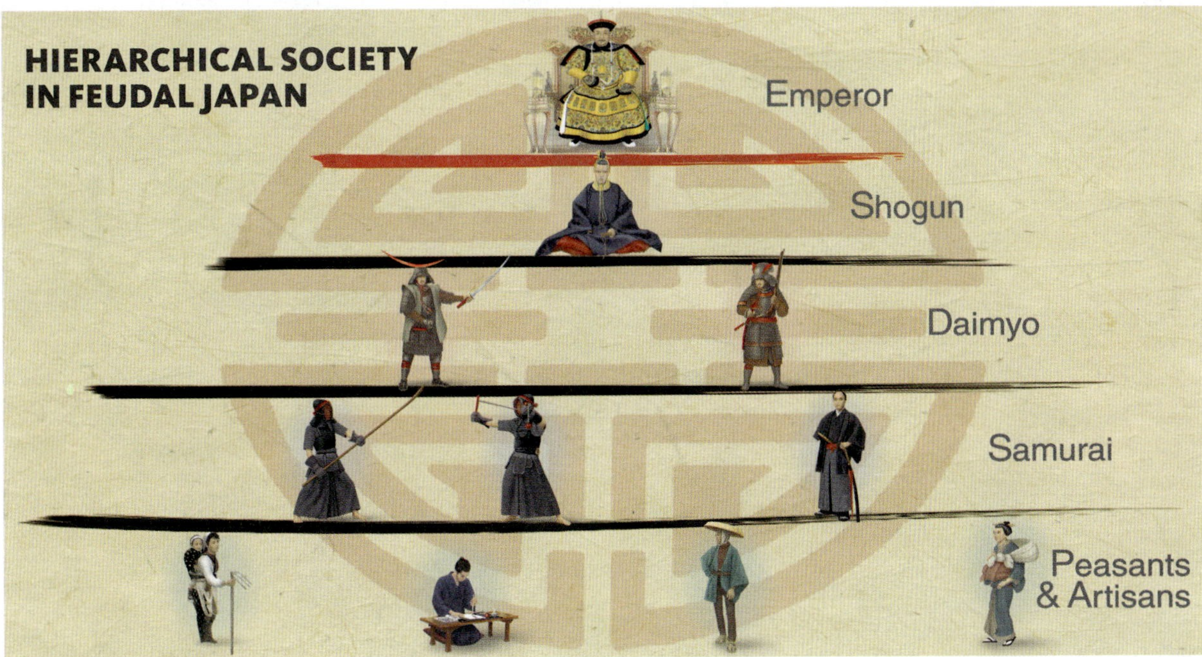
HIERARCHICAL SOCIETY IN FEUDAL JAPAN
Emperor
Shogun
Daimyo
Samurai
Peasants & Artisans

23. Who held the real power in feudal Japan's military society?

24. Which class of people probably created the most wealth for feudal Japan? Why?

ANALYZE SOURCES

Read the following haiku written by a modern Japanese poet. Then answer the question that follows.

> I kill an ant . . .
> and realize my three children
> were watching
> —Shuson Kato (1905–1993)

25. What enduring values of Japanese culture are reflected in this haiku?

WRITE ABOUT HISTORY

26. INFORMATIVE Write a short encyclopedia article for fellow students comparing or contrasting the rule of Prince Shotoku and the rule of Tokugawa Ieyasu.

TIPS

- Take notes on each ruler from Lessons 1.3 and 3.3.
- State your main idea about the similarities or differences between the two rulers in your beginning sentence.
- Develop the main idea with relevant facts, details, or examples about the rule of each leader.
- Use transitions, such as "in a similar way" or "unlike," to clarify the relationships between ideas.
- Provide a concluding statement that follows from and supports the information presented.

CHAPTER

20 KOREA AND SOUTHEAST ASIA

600 – 1910

SECTION 1

KOREA'S EARLY HISTORY

KEY VOCABULARY	NAMES & PLACES
adapt	Choson
celadon	Koguryo
hanbok	Koryo
kimchi	Paekche
ondol	Silla
rivalry	Tripitaka Koreana

SECTION 2

SOUTHEAST ASIAN CIVILIZATIONS

KEY VOCABULARY	NAMES & PLACES
bas-relief	Angkor Wat
cultivate	Dai Viet
impose	Khmer
	Nam Viet
	Trung Nhi
	Trung Trac

READING STRATEGY

DETERMINE WORD MEANINGS When you come across an unfamiliar word in a text, you can use context clues to help you figure out the word's meaning. Signal words like *or*, *is*, and *such as* often indicate that a word is going to be defined in the text. As you read the chapter, use a chart like this one to keep track of vocabulary words and their definitions.

Word	Definition	Example from My Life

Sokkuram, a cave temple in Korea, is home to this huge statue of Buddha.

1.1 The Three Kingdoms

What might happen if your teachers lost control of your school? Groups of friends would stick together and do their own thing. Some small groups might band together to form larger ones based on shared friends and interests. In time, the whole school might be split into a few large groups ruling themselves and maybe even trying to control their rivals. This is what happened in Korea.

MAIN IDEA

Three kingdoms with strong Chinese cultural influences ruled early Korea.

FORMATION OF KOREA

Korea is a large, mountainous peninsula that juts out from the Asian continent. Its population became concentrated in the coastal plains and river valleys, where the land was fertile and could be cultivated.

Korea's nearest neighbors are China and Japan. The three countries have always influenced one another, both culturally and politically. In 108 B.C., the Chinese Han dynasty conquered northwest Korea. Chinese settlers followed, bringing their culture with them. But as the Han dynasty declined, its grip on Korea weakened. Korea's scattered native tribes began taking control of their lands and gradually formed three kingdoms.

Tradition claims that the **Silla** (SIHL-uh) kingdom was formed in southeast Korea around 57 B.C. About 37 B.C., the **Koguryo** (koh-gur-YOO) kingdom emerged in the north. Then, around 18 B.C., the **Paekche** (pahk-chay) kingdom was founded in the southwest. For centuries, the three kingdoms grew, developed, and fought one another for control of Korea. At first, Koguryo was by far the strongest, even as it fought off Chinese invasions. But by the A.D. 300s, Koguryo had managed to dominate most of the peninsula. Paekche's strength was largely economic due to extensive trade. Over time, Silla increased its political, military, and economic power.

RIVALRY

Despite their bitter **rivalry**, or competition, the three kingdoms had very similar cultures. They each developed feudal-style societies, with kings commanding a warrior aristocracy and an educated bureaucracy. Poor peasants provided the labor for agriculture. The kingdoms shared a common language and adopted Chinese writing. Their economies were similar as well. All three exported leather goods, tools, and wool clothing in exchange for Chinese paper, porcelain, silk, and weapons.

Chinese culture greatly influenced Korea in the areas of art, architecture, literature, government, and religion. From China, the kingdoms imported the Buddhist religion, as well as Confucian ideas for government and society. They also adopted Chinese writing. Despite these strong Chinese influences, Korea managed to maintain its own distinct culture.

In A.D. 660, the Silla king entered into an alliance with the Tang dynasty in China. Together, Silla and the Tang conquered Paekche in A.D. 660 and Koguryo in A.D. 668. For the first time, Korea was unified.

THE THREE KINGDOMS OF KOREA, A.D. 500s
CHINA
KOGURYO
Sea of Japan
(East Sea)
40°N
N
W
E
S
0
100
200 Miles
0
100
200 Kilometers
Yellow
Sea
Kongju
SILLA
Kyongju
PAEKCHE
JAPAN
Kyoto
Osaka
35°N
125°E
130°E
135°E

Some historians see Silla's alliance with Tang China as a national betrayal that encouraged China's ambition to control the peninsula. Nevertheless, the alliance turned out to be a brilliant move for Silla. After the two allies conquered Paekche, the Tang seized complete control of the conquered lands and reduced the Silla king's powers. Silla waited patiently for revenge. It did not have long to wait.

Following the alliance's defeat of Koguryo, Silla took control of Paekche. Then China tried to depose the Silla king, an action that led to war between the two former allies. After a series of battles, Silla defeated the Chinese army in A.D. 675 and then fought off the Chinese navy the following year. China withdrew from the peninsula in A.D. 676, leaving Silla in control of a unified Korean kingdom.

REVIEW & ASSESS

1. **READING CHECK** How did China influence early Korea?
2. **SYNTHESIZE** What political goal did Silla, Koguryo, and Paekche have in common?
3. **INTERPRET MAPS** Why has human movement between China and Korea been relatively easy throughout history?

HISTORY THROUGH OBJECTS

1.2 KOREAN ARTIFACTS

Archaeologists have discovered many beautiful artifacts from early Korea. These artifacts range from pottery to jewelry to religious figures. In Silla, sometimes called "the land of gold," artisans often used gold to create precious objects, including a number of gold crowns. Uniquely Korean, the crowns' designs incorporate chains with mirrors or jewels as well as elements of trees and antlers.

Tile
The monster mask on this roof tile was thought to ward off evil spirits.

Gogok
This jade teardrop, or *gogok*, probably once adorned a crown, belt, or bracelet.

Earrings
This pair of gold earrings from the early 400s were probably worn by a Silla noblewoman.

Crown of Silla
This ornate crown of gold was discovered in the tomb of a Silla king and queen.

Necklace
This ornate gold necklace is adorned with a jade gogok.

Vase
Tiny figures of animals decorate this gray stoneware vase.

Bodhisattva
This statue of an enlightened being, or bodhisattva, is made of gilded bronze.

Dragon's Head
This gilded bronze dragon's head reflects the skill of Silla artisans.

1.3 Koryo and Choson Dynasties

After the decline of Silla in the 700s, two new dynasties rose to power. During the Koryo and Choson dynasties, Korea enjoyed proud independence. Then new rulers forbade Koreans from meeting freely, speaking their mind, practicing their culture, or even using their family name.

MAIN IDEA

Two great dynasties ruled for nearly a thousand years before Korea lost its independence.

KORYO

In the 700s, after a golden age, Silla began to decline. Its rulers fought among themselves. Nobles seized large areas of farmland, while peasants rebelled against poor government. In A.D. 918, General Wang Kon founded a rival dynasty called the **Koryo**. After a long war, the Silla king surrendered in 935. Then, for more than 450 years, Korea was ruled by the Koryo, from which Korea takes its name.

Chinese ideas and practices continued to flow south, although they were **adapted**, or changed, to meet Koryo's own needs. For example, Koryo adapted Chinese-style centralized government but gave special preference to aristocrats. As a result, Koryo's professional bureaucracy came almost entirely from its hereditary nobility. Koryo potters also imported advanced Chinese techniques but again developed a uniquely Korean style.

Yet Chinese influence remained strong. As in China, Buddhism greatly inspired art. Korea's literary language remained Chinese for centuries, and Chinese poetry was much imitated. Even the oldest surviving book on Korea's history, the *Samguk Sagi*, mentions almost twice as many Chinese sources as Korean.

CHOSON

In 1231, the Mongols invaded Koryo and took control. The Mongols were harsh rulers. They demanded tribute from the Koryo rulers, who had to send them a million soldiers and 20,000 horses. Mongol domination ended in 1336. Soon, a new dynasty arose.

In 1392, the **Choson** dynasty replaced the Koryo dynasty. Choson ruled Korea for the next 518 years. Like Koryo, Choson adapted many elements of Chinese culture. Choson rulers created a strong, centralized Confucian-style government with a strict political and social hierarchy. However, over the following centuries, Korea developed its own alphabet, artistic styles, and other distinctive cultural characteristics.

Then, in 1894, disaster struck. Both China and Japan invaded Korea to help crush a people's rebellion. The rebels quickly surrendered, but Japan fought on and won control of the peninsula. In 1910, Korea was formally made part of Japan, which imposed a harsh military rule.

The Japanese occupied Korea until 1945. During this occupation, life in Korea contrasted sharply with life during the Choson dynasty. The Japanese required Koreans to adopt Japanese culture and even to use Japanese-style names. Koreans considered this a heartbreaking betrayal of their ancestry and a bitter end to Korean independence.

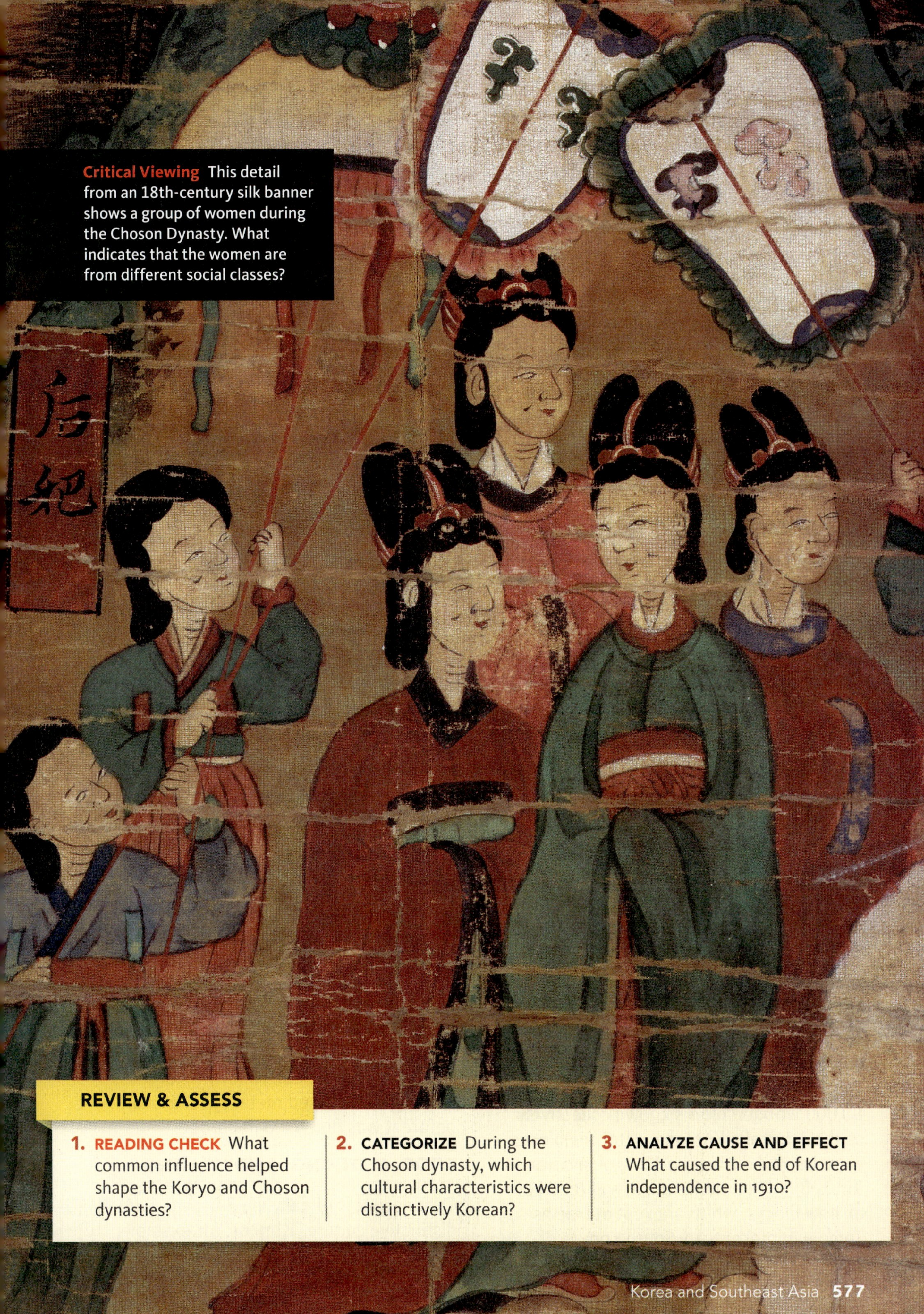
后妃

Critical Viewing This detail from an 18th-century silk banner shows a group of women during the Choson Dynasty. What indicates that the women are from different social classes?

REVIEW & ASSESS

1. **READING CHECK** What common influence helped shape the Koryo and Choson dynasties?
2. **CATEGORIZE** During the Choson dynasty, which cultural characteristics were distinctively Korean?
3. **ANALYZE CAUSE AND EFFECT** What caused the end of Korean independence in 1910?

1.4 Korean Culture

When we pose for a picture, we say "cheese" to produce a smile. In Korea, they say "kimchi"—a word that ends with a similar sound. Koreans have been making kimchi for hundreds of years. It is one of many examples of Korea's distinctive culture.

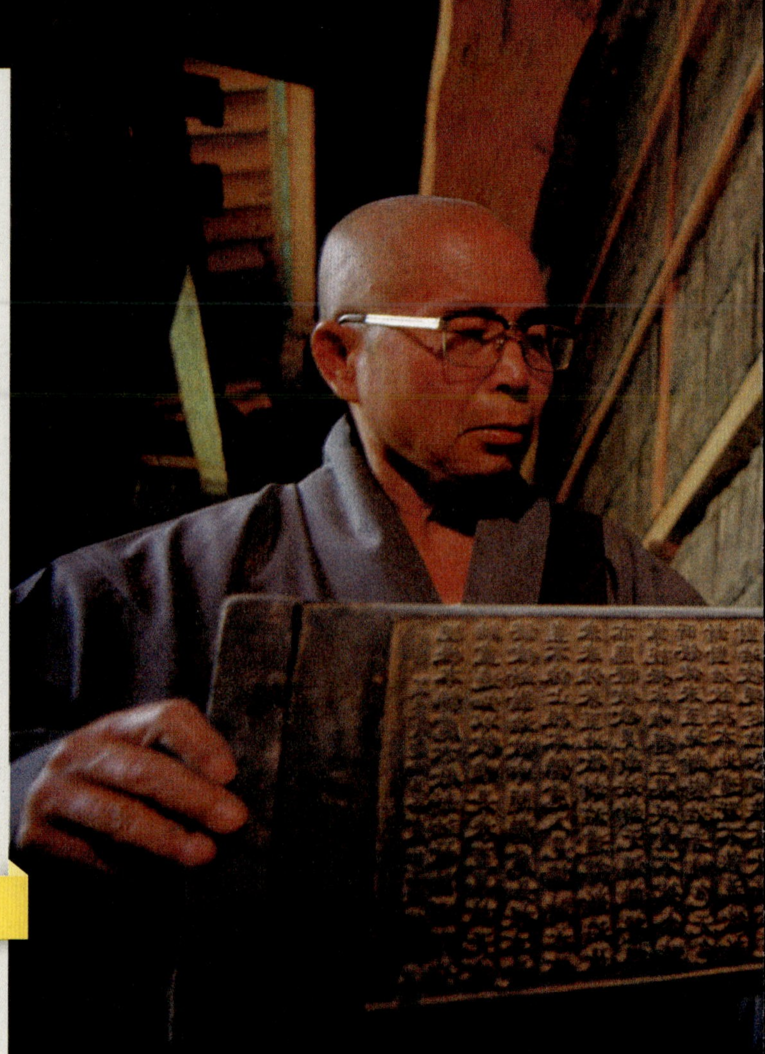

MAIN IDEA

Korea developed their own culture despite many Chinese influences.

RELIGION, POTTERY, AND PRINTING

While Chinese ideas and practices were certainly influential, Korea developed its own culture. Chinese Confucianism and Buddhism were adapted to Korean needs. Inspired by Song China's advanced glazed ceramics, Korean potters developed **celadon** (SEH-luh-dahn), a type of pottery with a unique blue-green color. Korean celadon is considered among the finest porcelain in the world.

Similarly, Chinese woodblock printing reached new heights in Korean hands. Korean monks spent years painstakingly carving Buddhist teachings onto more than 80,000 wooden blocks known collectively as the **Tripitaka Koreana**. After the blocks were burned during the Mongol invasion in 1231, Buddhist monks made and recarved all new blocks, which are kept at Haeinsa Temple in present-day South Korea.

Built in the 1400s, the complex of four buildings that house the Tripitaka Koreana is also remarkable. These structures create an environment that has preserved the woodblocks for centuries. The floor contains a mixture of soil, charcoal, salt, clay, sand, and plaster powder that regulates moisture, while strategically placed windows ensure consistent air quality.

In 1377, Korea produced *Jikji*, the world's oldest book printed with movable metal type. Reusable metal characters arranged on a board created a printing plate that was tough and flexible, allowing for mass printing. Korea used metal type 78 years before it was first used in Europe.

FOOD, CLOTHING, AND HEATING

Other aspects of daily life illustrate Korea's distinctive culture. **Kimchi**, for example, is Korea's national dish. This dish is made

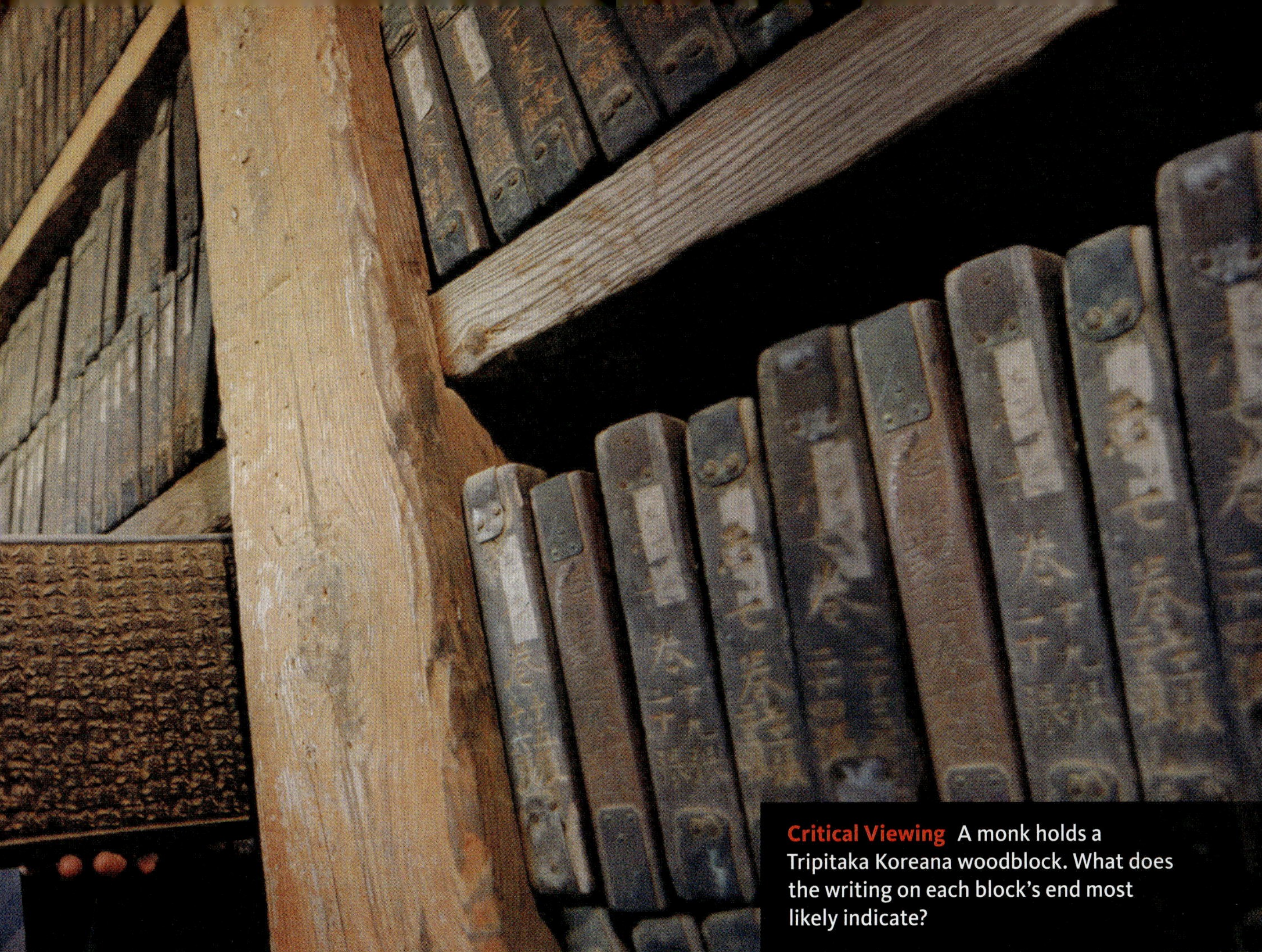

Critical Viewing A monk holds a Tripitaka Koreana woodblock. What does the writing on each block's end most likely indicate?

of spicy pickled vegetables and is as full of flavor as it is rich in vitamins and minerals. People began making kimchi as a way of preserving vegetables, especially cabbage. Once sliced and seasoned, the vegetables were placed in large jars of salt water and buried. About a month later, the kimchi was ready to eat. Today, there are more than 160 varieties of kimchi.

For centuries, Koreans wore traditional clothing called **hanbok**. A woman's hanbok included seven layers of undergarments covered by a long billowing skirt and a short, tight-fitting jacket. Men wore full-length pants and a long jacket with wide sleeves. The material ranged from hemp to silk but was usually brightly colored with beautiful designs. Today, most Koreans wear hanbok only on special occasions.

From as early as the first century, Korean homes benefited from a unique system of heating called **ondol**. Hot air from fireplaces was drawn through passageways beneath the floors. The heated air warmed both the floors and the rooms above. Even today, Koreans use an updated version of ondol.

REVIEW & ASSESS

1. **READING CHECK** What aspects of Chinese culture did Koreans adapt to develop their own distinct culture?
2. **ANALYZE CAUSE AND EFFECT** Why were the Tripitaka woodblocks carved a second time?
3. **DETERMINE WORD MEANINGS** In the phrase "the complex of four buildings," what does the word *complex* mean?

2.1 Vietnamese Kingdoms

Are there people you admire but also dislike? Perhaps you appreciate their skill in sports but dislike their superior attitude in the classroom. Vietnam appreciated Chinese culture but hated Chinese domination.

MAIN IDEA

Vietnam followed more than a millennium of foreign occupation with a thousand years of independence.

CHINESE RULE

Although the origins of modern Vietnam are shrouded in myth, Vietnamese history most likely began with the migration of settlers from southern China into the Red River delta. As in Korea, Vietnam's challenge was maintaining political and cultural independence from China, its powerful neighbor.

In 207 B.C., an ambitious Chinese governor incorporated the Red River delta into his breakaway kingdom of **Nam Viet**. Barely a century later, in 111 B.C., the Han Chinese seized control of Nam Viet, and it became a Chinese-ruled province for more than a thousand years. The province provided China with valuable ports for traders sailing to India and Southeast Asia.

Nam Viet's Chinese rulers increasingly **imposed**, or forced, Chinese culture onto the Nam Viet people. Yet the harder China pushed, the more the people resisted, which led to many violent uprisings. The most famous was in A.D. 39, when sisters **Trung Trac** and **Trung Nhi** led a rebellion against Chinese rule. Having raised an army, the sisters rode into battle on the backs of elephants. Within a year, the two women and their allies had driven out the Chinese. The sisters ruled for three years before being defeated by Chinese forces. Today the Trung sisters are still honored as national heroes.

DAI VIET

In A.D. 938, Ngo Quyen (noh kwehn) led an uprising that finally defeated the Chinese. In a decisive battle, he sank China's warships by planting iron-tipped stakes in a riverbed. China acknowledged the independence of the new **Dai Viet** state in exchange for tribute payments. This began a thousand years of independence for Vietnam.

The Ly dynasty's strong leadership from 1009 to 1225 moved the Vietnamese capital to what is now Hanoi, established a strong central government, and built an effective road network. Ly rulers reinforced Buddhism as the state religion and promoted Confucian values in government and society. They developed a code of law and recruited a professional army.

From 1225 to 1400, the equally dynamic Tran dynasty further reformed the administration, agriculture, and economy. Tran rulers succeeded in fighting off a major Mongol invasion in 1257 and expanded south into the rival kingdom of Champa. Then, in 1407, the Ming Chinese invaded and brutally enforced Chinese culture.

When, in 1428, Le Thanh Tong restored native rule, he actively promoted China's government systems as well as its language, art, and literature. His reforms may have had a greater effect on making Vietnam Chinese than a thousand years of occupation. In 1471, Dai Viet reconquered Champa, creating what is now recognized as Vietnam.

EARLY CHINESE INFLUENCE IN ASIA
CHINA
KOREA
JAPAN
DAI VIET
KHMER
Sea of Japan
(East Sea)
Yellow
Sea
East
China
Sea
PACIFIC
OCEAN
South
China
Sea
50°N
40°N
30°N
20°N
10°N
100°E
120°E
130°E
Exam
Buddhism
Civil service
Agriculture
Porcelain
Printing
System of
writing
N
E
S
W
0
300
600 Miles
0
300
600 Kilometers

REVIEW & ASSESS

1. **READING CHECK** Why did the Han Chinese want to occupy and control Nam Viet?

2. **COMPARE AND CONTRAST** How was Le Thanh Tong's rule similar to the Ming Chinese rule of Vietnam?

3. **INTERPRET MAPS** Where did Buddhism spread from China?

2.2 The Khmer Empire

Dark and threatening skies mean the monsoon is coming. However, you are confident that the efficient network of dams, dikes, and canals will save your rice paddy from flood damage. Rice is the backbone of the Khmer economy.

MAIN IDEA

Rice agriculture helped the Khmer dominate Southeast Asia for centuries.

INDIAN AND CHINESE INFLUENCES

Present-day Cambodia was the heartland of one of Southeast Asia's most powerful states. The **Khmer** (kuh-MAIR) people migrated south from China. By A.D. 500, they were founding small city-states known collectively as Chenla. To their south lay the powerful trading kingdom of Funan, which was probably founded by Indian traders who valued its strategic location between India and China. Funan introduced many Indian influences to Cambodia, including irrigation, centralized government, the Sanskrit language, and the Hindu religion.

In the mid-600s, Chenla extended into Funan. Threatened by strong island nations like Java, the Chenla kingdoms rallied together for protection. In 802, they formally united under the "universal ruler" Jayavarman II (JEYE-ah-var-mahn). This was the beginning of the Khmer Empire, which dominated Southeast Asia until 1431.

THE ANGKOR ERA

The Khmer established their capital in Angkor, which means "city." The city's art and architecture were Indian in style, and the layout reflected the Hindu vision of the universe. Khmer religious beliefs were a complex mixture of Hinduism, Buddhism, and native religions. The Khmer adopted the Indian idea of kings as gods who ruled with divine authority.

A large central bureaucracy governed the Khmer Empire, which included vassal states. These states paid tribute, which, along with trade, contributed to the empire's economy. Yet the mainstay of the Khmer economy was rice.

The Khmer were skilled rice farmers, having learned how to grow rice from the Chinese. The Khmer region's many wet and fertile river deltas were ideal for **cultivating**, or growing, rice. Khmer farmers built a brilliant water-management system to control and harness the heavy monsoon rains. The system combined immense storage tanks with canals, dikes, and dams. As a result, farmers were able to produce three or four rice harvests a year. By 1250, rice fed Angkor's population of 1.5 million and produced a huge surplus for export. This intensive rice cultivation was the foundation of Khmer prosperity, stability, and power, which expanded across Southeast Asia.

The Khmer Empire reached its peak under Jayavarman VII, who ruled from 1181 to 1218. Jayavarman VII built roads and a new capital city called Angkor Thom. He also supported Buddhism by building an estimated 20,000 Buddhist shrines. Under his rule, the state supported 300,000 monks and priests. Pouring resources into religious monuments strained the economy to the breaking point. Over the next two centuries, wars further weakened the Khmer Empire. In 1431, a Thai army seized Angkor itself. Though the empire shifted south, its power declined and its capital was abandoned.

A farmer in Cambodia harvests rice by hand.

REVIEW & ASSESS

1. **READING CHECK** How did rice agriculture lead to prosperity and power for the Khmer Empire?

2. **ANALYZE CAUSE AND EFFECT** How did India influence the culture of the Khmer?

3. **IDENTIFY MAIN IDEAS AND DETAILS** What two factors led to the downfall of the Khmer Empire?

2.3 Angkor Wat

With its dramatic jungle setting and fantastic architecture, the temple city of Angkor Wat is the classic image of a lost city. Remote and mysterious, it has been the spectacular backdrop for many Hollywood movies.

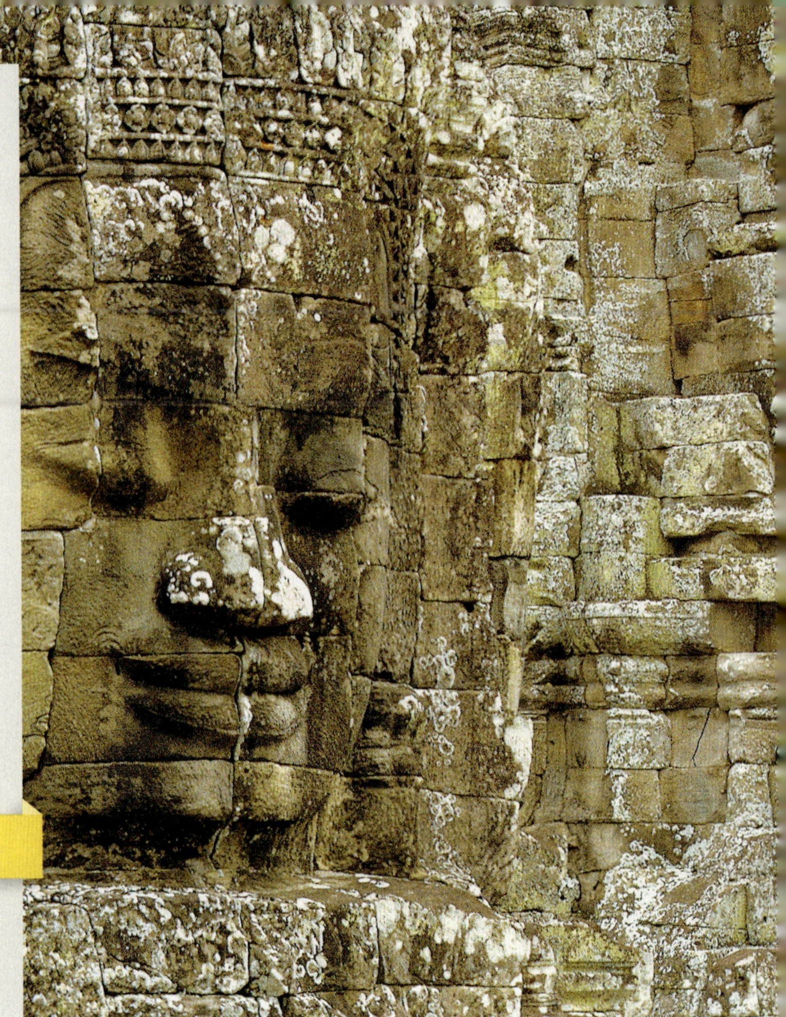

MAIN IDEA

Khmer culture peaked with the building of Angkor Wat.

A GREAT TEMPLE COMPLEX

The Khmer capital city of Angkor is actually a series of cities and temples spread over more than 300 square miles. For almost 500 years, Angkor was the political and religious heart of the Khmer Empire and the largest city in the world. Each king added to its glory by building beautiful temples and even a whole new city within the city. In the 1100s, however, King Suryavarman II built Angkor's most celebrated addition—the temple complex of **Angkor Wat**.

Angkor Wat means "city that is a temple." Its complex of interconnected buildings covers 244 acres, making it the largest religious monument in the world. Built to honor the Hindu god Vishnu, the temple has at its center a vast five-towered pyramid. Each tower is shaped like a lotus bud. In Hinduism, the lotus flower represents beauty and purity while the tower symbolizes the legendary home of the Hindu gods. An outer wall and a wide moat represent mountains at the edge of the world and the ocean that lies beyond. Indeed, every feature of Angkor Wat has a symbolic meaning.

The temple represents the peak of Khmer artistic achievement. Among its most admired features are its extraordinarily intricate carvings. These include hundreds of dancers, each one unique. Another outstanding feature is a 1,970-foot stretch of **bas-reliefs** (slightly raised figures on a flat background) that show scenes from Hindu legends.

Angkor Wat was also built to be Suryavarman's tomb and possibly an astronomical observatory as well. There is some evidence that it is oriented to align with certain stars. Unlike most other Khmer temples, Angkor Wat faces west, toward the setting sun, which symbolizes death.

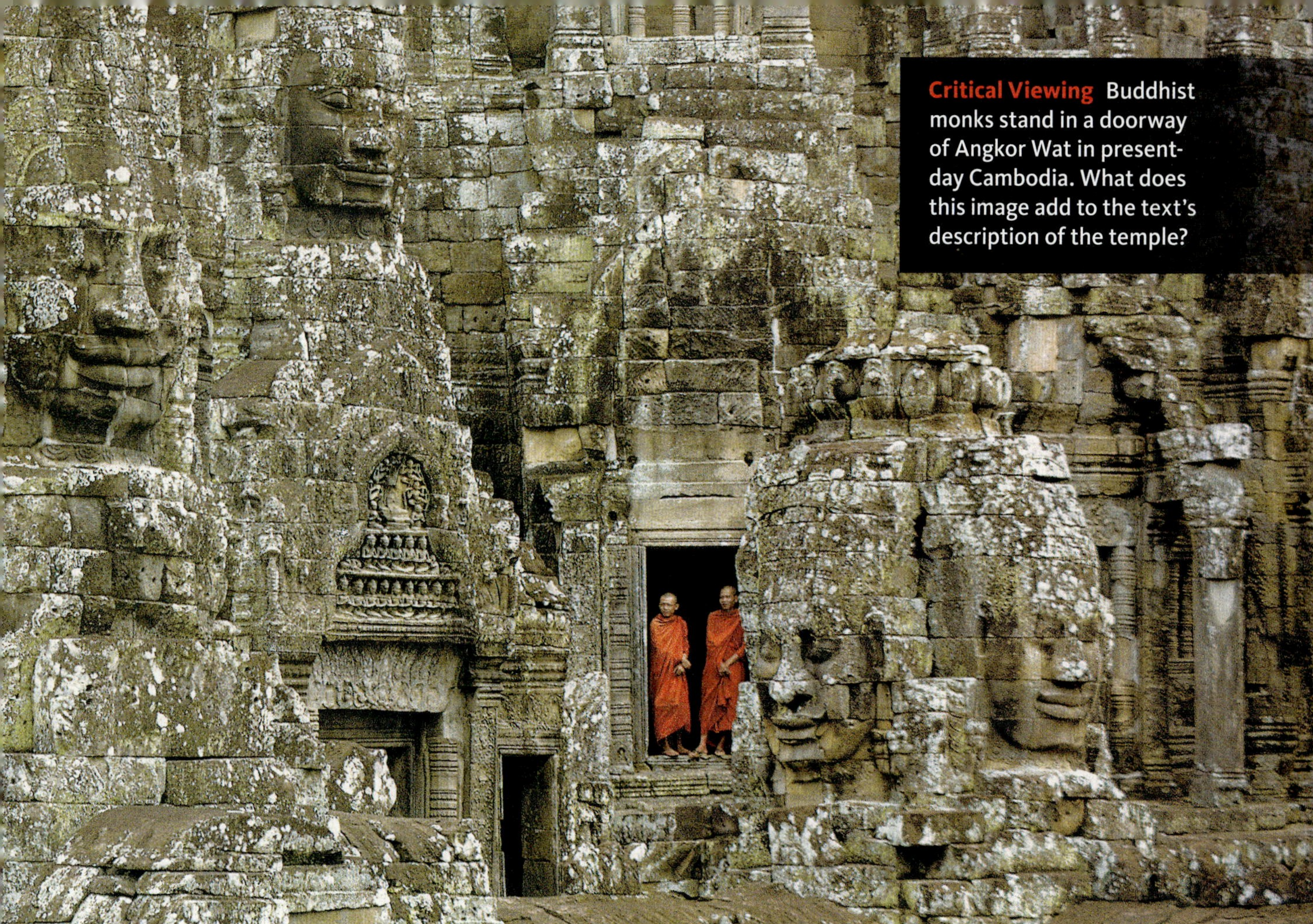

Critical Viewing Buddhist monks stand in a doorway of Angkor Wat in present-day Cambodia. What does this image add to the text's description of the temple?

CHANGES AND RESTORATION

After the Khmer's switch to Buddhism, Angkor Wat became a Buddhist shrine. When the Khmer Empire collapsed, Angkor fell to its enemies. By the 1600s, it was largely abandoned. The jungle quickly consumed its wooden structures and covered its stone buildings.

Then, in 1860, the French explorer Henri Mouhot encountered the "lost" world of Angkor and Angkor Wat. Mouhot brought the site to the attention of westerners. Sadly, visitors and thieves began removing its treasures. Indeed, Angkor Wat has suffered terribly from looters, uncontrolled tourism, and even poorly performed restoration.

Fortunately, in 1992, it became a UNESCO World Heritage Site with carefully planned measures to protect it for future generations. Today Angkor Wat is Cambodia's main tourist attraction with over 2 million visitors every year. It is so important to the country that it forms the centerpiece of the Cambodian flag.

REVIEW & ASSESS

1. **READING CHECK** Why was Angkor Wat built?
2. **IDENTIFY MAIN IDEAS AND DETAILS** Why is Angkor Wat often thought of as representing the peak of Khmer artistic achievement?
3. **SEQUENCE EVENTS** What changes did Angkor Wat undergo during its long history?

CHAPTER 20 Review

VOCABULARY

On your paper, write the vocabulary word that best completes each of the following sentences.

1. Korea's three early kingdoms had a bitter ______, so they fought one another for control of Korea.
2. Korean potters developed ______, which was known for its bluish-green color.
3. The Korean national dish is called ______, which is made with spicy pickled cabbage and other vegetables.
4. For centuries, the traditional ______ worn by Korean men included full-length pants and a long jacket with wide sleeves.
5. Early Koreans invented a unique system of heating called ______, which is still used in Korean homes today.
6. As Chinese rulers tried to ______ Chinese culture on the people of Nam Viet, violent uprisings occurred.
7. The Khmer took advantage of the wet and fertile river deltas to ______ rice successfully, which led to their prosperity.

READING STRATEGY

8. **DETERMINE WORD MEANINGS** If you haven't already, complete the chart for at least three vocabulary words. Then use each word in a paragraph about the history of Korea or Southeast Asia.

Word	Definition	Example from My Life
rivalry	competition	

MAIN IDEAS

Answer the following questions. Support your answers with evidence from the chapter.

9. How did the Silla kingdom triumph to unify Korea? **LESSON 1.1**
10. What borrowed aspects of Chinese culture helped the Koryo and Choson dynasties rule Korea for nearly a thousand years? **LESSON 1.3**
11. Despite strong Chinese influences, how did Korea develop a distinct culture? **LESSON 1.4**
12. Why did the Han Chinese want to occupy and control Nam Viet? **LESSON 2.1**
13. Why was rice farming important to the Khmer people? **LESSON 2.2**
14. What purposes did Angkor Wat serve? **LESSON 2.3**

CRITICAL THINKING

Answer the following questions. Support your answers with evidence from the chapter.

15. **COMPARE AND CONTRAST** How were the cultures of the three early Korean kingdoms—Silla, Koguryo, and Paekche—alike?
16. **ANALYZE CAUSE AND EFFECT** What effect did the Japanese occupation have on Korea?
17. **DRAW CONCLUSIONS** Why was the Korean invention of movable metal type a pioneering breakthrough in printing?
18. **MAKE INFERENCES** How did the Khmer's hierarchical society reflect the influence of Indian ideas?
19. **ANALYZE CAUSE AND EFFECT** What factors led to the Khmer's success in growing rice?
20. **YOU DECIDE** Which do you think was the greater Korean cultural achievement, the development of celadon or the creation of the Tripitaka Koreana? Support your opinion with evidence from the chapter.

INTERPRET MAPS

Study the map of Southeast Asia as it was in 1895. Then answer the questions that follow.

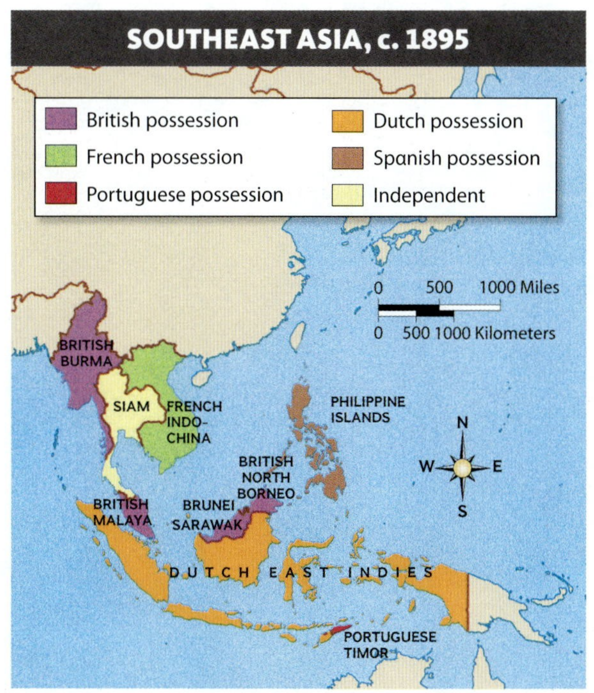
SOUTHEAST ASIA, c. 1895
British possession
French possession
Portuguese possession
Dutch possession
Spanish possession
Independent
0 500 1000 Miles
0 500 1000 Kilometers
BRITISH BURMA
SIAM
FRENCH INDO-CHINA
PHILIPPINE ISLANDS
BRITISH NORTH BORNEO
BRITISH MALAYA
BRUNEI
SARAWAK
DUTCH EAST INDIES
PORTUGUESE TIMOR
N
S
E
W

21. Based on the map, how would you describe foreign rule of Southeast Asia around 1895?

22. Which European countries held the most territory in Southeast Asia around 1895?

23. **MAP ACTIVITY** Sketch a map of Southeast Asia as it is today. Then compare it with Southeast Asia as it appeared in 1895. What similarities and diferences do you notice between borders of territories in 1895 and countries in the present day?

ANALYZE SOURCES

Read the following paragraph about the Trung sisters. Then answer the question that follows.

> In A.D. 40, the Trung sisters set up an army with the aid of the Vietnamese lords. Fighting fearlessly, they expelled the Chinese and established their own kingdom. In A.D. 43, however, the Chinese quelled [put down] the rebellion. To avoid capture, the sisters committed suicide by jumping into the Hat River. Centuries later, stone figures of two women washed up on a sandbank in the Red River. Believed to be the earthly remains of the Trung Sisters, petrified and turned into statues, they were taken to Dong Nhan village and installed in a temple there.

24. The Trung sisters are still honored today in Vietnam. What qualities do you think the Vietnamese admire in the two sisters?

WRITE ABOUT HISTORY

25. **NARRATIVE** Suppose you are taking tourists on a tour of Angkor Wat. Write a paragraph in which you explain to them how Angkor Wat represents the peak of Khmer artistic achievement.

TIPS

- Take notes from the lesson about Angkor Wat.
- Introduce the topic clearly.
- Develop the topic with supporting details and examples about the temple and its layout, relationship to Hinduism, and artistic features and symbolic meanings.
- Use two or three vocabulary terms from the chapter.
- Provide a concluding statement that summarizes the significance of the temple.

ON **LOCATION** WITH

Albert Lin

Research Scientist/Engineer and National Geographic Emerging Explorer

Check out more on myNGconnect

Albert Lin, pictured here in the forests of Mongolia, teams up with other National Geographic Explorers as part of the Valley of the Khans Project to hunt for the tomb of Genghis Khan.

TWO PATHS

Society often encourages us to choose a single path in life, but I've always been interested both in the sciences and the humanities. Turning my education in engineering into one of the greatest adventures of my life has been a huge journey. The idea to search for the tomb of Genghis Khan occurred to me while backpacking in Mongolia. I wanted to do something that everyone thought was impossible.

Genghis Khan united Mongolia's feuding tribes and led them on a campaign of conquest unequalled in world history. He died in 1227, but the location of his tomb remains a mystery. In fact, Mongolian custom warns that disturbing Genghis Khan's burial site will unleash a curse that could end the world. With a cultural taboo as strong as that, you can't just start digging—you have to get smart.

Albert Lin examines a digital projection of northern Mongolia from inside the StarCAVE, a 3-D virtual environment.

USING TECHNOLOGY

There are many ways to look under the ground without having to touch it. I use non-invasive computer-based technologies to gather, synthesize, and visualize data without ever digging a hole. Satellite imagery, ground-penetrating radar, and remote sensors let me explore places and make archaeological discoveries while respecting the traditional beliefs of indigenous people.

The real trick is synthesizing the vast amounts of information we collect into something that can be understood. We program billions of individual data bits into a file that allows us to re-render it into a digital 3-D world. And then we have some fun in the StarCAVE, a virtual reality room that lets us manipulate our way through images projected on the ground, walls, and on every surface. Special glasses create the 3-D effect so we can "fly" over the landscape. For example if a mountain is described in an old text, I can go into the StarCAVE and travel around that region to see if it actually exists. Technology like this lets us conduct a non-invasive search for Genghis Khan in a way that is respectful to the Mongolians. We can try to solve this ancient mystery without overstepping cultural barriers.

WHY STUDY HISTORY ?

"The Mongols created a lot of what we know of as our modern history, but their story hasn't been fully told and their contributions have been underestimated. *Sharing the true history of the foundation of our cultural past is crucial.*" —Albert Lin

NATIONAL GEOGRAPHIC

Divining Angkor

BY RICHARD STONE

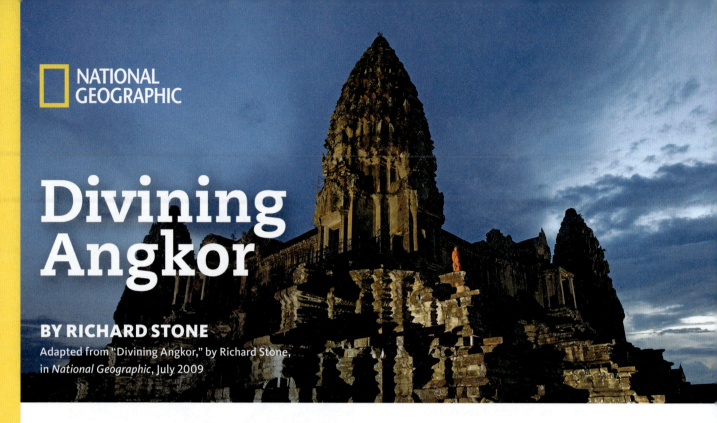

Adapted from "Divining Angkor," by Richard Stone, in *National Geographic*, July 2009

The Khmer kingdom lasted from the 9th to the 15th centuries. At its height it dominated a wide swath of Southeast Asia. Angkor, its capital, was the most extensive urban complex of the preindustrial world. As many as 750,000 people lived there. By the late 16th century, the once-magnificent capital was in decline.

Angkor became a powerhouse thanks to a sophisticated system of canals and reservoirs. Over several centuries, teams of laborers constructed hundreds of miles of canals and dikes. The city could hoard water in dry months and get rid of excess water during the rainy season.

The ability to divert and collect water would have afforded a measure of protection from floods, as well as a steady water supply. But forces beyond Angkor's control threw this system into disarray. Archaeologist Roland Fletcher was baffled when his team unearthed a vast structure in the waterworks and found that it had been destroyed, apparently by Angkor's own engineers.

These ruins are a vital clue to an epic struggle that unfolded as generations of Khmer engineers coped with an increasingly complex water system. "They probably spent vast portions of their lives fixing it," says Fletcher. Any deterioration of the waterworks would have left Angkor vulnerable to a natural disaster.

Starting in the 1300s, Europe endured a few centuries of unpredictable weather marked by harsh winters and chilly summers. Now it appears that Southeast Asia, too, experienced climatic upheaval. Extreme weather could have been the final blow to a vulnerable civilization. Prolonged and severe droughts, punctuated by torrential downpours, "would have ruined the water system," says Fletcher.

Angkor's end is a sobering lesson in the limits of human ingenuity. "Angkor's hydraulic system was an amazing machine," Fletcher says. Its engineers managed to keep the civilization's signal achievement running for six centuries—until, in the end, a greater force overwhelmed them.

For more from National Geographic
Check out "The Forgotten Road" on myNGconnect

UNIT INQUIRY: LEAVE A LEGACY OF INNOVATION

In this unit, you learned about Chinese, Japanese, and Korean civilizations. Based on your understanding of the text, what new products, methods, and ideas did these civilizations invent or develop? Which of these innovations do you think has made a lasting legacy on the modern world?

ASSIGNMENT Choose an innovation that you think our modern civilization will leave as a legacy for a future civilization. The innovation you choose should come from the 20th or 21st century. Be prepared to present your legacy to the class and explain why you chose it.

Plan As you choose your innovation, think about how other innovations—such as the Chinese invention of paper—dramatically changed and influenced many civilizations past and present. Make a list of the ways in which the innovation you selected has affected or changed the modern world. You might want to use a graphic organizer to help organize your thoughts. ▶

Produce Use your notes to produce detailed descriptions of the impact your innovation has made on modern civilization and what impact you envision it having on a future civilization. You might want to write your descriptions in outline or paragraph form.

Present Choose a creative way to present your innovation to the class. Consider one of these options:

- Create a multimedia presentation using photos to illustrate different ways your innovation has affected or changed modern civilization.
- Design an advertisement for your innovation, providing a "before" and "after" view of our civilization with and without the innovation.
- Write a paragraph describing how you envision this innovation will impact a future civilization and why.

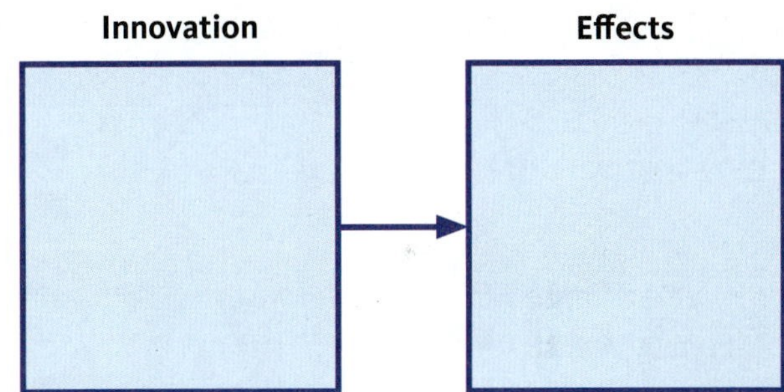

Innovation
Effects

RAPID REVIEW
UNIT 8

EMPIRES OF ASIA

TOP TEN

1. Genghis Khan united the Mongol tribes and conquered Central Asia.
2. Traditionalist forces in China imposed centuries of isolationism to protect China's culture from foreign influence.
3. Chinese inventions spread worldwide, especially printing, paper money, magnetic compasses, gunpowder, and porcelain.
4. Japan's emperors were replaced by the military rule of shoguns and a feudal system of daimyo warlords and samurai warriors.
5. Vietnam overthrew Chinese rule and built an independent nation in Southeast Asia.

6-10. **NOW IT'S YOUR TURN** Complete the list with five more things to remember about empires of Asia.

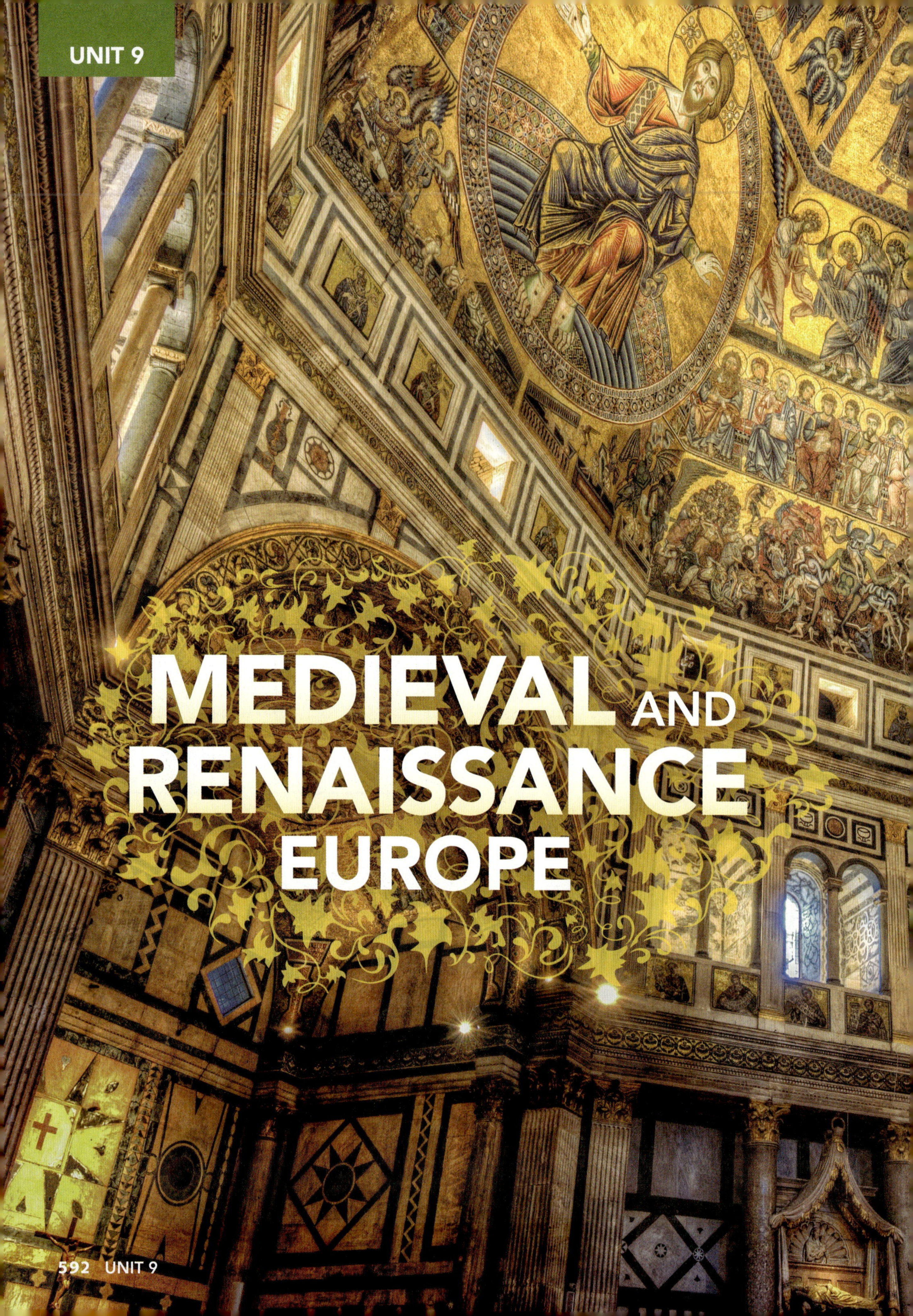

MEDIEVAL AND RENAISSANCE EUROPE

NATIONAL GEOGRAPHIC

ON **LOCATION** WITH

Maurizio Seracini

Cultural Heritage Engineer

Europe experienced a “rebirth” around the 1300s, a time when writing, thinking, and the arts flourished. This movement, known as the Renaissance, began in Italy, and artists like Leonardo da Vinci, Raphael, and Michelangelo were hugely influential. I’m Maurizio Seracini, and I use technology to study priceless European works of art—and seek out ones that haven’t been seen for centuries. Join me on an exploration of medieval and Renaissance Europe.

‹ **CRITICAL VIEWING** The Baptistery of Saint John in Florence, Italy, dazzles visitors with its mosaics and fine artwork. What types of imagery can you identify and what does it reveal about this time period?

Medieval and Renaissance Europe

700

768
Charlemagne becomes king of the Franks and, in time, unites much of Western Europe. *(bust of Charlemagne)*

1096
The Crusades begin. *(illustration of Crusaders in Jerusalem)*

1200

1215
King John seals the Magna Carta.

c. 1300
The Renaissance begins in Italy.

The World

610
ASIA
Muhammad begins to spread Islam.

1192
ASIA
Military rule under leaders called shoguns begins in Japan.

1325
THE AMERICAS
Aztecs establish their capital in Tenochtitlán, present-day Mexico City. *(Aztec calendar)*

COMPARE TIME LINES

What explorations took place in the 1400s?

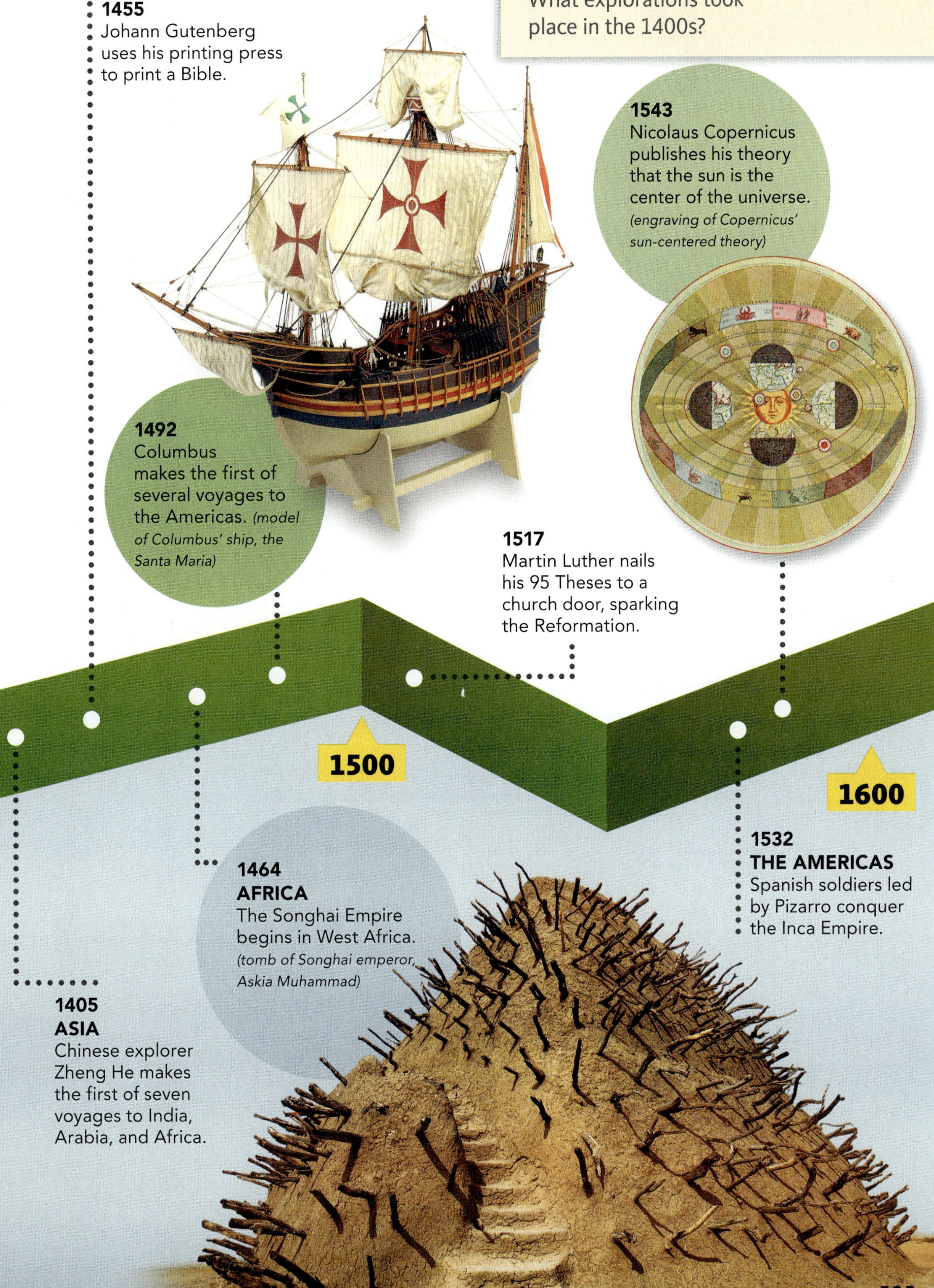

1500
1600

1455
Johann Gutenberg uses his printing press to print a Bible.

1492
Columbus makes the first of several voyages to the Americas. *(model of Columbus' ship, the Santa Maria)*

1517
Martin Luther nails his 95 Theses to a church door, sparking the Reformation.

1543
Nicolaus Copernicus publishes his theory that the sun is the center of the universe. *(engraving of Copernicus' sun-centered theory)*

1405
ASIA
Chinese explorer Zheng He makes the first of seven voyages to India, Arabia, and Africa.

1464
AFRICA
The Songhai Empire begins in West Africa. *(tomb of Songhai emperor, Askia Muhammad)*

1532
THE AMERICAS
Spanish soldiers led by Pizarro conquer the Inca Empire.

UNIT 9
GEOGRAPHY IN HISTORY

Europe
c. 1600

By the 1600s, Europe was divided into many states. One of these, the Holy Roman Empire, began in the 800s, when a Germanic king named Charlemagne united many other kingdoms under his rule. Charlemagne was a Christian and a strong supporter of the pope in Rome. He spread his faith throughout his empire.

However, over time, a revolution in thought led people to question the Roman Catholic Church. Some Europeans broke away from the Church and developed their own Christian religions, which soon spread over Europe.

What religions were practiced in the Holy Roman Empire?

0 100 200 300 400 kilometers
0 100 200 300 400 miles

EUROPEAN STATES
Europe, c. 1600
Austrian-Habsburg possessions
Spanish-Habsburg possessions
Papal states
Holy Roman Empire
SWEDEN
RUSSIA
DENMARK-NORWAY
Baltic Sea
SCOTLAND
North Sea
IRELAND
ENGLAND
London
Prussia
POLAND-LITHUANIA
NETHERLANDS
Elbe
BRANDENBURG
SMALL STATES
SAXONY
Wittenberg
HOLY ROMAN EMPIRE
Rhine
Worms
BAVARIA
Danube
AUSTRIA
HUNGARY
WALLACHIA
Seine
FRANCE
SWISS CONFEDERATION
Trent
SAVOY
REPUBLIC OF VENICE
Adriatic Sea
OTTOMAN EMPIRE
Avignon
REP. OF GENOA
TUSCANY
PAPAL STATES
Corsica
Rome
BENEVENTO
PONTECORVO
Naples
Aegean Sea
PORTUGAL
Madrid
SPAIN
Sardinia
Balearic Islands
Sicily
REPUBLIC OF VENICE
Crete
Mediterranean Sea

Renaissance Gallery

In the 1300s, an explosion in art called the Renaissance began in Italy and spread through Europe. Some of the greatest Renaissance artists created the works shown here.

Giotto: The Mourning of Christ (c. 1305)

Jan van Eyck: The Arnolfini Portrait (c. 1434)

CHRISTIANITY IN EUROPE
Christianity in Europe, c. 1600
Church of England
Calvinist
Lutheran
Roman Catholic
Holy Roman Empire
0 100 200 300 400 kilometers
0 100 200 300 400 miles
SCOTLAND
IRELAND
ENGLAND
London
North Sea
ATLANTIC OCEAN
SWEDEN
DENMARK-NORWAY
Baltic Sea
RUSSIA
Prussia
POLAND-LITHUANIA
Elbe
BRANDENBURG
SMALL STATES
SAXONY
Wittenberg
NETHERLANDS
HOLY ROMAN EMPIRE
Rhine
Worms
Augsburg
BAVARIA
Danube
AUSTRIA
HUNGARY
Seine
FRANCE
SWISS CONFEDERATION
Trent
SAVOY
Avignon
OTTOMAN EMPIRE
Danube
Adriatic Sea
PAPAL STATES
Rome
Naples
Corsica
Sardinia
Sicily
Aegean Sea
Crete
Madrid
SPAIN
PORTUGAL
Balearic Islands
Mediterranean Sea

Leonardo da Vinci: The Last Supper (c. 1498)

Durer: Four Horsemen of the Apocalypse (c. 1498)

Michelangelo: Moses (c. 1515)

CHAPTER
21

FEUDALISM AND THE MIDDLE AGES

500 – 1453

SECTION 1

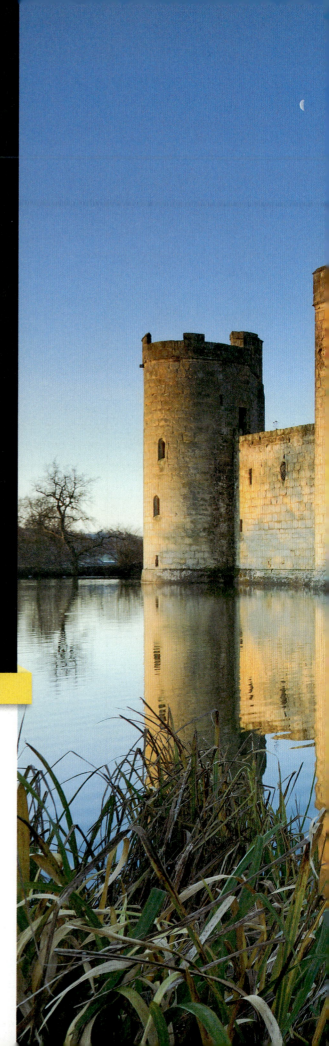

FEUDALISM DEVELOPS

KEY VOCABULARY	NAMES & PLACES
chivalry	Charlemagne
convert	Franks
feudalism	Middle Ages
knight	
lord	
manor	
medieval	
serf	
vassal	

SECTION 2

POLITICAL AND SOCIAL CHANGE

KEY VOCABULARY	NAMES & PLACES
bubonic plague	Crusades
burgher	Hundred Years' War
cathedral	Inquisition
clergy	Joan of Arc
common law	King John
guild	Magna Carta
longbow	Reconquista
monastery	
parliament	

READING STRATEGY

DRAW CONCLUSIONS Drawing conclusions means using the facts in a text to make educated guesses. Use a chart like this one to jot down your conclusions about how feudalism and Christianity affected people during the Middle Ages.

Middle Ages

Feudalism	Christianity

During the Middle Ages, kings and nobles built thick-walled castles to keep out invaders. Some castles, like this one in England, were also surrounded by a moat to discourage the enemy.

1.1 Medieval Europe

The Germanic tribes that caused the fall of the Western Roman Empire in A.D. 476 didn't just devastate towns and kill many of their inhabitants. They destroyed a way of life. For hundreds of years, the Roman Empire had united much of Europe. With the empire no longer in control, "Now what?" could well have been the question on almost everyone's mind.

MAIN IDEA

After Rome fell, Western Europe underwent many political and cultural changes.

AFTER THE FALL OF ROME

What came next is a period historians call the **Middle Ages**. This era lasted from about 500 to 1450 in Western Europe and is also called the medieval period. **Medieval** comes from the Latin words *medium*, meaning "middle," and *aevum*, meaning "age."

During the early part of this period, Western Europe was very different from what it had been under Rome's strong central government and powerful army. After Rome fell, Germanic leaders seized power, and much of the region became divided into small kingdoms that were almost constantly at war. As a result of this widespread warfare, one of the greatest challenges facing leaders was to keep their people safe and secure. This challenge would help shape stronger governments over time.

It was a violent time, yet many kingdoms thrived. Thanks to the region's mostly moderate climate and rich soil, farmers could grow crops and feed themselves and their livestock. Abundant forestland provided wood for building, and mountains containing a wealth of minerals—particularly iron—allowed the Germanic peoples to make all the weapons they needed to fight their foes. In addition, Western Europe's long coastline and major rivers gave people access to the sea and plentiful supplies of fish.

POLITICAL AND CULTURAL CHANGES

The region's many waterways offered ideal routes and networks for trading. However, unlike the Romans, the Germanic peoples who migrated to Western Europe were not interested in trade. The tribes that settled in Roman lands in the early part of the Middle Ages preferred their own traditions to Roman ways.

For example, the new settlers had their own ideas about government. Tribes such as the **Franks** united to form powerful kingdoms but didn't create large centralized governments or write down their laws, as the Romans had. Instead, the people obeyed the unwritten rules and traditions of their king. They lived in small villages where they worked the land and tended their herds. As trade began to disappear in the region, so did many cities.

Just about the only force that helped unite Western Europe in the early Middle Ages was Christianity, which survived the fall of Rome. Before the 500s, most Germanic peoples, including the Angles, Jutes, and Saxons, practiced their traditional religions and worshipped many gods. After the Germanic leaders came to power, however, many of them **converted**, or changed their religion, to Christianity.

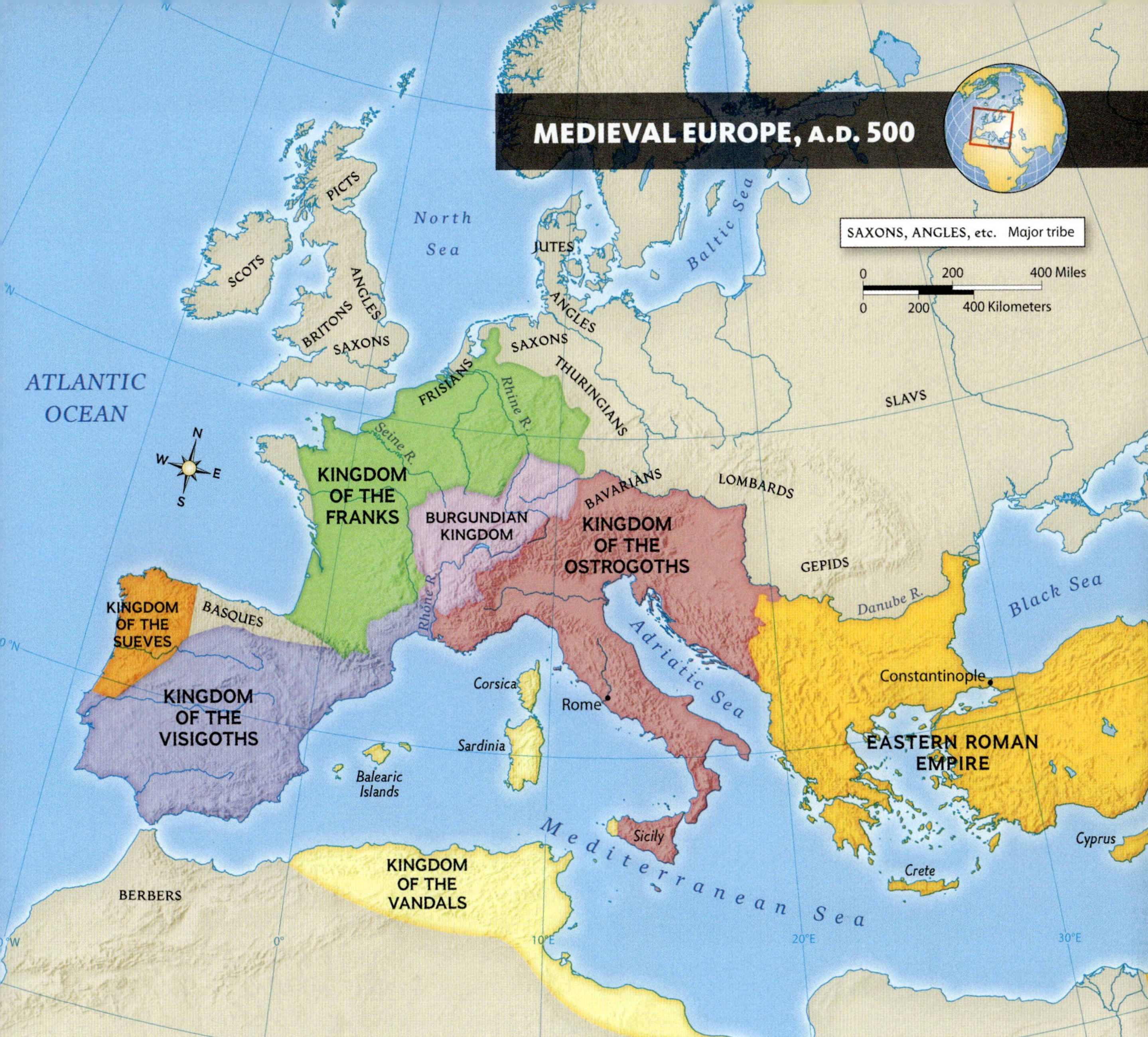
MEDIEVAL EUROPE, A.D. 500
SAXONS, ANGLES, etc. Major tribe
0 200 400 Miles
0 200 400 Kilometers
ATLANTIC OCEAN
North Sea
Baltic Sea
SCOTS
PICTS
ANGLES
BRITONS
SAXONS
JUTES
ANGLES
SAXONS
THURINGIANS
FRISIANS
Rhine R.
Seine R.
SLAVS
KINGDOM OF THE FRANKS
BURGUNDIAN KINGDOM
BAVARIANS
LOMBARDS
KINGDOM OF THE OSTROGOTHS
GEPIDS
Danube R.
Black Sea
KINGDOM OF THE SUEVES
BASQUES
Rhône R.
KINGDOM OF THE VISIGOTHS
Corsica
Rome
Adriatic Sea
Constantinople
EASTERN ROMAN EMPIRE
Sardinia
Balearic Islands
Sicily
Mediterranean Sea
Cyprus
Crete
KINGDOM OF THE VANDALS
BERBERS
0°
10°E
20°E
30°E

The first leader to convert was Clovis, who ruled the Franks. After Clovis defeated Roman Gaul (now France) in 486, he went on to conquer other weaker kingdoms. When he converted to Christianity, many of his subjects did, too. As a result of his conversion and that of other rulers, Christianity spread and increased in influence. Even though the Western Roman Empire had disappeared, the city of Rome itself retained a certain amount of power and strength. It remained the home of the pope as well as the center of Christianity.

REVIEW & ASSESS

1. **READING CHECK** How did government change in Western Europe after the fall of Rome?
2. **INTERPRET MAPS** Which of the six kingdoms labeled on the map might have been most exposed to attack from other kingdoms? Explain why.
3. **COMPARE AND CONTRAST** How did Western European culture in the early Middle Ages differ from culture during the Roman Empire?

CHARLEMAGNE c. 742 – 814

He was a man of contrasts. He ruthlessly destroyed his enemies but loved learning. He was a tall, commanding figure but usually wore simple clothing. He received fabulous gifts from foreign kings but collected songs of ancient Germanic heroes. In spite of—or maybe because of—these contradictions, he became the first emperor in Western Europe since the fall of the Western Roman Empire. They didn't call this king of the Franks Charlemagne—or Charles the Great—for nothing.

Job: First emperor of the Holy Roman Empire

Home: Kingdom of the Franks

FINEST HOUR

After Charlemagne conquered and united the Germanic kingdoms of Western Europe, the pope placed a crown on Charlemagne's head, proclaiming him emperor of the Romans.

HOBBIES

He enjoyed hunting and swimming and often made his friends and nobles swim with him.

TRIVIA

He could get by on little sleep and sometimes woke his officials to hear the latest report or charge them with a new task.

DEATH

After swimming in one of his favorite springs, he came down with a fever and died a week later.

A MIGHTY RULER

More than 200 years after Clovis died, **Charlemagne** (SHAHR-luh-mayn) became the Frankish king in 768 and proved to be a natural leader. He had a vision for his reign. Charlemagne wanted to unite under his rule all of the Germanic kingdoms shown on the map in the previous lesson. To achieve that goal, the Frankish king battled such tribes as the Slavs, the Lombards, and the Saxons, who reigned in what is now Germany. In the end, Charlemagne succeeded. He brought many of the Germanic tribes together as one people and became the strongest leader in Western Europe.

While Charlemagne was doing battle with the Saxons and other powerful Germanic tribes, he ably administered his kingdom. He established new laws to keep order and appointed officials to run faraway regions of his realm. Each year, Charlemagne called the officials to his court to keep tabs on them. He also took care of his subjects. He founded

In this painting, Pope Leo III crowns Charlemagne emperor of the Romans before an audience of Church officials.

Coronation of Charlemagne, Raphael Sanzio, 1516–1517

schools and protected the weak against injustice. Above all, he wanted to strengthen Christianity throughout his kingdom.

A CHRISTIAN EMPIRE

Like all Frankish kings since the 500s, Charlemagne was a Christian. In fact, his wars against the Germanic tribes had been fought not only to unite the tribes but also to spread his faith. After he conquered the Saxons, he declared that he would put to death anyone who refused to convert to Christianity. Since Charlemagne had already proved how ruthless he could be by slaughtering more than 4,000 Saxons who had fought against him, those who remained offered no further resistance.

Charlemagne was also a loyal defender of the pope at the time, Pope Leo III. After the pope passed laws that chipped away at the power of the nobles of Rome, they rebelled against him in 800. Leo asked for Charlemagne's help, and the king put the uprising down.

To express his gratitude, Leo crowned Charlemagne emperor of the Romans during a Christmas service in Rome. Charlemagne became the first German emperor of what would later be called the Holy Roman Empire. The title recognized Charlemagne as a guardian of Christianity. It also fueled his passion to strengthen the Church. By the time Charlemagne died in 814, he had created a strong Christian empire.

REVIEW & ASSESS

1. **READING CHECK** What were Charlemagne's two main goals during his reign?
2. **SEQUENCE EVENTS** What happened after Charlemagne put down the uprising in Rome?
3. **MAKE INFERENCES** How was Charlemagne a stabilizing, or steadying, force in Western Europe?

1.3 NATIONAL GEOGRAPHIC WRITER CAROLINE ALEXANDER

Investigating a Mysterious Treasure

People carefully combing every inch of a stretch of beach with a metal detector may dream of striking it rich, but they usually just find a few dollars in change. Who knows what Terry Herbert dreamed of finding with his metal detector as he searched a field in the English county of Staffordshire in 2009? The farmer who owned the land hoped Herbert would uncover his missing wrench. Instead, as **Caroline Alexander** has reported, he found a mysterious stash of long-ago buried treasure.

^ This gold sword hilt, or handle, was among the treasure found in Staffordshire. The hilt is inlaid with red gemstones called garnets. If you look closely, you can see traces of soil on the gems.

MAIN IDEA

Archaeologists are trying to figure out who buried a great treasure in England in the late 600s and why.

BURIED TREASURE

Remember reading about the Angles and Saxons in the first two lessons of this chapter? Not all members of these powerful tribes lived in Germany. The Anglo-Saxons—made up mostly of Angles, Saxons, and Jutes—settled in England in the 400s and ruled there for about 600 years. Archaeologists know that the treasure Herbert uncovered in Staffordshire was buried during the Anglo-Saxons' rule. They have also determined that most of the Staffordshire Hoard, as it came to be called, consists of military items. (*Hoard* is just another word for a mass or collection of something.) The only nonmilitary items are a quotation from the Bible, inscribed on a thin strip of gold, and two golden crosses.

STAFFORDSHIRE, ENGLAND

10°W
5°W
0°
0 50 100 Miles
0 50 100 Kilometers
ATLANTIC OCEAN
SCOTLAND
North Sea
NORTHERN IRELAND
N
W
E
S
55°N
Irish Sea
IRELAND
WALES
ENGLAND
STAFFORDSHIRE
50°N

What archaeologists don't know is who hid the hoard and why. Was the treasure buried by Anglo-Saxon soldiers or thieves? Did those who hid the treasure want to keep it safe from enemy hands? Did they plan to come back for it? Questions like these captured the imagination of National Geographic writer Caroline Alexander. As she points out in a 2011 issue of *National Geographic* magazine, "The Staffordshire Hoard was thrilling and historic—but above all it was enigmatic [mysterious]."

MYSTERIES AND MAGIC

Alexander believes the key to understanding the mystery of the hoard lies in understanding the importance of magic at that time. The Anglo-Saxons deeply believed in magic and certain supernatural creatures. For example, as Alexander writes, "Misfortune was commonly attributed to tiny darts fired by elves." Gold was thought to have magical properties that could please these creatures. So the hoard might also have been meant to ward off misfortune—particularly in battle.

But what about the Christian items? You've learned that many Germanic peoples converted to Christianity after the fall of Rome. This may explain the quotation from the Bible on the strip of gold and the two crosses. However, many of the new converts blended Christianity with their traditional beliefs. Some early Germanic Christian kings called on God to help them in battle. They also believed that biblical quotations could give them magical power in battle.

So was the hoard buried as an offering for the gods, the Christian God, or supernatural creatures? Perhaps it was a combination of all three. Or maybe it was none of the above. As Alexander admits, "Odds are we will never know the story behind the Staffordshire Hoard, but in a world without magic spells or dragons, would we understand it if we did?"

REVIEW & ASSESS

1. **READING CHECK** What treasure was discovered in a field in Staffordshire?
2. **IDENTIFY MAIN IDEAS AND DETAILS** Who were the Anglo-Saxons?
3. **DRAW CONCLUSIONS** Why does Caroline Alexander think we may never understand the story behind the Staffordshire Hoard?

FEUDAL SOCIETY

In feudal society, everyone knew his or her place. Feudalism created an economy based on the possession of land. The upper three classes held all the power, and peasants and serfs had few rights.

King
Most kings inherited their position, but none could rule without the support of the noblemen.
Church Officials and Noblemen
Church officials and high-ranking nobles often exercised more power than the king.
Knights
Knights guarded their lord's castle and fought for him according to a strict code of conduct.
Peasants and Serfs
Peasants and serfs both worked the land, but serfs needed their lord's permission to travel, marry, or own property.

1.4 Feudal Society

The united Europe that Charlemagne had fought so hard to establish didn't last very long. About 30 years after his death in 814, his empire was divided into three kingdoms. Frankish rule grew weak, and Western Europe fell back into disorder. Once again, the Germanic kingdoms competed for power.

MAIN IDEA

In the Middle Ages, feudalism grew out of the need to provide security and defense.

A NEW SYSTEM

Kings in Western Europe and England could not defend their vast kingdoms on their own. To help them hold on to their land and protect their subjects, a political and social system called **feudalism** developed by the 800s. In this system, kings gave pieces of their land to noblemen known as **lords**. A lord, in turn, granted parts of this land, called fiefs (feefs), to lesser noblemen called **vassals**. The vassals paid taxes on the land and pledged their military service to the lord. This meant that a vassal had to organize his own army of fighting men. Many vassals were themselves soldiers in the army and served as **knights**, who were warriors on horseback. The lord protected his vassals in exchange for their service.

Vassals were supposed to be loyal to the king, but many vassals switched their allegiance to their lord. This was the man who guarded their families, after all. As a result, lords were supreme rulers in their own territory.

A NEW SOCIAL ORDER

The new system created a social order that was as tightly structured as a pyramid. At the very top sat the king. Next came the church officials and noblemen, who included lords and some vassals. Lords lived in fortified castles that were guarded by knights, the third class in feudal society.

Relatively few people belonged to the upper three classes. The great majority of people in the Middle Ages found themselves at the bottom of the social heap. This class included peasants and serfs. Although some peasants worked as artisans and merchants, most were farmers and laborers. **Serfs**, however, were tied to the land and gave their lord most of whatever they produced. In return, their lord gave them shelter and protection. Serfs weren't quite slaves. They were allowed to buy their freedom. Yet with no skills or education to help them earn money, they were basically powerless to change their condition.

REVIEW & ASSESS

1. **READING CHECK** What role did vassals play in the feudal system?
2. **INTERPRET VISUALS** How does the illustration show that peasants and serfs made up the largest class in society and had little power?
3. **MAKE INFERENCES** How did the relationship between a lord and his vassals affect that between vassals and the king?

1.5 HISTORY THROUGH OBJECTS

MEDIEVAL KNIGHTS

Knights galloped into battle, striking terror into the hearts of enemy foot soldiers. But a knight not only learned how to ride and fight. He also learned to live by a code of **chivalry**. This code of conduct demanded that a knight be brave and courteous and never shrink from a challenge. Around the 1400s, warfare began to change. But before that, here's what the best-dressed knight wore and carried into battle. What might have been a drawback of wearing this armor?

Helmet
Helmets had air holes and eye slits that provided a very narrow f eld of vision.
Pauldron
This shoulder armor helped protect the knight's head from sword strikes.
Breastplate
This chest armor was often flared at the bottom for greater flexibility.

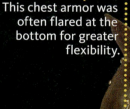

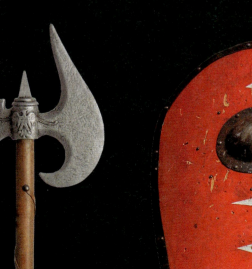

Halberd
This weapon consisted of an ax with a spike and hook mounted on a long wooden pole.
Shield
Shields were used as weapons as well as for defense. The decoration on a shield identified the knight.
Gauntlet
This metal glove protected the knight's hand and was flexible enough to allow him to grip his weapons.
Horse Armor
A knight's warhorse wore armor, too, and was trained for battle.
Longsword
This deadly double-edged sword could be held in one hand or wielded in two during combat.
Sabatons
These metal shoes protected the knight's feet and were the first pieces of armor he put on.

1.6 The Manor System

You're cold, tired, hungry, and dirty before you even start work. And no wonder. You get up before dawn to work the land, haul rocks, or do whatever your lord tells you to do. About 16 hours later, you retire to the comforts of your one-room home and huddle with your family around a smoky fire pit. Finally, you call it a night and fall asleep on the floor. At least you've got a sack for a blanket.

MAIN IDEA

Life on the manor was hard for most people but provided nearly everything they needed, including security.

A SELF-CONTAINED WORLD

The rough accommodations of peasants and serfs were part of everyday life in Europe's feudal society. The homes were part of the manor system, which tied the lowest class of people to the land and their lord. The **manor** was the system's basic unit, a walled-in, self-contained world located on land belonging to a lord.

A typical manor included a manor house, a church, a village, and lands with meadows, forests, pastures, and farms. The village provided such necessary businesses as a a mill, bakery, and forge where metal was worked into tools. The manor's farmland was divided into strips: one for the lord, one for the church, and the rest for the peasants and serfs. These laborers farmed the lord's lands as well as their own. They paid the lord rent for their land and fees for almost everything they used on the manor, including the woods and meadows.

LIFE ON THE MANOR

Life for peasants and serfs on the manor was hard. Their average lifespan was 30 years, and that was if they survived infancy. One out of six children did not. Those who grew into adulthood spent their lives performing hard physical labor and got by on a diet of bread, cheese, and vegetables. Peasants and serfs did get time off, though, on Sundays and religious holidays. With the lord's permission, they could even attend nearby fairs and markets.

While workers lived in one-room huts with dirt floors, the lord and his family lived much more comfortably in the manor house. The rooms in this fortified stone house had tiled floors, tapestries on the walls, and fine furnishings. After managing his lands, judging court cases, or hunting wild game, the lord would feast on meat, fish, bread, cheese, and fruit in his large dining room.

Peasants and serfs were sometimes admitted to the manor house on holidays or when the estate was under attack, but the church was the center of life on the manor. Church officials conducted religious services and also cared for the sick and needy. Some educated priests even instructed children in the Bible. The church required peasants and serfs to work its land for free and give one-tenth of their produce to the church, but workers did this willingly. They believed that doing these things was the key to escaping eternal punishment and attaining a better life after death.

MANOR IN THE MIDDLE AGES

This illustration shows a simplified view of a feudal manor in the 800s. Meadows, forests, pastures, and farmland lay outside the manor's walls.

A castle often served as the manor house.
Peasants, serfs, and the lord and his family regularly attended church.
Windows in the huts were so small that little natural light could enter the dwellings.
Guards were positioned along the wall to protect the manor from rival lords and invaders.

REVIEW & ASSESS

1. **READING CHECK** What was the role of the manor in feudal society?
2. **INTERPRET VISUALS** Based on the illustration, what measures were taken to protect those who lived on the manor?
3. **MAKE INFERENCES** Why might peasants and serfs have been willing to do almost anything to attain "a better life after death"?

2.1 Church and Crown

Light streams through stained-glass windows in the great church, inspiring worship. The ceiling seems to rise to heaven. It took decades and even centuries to construct cathedrals in the Middle Ages—some bigger than a king's castle. They were built for the greater glory of God. But they were also meant to inspire awe in the wealth and power of the Church.

MAIN IDEA

In the Middle Ages, the Church controlled lives and challenged the authority of kings.

THE ROLE OF THE CHURCH

It is hard for people today to understand the extraordinary power Christianity had in the Middle Ages. The Roman Catholic Church dominated people's lives from the cradle to the grave. It was the strongest unifying force in medieval Europe. The Church baptized, married, pardoned, and buried everyone from serfs to kings. It promised that good people would go to heaven and the wicked would be punished after death.

The religious leaders who oversaw these ceremonies and delivered the teachings formed the **clergy**. The pope led this group, which included bishops and priests. While a priest was in charge of a single church, a bishop oversaw a group of churches. Bishops exercised their authority from towering churches called **cathedrals**, the skyscrapers of their day.

Some Christians withdrew from medieval society to live in religious communities called **monasteries**. Monks, the people who lived in a monastery, spent much of their day praying, reading the Bible, and meditating. In addition, rulers and high-ranking clergy sometimes had monks make copies of ancient Greek and Roman texts. As a result, monks helped keep knowledge alive, and monasteries became centers of learning.

STRUGGLE FOR POWER

If anything, the power and wealth of the Church began increasing in the 1000s—in part because it received free land from nobles. At the same time, however, kings began to regain their former authority. The kings' return to power was largely because of the growth of towns and trade, which you will learn more about later. The kings' rise weakened the feudal structure, but it also led to a power struggle between kings and the Church.

The struggle came to a head in 1075. The German king Henry IV was next in line to become Holy Roman Emperor. Like Charlemagne, the first Holy Roman Emperor, Henry ruled over a multi-ethnic group of territories in central Europe, an empire that would continue until it dissolved in 1806. Henry had appointed his own priests to become bishops, but Pope Gregory VII claimed that these were religious appointments and should be his decision.

The conflict raged until Gregory shut Henry out of the Church, forcing the king to back down. Henry knew that if he did not, he would lose his throne. In those days, no one would have anything to do with a king who had been banished from the Church. Gregory got his way and lifted the ban. He then regained full control of religious appointments.

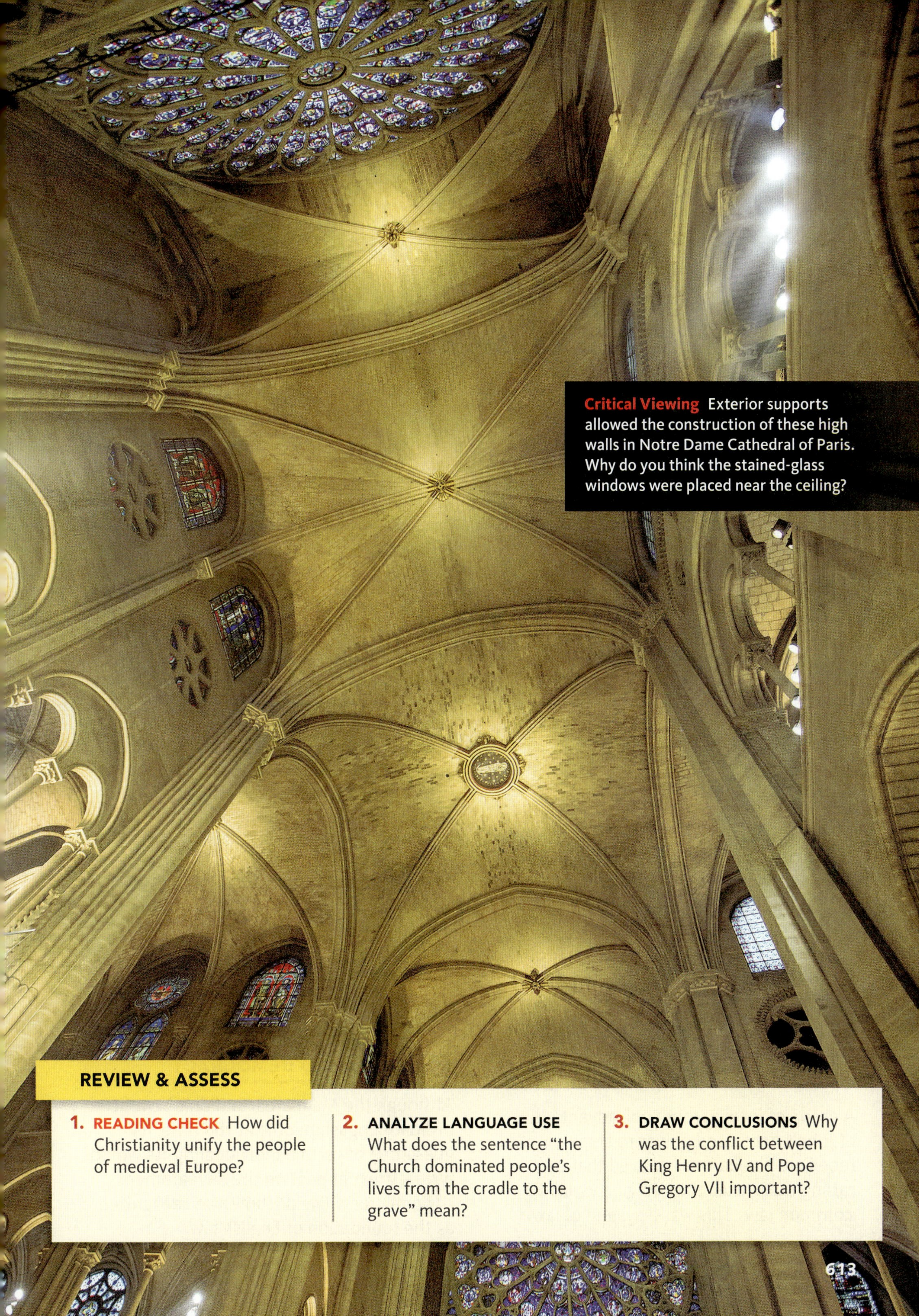

Critical Viewing Exterior supports allowed the construction of these high walls in Notre Dame Cathedral of Paris. Why do you think the stained-glass windows were placed near the ceiling?

REVIEW & ASSESS

1. **READING CHECK** How did Christianity unify the people of medieval Europe?
2. **ANALYZE LANGUAGE USE** What does the sentence "the Church dominated people's lives from the cradle to the grave" mean?
3. **DRAW CONCLUSIONS** Why was the conflict between King Henry IV and Pope Gregory VII important?

2.2 King John and the Magna Carta

Here's a joke told by English schoolchildren: Where did King John sign the Magna Carta? At the bottom. Actually, he was in a meadow called Runnymede, and he didn't sign it—he placed his seal on it. And it was called the Articles of the Barons then. The barons—a group of noblemen—were not amused by the growing authority of the king.

MAIN IDEA

The Magna Carta marked a major step toward democratic government in Western Europe.

THE GREAT CHARTER

In the last lesson, you read that kings were regaining their power. **King John** was one in a long line of powerful English kings that began in 1066. In that year, William, Duke of Normandy—a region in France—invaded England and established a strong, centralized monarchy there. When John rose to the throne in 1199, he ruled England and half of present-day France. However, the king soon weakened his position by waging a series of failed, expensive wars.

A group of local barons took advantage of John's decreased power to stage a rebellion. The barons believed that by raising their taxes the king had violated **common law**. This was a system of law established in the 1100s that sought to ensure that people throughout England received equal treatment.

So, in 1215, the barons forced John to place his seal on their document, which came to be known as the **Magna Carta**, or "Great Charter." It was meant to be just a contract between the king and his nobles. However, the Magna Carta made the king subject to the law of the land and limited his authority.

A STEP TOWARD DEMOCRACY

Although the Magna Carta didn't benefit ordinary English people at the time, its guarantee of certain individual rights would have a great impact on the development of democracy. The document is recognized as the foundation of English law.

Since the 1200s and the sealing of the Magna Carta, Britain's Parliament has met on this site on the Thames River in London. Today, representatives meet in the Houses of Parliament, shown here, next to the clock tower called Big Ben.

A further step toward democracy—in the form of representative government—took place in 1258. Henry III, John's son, was king of England at the time. Like his father, he had angered a group of nobles. The nobles overruled Henry's authority and put together a council of 15 men to advise the king and limit his power. This group of representatives would come to be called a **parliament**.

After King Henry died in 1272, his son Edward I rose to the throne. In 1295, Edward assembled what is considered the first truly representative parliament. The group included two knights from every county and two residents from each town. They passed laws, imposed taxes, and discussed political and judicial matters. From that point on, English kings would have to share their power—whether they liked it or not.

REVIEW & ASSESS

1. **READING CHECK** In what way did the Magna Carta limit the king's authority?
2. **ANALYZE CAUSE AND EFFECT** How did the establishment of a parliament change the government of England?
3. **MAKE INFERENCES** Do you think the Magna Carta affected the lives of ordinary people? Why or why not?

2.3 DOCUMENT-BASED QUESTION

Charters of Freedom

By setting down individual rights in the Magna Carta, the barons—unknowingly—laid the groundwork for the development of democracy. The Parliament members who penned the English Bill of Rights and the American Founders who wrote the U.S. Bill of Rights found inspiration in the Great Charter. So the next time you speak your mind or celebrate a religious holiday, you might remember the documents on the next page. They helped make such freedoms possible.

This painting, like many others that illustrate the event, mistakenly shows King John signing the Magna Carta rather than setting his seal to it.

***King John Signs the Magna Carta*, A.C. Michael, 1903–1928**

DOCUMENT ONE

Primary Source: Legal Document

from the Magna Carta

Most of the Magna Carta's 63 articles deal with the relationships among the king, nobles, and clergy and largely ignore the rights of the lower classes. However, the principles expressed in the following article are significant today for all free men—and women.

CONSTRUCTED RESPONSE What individual rights are protected in this article from the Magna Carta?

> 39. No freeman shall be taken, imprisoned, disseised [stripped of property], outlawed, banished, or in any way destroyed, nor will We proceed against or prosecute him [put him on trial], except by the lawful judgment of his peers [equals] or by the law of the land.

DOCUMENT TWO

Primary Source: Legal Document

from the English Bill of Rights

Concern over the increasing power of monarchs led Parliament to pass the English Bill of Rights in 1689. However, instead of focusing on the rights of nobles, the English Bill of Rights focuses on the rights of Parliament.

CONSTRUCTED RESPONSE Why do you think Parliament insisted on the free election and free speech of its members?

> 8. That election of members of Parliament ought to be free.
>
> 9. That the freedom of speech, and debates or proceedings in Parliament, ought not to be impeached [charged as a crime] or questioned in any court or place out of Parliament.

DOCUMENT THREE

Primary Source: Legal Document

from the U.S. Bill of Rights

The U.S. Bill of Rights took the documents above a step or two further. Adopted in 1791, the Bill of Rights—the first ten amendments to the Constitution—guarantees personal freedoms, like these, that had previously not been clearly stated.

CONSTRUCTED RESPONSE Why do you think the American Founders insisted on having these freedoms clearly stated in the Bill of Rights?

> 4. The right of the people to be secure in their persons, houses, papers, and effects, against unreasonable searches and seizures, shall not be violated . . .
>
> 6. In all criminal prosecutions, the accused shall enjoy the right to a speedy and public trial, by an impartial [fair to both sides] jury . . .

SYNTHESIZE & WRITE

1. **REVIEW** Review what you have learned about the Magna Carta and the development of democratic ideas in England.
2. **RECALL** On your own paper, write down the main idea expressed in each document.
3. **CONSTRUCT** Write a topic sentence that answers this question: How do the Magna Carta, English Bill of Rights, and U.S. Bill of Rights promote democratic ideas?
4. **WRITE** Using evidence from the documents, write a short essay to support your answer to the question in Step 3.

2.4 The Crusades

In 1095, Pope Urban II condemned a group of people who had "invaded the lands of the Christians." The people Urban referred to were Muslims, and he called on Christians to wage war against them. Kings had regained a good bit of their authority, but the Church and the pope still had plenty of power—certainly enough for the pope to gather armies to fight the spread of Islam.

MAIN IDEA

Christians in Europe fought non-Christians to conquer Palestine and retake Spain.

BATTLE FOR PALESTINE

Specifically, the people Urban had condemned were Seljuk Turks, Muslim rulers who had seized control of Jerusalem in 1071. Their takeover had made Christian pilgrimages to the Holy Land—also called Palestine—almost impossible. The Holy Land included Jerusalem and the area around the city, sites that were sacred to Christians, Jews, and Muslims.

The Seljuks had also begun to attack the Christian Byzantine Empire, once the eastern half of the Roman Empire. When the Byzantine emperor asked for help, Pope Urban seized his chance to rally Christians against the growing power of Islam. His words had the desired effect. In 1096, Christian armies set off to fight a series of wars called the **Crusades** to reclaim the Holy Land. Christian leaders and soldiers were motivated by a desire to protect Christians and to slow the spread of Islam.

Peasants, knights, and foot soldiers joined the fight, and they achieved victory. In 1099, the army retook Jerusalem and divided the Holy Land into four Crusader states. But the triumph was short-lived. In 1144, the Muslims fought back and conquered Edessa, one of the Crusader states. Soon after, a new pope launched the Second Crusade, but this ended in disaster for the Europeans. A Third and Fourth Crusade were fought, but these also failed to defeat the enemy. By 1291, the Muslims had defeated the Crusaders and taken control of Palestine. The Crusades were over.

A SPANISH CRUSADE

The Crusades had an unexpected impact on Europe. During the wars, trade between Europe and the eastern Mediterranean region greatly increased because of greater contact between the two regions. After the wars, ideas as well as goods were exchanged. The trade led to the rise of a merchant class in Europe and the further decline of feudalism.

Still, crusading fever didn't die, and hostility toward any non-Christians increased. As soldiers galloped toward the Holy Land, they killed Jews in Europe as well as those in Palestine. After the Crusades, many Jews were expelled from England and France. The greatest expulsion effort, however, took place on the Iberian Peninsula, which includes present-day Spain and Portugal. In the 700s, Muslims had conquered almost the entire peninsula. When Islamic rule weakened in the 1000s, Christian kings began a long war, called the **Reconquista** (ray-cone-KEY-stah), to drive the Muslims off the peninsula.

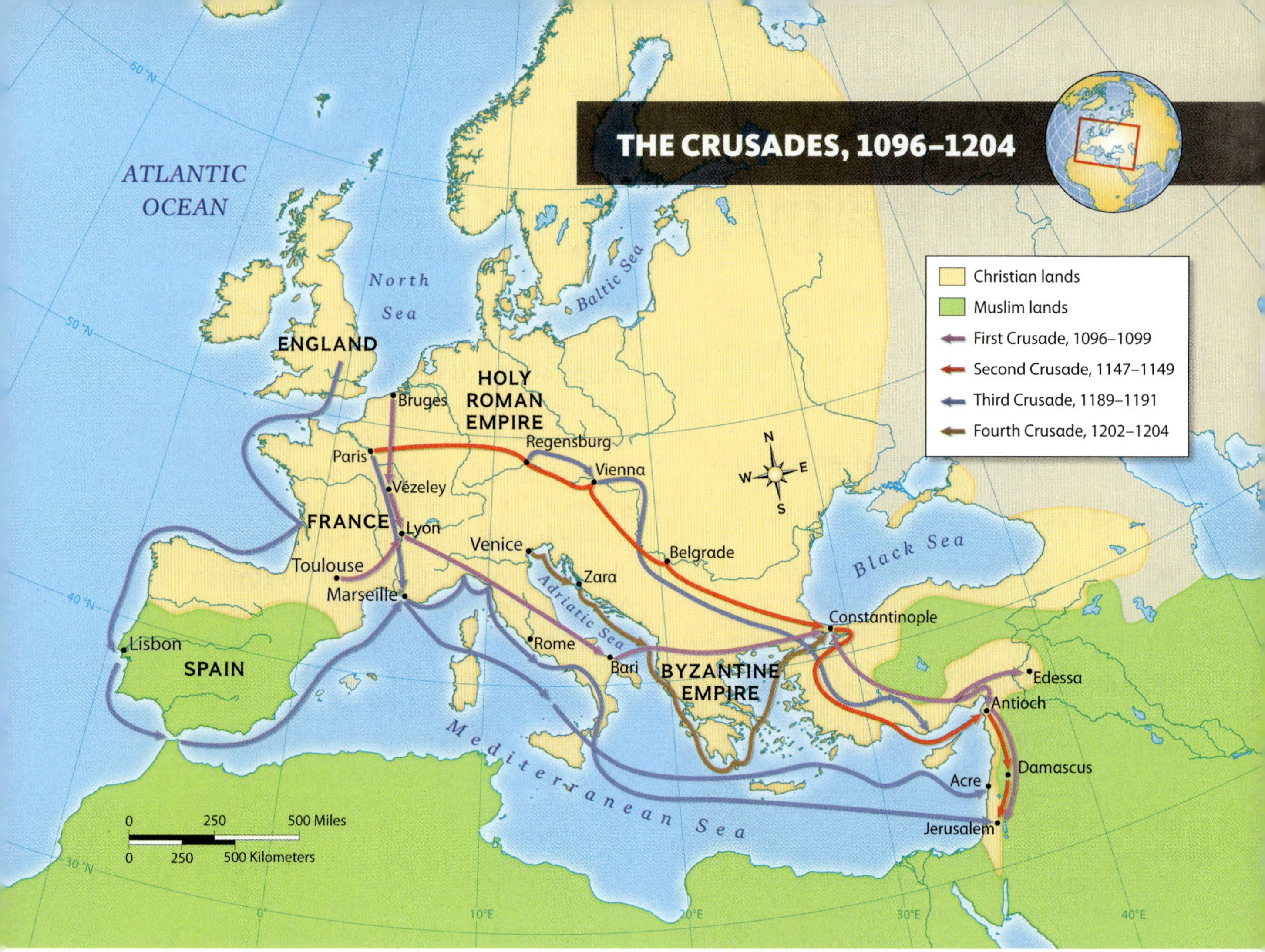

THE CRUSADES, 1096–1204

- Christian lands
- Muslim lands
- First Crusade, 1096–1099
- Second Crusade, 1147–1149
- Third Crusade, 1189–1191
- Fourth Crusade, 1202–1204

King Ferdinand and Queen Isabella of Spain stepped up the war. They used a powerful court known as the **Inquisition** to punish non-Christians. The court ordered the torture and execution of many Muslims and Jews who would not convert or who had converted but secretly practiced their former religion. In 1492, Ferdinand and Isabella finally defeated and expelled the last of the Muslim rulers and their followers from Spain and Portugal. They also drove out about 200,000 Jews. Unlike the Crusades, the Reconquista had achieved its goal—but at the cost of many human lives.

FERDINAND AND ISABELLA

The Reconquista ended when the Spanish army conquered Granada, a city in Spain. When the Muslim ruler handed over the keys to his palace, the Alhambra, Ferdinand and Isabella swore that Muslims would always be able to follow their faith in Spain. They broke that promise a few years later when they ordered Muslims to convert to Christianity or leave the country.

REVIEW & ASSESS

1. **READING CHECK** Why did Pope Urban II encourage Christians to begin a series of wars against Muslims?
2. **INTERPRET MAPS** Which Crusade involved much of Western Europe?
3. **SEQUENCE EVENTS** What efforts to drive Muslims from Europe were undertaken after the Crusades ended?

2.5 War and Plague

Shattered buildings and churches, deserted villages, and abandoned fields—these formed the landscape of Europe after war and disease swept through the continent in the 1300s. Both catastrophes brought suffering and death to millions and, like the Crusades, greatly weakened the feudal way of life.

MAIN IDEA

War and disease devastated Europe in the 1300s and brought about fundamental changes to society.

WAR BETWEEN ENGLAND AND FRANCE

The roots of the war were established long before the 1300s. As you may remember, William, Duke of Normandy, conquered England in 1066 and became its king. William and the Norman kings who came after him were vassals to the French kings. However, they also ruled over England in their own right. This created a tense relationship between England and France. Kings from both countries were very powerful and competed for territory in France. In time, they also competed over who would be king of France.

The situation came to a head in 1328 when the king of France died. Edward III of England believed he should succeed him, but French nobles crowned a Frenchman instead. In 1337, Edward invaded France to claim the throne. His actions began the **Hundred Years' War** between England and France. This was not a continuous conflict but rather a series of wars that dragged on for 116 years.

Between the beginning of the war in 1337 and its end in 1453, the English won many important victories. The French cause seemed hopeless until rescue came from an unexpected source. A French peasant girl called **Joan of Arc** claimed that Christian saints had told her to save her country. She impressed Charles, the ruler of France, and was given command of his army in 1429. Her religious and patriotic passion inspired her soldiers to win a battle that turned the tide of the war. The English captured and executed Joan, but they had lost the war. By 1453, the French had driven the English out of their lands.

Both sides were aided in their fight by deadly new weapons. The powerful **longbow** allowed archers to fire arrows with enough force to pierce a knight's armor. Cannons, made possible by the invention of gunpowder, could blast through castle walls. These weapons changed the nature of European warfare and made knights and castles, the symbols of feudalism, almost powerless.

DISEASE SPREADS OVER THE WORLD

As if war and its new weapons weren't enough, medieval Europeans suffered from widespread disease. Poor diet, filthy living conditions, and a lack of medicine made sickness common.

In 1347, however, a devastating disease known as the **bubonic plague** swept through Europe. Infected rats carried fleas that spread the disease to humans along land and sea trade routes from Asia to Europe and Africa. Unfortunately, no one at the time understood that the plague was caused by bites from these fleas.

Death of Bertrand du Guesclin, Chronique d'Angleterre, late 15th century

Critical Viewing In this 15th-century painting, English soldiers use longbows and cannon fire to fight for control of a French castle during the Hundred Years' War. What different actions does the painting illustrate?

Instead, many people believed the plague was a punishment from God. Some Christians believed the Jews had caused the plague by poisoning town wells. As a result, they destroyed entire Jewish communities. By the early 1350s, the worst of the plague was over in Europe, but by then it had killed about one-third of the continent's population. The deaths of so many people—from disease and war—led to major social and economic changes that would finally bring an end to feudalism.

JOAN OF ARC

After the English captured Joan of Arc, she was tried by the Inquisition and found guilty of being a witch. The court believed that the voices she claimed to hear were those of the devil. In 1431, Joan was burned at the stake. She was about 19 years old. Twenty-five years later, another court pardoned her. In 1920, the Catholic Church declared Joan a saint.

REVIEW & ASSESS

1. **READING CHECK** What impact did the Hundred Years' War and the bubonic plague have on medieval Europe?
2. **ANALYZE CAUSE AND EFFECT** How did events in 1066 lead to the Hundred Years' War?
3. **MAKE INFERENCES** How did the rats that carried plague-infected fleas probably travel along the trade routes?

2.6 MOMENTS IN HISTORY
The Bubonic Plague

The Triumph of Death, Pieter Bruegel the Elder, c. 1562

OCTOBER 1347

In a port in Italy, workers unload a ship's cargo and also release rats covered in fleas carrying the bubonic plague. According to an old legend, a childhood rhyme was said to describe the plague. The rhyme begins with "Ring around the rosie," which may refer to the red blisters caused when the fleas bit their victims. "A pocket full of posies" was said to be the flowers people carried to ward off the disease. When the flowers failed as a cure, "we all fall down," or die. In this painting, called *The Triumph of Death*, death is represented by skeleton figures. What generalization can you make about death's victims?

2.7 Growth of Towns

In the late Middle Ages, a saying started making the rounds: Town air makes you free. In the towns, you could work at a job and keep all your wages. You could go where you wanted without having to ask anyone's permission because you were no longer bound to a landowning lord or vassal. In fact, you answered to no one but the king.

MAIN IDEA

The growth of towns and trade led to economic, political, and cultural changes that brought the Middle Ages to an end.

ECONOMIC OPPORTUNITIES ARISE

People had been moving to towns since about 1000, but the bubonic plague greatly accelerated this movement. With about a third of the workforce wiped out by the disease, employers desperate for help increased wages to attract workers. Many peasants, and many serfs as well, left the manor to apply for jobs in the towns. As a result, the manor system began to fall apart.

After life on the manor, the bustling, exciting towns might have made a welcome change. Towns held weekly markets where local produce was sold, while town fairs brought in trade goods from other places. In time, a merchant class composed of traders and craftspeople arose. Wealthy town-dwelling merchants, known as **burghers**, could be elected to sit on governing councils. Groups of craftspeople, such as shoemakers or silversmiths, joined together to form **guilds**, which helped protect and improve the working conditions of their members.

THE MIDDLE AGES END

The growth of towns and their prosperous trade further helped kings regain their authority. By taxing the towns within his realm, a king earned money to pay for his army. A strong army brought peace

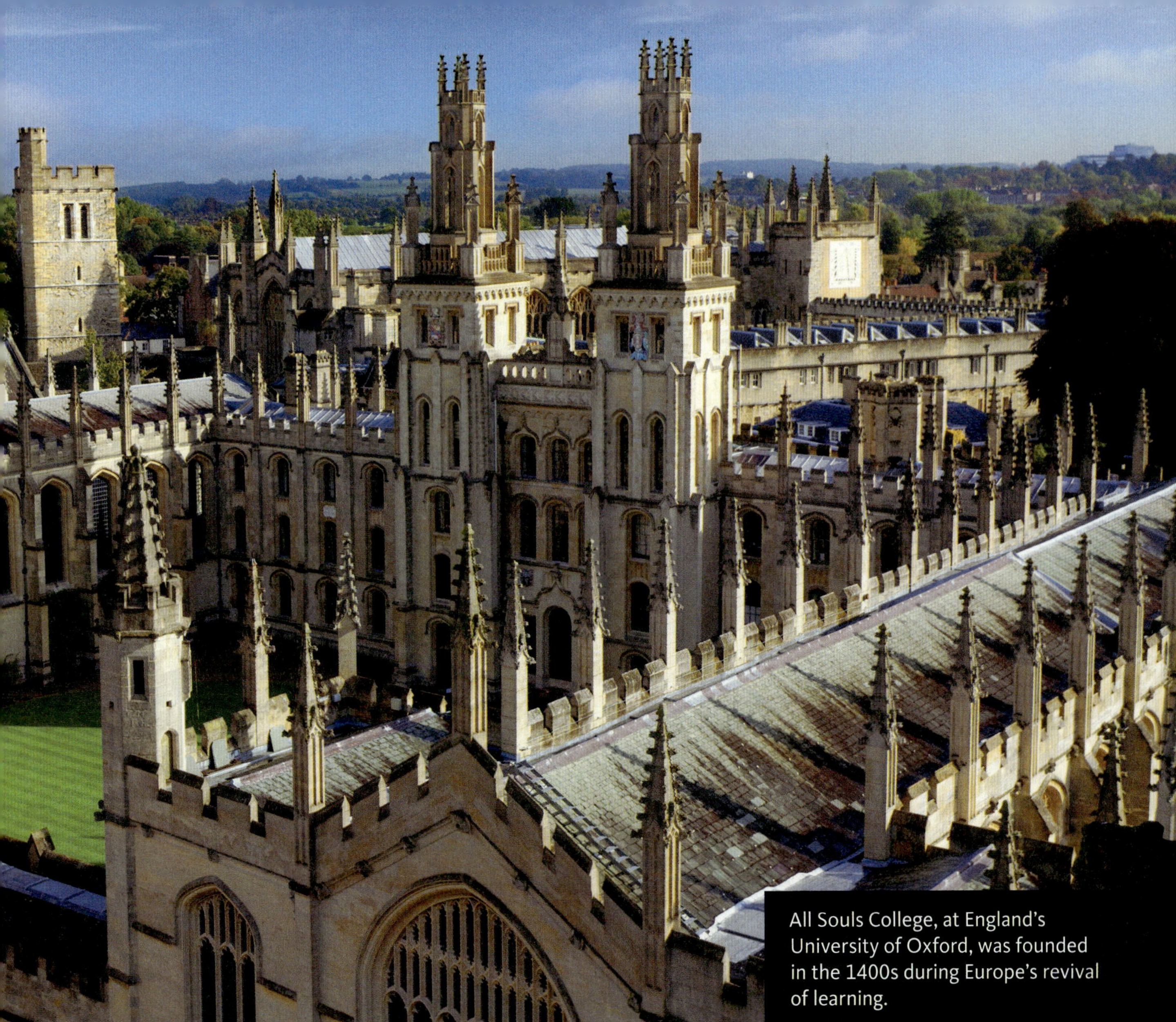

All Souls College, at England's University of Oxford, was founded in the 1400s during Europe's revival of learning.

and stability to his land. Increasingly, power and people's loyalty shifted from local lords to their king.

Europe experienced cultural changes as well as economic and political ones. You may remember that the Crusades brought European traders into contact with the civilizations of Islam and Byzantium. These civilizations had preserved the writings of ancient Greek and Roman philosophers in their libraries. As the Middle Ages came to a close, people became eager to gain knowledge. Universities were founded to satisfy this desire for learning. Monasteries were no longer the only centers of education. After centuries of war, instability, and fear, Europe was more than ready to embark on a new age of creativity.

REVIEW & ASSESS

1. **READING CHECK** What economic opportunities did towns offer ordinary people?
2. **ANALYZE CAUSE AND EFFECT** How did the growth of towns affect monarchs?
3. **MAKE INFERENCES** Why do you think learning was revived at the end of the Middle Ages?

CHAPTER 21 Review

VOCABULARY

Use each of the following vocabulary words in a sentence that shows an understanding of the word's meaning.

1. **medieval**
   The Middle Ages is also known as the medieval period, which was a time of many political, economic, and cultural changes in Western Europe.
2. **monastery**
3. **feudalism**
4. **manor**
5. **serf**
6. **parliament**
7. **cathedral**
8. **longbow**
9. **bubonic plague**
10. **guild**

READING STRATEGY

11. **DRAW CONCLUSIONS** If you haven't already, complete your chart to draw conclusions about how feudalism and Christianity affected people during the Middle Ages. Then answer the question.

Middle Ages

Feudalism	Christianity
People's loyalties were divided between their king and their lord.	*The Church dominated people's lives.*

What impact did the power struggles between kings and lords and between kings and the Church have on people during the Middle Ages?

MAIN IDEAS

Answer the following questions. Support your answers with evidence from the chapter.

12. What helped many small kingdoms thrive after the fall of Rome? **LESSON 1.1**
13. Why did the pope crown Charlemagne emperor of the Romans? **LESSON 1.2**
14. What led to the emergence of feudalism in Europe? **LESSON 1.4**
15. What did a typical manor include? **LESSON 1.6**
16. How did the Church become more powerful and wealthy in the 1000s? **LESSON 2.1**
17. How did the Magna Carta affect the development of democracy in Western Europe? **LESSON 2.2**
18. In what way did the Crusades help weaken feudalism? **LESSON 2.4**
19. How did the bubonic plague contribute to the growth of towns? **LESSON 2.7**

CRITICAL THINKING

Answer the following questions. Support your answers with evidence from the chapter.

20. **EVALUATE** How did a code of conduct help the knights do their job?
21. **COMPARE AND CONTRAST** How did manor life differ for workers and the lord of the manor?
22. **ANALYZE CAUSE AND EFFECT** What happened as a result of King John's weakened power?
23. **MAKE INFERENCES** Why do you suppose the ruler of France and his soldiers believed Joan of Arc could save their country?
24. **YOU DECIDE** Do you think feudalism benefited the lives of ordinary people or made them worse? Support your opinion with evidence from the chapter.

INTERPRET CHARTS

Study this chart, which compares the feudal structure in medieval Europe with that in medieval Japan. Then answer the questions that follow.

Feudal Structure in Europe and Japan	Europe	Japan
Ruler	King	Emperor
Landowners	Nobles and Church	Daimyo
Warriors	Knights	Samurai
Lower Classes	Peasants and serfs	Peasants, artisans, and merchants

25. How was the feudal structure in Europe similar to that in Japan?

26. How did the makeup of the lower classes in the two regions differ?

ANALYZE SOURCES

A Frankish scholar named Einhard was a trusted friend and adviser of Charlemagne and wrote a biography about his king. Read this excerpt from Einhard's biography of Charlemagne. Then answer the question that follows.

> He cherished the Church of St. Peter the Apostle at Rome above all other holy and sacred places, and heaped its treasury with a vast wealth of gold, silver, and precious stones . . . [T]hroughout his whole reign the wish that he had nearest at heart was to re-establish the ancient authority of the city of Rome . . . and protect the Church of St. Peter.

27. What does the excerpt suggest about Charlemagne's feelings toward the Church?

WRITE ABOUT HISTORY

28. INFORMATIVE What events brought about the downfall of feudalism and ended the Middle Ages? Write a paragraph for a children's encyclopedia, summarizing these events and explaining how they brought about the end of feudalism and the Middle Ages. You might create a chart or web diagram to organize your ideas and details.

TIPS

- Take notes from the lessons on the Crusades, the increasing power of the Church, the Hundred Years' War, and the growth of towns.
- State your main idea clearly at the beginning of the paragraph.
- Support your main idea with relevant facts, details, and examples.
- Use vocabulary from the chapter.
- Provide a concluding statement about the end of feudalism and the Middle Ages.

CHAPTER

22 RENAISSANCE AND REFORMATION

1300 – 1600

SECTION 1
THE ITALIAN RENAISSANCE

KEY VOCABULARY
classical
humanism
patron
perspective
Renaissance man
secular
vernacular

NAMES & PLACES
Borgias
Leonardo da Vinci
Medici
Michelangelo
Renaissance

SECTION 2
THE NORTHERN RENAISSANCE AND LEGACY

KEY VOCABULARY
cartography
printing press
woodcut

NAMES & PLACES
Elizabethan Age
Johann Gutenberg
William Shakespeare

SECTION 3
THE REFORMATION

KEY VOCABULARY
denomination
heresy
indulgence
missionary
nation-state

NAMES & PLACES
Council of Trent
Counter Reformation
Great Schism
Jesuits
Martin Luther
Protestant
Reformation

READING STRATEGY

ANALYZE LANGUAGE USE
When you analyze language use, you note how word choices indicate the author's purpose. Some word choices involve figurative language, such as personification. As you read the chapter, use a concept cluster like this one to help you analyze figurative language.

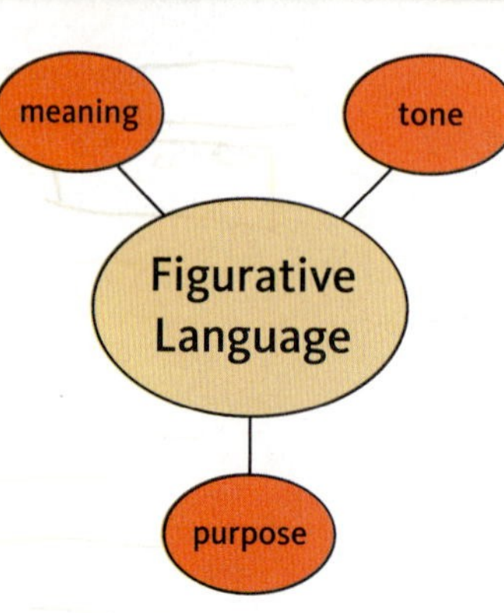
meaning
tone
Figurative Language
purpose

Construction of the Duomo, or cathedral, of Florence, Italy—shown here— began in 1296. Its dome came to symbolize the Renaissance.

1.1 Rise of the Individual

In the 1300s, a revolution began to brew in Europe. But this revolution didn't involve weapons and war. This was a movement of ideas. People decided they wanted to enjoy life on Earth—and not just look forward to their reward in heaven. They focused on the individual and believed every person had unlimited possibilities. This was not what the Church had taught in the Middle Ages. The movement was, indeed, revolutionary.

MAIN IDEA

The growth of humanism, with its emphasis on the individual, led to a rebirth of the arts and learning.

THE GROWTH OF HUMANISM

The new movement was called **humanism**. Instead of blindly obeying the authority of a king or the teachings of the Church, the followers of this movement wanted to be independent and think for themselves. Humanists stressed living a Christian life but also sought to explore a new understanding of the individual in relation to God. Humanism inspired a new sense of possibility. People suddenly felt as if they could do anything they chose.

The movement's followers found inspiration in **classical**, or ancient Greek and Roman, writings. Scholars in the Muslim empires had obtained and preserved many classical writings. Growing trade with these empires brought Europeans into greater contact with the texts. Humanists admired what the people of those ancient times had done and said and built.

An Italian poet named Petrarch became an early humanist leader and collected around 200 classical manuscripts. Some of these manuscripts had been hidden away in monastery libraries for centuries. People learned Greek just so they could read them. They began to forget about Charlemagne and wanted to learn more about the great leaders of ancient Greece and Rome.

REBIRTH OF THE ARTS

This rebirth of classical learning led to a movement of great creativity in the arts, writing, and thinking. Historians call the movement the **Renaissance**, which actually means "rebirth" in French. The Renaissance lasted from about 1300 to 1600 and began in Italy.

As the center of the ancient Roman Empire, Italy was well positioned to become the movement's birthplace. In addition, many of its cities—including Florence, Venice, Rome, and Milan—had become wealthy from trade. Ideas as well as goods were traded in these cities, which attracted artists, writers, and scientists.

Italian cities particularly benefited from the reopening of the ancient trade routes of the Silk Roads between Europe and China. Interest in Asian markets had been sparked, in part, by Venetian merchant Marco Polo. He wrote about the wonders he saw as he traveled the Silk Roads from Europe to Central Asia, China, and India.

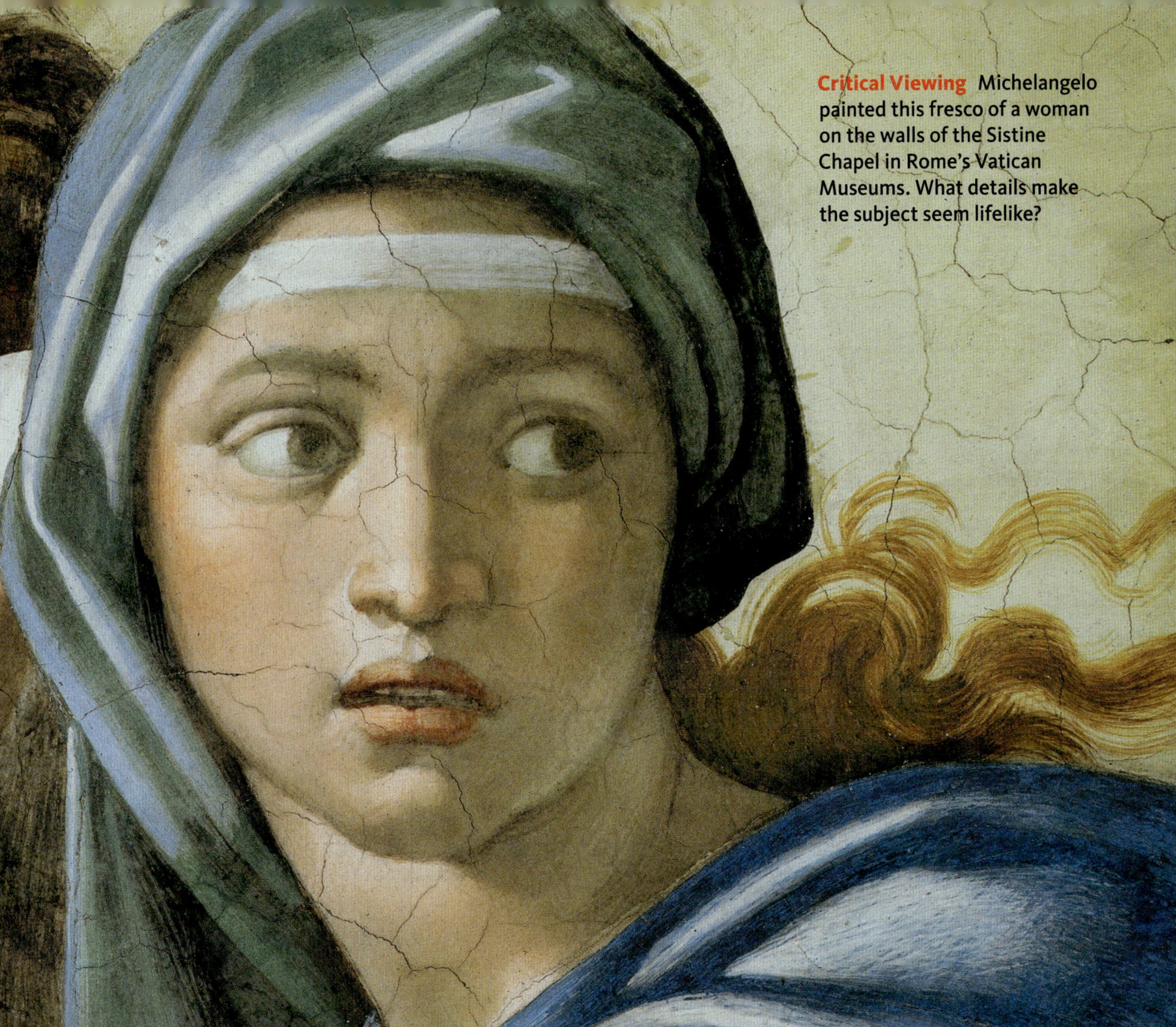

Critical Viewing Michelangelo painted this fresco of a woman on the walls of the Sistine Chapel in Rome's Vatican Museums. What details make the subject seem lifelike?

No city in Italy was more influential during the Renaissance than Florence. Artists like **Leonardo da Vinci**, Raphael, and **Michelangelo** came to Florence hoping to make a name for themselves—and they certainly did. Leonardo excelled as a painter, an inventor, and a scientist. You'll read more about the genius of Leonardo later in the chapter. Raphael came to Florence to study the great masters, including Leonardo, and created his own masterpieces. Michelangelo was a painter and sculptor whose muscular subjects convey great intensity and power. These artists and many, many others are counted among the greats of the Italian Renaissance. They were all part of an earthshaking cultural shift that transformed Europe.

REVIEW & ASSESS

1. **READING CHECK** What inspired the development of humanism?
2. **IDENTIFY MAIN IDEAS AND DETAILS** Why did the Renaissance begin in Italy?
3. **ANALYZE LANGUAGE USE** What does the phrase "an earthshaking cultural shift" suggest about the impact of the Renaissance in Europe?

1.2 New Styles and Techniques

Remember reading in the last chapter about the great stained-glass-filled cathedrals built during the Middle Ages? The walls of these churches seemed to stretch to the sky. But heavy brick blocks were often placed on the outside of a cathedral to support its soaring walls. As you'll see, Renaissance architects would try to find another, less visible means of support.

MAIN IDEA

The Renaissance inspired new forms of expression in art, literature, and architecture.

ART AND LITERATURE

Renaissance architects came up with new building strategies. However, the movement demanded new forms of expression from artists as well. For example, they found ways to show landscapes in a realistic manner by developing a technique called **perspective** to produce an impression of depth and distance. While art during the Middle Ages appeared flat, perspective allowed Renaissance artists to produce works that looked three-dimensional.

The subjects of the artwork changed, too. Artists including Titian (TIH-shun), a great painter in Venice, still drew inspiration from religious subjects. But **secular**, or nonreligious, subjects also became popular. For example, Sandro Botticelli of Florence painted *La Primavera*, which celebrates the arrival of spring.

New styles in the arts weren't limited to painters and sculptors. Renaissance writers got in on the act as well. Instead of using Latin, the language of the Church, many wrote in the **vernacular**, or their native language. One of the first to do so was the poet Dante, who wrote his masterpiece, *The Divine Comedy*, in Italian in the early 1300s. The work describes Dante's long journey to heaven led in part by the ancient Roman poet Virgil.

ARCHITECTURE

During the Renaissance, architects found inspiration by studying the buildings of ancient Rome. They incorporated classical Roman engineering features such as arches and domes in their own creations. One of the greatest of these architects was Filippo Brunelleschi (brew-nuhl-LESS-key) of Florence, whose impressive dome is illustrated on the opposite page.

It all began with a contest. In 1418, architects were challenged to build a self-supporting dome for the cathedral of

PERSPECTIVE

Renaissance artists often included perfectly proportioned buildings in their paintings. As you can see in this painting, *The Ideal City* by Piero della Francesca, the larger buildings in the foreground and the smaller ones in the background provide the illusion of depth and distance.

BRUNELLESCHI'S DOME

When the dome was completed in 1436, it soared to a height of about 374 feet. Engineers today still do not fully understand how Brunelleschi constructed his masterpiece. It remains the largest brick dome ever built.

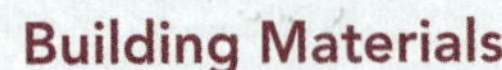

Nesting Domes
To prevent the base of the dome from bulging outward, Brunelleschi constructed an inner and an outer dome connected by vertical and horizontal brick ribs.

Building Materials
Beneath the tiles on the dome's exterior lie several million bricks made of different shapes and set either horizontally or vertically depending on where they were used.

Supporting Rings
Experts know that this wooden ring helped hold the dome in place. They believe the two stone rings above may also have been used.

Florence. Brunelleschi won the competition, but at first even he wasn't sure how to build the dome, which had to sit on a base that was about 150 feet wide. Without internal support, how could the dome be prevented from sagging and collapsing? Eventually, inspiration struck. Instead of constructing massive visible supports, Brunelleschi proposed building two domes, one nested inside the other. The effect would be of a dome rising effortlessly in the air. The dome would come to symbolize the freedom of the Renaissance and of the human spirit. It also inspired other architects and helped make Florence the center of the Renaissance.

REVIEW & ASSESS

1. **READING CHECK** What new techniques did Renaissance artists use?
2. **MAKE INFERENCES** Why do you think some Renaissance writers began expressing themselves in the vernacular?
3. **INTERPRET VISUALS** What difficulties do you think the builders of the dome encountered during its construction?

1.3 MOMENTS IN HISTORY

Raphael's *School of Athens*

School of Athens, Raphael Sanzio, 1511

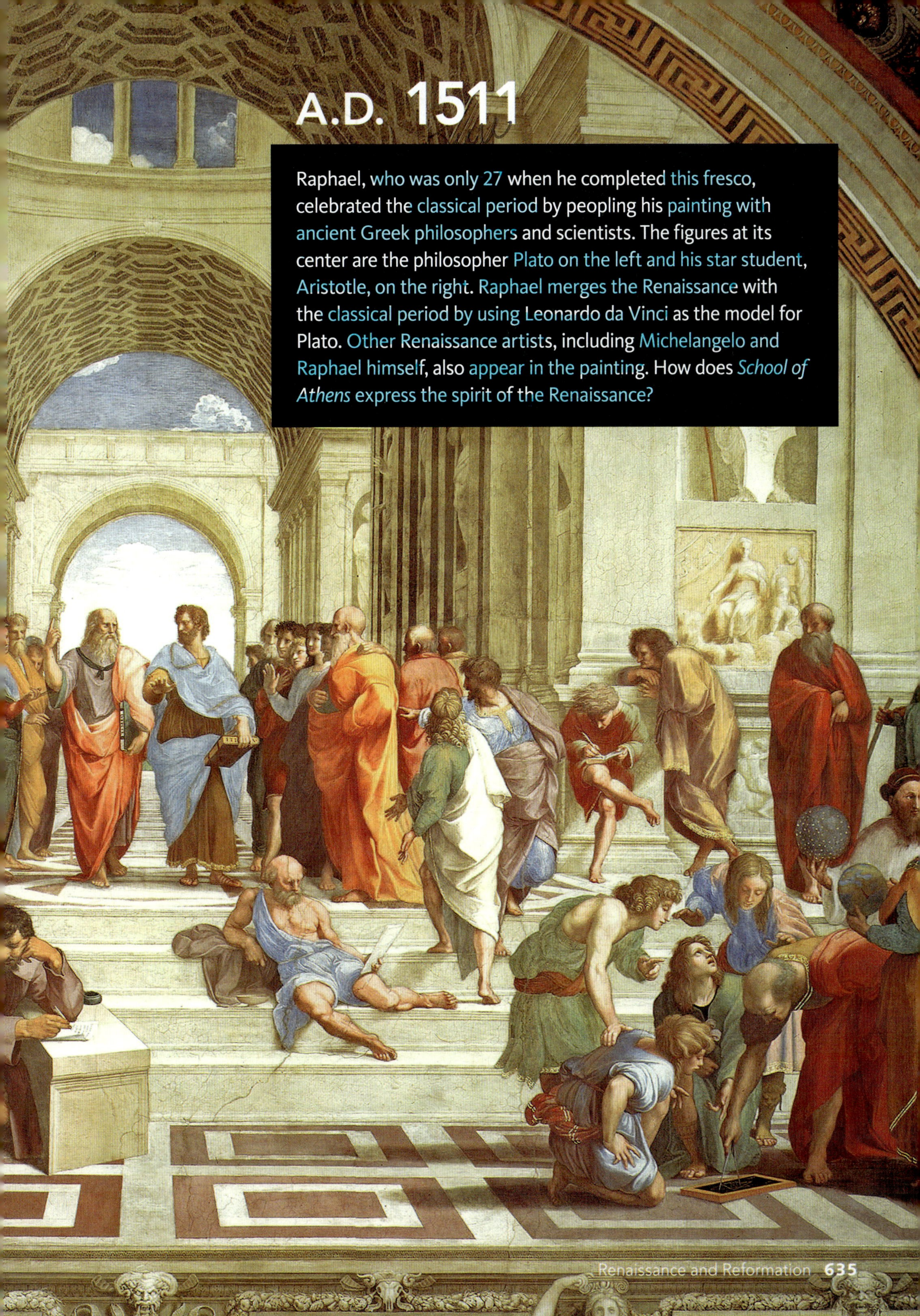

A.D. 1511

Raphael, who was only 27 when he completed this fresco, celebrated the classical period by peopling his painting with ancient Greek philosophers and scientists. The figures at its center are the philosopher Plato on the left and his star student, Aristotle, on the right. Raphael merges the Renaissance with the classical period by using Leonardo da Vinci as the model for Plato. Other Renaissance artists, including Michelangelo and Raphael himself, also appear in the painting. How does *School of Athens* express the spirit of the Renaissance?

1.4 The Medici and the Borgias

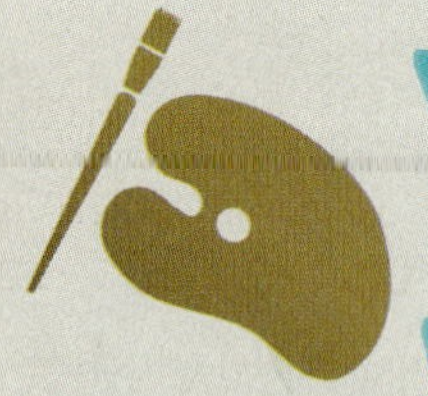

The Medici were like the godfathers, or crime bosses, of the Renaissance. They defeated their rivals by whatever means necessary—including murder. But the Medici family used its wealth and power to support some of the greatest artists in Florence.

MAIN IDEA

Wealthy and powerful families supported Renaissance artists and thinkers in many Italian cities.

WEALTHY FLORENCE

There were other rich families in Florence, but it was the **Medici** (MEH-dee-chee) who clawed their way to the top. Like other great families in the city, the Medici built their fortune as bankers and textile merchants. They were part of a wealthy merchant class that had developed in Italy and gained great power. The family's money bought them so much political power that the Medici ruled Florence during the Renaissance.

But the Medici weren't all about money and political gain. The Renaissance had brought about a renewed sense of pride throughout Italy. Rich families competed to restore the glory of ancient Rome's civilization to their cities and so became patrons of the arts. **Patrons** used some of their wealth to encourage and support artists. This support allowed the artists to create and work full-time on their masterpieces.

The Medici family made sure that Florence became the place to be for the great artists and scholars of the day. They spent fortunes attracting the best and brightest to their city. No member of the Medici family was more successful at bringing artists and scholars to Florence than Lorenzo de Medici, also known as Lorenzo the Magnificent. A poet himself, Lorenzo supported some of the most important artists of the Renaissance, including Leonardo da Vinci and Michelangelo.

POWERFUL ROME

Florence got a head start, but eventually Renaissance ideas and a new flood of people made their way to Rome. The pope, who ruled both Rome and the Catholic Church, rebuilt the city and brought back its authority and importance. In time, Rome became almost as powerful as Florence, and the two cities competed for dominance. When Michelangelo created his statue of the biblical hero David, it was originally placed outside the center of Florence's government. The towering, muscular David stood there, tense and ready for battle, with his eyes looking warningly in the direction of Rome.

The pope had authority over Rome, but the city, like Florence, had its share of patrons. The **Borgia** (BOR-gee-ah) family, originally from Spain, was the most powerful group of patrons in Rome. The Borgias were even more ruthless than the Medici. Since the Church controlled Rome, the Borgias attempted to control the Church. In the 1400s, two members of the family became popes. Another Borgia named Cesare (CHAY-suh-ray) was made a cardinal, a high-ranking member of the clergy, at the age of 17. Like many of the Borgias, Cesare used political methods that were less than honest. However, he did do one thing right: He briefly brought Leonardo da Vinci to Rome.

This museum in Florence, called the Pitti Palace, was built in 1472 for Luca Pitti. However, the palace became the official residence of the Medici in 1550.

REVIEW & ASSESS

1. **READING CHECK** What roles did the Medici play in Florence?
2. **ANALYZE CAUSE AND EFFECT** How did the Medici family become wealthy?
3. **MAKE INFERENCES** Why did some members of the Borgia family want to join the clergy?

1.5 BIOGRAPHY

LEONARDO DA VINCI

1452–1519

According to legend, Leonardo's father asked his teenage son to paint a wooden shield. The boy decided to paint a face on the shield—but not a human face. Instead, he collected an assortment of dead animals, including maggots, bats, and lizards, to create the head of a monster belching smoke. When Leonardo's father saw the painting, he was so stunned by its realism that he knew his son would be a painter. He was right. But Leonardo would be so much more.

Jobs: Painter, sculptor, engineer, scientist, and inventor

Home: He was born near Vinci but made his home wherever he found work—mostly Florence and Milan.

FINEST HOUR

Perhaps the acclaim received by his great painting, the *Mona Lisa*

WORST MOMENT

Seeing his bitter rival, Michelangelo, given the honor of decorating the Vatican, the palace of the pope in Rome

TRIVIA

He was left-handed and wrote backward, either because it was easier or to prevent the curious from reading his notebooks. His writing had to be held up to a mirror to be read.

LEONARDO THE ARTIST

Because of Leonardo da Vinci's obvious talent, he was sent to apprentice under Andrea del Verrocchio (vehr-OAK-ee-oh), a great painter in Florence. Eventually, Leonardo was given the honor of painting an angel in one of his teacher's paintings. It turned out to be the best part of the painting. Soon after, Leonardo left his teacher's studio to strike out on his own.

Word quickly spread about the young painter. Soon, nobles, patrons, and popes engaged Leonardo's services. He would produce several great works, including two very celebrated paintings. One is the *Mona Lisa*, shown here and arguably the most famous painting in the world. The other is *The Last Supper*, one of the best-known frescoes in history. The fresco depicts the final meal that, according to Christian belief, Jesus and his followers ate together. It is admired for the different emotions expressed by the followers and for the use of light and angles to draw attention to Jesus, the central figure.

LEONARDO'S *MONA LISA*

Many mysteries surround the *Mona Lisa*. For one thing, no one really knows the subject's identity, although she is believed to be Lisa Gherardini (gehr-ahr-DEE-nee), the wife of a merchant. (*Mona* means "madame.") But it is her mysterious smile that has captured people's imagination for centuries. What is she smiling about? And what's going on behind those eyes? Leonardo never gave the painting to whoever commissioned it. Instead, he kept it with him all his life. Today the painting hangs in the Louvre, a museum in Paris.

Mona Lisa, Leonardo da Vinci, 1503–1506

ULTIMATE RENAISSANCE MAN

Unfortunately for the world, Leonardo produced relatively few paintings—only about 17. He began many other paintings and other works of art but failed to finish them. This failure was probably due to his interest in so many other fields, including engineering and anatomy, or the study of the human body. Leonardo dissected, or cut up, the bodies of dead people, and used what he learned to make remarkably accurate anatomical sketches. These sketches helped him portray people more realistically. He also designed machines, including early forms of a flying machine and a submarine.

Leonardo studied whatever interested him and recorded his observations and sketches in a collection of notebooks. These are works of art themselves but were not widely known until more than 100 years after his death. Many people had considered Leonardo to be solely an artist and so were amazed at the breadth of his knowledge. In fact, with all his talents, Leonardo embodied the well-rounded ideal of Renaissance and humanist thinking. He could do it all. He was a painter, an architect, an inventor, an engineer, and a scientist. All these qualities and many more made Leonardo the ultimate **Renaissance man**.

REVIEW & ASSESS

1. **READING CHECK** Why is Leonardo da Vinci considered a true Renaissance man?
2. **INTERPRET VISUALS** The *Mona Lisa* is said to represent the idea of happiness. What details in the painting do you think make Mona Lisa appear happy?
3. **MAKE INFERENCES** Why do you think Leonardo decided to keep the *Mona Lisa* for himself?

1.6 NATIONAL GEOGRAPHIC PHOTOGRAPHER DAVE YODER

Searching for a Lost da Vinci

What if there were a painting by Leonardo that was just waiting to be uncovered? Italian engineer Maurizio Seracini is convinced one exists, and he thinks he knows where it is. His obsession has taken him to Florence, where he has conducted extensive research and experienced both triumphs and defeats. Seracini has also gathered a team, including photographer Dave Yoder, to help him find the hidden masterpiece. The question is: Will they find the lost da Vinci?

^ A member of Seracini's team looks on nervously as a probe is inserted in this painting by Giorgio Vasari. Seracini believes Leonardo's missing painting lies hidden behind Vasari's work.

MAIN IDEA

Researchers are trying to find a long-lost painting by Leonardo da Vinci.

A CENTURIES-OLD MYSTERY

The object of Seracini's search dates back about 500 years. Around 1505, Leonardo painted a fresco called *The Battle of Anghiari* (ahn-ghee-AHR-ee) on the wall of a room in the Palazzo Vecchio, the town hall of Florence. The fresco depicts four men on horseback, engaged in an intense battle. Leonardo had completed the *Mona Lisa*, but it was *The Battle of Anghiari* that other artists came to admire and copy.

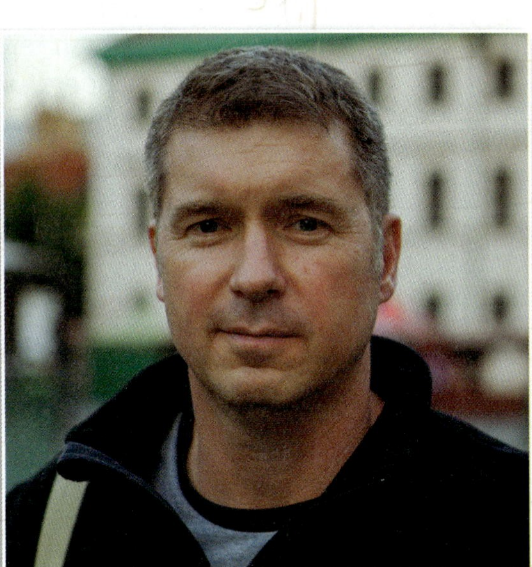

Photojournalist Dave Yoder

About 50 years later, a Renaissance artist and writer named Giorgio Vasari was asked to redecorate the town hall. However, legend has it that rather than destroy Leonardo's fresco, Vasari built a wall over the painting. He then painted his own battle scene on the new wall. Vasari had preserved other great works in a similar way.

An expert on Leonardo first told Seracini about the lost painting and suggested that he gather a team to look for it. As part of the team, National Geographic photojournalist Dave Yoder said his challenge was "to find things to photograph about a painting that might or might not be behind a wall." They also weren't sure which wall to look behind.

CLUES AND FINDINGS

But Seracini believes Vasari provided a clue to the painting's whereabouts. On a small flag in his painting, the artist wrote in tiny letters the Italian words *Cerca trova*, which mean "Seek and you shall find." At first Seracini used noninvasive methods to reveal what he called "a subtle gap behind the wall on which Vasari painted, which could have been constructed by Vasari himself to protect Leonardo's masterpiece."

Soon after this discovery, however, officials in Florence had Seracini's team use an endoscope, a more invasive method, to explore the painting. An endoscope is a lighted instrument that can be inserted inside an object to examine it. To reduce the damage, Seracini mostly inserted the endoscope into holes that had already opened in Vasari's painting. Material taken from one hole revealed traces of colors that only Leonardo had used. One black pigment was believed to be the same type used in painting the *Mona Lisa*.

Despite this promising finding, Italian authorities called a halt to further exploration in 2012. Restorers protested the invasion of Vasari's masterpiece. They also didn't believe Seracini's theory. As a result, the holes were filled in, and the scaffolding was taken down. So, is the lost da Vinci lost for good? Both Seracini and Yoder hope not. "I think it's likely that there is at least part of Leonardo's fresco somewhere in the room," says Yoder. "But given the technology we're limited to, we could easily miss it by a few inches, and then the world would never know."

REVIEW & ASSESS

1. **READING CHECK** What does Seracini think is hidden behind Vasari's fresco?
2. **ANALYZE CAUSE AND EFFECT** What event brought the search to a halt?
3. **FORM AND SUPPORT OPINIONS** Do you think the search for the lost da Vinci should continue? Explain why or why not.

2.1 The Renaissance Moves North

You've heard about the wonders in Italy, but you still can't believe your eyes and ears. In Florence, you marvel at the lifelike, muscular statue of David. You stop on the street in Rome to listen to people discuss the limitless possibility of the individual. In Milan, you gaze at *The Last Supper* and admire its depth and emotional power. You can't wait to get back home to northern Europe and tell everyone what you've seen and heard.

MAIN IDEA

Renaissance ideas spread from Italy and influenced art and literature across northern Europe.

ARTISTIC STYLES

Great ideas cannot be contained. This was true even in the 1400s and 1500s. In time, Italian Renaissance ideas began to influence northern Europe. Trade and the growth of cities spread the ideas to countries such as France, Belgium, the Netherlands, Germany, Spain, and England.

Artists from these countries visited Italy's cities to soak up their rebirth of culture firsthand. Powerful rulers in countries like France and England brought Italian artists to their courts. The kings and queens became the artists' patrons and paid them to create works that became a source of national pride.

While northern European artists were inspired by the Italian Renaissance, many put their own spin on artistic styles. For instance, instead of focusing on classical subjects, artists of the Northern Renaissance often painted scenes of everyday life. A Flemish artist named Pieter Bruegel (BROY-guhl) the Elder demonstrated this style. (*Flemish* refers to people from a region called Flanders, which is in present-day Belgium.) As the painting on the opposite page illustrates, Bruegel often depicted the lives of peasants with remarkable realism.

Another Flemish artist, Jan van Eyck (yahn van EHK), painted detailed, colorful portraits and images of religious subjects. The rich color in his paintings was largely due to his use of oil paint. Artists of the Italian Renaissance had mostly used water-based paints that often faded quickly. When Italian artists visited northern Europe, they eagerly adopted van Eyck's use of oils and brought the style back to Italy. The trade of ideas didn't go in only one direction.

The German artist Albrecht Dürer (DYUR-uhr) is often considered to be the greatest artist of the Northern Renaissance. Dürer had visited Italy and absorbed the styles there. He combined classical ideas, perspective, and great attention to detail to create realistic paintings and **woodcuts**, or images carved on blocks of wood.

SCHOLARS AND WRITERS

The Italian Renaissance and its humanist ideals also influenced the intellectual thinking of northern Europe. As you may recall, Petrarch was an early humanist leader of the Italian Renaissance. The Dutch scholar and priest Desiderius Erasmus (dehz-ih-DEHR-ee-uhs ir-RAZ-muhs) was a key humanist leader of the Northern

The Peasant Dance, Pieter Bruegel the Elder, 1567

Critical Viewing In this painting by Bruegel, peasants dance in a village square. What can you learn about the peasants' way of life from the painting?

Renaissance. Erasmus focused on making classical works and Christian texts more accessible to ordinary people. He also criticized some Church practices and called for reform. As you will see later in the chapter, the writings of Erasmus and others would have a big impact on the Church. Another humanist, the English statesman Thomas More, promoted free education for men and women, which was a radical idea at the time.

Unlike Erasmus and More, the best-known writer of the Northern Renaissance did not try to reform society. This author wrote tragic, comic, and historical plays filled with characters that spring to life off the page. Their passions, humor, personalities, and conflicts still capture our imagination today. Many people believe that the man who created these characters—William Shakespeare—is the greatest writer in the English language.

REVIEW & ASSESS

1. **READING CHECK** How did Renaissance ideas spread from Italy to northern Europe?
2. **COMPARE AND CONTRAST** In what ways did the artistic styles of the Northern Renaissance differ from those of the Italian Renaissance?
3. **SYNTHESIZE** Based on what you have learned about humanism, how did the scholars and writers of the Northern Renaissance reflect its ideals?

2.2 BIOGRAPHY

WILLIAM SHAKESPEARE 1564–1616

Some people don't believe William Shakespeare wrote the works credited to him, in part because he didn't have a university education. These doubters have identified other writers of the time as the authors of Shakespeare's work, but they've never been able to prove their theories. Maybe some people can't believe that a man of humble background could pen some of the greatest plays ever written. But that seems to have been exactly what happened.

Jobs: Playwright, poet, actor

Home: Stratford upon Avon; married to Anne Hathaway, with whom he had three children

FINEST HOUR

Writing and performing for his patrons—first Queen Elizabeth I and later King James I of England

WORST MOMENT

Perhaps the death of his son, Hamnet, at age 11

DEATH

Unlike many writers of his day, he died a rich man and left most of his possessions to his daughter Susanna.

TRIVIA

Some of the writers of his time didn't respect him and referred to him as an "upstart crow."

THE BARD

The Northern Renaissance was well established in England by the time **William Shakespeare** went to seek his fortune in London around 1585. He began as an actor and apparently had a successful career. In time, he became part owner of a theatrical company known as the Lord Chamberlain's Men and began writing his own plays. By around 1594, the company was mainly performing only Shakespeare's plays, and the playwright acted in many of them himself.

The Bard—or poet—as he is often called, wrote more than 150 poems and 37 plays, including tragedies such as *Romeo and Juliet* and comedies such as *A Midsummer Night's Dream*. Shakespeare's plays have stood the test of time largely because of their insight into human nature. Shakespeare created complex characters with deep emotions and used clever wordplay to make his audience laugh or cry. The plays also reflected the Renaissance mindset.

Romeo and Juliet is a timeless work. Its themes can be interpreted and expressed in many ways, and the story can be set in many different eras. This film version takes place in the present day and features actors Leonardo DiCaprio and Claire Danes.

They dealt with human life rather than religious themes. And many of the plays were based on stories and characters from classical Greek and Latin works.

THE ELIZABETHAN AGE

Most of Shakespeare's plays were written during the **Elizabethan Age**, or the reign of Queen Elizabeth I, which lasted from 1558 to 1603. Elizabeth spoke many languages, wrote poetry, and was a gifted musician. The queen supported the Globe Theater, where many of Shakespeare's plays were performed before people from all walks of life. After Elizabeth died, her cousin James I rose to the throne. James soon became the patron of Shakespeare's theatrical company, which then changed its name to the King's Men. Shakespeare wrote some of his greatest plays, including *Macbeth*, under the king's patronage.

Shakespeare retired from the theater when he was 49 and died three years later. Several years after his death, his plays were collected in a volume. The English playwright Ben Jonson, who had known Shakespeare, understood his friend's genius. In an introduction to the volume, Jonson wrote that Shakespeare "was not of an age, but for all time."

REVIEW & ASSESS

1. **READING CHECK** How did Shakespeare's plays reflect Renaissance ideas?
2. **MAKE INFERENCES** Why do you think Shakespeare's plays appealed to all people, from the very wealthy to the very poor?
3. **ANALYZE LANGUAGE USE** What does the phrase "not of an age, but for all time" suggest about Shakespeare's legacy?

2.3 The Printing Press

Today, ideas can fly around the world at the push of a button or the click of a mouse. In the early days of the Renaissance, however, ideas mostly spread by word of mouth as traders and travelers made their slow way from place to place. But then a German printer came up with an invention that sped up the exchange of ideas. In many ways, it was the Internet of its day.

MAIN IDEA

The printing press greatly quickened the spread of Renaissance ideas and information.

TECHNOLOGICAL ADVANCE

The invention was the **printing press**, and it was developed around 1450 by the German blacksmith, goldsmith, publisher, and printer **Johann Gutenberg**. He developed the press by improving on the Chinese technology of woodblock printing. Chinese printers had carved text onto a wooden block, inked the block, and then pressed it onto paper. Gutenberg developed movable metal type, with a separate piece of type for each letter. Using this technology, printers could arrange the letters any way they liked. They could also use and reuse the pieces. The diagram on the opposite page shows how the printing press worked.

Around the same time, a new technique for making paper was developed, which made paper easier to manufacture. Gutenberg used this paper and his new press to print a Latin Bible in 1455. He tried to keep his printing technique a secret, but his beautiful Bible caught people's attention. Like Renaissance culture, the technology of the new printing press spread quickly.

IMPACT OF PRINTING

It's hard to overestimate the impact of the printing press. It resulted in an information explosion throughout Europe. Before the press, most printers made every copy of a book by hand, which could take a full month. In the same amount of time, Gutenberg's press could produce 500 books. These books were far cheaper than the handmade copies. They also spread ideas much more quickly.

As you know, people had become eager for knowledge by the time of the Renaissance. The printing press only fueled this demand. As more books became available, more people learned to read, and more universities were founded. In addition, libraries became better stocked with reliable information, which helped in the advancement of science, technology, and scholarship.

Many of the first printed books were religious and classical works, but a demand for less scholarly reading soon grew. In response, publishers printed poetry, plays, travel books, and histories. People also wanted to read books in their native language, instead of Latin. Remember that Dante began this trend when he wrote *The Divine Comedy* in Italian. As a result, books began to be printed in the vernacular—even the Bible. This allowed many more people to read the Bible and interpret its teachings for themselves for the first time. As you'll see in the next section, this trend would cause trouble for the Catholic Church. Soon Gutenberg's invention would be printing pamphlets that would question the authority of the pope himself.

PRINTING ON GUTENBERG'S PRESS, STEP BY STEP

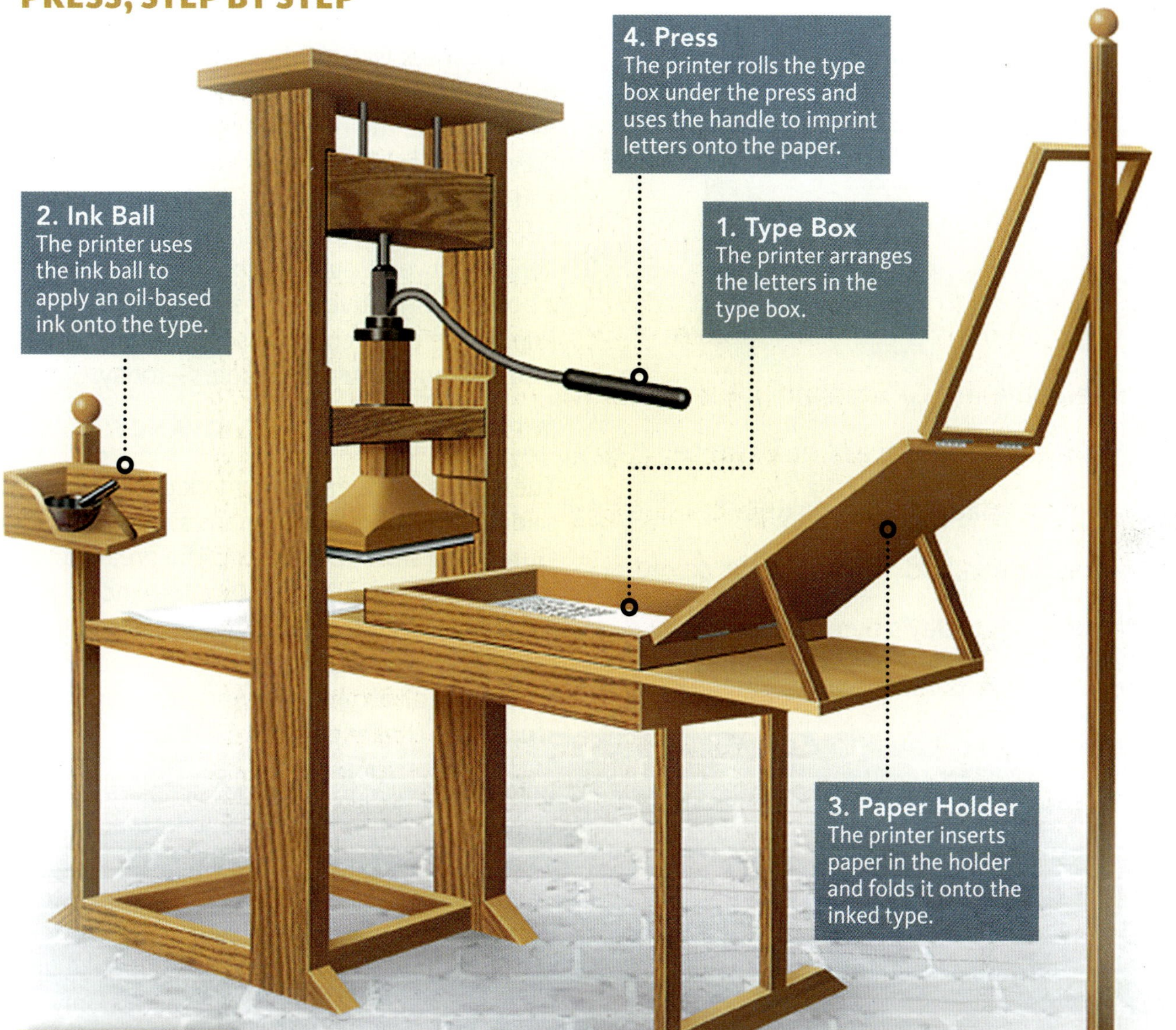

4. Press
The printer rolls the type box under the press and uses the handle to imprint letters onto the paper.

2. Ink Ball
The printer uses the ink ball to apply an oil-based ink onto the type.

1. Type Box
The printer arranges the letters in the type box.

3. Paper Holder
The printer inserts paper in the holder and folds it onto the inked type.

GUTENBERG'S BIBLE

The Gutenberg Bible, as it came to be called, contained 1,286 pages with about 42 lines on each page. It was remarkable for its neat, even letters and hand-painted illustrations of nature. Gutenberg printed 200 copies of his Bible, of which about 50 survive today.

REVIEW & ASSESS

1. **READING CHECK** How did the printing press help spread information?
2. **INTEGRATE VISUALS** Based on the diagram and what you have learned about the printing press, how do you think the new invention improved printers' lives?
3. **ANALYZE CAUSE AND EFFECT** What happened once the printing press made books more widely available?

2.4 Legacy in the Arts and Sciences

Did you know that the Renaissance influenced many modern developments? GPS technology owes a debt to the advances Renaissance scientists made in mapmaking. Studies of the human body in the 1500s paved the way for today's medical-imaging techniques. As for the arts, if you travel to almost any state capitol, you'll see a dome that resembles Brunelleschi's. The Renaissance left us a living legacy.

MAIN IDEA

Renaissance advances in the arts and sciences continue to influence thinking today.

THE ARTS AND ARCHITECTURE

As you have learned, Renaissance architects revived ancient Greek and Roman ideas to build and perfect such structures as domes, arches, and columns. These structures continue to be important elements in architecture today. Similarly, Renaissance artists' realistic portrayal of individuals and use of perspective have influenced modern and contemporary artists.

You've read about William Shakespeare, but the Renaissance also produced such literary figures as Spanish writer Miguel de Cervantes (sehr-VAHN-tez) and Italian historian Niccolò Machiavelli. In Cervantes' masterpiece, the novel *Don Quixote* (key-HOE-tay), the author used humor and insight to tell his tale. The novel has influenced other writers since its publication about 400 years ago. Machiavelli wrote a book on effective leadership called *The Prince*. The book continues to influence leaders—and would-be leaders—today.

IMPACT OF SCIENTIFIC ADVANCES

The Renaissance made its mark on the sciences, too. Some historians say that Gutenberg's printing press is the greatest invention of the past 1,000 years—more significant than the computer or the Internet. The printing press made it possible for people all around the world to share, study, and challenge others' ideas.

In mathematics, Renaissance scholars came up with the idea of using letters in algebraic equations; for example, $x + y = 5$. Renaissance thinkers also became interested in the natural world. Some scientists learned about the metals and minerals that make up Earth's surface. Others studied astronomy and gained new understanding of the wider universe and Earth's place in it.

You've learned about Leonardo da Vinci's anatomical sketches. In 1543, the Belgian physician Andreas Vesalius (vuh-SAHL-ee-us) dissected the bodies of executed criminals and published his findings. As a result of his accurate drawings of the human body, anatomy became a scientific discipline.

Scientific ideas were also applied to **cartography**, or mapmaking, during the Renaissance. Using these new ideas, exploration by men such as Christopher Columbus continued to improve the accuracy of maps. Exploration also opened up new lands to colonization and settlement. The legacy of these events is still felt today.

Statue of Martin Luther King, Jr., at his memorial

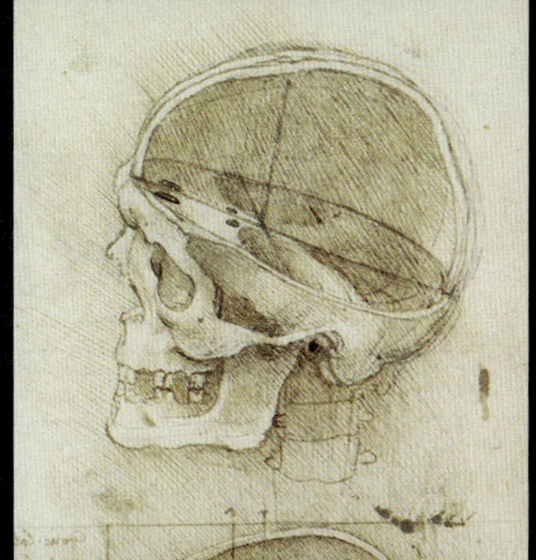
Drawing of the skull by Leonardo

THEN AND NOW

These images demonstrate the legacy of the Renaissance. Find each work created during the Renaissance and compare it to its modern counterpart. What similarities and differences do you see in each pair?

Michelangelo's *David*

Dome of St. Peter's Basilica in Rome

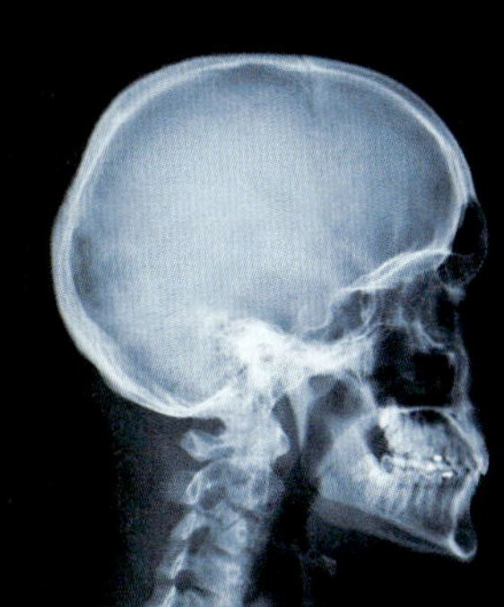
X-ray of the skull

Capitol Building dome in Washington, D.C.

REVIEW & ASSESS

1. **READING CHECK** What were some of the important scientific advances made during the Renaissance?
2. **COMPARE AND CONTRAST** In what way was the impact of Gutenberg's printing press similar to that of the Internet?
3. **MAKE CONNECTIONS** How have Renaissance advances in cartography affected modern life?

3.1 Protests Against the Catholic Church

Thanks to Gutenberg's new printing press, the printers quickly finish making copies of the pamphlet a customer brought in. But they're a bit nervous about its contents. The pamphlet, by Martin Luther, contains a list of items criticizing the Church. The printers are used to seeing old ideas challenged, but this list seems to go too far.

MAIN IDEA

In the 1500s, Martin Luther's protests against the Roman Catholic Church led to the Reformation.

HENRY VIII

King Henry VIII of England formed a new branch of Protestantism when the Church refused to grant him a divorce. The king wanted to divorce and marry a woman he hoped would give him a son.

MARTIN LUTHER

As you know, some people had begun to criticize the Church and call for reforms during the Renaissance. In the last chapter, you also learned that the Church became weaker as the authority of kings increased. In 1305, a powerful French king moved the center of the Church from Rome to Avignon (ah-veen-YOHN), in France, and appointed a French pope. Following a struggle for power, two popes were elected in 1378: one in Rome and the other in Avignon. This split in the Church is known as the **Great Schism** (*schism* means "split"). Although the Church was unified once again in 1417 and Rome restored as the center of Christianity, the Church had been weakened even further.

The Church needed money to regain its former strength, but some people believed the Church used questionable practices to obtain it. For example, Church officials sold **indulgences**, which relaxed the punishment for a sin. However, sometimes the officials sold an indulgence as forgiveness for a sin, with no punishment imposed. Many people, though, believed that only God could forgive sins. People also objected to paying one-tenth of their income to the Church every year in taxes.

A German monk named **Martin Luther** actively protested against these practices. On October 31, 1517, Luther nailed a list of protests, known as the 95 Theses, to a church door in Wittenberg, Germany. The list included the idea that the Bible was the only source of religious truth and that priests were not needed to interpret its words. Luther further suggested that salvation came through faith in Christ alone. Those who supported Luther's ideas would be called **Protestants**, which comes from the word *protest*. The reform movement Luther began is known as the **Reformation**.

PROTESTANTISM GROWS

After Luther made the 95 Theses public, Pope Leo X demanded that the monk take back his statements. Luther refused and was excommunicated, or cut off, from the Church. Nevertheless, pamphlets containing Luther's theses were soon printed, and his ideas spread rapidly.

SPREAD OF PROTESTANTISM, 1500s
ATLANTIC OCEAN
North Sea
SCOTLAND
IRELAND
ENGLAND
London
DENMARK
SWEDEN
Anglican
Calvinist
Lutheran
0 200 400 Miles
0 200 400 Kilometers
Wittenberg
POLAND-LITHUANIA
HOLY ROMAN EMPIRE
SWISS CONFEDERATION
FRANCE
AUSTRIA
Geneva
HUNGARY
ITALIAN STATES
OTTOMAN EMPIRE
PAPAL STATES
Adriatic Sea
Black Se
SPAIN
Mediterranean Sea
N
E
W
S

In response, peasants throughout Europe used Luther's teachings to stage revolts for better wages and living conditions.

Luther's teachings also had a great impact on Christianity. As people interpreted the Bible for themselves, their differing beliefs led to the development of many branches, or **denominations**, of Protestant religions. One branch, called Lutheranism, was inspired by Luther's teachings. Another, called Calvinism, was led by a French reformer named John Calvin who believed that God chose people for salvation. They could do nothing to earn it. A third branch, called Anglicanism or the Church of England, was begun in England by King Henry VIII. Protestantism would have a lasting impact on Europe. But in the meantime, the Catholic Church began to look for ways to stop its spread.

REVIEW & ASSESS

1. **READING CHECK** What Church practices did Martin Luther protest against?
2. **INTERPRET MAPS** How did the spread of the Lutheran and Calvinist branches of Protestantism differ from that of the Anglican branch?
3. **IDENTIFY MAIN IDEAS** Why did many branches of Protestantism develop?

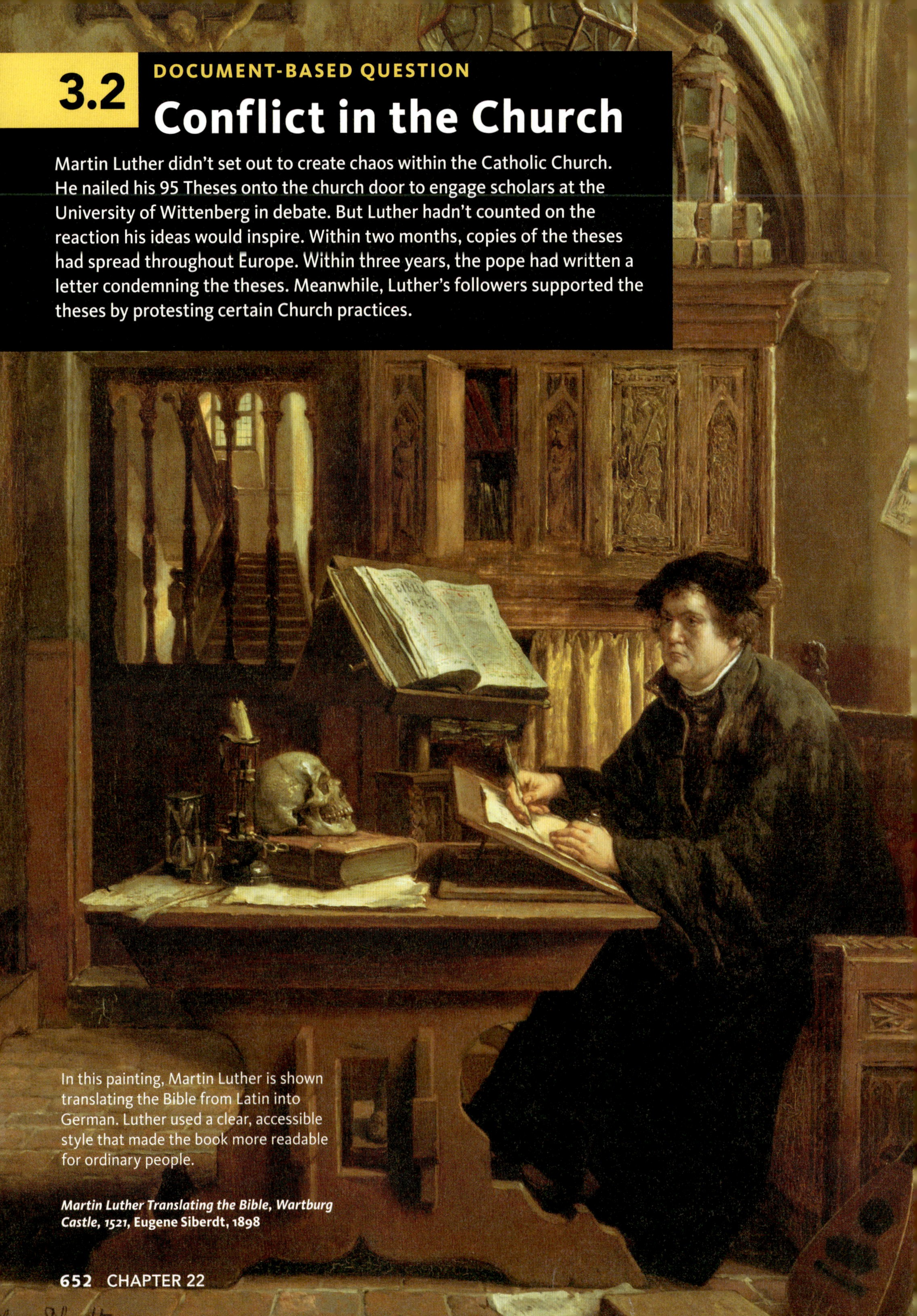

3.2 DOCUMENT-BASED QUESTION

Conflict in the Church

Martin Luther didn't set out to create chaos within the Catholic Church. He nailed his 95 Theses onto the church door to engage scholars at the University of Wittenberg in debate. But Luther hadn't counted on the reaction his ideas would inspire. Within two months, copies of the theses had spread throughout Europe. Within three years, the pope had written a letter condemning the theses. Meanwhile, Luther's followers supported the theses by protesting certain Church practices.

In this painting, Martin Luther is shown translating the Bible from Latin into German. Luther used a clear, accessible style that made the book more readable for ordinary people.

***Martin Luther Translating the Bible, Wartburg Castle, 1521*, Eugene Siberdt, 1898**

DOCUMENT ONE

Primary Source: Pamphlet

from the 95 Theses

In his 95 Theses, Luther expresses his criticism of the Church in statements that sum up his interpretation of teaching found in the Bible. In the following two theses, Luther presents his idea that letters of pardon, or indulgences, do not make people better and cannot ensure salvation.

CONSTRUCTED RESPONSE Why might the Church have taken offense at these statements?

> 44. . . . Love grows by works of love, and man becomes better; but by pardons man does not grow better, only more free from penalty.
>
> 52. The assurance of salvation by letters of pardon is vain [useless], even though . . . the pope himself were to stake his soul upon it.

DOCUMENT TWO

Primary Source: Letter

from the Papal Bull of Pope Leo X

In 1520, Pope Leo X issued a papal bull, or official letter, giving Luther 60 days to take back his theses. In the following excerpt from the bull, Leo condemns Luther's ideas and tells followers of Catholicism ("the faithful") how to handle them.

CONSTRUCTED RESPONSE According to the pope, how should Catholics deal with Luther's ideas?

> With the advice and consent of these our venerable [respected] brothers, . . . we condemn, reprobate [disapprove], and reject completely each of these theses. . . . We forbid each and every one of the faithful . . . to read, assert, preach, praise, print, publish, or defend them.

DOCUMENT THREE

Primary Source: Leaflet

Leaflet Against Johann Tetzel

Luther's followers distributed this leaflet to protest against the practices of Johann Tetzel, a monk who sold indulgences. Tetzel is said to have written the last two lines in the leaflet:
"As soon as gold in the cashbox rings,
The rescued soul to heaven springs."

CONSTRUCTED RESPONSE Why do you think the people shown in the leaflet are happy to see Tetzel?

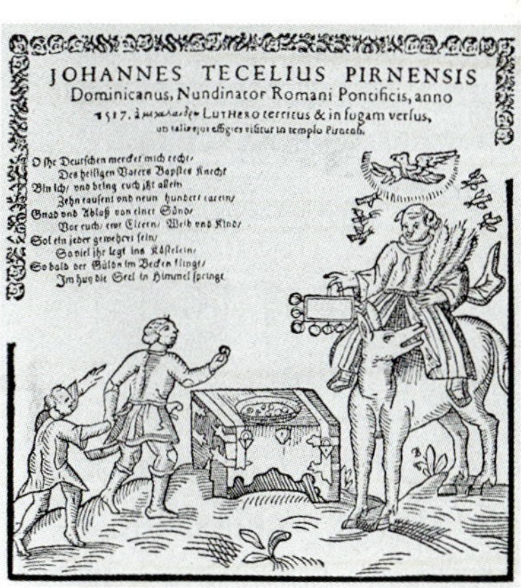
JOHANNES TECELIUS PIRNENSIS
Dominicanus, Nundinator Romani Pontificis, anno

SYNTHESIZE & WRITE

1. **REVIEW** Review what you have learned about the Reformation and protests against the Catholic Church.
2. **RECALL** On your own paper, write down the main idea expressed in each document.
3. **CONSTRUCT** Write a topic sentence that answers this question: How did the Church and Luther's followers react to the 95 Theses?
4. **WRITE** Using evidence from the documents, write a short paragraph to support your answer to the question in Step 3.

3.3 The Counter Reformation

After the Reformation, the Catholic Church was down but certainly not out. Millions of faithful followers remained loyal. They continued to recognize the pope as their leader and trusted their priests' interpretation of the Bible. But Church officials knew that to keep their members and bring Protestants back to the fold, they had to stop the spread of Protestantism. To do that, they had to make some changes.

MAIN IDEA

Reforms and a new religious order established during the Counter Reformation helped strengthen Catholicism.

REFORM FROM WITHIN

The changes the Catholic Church made were part of a movement called the Catholic Reformation—sometimes also called the **Counter Reformation**. (In this use of the word, *counter* means "against.") A meeting of Church officials and scholars summoned by the pope in 1545 was a key element of the movement.

The meeting, which came to be known as the **Council of Trent**, met for 26 sessions over 18 years, mostly in the northern Italian city of Trent. During that time, the council worked to define Catholic beliefs and practices and determine how the Church needed to change. Council members also sought to clarify how Catholicism differed from Protestantism. For example, while Protestants believed that the Bible could be understood directly by individuals, the Church taught that it must be interpreted and understood in light of tradition.

To make sure Catholics didn't stray from their faith, the Church also established a Roman Inquisition. Like the Spanish Inquisition discussed in the previous chapter, the Roman Inquisition used harsh methods, including torture, to force a confession and punish **heresy**, or a denial of Church teachings. Protestants were, of course, considered to be guilty of heresy.

In addition, Church officials created a list of books they objected to. Followers of Catholicism were forbidden to read the books, which included Bibles in the vernacular as well as most anything written by Luther, Calvin, and Erasmus. The books were collected by Church clergy and burned.

On the other hand, the Church also applied gentler methods to broaden its appeal. It built new, larger churches to hold more worshippers. In addition, priests sometimes delivered sermons in the vernacular.

A NEW RELIGIOUS ORDER

The struggle to revive Catholicism was aided by the development of a new religious order called the Society of Jesus, whose followers were known as **Jesuits** (JEHZH-oo-ihts). A former Spanish knight named Ignatius of Loyola formed the order, and he insisted on strict obedience.

Beginning in 1540, Ignatius commanded his followers as their "Superior General," and the Jesuits carried out their duties with great discipline. They also took vows of poverty and obedience, promising to fight "for the greater glory of God."

CHRISTIAN MISSIONS, 1600s

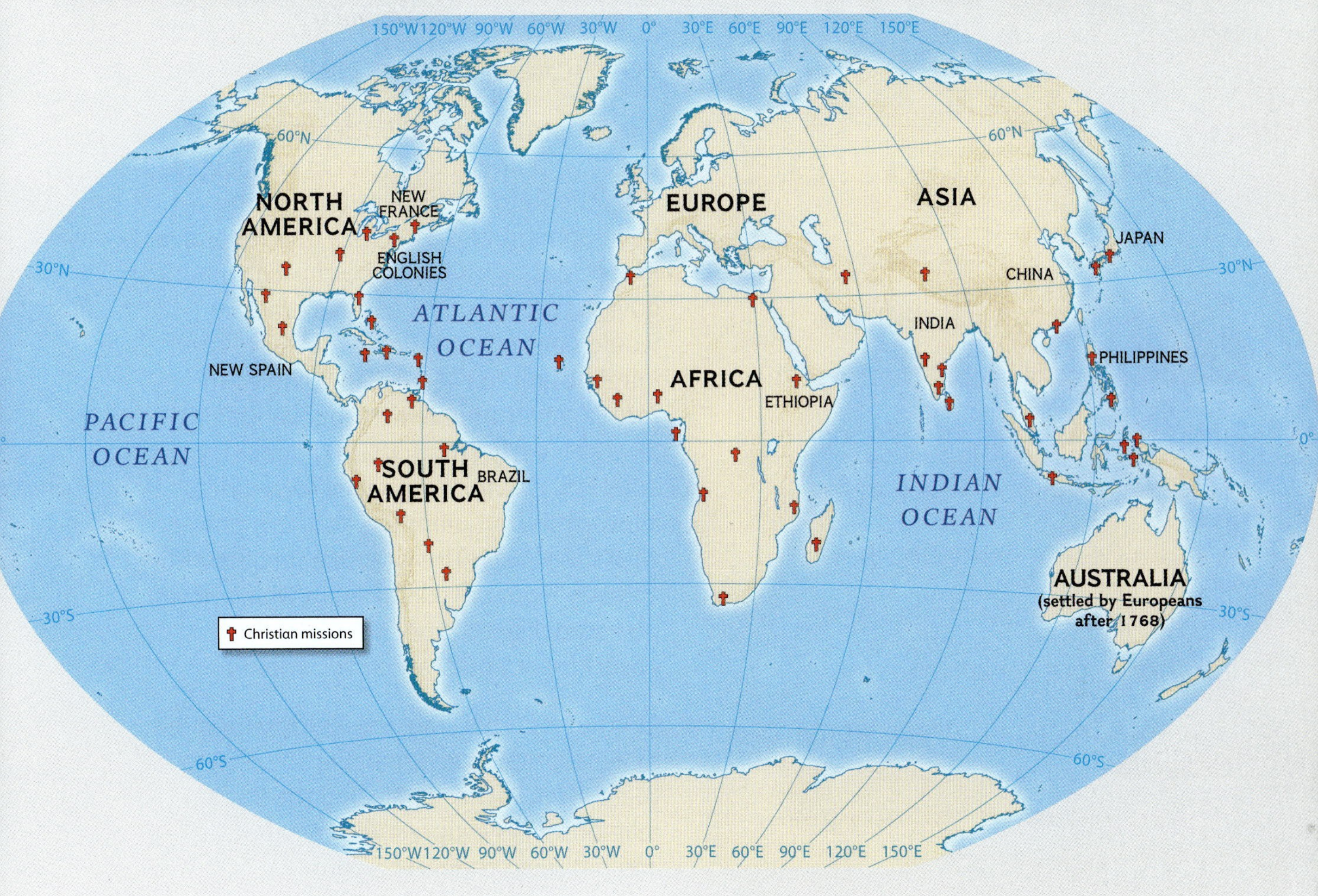

NORTH AMERICA
NEW FRANCE
ENGLISH COLONIES
NEW SPAIN
ATLANTIC OCEAN
PACIFIC OCEAN
SOUTH AMERICA
BRAZIL
EUROPE
AFRICA
ETHIOPIA
ASIA
CHINA
JAPAN
INDIA
PHILIPPINES
INDIAN OCEAN
AUSTRALIA (settled by Europeans after 1768)
Christian missions
150°W 120°W 90°W 60°W 30°W 0° 30°E 60°E 90°E 120°E 150°E
60°N
30°N
0°
30°S
60°S

From the start, the Jesuits' purpose was to obey the pope and go wherever he thought they were most needed. In time, this meant establishing schools and universities throughout Europe and the world. The Jesuits provided a good education to thousands of men and inspired many to dedicate their lives to the Church.

The Jesuits also worked as **missionaries** by spreading Catholicism to people in Africa, Asia, and the Americas. To prepare for this task and enable them to communicate their faith to people in other parts of the world, Jesuit priests studied many different languages.

Through their support of the Counter Reformation, the Jesuits and other Catholic reformers helped revitalize the Church. By the end of the 1500s, the Church had regained much of its power. The Church was ready to play an important role in the coming century.

REVIEW & ASSESS

1. **READING CHECK** What were some of the methods used during the Counter Reformation to stop the spread of Protestantism?
2. **MAKE INFERENCES** Why do you think the Church burned certain books?
3. **DRAW CONCLUSIONS** Why was it important to the Catholic Church to establish its own schools and universities?

3.4 The Impact of the Reformation

The Reformation resulted in a cultural shift. Once people could interpret the Bible for themselves, they formed new ideas about the Christian religion. More Protestant denominations formed as differences in beliefs developed, and new Protestant churches sprang up. Europe would never be the same.

MAIN IDEA

The Reformation had a long-lasting religious, social, and political impact on Europe.

RELIGIOUS EFFECTS

Protestantism flourished. Like Catholics, Protestants founded universities and parish schools to teach their beliefs and gain new followers. As a result, because both Protestants and Catholics wanted to read the Bible, the Reformation increased literacy.

In England, many Anglicans learned to read the Bible but not in the vernacular. They followed the Catholic belief that prohibited reading the Bible in translation. However, reformer William Tyndale believed that Anglicans should reject all Catholic beliefs and practices and so began to prepare an English translation of the New Testament. Tyndale completed his work in Germany. In time, however, Catholic officials there arrested and executed him for his beliefs.

POLITICAL EFFECTS

The Reformation had both positive and negative political effects. On the positive side, the Reformation influenced the development of democracy and federalism. Protestants who formed a church sometimes governed it themselves. This practice would later encourage religious groups immigrating to the English colonies to form a government with equal and fair laws—an early step toward democracy. In addition, Calvinist churches sometimes allowed church members to share power with the clergy. This practice represented an early form of federalism in which power is shared, like that between a national government and state governments.

On the negative side, the Reformation led to widespread warfare in Europe. In the years after Luther published the 95 Theses, religious wars erupted within countries and between them. The Thirty Years' War, for example, started as a conflict between Catholics and Protestants in Central Europe. The war, which lasted from 1618 to 1648, devastated the German states, killing an estimated seven million people.

Although the Catholic Church had partly recovered from the Reformation, its power in Europe would come to be challenged by powerful kings. These kings worked to bring all of the people within their territory under a unified rule. As a result, powerful modern **nation-states** began to emerge, with their own independent governments and populations united by a shared culture, language, and national pride.

The Catholic Church would also face challenges from another source. Scientists influenced by humanism would begin to question accepted views—including those of the Church. Their discoveries would change the way people looked at the world.

Church towers in the northern European country of Latvia represent three different Christian denominations: (from left to right) Lutheranism, Catholicism, and Anglicanism.

REVIEW & ASSESS

1. **READING CHECK** What were some of the religious effects of the Reformation?

2. **DETERMINE WORD MEANINGS** In the sentence "Because more people wanted to read the Bible, the Reformation also increased literacy," what does *literacy* mean?

3. **ANALYZE CAUSE AND EFFECT** What led to the rise of nation-states?

CHAPTER

22 Review

VOCABULARY

Complete each of the following sentences using one of the vocabulary words from the chapter.

1. A movement called ______ focused on the potential of the individual.
2. During the Renaissance, artists often painted nonreligious, or ______, subjects.
3. Artists use ______ to produce an impression of depth and distance.
4. Instead of Latin, some Renaissance writers wrote in the ______.
5. Wealthy ______ often supported artists during the Renaissance.
6. Gutenberg's development of the ______ helped spread ideas quickly.
7. The Roman Inquisition punished ______, or a denial of Church policy.

READING STRATEGY

8. **ANALYZE LANGUAGE USE** If you haven't already, complete at least three concept clusters that analyze figurative language. Then use each example of the language in a sentence of your own.

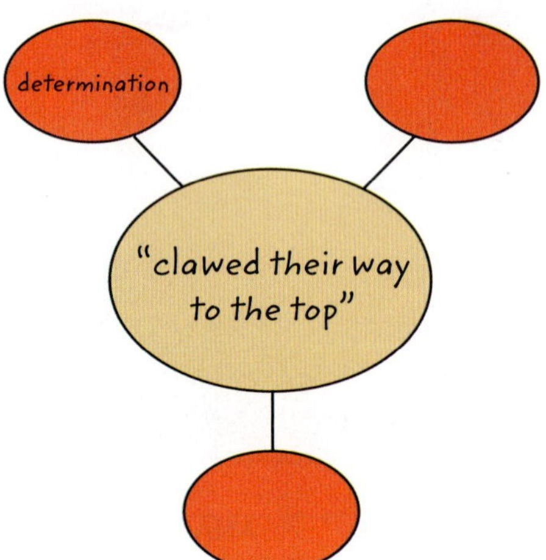
determination
"clawed their way to the top"

MAIN IDEAS

Answer the following questions. Support your answers with evidence from the chapter.

9. What was the Renaissance? **LESSON 1.1**
10. What artistic subjects became popular during the Renaissance? **LESSON 1.2**
11. Why were the best artists and scholars attracted to Florence during the Renaissance? **LESSON 1.4**
12. Who often served as patrons of Northern Renaissance artists? **LESSON 2.1**
13. How did Gutenberg's printing press improve on Chinese woodblock printing? **LESSON 2.3**
14. Which event triggered the Reformation? **LESSON 3.1**
15. What was the purpose of the Counter Reformation? **LESSON 3.3**

CRITICAL THINKING

Answer the following questions. Support your answers with evidence from the chapter.

16. **COMPARE AND CONTRAST** How did the ideas of humanism differ from those of the Middle Ages?
17. **MAKE PREDICTIONS** What might have happened if wealthy patrons had not supported Renaissance artists?
18. **MAKE INFERENCES** Why do you think art experts become so excited over the prospect of finding a new painting by Leonardo da Vinci?
19. **DRAW CONCLUSIONS** What conclusions can you draw about Shakespeare's career based on the fact that he died a rich man?
20. **SEQUENCE EVENTS** What chain of events followed Martin Luther's publication of his 95 Theses?
21. **YOU DECIDE** What do you think was the most important achievement of the Renaissance? Support your opinion with evidence from the chapter.

INTERPRET VISUALS

Study the paintings below from the Middle Ages and the Renaissance. Then answer the questions that follow.

Medieval painting from Catalan School, Spain

Renaissance painting by Raphael

22. In what ways are the two paintings alike?

23. How do the artistic styles differ in the two paintings?

ANALYZE SOURCES

In 1568, Giorgio Vasari wrote a collection of biographies about the great artists of his day, including Michelangelo. In this excerpt, a high-ranking government official named Piero Soderini has a suggestion for improving Michelangelo's famous sculpture of David.

> While Michelangelo was giving it the finishing touches, [Soderini] told Michelangelo that he thought the nose of the figure was too large. Michelangelo, . . . having quickly grabbed his chisel in his left hand along with a little marble dust, . . . began to tap lightly with the chisel, allowing the dust to fall little by little without retouching the nose from the way it was. Then, looking down at [Soderini] who stood there watching, he ordered: "Look at it now." "I like it better," replied [Soderini]: "you've made it come alive."

24. Based on this story, what were some of Michelangelo's personality traits?

WRITE ABOUT HISTORY

25. EXPLANATORY How did the Renaissance affect Europe? Write a paragraph designed to inform museumgoers about the ways in which Renaissance ideas about art, literature, and thinking changed Europe.

TIPS

- Take notes from the lessons on how the Renaissance affected people and events in Europe. You might use a web diagram to organize your notes.
- State your main idea clearly at the beginning of the paragraph.
- Support your main idea with relevant facts, details, and examples.
- Use two or three vocabulary terms from the chapter in your paragraph.
- Provide a concluding statement about the ways in which the Renaissance changed Europe.

CHAPTER

23 THE AGE OF SCIENCE AND EXPLORATION

1400 – 1700

SECTION 1

THE SCIENTIFIC REVOLUTION

KEY VOCABULARY	NAMES & PLACES
elliptical	Galileo Galilei
geocentric theory	Isaac Newton
heliocentric theory	Nicolaus Copernicus
hypothesis	René Descartes
scientific method	Robert Hooke
scientific rationalism	Scientific Revolution
theory	Sir Francis Bacon

SECTION 2

THE AGE OF EXPLORATION

KEY VOCABULARY	NAMES & PLACES
caravel	Christopher Columbus
colony	Columbian Exchange
exploit	Dutch East India Company
quinine	Ferdinand and Isabella
rivalry	Prince Henry the Navigator
smallpox	

SECTION 3

EUROPEAN EMPIRES

KEY VOCABULARY	NAMES & PLACES
conquistador	Atahualpa
plantation	Francisco Pizarro
racism	Hernán Cortés
triangular trade	Middle Passage
	Pedro Álvares Cabral
	Tenochtitlán

READING STRATEGY

MAKE INFERENCES
When you make inferences, you "read between the lines" to find information that isn't stated directly. As you read the chapter, use a chart like this one to make inferences about the relationship between the Scientific Revolution and European exploration.

I Learned	My Inference

A giant collection of telescopes in Chile scans the night sky. During the Age of Exploration, observations of the stars and planets led to changes in scientific views of the universe.

1.1

Roots of the Revolution

The period following the Middle Ages was one of major changes in Europe. The Renaissance brought an explosion of creativity in art, literature, and architecture. The Reformation transformed people's religious ideas. Another important movement introduced great advances in science. This movement is called the **Scientific Revolution**, and it began in Europe around the mid-1500s.

MAIN IDEA

Before the Scientific Revolution, Europeans generally relied on the works of ancient Greek thinkers and medieval Muslim scholars to answer scientific questions.

ANCIENT GREEK SCIENTISTS

Since earliest times, people have attempted to understand and explain the natural world—sometimes through religion, sometimes through science, and sometimes by combining the two. Early scientists called themselves "natural philosophers," and their methods differed greatly from those of modern scientists.

The ancient Greeks were great thinkers, and they often based their scientific explanations on reasoning rather than evidence. Indeed, some famous Greek philosophers rejected the need for scientific experiments. They believed that if enough clever men thought for long enough, they would discover the truth. This belief led to some incorrect theories. A **theory** is a proposed explanation for a set of facts.

Two ancient Greek thinkers, Aristotle and Ptolemy, promoted the **geocentric theory**, which placed Earth at the center of the universe. According to this theory, the sun, moon, and planets all moved in a circular path around Earth. This theory later supported the Christian belief that God had created Earth at the center of the universe. Even though the theory was wrong, it influenced scientific ideas about the universe for hundreds of years.

In other areas, however, the ancient Greeks made some valuable contributions to scientific knowledge. For example, the Greek mathematicians Pythagoras, Euclid, and Archimedes (ahr-kuh-MEE-deez) developed theories on which modern mathematics is based.

MEDIEVAL MUSLIM SCHOLARS

After the collapse of the Roman Empire in A.D. 476, most classical knowledge was lost to western Europe. However, it survived in the Muslim empire. Between the 600s and 1100s, Muslim scholars studied Greek scientific theories and combined them with ideas from other regions. From India, for example, they adopted such mathematical concepts as the decimal system, the number zero, and the ten Arabic numerals commonly used today. By bringing together learning from different cultures, Muslim scholars advanced mathematical understanding.

Muslim scholars also made significant advances in astronomy. They developed special buildings called observatories for studying the stars. These buildings had scientific instruments that allowed astronomers to accurately plot the locations of stars. As a result, scientists

SCENO
SYSTEMATIS
PTOLE
GRAPHIA
MVNDANI
MAICI.
SATVRNVS
MARS
LVNA
VENVS
SOL
OCCIDENS
ORIENS

Scenographia Systematis Mundani (Harmonia Macrocosmica or Atlas Coelestis), 1660

were able to develop more accurate calendars and methods of navigation.

The advanced knowledge of the Muslims spread throughout their vast empire and beyond, eventually reaching western Europe after the 1200s. Beginning in the 1500s, European scientists combined this knowledge with new technology and a willingness to challenge long-accepted ideas. These actions sparked a revolution in scientific thinking.

GEOCENTRIC THEORY ^

This illustration from the 1600s depicts the geocentric theory, which incorrectly placed Earth at the center of the universe. The illustration shows the sun, moon, and other planets revolving around a much larger Earth. The surrounding band shows the signs of the zodiac, an imaginary belt in the heavens that encircles the orbits of the planets. The zodiac plays a major role in astrology, the study of how the stars and planets supposedly influence people's lives and events on Earth. In the Middle Ages, astronomy and astrology were closely linked.

REVIEW & ASSESS

1. **READING CHECK** What sources of knowledge did scholars turn to before the Scientific Revolution?
2. **DETERMINE WORD MEANINGS** How do the roots of the words *geocentric* and *observatory* help clarify their meanings?
3. **ANALYZE CAUSE AND EFFECT** How did medieval Muslim scholars help advance the field of mathematics?

1.2 Discoveries and Inventions

You are a scientist living in the early 1600s. You spend many hours looking through a telescope, studying the stars and planets. Your observations lead you to believe the planets revolve around the sun. But you are afraid to publicly state this view because it conflicts with the teachings of the powerful Catholic Church. There could be serious consequences if you publish your findings.

MAIN IDEA

Improved technology and a focus on direct observation led to important scientific discoveries from the 1500s through the 1600s.

STRUCTURE OF THE UNIVERSE

The geocentric theory placed Earth at the center of the universe. According to this theory, the sun, planets, and stars revolved around Earth in perfect circles. Some scientists began to doubt this theory, however.

In the early 1500s, a Polish scientist named **Nicolaus Copernicus** was studying the locations of the stars to create a more accurate calendar. He noticed that his mathematical calculations worked better if he assumed that Earth revolved around the sun. He proposed the **heliocentric theory**, stating that the sun was the center of the universe. Copernicus published his theory in 1543, the year he died. His theory challenged the long-held view of Earth as the center of the universe.

The research of other scientists supported the heliocentric theory. The German scientist Johannes Kepler concluded that Copernicus's basic ideas were correct. Kepler added that the planets had **elliptical**, or oval, orbits rather than perfect circular ones.

Using more powerful telescopes, the Italian scientist **Galileo Galilei** (gal-uh-LAY-oh gal-uh-LAY-ee) made observations that further supported Copernicus's theory. In 1633, the Catholic Church condemned Galileo's discoveries and put him on trial. The church required Galileo to deny support for Copernicus's theory and kept Galileo under house arrest for the rest of his life. Over time, however, the heliocentric theory gained acceptance.

The English scientist **Isaac Newton** further expanded scientific understanding of the universe in the 1600s. He proposed the law of universal gravitation, which holds that all objects in the universe attract one another. With this law and his three laws of motion, Newton created a complete mechanical explanation of motion in the universe. The Royal Society of London, an organization dedicated to advancing and sharing scientific knowledge, helped spread Newton's ideas. His work would provide the foundation of modern physics and lead to scientific advances ranging from steam engines to space rockets.

BIOLOGY AND CHEMISTRY

While some scientists explored the universe, others focused on life on Earth. The invention of the microscope around 1590 allowed biologists to explore a new microscopic world and to observe things that had previously been invisible to them.

TECHNOLOGY OF THE 1600s

Scientists developed new tools and instruments as the Scientific Revolution spread in the 1600s.

Galileo's Pendulum Clock
Galileo Galilei designed a clock operated by a pendulum. This model of Galileo's design was built in the 1800s.
Hooke's Microscope
Robert Hooke was among the first to build a practical compound microscope, which had more than one lens.
Newton's Color Wheel
Isaac Newton experimented with light and invented the first color wheel.

The English scientist **Robert Hooke** used his microscope to produce detailed drawings of tiny creatures, such as fleas. In 1665, Hooke coined the word *cell* to name the microscopic structures he observed in thin slices of cork. Hooke was the first scientist to describe cells.

Hooke worked closely with Irish scientist Robert Boyle. Together, they discovered that air is made up of gases and determined how changes in the volume of a gas affect the gas's pressure. They formed Boyle's Law to describe this relationship. Boyle's work with gases led him to propose that all matter is made up of smaller particles that join together in different ways. Boyle's theory challenged the ideas of Aristotle, who stated that the physical world consisted of the four elements of earth, fire, air, and water. The experimental work and writings of Hooke and Boyle greatly advanced the fields of biology and chemistry.

REVIEW & ASSESS

1. **READING CHECK** How did technology and direct observation help advance science in the 1500s and 1600s?
2. **MAKE INFERENCES** Why did the Catholic Church condemn Galileo's ideas?
3. **DRAW CONCLUSIONS** How did Robert Hooke advance the field of biology?

1.3 The Scientific Method

For more than 2,000 years, European scientists believed that a person's health depended on a balance of four body fluids called *humors*. They thought diseases were caused by an imbalance in these fluids. Even though no evidence supported the theory, European scientists did not question it.

MAIN IDEA

Two European philosophers, Sir Francis Bacon and René Descartes, helped advance a new approach to science in the 1600s.

SIR FRANCIS BACON

How do scientists develop knowledge? Most people would answer that scientists make observations and conduct experiments. But, surprisingly, that approach is relatively new. Before the 1600s, European scholars mainly referred to ancient Greek or Roman writers or to the Bible to decide what to believe. They did not seek answers by carefully observing nature themselves. The Scientific Revolution changed that approach. Scholars began to rely on observations, experiments, evidence, and reasoning in order to understand the natural world.

Galileo was one of the first scientists to actually test scientific ideas through experiments. Along with Copernicus and Kepler, he started a revolution in scientific thinking.

Two important thinkers of the 1600s—**Sir Francis Bacon** and **René Descartes** (reh-NAY day-KAHRT)—promoted ideas that eventually led to an entirely new approach to science. This approach, called the **scientific method**, is a logical procedure for developing and testing ideas. One of the key steps in the procedure is forming a **hypothesis**, an explanation that can be tested.

Sir Francis Bacon was an English philosopher, politician, and writer who had a strong interest in science. He pioneered a different approach to science in 1620 in the book *New Instrument*. Bacon urged scientists to gather data by following specific steps. Bacon's insistence on observation and experimentation as the keys to scientific accuracy became the cornerstone of modern science.

RENÉ DESCARTES

René Descartes was a brilliant French philosopher who shared Bacon's interest in science. But instead of emphasizing experimentation, Descartes relied on logic and mathematics to learn about the world. He agreed with Bacon on the need for proof in answering questions. In fact, Descartes believed that everything should be doubted until it was proved by reason.

Descartes went so far as to declare that the only thing he knew for certain was that he existed. He reasoned, "I think, therefore I am." From this starting point, Descartes used mathematical reasoning and logic to establish other certainties. Descartes argued that in mathematics, the answers were always correct because you began with simple, provable principles and then used logic to gradually build on them.

This painting shows Galileo Galilei explaining his theories at the University of Padua in Italy.

***Portrait of Galileo Galilei*, Félix Parra, 1873**

THE SCIENTIFIC METHOD

The scientific method is a logical approach for forming and testing ideas. The steps shown here describe the general approach. However, not all scientific inquiries follow the steps in this exact order.

Step One: Observe and Question

A scientist makes observations and gathers information on a subject. The scientist forms a question about the subject.

Step Two: Hypothesize

The scientist proposes a hypothesis, an idea or explanation that answers the question.

Step Three: Experiment

The scientist designs and conducts an experiment to test the hypothesis.

Step Four: Analyze Data

The scientist records and carefully examines the data from the experiment.

Step Five: Evaluate and Share Results

The scientist judges whether the data do or do not support the hypothesis and publishes an article describing the experiment and results.

The ideas of Bacon and Descartes became known as **scientific rationalism**. In this school of thought, observation, experimentation, and mathematical reasoning replaced ancient wisdom and church teachings as the source of scientific knowledge. Scientific rationalism provided a procedure for establishing proof for scientific theories. It laid a foundation for formulating theories on which other scientists could build.

The influence of scientific rationalism extended beyond science. Bacon was active in politics and government, and he applied the principles of scientific rationalism to government. He argued that the direction of government should be based on actual experience.

Other writers argued that scientific rationalism encouraged people to think for themselves, so people should be allowed to take more control of their own lives. This thinking undermined the authority of the Catholic Church and contributed to the development of democratic government.

REVIEW & ASSESS

1. **READING CHECK** According to Bacon and Descartes, what are the best ways to build knowledge?
2. **EVALUATE** Why is it important to share the results of experiments?
3. **MAKE CONNECTIONS** How has the development of the scientific method affected your life?

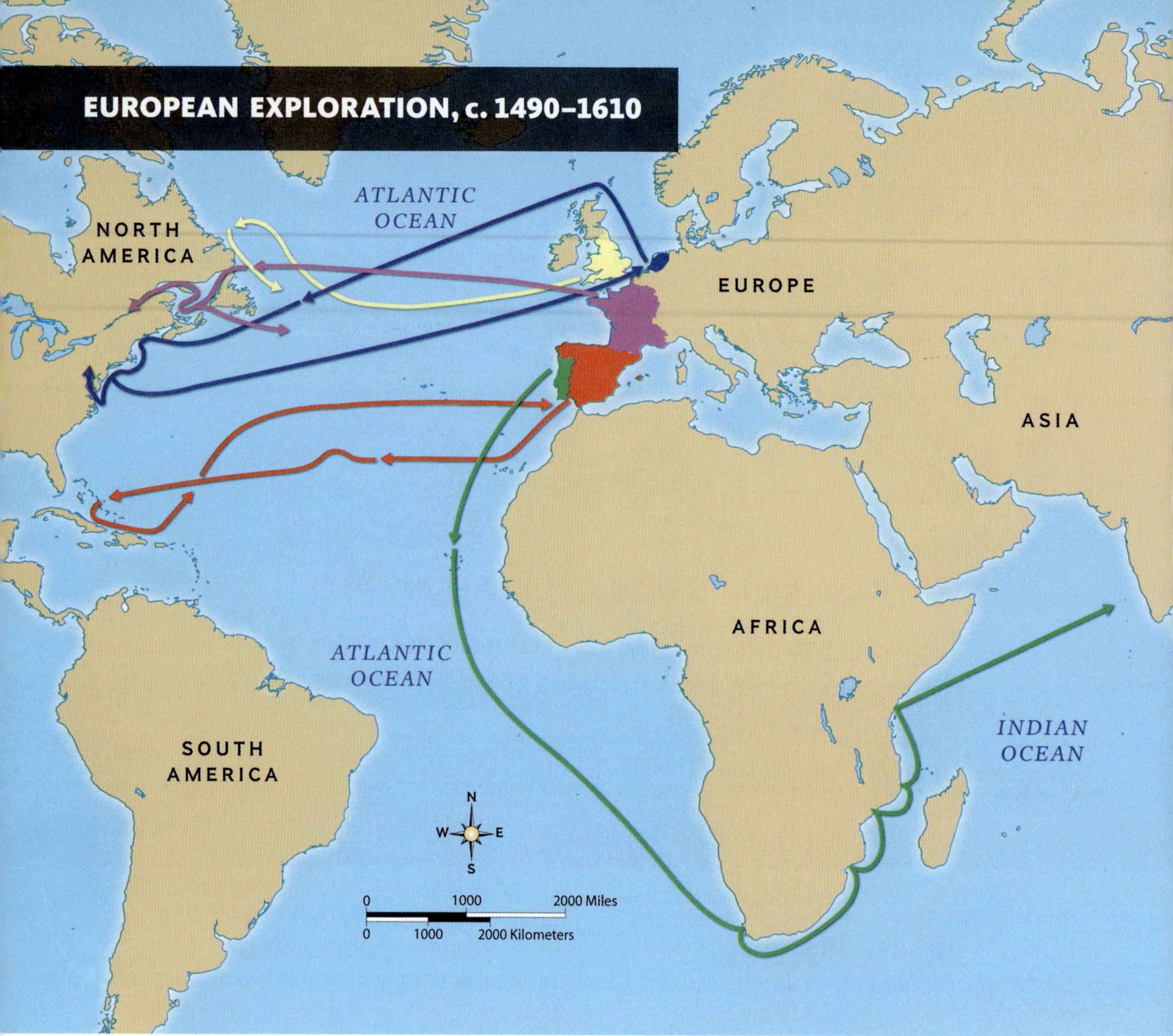
EUROPEAN EXPLORATION, c. 1490–1610
ATLANTIC OCEAN
NORTH AMERICA
EUROPE
ASIA
AFRICA
ATLANTIC OCEAN
INDIAN OCEAN
SOUTH AMERICA
N
W
E
S
0
1000
2000 Miles
0
1000
2000 Kilometers

The map above shows a few of the many voyages of exploration that European countries sponsored between the 1400s and 1700s. The chart below describes the voyages shown on the map.

Sponsoring Country	Voyage
Spain	**1492** Italian navigator Christopher Columbus lands in the Americas while searching for a western sea route to Asia.
Portugal	**1497–1498** Portuguese explorer Vasco da Gama sails to India, establishing a direct sea route to Asia.
England	**1497** Italian explorer John Cabot tries to find a northwest passage through North America to Asia. He paves the way for England's colonization of North America.
France	**1535** French navigator Jacques Cartier explores the St. Lawrence River, in what is now Canada, hoping it will lead to Asia.
Netherlands	**1609** English explorer Henry Hudson sails to the New World and explores the river that will later be named after him.

2.1

An Expanding World

The key to successful trading is being able to supply what people want. In the 1400s, Europeans wanted Asian spices. But Ottoman Turks controlled the trade routes to Asia, and they charged high prices. European rulers and merchants knew that whoever found an alternative sea route to Asia would become fabulously wealthy.

MAIN IDEA

The desire to control trade encouraged Europeans to explore the world.

THE PUSH TO EXPLORE

For about a thousand years after the fall of the Roman Empire, western Europeans tended to view the rest of the world with hostility and fear. By about 1450, however, the time was right for change. The Renaissance encouraged a spirit of adventure and inspired curiosity about the world. Western Europe's population was booming. Above all, merchants were impatient to find new trading opportunities—and new markets.

In the 1400s, many of Europe's most valuable luxuries, including silk and spices, came from Asia. However, the Ottoman Empire controlled the trade routes. Europe's leaders and merchants wanted a share of this profitable trade, so they sponsored numerous sailing expeditions to search for an alternative sea route to Asia.

AIDS TO EXPLORATION

By 1450, important advances in shipbuilding had made longer sea journeys possible. The Portuguese had pioneered ocean-going ships called **caravels**, which were fast, sturdy, and easy to maneuver. The caravel had triangular sails that enabled it to sail effectively against the wind, which earlier sailing ships could not do.

Along with advances in shipbuilding came improvements in navigational techniques. Greater knowledge of astronomy allowed sailors to steer a course by the stars. In addition, such technological tools as the astrolabe, quadrant, and magnetic compass further improved navigation. These tools also helped explorers draw more accurate maps of their travels.

With the new ability to travel to distant parts of the world, European explorers undertook numerous expeditions in a period of time that came to be known as the Age of Exploration. In less than a century, Europeans greatly extended their geographic knowledge of the continents of Europe, Africa, and Asia—and then North and South America. Their travels brought together the people of many different lands.

REVIEW & ASSESS

1. **READING CHECK** Why did Europeans want to find a sea route from Europe to Asia?
2. **IDENTIFY MAIN IDEAS AND DETAILS** What advances made long sea voyages possible in the 1400s?
3. **INTERPRET MAPS** Which explorer found a direct sea route to Asia? Describe the route.

2.2 Exploration and Colonization

Pedro is just 16 years old when he joins an expedition to sail across the Atlantic Ocean. Bringing just the clothes he's wearing, he climbs aboard a wooden ship to sail off to . . . he's not sure exactly where. He has no idea when he will return. He's excited—and scared, much like the other sailors on European expeditions.

MAIN IDEA

During the Age of Exploration, five western European nations competed for trade, land, and riches.

COMPETITION AMONG NATIONS

Portugal, a great seafaring nation, took the lead in European exploration. In 1419, **Prince Henry the Navigator**, the son of Portugal's king, established a navigation school in Portugal. He began encouraging sailors to explore Africa's western coast, where they soon established trading posts. The Portuguese discovered an eastern sea route to India in 1498 and eventually established a profitable Asian trade.

In 1492, Spain's monarchs **Ferdinand and Isabella** funded an expedition, led by the Italian navigator **Christopher Columbus**, to find a sea route to Asia by sailing west across the Atlantic Ocean. Although the expedition failed to achieve its goal, reaching the Americas proved to be of great benefit to Spain. The Spanish established colonies in the Caribbean and conquered large areas of the Americas. As you know, a **colony** is a group of people who settle in a new land but keep ties to their native country.

Portugal and Spain developed a heated **rivalry**, or competition, over who would control the newly encountered lands. In 1494, Portugal and Spain agreed to the Treaty of Tordesillas (tawr-day-SEE-yahs) to settle their dispute. The treaty drew an imaginary line through the Atlantic Ocean from north to south. Portugal received the easterly lands, including Brazil, while Spain would receive any newly encountered lands to the west.

The English, Dutch, and French entered the competition for trade and new lands later. The English formed the East India Company in 1600 and established trading posts in India. They established colonies in North America as well. In 1602, the Dutch founded the **Dutch East India Company** to compete for trade in the Indian Ocean. The French joined the exploration race largely to compete with their English rivals.

IMPACT OF EXPLORATION

European exploration changed the world. Trade increased greatly. At trading posts, both goods and ideas were readily exchanged. As trading posts developed into colonies, more and more people moved from Europe to establish farms, towns, and cities in Asia, Africa, and the Americas. These colonies enriched the mother countries, which claimed land and **exploited**, or used to their own advantage, local resources and native people. The colonists brought European culture to places all over the world. As the Age of Exploration turned into a competition for land and riches, Europeans ended up controlling much of the world.

SAILING ON A CARAVEL

The caravel was one kind of ship used by early explorers, including Christopher Columbus. The ship was small, fast, and easy to maneuver. It could sail about 100 miles a day and held a crew of about 20 sailors.

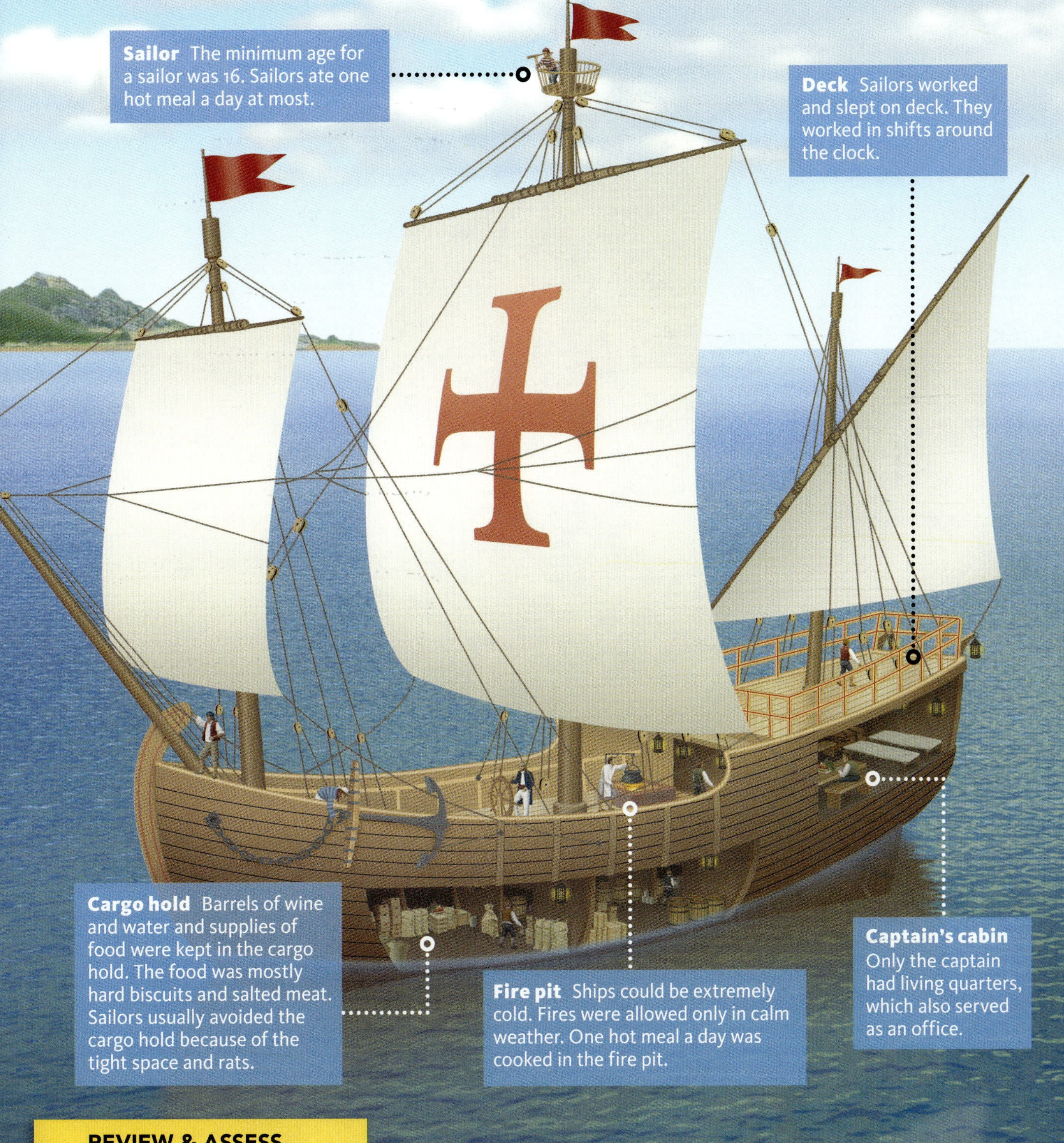

Sailor The minimum age for a sailor was 16. Sailors ate one hot meal a day at most.
Deck Sailors worked and slept on deck. They worked in shifts around the clock.
Cargo hold Barrels of wine and water and supplies of food were kept in the cargo hold. The food was mostly hard biscuits and salted meat. Sailors usually avoided the cargo hold because of the tight space and rats.
Fire pit Ships could be extremely cold. Fires were allowed only in calm weather. One hot meal a day was cooked in the fire pit.
Captain's cabin Only the captain had living quarters, which also served as an office.

REVIEW & ASSESS

1. **READING CHECK** How did the reasons for European exploration change over time?
2. **ANALYZE CAUSE AND EFFECT** What were some major effects of European exploration?
3. **INTERPRET VISUALS** What do you think were the best and worst parts of a sailor's life on a caravel?

2.3 MOMENTS IN HISTORY
Columbus Discovers the New World

OCTOBER 12, 1492

Around 2:00 a.m. on a moonlit night, the Spanish sailor Rodrigo de Triana yelled out the words his fellow sailors were so desperate to hear: "Land! Land!" The three small ships of Christopher Columbus's fleet had finally reached land. But what land? Columbus was aiming for Asia. Convinced that he'd reached it, he called the lands the West Indies and the natives Indians. In fact, Columbus had massively underestimated the size of the planet. He had unexpectedly found an area unknown to Europeans: the Americas or New World. The precise location of this landfall remains a mystery. One possibility is an island in the Bahamas called Samana Cay, which is shown above.

2.4 DOCUMENT-BASED QUESTION

A New World

During the European Age of Exploration, the leaders of many expeditions kept journals, in which they wrote detailed accounts of their voyages. Christopher Columbus kept such a journal. The voyages of Columbus and other explorers changed Europeans' view of the world—and their maps.

These ships are replicas of the *Pinta*, the *Santa María*, and the *Niña*, the three ships that made up Columbus's expedition in 1492.

DOCUMENT ONE

Primary Source: Journal

from *The Journal of Christopher Columbus*

Christopher Columbus's original journal from his historic voyage in 1492 was lost. Then, in 1790, a full copy was found in the writings of the Spanish historian Bartolomé de Las Casas. In this excerpt from the journal, Columbus addresses his sponsors, the Spanish monarchs Ferdinand and Isabella. He discusses the direction of his voyage and how he intends to record the voyage.

CONSTRUCTED RESPONSE What land was Columbus trying to reach, and what was unusual about his route?

> Your Highnesses . . . determined to send me, Christopher Columbus, to the above-mentioned countries of India . . . and furthermore directed that I should not proceed by land to the East, as is customary, but by a Westerly route, in which direction we have hitherto no certain evidence that any one has gone . . . Moreover, Sovereign Princes, besides describing every night the occurrences of the day, and every day those of the preceding night, I intend to draw up a nautical chart, which shall contain the several parts of the ocean and land in their proper situations; and also to compose a book to represent the whole by picture with latitudes and longitudes.

DOCUMENT TWO

Primary Source: Map

Map from 1513

This map by the German mapmaker Martin Waldseemüller was published in 1513. It was the first printed map to include a part of the New World. It highlights the importance of the islands of the Caribbean. The area labeled with the Latin words *terra incognita*, meaning "unknown land," is present-day Brazil.

CONSTRUCTED RESPONSE What does this map demonstrate about European knowledge of the Western Hemisphere in 1513?

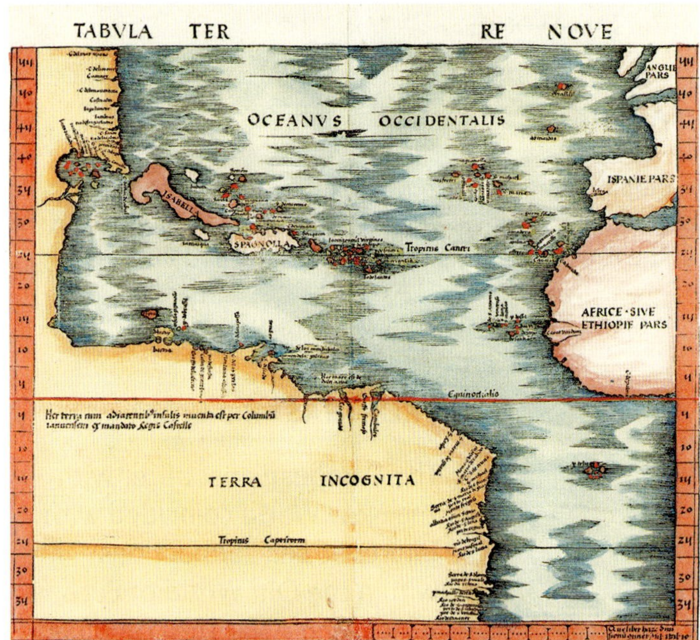

TABVLA TER RE NOVE
OCEANVS OCCIDENTALIS
ANGLIE PARS
ISPANIE PARS
ISABELLA
SPAGNOLLA
Tropicus Cancri
AFRICE·SIVE ETHIOPIE PARS
Equinoctialis
TERRA INCOGNITA
Tropicus Capricorni

SYNTHESIZE & WRITE

1. **REVIEW** Review what you have learned about the Age of Exploration.
2. **RECALL** Think about your responses to the constructed response questions above.
3. **CONSTRUCT** Write a topic sentence that answers this question: How did European voyages lead to unexpected results?
4. **WRITE** Using evidence from the documents, write an informative paragraph that supports your topic sentence.

2.5 The Columbian Exchange

For lunch, a girl in the United States eats an apple and a roast beef sandwich on wheat bread. A boy in Ireland chows down on a turkey-and-tomato sandwich and some french fries. In 1500, neither person could have eaten this lunch. The two meals are a result of the **Columbian Exchange**—a transfer of foods, plants, animals, and diseases between the Old and New Worlds.

MAIN IDEA

A global exchange of foods, plants, animals, and diseases occurred in the period after Columbus arrived in the Americas, bringing both benefits and disaster.

EUROPEAN DISEASES

European diseases killed more Native Americans than warfare. The native population of Central America fell from about 25 million to 2.5 million between 1519 and 1565 due to disease.

FROM EAST TO WEST

The European encounter with the New World coincided with improved sea connections within the Old World of Europe, Africa, and Asia. The combined impact was enormous. Places and people that were once isolated from one another became part of a global exchange network. The contact and trade between these far-flung lands helped some people—and harmed others.

European explorers and colonists wanted to re-create their European lifestyles in the New World. They introduced such familiar foods as wheat, barley, oats, grapes, apples, citrus fruits, and olives. They also brought cattle, sheep, pigs, goats, chickens, and horses. These plants and animals flourished in the Americas. Wheat could be grown in places where native crops could not, and it became one of North America's most important crops. The use of horses changed warfare and transportation in the Americas, while other livestock provided new sources of food.

Europeans also brought crops from Africa and Asia to the Americas. These crops included bananas, coffee beans, and sugarcane. Sugarcane grew especially well in the Caribbean climate. Using slave labor, European growers were able to harvest the sugar and sell it at a huge profit in Europe.

Unfortunately, Europeans also introduced deadly new diseases to the Americas. Native people had no resistance against such diseases as measles, malaria, and **smallpox**. Smallpox proved to be especially deadly, killing millions of native people across the Americas. Caused by a virus, smallpox is highly contagious. It produces a high fever and small blisters on the skin that leave pitted scars. The virus would finally be eradicated, or eliminated, in the United States in the 1900s.

FROM WEST TO EAST

In the Columbian Exchange, animals and plants also traveled from the Americas to Europe and Africa. Explorers returned to Europe with such exotic foods as turkeys, peppers, corn, tomatoes, potatoes, beans, and squashes. Many of these foods eventually became

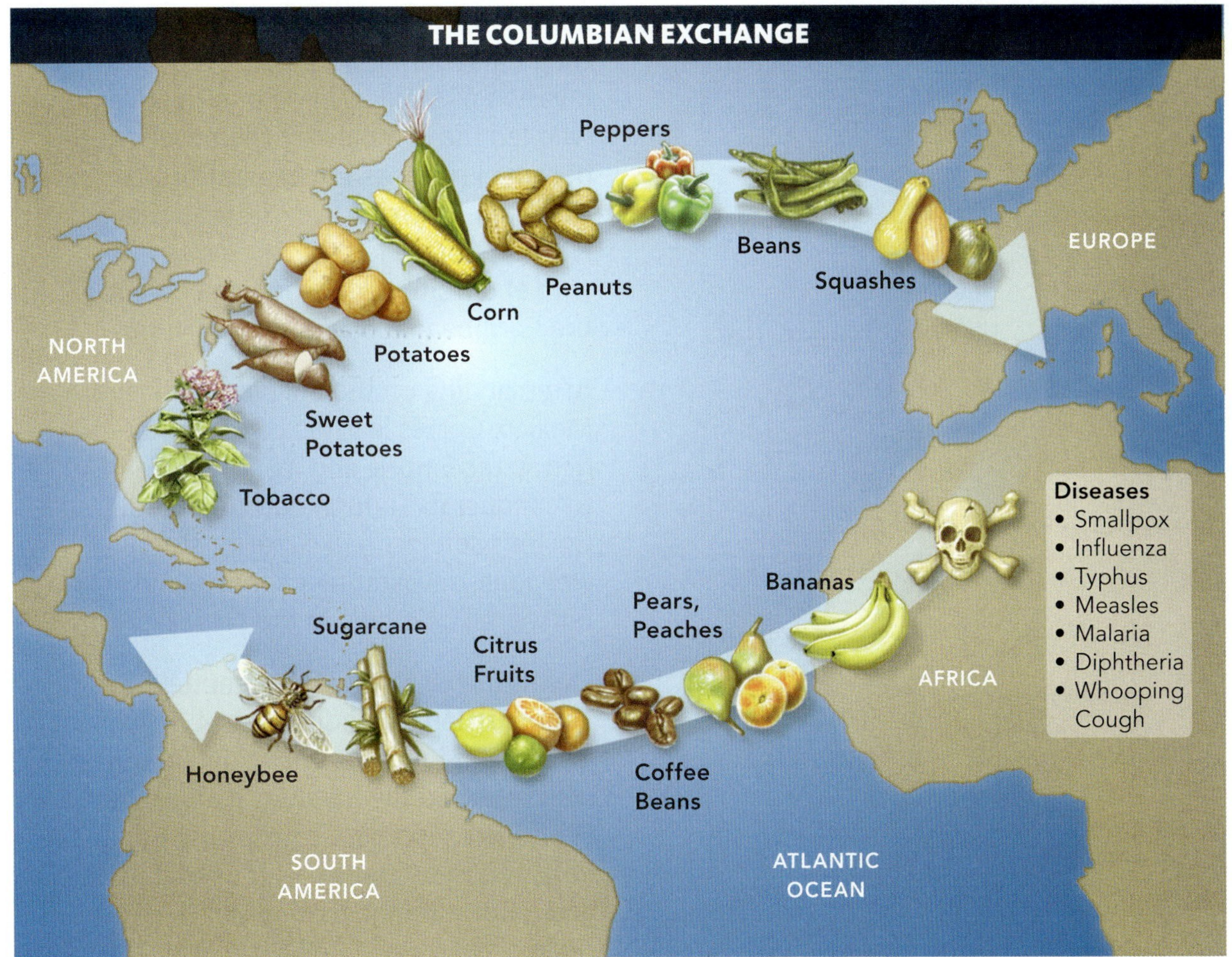
THE COLUMBIAN EXCHANGE
Peppers
Peanuts
Corn
Potatoes
Sweet Potatoes
Tobacco
Beans
Squashes
EUROPE
NORTH AMERICA
Diseases
• Smallpox
• Influenza
• Typhus
• Measles
• Malaria
• Diphtheria
• Whooping Cough
Bananas
Pears, Peaches
Citrus Fruits
Sugarcane
Honeybee
Coffee Beans
AFRICA
SOUTH AMERICA
ATLANTIC OCEAN

a regular part of European diets. Other imports were considered luxuries, including tobacco, vanilla, and cacao beans. Vanilla was used as a flavoring, while cacao beans were used to make chocolate drinks, which were sweetened with imported sugar.

The New World also contributed an important medicine called **quinine** to the Old World. Europeans learned about quinine, which comes from the bark of a tree in South America, in the 1600s. For about 300 years, it served as the only effective remedy for malaria, which is carried by mosquitoes. Quinine's use as a treatment for malaria benefitted millions of people and allowed Europeans to colonize malaria-ridden areas of the world.

For better or worse, the Columbian Exchange affected the lives of people throughout the world. About 30 percent of the foods eaten today originated in the Americas. A greater variety of foods helped improve the nutrition of people around the world. However, the effect of the Columbian Exchange on native populations in the Americas was disastrous.

REVIEW & ASSESS

1. **READING CHECK** How did the Columbian Exchange benefit Europeans?
2. **ANALYZE CAUSE AND EFFECT** Why was the Columbian Exchange disastrous for Native Americans?
3. **INTERPRET MAPS** What foods do you eat that came to the Americas in the Columbian Exchange?

3.1 The Spanish Conquest

Two Aztec messengers run to carry an important message to their king: Strangers have invaded their land. The invaders have white skin that looks like that of a ghost. They wear clothes that cover their entire bodies. They sit on deer that carry them wherever they want to go. They have a weapon that shoots a ball of stone, which comes out raining fire and shooting sparks. The messengers' report fills the Aztec king with terror.

MAIN IDEA

Spain created a large American empire that covered parts of the Caribbean and Central and South America by the mid-1500s.

CORTÉS AND THE AZTEC

As you learned earlier, the Treaty of Tordesillas divided the New World between Spain and Portugal. Spain was quick to explore and exploit its new territory. The Spanish established important colonies on several Caribbean islands, including what are now Haiti, the Dominican Republic, and Cuba. Although these islands provided valuable agricultural land, they did not supply the gold so coveted by the Europeans.

Seeking gold, in 1519 the Spanish launched their most daring conquest ever—the invasion of Mexico. The Spanish adventurers who led the conquest of the Americas became known as **conquistadors** (kahn-KEES-tuh-dawrs). A conquistador named **Hernán Cortés** led the invasion of Mexico with about 500 men who had come to the Caribbean to make their fortunes.

After landing on the uncharted coast of Mexico, Cortés learned of the fabulously rich Aztec Empire and marched inland to conquer it. Though outnumbered, Cortés's soldiers had superior steel weapons, devastating cannons, and horses, all unknown in the New World.

On his march to the Aztec capital of **Tenochtitlán** (tay-nohch-teet-LAHN), Cortés was joined by many native tribes who resented the harsh rule of the Aztec. With their support, Cortés fought and defeated the Aztec in a series of battles and a final dramatic siege that destroyed the magnificent city of Tenochtitlán. Its ruins lie buried under what is now Mexico City. The Spanish gained what they wanted—Aztec gold and silver—and they ruled Mexico for the next 300 years.

PIZARRO AND THE INCA

With Mexico conquered, the Spanish then pushed into South America. Sometime between 1530 and 1532, the conquistador **Francisco Pizarro** set off to invade the reportedly rich land of Biru, or what is now Peru. The huge and well-organized Inca Empire was based in Peru.

Pizarro's army had fewer than 200 men, but their steel weapons and horses gave them a deadly advantage. So did their cruelty. When Pizarro arrived, he found the Inca Empire weakened by smallpox and a bitter civil war. Pizarro arranged a meeting with the newly appointed Inca emperor, **Atahualpa** (ah-tah-WAHL-pah), but he had laid a dangerous trap.

Landing of the Spanish in Veracruz, Diego Rivera, 1951

Critical Viewing This mural by the Mexican artist Diego Rivera depicts the Spanish conquest of Mexico. How would you describe the Spaniards' treatment of the native people?

Although Atahualpa was accompanied by between 3,000 and 5,000 attendants, the Spanish cavalry cut a path to the Inca emperor and captured him. They then slaughtered many of his stunned and unarmed followers.

Atahualpa offered the Spanish a roomful of gold and two rooms of silver in exchange for his release. However, after obtaining the gold and silver, the Spanish killed the Inca ruler.

The Spanish went on to conquer much of the vast Inca Empire, which stretched from Ecuador into central Chile. The Inca continued to resist the Spanish until 1572, when the Spanish executed the last Inca ruler. Through military conquest, the Spanish built a large empire that helped make Spain the richest and most powerful country in the world in the 1500s. The Spanish continued to rule over much of South America for centuries.

REVIEW & ASSESS

1. **READING CHECK** What drove the Spanish to invade and conquer large areas of the Americas?
2. **COMPARE AND CONTRAST** How was Pizarro's conquest of the Inca similar to Cortés's conquest of the Aztec?
3. **MAKE INFERENCES** Why were small numbers of the Spanish able to conquer large areas of the Americas?

3.2 Portugal's Empire

On the sand of an African beach, your crew carries a huge stone cross and sets it upright. Its design and words stake Portugal's claim to this land where your crew has arrived. Almost all Portuguese explorers carry crosses like the one you've just erected here. These crosses dot the coasts of Africa and other lands.

MAIN IDEA

Portugal built a powerful trading empire that extended along the coast of Africa and reached into areas of the Indian Ocean and South America.

A TRADE NETWORK

In the Middle Ages, Portugal was a relatively small and undeveloped country. However, by focusing on maritime exploration and trade, the country developed a powerful commercial empire by the 1500s.

Beginning in 1415, Portugal's kings encouraged seafarers to explore the west coast of Africa, hoping to find an easterly sea route to tap into the spice trade with Asia. Portuguese explorers systematically advanced along Africa's coastline. By 1460, they had established trading posts that were sending spices, gold, and slaves to European markets.

Portugal's explorers continued around the southern tip of Africa, along its eastern coast, and across the Indian Ocean. They reached India itself in 1498. However, the Muslim merchants who had controlled the region's trade for centuries did not welcome the Portuguese. Portugal fought to gain access to the Indian Ocean trade. With bigger, stronger, and better-armed ships, the Portuguese defeated the Muslim traders.

The Portuguese built strongly fortified trading posts to control important areas, including Goa and Calicut in India and Macao in China. By the 1540s, the Portuguese had reached Japan and completely dominated the Indian Ocean trade. They were unrivaled until the Dutch and English muscled into the Indian Ocean trade in the early 1600s.

SUGAR, GOLD, AND DIAMONDS

The Portuguese stumbled across Brazil when they sailed too far west on a trip to India. In 1500, the Portuguese explorer **Pedro Álvares Cabral** sighted the coast of Brazil and landed for a short time to stake Portugal's claim to the area.

At first, Portugal had limited interest in Brazil, which provided little more than brazilwood, a source of red dye. But after the French began trading with Brazil's native people, Portugal decided to establish a colony to assert its authority over the area. Brazil's scattered tribes offered no organized resistance. Portugal established its first Brazilian colony in 1532 and divided the colony into administrative districts with a governor in charge.

The Portuguese kings encouraged Brazilian colonists to set up large farms, called **plantations**, for growing sugarcane, a plant used to make sugar. In the 1500s, sugar was a rare luxury in Europe, and Portugal expected to make huge profits from its import. However, growing and processing sugarcane was complex and labor-intensive. Sugarcane producers used a huge number of slaves to perform the

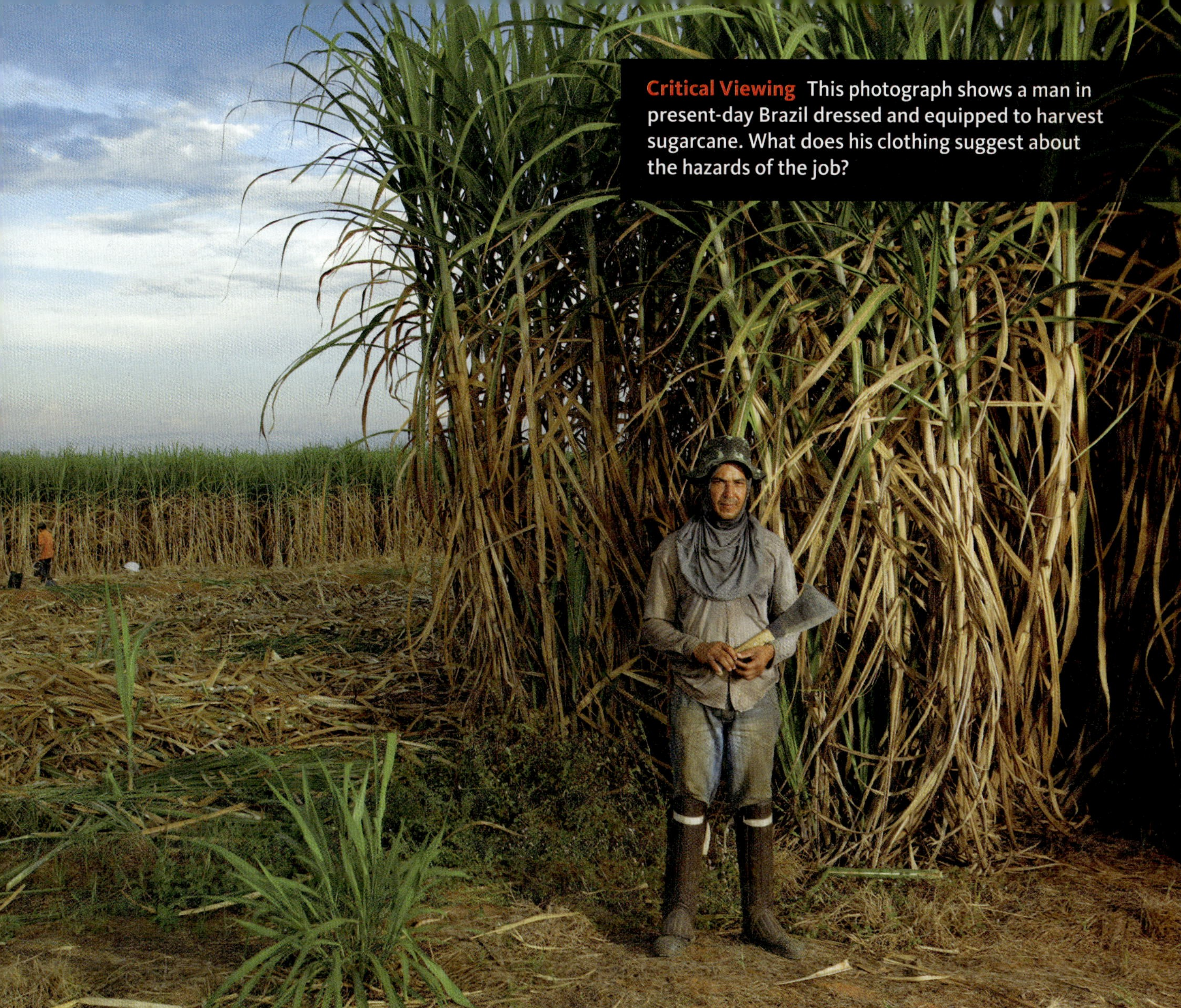

Critical Viewing This photograph shows a man in present-day Brazil dressed and equipped to harvest sugarcane. What does his clothing suggest about the hazards of the job?

hard and often dangerous work. Over the course of 300 years, Brazil would import nearly 4 million slaves from West Africa.

Then, in 1695, huge quantities of gold were discovered in Brazil, sparking a gold rush. By 1760, gold rivaled sugar as Brazil's main export. The search for gold led to the discovery of diamonds in the 1720s, adding to the wealth that Portugal gained from Brazil. Almost all the wealth was made possible through a much bigger trade, however—the slave trade. You'll learn more about the Atlantic slave trade in the next lesson.

REVIEW & ASSESS

1. **READING CHECK** How was the relatively small country of Portugal able to build a powerful trading empire?
2. **DRAW CONCLUSIONS** Why did Portuguese kings encourage colonists in Brazil to establish plantations for growing sugarcane?
3. **ANALYZE CAUSE AND EFFECT** How did the sugar trade contribute to the development and growth of the slave trade?

3.3 The Atlantic Slave Trade

You are young and strong. You work more than 18 hours a day, chopping stalks of sugarcane with a machete and loading the stalks onto carts. If you stop to rest, you will be beaten. You're thirsty, but you cannot ask for water. All your muscles ache, and your hands are blistered. You are a slave on a sugarcane plantation in Brazil in 1588. You have no way to escape.

MAIN IDEA

To supply labor on plantations in the New World, Europeans imported and enslaved millions of Africans.

SLAVE LABOR

To increase their profits, the European plantations in the New World wanted a large supply of cheap workers. At first, Europeans believed they could use Native Americans to meet their labor needs. But disease and warfare killed millions of Native Americans, and many who were forced into labor easily escaped into the familiar countryside.

Beginning in the mid-1450s, the Portuguese and Spanish solved the labor-shortage problem by buying and transporting slaves from West Africa. The West Africans were more resistant to European diseases, and they could not easily escape into lands that were largely unknown to them.

Slavery was common in West Africa, and local rulers grew rich by kidnapping and selling their enemies to Europeans. In return for the captives, the rulers received gold, trinkets, and guns. They used the guns to capture more slaves. By 1650, more than 40 trading posts on Africa's west coast were sending slaves to the New World.

These trading posts formed part of a transatlantic trading network known as the **triangular trade**. On the first leg of the triangle, European ships carried cheap manufactured goods to West Africa, where they were used to buy slaves. On the second or middle leg of the triangle, these slaves were brought to the Americas, where they were sold for a huge profit. On the third leg of the triangle, the slave ships returned to Europe laden with valuable sugar, tobacco, coffee, and cotton.

The triangular trade was a massive moneymaking business. Major participating countries—such as Portugal, Spain, Great Britain, France, and the Netherlands—were prepared to fight wars to secure their share of the trade.

IMPACT OF THE SLAVE TRADE

Europeans treated African slaves as property, not people. The slaves had no rights, and their owners could treat them any way they wanted. This system of slavery was based on both custom and **racism**, the belief that some races are better than others. Europeans genuinely believed that they were superior to Africans in every way. Indeed, they justified slavery as a way of civilizing Africans.

The conditions on the slave ships were especially brutal. Up to 600 slaves were chained together in dark, overcrowded holds, where it was impossible to move and difficult to even breathe. The crossing from Africa to the Americas took at least

THE MIDDLE PASSAGE

This illustration shows how enslaved Africans were transported from Africa to the Americas on a European slave ship. The journey could take up to 90 days, depending on the weather.

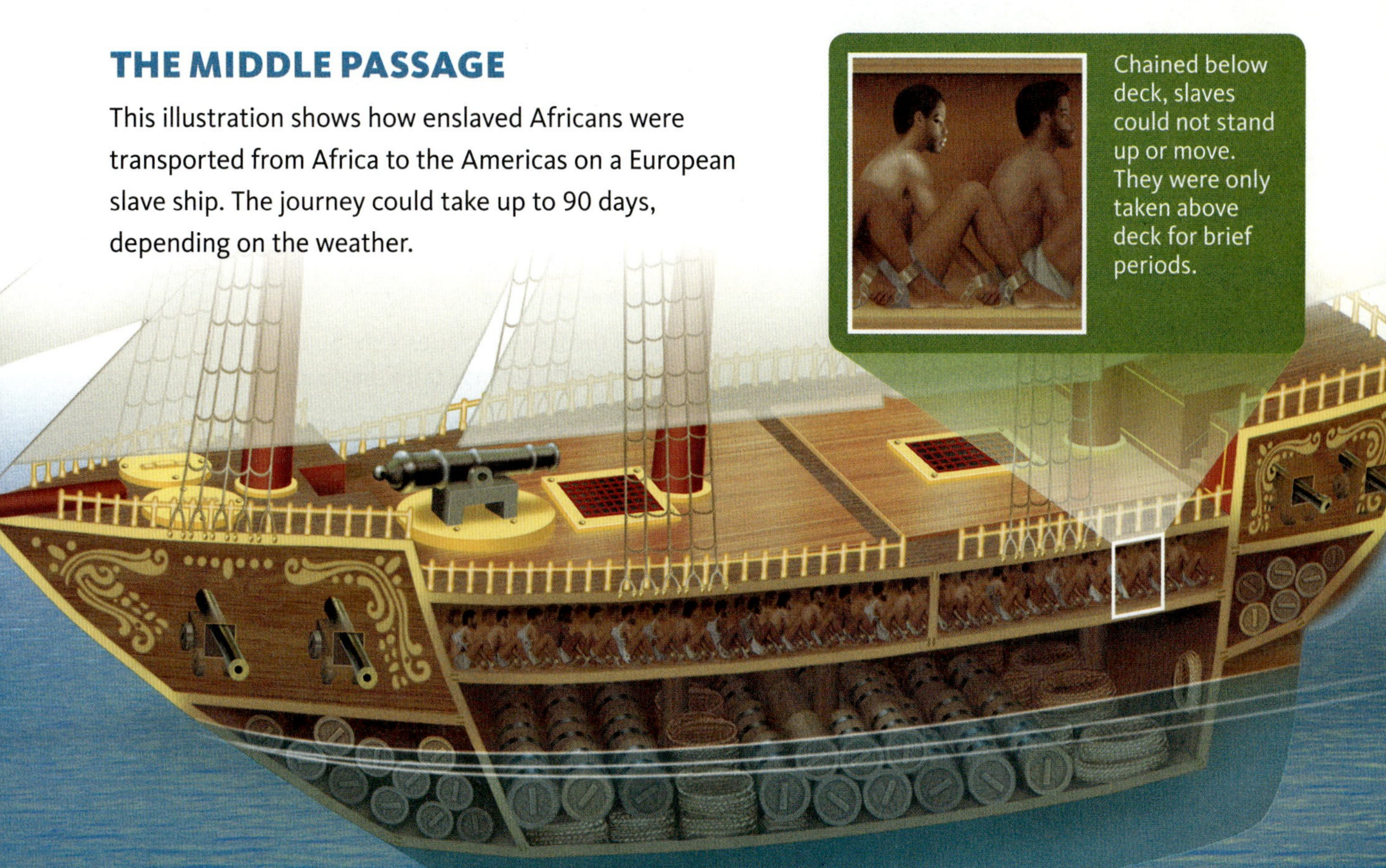

Chained below deck, slaves could not stand up or move. They were only taken above deck for brief periods.

three weeks and often as long as three months. The trip became known as the **Middle Passage** because it was considered the middle leg of the triangular trade. An estimated 13 to 20 percent of slaves died on the voyage from hunger, thirst, disease, suffocation, drowning, and abuse.

For many slaves, conditions in the colonies were little better than on the ships. Some slaveholders believed it was more cost-effective to replace overworked slaves who died than it was to improve conditions so that slaves lived and worked longer. On sugar plantations, death rates were especially high due to overwork, poor nutrition, harsh treatment, and disease. But colonists grew rich by using slaves to produce sugar, tobacco, coffee, and cotton and to mine gold, silver, and diamonds.

The number of people forced into slavery in the transatlantic slave trade is staggering. Slave traders took entire villages and ethnic groups in Africa, destroying whole communities and cultures. Over a period of about 360 years, from 1501 to 1867, more than 12 million Africans were forced into slavery. It was the largest forced migration of people in history.

REVIEW & ASSESS

1. **READING CHECK** How did the transatlantic slave trade affect Africans and Europeans?
2. **IDENTIFY PROBLEMS AND SOLUTIONS** Instead of using slaves, how might Europeans have solved their labor-shortage problem in the New World?
3. **ANALYZE VISUALS** What hardships did African slaves endure on the Middle Passage?

CHAPTER

23 Review

VOCABULARY

Write the vocabulary word that completes each of the following sentences.

1. The ______ incorrectly states that Earth is at the center of the universe.
2. In 1543, Copernicus published the controversial ______, which stated that the sun was the center of the universe.
3. The purpose of an experiment is to test an explanation that is called a ______.
4. Many European explorers sailed on fast, maneuverable ships called ______.
5. Spanish ______ defeated the Aztec and Inca empires.
6. Portuguese colonists in Brazil grew sugarcane on large farms called ______ .
7. In the ______, trade ships traveled from Europe to West Africa to the Americas and back to Europe.

READING STRATEGY

8. **MAKE INFERENCES** Complete your chart to make inferences about the relationship between the Scientific Revolution and European exploration. Then answer the question.

I Learned	My Inference
Observatories helped astronomers accurately plot the locations of stars, which led to better navigation.	Better navigation made it easier for ships to travel far from home.

How did the Scientific Revolution influence European exploration?

MAIN IDEAS

Answer the following questions. Support your answers with evidence from the chapter.

9. What were the scientific theories of the ancient Greeks based on? **LESSON 1.1**
10. What impact did the invention of the microscope have on scientific discovery? **LESSON 1.2**
11. How did the ideas of Sir Francis Bacon affect the practice of science? **LESSON 1.3**
12. What motivated Europeans to explore the world in the mid-1400s? **LESSON 2.1**
13. How did Prince Henry the Navigator promote exploration in the 1400s? **LESSON 2.2**
14. What were some of the new foods introduced to Europe as part of the Columbian Exchange? **LESSON 2.5**
15. Why did the Spanish invade and conquer large areas of Central and South America? **LESSON 3.1**
16. Why did Europeans ship millions of enslaved Africans to the New World? **LESSON 3.3**

CRITICAL THINKING

Answer the following questions. Support your answers with evidence from the chapter.

17. **COMPARE AND CONTRAST** How did the geocentric and heliocentric theories of the universe differ?
18. **MAKE INFERENCES** What did Descartes mean when he said, "I think, therefore I am"?
19. **DRAW CONCLUSIONS** Why was the first voyage of Christopher Columbus important?
20. **ANALYZE CAUSE AND EFFECT** How did the Atlantic slave trade affect African families, communities, and cultures?
21. **YOU DECIDE** Was the Columbian Exchange mainly good or bad for the native people in the Americas? Explain your opinion.

INTERPRET VISUALS

Look closely at the triangular trade map. Then answer the questions that follow.

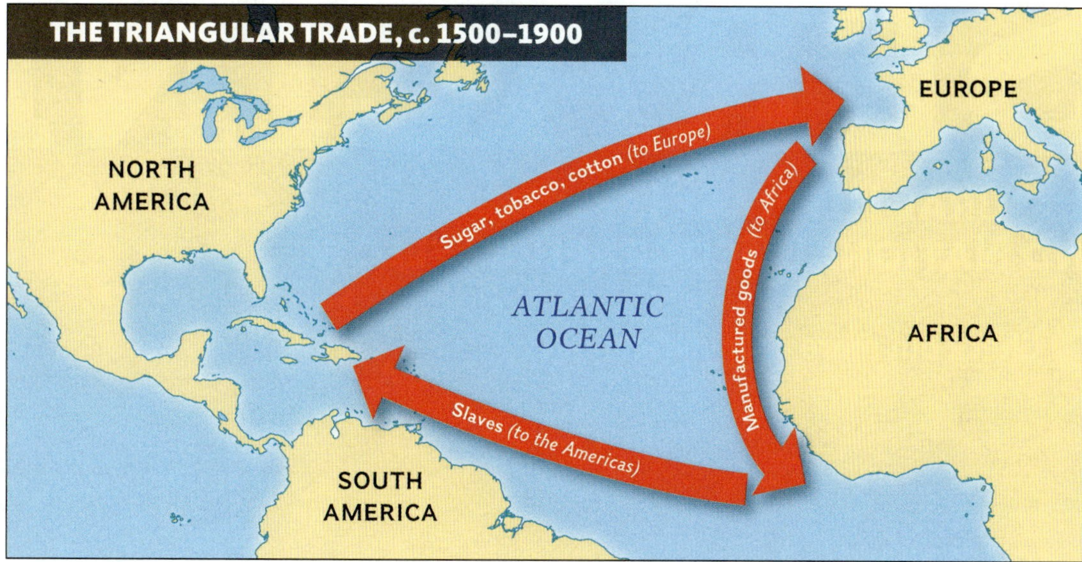
THE TRIANGULAR TRADE, c. 1500–1900
EUROPE
NORTH AMERICA
Sugar, tobacco, cotton (to Europe)
Manufactured goods (to Africa)
ATLANTIC OCEAN
AFRICA
Slaves (to the Americas)
SOUTH AMERICA

22. What goods were shipped from Europe to Africa and exchanged for slaves?

23. Why is the route shown on the map referred to as the triangular trade?

ANALYZE SOURCES

Olaudah Equiano, the son of a village leader in the African kingdom of Benin, was captured and sold into slavery at the age of 11. He later gained his freedom and, in 1789, wrote his autobiography, *The Interesting Narrative of the Life of Olaudah Equiano.* In this excerpt from the autobiography, Equiano describes his voyage on the Middle Passage.

> The closeness of the place, and the heat of the climate, added to the number in the ship, which was so crowded that each had scarcely room to turn himself, almost suffocated us. This produced copious perspirations [a lot of sweat], so that the air soon became unfit for respiration, from a variety of loathsome smells, and brought on a sickness among the slaves, of which many died.

24. How would you describe the treatment of enslaved Africans on the Middle Passage?

WRITE ABOUT HISTORY

25. INFORMATIVE Write an informative paragraph for other students explaining how scientific rationalism changed Europeans' basic approach to science.

TIPS

- Take notes from Lessons 1.1, 1.2, and 1.3 on early Europeans' approach to science.
- State a main idea on how scientific rationalism affected Europeans' practice of science.
- Develop the paragraph with relevant, well-chosen facts, concrete details, or examples about early Europeans' approach to science.
- Use appropriate transitions, such as *because, in contrast,* or *as a result,* to clarify the relationships among ideas.
- Use at least two vocabulary terms from the chapter.
- Provide a concluding sentence that follows from and supports the information presented.

ON LOCATION WITH

Maurizio SERACINI

CULTURAL HERITAGE ENGINEER AND NATIONAL GEOGRAPHIC FELLOW

Check out more on myNGconnect

It's not just about the art in museums for Maurizio Seracini, an Italian art expert who uses technology to seek out long-hidden masterpieces no one has seen for centuries.

BELOW THE PAINT

I love the way that technology is helping to write new pages of our history, find hidden treasures, and prove or disprove theories. In art history, for example, new technology has shown that Leonardo da Vinci's acclaimed painting *The Adoration of the Magi* is much more than it appears. It proves that while Leonardo drew the painting's original design, it was actually painted much later by an unknown and inferior artist who changed Leonardo's layout considerably. Technology allows us to peer through the layers of brown paint to reveal over 70 wonderful new images sketched by Leonardo that have not been seen for centuries.

Seracini carefully uses a scope with a tiny camera to examine the surface behind a fresco painted by Vasari.

EVOLVING TECHNOLOGY

Momentous discoveries like this take time and patience. In 1975, I was asked to use technology to solve a 500-year-old mystery about a lost Leonardo da Vinci masterpiece, *The Battle of Anghiari*. This mural painting was supposed to have been painted on the wall of a hall in the Palazzo Vecchio in Florence, Italy. Decades later, the hall was rebuilt and redecorated by another artist, Vasari, and Leonardo's celebrated masterpiece disappeared. We wanted to know if it was gone or if some of it was still there, but the technology of the 1970s wasn't sophisticated enough to tell.

In 2000, we were able to use 3-D modeling and thermography to reconstruct the hall at the time of Leonardo. We also learned that in similar projects, Vasari had saved existing artworks by constructing a brick wall in front of them and leaving a small air gap. Maybe Vasari had done the same thing for *The Battle of Anghiari*? We used sophisticated radio antennas to find air gaps in the area where we believed the mural was painted—directly behind a wall with a Vasari fresco on it. But the need to preserve Vasari's work stopped any further investigation.

We returned with new technology in 2011: an endoscope with a 4mm camera, to explore the wall behind the Vasari fresco. We found fragments of red, black, and beige paint. Since we know that no other artist painted on that wall before Vasari sealed it up, those pigments are likely related to mural painting and most likely to da Vinci. If so, we have found one of the most highly praised works of art ever—by far Leonardo's most important commission and the one that made him the top artistic influence of his time.

WHY STUDY HISTORY ?

“What we are doing is rediscovering the spirit of the Renaissance; we are blending art and science. As long as we live a life of *curiosity and passion*, there is a bit of Leonardo in all of us.” —Maurizio Seracini

NATIONAL GEOGRAPHIC

Brunelleschi's Dome

BY TOM MUELLER

Adapted from "Brunelleschi's Dome," by Tom Mueller, in *National Geographic*, February 2014

In 1418, the town fathers of Florence finally addressed a problem they'd been ignoring for decades: the enormous hole in the roof of their cathedral. They announced a contest to design the ideal dome, which would be the cathedral's crowning glory. Leading architects flocked to Florence and presented their ideas. One candidate named Filippo Brunelleschi promised to build not one but two domes, one nested inside the other. He refused to explain how he'd do this because he was afraid that a competitor would steal his ideas. Nevertheless, in 1420 the town fathers agreed to put Brunelleschi in charge of the dome project.

After he assembled the necessary tool kit, Brunelleschi began work on the dome, which he shaped with a series of stunning technical innovations. His double-shell design produced a structure that was far lighter than a solid dome of such size would have been. He also wove regular courses of herringbone brickwork, little known before his time, into the texture of the dome.

Throughout the years of construction, Brunelleschi oversaw the production of bricks of various dimensions and attended to the supply of choice stone and marble. He led an army of masons and stonecutters, carpenters, blacksmiths, and other craftsmen. When they were puzzled by some tricky construction detail, he'd shape a model out of wax or clay or carve up a turnip to illustrate what he wanted.

Brunelleschi and his workmen eventually did their victory dance. On March 25, 1436, the pope blessed the finished cathedral to the tolling of bells and cheering of proud Florentines. A decade later, workmen laid the cornerstone of the lantern, the decorative marble structure that Brunelleschi designed to top his masterpiece.

On April 15, 1446, the great architect died. He was buried in the crypt of the cathedral. A memorial plaque nearby celebrated his "divine intellect." These were high honors but fitting for the architect who had paved the way for the cultural and social revolutions of the Renaissance.

For more from National Geographic
Check out "Lady with a Secret" on myNGconnect

UNIT INQUIRY: MAP THE NEW WORLDVIEW

In this unit, you learned about Europe during the Middle Ages and the Renaissance. Based on your understanding of the text, what new ideas emerged during the Renaissance? How did these new ideas transform, or change, European culture?

ASSIGNMENT Create an idea map of the new worldview that emerged during the Renaissance because of humanism, an intellectual movement that emphasized the individual. The idea map should illustrate how humanism transformed medieval ideas about religion, philosophy, science, art, literature, and education. Be prepared to present your idea map and explain the overall impact of humanism to the class.

Plan As you create your idea map, think about European culture during the Middle Ages. Then think about how Renaissance humanism shifted the focus of European culture from divine matters to human beings and their needs. You might want to use a graphic organizer to help organize your thoughts. ▶

Produce Use your notes to produce detailed descriptions of how humanism transformed European culture. You might want to write the descriptions in outline or paragraph form.

Present Choose a creative way to present your idea map to the class. Consider one of these options:

- Create a multimedia presentation using paintings from the Middle Ages and Renaissance to illustrate how humanism transformed ideas about art.
- Write a monologue for a "Renaissance Man" that describes a day in his/her life.
- Design a brochure for a school that describes all the "new thinking" that will be taught to students.

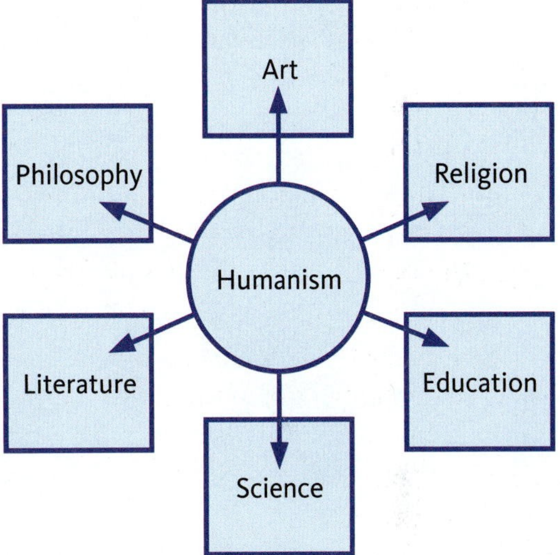
Art
Philosophy
Religion
Humanism
Literature
Education
Science

RAPID REVIEW
UNIT 9

MEDIEVAL AND RENAISSANCE EUROPE

TOP TEN

1. The collapse of the Roman Empire began a 1,000-year-long period called the Middle Ages in western Europe.
2. Humanism led to a rebirth in classical learning, stimulating a period of great creativity known as the Renaissance.
3. Johann Gutenberg developed the printing press.
4. Martin Luther wrote the 95 Theses, which criticized church practices and launched the Reformation.
5. Europeans explored and colonized much of Africa, Asia, and the Americas, which prompted the exchange of goods, ideas, people, plants, animals, and diseases.

6-10. **NOW IT'S YOUR TURN** Complete the list with five more things to remember about medieval and Renaissance Europe.

WHY STUDY HISTORY ?

TO IDENTIFY INNOVATIONS AND TECHNOLOGIES THAT SET THE STAGE FOR THE MODERN WORLD

New inventions and technologies are finding their way around the globe, and new trade relationships are beginning to make the world, as shown in Units 8 and 9, more recognizable for us. Understanding the events and developments that laid the groundwork for our society will help you, as global citizens, understand its complexity, promise, and challenges.

Fred Hiebert

Watch the Why Study History video

WHAT COMES NEXT? PREVIEW UNITS 10–11

10

ARC DE TRIOMPHE

REVOLUTIONS AND EMPIRES

Rapid and sometimes dramatic change has its pros and cons. See how revolutionary change in philosophy, governments, and economics impact Europe and the rest of the world.

11

SATELLITE VIEW OF EARTH

THE MODERN WORLD

Learn about the forces that shape our world—and what role you can play as a global citizen.

KEY TAKEAWAYS UNITS 8–9

PATTERNS IN HISTORY: SIMILAR DEVELOPMENTS ACROSS LOCATIONS

- Changes in religion, the arts, government, and economics begin to leapfrog each other—a change in one area brings change in others.
- The world economy begins to globalize as communication expands and trade patterns develop.
- With new economic relationships comes increasing conflict between countries and political groups.

GOVERNMENT

- New empires, including the Mongol in East Asia and the Khmer in Southeast Asia, rise to power.
- In Europe, modern nation-states emerge and extend their power.

MOVEMENT OF PEOPLE AND IDEAS

- Trade develops along the Silk Roads during the Mongol Empire.
- The Columbian Exchange is established among Europe, Africa, and the Americas.

ARTISTIC EXPRESSION

- Art reflects changing ideas of human identity.
- Renaissance artists revive classical ideals and depict their subjects more realistically, reflecting the humanist ideal of the individual.

TECHNOLOGY & INNOVATION

- Chinese inventions, including movable type, the compass, and gunpowder, lay the groundwork for European innovations.
- As a result, the invention of the printing press enables widespread communication, while new sailing ships put more explorers on the high seas.
- New weapons like cannons and longbows make conflict more deadly.

Terra cotta statues surround Chinese emperor Shi Huangdi's tomb and are thought to have helped guide him into the afterlife.

AS YOU READ ON

You're heading into the final chapters in the history of our world so far—that is, until you and your peers write new ones. These new chapters will no doubt reflect technological advances and, with luck, stronger positive relationships across the globe.

Think back over what you've learned about the human epic over the course of this world history program. Then think about what you would hope to add to the story.

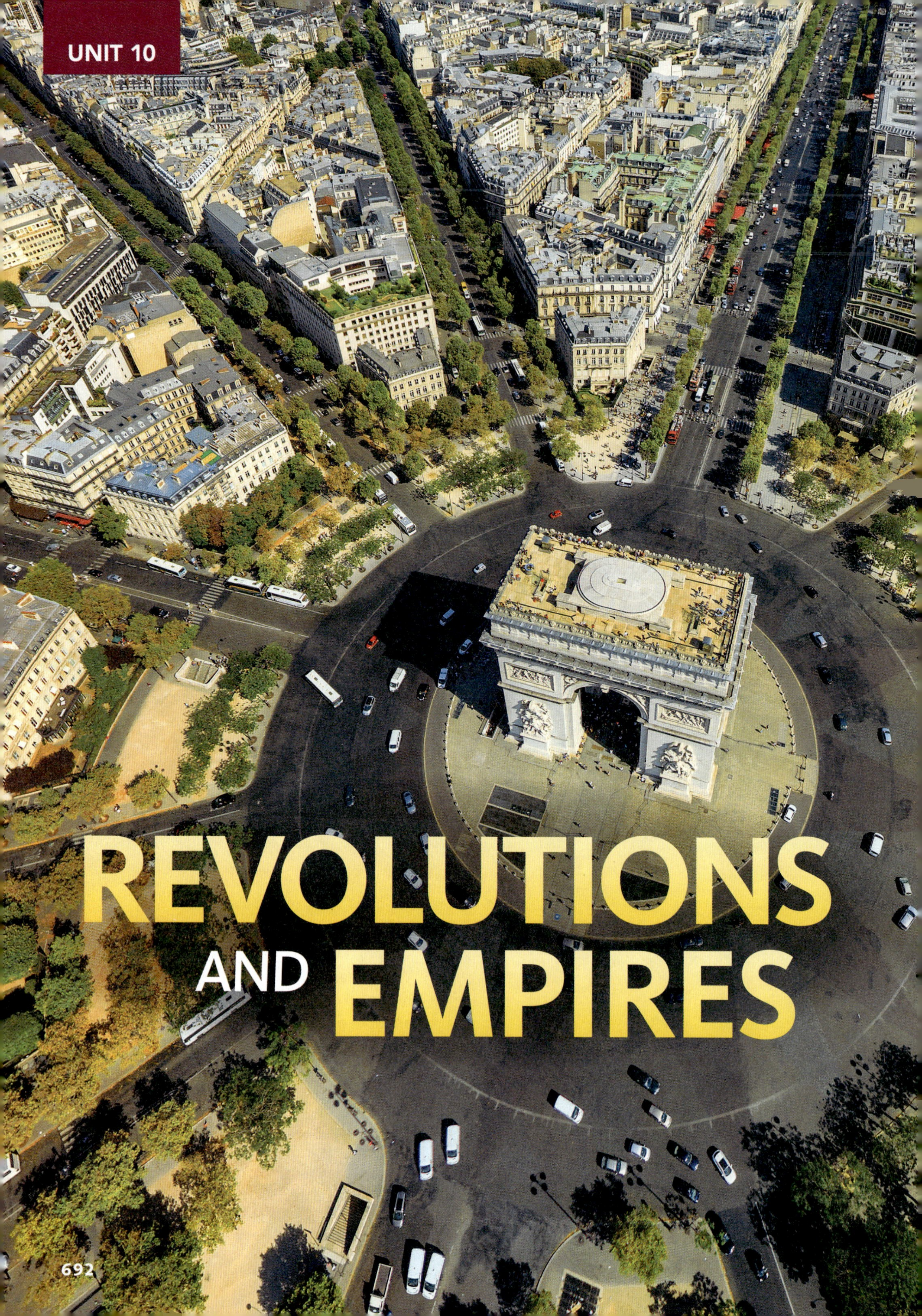

REVOLUTIONS AND EMPIRES

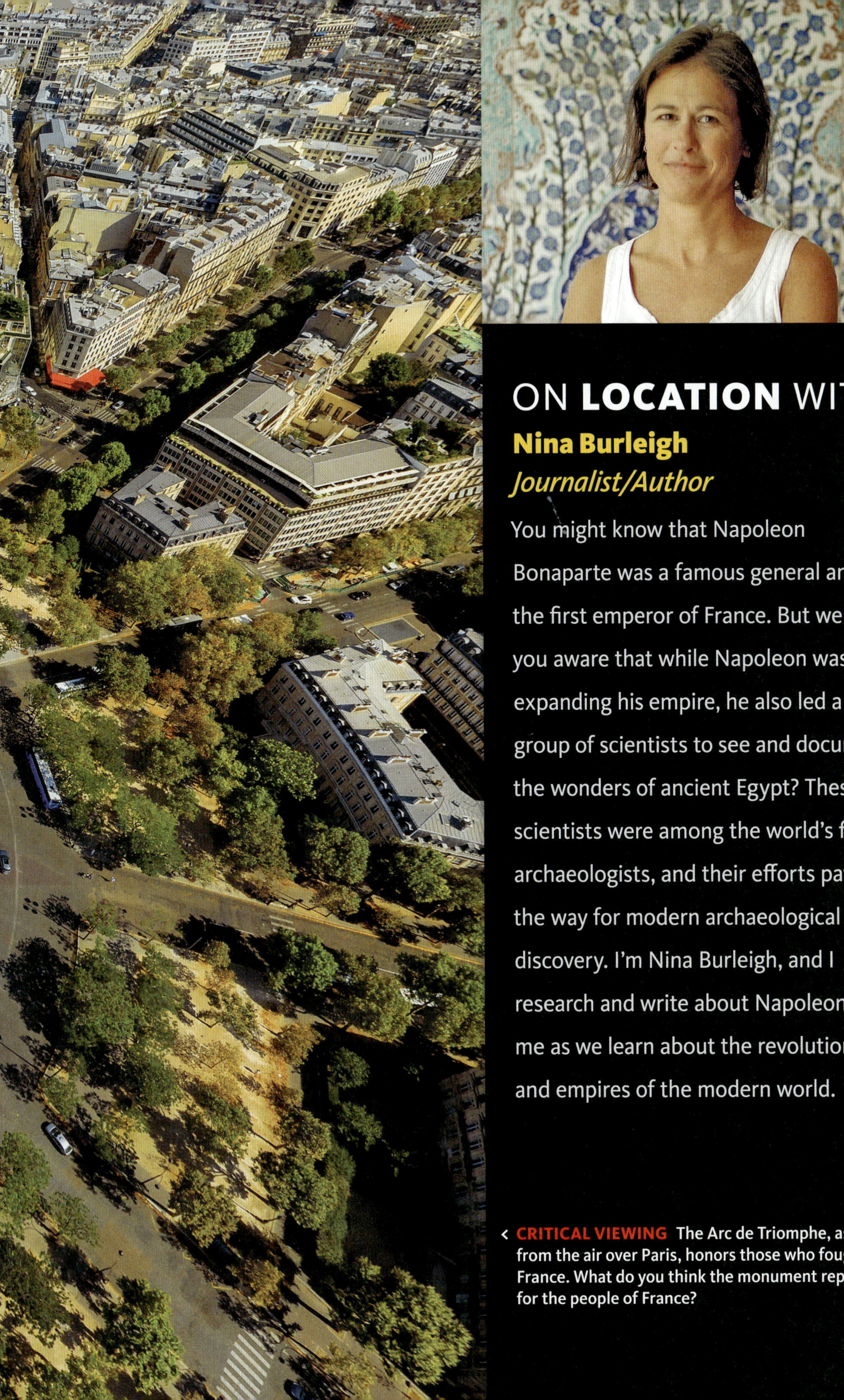

ON **LOCATION** WITH

Nina Burleigh

Journalist/Author

You might know that Napoleon Bonaparte was a famous general and the first emperor of France. But were you aware that while Napoleon was expanding his empire, he also led a group of scientists to see and document the wonders of ancient Egypt? These scientists were among the world's first archaeologists, and their efforts paved the way for modern archaeological discovery. I'm Nina Burleigh, and I research and write about Napoleon. Join me as we learn about the revolutions and empires of the modern world.

‹ **CRITICAL VIEWING** The Arc de Triomphe, as seen from the air over Paris, honors those who fought for France. What do you think the monument represents for the people of France?

Revolutions and Empires

1600

1643
EUROPE
Louis XIV begins his reign as king of France and rules as an absolute monarch. *(Louis XIV depicted as the Sun King on a gate at Versailles)*

1690
EUROPE
Englishman John Locke publishes *Two Treatises of Government*, declaring that humans are born free and equal.

c. 1750
EUROPE
The Industrial Revolution begins.

1762
EUROPE
Catherine the Great begins her reign of Russia as an enlightened despot.

1776
AMERICAS
The American colonies declare their independence from British rule.

IN CONGRESS, JULY 4, 1776.
The unanimous Declaration of the thirteen united States of America,

1780

1789
EUROPE
France explodes into revolution against King Louis XVI, and the *Declaration of the Rights of Man and of the Citizen* is adopted.

1799
EUROPE
Napoleon Bonaparte seizes control of the French government.

1804
AMERICAS
Haiti wins independence from France.

COMPARE TIME LINES

How are the events that took place in the Americas similar?

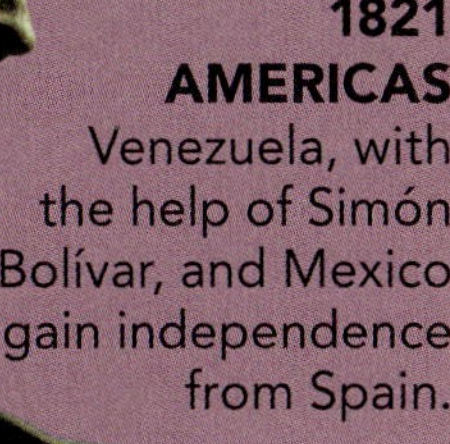

1821
AMERICAS
Venezuela, with the help of Simón Bolívar, and Mexico gain independence from Spain.

1848
EUROPE
Nationalism stirs unrest and revolution across Europe.

1857
ASIA
Indian soldiers revolt against British rule in India. *(painting of Indian soldiers rebelling in Delhi)*

1858
ASIA
France begins colonizing cities in Vietnam and eventually expands its control over Cambodia and Laos.

1867
ASIA
Meiji rule brings a period of modernization in Japan.
(Japanese print of a steam engine in a Tokyo station)

1870

1870s
ASIA
Britain begins colonizing the Malay Peninsula in Southeast Asia.

1884–1885
AFRICA
The Berlin Conference triggers a race for territory in Africa among European powers.
(political cartoon showing Cecil Rhodes standing on a map of Africa)

THE RHODES COLOSSUS
STRIDING FROM CAPE TOWN TO CAIRO.

1900

COLONIAL POWERS in 1900

COLONIES DES PUISSANCES EUROPÉENNES - FRANCE.
VÉRITABLE EXTRAIT DE VIANDE LIEBIG.
VOIR L'EXPLICATION AU VERSO.

This card from the late 1800s shows some of France's colonies in Africa and Southeast Asia.

Many colonial powers flexed their muscles in the 1800s and 1900s, but those in Europe had the most territory. By the late 1800s, European leaders had divided up nearly all of Africa and seized colonies in many parts of Asia. After the Industrial Revolution, the leaders needed increasing supplies of raw materials for their new industries, which many of their new colonies could provide. By the early 1900s, European power extended over most of the world.

The image below shows a British city transformed by the power of the Industrial Revolution. The other images illustrate the impact of European colonialism on the people and economies of Asia and Africa.

Which continent contained the most independent states?

Territory controlled by:

- Denmark
- France
- German Empire
- Great Britain
- Italy
- Japan
- The Netherlands
- Ottoman Empire
- Portugal
- Russian
- Spain
- United States
- Independent states

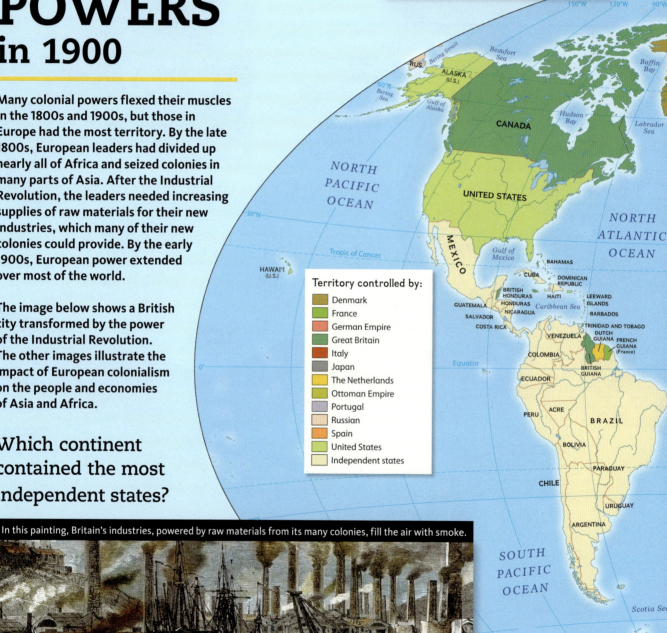

In this painting, Britain's industries, powered by raw materials from its many colonies, fill the air with smoke.

ARCTIC OCEAN
GREENLAND
ICELAND
Arctic Circle
Norwegian Sea
Barents Sea
Kara Sea
Laptev Sea
East Siberian Sea
Bering Sea
Sea of Okhotsk
NORWAY
SWEDEN
FINLAND
RUSSIAN EMPIRE
Lake Baikal
North Sea
DENMARK
Baltic Sea
NETHERLANDS
BRITAIN
BEL.
GERMAN EMPIRE
AUSTRO-HUNGARIAN EMPIRE
SWITZ.
FRANCE
ROMANIA
SERBIA
BULGARIA
Black Sea
MONTENEGRO
ITALY
SPAIN
PORTUGAL
Mediterranean Sea
GREECE
MALTA
CYPRUS
OTTOMAN EMPIRE
TUNIS
MOROCCO
ALGERIA
EGYPT
Lake Balkhash
Caspian Sea
KHIVA
BUKHARA
AFGHANISTAN
PERSIA
KUWAIT
BAHRAIN
Arabian Peninsula
OMAN
CHINA (QING EMPIRE)
Sea of Japan (East Sea)
JAPAN
KOREA
Yellow Sea
East China Sea
TAIWAN
NEPAL
BHUTAN
INDIA
BURMA
Bay of Bengal
Arabian Sea
Hong Kong (Br.)
Macao (Port.)
FRENCH INDOCHINA
SIAM
South China Sea
Philippine Sea
PHILIPPINES
BRITISH BORNEO
BRUNEI
SARAWAK
MALAYA
SINGAPORE
Celebes Sea
Borneo
Sumatra
DUTCH EAST INDIES
Java Sea
Java
New Guinea
KAISER WILHELM'S LAND
PAPUA
PORTUGUESE TIMOR
Arafura Sea
Timor Sea
Coral Sea
NORTH PACIFIC OCEAN
30°N
0°
30°S
RIO DE ORO
CAPE VERDE
FRENCH WEST AFRICA
SUDAN
Red Sea
ERITREA
GAMBIA
PORTUGUESE GUINEA
SIERRA LEONE
LIBERIA
GOLD COAST
TOGO
NIGERIA
KAMERUN
LADO
ABYSSINIA
HADHRAMAUT
FRENCH SOMALILAND
BRITISH SOMALILAND
ITALIAN SOMALILAND
BRITISH EAST AFRICA
CEYLON
SAO TOME AND PRINCIPE (Port.)
RIO MUNI
CONGO FREE STATE (Belgium)
GERMAN EAST AFRICA
NORTHEASTERN RHODESIA
BRITISH CENTRAL AFRICA
COMOROS
ANGOLA
NORTHWESTERN RHODESIA
GERMAN SOUTHWEST AFRICA
SOUTHERN RHODESIA
PORTUGUESE EAST AFRICA
MADAGASCAR
MAURITIUS
Réunion (Fr.)
Tropic of Capricorn
WALVIS BAY
BECHUANALAND
SOUTH AFRICAN REPUBLIC
ORANGE FREE STATE
NATAL
CAPE COLONY
HASUTOLAND
SOUTH ATLANTIC OCEAN
INDIAN OCEAN
AUSTRALIAN COLONIES
Great Australian Bight
Tasman Sea
NEW ZEALAND
0 1,000 2,000 kilometers
0 1,000 2,000 miles
Winkel Tripel projection
Prime Meridian
Antarctic Circle
Weddell Sea
ANTARCTICA
60°W 30°W 0° 30°E 60°E 90°E 120°E 150°E

In this early 1900s photo, Ceylonese men transport two Europeans in rickshaws.

In this illustration, European colonists collect diamonds in South Africa.

CHAPTER 24

ENLIGHTENMENT AND REVOLUTION

1600 – 1815

SECTION 1

THE AGE OF REASON

KEY VOCABULARY

absolute monarch
contract
divine right
enlightened despot
free enterprise
laissez-faire
natural right
philosophe
reason

NAMES & PLACES

Adam Smith
Catherine the Great
Frederick the Great
Jean-Jacques Rousseau
John Locke
Joseph II
Louis XIV
Mary Wollstonecraft
Montesquieu
Voltaire

SECTION 2

REVOLUTIONS ON THREE CONTINENTS

KEY VOCABULARY

bourgeoisie

NAMES & PLACES

Declaration of Independence
Declaration of the Rights of Man and of the Citizen
Jacobins
José de San Martín
Louis XVI
Napoleon Bonaparte
Simón Bolívar
Thomas Jefferson
Toussaint L'Ouverture

READING STRATEGY

DETERMINE WORD MEANINGS When you determine the meaning of an unfamiliar word, you may think of similar words that you already know, such as *light*, to help you understand the word *Enlightenment*. As you read the chapter, use a word map like this one to help you remember the meaning of unfamiliar words.

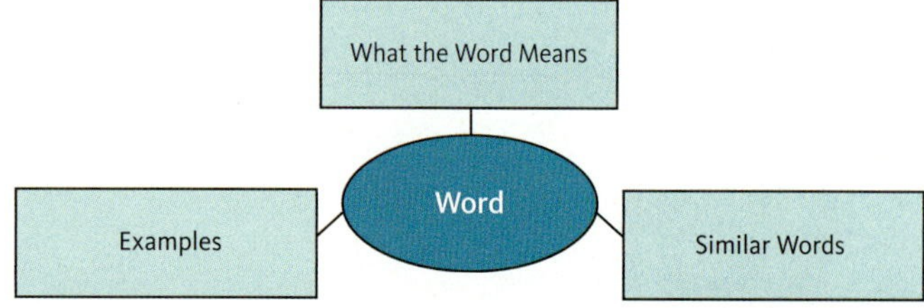
What the Word Means
Word
Examples
Similar Words

Several years after the French Revolution, the emperor Napoleon had this monument, the Arc de Triomphe, erected in Paris to celebrate his military victories.

1.1 The Enlightenment

It takes courage to oppose ideas that your rulers accept and enforce. But when you passionately believe you are right, it is possible to change the world. That's what a group of European thinkers did in the 1700s.

MAIN IDEA

Influential thinkers in the 1700s believed human reason was the best way to solve problems.

WHAT WAS THE ENLIGHTENMENT?

Starting in the late 1600s, Europe was swept by a cultural and intellectual movement that became known as the Enlightenment or the Age of Reason. (**Reason** is the power of the human mind to think and understand in a logical way.) As you've already learned, ancient Greek and Roman philosophers used logic and reason to explain the world around them. This way of thought was rediscovered during the Renaissance and was expanded on during the Scientific Revolution.

Enlightened thinkers were often known as **philosophes** (fee-loh-ZOHFS), the French word for "philosophers." They applied the logical thinking used in science to other areas, especially government and society. The name *Enlightenment* came from the philosophes' belief that the "light" of human reason would shatter the "darkness" of ignorance, superstition, and unfair authority.

At the heart of the Enlightenment was its open-mindedness and focus on what it means to be human. Enlightenment thinkers questioned and often opposed long-established institutions, beliefs, and social order. Philosophes also felt that the justice system was frequently unfair. Many claimed that rulers had too much power and that they kept their subjects uneducated and in poor conditions. By challenging established authority, the philosophes proved their courage as well as their independent thinking.

IDEAS AND INFLUENCES

The Enlightenment did not have a single set of clearly defined beliefs. Still, most philosophes shared some common ideas. Most important was the idea that human reason, not tradition or religious faith, should guide the actions of individuals and rulers. Philosophes argued that all knowledge should be based on reason. They also believed that civilization was becoming more and more advanced and that human reason could make further improvements.

A third common belief was that the "natural" state for any system was a rational and orderly arrangement, like the systems found in nature. This way of thinking extended to natural laws and **natural rights**, including life, liberty, and property. According to the philosophes, these laws and rights automatically applied to everyone and could be explained through reason.

Liberties such as freedom of speech were especially important to the philosophes. They held that people, regardless of class, have basic human rights. Some philosophes argued that natural rights applied to people who were often thought to be inferior. Slaves, they claimed, should be freed. Female thinkers argued that women should have equal rights with men. Further, the philosophes reasoned that no person has the automatic right to rule others. As a result of these beliefs, the philosophes

Critical Viewing This painting depicts a *salon*. What does the image suggest about women's participation in Enlightenment discussions?

An Evening at Madame Geoffrin's, Anicet-Charles Lemonnier, 1812

opposed rulers who did not respect or protect their subjects' natural rights.

The Enlightenment touched every area of people's lives, including politics, religion, society, science, culture, education, and economics. It influenced the way people were ruled and how they worshipped, interacted, and traded. Writers, poets, and artists all helped spread enlightened ideas east to Russia and west to the Americas. Ultimately, Enlightenment ideas would help shape the world we know today.

Portrait of the Marquise de Pompadour, Maurice-Quentin Delatour, 1748–1755

SALONS

The Enlightenment *salons* were gatherings organized by wealthy women. Salon hostesses would invite thinkers, writers, and artists to discuss their opinions. These lively conversations helped the philosophes refine and spread their ideas. Madame de Pompadour (at left) was one of the best-known hostesses.

REVIEW & ASSESS

1. **READING CHECK** What was the Enlightenment?
2. **ANALYZE CAUSE AND EFFECT** How did the Scientific Revolution inspire the Enlightenment?
3. **IDENTIFY MAIN IDEAS AND DETAILS** What natural rights did the philosophes and other thinkers believe people had?

1.2

Enlightenment Thinkers

The enlightened thinkers of the 1700s helped develop and promote new ideas about government that involved both rulers and those they ruled. Thanks to these great minds, we enjoy the freedoms we have today.

MAIN IDEA

Enlightened ideas gave people a greater voice in government and society.

POLITICAL THINKERS

In 1690, an Englishman named **John Locke** published *Two Treatises of Government*. Locke asserted that humans were born free and equal with natural rights including life, liberty, and property. He also claimed that a leader could rule only with the consent of the people. As a result, Locke proposed the idea of a **contract**, or agreement, between rulers and the ruled with clearly defined rights and responsibilities for each. People, he believed, had the right to overthrow rulers who broke this contract. This idea would prove hugely influential in North America, France, and Latin America.

Like Locke, a Frenchman known as **Montesquieu** (mohn-tehs-KYOO) believed that liberty was a natural right. In 1748, he expressed his opposition to rule by a single all-powerful individual. Instead, he proposed the separation of government powers into three branches—legislative, judicial, and executive. Montesquieu believed his plan would limit government power and preserve individual freedom. As you will see later in the chapter, the ideas of these political thinkers helped form the foundations of the United States government.

SOCIAL THINKERS

During the same period, several European writers were proposing new ideas about humans and society. The popular French writer **Voltaire** used his books and plays to promote enlightened ideas of social reform. He was especially outspoken about limiting the power of the Church and encouraging tolerance of all religions.

The philosophe **Jean-Jacques Rousseau** (roo-SOH) believed that all people are born free and good. He stressed government's responsibility to protect both individual rights and society as a whole. He proposed a social contract between individuals and the society in which they live. In the contract, individuals would agree to work toward the good of the country rather than pursuing only their personal interests.

A few philosophes also supported equality for women. In 1792, an English writer and thinker named **Mary Wollstonecraft** published *A Vindication of the Rights of Woman*. Wollstonecraft argued that because women have the ability to reason, they deserve equal rights to men.

Enlightenment thinkers also influenced economics. At the time, most governments closely controlled and regulated commerce. An enlightened Scottish economist named **Adam Smith** described a freer economy called **laissez-faire** (LEHS-ay FAYR), which is French for "leave it alone." He argued for a system of **free enterprise**. In this system, people selling and buying products in markets would determine what products were needed and what price should be paid for them. Smith's 1776 book, *The Wealth of Nations*, influenced people's ideas about the economy for the next hundred years.

KEY ENLIGHTENMENT THINKERS

Portrait of Voltaire, Nicolas de Largillière, after 1718

Voltaire

- Outspoken social reformer and defender of civil liberties
- Proposed religious tolerance and limiting the power of the Catholic Church

Portrait of Montesquieu, 1728

Montesquieu

- Believed the power of government should be limited
- Advocated the separation of government powers (legislative, judicial, and executive)

Portrait of John Locke, Sir Gotfrey Kneller, 1697

Locke

- Proposed the idea of a contract between the ruler and the ruled
- Believed governments that fail to uphold their subjects' natural rights should be overthrown
- Believed government power came only from the people

Portrait of Mary Wollstonecraft, John Opie, c. 1797

Wollstonecraft

- Stated that women are rational human beings
- Argued that natural rights extend to women as well as men
- Insisted women deserve equal rights in education and society

REVIEW & ASSESS

1. **READING CHECK** According to the philosophes, what right did the people have if rulers broke the social contract?

2. **COMPARE AND CONTRAST** What ideas did the political and social thinkers have in common?

3. **MAKE INFERENCES** How did Mary Wollstonecraft use reason to argue for women's equal rights?

1.3 Europe's Rulers and the Enlightenment

Being an absolute ruler would be pretty tempting if you were a king or queen. You could keep all the government's wealth and power to yourself. In the 1600s and 1700s, many rulers did just that, but the Enlightenment influenced some kings and queens to try a new path.

MAIN IDEA

Enlightenment ideas changed the way Europe was ruled.

THE RISE OF ABSOLUTE MONARCHY

To understand why Enlightenment thinkers argued that people should have rights and freedoms, it is important to know how governments changed over time in Europe. In medieval Europe, influential groups such as the nobility and the Church limited the power of kings and queens. As medieval order broke down, however, monarchs took more power for themselves. By 1600, some ruled as **absolute monarchs**. They had unlimited authority and almost no legal limits. They claimed to rule by **divine right**, meaning that their power came directly from God.

During the 1600s and 1700s, absolute monarchs ruled the European kingdoms of Russia, Austria, and Prussia (part of what is now Germany). The greatest of all was **Louis XIV** of France. For most of his 72-year reign, Louis ignored all of France's traditional institutions. He excluded the nobles from government and enforced his will through government officials. At Versailles (vair-SY), near Paris, he built a massive palace to show off his power. Louis became known as the Sun King because he chose the sun as his symbol. Indeed, all France revolved around him, like the planets around the sun.

Yet at the same time, a growing middle class was pressing for a voice in the policies that affected them. In England, as you may recall, this trend led to the creation of the Magna Carta and a parliament made up of nobles and elected commoners. Attempts to restore absolute monarchy in England were defeated in England's civil war of 1642 to 1651 and by a revolution in 1688. The subsequent English Bill of Rights of 1689 guaranteed basic rights to English citizens.

ENLIGHTENED DESPOTS

As the ideas of the Enlightenment spread in the 1700s, some monarchs applied reforms in their countries. Because they never surrendered their complete authority, they became known as **enlightened despots**, absolute monarchs who applied certain Enlightenment ideas. One was **Frederick the Great**, who ruled Prussia from 1740 to 1786. He introduced religious tolerance and legal reforms. He also banned torture and helped peasants improve their farms. However, Frederick refused to change the social hierarchy in Prussia.

Joseph II of Austria oversaw enlightened reforms between 1780 and 1790. He introduced religious tolerance, freedom of the press, and various law reforms. Joseph firmly believed in social equality. He promoted elementary education for all children. He abolished serfdom and tried to introduce a new system of taxes on the land that would be more fair to different social classes.

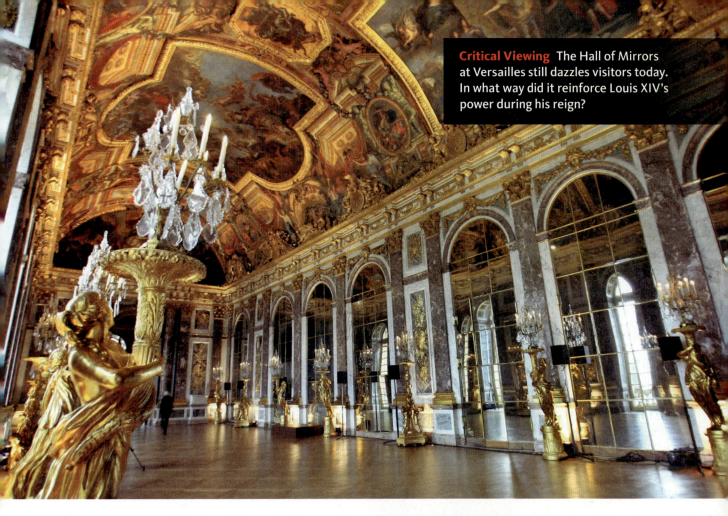

Critical Viewing The Hall of Mirrors at Versailles still dazzles visitors today. In what way did it reinforce Louis XIV's power during his reign?

Catherine the Great ruled Russia from 1762 to 1796. Although Catherine favored enlightened ideas, she struggled to introduce reforms. She considered freeing the serfs, but changed her mind when she realized she needed the support of serf-owning nobles to keep herself in power. Similarly, when Catherine called together elected representatives from all classes to suggest reforms, the meeting failed because of each group's self-interest. However, Catherine did succeed in expanding education, science, and the arts in Russia.

Louis XIV King of France, Andry (from a 1701 portrait by Hyacinthe Rigaud), 18th century

VERSAILLES

In modern numbers, Louis XIV's Versailles cost more than two billion dollars to build and involved more than 36,000 workers. It was the largest and most luxurious palace in Europe, with 700 rooms and 2,000 windows. Its rich decorations included 6,000 paintings, 2,000 sculptures, and the famous Hall of Mirrors, which was lit by 20,000 candles.

REVIEW & ASSESS

1. **READING CHECK** How were absolute monarchs and enlightened despots similar and different?
2. **MAKE CONNECTIONS** In what ways did the enlightened despots reflect the ideas of the philosophes? In what ways did they fail to reflect those ideas?
3. **ANALYZE CAUSE AND EFFECT** What effect did the Enlightenment have on monarchs such as Frederick the Great, Joseph II, and Catherine the Great?

2.1

The American Revolution

The Enlightenment lit a flame that could be seen not just in Europe, but across the Atlantic. Visions of liberty and equality would spark revolutions throughout the Americas and in France. The first to rebel were Britain's 13 colonies.

MAIN IDEA

The American Revolution followed the ideas of the Enlightenment and inspired other revolutions.

THE COLONIES REVOLT

The American Revolution was a key event for the development of the United States. It was also extremely influential in terms of world history.

Taxes were one important cause of the American Revolution. In the 1760s and 1770s, Britain's Parliament introduced a series of new taxes in its American colonies. The colonists protested that the British government could not tax them because they were not represented in Parliament. Tensions between Britain and the colonists grew. Then, on April 19, 1775, British soldiers and colonists exchanged shots at Lexington, Massachusetts. Parliament sent an army to North America to crush the rebellion against Britain.

On July 4, 1776, representatives of the 13 American colonies approved the **Declaration of Independence**. This document, written by **Thomas Jefferson**, drew on the Enlightenment ideas of John Locke and the basic concepts in the Magna Carta. It stated that rulers had a contract with their subjects to protect the people's natural rights. Jefferson listed all the ways in which Britain's king had broken this contract with the colonies.

After years of war against the British army, the colonists prevailed. In 1783, Britain officially recognized the independence of the United States of America. The country's first constitution was the Articles of Confederation. This document did not create a strong government, and in 1787, the country's leaders met in Philadelphia to revise it. Instead, they wound up writing a new Constitution. It went into effect in 1789.

Several Enlightenment ideas were reflected in the U.S. Constitution. For example, the executive, legislative, and judiciary branches were separated and assigned different powers. This measure ensured that no single person or government branch could achieve absolute control. A Bill of Rights listed individual rights that the government could not violate, such as freedom of speech and freedom of worship.

THE WORLD FOLLOWS

The American Revolution had an immediate effect in Europe. All people, not just the philosophes, could see the ideas of the Enlightenment turned into the reality of an elected government.

France had sent soldiers and aid to the colonists in fighting France's long-time enemy, Britain. Now French soldiers returned home and shared what they had learned about individual freedoms. These ideas helped sow the seeds of revolution in France. In the decades that followed, other European colonies also set out on the path to independence.

Critical Viewing Modern-day reenactors portray British troops in a battle from the American Revolution. Why do Americans commemorate the war with events like this one?

REVIEW & ASSESS

1. **READING CHECK** How did taxes affect the course of U.S. history?
2. **MAKE INFERENCES** How does the Declaration of Independence reflect Enlightenment ideas?
3. **SYNTHESIZE** What idea of Montesquieu's does the U.S. Constitution embody?

2.2 The French Revolution

Some events are so momentous that they can change the course of history. The French Revolution was one such turning point. It shattered established ideas about government and society and its effects were felt throughout Europe for the next 25 years.

MAIN IDEA

Long-oppressed French commoners seized power from the upper classes.

THE THREE ESTATES

In 1789, France exploded into revolution. The reasons were a mix of social and political problems that provoked people to action.

Prerevolutionary France suffered from inequality among its three main social classes, called estates. The First Estate was the Catholic clergy, who had significant powers and privileges such as paying very few taxes. The Second Estate was the nobility, who lived in privileged isolation at the king's court in Versailles. The nobles enjoyed lavish lifestyles and, like the members of the First Estate, were only lightly taxed.

The Third Estate was the common people, the vast majority of France. The Third Estate had its own hierarchy. At the top was the **bourgeoisie** (boor-jwah-ZEE), or middle class, made up of relatively prosperous and educated professionals and merchants. Beneath the bourgeoisie were the peasants, who made up the majority of the population. Hard work, hunger, and poverty were the norm for most of these people. The Third Estate paid the largest share of the nation's taxes but had no say in government.

At the top of society was the French king, **Louis XVI**. Louis ruled as an absolute monarch, but he was not an effective ruler. Instead, he was weak and manipulated by clever nobles and his unpopular Austrian wife, Marie Antoinette.

Louis lived in great splendor and did little to help his long-suffering subjects. In addition, a series of wars, including Louis's support of the American Revolution, had left the nation almost bankrupt. France's outdated economy favored the rich nobles, who prevented attempts at economic reform. The result was a major financial crisis and even higher taxes for the Third Estate. Making things still worse, France experienced a disastrous grain harvest in 1788. All across the country, the Third Estate was plunged into crippling poverty and deadly hunger.

THE END OF THE MONARCHY

To deal with the crisis, Louis was forced to summon a representative assembly called the Estates-General, which had not met since 1614. As the name implies, delegates to the Estates-General represented the estates to which they belonged.

At the meetings in the town of Versailles, the First and Second Estates combined had approximately the same number of delegates as the Third Estate. These wealthier estates worked to promote their own interests. Frustrated and angry, the Third Estate established a new representative body called the National Assembly. The National Assembly gave the Third Estate more power and was defended by armed mobs that were formed into a national guard.

Taille, Impots et Corvees

Critical Viewing This political cartoon from the 1700s shows the three estates. What view does it convey of the First and Second Estates?

All across France, peasants rose up in support of the National Assembly. Louis was forced to accept its authority. The National Assembly abolished the privileges of the nobles and effectively made Louis a prisoner. In August 1789, the assembly issued the **Declaration of the Rights of Man and of the Citizen**, which proclaimed the liberty and equality of all people. The assembly tried to form a new government in which Louis would share power with an elected legislature. However, the king refused to cooperate.

REVIEW & ASSESS

1. **READING CHECK** How did the revolution change relations among France's three estates?
2. **COMPARE AND CONTRAST** In what ways were conditions for the three estates similar and different?
3. **IDENTIFY PROBLEMS AND SOLUTIONS** How did the Third Estate seek to improve its conditions?

2.3 MOMENTS IN HISTORY

The Storming of the Bastille

JULY 14, 1789

The Bastille, a fortress prison in Paris, was seen as a symbol of the royalist tyranny that the French revolutionaries wanted to overthrow. On the morning of July 14, revolutionary leaders tried to negotiate the surrender of the arms and ammunition stored in the Bastille. As the day went by, the crowd outside grew increasingly restless and finally surged into the fortress courtyard. This painting illustrates the violence that followed when the revolutionaries clashed with the prison officers. How are the revolutionaries and officers portrayed in the painting?

***Storming of the Bastille, July 14, 1789*, Charles Thévenin, c. 1790**

2.4 From Republic to Empire

Imagine living in constant fear that your friends or even your family would accuse you of a crime. And what if the government would then torture and execute you, even if you were innocent? Revolutionary life was dangerous.

MAIN IDEA

Revolutionary France grew more and more unstable until Napoleon Bonaparte seized power.

THE GUILLOTINE

One of the most striking images of the French Revolution is the guillotine (GEE-yuh-teen), the machine used to execute thousands, including Louis XVI.

The guillotine had a blade that plunged down grooves in two upright posts to slice through the victim's neck, beheading him or her in one stroke.

REIGN OF TERROR

Louis XVI was forced to surrender most of his remaining powers in 1791. Then, in 1792, the absolute monarchs of Austria and Prussia invaded France, aiming to restore Louis to power. The French defeated the invasion, but it led to a drastic reaction from the new government. Thousands of suspected royalists were massacred. Then, in September 1792, France declared itself a republic. In 1793, Louis XVI and Marie Antoinette were publicly executed in Paris.

Their deaths did little to restore order. Rival political groups argued over how to run the country. Faced with internal disorder and threats from abroad, the revolutionary government grew more radical. Eventually, an extremist group called the **Jacobins** took control. The group was led by a former lawyer called Robespierre, who began a bloody period called the Reign of Terror.

Using the excuse of defending the republic, Robespierre's followers imprisoned, tortured, and murdered tens of thousands. Nobody was safe. In 1794, the mob turned against Robespierre himself and executed him.

NAPOLEON'S RISE TO POWER

Because of the chaos, France was ready for a strong leader—and one emerged. **Napoleon Bonaparte** was an ambitious and brilliant young military officer who rose to fame fighting the royalists in 1795. Napoleon's military successes and popularity gave him political influence, and, in 1799, he seized control of the government.

Napoleon was granted total control. With this power, he brought much-needed stability to the country. Although he ruthlessly crushed political opponents, Napoleon preserved revolutionary ideals and enlightened values, including equality, liberty, religious tolerance, and the rule of law. His most lasting contribution may be the Napoleonic Code, a clear and organized system of laws for France.

Napoleon defeated many other European nations in battle and crowned himself emperor in 1804. In 1814, however, Britain and its allies defeated France and restored the French monarchy. Just a year later, Napoleon returned and briefly retook power before being defeated at the Battle of Waterloo.

Napoleon Crossing the Alps, Jacques-Louis David, c. 1800

Critical Viewing This painting shows Napoleon crossing the Alps on his way to conquer Italy. Why would Napoleon choose to have himself portrayed in this way?

REVIEW & ASSESS

1. **READING CHECK** How was Napoleon able to seize control of France's government?
2. **ANALYZE CAUSE AND EFFECT** What were the effects of the invasion from Austria and Prussia?
3. **EVALUATE** Could Napoleon be described as an enlightened despot? Why or why not?

2.5 Revolutions in Latin America

In the early 1800s, most parts of Central and South America were colonized by European powers. After the American and French Revolutions, however, the idea of independence became unstoppable. Within decades, nearly all the American colonies were free.

MAIN IDEA

Mexico and colonies in the Caribbean and South America gained independence from European countries during the early 1800s.

HAITI AND MEXICO

In 1791, the Caribbean colony of Haiti was ruled by France. That year, a former slave in Haiti named **Toussaint L'Ouverture** (too-SAN loo-vair-TOOR) led a rebellion against this European domination. The French imprisoned L'Ouverture, but his followers would not give up. In 1804, Haiti gained independence from France.

The people of Mexico witnessed the extraordinary events in the United States, France, and Haiti—and were inspired by them. On September 16, 1810, a Mexican priest named Father Miguel Hidalgo y Costilla (mee-GEHL ee-DAHL-goh EE kohs-TEE-yah) preached a message of freedom to his parish. Inspired by the priest's words, his followers set out to overthrow Spanish rule. But they were armed only with machetes (long, heavy knives) and a few guns, and Spanish troops easily defeated them. They then executed Father Hidalgo.

But the desire for independence did not die. In 1821, creoles (KREE-ohlz), well-educated people who had been born in Mexico, led another revolution against Spain. This time, an experienced army officer named Agustín de Iturbide (ah-goos-TEEN day ee-toor-BEE-day) was better prepared. He led an uprising against the Spanish government, and that year Mexico gained independence from Spain.

SOUTH AMERICA

In the early 1800s, Spain ruled most of South America, but two great generals led the colonies to independence. One was **Simón Bolívar** (see-MONH boh-LEE-var), born to a wealthy family in Venezuela, in the northern part of South America. The other was **José de San Martín** (sahn mar-TEEN), who was from Argentina.

In 1811, Venezuela declared independence from Spain, but Spain fought to keep this valuable colony. For the next ten years, Bolívar led the struggle against Spanish troops. Finally, in 1819, he surprised Spanish soldiers after a courageous march through the Andes Mountains. In 1821, Venezuela gained its independence. During his struggles, Bolívar had carried the revolution into Colombia. In 1822, he also liberated Ecuador. There, he met José de San Martín.

While Bolívar had been liberating the northern part of South America, San Martín had been leading rebellions in the central and southern parts of the continent. Under San Martín's leadership, Argentina declared its independence in 1816, but Spanish loyalists remained a threat. It seemed that independence could be assured only if all of South America were liberated.

In 1817, San Martín liberated neighboring Chile by leading a brilliant campaign across the high Andes Mountains. From Chile, San Martín attacked the Spanish loyalist

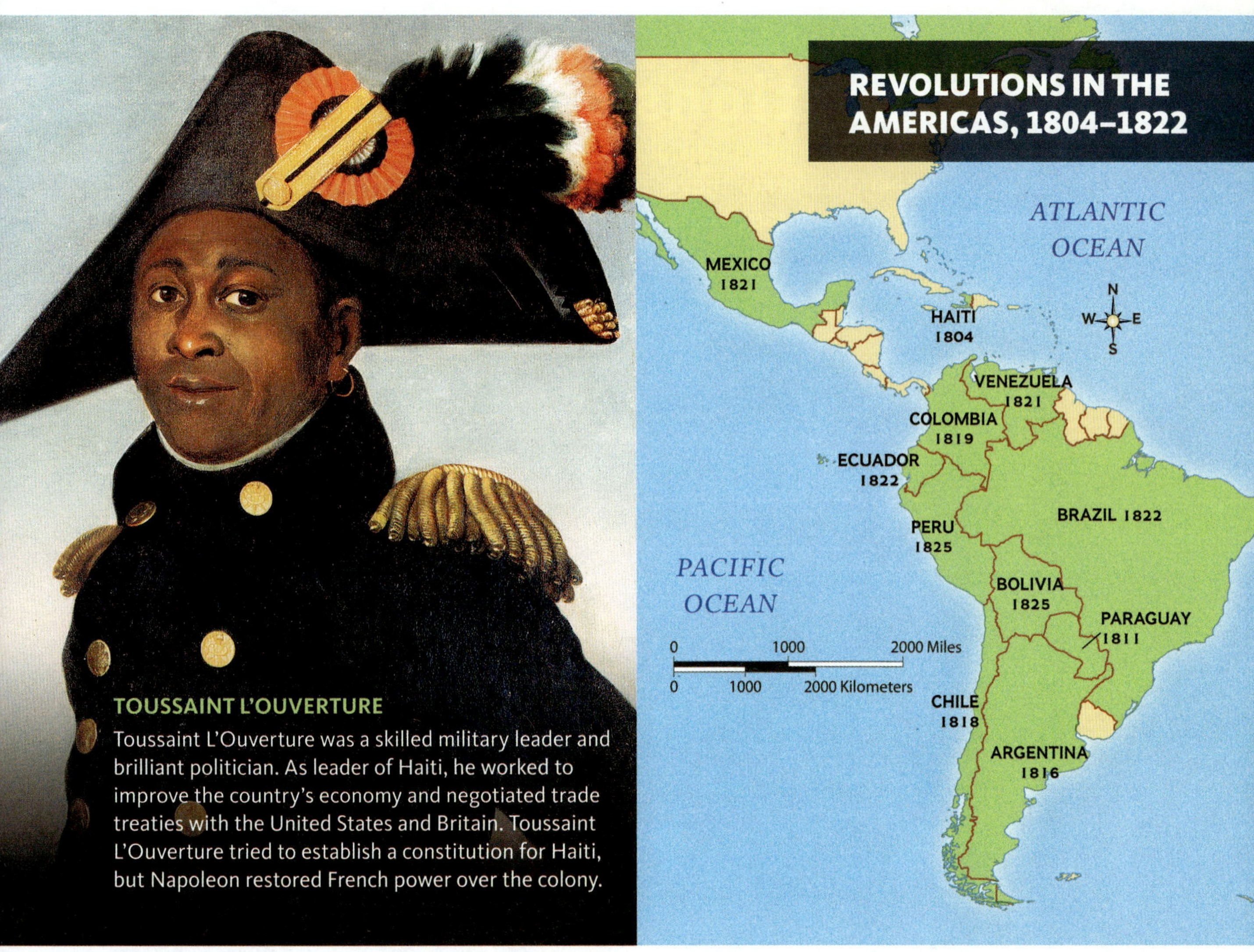
REVOLUTIONS IN THE AMERICAS, 1804–1822
ATLANTIC OCEAN
PACIFIC OCEAN
MEXICO 1821
HAITI 1804
VENEZUELA 1821
COLOMBIA 1819
ECUADOR 1822
PERU 1825
BRAZIL 1822
BOLIVIA 1825
PARAGUAY 1811
CHILE 1818
ARGENTINA 1816
N
W
E
S
0
1000
2000 Miles
0
1000
2000 Kilometers

TOUSSAINT L'OUVERTURE

Toussaint L'Ouverture was a skilled military leader and brilliant politician. As leader of Haiti, he worked to improve the country's economy and negotiated trade treaties with the United States and Britain. Toussaint L'Ouverture tried to establish a constitution for Haiti, but Napoleon restored French power over the colony.

heartland of Peru. By 1821, he had captured Peru's capital but still faced stiff resistance.

In 1822, San Martín resigned, and Bolívar was asked to complete the liberation of Peru. Bolívar finally achieved this feat in 1825. Part of Peru was renamed Bolivia in his honor. By 1826, Spain's vast colonial empire was reduced to the islands of Cuba and Puerto Rico.

The large colony of Brazil, which was ruled by Portugal, followed a more peaceful path to independence. France invaded Portugal in 1807, and Portugal's ruler, John VI, fled to Brazil. When France was defeated in 1814, John VI stayed on in Brazil. Despite attempts to reassert Portugal's authority, Brazil became independent in 1822 and established itself as a constitutional monarchy in 1824.

REVIEW & ASSESS

1. **READING CHECK** How did Simón Bolívar and José de San Martín contribute to the end of European control of the Americas?
2. **DETERMINE WORD MEANINGS** How does knowing that *liberated* derives from the Latin word *liberare*, which means "free," help to clarify its meaning?
3. **INTERPRET MAPS** Based on this map, what conclusion can be drawn about Latin America in the late 1700s and early 1800s?

2.6 DOCUMENT-BASED QUESTION

Declarations of Freedom

Many Enlightenment thinkers were also gifted writers. Through books, essays, and other documents, they explained their ideas about rights and liberties to the world. These writings set the stage for revolution.

Declaration of Independence, July 4th, 1776, John Trumbull, 1817–1819

In this detail from a painting that hangs in the United States Capitol Building, Thomas Jefferson (in the red vest) presents the Declaration of Independence to committee members.

DOCUMENT ONE

Primary Source: Legal Document

The Declaration of Independence (1776)

This famous document proclaims the independence of the British colonies and the founding of the United States of America. It was adopted by the Continental Congress on July 4, 1776. The declaration was largely created by Thomas Jefferson, a delegate from Virginia. He drew heavily on the political theories of John Locke. These ideas are most apparent in this passage asserting human equality and natural rights.

CONSTRUCTED RESPONSE How did the ideas of John Locke influence the creation of the Declaration of Independence?

We hold these truths to be self-evident, that all men are created equal, that they are endowed by their Creator with certain unalienable Rights, that among these are Life, Liberty, and the pursuit of Happiness.—That to secure these rights, Governments are instituted among Men, deriving their just powers from the consent of the governed,—That whenever any Form of Government becomes destructive of these ends, it is the Right of the People to alter or to abolish it, and to institute new Government.

DOCUMENT TWO

Primary Source: Legal Document

The Declaration of the Rights of Man and of the Citizen (1789)

This French Revolutionary document is a basic charter of human liberties. Its 17 articles build on the idea of equality and rights for all. Article 6 emphasizes every citizen's equality before the law. This article reflects the ideas of French philosophe Jean-Jacques Rousseau by stating that laws should reflect the will of the people. It further stresses that every citizen has the right to take part in government.

CONSTRUCTED RESPONSE Why do you think the Declaration of the Rights of Man and of the Citizen emphasized the Enlightenment idea of equality?

Law is the expression of the general will. Every citizen has a right to participate personally, or through his representative, in its foundation. It must be the same for all, whether it protects or punishes. All citizens, being equal in the eyes of the law, are equally eligible to all dignities [high offices] and to all public positions and occupations, according to their abilities, and without distinction except that of their virtues and talents.

SYNTHESIZE & WRITE

1. **REVIEW** Review what you have learned about the Enlightenment and the influence of its ideas.
2. **RECALL** On your own paper, write down the main idea expressed in each document.
3. **CONSTRUCT** Write a topic sentence that answers this question: What basic human rights were claimed by people following the Enlightenment?
4. **WRITE** Using evidence from the documents, write an essay to support your answer to the question in Step 3.

CHAPTER 24 Review

VOCABULARY

Use each of the following vocabulary words in a sentence that shows an understanding of the term's meaning.

1. **contract**
   Jefferson said Britain had broken the terms of the contract, or agreement, between the ruler and the people.
2. **laissez-faire**
3. **absolute monarch**
4. **divine right**
5. **enlightened despot**
6. **reason**
7. **bourgeoisie**

READING STRATEGY

8. **DETERMINE WORD MEANINGS** If you haven't already, complete at least three word maps for unfamiliar words from the chapter.

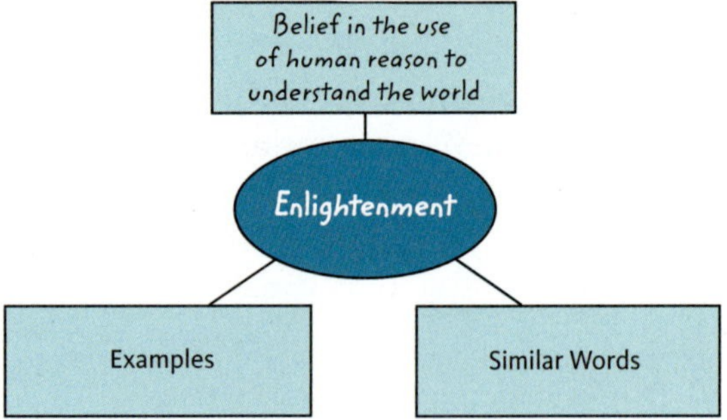

Belief in the use of human reason to understand the world
Enlightenment
Examples
Similar Words

Use each of the three words in a sentence that shows an understanding of the word's meaning.

MAIN IDEAS

Answer the following questions. Support your answers with evidence from the chapter.

9. Why is the Enlightenment also referred to as the Age of Reason? **LESSON 1.1**
10. Explain John Locke's idea about a contract between rulers and the ruled. **LESSON 1.2**
11. Why did some absolute monarchs introduce reforms in their countries? **LESSON 1.3**
12. Why did the American colonies rebel against Britain? **LESSON 2.1**
13. What were living conditions like for the Third Estate in France before the French Revolution? **LESSON 2.2**
14. What was the Reign of Terror? **LESSON 2.4**

CRITICAL THINKING

Answer the following questions. Support your answers with evidence from the chapter.

15. **SYNTHESIZE** Why would an absolute monarch like Louis XIV oppose the idea of natural rights?
16. **COMPARE AND CONTRAST** In what ways were the American and French Revolutions the same and different?
17. **MAKE INFERENCES** What did the Declaration of Independence do for the colonists of British North America?
18. **IDENTIFY MAIN IDEAS AND DETAILS** What political reforms did the National Assembly establish in France?
19. **DRAW CONCLUSIONS** Why was Napoleon granted absolute power as leader of the French Republic?
20. **YOU DECIDE** Which of the Enlightenment thinkers do you think had the greatest impact on the revolutions of the 1700s and 1800s? Explain your choice.

INTERPRET MAPS

This map shows Napoleon's empire in 1812. Look closely at the map and answer the questions that follow.

NAPOLEON'S EMPIRE, 1812
French Empire
Controlled by Napoleon
Allies of Napoleon
At war with Napoleon
Neutral
Napoleon's route into Russia
Napoleon's route out of Russia
ATLANTIC OCEAN
North Sea
Baltic Sea
Black Sea
Mediterranean Sea
UNITED KINGDOM
London
KINGDOM OF NORWAY & DENMARK
SWEDEN
Moscow
RUSSIAN EMPIRE
PRUSSIA
Berlin
GRAND DUCHY OF WARSAW
CONFEDERATION OF THE RHINE
Paris
Versailles
FRENCH EMPIRE
SWITZERLAND
Vienna
AUSTRIAN EMPIRE
KINGDOM OF ITALY
ILLYRIAN PROVINCES
OTTOMAN EMPIRE
PORTUGAL
Madrid
SPAIN
Rome
KINGDOM OF NAPLES
N
W
E
S
0 250 500 Miles
0 250 500 Kilometers

21. What European countries were under the influence of France in 1812?

22. What challenges would Napoleon face in trying to conquer Russia?

ANALYZE SOURCES

On the way to his inauguration in Washington, D.C., in 1861, Abraham Lincoln stopped in Philadelphia. While there, he gave a speech at Independence Hall, where the Declaration of Independence was signed in 1776. Read the following excerpt from that speech about the Declaration of Independence. Then answer the question.

> [The Declaration of Independence] gave liberty, not alone to the people of this country, but, I hope, to the world, for all future time.

23. Do you agree with Abraham Lincoln's assessment of the significance of the Declaration of Independence? Explain.

WRITE ABOUT HISTORY

24. EXPOSITORY Write a speech for an Independence Day celebration in your town. Your speech should explain the Enlightenment, its main ideas, and how it helped shape the government and society we have today.

TIPS

- Take notes from the lessons about the Enlightenment, its ideas, and its influences.
- Begin the speech with an introductory paragraph defining the Enlightenment.
- Develop the speech with ideas that were central to the Enlightenment.
- Use two or three vocabulary terms from the chapter in your speech.
- Conclude the speech by explaining how the Enlightenment influenced society and government.

CHAPTER 25 FACTORIES, NATIONS, AND EMPIRES

1700 – 1914

SECTION 1
THE INDUSTRIAL REVOLUTION

KEY VOCABULARY
communism
immigrate
industrialize
labor union
middle class
push-pull factor
socialism
urbanization
woman suffrage

NAMES & PLACES
Adam Smith
Eli Whitney
Ellis Island
Industrial Revolution
Karl Marx

SECTION 2
NATIONALISM AROUND THE WORLD

KEY VOCABULARY
confederation
dictator
militarism
nationalism
nation-state
republic

NAMES & PLACES
Giuseppe Garibaldi
José de San Martín
Meiji
Otto von Bismarck
Simón Bolívar

SECTION 3
THE NEW IMPERIALISM

KEY VOCABULARY
direct rule
imperialism
missionary
racism
sepoy

NAMES & PLACES
Berlin Conference
East India Company
French Indochina
Raj

READING STRATEGY

ORGANIZE IDEAS: SEQUENCE EVENTS As you read, use a time line like this one to record events of the Industrial Revolution and organize them in the order in which they occurred. Include a date for each event.

Events of the Industrial Revolution

63395
YORKSHIRE
COAST
EXPRESS

Built in 1918, a steam-powered locomotive chugs its way through Yorkshire, England.

1.1 Factories and Labor

"We remove mountains, and make seas our smooth highway; nothing can resist us," wrote one proud Englishman of his country's industrial achievements. But the changes he admired came with a human cost.

MAIN IDEA

In the mid-1700s, manufacturing began to replace farming as the main form of work.

A NEW WAY TO WORK

The changes that the Englishman referred to are known as the **Industrial Revolution**. This was a period starting around 1750, when businesses began to **industrialize**, or build and operate factories to produce goods. The revolution had an enormous impact on people and society. It led to the growth of cities and made countries more prosperous. It eventually improved people's standard of living, although it widened the gap between the rich and the poor. The revolution also led to the use of new sources of energy and improved systems of transportation.

As part of the manufacturing process, power-driven machines replaced skilled craftspeople working alone. New and better materials and new power sources made the machines possible. Improvements in making iron and steel enabled the building of machines that were stronger and bigger. The machines were powered by the new steam engine perfected by James Watt in the mid-1780s. Later, machines would run on electricity and petroleum.

Businesses built large factories to hold the new machines, which were operated by workers. Instead of one worker making an entire item, the production process was divided into a series of individual tasks. A different worker was assigned to each task. This division of labor, along with the new machines and the new sources of power, increased the rate at which goods were produced. As a result, products became cheaper.

New and improved transportation systems moved raw materials and finished goods farther, faster, and more cheaply. These included better roads and networks of canals that linked rivers, cities, and seas. Steam trains carried goods thousands of miles on newly built track, while steamships carrying huge cargoes crossed the oceans.

Great Britain's textile industry was the first to be industrialized. The use of machines like the spinning jenny and the power loom produced high quality cloth at record rates. By 1815, Britain produced more textiles than all other European countries combined. Between 1760 and 1830, the Industrial Revolution was largely limited to Great Britain, where industrial secrets were closely guarded. Even so, after 1830, industrialization spread across western Europe, especially to Belgium, France, and Germany, and across the Atlantic to the United States.

There, **Eli Whitney**'s cotton gin, which separated the seeds from cotton fibers, made it easier to produce cotton cloth. It also led to an increase in the growth of cotton. By 1860, the southern United States was producing two-thirds of the world's cotton. Textile mills in New England and Great Britain turned the cotton into cloth. By 1900, the United States had become a major industrial power with a thriving economy.

Women process wool at a British blanket factory in 1897.

WORKING CLASS LABORERS

The Industrial Revolution led to a rapid increase in the middle class. However, this extraordinary increase in production also had a human cost. Employers mistreated factory workers, who were forced to work long hours for low wages. Because of unsafe conditions, many workers suffered injuries and ill health. Employers used women and young children for cheap labor, often working them six days a week for 14 hours a day.

Shared hardships led workers to form organizations called **labor unions**, which worked to protect the rights and interests of their members. Female workers formed unions known as "trade societies." Unions had more power than individuals did to negotiate better conditions. Employers and governments opposed the unions and even made them illegal, but the union movement continued to grow. By the late 1800s, unions had succeeded in pressuring governments to begin improving conditions for the new industrial working class.

REVIEW & ASSESS

1. **READING CHECK** What was the Industrial Revolution?
2. **ANALYZE CAUSE AND EFFECT** How did the Industrial Revolution change the economy of participating countries?
3. **MAKE INFERENCES** Why did labor unions continue to grow in spite of opposition from governments?

1.2 HISTORY THROUGH OBJECTS

INDUSTRIALIZATION

Like the agricultural revolution that occurred more than 10,000 years before it, the Industrial Revolution changed many people's way of life. As you can see from the items shown here, industrialization transformed how they worked and traveled. It also cast a bright, new light on indoor living. Many of these items would pave the way for another revolution you may have heard of—the electronic revolution. Which of the items shown do you think had the greatest impact on people's lives?

Steam Locomotive
Powered by the steam engine, the first steam locomotive in America was tested in 1830. It carried 35 passengers and traveled at 18 miles per hour.

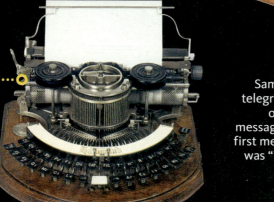

Typewriter
The first practical typewriter was an American invention. It featured the qwerty keyboard we're familiar with today.

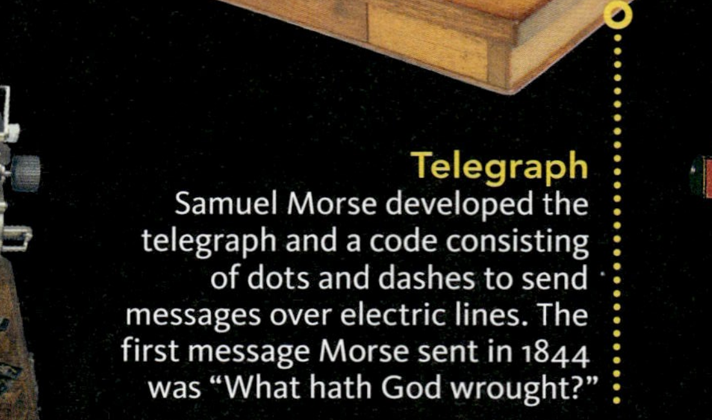

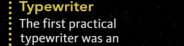

Telegraph
Samuel Morse developed the telegraph and a code consisting of dots and dashes to send messages over electric lines. The first message Morse sent in 1844 was "What hath God wrought?"

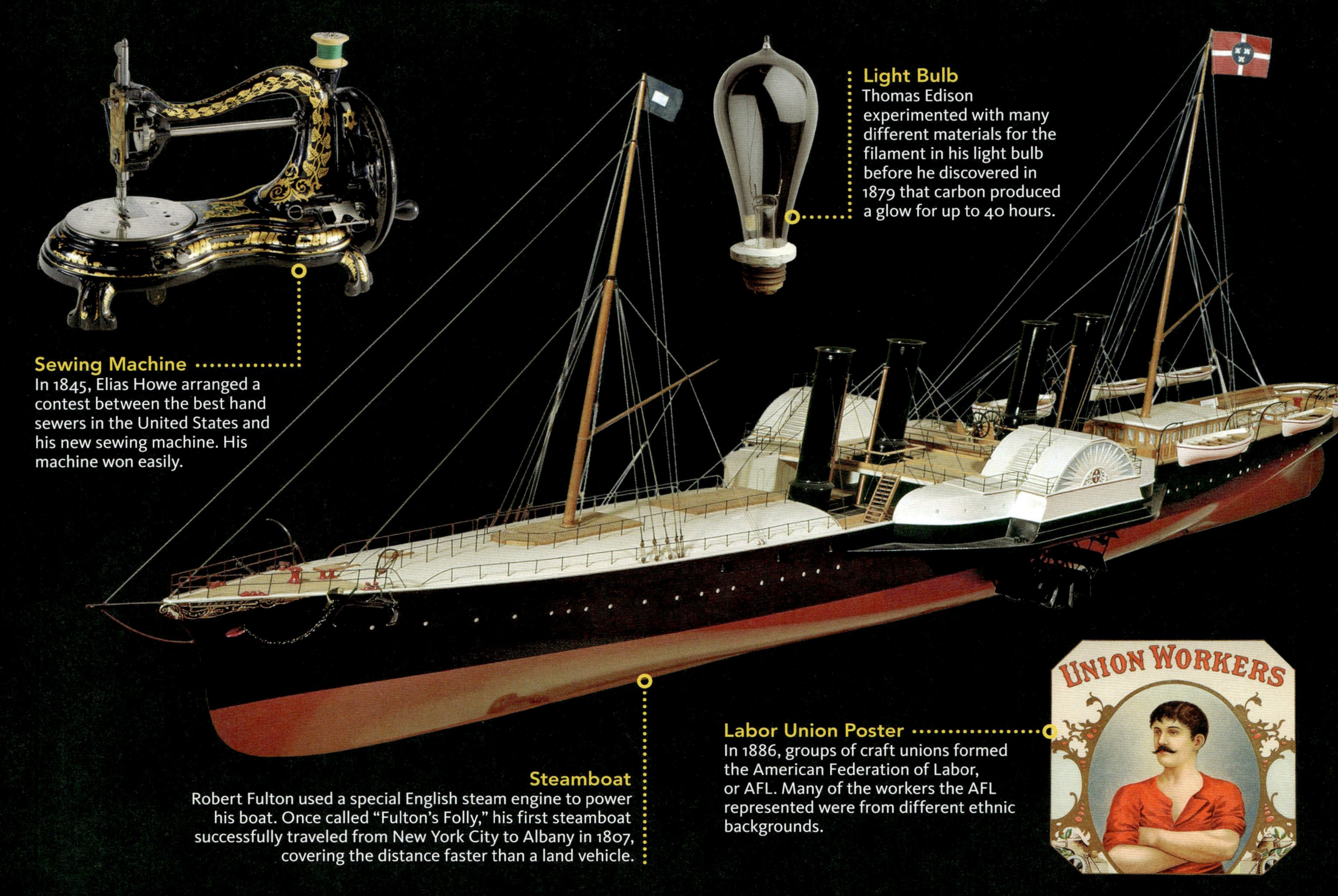
UNION WORKERS

Sewing Machine
In 1845, Elias Howe arranged a contest between the best hand sewers in the United States and his new sewing machine. His machine won easily.

Light Bulb
Thomas Edison experimented with many different materials for the filament in his light bulb before he discovered in 1879 that carbon produced a glow for up to 40 hours.

Steamboat
Robert Fulton used a special English steam engine to power his boat. Once called "Fulton's Folly," his first steamboat successfully traveled from New York City to Albany in 1807, covering the distance faster than a land vehicle.

Labor Union Poster
In 1886, groups of craft unions formed the American Federation of Labor, or AFL. Many of the workers the AFL represented were from different ethnic backgrounds.

1.3 Life in the Industrial City

A report on working class living conditions in France in the 1800s makes for miserable reading: "In their rooms . . . the air is never renewed, it is infected; the walls are plastered with garbage . . . the furniture is dislocated [out of place], worm-eaten, covered with filth . . . the windows . . . are so smoke-encrusted, that the light is unable to penetrate."

MAIN IDEA

Industrialization drew people to cities, where living conditions could be terrible for the working classes and the poor.

FROM COUNTRY TO CITY

Urbanization, or the growth of cities, followed in the footsteps of industrialization. Factories, mines, and mills attracted hordes of workers looking for jobs. Villages rapidly grew into towns and cities.

Major changes in agriculture also contributed to urbanization. In Europe, poor farmers relied on farming common land, which traditionally belonged to everyone. In the 1800s, however, landowners seized millions of acres of common land for their private use. The landowners enclosed the land by building fences around it. They created larger and more efficient farms, where new methods and technology produced more food more cheaply. The larger farms fed the industrial workers but also forced thousands of farming families off their lands and into cities.

During the early 1800s, Europe's cities boomed. For example, the population of London more than doubled, from 1 million to 2.5 million between 1801 and 1851. By that time, 50 percent of Great Britain's population lived in urban areas. Elsewhere, cities such as Berlin, Paris, and New York also doubled or tripled in size. However, most families that moved to cities were simply swapping rural poverty for urban conditions that could be even worse.

URBAN PROBLEMS

Urbanization concentrated large numbers of poor people in small areas. Cities grew uncontrollably and were almost completely unregulated. This resulted in living conditions that were crowded, polluted, and unhealthy. Towns of makeshift huts sprang up. Houses were usually badly built and were cold, damp, and unsafe. And families were charged high prices to live in them.

High rents meant that several families shared a single room. They had no privacy, no running water, and no sanitation or waste disposal. Garbage and sewage piled up in the streets. The smoke from factories polluted the air and blocked out the sun. People survived on a poor diet and lacked clean drinking water.

In these conditions, disease was common and spread quickly. Tuberculosis, typhoid, and cholera killed hundreds of thousands. Movements arose to reform, or improve, conditions. Governments enacted laws to ensure clean water, better sanitation, and safer housing.

Meanwhile, labor unions tried to improve working conditions. Employers and governments had failed to suppress the unions, which grew steadily and

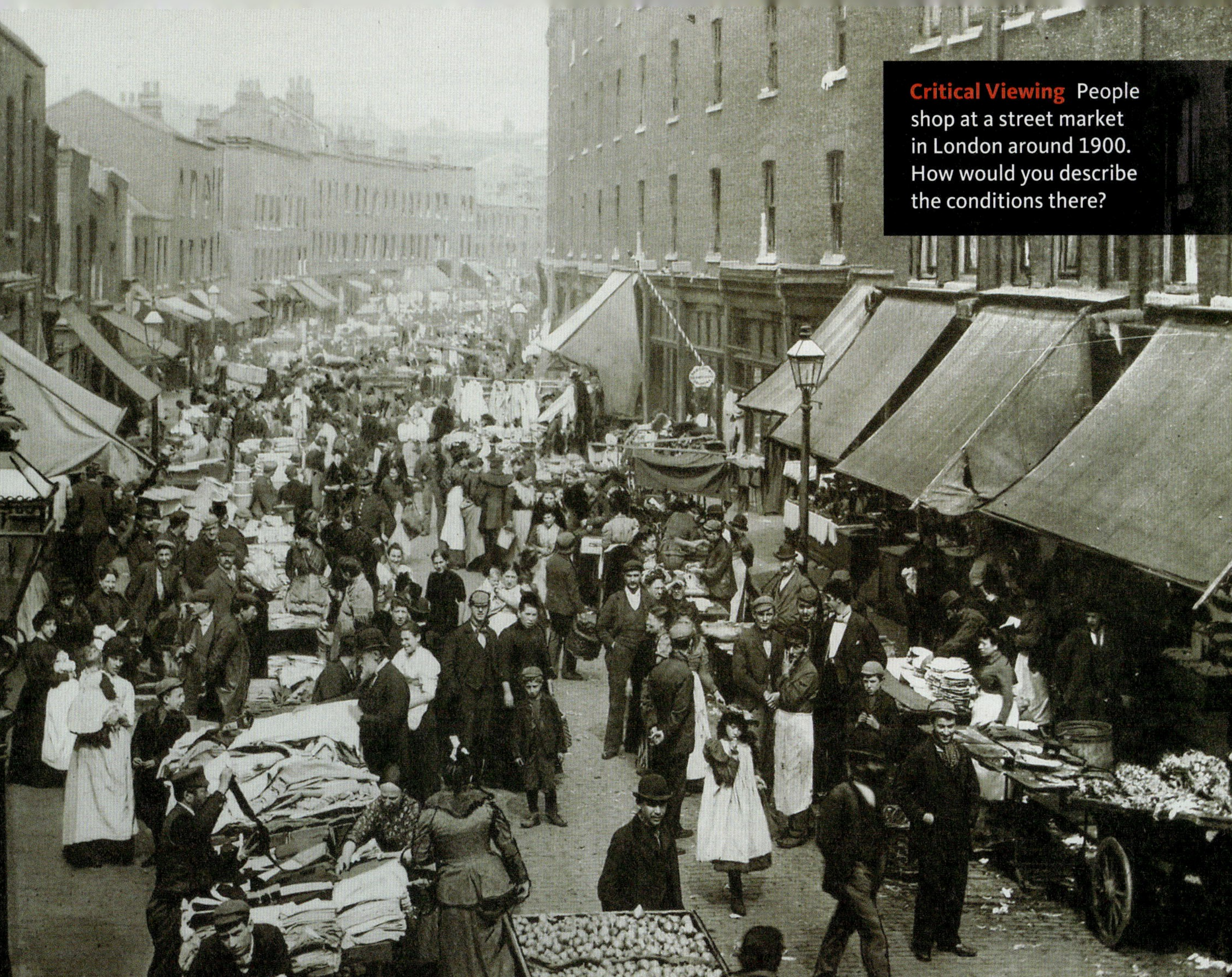

Critical Viewing People shop at a street market in London around 1900. How would you describe the conditions there?

began to have real power. In Great Britain alone, union membership had grown to around one million by 1874.

In the United States, unions banded together to create the American Federation of Labor, or the AFL. The AFL used its bargaining power to win improved wages, hours, benefits, and working conditions for its members. The threat of strike action and social unrest led to important improvements, including higher wages, increased safety, and regulated hours.

The AFL, in part, followed the example set by Great Britain. Britain's Factory Act of 1833 banned children younger than nine years old from working. The 1847 Ten Hours Act stated that women and older children could not work more than ten hours per day on weekdays and Saturdays. The act also required employers to provide children under 13 years of age with at least 2 hours of education every day. These laws served to reduce the unfair treatment of women and children in the workplace.

REVIEW & ASSESS

1. **READING CHECK** Why did industrialization lead to urbanization?
2. **DRAW CONCLUSIONS** Why were diseases common in large cities during the early 1800s?
3. **ANALYZE CAUSE AND EFFECT** What were the effects of the workers' threats to strike?

1.4 Effects on Society

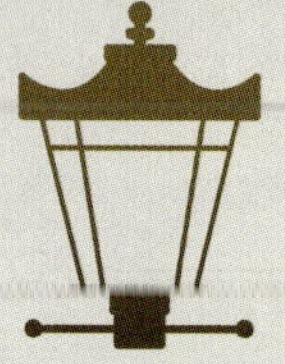

The yellow gaslights glow as you walk home along your respectable city street. Hanging up your top hat and coat, you warm yourself by the roaring fire in the cozy living room. You wonder what the cook has prepared for dinner and pour yourself something to drink. Middle-class life is very comfortable.

MAIN IDEA

Industrialization led to social and political changes that were long-lasting.

DICKENS AND THE URBAN POOR

Charles Dickens was one of the greatest English authors of the 19th century. He sharply criticized a law that made it a crime to be poor. He spoke out against the inhumane treatment of the poor and the wretched conditions in which they were living.

THE MIDDLE CLASS

The Industrial Revolution changed Europe enormously. It affected where people lived and how they lived. It transformed how different economic classes related to one another. Manufacturing and trade replaced land and agriculture as the most important sources of wealth. The number of farm workers shrank and the number of industrial workers grew. The revolution created a new working class of city dwellers, many of whom were poor. Meanwhile, the people who owned the mills, mines, and factories grew rich and powerful. Over time, industrialists became the new ruling class.

Between the super-rich upper class and the super-poor working class, a large **middle class** emerged. The middle class included businesspeople, bankers, merchants, accountants, managers, and engineers. Industry needed lots of skilled specialists, providing clever workers with the chance to move up into the middle class. As the middle class expanded, it sifted its members into a hierarchy of lower, middle, and upper-middle classes.

Life was better at all levels of the middle class. Its members were able to afford new products that increased comfort and convenience. They enjoyed improved housing, diet, education, and health care. The middle class might not have had the luxurious lifestyles of the upper class, but its members had escaped the horrific poverty of the working class.

Not everyone agreed that the rise of the middle class was beneficial to society. The Scottish economist **Adam Smith**, whom you read about in the previous chapter, analyzed the changing nature of the social classes. Division of labor, he believed, would lead to economic growth but would have a negative impact on society if it became too extreme. He worried that workers who did only a single task would be overwhelmed by boredom.

The German philosopher **Karl Marx** wanted social equality. He favored **socialism**, a movement that developed throughout Europe during the Industrial Revolution. In a socialist society, the public or the state owns or controls many or most of the means of production, such as factories. Marx took socialism to an extreme, however. He believed that equality could be

FREE
VOTES FOR WOMEN
WOMEN
AT 8
FREE
General Election, January 1910 - St Pancras

Women display posters and sell newspapers to promote woman suffrage in London in 1910.

achieved only through a workers' revolution to create a classless society with no private property. Marx's theory is known as **communism**. The central idea of this system is "from each according to his ability, to each according to his needs." In the next chapter, you will see how communism affected several European countries.

NEW ROLES FOR WOMEN

The Industrial Revolution also transformed family life. Traditionally, families had worked together at home or in nearby fields, with a woman's main responsibility being her family. Factories separated home and the workplace. Women often became key earners because employers favored their cheap labor. Some working-class women were able to improve their income by working as maids, cooks, cleaners, or child-care workers. Middle-class women had greater access to education and therefore to new opportunities for work.

The changing role of women led to calls for greater equality with men. Women in Great Britain and the United States passionately fought for **woman suffrage**, or the right to vote and participate in politics. Finally, in the 1920s, women in both Great Britain and in the United States gained equal voting rights with men.

REVIEW & ASSESS

1. **READING CHECK** In what ways did industrialization change Europe's social classes?
2. **SEQUENCE EVENTS** Following the Industrial Revolution, how did the role of women change?
3. **COMPARE AND CONTRAST** What were one advantage and one disadvantage of the division of labor?

1.5

Shifting Populations:
Immigration

The immigrants stagger awkwardly onto the bustling dock. Finally they're free from the cramped, foul-smelling, and constantly rolling ship. Activity swirls around them, and the noise is a babble of many languages. Most of the newcomers are pale. They wear ill-fitting rags and carry sacks containing all their worldly goods. Babies scream, children cling to their parents, and adults look bewildered at their first glimpse of life in the New World.

MAIN IDEA

In the 1800s, millions of Europeans began a new life in the United States.

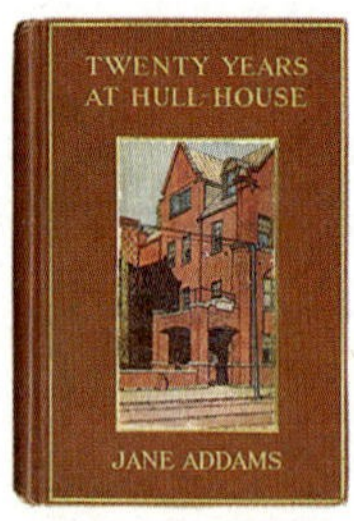

TWENTY YEARS AT HULL-HOUSE
JANE ADDAMS

HULL HOUSE
Hull House was the most influential settlement house in the United States. Established by Jane Addams and Ellen Gates Starr, Hull House served as a hub for Chicago's immigrants.

CAUSES AND EFFECTS

Between 1820 and 1900, about 30 million people **immigrated**, or permanently moved, to the United States. This immigration was driven by many different reasons, or **push-pull factors**. Most people were *pushed* to leave their countries to escape poverty, hunger, a lack of economic opportunity, political and religious oppression, or racial discrimination. Europe's constant wars caused many young men to flee abroad to avoid being forced into the army. Meanwhile, immigrants were *pulled* to new countries like the United States by the promise of rich economic opportunities, better lives, and a tolerant society.

Languages, customs, beliefs, and values from across Europe were transplanted to the United States. Eventually, the country became a blend of many cultures and nationalities. Along with their culture, immigrants brought their technical skills and their ambitions. These were powerful driving forces for U.S. economic growth.

TWO WAVES

Immigration to the United States in the 1800s happened in two major waves. From 1820 to 1870, around 7 million immigrants arrived, mostly from the British Isles, Germany, and Scandinavia. In the 1840s, a disease wiped out Ireland's potato harvest, which was the staple food for the poor. The resulting Irish Potato Famine pushed about 25 percent of Ireland's starving population to leave the country.

After 1870, a second wave of immigration brought roughly 23 million Europeans to the United States. They came mostly from southern and eastern Europe and provided the cheap labor needed to fuel the country's rapid industrialization. After landing on **Ellis Island**, where most immigrants were processed, many stayed in New York. In 1892, around 42 percent of New Yorkers were foreign-born. Others flocked to Chicago and other growing industrial cities. Meanwhile, Chinese immigrants moved west to work on the railroads connecting cities across the country. By 1900, around half of the United States' 76 million people lived in cities.

Critical Viewing An Italian woman arrives with her children at Ellis Island. What challenges did this family probably face?

REVIEW & ASSESS

1. **READING CHECK** Why did millions of Europeans immigrate to the United States in the 19th century?

2. **ANALYZE CAUSE AND EFFECT** How did European immigrants contribute to U.S. economic growth?

3. **IDENTIFY MAIN IDEAS AND DETAILS** Which groups made up the two waves of immigration to the United States in the 1800s?

2.1 Nationalism in Europe

Feeling a sense of pride and loyalty to your nation is an expression of nationalism, a force that unites people who share a culture. Nationalism created whole new countries, including the nations of Italy and Germany.

MAIN IDEA

Nationalism redrew the political map of Europe.

NATIONALISM DEFINED

Nationalism is a feeling of pride shared by people with the same history, language, and customs. This powerful idea generates loyalty to a person's **nation-state**, which is a political unit in which people have a common culture and identity. Nationalism is also a modern concept. Throughout much of history, people were not defined by nationality but by other loyalties, such as to a family, a city-state, or a dynasty.

The roots of nationalism are found in the American and French Revolutions, which you read about in the previous chapter. After these revolutions, people increasingly wanted to identify with and show loyalty to their own nation. The idea spread through the colonies of South America and emerged in Europe during the early 1800s. Nationalist uprisings occurred across Europe, but most were suppressed until 1848, a year of revolutions.

NATIONALISM EMERGES

In February 1848, France was again plunged into revolution. King Louis-Philippe was a moderate monarch, but he supported the rich middle class over the needs of the working class. Hungry and desperate after a bad harvest, the poor rebelled and replaced the king with a **republic**, or government in which the people vote for their leaders. Napoleon Bonaparte's nephew, Louis-Napoleon, was elected president. However, he dissolved the republic and ruled as an emperor. But another revolution in 1875 firmly established France as a republic, which it remains to this day.

The 1848 revolution sparked nationalist unrest across Europe. At that time, Italy was a patchwork of independent city-states, with Austria controlling the north. After 1848, some northern states briefly declared themselves republics, but only Sardinia's constitutional government lasted. Sardinia's nationalist prime minister, Camillo di Cavour, and King Victor Emmanuel began unifying northern Italy. In 1859, Sardinia's defeat of Austria prompted most northern Italian states to join a united Italy.

Meanwhile, a fiery nationalist named **Giuseppe Garibaldi** emerged. He put together an army that invaded southern Italy. He conquered Sicily and Naples and convinced them to unify with Italy. By 1861, the self-governing kingdom of Italy was established, and by 1870, all of Italy was united as a single nation.

Germans had also experimented with nationalism after 1848, but initially the many independent German states refused to unite. The most powerful state was Prussia, ruled by Wilhelm I and Prime Minister **Otto von Bismarck**. Realizing that nationalism was unstoppable, Bismarck began unifying Germany under Prussian leadership in the 1860s. Bismarck created a **confederation**, or group, of northern German states and won huge support by

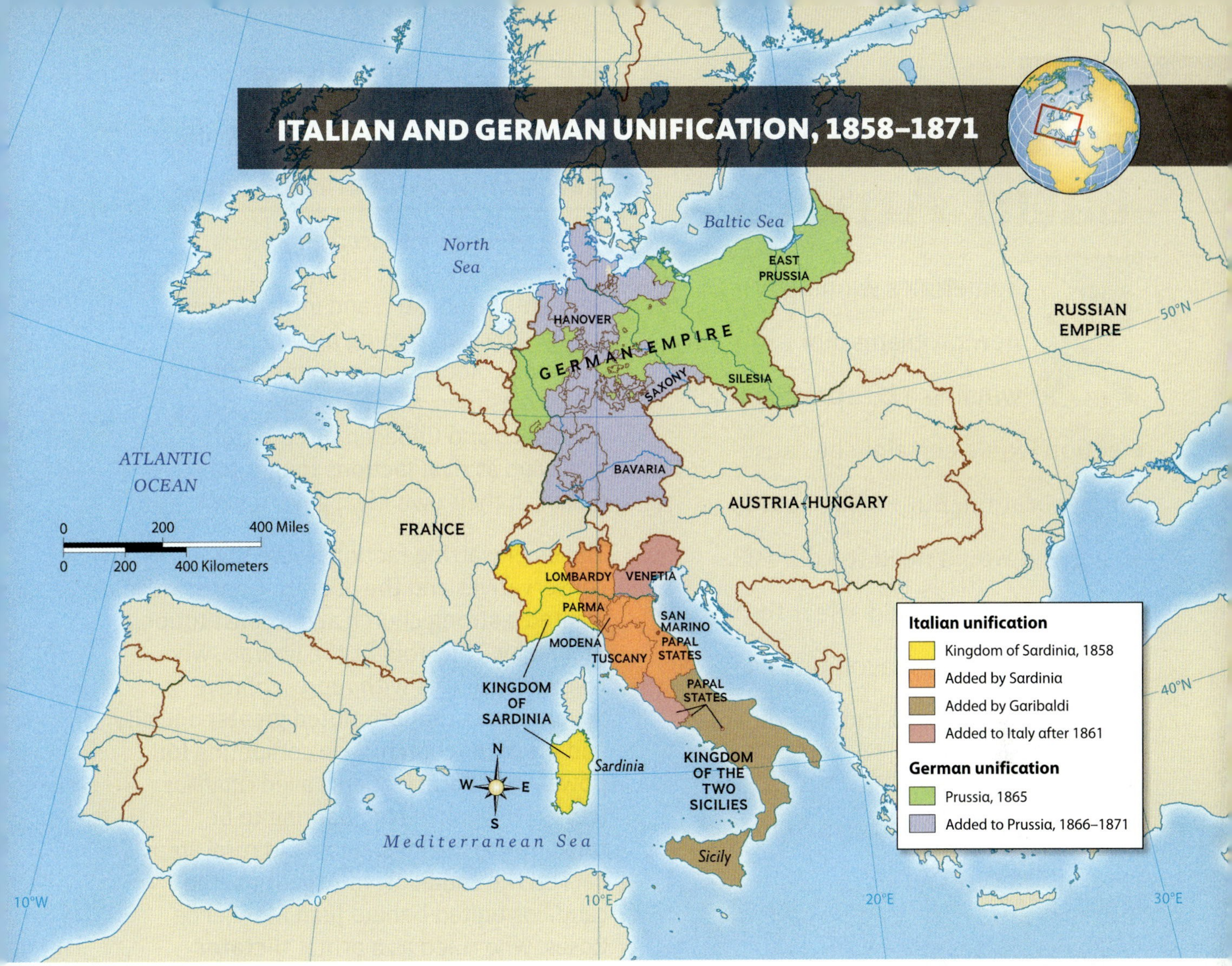

ITALIAN AND GERMAN UNIFICATION, 1858–1871

Baltic Sea
North Sea
EAST PRUSSIA
RUSSIAN EMPIRE
HANOVER
GERMAN EMPIRE
SAXONY
SILESIA
ATLANTIC OCEAN
BAVARIA
AUSTRIA-HUNGARY
FRANCE
0 200 400 Miles
0 200 400 Kilometers
LOMBARDY
VENETIA
PARMA
MODENA
TUSCANY
SAN MARINO
PAPAL STATES
KINGDOM OF SARDINIA
Sardinia
KINGDOM OF THE TWO SICILIES
Sicily
Mediterranean Sea
N S E W
10°W 0° 10°E 20°E 30°E 40°N 50°N

Italian unification
- Kingdom of Sardinia, 1858
- Added by Sardinia
- Added by Garibaldi
- Added to Italy after 1861

German unification
- Prussia, 1865
- Added to Prussia, 1866–1871

giving men of all economic classes the vote. Prussia's armies defeated Austria, securing more territory. Bismarck's popular policies encouraged many southern German states to join Prussia. In 1870, following France's declaration of war, Prussia spectacularly crushed the French army in the Franco-Prussian War, and Germany's remaining states joined the confederation. In January 1871, a unified and self-ruling German Empire was proclaimed under Bismarck's leadership.

OTTO VON BISMARCK

Bismarck was a clever and flexible leader. He understood what people wanted and was realistic enough to give it to them whenever possible. Bismarck's liberal and modernizing policies won him much popularity. Because he was respected and well liked, people sometimes underestimated him, which Bismarck used to his advantage. But his real power was his steadfast determination, earning him the nickname the Iron Chancellor.

REVIEW & ASSESS

1. **READING CHECK** In what way did nationalism change the political map of Europe?
2. **SEQUENCE EVENTS** Where and when did the roots of nationalism first take hold?
3. **INTERPRET MAPS** What was one effect of adding Hanover, Saxony, and Bavaria to Prussia?

2.2 Nationalism in Latin America

Sometimes winning brings new problems. For example, winning a U.S. presidential election would certainly be cause for celebration. But for the next four years, you would need to address many issues that could affect the entire world. When revolutionaries in Latin America won independence, they faced tremendous challenges to make their new nations succeed.

MAIN IDEA

Nationalist revolutions created the countries of modern Latin America.

END OF EUROPEAN RULE

As you learned earlier, a spirit of revolution swept through Latin America in the early 1800s. With Spain and Portugal defeated by France, oppressed Spanish and Portuguese colonial subjects claimed independence. Early nationalist revolutions in Haiti, Paraguay, Argentina, and Chile encouraged other colonies to rebel. In the north, **Simón Bolívar** (see-MONH boh-LEE-var) led the liberation of Venezuela, Colombia, Panama, Ecuador, and Bolivia. In the south, **José de San Martín** (hoh-SAY duh san-mahr-TEEN), an Argentinian soldier and statesman, helped liberate Argentina, Chile, and Peru. By 1850, almost all of South America was free of European rule, and independent, self-governing nations had taken the place of colonies.

NEW NATIONS IN LATIN AMERICA

These new nations faced enormous challenges. The fight for independence left agriculture, industry, and infrastructure ravaged by war. Fleeing members of defeated colonial governments looted state treasuries. Many countries, such as Mexico and Chile, endured bitter civil wars as rival factions fought to establish their own ideal government.

The chief warring factions were the conservatives and the liberals. Conservatives wanted a strong church and a constitutional monarchy. They fought the liberals, who favored republics with representative governments that promoted greater equality and a weaker church. Also competing for power were local leaders called *caudillos* (kow-THEE-yohz). Not wanting to be ruled by urban elites, people in rural areas backed the caudillos. In Argentina, the caudillos united behind Juan Manuel de Rosas, who ruled as a brutal **dictator** for more than 20 years. A dictator is a person who rules with total authority.

Independence did little to fulfill the expectations of poor revolutionaries. Governments had no money to rebuild economies, leaving many people worse off than ever. In time, foreign investment flowed in to secure raw materials for overseas industrialization. But much of the wealth went to a few rich businessmen and corrupt officials, rather than to the poor.

Meanwhile, liberal policies allowed businessmen to buy native lands, forcing native people to leave or become tenant farmers. Even freed slaves had little choice but to keep working for their former slaveholders for pitifully low wages. Despite independence, the poor majority grew poorer and the rich minority grew richer across most of Latin America.

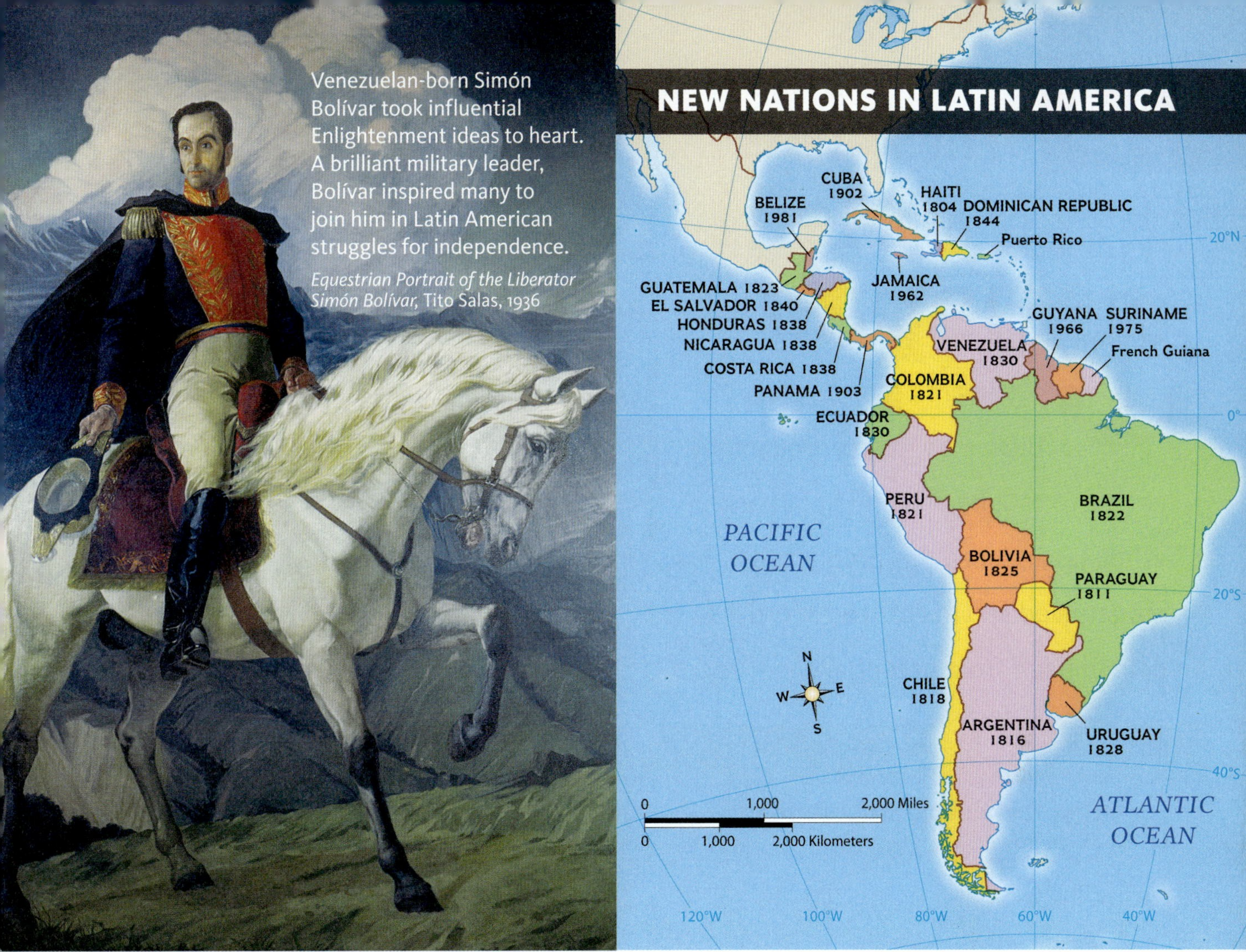
NEW NATIONS IN LATIN AMERICA
CUBA 1902
BELIZE 1981
HAITI 1804
DOMINICAN REPUBLIC 1844
Puerto Rico
JAMAICA 1962
GUATEMALA 1823
EL SALVADOR 1840
HONDURAS 1838
NICARAGUA 1838
COSTA RICA 1838
PANAMA 1903
GUYANA 1966
SURINAME 1975
French Guiana
VENEZUELA 1830
COLOMBIA 1821
ECUADOR 1830
PERU 1821
BRAZIL 1822
BOLIVIA 1825
PARAGUAY 1811
CHILE 1818
ARGENTINA 1816
URUGUAY 1828
PACIFIC OCEAN
ATLANTIC OCEAN
N
S
E
W
0
1,000
2,000 Miles
0
1,000
2,000 Kilometers
20°N
0°
20°S
40°S
120°W
100°W
80°W
60°W
40°W

Venezuelan-born Simón Bolívar took influential Enlightenment ideas to heart. A brilliant military leader, Bolívar inspired many to join him in Latin American struggles for independence.

Equestrian Portrait of the Liberator Simón Bolívar, Tito Salas, 1936

The new nations fought one another over boundaries. For example, Argentina, Brazil, and Uruguay conquered large areas of Paraguay. Chile seized mineral-rich deserts from Peru and Bolivia.

The United States also gained territory from Latin America after fighting and winning a war against Mexico. The Mexican-American War lasted from 1846 to 1848 and was the result of a dispute over the boundary of Texas. By treaty, the United States acquired vast areas from Mexico, including all of present-day California, Nevada, Utah, and most of New Mexico and Arizona. The 1823 Monroe Doctrine stated that the United States would militarily oppose European attempts to retake Latin America. Later, U.S. president Theodore Roosevelt expanded the doctrine, which paved the way for U.S. involvement in Latin American affairs. The United States increasingly used military force to stabilize unrest in the region, especially in Haiti, Nicaragua, the Dominican Republic, and Cuba. For the most part, the newly established nations viewed such intervention as unwelcome.

REVIEW & ASSESS

1. **READING CHECK** How did colonies in Latin America gain independence and become self-governing nations?
2. **IDENTIFY MAIN IDEAS AND DETAILS** What challenges did new nations in Latin America face?
3. **INTERPRET MAPS** What was the first new nation in Latin America? What was the last?

2.3 The Rise of Meiji Japan

If you are pestered and bullied by people, you might decide to toughen up and fight back. When Japan faced this problem, it modernized and militarized in order to defend itself from potential enemies.

MAIN IDEA

Japan's rapid modernization transformed it into a world power.

MODERNIZATION

As you may recall, Japan's Tokugawa government isolated the country in the 1630s. Although the Japanese emperor was the head of government, he was only a figurehead. The real power lay with the shogun, the military leader. Fearing that outside influences would weaken Japanese culture, the shoguns closed Japan to foreigners for more than 200 years, which severely limited trade.

Then, in 1853, the United States sailed four ships into Tokyo Bay. They forced the shogun to open Japanese ports to U.S. trade. Soon Britain, France, and Russia also forced Japan to trade, with terms that were often unfair. The Japanese eventually overthrew the Tokugawa government, and the emperor was restored as leader. In 1868, the emperor took the name **Meiji** (MAY-jee) in what became known as the Meiji Restoration.

The Meiji government transformed Japan into a modern industrial state. Western experts, machines, and materials helped fast-track Japan's industrialization, especially in textile production. Japan updated its infrastructure, while its factories soon created a booming economy that decreased dependence on foreign imports. The government also introduced European-style banking and a modern education system. By 1900, Japan had achieved the highest literacy rate in Asia.

These reforms brought radical change to Japan's political and social structure. The traditional feudal hierarchy was abolished, and the daimyo and samurai disbanded. Everyone was now considered socially equal. In 1889, a Western-style constitution was introduced with a limited representative government. The constitution also gave considerable political power to the military, which would

Japanese soldiers stand at attention on graduation day at the Army University in Tokyo around 1900.

influence future policy. By the 1890s, Japan was strong enough to renegotiate its trade deals on more favorable terms.

NATIONALISM AND MILITARISM

Militarism, or the belief in a strong and aggressive military, went hand in hand with Japanese nationalism. Military power was considered essential in keeping Japan free of foreign rule. Japan used Western ideas and experts to build a European-style army and a modern navy. A strong military enabled Japan to quickly expand its empire. In 1895, Japan's modernized military defeated China in the Sino-Japanese War. With this victory, the Japanese gained trading privileges on Chinese territory and were allowed to run factories in China. Japan also gained influence over Taiwan and other important territories. Then Japan defeated Russia in the Russo-Japanese War (1904–1905). To the horror of Western powers, an Asian nation had defeated a European one. In 1910, Japan annexed Korea as a colony. In just 50 years, Japan had become a world power and a force to be reckoned with.

REVIEW & ASSESS

1. **READING CHECK** How did the Meiji Restoration modernize Japan?
2. **SEQUENCE EVENTS** What events led to the collapse of Japan's Tokugawa government?
3. **ANALYZE LANGUAGE USE** The text uses the word *figurehead* to describe the Japanese emperor. What does the word suggest about the emperor's role in government?

3.1 Factors Behind Imperialism

The modern world map is a colorful patchwork of nearly 200 independent countries. But in the 1800s, a few European countries painted most of the world in the colors of their empires.

MAIN IDEA

In the 1800s, Europe's major powers competed to rule the world.

RAW MATERIALS AND MARKETS

Imperialism is a system in which a stronger nation controls weaker nations or territories beyond its own borders. These dependent territories, often called colonies, make up the nation's empire. Empires have existed throughout history, but in the 1800s, European imperialism reached extraordinary levels. Europe's major powers expanded their empires by around 83,000 square miles a year. And from 1875 to 1914, that rate doubled. By 1914, Europe had controlled or conquered most of the world.

Industrialization motivated European imperialism. Each nation's industry needed mounting quantities of increasingly varied raw materials, such as oil, rubber, and copper. European governments exerted influence over regions where these materials were found. Eventually, such regions came under direct rule of European nations. These colonies also provided a valuable market for the sale of an empire's manufactured goods.

The Industrial Revolution gave Europe a huge technological advantage over the territories it exploited. Fast-firing guns, steam-powered warships, and new medicines all allowed small European forces to conquer vast areas. What's more, Europe's industrialization led to rapid population growth, which provided the workers needed for imperial expansion. In 1800, one-fifth of the world's population was European. But by 1914, that ratio had increased to one-third. As many as two million Europeans emigrated each year. Many departed for imperial colonies. Some politicians encouraged imperialism as a useful outlet for surplus populations.

Similarly, building exotic overseas empires created a national pride that united people and distracted them from their problems. Indeed, some imperial conquests were undertaken almost purely to boost national pride. The intense rivalries among European nations—especially among Britain, France, Germany, and Russia—resulted in competition for control of distant lands. Such control was a measure of national superiority and provided an advantage in European politics.

CULTURAL IMPERIALISM

Racism, the belief that one race is better than others, also drove imperialism. The Europeans, who were mostly white, believed it was their duty to "civilize" the native peoples, who were mostly nonwhite. This involved replacing local traditions with European ideas of society and morality, which affected everything from clothing to laws to religion.

Imperialism also brought a surge of **missionaries**, or Christian preachers, who attempted to convert the native people to Christianity. Most governments supported missionary work, which was usually peaceful and included beneficial elements such as education and medicine. Nonetheless, missionaries reinforced the notion of European racial and religious superiority over indigenous peoples.

European Imperialism by Region

Region	European Colonizers	Resources
India	Great Britain	Cotton, tea
Africa	France	Gold, slaves
	Great Britain	Cotton, gold
Southeast Asia	Netherlands	Spices, coffee, sugarcane, rubber, tin
	Great Britain	Timber
	France	Coffee, tea

This image shows a South African sugar plantation around 1910.

REVIEW & ASSESS

1. **READING CHECK** Why did European countries dramatically expand their empires in the 1800s?

2. **DRAW CONCLUSIONS** Why did Europeans believe they had a duty to "civilize" native peoples?

3. **MAKE INFERENCES** Why do you think most governments supported missionary work?

3.2

British India

By 1914, Great Britain ruled 20 percent of the world's land and dominated its seas. Of the 400 million people living in the British Empire, over three-quarters lived in its most valued colony. That colony was India.

MAIN IDEA

The British conquered and ruled India to exploit its raw materials and manpower.

INDIA AS A COLONY

The British set out to trade with India, not to conquer it. In the 1600s, the **East India Company**, an important British trading organization, established trading posts across India. The Company was made up of merchants who invested in a trading mission and shared its profits. To defend or expand its commercial activity, the Company used its private armies to take control of important areas.

India had been weakened by the decline of its mighty Mughal Empire, which left a patchwork of self-governing states. This made it easier for the Company to take advantage of political rivalries and conquer India bit by bit. It ruled Indian states either directly or through an allied Indian prince. By 1750, the Company had pushed out other European powers, such as Portugal, and was governing most of the subcontinent as a colony.

The Company was not an understanding ruler. It banned traditional customs and introduced Western-style administration, education, and legal systems. It allowed Christian missionaries to aggressively convert Indians and instituted English as the official language. Meanwhile, it exploited India's vast supply of raw materials and labor. It also made the colony a major market for British imports. The Company built an extensive rail network, improved roads, and introduced a postal service. However, these improvements were primarily to help the Company rather than the people of India.

Many Indians deeply resented British rule. In 1857, that resentment exploded into a violent rebellion by the **sepoys**, native Indian soldiers employed by the Company. The Sepoy Rebellion spread across central and northern India. Although the rebellion was defeated, it showed the limits of Company power.

Following a series of laws passed by Parliament to establish some control over the Company and regulate its activities, the British government took direct control, or rule, of India in 1858. As a result, India became an official British colony, and the East India Company was dissolved soon after.

THE JEWEL IN THE CROWN

The period of Britain's **direct rule** in India is known as the **Raj**, meaning "rule." Although the British government introduced some reforms, much continued as before. The focus on extracting raw materials left India's industry underdeveloped. What's more, imported British clothing and other manufactured goods damaged India's textile industry and other industries as well. By the 1880s, about 20 percent of British exports were sent to India.

Britain's development of infrastructure, education, and administration systems continued, but taxes went directly to Parliament in London. Meanwhile, Indians

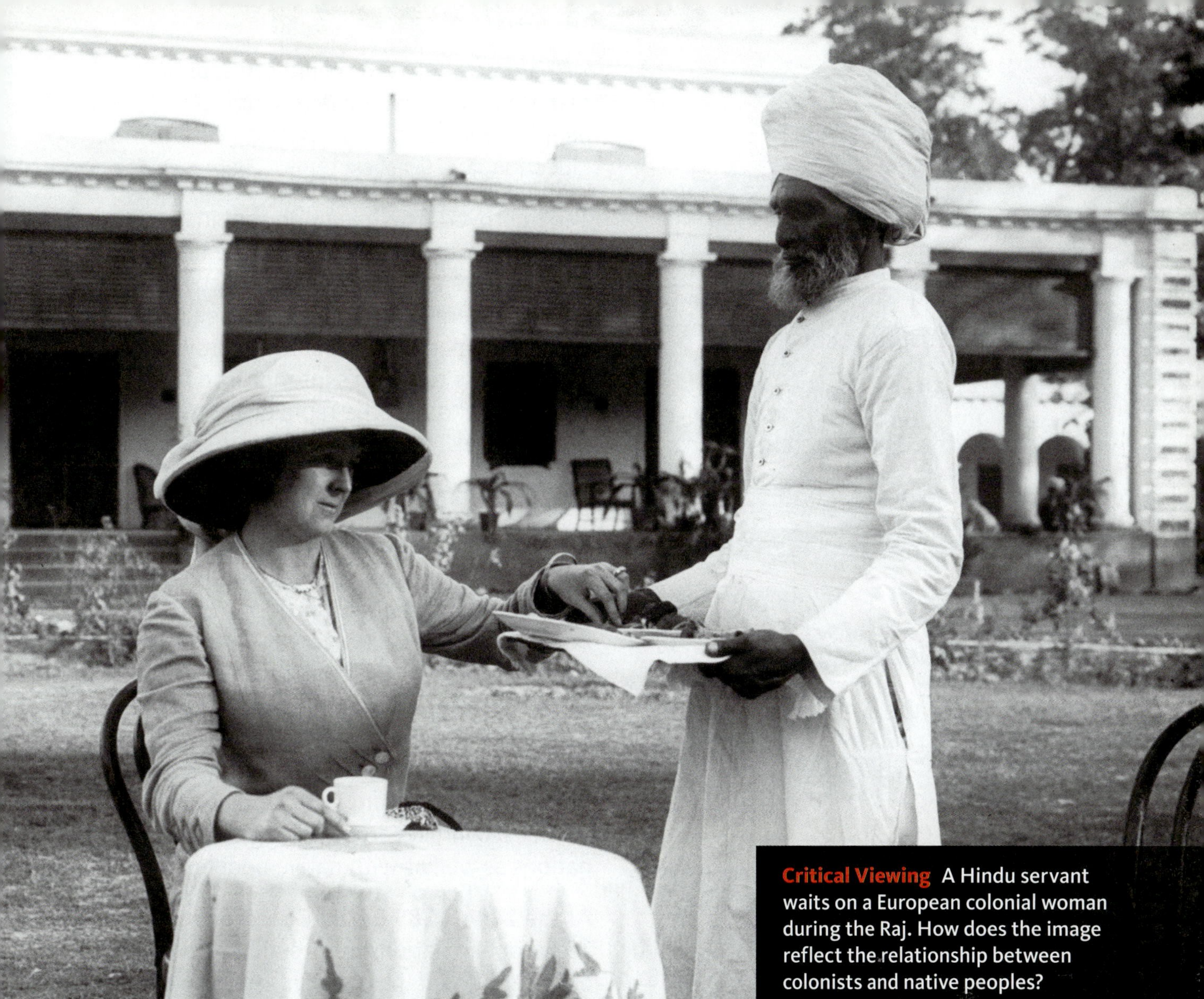

Critical Viewing A Hindu servant waits on a European colonial woman during the Raj. How does the image reflect the relationship between colonists and native peoples?

were actively excluded from any real power. This caused resentment among India's Western-educated middle class.

At the same time, Britain's rule laid the groundwork for an independence movement in India. Britain forced India to unify, and a sense of national unity began to emerge. Britain also exposed India to democracy, leading Indians to start calling for participation in government and for self-rule. In 1885, local leaders formed the Indian National Congress to promote Indian rights. The Congress became a powerful voice for Indian nationalism and the driving force behind India's independence. Finally, in 1947, India gained its independence from Britain and split into two countries: India, dominated by Hindus, and Pakistan, dominated by Muslims.

REVIEW & ASSESS

1. **READING CHECK** How did the British come to rule India?
2. **ANALYZE CAUSE AND EFFECT** Why was the East India Company able to become so powerful in India?
3. **SEQUENCE EVENTS** What events led to the Sepoy Rebellion?

3.3 The Scramble for Africa

For centuries, Europeans knew very little about the interior of Africa. That all changed in the 1800s, when new technologies allowed Europeans to travel to this uncharted territory. Their adventures captivated people's imaginations. They also paved the way for Europe's domination of resource-rich Africa.

MAIN IDEA

Technological superiority allowed European nations to divide up Africa.

TECHNOLOGY AND IMPERIALISM

By the 1800s, Europeans had colonized much of the African coast. However, the huge size, harsh terrain, and deadly diseases of the continent's interior made exploration difficult. But during the 1800s, improved navigation and mapmaking enabled explorers to more accurately pinpoint their position. Medical advances helped protect Europeans from African disease and infection. The discovery of quinine as an effective treatment for malaria was especially important. Quinine enabled Europeans to survive in Africa.

Europeans also armed themselves with modern guns that were fast and accurate. The invention of the machine gun made a single soldier deadlier than ever. A few well-armed Europeans could confidently defeat a vast force of indigenous people armed only with spears.

Communications and transportation also improved. The telegraph sent instant messages over long distances, which allowed Europeans to act quickly and collectively. Steam-powered ships carried Europeans up Africa's many rivers. Railways provided direct access to Africa's interior. The rails also brought about the rapid distribution of raw materials, goods, and Western culture.

THE BERLIN CONFERENCE

When slavery was abolished in the mid-1800s, Europeans became less interested in Africa as a potential source of wealth. But the explorers' discovery of valuable raw materials brought the continent back to Europe's attention. Competition to exploit Africa's resources grew dangerously political. With Britain, France, Germany, Italy, Spain, Portugal, and Belgium all extending their colonies, conflicts arose among these nations as well as with native peoples.

At the 1884–1885 **Berlin Conference**, 13 European nations met to divide up the entire continent. No African nations were invited to attend, and no attention was paid to traditional ethnic or cultural boundaries. According to the conference, nations in attendance could snatch up an unclaimed area of Africa as long as they occupied and administered it. This started a race for territory known as the Scramble for Africa. Britain won the lion's share, which stretched from South Africa to Egypt.

Aided by superior technology, European nations soon subdued their colonies. They then subjected Africa to the full force of cultural imperialism by imposing Western laws, economics, languages, values, and religion. European exploitation and ideas of racial superiority severely damaged the continent. Africa is still working to recover from the effects of European imperialism today.

IMPERIALISM IN AFRICA, 1914
30°W
20°W
10°W
0°
10°E
20°E
30°E
40°E
50°E
40°N
30°N
20°N
10°N
0°
10°S
20°S
30°S
Equator
Tropic of Cancer
Tropic of Capricorn
Mediterranean Sea
ATLANTIC OCEAN
SPANISH MOROCCO
Madeira I. (Portugal)
FRENCH MOROCCO
Canary Islands (Spain)
IFNI
TUNISIA
ALGERIA
LIBYA
EGYPT
RÍO DE ORO
FRENCH WEST AFRICA
FRENCH EQUATORIAL AFRICA
ANGLO-EGYPTIAN SUDAN
ERITREA
BRITISH SOMALILAND
FRENCH SOMALILAND
ETHIOPIA
THE GAMBIA
PORTUGUESE GUINEA
TOGOLAND
NIGERIA
SIERRA LEONE
LIBERIA
GOLD COAST
CAMEROON
Fernando Po (Spain)
SPANISH GUINEA (RÍO MUNI)
ITALIAN SOMALILAND
UGANDA
BRITISH EAST AFRICA
BELGIAN CONGO
GERMAN EAST AFRICA
Cabinda (PORT.)
N
S
E
W
ANGOLA
NYASALAND
NORTHERN RHODESIA
SOUTHERN RHODESIA
MOZAMBIQUE (PORTUGUESE EAST AFRICA)
MADAGASCAR
GERMAN SOUTH-WEST AFRICA
WALVIS BAY (U.K.)
BECHUANA-LAND
UNION OF SOUTH AFRICA
SWAZILAND
BASUTOLAND
0
500
1,000 Miles
0
500
1,000 Kilometers
Territorial claims
Belgium
France
Germany
Italy
Portugal
Spain
Great Britain

REVIEW & ASSESS

1. **READING CHECK** How did technology help Europeans take possession of Africa's interior?

2. **MAKE PREDICTIONS** If the Berlin Conference had not taken place, how do you think African countries might have developed differently?

3. **INTERPRET MAPS** Which countries controlled the most colonies in Africa? Which countries controlled the least?

3.4 Western Powers in Southeast Asia

Competition for colonial resources was so intense that in 1664, the Dutch swapped Manhattan Island for a British island in Southeast Asia. This trade gave the Dutch complete control of the world's supply of nutmeg. Partly because of its rarity, nutmeg was extremely valuable. However, the British managed to sneak out a few seedlings and were soon growing nutmeg across Southeast Asia.

MAIN IDEA

To gain trade resources, Europe colonized most of Southeast Asia by 1914.

DUTCH AND BRITISH CONTROL

During the 1500s, European countries fought to gain control of the valuable spice trade with Southeast Asia. Then, in the 1600s, the Dutch East India Company forced the Portuguese from the region. This powerful trading company backed up business with military might. It built fortresses and used armed ships and soldiers to dominate the Dutch East Indies (present-day Indonesia). First, the company seized the territory of Malacca and then the island of Java. The company steadily expanded its control to eventually include a 3,000-mile-long chain of islands. For around 300 years, the Dutch controlled the region's supply of major resources, which included spices, coffee, cocoa, sugarcane, pineapple, coconuts, bananas, and, later, rubber.

In 1795, the British took Malacca from the Dutch. Attracted by Southeast Asia's rich resources, Britain also wanted to protect its own trade routes with China. To do so, the British steadily took control of the strategically important Strait of Malacca. Then they colonized Singapore at the southern end of the strait. Singapore became one of the world's busiest trading ports.

To protect British interests in India, Britain extended its control over neighboring Burma, which eventually became part of British India. The British also took control of parts of Borneo, New Guinea, and other Southeast Asian islands. In the 1870s, Britain began colonizing Malaya. The British encouraged Chinese immigration as a source of cheap labor for the rubber and tin industries. In time, the Malays became an ethnic minority in their own country.

FRENCH INDOCHINA

Since the 1700s, France had operated trading posts and Christian missions in what is now Vietnam. But native people's attacks on Christian missionaries, as well as France's growing demand for resources and markets, led France to begin colonizing Vietnam. In 1858, France took the city of Da Nang. The following year, France took the city of Saigon. French control eventually expanded to include Vietnam, Cambodia, and Laos, countries that collectively became **French Indochina**.

The French governed Indochina by direct rule, meaning that the French themselves made up the government and administration. Native people had almost no political power. Social and economic

IMPERIALISM IN SOUTHEAST ASIA, 1914
Territorial claims
Netherlands
France
Germany
Portugal
Great Britain
United States
BURMA
SIAM (THAILAND)
FRENCH INDOCHINA
South China Sea
PHILIPPINES
PACIFIC OCEAN
BRUNEI
NORTH BORNEO
MALAYA
SARAWAK
Strait of Malacca
SINGAPORE
Borneo
Sumatra
Celebes
DUTCH EAST INDIES
New Guinea
GERMAN NEW GUINEA
PAPUA
INDIAN OCEAN
Java
PORTUGUESE TIMOR
Tropic of Cancer
Equator
20°N
10°N
0°
10°S
100°E
110°E
120°E
130°E
140°E
150°E
0 400 800 Miles
0 400 800 Kilometers
N
S
E
W

policies benefited the colonists and a small group of wealthy native people while making the lives of the poor more miserable. In Vietnam, for example, the government constructed irrigation works to create more farmland, which was then sold to the highest bidder. Although rice production increased fourfold, peasants had even less land on which to raise food. Many became tenant farmers whose rent was paid with high percentages of the rice they raised. Their landlords then exported the rice for profit.

With French Indochina under its control, France had become Europe's second largest imperial power. France had secured a large share of Asia's resources and markets, including trade with China. By 1914, almost all of the Philippines and Dutch East Indies were under the control of Europe or the United States. However, nationalist movements were growing. Small-scale farmers resented high taxes. And the emergence of a Western-educated native professional class in these countries led to sometimes violent calls for independence.

REVIEW & ASSESS

1. **READING CHECK** What did Southeast Asia have that European countries wanted for themselves?

2. **IDENTIFY PROBLEMS AND SOLUTIONS** How did the British acquire cheap labor for their tin and rubber industries?

3. **INTERPRET MAPS** Which area of Southeast Asia did the United States colonize?

CHAPTER 25 Review

VOCABULARY

For each pair of vocabulary words, write one sentence that explains the connection between the two words.

1. **industrialize; labor union**
   After countries industrialized, workers began to form labor unions.
2. **urbanization; middle class**
3. **immigrate; push-pull factors**
4. **communism; socialism**
5. **nationalism; nation-state**
6. **imperialism; racism**
7. **republic; direct rule**
8. **militarism; dictator**
9. **confederation; nationalism**
10. **missionary; racism**

READING SKILL

11. **ORGANIZE IDEAS: SEQUENCE EVENTS**
    If you haven't already, complete your time line of events of the Industrial Revolution using a graphic organizer like the one shown here. Provide a date for each event and list the events in the order in which they occurred. Then answer the question below.

Events of the Industrial Revolution

1750
Beginning of Industrial Revolution

Which event do you think was the most significant of the Industrial Revolution? Explain your answer.

MAIN IDEAS

Answer the following questions. Support your answers with evidence from the chapter.

12. What was the Industrial Revolution? **LESSON 1.1**
13. What kinds of work did members of the middle class perform? **LESSON 1.4**
14. Why did millions of Europeans immigrate to the United States in the 1800s? **LESSON 1.5**
15. How did nationalism change the political map of Europe? **LESSON 2.1**
16. Which Latin American groups opposed each other after the Portuguese and Spanish left? **LESSON 2.2**
17. How did the Meiji government transform Japan into a world power? **LESSON 2.3**
18. What caused European countries to expand their empires in the 1800s? **LESSON 3.1**
19. How did technology enable Europeans to divide up Africa? **LESSON 3.3**
20. How did the Dutch East India Company establish control of the Dutch East Indies? **LESSON 3.4**

CRITICAL THINKING

Answer the following questions. Support your answers with evidence from the chapter.

21. **COMPARE AND CONTRAST** How were goods made before the Industrial Revolution? How were they made after the Industrial Revolution?
22. **ANALYZE CAUSE AND EFFECT** How did the seizure of common lands affect farming families?
23. **DRAW CONCLUSIONS** Why was Otto von Bismarck important in Germany's unification?
24. **MAKE INFERENCES** Why did Japan's victory in the Russo-Japanese War shock the world?
25. **YOU DECIDE** What do you think are the most positive and negative outcomes of nationalism? Support your opinion with evidence from the chapter.

63395
YORKSHIRE
COAST
EXPRESS

INTERPRET CHARTS

Study this chart, which shows the miles of railway track some European countries built during the Industrial Revolution. Then answer the questions that follow.

Miles of Railway Track in Selected European Countries (1840–1880)

	1840	1860	1880
Austria-Hungary	144	4,543	18,507
Belgium	334	1,730	4,112
France	496	9,167	23,089
Germany	469	11,089	33,838
Great Britain	2,390	14,603	25,060
Italy	20	2,404	9,290
Netherlands	17	335	1,846
Spain	0	1,917	7,490

Source: Modern History Sourcebook

26. Which country had laid the most railway tracks in 1880? Which had laid the least?

27. What might account for the increase in railway track in Germany between 1840 and 1880?

ANALYZE SOURCES

Look at the following political cartoon that appeared in *Punch* magazine in 1848. The caption reads: "Here and There; or, Emigration a Remedy." Then answer the question that follows.

HERE AND THERE;
Or, Emigration a Remedy.

28. Why might this cartoon have persuaded Irish people to immigrate to America?

WRITE ABOUT HISTORY

29. EXPLANATORY Write an essay explaining to other students how the mass migration in the 1800s of millions of Europeans to the United States affected the U.S. culture and economy.

TIPS

- Take notes from the lesson about shifting populations and immigration.
- Begin the essay with an introductory paragraph describing the two major waves of immigration to the United States in the 1800s and the push-pull factors behind those waves of immigration.
- Develop the essay explaining where these immigrants settled, and providing examples of how they affected the U.S. culture and economy.
- In your essay, use two or three vocabulary words that you learned.
- Conclude the essay by explaining the effects of the mass migration of millions of people to the United States.

NATIONAL GEOGRAPHIC
ON LOCATION WITH Nina BURLEIGH
JOURNALIST AND AUTHOR
Check out more on myNGconnect

Journalist and author Nina Burleigh explores the city of Siena, Italy. With its gothic appearance, Siena is the embodiment of a medieval city.

A LIBRARY DISCOVERY

I am fascinated by accounts of the past written by people who were actually there. Journals, notes, letters, and diaries—no matter how poorly they are written—provide a unique and personal insight into how people felt about events that took place during their lifetime.

While studying in a library in Paris, a librarian wheeled a cart past me, loaded high with volumes of old books. They were books about Egypt written over 200 years ago by French scientists who were traveling on a campaign of conquest for the great French general Napoleon Bonaparte, and I was instantly fascinated. I just had to write a book about this extraordinary story.

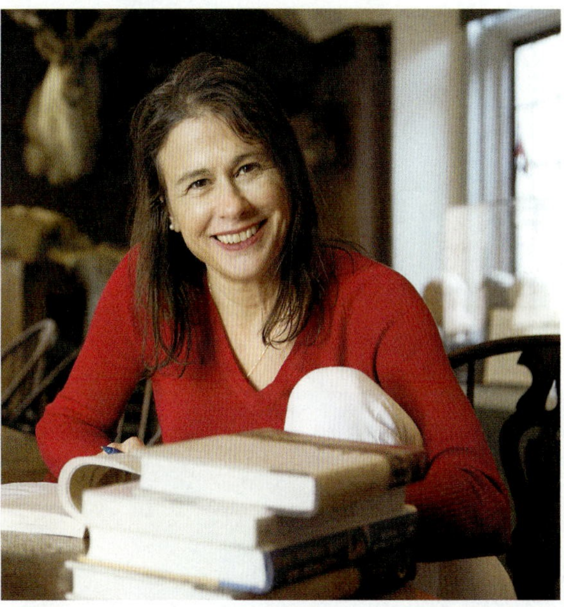

Having lived in France and Italy helps Nina Burleigh write about European history.

NAPOLEON AND EGYPT

In 1798, Napoleon set out to conquer Egypt because it was part of an important trade route. There was little known at this time about the country's mysterious history. Because science was beginning to compete with religion in terms of explaining how the world works, Napoleon assembled a group of the best mathematicians, engineers, artists, naturalists, and scholars in France to join him in Egypt. While he fought battles and was eventually defeated, his team studied Egypt. They explored and mapped ancient ruins, dug up artifacts, and made detailed drawings of everything they found. Then they housed their findings in a museum called the Institut d'Égypte in Cairo.

The French team's systematic and scientific approach to exploring Egypt's history makes them some of the world's first archaeologists. Until then, studies of the past usually consisted of wealthy gentlemen traveling around collecting old objects. But Napoleon's team looked at Egypt's ruins and artifacts in an entirely new way, sparking a worldwide obsession with ancient Egypt, and fundamentally establishing the field of study that we now call archaeology.

Obviously we've learned a lot about Egyptian history since Napoleon's time. And like these early French researchers, most people who make discoveries never live to see how their findings affect the future. It is a noble thing, to add a bit of knowledge to the chain, never knowing whether or how your contribution will alter human life and enable future discoveries. The work of Napoleon's team certainly did.

WHY STUDY HISTORY ?

"History feeds our imaginations and helps us understand that human beings were just like us, whether in 1800 or 1800 B.C. Even though their houses and technology and cultures were different, when you read their writings, you find that *humans throughout history are just that—human.*" —Nina Burleigh

NATIONAL
GEOGRAPHIC

Catherine the Great

BY ERLA ZWINGLE

Adapted from "Catherine the Great," by Erla Zwingle, in National Geographic *Exploring History*, 2014

Catherine—named Sophie at birth—was born on April 21, 1729. She was the first child of an obscure German prince connected with the Russian royal family. Sophie's mother managed to have her daughter introduced to Duke Karl Peter Ulrich—the only living grandson of Peter the Great of Russia. In time, Sophie and Peter were engaged.

The pair was mismatched. Peter was feebleminded, childish, and cruel. Still, Sophie embraced Russia. She studied hard and learned the language. The German Sophie became Ekaterina, or Catherine, the name given to her when she was accepted into the Russian Orthodox Church. All the while, her eyes were on the prize. "I had in my heart a strange certainty that one day I should, by my own efforts, become empress of Russia," she wrote in her memoirs.

Catherine and Peter were married on August 21, 1745, in St. Petersburg. Catherine was 16 years old, and the marriage was not a happy one. Her husband finally became tsar in 1761, but Peter was an unpopular ruler. He was overthrown in 1762, and within hours of the coup, Catherine had herself declared empress.

From the beginning of her rule, Catherine wanted to be admired as a reformer, and she labored on issues such as the legal code, schools and orphanages, town planning, and agriculture. She asserted that Russia was a European state and needed to adopt laws and attitudes to reflect that position.

Ending serfdom was part of Catherine's plan. However, she knew that her reforms would require the support of the nobility. As a result, she extended their authority at the expense of the serfs. Nine million male serfs (females weren't counted) lived in Russia, more than half the male population. Catherine's measures ended in revolt.

In 1773, rebels looted estates and murdered nobles. They had neared Moscow when the army stopped them. Catherine was never the same again. She died in 1796 at age 67.

For more from National Geographic
Check out "Our Wall" on myNGconnect

UNIT INQUIRY: CREATE A NEGOTIATION STRATEGY

In this unit, you learned about revolutions that took place in Europe. Based on your understanding of the text, what new ideas about human rights and government caused people to revolt? What changes did people hope to achieve through revolution?

ASSIGNMENT Create a strategy that you think could have been successful in negotiating a peaceful end or transition for one of the revolutions that took place in Europe. Since you have knowledge of how events unfolded, your strategy should take into consideration the factors that sparked the revolution. Be prepared to present and defend your strategy to the class.

Plan As you create your negotiation strategy, think about the new ideas about human rights and government that sparked revolution. Also think about what ordinary people hoped to achieve through revolution and how powerful governments did not address the concerns of their citizens. Make a list of factors that caused revolution and address the most significant ones in your strategy. You might want to use a graphic organizer to help organize your thoughts. ▶

Produce Use your notes to produce detailed descriptions of the factors that caused one of Europe's revolutions. You might want to write the descriptions in outline or paragraph form.

Present Choose a creative way to present your negotiation strategy to the class. Consider one of these options:

- Play the role of a diplomat and explain why a peaceful solution or compromise is preferable to a full-scale revolution.
- Write a dialogue between two people of different social classes that describes their different perspectives on revolution.
- Create a multimedia presentation using paintings from the Enlightenment to illustrate new ideas about human rights, government, and revolution.

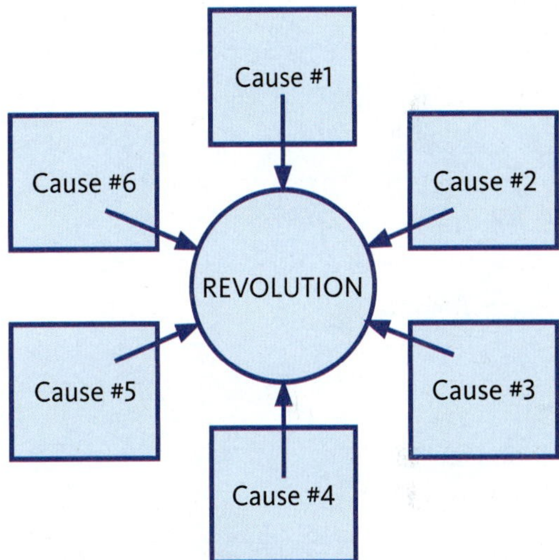
Cause #1
Cause #6
Cause #2
REVOLUTION
Cause #5
Cause #3
Cause #4

RAPID REVIEW
UNIT 10

REVOLUTIONS AND EMPIRES

TOP TEN

1. Enlightenment ideas spread across Europe, influencing politics, society, economics, religion, and the arts.
2. The Industrial Revolution began in 18th-century England.
3. The French and American revolutions overthrew colonial rule and inspired revolutions in South America.
4. Industrialization stimulated urbanization as populations grew and people left farming to work in factories in cities.
5. European nations built colonial empires in Africa and Asia to secure raw materials and to create new markets for industrial goods.

6-10. **NOW IT'S YOUR TURN** Complete the list with five more things to remember about revolutions and empires.

THE MODERN WORLD

NATIONAL GEOGRAPHIC

ON **LOCATION** WITH

Aziz Abu Sarah

Cultural Educator

There are more than seven billion people in the world, and we have more in common with each other than the news sometimes reflects. I know because I've seen firsthand the power of bringing together people who have different points of view. In our increasingly global community, cultural understanding is more important than ever. My name is Aziz Abu Sarah, and I am a cultural educator. Join me as we explore our modern world.

‹ **CRITICAL VIEWING** This NASA satellite image shows Earth at night and reveals the light of wildfires, city lights, and reflected moonlight. Which countries and continents can you identify?

UNIT 11

TIME LINE OF WORLD EVENTS

The Modern World

1919
The Treaty of Versailles is signed. *(illustration of the Allied leaders signing the treaty at Versailles)*

1947
India gains independence and separates into two countries, Pakistan and India. *(flags of India, in the front, and Pakistan)*

1900

1914
The Great War, the "war to end all wars," begins.

1917
The Russian Revolution begins.

1929
Global economic depression begins when U.S. stock market crashes.

1940

1939
Germany invades Poland, and World War II begins.

1945
World War II ends; atomic bombs are dropped on Hiroshima and Nagasaki, Japan. *(newspaper headline announcing Japanese surrender)*

The Evening News

LATE EXTRA

WORLD'S LARGEST EVENING NET SALE

INDIGESTION

This is the Gin Gordon's

JAPAN SURRENDERS

They ask only to keep the Mikado

Attlee and Truman Call Immediate Cabinet Meetings

BIG 4 TERMS ACCEPTED: MINISTERS GET "SHOCK"

JAPAN has offered unconditional surrender to the Allies with one reservation—that Emperor Hirohito retains his prerogatives as sovereign ruler.

In Washington this is interpreted as meaning simply that Japan will get out if the Mikado is allowed to stay on the throne—and unofficial but well informed quarters in Washington expect no difficulties over that point.

EMPEROR'S "BID TO END SUFFERINGS"

No Prejudice to Rights

PICCADILLY GOES WILD: BIG CROWDS CELEBRATE VICTORY

River Tugs Give VJ-Sign

JAPAN DESIRES "SPEEDY CONCLUSION"

1948
Modern Israel is founded.

COMPARE TIME LINES

What three countries became self-governing in the 1940s?

MARINES
YF-9

1975
Saigon falls, and U.S. troops leave Vietnam. *(American personnel leave Saigon.)*

2001
Terrorists attack the United States on September 11. *(helmet of firefighter who fought to rescue survivors)*

1963
Kenya is granted independence from Britain, and Jomo Kenyatta becomes its first president.

1994
Nelson Mandela is elected president of South Africa.

1989
The Berlin Wall falls.

2000

2011
Arab Spring begins in Tunisia and spreads to other countries in North Africa and Southwest Asia. *(photo of protestors in Tahir Square in Cairo, Egypt)*

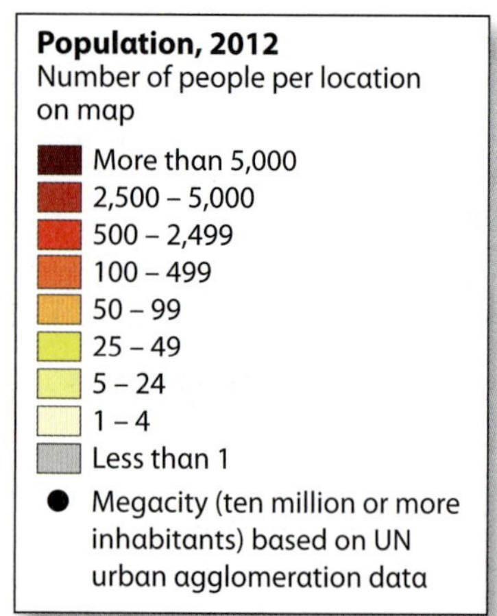
Population, 2012
Number of people per location on map
More than 5,000
2,500 – 5,000
500 – 2,499
100 – 499
50 – 99
25 – 49
5 – 24
1 – 4
Less than 1
Megacity (ten million or more inhabitants) based on UN urban agglomeration data

NORTH AMERICA
New York
Los Angeles
Mexico City

POPULATION

Life on a Crowded Planet

Throughout most of history, wars, disease, and natural disasters have kept the world's population in check. Over time, however, advancements in medicine and industrialization allowed people to live longer and eased their workload. As you can see on the time line below, the world's population began to grow after 1500, the time of the Scientific Revolution, and exploded after 1900. In 2014, the world population numbered 7.2 billion people.

Although the number of people in the world keeps growing, Earth remains the same size, and we are putting a greater strain than ever on the planet's natural resources. In densely crowded areas, people often don't have adequate access to clean water and good farmland. And the situation may only get worse. As the population continues to grow, these areas are the ones that will likely be most affected by the increase.

SOUTH AMERICA
Rio de Janeiro
São Paulo
Buenos Aires

Which continent has the most densely populated cities?

Year
A.D. 1

1000

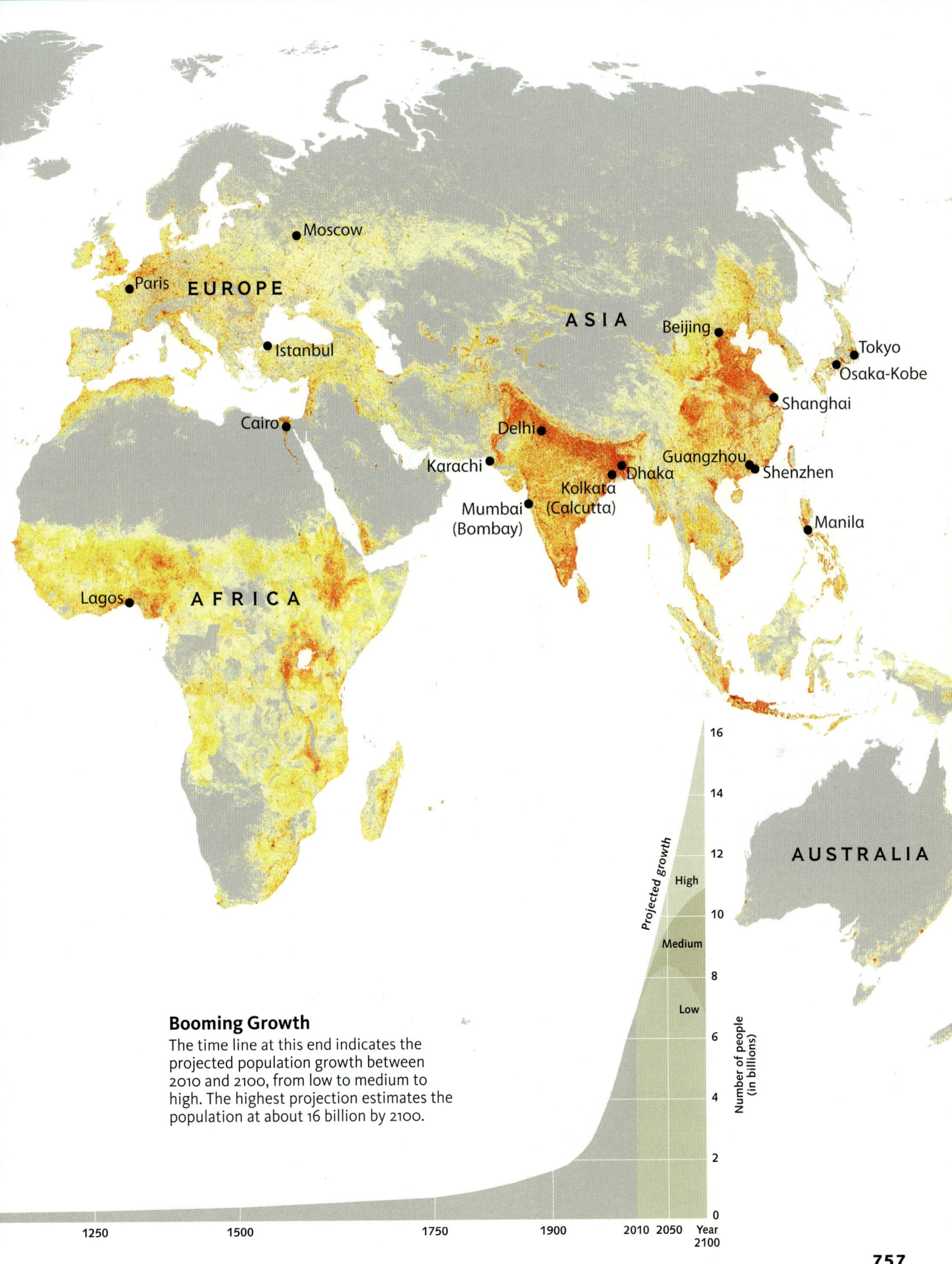
Moscow
Paris
EUROPE
ASIA
Beijing
Tokyo
Osaka-Kobe
Istanbul
Shanghai
Cairo
Delhi
Karachi
Guangzhou
Shenzhen
Dhaka
Kolkata
(Calcutta)
Mumbai
(Bombay)
Manila
Lagos
AFRICA
AUSTRALIA
Projected growth
High
Medium
Low
Number of people
(in billions)
16
14
12
10
8
6
4
2
0
1250
1500
1750
1900
2010
2050
Year
2100

Booming Growth

The time line at this end indicates the projected population growth between 2010 and 2100, from low to medium to high. The highest projection estimates the population at about 16 billion by 2100.

CHAPTER

26 THE WORLD AT WAR

1900 – 1945

SECTION 1
WAR AND REVOLUTION

KEY VOCABULARY
alliance
capitalism
communism
proletariat
stalemate
trench warfare
U-boat

NAMES & PLACES
Bolsheviks
Karl Marx
League of Nations
Treaty of Versailles
Triple Alliance
Triple Entente
Vladimir Lenin

SECTION 2
BETWEEN THE WARS

KEY VOCABULARY
economic depression
fascism
inflation
propaganda
reparations
totalitarian

NAMES & PLACES
Adolf Hitler
Benito Mussolini
Franklin Roosevelt
Great Depression
Joseph Stalin
Nazi Party

SECTION 3
WORLD WAR II

KEY VOCABULARY
appeasement
atomic bomb
blitzkrieg
genocide
ration

NAMES & PLACES
Hiroshima
Holocaust
Nagasaki
Pearl Harbor
Winston Churchill

READING STRATEGY

ANALYZE LANGUAGE USE

When you analyze language use, you note how specific word choices shape the meaning or tone of a text. As you read the chapter, use a graphic organizer like this one to analyze how word choices help convey the horrors of war.

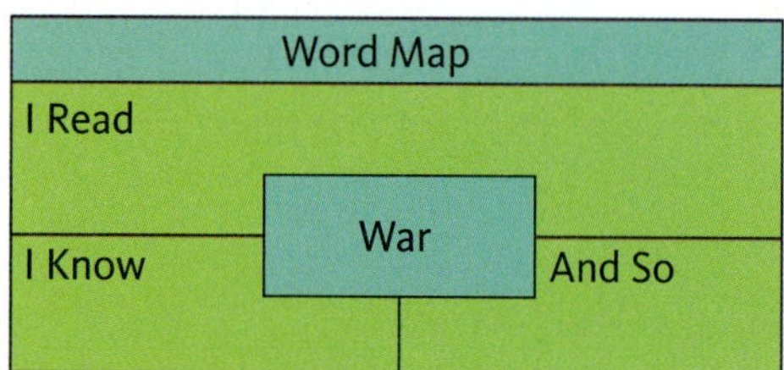
Word Map
I Read
War
I Know
And So

British troops rest in a trench in France on the first day of the Battle of the Somme during World War I.

1.1

The Great War

As you join the long line at the army recruitment office, you laugh with friends. You're filled with national pride. You are excited. You expect the conflict to be short, glorious, and fun. But the Great War of 1914–1918, eventually known as World War I, will be none of those things.

MAIN IDEA

European conflicts brought the world into the deadliest war ever known up to that time.

CAUSES AND ALLIANCES

During the late 1800s, European nations' competition for trade, resources, and colonies grew more intense. At the same time, nationalism threw whole regions of Europe into conflict. As tensions grew, nations expanded their armies and navies to defend themselves and attack their enemies. They also formed **alliances**, or agreements, which in this case were to fight one another's enemies.

By 1914, these alliances had created two hostile groups. Germany, Austria-Hungary, and Italy formed the **Triple Alliance**, while Britain, France, and Russia formed the **Triple Entente** (ahn-TAHNT). If any one of these nations went to war, its allies were bound to join. Trouble started in the politically unstable Balkan region of eastern Europe. On June 28, 1914, a Bosnian Serb assassinated Archduke Franz Ferdinand of Austria-Hungary and his wife. Austria-Hungary called on its allies to attack Serbia. But Serbia was protected by Russia, which called on the support of its allies. Most of Europe rapidly went to war, including their many imperial colonies with them. A world war had started.

WESTERN AND EASTERN FRONTS

New alliances formed as more countries entered the war. The Ottoman Empire and Bulgaria joined Germany and Austria-Hungary to form the Central Powers. Italy joined Britain, France, and Russia, forming the Allies. Most fighting took place in Europe, on the Western Front in France and on the Eastern Front around Russia. Germany's invasion of France stalled, and the Western Front quickly became a **stalemate**, meaning neither side was able to win. On the Eastern Front, the armies were more mobile, but still neither side could win a decisive advantage. Battles were also fought across Africa and Southwest Asia.

Defenders in battles usually held the advantage because of advances in military technology. One innovation was **trench warfare**, in which long ditches were dug deep into the ground. These trenches were protected by barbed wire and machine guns, making them nearly impossible to attack. In 1916, the Allies launched a major attack at a region in France called the Somme (sahm). Approximately 60,000 British soldiers died on the first day of battle alone. By the end of the battle, 600,000 soldiers were killed—and the Allies advanced just seven miles.

World War I was the first total war. That is, countries poured all their resources into the war, which directly affected those countries' populations. Nations mobilized their entire civilian populations to work for the war effort. Winning proved harder than anyone had imagined.

WORLD WAR I
NETH.
BELGIUM
Meuse
FRANCE
LUX.
Paris
Seine
Marne
Meuse
Moselle
GER.
1. Battles of Ypres (Oct.12–Nov. 11, 1914; April 22–May 25, 1915; July 31–Nov. 6, 1917)
2. First Battle of the Marne (Sept. 6–12, 1914)
3. Second Battle of the Marne (July 15–18, 1918)
4. Battles of the Meuse-Argonne (Sept. 26–Nov. 11, 1918)
5. First Battle of the Somme (July 1–Nov. 13, 1916)
6. Second Battle of the Somme (March 21–April 5, 1918)
7. Battle of Verdun (Feb. 21–July, 1916)
Battle of Jutland (May 31–June 1, 1916)
GREAT BRITAIN
North Sea
DENMARK
SWEDEN
Baltic Sea
Moscow
London
NETHER-LANDS
BELGIUM
Rhine
Elbe
Berlin
GERMANY
Battle of Tannenberg (Aug. 26–30, 1914)
RUSSIA
LUXEMBOURG
Paris
Seine
Loire
FRANCE
SWITZERLAND
AUSTRIA-HUNGARY
Dnieper
Dniester
Battle of Caporetto (Oct. 24, 1917)
Battles of the Isonzo (1915–17)
Battle of Cambrai (Nov.–Dec. 1917)
Danube
ROMANIA
Black Sea
Rhône
PORTUGAL
SPAIN
ITALY
Adriatic Sea
SERBIA
MONTE-NEGRO
BULGARIA
ALBANIA
Dardanelles Campaign (Feb. 1915–Jan. 1916)
GREECE
OTTOMAN EMPIRE
Mediterranean Sea
Central Powers
Allies
Neutral countries
Major battles
N
W
E
S
0 250 500 Miles
0 250 500 Kilometers

In 1917, the United States joined the Allies. More than 4 million U.S. troops served in the war. Exhausted, the Central Powers finally surrendered on November 11, 1918.

The loss of life was terrible. An estimated 9 million soldiers were killed, 21 million were wounded or missing, and 13 million civilians were killed or wounded. The Treaty of Versailles, signed in 1919, required Germany to accept sole blame for the war and to pay unrealistically huge sums of money to the Allies. To try to prevent more wars, the Treaty of Versailles also created the **League of Nations**. This group of nations would work to solve conflicts peacefully, rather than through war. The league proved to be ineffective, partly because the U.S. Congress refused to join for fear of being drawn into Europe's problems again. The **Treaty of Versailles** left many Germans feeling angry and desperate. Their resentment helped set the stage for another world war.

REVIEW & ASSESS

1. **READING CHECK** What major factors contributed to the Great War?
2. **ANALYZE CAUSE AND EFFECT** Why did European nations form alliances?
3. **INTERPRET MAPS** What battle was in progress when the Central Powers surrendered?

1.2 Technology and the War

In World War I, European powers turned their vast collection of technologically advanced weapons on one another—with devastating results. It was the first modern war fought on a global scale with powerful new weapons such as machine guns, artillery, tanks, submarines, and poison gas.

MAIN IDEA

Powerful new weapons made World War I the deadliest war yet.

MODERN WEAPONS

War often generates technological advances, and the Great War was no exception. Britain developed the tank and first used it in 1916. It could cross rough ground, and heavy armor protected the crew from bullets. Tanks also provided protection for infantry that followed them. Armed with cannon or machine guns, tanks helped capture enemy trenches. However, not many tanks were available, and they reached their full effectiveness only toward the end of the war.

Poison gas was another modern weapon used in the war. The Germans first used this frightening weapon in 1915, but soon both sides were firing shells of lethal gas at enemy trenches. Drifting clouds of poison gas killed nearly 100,000 soldiers and injured many more, despite the introduction of gas masks.

At sea, expensive battleships fell prey to cheap but destructive floating explosives. As a result, large ships rarely took part in combat. Instead, Germany used its submarines, known as **U-boats**. Germany's U-boats would sink any ship in the war zone, including passenger ships suspected of carrying military supplies. One such ship was the British *Lusitania*. Germany attacked and sank it as it sailed from New York to Liverpool, England, in 1915. Nearly 1,200 people were killed, including 128 Americans. German attacks on civilian ships were one of the reasons the United States finally entered the war in 1917.

In the air, planes were a new technology, but they developed quickly during the war. They were used mostly for studying enemy positions and movements. Soon, however, dedicated fighters and bombers were being built. By 1918, the importance of air power was apparent to military leaders.

NO-MAN'S-LAND

Some new technologies created an unusual battlefield. Machine guns could fire around 600 bullets a minute, making attacks against them difficult. Similarly, artillery guns could blast apart a battlefield from a distance. Massive artillery bombardments that could last for days usually came before ground attacks.

The deadliness of machine guns and artillery forced both sides to stop advancing and dig in. Trenches made difficult targets for artillery, keeping the defenders relatively safe. Yet trenches were horrific places to live. They were dirty, cold, and filled with muddy water. Disease spread easily.

Between the trenches of the opposing armies was an area that neither side controlled, called no-man's-land. This was a field of mud filled with artillery craters and covered in barbed wire. To launch an attack, soldiers climbed out of trenches and into a hail of enemy fire that made no-man's-land the deadliest place on Earth.

MILITARY TECHNOLOGY OF THE GREAT WAR

U.S. tanks in France

Tank

- Heavily armored
- Effective against ground troops
- Limited numbers at the beginning of the war

German U-boat

U-boat

- Made large warships less effective
- Used torpedoes to attack without surfacing
- Short for *Unterseeboot* (meaning: undersea boat)

American pilot Eddie Rickenbacker and his plane

Airplane

- Early combat pilots used handheld pistols.
- The first bomber was an Italian pilot who dropped grenades out of his plane.

German machine gunners wearing their gas masks

Machine Gun/Gas Mask

- Machine guns were deadly for enemy soldiers.
- Gas masks were developed to protect soldiers from poison gas attacks.

REVIEW & ASSESS

1. **READING CHECK** How did new technology influence World War I?
2. **ANALYZE CAUSE AND EFFECT** Why was poison gas such an effective weapon?
3. **COMPARE AND CONTRAST** What were the advantages and disadvantages of trench warfare?

1.3

DOCUMENT-BASED QUESTION

Memories of World War I

There are now no surviving veterans from World War I. Yet many firsthand accounts are available, capturing the memories of those who served. Increased literacy allowed many men of all ranks and nationalities to keep diaries and write letters home. This moving correspondence reveals what life was like for those along the battle lines. Those who had witnessed it firsthand also wrote many poems and books about the war. Artists sketched and painted vivid scenes, while increasingly portable still cameras and movie cameras captured moments and events in ways that were never before possible.

Critical Viewing This painting shows British soldiers defending against a German attack. What mood has the artist captured in this painting?

DOCUMENT ONE

Primary Source: Diary

from the Diary of Harry Frieman, 313th Machine Gun Company, 79th Division

Many soldiers kept diaries of their time in the war, including Russian-born American Harry Frieman. He served on the Western Front in France and experienced the full horror of trench warfare. Here he describes the hardships and dangers that he and his fellow soldiers suffered in the last few weeks of the war.

CONSTRUCTED RESPONSE Why do you think some soldiers took chances by drinking water and not wearing their gas masks?

September 30, 1918

[M]ost of the men were drinking water out of shell holes, taking a chance, as most of the holes were full of gas. We had many gas attacks. We wore our masks at times when the gas was heavy. At times we would go right on without them. The weather was cold and raining nearly every day. We had hardly any sleep as we had to lay in water and mud—Cold out and no cover of any kind.

DOCUMENT TWO

Primary Source: Novel

from *All Quiet on the Western Front* by Erich Maria Remarque

Erich Maria Remarque was a German veteran who wrote this semiautobiographical novel in 1929. It follows the experiences of a young German soldier and dwells on the inhumanity and destructiveness of the war—both physically and emotionally. This passage explains how battle changed the main character's perception of the world and its values.

CONSTRUCTED RESPONSE How did the war change this young man's view of the world?

We were eighteen and had begun to love life and the world; and we had to shoot it to pieces. The first bomb, the first explosion, burst in our hearts. We are cut off from activity, from striving, from progress. We believe in such things no longer, we believe in the war.

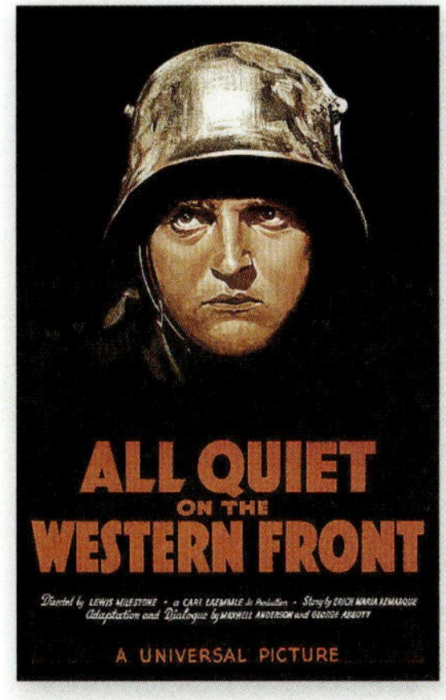
ALL QUIET
ON THE
WESTERN FRONT
A UNIVERSAL PICTURE

In 1930, Hollywood made *All Quiet on the Western Front* into a movie. This is the promotional poster for the film.

SYNTHESIZE & WRITE

1. **REVIEW** Review what you have learned about World War I.
2. **RECALL** On your own paper, write down the main idea expressed in each document.
3. **CONSTRUCT** Write a topic sentence that answers this question: How did World War I affect those who fought in it?
4. **WRITE** Using evidence from the documents, write a paragraph to support your answer to the question in Step 3.

1.4 The Russian Revolution

In 1914, Russia was still a monarchy ruled by a czar (zahr) with absolute power. The czar neglected millions of peasants who had too little land to feed themselves but still had to pay high taxes. At the same time, Russia's rapid industrialization had created a very large urban working class whose living conditions were among the worst in Europe.

MAIN IDEA

War led to revolution in Russia, which became the first communist state.

IMPACT OF WORLD WAR I

The Russian Empire fought against the Central Powers during World War I. But Russia's war went badly and made many existing problems worse. Russia could not support a war. Its soldiers didn't have enough weapons, ammunition, or food to fight effectively. They were also poorly led, and Germany constantly outfought Russia. By October 1916, millions of Russian soldiers had been killed, captured, or wounded. The army broke down. Similarly, Russia's factory and farm production collapsed, creating terrible shortages of fuel and food. Most Russians blamed their suffering on Czar Nicholas II.

THE BOLSHEVIKS TAKE POWER

Conditions in Russia led many different political groups to call for revolution. One group was influenced by the ideas of the German philosopher **Karl Marx**. As you've already learned, Marx believed the **proletariat** (proh-luh-TEHR-ee-uht), or workers, should violently overthrow the government, which he saw as controlled by the upper classes. He attacked **capitalism**, which is an economic system in which factories and other means of production are privately owned.

As an alternative to capitalism, Marx proposed **communism**. Under communism, workers would run a government that owned the means of production, such as factories, farms, mines, and transportation. In theory, wealth and property would be shared and used for the common good. Marx also believed that, eventually, there would be no need for government at all.

In February 1917, protests against food shortages in Russia's capital, Petrograd, grew rapidly into a revolution. Petrograd established a soviet, or elected council, to represent the rights of workers and soldiers. These developments put tremendous pressure on Czar Nicholas II, and in March he resigned. A temporary government called the Petrograd Soviet took over. It had a great deal of influence, and soon other soviets sprang up across Russia—even in the army.

The soviets' most radical members were the **Bolsheviks** (BOHL-shuh-vihks), led by **Vladimir Lenin**. The Bolsheviks believed in the ideas of Marx and soon dominated the soviets. In October 1917, the Bolsheviks seized Petrograd and overthrew the government. They quickly negotiated peace with Germany and won much support across Russia. The Bolsheviks killed people who opposed them and renamed their party the Communist Party. After nearly three years of civil war, Lenin and the Bolsheviks controlled the Russian Empire.

ПЕТРОГРАДА
НЕ
ОТДАДИМ

Critical Viewing This Russian Bolshevik poster from 1917 says, "Petrograd, No Surrender." What do you believe was the purpose of this poster?

REVIEW & ASSESS

1. **READING CHECK** What factors led to revolution in Russia?
2. **COMPARE AND CONTRAST** What are the similarities and differences between capitalism and communism?
3. **SEQUENCE EVENTS** How did Russia's government change between 1914 and 1917?

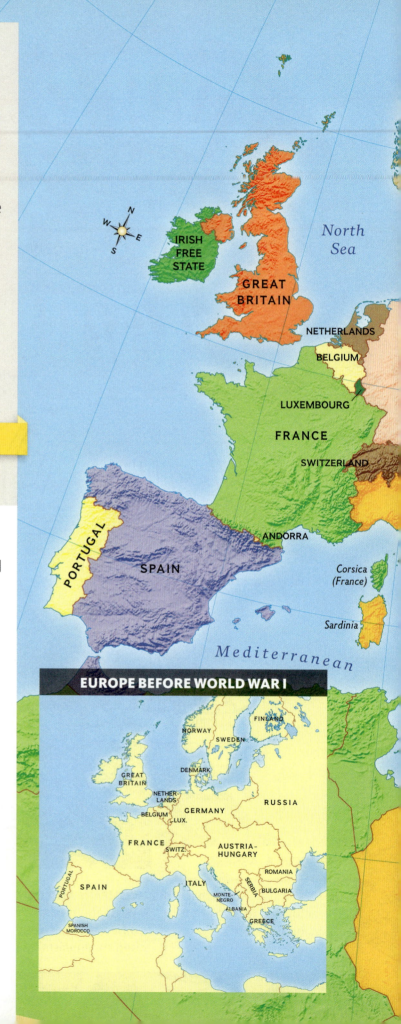

1.5 Europe After World War I

U.S. president Woodrow Wilson and others called the Great War "the war to end all wars." The Allies paid a heavy price for victory during the war. When they finally defeated the Central Powers, they were determined to make their enemies pay—literally.

MAIN IDEA

The Great War changed Europe forever.

THE IMPACT OF WORLD WAR I

The Treaty of Versailles redrew the political map of Europe. Newly independent nations replaced some long-established empires. Around 9 million soldiers had been killed, and 21 million were missing or wounded. An additional 13 million civilians died because of the war. Between 1918 and 1919, 25 to 50 million more people died from an outbreak of flu that spread around the world. The Central Powers were financially ruined, and the Allies had huge debts from the war.

Five separate peace treaties ended the war, but the most famous is the Treaty of Versailles, signed between the Allies and Germany. The treaty divided Germany's overseas empire among the Allies, reduced its borders in Europe, and required Germany to pay money to the Allies. Many people, not just Germans, felt the treaty went too far.

IRISH FREE STATE
GREAT BRITAIN
North Sea
NETHERLANDS
BELGIUM
LUXEMBOURG
FRANCE
SWITZERLAND
ANDORRA
PORTUGAL
SPAIN
Corsica (France)
Sardinia
Mediterranean
EUROPE BEFORE WORLD WAR I
NORWAY
SWEDEN
FINLAND
DENMARK
GREAT BRITAIN
NETHER-LANDS
BELGIUM
LUX.
GERMANY
RUSSIA
FRANCE
SWITZ.
AUSTRIA-HUNGARY
ROMANIA
PORTUGAL
SPAIN
ITALY
SERBIA
BULGARIA
MONTE-NEGRO
ALBANIA
GREECE
SPANISH MOROCCO

EUROPE AFTER WORLD WAR I
0 250 500 Miles
0 250 500 Kilometers
NORWAY
SWEDEN
FINLAND
ESTONIA
LATVIA
LITHUANIA
ENMARK
Baltic Sea
DANZIG
GERMANY (East Prussia)
GERMANY
POLAND
CZECHOSLOVAKIA
AUSTRIA
HUNGARY
ROMANIA
KINGDOM OF SERBS, CROATS, AND SLOVENES
BULGARIA
ALBANIA
ITALY
GREECE
Sicily
Sea
Malta (Britain)
Crete
Dodecanese Is. (Italy)
Cyprus (Britain)
SOVIET UNION
Caspian Sea
TURKEY
IRAN
SYRIA (France)
IRAQ (Britain)
PALESTINE (Britain)
TRANSJORDAN (Britain)
SAUDI ARABIA
In 1922, Lenin declared Russia to be the Union of Soviet Socialist Republics, or U.S.S.R.—the world's first communist country.
The territories of Finland, Latvia, Lithuania, and Estonia were all made nations independent of Russia.
Poland became a country again (taking land from Germany and Russia) after having been virtually eliminated more than 100 years earlier.
The Ottoman Empire had ruled all of Turkey and large areas of the Middle East and Balkans. This once large empire was now reduced to a single country—the Republic of Turkey.
Austria and Hungary were established as separate and independent republics. Former Austro-Hungarian provinces were merged to create the countries of Yugoslavia and Czechoslovakia.

REVIEW & ASSESS

1. **READING CHECK** How did Europe change as a result of the war?

2. **IDENTIFY** Name three countries that appear on the "Europe After World War I" map that are not on the "Europe Before World War I" map.

3. **INTERPRET MAPS** Based on the map, what problems do you think the new borders might have caused?

2.1 Economic Collapse

If you loaned your friend a dollar, you'd expect him to pay you back. But if he loses that dollar, you've lost it, too. After the end of World War I, American banks loaned millions of dollars to people who invested in stocks. When stocks went down, everyone lost money.

MAIN IDEA

World War I helped bring about the world's greatest economic collapse.

POSTWAR STRESSES

World War I left Europe weakened socially, economically, and politically. It sounds odd, but peace brought widespread anger, resentment, and poverty. It was a dangerously unstable situation. Every country had trouble paying off its huge war debts and switching its economy back to peacetime production.

Germany was in the most trouble. It also had to pay the Allies the impossible sum of more than $30 billion in **reparations**, or payments for wrongdoing. Germany's economy collapsed, which brought further hardship for the German people. France was relying on Germany's payments to support its own economy. In 1923, French and Belgian troops captured Germany's industrial heartland and took resources directly from its mines and factories. Not surprisingly, Germany shut down the factories, which did not help the economy. The Allies agreed that rebuilding Germany's economy was in everyone's interest. In 1924, the Allies developed the Dawes Plan, which reduced reparations and loaned Germany millions of dollars. But it was too little, too late. Desperate and resentful, Germans turned against their newly appointed democratic government, known as the Weimar Republic, and looked for stronger, more effective leadership.

WORLDWIDE DEPRESSION

By comparison, the U.S. economy bounced back quickly after World War I. Soon, a wide variety and number of consumer goods were available that raised living standards. By 1930, the United States had 26 million cars on its roads. U.S. banks made more loans to Europe, stimulating the European economy. But the continued growth of the U.S. economy created an unrealistic belief that the growth would never stop. Everyone wanted a part of the economic success. Many ordinary people invested in companies by buying a share, or piece, of the company through the stock market. Most borrowed money from banks to buy their shares. High demand inflated the value of shares far beyond their true worth. Then trouble struck.

Too many goods were being produced, and many Americans did not earn enough to buy the goods. By the late 1920s, many goods remained on shelves in stores throughout the country. Factories had to reduce production and started laying off workers. Investors began to realize that stocks were massively overpriced and began selling their stocks. On October 24, 1929, panic hit. That day is now known as Black Thursday. Nearly 13 million shares were sold at rapidly falling prices. Suddenly everyone was selling shares before they became worthless. This event is known as a stock market collapse. Millions of people lost everything they owned, and hundreds of banks went out of business.

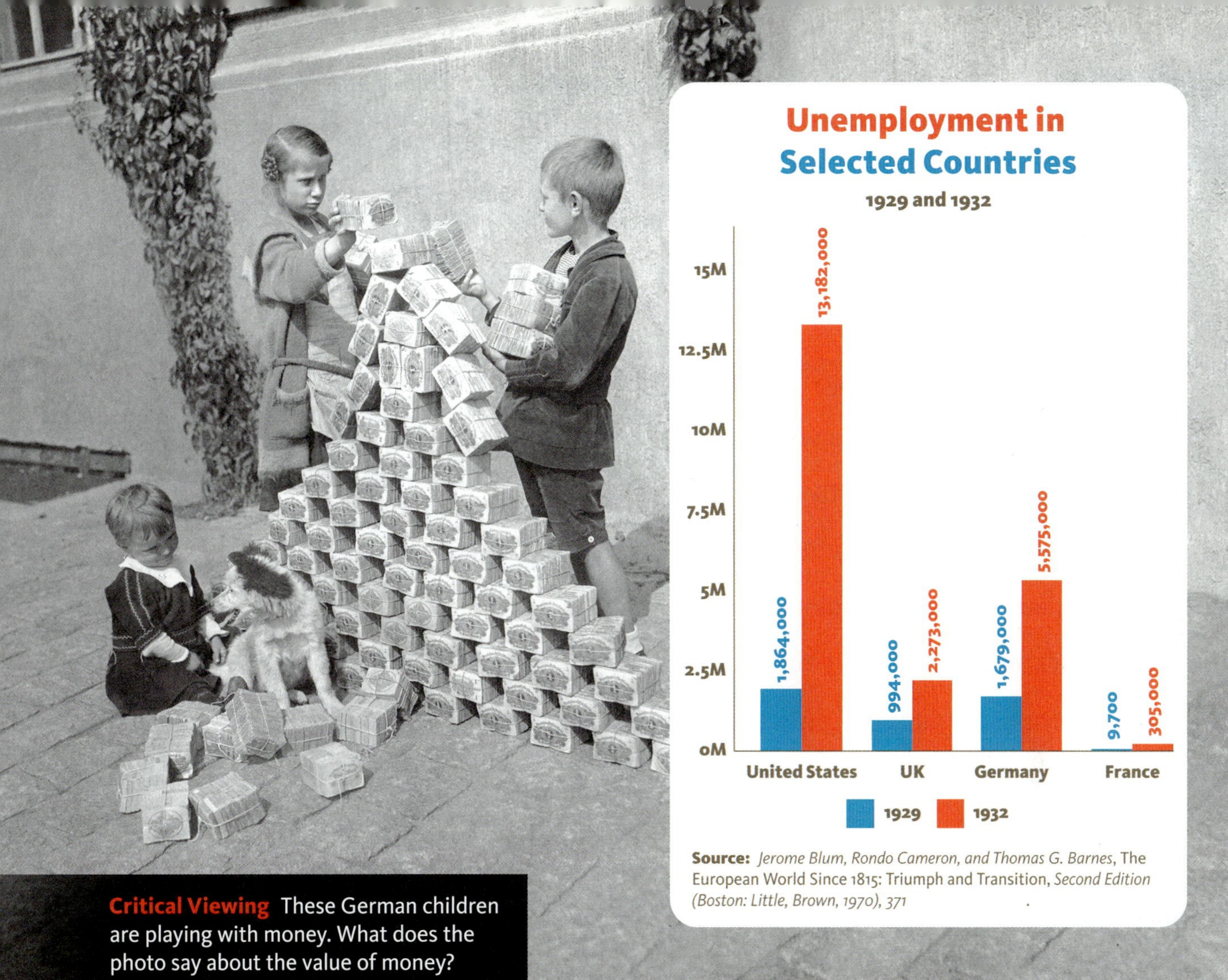
Unemployment in Selected Countries
1929 and 1932
15M
12.5M
10M
7.5M
5M
2.5M
0M
1,864,000
13,182,000
994,000
2,273,000
1,679,000
5,575,000
9,700
305,000
United States
UK
Germany
France
1929
1932
Source: Jerome Blum, Rondo Cameron, and Thomas G. Barnes, The European World Since 1815: Triumph and Transition, Second Edition (Boston: Little, Brown, 1970), 371

Critical Viewing These German children are playing with money. What does the photo say about the value of money?

National economies around the world were so connected that the financial crisis soon spread around the world. U.S. banks quickly withdrew loans to foreign countries, and the money that had once lifted Europe's economy suddenly disappeared. European banks, industry, and businesses collapsed. Unemployment rose dramatically across the continent. **Inflation**, an increase in the price of goods and services in a country, also rose. All this meant that people had less money to buy more expensive goods and services.

An **economic depression**, or period of low economic activity and high unemployment, took hold in countries around the world. In Germany, large sums of money were needed to buy a single loaf of bread. The economic crisis hit the United States especially hard. This period has become known as the **Great Depression**. At the Depression's peak in 1932, more than 20 percent of Americans were unemployed, millions were homeless, and nearly everyone was desperate.

REVIEW & ASSESS

1. **READING CHECK** Why did France send troops to occupy Germany's industrial heartland?
2. **SUMMARIZE** How did the economic crisis in the United States spread around the world?
3. **DRAW CONCLUSIONS** Why did the U.S. economy experience a boom right after the end of World War I?

2.2 Life in the Great Depression

You carry a sign saying "Will work for a dollar a week." A dollar isn't much to support your family, but you'll be grateful to get it. You feel miserable looking at the desperate faces around you. No wonder people are calling this time the Great Depression.

MAIN IDEA

The Great Depression pushed millions of people into poverty.

SOCIAL IMPACT

The Great Depression lasted from 1929 until about 1939. It was the longest and deepest economic downturn the world had ever seen. By 1932, tens of millions workers were unemployed worldwide, and about a quarter of the U.S. workforce was jobless. Many historians argue that the Great Depression was felt most sharply in the United States.

In 1929, a large percentage of Americans lived at or below the poverty level. People lost their homes because they could not make the payments and sold their possessions for food. Many blamed President Herbert Hoover for the crisis. Whole families traveled to cities to find work. Many lived in communities of tents, crates, and even old cars. The areas were nicknamed Hoovervilles, after the unpopular president. People relied on soup kitchens and breadlines for food. Hundreds of people would line up to apply for a single job. Protest marches and riots became common.

In the central United States, a long drought made the economic hardship even worse. Over-farmed land became unproductive, and winds blew the dry dirt into giant dust storms. The Great Plains came to be known as the Dust Bowl. Thousands abandoned their farms and migrated west, seeking whatever work they could find.

FEDERAL RESPONSE

In the 1932 presidential election, **Franklin Roosevelt** easily defeated Hoover. Hoover had opposed government intervention in the economic crisis, but Roosevelt led the government in taking swift and decisive action. He proposed a series of government programs known as the New Deal.

New Deal programs were aimed at lessening people's suffering, stimulating the economy, and protecting against future disasters. To create jobs, the government employed people for projects that benefited communities, such as building roads, bridges, and schools. The government helped restore public trust in banks by guaranteeing people's savings. The Social Security Act created a federal tax to be paid back to workers after they retired. These and many more reforms steadily stabilized and restored the U.S. economy.

The Great Depression affected other countries in different ways. Many Latin American countries relied on exports to the United States, which slowed or stopped during the Depression. Their economies became unstable and they turned to military dictators for leadership. In some European and Asian countries, dictators seized power, as you will explore in the next lesson. The United States was back on its feet by 1939, but the effects of the Great Depression continued to be felt around the world.

Critical Viewing Photographer Dorothea Lange took this photo of a family during the Great Depression. How does the photo reflect conditions during the Depression?

REVIEW & ASSESS

1. **READING CHECK** What effect did the Great Depression have on millions of people in the United States?
2. **ANALYZE CAUSE AND EFFECT** Why was economic hardship especially difficult in the Great Plains of the United States?
3. **MAKE INFERENCES** Do you think the Great Depression damaged the image of the United States with other countries? Why or why not?

2.3 The Rise of Authoritarianism

Hard times can make desperate people turn to extreme solutions. World War I and the Great Depression encouraged the rise of extreme political parties in many countries around the world.

MAIN IDEA

War and depression allowed powerful dictators to seize complete control of some European countries.

Baut
Jugendherbergen
und Heime

NAZI PROPAGANDA

Nazi propaganda was effective and powerful. Posters, newspapers, films, radio broadcasts, and even school books projected an image of German superiority.

TOTALITARIANISM

A **totalitarian** government controls all aspects of life. There is usually only one, all-powerful political party. Totalitarian governments use violence, fear, and **propaganda** to control their citizens. Propaganda occurs when a government deliberately manipulates information to make people think in a particular way. After World War I, totalitarian states emerged in several countries. People wanted order, power, and prosperity.

The U.S.S.R., which was also known as the Soviet Union, developed into a communist totalitarian state under the long and brutal leadership of **Joseph Stalin**. Stalin eliminated his political rivals to become a dictator by 1929. In an effort to turn the U.S.S.R. into a global power, his government took control of industries and factories. Fear of failure under Stalin's regime was a strong motivator for everyone, and the result was rapid industrialization. The government focused on heavy industries like coal, steel, oil, and electricity, rather than on consumer goods like clothing and housing. This caused terrible shortages and hardship for millions.

To feed the industrial workforce, the Soviet government also took control of agriculture. The government seized private farms and forced peasants to work on them. Food production fell, resulting in famines that killed millions of people.

The government executed people suspected of opposing Stalin or imprisoned them in labor camps. The victims included top government officials, army officers, and even many Bolsheviks who had fought in the 1917 revolution.

FASCISM AND NAZISM

Meanwhile, Italy developed a different form of totalitarianism —**fascism**. Fascism promotes extreme nationalism, militarism, and racism in an attempt to establish the superiority of a particular people over all others. In 1919, **Benito Mussolini** founded the fascist movement in Italy.

Fascism won support among many Italians, who were suffering during the Great Depression. Mussolini openly used violence to achieve his goals and took control of the Italian government in 1925. Determined to make Italy a strong military power, Mussolini outlawed political opposition and used propaganda to promote his fascist ideals.

Critical Viewing Adolf Hitler marches through a Nazi rally with other members of his party in Germany in 1934. What kind of impression do you think Hitler and the Nazis are trying to make?

In Germany, the **Nazi Party** and its leader, **Adolf Hitler**, admired Mussolini's ideas and put them into practice. The Nazis promised to rebuild Germany's economy and military and to take back territory lost after World War I. The Nazis won support from Germans who were, like the Italians, suffering from the effects of the Great Depression. By 1932, the Nazis were Germany's largest political party, and in 1933, the Nazis won an election and took control of the government. Hitler savagely crushed all opposition, seized government powers for himself, and became a dictator. The Nazis promoted the idea of a German master race and persecuted Jewish people and anyone else they believed to be inferior. Hitler had ambitions to rule all of Europe, as you will soon learn.

REVIEW & ASSESS

1. **READING CHECK** What were the differences between the governments of the Soviet Union, Italy, and Germany?
2. **ANALYZE CAUSE AND EFFECT** Why did Stalin force peasants to work on government farms?
3. **DRAW CONCLUSIONS** What factors led to the rise of totalitarian governments in Italy and Germany?

3.1 War in Europe

Winston Churchill became Britain's prime minister on May 10, 1940. Three days later, he delivered a powerful speech to the House of Commons. Churchill described Britain's goal in the fight against Nazi Germany: "It is victory, victory at all costs, victory in spite of all terror, victory, however long and hard the road may be; for without victory, there is no survival."

MAIN IDEA

Between 1939 and 1945, the world was devastated by World War II.

ALLIED VS. AXIS POWERS

The rise of totalitarian states created great tension in Europe. Desperate to avoid war, Britain and France ignored aggressive actions by Italy and Germany. Hitler was allowed to seize some territories in the hope that it would satisfy him. This policy came to be known as **appeasement**. But it wasn't enough. In 1939, Germany and the Soviet Union agreed not to attack each other. They were enemies, but each got something from the deal. Germany could focus on conquering western Europe, and the Soviet Union bought time to build more weapons before it fought Germany. September 1, 1939, German tanks rolled into Poland. Britain and France finally declared war on Germany. Two sides developed. The Allied forces ultimately included Britain, France, the United States, and the Soviet Union. The Axis powers were Germany, Italy, and Japan. Many other nations eventually joined World War II, which became even more global and destructive than the first world war.

GERMANY'S BLITZKRIEG

Germany had built a powerful military with advanced weapons and effective new tactics, including **blitzkrieg** (BLIHTS-kreeg), or "lightning war." Blitzkrieg involved fast-moving tanks, motorized infantry, and bombers that overwhelmed enemies before they could recover. Germany conquered Poland in three weeks. Hitler's forces also quickly overran France. Hitler expected Britain, now on its own, to surrender. But Churchill pledged that the British Empire would fight on.

In summer 1940, Germany sought to weaken Britain by launching a heavy bombing campaign. The air war, known as the Battle of Britain, was one of the most intense in history. British cities were flattened, killing thousands. Yet Britain's Royal Air Force heroically defended its country, ultimately defeating the German air force. Meanwhile, German U-boats continued to sink ships at an alarming rate, denying Britain much needed supplies. Still, Britain held out.

With the air attack on Britain stalled, Germany turned on the Soviet Union. In June 1941, Hitler launched an invasion. The Soviet leader Joseph Stalin was surprised, and the Germans quickly advanced. But Hitler underestimated the U.S.S.R.'s size, resources, and harsh winters. German armies became overstretched as they fought to capture the cities of Leningrad and Stalingrad. Meanwhile, the Soviet Union mobilized its vast resources and sent millions of soldiers against the enemy.

WORLD WAR II IN EUROPE
Axis countries, 1942
Axis-controlled areas, 1942
Allied- and Allied -controlled areas, 1942
Neutral countries
Axis offensives, 1940–42
Allied offensives, 1942–45
Farthest Axis advance, 1942
Major battle
ATLANTIC OCEAN
North Sea
Baltic Sea
Black Sea
Mediterranean Sea
Adriatic Sea
Aegean Sea
FINLAND
NORWAY
SWEDEN
SOVIET UNION
Leningrad (besieged Sept. 1941–Jan. 1944)
Moscow
Kursk (July 1943)
Stalingrad (Aug. 1942–Feb. 1943)
Kiev
Warsaw
Danzig
DENMARK
GREAT BRITAIN
London
NETHERLANDS
Dunkirk
BELG.
Battle of the Bulge (Dec. 1944)
Berlin
Elbe R.
GERMANY
Normandy (June 1944)
Paris
Seine R.
Rhine R.
Rhône R.
Munich
SWITZ.
Vichy
FRANCE
SLOVAKIA
HUNGARY
ROMANIA
Danube R.
CROATIA
SERBIA
BULGARIA
MONTENEGRO
ALBANIA
ITALY
Corsica
Rome
Anzio (Jan. 1944)
Monte Cassino (Jan.–May 1944)
Sardinia
Sicily
Balearic Islands
PORTUGAL
SPAIN
TURKEY
GREECE
Crete
Cyprus
SYRIA
LEBANON
PALESTINE
TRANS-JORDAN
SPANISH MOROCCO
Casablanca
MOROCCO
Oran
Algiers
ALGERIA
Tunis
Kasserine Pass (Feb. 1943)
TUNISIA
MALTA
LIBYA
El Alamein (Oct.–Nov. 1942)
Cairo
EGYPT
0 200 400 Miles
0 200 400 Kilometers
N S E W

The Battle of Stalingrad is considered by many historians to be the defining battle of the entire war. German troops began their attack in late summer, 1942. Soviet troops were driven farther and farther back into the city, but they refused to surrender. As the battle extended into October, the German troops continued to suffer heavy losses. In late November, the Soviets launched a counterattack that surrounded the German army.

The year 1943 was a turning point for the Allies. The German army at Stalingrad surrendered, and the Soviets went on the offensive. The Allies began winning the war at sea. British forces halted Axis attempts to conquer North Africa. In July, Britain, joined by the United States, invaded Italy. Italian Communists captured and killed Italy's leader, Benito Mussolini. Italy soon surrendered, but German soldiers fought fiercely as they retreated toward Germany.

REVIEW & ASSESS

1. **READING CHECK** In what order did early events of the war occur?
2. **ANALYZE CAUSE AND EFFECT** Why were German forces able to quickly conquer countries such as Poland and France?
3. **INTERPRET MAPS** How far into the Soviet Union were German armies able to advance between 1941 and 1943?

3.2 War in the Pacific

The enemy is hidden in the shadowy tangle of jungle ahead—but you can't see him. Despite the intense heat and a raging thirst, you remain absolutely still and barely breathing. One wrong move and you're dead. You're in the jungles of the Pacific islands, where some of the fiercest battles of World War II were fought.

MAIN IDEA

While the war in Europe raged on, the United States also fought to deny Japan's imperial ambitions in the Pacific.

JAPANESE AGGRESSION

In the 1920s, Japan's booming industrial economy declined, and the Great Depression brought severe economic hardships. Japan invaded the Chinese province of Manchuria in 1931 in an effort to gain more natural resources. Japan made the province an independent state, which it controlled completely.

By 1936, the military was in control of the Japanese government. It was very nationalistic and packed with army officers. Japan began an expanded effort to capture new land and resources. Japanese leaders sought to build a strong and lasting Japanese empire.

Japan renewed its attacks against China in 1937. Just six months later, Japanese forces controlled all of northern China, including Beijing, Shanghai, and the Chinese capital of Nanking. Japanese forces committed horrific war crimes in Nanking, massacring as many as 300,000 Chinese civilians.

Japan formally joined the Axis powers in September 1940. Japan seized European colonies in Asia that were rich in resources. By 1941, Japan occupied French Indochina. Japan's aggressions deeply worried the United States, which had interests in the Pacific. Japan's prime minister, Hideki Tojo, saw the United States as the last barrier to a new Japanese empire and prepared for war.

THE UNITED STATES ENTERS THE WAR

On December 7, 1941, Japanese planes made a surprise attack on the U.S. naval base at **Pearl Harbor**, Hawaii. The attacks killed more than 2,300 Americans and destroyed nearly 200 ships. But the main Japanese targets, U.S. aircraft carriers, were not in the harbor. The next day, the United States joined the Allies and declared war on Japan, Germany, and Italy. Japanese forces continued their advance, but the U.S. Navy stopped them at the Battle of the Coral Sea in May 1942. The U.S. Navy was victorious again a month later at the Battle of Midway. Both these battles were fought entirely by aircraft launched from aircraft carriers—the key weapon in the Pacific.

The Allies began pushing Japan back in a process called island-hopping. The United States planned to reach Japan by attacking only the weaker islands, "hopping" from one to the next, across the Pacific. The fighting was brutal because the Japanese soldiers had sworn to fight to the death. At the Battle of Guadalcanal, soldiers on both sides fought in hot and unhealthy jungle conditions. It took six months and thousands of U.S. lives to drive the Japanese off the island. It was a terrible warning of the enormous struggle ahead.

WORLD WAR II IN THE PACIFIC
SOVIET UNION
MONGOLIA
MANCHUKUO
Beijing
KOREA
JAPAN
CHINA
Hiroshima
Nagasaki
Tokyo
Nanking
Shanghai
PACIFIC OCEAN
Midway
(June 3, 1942)
Iwo Jima
(Feb. 19, 1945)
Pearl Harbor
(Dec. 7, 1941)
HAWAIIAN IS. (U.S.)
INDIA
Hong Kong
BURMA
Rangoon
Okinawa
(Apr. 1, 1945)
THAILAND
Bangkok
Manila
PHILIPPINES
(U.S.)
Guam
(Aug. 11, 1944)
FRENCH INDOCHINA
Tarawa
(Nov. 1943)
Leyte Gulf
(Oct. 20, 1944)
MALAYA
Singapore
SUMATRA
BORNEO
NEW GUINEA
DUTCH EAST INDIES
Guadalcanal
(Aug. 7, 1942)
INDIAN OCEAN
Coral Sea
(May 4, 1942)
AUSTRALIA
0 1000 2000 Miles
0 1000 2000 Kilometers
Areas under Japanese control
Areas under Allied control
Battles
Allied forces

Rescue boats move toward the battleships U.S.S. *West Virginia* (foreground) and U.S.S. *Tennessee* after the attacks on Pearl Harbor.

REVIEW & ASSESS

1. **READING CHECK** What factors fueled Japan's imperial ambitions in the Pacific?

2. **ANALYZE CAUSE AND EFFECT** Why did the Japanese bomb Pearl Harbor?

3. **DRAW CONCLUSIONS** What strategies did the United States use against Japan?

3.3 On the Home Front

After a hard day's work, you change into your uniform and grab your tin hat. It's time to do your patriotic duty as a volunteer firefighter in a city targeted by enemy bombers. It will be a long night before you're back to work in the morning.

MAIN IDEA

Civilians participated in World War II in large numbers.

TOTAL WAR

World War II was a total war, meaning it involved a large part of many countries' populations. While soldiers were engaged in combat on the battlefields, civilians on the home front were critical to the success of the war effort. They kept their countries running and provided supplies crucial to the fight. Civilians also made many sacrifices and endured terrible suffering. In the Soviet Union, the government had to move 1,500 factories and 6 million workers hundreds of miles so that they were beyond the reach of German bombers. Even so, around 11 million Russian civilians died from fighting, cold, disease, or starvation.

Between 1940 and 1941, Britain suffered more than 100 massive air attacks on its cities. London was frequently targeted. Hitler's "Blitz," as the bombing campaign was called, aimed to break civilian spirit and destroy infrastructure and factories. Thousands of civilians died. Beginning in 1942, Allied bombers targeted German cities with even more devastating effect. During three days of bombing, Allied bombs utterly destroyed the city of Dresden. Between 25,000 and 35,000 civilians were killed. The attacks on civilians throughout the war are still criticized today.

In such a total war, propaganda was considered essential to victory. Newspapers, posters, leaflets, films, and radio broadcasts were manipulated to inspire, motivate, anger, or dishearten the population. Both sides exaggerated the truth and even lied, especially in totalitarian states.

Even U.S. propaganda unfairly treated Japanese, Italian, and German Americans. Many Americans of Japanese descent were forced to sell their homes and possessions and live in internment camps against their will. Ten of these camps had been built in remote areas of seven western states to house Japanese families, who were unjustly considered a security risk during the war.

PATRIOTIC RESPONSE

Propaganda encouraged millions on both sides to join the war effort. Many gave up their spare time to build defenses, guard coastlines, and nurse the wounded. The war also brought about a major shift in the workforce. With millions of men away at war, women took their places in the fields, factories, and service sectors of most countries. In the United States, Britain, and other countries, women formed the bulk of the national workforce. In Germany, though, women were still discouraged from such work.

In the United States, Rosie the Riveter was a fictional female factory worker who came to symbolize women's contributions to the U.S. war effort. Rosie made her first appearance in a popular 1942 song, and many artists, including famous illustrator Norman Rockwell, painted

Critical Viewing This color photograph from 1942 shows a worker assembling an airplane engine. What skills can you conclude that she needed for the work?

images of her. Rosie inspired millions of American women to join the war effort.

The war demanded the complete dedication of each nation's resources. Factories were transformed to make weapons, ammunition, and military supplies. In Europe and the United States, most goods were **rationed**, or distributed in limited quantities by the government. Governments issued ration coupons, which people exchanged for goods like meat, sugar, clothes, and gasoline. People would repair and recycle what they couldn't replace. Any scrap metal was collected and sent to factories to be turned into tanks, planes, and other military hardware. In Britain, every inch of land was used for growing fruit and vegetables, which became known as "Digging for Victory."

REVIEW & ASSESS

1. **READING CHECK** How were civilians involved in World War II?
2. **IDENTIFY MAIN IDEA AND DETAILS** What role did propaganda play in the war?
3. **ANALYZE CAUSE AND EFFECT** Why did governments ration supplies, including food and gasoline, on the home front during the war?

3.4 The Holocaust

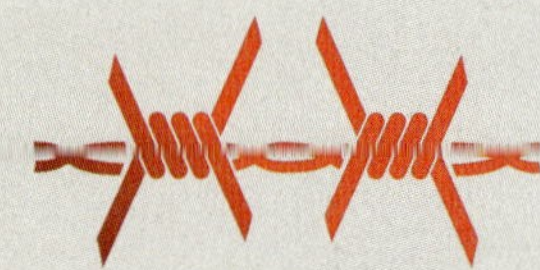

World War II lasted six years and was the bloodiest conflict in history. Estimates vary, but up to 60 million people died, including millions of civilians. In the Soviet Union alone, 11 million people died. Yet the inhuman nature of the war emerged most horribly during the events of the Holocaust.

MAIN IDEA

The Nazis tried to exterminate Europe's Jews.

Jude

THE STAR OF DAVID

The Star of David is a symbol of the Jewish people. All Jews in Nazi-occupied Europe were forced to sew a yellow Star of David onto their clothes. It was intended to be a badge of shame, but over time, it has become a symbol of heroism.

ANTI-SEMITISM IN EUROPE

Anti-Semitism, a hostility toward or discrimination of the Jewish people, has existed since ancient times. During the late 1800s, some political parties in Germany and Austria used anti-Semitism to win votes by claiming Jews caused the countries' various problems. Hitler exploited this anti-Semitism and blamed the Jews for Germany's problems.

Many non-Jewish Germans, looking for someone to blame for their problems, supported this unjustified position. Hitler went further and claimed that the Jews were racially inferior to Germans, whom he described as a "master race" destined to rule over Europe.

When the Nazis came to power in 1933, they turned their anti-Semitic beliefs into government policy. They banned Jews from civil service, education, and medicine, and they encouraged a boycott of Jewish businesses. On November 9, 1938, a violent outburst of government-approved anti-Semitism swept across Germany and Austria. Jewish homes, shops, and synagogues were attacked. This became known as *Kristallnacht* (krees-TAHL-nahkht), or "Night of the Broken Glass." Many Jews were killed. Yet much worse was to come.

NAZI BRUTALITY

World War II allowed the Nazis to extend their anti-Semitic policies to all of occupied Europe. The Nazis forced millions of Jews into slum-like areas called ghettos, where many starved or died of disease. They sent other Jews to work as slaves in brutal concentration camps. A few of the prisoners escaped, hid, or fought back in organized groups. After 1941, Nazi policies against Jews shifted from imprisonment to extermination. Special units followed the German army into Russia, rounding up and shooting all the Jews. By spring 1942, hundreds of thousands of Jews had been executed. But Nazi leaders, committed to **genocide**, or total elimination of a race, demanded more efficient methods of murder.

The Nazis built six death camps to carry out the mass murder of Jews. Indeed, any group that the Nazis found "undesirable" would be sent to the death camps. Across Europe, the Nazis packed Jews into train cars designed to move livestock and transported them to the death camps. German soldiers unloaded the prisoners, and Nazi

These people have just arrived at the German concentration and extermination camp *Auschwitz-Birkenau*.

doctors selected the healthiest to be worked to death in concentration camps or used for cruel medical experiments. Most of the prisoners, though, were chosen for immediate death. The prisoners had to strip, and soldiers herded them into poison gas chambers. After the gas was turned on, it took only 20 minutes to kill all the prisoners in a chamber. Soldiers then pillaged the bodies for jewelry and pulled out teeth with gold fillings. Finally, the Nazis tossed the bodies into giant furnaces that burned them to ash. At the most efficient death camps, it took only 90 minutes for a prisoner to travel from arrival to cremation. Six million Jews—two-thirds of Europe's Jewish population—were murdered in what is known as the **Holocaust**.

REVIEW & ASSESS

1. **READING CHECK** Why did the Nazis try to exterminate Europe's Jews?
2. **SEQUENCE EVENTS** What steps did the Nazis take to turn their anti-Semitic beliefs into action?
3. **DETERMINE WORD MEANINGS** The word *Holocaust* comes from the Greek terms *holos*, which means "whole," and *kaustos*, which means "burned." How does knowing that clarify its meaning?

3.5 MOMENTS IN HISTORY

D-Day

A13-13

JUNE 6, 1944

On this date, known as D-Day, the Allies landed around 150,000 soldiers on five beaches across the Normandy region of France. The invasion began the push to liberate Europe. Despite poor weather, more than 5,000 ships and 13,000 aircraft headed for France. The night before, paratroopers seized key enemy positions, and French fighters caused confusion behind enemy lines. The attack took the Germans completely by surprise. Even so, German resistance was fierce, especially at Omaha Beach, where U.S. troops suffered more than 2,000 casualties. By nightfall, the Allies had secured a series of positions, and reinforcements were arriving. Over the next few weeks, the various units linked up, fought off German counterattacks, and pushed into France toward Germany.

3.6 Allied Victories

World War II ended with a blinding flash and the mushroom cloud of an atomic bomb. The most destructive weapon ever created ended the bloodiest conflict in history. It's a weapon that continues to affect global politics to this day.

MAIN IDEA

The Allies defeated the Axis powers, but at an enormous cost.

VICTORY IN EUROPE

After the Battle of Stalingrad in 1943, the Soviets took the offensive and began driving the Germans back. At the Battle of Kursk, the Soviets beat the Germans decisively, and the Axis powers lost all offensive capability on the Eastern Front. In January 1944, the Soviets fought their way to Leningrad, which had been under German siege for 872 days. The Soviet Union now advanced on all fronts, occupying Bulgaria, Romania, Hungary, and Poland. The Soviet soldiers proved unstoppable, and in January 1945, they entered eastern Germany.

At the same time, the Allies were advancing in the west. After D-Day, the Allies broke down the German defenses and pushed toward Germany. With considerable effort, they crossed heavily fortified rivers into western Germany. In December 1944, Hitler launched a surprise offensive in Belgium, beginning a battle known as the Battle of the Bulge. Under the cover of bad weather, German tanks pushed Allied forces into retreat. Then the weather cleared, and Allied planes crushed the German attack—and Hitler's last hope.

The Allies then advanced rapidly on both fronts until, in April 1945, the Soviets surrounded Berlin. Soviet troops took revenge for their nation's suffering and committed numerous atrocities as they captured Berlin. Hitler and his top commanders retreated to an underground bunker in the heart of Berlin. Surrounded, Hitler committed suicide on April 30. On May 7, 1945, Germany surrendered.

VICTORY IN THE PACIFIC

Japan, however, continued to fight. After the Battles of the Coral Sea and Midway, Japan struggled to replace its lost ships and aircraft and began a long and increasingly desperate retreat. By July 1944, the U.S. strategy of island-hopping had won bases from which Allied airplanes bombed Japan. Instead of surrendering, Japanese forces fought even harder. Japan used more and more *kamikaze* (kah-mih-KAH-zee) pilots. These pilots flew planes packed with explosives directly into U.S. ships, inflicting severe casualties.

In February 1945, some 70,000 U.S. troops attacked the tiny island of Iwo Jima. Of 21,000 Japanese soldiers defending the island, only 212 surrendered. The rest died fighting. In April, the United States attacked the Japanese island of Okinawa. The United States suffered more than 45,000 casualties while kamikaze attacks sank or damaged nearly 400 ships. By now, Japan knew it could not win, but Japanese leaders hoped the strong resistance shown during the island battles would force peace negotiations. President Roosevelt died in April 1945, and his successor, President Harry Truman, chose to use the most destructive weapon the world had ever seen.

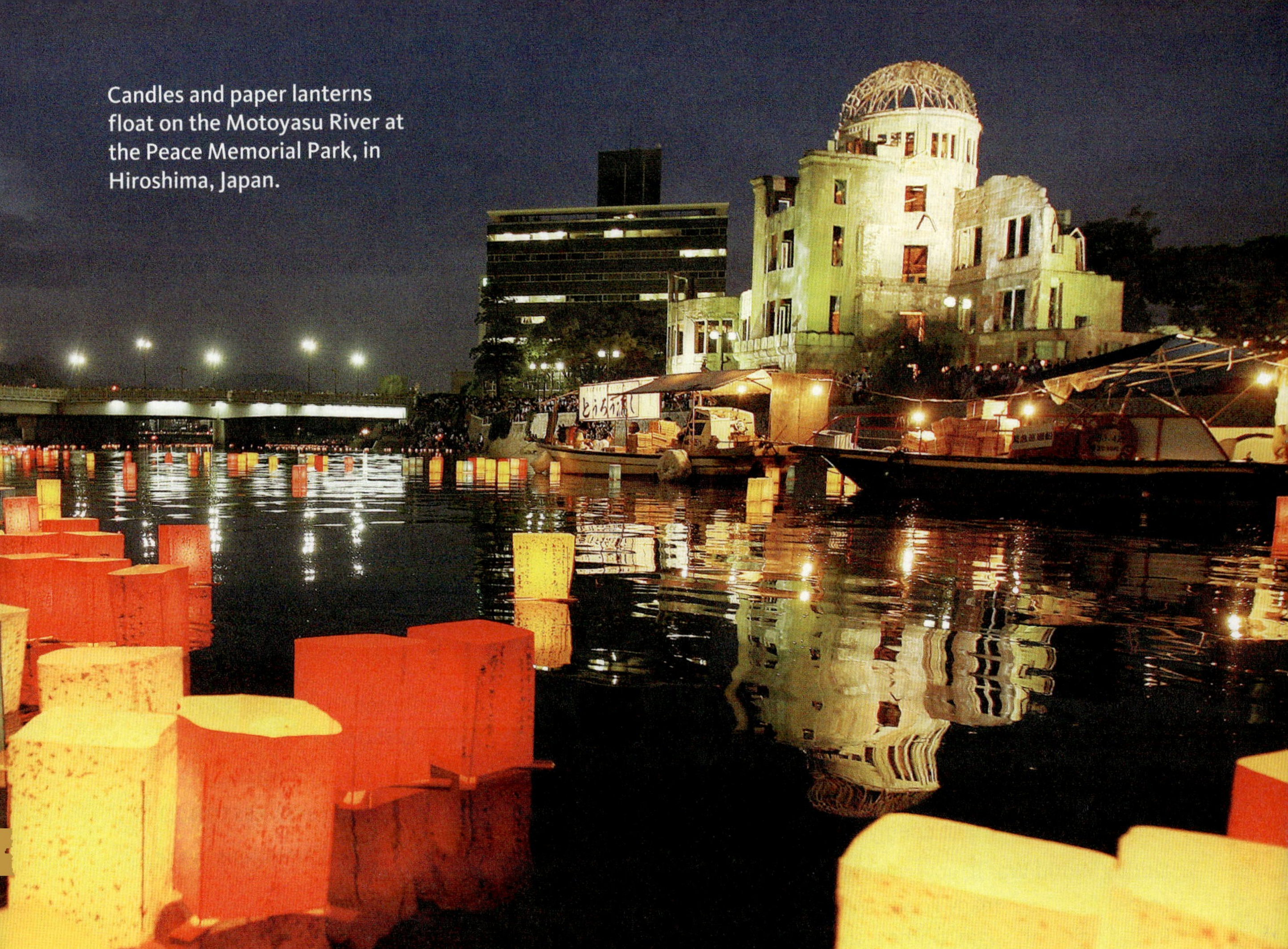

Candles and paper lanterns float on the Motoyasu River at the Peace Memorial Park, in Hiroshima, Japan.

THE ATOMIC BOMB

Early in the war, President Roosevelt was worried that Germany was developing nuclear weapons. He authorized the U.S. effort to build an **atomic bomb**, a bomb that would create a massive explosion by splitting atoms. In July 1945, the world's first atomic device was tested in the New Mexico desert. Truman was president by this time, and the Japanese ignored his demands for a complete surrender. He decided to use atomic weapons on Japanese civilians rather than sacrifice U.S. soldiers in an invasion.

On August 6, 1945, a U.S. bomber called *Enola Gay* carried an atomic bomb toward Japan. The bomb obliterated well over half of the Japanese city of **Hiroshima**. Some 70,000 Japanese civilians died instantly, and thousands more died later of radiation poisoning. On August 9, a second bomb left the city of **Nagasaki** in ruins and killed another 40,000 people instantly. On August 15, 1945, Japan's emperor, Hirohito, forced his government to surrender rather than have more Japanese cities reduced to rubble and more civilians killed. World War II had finally ended.

REVIEW & ASSESS

1. **READING CHECK** How were Allied victories in Europe and the Pacific alike and different?
2. **SEQUENCE EVENTS** What series of events led to Japan's surrender in World War II?
3. **FORM OPINIONS** Was the use of atomic bombs justified? Why or why not? Use evidence to support your opinion.

CHAPTER 26 Review

VOCABULARY

On your own paper, write the vocabulary word that completes each of the following sentences.

1. Karl Marx called on the _______ to overthrow the elite and establish a communist state.

2. After World War I, Germany's economy collapsed because of the high _______ Germany had to pay to the Allies for war damages.

3. In Italy, Mussolini founded the political movement of _______, which promoted extreme nationalism and militarism.

4. Germany's effective tactic of _______ used fast-moving tanks, motorized infantry, and bombers to overwhelm enemy defenses.

5. During World War II, governments were forced to _______ many goods and supplies, including meat, sugar, clothes, and gasoline.

READING STRATEGY

6. **ANALYZE LANGUAGE USE** If you haven't already, complete your graphic organizer to analyze how word choices throughout the text help convey the horrors of war. Then answer the question.

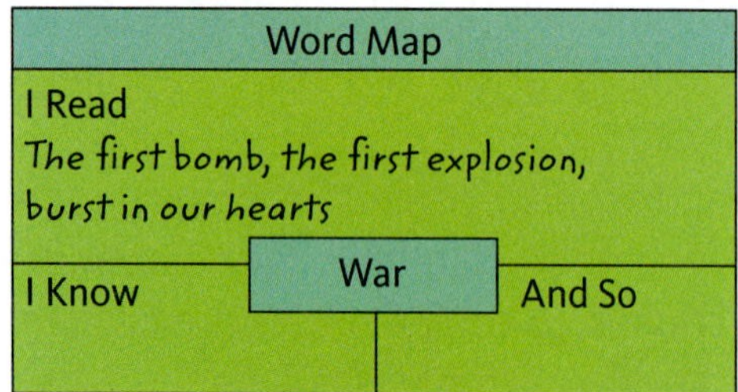
Word Map
I Read
The first bomb, the first explosion, burst in our hearts
War
I Know
And So

How do the words used by Harry Frieman and Erich Maria Remarque in Lesson 1.3 help you understand how it felt to be in the middle of a war?

MAIN IDEAS

Answer the following questions. Support your answers with evidence from the chapter.

7. What powerful new weapons were introduced in World War I? How did they affect the war? LESSON 1.2

8. What factors led to revolution in Russia? LESSON 1.4

9. What impact did World War I have on Europe? LESSON 1.5

10. What factors contributed to instability in Europe after World War I? LESSON 2.1

11. Why did powerful dictators and totalitarian states emerge after World War I? LESSON 2.3

12. What fueled Japan's imperial ambitions in the Pacific? LESSON 3.2

13. What role did women play in the civilian war effort on the home front? LESSON 3.3

14. What brought about the end of World War II? LESSON 3.6

CRITICAL THINKING

Answer the following questions. Support your answers with evidence from the chapter.

15. **DRAW CONCLUSIONS** Why was World War I called a "total war"?

16. **ANALYZE CAUSE AND EFFECT** Why did the U.S. stock market crash in 1929 affect the global economy as well?

17. **ANALYZE CAUSE AND EFFECT** What was the result of the U.S. aircraft carriers not being present at the attack on Pearl Harbor?

18. **DRAW CONCLUSIONS** Why is it important to remember the Holocaust?

19. **YOU DECIDE** Was the Treaty of Versailles, signed between the Allies and Germany, fair or unfair? Support your opinion with evidence from the chapter.

INTERPRET MAPS

Look closely at the map of the Soviet Union in 1939. Then answer the questions that follow.

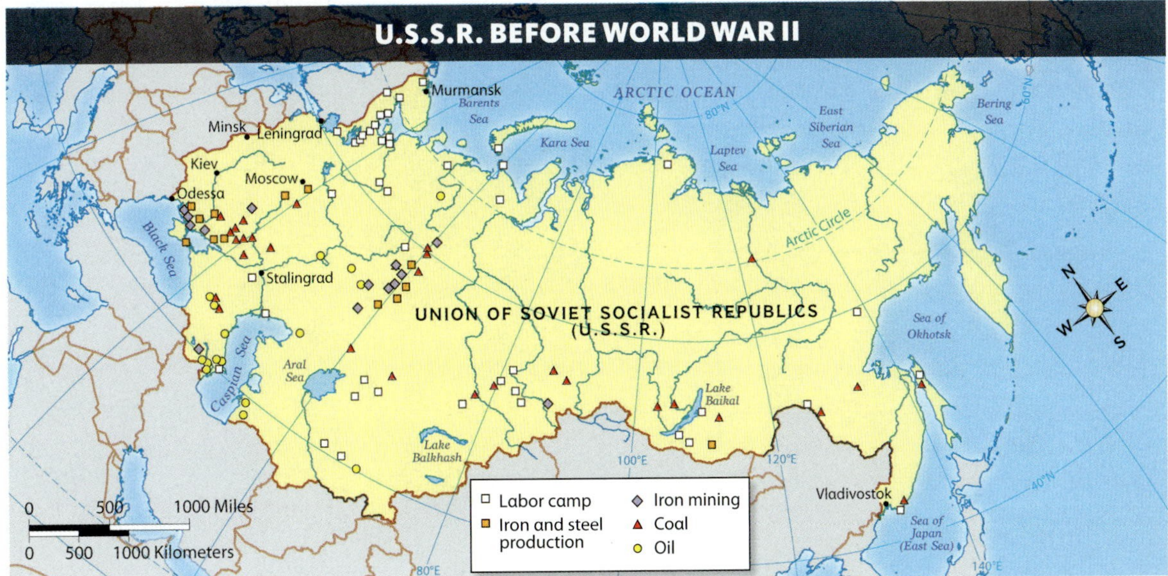

U.S.S.R. BEFORE WORLD WAR II
Murmansk
Barents Sea
ARCTIC OCEAN
Kara Sea
Laptev Sea
East Siberian Sea
Bering Sea
Minsk
Leningrad
Kiev
Moscow
Odessa
Black Sea
Stalingrad
Arctic Circle
UNION OF SOVIET SOCIALIST REPUBLICS (U.S.S.R.)
Sea of Okhotsk
Caspian Sea
Aral Sea
Lake Baikal
Lake Balkhash
Vladivostok
Sea of Japan (East Sea)
100°E
120°E
80°E
140°E
0 500 1000 Miles
0 500 1000 Kilometers
Labor camp
Iron and steel production
Iron mining
Coal
Oil
N
E
S
W

20. Why was the area near Odessa important to Stalin's industrialization plan?

21. What area of the U.S.S.R. had the fewest natural resources?

ANALYZE SOURCES

Read the following eyewitness account written by a Nazi SS officer at the Belzec death camp in Poland. Then answer the questions.

> The people were still standing like columns of stone, with no room to fall or lean. Even in death you could tell the families, all holding hands. It was difficult to separate them while emptying the room for the next batch . . . Two dozen workers were busy checking mouths which they opened with iron hooks . . . Dentists knocked out gold teeth, bridges and crowns with hammers.
>
> Kurt Gerstein, Nuremberg Trial Document 1553-PS

22. What is particularly chilling about the tone used in this eyewitness account? What impact would such a description have on Europe and the rest of the world?

WRITE ABOUT HISTORY

23. INFORMATIVE TEXT Write an essay explaining how President Roosevelt's New Deal programs addressed problems that the Great Depression created in the United States.

TIPS

- Take notes from the lessons about the Great Depression.
- Begin the essay with an introductory paragraph describing the problems created by the Great Depression, particularly in the United States.
- Develop the essay, explaining the impact the Great Depression had on the lives of millions of Americans.
- Explain what President Roosevelt's New Deal was and describe what these government programs aimed to do for the American people.
- Conclude the essay by explaining how the New Deal programs helped address problems created by the Great Depression.

CHAPTER

27 GLOBAL CONNECTIONS

1945 TO THE PRESENT

SECTION 1
A POSTWAR WORLD

KEY VOCABULARY	NAMES & PLACES
apartheid	Achmed Sukarno
civil disobedience	Aung San Suu Kyi
guerrilla	Ho Chi Minh
intifada	Jomo Kenyatta
nonviolent	Kwame Nkrumah
partition	Mohandas Gandhi

SECTION 2
THE COLD WAR

KEY VOCABULARY	NAMES & PLACES
collective	Berlin Wall
containment	Cold War
domino theory	Cultural Revolution
ethnic cleansing	Joseph Stalin
glasnost	Mao Zedong
perestroika	Marshall Plan

SECTION 3
INTO THE 21ST CENTURY

KEY VOCABULARY	NAMES & PLACES
free trade	al Qaeda
global citizen	Arab Spring
globalization	Lech Walesa
petroleum	Nelson Mandela
refugee	Osama bin Laden
surveillance	
terrorism	

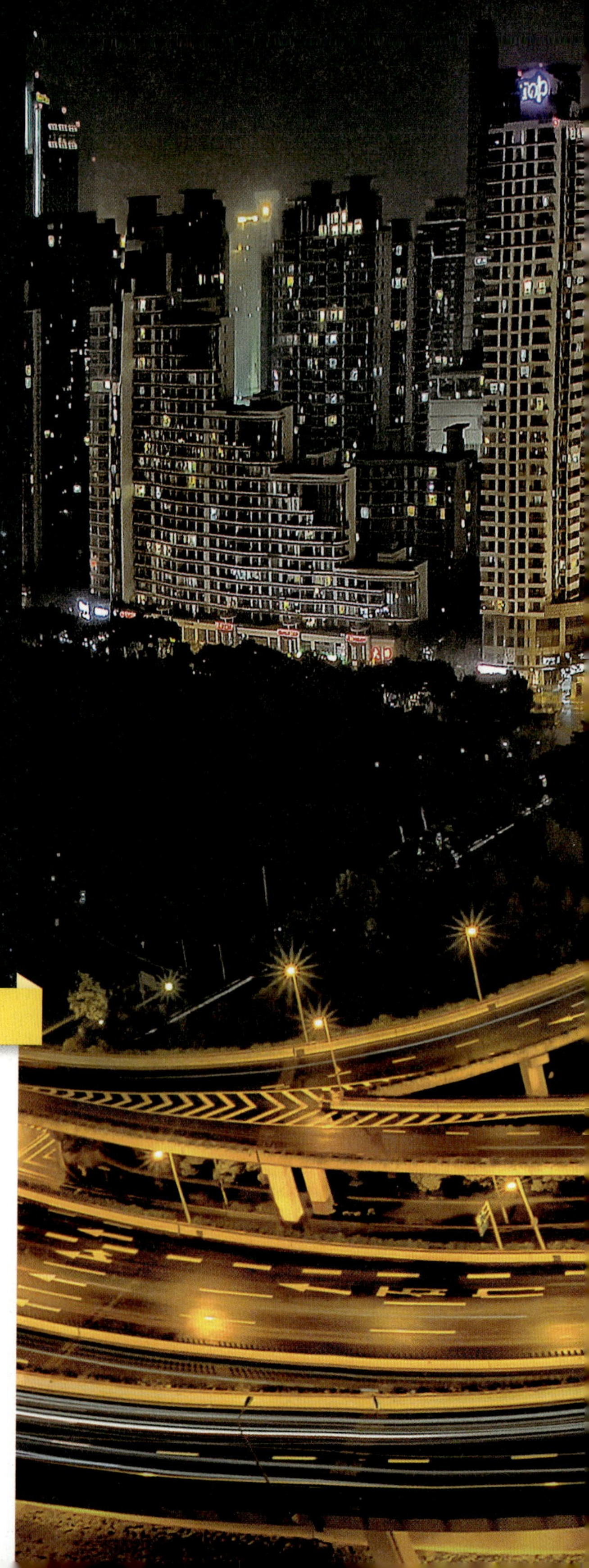

READING STRATEGY

DRAW CONCLUSIONS When you come to a conclusion, you decide that something is true after you have considered all the facts. As you read the chapter, use a chart like this one to help you draw a conclusion about the impact of globalization on the modern world.

GLOBALIZATION	
PROS:	CONS:
CONCLUSION:	

Shanghai, China, represents the global city. With more than 24 million people, it is one of the world's most influential technological, cultural, and economic centers.

1.1 The Partition of India

The world was not the same after World War II. Colonial powers lost influence and eventually their colonies. Change came swiftly in some parts of the world, but painfully slowly in others. One thing was for sure: There was no turning back to prewar realities.

MAIN IDEA

In 1947, India achieved independence from Great Britain after decades of resistance against colonial rule.

NATIONALISM AND CONFLICT

India was the "Jewel in the Crown" of the British Empire—a valuable colony the British wanted to keep. However, in the 1880s, British rule came under growing pressure from Indian nationalists demanding independence. The Indian National Congress, made up mostly of Hindus and founded in 1885, soon led a campaign for independence. The Muslim League, founded in 1906, supported independence but focused on protecting Muslims' interests.

In the early 1900s, nationalist actions forced the colonial government to make some reforms. British forces responded to nationalists' additional demands with brutal acts of suppression. In 1919, British soldiers fired on unarmed protestors in the city of Amritsar, killing nearly 400.

In 1920, **Mohandas Gandhi** became leader of the Indian National Congress. Gandhi, also called *Mahatma*, meaning "Great Soul," was a Hindu lawyer who wanted India to win independence peacefully. Throughout the 1920s and 1930s, Gandhi organized **nonviolent** protests such as strikes, boycotts of British goods, and noncompliance with British laws and taxes. British rulers offered some reforms but refused to give India full independence.

When Britain entered World War II in 1939, India, as a colony, became involved in the war, too. Because Indian leaders were not consulted about India's entrance into the war, many resigned in protest. Three years later, Gandhi organized the Quit India Movement to pressure Britain to grant independence. Members of this movement refused to support the war and threatened widespread **civil disobedience**, or refusal to follow certain laws. Gandhi was imprisoned, and nationalist violence increased.

INDIA AND PAKISTAN

Despite tensions and occasional violence, Hindus and Muslims generally worked together for independence. Both groups were geographically spread out, but most Muslims lived in the northern part of the subcontinent. Hindus were the majority population, numbering about 225 million. As a minority population of about 92 million, Muslims had long worried that Hindus would dominate an independent India. After the 1937 elections, in which Muslims did not feel represented, the Muslim League demanded the creation of a separate Muslim state.

After World War II, the British government finally agreed to grant India independence. However, independence did not resolve tensions among Indians themselves. As violence between Hindus and Muslims escalated toward civil war, Indian leaders reluctantly agreed to **partition**, or divide, India. On August 15, 1947, India became independent, and a new country,

Critical Viewing Muslim refugees trying to flee to Pakistan crowd onto a train near New Delhi, India, in September 1947. What do details in the photo reveal about possible conditions on their journey?

Pakistan, was established. The partition was meant to be a peaceful solution. However, one million people died in violent clashes as Hindus fled the newly created Pakistan and Muslims fled India.

Gandhi agreed to the creation of Pakistan but had doubts about partition as a solution. In the months following partition, he devoted his energies to restoring peace. In 1948, Gandhi was assassinated by a Hindu extremist who accused him of being too sympathetic to Muslims. Though he died a violent death, Gandhi's legacy of nonviolent resistance influenced leaders who came after him, including Martin Luther King, Jr., and Nelson Mandela.

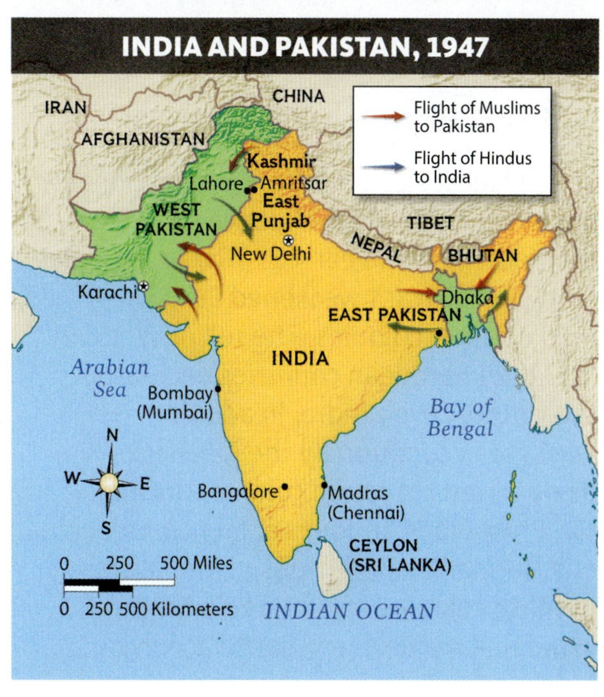

INDIA AND PAKISTAN, 1947
Flight of Muslims to Pakistan
Flight of Hindus to India
IRAN
CHINA
AFGHANISTAN
Kashmir
Lahore
Amritsar
East Punjab
WEST PAKISTAN
TIBET
NEPAL
BHUTAN
New Delhi
Karachi
Dhaka
EAST PAKISTAN
INDIA
Arabian Sea
Bombay (Mumbai)
Bay of Bengal
N
W
E
S
Bangalore
Madras (Chennai)
CEYLON (SRI LANKA)
0 250 500 Miles
0 250 500 Kilometers
INDIAN OCEAN

REVIEW & ASSESS

1. **READING CHECK** What nonviolent methods did Gandhi use to help win India's independence from Great Britain?

2. **ANALYZE CAUSE AND EFFECT** Why was India divided into two separate countries?

3. **INTERPRET MAPS** From what areas of India did most Muslims flee to Pakistan?

1.2 Independence in Southeast Asia

Colonies in Southeast Asia took advantage of the destabilizing effects of World War II to overthrow European rule. But no country in the region achieved independence without a struggle.

MAIN IDEA

After World War II, several Southeast Asian colonies gained independence from different European powers.

THE PHILIPPINES AND INDONESIA

In Southeast Asia, as elsewhere, nationalist movements for independence gained momentum in the early 1900s. As you have read, World War I weakened Europeans' hold on their colonies. The toll of World War II on European countries decreased their power even more. In addition, wartime occupation by the Japanese destabilized European colonies, including the Philippines, Indonesia, French Indochina, and Burma. In some cases, nationalists in these colonies cooperated with the invading Japanese in order to achieve independence from European rule.

The United States took control of the Philippines in the 1890s, but never formally recognized it as a colony. The United States approved a 10-year transition plan for Philippine independence in 1935. Filipino and U.S. forces fought together against Japan during the war. In 1946, the United States granted independence to the Philippines, but continues to exert an economic influence on the country.

Unlike the United States, the Dutch were far less willing to surrender their profitable colony, Dutch East Indies, which they had ruled since the 1800s. A powerful independence movement was already in place when Japan seized the colony during the war. At first, many Indonesians welcomed the Japanese as liberators, but later experienced harsh treatment under Japanese rule.

After the war and Japanese surrender, **Achmed Sukarno** emerged as the independence movement's leader. Sukarno seized power and established an independent republic in Indonesia before the Dutch could return. The United States of Indonesia was founded in 1949. Sukarno named himself a "lifetime president," but he was unable to hold onto power in this populous and economically troubled country. He was replaced in 1967 after a military coup, or takeover.

FRENCH INDOCHINA AND BURMA

Colonial rule and power struggles after independence caused problems even decades after nationalists forced Europeans out. One example of this pattern was French Indochina, which included the present-day countries of Cambodia, Laos, and Vietnam. Nationalists in French Indochina did not welcome occupying Japanese forces during World War II as their liberators from French rule. Instead, a group called the Viet Minh, under the leadership of **Ho Chi Minh**, led the fight against the French.

The French wanted to re-establish power after the war, but they had to face the Viet Minh, who wanted them out. The Viet Minh forced the French to withdraw from Vietnam and Laos in 1954. However, the region's troubles were far from over.

Achmed Sukarno of Indonesia attends a conference of world leaders in 1961, six years before he was forced out of office.

Ho Chi Minh, shown here in 1954, led the nationalist movement for three decades. He served as the president of North Vietnam from 1945 to 1969.

Aung San Suu Kyi won the Nobel Peace Prize in 1991 for her nonviolent work in democracy and human rights.

The peace agreement that followed, called the Geneva Accords, divided Vietnam into two parts: North Vietnam, a communist state led by Ho Chi Minh, and South Vietnam, a democratic republic backed by the United States. Ten years later, full-scale war broke out between North and South Vietnam.

Burma is another example of the troubles left behind by colonialism. During World War II, nationalists in Burma welcomed the invading Japanese and joined with them to overthrow British rule. Later, the nationalists, led by Aung San, switched sides and fought with the British in exchange for independence after the war. Aung San was assassinated in 1947, so he did not live to see Burmese independence in 1948. Struggles over power in Burma resulted in an unstable and repressive regime for the next several decades.

Forty years after Burma achieved independence, Aung San's daughter, **Aung San Suu Kyi**, returned to Burma after living abroad since 1960. She soon became the leader of a nonviolent movement of monks, students, and workers advocating for peaceful democratic reform. The army suppressed the demonstrations and seized power in a coup in September 1988. Under the new regime, Burma became Myanmar. The government placed Suu Kyi under house arrest on numerous occasions. Restrictions on her were finally lifted in 2010.

REVIEW & ASSESS

1. **READING CHECK** How did many Southeast Asian colonies gain independence?
2. **ANALYZE CAUSE AND EFFECT** During World War II, why did some Southeast Asians welcome the Japanese?
3. **DRAW CONCLUSIONS** Why were the Viet Minh important?

1.3 Postcolonial Africa

Nationalist movements achieved success in Africa after the war as they had in India and Southeast Asia. In the 1950s and 1960s, most African nations established independence from European rule. Some transitions to independence were peaceful, and some were violent.

MAIN IDEA

After World War II, countries in Africa gained independence from European powers.

INDEPENDENT AFRICA

Unlike other countries in Africa, South Africa had been independent from European rule since 1910. However, as nationalism spread throughout the continent, South Africa's white minority rulers solidified their power over the black majority. In 1948, they imposed **apartheid**. Apartheid was a system of racial segregation that discriminated against nonwhite South Africans socially, politically, and economically.

For decades, the white minority government refused to work with the African National Congress (ANC), founded in 1912. The ANC worked for black rights and fought against apartheid. The white minority government tried to silence the ANC by banning the organization in 1960.

As the maps to the right show, most African countries did not achieve independence until after 1950. The dramatic shift in power on the continent came quickly, but not easily.

One of the first colonies in Africa to win independence after World War II was the Gold Coast. There, nationalists opposed British rule. **Kwame Nkrumah** (KWAH-mee uhn-KROO-mah) had been educated in the West. He and other leaders used nonviolent tactics to force the British out, as Gandhi had done in India. The Gold Coast won independence in 1957 and renamed itself Ghana. Nkrumah became Ghana's first president. However, his ambitious plans for a modernized Ghana did not materialize, and political instability became the norm between 1966 and 2001.

In the British colony of Kenya, the struggle for independence was more violent. The Mau Mau (MAOW MAOW) was a **guerrilla** group, or a group of organized resistance fighters, who used violence to try to force the British to leave. In 1963, the country achieved independence from Britain, and **Jomo Kenyatta** became its first president.

Some struggles for independence were quite violent, as in Algeria, part of French North Africa. More than one million French citizens lived there, along with nine million Arabs and Berber Muslims. After World War II, the French colonists vigorously opposed self-rule for Algeria. Algerians began a guerrilla war against the French. High casualties and the cost of the war forced the French to grant independence in 1956.

POSTCOLONIAL LEGACY

By 1975, most African nations had won independence. However, self-rule brought many challenges. Newly established countries struggled to form stable governments that could provide security and bring prosperity. Military dictatorships, corruption, and one-party rule dominated some African nations.

One country that had a rocky beginning was Congo, which had been ruled by Belgium. In 1965, five years after independence, an army officer named Mobutu Sese Seko (moh-BOO-too say-say SAY-koh) seized power and ruled a one-party state for more than 30 years. His plans for Congo's economic development failed. Yet he became one of the world's wealthiest men—and was often accused of corruption.

In addition to political instability, military rule, and corruption, postcolonial African countries also faced the problem of national boundaries. The British, French, and other European rulers had ignored ethnic homelands when they created the boundaries for their colonies.

Postcolonial governments inherited these artificial boundaries, which put many ethnic groups into the same countries. Over time, tensions among rival ethnic groups exploded into violence and civil war. For example, Nigeria was torn apart by civil war in the 1960s, and Somalia and Rwanda experienced violence during the 1990s.

The effects of artificial colonial boundaries persisted even into the 21st century. Sudan won independence from British rule in 1956, but the country endured decades of violence because of ethnic, tribal, and religious divisions. In addition, a massive drought caused widespread famine. More than two million people died because of war and starvation. In 2011, South Sudanese people voted to break away from Sudan to establish an independent nation. South Sudan has since struggled with an ineffective government, a weak economy, and continued violence.

INDEPENDENCE IN AFRICA, 1955–1975

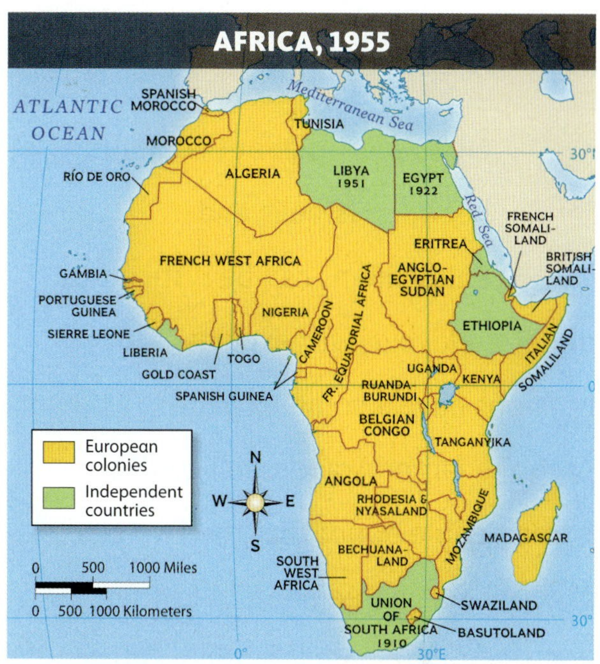

AFRICA, 1955
ATLANTIC OCEAN
Mediterranean Sea
SPANISH MOROCCO
MOROCCO
TUNISIA
RÍO DE ORO
ALGERIA
LIBYA 1951
EGYPT 1922
Red Sea
FRENCH SOMALI-LAND
ERITREA
BRITISH SOMALI-LAND
GAMBIA
FRENCH WEST AFRICA
ANGLO-EGYPTIAN SUDAN
PORTUGUESE GUINEA
NIGERIA
CAMEROON
FR. EQUATORIAL AFRICA
ETHIOPIA
SIERRE LEONE
LIBERIA
TOGO
GOLD COAST
SPANISH GUINEA
UGANDA
KENYA
ITALIAN SOMALILAND
RUANDA-BURUNDI
BELGIAN CONGO
TANGANYIKA
European colonies
Independent countries
N
W
E
S
ANGOLA
RHODESIA & NYASALAND
MOZAMBIQUE
MADAGASCAR
BECHUANA-LAND
SOUTH WEST AFRICA
0 500 1000 Miles
0 500 1000 Kilometers
UNION OF SOUTH AFRICA 1910
SWAZILAND
BASUTOLAND
0°
30°E
30°N
30°S

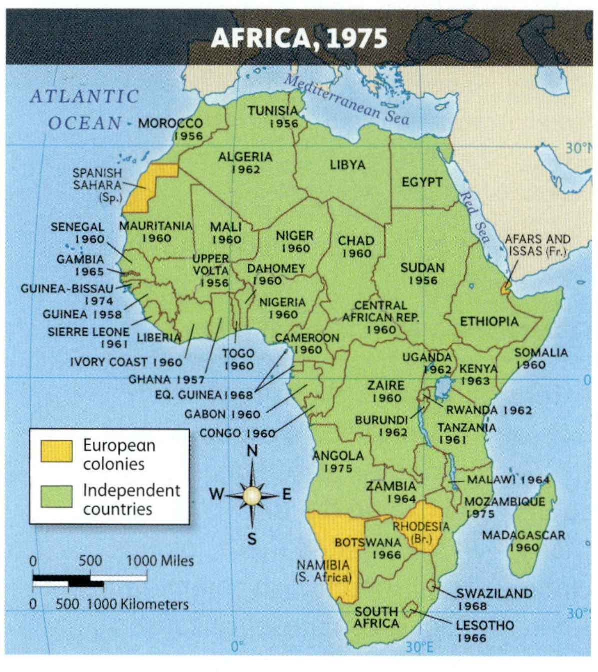

AFRICA, 1975
ATLANTIC OCEAN
Mediterranean Sea
MOROCCO 1956
TUNISIA 1956
ALGERIA 1962
LIBYA
EGYPT
Red Sea
SPANISH SAHARA (Sp.)
SENEGAL 1960
MAURITANIA 1960
MALI 1960
NIGER 1960
CHAD 1960
AFARS AND ISSAS (Fr.)
GAMBIA 1965
UPPER VOLTA 1956
DAHOMEY 1960
SUDAN 1956
GUINEA-BISSAU 1974
NIGERIA 1960
GUINEA 1958
CENTRAL AFRICAN REP. 1960
ETHIOPIA
SIERRE LEONE 1961
LIBERIA
CAMEROON 1960
SOMALIA 1960
IVORY COAST 1960
TOGO 1960
UGANDA 1962
KENYA 1963
GHANA 1957
EQ. GUINEA 1968
ZAIRE 1960
RWANDA 1962
GABON 1960
BURUNDI 1962
TANZANIA 1961
CONGO 1960
European colonies
Independent countries
N
W
E
S
ANGOLA 1975
ZAMBIA 1964
MALAWI 1964
MOZAMBIQUE 1975
RHODESIA (Br.)
MADAGASCAR 1960
BOTSWANA 1966
NAMIBIA (S. Africa)
0 500 1000 Miles
0 500 1000 Kilometers
SWAZILAND 1968
SOUTH AFRICA
LESOTHO 1966
0°
30°E
30°N
30°S

REVIEW & ASSESS

1. **READING CHECK** What effect did the spread of nationalist movements after World War II have on the continent of Africa?

2. **ANALYZE CAUSE AND EFFECT** Why did South Africa's white minority rulers impose the policy of apartheid?

3. **INTERPRET MAPS** Which countries were independent in 1955? In which decade did most African nations gain independence?

1.4 Shifts in Southwest Asia

News stories about conflicts between Israelis and Palestinians can be difficult to understand, even for experts. Today's tensions have a complex history as part of a larger Arab-Israeli conflict. Some people doubt that the two sides can reach an agreement, but others are hopeful for a diplomatic solution.

MAIN IDEA

Israel, Arab states, and Palestinians have struggled with issues of land, security, and self-rule for many decades.

FOUNDING MODERN ISRAEL

After World War I, the area of present-day Jordan, Israel, the West Bank, and the Gaza Strip was placed under British control and named the British Mandate. Many Jews immigrated there, joining already established Jewish communities. An increased Jewish presence caused resentment among Palestinian Arabs.

The experience of the Holocaust prompted the United Nations (UN) to create a state for the Jewish people. In 1947, the UN voted to divide the mandate into two parts, Arab and Jewish. The Arab states and the Palestinian Arabs rejected the division as unfair. However, Jews who desired an independent nation accepted the plan. In 1948, the State of Israel was founded. Immediately, five Arab countries—Egypt, Iraq, Jordan, Syria, and Lebanon—declared war against Israel. Troops from Saudi Arabia also joined the war on the Arab side. Israel won the war, while Jordan took control of the West Bank and East Jerusalem, and Egypt took control of the Gaza Strip. A Palestinian Arab state never formed.

Before and during the war in 1948–1949, around 700,000 Palestinians had fled to neighboring countries or Arab towns in the West Bank and Gaza. They were not allowed home when the war ended. At about the same time, approximately 800,000 Jews were forced to flee Muslim countries in Southwest Asia and North Africa. Most of these Jews sought refuge in Israel.

BORDERS AND CONFLICTS

In the next few decades, Israelis, Palestinians, and Arabs from surrounding countries fought several wars over security and territory. During the Six-Day War of 1967, Israel took control of the Golan Heights from Syria, the Sinai Peninsula and Gaza Strip from Egypt, and the West Bank and East Jerusalem from Jordan.

Israel expected to trade captured lands for peace, but shortly after the 1967 War, the Arab League met in Khartoum, Sudan, and adopted the "3 NOs" policy—no peace with Israel, no recognition of Israel, and no negotiations with Israel.

During the Yom Kippur War of 1973, Egypt and Syria attacked Israel in a failed attempt to regain territory. Meanwhile, the Israeli government began building Jewish settlements in disputed areas, resulting in sometimes violent protest by Palestinians.

In the 1960s, Palestinian leaders created the Palestine Liberation Organization (PLO). The PLO supported the creation of a Palestinian state. However, the PLO's formal position focused on the elimination of the state of Israel. Israel fought back against anti-Israeli violence.

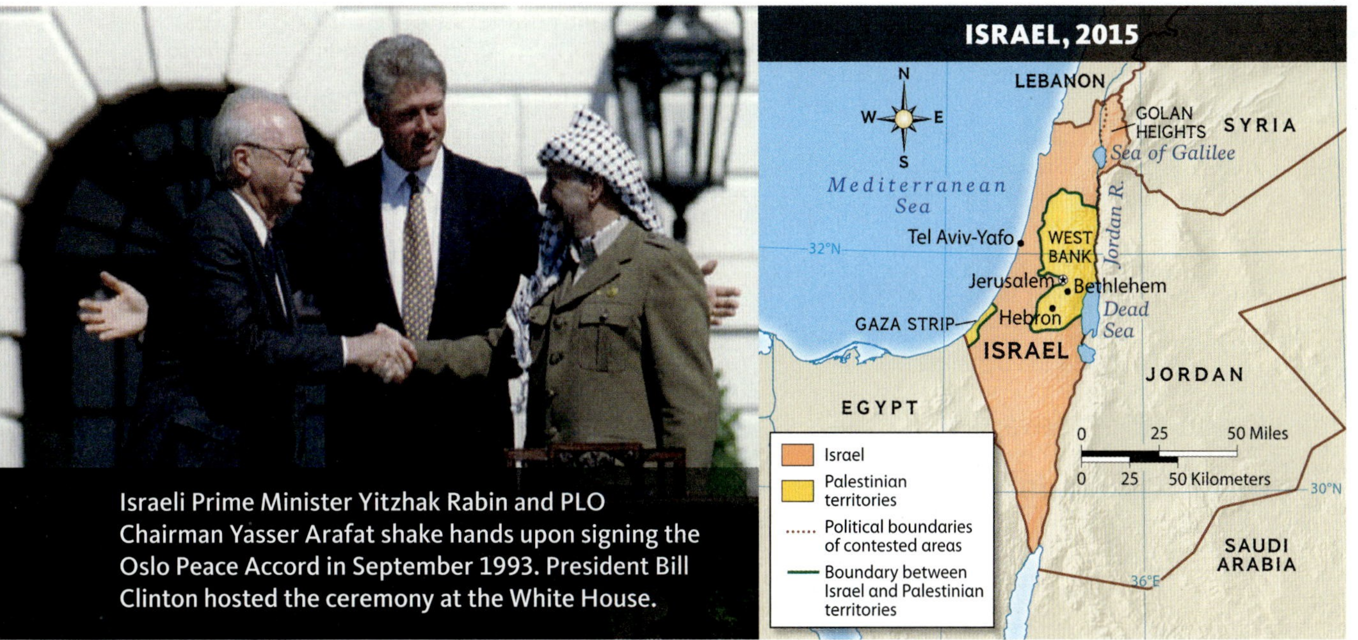
ISRAEL, 2015
N
W
E
S
LEBANON
GOLAN HEIGHTS
SYRIA
Sea of Galilee
Mediterranean Sea
Tel Aviv-Yafo
WEST BANK
Jordan R.
32°N
Jerusalem
Bethlehem
Dead Sea
GAZA STRIP
Hebron
ISRAEL
JORDAN
EGYPT
0
25
50 Miles
0
25
50 Kilometers
30°N
Israel
Palestinian territories
Political boundaries of contested areas
Boundary between Israel and Palestinian territories
SAUDI ARABIA
36°E

Israeli Prime Minister Yitzhak Rabin and PLO Chairman Yasser Arafat shake hands upon signing the Oslo Peace Accord in September 1993. President Bill Clinton hosted the ceremony at the White House.

Continuing conflict led the United States to pressure Israel and Egypt into peace talks. In the 1978 Camp David Accords and 1979 Israel-Egypt Peace Treaty, Israel agreed to withdraw from Sinai, and Egypt recognized Israel's right to exist. It was an important step toward peace, but violence continued in other parts of the region.

In 1987, Palestinians launched a mass uprising, called an **intifada**. They were protesting Israeli control of the West Bank and Gaza Strip. Peace talks in the 1990s led to some agreements. The Oslo Peace Accord in 1993 was an important first step. Israel agreed to give self-rule to Palestinians in the Gaza Strip and in Jericho in the West Bank. The PLO recognized the right of the state of Israel to exist and renounced violence against Israel.

Efforts toward peace stalled, though. Israelis and Palestinians could not agree on other issues, including the status of Jerusalem. Both sides wanted this city for their capital. Peace talks collapsed. Palestinians began a second intifada in 2000, and Israel withdrew from Gaza in 2005.

Conflict between Palestinian factions since 2007 has produced two Palestinian governments. Hamas controls Gaza, and the Palestinian Authority controls the West Bank. Hamas does not accept previous Palestinian-Israeli agreements and calls for the destruction of Israel. More violence occurred in 2014 when Israel invaded the Gaza Strip to stop Palestinian rocket attacks from Gaza.

Today, most Palestinians live in the self-governing regions of Gaza and the West Bank, but the permanent status of these areas is undecided. Progress toward peace and resolution to the issue of Palestinian statehood is slow.

REVIEW & ASSESS

1. **READING CHECK** What is the main issue over which different groups in Israel and bordering states have fought since 1948?
2. **DRAW CONCLUSIONS** Why did Jews around the world want to establish a Jewish state?
3. **INTERPRET MAPS** Which Arab states border Israel?

2.1 The Iron Curtain

After World War II, some countries struggled to rebuild and move forward, and others became more powerful than ever. Lines drawn in the immediate years after the truce would shape world events for the next 50 years.

MAIN IDEA

The United States and the Soviet Union competed for influence around the world in the decades after World War II.

TWO SUPERPOWERS SQUARE OFF

In a 1946 speech, British Prime Minister Winston Churchill warned that the Soviet Union was establishing communist governments throughout Eastern Europe, effectively hanging an "Iron Curtain" that divided Europe into two hostile parts. Churchill cautioned Western leaders that unless they stopped the Soviets from extending this practice beyond Eastern Europe, another war would be unavoidable.

After the war, the Soviets had indeed created communist governments throughout Eastern Europe, sometimes referred to as the Eastern Bloc. Fearing the spread of communism, U.S. president Harry Truman announced the Truman Doctrine in 1947. This doctrine committed the United States to a policy of **containment**, or stopping the spread of communism by providing financial and military assistance to specific countries.

Some policymakers in the United States, including Secretary of State George C. Marshall, believed that communism thrived among poor populations and that the United States should offer aid to vulnerable countries. In 1948, the U.S. Congress passed the Economic Cooperation Act, which became known as the **Marshall Plan**.

The Marshall Plan provided 13 billion dollars in U.S. aid to rebuild Europe's postwar economies and to restore prosperity. The Soviet Union's leader, **Joseph Stalin**, forbade communist governments from taking this aid. The United States and other Western nations also formed the North Atlantic Treaty Organization (NATO), a defensive alliance against potential Soviet aggression. In 1955, the Soviet Union and other communist states formed an alliance of their own, called the Warsaw Pact.

Between 1945 and 1990, the United States and the Soviet Union were divided by very different ideals. The United States favored democracy and free enterprise, or capitalism. The Soviet Union attempted to spread communism. As a result, the two countries became heated rivals. This period of rivalry and aggression is known as the **Cold War**. During this tense time in international relations, two military superpowers—the United States and the Soviet Union—competed for global influence and dominance.

RACE FOR FIREPOWER

During the Cold War, both the United States and the Soviet Union spent millions of dollars building up their militaries with more soldiers, tanks, planes, and ships. Both superpowers also engaged in an expensive arms, or weapons, race, including nuclear weapons. At the height of the arms race in the 1960s, each superpower possessed the ability to destroy the planet several times over. The arms race fueled fears of nuclear war in the United States and around the world. Attempts by both sides

COLD WAR EUROPE AND THE SOVIET UNION

Members of the Warsaw Pact
Members of NATO
Other communist countries
Non-aligned countries
Iron Curtain

to agree to limit nuclear weapons had varied success. During the 1970s, both sides agreed to nuclear test ban treaties and limits on weapons production.

Another race also occupied the superpowers during the Cold War: the "space race" of the 1950s and 1960s. Getting to outer space first became a matter of national pride. In 1957, the Soviets launched *Sputnik*, a satellite that successfully orbited Earth. The United States responded with the creation of the National Aeronautics and Space Administration (NASA) just a year later.

ONE GIANT LEAP

On July 20, 1969, more than half a billion people worldwide tuned in to their black-and-white televisions to watch U.S. astronaut Neil Armstrong (shown here) become the first human to set foot on the moon.

"That's one small step for a man, one giant leap for mankind," Armstrong exclaimed. He and fellow astronaut Buzz Aldrin explored the moon for a few hours and left behind a firmly-planted U.S. flag before returning to Earth.

REVIEW & ASSESS

1. **READING CHECK** Which two superpowers competed for influence around the world during the Cold War?
2. **COMPARE AND CONTRAST** How did the primary political aims of the United States and Soviet Union differ after World War II?
3. **INTERPRET MAPS** Which countries were located behind the "Iron Curtain"?

2.2 A Divided Berlin

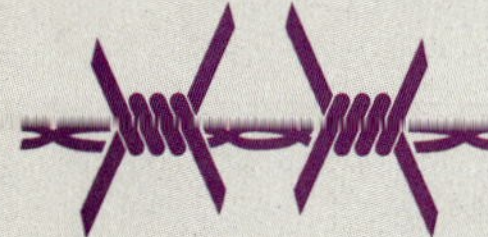

Searchlights sweep across the concrete wall, and soldiers with machine guns guard the open ground between you and a new life in the West. Like many Germans living in Soviet-controlled East Berlin, you look longingly over the wall, but escape is almost impossible. You are in one of the hot spots of the Cold War—Berlin, Germany.

MAIN IDEA

During the Cold War, Germany was divided into East Germany and West Germany.

GERMANY DIVIDED

After World War II, the Allies divided the defeated Germany into four sectors, or parts. The United States, Britain, and France governed sectors in western Germany, and the Soviet Union occupied large areas of eastern Germany. The postwar division was complicated by Berlin, Germany's capital city, because it was located deep inside the Soviet-controlled sector.

The Allies did not want to allow the Soviets to control Germany's capital, so they divided Berlin as they had divided Germany. The United States, Britain, and France controlled West Berlin, and the Soviet Union took charge of East Berlin. It was an awkward solution, and it led to some dramatic consequences.

Tensions in the divided Berlin grew. In June 1948, the Allies proposed combining their three sectors of Germany into a new democratic republic, which would also include West Berlin. The Soviets opposed this move and closed off all road, rail, and canal links into West Berlin. With their supply routes blockaded, two million West Berliners suddenly found themselves effectively under siege by the Soviets. Stalin hoped the Allies would abandon Berlin. They did the opposite.

Instead, President Harry Truman ordered the Berlin Airlift. Between June 1948 and September 1949, Allied cargo planes flew every necessary item into West Berlin. Through even the worst weather, planes delivered more than 2 million tons of food, fuel, and medicine to keep West Berlin running.

Stalin ended the 11-month blockade in May 1949. In October 1949, the Allies established a separate West Germany, which included West Berlin. Soon after, the state of East Germany was also established. The Berlin Crisis of 1948–1949 was resolved, but it solidified a division between East and West. Not surprisingly, more trouble lay ahead.

THE BERLIN WALL

Once Germany and Berlin were divided, they became very different places to live. Thanks to Western aid, the economy of West Germany improved dramatically. However, the economy—and the living standards—in East Germany fell behind. The stark differences between life in the East and the West became more than many Germans could stand.

Between 1945 and 1961, nearly 3 million East Germans, or 20 percent of the population, fled to West Germany and other democratic countries. These East Germans

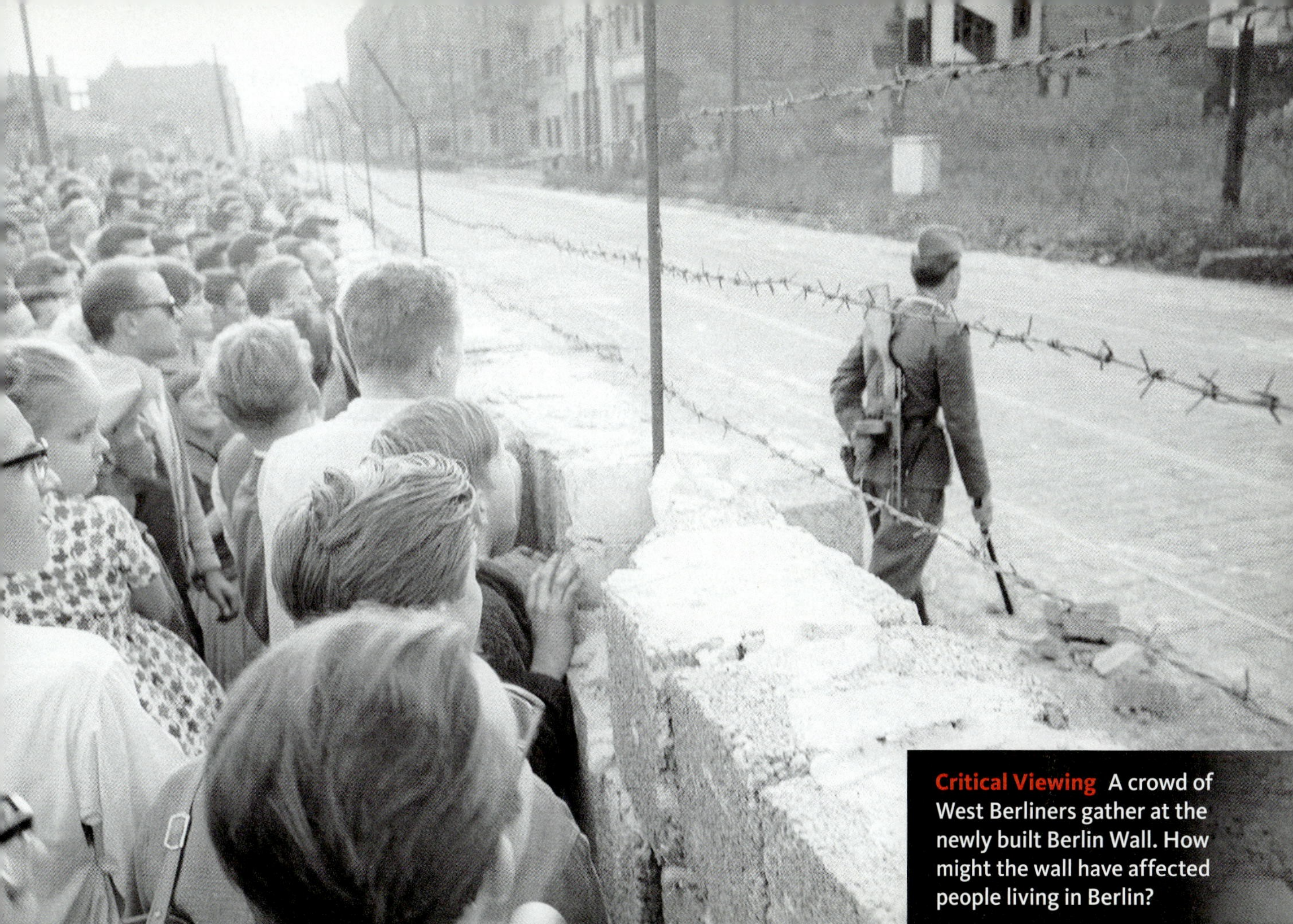

Critical Viewing A crowd of West Berliners gather at the newly built Berlin Wall. How might the wall have affected people living in Berlin?

were looking for better opportunities. The desperate migration out of the country embarrassed the East German government and led to severe labor shortages. In August 1961, the government ordered that barbed wire be put up to separate East Berlin from West Berlin and to stop the flow of Germans out of East Germany. The two parts of the city were completely cut off from each other.

The **Berlin Wall** eventually measured more than 100 miles long and included cinder block walls and guard towers. Once it was in place, it restricted movement into East Berlin from West Berlin through checkpoints along the heavily guarded wall. Traveling from East Berlin into West Berlin became almost impossible, but many people still tried.

During its 28-year existence, fewer than 5,000 people managed to escape East Germany across the Berlin Wall. The East German government captured at least 5,000 people and killed nearly 200 people who were trying to escape. The Berlin Wall became a powerful symbol of Cold War tensions.

REVIEW & ASSESS

1. **READING CHECK** How was Germany divided after World War II?
2. **ANALYZE CAUSE AND EFFECT** What caused President Truman to organize the Berlin Airlift?
3. **DRAW CONCLUSIONS** In what way was the Berlin Wall a symbol of the Cold War?

2.3 Mao's China

At the beginning of the 20th century, China was a mere shadow of the great imperial civilization it had once been. In 1912, the last imperial dynasty came to an end. However, in less than 100 years, China transformed itself into an industrial and commercial powerhouse with a major role in the world economy.

MAIN IDEA

Despite its oppressive policies, China grew into a major world economy.

CHAIRMAN MAO

In 1949, the Chinese Communist Party emerged victorious from a long and bloody civil war with Chinese nationalists. Their leader, **Mao Zedong** (MOW dzuh-dahng), established the People's Republic of China. Like Stalin in the Soviet Union, Mao ruled as a totalitarian dictator. He established a terrifying control over the Chinese people. Until his death in 1976, Mao led China through many massive changes in an effort to make it a world power.

Mao modeled his methods on Stalin's plans for the Soviet Union. The government took over industrial and agricultural production to stimulate rapid growth. To speed up modernization, Mao established the Great Leap Forward in 1958. He believed he could force the modernization of China's industry and economy quickly, despite a lack of money and technology.

During the Great Leap Forward, Mao combined farms into vast **collectives**, or huge, factory-like farms. He also ordered peasants to neglect their own crops in order to produce steel in backyard furnaces. A devastating famine resulted, in which 20 to 30 million people died. The government killed another 20 million people who opposed Mao's policies. By 1962, Mao admitted failure, and he abandoned the Great Leap Forward.

CULTURAL REVOLUTION

By the late 1950s, Mao believed the Soviet Union lacked commitment to a worldwide communist revolution. Mao wanted China to lead the way. So in 1966, he launched the **Cultural Revolution**.

Armed groups of militant, radical students called the Red Guard carried out Mao's plan. The Red Guard arrested, tortured, and killed millions of people. It targeted government officials, factory managers, teachers, scientists, artists, and especially intellectuals. Anyone suspected of doubting communism or Mao or even accused of "bourgeois values" could be sent to rural areas to be "re-educated."

During the Cultural Revolution, education and industry collapsed as people stopped working. Fighting among Red Guard factions edged China toward civil war. In 1968, Mao sent in the army to stop the bloodshed and disband the Red Guard.

In the early 1970s, China began opening up relations with the outside world. After Mao's death in 1976, more moderate leaders took power in China. They improved relations with countries such as the United States and Japan. The resulting economic growth transformed China into one of the world's largest economies.

Critical Viewing Children read the "Little Red Book," a collection of Mao's teachings, in front of a portrait of Mao in 1968. What do you notice about how they are dressed?

REVIEW & ASSESS

1. **READING CHECK** How did Mao Zedong attempt to transform China into a modernized world power?

2. **ANALYZE CAUSE AND EFFECT** Why did the Great Leap Forward fail?

3. **DRAW CONCLUSIONS** After Mao's death, why might some communist leaders in China have been willing to improve relations with Western countries?

2.4 Cold War Hot Spots

During the Cold War, the United States and the Soviet Union never fired directly on each other—and that's what kept the Cold War "cold." However, many terrifying moments made a "hot" war seem likely. At times, even the horrors of nuclear war seemed possible.

MAIN IDEA

The United States and the Soviet Union avoided direct warfare by supporting opposing sides in other countries' conflicts.

STANDOFFS IN KOREA AND CUBA

During the Cold War, the United States and the Soviet Union formed alliances and used their allies to fight wars on their behalf. The Soviets actively supported the spread of communism around the world. U.S. policymakers wanted to contain the spread of communism—especially in Latin America and Southeast Asia—and to protect U.S. economic interests there. They argued that when one country fell to communism, its neighbors would fall, too. This **domino theory** convinced decision makers in the United States to get involved in Cold War hot spots around the world.

After World War II, the Allies split Korea, which the Japanese had occupied, into two parts. This division was meant to be temporary, but Korean leaders formally established a communist North Korea and a democratic South Korea.

In 1950, North Korea invaded South Korea. The United Nations and the United States supported South Korea and communist China supported North Korea. The war reached a stalemate after three years and 2.5 million deaths. North Korea and South Korea remain divided today, and the two nations are still technically at war.

The Cold War nearly turned nuclear in another hot spot during the Cuban Missile Crisis. Cuba had become a communist state after a revolution in 1959. In October 1962, Cuba's new leader, Fidel Castro, allowed the Soviets to place nuclear missiles in Cuba. U.S. president John F. Kennedy demanded the missiles be removed, but the Soviet leader, Nikita Khrushchev, refused.

Kennedy ordered a U.S. naval blockade to prevent Soviet ships carrying the missiles from reaching Cuba. For six days, the world held its breath as the two countries moved closer to war. At the last minute, they reached an agreement. The Soviets turned their ships around and took apart their missile bases. In exchange, the United States promised not to invade Cuba.

WAR IN VIETNAM

As you have read, in 1954, Vietnam had been divided into two separate countries. Ho Chi Minh was determined to reunite Vietnam by force. In 1956, he sent North Vietnamese troops into South Vietnam. Communist forces in the South, the Viet Cong, fought with North Vietnamese troops.

By 1964, the United States began sending troops to stop the Viet Cong and North Vietnamese troops. After almost 10 years, U.S. forces withdrew, and in 1975, Vietnam united under communist rule. Laos and Cambodia also became communist.

The Vietnam War caused immense suffering and death for millions of ordinary Vietnamese, Laotians, and Cambodians. Nearly 60,000 American soldiers died.

U.S. soldiers eat a quick meal in front of their Huey helicopter, six miles inside the Cambodian border with Vietnam in 1970. During the Vietnam War, Americans saw the reality of war on television for the first time, which made it extremely unpopular. As a result, returning veterans were often ignored and treated unfairly.

REVIEW & ASSESS

1. **READING CHECK** Why did hot spots between the United States and the Soviet Union flare up in different locations during the Cold War?

2. **DRAW CONCLUSIONS** Why was the Cuban Missile Crisis such a dangerous event?

3. **ANALYZE CAUSE AND EFFECT** How did the domino theory shape U.S. involvement in Cold War conflicts?

2.5 The Fall of Communism

The Cold War seemed like the new normal for the people who lived through it. The period brought constant tension and competition between the governments of the United States and the Soviet Union. But nearly 50 years after the Cold War started, communism began to crumble.

MAIN IDEA

Economic pressures and a popular desire for political reform ended the Cold War.

REFORM AND COLLAPSE

Since the 1950s, both the United States and the Soviet Union had spent massive amounts of money on arms. The United States, because of its robust economy, could afford the spending. By the 1980s, though, the Soviet Union could not, and it was near economic collapse.

In 1985, a new Soviet leader, Mikhail Gorbachev, wanted to modernize the Soviet Union and open it up to the West. In order to do so, he proposed drastic reforms called **glasnost**, which means "openness," and **perestroika**, or "restructuring."

These reforms included freedom of the press and political expression, multiparty elections, and some level of free enterprise.

As part of his new strategy, Gorbachev also began to pull Soviet troops from communist countries in Eastern Europe. In June 1989, he declared Eastern Bloc countries free to choose their own political paths. The most symbolic fall of Soviet power came with the destruction of the Berlin Wall in November 1989. East and West Germany were formally reunited in 1990.

Gorbachev was very popular with Western leaders. However, at home his popularity faded as the economy failed to improve and living standards declined. Some criticized his reforms for betraying communism. Others attacked him for not reforming enough.

Protestors in several Soviet republics, such as Georgia, demanded independence from the Soviet government. The Soviet Union was falling apart. In 1991, Communist Party hard-liners attempted a military coup in Moscow. Ordinary people took to the streets and stopped the coup, but Gorbachev was finished. The former superpower split into 15 different countries with many challenges ahead.

ETHNIC CONFLICTS

In many former Soviet republics and communist countries, the collapse of communism resulted in a lack of clarity about who was in charge. A scramble for power followed as countries struggled to establish new governments and improve their economies. In some cases, ethnic tensions that had been suppressed for decades under communist rule erupted into violent conflicts.

One such conflict developed in Yugoslavia. From 1945 until his death in 1980, Josip Tito was the communist ruler of Yugoslavia. After his death, several different groups in Yugoslavia struggled for power. In 1991, a number of ethnic and religious groups sought independence. Ethnic conflicts and long-held tensions came to the surface. These conflicts are called the Balkan Wars.

Critical Viewing West German citizens destroy a section of the Berlin Wall in November 1989. Why was the fall of the Berlin Wall an important event?

Slovenia was able to break away fairly easily, but long-held resentments brewing in other parts of Yugoslavia exploded into vicious fighting. All sides of the conflict committed horrific atrocities, including **ethnic cleansing**, or mass murder of an ethnic or religious group. Serbs massacred thousands of Muslims in Bosnia. Croatians killed Serbs in large numbers in Croatia.

In 1994, NATO intervened in the conflict, providing combat and peacekeeping forces for the first time in its history. The United States helped negotiate a peace agreement among the various groups involved in 1995. Yugoslavia then split into the independent countries of Slovenia, Croatia, Bosnia and Herzegovina, Serbia, Montenegro, and Macedonia.

REVIEW & ASSESS

1. **READING CHECK** What major factors contributed to the collapse of the Soviet Union?
2. **DRAW CONCLUSIONS** What was new about Gorbachev's policies of glasnost and perestroika?
3. **MAKE GENERALIZATIONS** What can happen in countries when ethnic tensions are suppressed?

3.1 Transitions to Democracy

When the Berlin Wall fell, anything seemed possible. The 1990s were years of swift change in many countries. The decade brought a transition from Cold War alliances to a new world order. These changes reached from Eastern Europe all the way to South Africa.

MAIN IDEA

In the 1990s, new, more democratic governments replaced repressive ones.

EASTERN EUROPE

With the break up of the Soviet Union, democratic movements emerged across Eastern Europe. Most communist governments were in financial ruin and could no longer resist the will of their citizens.

In 1989, Czechs wanted a new Czechoslovakia. In the capital city of Prague, thousands of people marched in favor of democracy. When the Czech police attacked the marchers, Czech citizens united in a nationwide general strike. They also called for free multiparty elections.

Facing widespread unrest, and without Soviet support, the Czech government agreed to free elections. Fewer than six weeks after the first protests, Czechs demanding democracy and freedom elected Václav Havel president. It was such a rapid and mostly peaceful transition that it was called the Velvet Revolution.

In Poland, widespread strikes in 1980 led the government to legalize the Eastern Bloc's first independent labor union, called Solidarity. Led by **Lech Walesa**, Solidarity soon had nearly 10 million members.

Solidarity began organizing labor strikes to force the government to change its policies. Under Soviet pressure, the Polish government banned Solidarity. However, the union continued as an underground movement with widespread secret support.

In 1989, striking workers and protestors brought Poland's economy to a standstill. Solidarity came out of hiding. Without Soviet support and under pressure from the West, Poland's government gave in and allowed free elections. In a stunning result, Polish citizens elected Solidarity candidates for every single political seat except one. Lech Walesa became Poland's president in 1990.

SOUTH AFRICA

For several decades during the 20th century, black South Africans suffered under a different kind of tyranny—apartheid, which you learned about earlier in the chapter. Whites and nonwhites were separated in every area of society: housing, work, education, religion, and even sports. Nonwhites were denied basic rights, including voting. Police attacked anti-apartheid protestors, violating human rights in the process.

In the 1960s, the system of apartheid came under fire, both from within and outside of South Africa. In South Africa, anti-apartheid movements such as the African National Congress (ANC) fought the government, sometimes turning to violence.

A young lawyer, **Nelson Mandela**, had worked in the ANC since he joined in 1944. He led the ANC's campaigns against discriminatory laws. His activism was nonviolent, and it focused on changing laws. However, after the 1960 Sharpeville massacre in South Africa, during which 69 unarmed protestors were killed, Mandela turned away from nonviolent activism. He became the leader of the ANC's military wing. Mandela was eventually tried and convicted of sabotage and then sentenced to life in prison in 1964. His case drew world attention and criticism, much to the displeasure of the South African government.

Starting in the 1960s, countries around the world condemned apartheid and placed an economic and cultural boycott on South Africa. In 1962, the country was barred from the Olympic Games. By 1989, many whites in South Africa wanted change and elected a moderate president, F.W. de Klerk. De Klerk took steps to end apartheid. He also prepared the way for multiracial elections. De Klerk freed a number of political prisoners, including Nelson Mandela, in 1990.

As leaders, both elected and symbolic, de Klerk and Mandela formed a unique partnership, and they worked together closely as South Africa faced a new future. Their goal was to end apartheid and to build a foundation for a peaceful transition to a democratic South Africa.

In 1993, Mandela and de Klerk were both awarded the Nobel Peace Prize for their exceptional efforts to promote equality. One year later, white and black South Africans lined up together to vote in the country's first multiracial elections. Nelson Mandela became the first black president of South Africa.

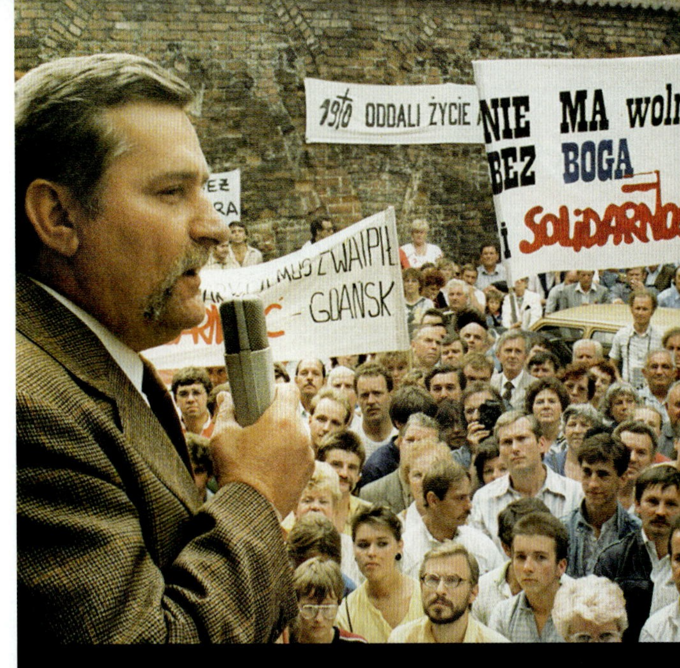
1970 ODDALI ŻYCIE
NIE MA
BEZ BOGA
GDANSK
Solidarity leader Lech Walesa addresses 10,000 striking shipyard workers in Gdansk, Poland, in 1988.

IEC
Nelson Mandela celebrates as he casts his historic vote on April 27, 1994, near Durshan, South Africa.

REVIEW & ASSESS

1. **READING CHECK** What factors contributed to the rise of democratic movements in countries across Eastern Europe?
2. **DRAW CONCLUSIONS** Why was Poland's Solidarity movement successful?
3. **ANALYZE CAUSE AND EFFECT** What prompted the international community to impose an economic and cultural boycott of South Africa in the 1960s?

3.2 Oil and Conflict in Southwest Asia

The modern world depends on oil for everything from fuel to plastic to medicine. Whoever controls the oil is not only rich, but also powerful. It is not surprising, then, that conflicts over oil have become more and more common.

MAIN IDEA

Many countries compete to control the world's oil supply.

GULF STATES AND OIL

Petroleum, or oil in its unrefined form, was discovered in Southwest Asia in the early 1900s. Since the 1930s, oil has become increasingly important in the global economy. Oil fuels the world's cars, planes, and ships, and keeps the wheels of industry turning.

Guaranteeing a steady supply of oil is a priority in industrialized countries such as the United States. However, the world's largest and most accessible petroleum deposits lie in the politically unstable region of Southwest Asia.

In the years following World War II, competition for oil resources has created tension and conflict. Arab countries in the region felt that Western countries had too much influence. To protect their interests and to coordinate oil policies and prices, most Arab states agreed to work together. They formed organizations such as OAPEC—the Organization of Arab Petroleum Exporting Countries.

Oil-producing countries such as Saudi Arabia, Kuwait, Qatar, and the United Arab Emirates (UAE) became some of the wealthiest nations in the world. Yet that wealth remains unevenly distributed across the region as a whole. As a result, several countries in the region experienced widening income gaps, mass migration to cities, and growing resentment, especially among the young. Today, some oil-producing nations are investing more money in industry and infrastructure.

CONFLICTS IN THE REGION

Competition for oil intensified existing rivalries. For example, during the Cold War, both the Soviet Union and the United States took advantage of the region's conflicts. Iraq and Syria established Soviet-backed socialist regimes. These governments clashed with the authoritarian monarchies of Saudi Arabia, Iran, and Jordan—three governments the United States supported. In addition, because of concerns over oil security, the United States established a military presence in the region.

The region also experienced tensions between Sunni and Shi'ite Muslims. These two religious identities emerged centuries ago. Most Muslims are Sunnis. They believe a qualified member of the community can be a leader. Shi'ite Muslims believe that only a direct descendant of Muhammad should be the head of the community.

In 1980, war broke out between two major oil producers—Iraq and Iran. The Iranian Revolution the previous year had brought the country under Shi'ite religious rule. Iraq's dictator, Saddam Hussein, fearing Iraqi Shi'ites would be inspired by Iran, suppressed them. He also invaded oil fields along the border with Iran. Both sides were well funded and heavily armed.

OIL AND GAS, GULF STATES, 2015

Oil field
Gas field
Oil pipeline
Gas pipeline
Refinery

0 250 500 Miles
0 250 500 Kilometers

They fought to a stalemate, despite Iraq's use of horrific chemical weapons. The Iran-Iraq War ended in 1988 with no clear victory on either side. It lasted eight years and cost more than one million lives.

The Iran-Iraq War also left Iraq bankrupt and desperate for power. Hussein's response was to invade oil-rich Kuwait in 1990, which started the first Gulf War. A U.S.-led coalition, or alliance, of armies drove Iraqi forces out of Kuwait. Though defeated, Hussein remained Iraq's dictator.

OIL ALTERNATIVES

Global dependence on oil and conflicts in Southwest Asia have spurred the development of alternative forms of energy, such as solar, hydroelectric, and wind.

Wind turbines like these convert wind into electricity. Unlike petroleum, wind is an energy source that will never run out.

REVIEW & ASSESS

1. **READING CHECK** Why are countries in Southwest Asia important to the global economy?
2. **ANALYZE CAUSE AND EFFECT** What factors led to armed conflicts in the Gulf States?
3. **INTERPRET MAPS** Which body of water is critical to the production of oil exports in Southwest Asia?

3.3 MOMENTS IN HISTORY

The Attacks on September 11

Smoke rises from the wreckage of the World Trade Center two days after its two main towers were destroyed.

SEPTEMBER 11, 2001

On September 11, 2001, at 8:46 a.m., American Airlines Flight 11 crashed into the North Tower of the World Trade Center in New York City. Horrified onlookers watched as smoke billowed from the building. Just 17 minutes later, United Airlines Flight 175 crashed into the South Tower. Emergency responders rushed into the buildings to help. At 9:37 a.m., American Airlines Flight 77 crashed into the Pentagon in Washington, D.C. At 10:03 a.m., United Airlines Flight 93, likely headed for the White House, crashed in a field in Pennsylvania.

That morning, the 19 men who had hijacked the four planes killed nearly 3,000 people. The events of September 11 were a defining moment in modern history. They changed the way people and their governments thought and acted, from increased security on public transportation to the invasion of countries that supported those who would harm others.

3.4 Confronting Terrorism

September 11 had far-reaching consequences. The response of the United States and the international community reached new levels of outrage and action. An effort to confront terrorism had begun.

MAIN IDEA

The events of September 11 initiated a military and political response to terrorism.

RESPONDING TO SEPTEMBER 11

In the days following September 11, an Islamic extremist group called **al Qaeda** (ahl KAI-dah) claimed responsibility for the attacks. Al Qaeda relies on **terrorism**, or the use of violence against civilians to achieve political goals. Terrorism has been used by groups around the world who oppose the political situation in their countries or more globally. The United States became a target of al Qaeda in the late 20th century.

Such political violence stems from extreme expressions of ethnic or religious identity. Islamic fundamentalism increased in the late 20th century. It emphasized a return to a more literal interpretation of scripture and a rejection of Western influence. In 1996, an Islamic fundamentalist group called the Taliban seized control of Afghanistan. It imposed shari'a, a strict interpretation of Islamic law. Shari'a law restricted women from education, work, and free movement and destroyed non-Islamic art, including priceless historical pieces. The Taliban allowed other terrorist groups to use Afghanistan as a base from which to launch terror attacks. One of those groups was al Qaeda. After September 11, the Taliban refused U.S. requests to hand over al Qaeda's leader, **Osama bin Laden**.

In October 2001, the United States and its allies launched airstrikes against al Qaeda camps in the mountains of Afghanistan. They also provided military support to Afghan rebels fighting the Taliban. The Taliban weakened, and U.S. and allied forces captured their final stronghold in December 2001. However, bin Laden and the Taliban leadership escaped. The Taliban continue to fight a guerrilla war against Afghanistan's democratically elected government. The international community supports Afghanistan, but the country's future remains uncertain.

WAR AGAINST IRAQ

The United States was concerned about Iraq's ability to attack neighboring countries. Some U.S. intelligence officials believed that Saddam Hussein's government was hiding weapons of mass destruction, or WMDs, which could be sold to terror groups. In 2003, the threat of chemical, biological, or even nuclear attacks on major cities led the United States and some allies to invade Iraq. They defeated Hussein's government, located Hussein, and handed him over to the Iraqi government, which executed him in 2006.

The war became controversial in the United States when the United Nations could not find the suspected WMDs. In addition, U.S. and allied troops faced continued attacks by forces that wanted to take over the Iraqi government. Despite democratic elections and international support, Iraq continues to face conflict, especially from extremist groups.

After September 11, al Qaeda launched other attacks against Western targets in Bali, Madrid, London, Jordan, and Algeria.

Critical Viewing Iraqis celebrate as a statue of Saddam Hussein topples in the capital city of Baghdad in April 2003. Why might citizens want to take down statues of former leaders?

Other terrorist groups are also highly active, including more extreme groups known as the Islamic State of Iraq and Syria, or ISIS.

Faced with constant threats, many countries have increased domestic security at government buildings, large public gatherings, airports, and train stations. Governments also gather intelligence on terror groups to prevent possible attacks. This intelligence involves surveillance of civilian populations. **Surveillance** means keeping watch over a person or a group. Critics argue, though, that surveillance threatens the right to privacy that people in democracies expect.

OSAMA BIN LADEN

Osama bin Laden was born in Saudi Arabia to a wealthy family. In 1984, while fighting the Soviets in Afghanistan, he gained a reputation for bravery and devotion to Islam, and he attracted a number of like-minded followers. He accused the United States of interfering in the Muslim world and adopted an extremist attitude.

In 1990, Saudi Arabia turned to the United States, not bin Laden, for protection against Iraq. Outraged, bin Laden plotted attacks against U.S. interests through his network of followers. Bin Laden masterminded many terrorist attacks, including September 11. After nearly 10 years of searching for him, U.S. special forces killed him at his hideout in Pakistan in May 2011.

REVIEW & ASSESS

1. **READING CHECK** What event caused the international community to launch a worldwide effort to fight terrorist groups?
2. **ANALYZE CAUSE AND EFFECT** Why did Afghanistan become a key target for the United States and its allies in October 2001?
3. **DRAW CONCLUSIONS** Why has it been difficult to establish a stable, democratic government in Iraq?

3.5 The Arab Spring

Sometimes, historic change comes swiftly. In the spring of 2011, long-brewing tensions in several Arab countries led to a series of revolutions. In some countries, the success of the revolutions remains uncertain.

MAIN IDEA

Uprisings in Arab countries led to revolutions and new governments, but also civil war.

REVOLUTION

Late 20th-century democratic movements transformed South Africa and Eastern Europe. However, in some Arab countries, authoritarian governments kept an iron grip on their populations for another 25 years. In 2011, pro-democracy movements emerged in North Africa and Southwest Asia. Anti-government demonstrations evolved into revolutions called the **Arab Spring**. In some countries, oppressive regimes were replaced with ineffective new governments. In others, revolution led to civil war.

In Tunisia in December 2010, a street vendor's protest against mistreatment by local officials sparked protests against poverty and repression. The authoritarian government responded with a few political and economic reforms but collapsed within a month. By December 2011, Tunisia had a new democratic constitution and a democratically elected government.

One of the most dramatic revolutions of the Arab Spring began in January 2011. Demonstrators were demanding the resignation of Egypt's president, Hosni Mubarak, who had ruled for nearly 30 years. After much violence, the army announced it would no longer fight the protestors, and Egypt's government collapsed. A democratically elected government took power in January 2012. However, this government was too divisive for many and was overthrown by the army. The country remains divided today.

CIVIL WAR

Protests against the 40-year rule of Libyan dictator Muammar Qaddafi in February 2011 rapidly grew into a civil war. Qaddafi used tanks, artillery, and warplanes against his own citizens. A NATO-led coalition stepped in to help the rebels, who seized Tripoli, the Libyan capital, and killed Qaddafi. Democratic elections took place in 2012, but the new government has been unable to rebuild the economy or control infighting among militia groups. Libya remains highly unstable.

Mass protests erupted in Syria in early 2011. Protestors demanded the resignation of Bashar al-Assad, Syria's dictator since 2000. The demonstrators armed themselves, and the uprising became a long and bloody civil war. Assad's brutal response to the protestors included the use of chemical weapons, mass murder, and torture. World leaders and the United Nations pressed Assad to show restraint against his own citizens. However, he has refused to resign.

The civil war in Syria caused tremendous suffering, including more than 200,000 deaths. More than 6 million people have been forced from their homes. Four million more Syrians have fled to neighboring countries as **refugees**, or people forced to leave their country because of wars, persecution, or natural disasters. The war in Syria continues with no sure end in sight.

CONFLICT PHOTOGRAPHY
National Geographic photographer Lynsey Addario uses her skillful lens to raise awareness about people living in war zones and refugees struggling to survive.

Addario photographed this Syrian mother tending to her family in their tent at the Killis refugee camp in Turkey. Syrian refugees face many challenges, including lack of food, water, and shelter, unemployment, and no schools for children.

REVIEW & ASSESS

1. **READING CHECK** What was the Arab Spring?
2. **SUMMARIZE** What fueled large-scale anti-government protests in Tunisia, Egypt, Libya, and Syria?
3. **MAKE INFERENCES** What kinds of challenges do refugees from civil war face?

3.6 Global Citizens in a Global Economy

The transformative power of technology is undeniable. The invention of the wheel, the printing press, the automobile, and the computer changed lives of ordinary people and the course of world history. Thanks to technology, people in today's world are more connected than ever before.

MAIN IDEA

Advances in technology make a global economy possible and shape global citizenship.

TECHNOLOGY AND TRADE

Today's technological advancements are built on the foundation of centuries of innovation. New technologies and communications networks from the Internet to smart phones allow immediate communication and access to information. New medicines and disease detection technologies save and improve lives every day. Faster planes and high-speed trains mean people are never more than 24 hours from a major city.

These technological advances, combined with the spread of democracy and growth of global markets, have increased international commerce and interaction. The nations of the world have become increasingly interconnected through a process called **globalization**. Some countries have become new economic powers.

One important aspect of globalization is **free trade**. Free trade is a form of commerce in which groups of nations agree to trade with one another on equal terms, with fewer taxes and tariffs. Free trade boosts commerce among member countries. Recent free trade agreements include the North American Free Trade Agreement (NAFTA), the Asia-Pacific Economic Cooperation (APEC), and the Trans-Pacific Partnership (TPP).

Globalization has its critics, however. Some say it destroys national identities by weakening unique cultures. Critics also claim that globalization widens the gap between wealthy and poor countries. Today, the six richest countries hold more than half of the world's wealth. At the same time, half the world's population lives on less than $2.50 a day.

GLOBAL CITIZENSHIP

When countries become involved with one another, they become interdependent, which means they depend more on each other. People are citizens of the countries they live in, but also of the world. We are all **global citizens**. Being a global citizen means learning about the world we live in, advocating for a healthy environment, and learning the technological skills necessary to succeed in our interdependent world.

Global citizenship also involves empathy for other cultures and working together to solve problems around the world. The United Nations promotes international cooperation on reducing poverty, curing diseases, and addressing climate change. Other issues facing the global community include ending wars, fighting terrorism, and limiting nuclear weapons.

As the world's population rises to more than seven billion people, enormous challenges and opportunities lie ahead. With continued cooperation among nations, who knows what people can achieve?

GLOBAL CONVERSATIONS

PREVENTING NUCLEAR WAR: IRAN

During a 15-minute conversation on September 27, 2013, President Barack Obama and Iranian president Hassan Rouhani agreed to work together to resolve issues regarding Iran's nuclear program. It was the first time leaders of Iran and the United States had spoken in more than 30 years. While supporting Iran's right to develop nuclear energy, the United States and other countries want to prevent Iran from building nuclear weapons. Critics warn that Iran is not interested in limiting nuclear weapon development. The issue remains far from resolved, but this conversation may be a first step in the right direction.

NORMALIZING RELATIONS: CUBA

In December 2013, U.S. president Barack Obama and Cuban president Raúl Castro surprised the world by shaking hands at Nelson Mandela's funeral in South Africa. For more than 50 years, the leaders of these two countries had not acknowledged each other. Because of Cuba's ties with the Soviet Union, the United States instituted a trade embargo, or ban, in 1960 and cut off diplomatic ties in 1961. A year after the handshake that made headlines, Obama and Castro announced that the United States and Cuba were reestablishing full diplomatic relations. This dramatic development came after months of high-level talks between U.S. and Cuban representatives.

PROTECTING THE ENVIRONMENT: CHINA

In November 2014, President Xi Jingping of China and President Barack Obama announced that China and the United States had agreed to reduce carbon dioxide emissions and coal consumption. The leaders' commitment to concrete goals stood in dramatic contrast to the position both countries took in 1997 with the world's first climate change treaty, the Kyoto Protocol. At that time they refused to sign the deal, which encouraged other governments to avoid action, too. Because the United States and China are the two top carbon polluters, environmental advocates cheered the 2014 agreement as a significant move forward for international cooperation on climate change.

REVIEW & ASSESS

1. **READING CHECK** How does globalization affect people's lives?
2. **DRAW CONCLUSIONS** Why is free trade important to the global economy?
3. **ANALYZE CAUSE AND EFFECT** What has led to the world's nations becoming more interconnected?

3.7 NEW FACES

People who make history take risks, try out fresh ideas, and dare to imagine new solutions. An exciting new generation of empowered global citizens is full of promise. These 21st-century faces point to a bright future.

MAIN IDEA

Inventive and brave young people around the world are solving problems, helping others, and forging new paths.

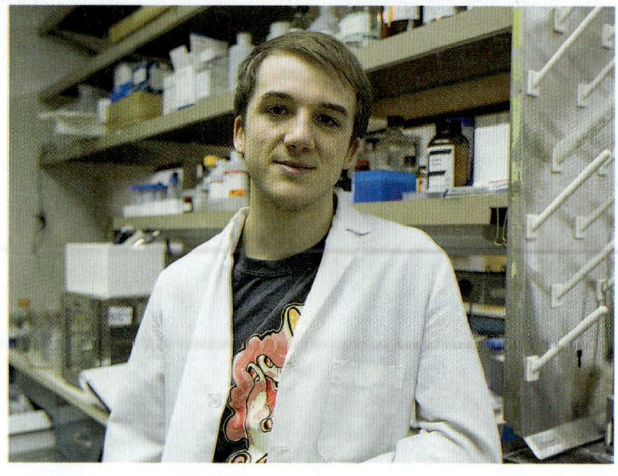

JACK ANDRAKA, INVENTOR

National Geographic Emerging Explorer Jack Andraka did more than win a high school science fair. He invented a prototype for a new diagnostic test for pancreatic cancer when he was just 15. Though it needs further study, his invention, a type of biosensor, has great potential as a fast, accurate, and inexpensive test for the disease.

KELVIN DOE, ENGINEER

Kelvin Doe of Freetown, Sierra Leone, sees solutions where other people see trash. He started by building batteries that would help provide nighttime light for homes in his neighborhood. By the time he was 16, he had built a radio station for his community out of recycled electronic parts. Today he broadcasts news and music at that station under the name "DJ Focus."

ERIKA BERGMAN, OCEANOGRAPHER

As a submarine pilot, National Geographic Young Explorer Erika Bergman studies ocean life 2,000 feet below the surface of the ocean. She shares her dives with classrooms around the world via internal and external cameras mounted to her sub. She has explored coral reefs in the warm waters of the Carribbean Sea as well as sea ice shrinkage in the Arctic Ocean.

MALALA YOUSAFZAI, ACTIVIST

As a 14-year-old living in the Swat Valley of Pakistan, Malala Yousafzai advocated for education for girls and women. In 2009, Taliban gunmen boarded a bus and shot her. She survived and, after a long recovery, she returned to her work with even more determination. In December 2014, Malala Yousafzai became the youngest person ever to win the Nobel Prize for Peace.

RICHARD TURERE, INNOVATOR

Richard Turere lives in Kitengela, Kenya. When he was just 11 years old, he invented "lion lights" to help save his cattle from lion attacks while making sure the lions themselves stayed safe. Everyone wins: people, cattle, and lions.

ALIZÉ CARRÈRE, ENVIRONMENTALIST

National Geographic Young Explorer Alizé Carrère studies how humans adapt to changing environments. Her research in Panama, Madagascar, Norway, and China reveals that people are turning hardships into opportunities.

REVIEW & ASSESS

1. **READING CHECK** What kinds of changes are young people making in the world today?
2. **DRAW CONCLUSIONS** In what ways did some of these young people's experiences shape their actions?
3. **MAKE INFERENCES** How might the actions of people like these make a difference for future generations?

CHAPTER

27 Review

VOCABULARY

Use each of the following vocabulary words in a sentence that shows an understanding of the term's meaning.

1. nonviolent
   In the 1930s and 1940s, Mohandas Gandhi organized nonviolent protests against British rule.
2. globalization
3. partition
4. apartheid
5. containment
6. ethnic cleansing
7. domino theory
8. glasnost
9. civil disobedience
10. terrorism

READING STRATEGY

11. **DRAW CONCLUSIONS** If you haven't done so already, complete your graphic organizer to identify pros and cons of globalization. Then answer the question to draw your conclusion.

GLOBALIZATION	
PROS: *Countries are more connected.*	CONS:
CONCLUSION:	

How has increased globalization impacted the modern world?

MAIN IDEAS

Answer the following questions. Support your answers with evidence from the chapter.

12. Why did Gandhi organize nonviolent protests in India? **LESSON 1.1**
13. How did World War II help bring independence to Southeast Asian colonies? **LESSON 1.2**
14. What was the Cold War? **LESSON 2.1**
15. How was Germany divided after World War II? **LESSON 2.2**
16. In what ways did Mao try to modernize China? **LESSON 2.3**
17. What were some of the factors that helped end the Cold War? **LESSON 2.5**
18. What was the Arab Spring? **LESSON 3.5**
19. How do technological advancements encourage globalization? **LESSON 3.6**

CRITICAL THINKING

Answer the following questions. Support your answers with evidence from the chapter.

20. **SUMMARIZE** What challenges did self-rule bring to newly independent countries in Africa between 1950 and 2011?
21. **ANALYZE CAUSE AND EFFECT** Why did Palestinians launch an intifada in 1987?
22. **DRAW CONCLUSIONS** Why was control of Berlin important to the Allies and to the Soviets?
23. **MAKE INFERENCES** How did Mao's Cultural Revolution affect Chinese society?
24. **YOU DECIDE** Does government surveillance of civilians protect national security or invade personal privacy? Support your opinion with evidence from the chapter.

INTERPRET MAPS

Look closely at the map of the breakup of the Soviet Union. Then answer the questions that follow.

BREAKUP OF THE SOVIET UNION, 1989
RUSSIA
LITHUANIA
Vilnius
Riga
Tallinn
ESTONIA
LATVIA
Minsk
BELARUS
MOLDOVA
Chişinău
Kiev
UKRAINE
Moskva
EUROPE
Black Sea
GEORGIA
T'Bilisi
ARMENIA
Yerevan
Baki
AZERBAIJAN
Caspian Sea
Aral Sea
Astana
KAZAKHSTAN
Lake Balkhash
TURKMENISTAN
UZBEKISTAN
Aşgabat
Toshkent
Bishkek
KYRGYZSTAN
TAJIKISTAN
Dushanbe
RUSSIA
ASIA
Lake Baikal
CHINA
Barents Sea
Kara Sea
ARCTIC OCEAN
Laptev Sea
East Siberian Sea
Bering Sea
Sea of Japan (East Sea)
Border of the former Soviet Union
0 500 1000 Miles
0 500 1000 Kilometers

25. Which newly independent nations were located in Asia, east of the Caspian Sea?

26. Which new nations might look to China as a potential trade partner, based on their locations?

ANALYZE SOURCES

Read the following excerpt from the 9/11 Commission Report, which contains the commission's findings and recommendations following the events of September 11.

> None of the measures adopted by the U.S. government from 1998 to 2001 disturbed or even delayed the progress of the al Qaeda plot. Across the government, there were failures of imagination, policy, capabilities, and management.

27. What do you think the commissioners meant by their use of the phrase "there were failures of imagination"?

WRITE ABOUT HISTORY

28. INFORMATIVE Write an essay to share with other students that explains democratic transitions as globalization increased.

TIPS

- Take notes from the lessons about the regions that experienced democratic changes.
- Begin the essay by describing nationalist and independence movements in the postwar years.
- Develop the essay by explaining how groups competed within several regions to create independent nations.
- Explain how the world governments are working together as the world becomes more interconnected.
- Conclude the essay by explaining both the positive and negative ways in which globalization is changing the world.

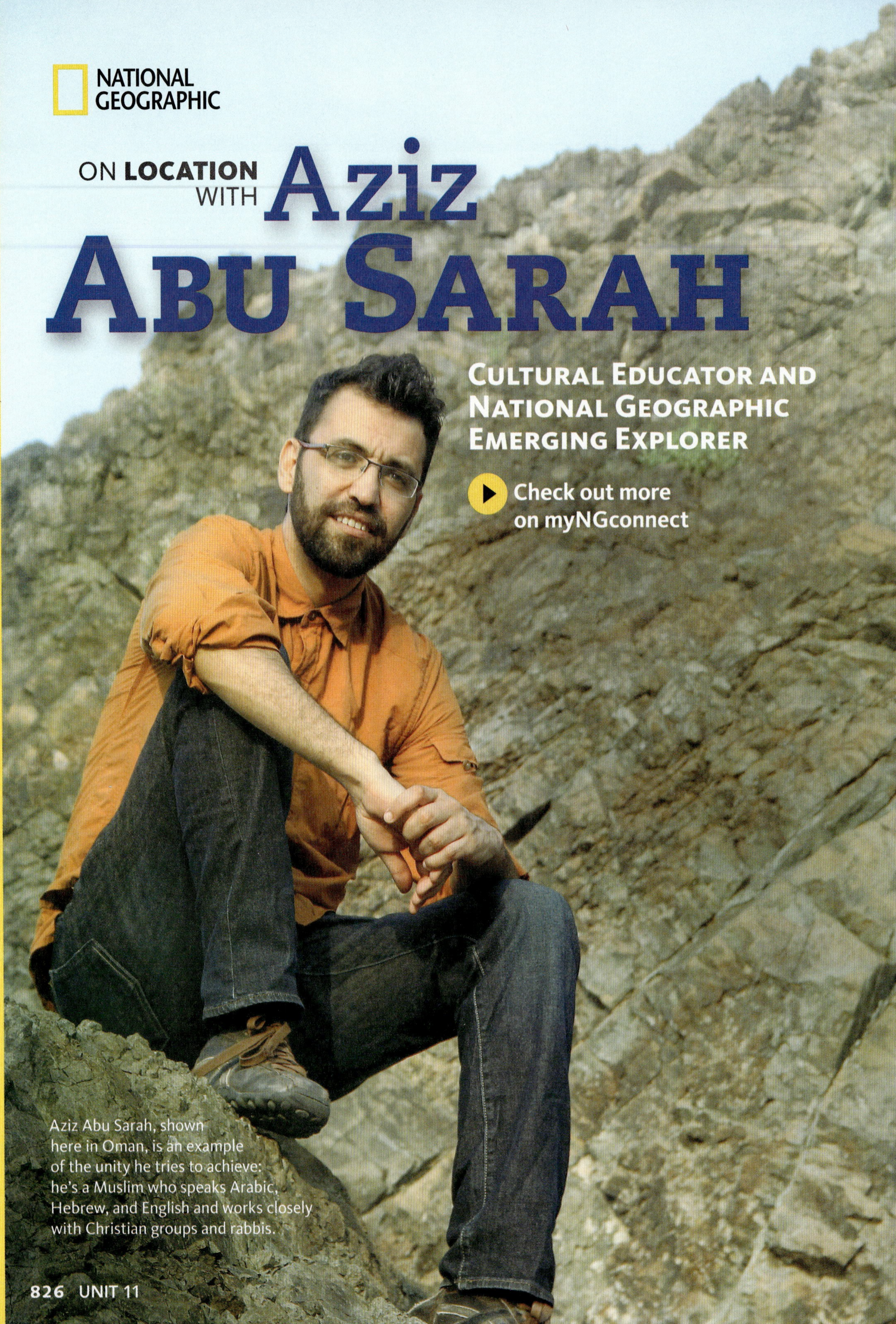

NATIONAL GEOGRAPHIC

ON LOCATION WITH Aziz ABU SARAH

CULTURAL EDUCATOR AND NATIONAL GEOGRAPHIC EMERGING EXPLORER

Check out more on myNGconnect

Aziz Abu Sarah, shown here in Oman, is an example of the unity he tries to achieve: he's a Muslim who speaks Arabic, Hebrew, and English and works closely with Christian groups and rabbis.

YEARS OF CONFLICT

The 20th century was filled with conflict. Along with two world wars and the Cold War, religious and ethnic troubles flared up all over the world, including in my homeland of Palestine. The conflict between Arabs and Israelis that still rages here has its roots buried deep in history. This small area of land, including the holy city of Jerusalem, is claimed by both Israelis and Palestinian Arabs, and both sides can point to strong historical justifications for their claim—and strong moral arguments too. The struggles over this land have fueled hatred and distrust for centuries.

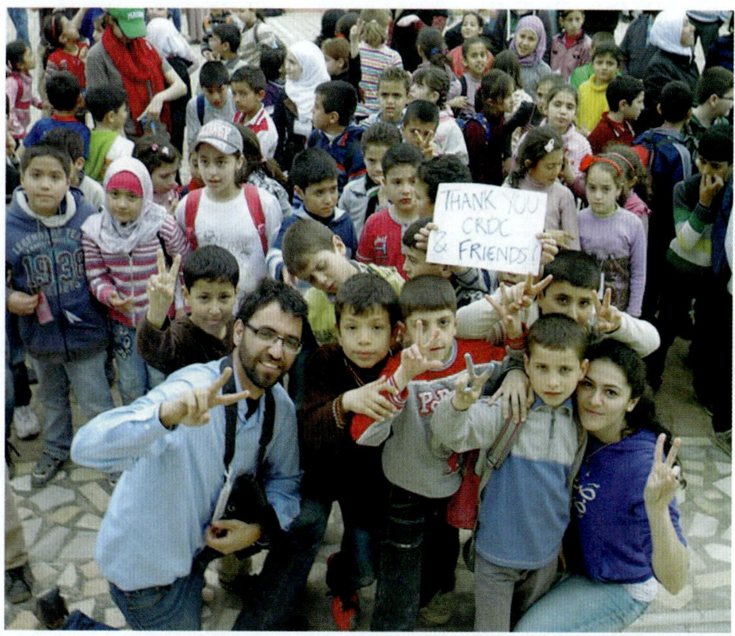
THANK YOU
CRDC
& FRIENDS!
One of Aziz Abu Sarah's missions is getting the children of Syrian refugee camps the education and support they deserve.

As a Palestinian boy in Jerusalem, my life was shattered when my brother was killed by the Israelis. I devoted myself to spreading hate, seeking revenge, and opposing the peace process. But in Jerusalem, if you want a good job, you have to learn Hebrew, so I found myself in a Hebrew class full of Jewish newcomers to Israel. These were the first Jewish people I had ever met besides soldiers with guns at checkpoints. Suddenly, I began developing friendships with people I had called enemies all my life. When I saw they were ordinary human beings just like me, I made a difficult decision: I decided not to remain a victim fueled by rage, but to take a harder path and work for peace. Meeting Jews for the first time challenged everything I believed; now I use that as a framework to help people question what they think.

MANY PERSPECTIVES

Jerusalem is a city divided by walls of fear and anger. I try to understand why. Walls that separate people are often built on ignorance, hatred, and fear. I try to put cracks in those walls by helping people towards understanding. I write and lecture to help people consider the complexity of the Arab-Israeli situation and appreciate both sides of the conflict. I expose people to ideas they've never considered. When people realize they feel the same pain, they see how much we all have in common. I even run tours of Jerusalem that explore the true complexity of the situation from every point of view—Israeli, Palestinian, Jewish, Muslim, and secular. I believe diversity fosters understanding, and when you explore a region's history, you need to know all points of view or you'll go home with a distorted picture.

WHY STUDY HISTORY ?

“The world we live in today, the good and the bad, is built on the events and actions of history. By studying the past we can understand the present, try to learn from the mistakes that were made, and *build a better future.*” —Aziz Abu Sarah

NATIONAL GEOGRAPHIC
EAT

A Five-Step Plan to Feed the World

BY JONATHAN FOLEY

Adapted from "A Five-Step Plan to Feed the World," by Jonathan Foley, in *National Geographic*, May 2014

In May 2014, National Geographic launched "The Future of Food: How to Feed Our Growing Planet." This initiative addresses population growth and sustainable agriculture. How can the world increase food production while reducing the environmental harm caused by agriculture? Here are five steps that could solve the world's food dilemma.

Step 1: Freeze Agriculture's Footprint In the past, whenever we've needed to produce more food, we've cut down forests or plowed grasslands to make farmland. But we can no longer afford this approach. Trading forests for farmland is destructive and it rarely benefits the 850 million people in the world who are still hungry.

Step 2: Grow More on Farms We've Got Starting in the 1960s, the green revolution increased yields in Asia and Latin America using better crop varieties and more fertilizer, irrigation, and machines. The world can now turn its attention to increasing yields on less productive farmlands.

Step 3: Use Resources More Effectively Some farmers are finding ways to apply fertilizers and pesticides. Others have replaced inefficient irrigation systems with more precise ones. These advances can give us more "crop per drop" from our water and nutrients.

Step 4: Shift Diets It would be easier to feed nine billion people by 2050 if more of the crops we grew ended up in human stomachs. Finding more efficient ways to grow meat and eating less meat could free up food for hungry people.

Step 5: Reduce Waste In rich countries, most food waste occurs in homes, restaurants, or supermarkets. In poor countries, food is often lost between farm and market, due to unreliable storage and transportation. Tackling waste is one of the best options for boosting food availability.

These five steps could more than double the world's food supplies, reduce the environmental impact of agriculture, and sustain the planet for future generations.

For more from National Geographic
Check out "The Visual Village" on myNGconnect

UNIT INQUIRY: PREPARE AN ARGUMENT

In this unit, you learned about the modern world and how its countries, cultures, and economies have become more and more connected. Based on your understanding of the text, what are some of the positive aspects of interdependency? What are some of the negative aspects?

ASSIGNMENT Prepare an argument for or against interdependency in the modern world. Your argument should support either the positive or negative impact of interdependency on the world's countries, cultures, and economies. Be prepared to present and defend your argument to the class.

Plan As you prepare your argument, think about both the positive and negative ways that interdependency has affected the modern world. Make a list of these positive and negative aspects and try to incorporate them into your argument. You might want to use a graphic organize to help organize your thoughts. ▶

Produce Use your notes to produce detailed descriptions of the positive and negative aspects of interdependency in the modern world. You might want to write the descriptions in paragraph form on individual index cards and label each as positive or negative.

Present Choose a creative way to present your argument to the class. Consider one of these options:

- Create a multimedia presentation using photos to support your argument for or against interdependency.
- Identify unique challenges that interdependency will present to future generations.
- Organize teams and hold a classroom debate on the topic of interdependency.

Interdependency

Positive Aspects	Negative Aspects

RAPID REVIEW UNIT 11

THE MODERN WORLD TOP TEN

1. World War I broke up old empires and established new nations.
2. The Russian Revolution overthrew the Russian tsar and established a communist government.
3. A global economic crisis called the Great Depression caused inflation and widespread unemployment in the 1930s.
4. World War II brought an end to colonial empires and independence to India and countries in Africa and Asia.
5. Revolutions during the Arab Spring overthrew some repressive regimes in Southwest Asia and North Africa.

6-10. **NOW IT'S YOUR TURN** Complete the list with five more things to remember about the modern world.

IT'S ABOUT BEING A GLOBAL CITIZEN.

You've read about many great civilizations, and you've seen what happens when people come into conflict. Despite those struggles, our shared human experience allows us to draw the best from all of humanity.

As a global citizen, you are empowered to act responsibly in the 21st century by showing empathy and respect for others; making informed decisions and finding your own voice; and actively participating in a rich and diverse environment. Go for it!

Fred Hiebert

Watch the Why Study History video

◄ WHITE ASPARAGUS, PERU

DRAGON FRUIT, VIETNAM ►

◄ CHESTNUTS, ITALY

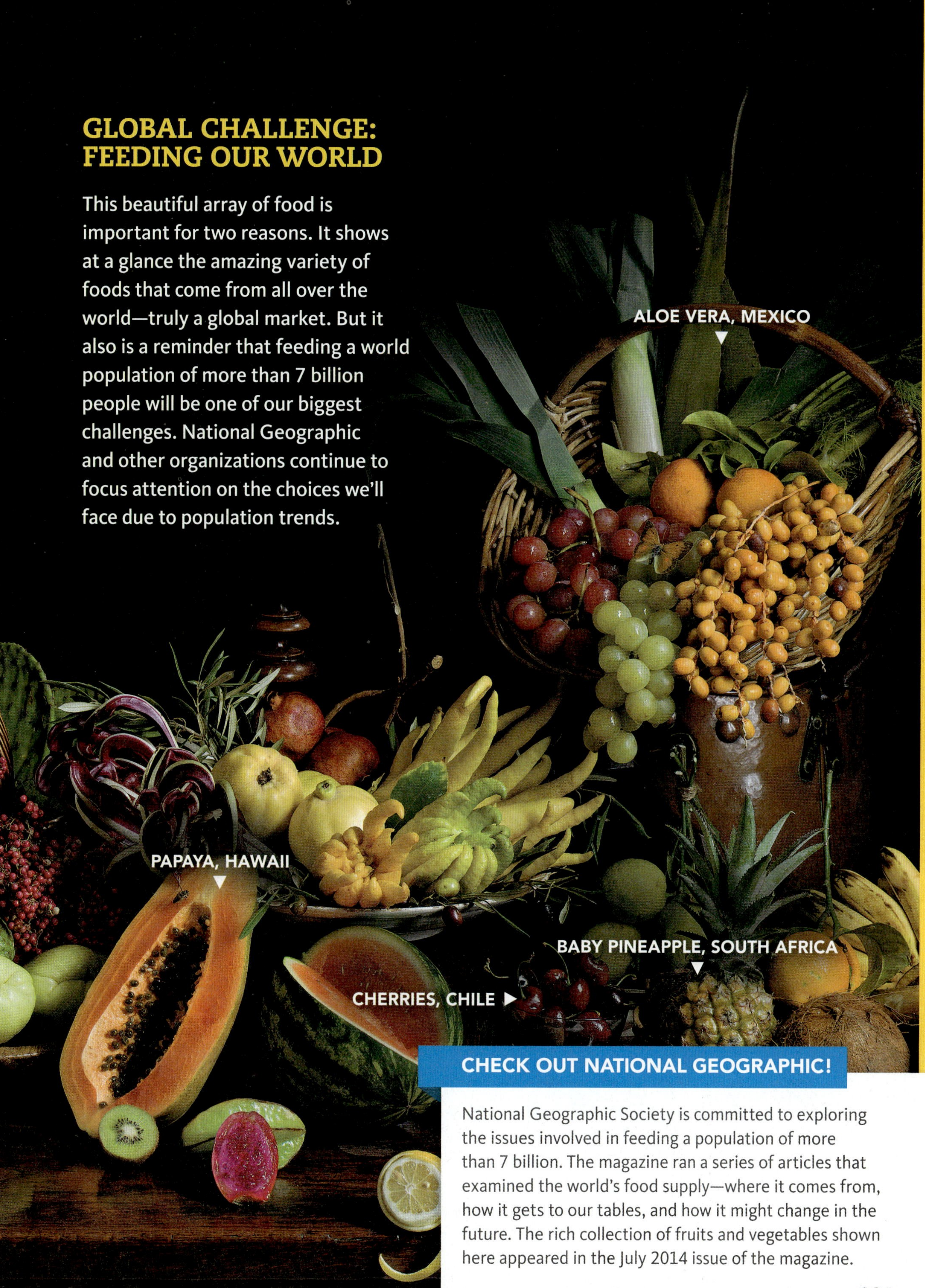
ALOE VERA, MEXICO
PAPAYA, HAWAII
BABY PINEAPPLE, SOUTH AFRICA
CHERRIES, CHILE

GLOBAL CHALLENGE: FEEDING OUR WORLD

This beautiful array of food is important for two reasons. It shows at a glance the amazing variety of foods that come from all over the world—truly a global market. But it also is a reminder that feeding a world population of more than 7 billion people will be one of our biggest challenges. National Geographic and other organizations continue to focus attention on the choices we'll face due to population trends.

CHECK OUT NATIONAL GEOGRAPHIC!

National Geographic Society is committed to exploring the issues involved in feeding a population of more than 7 billion. The magazine ran a series of articles that examined the world's food supply—where it comes from, how it gets to our tables, and how it might change in the future. The rich collection of fruits and vegetables shown here appeared in the July 2014 issue of the magazine.

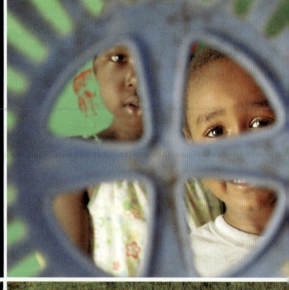

NATIONAL GEOGRAPHIC

STORIES MAKING HISTORY

History is a living thing, and you are part of it.

You've just read about centuries and centuries of events that may seem like they have little connection to your life—but you might be surprised. Those long-gone people and dramatic occurrences have brought us to where we are today, and the things happening all over the world while you sit in class each day will shape your life for years to come. If you don't keep an eye on the issues that will someday become the history of your generation, who will?

As this *World History* book went to the printer, important new National Geographic stories were just hitting the news. So we narrowed them down to the five stories that follow. Remember: These are just a few of the many intriguing stories surfacing around the world, and they're still developing. As a global citizen, it's up to you to ask yourself: What happened next? How did this turn out? **Go find out!**

Renewing Relationships: Cuba and the United States

Serving as The Geographer for National Geographic's Maps Division is an epic job. On any given day, Juan José Valdés and his team have the monumental task of creating and updating maps in a world where borders change frequently and sometimes without much notice. In 2011, Valdés stood expectantly outside a house in Havana, Cuba; but he wasn't in the country to make a map. He was visiting the place where he was born in 1953, and attempting to reconnect to a country he hadn't entered in 50 years.

^ The national flags of the United States and Cuba fly outside the Cuban hotel where the first U.S. congressional delegation to Cuba stayed in 2015.

Juan José Valdés

A year later, Juan visited Cuba again and reunited with his remaining family. A cousin approached him saying, "You are Cuban."

"Yes, I am Cuban," Juan answered, his voice trembling with emotion.

Like so many Cuban-Americans, Juan's life has been marked by enormous changes. When he was a child in Havana during the 1950s, a dictator named Fulgencio Batista ruled the country with an iron hand. A young law student and activist named Fidel Castro led rebels who waged a war to end Batista's rule. In 1959, Castro and his forces overthrew Batista.

Castro had promised free elections and other reforms. Yet once he took power, he quickly established a Communist government, in which the state owns or controls factories and other businesses. Castro refused to hold free elections, and he denied Cuban citizens freedom of speech and other rights most Americans take for granted. Castro also formed an alliance with the Soviet Union, in spite of the fact that the United States was in the middle of a Cold War with the Soviets. The U.S. response was swift and severe: diplomatic relations and trade with Cuba ended, and no one could travel between Cuba and the United States.

Hundreds of thousands of Cubans desperately wanted to leave Cuba for other countries like the United States. They didn't want to live in a Communist country. Juan's family could not leave right away, but they managed to get an airline ticket for Juan in 1961. At the age of seven, he traveled alone on an airplane to Miami, Florida. He lived with an elderly couple in Miami, until several months later, when his parents were able to leave Cuba and join him. Their family was reunited and built a life together in the United States.

Meanwhile, Cuba and the United States remained locked in tension. In April 1961, President John F. Kennedy authorized a group of American-trained Cuban exiles to attack Cuba at the Bay of Pigs and try to overthrow Castro. The invasion was a disaster for the United States. The Cuban exiles were outnumbered and many were captured. In October 1962, the Soviet Union tried to set up missiles with nuclear warheads in Cuba. This dangerous situation, known as the Cuban Missile Crisis, ended only when President Kennedy confronted the Soviets and forced them to remove the missiles.

But the world changes daily. On December 17, 2014, President Barack Obama announced that the United States would work to restore diplomatic and trade relations with Cuba and move to open an embassy in Havana, with Congressional approval. On April 11, 2015, President Obama met with Cuban President Raúl Castro in Panama in the first face-to-face discussion between the leaders of the two countries in more than 50 years. Both leaders expressed hope that the two countries will be able to interact without the tension and restrictions of the past.

This change is important for both nations, but it's also important for people like Juan Valdés who have roots in Cuba. As tensions between the countries continue to subside, Cuban-Americans will be able to travel more easily to Cuba and reconnect with relatives they left behind long ago. Yet change is never without complication. Cubans will have to adjust to the impact the lifted trade embargo has on the local economy they are used to. Others may find it unusual to welcome American tourists to their country after so many decades without them. It's likely that the Cuban people will find themselves and their country in a period of transition and adjustment for years to come.

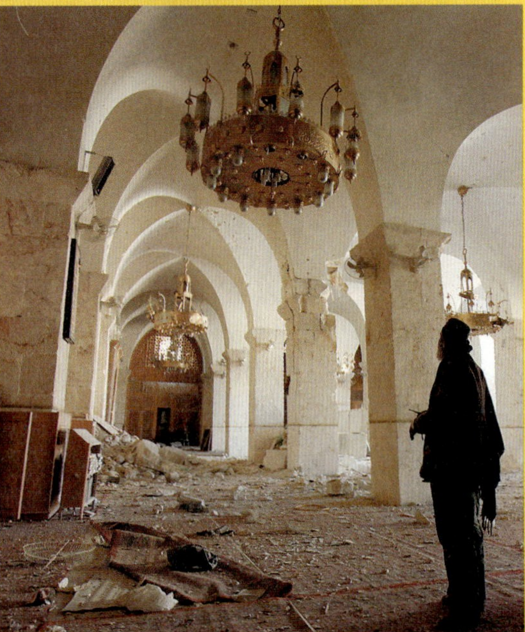

Saving Cultural Heritage

Home to some of the oldest cultures on earth and six UNESCO World Heritage sites, modern-day Syria lies along the eastern coast of the Mediterranean Sea with Iraq to the east, Turkey to the north, and Jordan to the south—at the heart of the region referred to as the Middle East. Syria's modern borders were drawn in the 20th century, and crossed diverse cultures. This diversity makes it a place where people from all faiths gather, where cultural heritage is a part of people's identity, and greatly influences their way of life.

^ Destruction and looting have drastically altered the Umayyad Mosque in Aleppo, Syria, as seen in these before and after shots of its exterior and interior.

Salam Al Kuntar
2015 Emerging Explorer

Dr. Salam Al Kuntar, an archaeologist who grew up in Syria, can tell you all about what it's like to live in a place so rich in cultural heritage.

As a young girl picking olives, pistachios, and almonds in her family's orchard in Syria, Al Kuntar also collected pottery shards left behind by ancient cultures. At the time, she dreamed of becoming an astronaut. Today, she laughs as she admits that instead of taking her up into the sky, her career sends her digging below the ground!

Named a National Geographic Emerging Explorer in 2015, Al Kuntar's work has taken on an unexpected urgency. She and a team of experts are working to save ancient evidence of Syria's diverse heritage from the ravages of war. Since civil war erupted in Syria in 2011, violence has sent millions of Syrians fleeing from their homes to live in refugee camps. Years into the conflict, millions of Syrian children are unable to go to school. Instead of focusing on homework assignments, they think about their family's safety and whether or not they'll have enough to eat.

Syria's ancient monuments and museums, too, have been the victims of careless government airstrikes as well as bombing and shelling by various opposition groups.

In the city of Aleppo in April 2013, for example, the minaret, or tower, on the Umayyad Mosque dating from 1090 A.D. was completely destroyed. Other fragile archaeological sites have been damaged, and thieves have been looting antiquities—objects or works of art from the ancient past—and selling them illegally outside of Syria.

Syria's Ma'arra Mosaic Museum, southwest of Aleppo, was once a *caravanserai*, or inn. It holds a collection of Roman and Byzantine mosaics more impressive than any other in the Middle East. The museum was near collapse from damages sustained because of the war until preservationists and volunteers stepped in. Their efforts saved the collection.

The physical destruction of something tangible like Syria's historical monuments actually is intended to rob people of something intangible—their cultural heritage and identity. The impact is deeply felt when people can no longer visit a place or a monument that they have memories of visiting with their grandparents. The stories they've carried with them since childhood become harder to remember and share. Al Kuntar warns that the war "is killing the hope for the future."

But there is still hope even under these difficult circumstances. Salam Al Kuntar's team works closely with local activists to document the destruction of monuments. They map and identify damage, apply a harmless glue to keep the tesserae, or small cubes that make up the mosaics, intact, and use sandbags and wrapping materials to protect them. People sometimes try to escape from the war and seek refuge inside some of the remote ruins. Al Kuntar's team does emergency repairs to shore up crumbling stone so it doesn't crush these frightened and exhausted guests.

As an archaeologist, Al Kuntar knows something very important that keeps her going under dangerous and discouraging conditions: this effort to destroy Syria's cultural heritage ultimately is not going to work. The fact is that their cultural heritage is embedded in the hearts and minds of the Syrian people—in their memories of family and country—and it cannot be destroyed. Salam Al Kuntar describes Syria's diversity as "precious," and is determined to protect it for future generations.

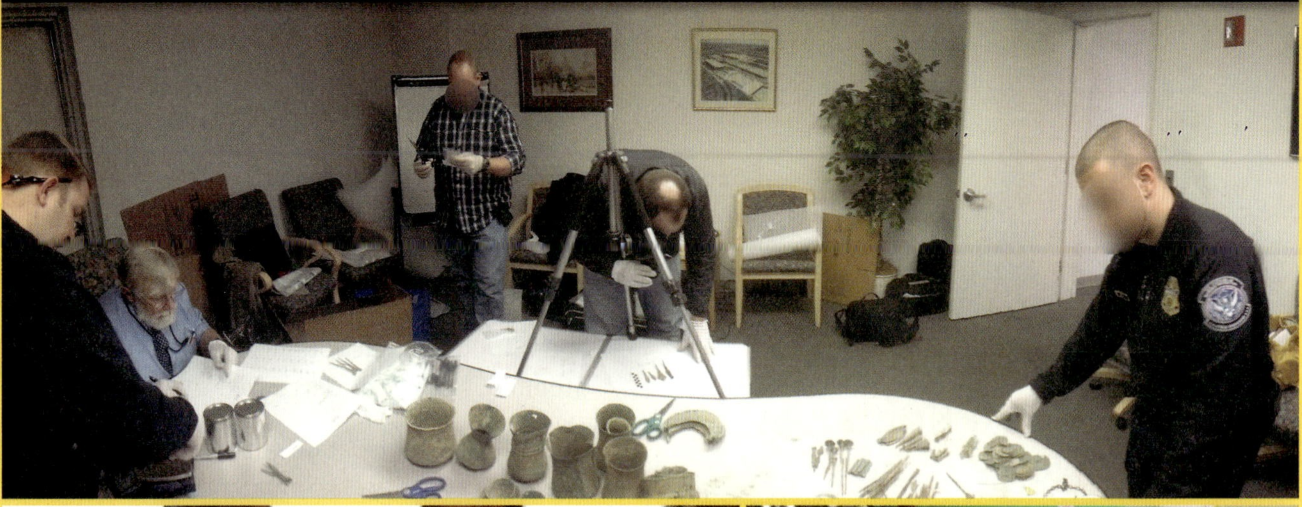

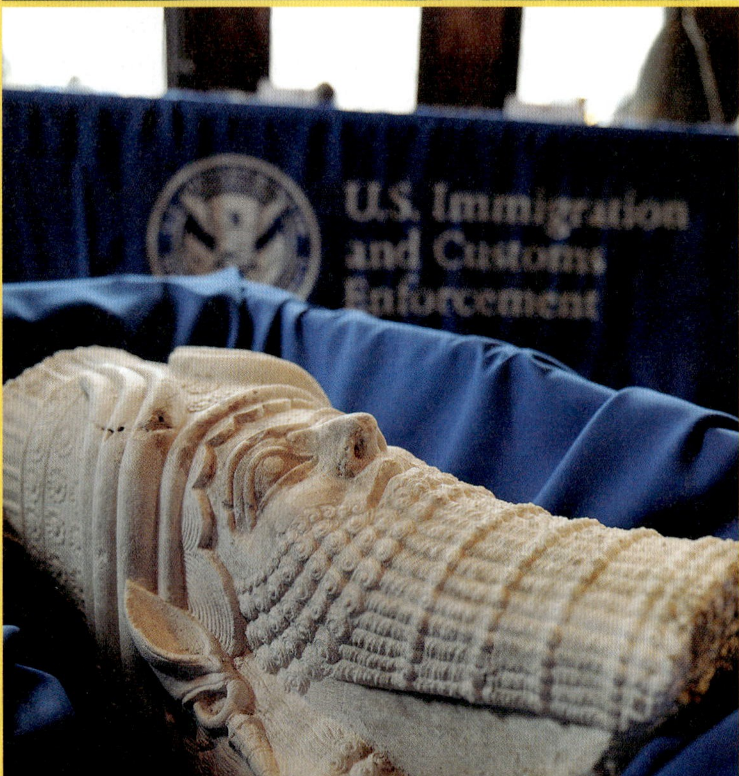
U.S. Immigration
and Customs
Enforcement

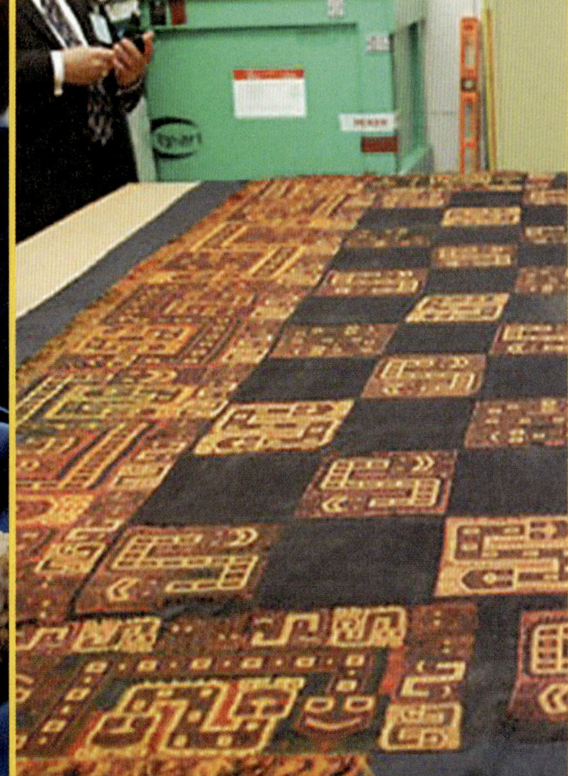

Our Shared History

Imagine if a symbol of the United States—for example, the Statue of Liberty—was stolen from New York Harbor and whisked away to another country. Most Americans would be angry that part of their history was lost to them. Across the world, this theft of the past happens regularly in areas that have been centers of civilization and are rich with archaeological sites and cultural artifacts. And it results in the same feeling of loss.

Top U.S. Customs agents at Dulles Airport in Washington, D.C., examine illegally shipped artifacts.

Bottom Left Head of a lamassu repatriated to Iraq

Bottom Right Paracas textile repatriated to Peru

Cultural artifacts are the little pieces of humanity left behind. They add to what we know of the human record, a non-renewable resource that we all share. When a cultural artifact is damaged or stolen, it is robbed of its identity and can never be replaced. The more conflict a region experiences, the less stable it becomes and the more vulnerable it is to looting, the illegal excavation and smuggling of cultural artifacts.

Fred Hiebert

Some experts now work to help keep artifacts and identities where they belong. Dr. Fredrik Hiebert, National Geographic's Archaeology Fellow and an expert in documenting endangered collections around the world, calls these people "culture heroes" for their dedication to preserving the past. These historians, archaeologists, and anthropologists often support the goal of repatriation, the official returning of looted artifacts to their country of origin. National Geographic has helped bring about repatriations to Afghanistan, Egypt, and Peru.

Afghanistan 2009 Afghanistan was a gathering place for cultures that traded along the Silk Roads. Invasion by the Soviet Union in 1979 began more than three decades of violence that continues today. As a result, Afghanistan's archaeological sites and museums suffered rocket attacks that destroyed cultural artifacts. Such unintended damage is called collateral damage. Other damage is caused intentionally. In 2001, for example, the Taliban used explosives to blow up giant sandstone Buddha statues dating from the 6th century A.D. For years, looting was widespread. More than 1,500 objects spanning thousands of years were confiscated at Heathrow Airport in London and repatriated to Afghanistan in 2009.

Peru 2015 Sometimes what happens to an artifact isn't necessarily the result of violence or war. The 2,300-year-old textile shown on the opposite page has had numerous adventures on its journey home—yet is still in perfect condition. It was discovered as part of a necropolis, or ancient cemetery, in the 1920s and excavated by the founder of Peruvian archaeology, Julio Tello. The textile was stolen from the National Museum in Lima, Peru, not once, but twice. The second time, it found its way to Texas, where U.S. Customs agents recognized the illegal shipment and returned it to the Peruvian embassy. National Geographic helped return the textile in good condition to the museum in 2015.

Egypt 2010 and 2015 In 2008, U.S. Customs agents in Miami, Florida, became suspicious about a shipment with inconsistencies in the paperwork accompanying it. Two years later, the sarcophagus of a man named Imesy who lived during the 21st dynasty of Egypt was repatriated to the Grand Egyptian Museum in Cairo.

In April 2015, National Geographic hosted a ceremony for dozens more illegally shipped artifacts being repatriated from the United States back to Egypt, including a rare nesting sarcophagus from the 26th dynasty and even some mummy parts. Attended by both the U.S. Customs officers and archaeologists involved in solving the case, the ceremony was a moving recognition of an international effort to stop the looting of cultural artifacts and preserve them for future generations.

Fred Hiebert believes that every country is entitled to its own history. He is part of an effort to develop an "antiquities protocol," a process that can be deployed when smuggled artifacts are discovered in the world's ports. Hiebert conducts emergency inventories of looted artifacts, creating a "passport" or permanent record for these objects. But he claims that education is just as important: training customs agents to safely handle artifacts and teaching local residents to become better stewards for the objects that represent their heritage. "Who owns the past?" Fred Hiebert asks, and he has a ready answer: "All of us."

Into the Okavango Delta: A Live-Data Expedition

Located on the continent of Africa in the northwestern part of Botswana, the Okavango Delta is one of the richest wildlife areas on Earth. Unlike most deltas, it doesn't flow into an ocean or sea—it's an inland delta made up of flat, grassy savannas that are flooded by the Okavango River during the winter. This miraculous ecosystem was declared the 1000th UNESCO World Heritage Site in 2015, in part because its unique, seasonal wetlands give many endangered large mammals salvation after their long migration across the Kalahari Desert.

^ National Geographic Emerging Explorers Steve Boyes and Shah Selbe and their team document and share their experiences with the species of the Okavango Delta.

Visible from space, the Okavango Delta is huge—the size of the state of Texas. It's one of Africa's last truly wild landscapes, like the Sahara, the Serengeti, and the Congo. 100,000 elephants roam free across the land. Lions, leopards, hyenas, rhino, cheetahs, crocodiles, and wild dogs also thrive here, as well as nearly 500 bird species and over 1,000 plants.

Since 2011, an expedition team made up of Ba Yei river bushmen and National Geographic Emerging Explorers Steve Boyes and Shah Selbe and their team has been making annual visits to the remote land of the delta in one of the first "live-data" expeditions. That means the team constantly uploads data from the field to their website—intotheokavango.org—via satellite. This data is also available through a public API, or application program interface, which allows anyone to analyze and examine the collected information. "We're connecting society with the wilderness," explains conservation biologist, and Into the Okavango expedition leader, Steve Boyes.

Every ten seconds, state-of-the-art sensors record personal data about expedition members, including heart rate, the amount of energy they are using, and GPS positional data. Cameras automatically take pictures of the team's current location and record sound clips every ten minutes. Team members also post water quality data, and document their animal and bird sightings. They tweet progress updates constantly for people who are tracking their movements online and analyzing the expedition's data.

This mobile computer station allows sensors to be programmed and data to be posted from the field.

Team members also respond to questions and suggestions from their followers.

The team has crossed the Okavango Delta five times so far in dug-out canoes, the traditional mode of transportation for Ba Yei river bushmen. Their goal is to continue conducting in-depth biodiversity surveys in this delicate ecosystem so that any major changes can be noted and addressed.

"We have unprecedented opportunities to improve the world. But only if we act in time." –Shah Selbe

In 2015, the team's two-month "Source to Sand" expedition includes plans to cover the entire Okavango River system. They'll start at the river's source in Angola and travel 1,000 miles down the river through Namibia's Caprivi Strip, into untouched wilderness in the heart of the Okavango Delta in Botswana.

NATIONAL
GEOGRAPHIC
SOCIETY

The team gathers in Okavango after a long trek in 2014.

This Okavango Delta exploration team has made an exciting step forward into expedition technology. For the first time, National Geographic explorers can share their movements, findings, and the sights and sounds of their surroundings, as well as their personal data, thoughts, and emotions in real-time while exploring one of the world's richest wilderness areas. This ground-breaking expedition gives people everywhere the chance to experience—and hopefully support—one of the world's most vibrant and important ecosystems.

Peacemaking Through Photography

The shifting nature of national boundaries is a theme throughout history as well as in current news stories. The world's newest nation is one of those stories. In July 2011, South Sudan became an independent country after citizens voted to break away from Sudan. Why did one country become two?

^ Photos taken by the students of National Geographic's South Sudan Photo Camp capture friends, family members, and daily life.

For the first half of the 20th century, Sudan was a British colony. During British rule, English-speaking Christians and members of many different tribes lived in the southern part of the country. Arabic-speaking Muslims lived in the northern part. When the British left in 1956, two civil wars took place: one in the 1960s and another in the 1980s. War finally ended, but old wounds and animosities did not disappear. A 2005 peace agreement included an option for independence. In January 2011, southern Sudanese people voted to split from Sudan. South Sudan became the world's newest country in July 2011, with the city of Juba as its capital.

Immediately, the new country faced a number of problems, including border disputes with Sudan. Then, in December 2013, widespread violence broke out between rival political groups. Since then, more than 10,000 South Sudanese have been killed, and 2 million have been internally displaced, or forced to leave their homes. Tens of thousands of South Sudanese have fled the country altogether, and many now live in neighboring Ethiopia as refugees. Both sides are responsible for violence committed against others based on their ethnic and tribal background. The fighting in South Sudan also disrupted farming, and now 11 million people face a serious food crisis.

In September 2014, National Geographic responded to the situation in South Sudan with an outreach program called Photo Camp. This program empowers young people to tell their own stories about their life and community through photography, guided by the mentorship of National Geographic photographers. Over a period of five days, 20 University of Juba students from different ethnic backgrounds learned photography from National Geographic photographers and photo editors. This lively group took nearly 32,000 images, including the ones you see on the left. They also engaged in cross-tribal peace-building activities.

Why photography? National Geographic photographers Ed Kashi, Matt Moyer, and Amy Toensing explain. According to Toensing, the students at Photo Camp are eager to learn about cameras and photography. Moyer observes, "To see the students take the cameras and go into their communities, document positive things, and see their world with new eyes is just really inspiring."

National Geographic Photo Camp teaches photography skills, but it also encourages storytelling. Ed Kashi says, "I believe in the power of storytelling. And I believe in the importance of bridging these gaps of misunderstanding. Photo Camp represents that spirit, that desire to bring people together to share stories and to try to make the world a better place."

Participants in National Geographic's South Sudan Photo Camp examine the photos they took.

"We are the same—we are all South Sudanese."

–Mabil Dau Mabil, student

South Sudan participants responded to Photo Camp in a number of ways. For Catherine Koro, the benefits reached far beyond photography. She said, "It's about how you can look into something differently." Students saw their communities and each other with new eyes. Mabil Dau Mabil said they purposely avoided identifying themselves as belonging to the Dinka, Bari, Kuku, or Madi tribes.

These budding photographers understand that the story of South Sudan is just beginning. Even in the midst of the country's current turmoil, they remain hopeful. Akuot Chol Mayak predicts, "The world's eyes are on this nation, not because it's special, but because it is the newest. We are still on the move, but we shall reach there."

Think It Through

The articles in this section focus on history-making events and issues that have a profound effect on people and cultures across the globe. Consider and discuss the questions below to further your understanding of these important topics.

1. Choose one article that connects to your own life and experiences in some way and explain why. How does this article relate to your own personal history?
2. Which of the five articles would be most likely to motivate you to take action as a global citizen? How might you get involved?
3. Which topic are you most interested in finding out more about, and why? How might you seek additional information or updates?

Inquiry Project: Roundtable

Consider each of the newsworthy issues discussed in this section and select the one you feel is the most important or impactful within the world today. Why do you feel your chosen global issue is the most important one?

Assignment Become an expert on the issue you have chosen alongside others who have also chosen that issue. Participate in a roundtable discussion. Articulate why you feel your chosen issue is the most important one, and support your argument.

Plan Connect with other students in your class who share your opinion and discuss what you already know about this issue and what you would like to know. Through research and discussion, develop a solid understanding of the topic.

Produce From your research, develop a list of reasons and arguments to support the notion that your chosen topic has the most impact on the world.

Present Participate in a classroom-wide roundtable discussion. Along with others who share your opinion about the topic you have chosen, work to explain why your topic has the most world impact. Listen respectfully as others present their viewpoints.

STUDENT REFERENCES

AVAILABLE ONLINE

GLOSSARY

A

absolute monarch *n.* a ruler who has unlimited authority

acropolis *n.* the highest point in an ancient Greek city

adapt *v.* to change

adobe *n.* a kind of clay that when dried is used as a building material

agora *n.* an open space in an ancient Greek city that served as a marketplace and social center

agriculture *n.* the practice of growing plants and rearing animals for food

alliance *n.* an agreement between nations to fight each other's enemies; a partnership

anthropologist *n.* a scientist who studies the cultural development of humans

apartheid *n.* a form of racial segregation in South Africa that discriminated against nonwhite citizens

appeasement *n.* a policy in which an aggressor is given concessions to keep the peace

aqueduct *n.* a long stone channel that carries clean water

arabesque *n.* an abstract design made up of patterns of flowers, leaves, vines, and geometric shapes

arch *n.* a curved structure over an opening

archaeologist *n.* a scientist who studies past human life by analyzing fossils and artifacts

archipelago *n.* a collection of islands

aristocracy *n.* an upper class that is richer and more powerful than the rest of society

artifact *n.* an object made by humans from a past culture

artisan *n.* a person skilled at making things by hand

atomic bomb *n.* a bomb that causes an extremely dangerous explosion by splitting atoms apart

B

barbarian *n.* in this context, a person who lived outside the Roman Empire

barter *v.* to exchange goods

bas-relief *n.* a realistic sculpture with figures raised against a flat background

blitzkrieg *n.* a form of warfare conducted with great speed and force

bourgeoisie *n.* the middle class

bubonic plague *n.* a disease that killed more than a third of Europe's population during the Middle Ages

bureaucracy *n.* a system of government in which appointed officials in specialized departments run the various offices

burgher *n.* a wealthy, town-dwelling merchant during the Middle Ages

bushido *n.* a strict code of behavior followed by the samurai in feudal Japan

C

cacao *n.* a bean used to make chocolate

caliph *n.* the title of the chief Muslim leader who was regarded as a successor of Muhammad from A.D. 632 to 1924

calligraphy *n.* a form of elegant writing

capitalism *n.* an economic system in which factories and other means of production are privately owned

caravan *n.* a group of people that travels together

caravel *n.* a small, fast ship used by Spanish and Portuguese explorers

cartography *n.* the study of maps and mapmaking

caste system *n.* a rigid social hierarchy in India that divides people into hereditary classes

catacomb *n.* a hidden underground chamber where people are buried

catapult *n.* a weapon that hurls large stones

cataract *n.* a rock formation that creates churning rapids; also, a large waterfall

cathedral *n.* a towering church built during the Middle Ages; often the place from which a bishop ruled

celadon *n.* a type of Chinese pottery with a unique blue-green color

chinampa *n.* a floating field that supported agriculture

chivalry *n.* a code of conduct for knights

city *n.* a political, economic, and cultural center with a large population

city-state *n.* a self-governing unit made up of a city and its surrounding lands and settlements; a city that controls the surrounding villages and towns

civil disobedience *n.* the refusal to obey laws in order to make the government change something

civil war *n.* a war between groups in the same country

civilization *n.* a society with a highly developed culture and technology

clan *n.* a group of families that shares a common ancestor

classical *adj.* relating to ancient Greek and Roman culture

clergy *n.* the religious leaders who oversee ceremonies and deliver teachings of the Christian Church

codex *n.* a folded book made of tree bark paper

collective *n.* a farm or other enterprise run and owned by the government

colony *n.* a group of people that settles in a new land but keeps ties to its native country

comedy *n.* a humorous form of Greek drama that often mocked famous people

commerce *n.* the buying and selling of goods

commodity *n.* a trade good

common law *n.* a system of law established in England to make sure people received equal treatment

communal *adj.* shared

communism *n.* a belief in a classless society in which there is no private property and the state owns all the means of production; an economic system in which the state owns the means of production

confederation *n.* a group of allies

conquistador *n.* a Spanish conqueror who sought gold and other riches in the Americas

consul *n.* one of two chief leaders elected yearly in ancient Rome

containment *n.* a policy to stop the spread of communism by providing financial and military assistance to specific countries

contract *n.* an agreement between two or more people

convert *v.* to change one's religion

cosmopolitan *adj.* worldly

covenant *n.* a religious agreement

creation story *n.* an account that explains how the world began and how people came to exist

creed *n.* a statement of belief

crossroads *n.* the place where two roads meet

cultivate *v.* to grow a crop

cultural diffusion *n.* the process by which cultures interact and ideas spread from one area to another

cultural hearth *n.* a place from which new ideas, practices, and technology spread

culture *n.* a group's way of life, including types of food, shelter, clothing, language, religion, behavior, and ideas

cuneiform *n.* the earliest form of writing, invented by the Sumerians

D

daimyo *n.* a class of large landowning families in medieval Japan

delta *n.* an area where a river fans out into various branches as it flows into a body of water

democracy *n.* a form of government in which citizens have a direct role in governing themselves or elect representatives to lead them

denomination *n.* a branch of one type of religion

deplete *v.* to use something up, such as a resource

desertification *n.* the process by which once fertile land is transformed into a desert

dharma *n.* the Buddha's teachings; divine law

dhow *n.* a ship with a long, thin hull and triangular sails

dictator *n.* a person who rules with total authority

direct democracy *n.* a form of democracy in which citizens gather together to vote on laws and policies

direct rule *n.* a form of rule in which an imperial power makes up the entire government and administration of its colony

diversity *n.* a range of different things; a variety

divine *adj.* having the nature of a god

divine right *n.* a right to rule believed to be given by God to a king or queen

domestication *n.* the raising of plants and animals to make them useful to humans

domino theory *n.* the theory that if one country becomes communist, its neighbors will also become communist

drought *n.* a long period of dry, hot weather

dynastic cycle *n.* the pattern of the rise and fall of dynasties in ancient and early China

dynasty *n.* a series of rulers from the same family

E

economic depression *n.* a period of low economic activity and high unemployment

elliptical *adj.* oval

embassy *n.* a group of people who represent their nation in a foreign country

emperor *n.* the supreme ruler of an empire

empire *n.* a group of different lands and people governed by one ruler

enlightened despot *n.* an absolute ruler who applied Enlightenment principles to his or her reign

epic poem *n.* a long story in the form of a narrative poem

epistle *n.* a letter

ethnic cleansing *n.* the mass murder of an ethnic or religious group

excommunicate *v.* to officially exclude a member of a church from its rituals and membership

exile *n.* the forced removal from one's native country

exploit *v.* to mistreat

F

famine *n.* an extreme lack of crops or food causing widespread hunger

fascism *n.* a political movement based on extreme nationalism, militarism, and racism promoting the superiority of a particular people over all others

fertile *adj.* encouraging the growth of crops and plants

feudalism *n.* a political and social system in which a vassal receives protection from a lord in exchange for obedience and service

filial piety *n.* the belief that children owe their parents and ancestors respect

fossil *n.* the remains of organisms that lived long ago

free enterprise *n.* an economic system in which people buying and selling products determine what products are needed and what price should be paid for them

free trade *n.* a form of commerce in which groups of nations agree to trade with one another on equal terms without taxes or tariffs

fresco *n.* a picture painted directly onto a wall

G

genocide *n.* the total elimination of a group of people

geocentric theory *n.* a theory that places Earth at the center of the universe

geoglyph *n.* a large, geometric design or shape drawn on the ground

gladiator *n.* a man in ancient Rome who fought others for entertainment

glasnost *n.* in the former Soviet Union, a policy of openness in communication

global citizen *n.* a person who functions effectively in the interdependent, modern world

globalization *n.* the process through which the world has become increasingly interconnected

glyph *n.* a symbolic picture used to represent a word, syllable, or sound

golden age *n.* a period of great cultural achievement

government *n.* an organization set up to make and enforce rules in a society

griot *n.* a West African storyteller who relates stories through the oral tradition

guerrilla *n.* a member of a group of organized resistance fighters

guild *n.* a group of craftspeople that helped protect and improve the working conditions of its members

H

haiku *n.* a form of Japanese poetry that has 17 syllables in three unrhymed lines of 5, 7, and 5 syllables

hanbok *n.* a traditional Korean jacket and skirt or pant combination

heliocentric theory *n.* a theory that places the sun at the center of the universe

Hellenistic *adj.* relating to Greek history or culture

helot *n.* a state-owned slave who was part of the lowest class of ancient Greek society

heresy *n.* beliefs contrary to Church teachings; opposition to Church policy

hero *n.* a character who faces a challenge that demands courage, strength, and intelligence

hierarchy *n.* a system in which people belong to social classes of different ranks

hieroglyph *n.* a picture representing an object, sound, or idea that was part of the ancient Egyptian writing system

highland *n.* a type of land that is high above the sea

hub *n.* a center

humanism *n.* a movement that focused on the importance of the individual

hunter-gatherer *n.* a human who hunts animals and gathers wild plants to eat

hypothesis *n.* an explanation that can be tested

I

icon *n.* an image of Jesus or a saint

imam *n.* a Muslim religious leader

immigrate *v.* to permanently move to another country

immortal *adj.* able to live forever

imperialism *n.* a system in which a stronger nation controls weaker nations or territories

impose *v.* to force someone to do something

indulgence *n.* the release from punishment for sins, sold by papal officials

industrialize *v.* to build and operate factories to produce material goods

inflation *n.* an increase in the price of goods and services compared to the value of money

inoculation *n.* a vaccine containing a mild form of a disease to prevent the development of that disease

intifada *n.* an uprising of Palestinians against the Israeli occupation of the West Bank and the Gaza Strip

iron *n.* a metal that is found in rock

irrigation *n.* the supply of water to fields using human-made systems

isolate *v.* to cut off from the rest of the world

isolationism *n.* a rejection of foreign contact and outside influences

J

janissary *n.* a highly trained and disciplined soldier in the Ottoman army

jury *n.* a group of people chosen to make a decision based on evidence presented in a trial

K

kabuki *n.* a form of Japanese drama that involves luxurious costumes and elaborate makeup

karma *n.* in Hinduism, a state of being influenced by a person's actions and conduct; determines the kind of life into which a person will be reborn

khanate *n.* a region of the Mongol empire

kimchi *n.* a spicy pickled vegetable mix that serves as Korea's national dish

kiva *n.* a circular-shaped chamber built in the ground by the ancient Pueblo

knight *n.* a warrior in medieval Europe

kosher *adj.* specially prepared according to Jewish dietary laws

L

labor union *n.* a voluntary association of workers that uses its power to negotiate better working conditions

labyrinth *n.* a maze

laissez-faire *n.* a policy that calls for less government involvement in economic affairs

land bridge *n.* a strip of land connecting two landmasses

legacy *n.* the things, both cultural and technological, left to us from past cultures

legend *n.* a story from the past that is accepted as truth but cannot be proven

legionary *n.* a professional soldier in ancient Rome

lingua franca *n.* a language commonly used by many different groups of people

longbow *n.* a weapon that allowed archers to fire arrows

lord *n.* a nobleman who received land from a king in medieval feudal society

lowland *n.* a type of land that is low and level

M

maize *n.* a type of corn first domesticated by early Mesoamericans

manor *n.* a self-contained world located on land belonging to a lord

mansa *n.* a West African king

mariner *n.* a sailor

maritime *adj.* relating to the sea

matrilineal *adj.* relating to descendants traced through the mother

medieval *adj.* a period in history that spanned from the A.D. 500s to the 1500s; from the Latin *medieum* (middle) and *aevum* (age)

meditation *n.* the act of achieving inner peace and an enlightened realization of the divine aspect in each person

megafauna *n.* the large animals of a particular region, habitat, or geological period

mercenary *n.* a hired soldier

metallurgy *n.* the science of obtaining metals in their natural form and preparing them for use

middle class *n.* a social class made up primarily of workers that emerged between the upper and lower classes during the Industrial Revolution

migration *n.* the movement from one place to another

militarism *n.* the belief that a country should maintain a strong and aggressive military

minaret *n.* a tall, slender tower that is part of a mosque

missionary *n.* a person who goes to another country to do religious work; a person who tries to spread Christianity to others

monarchy *n.* a government ruled by a single person, such as a king

monastery *n.* a Christian religious community

monotheism *n.* the worship of a single God

monsoon *n.* a strong seasonal wind in South and Southeast Asia

mosaic *n.* a grouping of tiny colored stone cubes set in mortar to create a picture or design

mosque *n.* a Muslim place of worship

mother culture *n.* a civilization that greatly influences other civilizations

mound builder *n.* a Native American culture that built mounds and cities in the Mississippi River Valley region between 1000 B.C. and A.D. 500

movable type *n.* the individual clay tablets that could be arranged on a board to form text

mummy *n.* the preserved body of a pharaoh or other powerful person in ancient Egypt

myth *n.* an old story told to explain an event or justify a belief or action

mythology *n.* a collection of stories that explains events, beliefs, or actions

N

nationalism *n.* a feeling of pride shared by people with the same history, languages, and customs

nation-state *n.* a country with an independent government and a population united by a shared culture, language, and national pride; a political unit in which people have a common culture and identity

natural right *n.* a right, such as life or liberty, that a person is born with

nirvana *n.* in Buddhism, a state of bliss or the end of suffering caused by the cycle of rebirth

noble *n.* a member of a high class in society who inherits his or her status

noh *n.* a form of drama that grew out of Japanese Shinto rituals and often retells well-known folktales

nomad *n.* a person who moves from place to place

nonviolent *adj.* free from violence

O

oasis *n.* a fertile place with water in a desert

oligarchy *n.* a government ruled by a few powerful citizens

ondol *n.* a Korean system of heating in which an outside fire heats thick stones set into a floor

oracle bone *n.* an animal bone used to consult with the many gods worshipped by the Shang people

oral history *n.* an unwritten account of events, often passed down through the generations as stories or songs

oral tradition *n.* the passage of spoken histories and stories from one generation to the next

oratory *n.* the art of public speaking

P

pantheon *n.* the gods of a group of people, a religion, or a civilization

papyrus *n.* a paperlike material made from reeds

parable *n.* in the Bible, a simple story to illustrate a moral or spiritual lesson

parliament *n.* a group of representatives who shared power with the English monarch

partition *v.* to divide something

patriarch *n.* the leader of the Eastern Orthodox Church

patriarchy *n.* a society in which men hold all the power

patrician *n.* a wealthy landowner in ancient Rome

patron *n.* a wealthy person who financially supports and encourages an artist

peasant *n.* a poor farmer

peninsula *n.* a piece of land surrounded by water on three sides

perestroika *n.* in the former Soviet Union, a policy of economic and governmental reform

perspective *n.* an artistic technique that produces an impression of depth and distance

petroleum *n.* the raw material that is used to produce refined oil

phalanx *n.* in ancient Greece and Rome, a battle formation in which soldiers stood close together to protect themselves from enemy attack

pharaoh *n.* an ancient Egyptian ruler

philosophe *n.* an Enlightenment thinker

philosophy *n.* the study of the universe and our place in it

pilgrimage *n.* a journey to a holy place

plague *n.* a disease that causes many deaths

planned city *n.* a city built with a specific layout in mind

plantation *n.* a large farm where slaves worked to grow and harvest crops

plebeian *n.* a common person in ancient Rome

polis *n.* a Greek city-state

polytheism *n.* a belief in many gods

pope *n.* the leader of the Roman Catholic Church

porcelain *n.* a strong, light, and translucent ceramic

potlach *n.* a gift-giving ceremony practiced by the Kwakiutl and Haida Native American tribes

primary source *n.* an artifact or piece of writing that was created by someone who witnessed or lived through a historical event

printing press *n.* an invention that used movable metal type to print pages

proletariat *n.* in communism, the working class

propaganda *n.* the information used by a government to make people think or act in a particular way

prophet *n.* a teacher believed to be inspired by God

province *n.* an administrative district of a larger empire or country

push-pull factor *n.* a reason why people immigrate, such as lack of economic opportunity or freedom in one country and the promise of a better life in another

pyramid *n.* a massive monumental tomb for a pharaoh

Q

quarry *v.* to extract stone from the earth

quinine *n.* a substance from the bark of a tree that is an effective remedy for malaria

quinoa *n.* a high-protein grain native to the Andes Mountains in South America

R

rabbi *n.* a Jewish spiritual leader

racism *n.* the belief that one race is better than others

ration *v.* to distribute something in limited quantities

raw material *n.* a substance from which other things are made

reason *n.* the power of the human mind to think and understand in a logical way

record keeping *n.* the practice of organizing and storing information

reform *n.* a change to make a situation better

refugee *n.* a person forced to leave his or her country because of wars, persecution, or natural disasters

regent *n.* a person who rules when a monarch or emperor is unable to do so

reincarnation *n.* in Hinduism, the rebirth of a person's soul into another body after death

religion *n.* the belief in and worship of one or more gods and goddesses

Renaissance man *n.* a person who has a wide variety of skills and knowledge

reparations *n.* the money paid to the victors by the losing side in a war

representative democracy *n.* a form of democracy in which people are elected to vote on the citizens' behalf

republic *n.* a type of government in which citizens vote for their leaders

reunify *v.* to join together again

ritual *n.* a formal series of acts always performed in the same way; a religious ceremony

rivalry *n.* a competition

S

samurai *n.* a hired warrior in medieval Japan

satrap *n.* a governor of a province in the Persian Empire

savanna *n.* an area of lush tropical grasslands

scarcity *n.* a small supply of something

schism *n.* a separation

scientific method *n.* a logical procedure for developing and testing ideas

scientific rationalism *n.* a school of thought in which observation, experimentation, and mathematical reasoning replace ancient wisdom and church teachings as the source of scientific truth

scribe *n.* a professional writer who recorded official information

secondary source *n.* an artifact or writing created after an event by someone who did not see it or live during the time when it occurred

secular *adj.* nonreligious

sepoy *n.* a native Indian soldier employed by the East India Company

serf *n.* a person who lived and worked on the private land of a noble or medieval lord

shah *n.* a ruler of the Safavid Empire; the Persian title for "king"

shaman *n.* a medicine healer in Native American cultures

shari'a *n.* an Islamic system of law that covers all aspects of human behavior

shogun *n.* the military ruler of medieval Japan

shogunate *n.* the rule by a shogun

siege *n.* a military tactic in which troops surround a city with soldiers in an attempt to take control of it

silk *n.* a textile made from the cocoons of silkworms

silt *n.* an especially fine and fertile soil

slash-and-burn agriculture *n.* a method of clearing fields for planting

smallpox *n.* a deadly virus that causes a high fever and small blisters on the skin

social class *n.* a category of people based on wealth or status in a society

socialism *n.* a belief in a society in which the government owns or controls the means of production

specialized worker *n.* a person who performs a job other than farming, such as metalworking or toolmaking

stalemate *n.* a situation in which neither side in a conflict is able to win

staple *n.* a main crop produced in a specific place

steppe *n.* a vast, grassy plain

subcontinent *n.* a large, distinct landmass that is part of a continent

sultan *n.* a ruler of the Ottoman Empire

surplus *adj.* more than is required or necessary; extra

surveillance *n.* the act of keeping watch over a person or a group

synagogue *n.* a Jewish place of worship

T

technology *n.* the application of knowledge, tools, and inventions to meet people's needs

temple *n.* a place of worship

terra cotta *n.* a fire-baked clay

terrace *n.* a stepped platform built into a mountainside

terrace farming *n.* a type of farming in which flat steps are cut into a mountain to provide farmland

terrorism *n.* the use of violence against civilians to achieve political goals

tetrarchy *n.* a system of rule by four emperors

theory *n.* a proposed explanation for a set of facts

tolerance *n.* the sympathy for the beliefs and practices of others

totalitarian *adj.* completely controlling all aspects of public and private life

totem pole *n.* a tall, elaborately carved and painted tree trunk common in Northwest Coast native cultures

trade *n.* the exchange of goods

tragedy *n.* a serious form of Greek drama in which characters endure suffering before an unhappy ending

trans-Saharan *adj.* across the Sahara

trench warfare *n.* a type of warfare in which long ditches dug deep in the ground provided a fortress for soldiers

triangular trade *n.* a transatlantic trade network formed by Europe, West Africa, and the Americas

tribe *n.* an extended family unit

tribune *n.* a representative who fought to protect the rights of ordinary citizens in ancient Rome

tribute *n.* a tax paid or goods and services rendered in return for protection

trireme *n.* an ancient Greek warship

truce *n.* an agreement to stop fighting

tyrant *n.* in ancient Greek city-states, a ruler who took power illegally

U

U-boat *n.* a German submarine used during both World War I and World War II

urbanization *n.* the growth of cities

V

vassal *n.* a person, usually a lesser nobleman, who received land and protection from a feudal lord in exchange for obedience and service

vernacular *n.* a person's native language

veto *v.* to reject a decision or proposal made by another government body

vizier *n.* a chief official in ancient Egypt who carried out much of the day-to-day work of governing

W

wigwam *n.* a domed tent used as housing by the Algonquin in North America

woman suffrage *n.* the right of women to vote and to participate in politics

woodcut *n.* an image carved on a block of wood

Y

yoga *n.* a series of postures and breathing exercises

Z

ziggurat *n.* a pyramid-shaped temple in Sumerian city-states

ACADEMIC VOCABULARY

abandon *v.* to leave behind and never return to (page 772)

absolute *adj.* complete (page 360)

accuracy *n.* the freedom from errors (page 666)

accurate *adj.* without mistakes or errors (page 472)

advance *v.* to move forward (page 238)

ambitious *adj.* having a desire for fame or success (page 530)

appoint *v.* to give someone a particular job or duty (page 354)

benefit *v.* to be helpful to someone or something (page 677)

capacity *n.* the ability to do something (page 15)

civilian *adj.* of the general public, as opposed to the military (page 762)

coexist *v.* to live peacefully together (page 440)

collide *v.* to crash together (page 145)

commerce *n.* the buying and selling of goods and services (page 282)

commit *v.* to promise to do something (page 306)

communal *adj.* used or shared by a group of people (page 490)

concentrate *v.* to focus on (page 74)

constant *adj.* happening all the time (page 422)

creation *n.* the act of making something that did not exist before (page 704)

crucial *adj.* extremely important or necessary (page 390)

decade *n.* a period of ten years (page 794)

decline *v.* to worsen in terms of condition or quality (page 434)

depose *v.* to remove someone from power (page 573)

determination *n.* the quality that makes someone continue to try doing a difficult task (page 284)

distinct *adj.* noticeably different or unique (page 496)

distinctive *adj.* different in a noticeable way (page 41)

dominate *v.* to have power over someone or something (page 112)

elaborate *adj.* made with great detail and effort (page 556)

emerge *v.* to rise or appear (page 36)

emphasis *n.* the additional importance given to something (page 380)

enable *v.* to make it so something can be done (page 722)

ensure *v.* to make something certain (page 386)

eternal *adj.* existing at all times; lasting forever (page 150)

ethical *adj.* following accepted rules or behaviors (page 522)

excel *v.* to be or do better than others (page 631)

flourish *v.* to be successful (page 270)

fortified *adj.* strong, strengthened (page 607)

influence *v.* to affect or change someone or something indirectly (page 170)

interact *v.* to do things with others (page 701)

interval *n.* the period of time between events (page 308)

intricate *adj.* having many parts or details (page 584)

loyalty *n.* a strong feeling of support for someone or something (page 732)

luxury *adj.* expensive and unnecessary (page 434)

massive *adj.* extremely large in size (page 808)

observation *n.* the written descriptions based on something you have watched or seen (page 639)

policy *n.* a set of rules or ideas about how things should be done (page 127)

possession *n.* a personal article or possession (page 181)

predict *v.* to say that something will happen in the future (page 467)

privilege *n.* a right or benefit that only some people receive (page 114)

profit *n.* the money that is made through doing business (page 416)

promote *v.* to encourage (page 154)

prosperous *adj.* successful, usually by making a lot of money (page 209)

protest *n.* an event during which people gather to show dislike or disapproval toward something (page 810)

radical *adj.* different from what is typical or ordinary (page 643)

reluctantly *adv.* with hesitation or doubt (page 245)

retain *v.* to keep or continue to have (page 601)

revolve *v.* to move or turn around something (page 664)

supervise *v.* to watch and oversee someone or something (page 69)

transform *v.* to dramatically change (page 26)

undermine *v.* to make someone or something weaker (page 566)

unrest *n.* a situation in which many people in a group or region are upset and unsettled (page 732)

wage *n.* the amount of money a worker is paid (page 221)

A

acrópolis *s.* punto más alto en una ciudad griega de la antigüedad

acueducto *s.* canal largo de piedra que transporta agua limpia

adaptar *v.* cambiar

adobe *s.* tipo de arcilla que cuando se seca se usa como material de construcción

ágora *s.* espacio abierto en una ciudad griega de la antigüedad que servía como mercado y centro social

agotar *v.* consumir algo por completo, por ejemplo, un recurso

agricultura *s.* práctica de cultivar plantas y criar animales para obtener alimento

agricultura de tala y quema *s.* método de limpiar los campos para sembrar cultivos

aislacionismo *s.* rechazo al contacto extranjero y a las influencias externas

aislar *v.* apartar del resto del mundo

alianza *s.* acuerdo entre naciones para colaborar en la lucha contra los enemigos; asociación; pacto religioso

alminar *s.* torre alta y angosta que es parte de una mezquita

antropólogo *s.* científico que estudia el desarrollo cultural de los seres humanos

apaciguamiento *s.* política en que a un agresor se le otorgan concesiones para mantener la paz

apartheid *s.* forma de segregación racial establecida en Sudáfrica que discriminaba a los ciudadanos no blancos

arabesco *s.* diseño abstracto que consiste en patrones o flores, hojas, enredaderas o figuras geométricas

archipiélago *s.* conjunto de islas

arco largo *s.* arma que permitía que los arqueros dispararan sus flechas

arco *s.* estructura curva colocada sobre una abertura

aristocracia *s.* clase alta que es más adinerada y más poderosa que el resto de la sociedad

arqueólogo *s.* científico que estudia el pasado de la vida humana mediante el análisis de fósiles y artefactos

artefacto *s.* objeto hecho por humanos pertenecientes a una cultura del pasado

artesano *s.* persona que se dedica a fabricar objetos de forma manual

B

bajorrelieve *s.* escultura realista que contiene figuras realzadas sobre un fondo plano

bancales *s.* tipo de agricultura en que se cortan escalones planos en una montaña para brindar terrenos de cultivo

bárbaro *s.* en este contexto, una persona que vivía fuera del Imperio Romano

blitzkrieg *s.* forma de conflicto armado que se lleva a cabo con gran velocidad y fuerza

bomba atómica *s.* bomba que causa una explosión extremadamente peligrosa mediante la división de los átomos

burgués *s.* comerciante rico, citadino, durante la Edad Media; miembro de la clase media

burocracia *s.* sistema de gobierno en que funcionarios designados en departamentos especializados están a cargo de distintas oficinas

bushido *s.* estricto código de comportamiento seguido por los samurái en el Japón feudal

C

caballero *s.* guerrero de la Europa medieval

cacao *s.* grano que se usa para hacer chocolate

califa *s.* título del líder musulmán que era considerado sucesor de Mohammed, desde 632 a 1924 D.C.

caligrafía *s.* forma de escritura elegante

campesino *s.* granjero pobre

capitalismo *s.* sistema económico en que las fábricas y otros medios de producción están en manos de privados

carabela *s.* nave pequeña y rápida usada por los exploradores españoles y portugueses

caravana *s.* grupo de personas que viajan juntas

cartografía *s.* estudio de los mapas y de la creación de mapas

catacumba *s.* cámara escondida bajo la superficie en donde se entierra a los muertos

catapulta *s.* arma que lanza piedras enormes

catarata *s.* formación rocosa que crea rápidos agitados; además, una cascada grande

catedral *s.* iglesia alta construida durante la Edad Media; a menudo el lugar en donde gobernaba un obispo

cazador-recolector *s.* ser humano que caza animales y que cosecha plantas silvestres para alimentarse

celadón *s.* tipo de cerámica china con un peculiar color verdeazulado

centro de comercio *s.* núcleo comercial

chamán *s.* curandero de las culturas nativo-americanas

chinampa *s.* campo flotante que sustenta la agricultura

ciclo dinástico *s.* patrón del surgimiento y la caída de las dinastías de la China ancestral y antigua

cieno *s.* suelo especialmente fino y fértil

cipayo *s.* soldado nativo de la India empleado por la Compañía Británica de las Indias Orientales

cisma *s.* separación

ciudad *s.* centro político, económico y cultural con una población grande

ciudad-estado *s.* unidad que se gobierna a sí misma, formada por una ciudad y sus territorios y asentamientos circundantes; ciudad que controla las aldeas y pueblos circundantes

ciudad planificada *s.* ciudad construida con un diseño específico en mente

ciudadano global *s.* persona que funciona efectivamente en el mundo interdependiente moderno

civilización *s.* sociedad con una cultura y tecnología altamente desarrolladas

clan *s.* grupo de familias que comparten un ancestro en común

clase media *s.* clase social compuesta principalmente por trabajadores, que emergió entre las clases alta y baja durante la Revolución Industrial

clase social *s.* categoría de personas basada en las riquezas o estatus en una sociedad

clásico *adj.* relacionado con la cultura griega y romana antiguas

clérigo *s.* líder religioso que dirige las ceremonias e imparte las enseñanzas de la iglesia cristiana

códice *s.* libro plegado hecho de papel de corteza de árbol

colectivo *s.* granja u otro tipo de empresa que el gobierno posee y maneja

colonia *s.* grupo de personas que se asientan en un nuevo territorio, pero que mantienen sus lazos con su país nativo

comedia *s.* obra de teatro griega con un formato humorístico que solía burlarse de las personas famosas

comercio *s.* intercambio de productos; compra y venta de bienes

comercio triangular *s.* red de comercio transatlántico formado por Europa, África Occidental y las Américas

comunal *adj.* compartido

comunismo *s.* creencia en una sociedad sin clases sociales y sin propiedad privada, en la que el estado es dueño de todos los medios de producción; sistema económico en que el estado es dueño de todos los medios de producción

confederación *s.* grupo de aliados

conquistador *s.* explorador español que buscaba oro y otras riquezas en Centroamérica y América del Sur

constructores de montículos *s.* cultura nativo-americana que construyó montículos y ciudades en la región del valle del río Mississippi entre los años 1000 A.C. y 500 D.C.

cónsul *s.* uno de los dos jefes líderes elegidos cada año en la Antigua Roma

contención *s.* política para detener el avance del comunismo al proporcionar asistencia financiera y militar a países específicos

contrato *s.* acuerdo entre dos o más personas

convertirse *v.* cambiar la propia religión

cosmopolita *adj.* internacional

credo *s.* declaración de creencia

crisol cultural *s.* lugar desde el cual se difunden nuevas ideas, prácticas y tecnología

cultivar *v.* sembrar cultivos

cultivo básico *s.* cultivo principal producido en un lugar específico

cultura madre *s.* civilización que tiene una gran influencia sobre otras civilizaciones

cultura *s.* forma de vida de un grupo, que incluye tipos de alimento, vivienda, vestimenta, idioma, religión, comportamiento e ideas

cuneiforme *s.* primera forma de escritura conocida, inventada por los sumerios

D

daimio *s.* clase de familias terratenientes grandes del Japón medieval

delta *s.* área donde un río se divide en distintos brazos a medida que fluye hacia una masa de agua

democracia *s.* forma de gobierno en que los ciudadanos tienen un papel directo para gobernarse a sí mismos o para elegir a representantes que los gobiernen

democracia directa *s.* forma de democracia en que los ciudadanos se reúnen para votar sobre las leyes y las políticas

democracia representativa *s.* forma de democracia en que se eligen personas para que voten en representación de los ciudadanos

denominación *s.* rama de una religión determinada

depresión económica *s.* período de baja actividad económica y de alto desempleo

derecho consuetudinario *s.* sistema legal establecido en Inglaterra para asegurarse de que todas las personas fueran tratadas con igualdad

derecho divino *s.* derecho a gobernar que se creía que Dios daba a un rey o reina

derecho natural *s.* derecho, tal como la vida o la libertad, con los que nace una persona

desertificación *s.* proceso mediante el cual las tierras fértiles se convierten en un desierto

desobediencia civil *s.* rehusar obedecer las leyes para lograr que el gobierno realice cambios

despotismo ilustrado *s.* gobernante absolutista que aplicó los principios de la Ilustración a su propio reino

dharma *s.* enseñanzas de Buda; ley divina

dhow *s.* nave con un casco largo y delgado y velas triangulares

dictador *s.* persona que gobierna con total autoridad

difusión cultural *s.* proceso mediante el cual las culturas interaccionan y las ideas se propagan de un área a otra

dinastía *s.* serie de gobernantes de la misma familia

diversidad *s.* rango de cosas diferentes; variedad

divino *adj.* tener la naturaleza de un dios

domesticación *s.* cultivo de plantas y animales de manera que fueran útiles para los humanos

E

edad de oro *s.* período de grandes logros culturales

elíptico *adj.* ovalado

embajada *s.* grupo de personas que representa a su nación en un país extranjero

emperador *s.* gobernante supremo de un imperio

epístola *s.* carta

escasez *s.* suministro pequeño de algo

escriba *s.* escritor profesional que anotaba información oficial

estancamiento *s.* situación en la que ninguno de los lados de un conflicto es capaz de ganar

estepa *s.* planicie vasta y cubierta de hierbas

excedente *adj.* más de lo que se requiere o necesita; extra

excomulgar *s.* excluir oficialmente a un miembro de una iglesia de sus rituales y membresía

exilio *s.* expulsión forzada del propio país de origen

explotar *v.* maltratar

extraer *v.* sacar piedras de la tierra

F

factores de atracción y repulsión *s.* razón por la cual las personas inmigran, tal como la falta de oportunidades económicas o de libertad en un país y la promesa de una mejor vida en otro país

falange *s.* en la Antigua Grecia y Roma, formación de batalla en que los soldados se formaban juntos unos de otros para protegerse de los ataques de los enemigos

faraón *s.* gobernante egipcio de la antigüedad

fascismo *s.* movimiento político que promueve el nacionalismo extremo, el militarismo y el racismo, promoviendo a la vez la superioridad de un pueblo en particular

fértil *adj.* que sustenta el crecimiento de cultivos y plantas

feudalismo *s.* sistema político y social en que el vasallo recibe protección de un señor a cambio de obediencia y servicio

filosofía *s.* estudio del universo y de nuestro lugar en él

filósofo *s.* pensador de la Ilustración

fósil *s.* restos de organismos que vivieron hace mucho tiempo atrás

fresco *s.* arte que se pinta directamente sobre una muralla

fuente primaria *s.* artefacto o texto escrito creado por alguien que presenció o vivió un acontecimiento histórico

fuente secundaria *s.* artefacto o texto escrito creado después de un acontecimiento por alguien que no lo vio o presenció durante el tiempo en que ocurrió

G

genocidio *s.* total eliminación de un grupo de personas

geoglifo *s.* diseño o forma geométrica grande dibujado sobre el suelo

gladiador *s.* hombre de la Antigua Roma que luchaba contra otros como espectáculo de entretención

glasnost *s.* en la ex Unión Soviética, una política de apertura a la comunicación

glifo *s.* dibujo simbólico usado para representar una palabra, sílaba o sonido

globalización *s.* proceso mediante el cual el mundo está más interconectado

gobierno *s.* organización establecida para hacer y reforzar las reglas de una sociedad

gobierno directo *s.* forma de gobierno en que un poder imperial conforma todo el gobierno y la administración de su colonia

gremio *s.* grupo de artesanos que ayudaron a proteger y a mejorar las condiciones laborales de sus miembros

griot *s.* cuentacuentos del África Occidental que cuenta historias a través de la tradición oral

guerra civil *s.* guerra entre grupos de un mismo país

guerra de trincheras *s.* tipo de conflicto armado en que se excavaban zanjas largas y profundas que brindaban una fortaleza para los soldados

guerrilla *s.* miembro de un grupo de guerreros de la resistencia organizada

H

haikú *s.* forma de poesía japonesa que consiste en 17 sílabas organizadas en tres versos no rimados de 5, 7 y 5 sílabas respectivamente

hambruna *s.* escasez extrema de cultivos o de alimentos que causa hambre generalizada

hanbok *s.* combinación coreana de vestimenta tradicional que consiste en una chaqueta con falda o pantalón

helenístico *adj.* relacionado con la historia o cultura griega

herejía *s.* creencias contrarias a las enseñanzas de la iglesia; oposición a las políticas de la iglesia

héroe *s.* personaje que enfrenta un desafío que requiere valentía, fuerza e inteligencia

hidalguía *s.* código de comportamiento de los caballeros

hierro *s.* metal que se encuentra en la roca

hipótesis *s.* explicación que puede ponerse a prueba

historia de la creación *s.* narración que explica cómo comenzó el mundo y cómo nacieron las personas

historia oral *s.* registro no escrito de acontecimientos, que a menudo se transmite de una generación a otra a través de historias o canciones

hombre renacentista *s.* persona con una amplia variedad de destrezas y conocimientos

hueso oracular *s.* hueso de animal usado para consultar a los muchos dioses adorados por el pueblo Shang

humanismo *s.* movimiento que se enfoca en la importancia del individuo

I

ícono *s.* imagen de Jesús o de un santo

ilota *s.* esclavo que poseía el estado que era parte de la clase social más baja en la sociedad griega de la antigüedad

imam *s.* líder religioso musulmán

imperialismo *s.* sistema en que una nación más poderosa controla naciones o territorios más débiles

imperio *s.* conjunto de diferentes tierras y pueblos liderados por un gobernante

imponer *v.* forzar a alguien a hacer algo

imprenta *s.* invento que usaba tipos móviles de metal para imprimir páginas

indemnización *s.* dinero que quienes perdieron una guerra le pagan a los ganadores

indulgencia *s.* liberación de los castigos causados por los pecados, vendida por funcionarios papales

industrializar *v.* construir y operar fábricas para producir bienes materiales

inflación *s.* aumento en el precio de los bienes y servicios en comparación con el valor del dinero

inmigrar *s.* mudarse permanentemente a otro país

inmortal *adj.* que puede vivir para siempre

inoculación *s.* vacuna que contiene una forma leve de una enfermedad para prevenir el desarrollo de dicha enfermedad

intersección *s.* lugar en donde se juntan dos caminos

intifada *s.* rebelión de los palestinos contra la ocupación israelita de Cisjordania y la Franja de Gaza

irrigación *s.* suministro de agua para los campos mediante el uso de sistemas hechos por el hombre

J

jenízaro *s.* soldado altamente entrenado y disciplinado del ejército otomano

jerarquía *s.* sistema en que las personas pertenecen a distintas clases sociales que tienen distintos rangos en la sociedad

jeroglífico *s.* imagen que representa un objeto, sonido o idea y que era parte del antiguo sistema de escritura egipcio

jurado *s.* grupo de personas escogidas para tomar una decisión con base en la evidencia presentada en un juicio

K

kabuki *s.* forma de obra teatral japonesa que incluye disfraces lujosos y maquillaje elaborado

kanato *s.* región del Imperio Mongol

karma *s.* en el hinduismo, estado de estar influenciado por las acciones y el comportamiento; determina el tipo de vida en que una persona volverá a nacer

kimchi *s.* plato nacional de Corea, que consiste en una mezcla de verduras bien condimentadas

kiva *s.* cámara de forma circular construida en el suelo por los indígenas pueblo del pasado

kosher *adj.* preparado especialmente según las leyes dietéticas judías

L

laberinto *s.* lugar formado por encrucijadas, del cual es difícil salir

laissez-faire *s.* política que exige menos participación del estado en asuntos económicos

legado *s.* cosas, tanto culturales como tecnológicas, que nos quedan del pasado

legionario *s.* soldado profesional de la Antigua Roma

lengua franca *s.* idioma que se usa comúnmente entre distintos grupos de personas

leyenda *s.* historia del pasado que se acepta como verdad, pero que no puede probarse

libre comercio *s.* forma de comercio en que grupos de naciones acuerdan comercializar entre sí en términos igualitarios, sin impuestos o aranceles

libre mercado *s.* sistema económico en que la compra y venta de productos determina qué productos se necesitan y qué precio deben tener

limpieza étnica *s.* asesinato en masa de un grupo étnico o religioso

M

maíz *s.* tipo de elote que fue domesticado por los primeros mesoamericanos

mansa *s.* rey de África Occidental

marinero *s.* marino

marítimo *adj.* relacionado con el mar

materia prima *s.* sustancia a partir de la cual se fabrican otras cosas

matrilineal *adj.* relacionado con los descendientes que provienen de la madre

mecenas *s.* persona adinerada que apoya financieramente y promueve a un artista

medieval *adj.* período de la historia que se expandió desde el siglo VI al siglo XVI; del latín *medieum* (medio) y *aevum* (edad)

meditación *s.* acto de alcanzar la paz interior y el entendimiento del aspecto divino en cada persona

megafauna *s.* animales grandes de una región, hábitat o período geológico en particular

mercancía *s.* producto de comercio

mercenario *s.* soldado asalariado

metalurgia *s.* ciencia que consiste en obtener materiales en su forma natural y prepararlos para el uso

método científico *s.* procedimiento lógico para desarrollar y poner a prueba las ideas

mezquita *s.* lugar musulmán de adoración

migración *s.* mudarse de un lugar a otro

militarismo *s.* creencia de que un país debe mantener una milicia fuerte y agresiva

misionero *s.* persona que va a otro país para realizar labores religiosas; persona que trata de divulgar la cristiandad a otros

mito *s.* historia antigua contada para explicar un acontecimiento o justificar una creencia o acción

mitología *s.* colección de historias que explica acontecimientos, creencias o acciones

momia *s.* cuerpo preservado de un faraón u otra persona poderosa del Antiguo Egipto

monarca absoluto *s.* gobernante con autoridad ilimitada

monarquía *s.* gobierno liderado por una sola persona como, por ejemplo, un rey

monasterio *s.* comunidad religiosa cristiana

monoteísmo *s.* alabanza a un solo Dios

monzón *s.* vientos estacionales fuertes en el Sudeste Asiático

mosaico *s.* agrupación de cubitos de piedra coloridos que se colocan sobre argamasa para crear un dibujo o diseño

N

nación-estado *s.* país con un gobierno independiente y una población unida por una cultura compartida, un idioma común y orgullo nacional; unidad política en que las personas tienen una cultura e identidad en común

nacionalismo *s.* sentimiento de orgullo compartido por personas que comparten la misma historia, idiomas y costumbres

nirvana *s.* en el budismo, un estado de dicha o del final del sufrimiento causado por el ciclo del renacer

noviolencia *adj.* libre de violencia

noble *s.* miembro de la clase alta de la sociedad que hereda su estatus de sus antepasados

noh *s.* forma de obra teatral que surgió a partir de los rituales japoneses Shinto y que a menudo relata cuentos folclóricos conocidos

nómada *s.* persona que se muda de un lugar a otro

O

oasis *s.* lugar fértil con agua en un desierto

oligarquía *s.* gobierno liderado por unos pocos ciudadanos

ondol *s.* sistema coreano de calefacción en que una fogata al exterior calienta piedras gruesas que se colocan en el suelo

oratoria *s.* arte del discurso público

P

panteón *s.* dioses de un grupo de personas, una religión o una civilización

papa *s.* líder de la Iglesia Católica Romana

papiro *s.* material parecido al papel que se hace a partir de juncos

parábola *s.* en la Biblia, un relato sencillo que ilustra una moraleja o una lección espiritual

parlamento *s.* grupo de representantes que comparten el poder con el rey inglés

partición *s.* dividir algo

patriarca *s.* líder de la Iglesia Ortodoxa oriental

patriarcal *adj.* dicho de una sociedad en que los hombres tienen todo el poder

patricio *s.* terrateniente rico de la Antigua Roma

península *s.* porción de tierra rodeada por agua en tres de sus costados

peregrinación *s.* viaje a un lugar sagrado

perestroika *s.* en la ex Unión Soviética, una política de reformas económicas y gubernamentales

permutar *v.* intercambiar productos

perspectiva *s.* técnica artística que produce una impresión de profundidad y distancia

peste bubónica *s.* enfermedad que mató a más de un tercio de la población de Europa durante la Edad Media

petróleo *s.* materia prima que se usa para producir un aceite refinado

piedad filial *s.* creencia de que los niños le deben respeto a sus padres y ancestros

pirámide *s.* tumba masiva y monumental construida para un faraón

plaga *s.* enfermedad que causa muchas muertes

plantación *s.* granja grande en donde trabajan esclavos para producir y cultivar las siembras

plebeyo *s.* persona común de la Antigua Roma

poema épico *s.* historia larga escrita como un poema narrativo

polis *s.* ciudad-estado griega

politeísmo *s.* creencia en muchos dioses

porcelana *s.* cerámica resistente, liviana y translúcida

potlach *s.* ceremonia de entrega de obsequios practicada por las tribus nativo-americanas kwakiutl y haida

profeta *s.* maestro que se cree es inspirado por Dios

proletariado *s.* en el comunismo, la clase trabajadora

propaganda *s.* información usada por un gobierno para hacer que las personas piensen o actúen de una forma determinada

provincia *s.* distrito administrativo de un imperio grande o de un país

puente terrestre *s.* franja de territorio que conecta dos masas terrestres

Q

quinina *s.* sustancia de la corteza de un árbol que es un antídoto efectivo para la malaria

quínoa *s.* grano alto en proteínas originario de las montañas de los Andes en América del Sur

R

rabino *s.* líder espiritual judío

ración *s.* distribuir algo en cantidades limitadas

racionalismo científico *s.* escuela de pensamiento en que la observación, experimentación y razonamiento matemático reemplazan el conocimiento ancestral y las enseñanzas de la iglesia como fuente de la verdad científica

racismo *s.* creencia de que una raza es mejor que las otras

razón *s.* poder de la mente humana para pensar y comprender de una manera lógica

reencarnación *s.* en el hinduismo, el renacer del alma de una persona en otro cuerpo después de la muerte

reforma *s.* cambio hecho para mejorar una situación

refugiado *s.* persona que es forzada a dejar su país a causa de guerras, persecución o desastres naturales

regente *s.* persona que gobierna cuando un monarca o emperador no puede hacerlo

registros *s.* práctica que consiste en organizar y almacenar la información

religión *s.* creencia en y alabanza de uno o más dioses y diosas

república *s.* tipo de gobierno en que los ciudadanos votan por sus líderes

reunificar *v.* volver a unir

ritual *s.* serie de actos formales que siempre se realizan de la misma manera; ceremonia religiosa

rivalidad *s.* competencia

S

sabana *s.* área de praderas tropicales exuberantes

samurái *s.* guerrero asalariado del Japón medieval

sátrapa *s.* gobernante de una provincia en el Imperio Persa

secular *adj.* no religioso

seda *s.* textil hecho de los capullos de los gusanos de la seda

señor *s.* miembro de la nobleza que recibía tierras de un rey en la sociedad feudal medieval

señorío *s.* mundo autosuficiente ubicado en las tierras que pertenecían a un señor

sequía *s.* período largo de estado del tiempo seco y caluroso

shah *s.* gobernante del Imperio Safávida; título persa para "rey"

shari'a *s.* sistema islámico de leyes que cubre todos los aspectos del comportamiento humano

siervo *s.* persona que vivía y trabajaba en los terrenos privados de un noble o de un señor medieval

sinagoga *s.* lugar de reunión religiosa para los judíos

sindicato *s.* asociación voluntaria de trabajadores que usa su poder para negociar mejores condiciones laborales

sistema de castas *s.* jerarquía social rígida en India que divide a las personas en clases sociales hereditarias

sitio *s.* táctica militar en que las tropas rodean una ciudad con soldados en un intento por controlarla

socialismo *s.* creencia en una sociedad en que el gobierno es dueño de o controla los medios de producción

sogún *s.* gobernante militar del Japón medieval

sogunato *s.* gobierno de un sogún

subcontinente *s.* gran masa de tierra que es parte de un continente

sultán *s.* gobernante del Imperio Otomano

T

tecnología *s.* aplicación de conocimiento, herramientas e inventos para satisfacer las necesidades de las personas

templo *s.* lugar de alabanza

teoría *s.* explicación propuesta para un conjunto de hechos

Teoría de Dominó *s.* teoría que declara que si un país se vuelve comunista, sus vecinos también lo harán

teoría geocéntrica *s.* teoría que posiciona a la Tierra en el centro del universo

teoría heliocéntrica *s.* teoría que posiciona al Sol como el centro del universo

terracota *s.* arcilla cocida al fuego

terrazas *s.* plataformas de estepa construidas en la ladera de una montaña

terrorismo *s.* uso de violencia contra los ciudadanos para alcanzar objetivos políticos

tetrarquía *s.* sistema de gobierno de cuatro emperadores

tierras altas *s.* terrenos que están sobre el mar

tierras bajas *s.* tipo de terrenos nivelados de poca altura

tipos móviles *s.* tablas de arcilla individuales que podían organizarse sobre un tablero para formar un texto

tirano *s.* en las ciudades-estado de la Antigua Grecia, gobernante que obtenía el poder de forma ilegal

tolerancia *s.* respeto por las creencias y las prácticas de otros

totalitario *adj.* que tiene control absoluto de todos los aspectos de la vida pública y privada

tótem *s.* tronco de árbol alto y elaboradamente tallado y pintado, común en las culturas nativas de la costa noroeste

trabajador especializado *s.* persona que realiza un trabajo que no está relacionado con la agricultura, como en la metalurgia o en la producción de herramientas

tradición oral *s.* transmisión verbal de historias y relatos de una generación a la siguiente

tragedia *s.* obra de teatro griega con un formato serio en que los personajes sufren antes de enfrentar un final triste

transahariano *adj.* que va a través del Sahara

tregua *s.* acuerdo para detener un conflicto

tribu *s.* unidad familiar extendida

tribuno *s.* representante que luchó para proteger los derechos de los ciudadanos comunes en la Antigua Roma

tributo *s.* impuesto pagado o bienes y servicios proporcionados a cambio de protección

trirreme *s.* antigua nave de guerra griega

U

U-boat *s.* submarino alemán usado en la Primera y Segunda Guerra Mundial

urbanización *s.* crecimiento de las ciudades

V

vasallo *s.* persona, usualmente un hombre noble menor, que recibía tierras y protección de un señor feudal a cambio de obediencia y servicio

vernáculo *s.* idioma nativo de una persona

vetar *v.* rechazar una decisión o propuesta hecha por otro cuerpo gubernamental

vigilancia *s.* acto de poner atención directa a una persona o a un grupo

viruela *s.* virus mortal que causa una fiebre alta y ampollas pequeñas en la piel

visir *s.* oficial jefe en el Antiguo Egipto que realizaba la mayor parte del trabajo de gobernar cotidiano

voto femenino *s.* derecho de la mujer a votar y participar en la política

W

wigwam *s.* tipo de choza con techo en forma de cúpula usada como vivienda por los indígenas algonquinos de América del Norte

xilografía *s.* imagen tallada en un bloque de madera

Y

yoga *s.* serie de posturas y ejercicios de respiración

Z

zigurat *s.* templo con forma de pirámide en las ciudades-estado de Sumeria

abandonar *v.* dejar atrás y nunca más regresar a ese lugar (pág. 772)

absoluto *adj.* completo (pág. 360)

ambicioso *adj.* que desea la fama o el éxito (pág. 530)

asegurar *v.* garantizar algo (pág. 386)

avanzar *v.* moverse hacia adelante (pág. 238)

beneficiar *v.* ayudar a alguien o a algo (pág. 677)

capacidad *s.* habilidad de hacer algo (pág. 15)

civil *adj.* perteneciente al público en general, opuesto a la milicia (pág. 762)

coexistir *v.* vivir en paz en conjunto (pág. 440)

colisionar *v.* chocar (pág. 145)

comercio *s.* compra y venta de bienes y servicios (pág. 282)

comprometerse *v.* prometer hacer algo (pág. 306)

comunal *adj.* usado o compartido por un grupo de personas (pág. 490)

concentrar *v.* enfocarse en algo (pág. 74)

constante *adj.* que ocurre todo el tiempo (pág. 422)

creación *s.* acción de hacer algo que no existía antes (pág. 704)

crucial *adj.* extremadamente importante o necesario (pág. 390)

década *s.* período de diez años (pág. 794)

decaer *v.* empeorar en términos de condición o de calidad (pág. 434)

designar *v.* dar a alguien un trabajo o responsabilidad determinado (pág. 354)

destituir *v.* remover a alguien del poder (pág. 573)

determinación *s.* cualidad que hace que alguien continúe intentando realizar una labor difícil (pág. 285)

distintivo *adj.* notoriamente diferente o único (pág. 496)

dominar *v.* tener poder sobre alguien o algo (pág. 112)

elaborado *adj.* hecho con mucho detalle y esfuerzo (pág. 556)

énfasis *s.* importancia adicional que se otorga a algo (pág. 380)

eterno *adj.* que existe en todo momento; que dura para siempre (pág. 150)

ético *adj.* que sigue las reglas o comportamientos aceptados (pág. 522)

florecer *v.* tener éxito (pág. 270)

fortificado *adj.* fuerte, resistente (pág. 607)

ganancia *s.* dinero que se gana al hacer negocios (pág. 416)

girar *v.* moverse o rotar alrededor de algo (pág. 664)

habilitar *v.* activar para que pueda hacerse algo (pág. 722)

influenciar *v.* afectar o cambiar alguien o algo de manera indirecta (pág. 170)

inquietud *s.* situación en la que muchas personas en un grupo o región están molestas y agitadas (pág. 732)

interaccionar *v.* hacer cosas con otros (pág. 701)

intervalo *s.* período de tiempo entre los acontecimientos (pág. 308)

intricado *adj.* que contiene muchas partes o detalles (pág. 584)

lealtad *s.* sentimiento fuerte de apoyo por alguien o algo (pág. 732)

lujoso *adj.* costoso e innecesario (pág. 434)

masivo *adj.* de tamaño extremadamente grande (pág. 808)

observación *s.* descripción escrita con base en lo observado o visto (pág. 639)

peculiar *adj.* diferente de una manera perceptible (pág. 41)

política *s.* conjunto de reglas o ideas sobre cómo deben hacerse las cosas (pág. 127)

posesión *s.* artículo o propiedad personal (pág. 181)

precisión *adj.* sin faltas ni errores (pág. 472)

preciso *s.* libre de errores (pág. 666)

predecir *v.* decir qué sucederá en el futuro (pág. 467)

privilegio *s.* derecho o beneficio que sólo reciben algunas personas (pág. 114)

promover *v.* animar (pág. 154)

próspero *adj.* exitoso, usualmente por ganar mucho dinero (pág. 209)

protesta *s.* acontecimiento en que las personas se reúnen para demostrar su descontento o desaprobación de algo (pág. 810)

radical *adj.* diferente de lo que es típico u ordinario (pág. 643)

reaciamente *adv.* con incertidumbre o dudas (pág. 245)

retener *v.* mantener o seguir teniendo (pág. 601)

salario *s.* cantidad de dinero que recibe un trabajador (pág. 221)

sobresalir *v.* ser o desempeñarse mejor que el resto (pág. 631)

socavar *v.* debilitar a alguien o a algo (pág. 566)

supervisar *v.* vigilar y monitorear algo o alguien (pág. 69)

surgir *v.* emerger o aparecer (pág. 36)

transformar *v.* cambiar dramáticamente (pág. 26)

A

B

C

D

H

I

N

O

P

Q

R

T

X

Z

A

C

D

E

F

I

ACKNOWLEDGMENTS

Text Acknowledgments

545 Li Po, "Zazen on Ching-t'ing Mountain" from Crossing the Yellow River: Three Hundred Poems from the Chinese, translated by Sam Hamill. Copyright ©2000 by Sam Hamill. Reprinted with the permission of The Permissions Company, Inc., on behalf of Tiger Bark Press, www.tigerbarkpress.com.

559 Matsuo Basho, "The Quiet Pond..." from The Classic Tradition of Haiku: An Anthology by Faubion Bowers (editor). Dover Publications, Inc., 1996. (Poem translated by Edward G. Seidensticker)

569 Shuson Kato, "I kill and Ant..." from Haiku Mind: 108 Poems to Cultivate and Open Your Heart, by Patricia Donegan, ©2008 by Patricia Donegan. Reprinted by arrangement with The Permissions Company, Inc., on behalf of Shambhala Publications Inc., Boston, MA. www.shambhala.com.

NATIONAL
GEOGRAPHIC
LEARNING

CENGAGE Learning

National Geographic Learning gratefully acknowledges the contributions of the following National Geographic Explorers and affiliates to our program:

Lynsey Addario, National Geographic Photographer
Salam Al Kuntar, National Geographic Emerging Explorer
Caroline Alexander, National Geographic Writer/Journalist
Nicole Boivin, National Geographic Grantee
Steve Boyes, National Geographic Emerging Explorer
Nina Burleigh, Journalist/Author
Michael Cosmopoulos, National Geographic Grantee
Christopher DeCorse, National Geographic Grantee
Steven Ellis, National Geographic Grantee
Francisco Estrada-Belli, National Geographic Grantee
Beverly Goodman, National Geographic Emerging Explorer
Jeff Gusky, National Geographic Photographer
Fredrik Hiebert, National Geographic Archaeology Fellow
Patrick Hunt, National Geographic Grantee
Louise Leakey, National Geographic Explorer-in-Residence
Christine Lee, National Geographic Emerging Explorer
Albert Lin, National Geographic Emerging Explorer
Jodi Magness, National Geographic Grantee
Sarah Parcak, National Geographic Fellow
Thomas Parker, National Geographic Grantee
William Parkinson, National Geographic Grantee
Matt Piscitelli, National Geographic Grantee
Jeffrey Rose, National Geographic Emerging Explorer
Max Salomon, National Geographic Producer
Aziz Abu Sarah, National Geographic Emerging Explorer
William Saturno, National Geographic Grantee
Anna Secor, National Geographic Grantee
Shah Selbe, National Geographic Emerging Explorer
Maurizio Seracini, National Geographic Fellow
Hayat Sindi, National Geographic Emerging Explorer
Christopher Thornton, National Geographic Lead Program Officer of Research, Conservation, and Exploration
Soultana Maria Valamoti, National Geographic Grantee
Juan José Valdés, National Geographic Geographer
Simon Worrall, National Geographic Writer
Xiaobai Angela Yao, National Geographic Grantee
Dave Yoder, National Geographic Grantee

Photographic Credits

COVER ©Neale Clark/Robert Harding World Imagery/Alamy i (bg) ©Neale Clark/Robert Harding World Imagery/Alamy. iii (bl) ©Winn Brewer/National Geographic Learning. (bc) ©Winn Brewer/National Geographic Learning. (br) ©Chad Cohen/National Geographic Studio. iv (bl) ©Donnelly Photography/National Geographic Learning. (bc) ©Mary Lynne Ashley Photography/National Geographic Learning. (br) ©Andrew Faulds/National Geographic Learning. v (tl) ©Jeanine Childs/National Geographic Learning. vi (tl) ©Louise A. Hitchcock. (tcl) ©Erin West Kephart/National Geographic Learning. (tcr) ©Steven Ellis. (tr) ©Kenneth Garrett/National Geographic Creative. (cl) ©Rebecca Hale/National Geographic Creative. (ccl) ©Sora Devore/National Geographic Creative. (ccr) ©Mark Thiessen/National Geographic Creative. (cr) ©Jim Haberman. (bl) ©2011 The Field Museum, Photo by John Weinstein. (bcl) ©Mark Thiessen/National Geographic Creative. (bcr) ©Mark Thiessen/National Geographic Creative. (br) ©Christopher Thornton. vii (tcr) ©Rebecca Hale/National Geographic Creative. (tl) ©George Butler. (tcl) ©Rebecca Hale/National Geographic Creative. (tr) ©Frank Wing. (cl) ©Mark Thiessen/National Geographic Creative. (ccl) ©Mark Thiessen/National Geographic Creative. (ccr) ©Mark Thiessen/National Geographic Creative. (cr) ©Mark Thiessen/National Geographic Creative. (bl) ©Rebecca Hale/National Geographic Creative. (br) ©Eric Kruszewski/National Geographic Creative. viii (tc) ©Sora DeVore/National Geographic Creative. (tcl) ©Nicole Boivin. (tcr) ©G. Vdokakis/Michael Cosmopoulos. (tr) ©Marty Perlman. (tl) ©Marcie Goodale/National Geographic Learning. (cl) ©Mark Thiessen/National Geographic Creative. (ccl) ©Grace Parker. (c) ©Matthew Piscitelli. (ccr) ©Ryan Hill/Still Life Projects. (cr) ©Brian Conners Manke Photography. (bl) ©Benjamin Grimes/National Geographic Creative. (bcl) ©Georgios-Villy Kapetanakis. (bcr) ©Adrian Sherratt. (br) ©Angelo Yao. ix (t) ©Nigel Pavitt/JWL/Aurora Photos. x (t) ©Kenneth Garrett/National Geographic Creative. xii (t) ©Herbert Esser/Panther Media/age footstock. xiii (t) ©Roger Ressmeyer/Corbis. xiv (t) ©Jim Haberman. xv (t) ©Scott Carr/500Prime. xvi (t) ©Kenneth Garret/National Geographic Creative. xvii (t) ©Hakbong Kwon/Alamy. xviii (t) ©Terence Kong/500Prime. xix (t) ©Sergey Semenov/AirPano.com. xx (t) ©NASA Earth Observatory image by Robert Simmon, using Suomi NPP VIIRS data provided courtesy of Chris Elvidge (NOAA National Geophysical Data Center). xxi (tl) ©Stringer/REUTERS. (tcl) ©Molhem Barakat/REUTERS. (cl) ©Frederik Hiebert. (bcl) ©Shah Selbe. (bl) ©2014 Holly Moses Edward/National Geographic Photo Camp South Sudan. xxii (cl) ©Jonathan Torgovnik/Contour by Getty Images. xxiii (cr) ©Murat Taner/Corbis. (cl) ©Erik S. Lesser/epa/Corbis. xxv (cr) ©O. LOUIS MAZZATENTA/National Geographic Creative. xxviii (bg) ©Joe Scherschel/National Geographic Creative. (bl) ©Superstock/Getty Images. (br) ©Werner Forman/Art Resource, NY. 1 (tl) ©Winn Brewer/National Geogrpahic Learning. (bl) ©Fredrik Hiebert. 2 (bg) ©Sisse Brimberg/National Geographic Creative. (cl) ©Sora DeVore/National Geographic Creative. (c) ©William Saturno. (cr) ©G. Vdokakis/Michael Cosmopoulos. 3 (tr) ©Steven Ellis. (cl) ©Sarah Parcak. 4 (bg) ©Nigel Pavitt/JWL/Aurora Photos. 5 (tr) ©Kenneth Garrett/National Geographic Creative. 6 (tr) ©Raul Martin/National Geographic Creative. (tl) ©Keenpress/National Geographic Creative. (b) ©Berthold Steinhilber/laif/Redux. 7 (bc) ©Metta image/Alamy. (tl) ©Erich Lessing/Art Resource, NY. (tr) ©O. Lewis Mazzatenta/National Geographic Creative. 8 (tc) ©Wildnerdpix/iStock/Getty Images. (tr) ©LuismiX/MomentOpen/Getty Images. 9 (tr) ©Ronald Naar/ANP Photo/age footstock. (tc) ©Catalin Petolea/Alamy. (tl) ©Gertjan Hooijer/Shutterstock. 10 ©Paule Seux/Latitude/Corbis. 13 ©Wil Matthews/500Prime. 14 ©Enguang Zhu/TAO Images Limited/Alamy. 16 ©Joel Sartore/National Geographic Creative. 16 (cll) ©Bridgeman-Giraudon/Art Resource, NY. (clr) ©Erich Lessing/Art Resource, NY. 20 ©National Geographic Studios. 23 ©Paul Franklin/World Illustrated/Photoshot . 25 ©Alexander Maleev/National Geographic. 26 ©Matthieu paley/National Geographic Creative. 28 ©Gianni Dagli Orti /The Art Archive at Art Resource, NY. 31 (bg) ©Album/Prisma/Newscom. (tr) ©The Trustees of the British Museum/Art Resource, NY. (cr) ©Album/Art Resource, NY.

(br) ©Album/Art Resource, NY. 33 (bl) ©C M Dixon/AAA Collection/Ancient Art & Architecture Collection Ltd/ Alamy. (t) ©Paule Seux/Latitude/Corbis. 34 ©Dmitry Ovcharov/500Prime. 41 (t) ©Aldo Pavan/Terra/Corbis. (br) ©De Agostini Picture Library/akg-images. 43 ©Nicolle Rager Fuller, National Science Foundation. 44 ©Guido Alberto Rossi/AGE Fotostock. 47 ©Vincent J. Musi/National Geographic Society/Corbis. 49 (cl) ©Kenneth Garrett/ National Geographic Creative. (b) ©Balage Balogh /Art Resource, NY. (tr) ©DeA Picture Library/Art Resource, NY. (cr) ©Louvre, Paris, France/Bridgeman Images. (tl) ©Manuel Cohen/The Art Archive at Art Resource, NY. 50 (br) ©PjrStudio/Alamy. (tr) ©Vanni Archive/Art Resource, NY. (t) ©CDA/Guillemot/akg-images. (cr) ©Gianni Dagli Orti/The Art Archive at Art Resource, NY. (cr) ©Erich Lessing/Art Resource, NY. (b) ©Dagli Orti/De Agostini/Getty Images. 51 (c) ©Nathan Benn/Encyclopedia/Corbis. (bc) ©Phil Cawley/ Alamy. (b) ©Erich Lessing/Art Resource, NY. (tl) ©Z. Radovan/Bible Land Pictures/akg-images. (tr) ©Kenneth Garrett/National Geographic Creative. (c) ©Nathan Benn/ Ottochrome/Corbis. (bcr) ©The Metropolitan Museum of Art/ Art Resource, NY. (br) ©Alfredo Dagli Orti/The Art Archive at Art Resource, NY. 53 (bl) ©Nathan Benn/ Ottochrome/Corbis. (t) ©Dmitry Ovcharov/500Prime. 54 (bg) ©Kenneth Garrett/National Geographic Creative. 55 (tr) ©Kenneth Garrett/National Geographic Creative. 56 (t) ©Jim Richardson/National Geographic Creative. 58 (bg) ©Kenneth Garrett/National Geographic Creative. 59 (tr) ©Christopher Thornton. 60 (bc) ©François Guenet/Art Resource, NY. (tl) ©The Trustees of the British Museum/Art Resource, NY. (tr) ©Bridgeman Images. 61 (tr) ©Dinodia Photo/age footstock. (br) Digital Image © 2014 Museum Associates/LACMA. Licensed by Art Resource, NY. (tl) ©Fitzwilliam Museum, Cambridge/Art Resource, NY. 62 (bl) ©Bilderbuch/Design Pics/Corbis. (br) ©Catherine Leblanc/ Godong/Corbis. (tr) ©Ruggero Vanni/Corbis. 63 (bl) ©Lindsay Hebberd/Corbis. (tr) ©Aaron Geddes Photography/ Moment/Getty Images. 64 ©Iain Masterton/Photographer's Choice RF/Getty Images. 70 ©Gianni Dagli Orti/Fine Art/ Corbis. 71 ©FranÃ§ois GuÃ/©net/akg-images. 72 ©Mary Evans Picture Library/The Image Works. 73 ©Bible Land Pictures/Zev Radovan/B/akg-images. 75 ©Scala/Art Resource, NY. 77 ©DeAgostini/Getty Images. 79 ©GraphicaArtis/Fine Art/Corbis. 83 ©James P. Blair/ National Geographic Society. 85 (bc) ©Andy Crawford/ Dorling Kindersley. (c) ©Tono Balaguer/easyFotostock/Age Fotostock. (tr) ©Photograph courtesy of Dr. Timothy Matney, Ziyaret Tepe Archaeological Expedition.. (tl) ©Alex Segre/ Alamy. (cr) ©Imanhakim/Shutterstock.com. (tr) ©Gianni Dagli Orti /The Art Archive at Art Resource, NY. (bl) ©Dan Barnes/ Vetta/Getty Images. (tc) ©Blackbirds/Age Fotostock. 87 ©Iain Masterton/Photographer's Choice RF/Getty Images. 88 ©Dorothea Schmid/laif/Redux. 90 ©ImageBroker/Alamy. 95 ©Prisma/SuperStock. 96 Courtesy of Sarah Parcak. 97 ©AP Images/Space Imaging. 98 ©Sami Sarkis/Photolibrary/ Getty Images. 101 ©De Agostini Picture Library/G. Dagli Orti/Bridgeman Images. 102 ©Scala/Art Resource, NY. 103 ©Gianni Dagli Orti/The Art Archive at Art Resource, NY. 105 ©Alfredo Dagli Orti/Fine Art/Corbis. 106 ©Kenneth Garrett/National Geographic Creative. 108 (tr) ©De Agostini Picture Library/A. Vergani/Bridgeman Images. (t) ©O. Louis Mazzatenta/National Geographic Creative. (bl) ©O. Loius Mazzatenta/National Geographic Creative. 110 (tl)©Kenneth Garrett/National Geographic Creative. (br) ©CULTNAT, Dist. RMN-GP/Art Resource, NY. (cr) ©FranÃ§ois Guenet/ Art Resource, NY. (tr) ©Bpk, Berlin/Art Resource, NY. 111 (bl) ©FranÃ§ois Guenet/Art Resource, NY. (cl) ©DeAgostini/ SuperStock. (tl) ©FranÃ§ois Guenet/Art Resource, NY. (br) ©DeAgostini/SuperStock. (cr) ©FranÃ§ois Guenet/Art Resource, NY. (tcr) ©CULTNAT, Dist. RMN-GP/Art Resource, NY. (tr) ©FranÃ§ois Guenet/Art Resource, NY. 113 ©Kenneth Garrett/National Geographic Creative. 114 ©Gianni Dagli Orti/The Art Archive at Art Resource, NY. 116 ©The Trustees of the British Museum/Art Resource, NY. 117 ©O. Loius Mazzatenta/National Geographic Creative. 118 ©DEA/G Dagli Orti/De Agostini Editore/Age Fotostock. 121 ©Dorothea Schmid/laif/Redux. 122 ©Duby Tal/ Albatross Aerial Perspective (Duby Tal)/AGE Fotostock. 125 ©De Agostini Picture Library/G. Nimatallah/Bridgeman Images. 126 (t) ©Hanan Isachar/Superstock. (cl) ©Colin Underhill/Alamy. 129 ©Grotesques, illustration from the Jewish Cervera Bible, 1299 (vellum), Asarfati, Joseph (fl.1299)/Instituto da Biblioteca Nacional, Lisbon, Portugal/ Bridgeman Images. 130 ©cala/Ministero per i Beni e le AttivitÃ culturali/Art Resource, NY. 131 ©The Israel Museum, Jerusalem, Israel/Shrine of the Book/ Photo ©The Israel Museum, by Ardon Bar Hama/Bridgeman Images. 133 ©2008 by Crossway Bibles, a publishing ministry of Good News Publishers. Used by permission. All rights reserved. 134 ©Boris Diakovsky/Alamy. 137 ©BrAt82/Shutterstock.com. 138 ©Beverly Goodman. 139© Duby Tal/Albatross Aerial Perspective (Duby Tal)/AGE Fotostock. 141 (cr) ©Bettmann/Corbis. (t) ©Duby Tal/Albatross Aerial Perspective (Duby Tal)/AGE Fotostock. 142 ©Danish Siddiqui/Reuters. 147 ©Ursula Gahwiler/Robert Harding Picture Library Ltd/Alamy. 148 ©De Agostini Picture Library /A. Dagli Orti/Bridgeman Images. 149 (tl) ©Schoyen Collection. (t) ©Schoyen Collection. (tcl) ©Schoyen Collection. 151 (bl) © The Metropolitan Museum of Art. Image source: Art Resource, NY. (bc) ©V&A Images, London/ Art Resource, NY. (br) © Smart-foto/Shutterstock.com. (t) ©Vivek Prakash/Reuters. 152 ©Helene Rogers/Art Directors & Trips Photo/Age Fotostock. 154 ©Sanjeev Gupta/epa/ Corbis Wire/Corbis. 157 ©Dinodia/Dinodia Photo/Age Fotostock. 158 ©Moustafellou/IML/ Icarus/Age Fotostock. 161 (tl) ©Dinodia Photos/Hulton Archive/Getty Images. (cr) ©Leigh Prather/Shutterstock.com. (cl) ©Hero/Fancy/Age Fotostock. (tr) ©Rhimage/Shutterstock.com. 163 ©Danish Siddiqui/Reuters. 164 ©Xinhua/eyevine/Redux. 169 ©Roman Sigaev/ShutterStock.com. 170 ©Philip Lange/ Panther Media/AGE Fotostock. 172 ©China Photos/Getty Images News/Getty Images. 174 (tr) ©The Art Archive/ British Library. (tcr) ©Pure Rendereing Gmbh/National Geographic Creative. 176 ©Dave Porter Peterborough Uk/ Photolibrary/Getty Images. 178 ©O. Louis Mazzatenta/ National Geographic Image Creative. 179 ©O. Louis Mazzatenta/National Geographic Image Creative. 182 (c) ©Yi Lu/Viewstock/Collage/Corbis. (bl) ©Stockbyte/Getty Images. (bc) ©Smithsonian Institution, National Air and Space Museum. (br) ©Jeff Metzger/ShutterStock.com. 187 ©Adstock/UIG/age fotostock. 188 (b) ©bakelyt/age fotostock. (t) ©Private Collection/Art Resource, NY. (cr) ©Steshkin Yevgeniy11/ShutterStock.com. (br) ©Erich Lessing / Art Resource, NY. 189 (bl) ©photosindia/Getty Images. (cr) ©Hanyang University Museum, South Korea/Bridgeman Images. (tr) ©Senol Yaman/ShutterStock.com. 190 ©Danita Delimont/Alamy. 191 ©Leonid Bogdanov/Superstock. 193 (bl) ©DEA/E.Lessing/De Agostini Picture Library/Getty Images. (t) ©Xinhu/eyevine/Redux. 194 (bg) ©Christopher Thornton. 195 (tr) ©Christopher Thornton. 196 (t) ©Zhao jian kang/Shutterstock.com. 198 (bg) ©Joe Scherschel/ National Geographic Creative. (tr) ©Winn Brewer/National Geogrpahic Learning. (bl) ©Herbert Esser/Panther Media/ age footstock. (br) ©Jim Haberman. (bc) ©Roger Ressmeyer/ Corbis. 199 (bl) ©Scott Carr/500Prime. (bc) ©Kenneth Garret/National Geographic Creative. 200 (bg) ©Herbert Esser/Panther Media/age footstock. 201 (tr) ©William Parkinson. 202 (bc) ©Werner Forman/UIG/age footstock. (tr) ©Hercules Milas/Alamy. (tl) ©Werner Forman Archive/ Bridgeman Images. 203 (tl) ©Ashmolean Museum, University of Oxford, UK/Bridgeman Images. (bl) ©Zhang Shui Cheng/Bridgeman Images. (tr) ©Hoberman/UIG/ Bridgeman Images. 206 ©Vasilis Protopapas. 209 ©National Archaeological Museum, Athens, Greece/Bridgeman Images. 211 ©De Agostini Picture Library/Bridgeman Images. 213 ©Bettmann/Corbis. 214 ©J.D. Dallet/Age Fotostock. 217 ©Akg-images/De Agostini Picture Lib./A. De Gregorio. 218 ©The Trustees of the British Museum/Art Resource, NY. 219 © Anastasios71/Shutterstock.com. 220 (tc) ©Erich Lessing/Art Resource, NY. (cl) ©Erich Lessing/Art Resource, NY. (tr) ©Alinari / Art Resource, NY. (br) ©Scala/ Art Resource, NY. (bl) ©Ashmolean Museum/The Art Archive at Art Resource, NY. (tl) ©Leemage/Universal Images Group/Getty Images. 224 ©Warner Bros/Legendary

Pictures/The Kobal Collection/Picture Desk. 227 ©Vasilis Protopapas. 228 ©Hercules Milas/Alamy. 230 ©John Hios/ akg-images. 231 ©De Agostini Picture Library/G. Nimatallah/akg-images. 235 ©Mary Evans Picture Library / Alamy. 237 (bc) ©Orestis Panagiotou/EPA/Newscom. (bl) ©Yiorgos Karahalis/Reuters /Landov. 239 ©Howard David Johnson. 240 ©Phillipp von Foltz/akg-images. 241 ©Gianni Dagli Orti / The Art Archive at Art Resource, NY. 243 ©Erich Lessing/Art Resource, NY. 244 (tr) ©Dea/G. Dagli Orti/De Agostini Picture Library/Getty Images. 246 ©Dea/G. Dagli Orti/De Agostini/Getty Images. 249 ©Fine Art Images/ Age Fotostock. 250 (t) ©Antonino Bartuccio/Grand Tour/ Terra/Corbis. (cl) ©Dea/G. Dagli Orti/De Agostini Picture Library/Getty Images. 251 ©mart/Shutterstock.com. 252 ©Stelios Kritikakis/500px. 255 ©Lucas Jackson/Reuters. 257 ©Hercules Milas/Alamy. 258 (bg) ©William Parkinson. 259 (tr) ©William Parkinson. 260 (t) ©Thanassis Stavrakis/AP Images. 262 (bg) ©Roger Ressmeyer/Corbis. (t) ©James L. Stanfield/National Geographic Image Collection. 263 (tr) ©Steven Ellis. 264 (tr) ©Atlantide Phototravel/Corbis. (tl) ©Universal Images Group/Getty Images. (br) ©G. Dagli Orti/ De Agostini Picture Library/Getty Images. 265 (tl) ©The Trustees of the British Museum/Art Resource, NY. (b) ©Jean-Pierre Lescourret/Corbis. (tr) ©Bridgeman Images. 266 (tr) ©Stephan Goerlich/imageBROKER/agefotostock. 267 (tr) ©DEA/G DAGLI ORTI/De Agostini Editore/agefotostock. (tl) ©Ivern Photo/agefotostock. (br) ©Robert Clark/National Geographic Creative. 268 (bg) ©Ruggero Vanni/ Encyclopedia/Corbis. (cl) ©Cephas Picture Library/Alamy. 269 (cr) ©Glyn Thomas Photography/Alamy. (tr) ©Bettmann/ Corbis. 270 ©Tantoon Studio/istock/Getty Images Plus/Getty Images. 272 (tl) ©Mystockicons/Digital Vision Vectors/Getty Images. (t) ©Gaertner/Alamy. 274 ©Tantoon Studio/istock/ Getty Images Plus/Getty Images. 275 ©Ancient Art and Architecture Collection Ltd. / The Bridgeman Art Library. 276 ©Caroline Seidel/dpa/Corbis Wire/Corbis. 278 ©Tantoon Studio/istock/Getty Images Plus/Getty Images. 279 ©James L. Stanfield/National Geographic Image Creative. 280 ©Mystockicons/Digital Vision Vectors/Getty Images. 281 ©Peter Connolly/akg-images. 282 ©Mystockicons/Digital Vision Vectors/Getty Images. 283 ©James Hardy/PhotoAlto/ Corbis. 284 ©Bogdan Cristel/X00337/Reuters/Corbis. 285 ©Taylor S. Kennedy/National Geographic Society/Corbis. 286 ©Gary Ombler/Dorling Kindersley. ©Gary Ombler/ Dorling Kindersley. 287 (t) ©Gary Ombler/Dorling Kindersley. (tcl) ©Gary Ombler/Dorling Kindersley. (cl) ©Gary Ombler/Dorling Kindersley. (c) ©Gary Ombler/ Dorling Kindersley. (cr) ©Dorling Kindersley. (tl) ©Gary Ombler/DK Images. (tr) ©Gary Ombler/Dorling Kindersley. 288 (cl)©Mystockicons/Digital Vision Vectors/Getty Images. (t)©Bridgeman-Giraudon/Art Resource, NY. 290 ©Patrick Hunt. 292 (tl) ©Mystockicons/Digital Vision Vectors/Getty Images. (cl) ©Bettmann/Corbis. 295 ©akg-images. 296 (tr) ©Murat Taner/Comet/Corbis. (bg) ©Photos 12/Alamy. (cl) ©Louvre, Paris, France/Bridgeman Images. 298 ©Fine Art Premium/Corbis. 299 ©The Trustees of the British Museum / Art Resource, NY. 300 ©De Agostini Picture Library/L. Romano/Bridgeman Images. 303 ©Ruggero Vanni/ Encyclopedia/Corbis. 304 ©Image Source/Aurora Photos. 307 ©Araldo de Luca/Fine Art/Corbis. 311 ©Hans Madej/ Gruppe28/Aurora Photos. 312 (b) ©USA-TV/Kristy Griffen/ The Kobal Collection/Picture Desk. (tl) ©Mystockicons/ Digital Vision Vectors/Getty Images. 314 (tl) ©Tantoon Studio/istock/Getty Images Plus/Getty Images. (t) ©Marc Dozier/Latitude/Corbis. 316 ©Roger Ressmeyer/Eureka Premium/Corbis. 318 ©Tantoon Studio/istock/Getty Images Plus/Getty Images. 319 ©Scala/Ministero per i Beni e le AttivitÃ culturali/Art Resource, NY. 322 ©Alfredo Dagli Orti/The Art Archive at Art Resource, NY. 323 ©Album/ Prisma/Album. 324 (tl) ©Tantoon Studio/istock/Getty Images Plus/Getty Images. (cl) ©Image Source/Corbis. (t) ©Michele Falzone/Alloy/Corbis. 325 ©Gallery with Loculus Tombs (fresco)./Catacombs of Priscilla, Rome, Italy/ Bridgeman Images. 326 ©Tantoon Studio/istock/Getty Images Plus/Getty Images. 327 (bl) ©Dea/G. Dagli Orti/De Agostini/Getty Images. (br) ©akg-images. (tr) ©Dea/G. Dagli Orti/De Agostini Picture Library/Getty Images. (tl) ©Stefano Bianchetti/Fine Art/Corbis. 330 ©Private Collection/Look and Learn/Bridgeman Images. 331 ©Tantoon Studio/istock/ Getty Images Plus/Getty Images. 332 ©Tantoon Studio/ istock/Getty Images Plus/Getty Images. 333 (tr) © Ensuper/ Shutterstock.com. (cl) © Ifong/Shutterstock.com. (br) ©Zoonar/A Maltsev/Age Fotostock. 334 (tl) ©Tantoon Studio/istock/Getty Images Plus/Getty Images. (t) ©Araldo de Luca/Corbis art/Corbis. 336 ©Guido Baviera/Terra/ Corbis. 339 ©Image Source / Aurora Photos. 340 (bg) ©Steven Ellis. 341 (tr) ©Steven Ellis. 342 (t) ©Sam Weber/ National Geographic Creative. 344 (bg) ©Jim Haberman. 345 (tr) ©Jim Haberman. 346 (tl) ©Ghigo Roli/Alinari/Alinari Archives/Getty Images. (br) ©Werner Forman/Universal Images Group/Getty Images. (tl) ©Pictures From History/ Bridgeman Images. (bl) ©Freer Gallery of Art, Smithsonian Institution/Bridgeman Images. 347 (tl) ©Rolf Richardson/ Alamy. (br) ©Eric SA House - Carle/SuperStock/Getty Images. (tr) ©Rudolf Tepfenhart/Shutterstock. 348 (br) ©Christie's Images Ltd/Corbis. 349 (bl) ©Laurie Chamberlain/Corbis. (br) ©Corbis. 350 ©Rabouan Jean-Baptiste/Latitude/Corbis. 355 ©Erich Lessing/Art Resource, NY. 356 ©Michele Burgess/Alamy. 361 © The Metropolitan Museum of Art. Image source: Art Resource, NY. 362 ©AGF Srl/Alamy. 363 (c) ©Gina Martin/National Geographic Creative. (tr) ©Erich Lessing/Art Resource, NY. (br) ©Cubo Images/Superstock. (tc) ©Dagli Orti/The Art Archive/ Picture Desk. (bc) ©James L. Stanfield/National Geographic Creative. 365 ©SuperStock. 367 ©Rabouan Jean-Baptiste/ Latitude/Corbis. 368 ©Tino Soriano/National Geographic Learning. 371 ©Jon Bower/Loop Images/Terra/Corbis. 372 ©The Thorburn Group/National Geographic Learning. 373 ©Kazuyoshi Nomachi/Latitude/Corbis. 374 ©The Thorburn Group/National Geographic Learning. 375 ©Bruno Zanzottera/Parallelozero/Aurora Photos. 376 ©Roland and Sabrina Michaud/Akg-Images. 378 ©Suhaib Salem SJS/GB/ Reuters. 381 ©Roland and Sabrina Michaud/Akg-Images. 382 ©Jose Antonio Moreno/Age Fotostock. 384 ©Sylvain Grandadam/Age Fotostock. 386 ©UniversalImagesGroup/ Getty Images. 389 ©Ivan Vdovin/Age Fotostock. 391 ©Sheila Terry/Science Source. 392 ©Jonathan Torgovnik/Contour by Getty Images/Getty Images. 393 ©Todd Heisler/The New York Times/Redux. 395 ©Glenn Beanland/Lonely Planet Images/Getty Images. 396 (b) ©Dea/G.Dagli Orti/De Agostini Picture Library/Getty Images. (t) ©The Metropolitan Museum of Art/Art Resource, NY. 397 (br) ©Bonhams, London, UK/Bridgeman Images. (tr) ©RMN-Grand Palais/ Art Resource, NY. (cr) ©bpk, Berlin/Museum fuer Islamische Kunst/Staatliche Museen/German/Art Resource, NY. (c) ©Michael Weber/Image Broker/Alamy. 399 ©Tino Soriano/National Geographic Learning. 400 (bg) ©Jim Haberman. 401 (tr) ©Jim Haberman. 402 (t) ©Michael Melford/National Geographic Creative. 404 (bg) ©Scott Carr/500Prime. 405 (tr) ©Christopher DeCorse. 406 (tr) ©Douglas Pearson/The Image Bank/Getty Images. (br) ©Universal History Archive/Universal Images Group/Getty Images. (tl) ©akg-images/De Agostini Picture Lib./G. Dagli Orti. 407 (bc) ©bpk, Berlin/Muenzkabinett, Staatliche Museen/Art Resource, NY. (tr) ©Bridgeman-Giraudon/Art Resource, NY. (tl) ©Ulrich Doering/Alamy. 408 (bl) ©Hoberman Collection/Corbis. (br) ©Bill Stormont/Corbis. 410 ©Joe Penney/Reuters. 413 ©Frans Lemmens/The Image Bank/Getty Images. 415 ©Fadel Senna/Getty Images. 416 ©Johnny Haglund/Lonely Planet Images/Getty Images. 418 ©Pictures From History/Bridgeman Images. 419 ©Ivern Photo/Age Fotostock. 420 (cr) ©Cleveland Museum of Art, OH, USA/Andrew R. and Martha Holden Jennings Fund/ Bridgeman Images. (br) ©Andrea Jemolo/akg-images. (bl) ©Andrea Jemolo/akg-images. (cl) ©Werner Forman/ akg-images. (tr) ©CDA/Guillemot/akg-images. 427 (c) ©Daniel Lain/Cosmos/Redux. (bl) ©F. Jimenez Meca/ Shutterstock.com. (br) ©Collection of the Lowe Art Museum, University of Miami/Gift of Professor and Mrs. Robert R. Ferens/Bridgeman Images. (bc) ©Fortune Fish/ Alamy. 428 ©Bibliotheque Nationale de France/National Geographic Creative. 429 ©Bibliotheque Nationale, Paris, France/Bridgeman Images. 431 ©Joe Penney/Reuters. 432 ©Jorgen Schytte/StillPictures/Aurora Photos. 434 ©Werner

Forman/Universal Images Group/Getty Images. 435 ©David Else/Getty Images. 437 ©John Warburton-Lee/ DanitaDelimont.com. 439 ©John Warburton Lee/SuperStock. 442 ©Stefano Gulmanelli/Marka/Age Fotostock. 443 ©Simon Colmer/Alamy. 444 ©DEA PICTURE LIBRARY/ Getty Images. 447 (cr) ©Gavin Hellier/AWL Images Ltd. (t) ©Jorgen Schytte/StillPictures/Aurora Photos. 448 (bg) ©Christopher DeCorse. 449 (tr) ©Christopher DeCorse. 450 (t) ©Jordi Cami/Cover/Getty Images. 452 (bg) ©Kenneth Garret/National Geographic Creative. 453 (tr) ©Kenneth Garrett/National Geographic Creative. 454 (br) ©APIC/Getty Images. (tr) ©Album/Art Resource, NY. 455 (tl) ©Michel Zabe/AZA/INAH/Bridgeman Images. (b) ©Andrea Fremiotti/Gallery Stock/Galeries/Corbis. (tr) ©Gonzalo Azumendi/age footstock. 458 ©Simon Norfolk/Institute. 462 ©Werner Forman/Universal Images Group/Getty Images. 463 ©Kenneth Garrett. 464 ©Gianni Dagli Orti/The Art Archive/Art Resource, NY. 467 ©The Trustees of the British Museum/Art Resource, NY. 470 ©Tyrone Turner/EPA/ Alamy. 471 ©Kenneth Garrett/National Geographic Creative. 472 ©Egmont Strigl/imagebroker/Age Fotostock. 474 ©Ethnologisches Museum, Staatliche Museen, Berlin, Germany/Art Resource, NY. 477 ©Universal History Archive/UIG/The Bridgeman Art Library. 478 ©Kenneth Garret/National Geographic Creative. 479 ©Gianni Dagli Orti/The Art Archive/Art Resource, NY. 481 ©Palazzo Pitti, Florence, Italy / Bridgeman Images. 483 (tr) ©Rahmo/ Shutterstock.com. (tl) ©f9photos/Shutterstock.com. (bl) ©Werner Forman/Universal Images Group/Getty Images. (t) ©Simon Norfolk/Institute. 484 ©Kenneth Garrett/National Geographic Society/Museos del Banco Central de Costa Rica. 487 ©Robert Clark/National Geographic. 488 (br) ©Museo Larco, Lima Peru. (tl) ©Kenneth Garrett/National Geographic Society/Museos del Banco Central de Costa Rica. 489 (br) ©Kenneth Garrett/National Geographic Society/Museos del Banco Central de Costa Rica. (t) ©Y. Yoshii/PAS. 492 ©Image Source/Getty Images. (bl) Kenneth Garrett/National Geographic Learning. 494 ©Mireille Vautier / Alamy. 497 ©Stuart Dee/Getty Images. 499 (b) ©Jason Langley/AGE Fotostock. (t) ©Richard A. Cooke/ Encyclopedia/Corbis. 501 ©Joel Sartore/National Geographic Creative. 503 (br) ©Ira Block/National Geographic Creative. (t) ©Wood Ronsaville Harlin Inc/ National Geographic Creative. 505 ©CharlineXia Ontario Canada Collection / Alamy. 507 (t) ©Kenneth Garrett/ National Geographic Society/Museos del Banco Central de Costa Rica. (c) ©Mike Theiss/National Geographic. 508 (bg) ©Bruce Smith. 509 (tr) ©Kenneth Garrett/National Geographic Creative. 510 (t) ©Kenneth Garrett/National Geographic Creative. 512 (tr) ©Winn Brewer/National Geographic Learning. (bl) ©Hakbong Kwon/Alamy. (br) ©Terence Kong/500Prime. 513 (bg) ©David Santiago Garcia/ Aurora Photos. 514 (bg) ©Hakbong Kwon/Alamy. 515 (tr) ©Erik Jepsen. 516 (br) ©Fine Art Images/Heritage Images/ Getty Images. (cl) ©akg-images/British Library. (tr) ©DeA Picture Library/Art Resource, NY. 517 (tl) ©akg-images/ Rabatti – Domingie. (b) ©INTERFOTO/Alamy. 518 (bl) ©Werner Forman/Universal Images Group/Getty Images. (br) ©Seattle Art Museum/Corbis. 520 ©Sean Pavone/Alamy. 525 ©Vidler Steve/Travelpix/Age Fotostock. 527 ©Private Collection/Paul Freeman/Bridgeman Images. 529 (bl) ©Science Source. (tr) ©RMN-Grand Palais/Art Resource, NY. (tl) ©Hjschneider/Shutterstock.com. (br) ©iBird/ Shutterstock.com. 530 ©GL Archive/Alamy. 533 ©Robert Harding Picture Library/SuperStock. 534 ©Dea/J e Bulloz/ AGE Fotostock. 535 ©Erik S. Lesser/epa/Corbis Wire/Corbis. 542 ©O. Louis Mazzatenta/National Geographic Creative. 543 ©Courtesy of Christine Lee. 545 (c) ©Ma Xiaoliang/TAO Images Limited/Alamy. (t) ©Sean Pavone/Alamy. 546 ©Masterfile. 550 ©Deco/Alamy. 552 ©Vanni Archive/Art Resource, NY. 555 ©Kazuhiro Nogi/Staff/Getty Images. 556 ©rodho/Shutterstock.com. 557 ©Quim Llenas/Cover/Getty Images. 558 ©Private Collection/Bridgeman Images. 561 ©Catherine Karnow/Corbis. 562 (t) ©Asian Art & Archaeology, Inc./Corbis. (cl) ©Warner Brothers/Everett Collection. 564 ©The Ann & Gabriel Barbier-Mueller Museum: The Samurai Collection, Dallas, Texas. Photograph by Brad Flowers. 565 ©The Ann & Gabriel Barbier-Mueller Museum: The Samurai Collection, Dallas, Texas. Photograph by Brad Flowers. 567 ©Newark Museum/Art Resource, NY. 569 ©Masterfile. 570 ©Topic Photo Agency In/Topic Photo Agency/AGE Fotostock. 574 (tc) ©DeA Picture Library/Art Resource, NY. (cr) ©The Metropolitan Museum of Art. Image source/Art Resource, NY. (c) ©De Agostini Picture Library/ Bridgeman Images. (br) ©Erich Lessing/Art Resource, NY. 575 (tr) ©DeA Picture Library/Art Resource, NY. (cl) ©DeAgostini/Superstock. (b) ©De Agostini Picture Library/ Bridgeman Images. (tl) ©De Agostini Picture Library/ Bridgeman Images. 577 ©De Agostini Picture Library/G. Dagli Orti/Bridgeman Images. 578 ©Eye Ubiquitous/Eye Ubiquitous/Superstock. 583 ©BODY Philippe/hemis.fr/ Getty Images. 584 ©W.E. Garrett/National Geographic Creative. 587 © Topic Photo Agency In/Topic Photo Agency/ AGE Fotostock. 588 (bg) ©Ben Horton. 589 (tr) ©Erik Jepsen. 590 (t) ©Robert Clark/National Geographic Creative. 592 (bg) ©Terence Kong/500Prime. 593 (tr) ©Rocco Rorandelli/ TerraProject/contrasto/Redux. 594 (tr) ©A.Dagli Orti/DEA/ De Agostini/Getty Images. (bc) ©Ronaldo Schemidt/AFP/ Getty Images. (tl) ©Gianni Dagli Orti/Corbis. 595 (tl) ©Science & Society Picture Library/SSPL/Getty Images. (tr) ©akg-images. (b) ©JTB Photo/JTB Media Creation/Alamy. 596 (bc) ©Universal History Archive/Universal Images Group/Getty Images. (br) ©National Gallery, London/Art Resource, NY. 597 (br) ©G. Nimatallah/De Agostini Picture Library/Getty Images. (bl) ©Scala/Ministero per i Beni e le Attività culturali/Art Resource, NY. (bc) © The Metropolitan Museum of Art. Image source: Art Resource, NY. 598 ©Slawek Staszczuk/500px. 602 ©Dea/A.Dagli Orti/De Agostini/Getty Images. 603 ©Stefano Baldini/Age Fotostock. 604 ©Robert Clark/National Geographic Creative. 608 (t) ©Dea/A.Dagli Orti/De Agostini Picture Library/Getty Images. (c) ©Ivan Smuk/Alamy. (b) ©Nikreates/Alamy. 609 (t) ©The Board of Trustees of the Armouries/Heritage-Images/The Image Works. (b) ©Dea/A.Dagli Orti/De Agostini/Getty Images. 613 ©Xavier Arnau Serrat/ Photographer's Choice/Getty Images. 614 ©Sebastian Wasek/ Age Fotostock. 616 ©Stapleton Collection/Corbis. 619 ©Scala/Art Resource, NY. 621 (t) ©British Library Board/ Robana/Art Resource, NY. (bc) ©Centre Historique des Archives Nationales, Paris, France/Archives Charmet/ Bridgeman Images. 622 ©Scala/Art Resource, NY. 624 ©Jon Bower/Loop Images/Age Fotostock. 627 ©Slawek Staszczuk/500px. 628 ©Francesco Riccardo Iacomino/500px. 631 ©Musei e Gallerie Pontificie, Musei Vaticani, Vatican City/Mondadori Portfolio/Bridgeman Images. 632 ©Scala/Art Resource, NY. 633 ©Fernando G. Baptista/National Geographic Creative. 634 ©Image Asset Management/World History Archive/age fotostock. 637 ©Alinari/Art Resource, NY. 638 ©SuperStock. 639 (tr) ©Louvre, Paris, France/Bridgeman Images. (tl) ©Louvre, Paris, France/Bridgeman Images. 640 ©David Yoder/ National Geographic Creative. 641 ©Eric Kruszewski/ National Geographic Creative. 643 ©Imagno/Getty Images. 644 ©Philip Mould Ltd, London/Bridgeman Images. 645 ©20th Century Fox/The Kobal Collection/Morton, Merrick/ Picture-Desk. 647 ©Lebrecht Music & Arts/Fine Art/Corbis. 649 (cr) ©Scala / Art Resource, NY. (tl) ©Charles Kogod/ National Geographic Creative. (bl) ©Brian Jannsen/age fotostock/Getty Images. (br) ©Konstantin L/Shutterstock. com. (tr) ©GraphicaArtis/Fine Art/Corbis. (bc) ©Itsmejust/ Shutterstock.com. 650 ©Philip Mould Ltd, London/ Bridgeman Images. 652 ©Fine Art Photographic Library/ Fine Art/Corbis. 653 ©Mansell/Getty Images. 657 ©Wojtek Buss/age fotostock. 659 (cl) ©Scala/Art Resource, NY. (cr) ©Nimatallah/Art Resource, NY. (t) ©Francesco Riccardo Iacomino/500px. 660 ©Dave Yoder/National Geographic Creative. 663 ©British Library, London, UK/British Library Board. All Rights Reserved/Bridgeman Images. 665 (tr) ©Science & Society Picture Library/Getty Images. (tc) ©Replica of Newton's colour wheel, 17th century/Dorling Kindersley/UIG/Bridgeman Images. (cl) ©Clive Streeter/ Dorling Kindersley/Science Museum, London/Science Source. 667 ©De Agostini Picture Library/G. Costa/ Bridgeman Images. 672 ©James L. Stanfield/National

Geographic Creative. 674 ©Reuters. 675 ©Ullstein Bild/akg-images. 679 (t) ©Diego Rivera/akg-images. (c) ©Diego Rivera/akg-images. 681 ©Robert Clark/National Geographic. 685 ©Dave Yoder/National Geographic Creative. 686 (bg) ©Dave Yoder/Aurora Photos/Alamy. 687 (tr) ©Dave Yoder/National Geographic Creative. 688 (t) ©Dave Yoder/National Geographic Creative. 690 (tr) ©Winn Brewer/National Geographic Learning. (bl) ©Sergey Semenov/AirPano.com. (br) ©NASA Earth Observatory image by Robert Simmon, using Suomi NPP VIIRS data provided courtesy of Chris Elvidge (NOAA National Geophysical Data Center). 691 (bg) ©O. Louis Mazzatenta/National Geographic Creative. 692 (bg) ©Sergey Semenov/AirPano.com. 693 (tr) ©Louise A. Hitchcock. 694 (bc) ©Imagno/Hulton Archive/Getty Images. (tr) National Archives and Records Administration. (tl) ©Jochen Schlenker/Robert Harding World Imagery/Corbis. 695 (tl) ©Krzysztof Dydynski/Lonely Planet Images/Getty Images. (bl) ©Culture Club/Hulton Archive/Getty Images. (br) ©Stock Montage, Inc./Alamy. (tr) ©Asian Art & Archaeology, Inc./Corbis. 696 (bl) ©Leemage/Corbis. 697 (tl) ©Lebrecht Music & Arts/Corbis. (br) ©Stefano Bianchetti/Corbis. (tr) ©Michael Maslan Historic Photographs/Corbis. 698 ©Rick Lacoume/500Prime. 701 (cr) ©DEA/G.Dagli Orti/Getty Images. (t) ©Leemage/Corbis. 703 (tl) ©After Nicholas de Largilliere/Getty Images. (cl) ©Fine Art Images/Heritage Images/Getty Images. (tr) ©De Agostini Editore/Age Fotostock. (cr) ©bpk, Berlin/Art Resource, NY. 705 (t) ©Charles Platiau/Reuters. (cr) ©Active Museum/Alamy. 707 ©H. Mark Weidman Photography / Alamy. 709 ©The Gallery Collection/Corbis. 710 © RMN-Grand Palais/Art Resource, NY. 713 ©Alfredo Dagli Orti/The Art Archive at Art Resource, NY. 715 ©Christie's Images/Corbis. 716 ©Capitol Collection, Washington, USA/Bridgeman Images. 719 ©Rick Lacoume/500Prime. 720 ©Quentin Bargate/Loop Images/Age Fotostock. 723 ©Heritage Images/Hulton Archive/Getty Images. 724 (tr) ©Science & Society Picture Library/Getty Images. (br) ©Hammond typewriter, with the ideal keyboard, c.1895, English School, (19th century) / Private Collection / Bridgeman Images. (c) ©Clive Streeter/DK Images. 725 (cl) ©High Impact Photography/Getty Images. (br) ©Science & Society Picture Library/Getty Images. (c) ©SSPL/The Image Works. (tr) ©Popperfoto/Getty Images. 727 ©Akg-Images. 728 ©Bettmann/Corbis. 729 ©Museum of London/Heritage Images/Hulton Archive/Getty Images. 730 ©Newberry Library, Chicago, Illinois, USA / Bridgeman Images. 731 ©Bettmann/Corbis. 733 ©Anonymous Person/Akg-Images. 735 ©Luis Marden/National Geographic Creative. 736 ©Jeffrey Thurnher/Underwood & Underwood/Historical/Corbis. 739 ©Popperfoto/Getty Images. 741 ©Underwood & Underwood/Historical/Corbis. 747 (bl) ©Mary Evans Picture Library/The Image Works. (t) ©Quentin Bargate/Loop Images/Age Fotostock. 748 (bg) ©Katja Meier. 749 (tr) ©Erik Freeland. 750 (t) ©Fine Art Images/Hulton Fine Art Collection/Getty Images. 752 (bg) ©NASA Earth Observatory image by Robert Simmon, using Suomi NPP VIIRS data provided courtesy of Chris Elvidge (NOAA National Geophysical Data Center). 753 (tr) ©Aziz Abu Sarah. 754 (tl) ©Imperial War Museum, London, UK/Bridgeman Images. (tr) ©Narinder Nanu/AFP/Getty Images. (bc) ©Heritage-Images/The Image Works. 755 (tr) ©Ira Block/National Geographic Creative. (tl) ©Dirck Halstead/Getty Images. (b) ©Dylan Martinez/REUTERS. 758 © Mary Evans/Robert Hunt Collection/The Image Works. 763 (tl) ©National Archives and Records Administration. (cr) ©SZ Photo/Scherl/The Image Works. (tr) ©Bain News Service/Interim Archives/Archive Photos/Getty Images. (cl) ©U.S. Air Force photo. 764 ©Private Collection/Peter Newark Military Pictures/Bridgeman Images. 765 ©Everet Collection. 767 ©Peter Newark Military Pictures/Bridgeman Images. 771 ©Akg-Images. 773 ©Library of Congress Prints and Photographs Division [LC-DIG-fsa-8b29516]/Dorothea Lange. 774 ©Fine Art Images/Heritage Images/Hulton Fine Art Collection/Getty Images. 775 ©Heinrich Hoffmann/Timepix/The LIFE Picture Collection/Getty Images. 779 ©Bettmann/Corbis. 781 ©Library of Congress Prints and Photographs Division[LC-DIG-fsac-1a35287]. 782 ©Heritage Image Partnership/ Fine Art Images/Alamy. 783 ©Iam/Akg-Images. 784 ©Hulton Archive/Archive Photos/Getty Images. 787 ©Junko Kimura/Getty Images News/Getty Images. 789 © Mary Evans/Robert Hunt Collection/The Image Works. 790 ©Clemens Geiger/500Prime. 793 ©AP Images. 795 (tl) ©AP Images/Sipa Press/Dalmas. (tc) ©Edouard Boubat/Gamma-Legends/Getty Images. (tr) ©Alison Wright/Robert Harding Picture Library Ltd/Alamy. 799 ©Gary Hershorn/Reuters. 801 ©courtesy of NASA/Houghton Mifflin Harcourt. 803 ©Paul Schutzer/The Life Picture Collection/Getty Images. 805 ©Hulton Archive/Getty Images. 807 ©AP Images/Mark Godfrey. 809 ©Tom Stoddart/Edit/Getty Images. 811 (cr) ©Walter Dhladhla/AFP/Getty Images. (tr) ©Marek Druszcz/AFP/Getty Images. 813 ©Cristovao. 814 ©Chris Hondros/Edit/Getty Images. 817 (t) ©Mirrorpix/Daily Mirror Gulf coverage/3rd Party - Misc/Getty Images. (c) ©AFP/Getty Images. 819 (t) ©Lynsey Addario/Getty Images. (c) ©Mark Thiessen and Rebecca Hale/National Geographic Creative. 821 (tl) ©Official White House Photo by Pete Souza. (bl) ©AP Images/Yomiuri Shimbun/Mitsuru Tamura. 822 (cl) ©Paula Aguilera. (cr) ©Courtesy of SubStation Curacao. (tr) ©Alexandra Verville/National Geographic Creative. 823 (t) ©Oli Scarff/AFP/Getty Images. (cl) ©Paula Kahumbu/Wildlife Direct. (cr) ©National Geographic Creative. 825 ©Clemens Geiger/500Prime. 826 (bg) ©Aziz Abu Sarah. 827 (tr) ©Aziz Abu Sarah. 828 (t) ©Nick Kaloterakis/National Geographic Creative. 830 (tr) ©Winn Brewer/National Geogrpahic Learning. (bg) ©Paulette Tavormina/National Geographic Creative. 832 (tr) ©2014 Dotjang Agany Awer/National Geographic Photo Camp South Sudan. (cl) ©ed nazarko/500px. (c) ©2014 Emmanuela Henry Andrew Kenyi/National Geographic Photo Camp South Sudan. (cr) ©Bobby Haas/National Geographic Creative. (bl) ©David Doubilet/National Geographic Creative. (bcr) ©Jose Luis Gonzalez/REUTERS. (br) ©Mahmoud Hebbo/REUTERS. 833 (tl) ©Alexandre Meneghini/REUTERS. (tcl) ©David Doubilet/National Geographic Creative. (bcl) ©Richard Drew/AP Images. (bl) ©JD Dallet/arabianEye/Getty Images. (tr) ©2014 National Geographic Photo Camp South Sudan. 834 (t) ©Stringer/REUTERS. 835 (tl) ©Erin West Kephart/National Geographic Learning. 836 (tl) ©Izzet Keribar/Lonely Planet Images/Getty Images. (tr) ©Molhem Barakat/REUTERS. (cl) ©Izzet Keribar/Lonely Planet Images/Getty Images. (cr) ©Molhem Barakat/REUTERS. 837 (tl) ©Marcie Goodale/National Geographic Learning. 838 (t) ©Frederik Hiebert. (cl) ©ICE/Handout/REUTERS. (cr) ©Frederik Hiebert. 839 (c) ©Rebecca Hale/National Geographic Creative. 840 (t) ©Bobby Haas/National Geographic Creative. (tcl, bcl, cr) ©Shah Selbe. 841 (bl, cr) ©Shah Selbe. 842 (tl) ©2014 Simon Odhol/National Geographic Photo Camp South Sudan. (tc) ©2014 Catherine Simon Arona Samuel/National Geographic Photo Camp South Sudan. (tr) ©2014 Dotjang Agany Awer/National Geographic Photo Camp South Sudan. (cl) ©2014 Holly Moses Edward/National Geographic Photo Camp South Sudan. (c) ©2014 Simon Odhol/National Geographic Photo Camp South Sudan. (cr) ©2014 Duku Stephen Savio/National Geographic Photo Camp South Sudan. (bl) ©2014 Duku Stephen Savio/National Geographic Photo Camp South Sudan. (bc) ©2014 Lisok James Moses/National Geographic Photo Camp South Sudan. (br) ©2014 Samuel Oyet Faustino/National Geographic Photo Camp South Sudan. 843 (cr) ©2014 Lisok James Moses/National Geographic Photo Camp South Sudan. 844 (tr) ©Beverly Joubert/National Geographic Creative. R1 (bg) ©Kenneth Garrett/National Geographic Creative.

Map Credits

Mapping Specialists, LTD., Madison, WI.
National Geographic Maps, National Geographic Society

Illustrator Credits

Unless otherwise indicated, all illustrations were created by Precision Graphics.

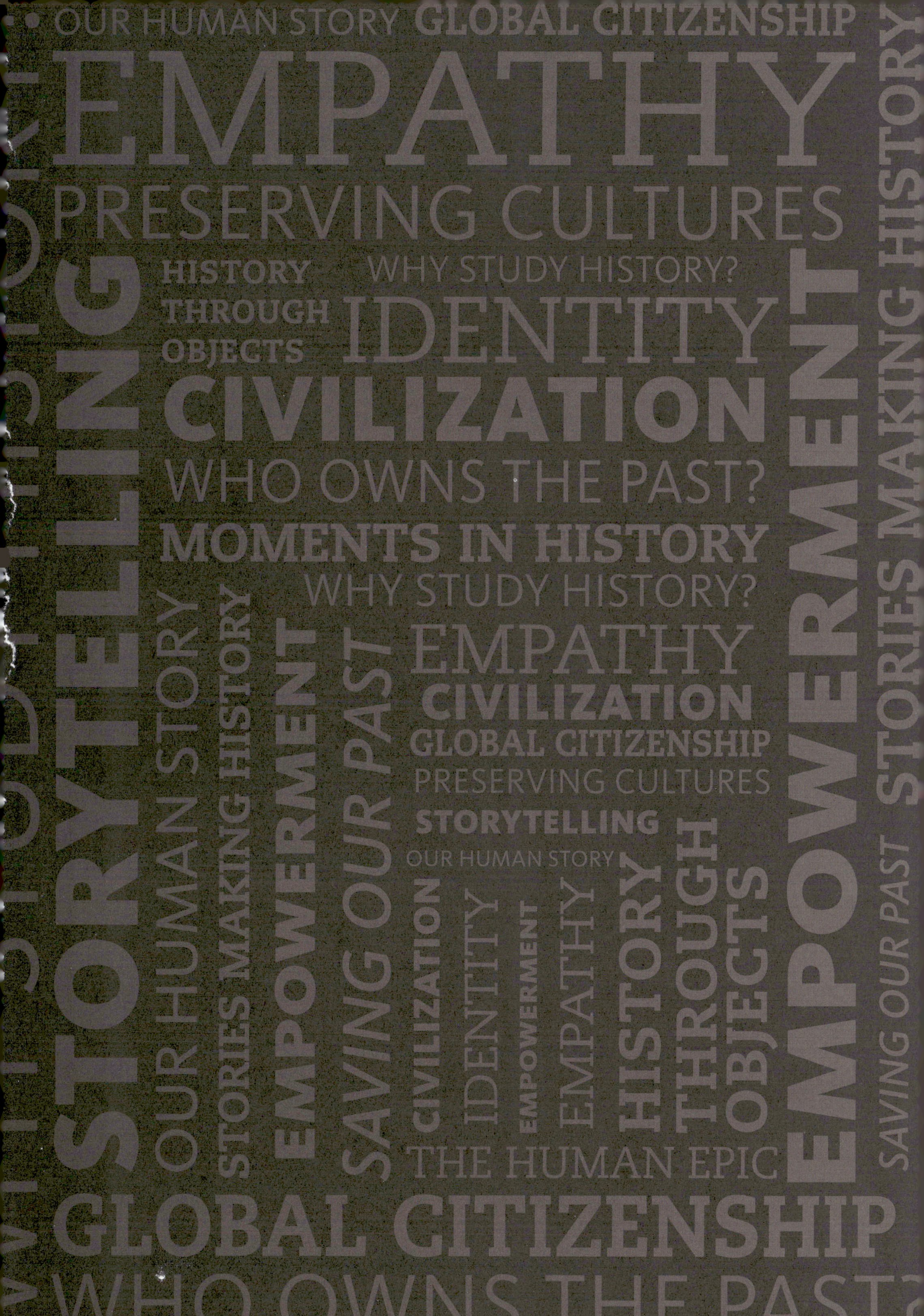
OUR HUMAN STORY
GLOBAL CITIZENSHIP
EMPATHY
PRESERVING CULTURES
HISTORY THROUGH OBJECTS
WHY STUDY HISTORY?
IDENTITY
CIVILIZATION
WHO OWNS THE PAST?
MOMENTS IN HISTORY
WHY STUDY HISTORY?
EMPATHY
CIVILIZATION
GLOBAL CITIZENSHIP
PRESERVING CULTURES
STORYTELLING
OUR HUMAN STORY
STORYTELLING
OUR HUMAN STORY
STORIES MAKING HISTORY
EMPOWERMENT
SAVING OUR PAST
CIVILIZATION
IDENTITY
EMPOWERMENT
EMPATHY
HISTORY THROUGH OBJECTS
EMPOWERMENT
STORIES MAKING HISTORY
SAVING OUR PAST
THE HUMAN EPIC
GLOBAL CITIZENSHIP
WHO OWNS THE PAST

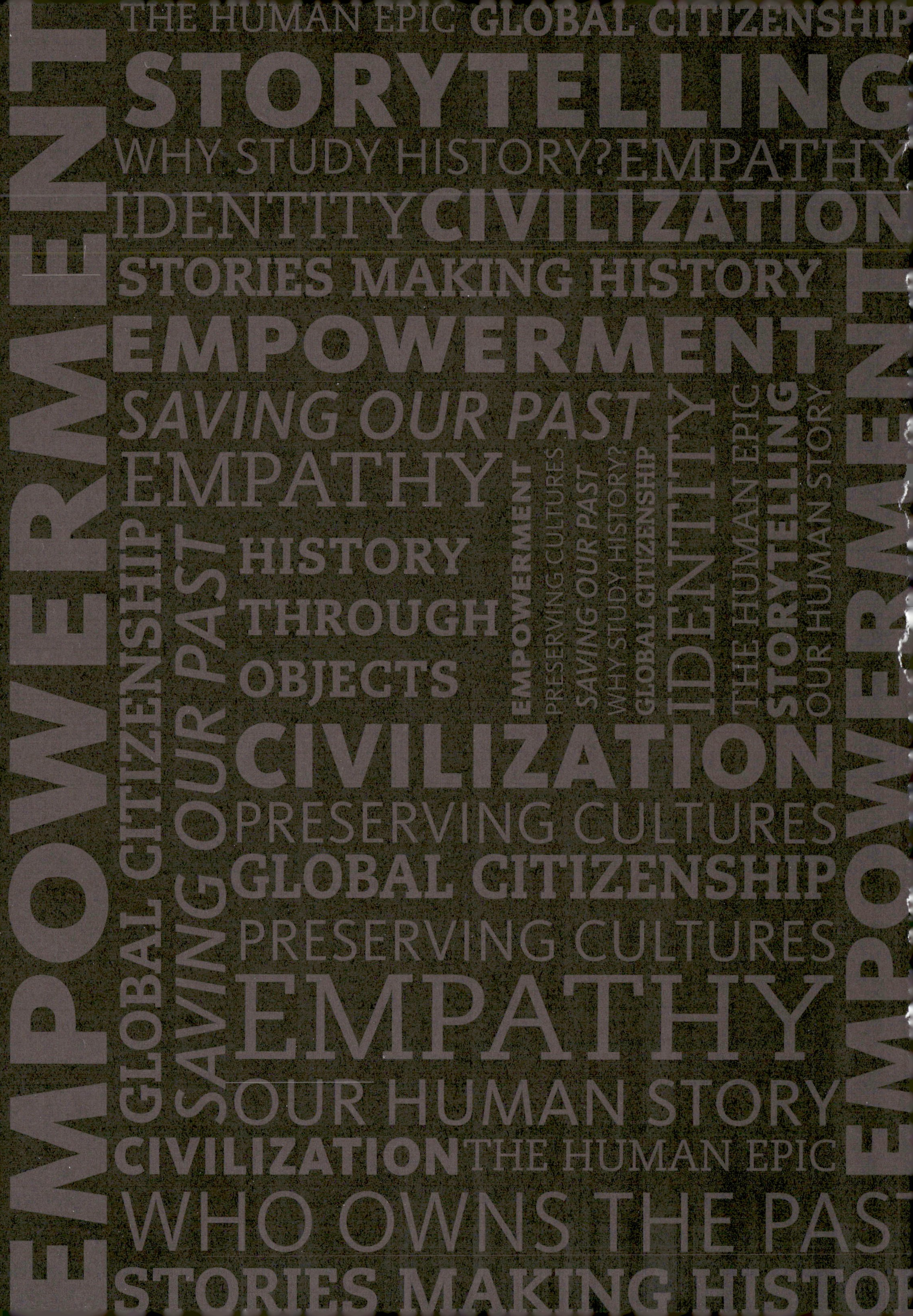
THE HUMAN EPIC GLOBAL CITIZENSHIP
STORYTELLING
WHY STUDY HISTORY? EMPATHY
IDENTITY CIVILIZATION
STORIES MAKING HISTORY
EMPOWERMENT
SAVING OUR PAST
EMPATHY
HISTORY
THROUGH
OBJECTS
EMPOWERMENT
PRESERVING CULTURES
SAVING OUR PAST
WHY STUDY HISTORY?
GLOBAL CITIZENSHIP
IDENTITY
THE HUMAN EPIC
STORYTELLING
OUR HUMAN STORY
CIVILIZATION
PRESERVING CULTURES
GLOBAL CITIZENSHIP
PRESERVING CULTURES
EMPATHY
OUR HUMAN STORY
CIVILIZATION THE HUMAN EPIC
WHO OWNS THE PAST
STORIES MAKING HISTORY
EMPOWERMENT
GLOBAL CITIZENSHIP
SAVING OUR PAST
EMPOWERMENT